Business Law

With UCC Applications

TWELFTH EDITION

Gordon W. Brown

PROFESSOR EMERITUS
NORTH SHORE COMMUNITY COLLEGE
DANVERS, MASSACHUSETTS

Paul A. Sukys

PROFESSOR OF LAW AND APPLIED PHILOSOPHY
NORTH CENTRAL STATE COLLEGE
MANSFIELD, OHIO

Boston   Burr Ridge, IL   Dubuque, IA   New York   San Francisco   St. Louis
Bangkok   Bogotá   Caracas   Kuala Lumpur   Lisbon   London   Madrid   Mexico City
Milan   Montreal   New Delhi   Santiago   Seoul   Singapore   Sydney   Taipei   Toronto

BUSINESS LAW WITH UCC APPLICATIONS
Published by McGraw-Hill/Irwin, a business unit of The McGraw-Hill Companies, Inc., 1221 Avenue of the
Americas, New York, NY, 10020. Copyright © 2009, 2006, 2001, 1997, 1993, 1989, 1983, 1978, 1972, 1966,
1961, 1953 by The McGraw-Hill Companies, Inc. All rights reserved. No part of this publication may be
reproduced or distributed in any form or by any means, or stored in a database or retrieval system, without
the prior written consent of The McGraw-Hill Companies, Inc., including, but not limited to, in any network
or other electronic storage or transmission, or broadcast for distance learning.

Some ancillaries, including electronic and print components, may not be available to customers outside the
United States.

This book is printed on acid-free paper.

2 3 4 5 6 7 8 9 0 WCK/WCK 0 9

ISBN 978-0-07-352494-8 (student edition)
MHID 0-07-352494-8 (student edition)
ISBN 978-0-07-334114-9 (annotated instructor's edition)
MHID 0-07-334114-2 (annotated instructor's edition)

Publisher: *Paul Ducham*
Sponsoring editor: *Dana L. Woo*
Developmental editor: *Megan Richter*
Marketing manager: *Sarah Schuessler*
Project manager: *Jim Labeots*
Production supervisor: *Gina Hangos*
Senior designer: *Cara Hawthorne*
Photo research coordinator: *Lori Kramer*
Photo researcher: *Ira C. Roberts*
Senior media project manager: *Kerry Bowler*
Cover design: *Cara Hawthorne*
Interior design: *Cara Hawthorne*
Typeface: *10/12 Times Roman*
Compositor: *Aptara*
Printer: *Quebecor World Versailles Inc.*

Library of Congress Cataloging-in-Publication Data

Brown, Gordon W.
    Business law : with UCC applications / Gordon W. Brown, Paul A. Sukys. -- 12th ed.
        p. cm.
    Includes index.
    ISBN-13: 978-0-07-352494-8 (student edition : alk. paper)
    ISBN-10: 0-07-352494-8 (student edition : alk. paper)
    ISBN-13: 978-0-07-334114-9 (annotated instructor's edition : alk. paper)
    ISBN-10: 0-07-334114-2 (annotated instructor's edition : alk. paper) 1. Commercial
law--United States. I. Sukys, Paul. II. Title.
    KF889.3.B76 2009
    346.7307—dc22
                                                                    2007048926

Dedication

This book is dedicated with much love and many thanks to our most understanding wives, Jane A. Brown and Susan E. Sukys, and to our respective issue and their spouses, of whom we are extremely proud:

Gordon and Jane Brown: Steven, Linda, Joshua, Kaleigh, Christopher, Matthew, Jan, Ryan, Corey, Emily, Deborah, Michael, Patrick, Connor, Camden, Melanie, Jennifer, Harbir, Millin, Kurrun, Timothy, Celeste, Nicholas, and David.

Paul and Susan Sukys: Jennifer, Dave, Ashley, and Megan.

About the Authors

Gordon W. Brown, Professor Emeritus, North Shore Community College, Danvers, Massachusetts, where he has taught for 30 years, is the author of *Legal Terminology* and *Administration of Wills, Trusts, and Estates* and the co-author, with Dr. Paul A. Sukys, of *Understanding Business and Personal Law.* Mr. Brown received his law degree from Suffolk University and practiced law in Beverly, Massachusetts, while teaching full time at North Shore Community College. He is a member of the Massachusetts and federal Bars.

Paul A. Sukys is a professor of law and applied philosophy at North Central State College in Mansfield, Ohio. He is co-author of *Understanding Business and Personal Law* and *Civil Litigation,* a textbook for paralegals. He is also the author of *Lifting the Scientific Veil: Science Appreciation for the Nonscientist,* which explores the relationships among science and other disciplines, focusing on the interaction of science and the law. He has a Ph.D. in applied philosophy from The Union Institute and University of Cincinnati. Dr. Sukys received his law degree from Cleveland State University. He is a member of the Ohio Bar.

Preface

The twelfth edition of *Business Law with UCC Applications* reflects the many changes that have taken place in the law over the past three years. As in previous editions, we've taken care to present business law concepts in the most coherent and accessible way and to provide up-to-date coverage of business law topics that are essential to today's students. All of the chapters for this edition have been updated, and we have continued to enhance our coverage of the important topics of e-commerce, signature requirements and electronic signatures, international law, identity theft, antispam law, the Uniform Anatomical Gift Act, the "kiddie tax," trade secrets, abandoned property, trade dress, video piracy, transportation security, eminent domain, hurricane insurance, mortgages and deeds of trust, bankruptcy, limited liability companies (LLC), ethics, and Alternative Dispute Resolution.

The popular format of the eleventh edition has been enhanced, with learning objectives identified in the margin where that material appears in the text. Each chapter begins with an outline followed by The Opening Case, with numbered questions and Chapter Objectives. Titles have been given to every example. Major headings and chapter summaries continue to be numbered, following the chapter outline. The popular case illustrations, presenting either hypothetical or actual situations based on well-founded court decisions, have been retained and updated. Our Quick Quiz feature appears in each chapter and allows students to test their knowledge of the chapter topics while they actively study the text. The Talking Points feature has been included in many chapters in this edition, giving both the instructor and the students an opportunity to discuss stimulating, provocative, and controversial topics suggested by the content in each chapter.

We also have retained case studies pertaining to each of the nine parts of the book, which summarize an actual litigated case, present a lengthy extract from the judge's decision, and provide follow-up questions that are pertinent to the cases and are appropriate as a review of the legal concepts involved. Activities at the end of each chapter, including Key Terms, Questions for Review and Discussion, Investigating the Internet, and Cases for Analysis, help students self-check their understanding of the terms and concepts presented in the chapter. We also have updated every Business Law in the News feature and expanded the Question of Ethics elements throughout the text. These features take excerpts from the weekly news magazine *BusinessWeek* and tie them directly to chapter material. Discussion questions for each article are also included. The U.S. Constitution appears in Appendix A. Included in Appendix B are four articles of the Uniform Commercial Code. Appendix C consists of the United Nations Convention for the International Sale of Goods (CISG). Marginal references within the chapters tie these specific documents to the content.

The twelfth edition of *Business Law with UCC Applications* thus offers a comprehensive package of materials to meet both instructors' and students' needs.

Acknowledgments

We are grateful to the following individuals for their review feedback. We appreciate their ideas and suggestions.

Carol Brady
Milwaukee Area Technical College

Cheryl Head
Central Piedmont Community College

Lynda Hodge
Guilford Technical Community College

Steve Kempisty
Bryant & Stratton College

Vonda Laughlin
Carson-Newman College

Brian Logan
Bryant & Stratton College

Jeffrey Sisley
Milwaukee Area Technical College

Henry Arnold
Aiken Technical College

Nancy Dempsey
Cape Cod Community College

Jeffrey Penley
Catawba Valley Community College

Deborah Sementa
Cape Cod Community College

Ron O'Brien
Fayetteville Technical Community College

Cathy Trecek
Iowa Western Community College

Traci Etheridge
Richmond Community College

Linda Sanders
Fayetteville Technical Community College

We also extend special thanks to Jane A. Brown for her assistance in proofreading and writing the Study Guide for the edition. Additional special thanks to Jennifer A. Bates for her excellent photograph of Dr. Sukys on the About the Authors page.

Special thanks are also extended to the Business Law classes for Fall Quarter 2003 and Winter Quarter 2004 at North Central State College for pilot testing the Mock Hearing Process found in the ancillary materials for *Business Law with UCC Applications, 12e.*

A Guided Tour

Business Law with UCC Applications, 12/e, is full of useful chapter features to make studying productive and hassle-free. The following pages show the kind of engaging, helpful pedagogical features that complement the accessible, easy-to-understand approach to teaching business law.

Chapter Outline

Each chapter features an outline that allows students to recognize the organization of the chapter at a glance. For reinforcement, the outline's numbering system is used throughout the body of the chapter and is repeated in the end-of-chapter Summary.

Chapter 3 — The Judicial Process

3-1 The Court System
The Federal Court System • Court Jurisdiction • State Court Systems • Electronic Jurisdiction

3-2 Civil Procedure
Commencement of the Action • Service of Process • The Pre-Answer Stage • The Answer • The Pretrial Stage • The Civil Trial • The Appeal • Execution of the Judgment

The Opening Case
Ruhrgas v. Marathon Oil Company

Marathon Oil, an American energy company, filed a fraud case in state court against a German corporation named Ruhrgas. Almost immediately after being served with process, Ruhrgas filed a motion to remove the case from state to federal court. Ruhrgas argued that the case belonged in federal court because the federal court held subject matter jurisdiction, based on diversity and federal law. Once the case was before a federal judge, Ruhrgas, using a very clever strategy, argued that the case should be dismissed entirely because though the federal court had subject matter jurisdiction, it did not have personal jurisdiction over the German corporation. The district court agreed with Ruhrgas and dismissed the case. Not to be outdone, Marathon Oil appealed, arguing that the federal court had no subject matter jurisdiction and the case should therefore be sent back to the state court. Ruhrgas asserted that the issue of subject ma

The Opening Case

A brief case opens each chapter and introduces the chapter concepts, followed by numbered questions addressing legal issues in the case. Every Opening Case is re-examined throughout the chapter in The Opening Case Revisited features.

Learning Objectives

Succinct, crisply written learning objectives follow The Opening Case at the beginning of each chapter. The numbered objectives describe what the students can expect to learn as a result of completing the chapter. Each objective is identified by a unique symbol in the margin where the material appears in the text.

LO Learning Objectives

1. Explain the fundamental nature of American cou
2. Determine in what circumstances the federal cou
3. Recognize which cases may be heard by the U.S
4. Identify the structure found in most state court sy
5. Determine the extent of electronic jurisdiction.
6. Define civil litigation.
7. List the most commonly used discovery techniqu
8. Explain the nature of electronically stored inform
9. Detail the nature of an appeal.
10. Describe the steps in a criminal prosecution.

Several boxed features elaborate on the chapter topics at hand and facilitate further research and understanding:

New and retained in the twelfth edition!

New! Appendix C

International trade has grown by leaps and bounds, and so, the twelfth edition includes the United Nations Convention on Contracts for the International Sale of Goods (CISG), which appears in the text as Appendix C. Marginal references within the text in the sales chapters refer to the CISG, similar to those referencing the UCC.

Appendix C — United Nations Convention on Contracts for the International Sale of Goods

THE STATES PARTIES TO THIS CONVENTION, BEARING IN MIND the broad objectives in the resolutions adopted by the sixth special session of the General Assembly of the United Nations on the establishment of a New International Economic Order, CONSIDERING that the development of international trade on the basis of equality and mutual benefit is an important element in promoting friendly relations among States, BEING OF THE OPINION that the adoption of uniform rules which govern contracts for the international sale of goods and take into account the different social, economic and legal systems would contribute to the removal of legal barriers in international trade and promote the development of international trade, HAVE AGREED as follows:

Article 3
(1) Contracts for the supply of good or produced are to be considere party who orders the goods un substantial part of the material manufacture or production.
(2) This Convention does not appl the preponderant part of the ob who furnishes the goods consi bour or other services.

Article 4 This Convention govern the contract of sale and the rights seller and the buyer arising from ticular, except as otherwise expr Convention, it is not concerned wi

Part I Sphere of Application

 BusinessWeek Business Law in the News

Global Warming: Here Come the Lawyers

Two days after Hurricane Katrina smashed into the Gulf Coast, F. Gerald Maples returned to his hometown of Pass Christian, Miss., to utter devastation. Most of his neighbors' houses were totally destroyed. His was in ruins. "It broke our hearts and absolutely changed our lives," he says. It also made Maples, a veteran asbestos plaintiffs' attorney in New Orleans, determined to fight back. "I couldn't stand by when my entire cultural history was destroyed by an event that could become more frequent because of global warming," he says.

So when friend and fellow trial lawyer Timothy W. Porter showed up to help with food and water, the two plotted a legal assault. Since Katrina's fury was powered by unusually warm Gulf water, and since such warmth could result from global warming, companies that have pumped the atmosphere full of greenhouse gases like carbon dioxide should be liable for damages, they figured. "To me, Katrina was a clear result of irresponsible behavior by the carbon-emissions corporate economy," says Maples. He re-

sents frustration with the White House's and Congress' failure to come to grips with the issue," says John Echeverria, executive director of Georgetown University's Environmental Law & Policy Institute. "So the courts, for better or worse, are taking the lead."

It's hardly the first time the judiciary has emerged as the forum for those who have felt stymied trying to address a broad social issue on other fronts. And it's possible that this legal assault will prove quixotic, akin to failed suits by cities to hold gunmakers responsible for gun violence or by African Americans to win reparations for slavery.

Sword of Damocles

But there's another example that's far more worrisome for polluters: tobacco. When state attorneys general began suing cigarette makers in the mid-1990s to recover smoking-related health-care costs, the litigation was widely dismissed as fanciful. Yet

---

Business Law in the News

uses articles from *BusinessWeek* to tie today's headlines with business law concepts. Each article is enhanced with Questions for Discussion.

A Question of Ethics

boxes challenge students' understanding of previously discussed chapter examples by asking questions specifically relating to ethical dilemmas. In addition, many articles by "Ask the Ethics Guy," Bruce Weinstein, are taken from *BusinessWeek* magazine and BusinessWeek.com.

About the Law

boxes provide additional clarification of chapter concepts.

About the Law

Unlike the United States Constitution, the British Constitution cannot be found in a single document. Rather, it is based on a group of implicit traditions

2-2 Constit

The law has been defined a mony, stability, and justice what limited. It does not e power to make those rules.

In some societies, the the establishment of a gove essary power to take contro ment was established by a

---

A Question of Ethics

Edward McDonough, assistant district attorney for the city of Middletown, has just left a session with Harold Harrison, a criminal defendant accused of armed robbery. During the session, acting under the advice of Jennifer Miller, his attorney, Harrison confessed to the crime and entered a plea bargain agreement that will place him in prison for 10 years. On his way back across the city square to his office, ADA McDonough is stopped by Sgt. Anne Wade, who confesses to him that neither she nor her partner, Sgt. Sam Newton, read Harrison his rights. McDonough knows that this admission means that the confession he just obtained is tainted and would be thrown out of court if it were challenged by Miller on behalf of Harrison. From an ethical point of view, what action should McDonough take now?

An Indictment The federal courts and many state courts bring formal charges against the defendant by issuing an indictment. An **indictment** is a set of formal

Did You Know? boxes are interesting factoids directly linked to the chapter concept being discussed.

instance, the discovery request seeks information protected by the a[ttorney-client privi]lege, the judge may refuse to compel the litigant to comply with the re[quest.]

If, however, the litigant cannot persuade the judge that the refusa[l is justified,] the judge may impose severe penalties on the litigant. For example, th[e judge may] dismiss the lawsuit completely. The judge may also decide to render [a judgment] against the uncooperative party. Reasonable expenses caused by the ref[usal to permit] discovery may also be assessed against the uncooperative party. Thes[e expenses in]clude attorney's fees. In many states, the rules allow the expenses to [be assessed to] either the attorney or the litigant.

Electronically Stored Information Rapid changes in co[mputers have] an impact on the discovery process. Until recently, the courts were sati[sfied with com]puterized data as if it was just another way of producing paper docu[ments. When] data stored in or produced by computers, they simply used a catchphra[se "documented col]lation" to cover all such evidence, whether it was on paper, on a co[mputer disk, or a] flash drive. This coverage is no longer enough. The Federal Rules of C[ivil Procedure now] refer to computerized evidence as *electronically stored information* ([ESI]). The rule makers have officially recognized that ESI can cause many diffi[culties not] covered by the old rules. For example, computers produce and store [evidence in] many different formats that even the most up-to-date computer exper[t, let] alone an unskilled lawyer or paralegal. This complexity makes coming [up with a] discovery plan that does not crash and burn on the first day of its imple[mentation]

---

dant admits or denies the allegations in the complaint. The defendant's answer can also include affirmative defenses. An **affirmative defense** is a set of circumstances that indicate that the defendant should not be held liable, even if the plaintiff proves all of the facts in the complaint. One affirmative defense is *assumption of the risk.*

EXAMPLE 3-3:   Assessing the Risk of a Risky Business

Carol Jennings took a cruise of the Mediterranean on the Underwood Cruise Line, a firm incorporated and doing business in the United States. While the cruise ship *Principia* was docked at a Greek island, Jennings joined a tour group. She was cautioned numerous times to remain with the tour group and not to wander off by herself because of the danger of being attacked and robbed. Nevertheless, Jennings ignored the warnings and left the tour group. While on her own, she wandered into a particularly dangerous part of the city where she was beaten and robbed. She later brought a lawsuit against the Underwood Cruise Line. In its answer to Jennings' complaint, the cruise line may wish to use the defense of assumption of the risk. Such a defense would argue that Jennings was aware of danger when she chose to abandon the tour group and wander off by herself. As a result, the cruise line might argue, she assumed the risk of being attacked and robbed.

Examples are titled and numbered throughout each chapter and use short vignettes to explain how concepts can be applied in real-life situations.

Talking Point boxes are found in many chapters in the book. The Talking Points feature takes concepts and ideas from leading scholars, philosophers, economists, writers, lawyers, politicians, and judges and offers them to students for further thought and discussion. Whenever feasible, the feature quotes contrasting ideas from two or three different perspectives and then asks students to defend one of those positions in a thoughtful and constructive way.

Quick Quiz boxes follow each numbered section and give students the chance to test themselves with three true/false questions. Answers are provided at the end of each chapter.

3-3 Criminal Procedure

The objectives of a criminal prosecution are to protect society and to punish the wrongdoer

Questions for Review and Discussion provide a means for students and the instructor to reexamine and discuss the key points of law. All objectives listed at the beginning of each chapter are also reviewed.

Summary

3.1 Courts are judicial tribunals that meet in a regular place and apply the laws in an attempt to settle disputes fairly. The federal court system is divided into three levels: the district courts, the courts of appeals, and the U.S. Supreme Court. State systems vary in structure but often consist of several levels, including lower-level limited jurisdiction trial courts, higher-level trial courts, intermediate appellate courts, and supreme courts.

3.2 Litigation begins when the plaintiff files [a] complaint with the appropriate trial court. The defendant must then be given a copy of the complaint and [a sum]mons. During the pre-answer stage, the defenda[nt may] attempt to dismiss the lawsuit by filing certain [an]swer motions. In the answer stage, the defenda[nt may] file an answer, which may contain affirmati[ve de]fenses, counterclaims, and/or cross-claims. The[n the]

jury then renders a verdict. Either party may appeal the case if that party believes that a legal error was made during the trial that influenced the verdict unfavorably. If a judgment is not paid, the court may issue a writ of execution.

3.3 The steps in a criminal prosecution include the

Summary Numbered to match the outline at the beginning of the chapter and the main heads within each chapter, the Summary provides an encapsulated review of the chapter's content.

Key Terms

administrative law, 42	constitution, 30
Articles of Confederation, 31	constitutional law, 30
binding precedent, 39	devolution, 35
code, 37	e-commerce, 38
Code of Federal Regulations (CFR), 42	embedded niches, 29
	Federal Register, 42
common law, 39	judicial review, 41
complex adaptive system, 28	law, 27

Key Terms Each key term is printed in boldface and defined when introduced in the text. A list of key terms and the page number of first usage appears at the end of each chapter. A glossary of the key terms is provided at the back of the text.

Cases for Analysis have been updated extensively for the twelfth edition and chosen for their relevance, ease of understanding, and interesting fact patterns. Many are abridgments of actual court decisions; some are taken from current news stories; and still others are hypothetical situations written to emphasize legal issues and concepts presented in the text.

Cases for Analysis

1. The State of Oregon passed a statute called the Oregon Death with Dignity Act (ODWDA) which permitted licensed physicians in Oregon to prescribe or administer drugs to patients who are terminally ill. However, according to the federal law known as the Controlled Substances Act (CSA), it is illegal for physicians to prescribe such drugs, except for a legitimate medical reason. The attorney general of the United States therefore sought to stop the administration of such drugs under the

ing a physician's intent to assist a terminally ill patient to commit suicide in this way. Is the attorney general or the state of Oregon correct here? Explain. *Alberto R. Gonzales, Attorney General, et al., Petitioners, v. Oregon, et al.* (U.S. Supreme Court).

2. Karen Silkwood was an employee at the Kerr-McGee Nuclear Power Plant in Oklahoma. During her employment there, she was apparently contaminated by exposure to plutonium. The contamina-

Investigating the Internet

Access the U.S. Historical Documents Archive on the Internet and write a research paper in which you trace the evolution of American political thought as represented in these major documents. In that report, answer the following questions: (1) Which of these documents is the most important in relation to shaping the nature of the law in the United States? (2) What are the major ideas that most people remember about each document? (3) What are some of the misconceptions that people have

Investigating the Internet activities encourage students to seek additional information on the Internet about subjects that appear in the text.

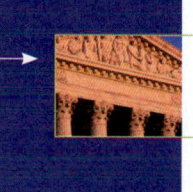

Part 1 Case Study

Kelo v. City of New London
United States Supreme Court
125 S.Ct. 2655

Summary

The case of Kelo v. City of New London is a fascinating exercise in case law for

The **Case Study** at the end of each of the nine parts begins with a summary of the facts of the case, is followed by an excerpt from the court's opinion, and concludes with a series of questions.

Three appendices provide critical material for the students: **The Constitution of the United States (Appendix A),** Articles 1, 2, 2a, and 3 of the **Uniform Commercial Code (Appendix B),** and the **United Nations Convention for the International Sale of Goods (Appendix C).** Marginal references throughout the text refer students to the page of the appendix where the original source of the law being discussed can be found.

Appendix A

Preamble

We the People of the United States, [in order to form a] more perfect Union, establish Justi[ce, insure domestic] Tranquility, provide for the common d[efence, promote the] general Welfare, and secure the Bles[sings of Liberty to] ourselves and our Posterity, do ordai[n and establish this] Constitution for the United States of A[merica.]

Article I

Section 1. All legislative Powers her[ein granted shall be] vested in a Congress of the United [States, which shall] consist of a Senate and House of Repr[esentatives.]

Section 2. [1] The House of Repr[esentatives shall be] composed of Members chosen every [second Year by the] People of the several States, and th[e]

Appendix B — Uniform Commer[cial Code] (Articles 1, 2, 2a[, 3])

Article 1: General Provisions

Part 1: Short Title, Construction, Application and Subject Matter of the Act

§1-101. Short Title. This act shall be known and may be cited as Uniform Commercial Code.

§1-102. Purposes; Rules of Construction; Variation by Agreement.
(1) This Act shall be liberally construed and applied to promote its underlying purposes and policies.
(2) Underlying purposes and policies of this Act are
   (a) to simplify, clarify and modernize the law governing commercial transactions;
   (b) to permit the continued expansion of commercial practices through custom, usage and agreement of the parties;
   (c) to make uniform the law among the various jurisdictions.
(3) The effect of provisions of this Act may be varied by agreement, except as otherwise provided in this Act and except that the obligations of good faith, diligence, reasonableness and care prescribed by this

to be impli[ed] construction [of]

§1-105. Te[rritorial] Po[licy]
(1) Except[transac]tions [and also] agree th[at] state or [] Failing[g] tions b[]
(2) Where [] specifi[] and a c[] tent per[] laws ru[] Rights []
   Applic[] 105 and 2A[] Applic[] Collections[] Bulk tr[] fers. Section[]

Student Study Guide

Each chapter in the Study Guide begins with an outline to be completed by the student. Corresponding with the outline at the beginning of each text chapter, this learning activity reinforces the subject matter being studied. When completed, it also serves as a study aid to the student. The outline is followed by true/false questions covering important legal concepts. Next, a section entitled "Language of the Law" gives students practice in matching key legal terms with their definitions. Finally, ten hypothetical cases give students an opportunity to apply the law to cases. Answers to the objective questions and hypothetical cases are found in the back of the Study Guide.

Instructor's Edition

This instructional tool features teaching tips, answers to end-of-chapter questions, analyses of chapter cases, and solutions to case studies. In addition, annotations on text pages provide background information, related cases, state variations of specific laws, vocabulary terms, methods to get students involved, interesting quotes, and suggested further readings.

Instructor's Manual

Printed Instructor's Test Bank

Instructor's Resource CD-ROM

Instructors are now able to choose between printed supplements or CD-ROMs. The Instructor material includes Lesson Plans, Lecture Notes and Outlines, Sample Syllabi, Test Bank (CD-ROM test bank written in ExamViewPro), and Conducting a Mock Trial. PowerPoint slides are also available on the Instructor's Resource CD-ROM.

Enhanced Cartridge

Do you already use WebCT or Blackboard? Or are you hoping to put more of your course materials online? Are you looking for an easy way to assign more materials to your students and manage a gradebook? If so, *Business Law with UCC Applications* comes with McGraw-Hill's new Enhanced Cartridge.

The Enhanced Cartridge is developed to help you get your course up and running with much less time and effort. The content, enhanced with more assignments and more study materials than a standard cartridge, is pre-populated into appropriate chapters and content categories. Now there's no need to cut and paste our content into your course—it's already there!

But you can still choose to hide content we provide and add your own—just as you have before in WebCT and Blackboard.

The twelfth edition of the enhanced cartridge for *Business Law with UCC Applications* includes:

- iPod/MP3 content
- Chapter pre- and post-tests
- **You Be the Judge Online** video segments, which include 18 hypothetical business law cases. All of the cases are based on real cases from our Business Law texts. Each case allows you to watch interviews of the plaintiff and defendant before the court-

Online Learning Center (OLC)
www.mhhe.com/brown12e

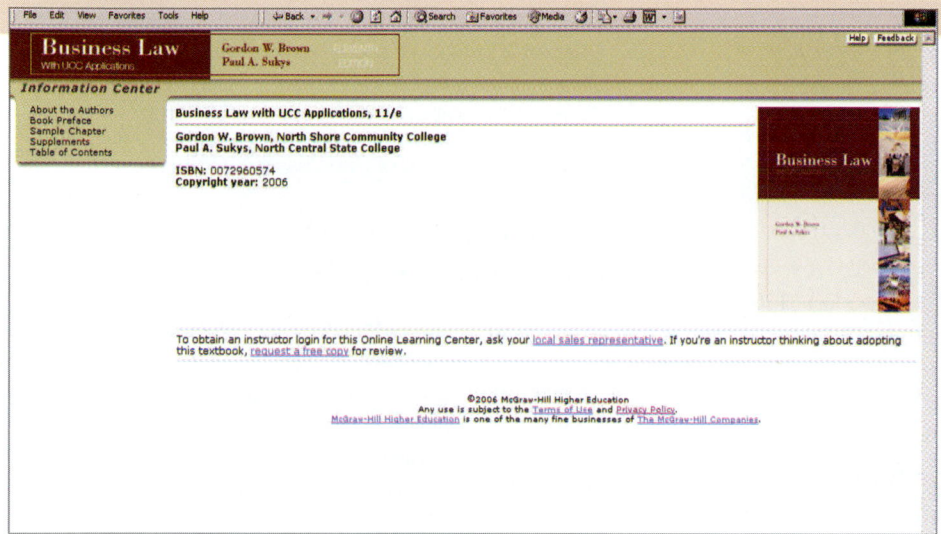

room argument, see the courtroom proceedings, view relevant evidence, read other actual cases relating to the issues in the case, and then create your own ruling. After your verdict is generated, view what an actual judge ruled (unscripted) in the case and then get the chance to defend or change your ruling.

You can choose to package a password card with your text, or students can buy access via e-commerce through the book's Web site for $10. Ask your McGraw-Hill sales representative on how to get the enhanced cartridge to accompany *Business Law with UCC Applications* for your course.

More and more students are studying online. That's why we offer an Online Learning Center that follows *Business Law with UCC Applications* chapter by chapter. It doesn't require any building or maintenance on your part—it's ready to go the moment you or your students type in the URL.

A secured Instructor Resource Center stores your essential course materials to save you prep time before class. The Instructor's Manual, Lesson Plans, Lecture Notes and Outlines, PowerPoint slides, and sample syllabi are only a couple of clicks away. You can even access the "Conducting a Mock Trial" feature with ease!

Contents in Brief

Part Eight

Business Organization and Regulation 767

Part Nine

Emerging Trends and Issues 859

Contents

Part Three

Part Four

Part Five
Negotiable Instruments 537

Part Six
Insurance, Secured Transactions,
and Bankruptcy 613

Part Seven

Agency and Employment   681

Part Eight

Business Organization and Regulation   767

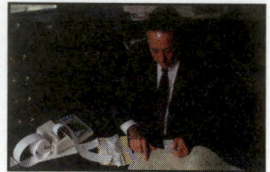

Part Nine
Emerging Trends and Issues   859

Part One

Ethics, Law, and the Judicial System

Chapter 1   Ethics

The Opening Case
The McNulty Memorandum

The document that came to be known as *The McNulty Memorandum* did not capture the attention of the public until it produced a heated conflict between the government and the corporate establishment. The memorandum, "Principles of Federal Prosecution of Business Organizations," dealt with certain problems that had surfaced in relation to the attorney–client privilege. However, the memo also included a section called, "Shielding Culpable Employees and Agents." Under this section, Deputy U.S. Attorney General Paul J. McNulty wrote that "a corporation's promise of support to culpable employees" would not be looked on favorably by the Department of Justice. Herein lies a serious legal and moral problem for business managers who find themselves under investigation by the Justice Department. The dilemma could be stated in the following way: "Should a corporate manager help an employee who has been accused of breaking the law by the Justice Department?" When a federal prosecutor has decided to pursue an indictment against an employee, that prosecutor has probably built a fairly substantial case against that employee. However, the court, not the prosecutor, determines a person's guilt or innocence. A prosecutor simply seeks an indictment by demonstrating that there is enough evidence of wrongdoing on the part of the accused to bring him or her to trial. The indictment, then, is not a determination of culpability and should never be treated as such. How should business managers treat employees who have been labeled "culpable" by the Justice Department? Should they support those employees under the rule that says everyone is innocent until proven guilty, or should they obey the Justice Department? As you read this chapter on ethics and social responsibility, ask yourself how you would deal with this problem. (See Paul J. McNulty, "Principles of Federal Prosecution of Business Organizations," *United States Department of Justice Memorandum*, 11; see also Richard Cooper, "Business Crime: McNulty Memorandum," *The National Law Journal,* March 5, 2007, p.13.)

Opening Case Questions

1. Was the Department of Justice justified in placing this warning in the McNulty Memo? Explain.

2. Would it be illegal for a business manager to disobey the McNulty Memo? Explain.

3. Would it be unethical for a business manager to disobey the McNulty Memo? Explain.

4. Would it be unethical for a business manager to fire a "culpable" employee? Explain.

5. What course of action should a business manager take in this case? Explain.

 Learning Objectives

1. Define law and morality.
2. Distinguish between natural law and positive law.
3. Explain ethical relativism.
4. Describe social contract theory.
5. Outline the steps in applying utilitarianism.
6. Define rational ethics.
7. Identify the ethical character traits reflected in role model ethics.
8. Outline the arguments supporting social responsibility.
9. Explore the need for law in our society.
10. Clarify how the law and ethics are usually in harmony with each other.

1-1 Defining the Law, Morality, and Ethics

In a perfect world, everyone would know what the law is and why the law is an important aspect of our lives. Similarly, in an ideal situation, everyone would know what the term "ethics" means and how it is different from the concept of morality. Of course, a quick glance at any daily newspaper or a brief look at the evening news will reveal that people hold widely diverse views on the difference between right and wrong. If this were not the case, if everyone thought exactly the same about right and wrong, there would have been no conflict over Saddam Hussein's refusal to cooperate with the United Nations, no dispute over the treatment of al-Qaeda and Taliban prisoners, and no disagreement over the removal of troops from Iraq. In fact, in a perfect world in which everyone held similar, if not identical, ethical values, there would have been no terrorist attack on 9/11 and no war in Iraq to begin with. Yet in each of these cases, and others like them, many people's various opinions clash not only on how to handle each situation but also on the ethical or moral nature of the actions themselves.

It is therefore no surprise that most legal textbooks and many treatises on ethics begin by defining these disciplines. This tradition stands in marked contrast to most other studies. Few physics textbooks pause to tell the reader what physics is. Fewer history books devote space to explaining the term history, and almost no math texts begin by defining math. However, that is as it should be. These disciplines and others like them are fixed in our minds as implacable fields of study. In history, for example, the fact that the Twin Towers of the World Trade Center were destroyed on September 11, 2001, is not open to debate. Nor is our understanding that such an event is historical fact. The same is true of the second law of thermodynamics in physics and the multiplication tables in mathematics. These facts are not debatable, except in the most esoteric way. (See Jeffrie G. Murphy and Jules L. Coleman, *The Philosophy of Law*. Boulder, CO: Westview Press, 1990, 6; John C. Calhoun, "A Disquisition on Government," in *Philosophy in America,* eds. Paul Russell Anderson and Max Harold Fisch. New York: Appleton-Century-Crofts, Inc., 1939, 356–357.)

LO1

The Law and Morality

Such is not the case with the law and morality. People *will* argue about whether the law is a form of civil management or a way to dictate individual behavior, whether it ought to be created by a national government or a regional state system, and whether it should change regularly or stay the same indefinitely. They will even argue about whether the rules made by the government demand absolute, unquestioned obedience or simply ask for occasional recognition as optional guiding principles. People will also argue about moral issues. They will argue about whether schools should censor student newspapers, whether capital punishment should be permitted, and whether waging a preventative war is morally correct. This is why we pause at the beginning of *Business Law with UCC Applications* to define the law and morality and to distinguish between ethics and morals, concepts that many of us usually do not think about on a daily basis.

The **law** consists of rules of conduct established by the government of a society to maintain harmony, stability, and justice. It accomplishes these objectives by defining the legal rights and duties of the people. The law also provides a way to protect the people by enforcing these rights and duties through the courts, the executive branch, and the legislature. The law is therefore a means of civil management. Certainly, the law usually cannot stop a person from doing wrong. However, the law can punish an individual who chooses to do that wrong, whatever it might be. The law then draws the line between conduct that is permissible and that which is not allowed, so people, at the very least, know that they can be punished if they choose to disobey the law.

In contrast, **morals** are values that govern a society's attitude toward right and wrong and toward good and evil. As a result, we ought to see morality as more fundamental than law. Therefore, morality ought to serve as a guide for those bodies within our society, such as the courts, the executive branch, the legislature, and the administrative agencies, that make, interpret, and enforce the law. Most of the time, these law-making, law-interpreting, and law-enforcing bodies will follow the belief that morality and legality ought to match up with each other. Indeed, there are even those philosophers of law who argue that morality is a necessary element of the law. They would say that you cannot have a philosophically valid law that is not grounded in morality.

Values and Ethics

So far we have defined **law** as a set of rules created by the government to establish a means of civil management that directs people to do what is right and avoid what is wrong. The purpose served by the law includes the creation of order, stability, and justice. The assumption is that if these purposes are met, right will be served and wrong defeated. Moreover, we have also defined **morals** as those fundamental values that tell us the difference between right and wrong in the first place. What we have not explained, however, is where those values come from. This is the job of ethics. **Ethics** is the attempt to develop a means of determining what these values ought to be and for formulating and applying rules that enforce those values.

Natural Law Theory

According to one system of legal thought, morality and the law are united in a common bond based on their intrinsic nature. This system of thought, which is generally known as **natural law**, sees law as originating from some objective, superior force that stands outside the everyday experience of most people. That superior force might be God, human nature, rational thought, or some other source of universal truth. Thus, according to natural law, there exists an unbreakable link joining morality to the law in a fundamental way. This link exists because a law must, in its most basic form, be moral. Otherwise, it is not lawful. A law with an immoral purpose is not a law at all. Instead it is an anomaly that does not fit into our concept of either law or the legal process. It is, of course, one thing to say that laws must be firmly grounded in morality and quite another to argue that legality and morality are always the same thing. There are, in fact, some laws that have no moral content whatsoever. Thus, a statute that requires a driver to have an operator's license has no intrinsic moral substance, though such a law is not immoral on its face either. The natural law theorist would say that a law must, at the very least, be morally neutral to have any integrity as a law. In a larger sense, it can also be argued that a law that says people must be licensed to drive, while not intrinsically moral, contributes to the orderly and stable functioning of society and is therefore moral because of its purpose and effect.

Positive Law Theory

Natural law is sometimes confused with positive law because both depend on an outside force for their understanding of law, morality, and human rights. The difference is that positive law says that the law comes from social institutions rather than from God, from human nature, or from human rationality. **Positive law**, then, is a legal theory that says that the law originates from an outside source that has emerged from within society. The process works something like this: The people of a society discover their rights as they live and work together. This discovery leads to commonly held rights that are described in a series of documents, such as the Magna Carta and the U.S. Constitution. Exactly why people discover rather than invent universal rights is not clear. One argument says that rights are intuitively understood to exist within the human character. So, when people write documents such as the Constitution, they include certain human rights such as the right to be treated fairly under the law. (See Alan Dershowitz, *Rights from Wrongs: A Secular Theory of the Origin of Rights,* New York: Perseus Books Group, 2004, 39-42.)

Some people say that human decency will ultimately triumph over human cruelty, giving rise to a just and moral society that will eventually abolish the worst sins of humanity. This brand of positive law is sometimes called the *Law of Peoples*. Not everyone agrees with this position, but such agreement is not necessary, so long as principles of decency and social justice can be found in certain universal documents such as the Bill of Rights in the United States Constitution or the United Nations Universal Declaration of Human Rights. Despite the differences between positive law and natural law, they hold one idea in common, namely, the belief that human values apply to all people at all times. Neither theory, however, tells us how to make ethical decision. For that reason, we now turn to the next topic, ethical decision making. (See John Rawls, *The Law of Peoples,* Cambridge, MA: Harvard University Press, 1999, 6-7.)

Ethical Decision Making

People make ethical decisions every day. However, how they make those decisions is not always clear. Some people say that they do not think about ethics but instead act instinctively when faced with a moral problem. Others say that they just do what they "believe" is right. Still others say that they follow the rules they learned in school, in their place of worship, or in their family setting. Some professions, businesses, and organizations develop guidelines, usually called rules of conduct or canons of professional responsibility. Such rules generally describe certain levels of behavior. Some behaviors are encouraged; others are discouraged. Punishments are often included in these guidelines.

While such rules are admirable, they are often so long and complex that they end up contradicting themselves. For example, Rule 2.1 of the ABA Model Code of Professional Conduct requires attorneys to "exercise independent professional judgment and render candid advice" to their clients. Moreover, the rule per-

Paul McNulty's refuted statement "that the White House played only a marginal role in the dismissals" of many U.S. attorneys in 2006 led to his resignation on July 26, 2007.

Opening Case Revisited, Part I

The McNulty Memorandum, Round 2

For a practical example of how these complicated guidelines sometimes contradict themselves, let's return to The Opening Case. Recall that the McNulty Memorandum tells business managers to abandon any employee who has been accused of breaking the law. Prosecutors, however, do not have the authority to determine an employee's guilt. That decision is up to the courts. Still, the McNulty Memorandum makes it clear that the manager has no choice. At this point, the manager's attorneys will find little help in the ethical code. Rule 8.4 tells them to avoid any conduct that might hinder the administration of justice. This implies that they had better do what the prosecutor says. Yet at the same time, Rule 2.1 encourages them to follow their moral conscience. This indicates that, rather than simply following the letter of the law, they ought to take a moral stand by defying the prosecutor. Clearly the professional rules, while helpful in the short run, cannot substitute for the development of an individual moral code. For this reason, we will now look at several ethical theories, each of which can help in the development of a personal code of conduct.

Did You Know?

The Greek word "ethos," which forms the root of the English word "ethics," means "character."

mits, and in fact encourages, attorneys to make legal decisions by using "moral, economic, social, and political factors." Yet at the same time, Rule 8.4 warns attorneys that they cannot "engage in conduct that is prejudicial to the administration of justice." What happens when a lawyer advises a client to break the law because it is the "morally correct" thing to do? Such advice simultaneously follows Rule 2.1 and violates Rule 8.4. Such contradictions, real or imagined, can cause confusion and will inevitably lead to unpredictable, uncertain, unreliable, and perhaps even unjust results. (See "Model Code of Professional Conduct." *American Bar Association*. Retrieved from <http://www. abanet.org> on April 10, 2007.)

Quick Quiz 1-1 True or False?

1. Natural law theory holds that there is no link between morality and law.   F

2. Law has nothing to do with civil management.   F

3. Ethical decisions are made in a variety of ways.   T

1-2 Ethical Theories

Throughout the history of philosophy, many scholars have offered techniques for determining those values that ought to guide all ethical decisions. Although these theories differ in their particulars, they all have one thing in common: Each theory is based on the assumption that people want to live ethical lives. If this were not the case, there would be no need to fashion these theories in the first place. Nevertheless, despite this common assumption, the theories differ greatly in their individual approaches to the problem of determining the nature of the values that underline ethical decision making.

Ethical Relativism

Ethical relativism says that there are no objective or absolute standards of right and wrong. Rather, the standards used to distinguish between right and wrong change from circumstance to circumstance and from person to person. Thus, ethical rules are relative; that is, the rules vary depending upon the actor, the circumstances, and countless other factors that may affect a person's ethical judgments. Because relativism emphasizes the highly individualized nature of ethical decision making, it is also called subjective ethics.

NO RIGHT OR WRONG

Ethical relativism is a very common position among Americans because the United States is a country of immigrants from a wide variety of cultures, many of which have different social values. Because many Americans want to respect these different cultures and their value systems, they often conclude that each culture is right within its own world, even when the values of those cultures clash with one another. Moreover, the United States was founded on a tradition that allows and even encourages a free exchange of ideas, feelings, and opinions on all subjects, including ethics.

Shortcomings of Ethical Relativism It should be instantly clear that ethical relativism cannot be reconciled with either natural law or positive law, because both of these two fundamental theories assume the existence of a universal standard of behavior. Natural law says that this universal standard originates on a superior plane of existence, perhaps with God or with human nature, while positive law says that it emerges from within certain documents such as the United Nations Universal Declaration of Human Rights or the Bill of Rights of the United States Constitution. In contrast, ethical relativism denies the existence of any universal standard of behavior. Thus, according to ethical relativism, no one can ever do, say, or think anything wrong. Moreover, no one can disagree with anyone just because another person holds a different view on the morality of an action. In fact, if we pursue ethical relativism to its logical end, neither natural law nor positive law can exist.

RELATIVISM NO EXISTENCE OF ANY UNIVERSAL STANDARD

Situational Ethics Still, certain aspects of relativism are appealing, including the notion that the ethical decisions of other individuals ought not to be judged without taking into consideration the special situation in which those individuals find themselves. This is why some people favor a variation of relativism that takes different situations into consideration but does not necessarily use those different situations to exonerate the actor completely. This theory, which is known as **situational ethics**, argues that each of us can judge a person's ethical decisions only by initially placing ourselves in the other person's situation. This technique allows us to be aware of the various factors that led to the other person's situation. Such an approach encourages people to look at others with tolerance and patience, an outlook that all of us would like to see practiced by those who might be inclined to judge our ethical decisions. However, it would be more satisfying if we agreed on a single ethical standard for making such moral judgments. Consequently, we must look elsewhere for a more consistent set of ethical values.

SITUATIONAL ETHICS SHOES

Social Contract Theory

Social contract theory holds that right and wrong are measured by the obligations imposed on each individual by an implied agreement among all individuals within a particular social system. At the most fundamental level, the social contract says that for

The Opening Case Revisited, Part II
The McNulty Memorandum, Round 3

If we apply these principles to the McNulty Memorandum, we can see that the document clearly violates the social contract. The social contract requires that everyone adhere to the law of the land. One law guarantees that all criminal defendants are presumed to be innocent. The rule is violated when employees are labeled "culpable" by the Department of Justice, without having their day in court. A rule that says people are to be presumed innocent might limit the freedom of the prosecutor to lock people up, but it helps ensure that people will be judged in court, not by overenthusiastic prosecutors. Rules like this help us feel secure in our own interactions and allow us to go about our daily activities without fear of retaliation by those in power.

people to live together harmoniously, they must give up certain freedoms to receive certain protections in return. Thus, all individuals give up the freedom to do as they please and in return receive a guarantee that other individuals will curb their behavior, thus protecting everyone else in that society from random and indiscriminate actions. The existence of the implied social contract permits us to live together in peace and harmony. For example, one rule that emerges from the social contract is that people should never make unsupported judgments about one another but should instead always investigate the facts in an effort to uncover the truth about the character of a person or the nature of a situation. Such a rule prevents people from avoiding one another, cheating one another, or, even worse, attacking one another simply because of the way another person looks, speaks, or acts.

Naturally, for the social contract to work, most people must adhere to its rules, and those who do not must be punished. If this were not the case, then the social contract would disintegrate, and the society would return to a "state of nature" in which people must fend for themselves. As is true of ethical relativism, there are problems with social contract theory. One problem is that social contract theory is descriptive rather than prescriptive. A **descriptive theory** simply describes the values at work within a social system, rather than explaining how the values originated in the first place. In contrast, a **prescriptive theory** explains how to come up with the values that permit a society to run smoothly. Of course, not everyone believes that social contract theory is descriptive only. Some ethical theorists argue that social contract ethics is a prescriptive theory because it places a value on the obligation itself. Thus, the benefits that people receive by knowing others will not judge them creates the obligation not to judge anyone else. Social contract ethics therefore concentrates on each individual's obligation to everyone else and on the belief that, as long as these obligations are met, social stability will be preserved.

Utilitarianism

Utilitarianism is an ethical theory that says that the morality of an action is determined by its ultimate effects. The more good that results, the more ethical is the action. Conversely, the more bad that results, the less ethical is the action. Unlike ethical relativism, which is constantly shifting, utilitarianism seeks only one stable goal: the greatest good for the greatest number. Determining the greatest good for the greatest number, however, is not as simple as it sounds. For one thing, we must resist the temptation to transform the greatest good for the greatest number principle into the "greatest good for me" principle. One way to avoid mistakes that can result from an improper application of utilitarianism is to follow these steps:

1. The action to be evaluated should be stated in unemotional, general terms. For example, "stealing another person's property" is emotional language; "confiscating property for one's own use" is somewhat less emotional.

2. Every person or class of people that will be affected by the action must be identified.

3. Good and bad consequences in the relation to those people affected must be considered.

4. All alternatives to the action stated in step 1 must be considered.

5. Once step 4 has been carried out, a conclusion must be reached. Whichever alternative creates the greatest good for the greatest number of people affected by the action is the one that ought to be taken.

Despite the systematic approach of the utilitarian theory, many people are uncomfortable with it. One questionable aspect of utilitarianism is that, in business at least, it can be confused with utility thinking. **Utility thinking**, which is also referred to as **cost-benefit thinking**, looks only at corporate benefits and problems rather than the benefits and problems that will result for others outside the boardroom.

EXAMPLE 1-1:   The Brocade Backdating Case

The Justice Department brought criminal charges against the CEO of Brocade Communications, Inc., for failing to record a series of backdating transactions. *Backdating* is a process that allows a corporate officer to issue stock options to employees based on the value of the stock at an earlier date when the stock was selling at a lower price. The result is an instantaneous gain for the employees. The practice of backdating is legal, but hiding the backdated transactions to avoid the cost involved in those transactions is illegal. Nevertheless, the backdating engineered by the CEO in this case hurt no one. In fact, the practice resulted in a gain for those employees who exercised their options. Moreover, due to the work of the CEO, the value of Brocade stock had increased by 17 percent. If we apply utilitarian principles here, it would seem that the CEO's actions produced the greatest good for the greatest number of people, even though technically speaking, the failure to record the backdating was illegal. After all, the company's stock rose in value, and the employees and shareholders were quite pleased with the entire deal. However, a closer look reveals that the focus of the CEO's decision was on maximizing profits, not on any long-term effects outside of the company. This may be effective utility thinking, but it is not pure utilitarianism. Pure utilitarianism would demand that the CEO consider other constituencies, such as the public at large, the financial community, and other CEOs who might engage in the same illegal conduct. Covering up the backdated transactions hurt the entire process, thus threatening a business practice that requires truthfulness for its continued success. (See Peter Burrows, "A Smaller Options Scandal?" *BusinessWeek*, March 5, 2007, 28-31.)

Talking Points

Read the following quotation on the nature of morality. As you read the quotation and reflect on the ideas that the author presents, ask yourself if the position represents your own point of view. Be prepared to defend your ideas with specific, well-drawn arguments. If you are not comfortable with these concepts, supply your own, but make sure to explain your position with a thoughtful and thorough defense.

From the American founding until World War II, there was a widespread belief in this country that there is a moral order in the universe that makes claims on us. This belief was not unique to Americans. It was shared by Europeans since the very beginning of Western civilization, and it is held even today by all the traditional cultures of the world. The basic notion is that morality is external to us and is binding on us. In the past, Americans and Europeans, being for the most part Christian, might disagree with Hindus and Muslims about the exact source of this moral order, its precise content, or how a society should convert its moral beliefs into legal and social practice. But there was little doubt across the civilizations of the world about the existence of such an order. Moreover, the laws and social norms typically reflected this moral consensus. During the first half of the twentieth century, the moral order generated some clear American social norms. . . . The point is not that everyone lived up to the dictates of the moral code, but that it supplied a standard, accepted virtually throughout society, for how one should act.

—Dinesh D'Souza, *The Enemy at Home* (New York: Doubleday, 2007), 19.

Thus, in *The Brocade Backdating Case,* the cover-up might be more cost effective for the employees and for other investors, but it undermines the long-term stability of the entire system. If the practice continued, it might, for example, prompt more corporations to cover up their backdating transactions. Eventually, what appears to be a small transgression that hurts no one will create a culture of deceit that makes it difficult for business-people to trust anyone or have any faith in the records kept by corporations. Certainly, not all utilitarian thinkers are prone to this type of short-sighted, self-serving analysis. Many are perfectly capable of considering not only all the people who might be affected by their actions but also the consequences that flow from those actions. Nevertheless, because utilitarian thinkers can sometimes be led astray by utility thinking, it is wise for us to look at two more ethical theories.

Rational Ethics

Rational ethics replaces the shifting standards of relativism, the prescriptive approach of social contract theory, and the result-oriented standard of utilitarianism with a system that is objective, logical, and relatively consistent. **Rational ethics** is a philosophical theory that says ethical values can be determined by a proper application of human reason. The theory assumes that, because all human beings are rational, all human beings will have the same ethical values. Therefore, rational ethics ought to establish universal rules of behavior that apply to all people at all times. For this reason, rational ethics is often referred to as *objective ethics*. Rational ethics begins with the premise that only human beings are morally responsible for their actions. Animals, plants, and inanimate objects may cause injury or harm, but they are never held morally responsible because they are incapable of making rational decisions. Therefore, we say that they are *amoral*. The only thing that separates moral beings from those that are amoral is the rationality of the moral beings.

The Golden Rule and Rational Ethics As rational beings, people think for themselves and, in doing so, recognize their own self-worth as individuals. Along with self-worth comes a belief in certain rights. These rights include the right to life, the right to be free from injury, the right to be treated fairly, the right to self-determination, and so on. Rational beings recognize that they do not want to be killed or cheated. They do not want their freedom taken away without just cause and due process. Because they believe in their own rights, they also recognize that all people share these same rights. Thus, each individual has a duty to refrain from violating the rights of all other human beings.

The Logical Premise of Rational Ethics As rational beings, people also realize that it is logical to establish rules that support the continued existence of society. A rule that destroys a society that tries to follow it would be an illogical rule. Consider the following rule: "False promises are morally correct as long as they are made to gain some advantage." A person who adheres to rational ethics would instantly recognize that such a rule is both illogical and immoral. If everyone in a society were to adopt such a rule, no one could make a promise, and no one would accept a promise, even if it were made. A society without promises would be a society without commerce, diplomacy, credit cards, religion, pizza deliveries, marriage, airline schedules, democracy, and baseball, all of which require promises in one way or another. Such a society would be illogical and therefore immoral.

EXAMPLE 1-2:   The Brocade Backdating Case
                   Reconsidered

Let's return momentarily to *The Brocade Case*. Recall that the CEO of Brocade altered the corporate records to hide certain backdating transactions, thus giving the employees the benefits of backdating without adding any expenses to the corporate books. The utility thinker argued that, though hiding the transactions was illegal, it hurt no one and benefited the employees to such an extent that it was ethically harmless. Rational ethics leads to a different conclusion. The Golden Rule of rational ethics states, "Act so that you treat others as you believe you would want to be treated. Be sure to respect others as ends in themselves, not as a means to an end." In this case, the CEO of Brocade should have asked, "Do I want other business executives to lie to me in the same way that I have lied to others?" Hopefully, most of us would have answered "no" to this question. The other question required by rational ethics asks, "Can a society that follows such a rule survive?" In other words, in this case, "Can a society that encourages lying survive?" If some people lie to gain financial advantage, as was done in *The Brocade Case,* soon most people will lie to make money. Eventually the concept of truthfulness disappears entirely. It is eroded to such an extent that no one trusts anyone in any transaction, even the simplest and most basic of transactions. For this reason, lying about backdating transactions is harmful because it promotes a culture of deceit that threatens the credibility of the business person who lies, the company that he or she lies to protect, and, eventually, the entire business environment.

Role Model Ethics

Role model ethics is a philosophical theory that encourages people to pattern their behavior after admirable individuals whose activities provide examples of the proper way to act. One advantage of the role model theory is that it provides concrete examples of how to behave rather than an abstract system for determining principles of behavior. A downside

Table 1-1	Ethical Characteristics
Trait	**Definition**
Honesty	Honesty allows a person to be open and truthful with other people.
Compassion	Compassion allows a person to care for others.
Fairness	Fairness allows a person to treat other people with justice and equality.
Integrity	Integrity allows a person to do what is right regardless of personal consequences.

to role model ethics is that it is still necessary to derive consistent characteristics from those role models. Sometimes extracting character traits from individual lives is difficult, contradictory, and controversial. Nevertheless, in most cases, the following ethical character traits can be distilled from these models: honesty, compassion, integrity, and fairness. Table 1-1 provides an overview of these character traits.

Honesty   The character trait of **honesty** means that a person is always open and truthful in his or her dealings with other people. Being honest is not always the easiest action to take in every situation. Yet most of us, if given the choice, would prefer to deal with an honest person rather than a dishonest one. To characterize someone as an honest person is the highest of compliments. After all, it's no accident that Abraham Lincoln was nicknamed "Honest Abe." Also encompassed by honesty is the requirement that people be faithful to their word. Thus, an honest person is not only one who tells the truth but also one who can be trusted to do what he or she has promised to do. Possessing an honest character and being truthful, however, are not always the same thing. A person can be truthful without being honest.

EXAMPLE 1-3:   Honesty and the "Truthfulness" Loophole

Velma Hite has a copy of an important deed locked in her safe deposit box at the First National Bank of Gotham City. When Fred Henry asks her if she has the deed, she tells him that she does not. Strictly speaking, she is being truthful because the deed is not in her immediate possession. Yet because the deed is in her safe deposit box and therefore under her control and because she could produce it for Henry if she wished, she is not being honest with him.

Compassion   The second ethical character trait is compassion. **Compassion** means that people should always act with the intent of doing good to one another. Another way of saying this is to note that people should always attempt to be kind to one another. Moreover, the trait of compassion means that people should respect other individuals and their right to make their own decisions regarding what is best for them. Individuals who have compassion would also try to preserve individual freedom and liberty. The ability to be understanding of other people's shortcomings and to be forgiving when they make mistakes would also be characteristics of the compassionate individual. Albert Schweitzer and Mother Teresa are often held up as models of compassion. This is because they both dedicated their lives to helping those in need.

EXAMPLE 1-4:   On-the-Job Compassion

Acting with compassion often requires seeing things from another person's point of view. Harriet Farmer, the director of the Research and Development Department at Lewis, Inc., has had a lot of trouble recently with Yale Zimmerman, one of her lab assistants, who has had an impeccable work record for years. But Zimmerman now is consistently late for work, often leaves early, and frequently takes long, unwarranted breaks. Farmer clearly has grounds for firing Zimmerman. Instead, she takes the time to discuss the situation with him. As a result, she discovers that Zimmerman's sister is very ill and that Zimmerman is the only one who can care for her. To help Zimmerman, Farmer arranges some flex-time scheduling to allow Zimmerman the time that he needs to care for his sister. By exercising compassion, Farmer has helped another person and has saved a valuable employee for the company.

Integrity   The third ethical character trait is integrity. A person with **integrity** has the courage to do what is right regardless of personal consequences. People with integrity may have to stand up for their convictions against the majority of the people. They may find themselves at great personal risk and may often suffer great personal loss. A person with integrity is often said to be a person with a high sense of duty to do what is right and to avoid doing what is wrong. At the very least, this would mean the duty not to violate the rights of all other people, regardless of the circumstances or the consequences. Gandhi had been a relatively well-to-do attorney when, because of his personal integrity and his deep sense of duty, he took up the cause of freedom and fought for the people of India. His unwavering dedication to the principle of nonviolent protest demonstrates his integrity.

EXAMPLE 1-5:   The Delahunty Controversy: Integrity in Action

To act with integrity, a person may be forced to place himself or herself in an unpopular position. When officials at the University of Minnesota Law School hired Robert Delahunty, they unwittingly touched off a firestorm of opposition that forced them to face questions of personal integrity. The controversy surrounding Delahunty emerged when several students and faculty members protested Delahunty's hiring because he had coauthored a memo written to President Bush that argued international conventions and federal law did not protect al Qaeda and Taliban prisoners being held by U.S. authorities. Significantly, there were no allegations of wrongdoing by Delahunty, nor any suggestion that he was not a competent teacher. The protest was based solely on the fact that certain faculty members and students disagreed with the political position that Delahunty had adopted in the memo. Fortunately, university officials stood by their decision despite its enormous unpopularity. The officials refused to be intimidated by the extreme pressure placed on them by the students and the faculty. This clearly demonstrated integrity. (See Tresa Baldas, "Law Professor's Hiring Sparks Uproar," *The National Law Journal,* December 11, 2006, 6.)

Fairness   The final ethical character trait is fairness. A fair person is one who treats people with justice and equality. A person who is fair minded can also be trusted to deal evenhandedly not only with friends and family but also with his or her enemies. Because everyone wants to be treated fairly, it stands to reason that they would admire a person who has the ability to exercise fairness. That is one reason why Martin Luther King Jr. is admired by millions of people. His campaign against segregation was, in its most basic form, a demand for the fair treatment of everyone, not just minorities.

Fairness is, perhaps, the most difficult of the character traits to follow because, unlike honesty, compassion, and integrity, which are individual characteristics, fairness involves the activities of an entire society. Thus, while it is important for each individual to be fair in his or her own personal dealings with others, it is also necessary for society at large to be fair to all people. Sometimes it is difficult for people to grasp the fundamental importance of developing a fair and equitable social system. To counteract this problem, John Rawls, a prominent legal philosopher, in his book *The Law of Peoples,* provides three key reasons for promoting social justice. Rawls notes that we should promote fairness to (1) reduce the unequal distribution of wealth, thus diminishing the difficulties and the distress associated with poverty; (2) prevent those people who are among the poorest in our society from being treated as second-class citizens; and (3) make certain that the political process is open to everyone. (See John Rawls, *The Law of Peoples,* Cambridge: Harvard University Press, 1999, 114-115.)

Quick Quiz 1-2 True or False?

1. Utilitarianism focuses on the consequences of an action.   T

2. Rational ethics is a form of ethical relativism.   F

3. A fair person is one who treats people with justice and equality.   T

1-3 Social Responsibility in the Business Sector

So far our study of ethics has focused on individuals. This is natural because ultimately all ethical decisions, even those that drive governmental regulations and corporate policies, are made by individuals. However, the decisions made by individuals affect the policies and procedures carried out by institutions that have the power to affect many parts of our social structure. Aside from the government, which has an enormous amount of power and which we will examine later, corporations carry a great deal of influence over the economy, the community, and the people. There are those who say that a corporation has no social responsibility beyond making a profit for its shareholders. This is, in fact, the traditional view of corporate responsibility. It is a view that has remained so ingrained in our system that, until recently, it was the only view built into statutory and common law. Recently, however, voices have been raised arguing that corporations have a high degree of social responsibility to those people affected by their decisions.

The Traditional Corporate Culture

Although all businesses affect the economy and the community, the greatest force in the American industrial state is the corporation, in general, and the multinational corporation,

Did You Know?

The Koran states that the equality of all humanity serves as the basic foundation for all human rights.

in particular. The reality of corporate power is revealed by the fact that philosophers on both ends of the political spectrum can point to the corporation as a guiding force in modern civilization. For instance, in his treatise, *Individualism Old and New,* the *pragmatic* American philosopher, John Dewey, notes, "The United States has steadily moved from an earlier pioneer individualism to a condition of corporate dominance." Similarly, the *theoretical* philosopher, Herbert Marcuse, once remarked that no one, not even the former enemies of capitalism, can escape the influence of corporate power. In fact, Marcuse goes so far as to say that in the modern global marketplace, "the socialist and communist systems are linked with capitalism." (See John Dewey, *Individualism: Old and New*. New York: Capricorn Books, 1962; Herbert Marcuse, *Five Lectures: Psychoanalysis, Politics, and Utopia,* trans. Jeremy J. Shapiro and Shierry M. Weber, Boston: Beacon Press, 1970.)

One reason that corporations have such power is that they are legal persons, created under the authority of federal and state statutes. This status as a "legal person" gives the corporation certain rights and abilities that other business entities do not always have. For instance, as legal persons they are accorded certain constitutional rights, such as the right not to be deprived of property without due process of law. They can also own property in their own name and have lawsuits filed to protect them or vindicate their rights. There are, of course, many types of corporations. Our focus will be on those corporations that are privately run to make a profit for their owners, who are referred to as shareholders. The traditional view says that privately owned corporations are created solely to make a profit for their shareholders. Consequently, the foremost job of any manager is to maximize those profits. In fact, under the traditional rule of shareholder dominance, the managers of a corporation could be held liable in a court of law for making decisions that do not guarantee that the shareholders would receive a maximum return on their investment.

EXAMPLE 1-6:   Corporate Culture and Utility Thinking

When Lynn Cummings discovered that the managers of a corporation in which she owned stock had made a decision that had caused shareholders to lose money in a merger plan, she sued, seeking a reversal of the merger or a suitable payment from the managers that would make up for her losses. Basically, Cummings second-guessed the way that the managers had made their decision, arguing that they had not properly researched the merger and had not placed the shareholders' profits first. The managers argued that they had made their decision based on the long-term benefits of the merger to everyone involved, including the local community and the economy of the nation and state. The court sided with Cummings, noting that the job of the managers was to look out for the shareholders' profits, not the long-term benefits to the community or the economy.

As defined previously, the type of thinking promoted by the court in Example 1-6 is referred to as utility thinking or cost-benefit thinking. Using utility thinking, a corporate manager simply looks at the action he or she is about to take and asks whether the benefit to the shareholders will outweigh the cost to the corporation. If the shareholders' benefits offset corporate costs, then the action is taken. If not, the action is abandoned. Proponents of this position justify cost-benefit thinking in three ways. First, the profits to the shareholders must always come first. Second, it would be unfair to divert funds that belong to the shareholders to activities that do not directly benefit the shareholders. Third, a corporation's managers are accountable to the shareholders and to no one else. The problem with utility thinking is that it often results in actions that are clearly unethical and potentially illegal.

EXAMPLE 1-7:   Maximum Corporate Irresponsibility

The managers of Taylor-Beechaum Pharmaceuticals, Inc., received a report that the corporation's latest weight loss drug, biomiocin, was having unpredicted side effects that caused problems for several people. The managers of Taylor-Beechaum ordered the accounting department to determine how much it would cost to recall all the biomiocin now on the market, suspend manufacturing, and conduct more tests on the drug's safety. The accountants reported that it would be more cost effective to simply leave the drug on the market and pay off anyone who might be injured and who might bring a lawsuit against Taylor-Beechaum. Keeping the drug on the shelves will allow the corporation to continue to pay dividends to the shareholders. In contrast, if the drug were taken off of the market, the payment of dividends would be suspended pending the outcome of the new testing program. Consequently, the corporate managers decided to leave biomiocin on the shelves. This decision not only violated virtually every ethical standard that we've studied thus far (except ethical relativism) but also evaded the corporation's social responsibility to consumers, to the government, to the shareholders, and to the public at large.

Reasons for Social Responsibility

The fact that corporate officers and directors have made such irresponsible decisions should not be surprising. Nor should it be surprising that, until recently, the law supported such decisions. The idea that a corporation is a legal person did not spring full grown into the law when the first corporations were formed. In fact, it took jurists quite some time to see that corporations were neither partnerships nor miniature democratic states but instead vehicles for making a profit. Once jurists recognized the unique position that corporations hold within the hierarchy of business associations, however, they easily granted certain privileges to corporate entities. Despite this, as the jurists entered the modern age, they began to see that there were a number of reasons that corporations, like Taylor-Beechaum in Example 1-7, should accept social responsibility for their actions. Some of these reasons are built on the legal advantages granted to corporations. Others are based on the idea that many corporations are powerful forces in their communities. Still others focus on the self-interest of the corporation. Whatever the case, these arguments are being voiced more loudly and with more conviction with each passing fiscal year.

Legal Advantages Granted to the Corporation
The first argument supporting corporate social responsibility is based on the premise that corporations are granted certain rights as a result of the incorporation process. For example, the corporate form offers limited liability to those who share in its ownership. This means that the personal assets of the corporate owners cannot be taken if the corporation defaults on a contract or commits a tort or a crime. In addition, under provisions of most incorporation statutes, a

corporation is considered an artificially created person. This means that, under provisions of the U.S. Constitution and those of most state constitutions, a corporation, like a natural person, cannot be deprived of life, liberty, or property without due process of law. This also means that a corporation can own property in its own name and bring a lawsuit to vindicate its rights. Because corporations have all these rights, they owe an obligation to the public and to the community at large to act responsibly. In practical terms, this means that the decisions of corporate managers must not be narrowly focused on the profits of the shareholders.

EXAMPLE 1-8:   The Andrean-Harrison Donation

As part of a downsizing campaign, the Andrean-Harrison Corporation was about to close down operations in Tulsa. The company owned an office building and a small laboratory on the outskirts of Tulsa that are adjacent to 30 acres of undeveloped land. The corporation had a chance to sell the land at a price that would have made a profit for the shareholders of the company. Rather than take advantage of this offer, Andrean-Harrison decided to donate the land to the city. The fact that the corporation was a legal person meant that it owned the land and could donate it to the city. Corporate officials acted responsibly in this case, taking advantage of the corporation's right to own land in its own name.

The Impact of Corporate Decision Making A second reason for demanding social responsibility from corporations is that corporate decision making clearly has an impact on more people than just the shareholders and the managers. Those who support corporate social responsibility often argue that many corporate decisions, such as the decision to open or close a factory, will affect everyone in the local community. Those affected by such decisions include suppliers, consumers, employees, support businesses, and community members. Consequently, the argument goes, all of these groups should be taken into consideration when corporate managers make decisions. Some individuals who support this form of extreme corporate social responsibility would like to see representatives from the employees' union, from consumer protection groups, from environmental protection groups, and from the local chamber of commerce on every corporation's board of directors. Others, however, argue that because corporate decisions affect more individuals and groups than just the shareholders and managers, those decisions should be made by an impartial group of corporate outsiders. Often the corporate outsiders named are governmental officials.

EXAMPLE 1-9:   Corporate Cooperation and Compromise

When the directors of Igar International Corporation were working on plans to diversify their operation, they considered opening a chemical plant in Santa Ana. Before making the decision, they sent a team of experts to Santa Ana to investigate the possibility of establishing an operation just within the city limits. Although the city officials promised Igar a tax abatement plan and agreed to donate several acres of land to the corporation, citizens' groups were against the plant because of environmental and health concerns. The corporation could have simply found a more receptive or, perhaps, a less vocal city in which to locate. However, instead of simply discarding their consideration of Santa Ana, they worked with the citizens' groups to meet their concerns. Ultimately the two sides agreed on modifications to the project and moved forward. The willingness of the company to discuss the proposed changes in its operation reflected an understanding of the corporation's social responsibility based on the fact that corporate decisions have a far-ranging impact.

Enlightened Corporate Self-Interest   Finally, there are those who argue, rather convincingly, that accepting social responsibility is actually in the long-term best interests of the corporation. This argument, which is generally referred to as enlightened self-interest, is based on the notion that socially responsible corporations benefit by creating goodwill for themselves, thus motivating consumers to purchase their products, investors to buy their stock, and lawmakers to grant them further legal advantages. In addition, the corporation benefits because the community at large gains from such decisions. If the community at large is healthy, the argument goes, then the corporation that relies on that community will be healthy also.

EXAMPLE 1-10:   Failed Negotiations Lead to Problems

The president of Pilder and Wesselkamper International, Inc., decided to suspend negotiations with union representatives when he learned that they were about to demand a salary increase that he believed was untenable given the corporation's financial health, or lack thereof. The union threatened to file a complaint with the National Labor Relations Board, charging that the president and his staff were not cooperating with the collective bargaining process. The union also indicated that it was considering publishing an advertisement in *The New York Times* denouncing the president's decision and eventually would authorize a strike. The president continued to resist further negotiations and simply shut down operations. Eventually, the company filed for bankruptcy and dissolved its operation. Neither of the parties involved in this case opted to pursue a course of enlightened self-interest, which resulted in the worst possible conclusion for all those involved.

Efforts to Promote Social Responsibility

As noted previously, the traditional view of a corporation says that its primary role is to make a profit for its shareholders. This means that corporate managers are obligated to make decisions that maximize those profits. Moreover, under the traditional role of corporate managers, those managers could be sued for making a decision that hurt the corporation's profits and thereby reduced or eliminated dividends. However, recent amendments to many corporate statutes have been designed to encourage corporate managers to make broader-based decisions. Thus, some statutes now permit managers to consider factors beyond profit in making corporate decisions. These factors include the economic well-being of the nation, the state, and the local community; the interests of employees, consumers, and suppliers; and the betterment of the environment, the economy, and the overall social structure. These statutes generally hold managers immune from shareholder lawsuits, which claim that the managers did not put the shareholders' profits first.

Business Law in the News
Analyze This

The Psychology of the Deal

I work in the investment business and want to understand more about the psychology of making deals. I notice that even seasoned negotiators, who have a knack for figuring out what makes a person tick, sometimes get it wrong. Can someone with psychological training analyze a target at a distance to provide an edge in talks?

—*A. G. Newmyer III*
Palm Beach Gardens, Fla.

The answer, in my view, is yes. My colleagues and I have been helping clients develop psychological profiles of executives involved in high-stakes mergers-and-acquisitions talks and other negotiations for many years. We find that having an understanding of the mind of the person sitting across the table can make all the difference.

Business talks are essentially psychological processes. Nobody ever says yes to the first offer. Why? Not just because it's bad business but because to do so would show weakness and submission, intolerable feelings for most people. When seasoned negotiators "get it wrong," it's often because they've miscalculated the other party's emotional attachment to what they're giving up, whether that's something they own or money itself. Or they assume their approach will lower the other party's resistance to saying yes, when in fact it increases it.

Applying dynamic insights, provided at a distance by a trained clinician, can unlock even the thorniest of business interactions. An analogous situation is that of a patient who describes his wife to his psychoanalyst. The analyst may never meet the wife, but as the analyst speaks with the husband, they jointly develop an understanding of what makes the wife tick, and this, in turn, can help the husband relate to her better.

Now substitute CEO A for the husband and CEO B (the potential acquiree) for the wife. CEO A has various interactions with CEO B in meetings, at industry events, on the golf course, or through phone and e-mail contact. In discussing those interactions with me, we can figure out how CEO A can better size up CEO B. The psychological portrait that emerges, while inevitably imperfect, is often good enough to make a difference in negotiations.

Your question touches on an interesting controversy: Psychiatrists got into trouble when one of them made a damning diagnosis from afar of Barry Goldwater during the 1964 Presidential race, deeming him unfit for office because of what was considered his paranoid behavior. The subsequent backlash caused the pendulum to swing too far in the other direction, with shrinks avoiding such bold pronouncements ever since.

That's too bad. A psychoanalytic assessment, even of someone you've never met, has a positive role to play not just in personal lives, but also in business dealings and even in helping to choose a president.

Questions for Analysis

1. From the point of view of utility thinking, can the hiring of a profiler like the one described in this article be justified? Explain. From a utilitarian perspective, is it ethical for a businessperson to hire a psychologist to produce a psychological profile of a business competitor? Explain.

2. Would a person who believes in rational ethics approve of the plan to produce a "diagnosis from afar" of a business competitor? Why or why not?

3. What ethical trait or traits might have been violated by CEO A when he hired a psychoanalyst to produce a long-distance diagnosis of CEO B? Explain.

4. Has CEO A broken any part of the social contract by commissioning a long-distance diagnosis of CEO B? Explain.

5. Suppose that CEO A is actually an agent of the Department of Justice. Would it be ethical under any theory other than ethical relativism (which can excuse any bad behavior) for a government agent to commission a psychological profile of a businessperson? Explain.

Source: Kerry J. Sulkowicz, M.D. "Analyze This: The Psychology of the Deal," *BusinessWeek,* April 9, 2007, 14.

EXAMPLE 1-11:   Corporate Trade-Offs Mean Corporate Survival

The directors of Chindi-Mowry Enterprises, Inc., were under fire because of a take-over bid against Chindi-Mowry engineered by an alien corporation known as Rixensart Industries. To stave off the assault, the directors invited a friendly bid from Sandoff, Inc., a firm that promised not to dismantle Chindi-Mowry after the deal was entered. The final amount of the offer from Sandoff was less than that offered by Rixensart, and so those shareholders who sold their stock received less on the sale to Sandoff than they would have received had the directors endorsed the Rixensart plan. However, in making their decision, the directors were persuaded that the deal offered by Sandoff would save jobs, help the community, boost the national and state economy, and eventually result in a long-term gain for the corporation and for those shareholders who remained with the company.

Quick Quiz 1-3 True or False?

1.   Cost-benefit thinking will always result in ethical decisions.   F

2.   Corporations are not allowed to own property.   F

3.   Some statutes allow corporate managers to consider factors beyond share-holder profits in making business decisions.   T

1-4 The Relationship Between Law and Ethics

Thus far, we have seen that ethics and morals can be distinguished from one another. We have also looked at the ethical character traits of honesty, fairness, compassion, and integrity. We have defined values, examined the causes of unethical conduct, and determined how to develop an ethical lifestyle. Some people determine an ethical lifestyle as simply doing what is legal. Such a course of action may often result in ethical conduct. However, that is not always the case. Even when most people know that a particular type of conduct is illegal, that does not prevent some people from engaging in that conduct. For example, everyone knows that killing is illegal. Yet that knowledge does not stop the national murder rate from remaining disturbingly high. Similarly, everyone knows that child abuse, spousal abuse, and elder abuse are immoral, but that consensus has not eliminated the problem of abuse from our society.

The Need for Law in Our Society

LO9

The law is needed because, though people know better, they do not always follow ethical principles. As noted previously, the law consists of rules of conduct established by the government of a society to maintain harmony, stability, and justice in that society. It does so by defining the legal rights and duties of the people. It also provides a way to protect the people by enforcing these rights and duties through the courts and the legislature. Ethical principles can tell us what is right, but they cannot stop us from doing that which is wrong.

The law also cannot stop us from doing wrong. However, the law can punish us if we choose to do wrong. The law draws the line between permissible and impermissible conduct, so that people, at the very least, are punished if they hurt or cheat one another or threaten society as a whole.

Of course the law also has other functions. For instance, the law serves as the ultimate rule maker, providing a sense of stability and harmony when order breaks down in any other area of society, from our schools and universities to the family itself. This is why each state has established a system of juvenile courts and a network of domestic relations courts to handle such disputes when they arise. The law also promotes economic growth by granting tax abatements, by rezoning certain urban areas for the establishment of stores and businesses, and by exercising the power of *eminent domain* to confiscate privately owned land for community purposes. In addition, the law guards property rights by enforcing contracts and other similar agreements and providing a forum for tort victims and their families. The law also protects the environment by regulating those industries that might overdevelop the land and those that dump waste materials and other pollutants on to the land and into the waterways. Finally, as noted, the law is responsible for advancing social justice and guaranteeing personal freedom by granting all people due process and equal protection and providing a system by which legitimate grievances can be resolved in an orderly and timely fashion.

Is the law perfect? Does the law always succeed in its goals and objectives? Certainly not. As is true of all institutions, the law is flawed. It is filled with loopholes, foolishness, red tape, and, at times, absolute idiocy, much of which is unintentional and most of which could be avoided if people just take the time to think coolly and rationally. For example, it makes very little sense for Congress to pass legislation to punish flag burners when it is quite clear that the Supreme Court will declare that legislation unconstitutional. Or, in a similar vein, it makes no sense for Congress to pass unfunded mandates that force the state governments to raise money to perform tasks that the federal government should have taken care of in the first place. Yet this type of thing happens all of the time. Nevertheless, having an imperfect but functioning legal system is always preferable to the alternative—anarchy and all the unpleasantness that would surround a descent into chaos.

Ethical and Legal Harmony

In a utopian society, ethics and the law would always coincide. Our society is not perfect however, and it is not likely to become perfect in the foreseeable future. Therefore, our society needs the law and the legal system to give it structure, harmony, predictability, and justice. However, ethical considerations should always form the foundation of law and the legal system. If the law is not founded on ethics, it will rarely succeed in reaching its objectives. Ethics can lead the way in difficult situations or in areas of the social structure into which the law has yet to venture.

Quick Quiz 1-4 True or False?

1. The law cannot stop us from doing wrong, but it can punish us if we choose to do wrong.   T

2. In a perfect society, ethics and law would always coincide.   T

3. The law and the legal system need not be founded on ethical considerations.   F

Summary

1.1 The law consists of rules of conduct established by the government of a society to maintain harmony, stability, and justice. Morals involve the values that govern a society's attitude toward right and wrong. Ethics, in contrast, attempt to develop a means for determining what those values ought to be and for formulating and applying rules in line with those values.

1.2 Ethical relativism holds that there are no fixed or stable standards of right and wrong. Social contract theory holds that right and wrong are measured by the obligations imposed on each individual by an implied social agreement. Utilitarianism determines right and wrong by looking at the consequences of a person's actions. According to rational ethics, actions are either right or wrong, regardless of the circumstances and regardless of the consequences. Role model theory encourages people to pattern their behavior after individuals whose activities provide a good example of how to act.

1.3 Corporations owe society a level of responsibility because the government has granted certain legal advantages to corporations. Another reason for expecting socially responsible decisions from corporate executives is that corporations have a great deal of power in the economic structure, and with power comes responsibility. Finally, corporations should act responsibly because it is in their own best interest to do so.

1.4 In a perfect society, ethics and the law would always coincide. Our society is not perfect and is not likely to become so in the foreseeable future. Therefore, our society needs the law and the legal system to give it structure, harmony, predictability, and justice.

Key Terms

compassion, 12
cost-benefit thinking, 9
descriptive theory, 8
ethical relativism, 7
ethics, 4
fairness, 14
honesty, 12

integrity, 13
law, 4
morals, 4
natural law theory, 4
positive law theory, 5
prescriptive theory, 8
rational ethics, 10

role model ethics, 11
situational ethics, 7
social contract theory, 7
utilitarianism, 8
utility thinking, 9

Questions for Review and Discussion

1. What is the difference between law and morality?
2. What is the difference between natural law and positive law?
3. What is ethical relativism?
4. What is social contract theory?
5. What are the steps in applying utilitarianism?
6. What is rational ethics?
7. What are the ethical character traits generally reflected in role model ethics?
8. What are the arguments supporting social responsibility?
9. Why is law needed in our society?
10. How is harmony established between the law and ethics?

Investigating the Internet

One ethical code that provides an interesting contrast to the detail-oriented Model Code of Professional Conduct written by the American Bar Association is the short and direct code written by the American Marketing Association. Access this code on the Internet and write a paper outlining its provisions. In the report, answer the following questions: (1) What level of conduct does the American Marketing Association identify as the standard of behavior? (2) What are the general norms that the American Marketing Association establishes for marketers? (3) What are the ethical values that the American Marketing Association lists as being essential to the marketing profession? (4) What subdisciplines does the American Marketing Association include within marketing? (5) What final suggestion does the American Marketing Association make for viewers of its ethics Web site?

Cases for Analysis

1. The Student Loan Xpress (SLX), a company that makes loans to college students for their college expenses, invited the director of student financial aid at the University of Texas at Austin to invest in the company when its stock was valued at $1 per share. About a year later, SLX appeared on a list of preferred lenders that was produced by the University and that was available to students in need of financial assistance. The director of financial aid, who stated quite unequivocally that his ownership of SLX stock had no effect on the placement of that firm on the preferred list, eventually sold all of his stock in that company. SLX, however, remained on the University's list of preferred lenders. Did the financial aid director breach his social responsibility by recommending a company in which he had a financial interest? Explain. Would it make a difference if the company had a solid reputation as a good source of assistance and financial support? Explain. (See Jonathan D. Glater, "College Officers Profited by Sale of Lender Stock," *The New York Times,* April 5, 2001, sec. A, p. 1 and sec. A, p. 17.)

2. The British Home Office installed closed circuit television cameras (CCTVC's) with loudspeakers at various strategic points in the city of Middlesbrough. Whenever a camera operator spotted an individual littering, vandalizing, or fighting, he or she would use the loudspeaker to order the perpetrator to stop the illegal, and somewhat distasteful, activity. The goal of the surveillance program was to cut crime and curb obnoxious and disruptive behavior by embarrassing people caught in the act. Initial results indicated that the crime rates in relation to the targeted behavior had dropped dramatically. Nevertheless, a civil rights group, called Liberty, labeled the new program an invasion into the private activities of everyday citizens. Liberty also charged that this activity was a giant leap toward the establishment of the United Kingdom as a "surveillance society." Is the use of these cameras by the Home Office ethical from a utilitarian point of view? Explain. Is the activity ethical from the perspective of rational ethics? Explain. Is the targeted behavior (i.e., littering, vandalism, and fighting) ethical? Explain. (*Note:* Make sure that all of your answers here are consistent with one another.) (See "British Miscreants Caught on Camera Face Loudspeaker Lectures," *The New York Times,* April 5, 2007, sec. A, p. 5.)

3. The Texas legislature passed a statute that institutionalized a long-standing tradition in the Longhorn State that permits an individual traveling in a private vehicle to possess a firearm, even one that is concealed from view. The exemption was designed to protect anyone traveling in a private vehicle who was not otherwise banned from carrying such a weapon and who was not involved in a criminal

act at the time of the possession. Nevertheless, the Texas District and County Attorneys Association (TDCAA), which opposed the measure, urged police officers to ignore the statute and to arrest private citizens found transporting firearms in their vehicles. The TDCAA relied on a loophole in the law that said that the courts would make the final determination on whether a person had violated the law. Thus, the TDCAA told police officers that they could, in good conscience, arrest travelers and then argue that the determination of their guilt or innocence was up to the courts. Both the National Rifle Association and the ACLU of Texas opposed the measures taken by the TDCAA and the police, arguing that such activities were not only clearly illegal but also violated the rights of Texas citizens. Applying the social contract theory to this case, is the action taken by the TDCAA ethical? Explain. Is there any ethical theory described in the chapter that might be used to defend the decision by the TDCAA to encourage the police to disobey the law? Explain. (See Ralph Blumenthal, "Unusual Allies in a Legal Battle Over Texas Drivers' Gun Rights," *The New York Times,* April 5, 2007, sec. A, p. 12.)

4. Philip Holden and Kurt Mueller were replacing the roof on Tom Harrelson's farmhouse when Mueller lost his balance and fell to the ground. When Holden could not revive Mueller, he placed his partner in their van and drove him to the Culver City Hospital. When they arrived at the hospital, while Mueller was being examined by the emergency room physician, Holden was questioned by the admissions clerk. During the admission process, Holden learned that Culver City Hospital has a policy of not treating patients who do not have health insurance. Neither Holden nor Mueller have such insurance. When the admissions clerk asked about insurance, Holden, who believed that his friend's life was hanging in the balance, told her that Mueller had insurance. When asked about Mueller's insurance card, Holden told the clerk that the card was back at Harrelson's farm. On the strength of Holden's answers, Mueller was admitted. He underwent extensive surgery and a long period of recovery at the hospital. Eventually, his hospital bills totaled $65,897.52. These expenses are not covered by insurance. Neither Holden nor Mueller can afford to pay the bill. Instead of suing Holden and Mueller, the hospital turned the case over to the district attorney, who charged both Holden and Mueller with fraud. Is the hospital's

policy of turning away people without health insurance ethical? Did Holden face a genuine conflict of duties? What two duties did he have to balance? How might Holden have solved this ethical dilemma? Was Holden's lie about the health insurance ethical? Is the hospital's decision to turn the case over to the district attorney ethical? Is the district attorney's decision to prosecute ethical? Defend your answers.

5. The accounting firm of Thompson, Myers, and Polis was hired by Greystone Industries to prepare the company's annual audit. During the course of the audit, Larry Kenton discovered several irregularities in the bookkeeping process conducted by Gary Wentworth, Greystone's treasurer. The irregularities did not involve any illegalities and were relatively minor. Moreover, they did not amount to very much in terms of a monetary loss for the company. Nevertheless, if allowed to continue, the questionable practices could cost the firm thousands of dollars. When Kenton informs Fred Thompson, the senior partner in the accounting firm, Thompson tells Kenton not to bring the matter up. Thompson argues that Wentworth has a volatile temper and is likely to cancel the accounting firm's contract with Greystone if his bookkeeping techniques are questioned. When Kenton objects to this course of action, Thompson tells him that the decision is final. Is it ethical for Thompson to order Kenton not to reveal the bookkeeping discrepancies? What should Kenton do now that he has been ordered not to bring the matter to Wentworth's attention? Defend your answers.

6. William Yurchak, vice president of production for Dragonfly Enterprises, was passed over for what he believed was a much deserved promotion to the presidency. Instead of promoting Yurchak, the board of directors of Dragonfly, a firm that specializes in the development and production of recreational aircraft, decided to hire an outsider. Clyde Kellor, the chair of the board of Vostok Incorporated, one of Dragonfly's chief competitors, offers Yurchak the presidency of Vostok. Although Yurchak still has three years to run on his contract with Dragonfly, he is tempted to take Kellor's offer because he feels that he has been badly treated by Dragonfly and because he could use the 50 percent raise that Kellor has offered him. Kellor has added one stipulation: He wants Yurchak to bring with him the plans for Dragonfly Six, the corporation's latest revolutionary aircraft. Was it ethical

for the board of Dragonfly to hire an outsider as president? Is Kellor's offer to Yurchak ethical? Would the offer be ethical if Kellor had not added the request for the Dragonfly Six plans? What is the ethical course of action for Yurchak? Explain all of your answers.

7. Barbara McMahon is a reporter for *The Lake County Press*. McMahon is approached by Julie Bryant, a research scientist for the International Chemical Corporation. Bryant, who asks for and receives a promise of confidentiality from McMahon, informs the reporter that International Chemical has been disposing of its chemical waste product by illegally dumping it in the Lake County River. On the strength of Bryant's word alone, *The Lake County Press* runs a series of articles on the illegal dumping. The district attorney of Lake County elects to prosecute the president and board members of International. At the trial, McMahon is called as a witness and asked to reveal her confidential news source. The state in which Lake County is located does not recognize any journalist–news source privilege. The judge tells McMahon that if she does not reveal her source, she will be placed in jail until she does so. Was it ethical for Bryant to go to McMahon with her confidential story in the first place? Was it ethical for McMahon to print the news stories on the basis of Bryant's word alone? Would it be ethical for the judge to place McMahon in jail? What is the ethical course of action for McMahon? What is the ethical course of action for Bryant? Defend all of your responses.

Quick Quiz Answers

1-1	1. F	1-2	1. T	1-3	1. F	1-4	1. T
	2. F		2. F		2. F		2. T
	3. T		3. T		3. T		3. F

Chapter 2

Sources of the Law

The Opening Case
When Congress Conducts Foreign Policy

Once the Democratic Party took control of Congress in the final years of the Bush presidency, it immediately challenged the Republican administration's foreign policy. As one challenge, the new Speaker of the House Nancy Pelosi engineered an official visit to the Midddle East during which she had an audience with Bashar Assad, the president of Syria. On the surface, such a visit sounds innocent. After all, legislators have had a long tradition of visiting foreign dignitaries. What made this visit different was the nature of the regime that Assad represented and the official position that the executive branch had taken toward that regime. Under Assad, the Syrian government had repeatedly jailed and tortured political opponents, given aid to terrorist organizations such as Hamas and Hezbollah, and allegedly engineered the assassination of Rafik Hariri, the former prime minister of Lebanon. To send a message to the world that the United States would not tolerate rogue nations like Syria, the administration refused any official contact with the Assad regime. Such actions are clearly within the president's authority under the Constitution. Article II, Section 1, gives the president all executive power, and Article II, Section 2, grants the president the exclusive power to negotiate treaties. This authority does not mean, however, that Congress has no checks on this power. On the contrary, Article II, Section 2, gives senators the power to ratify treaties. Pelosi, however, was not a senator, nor was she ratifying a treaty. She was instead violating a strategic policy that had been unequivocally declared by President Bush, who had the proper power to do so. These events underscore the complex interplay that occurs among the various levels of our government. In this case, the executive branch created a policy, under its power to do so, and a member of Congress openly defied that policy. Our government is a system of checks and balances. Sometimes those checks and balances work, and sometimes, as in this case, they do not. As you read this chapter, revisit these issues to see how the system works. (See "Pelosi in Syria: Is It Wrong to Talk to a Tyrant?" *The Week,* April 20–27, 2007, p. 6.)

Opening Case Questions

1. What powers are given to Congress by the Constitution in relation to foreign affairs?

2. Which article of the Constitution gives the president power in relation to foreign affairs?

3. Did the Speaker of the House violate the separation of powers doctrine in this case?

4. Would it make a difference if the visit had been engineered by a senator rather than a representative?

5. Did the Speaker of the House commit any ethical violations in her visit to Syria?

LO Learning Objectives

1. Enumerate the objectives of the law.
2. Clarify the operation of the law as a complex adaptive system.
3. Outline the content of the U.S. Constitution.
4. Distinguish between the principle of preemption and the doctrine of devolution.
5. Explain the role of statutory law in the legal system.
6. Defend the need to set up a system of uniform state laws.
7. State the role of common law in the legal system.
8. Describe how the principle of *stare decisis* provides stability to our legal system.
9. Differentiate between statutory interpretation and judicial review.
10. Account for the legislature's need to establish administrative agencies.

2-1 The Purpose and Operation of the Law

As explained in Chapter 1, the **law** consists of rules of conduct established by the government to maintain harmony, stability, and justice within a society. Ideally, the primary objectives of the law are to promote harmony, stability, and justice. In everyday life, the balance is not easy to maintain. Often justice must be sacrificed for harmony and stability. Sometimes the opposite is true.

LO1

The Law as a Balancing Act

The law is often a balancing act. One person's rights are enforced while another's are not. One group is allowed to act, which restrains the freedom of another group. One company's contract rights are upheld at the expense of another's. Balancing like this occurs frequently. Generally, the objectives of harmony, stability, and justice are kept in mind as such decisions are made. Because the law is made by people, it is not perfect. Legislators and judges bring their own personal prejudices and biases into the process. Nevertheless, most of them try to apply the law as objectively as possible. The law is made even more complex because it is not a fixed tradition but is instead a complex adaptive system that is constantly changing.

One of the reasons that such slip-ups occur is that the government that makes the law is not a deterministic system that runs according to predetermined, scientific rules that will accurately predict every action of every member of the system. However, that does not mean that there are no underlying principles that describe how the government works to make law, even if those principles are neither absolute nor infallible. The government is in fact a complex adaptive system that sometimes takes on a life of its own. Moreover, and more to the point, the law that results and the legal system that maintains the law are also complex adaptive systems. It is to that subject that we now turn.

The Opening Case Revisited, Part I

When Congress Conducts Foreign Policy, Round 2

After the unapproved audience that Speaker of the House Nancy Pelosi had with President Bashar Assad of Syria, many members of the U.S. foreign service in the Middle East found their lives in turmoil, at least temporarily. Pelosi's remarks had included an assertion that the prime minister of Israel was prepared to enter peace talks with Syria. Unfortunately, that declaration proved to be patently false. Pelosi's error caused American foreign policy personnel a moment or two of consternation, upset the White House, and forced Israel to issue a stern declaration that the prime minister had never said any such thing. This situation reveals the balancing act that the law and the government must engage in on a daily basis. In this case, the orderly lives of certain government officials were

disrupted by the comments of a well-meaning, if injudicious, member of Congress, who was probably trying to play fair with a foreign head of state but who instead caused an embarrassing situation, if not for herself or the United States government, then certainly for the Israeli prime minister. (See "Pelosi in Syria: Is It Wrong to Talk to a Tyrant?" *The Week,* April 20–27, 2006, 6; "Pelosi Steps out of Bounds on Ill-Conceived Trip to Syria," *USA Today,* April 6, 2007, sec. A, p. 10.)

U.S. Speaker of the House, Nancy Pelosi.

The Law as a Complex Adaptive System

The law acts as a constantly changing, complex adaptive system. A complex adaptive system is a network of interacting conditions that reinforce one another while at the same time adjusting to changes from agents both outside and inside the system. The entire purpose of a complex adaptive system is the survival and improvement of the system itself. Natural examples of complex adaptive systems include beehives, anthills, the neural network of the human brain, the operation of a cell, and any sufficiently advanced ecosystem. Social examples include the educational system, the technological community, the stock market, and the economy itself.

All complex adaptive systems, whether they are natural or social, share six basic attributes. First, every complex adaptive system operates as the result of the interaction of a variety of actors within the system itself. In an anthill, the actors are the various ranks of ants, each rank having its own independent yet interactive function. In an economic network, the actors include producers and consumers, as well as intermediaries such as bankers, transporters, sellers, lawyers, and so on. In the law, those agents include lawmakers, attorneys, judges, administrators, paralegals, executives, and so on. Each agent has his or her independent job to do within the system, yet each agent depends on all of the other agents to hold the entire system together as a functioning entity.

Second, in a complex adaptive system, there is no central controlling actor. Instead, control of the system is dispersed among various actors, any one of which can be replaced by another, equally effective actor. Even those actors designated as "chief " or central actors have only nominal control over the entire complicated system. Thus, despite its apparent power, even the United States Supreme Court does not control the entire legal system. The Supreme Court has no police power of its own. Therefore, it cannot force other agents in the system to follow its dictates. Yet most of the time, those dictates are followed, because the existence of the entire complex adaptive system depends on granting the Court a certain degree of autonomy.

Third, complex adaptive systems are just that; they are complex. This point means that multiple levels of organization exist within the network. To be a true adaptive system, however, each lower level must contribute to the existence of the upper levels, and vice versa. Thus, within the law, Congress depends on the president and the president's cabinet to carry out the law, while the organizational levels depend on the courts to interpret the law and make certain that it affects individuals according to a proper assessment of congressional and presidential intent.

Fourth, the more experienced a complex adaptive system becomes, the more change it undergoes. This aspect is the "adaptive" element within the complex system. As the system learns from the past, it changes to avoid making the same mistakes a second and third time. This learning is what happened, for instance, when states passed laws to deal with surrogate parenting contracts or when Congress created the Securities and Exchange Commission to deal with abuses in the sale of stock.

Fifth, as a part of this process, a complex adaptive system can infer the direction of future events and often adjust to those changing events. Often this anticipation is more intuitive than conscious, thus making adaptation an encoded part of the system. Such prediction is what happens when, anticipating problems with litigation, the law cooperates with the institution of alternative dispute resolution techniques and creates replacement approaches to the administration of justice.

Sixth, within each complex adaptive system, certain levels of influence, called **embedded niches**, exist, which permit individuals inhabiting those niches to exercise a certain degree of limited power. Each niche is populated by experts upon whom others, outside that level, depend. Within the law, attorneys depend on judges, who depend on law clerks, who depend on law professors, who depend on legal assistants, and so on. Or, on the legislative side of the aisle, the president or governor depends on legislators, who depend on legislative aides, who depend on lobbyists, who depend on clients, who depend on lawyers, who depend on paralegals, who depend on law professors, who depend on graduate assistants, and so on.

The point of demonstrating that the law is a complex adaptive system is to show that, like any complex adaptive system, the law has a life of its own. This status explains why certain things happen in the law and others do not, despite human attempts to promote or stop them. A key result of examining complex adaptive systems is the conclusion that out of the self-interaction of the levels within the system, order emerges. Thus, what appears to be aimless and random activity at the local level becomes organized and orderly when the system is viewed as a whole. Disorder in the courtroom, on the floor of Congress, or in the Oval Office, as well as among these embedded niches, is ultimately canceled out because an orderly process emerges from these lower-level interactions. Throughout the text, we will often remind ourselves that the law is a complex adaptive system, which will help us understand why certain objectives are met by the law while others are not. Thus, a complex adaptive system involves interdependent levels of influence. (See M. Mitchell Waldrop, *Complexity: The Emerging Science on the Edge of Chaos.* New York: Simon and Schuster, 1992, 145-147.)

Talking Points

Read the following quotations on the nature of the law. As you read the quotations and reflect on the ideas that they represent, ask yourself which of the positions best reflects the development of the law as a complex adaptive system.

The truth is, that the law is always approaching, and never reaching, consistency. It is forever adopting new principles from life at one end, and it always retains old ones from history at the other; which have not yet been absorbed or sloughed off. It will become entirely consistent only when it ceases to grow.

—Oliver Wendell Holmes, Jr., "Early Forms of Liability," in *The Common Law*

The multi-layered character of American law (legislation superimposed on common law, federal law superimposed on state law, and federal constitutional law superimposed on state and federal statutory and common law), the undisciplined character of our legislatures, the intricacy and complexity of our society, and the moral heterogeneity of our population combine to thrust on the courts a responsibility for creative lawmaking that cannot be discharged either by applying existing rules to the letter or by reasoning by analogy.

—Richard Posner, *Overcoming Law*

Americans are not accustomed to a political system that allows so much latitude to an elite in managing foreign policy, setting strategic priorities, committing national resources, and determining the workings of the political system. By dividing powers between the branches of government, the American system is, in Edwin Corwin's famous phrase, 'an invitation to struggle.'

—Kenneth Pyle, *Japan Rising: The Resurgence of Japanese Power and Purpose*

Quick Quiz 2-1 True or False?

1. The law consists of rules of conduct established by the government to maintain harmony, stability, and justice within a society. *T*

2. Often justice must be sacrificed for harmony and stability, but the opposite is never true. *F*

3. Legislators and judges bring their own personal prejudices and biases into the process. *T*

2-2 Constitutional Law

About the Law

Unlike the United States Constitution, the British Constitution cannot be found in a single document. Rather, it is based on a group of implicit traditions that arise from a number of diverse laws.

The law has been defined as rules of conduct created by the government to maintain harmony, stability, and justice within a society. This definition is adequate, but it is also somewhat limited. It does not explain where the government comes from or who gives it the power to make those rules.

In some societies, the government is represented by a hereditary monarchy. In others, the establishment of a government depends on which political faction can muster the necessary power to take control of that nation's resources. In the United States, the government was established by a constitution.

A **constitution** is the basic law of a nation or state. The United States Constitution provides the organization of the national government. Each state also has a constitution that establishes the state's governmental structure. The body of law that makes up a constitution and its interpretation is known as **constitutional law**.

The Articles of Confederation

The Constitution of the United States, as it exists today, is not the nation's first constitution. The first constitution was known as the Articles of Confederation. The Articles of Confederation were created to hold together a fragile coalition of states, each of which was determined to maintain its own independent existence. Although the Articles of Confederation fulfilled a much needed function during the first years in the life of the United States, they contained certain weaknesses.

One of the primary weaknesses was the fact that the Confederation Congress, as the national legislature was known under the Articles, could not impose taxes or tariffs. Although a common treasury was supposed to be supplied by the states in proportion to the value of the land within each state, the states retained the power to levy and collect taxes. In essence, this rule meant that the Confederation Congress had to rely on the goodwill of the states to obtain money. Such revenues were rarely forthcoming. Some states paid nothing at all; others turned over a portion of what they owed but rarely by the date the payments were due. Part of this problem was caused by the fact that the states were not about to trade one dictatorial central government for another and, therefore, simply ignored the national government.

Moreover, the desire to prevent the type of tyranny that the colonies had experienced under the rule of King George and the British Parliament led the framers of the Articles to include other limitations on the national government. For instance, the Articles made no provision for any sort of chief executive to run the national government. Instead, the administrative power of the confederation was to reside in a Committee of the States appointed by Congress to operate when Congress was not in session. Moreover, all delegates to the Congress were appointed by the state legislatures and served at their pleasure. Several times, the national government found itself powerless to act, because some of the legislatures did not even bother to send delegates to Congress. In addition, whereas the Confederation Congress had the authority to regulate the value of any money created under its own authority or under the authority of a state, the states retained the power to issue their own currency.

Eventually these weaknesses made the establishment of any effective national government impossible. Consequently, in the summer of 1787, twelve of the thirteen states organized under the Articles sent delegates to a Constitutional Convention held in Philadelphia. The purpose of the convention was to revise the nation's first constitution, the Articles of Confederation. However, the Articles were so weak that the delegates decided instead to come up with a brand new constitution.

The Principles of the United States Constitution

The Constitution of the United States is based on two fundamental principles that were supported by many of the delegates to the convention in Philadelphia. Those two principles promote, first, a separation of national powers among three distinct branches of government and, second, a system of checks and balances that allows each branch to oversee the operation of the other two branches. The principle of the separation of powers set up the now familiar three branches of the national government: the executive branch, the legislative branch, and the judicial branch. The principle of checks and balances allows each branch to share in the power of the other two branches.

The Structure of the United States Constitution

The U.S. Constitution is divided into two parts: the articles and the amendments. The articles establish the organization of the national government. The amendments change provisions in the original articles and add ideas that the framers did not include in those articles.

U.S. Const. Articles I–VII
(see pages 945–949)

The Opening Case Revisited, Part II
When Congress Conducts Foreign Policy, Round 3

As explained previously, our government is based on the separation of powers and on a system of checks and balances. Sometimes that separation and those checks work, and sometimes they do not. Recall that, in The Opening Case, the executive branch of the United States, in carrying out the orders of the president, refused to have any official contact with the Assad regime in Syria because of that regime's link to terrorist organizations, its abuse of its own citizens, and its alleged complicity in the assassination of the Lebanese prime minister. Despite this prohibition, the Speaker of the House conducted her own foreign policy visit to Syria. Such actions clearly defied the president's authority under the Constitution. Article II, Section 1, gives the president all executive power, and Article II, Section 2, grants the president the exclusive power to negotiate treaties. In contrast, Article I, Section 1, of the Constitution gives to Congress only those powers "herein granted." This phrase means that only those powers and abilities that are listed in the Constitution belong to Congress. The only powers given to Congress in foreign affairs, outside the powers to declare war and to raise and finance the army and navy, are the powers given to the Senate to ratify treaties and approve the appointment of ambassadors. Pelosi was not ratifying a treaty or approving the appointment of an ambassador. Perhaps more to the point, she was not even a senator. Many legal and political experts therefore labeled her audience with the president of Syria as a clear violation of the "separation of powers" guaranteed by the Constitution.

The Articles   The first three of the seven articles distribute the power of the government among the legislative, executive, and judicial branches. Article I establishes Congress as the legislative (statute-making) branch of the government. Article II gives executive power to the president, and Article III gives judicial power to the Supreme Court and other courts established by Congress. Article IV explains the relationships among the states, while Article V outlines the methods for amending the Constitution. Article VI establishes the U.S. Constitution, federal laws, and treaties as the supreme law of the land. Finally, Article VII outlines how the original 13 states would go about ratifying the new Constitution. Table 2-1 outlines the content of each article in the Constitution.

The Amendments   The amendments to the Constitution establish the rights that belong to the people, change some of the provisions in the original articles, and add ideas that the Framers did not include in those articles. Thus, the amendments are attempts to fine-tune the Constitution and update its provisions to meet the demands of a changing socioeconomic structure. The first 10 amendments of the Constitution compose the Bill of Rights. They were added soon after the ratification of the Constitution by the original 13 states. Other amendments that secure the rights of the people include the Thirteenth, which prohibits slavery; the Fourteenth, which guarantees equal protection of the law and due process; the Fifteenth, which guarantees voting rights; the Nineteenth, which extends voting rights to women; the Twenty-Fourth, which prohibits poll taxes; and the Twenty-Sixth, which extends the right to vote to eighteen-year-old citizens. Table 2-2 provides a more detailed look at the amendments.

Table 2-1   Articles of the U.S. Constitution

Articles	Content
Article I	Establishes the legislative branch of the federal government (the Congress)
	Defines the duties and powers of each house
	Outlines how Congress must conduct its business
	Lists legislative powers granted to Congress
	Lists powers denied to Congress
	Lists powers denied to the states
Article II	Gives executive power and responsibilities to the president
	Outlines the president's term of office, qualifications, and manner of election
	Identifies the president as commander in chief
	Gives the president power to make treaties
Article III	Establishes the Supreme Court and authorizes the establishment of other federal courts
	Provides for trial by jury for crimes
	Defines treason against the United States
Article IV	Defines interstate relations
	Sets up the full faith and credit clause obligating each state to recognize the public acts and proceedings of other states
	Provides for extradition of those accused of crimes in other states
Article V	Outlines the method of amending the Constitution
Article VI	Establishes the Constitution, federal laws, and federal treaties as the supreme law of the land
Article VII	Provides for the original ratification of the Constitution

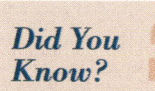

Did You Know?

Roman law was first codified into The Law of the Twelve Tables in 450 BC. The Twelve Tables declared that all free citizens had certain fundamental rights.

The Question of Democracy

The structure of the Constitution as described here does not set up a democracy. Instead, it establishes a republic. The difference between a democracy and a republic is that in a democracy, the people have direct control over the government, whereas in a republic, the people elect delegates to represent them. When the Framers wrote the Articles of Confederation in 1777 and designed the Constitution in 1787, they thought in terms of a republic rather than a democracy. Certainly to the Framers, the concept of republicanism meant that there would be no royalty in the American system. However, it also implied that the people would have some voice in the running of the government, even if it were an indirect voice. In fact, for the most part, the voice of the people was an indirect voice, because the only delegates that the people elected directly were those in the House of Representatives.

U.S. Const. Amendments 1–27 (see pages 949–953)

Today, when most people speak of democracy, it is likely that they mean a form of republicanism in which there is competition among political parties to elect representatives on a regular basis and in which the government's power to interfere in the rights of the people is limited. Despite the fact that democracy is a part of the rhetoric of politicians, not everyone agrees automatically that democracy is a good thing. Even American politicians are not as dedicated to democracy as it sometimes appears on the surface. For example, the first Constitution ratified for Iraq after Gulf War II limited the power of the Iraqi Congress to pass its own laws, something that is essential to democracy. In addition, some nations seem to prefer to have a less-than-democratic ruling process.

Even in the United States itself, many people express disillusionment with democracy, as evidenced by perennially low voter turnout. Still, most people seem to prefer the

Table 2-2 Amendments to the U.S. Constitution

The Bill of Rights	Pre–Civil War Amendments	Civil War Amendments	Early Twentieth-Century Amendments	Depression-Era Amendments	Modern Amendments
Amendment 1 Freedom of religion, speech, press, assembly	*Amendment 11* Lawsuits against the states	*Amendment 13* Slavery is abolished	*Amendment 16* The income tax is established	*Amendment 20* Terms of president, vice president, senators and representatives altered	*Amendment 22* President's terms limited to two
Amendment 2 The right to bear arms and set up a militia	*Amendment 12** President and vice president elected together	*Amendment 14* Equal protection of the law, due process, citizenship	*Amendment 17* Senators elected by direct election	*Amendment 21* Prohibition repealed	*Amendment 23* Washington, DC gets electors
Amendment 3 The quartering of soldiers in homes is prohibited		*Amendment 15†* Voting rights guaranteed	*Amendment 18‡* Prohibition established		*Amendment 24* Poll taxes outlawed
Amendment 4 Search and seizure by probable cause			*Amendment 19* Women given right to vote		*Amendment 25* Disability of the president; vacancies in the vice presidency
Amendment 5 Grand juries, double jeopardy, self-incrimination, due process, and eminent domain					*Amendment 26* Vote extended to 18-year-olds
Amendment 6 Procedures allowed in criminal cases					*Amendment 27* Congress prevented from voting itself instant pay raises
Amendment 7 Jury trials in common law cases guaranteed					
Amendment 8 Bill of Rights guaranteed, cruel and unusual punishment prohibited					
Amendment 9 People retain other rights					
Amendment 10 Powers reserved to states					

*Altered somewhat by the Twentieth Amendment. †Voting age changed by Twenty-sixth Amendment. ‡Repealed by Twenty-first Amendment.

democratic process, even if they are disillusioned by how democracy works in the "real" world. This loyalty to democratic ideals probably remains intact because, over the long haul, all other forms of government are even less satisfying than democracy. Part of it may be due to the fact that, in a democracy, there is always the opportunity to change leaders at election time, even if the opportunity is not often realized. It is also probably due to the fact that, in a democracy, the people's rights are recognized as an integral part of the governmental formula, even if the exercise of those rights is often imperfectly realized. (See R. B. Bernstein, *The Constitution of the United States with the Declaration of Independence and the Articles of Confederation.* New York: Barnes and Noble, 2002, 9; Anthony Giddens, *Runaway World: How Globalization Is Reshaping Our Lives.* New York: Routledge, 2000, 100; Steven R. Weisman, "White House Says Iraq Sovereignty Could Be Limited," *The New York Times,* April 23, 2004, sec. A, p. 1; Richard N. Rosenfeld, "What Democracy: The Case for Abolishing the United States Senate," *Harpers,* May 2004, 35ff.)

State Constitutions

Each state in the union adopts its own constitution. A state constitution establishes the state's government. It also sets down principles to guide the state government in making state laws and conducting state business. Most state constitutions are patterned after the U.S. Constitution. However, state constitutions tend to be longer and more detailed than the U.S. Constitution, because they must deal with local as well as statewide matters.

The Principle of Supremacy

A basic principle of constitutional law is that the U.S. Constitution is the supreme law of the land. This principle of constitutional supremacy means that all other laws must be in line with constitutional principles. If a law somehow conflicts with the Constitution, that law is said to be unconstitutional. If it does not conflict, it will be upheld by the court as constitutional.

U.S. Const. Article VI (see page 949)

The Principle of Preemption

The Constitution also says that all federal laws that are made in line with constitutional principles are to be considered the supreme law of the land. Cases that involve such conflicts, however, are not always as clear cut as those that involve state statutes that conflict with the Constitution. Preemption is the process by which the courts decide that a federal statute must take precedence over a state statute. The preemption of a state statute can occur in three situations. First, Congress can be very clear about its intent and explicitly state that the federal statute preempts any state statute that covers the same issues. If that is the case, then all that remains for the courts is to determine which statutes are covered by the preemption clause. Second, state statutes can be preempted by federal statutes when they conflict with the objectives of federal legislation. Third, the courts will preempt a state statute that has entered an area of the law that is traditionally an area that the federal government handles, such as foreign affairs or banking.

The Doctrine of Devolution

Devolution occurs when the courts redefine a right and shift the obligation to enforce a right from an upper level authority to a lower one. For instance, a court may decide that a state agency, rather than a federal one, can control what governmental employees, in the course of performing their duties, are permitted to talk or write about in relation to official policies, procedures, and programs. Such a prohibition might appear to violate the employee's Constitutional right of free speech as a U.S. citizen. However, in such cases, the court has decided that the duty and the power to define and enforce that right belongs to the state rather than to the federal government. It is important to note that the devolution of a right

A Question of Ethics

Ethics on Distant Shores and in High Places

In The Opening Case, the Speaker of the House of Representatives of the United States Congress took it upon herself to stage a formal visit with the president of Syria, a man whose record of involvement with terrorism, torture, and assassination led the administration to break official ties with his regime. Aside from the fact that the visit violated the separation of powers doctrine, was the speaker's decision to visit Syria ethical? Refer back to Chapter 1 and determine the extent of her ethical responsibility using all four of the major ethical theories discussed in that chapter: social contract ethics, utilitarianism, rational ethics, and role model ethics.

does not destroy that right. Rather, devolution simply redistributes the authority to define the nature of that right in certain situations.

Not everyone in the legal community believes that devolution is a good thing. Opponents argue that devolution may result in an uneven, unfair distribution of rights at the state level. Thus, some states might curtail the free speech of public employees while others might not, creating inconsistencies from state to state. This inconsistency might even lead to competition among the states to present the best package of rights to its citizens, thus encouraging people and businesses to relocate to their jurisdiction. In contrast, supporters of devolution note that state legislatures and state courts will offer different interpretations of legal rights and responsibilities only if their constituencies favor those different interpretations. Moreover, such variety is healthy because it reflects the open and free expression of differing political and social views. These supporters also assert that the transfer of responsibility for the interpretation and enforcement of rights and duties from a small number of federal bureaucrats to a large number of public officials will inspire ingenuity and originality, something that the original founders intended. (See Isidore Silver, "Recent Supreme Court Opinions: A Devolving Constitution," *The National Law Journal*, March 12, 2007, p. 22; Robert Tannenwald, "Devolution: The New Federalism—An Overview," *New England Economic Review*, May/June 1998, 1–7.)

Quick Quiz 2-2 True or False?

1. The present U.S. Constitution is the only constitution that the United States has ever had.   F

2. The principle of separation of powers was never adopted by the framers of the U.S. Constitution.   F

3. All legal authorities support the doctrine of devolution.   F

2-3 Statutory Law

Laws passed by a legislature are known as statutes. At the federal level, statutes are the laws made by Congress and signed by the president. At the state level, statutes are enacted by state legislatures, such as the Ohio General Assembly or the Oregon Legislative Assembly. Many statutes prohibit certain activities. Most criminal statutes are prohibitive statutes. For instance, Ohio criminal law prohibits hazing, which is defined as coercing someone into doing an act of initiation that has a substantial risk of causing mental or physical harm.

Other statutes demand the performance of some action. For instance, Ohio statutory law requires all motor vehicle drivers and passengers to wear safety belts. Some statutes, such as those that create governmental holidays or name state flowers, simply declare something.

Codes and Titles

Statutes must be arranged, cataloged, and indexed for easy reference. This is done by compiling state and federal codes. A **code** is a compilation of all the statutes of a particular state or the federal government. All federal statutes, for instance, are gathered in the United States Code (USC), while all Ohio statutory law is collected in the Ohio Revised Code (ORC). In general, codes are subdivided into **titles**, which are groupings of statutes that deal with a particular area of the law. Title 17 of the Ohio Revised Code, for example, covers corporations and partnerships. Often titles are subdivided into chapters, and chapters subdivided into sections. Thus, ORC 1701.03, *Purposes of a Corporation,* can be read from right to left as the third section of the first chapter of Title 17 of the ORC.

Uniform Laws

Because many different statutes are passed each year by the 50 state legislatures, statutory law differs from state to state. This lack of consistency can cause problems when legal matters cross state boundaries. One solution to the problem of inconsistent statutory law is for all the state legislatures to adopt the same statutes. The National Conference of Commissioners on Uniform State Laws (NCCUSL) was founded to write these uniform laws. The NCCUSL is composed of commissioners that come from every state, the District of Columbia, Puerto Rico, and the Virgin Islands. These commissioners are usually selected by the governor. Most of the commissioners serve for a term of years set by the state. Some however have no set term and therefore can be replaced by the governor at any time. The number of commissioners from each jurisdiction is established by that jurisdiction. Some jurisdictions decide to have a lot of commissioners, while others decide to send only a few. California, for example, appoints fourteen, while New Hampshire limits its number to three. The states are also responsible for sending money to the NCCUSL to support its activities. The more populated states generally pay more than the smaller states.

Just about anybody can submit a suggestion for a uniform law. However, most often, such suggestions come from the states, the American Bar Association, and those people in a particular profession or activity who have a specific interest in that area of the law. Recent topics that have been considered for uniform laws include genetic engineering, organ donation procedures, and the electronic discovery of evidence during lawsuits. Once a suggestion has been made, the NCCUSL's Committee on Scope and Program will appoint a committee to study the advisability of working on that uniform law. If the committee decides that such a law would be useful and appropriate, the committee members send the proposal back to the Scope and Program Committee, which then transmits the proposal to the executive committee and, eventually, to all of the commissioners. If everyone approves the proposal, they set up a drafting committee. As the name suggests, the job of the drafting committee is to write the actual uniform law, point by point. After the draft is written, it must be reviewed and voted upon. This can be a long and involved process that includes input from the states, legal experts, and those people, businesses, organizations, and institutions directly affected by a newly proposed law. Once the entire group of commissioners has voted to endorse a law, the state delegations must then vote to confirm it also. After a proposed uniform law is accepted by the state delegations within the NCCUSL, it is recommended to the state legislatures for adoption. Some states may adopt it, others may not. Remember that a uniform law does not become a binding statute until it has been officially passed by a state legislature.

LO6

UCC (see pages 954–1017)

The Uniform Commercial Code

The most significant development in uniform state legislation has been the Uniform Commerical Code. The Uniform Commercial Code (UCC) is a unified set of statutes designed to govern almost all commercial transactions. The basic principles of commercial law were not changed by the UCC provisions. By defining and clarifying often misunderstood business and legal terms, the UCC helps parties involved in commercial transactions prepare their contracts. Even the famed UCC, however, has been adjusted by various states, and not all states decide to the accept suggested amendments that come from the NCCUSL from time to time. Some states have even decided to eliminate some of the chapters and articles in the UCC that they have found obsolete or irrelevant or that do not fit within their established legal traditions. Louisiana, for example, which still uses the Napoleonic Code, has adopted only four of the nine articles. Nevertheless, the UCC remains one of the most successful achievements of the NCCUSL. The National Conference of Commissioners on Uniform State Laws maintains a Web site that includes the final drafts of all uniform acts that have been approved and recommended for adoption by the state legislatures.

Electronic Law Statutes

The advent of the Information Age has sparked the need for specific electronic law statutes that address the problems associated with e-commerce. E-commerce is the term applied to all electronic transactions. The NCCUSL has responded to this challenge by creating several new uniform laws. For example, the Uniform Computer Information Transactions Act (UCITA) is designed to deal directly with e-contracts that involve the sale or licensing of digital information. Another uniform e-law approved by the commissioners for enactment by state legislatures is the Uniform Electronic Transactions Act (UETA). This uniform e-law points out those principles that should be used in every state to make certain that e-contracts are enforceable.

Quick Quiz 2-3 True or False?

1. Laws passed by a legislature are known as amendments. _F_

2. Once the NCCUSL adopts a uniform law, it becomes binding in all states. _F_

3. E-commerce is the term that is applied to all electronic transactions. _T_

2-4 Court Decisions

When most people think of the law, they think of the Constitution or of statutes passed by Congress and the state legislatures. Although these two sources are important, they are not the only two sources of law in this country. The courts also make law in the following ways:

- Common law
- Interpretation of statutes
- Judicial review

Common Law

The term *common law* comes from the attempts of early English kings to establish a body of law that all the courts in the kingdom would hold in common. At that time, judges in towns and villages had instructions to settle all disputes in as consistent a manner as possible. The judges maintained this consistency by relying on previous legal decisions whenever they faced a similar set of circumstances. In this way, they established a body of common law. As the process continued, judges began to record their decisions and share them with other judges. **Common law** is the body of previously recorded legal decisions made by the courts in specific cases. The process of relying on these previously recorded legal decisions is called *stare decisis* (let the decision stand). The previously recorded legal decisions themselves are referred to as precedents.

The legal system of the United States, except Louisiana, is rooted in the common law of England. These roots derive from the early American colonists who came from England and were governed by the English monarchy. Over time, English common law has been eroded in the United States by the passing of state statutes and court decisions that better meet the needs of today's society. Nevertheless, parts of the common law as practiced in England still exist in the laws of the United States today. Courts still apply the common law when there are no modern court decisions or statutes dealing with an issue in dispute.

Today's judges make decisions in the same way as their counterparts from the Middle Ages. They rely on precedent according to the principle of *stare decisis*. A **precedent** is a model case that a court can follow when facing a similar situation.

Precedents, past decisions, form the basis of common law.

There are two types of precedent: binding and persuasive. **Binding precedent** is precedent that a court must follow. **Persuasive precedent** is precedent that a court is free to follow or ignore. Generally, whether a precedent is binding or persuasive is determined by the court's location. For instance, decisions made by the Florida Supreme Court would be binding in all Florida state courts but persuasive in all other states' courts.

The U.S. Supreme Court has frequently emphasized the crucial role that precedent plays in the American legal system. In emphasizing the importance of precedent, the Court has outlined a series of questions that judges should ask as they contemplate whether to overturn a rule of law established in an earlier case. These questions include the following:

- Is the established rule still practical?
- Have so many people relied upon the rule that overturning it would cause difficulty and injustice?
- Is the rule still legally viable, or has it become merely a relic of an outdated and deserted legal doctrine?
- Is the rule still up to date, or has it become obsolete because of changes in society?

Only if judges can answer these questions satisfactorily should they consider overturning an established precedent.

Statutory Interpretation

A second way that court decisions make law is in the interpretation of statutes. **Statutory interpretation** is the process by which the courts analyze those aspects of a statute that are unclear or ambiguous or that were not anticipated at the time the legislature passed the statute. When legislators enact a new statute, they cannot predict how people will react to the new law. Nor can they foresee all of its future ramifications and implications. Thus, when two or more parties have a dispute that challenges the statute, they may differ as to what the legislature had in mind when it wrote the statute. Also, legislators may have purposely made the language of a statute general. The job of reacting to unforeseen circumstances and making generalities fit specific circumstances falls to the courts. As a result, a judge may be called upon to determine how a certain statute should be interpreted.

Courts are not, however, free to interpret a statute at random. A court cannot interpret a statute unless it is faced with a case involving that statute. In interpreting a statute, a court looks to a variety of sources, including the legislative history of the statute and the old statute that the new statute replaced, if any. Naturally, the court also must review any binding

BusinessWeek **Business Law in the News**

Lighting a Fire Under Global Warming

The first fallout from the U.S. Supreme Court's dramatic 5–4 decision on global warming came swiftly. Just two days later, on Apr. 4, lawyers gathered in a Vermont courtroom. The Green Mountain State, one of 10 states that have adopted California's proposed limits on carbon dioxide emissions from vehicles, had been sued by automakers seeking to block the rules. At the Vermont hearing, environmental lawyers argued that Detroit no longer had much of a case— and the state now is expected to win. "The Supreme Court knocked the legs out from under all of the claims of the car-makers," says Natural Resources Defense Council attorney David D. Doniger.

The Supreme Court's decision is rippling through other courtrooms, statehouses, and even boardrooms across the nation. Even if, as most expect, the Environmental Protection Agency and White House do not use their court-sanctioned authority to impose greenhouse gas emission curbs, the ruling sweeps away much of the legal challenge to the auto regulations in California and the other states, which will force automakers to improve fuel economy. It also gives a boost to state suits against utilities for alleged harm from power plant emissions. "Since November, this issue has accelerated from 5 mph to 80 mph," says Peter A. Molinaro, director of government affairs at Dow Chemical Co. The ruling "just adds more momentum."

The heart of the high court's ruling is that carbon dioxide is a "pollutant" under the Clean Air Act and thus can be regulated by the EPA. Equally important, Justice John Paul Stevens dismissed the claim that Massachusetts and other states had no legal standing to bring the case because they hadn't suffered injuries from global warming. "The harms associated with climate change are serious and well-recognized," he wrote.

One Federal Rule

In making the decision on standing, the court removed a roadblock for key suits in federal courts. "It's hard to overstate its importance in the litigation arena," says J. Kevin Healy, a partner with law firm Bryan Cave. It improves the chances of existing lawsuits, like one led by Connecticut asking utilities to lower their emissions. And it could bring what Arnold & Porter partner Michael B. Gerrard calls a "forest fire of litigation" against business, which has been working hard to get the issue out of the courts.

The door is now open for new lawsuits against companies that emit carbon dioxide. However, the suits have always been a means to an end, a way to pressure companies into supporting mandatory national emissions limits. "Ultimately, the litigation is aimed at Congress and the White House," says Gerrard.

It's working. U.S. carmakers and their biggest supporter, Representative John D. Dingell (D.-Mich.), had long opposed boosting fuel economy standards. Now they have signed on to federal legislation. They'd rather have one national rule than the patchwork of state regulations. The justices' decision "provides another compelling reason why Congress must enact, and the President must sign, comprehensive climate change legislation," Dingell said in a statement.

Other groups and companies that once opposed mandatory carbon curbs, like the utility industry's Edison Electric Institute and Dow Chemical Co., have come to the table, too. Healy tells his corporate clients they can't ignore global warming any longer. "They have to think about it when planning for the future," he says.

In the wake of the Supreme Court decision and increasing international concern, there's even more pressure for national legislation. If Congress and the Bush White House cannot reach an agreement, business fears that the next Administration might impose tougher rules than the bills now under consideration. The top Presidential candidates from both parties have endorsed policies to limit carbon emissions.

Questions for Analysis

1. The article discusses a ruling by the United States Supreme Court. Does this ruling involve common law, statutory interpretation, or judicial review? Explain.

2. According to the author, what was the term in the Clean Air Act that the court defined? Why was this interpretation important? Explain.

3. The courts also determined that the states involved in the lawsuit had standing, that is, they had the right to be in court regarding the pollution issue. To decide this, however, the court had to believe that the states had been injured. How did the court indicate that the states had been injured?

4. One of the attorneys quoted in the article indicated that the lawsuits against companies that emit carbon dioxide had always been simply a

means to an end. What end does he have in mind? Is this a legitimate reason to bring a lawsuit? Explain.

5. Has this tactic, the one described in question #4, worked? Explain. How is this entire operation an example of the law working as a complex adaptive system? Explain.

Source: John Carey, *BusinessWeek,* April 16, 2007, 33.

---

precedent that interprets that statute. This requirement exists because the court must still rely upon previous cases when engaged in statutory interpretation, just as it does when deciding questions of common law.

Judicial Review

A third way that courts make law is through judicial review. Judicial review is the process of determining the constitutionality of various legislative statutes, administrative regulations, or executive actions. In exercising the power of judicial review, a court will look at the statute, regulation, or action and compare it with the Constitution. If the two are compatible, no problem exists. However, if they are contradictory, one of the two must be declared void. Because the Constitution is the supreme law of the land, the Constitution always rules, and the statute, regulation, or action is ruled unconstitutional.

Naturally, in exercising the power of judicial review, the court also must review any binding precedent involved in the constitutional issue, because the court still must rely upon previous cases in judicial review, just as it does in common law and statutory interpretation. The lower courts in this country have the capacity to review issues of constitutionality and interpret the meaning of provisions within the U.S. Constitution. However, the ultimate authority, and therefore the final word, on such issues rests with the United States Supreme Court.

Quick Quiz 2-4 True or False?

1. The process of relying on previous decisions is called *stare decisis.* T

2. Common law originated in France. F

3. Judicial review is another name for statutory interpretation. F

2-5 Administrative Regulations

Neither legislators nor judges can administer to all aspects of today's society. Moreover, legislators are generalists; they are rarely experts in all areas over which they have power. Because legislators are generalists and today's problems are so complex, statutory law, created by legislators, is very limited in what it can do. To broaden the power of statutory law, legislators delegate their power to others. They do this when they create administrative agencies.

Administrative Agencies

Federal administrative agencies administer statutes enacted by Congress in specific areas, such as communication, aviation, labor relations, working conditions, and so on. Similarly,

Fuel economy standards are rising, increasing the need for more fuel efficient vehicles to be produced.

agencies have been designated by the states to supervise intrastate activities. These agencies create rules, regulate and supervise, and render decisions that have the force of law. Their decrees and decisions are known as **administrative law**.

Administrative Procedures Act

Problems sometimes occur because administrative agencies have the power to make the rules, enforce the rules, and interpret the rules. To help prevent any conflict of interest that could arise from these overlapping responsibilities, Congress passed the federal Administrative Procedures Act. Similarly, most states have adopted a uniform law known as the Model State Administrative Procedures Act. Under these two acts, an administrative agency planning new regulations must notify the affected parties and hold hearings to allow those parties to express their views. These acts also allow the courts to review agency decisions and rulings.

The Federal Register and the Code of Federal Regulations

The **Federal Register** is a publication that produces a daily compilation of new regulations issued by federal administrative agencies. The Federal Register operates within the National Archives and Records Administration under the authority of the Office of the Federal Register. The Government Printing Office is responsible for actually printing the document, though today it is also available online. Most of the documents included within the Federal Register are directly related to the agencies. Those subdivisions devoted to the agencies include a section on rules and regulations, one on proposed rules, and one on notices of hearings, meetings, application deadlines, and administrative orders. There is also a section devoted to presidential orders and proclamations. Once a rule is finalized, it is included in the **Code of Federal Regulations (CFR)**, which is updated each year.

Quick Quiz 2-5 True or False?

1. Together, legislators and judges can administer all aspects of today's society. *F*

2. Most legislators are specialists. *F*

3. The decrees and decisions made by administrative agencies are known as administrative law. *F*

Summary

2.1 The law consists of rules of conduct established by the government to maintain harmony, stability, and justice within a society. Ideally, the primary objectives of the law are to promote harmony, stability, and justice. In everyday life, the balance is not easy to maintain. The law or, more properly, the entire legal framework is a complex adaptive system exhibiting each of the six attributes of such systems.

2.2 A constitution is the basic law of a nation or state. The United States Constitution provides the organization of the national government. Each state also has a constitution that determines the state's governmental structure. The body of law that forms a constitution and its interpretation is known as constitutional law.

2.3   The laws passed by a legislature are known as statutes. At the federal level, these are the laws made by Congress and signed by the president. At the state level, statutes are enacted by state legislatures. Statutes must be arranged, cataloged, and indexed for easy reference by compiling state and federal codes. Because many different statutes are passed each year by the 50 state legislatures, there are important differences in state statutory law throughout the nation. One solution to the problem of inconsistent statutory law is for the legislatures of all the states to adopt the same statutes. The National Conference of Commissioners on Uniform State Laws (NCCUSL) was founded to write these uniform laws.

2.4   Courts make law through common law, the interpretation of statutes, and judicial review. Common law is the body of previously recorded legal decisions made by the courts in specific cases. Statutory interpretation is the process by which the courts analyze those aspects of a statute that are unclear or ambiguous or that were not anticipated at the time that the legislature passed the statute, and judicial review is the process by which the courts determine the constitutionality of various legislative statutes, administrative regulations, or executive actions.

2.5   Federal administrative agencies administer statutes enacted by Congress in specific areas, such as commerce, communication, aviation, labor relations, and working conditions. Similar agencies have been designated by the states to supervise intrastate activities. These agencies create rules, regulate and supervise, and render decisions. To help prevent any conflict of interest that could arise from these overlapping responsibilities, Congress passed the federal Administrative Procedures Act. Similarly, most states have adopted a uniform law known as the Model State Administrative Procedures Act.

Key Terms

administrative law, 42

Articles of Confederation, 31

binding precedent, 39

code, 37

Code of Federal Regulations (CFR), 42

common law, 39

complex adaptive system, 28

constitution, 30

constitutional law, 30

devolution, 35

e-commerce, 38

embedded niches, 29

Federal Register, 42

judicial review, 41

law, 27

persuasive precedent, 39

precedent, 39

preemption, 35

statutes, 36

statutory interpretation, 39

titles, 37

Uniform Commercial Code (UCC), 38

Questions for Review and Discussion

1. What are the objectives of the law?
2. How is the law a complex adaptive system?
3. What are the functions of the articles and the amendments of the U.S. Constitution?
4. What is the difference between the principle of preemption and the doctrine of devolution?
5. What is the role of statutory law in the legal system?
6. Why does this country need to set up a system of uniform state laws?
7. What is the role of common law in the legal system?
8. How does the principle of *stare decisis* provide stability to our legal system?
9. What is the difference between statutory interpretation and judicial review?
10. Why does the legislature need to establish administrative agencies?

Investigating the Internet

Access the U.S. Historical Documents Archive on the Internet and write a research paper in which you trace the evolution of American political thought as represented in these major documents. In that report, answer the following questions: (1) Which of these documents is the most important in relation to shaping the nature of the law in the United States? (2) What are the major ideas that most people remember about each document? (3) What are some of the misconceptions that people have about these documents? (4) Which of these documents appears to make the clearest and most consistent statement of American rights? Why is this so? (5) Summarize a statement of "American Principles."

Cases for Analysis

1. The State of Oregon passed a statute called the Oregon Death with Dignity Act (ODWDA) which permitted licensed physicians in Oregon to prescribe or administer drugs to patients who are terminally ill. However, according to the federal law known as the Controlled Substances Act (CSA), it is illegal for physicians to prescribe such drugs, except for a legitimate medical reason. The attorney general of the United States therefore sought to stop the administration of such drugs under the ODWDA by issuing an Interpretive Rule saying that prescribing such drugs for terminally ill patients was not an acceptable medical practice and that the practice would therefore violate the CSA. The attorney general also argued that the CSA, as a federal law, ought to take precedence over the ODWDA, which was, after all, only a state statute. In answer, Oregon pointed out that the CSA contained a clause that stated that nothing in the act was to be "construed as indicating an intent on the part of the Congress to occupy the field in which that provision operates . . . to the exclusion of any State law on the same subject matter which would otherwise be within the authority of the state." Congress therefore had no intent to outlaw any state statutes related to the practice of medicine. As a result, because the ODWDA regulated the practice of medicine, such practices could not be outlawed by the CSA, and the state retained the power to regulate the practice of medicine, including a physician's intent to assist a terminally ill patient to commit suicide in this way. Is the attorney general or the state of Oregon correct here? Explain. *Alberto R. Gonzales, Attorney General, et al., Petitioners, v. Oregon, et al.* (U.S. Supreme Court).

2. Karen Silkwood was an employee at the Kerr-McGee Nuclear Power Plant in Oklahoma. During her employment there, she was apparently contaminated by exposure to plutonium. The contamination was so severe that she had to be sent to a special facility for an examination, and her personal belongings at her home had to be destroyed. After Silkwood died in an unrelated car accident, her father, as administrator of her estate, brought a lawsuit against the Kerr-McGee power plant. Under state tort law, Silkwood's estate was awarded actual damages of $505,000 ($500,000 for personal injuries, and $5,000 for property loss), and $10 million in punitive damages, that is, damages designed to punish the defendant for its wanton misbehavior. The power plant argued that when Congress passed the Atomic Energy Act, it intended to completely outlaw any state regulation of nuclear power plants. Permitting the plaintiff to receive punitive damages in this case would destroy that intent. Silkwood's father, as the plaintiff in the case, argued that there was no intent expressed by Congress to preempt tort law in the area of nuclear regulation. In fact, when the plain-

tiff searched the Congressional Record, he could find no evidence that Congress intended to replace state tort law by passing the Atomic Energy Act. He also found that whenever Congress passed statutes similar to the Atomic Energy Act, there was never any intention to replace state tort law. Therefore, the plaintiff concluded, Congress did not intend to preempt state tort law in this case either. Is the plaintiff correct? Explain. *Silkwood v. Kerr-McGee Corporation,* 464 U.S. 238 (U.S. Supreme Court).

3. Richard Ceballos worked as a deputy district attorney for the city of Los Angeles. Ceballos wrote a memo in which he criticized the accuracy of an affidavit in a case that he had been assigned to handle. In the memo, he expressed doubt about the truthfulness of another employee in the department. Ceballos also testified in court about his doubts in relation to the affidavit. Afterward, Ceballos was victimized by reassignments, transfers, and the loss of a promotion. He argued that the actions of his superiors violated his right to speak freely about this problem in his department. The district attorney's office argued that a public employee's right to free speech could be limited by a state agency when that speech was made in the exercise of his or her official duties. Ceballos argued that his free speech rights, as guaranteed by the First Amendment to the U.S. Constitution, trumped any state action. The district attorney argued that the power to control the right of free speech in relation to public employees had devolved to the states. Is the district attorney correct? Explain. *Garcetti, et al. v. Ceballos,* 126 S. Ct. 1951 (U.S. Supreme Court).

4. Barbara Rome entered Flower Memorial Hospital to undergo a series of X-rays. When she was ready for the X-rays, she was assisted by a student radiological intern. The intern placed Rome on the X-ray table and strapped her onto the table correctly. However, the intern did not properly fasten the footboard, which was located at the foot of the table. As a result of this error, Rome fell and was hurt when the table was raised. As a consequence, Rome brought a lawsuit against Flower Memorial Hospital alleging that the ordinary negligence of the intern had caused her injury. In contrast, the hospital argued that the lawsuit involved a medical claim, as defined under the state's medical malpractice statute. Whether a case involves ordinary negligence or a medical claim would determine whether the state's two-year statute of limitations for negligence or the state's one-year statute of limitations for medical claims would apply. This case clearly involves a difference of opinion on the interpretation of a statute. What sources might the court consider when interpreting the statute in question? *Rome v. Flower Memorial Hospital,* 635 N.E.2d 1239 (OH).

5. The Heart of Atlanta Hotel brought an action against the United States seeking a judgment that would declare Title II of the Civil Rights Act of 1964 unconstitutional. Congress's power to enact the Civil Rights Act is based upon Article I, Section 8, Clause 3, which gives Congress the power to regulate commerce among the states. The Heart of Atlanta Hotel argued that the statute was an unconstitutional extension of congressional power. The hotel also contended that the unconstitutional nature of the act especially applied to establishments like itself, which are incorporated and do business in only one state. However, because at any given time, three-fourths of the hotel's registered guests came from other states, the hotel clearly had an impact on interstate commerce. Do the lower federal courts have the authority to determine the constitutionality of Title II of the Civil Rights Act? What court has the ultimate authority to determine the constitutionality of the Civil Rights Act? Speculate on the outcome of this case. Do you think that the court should uphold the act? Explain. *Heart of Atlanta Hotel v. United States,* 370 U.S. 241 (U.S. Sup. Ct.).

Quick Quiz Answers

2-1	2-2	2-3	2-4	2-5
1. T	1. F	1. F	1. T	1. F
2. F	2. F	2. F	2. F	2. F
3. T	3. F	3. T	3. F	3. T

Chapter 3   The Judicial Process

The Opening Case
Ruhrgas v. Marathon Oil Company

Marathon Oil, an American energy company, filed a fraud case in state court against a German corporation named Ruhrgas. Almost immediately after being served with process, Ruhrgas filed a motion to remove the case from state to federal court. Ruhrgas argued that the case belonged in federal court because the federal court held subject matter jurisdiction, based on diversity and federal law. Once the case was before a federal judge, Ruhrgas, using a very clever strategy, argued that the case should be dismissed entirely because though the federal court had subject matter jurisdiction, it did not have personal jurisdiction over the German corporation. The district court agreed with Ruhrgas and dismissed the case. Not to be outdone, Marathon Oil appealed, arguing that the federal court had no subject matter jurisdiction and the case should therefore be sent back to the state court. Ruhrgas asserted that the issue of subject matter was irrelevant, because the court had no personal jurisdiction. Marathon then argued, and the appeals court agreed, that a federal court could not consider matters of personal jurisdiction until it had considered all issues related to subject matter jurisdiction, and therefore, the case should be sent back to federal court for a determination of subject matter jurisdiction. In a surprise move, the Supreme Court ruled that though it was common practice for courts to consider subject matter jurisdiction first, there was no procedural requirement that they do so. Therefore, the lower court's decision to dismiss the case for lack of personal jurisdiction was perfectly valid. This case demonstrates the central importance of procedural law. It also shows that cases can be lost even when a party has the substantive law on its side. (See *Ruhrgas AG v. Marathon Oil Co.*, 526 U.S. 574 (1999) and Georgene M. Vairo, "Forum Selection: A Jurisdiction Question," *The National Law Journal,* February 26, 2007, p. 13.)

Opening Case Questions

1. How can a party establish the jurisdiction of the federal court to hear a case?

2. In what circumstances can a party remove a case from state to federal court?

3. What is the difference between subject matter jurisdiction and personal jurisdiction?

4. How does a federal court determine the extent of its personal jurisdiction over a defendant?

5. What is the central lesson of the case of *Ruhrgas v. Marathon Oil*?

Learning Objectives

1. Explain the fundamental nature of American courts.
2. Determine in what circumstances the federal court has jurisdiction to hear a case.
3. Recognize which cases may be heard by the U.S. Supreme Court.
4. Identify the structure found in most state court systems.
5. Determine the extent of electronic jurisdiction.
6. Define civil litigation.
7. List the most commonly used discovery techniques.
8. Explain the nature of electronically stored information.
9. Detail the nature of an appeal.
10. Describe the steps in a criminal prosecution.

3-1 The Court System

LO1

The laws of the American government are interpreted and enforced by a system of courts authorized by either the federal or a state constitution and established by legislative authority. Courts are judicial tribunals that meet in a regular place and apply the law in an attempt to settle disputes by weighing the arguments presented by advocates for each party. Each of these official bodies is a forum for the party who presents a complaint, the party who answers the complaint, and the jury and/or judge who settles the dispute. As noted in the previous chapter, the courts are an integral part of the complex adaptive system that is the law. As is true of all complex adaptive systems, the law is an intricate network of interactive organizational levels, each of which depends on the others for the smooth operation of the entire network. The courts make up one of these key organizational levels. Thus, within the law, the executive branch (the president or the governor, and his or her executive assistants), the legislature (Congress or the various state assemblies), and the bureaucracy (those agencies charged with doing the "grunt work" of the law) depend on the courts to interpret the law and ensure the law is carried out according to legislative and executive intent.

Also, as in all complex adaptive systems, the more experienced the law becomes, the more readily it adjusts to a shifting social and economic climate. This "adaptive" attribute of the law is seen in the court's willingness to interpret statutory law, to uphold the Constitution, and to address tough contemporary issues by hearing controversial cases. It can also be seen when the United States Supreme Court decides to tackle landmark cases like *Kelo v. New London*, which is highlighted at the end of Part I in this text. As we shall see in *Kelo v. New London*, though the courts are usually thought of as the most stable of the embedded niches within the complex legal system, they will at times make radical moves that upset the entire network, at least temporarily. However, this tendency should not worry us. It is, after all, the unpredictability of the entire legal system that makes the law so much fun.

The Federal Court System

LO2

The federal court system is authorized by Article III of the U.S. Constitution, which states, "The Judicial Power of the United States shall be vested in one supreme court, and in such inferior courts as Congress may from time to time ordain and establish." The present federal court system includes the Supreme Court, courts of appeals, and federal district courts.

U.S. Const. Article III
(see page 948)

Court Jurisdiction

The authority of a court to hear and decide cases is called the court's jurisdiction. It is set by law and limited as to territory and type of case. A court of original jurisdiction has the authority to hear a case when it is first brought to court. Those courts that have the power to review a case for errors are courts of **appellate jurisdiction**. Most of the time courts with appellate jurisdiction will be empowered to determine whether the lower courts have made errors of law. This process is referred to as **plenary review**. Sometimes an appellate court will review the factual decisions made by the judge or the jury in lower courts. Such a review, however, only occurs when the appeals court determines that the decision made in the lower court was undeniably wrong, given the facts and evidence in the case. This determination relies on the **clearly erroneous standard**. Appellate courts also have the ability to determine whether the judge in the lower court has in some way misused his or her authority. This type of review is referred to as **abuse of discretion**.

Courts with the power to hear any type of case are said to exercise **general jurisdiction**. Those with the power to hear only certain types of cases have **special jurisdiction**. Examples of courts with special jurisdiction are probate courts and courts of claims. Courts also exercise subject matter jurisdiction and personal jurisdiction. **Subject matter jurisdiction** is the court's power to hear a particular type of case. **Personal jurisdiction** is the court's authority over the parties to a lawsuit.

Federal District Courts
Each state and territory in the United States has at least one federal district court. These courts are also known as *U.S. district courts*. The district courts are the courts of general jurisdiction in the federal system. They carry a very heavy caseload in the federal system. Recent figures indicate that the district courts handle more than 600,000 cases each year. Most federal cases begin in the federal district court. Not all cases belong there, however. The federal courts have subject matter jurisdiction over two types of cases: those involving federal law and those involving diversity.

Federal district courts have subject matter jurisdiction over cases that pertain to a federal question. A **federal question** could involve the U.S. Constitution, a federal statute or statutes, or a treaty. A state law issue can be included in a suit involving a federal question if the state claim is part of the same situation that created the federal question. If the federal claim is thrown out by the federal court, the state law issue usually cannot stand by itself. The people bringing the lawsuit would have to take their case to a state court.

Subject matter jurisdiction in federal court also arises in cases of diversity, even when no federal law is involved. **Diversity cases** include lawsuits that are (1) between citizens of different states, (2) between citizens of a state or different states and citizens of a foreign nation, and (3) between citizens of a state and a foreign government as the plaintiff. This last method of establishing jurisdiction usually applies only when a foreign government sues a citizen of a state. Congress has, however, provided an exception to this rule: Federal law now permits lawsuits in the federal courts against a foreign state when that state supports terrorism. The lawsuit must involve a request for damages arising from terrorist acts related to that support and as those acts are defined by law.

In diversity cases, and for other legal purposes, corporations are considered citizens of the state in which they are incorporated and the state where they have their principal place of business. In federal court, if even one defendant is a citizen of the same state as one of the plaintiffs, diversity cannot be established. In such a case, the law says that "diversity is not complete." Diversity cases also must involve an amount over $75,000.

Sometimes a case that begins in a state court can be transferred to the federal court. The process of moving a case from a state court to a U.S. District Court is called **removal**. Such requests are not granted on a whim. A defendant who wants to move a case from state court to federal court must have proper grounds for that removal. To convince the court to remove a case, a defendant must show that the case actually belonged in the federal court in the first case. This requirement means that the defendant will have to show that diversity exists or that a federal question was involved from the start. The defendant must file a motion to remove the case within 30 days of being served. It is also possible to remove a case to federal court even after the case has started, if circumstances change in the middle of a

Opening Case Revisited, Part I
Ruhrgas v. Marathon Oil Company, Round 2

In The Opening Case, a German corporation named Ruhrgas managed to get a case removed from state court to federal court by arguing that the federal court had subject matter jurisdiction based on both diversity and subject matter jurisdiction. Subject matter jurisdiction existed because the case involved a federal statute that allowed arbitration cases to be heard in federal court if the arbitration process related to the Convention on the Recognition and Enforcement of Foreign Awards. Diversity was a bit harder to see because the diversity in the case appeared to be incomplete; one plaintiff, Norge, and one defendant, Ruhrgas, were both citizens of a foreign country. Ruhrgas, however, argued that Norge was actually owned by Marathon. Ruhrgas also argued that Marathon had pulled Norge into the case just to force the lawsuit into state court. This effort, Ruhrgas argued, was fraud, because Norge was not involved in the case at all. Without Norge, diversity would be complete, and the case could proceed in federal court.

case, creating grounds for the removal. The statute of limitations on this type of move, however, is one year from the time that the case began, with the filing of the complaint.

Establishing subject matter jurisdiction will not be enough to get a case into federal court if the federal court does not have personal jurisdiction over a party. To establish personal jurisdiction, the court must look at the long-arm statute in the state in which the federal court is physically located. The court must then look to see if an appropriate level of contact has been made with the home state. A long-arm statute lists circumstances in which a court can exercise personal jurisdiction over an out-of-state defendant. Typically, these circumstances include the following:

- Owning real property in the state.
- Soliciting business in the state.
- Having an office or a store in the state.
- Committing a tort within the state.
- Transacting business in the state.

Some of the circumstances listed in the long-arm statute are relatively clear. Committing a tort in a state, for instance, leaves little room for misunderstanding. Other circumstances, however, such as "transacting business in the state," are not as precise. Therefore, personal jurisdiction under a state long-arm statute also requires meeting the required minimum contacts with the state. The concept of **minimum contacts** identifies the fewest number of contacts needed to allow the court to exercise jurisdiction over the out-of-state defendant. For example, let's say that a state allows the court to establish personal jurisdiction over any person who transacts business in the state. Now suppose a person buys a newspaper at an airport during a layover in the state. Does the purchase of that single newspaper constitute "transacting business" in the state?

The question turns on whether the purchase establishes a minimum contact with the state. In this case, the answer is probably "no." In general, the courts exclude contacts that are passive or that do not rise to a level that would permit the person transacting the business to reasonably foresee that he or she would come under the court's jurisdiction as a result of that transaction. It is difficult to conclude that the casual purchase of a newspaper at an airport kiosk would lead a person to foresee that he or she has voluntarily submitted

Opening Case Revisited, Part II
Ruhrgas v. Marathon Oil Company, Round 3

In The Opening Case, the defendant, Ruhrgas, filed a motion to remove the case from state to federal court. Marathon appealed, arguing that the federal court had no subject matter jurisdiction and that the case should be sent back to the state court. Ruhrgas counterattacked by contending that the issue of subject matter was beside the point, because the court had no personal jurisdiction in the case. Ruhrgas pointed out that the court had no personal jurisdiction because it, Ruhrgas, never achieved the required level of minimum contacts demanded by law. This point is crucial because if the U.S. District Court in the state did not have personal jurisdiction over the case under the state long-arm statute, the state court would also lack personal jurisdiction, and the lawsuit would end. If the federal court lacked subject matter jurisdiction however, it could be sent back to the state court. The district court agreed with Ruhrgas. Marathon appealed that ruling. The appeals court agreed with Marathon and reversed the case. The case then went to the United States Supreme Court. When presenting its case to the Supreme Court, Marathon asserted, quite convincingly, that a court must always consider subject matter jurisdiction before considering personal jurisdiction. The case should therefore be sent back to federal court for a determination of subject matter jurisdiction, and its ruling on personal jurisdiction was invalid. Ruhrgas argued that though considering subject matter jurisdiction first is a traditional procedure that most courts follow routinely, it is not required by law. The Supreme Court agreed with Ruhrgas and ruled that the court could consider personal jurisdiction first and that the dismissal was therefore legally sound.

to the jurisdictional power of a state. Something more would have to be involved. For instance, if the person in question specifically targeted the airport layover time to conduct negotiations with a client, and if a contract resulted from those negotiations, then the minimum contacts requirement would have been met and jurisdiction established.

Most of the time a court will determine subject matter jurisdiction before turning to the question of personal jurisdiction. Determining subject matter jurisdiction first, however, is not absolutely necessary. If the issue of personal jurisdiction is very obvious to the court, the court is free to dismiss the case before considering the question of subject matter jurisdiction. For example, this dismissal might happen if the defendant meets none of the categories in the long-arm statute or clearly does not meet the minimum contacts required by the case law of a state. In fact, if determining subject matter jurisdiction is especially difficult, the court is free to look at personal jurisdiction first, without even considering the question of subject matter jurisdiction.

U.S. Courts of Appeals
The judges at the appellate level must be guided by the standard of review that is appropriate to each case. The standard of review tells the appellate-level judges the degree to which they must remain faithful to the decision of the lower court judge. As noted previously, the three standards of review are *plenary, clearly erroneous*, and *abuse of discretion*. Although they do not hear as many cases each year as the district courts, there are fewer U.S. courts of appeals and therefore fewer judges to hear those cases. Currently, the appellate courts in the federal system hear over 60,000 cases annually (see Table 3-1). At present, there are 13 U.S. courts of appeals within the federal court system (see Figure 3-1). Eleven of these appellate courts cover geographical groupings of states. For example, the Sixth Circuit Court of Appeals includes Michigan, Ohio,

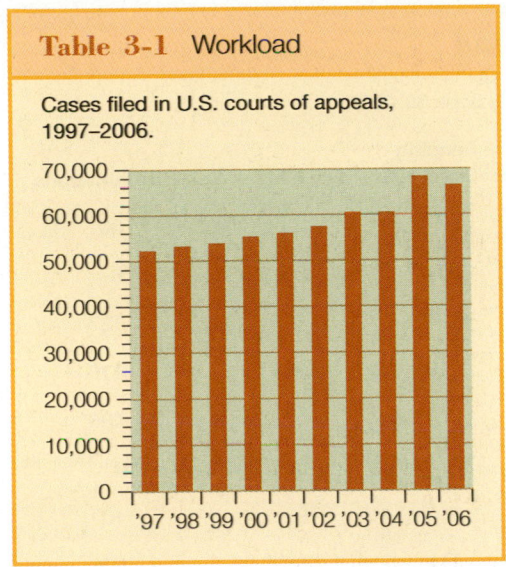

Table 3-1 Workload

Cases filed in U.S. courts of appeals, 1997–2006.

Source: Administrative Office of the U.S. Courts. Pamela A. MacLean, "U.S. Courts: Courts See Slight Easing of New Case Loads," *The National Law Journal,* March 19, 2007, p. 17.

Kentucky, and Tennessee. The Fifth Circuit includes Texas, Louisiana, and Mississippi. There is also a special appellate court for the District of Columbia called the U.S. Court of Appeals for the District of Columbia.

In addition to 12 appellate courts, organized on a geographical basis, there is a thirteenth appellate court that has special jurisdiction over certain types of cases. This court is

The Thirteen Federal Judicial Circuits

Figure 3-1   The U.S. federal court system is divided into thirteen circuits, including the Washington, D.C., and federal circuits. Each circuit has several district courts.

Table 3-2   Caseload of the Federal Circuit

By source of appeals, for 12-month period ending Sept. 30, 2006.

Source of appeals	Pending Oct 1, '05	Filed	Terminations	Pending Sept. 30, '06
Board of Contract Appeals	22	33	30	25
Court of International Trade	56	58	67	47
U.S. Court of Federal Claims	124	154	137	141
U.S. Court of Appeals for Veterans Claims	216	384	119	481
U.S. district courts	376	522	496	402
Department of Veterans Affairs	2	3	3	2
International Trade Commission	8	9	10	7
Merit Systems Protection Board	244	508	506	246
Office of Compliance	4	0	4	0
U.S. Patent and Trademark Office	39	72	60	51
Writs*	3	29	28	4
Total	1,094	1,772	1,460	1,406

*Includes writs of mandamus, other extraordinary writs, petitions for permission to appeal, and discretionary petitions for review.
Source: U.S. Court of Appeals for the Federal Circuit. Marcia Cole, "Critics Target Federal Circuit," *The National Law Journal,* October 16, 2006, pp. 1, 20–21.

known as the U.S. Court of Appeals for the Federal Circuit. The Federal Circuit was established by Congress primarily to streamline and unify patent law. However, the Federal Circuit was also given the power to hear appeals in cases that entail government contracts, trademark disputes, federal workers, veterans' benefits, and international trade, among others. Still, more than one-third of the appeals that end up in the Federal Circuit are patent cases that come either from the U.S. district courts or the U.S. Patent and Trademark Office (see Table 3-2). Critics of the Federal Circuit have argued that the court's approach to patent law has become too narrow and too formalistic. (See Marcia Cole, "Critics Target Federal Circuit," *The National Law Journal,* October 16, 2006, pp. 1, 20–21.)

The United States Supreme Court   Established by the Constitution, the U.S. Supreme Court is the court of final jurisdiction in all cases appealed from the lower federal courts and in cases coming from state supreme courts. It has original jurisdiction in cases affecting ambassadors or other public ministers and consuls and in cases in which a state is a party. The Supreme Court is composed of a chief justice and eight associate justices. They are appointed by the president with the consent of the Senate and hold office during good behavior.

U.S. Const. Article III
(see page 948)

In many situations, a case will reach the U.S. Supreme Court only if the court agrees to issue a writ of certiorari. A **writ of certiorari** is an order from the Supreme Court to a lower court to deliver its records to the U.S. Supreme Court for review. The Court will issue a writ of certiorari if several lower courts have dealt with an issue but cannot agree on how it should be handled. If the case involves an issue that affects a large segment of society, the Court is likely to grant a writ. Finally, the Court may also hear a case if it involves a constitutional issue.

Applicable Law When a federal court hears a case involving only federal law or the U.S. Constitution, it must follow that federal law, the Constitution, and/or any line of federal precedent that can be used to interpret the situation. Circumstances are different in diversity cases or federal law cases that also concern issues of state law. For instance, if a federal judge in Minnesota hears a diversity case between a Minnesota citizen and an Iowa citizen, would that judge use federal law, Minnesota law, or Iowa law? As a general rule, a federal court hearing a diversity case will apply the law of the state in which it is physically located.

EXAMPLE 3-1:   The Demise of "General Law"

While walking on a railroad track in Pennsylvania, Tompkins was injured when he was struck by an open door protruding from one of the passing freight trains. The federal court had diversity jurisdiction because Tompkins was a citizen of Pennsylvania and the railroad company was formed in New York. Under Pennsylvania common law, Tompkins would have been considered a trespasser and would therefore lose the case. Tompkins urged the court to ignore Pennsylvania law and apply what he called "general law." General law, according to Tompkins's attorneys, included principles of law that are of a universal nature and thus not tied to any one state. The trial court and the appellate court agreed with Tompkins. The U.S. Supreme Court did not. The Court held that attempts to enforce this unwritten "general law" were confusing and inconsistent. The Court concluded that federal courts in diversity cases must use state substantive law.

State Court Systems

The courts of each state are organized according to the provisions of the state constitution. Despite differences from state to state, such as the names for similar types of courts, there are basic similarities. For example, each state has an arrangement of inferior, or lower-level, courts that serve as limited jurisdiction trial courts. Higher-level trial courts with broader jurisdiction are also provided. In addition, each state has appellate courts to which questions of law (not questions of fact) may be appealed. Figure 3-2 provides a general outline of the federal and the state court systems.

State Trial Courts The state trial courts, also known as general jurisdiction courts, have the power to hear any type of case. They are often called superior courts, circuit courts, or courts of common pleas. Some states, notably New York, refer to them as supreme courts. These courts are usually organized around the counties of the state, so that each county has its own trial court of general jurisdiction. Most states also have other trial courts that are lower than the general jurisdiction courts. These limited jurisdiction courts usually hear only certain types of cases. For instance, a municipal court may be empowered to hear only those cases that involve municipal ordinances, criminal cases involving crimes within the city limits, and other cases that involve monetary claims of less than $10,000. Many localities have small-claims courts that hear civil cases involving small dollar amounts, ranging from $500 to $5,000, depending on state law.

State Intermediate Appellate Courts State court systems provide for a variety of appellate court structures. Still, the purpose of the appellate courts remains the same, that is, to hear appeals on questions of law from the lower courts. Usually, appeals are heard by a three-judge panel. The panel examines the records of the lower court, reads the written arguments submitted by the attorneys, studies the law on its own, and listens to the oral

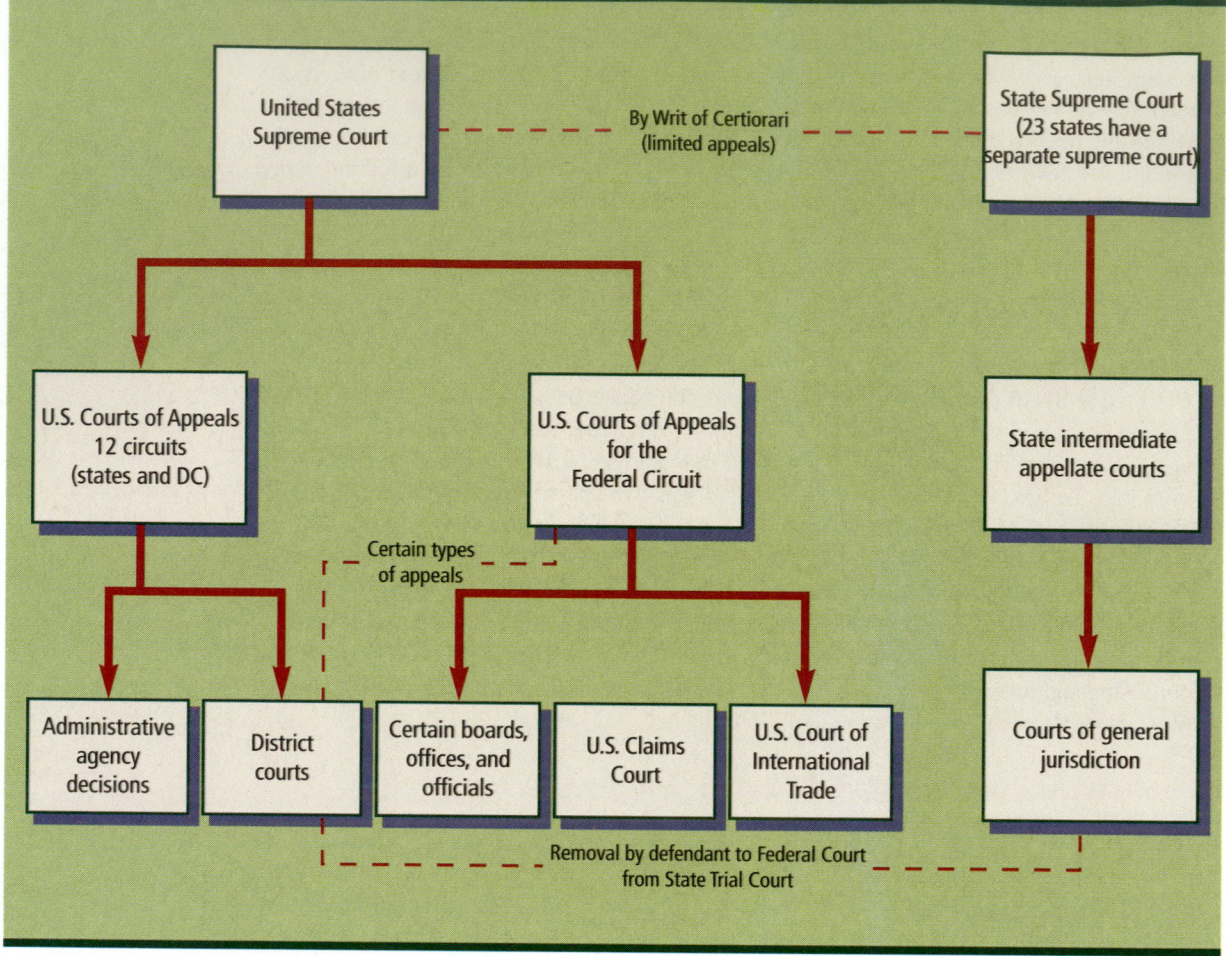

Figure 3-2   Federal and state court systems.

arguments of the attorneys. If the panel agrees with the lower court, it will affirm the decision of that court. However, if the panel disagrees with the lower court's decision, it can set aside or modify the decision of that court.

State Supreme Courts

Twenty-seven states rely on their supreme court as their only appellate court. These states have no intermediate appellate courts. The other 23 states have both intermediate appellate courts and state supreme courts. Most supreme courts consist of a panel of three to nine judges. As is true at the intermediate appellate level, the panel of judges examines the records of the lower court, reads the written arguments submitted by the attorneys, studies the law on its own, and listens to the oral arguments of the attorneys. The decisions of state supreme courts are final unless a federal issue or a constitutional right is involved.

Electronic Jurisdiction

LO5 Whether courts have jurisdiction over out-of-state defendants has been complicated by Internet business transactions. Using the Internet, sellers can solicit business, negotiate terms of a contract, enter the contract, receive payment, and deliver the goods without ever physically entering a state. Does this type of activity reach the level of a minimum contract required to establish personal jurisdiction? **Electronic jurisdiction (e-jurisdiction) is the authority of a court to hear a case based on Internet-related transactions.** While this area of law is still in its infancy, we can nevertheless extract at least one general principle: Because of its basic nature, e-jurisdiction is a moving target. To help attorneys and businesspeople hit this moving target, the courts have established a sliding scale on which several types of jurisdiction can be measured.

On one side of this scale are electronic transactions that involve minimum contacts. These would include e-transactions carried out from beginning to end on the Internet. Those e-transactions that involve solicitation, negotiation, payment, and delivery in cyberspace would therefore establish jurisdiction. On the other side of the scale are those cases that can establish that the defendant simply placed an inactive advertisement on the Web. Such inactive advertisements will usually not establish jurisdiction. The final type of case falls between the two extremes. These cases concern e-transactions that involve more than simple inactive advertising on the Internet. The courts have not established any single normative approach to such transactions, and so the matter must be handled on a case-by-case basis.

Cybertransactions must be handled on a case-by-case basis.

Quick Quiz 3-1 True or False?

1. Courts are judicial tribunals that meet in a regular place and apply the laws in an attempt to settle disputes fairly. *T*

2. The authority of a court to hear and decide cases is called the court's jurisdiction. *T*

3. The concept of minimum contacts identifies the fewest number of contacts needed to allow the court to exercise jurisdiction over the out-of-state defendant. *T*

3-2 Civil Procedure

In a civil lawsuit, one individual, organization, or corporation brings an action against another individual, organization, or corporation. The objective of a civil suit is usually to obtain money to compensate the victim. **Civil litigation** is another name for the process of bringing a case to court to enforce a right.

Commencement of the Action

The principal parties to a lawsuit are the plaintiff and the defendant. The **plaintiff** is the person who begins the lawsuit by filing a complaint in the appropriate trial court of general jurisdiction. The **defendant** is the person against whom the lawsuit has been brought and from whom a recovery is sought.

Filing the Complaint   The **complaint** sets forth the names of the parties to the lawsuit, identifying them as plaintiffs or defendants. Generally, the complaint includes the addresses of all parties. The complaint also sets forth the following:

- The facts in the case from the plaintiff's perspective.
- The alleged legal violations by the defendant.

- The injuries that the plaintiff suffered.
- The plaintiff's request for relief.

If the plaintiff wants a jury trial, this information must also be specified in the complaint. In federal court, the complaint must also include a statement of jurisdiction, which will tell the court whether the case has been brought in federal court because of a federal question or because of diversity among the plaintiffs and the defendants.

There are times when the filing of a complaint would be pointless because the amount of recovery that any single plaintiff might receive in the case would be so low that the effort and expense of carrying out the suit would not be worth the potential award. In some instances, however, the potential number of plaintiffs injured by a transgression is so high that the cost of entering the action would be justified if all of those plaintiffs joined together. A **class action** is a case in which one representative party files a lawsuit on behalf of all members of a group of plaintiffs who share a single, similar injury. Such a case is called a class action lawsuit. The courts will permit a class action lawsuit provided that (1) it is not feasible for the members of the group to bring the suit on their own, (2) the members of the group share common questions of law that can be tried together, and (3) the class action approach is far better than forcing the plaintiffs to file separate actions.

Service of Process

The complaint is presented to the appropriate court officer, usually the clerk of courts. The clerk will then see that the defendant is served with a copy of the complaint and a summons. The *summons* names the court of jurisdiction, describes the nature of the action, and demands that the defendant answer the complaint within a specified period of time, usually between 20 and 30 days, depending on the state rules of civil procedure. Giving the summons and the complaint to the defendant is called **service of process**.

The Pre-Answer Stage

As noted, once the defendant has been served, he or she has 20 to 30 days to file an answer. Usually, however, the defendant will ask for and receive an extension of that time period. The time between service and the answer is termed the *pre-answer stage*. During this stage, the defendant will take some time to examine the nature of the claim that has been filed by the plaintiff. The defendant may, as a result of this initial examination, decide to file one or more pre-answer motions. A *motion* is a request for the court to rule on a particular issue. One possible motion is a motion for dismissal of the case for failure to state a claim for which relief can be granted. Some states call this a **demurrer**. Other motions to dismiss may be based on the grounds that the court lacks subject matter jurisdiction, that the court lacks personal jurisdiction, or that the court cannot hear the case because the statute of limitations has passed.

EXAMPLE 3-2:   To Demurrer or Not to Demurrer

Lauren Jensen agreed to purchase a desk for $295 from the Stephens Sisters Furniture Store. During a management change at Stephens, Jensen's order was lost, and the furniture was never delivered. Jensen never contacted Stephens, but instead purchased a similar desk for $495 at another store. Five years later, Jensen decided to bring suit against Stephens for breach of contract. She wants to recover the extra $200 that she paid to the second store. Stephens' attorney realizes that the state statute of limitations for such contracts is four years. As a result, she files a motion to dismiss for failure to state a claim for which relief can be granted. Some states call this motion a demurrer. If Stephens's attorney is correct, the suit will be dismissed.

BusinessWeek **Business Law in the News**

Global Warming: Here Come the Lawyers

Two days after Hurricane Katrina smashed into the Gulf Coast, F. Gerald Maples returned to his hometown of Pass Christian, Miss., to utter devastation. Most of his neighbors' houses were totally destroyed. His was in ruins. "It broke our hearts and absolutely changed our lives," he says. It also made Maples, a veteran asbestos plaintiffs' attorney in New Orleans, determined to fight back. "I couldn't stand by when my entire cultural history was destroyed by an event that could become more frequent because of global warming," he says.

So when friend and fellow trial lawyer Timothy W. Porter showed up to help with food and water, the two plotted a legal assault. Since Katrina's fury was powered by unusually warm Gulf water, and since such warmth could result from global warming, companies that have pumped the atmosphere full of greenhouse gases like carbon dioxide should be liable for damages, they figured. "To me, Katrina was a clear result of irresponsible behavior by the carbon-emissions corporate economy," says Maples. He recruited suddenly homeless neighbors like Ned Comer and filed a class action on their behalf in federal court in Gulfport, Miss. The defendants? Dozens of oil companies, utilities, and coal producers, from Chevron and ExxonMobil to American Electric Power and Xcel Energy. "This is a heartfelt effort," Maples says. "I don't want to leave this global warming mess to my children."

Broad Assault

Neither, apparently, do a host of other lawyers, in what is becoming an ambitious legal war on oil, electric power, auto, and other companies whose emissions are linked to global warming. At least 16 cases, drawing on a variety of legal strategies, are pending in federal or state court. It may seem like an unconnected hodgepodge of initiatives, but whether it's a case now before the U.S. Supreme Court seeking to force the Environmental Protection Agency to crack down on greenhouse gases or the effort by a coalition of Texas cities to require cleaner plants than 17 now proposed by utilities, the challenges spring from a common concern: the lack of action in Washington. "This boomlet in global warming litigation represents frustration with the White House's and Congress' failure to come to grips with the issue," says John Echeverria, executive director of Georgetown University's Environmental Law & Policy Institute. "So the courts, for better or worse, are taking the lead."

It's hardly the first time the judiciary has emerged as the forum for those who have felt stymied trying to address a broad social issue on other fronts. And it's possible that this legal assault will prove quixotic, akin to failed suits by cities to hold gunmakers responsible for gun violence or by African Americans to win reparations for slavery.

Sword of Damocles

But there's another example that's far more worrisome for polluters: tobacco. When state attorneys general began suing cigarette makers in the mid-1990s to recover smoking-related health-care costs, the litigation was widely dismissed as fanciful. Yet before the decade was out, tobacco companies had agreed to fork over more that $300 billion and make big changes in the marketing of cigarettes.

What's more, plaintiffs can have an impact without prevailing in court. The mere threat of obesity lawsuits, for example, has sent soft drink and junk food purveyors scrambling to change their products and improve their public images. In fact, the ultimate goal for environmentalists isn't necessarily to win cases but to ratchet up the pressure on business and politicians to impose mandatory curbs on greenhouse gas emissions.

Business is fighting hard to toss the issue of global warming out of the courts entirely. "These kinds of judgments should be made by elected representatives," insists Quentin Riegel , vice-president for litigation at the National Association of Manufacturers. While industry lawyers don't fear any imminent liability, they are taking the litigation seriously. Three big law firms—Hunton & Williams, Jones Day, and Sidley Austin—are coordinating defense efforts on behalf of a group of utilities.

There are signs that others see the writing on the wall. Bryan Cave partner J. Kevin Healy says he advises corporate clients that they need to take "reasonable" steps to pare back emissions to reduce their legal exposure. And despite the strong opposition to mandatory limits from the White House and key lawmakers, many companies, some with an eye to potential litigation, are privately ready to sign on to such curbs. Louisiana utility Entergy Corp. even took the unusual step of filing a brief supporting the plaintiffs in the Supreme Court case.

As with tobacco, plaintiffs are trying out a variety of legal theories, some quite speculative. Judges and juries, however, particularly in hard-hit areas like the Gulf Coast, may be inclined to sympathize with even legally marginal claims. The Hurricane Katrina suit filed by Maples in Mississippi alleges that the emission of carbon dioxide is a "nuisance" under common law. That's a theory more typically relied on by those seeking to shut down noxious-smelling hog farms or rowdy nightclubs, though it has recently been used to win a big suit against paint manufacturers for lead contamination.

The claim that global warming is a nuisance is " a tough case to bring," says Arnold & Porter attorney Michael B. Gerrard, who is monitoring the Maples suit for a corporate client. That's because it will be tremendously difficult to prove that greenhouse gases caused Katrina and, if a jury finds that they did, apportion responsibility among polluters. Maples will have a major win if, in a decision expected within weeks, the judge even allows the trial to take place.

Questions for Analysis

1. The Katrina case filed in federal court is a class action case. What is a class action lawsuit?

2. Who are the plaintiffs in the Katrina class action case? Who are the defendants in the Katrina class action case?

3. What types of similar cases have failed to make their mark in the past? What cases have been more successful?

4. What is the real objective of many of these class action cases?

5. What unusual legal theory of liability is being used by the plaintiffs in the Katrina class action lawsuit?

Source: J. Carey and L. Woellert, "Global Warming: Here Come the Lawyers," *BusinessWeek,* October 30, 2006, 34–36.

The Answer

The **answer** is the defendant's official response to the complaint. In the answer, the defendant admits or denies the allegations in the complaint. The defendant's answer can also include affirmative defenses. An **affirmative defense** is a set of circumstances that indicate that the defendant should not be held liable, even if the plaintiff proves all of the facts in the complaint. One affirmative defense is *assumption of the risk.*

EXAMPLE 3-3:   Assessing the Risk of a Risky Business

Carol Jennings took a cruise of the Mediterranean on the Underwood Cruise Line, a firm incorporated and doing business in the United States. While the cruise ship *Principia* was docked at a Greek island, Jennings joined a tour group. She was cautioned numerous times to remain with the tour group and not to wander off by herself because of the danger of being attacked and robbed. Nevertheless, Jennings ignored the warnings and left the tour group. While on her own, she wandered into a particularly dangerous part of the city where she was beaten and robbed. She later brought a lawsuit against the Underwood Cruise Line. In its answer to Jennings' complaint, the cruise line may wish to use the defense of assumption of the risk. Such a defense would argue that Jennings was aware of danger when she chose to abandon the tour group and wander off by herself. As a result, the cruise line might argue, she assumed the risk of being attacked and robbed.

The defendant's answer may also contain counterclaims and cross-claims. A *counter-claim* is a claim that a defendant has against a plaintiff. A *cross-claim* is a claim filed by a defendant against another defendant in the same case. At this time, a defendant may also wish to file a *third-party complaint*, which is a complaint filed by the defendant against a third party not yet named in the lawsuit.

The Pretrial Stage

After the answer has been filed, the parties must await trial. During this waiting period, cleverly dubbed the pretrial stage, several activities can be carried out, including the pretrial conference, discovery, and the filing of pretrial motions.

Pretrial Conference Some courts require cases to go to a pretrial conference after the complaint and the answer have been filed. A pretrial conference usually has two purposes. One is to discuss the possibility of settling the case without the need for a trial. Another is to decide on the details involved in bringing the case to trial. Such a conference is generally called a *case management conference*. Issues that might be discussed at a case management conference include the way that the parties will conduct discovery or the need to place a limit on the number of expert witnesses that will be called at trial.

Pretrial Motions Several motions may be filed during the pretrial stage. One motion available at this time is a motion for summary judgment. A **summary judgment motion** is a motion that asks the court for an immediate judgment for the party filing the motion. This motion is filed when there is no genuine issue as to any material fact, and the party filing the motion is entitled by law to a favorable judgment. The motion cannot be filed without supporting legal arguments written out in a brief and accompanied by applicable supporting evidence.

Discovery **Discovery** is the process by which the parties to a civil action search for information that is relevant to the case. The objective is to simplify the issues and avoid unnecessary arguments and surprises in the subsequent trial. Discovery techniques and tools include the following:

LO7

Depositions are oral statements made out of court under oath by witnesses or parties to the action in response to questions from the opposing attorneys. The answers are recorded by a court stenographer and can be used for later reference.

Interrogatories are written questions that must be answered in writing under oath by the opposite party. Interrogatories cannot be given to witnesses. Only plaintiffs and defendants can be required to answer interrogatories.

Requests for real evidence ask a party to produce documents, records, accounts, correspondence, photographs, or other tangible evidence. The request may also seek permission to inspect land.

Requests for physical or mental examination ask a party to undergo a physical or a mental examination. Such requests can be made only if the physical or the mental condition of the party is in controversy; it must be a central concern to the lawsuit.

Requests for admissions are made to secure a statement from a party that a particular fact is true or that a document or set of documents is genuine. An admission eliminates the need to demonstrate the truthfulness of the fact or the genuineness of the documents at trial.

The discovery process cannot be taken lightly by the litigants. The rules of court provide severe penalties for those who fail to cooperate with discovery. Should a litigant withhold his or her cooperation, the other litigant can ask the court to compel the uncooperative party to respond to the discovery request. If the uncooperative party has a reason for not

Prospective jurors may be selected or rejected based on their ability to render an impartial judgment.

complying, then he or she may try to persuade the court of the validity of the refusal. If, for instance, the discovery request seeks information protected by the attorney–client privilege, the judge may refuse to compel the litigant to comply with the request.

If, however, the litigant cannot persuade the judge that the refusal is legally justified, the judge may impose severe penalties on the litigant. For example, the judge may elect to dismiss the lawsuit completely. The judge may also decide to render a default judgment against the uncooperative party. Reasonable expenses caused by the refusal to comply with discovery may also be assessed against the uncooperative party. These expenses may include attorney's fees. In many states, the rules allow the expenses to be assessed against either the attorney or the litigant.

Electronically Stored Information   Rapid changes in computer science have an impact on the discovery process. Until recently, the courts were satisfied to look at computerized data as if it was just another way of producing paper documents. To deal with data stored in or produced by computers, they simply used a catchphrase like "data compilation" to cover all such evidence, whether it was on paper, on a computer disk, or in a flash drive. This coverage is no longer enough. The Federal Rules of Civil Procedure now refer to computerized evidence as electronically stored information (ESI). Moreover, the rule makers have officially recognized that ESI can cause many difficulties that were not covered by the old rules. For example, computers produce and store so much ESI in so many different formats that even the most up-to-date computer expert cannot keep up, let alone an unskilled lawyer or paralegal. This complexity makes coming up with an effective discovery plan that does not crash and burn on the first day of its implementation a difficult challenge. Another difficulty is caused by the unavoidable fact that computers delete some material automatically and hold on to material that the user believed had been deleted months earlier.

Fortunately for practitioners, several new amendments have been added to the Federal Rules of Civil Procedure to overcome these difficulties and others like them. These changes were designed to meet several goals. First, attorneys must now get an early start on any discovery plan if they expect to comply with the time limits built into the rules. Second, attorneys must deal with the question of which electronic format will be used to request and deliver data. Third, problems that arise with ESI and privilege have been covered by the new rules. Fourth, the rules help in the recovery of ESI that might otherwise be difficult to find. Fifth, the new rules make certain that there is a fair apportionment of the money that has to be spent to locate hidden, deleted, or difficult-to-find ESI. Finally, the rules make clear that certain penalties exist for those who do not obey the new ESI rules.

The Civil Trial

Upon completion of discovery, the pretrial conference, and any hearings held on pretrial motions, the case is ready for trial. A trial by jury is an adversarial proceeding in which the judge's role is secondary to that of the jury's. Competition between attorneys permits the jury to sort out the truth and arrive at a just solution to the dispute.

Jury Selection   Once it is decided that the case will involve a jury, the process of *voir dire* (to speak the truth) begins. In this process, the lawyers for both parties question prospective jurors to determine whether they will be allowed to sit on the jury. Prospective jurors may be rejected if they are unable to render an impartial judgment. One reason for rejecting a prospective juror is if he or she had a personal relationship with the litigant or with a witness.

Prospective jurors may also be rejected if they have a financial interest in the outcome of the trial. However, the financial interest must be a direct, substantial interest. Remote financial interests in a trial will not disqualify a juror. Thus, the fact that the outcome of a trial may result in higher insurance rates would not disqualify a juror who has an insurance policy. Another reason might be if the prospective juror has had past experience that would prevent him or her from being impartial in the present case. Thus, a juror who has had a bad experience with a psychologist, for instance, might be unable to judge impartially the actions of a psychologist who has been sued for malpractice.

In most lawsuits, *voir dire* is conducted in the open, which means that the process is generally accessible to the press and the mass media. However, in cases that have attracted a lot of public attention, the judge may order that the media's access to the *voir dire* process be limited. Often news reporters will be limited to reading abridged copies of the transcript of the *voir dire* process after the process has been completed. The names of the jurors may also be censored, along with personal data about those jurors. This limit on the access to *voir dire* usually occurs in notorious criminal trials, but it could also happen in high-profile civil lawsuits.

Opening Statements At the beginning of the trial, both attorneys have the opportunity to make an opening statement. In the *opening statement,* an attorney presents the facts in the case and explains what he or she intends to show during the trial. Attorneys are not permitted to argue their case in the opening statement. There is widespread disagreement, however, as to what constitutes "arguing the case" during the opening statement. Consequently, the degree of argument permitted during the opening statement often depends on what the judge will allow.

The Plaintiff's Case in Chief The plaintiff's **case in chief** is the plaintiff's opportunity to present evidence that will prove his or her version of the case to the jury. The plaintiff's attorney calls witnesses and immediately subjects those witnesses to **direct examination**. Direct examination is designed to present the facts that will support the plaintiff's version of those facts. Opposing attorneys then have the chance to challenge the truthfulness of each piece of evidence presented. In this process of **cross-examination**, the witnesses answer questions of the defense attorney.

The Defendant's Case in Chief After the plaintiff has ended the presentation of his or her case in chief, the defendant has the opportunity to present his or her case in chief. The defendant's attorney calls witnesses for direct examination, and the plaintiff's attorney has an opportunity to cross-examine the defendant's witnesses.

The Rebuttal and the Surrebuttal Once the plaintiff and the defendant have presented their cases in chief, each attorney may present evidence to discredit the evidence presented by the opposition and reestablish the credibility of his or her own evidence. This step is called the **rebuttal**. The term **surrebuttal** is used in some states when referring to the defendant's rebuttal.

Closing Statements After the rebuttals are completed, each attorney makes a closing statement. In this statement, the attorneys emphasize aspects of the testimony and other evidence they believe will best persuade the judge or jury.

Jury Instructions Because juries comprise many people who are not familiar with particular aspects of the law, someone must explain the law to the jury. This is one of the duties of the judge. Although the attorneys may suggest to the judge what instructions ought to be used, the judge makes the decision. The judge's instructions explain the rules of law that the jurors are to apply to the facts in reaching their decision.

Verdict and Judgment   After receiving the judge's instructions, the members of the jury retire to a private room, where they apply the rules stated by the judge to the evidence presented by the witnesses. The jury eventually reaches a verdict. A **verdict** is a finding of fact. The verdict may be limited to the question of liability, or it can be extended to include the issue of damages. **Liability** means that the defendant is held legally responsible for his or her actions. The term **damages** refers to the money recovered by the plaintiff for the injury or loss caused by the defendant. The verdict is entered by the judge in the court records, and the case is said to be decided. According to the terms of the judgment, the defeated party either is required to pay the amount specified or do a specific thing, such as perform the terms of the contract. Court costs are usually paid by the losing party.

In some cases, money will not be adequate to satisfy the plaintiff. In such cases, the plaintiff may seek an equitable remedy. An **equitable remedy** requires a party to do something or to refrain from doing something beyond the payment of money. One equitable remedy is **specific performance**, which would require a party to a contract to go through with the terms of the contract. Usually, specific performance is permitted only in cases involving real estate or unique, one-of-a-kind goods such as art objects or rare antiques. Another equitable remedy is an injunction. An **injunction** stops a party from doing something. For instance, an employer may seek an injunction against a former employee to prevent that employee from using a trade secret on his or her new job if that trade secret is the property of the original employer.

The Appeal

An **appeal** is the referral of a case to a higher court for review. For an appeal to be successful, it must be shown that some legal error occurred. For example, a party could argue that some of the evidence that was admitted should have been excluded or that evidence that was not allowed should have been allowed. A party could also argue that the judge's instructions were erroneous or were stated in an inappropriate manner. Generally, an appeal is filed by the party that lost the case in the trial court. However, it is also possible that the party that prevailed at trial may wish to file an appeal. This step is referred to as a **cross-appeal**. For instance, if the trial court upheld most of the claims made by the plaintiff but denied one or two key claims, the plaintiff may wish to file a cross-appeal. It may also be advisable to file a cross-appeal if the trial court did not award the appropriate amount in damages, if it refused to grant attorney's fees, or if it allowed money damages but refused to permit equitable relief. (See Aaron S. Bayer, "Appellate Law: The Cross-Appeal," *The National Law Journal,* February 9, 2004, p. 13.)

Execution of the Judgment

In civil cases, if the judgment is not paid, the court will order the loser's property to be sold by the sheriff to satisfy the judgment. This order by the court is known as a **writ of execution**. Any excess from the sale must be returned to the loser. Execution of the judgment also may be issued against any income due to the loser, such as wages, salaries, or dividends. This process is known as execution against income, or garnishment, and the proceedings are known as garnishee proceedings. Checking accounts are also subject to garnishment.

3-3 Criminal Procedure

The objectives of a criminal prosecution are to protect society and to punish the wrongdoer by a fine or imprisonment. The steps in a criminal prosecution include the following:

- Arrest and initial appearance.
- Preliminary hearing.
- Formal charges.
- Arraignment.
- Trial.

The Arrest and Initial Appearance

A crime is an offense against the people. Once a law enforcement agency learns that a crime has been committed, the agency begins a criminal prosecution. The first step in a criminal prosecution is to gather evidence of the crime and identify all possible suspects. When the law enforcement agency is convinced that it has ample evidence of both the crime and the identity of the suspect, an arrest warrant is issued, and the suspect is arrested. At the time of arrest, the defendant must be informed of his or her rights. One of the principal rights of the accused is the right to be represented by counsel. This right is guaranteed by the Sixth Amendment to the Constitution. Another important right is the right to remain silent, which is protected under the Fifth Amendment, which states that a criminal defendant cannot be compelled to be a witness against him- or herself. The U.S. Supreme Court has ruled that the Fourteenth Amendment to the Constitution requires that both the right to remain silent and the right to representation by counsel must also be protected by state governments. The defendant is then brought before a judge or a magistrate for an initial appearance, where once again the defendant is reminded of his or her rights. At this time, a preliminary hearing is also scheduled.

Defendants must be informed of their rights at the time of arrest. Two important rights are the right to representation by counsel and the right to remain silent.

The Preliminary Hearing

A **preliminary hearing** is a court procedure during which the judge decides whether probable cause exists to continue holding the defendant for the crime. The government is represented by an attorney called the **prosecutor**. In some states, this government official is called the district attorney. During the preliminary hearing, the prosecution and the defendant are permitted to make arguments and call witnesses. The case will move on to the next step if there is probable cause to hold the defendant. If not, the defendant is set free.

The Formal Charges

In the United States, formal charges against the defendant may be brought either by indictment or by information. Some states do not have a grand jury system and therefore can bring formal charges only by an information. In those states that use both, the indictment is usually used to bring formal charges for serious crimes.

A Question of Ethics

Edward McDonough, assistant district attorney for the city of Middletown, has just left a session with Harold Harrison, a criminal defendant accused of armed robbery. During the session, acting under the advice of Jennifer Miller, his attorney, Harrison confessed to the crime and entered a plea bargain agreement that will place him in prison for 10 years. On his way back across the city square to his office, ADA McDonough is stopped by Sgt. Anne Wade, who confesses to him that neither she nor her partner, Sgt. Sam Newton, read Harrison his rights. McDonough knows that this admission means that the confession he just obtained is tainted and would be thrown out of court if it were challenged by Miller on behalf of Harrison. From an ethical point of view, what action should McDonough take now?

An Indictment   The federal courts and many state courts bring formal charges against the defendant by issuing an indictment. An **indictment** is a set of formal charges against a defendant issued by a grand jury. A *grand jury* consists of citizens who serve as jurors for a specified period of time to review a variety of criminal cases. The objective of a grand jury review is to determine whether probable cause exists to believe that a crime has been committed and that this particular defendant may have committed the crime. Grand jury proceedings are held in secret and are directed by the prosecutor or district attorney. If the grand jury finds probable cause exists, an indictment is issued.

An Information   An **information** is a set of formal charges against a defendant drawn up and issued by the prosecutor or district attorney. No grand jury is involved in this process. Nevertheless, an information does the same thing that an indictment does. If the prosecutor has found that probable cause exists to indicate that a crime has been committed and that this particular defendant committed the crime, an information is issued.

The Arraignment

The **arraignment** is a formal court proceeding, during which the defendant, after hearing the indictment or information read, pleads either guilty or not guilty. Should the defendant enter a guilty plea, a sentence may be imposed immediately. If the defendant enters a plea of not guilty, the case moves on to the trial.

The Criminal Trial

If the defendant has requested a jury trial, a jury is selected. After the jury has been seated, each side makes its opening statement. Opening statements are followed by the production of evidence by both the prosecution and the defendant. One very significant difference between a criminal trial and a civil trial is the burden of proof. In a civil trial, the plaintiff must prove his or her case by a preponderance of evidence. In contrast, in a criminal case, the prosecution must prove the defendant's guilt beyond a reasonable doubt. As is the case with civil procedure, the criminal trial is completed by the attorneys' closing statements and the judge's instructions to the jury. The jury members are then allowed to retire to deliberate and decide on a verdict. In most states, a defendant can be found guilty only by the unanimous agreement of all of the jurors. A defendant who is found not guilty is released. One who has been found guilty is sentenced by the judge.

Quick Quiz 3-3 True or False?

1. The objectives of a criminal prosecution are to protect society and to punish *T*
   the wrongdoer by a fine or imprisonment.

2. The steps in a criminal prosecution include the arrest and initial appearance, *T*
   the preliminary hearing, the formal charges, the arraignment, and the trial.

3. A crime is an offense against a single individual. *F*

Summary

3.1 Courts are judicial tribunals that meet in a regular place and apply the laws in an attempt to settle disputes fairly. The federal court system is divided into three levels: the district courts, the courts of appeals, and the U.S. Supreme Court. State systems vary in structure but often consist of several levels, including lower-level limited jurisdiction trial courts, higher-level trial courts, intermediate appellate courts, and state supreme courts.

3.2 Litigation begins when the plaintiff files a complaint with the appropriate trial court. The defendant must then be given a copy of the complaint and a summons. During the pre-answer stage, the defendant may attempt to dismiss the lawsuit by filing certain pre-answer motions. In the answer stage, the defendant will file an answer, which may contain affirmative defenses, counterclaims, and/or cross-claims. The defendant at this time may also file third-party complaints. During the pretrial stage, conferences may be held, motions may be made, and discovery conducted. The trial includes the opening statement, each side's case in chief, the opportunity for rebuttal and surrebuttal, the closing arguments, and the jury instructions. The jury then renders a verdict. Either party may appeal the case if that party believes that a legal error was made during the trial that influenced the verdict unfavorably. If a judgment is not paid, the court may issue a writ of execution.

3.3 The steps in a criminal prosecution include the arrest and initial appearance, the preliminary hearing, the formal charges, the arraignment, and the trial. At the time of the arrest, the defendant must be informed of his or her rights. Immediately following the arrest, the defendant is brought before a judge or a magistrate for an initial appearance, at which time the defendant is again reminded of his or her rights. A preliminary hearing is also scheduled. A preliminary hearing is a court procedure during which the judge will decide whether probable cause exists to continue to hold the defendant pending formal charges. Formal charges against the defendant may be brought either by indictment or by information. The arraignment is a formal court proceeding, during which the defendant pleads guilty or not guilty. The trial includes the opening statement, each side's case, the closing arguments, and the jury instructions. The jury then renders a verdict.

Key Terms

abuse of discretion, 48

affirmative defense, 58

answer, 58

appeal, 62

appellate jurisdiction, 48

arraignment, 64

case in chief, 61

civil litigation, 55

class action, 56

clearly erroneous standard, 48

complaint, 55

courts, 47

cross-appeal, 62

cross-examination, 61

damages, 62

defendant, 55

demurrer, 56

deposition, 59

direct examination, 61

discovery, 59

diversity cases, 48

electronic/e-jurisdiction, 55

electronically stored information (ESI), 60

equitable remedy, 62

federal question, 48

general jurisdiction, 48

indictment, 64

information, 64

injunction, 62

interrogatories, 59

jurisdiction, 47

liability, 62

minimum contacts, 49

original jurisdiction, 47

personal jurisdiction, 48

plaintiff, 55

plenary review, 48

preliminary hearing, 63

prosecutor, 63

rebuttal, 61

removal, 48

request for admissions, 59

request for a physical or mental examination, 59

request for real evidence, 59

service of process, 56

special jurisdiction, 48

specific performance, 62

subject matter jurisdiction, 48

summary judgment motion, 59

surrebuttal, 61

verdict, 62

writ of certiorari, 52

writ of execution, 62

Questions for Review and Discussion

1. What is the fundamental nature of an American court?
2. Under what circumstances might a federal court have jurisdiction to hear a case?
3. Under what circumstances might the Supreme Court hear a case?
4. What is the structure of a typical state court system?
5. What is the extent of e-jurisdiction?
6. What is civil litigation?
7. What are the most commonly used discovery tools?
8. What is ESI?
9. What is involved in an appeal?
10. What are the steps in a criminal prosecution, beginning with the arrest and up through the sentencing of the defendant?

Investigating the Internet

The Administrative Office of the United States Courts maintains a Web site that includes the latest press releases from the federal courts. Access one of the most recent press releases and write a report on the issues contained therein. As you write the report, make sure that you answer the following questions: (1) What is the subject of the news release? (2) When was the release issued by the court? (3) Who is affected by the information contained within the release? (4) Which level or levels of the federal court system are involved in the news release? (5) How do the issues discussed in the release relate to the information learned within this chapter?

Cases for Analysis

1. William Stevenson offered to help Rayford Le-Blanc remove his truck from the mud. At first, LeBlanc refused. However, later, when the towing company that LeBlanc had called proved to be unavailable, he accepted Stevenson's offer of assistance. LeBlanc then bought a towing strap from a nearby store to help in the removal of his truck from the mud. The first two attempts at removing the truck failed. On the third attempt, while LeBlanc was still in the process of connecting the straps to his truck, Stevenson, apparently without warning, pulled his vehicle forward. This movement caught LeBlanc by surprise. His hand was still wrapped up in the strap, and therefore, as Stevenson's vehicle moved forward, LeBlanc's hand was severely injured. LeBlanc sued Stevenson for damages related to the injuries to his hand. The jury decided that Stevenson was not at fault, and LeBlanc found himself on the losing end of the lawsuit. Accordingly, he appealed the case. The appellate court threw out the jury's factual finding and awarded LeBlanc over $190,000 in damages. Stevenson hollered "foul" and asked the Supreme Court of Louisiana to hear his request to have the decision reversed. The high court accepted the case. One of the central issues involved the question of whether, and under what circunmstances, an appellate court can overturn decisions of fact made by a jury. Should the supreme court uphold the appellate court's decision? What standard of review should be involved here? Explain. *LeBlanc v. Stevenson*, 770 So.2d 766 (Sup. Ct. LA).

2. On October 12, 2000, an American naval vessel, the U.S.S. *Cole*, was bombed while it was berthed in Aden Harbor in Yemen in the Middle East. The bombing, which killed 17 American sailors, was planned and executed by Al-Qaeda. Relatives of those 17 sailors brought a lawsuit in U.S. District Court against the foreign state of the Republic of Sudan, alleging that Sudan was responsible for the bombing because that government supported al-Qaeda in general and the terrorists who carried off this assault in particular. The government of the Republic of Sudan moved to dismiss the case, arguing that the court lacked subject matter jurisdiction. The argument was based on the fact that the case involved citizens of states of the United States in an attempt to sue a foreign government, something not permitted under federal law. Is the government of Sudan correct in this case? Explain. *Rux v. Republic of Sudan*, 461 F.3d. 461 (4th Cir. 2006).

3. The state of Alabama was required under the provisions of its own constitution to reapportion its electoral districts every 10 years. However, the state had failed to reapportion districts for more than half a century. Since then, the population of Alabama had grown to such an extent that severe inequalities existed among the electoral districts. The inequalities were so great in some cases that the votes of citizens in some parts of the state carried as much as 10 times the weight of the votes of citizens in other parts of the state. A suit was brought in federal court on the grounds that the inequalities in voting power violated certain guarantees found in the U.S. Constitution. The defendants argued that the federal court should not interfere in what is essentially a state matter and that by doing so, it would upset the delicate balance between the states and the federal government. Nevertheless, the federal district court struck down the apportionment scheme as unconstitutional. Does this case belong in the U.S. Supreme Court? Explain the reasons for your response. Should the Supreme Court uphold or overturn the federal district court's decision? Explain. *Reynolds v. Sims,* 377 U.S. 533 (U.S. Sup. Ct.).

4. Speculate on which of the following cases the U.S. Supreme Court might decide to review: a case involving a dispute over whether computer software can be copyrighted; a case involving an appeal of a zoning board's decision to limit the number of adult book stores on any single city block; a case involving the constitutionality of an abortion statute; a case involving an antitrust suit based on a violation of a federal antitrust statute between the National Football League and the United States Football League; a libel case against a small town newspaper involving allegations of the mayor's dishonesty; a case involving the placement of a religious scene on city property; a case brought by a steel company to enjoin employees from going on strike; a case involving the distribution of antiwar flyers at a private shopping mall; and a case involving the search of a high school student's locker without her permission. In each case, give reasons for your answer.

5. Eight limited partners filed a lawsuit in the Lucas County Court of Common Pleas, alleging that the general partners in 10 different limited partnerships had engaged in an extensive pattern of self-dealing that had involved converting partnership property for their own personal use. Also named in the lawsuit was the accounting firm of Donald J. Goldstein, CPA, a resident of Florida, and Goldstein, Lewis, and Company, a professional corporation located in Florida. The plaintiffs claimed that the accountant and the accounting firm had known of the general partners' misconduct and were therefore liable to the plaintiff for that malpractice. The accountant and the accounting firm decided to end the suit as quickly as possible. Consequently, they filed a motion for dismissal. The motion stated that the courts of Ohio lacked personal jurisdiction over them because they were from Florida. They further stated that they did not solicit business in Ohio, maintained no place of business in Ohio, had no license to act as accountants in Ohio, owned no property in Ohio, provided all services from Florida, and filed no documents with the state of Ohio. Thus, they concluded that they fell outside the power of Ohio's long-arm statute. Conversely, the plaintiffs argued that the defendants transacted business in the state of Ohio on a continuing and ongoing basis by regularly submitting financial statements to the limited partners in Ohio and by being actively involved in the decisions of the general partnership. Did the activities of the accountant and the accounting firm place them under the jurisdiction of the Ohio court, according to the state "long-arm" statute? Explain. *Goldstein v. Christiansen,* 638 N.E.2d 541 (OH).

6. The criminal defendant in this case, a man named Gideon, broke into a pool room in Florida with the objective of committing a minor crime. Because Gideon was without any means of financial support, he could not afford an attorney. He asked for but was denied representation by a court-appointed attorney. Consequently, he represented himself at trial. Ultimately, he was found guilty and sentenced to five years in prison. Gideon later challenged his conviction on the grounds that he had been deprived of his constitutional right to representation by an attorney. In opposition, Florida argued that, though all fundamental rights guaranteed by the federal government through the Bill of Rights should also be guaranteed by state governments, the right to legal representation was not such a fundamental right. In fact, the right to a court-appointed attorney arose only when the criminal defendant had been accused of a very serious crime. The U.S. Supreme Court agreed to hear the case. How should the Supreme Court rule in this case? Is the right to an attorney a fundamental right that should be guaranteed to criminal defendants by the states, regardless of the seriousness of the crime? Explain. Examine the Constitution and find the Amendment that guarantees the right to representation by an attorney. Examine the Constitution and find the Amendment that extends that right to defendants in state criminal actions. *Gideon v. Wainwright,* 372 U.S. 355 (U.S. Sup. Ct.).

7. Ernesto Miranda was arrested in his own home for a serious crime and held in an interrogation room. He was not informed of his right to remain silent, nor was he informed that he could be represented by an attorney. Eventually, after a two-hour interrogation conducted by two police officers, Miranda signed a statement that indicated he had voluntarily confessed to the crime of which he was accused. On the basis of the confession, Miranda was found guilty. He appealed to the Arizona Supreme Court, which affirmed the guilty verdict. Miranda asked the U.S. Supreme Court to hear his appeal. Is this the type of case that belongs in the U.S. Supreme Court? Explain the reasons for your response. Should the Supreme Court uphold or overturn the state court's conviction of Miranda? Explain the Constitution and find the Amendment that guarantees the right to remain silent when arrested for a criminal action. Examine the Constitution and find the Amendment that extends that right to defendants in state criminal actions. *Miranda v. Arizona,* 384 U.S. 436 (U.S. Sup. Ct.).

Quick Quiz Answers

3-1	1. T	3-2	1. F	3-3	1. T
	2. T		2. F		2. T
	3. T		3. F		3. F

Chapter 4

Alternative Dispute Resolution

The Opening Case

Natare Corp. v. D.S.I. Duraplastec Systems, Inc.

Two corporations, one named D.S.I. Duraplastec Systems and the other Natare, entered into an agreement, according to which each of the corporations promised the other that it would no longer make disparaging remarks about it. They also agreed that the best way to handle any disputes between them would be arbitration. Added to this arbitration clause was an agreement that the party that broke the agreement would pay the other party's attorney's fees. After a brief time during which no problems arose, Natare discovered that D.S.I. had broken the contract by making disparaging remarks about Natare. Accordingly, Natare activated the arbitration clause. The arbitrator agreed with Natare, and as a result, D.S.I. was ordered to pay Natare $5,000. However, the arbitrator decided not to award any attorney's fees to Natare. This upset the managers of Natare, who pointed to the clause in the non-disparagement agreement and asked again for attorney's fees. When this request did not work, Natare brought a claim in state court demanding that it be awarded attorney's fees as stipulated in the contract. Natare argued that by not ordering the payment of attorney's fees, the arbitrator had violated the limits of his power. The case went to trial court, and the judge upheld the award; however, when the case was appealed, the appellate court agreed with Natare. The case then went to the Indiana Supreme Court. The Indiana Supreme Court found no abuse of discretion on the part of the arbitrator, and the ruling stood. If two parties are supposed to use arbitration to escape the red tape, expense, and confusion of the court, why take the case to court when a party disagrees with the arbitrator's decision? It would appear that, in some cases at least, arbitration does not work the way it is supposed to work, or at least not as the parties expect it to work. As you read Chapter 4, consider this case and ask yourself whether ADR is as foolproof and effective as its supporters contend. (See *Natare Corporation v. D.S.I. Duraplastec Systems, Inc.*, 855 N.E. 2d 985 (Sup. Ct. Ind) and "Arbitrator Sustained in Denying Attorneys Fees," *The National Law Journal*, March 19, 2007, p. 18.)

Opening Case Questions

1. What is arbitration?

2. Why do many parties prefer arbitration to litigation?

3. Is an arbitration ruling always subject to an appeal?

4. What are some of the problems associated with arbitration?

5. If arbitration is supposed to be better than a civil trial, what went wrong in this case?

 Learning Objectives

1. Discuss the shortcomings of litigation.
2. List the advantages and disadvantages of ADR.
3. Identify the advantages of mediation.
4. Explain the nature of an arbitration hearing.
5. Outline the med-arb process.
6. Relate the role of an early neutral evaluator.
7. Describe the process of running a summary judgment trial.
8. Determine the advantages of a private civil trial.
9. Clarify the private options available under proactive ADR.
10. Specify the governmental options available under proactive ADR.

4-1 A Primer on Alternative Dispute Resolution

As we have seen at various points throughout this text, the law operates as a complex adaptive system that must adjust to rapid, unpredictable alterations in the socioeconomic-cultural context. Sometimes the juris-economic system must make internal, self-adapting changes to correct mistakes or redefine the mission of the system. A case in point involves the problems that have arisen within the litigation process. As we noted in Chapter 3, litigation is the process of bringing a case to court to enforce a right. The people involved in litigation are called litigants. Litigation has always been a part of the American legal system. Lately, however, things have begun to change. The complexity and expense of the litigation process have led many people to seek alternative dispute resolution techniques to redress their grievances. **Alternative dispute resolution (ADR)** occurs whenever people attempt to resolve disagreements by stepping outside the usual adversarial system and applying creative settlement techniques, many of which have fact finding and the discovery of truth as their goals.

Problems with Litigation

LO1

Many people choose a dispute resolution process that sidesteps the adversarial approach of civil litigation because they believe that it is the best way to achieve justice. Part of this belief is based on the suspicion that, with an adversarial approach, victory often depends not on who is in the right but on which advocate is the better tactician. Unfortunately, the best tactician is often one of the most expensive advocates available, which can mean that justice often goes to those who can afford it. For this reason, many people seek an alternative that is less costly to both sides.

Litigation can also be expensive because of the initial steps that lead to the filing of a lawsuit. For instance, before an attorney can file a medical malpractice lawsuit, he or she must obtain the client's medical records, which means paying an initial copying fee that can amount to hundreds or even thousands of dollars. The attorney must then hire an expert to evaluate the records to determine whether the information in the records indicates that the client has a viable claim. Again this expense can run into hundreds or thousands of dollars. All these expenses are encountered before the attorney even knows that a claim actually exists.

In addition to being expensive, litigation can be time consuming. The initial steps after the filing of a complaint can delay progress on a lawsuit for many months. For instance, should the defendant's motion for dismissal be granted by the court, a lengthy and time-consuming appeal process may ensue. In some cases, the appeal could even find its way to the highest court in the jurisdiction. In such a case, if the highest court reverses the lower court's dismissal of the action, the case quite literally returns to the starting line. Another time-consuming step in litigation is the process of discovery. Taking depositions, answering interrogatories, filing, and responding to requests for real evidence and handling requests for mental or physical examinations can tie up a lawsuit for months.

Moreover, some jurisdictions require litigants to submit to case management hearings and settlement hearings before they can secure a trial date. Even when a court date is secured, many court dockets, especially those in large urban areas, are backed up for months, or even years, which often means that the parties to a lawsuit must wait for long periods of time before having their day in court. Even once a trial has occurred and a decision rendered, recovery can be delayed as the parties enter a second phase of the lawsuit, the execution of the judgment phase. This process involves its own complex set of procedures which, like the actual lawsuit, can cause expensive and time-consuming delays.

The ADR Option

However, ADR can provide an economical and efficient alternative to litigation. Depending on the ADR technique employed, the time involved in settling a dispute can be shortened considerably and the expenses lowered significantly. Arbitration and mediation, for example, can be scheduled quickly, even before a lawsuit is filed. When scheduling either a mediation or an arbitration session, the parties need not consult the court's dockets or worry about any preliminary requirements, such as a case management conference. Moreover, even if the arbitration or mediation session does not end the dispute, it can save time by narrowing the issues or providing an evaluation of the strength of each side's case. The arbitration or mediation session may also, in some cases, provide a shortcut to discovery, thus saving time and lowering expenses.

Other ADR approaches, such as early neutral evaluation (ENE), can save money and time by providing an assessment of the issues at stake and the range of damages available, should the outcome of the case demand a remedy of some sort. Summary jury trials, private trials, and mini-trials can all be inexpensive and quick because they can be scheduled without regard to the court's docket and can be held without the expenses involved in hiring expert witnesses and providing travel and hotel accommodations for those witnesses. The cost and time involved in lengthy discovery processes can also be avoided by selecting any one of these ADR techniques.

ADR options provide a timely, cost-efficient method for resolving legal issues.

Private proactive ADR techniques such as drafting contract clauses and entering partnering agreements can help to make litigation unnecessary from the outset. The idea behind the proactive ADR approach is to anticipate and deal with disputes before they occur. By providing a solution to problems before those problems arise, proactive ADR eliminates the uncertainty and risk inherent within the litigation process.

Shortcomings of ADR

Yet ADR is not without problems. On the contrary, some critics of the alternative dispute resolution process have pointed out that the private administration of justice hampers the development of the law. Because many ADR techniques completely sidestep the courts, many critical social issues may never reach the judicial system, causing gaps in the evolution of case law and the progression of legislation. Another criticism of ADR involves its limited scope. Some legal conflicts, notably employment, contract, and tort cases, are especially well suited for ADR. However, other legal problems, primarily those involving constitutional law, civil rights, and criminal law, could never be brought before an ADR panel.

BusinessWeek Business Law in the News

Civil Suits: The Vanishing Trial

A towering state courthouse that opened in downtown Houston last year boasts 39 courtrooms and expansion space for more. But lawyers in that city say the new building, built to handle civil lawsuits, is often eerily empty. The reason: So few cases are going to trial.

The federal courthouses in the northern district of Florida, a sprawling region that includes Tallahassee, Pensacola, and Gainesville, have been similarly quiet in recent months. The four federal judges in the district presided over just 12 civil trials in 2006 and 5 in 2005.

Around the country, plenty of lawsuits are getting filed, but fewer and fewer are going to trial. The civil trial is one of the most iconic American institutions, a time-honored forum where disputes over injuries, divorces, and all manner of business disasters are resolved. Yet rising legal costs, decreasing judicial tolerance for weak lawsuits, and the surging use of alternative dispute resolution (ADR) are combining to make courtroom showdowns exceptional occurrences.

After peaking at 12,018 in 1984, the number of civil trials in all federal district courts has dropped precipitously, reaching a new low of 3,555 last year. That's almost half the number of federal trials that took place 40 years ago, even though the number of suits filed during the same period soared from 66,144 to 259,541. Now the U.S. Securities & Exchange Commission is considering a contentious proposal to allow federal shareholder lawsuits to be handled through arbitration, a move that could siphon additional lawsuits out of the court system.

University of Wisconsin law professor Marc Galanter has dubbed this trend the "vanishing trial." It has also played out in state courts. In 21 states for which data were available, the number of civil jury trials fell 40% from 1976 to 2004.

Is this development worrisome? Some in the legal community are happy that trials are becoming rarer. Courtroom litigation is "a very inefficient process" for most cases, says Victor Schachter, a lawyer in Mountain View, Calif., who represents companies in employment suits.

Yet others are worried, with concerns ranging from the profound to the practical. Nathan L. Hecht, a senior justice on the Texas Supreme Court, says that the drop in the number of trials is resulting in a reduction in the number of precedents—the broad rulings that tell people and businesses how to behave in changing and legally ambiguous circumstances. "I think it's a detriment if we lose the development of the common law through cases and appeals that have been the [basis of the] rule of law in this country since its founding," says Hecht. . . .

Companies began flocking out of the court system in the 1980s, steering disputes into alternative procedures such as mediation (nonbinding settlement discussions) or arbitration (in which a paid arbitrator or panel of three arbitrators decides a case). . . .

Still what amounts to private justice remains popular, partly because it is shielded from the public. In Seattle and surrounding King County, Wash., for example, a cottage industry of retired judges has risen up to resolve not just commercial disputes but also the divorce and child custody battles of the region's many high-tech millionaires in proceedings that are fast and confidential.

Other developments are also contributing to the trial drought. Changes to liability laws passed in many states have simply closed the door to many types of personal injury claims. Limits on damages, for example, have caused a sharp falloff in medical malpractice lawsuits in a number of states.

Judges themselves have also become much more aggressive about pruning their dockets, resolving cases through summary judgment, or pressuring parties to mediate or settle. That's not necessarily bad, but some says it's gone too far. "There's a divide in the judiciary," says William G. Young, a federal district judge in Boston. Some judges, he says, see their job as "managing" disputes and avoiding trial. Others, including himself, do not shy away from trials and think they play a critical role in American justice. . . .

David Berg, a longtime Houston trial lawyer, sees a future devoid of the courtroom dramas that have long captured the American imagination. In a manual on trial technique that he published last year, Berg wrote that he feared that "the great war stories of the next generation of trial lawyers would begin,

'And then, I looked the mediator in the eyes and I said . . . .'"

Questions for Analysis

1. What has caused a reduction in the number of trials in federal and state courts? Explain.

2. What are the effects on common law precedents as a result of the drop in the number of trials? Explain.

3. What are some of the reasons that legal experts give to defend the drop in the number of trials? Explain.

4. How have changes in the laws affected the number of trials? Explain.

5. According to the author, what are the two positions taken by judges in relation to the drop in the number of trials? Explain.

Source: Michael Orey, "Civil Suits: The Vanishing Trial," *Business-Week,* April 30, 2007, 38–39.

Other difficulties associated with ADR have also appeared in recent years. One problem is that ADR does not always save time and money the way it is supposed to. Typically, two of the advantages that supporters of ADR promote are the ideas that ADR is less expensive and less time consuming because such procedures do not get tangled up in the red tape of the court system. Unfortunately, this is not always the case. Sometimes even cases that are decided by arbitration end up in the court system. Most often this happens when one or more of the parties decide to challenge the decision of the arbitrator. When such challenges occur, there is only one place for the parties to go: to court.

Two additional advantages of ADR are that little discovery and very few motions are involved in the process, thus saving the litigants a lot of money. Although this argument sounds good in theory, it does not always play out in reality. Unfortunately, sometimes a case may actually take longer to resolve because there is no discovery or motion practice involved. Part of the delay is due to the fact that discovery and motion practice often help attorneys focus on the most crucial issues in a case. Also, discovery will sometimes reveal that it is necessary to settle a case rather than proceeding to trial. When there is no discovery or motion practice, the issues remain wide open. This gap means that attorneys must anticipate all the possible moves that their opponents might make. The lack of discovery also means that the small flaws in an argument may not be revealed, and a case that would have been settled during a conventional lawsuit might drag on in arbitration.

Admittedly, ADR is not intended as a replacement for the legal system. Rather, it is intended to provide potential litigants with a wider variety of choices when they are facing a legal dispute. As noted previously, because of the delays and the expense involved in litigation, many people would like to avoid that route altogether. Others would like to find a way to streamline the litigation process, so that, should the need for a trial finally present itself, the preliminary steps can be administered as painlessly as possible. With these facts in mind, we will proceed with an examination of ADR techniques.

Did You Know?

When mediation is used to settle cases of sexual harassment in the workplace, 85 percent of those cases are resolved successfully without having to go to court.

4-2 ADR Techniques

There are numerous ADR techniques that can be invoked once a dispute has arisen between parties. These include but are not limited to mediation, arbitration, med-arb, early neutral evaluation, summary jury trials, and private civil trials.

Mediation

Mediation is the process by which the parties to a dispute invite a third party, known as a **mediator**, to help find a solution to their problem. The job of a mediator is to convince the contending parties to adjust or settle their dispute. The mediator will try to persuade the parties to reach some sort of compromise but cannot decide what the parties will do.

Mediation is often more successful than litigation, because in mediation, the parties remain involved in the settlement of the dispute. Unlike litigation, which is decided by a judge or a jury, a mediation session is in the hands of the parties. The mediator does not decide the disagreement. Rather, he or she serves as an intermediary who attempts to understand what brought the parties into disagreement and what issues lie at the heart of the disagreement. The mediator does not act as a therapist, a judge, or an advocate. Rather, he or she acts as an impartial outsider who can serve as a source of ideas and suggest solutions that will please all the parties involved in the dispute. Often the mediator can cut to the center of a dispute in objective ways that are unavailable to the parties themselves.

> **EXAMPLE 4-1:**   Mediation: Practical Solutions
>   to Practical Problems
>
> Bruce Langton brought suit against David Winchester in small claims court after Winchester's daughter, Jackie, backed her car into Langton's truck, causing extensive damage to the front end of the vehicle. Langton wanted damages in the amount of $4,000. Langton's sister-in-law, Wendy Miller, suggested that the parties hire a mediator to try to reach a settlement. During the mediation session, the mediator saw that the real issue was the fact that Langton's truck was still damaged. Winchester's brother, who owned and operated an auto body shop, agreed to fix Langton's truck at no cost. This solution satisfied both parties. Langton had his truck fixed, and Winchester suffered no out-of-pocket expenses.

Arbitration

Arbitration is the process by which the parties invite a third party, called an **arbitrator**, to settle their dispute. The procedures involved in arbitration are generally more flexible than those followed in a lawsuit. The rules are either set by law or agreed to by an arbitration

agreement. The hearing may be relaxed, with the arbitrator or arbitrators receiving informal testimony from the parties, or it may be rigidly controlled, with the arbitrator or arbitrators following strict rules of evidence and requiring lengthy explanations. The parties may agree in advance to be bound by the arbitrator's decision. If they do not so agree, the arbitrator's decision can be appealed in court.

Some states require arbitration prior to trial in certain cases. Required arbitration is called *mandatory arbitration*. Some litigants have challenged government-imposed mandatory arbitration as an unconstitutional deprivation of their right to a trial by jury and equal protection under the law. Most states faced with this question have disagreed with these arguments as long as the arbitration requirement does not replace the jury trial and as long as the motives for requiring arbitration are reasonable.

An arbitration hearing can be planned and executed by the parties themselves. Generally, this step means that the parties set the ground rules for choosing the arbitrator or arbitrators, for conducting discovery, for presenting evidence, for determining the outcome, and for enforcing the reward. In addition, details such as setting the time and the place of the hearing, filling vacancies on the arbitration panel, recording the proceedings, handling objections, granting time extensions, and so on, must also be agreed upon. Because of the intricacies of such a process, many individuals who select arbitration prefer to use professional arbitration organizations such as the American Arbitration Association to handle the details of their arbitration proceeding.

Like most forms of ADR, arbitration is not without its difficulties. One shortcoming is that an arbitration hearing is run like a trial but without the safeguards that come with the rules of civil procedure, discovery, and motion practice. This characteristic may actually extend the time involved in arbitration because attorneys and negotiators must prepare a wide variety of legal arguments, some of which might have been eliminated during motion practice. Discovery also sometimes reveals facts that lead the parties into settlement negotiations that might not otherwise take place. Moreover, the wide discretion that is usually granted to arbitrators has, in some cases, led to unreasonable decisions and unjustifiable awards. Sometimes the decision made by an arbitrator comes under the review of the courts, which may result in a reversal of the arbitration order

The Opening Case Revisited

Natare Corp. v. D.S.I. Duraplastec Systems, Inc., Round 2

In the case of *Natare v. D.S.I. Duraplastec Systems, Inc.*, the arbitrator agreed that D.S.I. had violated the non-disparagement contract that had been negotiated between the two companies. Consequently, he ordered D.S.I. to pay Natare $5,000. However, the arbitrator did not order D.S.I. to pay Natare attorney's fees, something that the managers of Natare felt was due to them under the agreement. Natare then brought a claim in state court asking the court to overturn the decision of the arbitrator. The case went to the trial court, then to the appellate court, and finally to the Supreme Court of Indiana. The Indiana Supreme Court found no abuse of discretion on the part of the arbitrator, and the ruling stood. This ruling meant that Natare, which had hoped to use the arbitration clause to avoid the delays and the expense of the state court system, may have actually spent more time and money than it would have had the case started in the court system in the first place.

and thus frustrate the whole object of entering arbitration in the first place. Some of these difficulties can be overcome by stipulating that an arbitration award cannot be reversed by the courts except to correct a violation of the arbitration agreement itself. Sometimes, even that does not work, however, as demonstrated by The Opening Case at the beginning of this chapter.

The difficulties associated with discovery can be solved by streamlining the discovery process in arbitration, without going to the extremes represented by the way that discovery is conducted in litigation. Other problems can be solved by making sure that arbitrators follow the same rules in all hearings and insisting that they write down the reasons behind their decisions.

Med-Arb

Med-arb is an ADR process that combines mediation with arbitration. Under med-arb procedures, the parties first submit their dispute to a mediation session. If the dispute is settled via mediation, then all of the parties can leave satisfied. If, however, some matters are left undecided, the parties can move on to an arbitration hearing. During the hearing, the undecided issues would be placed before an arbitrator for final deliberation.

Early Neutral Evaluation

Early neutral evaluation (ENE) is an ADR process in which the parties permit a referee to assess their case on the basis of the facts and legal arguments alone. At the outset of an ENE process, an independent, objective referee is provided with an overview of the facts involved in the dispute and a summary of the legal arguments on which each side has built his or her case. The evaluator, after examining the facts and the law, renders an impartial assessment of the legal rights of each party and a determination of the amount of the award that should be rendered, if any. The parties can use this impartial evaluation to either settle the case or proceed to trial. Even if the ENE does not result in a final decision, it can be used to shape the issues, plan discovery, and guide any research that the attorneys must conduct as the case proceeds to trial.

Summary Jury Trials

A **summary jury trial** is a shortened version of a trial conducted in less than a day before an actual jury that then renders an advisory verdict in the case. The summary jury process offers litigants a chance to see how a jury would react to the facts of the case, as well as to the legal arguments that will be made by both sides at trial. On the day of the summary jury trial, lawyers from both sides present an abbreviated version of the case to an actual jury. The presentations are simplified, focusing on the essential facts and law. In this way, the summary jury trial eliminates much of the redundancy that occurs during a "real" trial and allows the judge and jury to focus on the essentials of the case.

As noted previously, the ultimate objective of a summary jury trial is to help both sides evaluate the effectiveness of their arguments in front of a judge and jury. This effort in turn helps the attorneys shape the issues and select the positions that are most advantageous to their case. This knowledge is enhanced by the fact that, after the trial, each side has the chance to interview the jurors to see why they reacted as they did.

The success or failure of a summary jury trial depends on several factors. First, only those cases that involve a *bona fide* dispute as to the facts or authentic questions of law should be considered for a summary jury trial. Second, advanced planning is necessary to ensure a successful summary jury trial. The judge must be consulted, issues should be settled, the facts should be composed properly, the jury instructions should be determined, and a date and time established before the trial begins.

BusinessWeek Business Law in the News

Arbitration Aggravation

Donald A. Burleson has a confession to make. He's general counsel of Jani-King International Inc., an Addison (Tex.) commercial-cleaning operation with 12,500 franchises worldwide. Because franchising is such a contentious business, companies in it frequently use arbitration agreements to keep disputes out of court. But Burleson doesn't like arbitration. One reason: These days, he says, it too closely resembles the courtroom litigation it was supposed to replace.

Burleson is not alone. Business attorneys say arbitration is losing its luster among a growing number of their clients. "There was this notion back in the 1980s that arbitration would be a more streamlined, more cost effective mechanism to resolve disputes," says J. Cary Gray, at Looper Reed & McGraw in Houston. "I'm telling you that it's not."

In arbitration proceedings, a single arbitrator, or sometimes a panel of three, considers evidence and then issues a ruling. The proceedings are conducted in private, and the decision in most cases is not subject to court review. As originally conceived, the system was supposed to be faster and cheaper than going to court.

But often as not, Gray says, arbitration clauses seem to generate litigation, not skirt it. Parties can go to court to battle over whether arbitration is required; then, if it is, they can end up back in court fighting over the award or trying to get it enforced.

Discovery, the protracted pretrial exchanging of documents and taking of depositions, is supposed to be sharply limited in arbitration. The reality, however, is that many arbitrators are allowing extensive and expensive discovery. Attorneys bear some of the blame, says Larry A. Jordan, a retired judge who now handles arbitration and mediation at a private Seattle firm, Judicial Dispute Resolution. "They're used to a complete discovery," he says. "They feel obligated to do that."

Jordan's services aren't free. While taxpayers pick up judicial salaries, arbitrators draw their big paychecks from the parties who appear before them. Houston litigator David E. Warden says that for an arbitration he has scheduled later this year, the three panel members are each asking for retainers of $40,000. Another concern is that arbitrators, who often specialize in areas such as construction claims, may have trouble being truly impartial because they are beholden to the industry they work for. The worry is that the arbitrators, who want repeat business, won't want to offend either side and so will essentially split the baby to resolve disputes. Warden says his firm, Yetter & Warden, has energy industry clients who now regret some of the mandatory arbitration clauses they are subject to. Says Warden, "They're looking around and saying, 'Maybe the court system isn't so bad—at least you get due process at some point.'"

Questions for Analysis

1. Why do some attorneys dislike arbitration? Explain.

2. How do arbitration clauses generate litigation? Explain.

3. Why are attorneys sometimes to blame for extended discovery? Explain.

4. Who pays the salaries of judges? Explain.

5. Why might arbitrators be more biased than judges? Explain.

Source: Michael Orey, "Out of Court: Arbitration Aggravation," *BusinessWeek*, April 30, 2007, 38–39.

Third, during the process, strict controls and ironclad time limits must be imposed on the parties. For instance, opening statements should last no more than 20 minutes. Both sides should have no more than one hour for the presentation of their case in chief and 30 minutes for their rebuttal. The closing arguments should also be limited to no more than 20 minutes. Finally, a conference should be held after the trial, during which the parties have the opportunity to discuss an immediate settlement. Such a conference should be held after the jury has been polled so that their input can be factored into the settlement discussion.

EXAMPLE 4-2:   Summary Jury Trials: A Post Trial, Pretrial Settlement

When Ashley Utalizar was discharged from her job with Solarpower Industries Inc., she was certain that the dismissal had been in direct violation of an implied contract that had been created by Solarpower's employee policy manual. When she brought a lawsuit against Solarpower, both parties decided to hold a summary jury trial. After the trial was held, both sides participated in a posttrial settlement conference. The results of the jury poll indicated that, though the jury had decided in favor of Utalizar, they were unable to agree on the amount of damages that should be awarded to her. As a result, both Solarpower and Utalizar decided that it would be in their best interests to settle the case immediately. The attorneys for Solarpower agreed to the settlement because they saw that the jury was sympathetic to Utalizar, while Utalizar's attorneys agreed that they could not be certain that Utalizar would receive an adequate award if the jury were permitted to decide the amount of damages.

Because one reason for holding a summary jury trial is to determine how the judge and jury will react to the facts and the arguments, it is helpful to have observers gauge how the judge and the jurors react to the points made by both sides. The observers, who are often students recruited from local law schools and paralegal institutes, will record the reactions of the judge and the jurors during the trial. As an alternative, the entire process can be recorded, so that reactions can be observed later.

Private Civil Trials

LO8

A **private civil trial** is an ADR technique by which the parties hire a retired judge or magistrate to hear their dispute, following the same rules used in an official trial. Many states now permit the parties to a lawsuit to have their cases tried in a private civil trial rather than an official court. One advantage of a private trial is that the parties can hold the trial at a time and a place of their own choosing. In addition, the parties have the opportunity to choose their own judge. Decisions rendered by a judge in a private civil trial are just as binding as those made by judges on the official court docket. Moreover, private trial decisions can be appealed in the same way that public decisions are appealed.

Private civil trials are not postponed nor are they interrupted because the court has more pressing duties to perform. In addition, a private trial receives the undivided attention of the judge, who is not sidetracked by the need to attend to other matters such as the sentencing of criminal defendants. Intricate, lengthy civil cases are ideally suited for private civil trials because, in such cases, time is money. Consequently, the shorter the trial, the less expensive the final bill facing the client.

In recent years, some private firms have appeared that specialize in setting up private civil trials. Such firms will make most of the arrangements for the litigants. These arrangements include securing a judge, providing the place for the trial, and providing all necessary administrative support. These firms can also provide a jury for the trial. Jurors for private trials are generally selected from a pool of individuals who have recently served on a jury in an official trial. Therefore, the jurors at the private civil trial are well acquainted with the trial procedures.

Quick Quiz 4-2 True or False?

1. The job of a mediator is to convince the contending parties to adjust or settle their dispute.

2. Some states require arbitration prior to trial in certain cases.

3. The early neutral evaluator process is similar to that of a settlement hearing.

4-3 Proactive ADR

All of the ADR techniques discussed thus far are invoked after a dispute has arisen. Since ADR has become so popular in recent years, some business people are taking a proactive approach to the situation by agreeing in advance to submit to one of the alternative dispute resolution tools should a disagreement between the parties arise at a later date. These proactive ADR techniques include, but are not limited to, partnering, ADR contract clauses, settlement week, negotiated rule making, post-appellate procedures, international arbitration agreements, and the science court proposal.

Partnering

Partnering is a process that establishes supportive relationships among the parties to a contract to head off disputes before they occur. Generally, partnering is best used when a contract involves complex interrelationships among a wide variety of different parties. Construction agreements are ideally suited to partnering arrangements, because construction contracts involve contractors and subcontractors, all of whom must perform in a cooperative manner to fulfill a contract that often takes a long period of time to complete.

Partnering attempts to deter the disorder that can arise during a dispute by drawing up certain ground rules that all the parties agree to observe. The entire process begins with a meeting held after the contract has been finalized but before the project has begun. The meeting is held at a location that is unrelated to the business of any party to the contract. In this way, the process can procede in an uninterrupted fashion.

Moreover, the meeting should be directed by an objective third party, whose job it is to help create an atmosphere of trust among the parties to the contract. The parties attempt to anticipate problems that may arise during the project as well as potential solutions to those problems. The parties agree to address all problems when they arise and to look for solutions that will mutually benefit all those involved in the project. Ultimately, the goal is to improve efficiency, ensure safety, and maximize profit by minimizing expenses, especially those that arise from cost overruns.

The parties agree to handle problems according to some ADR technique rather than by litigation. Finally, they agree to deal with one another in a fair manner within the confines of their legal relationships.

ADR Contract Clauses

An **ADR contract clause** will specify that the parties to the agreement have promised to use an alternative dispute resolution technique when a disagreement arises rather than litigating the issue. Like partnering, the drafting of ADR contract clauses is a proactive attempt to ensure that litigation will be avoided should a dispute arise. Unlike partnering, which is best suited to long-term construction contracts, ADR clauses can be included in just about any contract.

A Question of Ethics

Andrew Zapior, the president and CEO of Zapior Industries, and Oliver McMurray, the president of Georgetown Construction, have just finalized a contract for the construction of Zapior's new research facility in Cincinnati, Ohio. To minimize the problems that may arise, they agree to enter a partnering arrangement. At the end of a three-day meeting, the parties draw up an agreement, one clause of which states that they will submit any claim to mediation. In the third month of the contract, one of Georgetown's suppliers goes on strike, delaying an important shipment of material to the construction site. Zapior demands that McMurray and Georgetown find a different supplier. McMurray, who has done business with this supplier for 20 years, resists the suggestion and calls for a mediation session. Zapior refuses to comply, stating that there is no need to delay the project to maintain a contractual relationship with a supplier that can easily be replaced. Analyze the ethical stand taken by McMurray. Now do the same for Zapior. Which stand do you find easier to support? Explain.

These ADR clauses can take many shapes and forms. It is possible, for instance, to insert a clause that states merely that the parties have the option of using an ADR technique. Such a clause is weak, at best, serving only to remind the parties that they do not have to sue one another to gain satisfaction. One step beyond the optional clause is a compulsory clause. This clause states that the parties are required to submit all claims that arise under the contract to an ADR technique, most often mediation or arbitration, before filing a lawsuit. The final type of clause would require the parties to submit any claim to binding arbitration. This strictest type ADR clause forces the parties to abide by the decision of the arbitrator.

Regardless of the type of clause used by the parties, the language should include certain standard provisions. For instance, the clause should specify the types of disagreements that will be submitted to ADR, the ADR technique or techniques that can be used, the scope of discovery allowed, the substantive law and the procedural rules that will be followed in the proceeding, the remedies that will be authorized, the grounds for and the procedure to follow in an appeal, and the methods of enforcing an award. The failure to follow provisions specified in an ADR clause may be grounds for the court to revoke a ruling made by an arbitrator.

Such ADR clauses have several advantages. They are especially helpful when two or more parties have embarked on an extended affiliation that may involve numerous contracts, because ADR clauses clearly establish a reliable and predictable method of dealing with the disputes that will inevitably arise whenever two parties are involved in a lengthy association with each other. In addition, ADR clauses are very beneficial to those parties with the weakest position within a contractual relationship. Often, when a dispute does arise, the more powerful party will threaten litigation, secure in the knowledge that he or she can afford a lawsuit more easily than the weaker party. An ADR clause eliminates this leverage point.

EXAMPLE 4-3:   ADR Clause: Power to the Powerless

Audrey Kemmelman, a freelance photographer, entered a work-for-hire agreement with The Daily Montgomery Central Times Corporation. During the negotiation stages, Kemmelman asked that an ADR clause be added to the contract that would compel the signatories to submit any claim to ADR. The clause stated that, in the event of any dispute, the signatories to the contract would first discuss the points of conflict informally. If after 30 days, no satisfactory solution had been reached, the signatories agreed to submit the problem to the American Arbitration Association, which would assist in selecting an objective moderator who would help the signatories decide on an appropriate ADR method. This ADR clause would benefit Kemmelman because, as the weaker party, she might not have the resources to finance a lengthy and expensive lawsuit.

Because the parties to an ADR clause are agreeing, at least initially, to forgo the right to litigate any claims that arise among them, the courts prefer that such clauses be clear and precise. Clauses that are drafted in imprecise and ambiguous language may be invalidated by the court. If the parties intend to submit all the claims arising out of their contractual relationship to ADR, they should spell that out as precisely and completely as possible. Otherwise a party that, at a later date, wishes to invoke the clause, may find that the court is reluctant to support that position. When writing an ADR contract clause, it is best to use standard expressions that the court will recognize. Clauses that say that the parties agree to use ADR for "any controversy or claim arising out of or relating to the agreement" will convince the court to enforce the clause for most disputes between the parties. Anything less may meet with judicial resistance.

Settlement Week

Settlement week is a five-day period during which a court's docket is cleared of all business, except for settlement hearings. Prior to the opening of settlement week, all attorneys with cases pending before the court are asked to choose which of those cases might be best handled by a mediator. Judges are also permitted to nominate cases for mediation during settlement week. Also before the opening of settlement week, a list of volunteer mediators is compiled. Cases are then matched with mediators, and a schedule is established. Attorneys are required to be present for the mediation session.

A mediation session is then held for each case. Following each session, the mediator is required to file a report with the court, stipulating the results of the session and asking for the judge's approval. Occasionally, some cases, chiefly those that do not involve determining liability, are submitted to an arbitration panel rather than to a single mediator. In such a situation, the plaintiff chooses one of the arbitrators, the defendant chooses one, and the court names the final one. Not all cases scheduled for settlement week are actually resolved during that time. However, the technique is an effective way to lighten the court's docket and is becoming more and more popular.

Negotiated Rule Making

Negotiated rule making (reg-neg) is a process by which an agency invites the people and the organizations to be affected by a new rule to have input into the writing of that rule. A working team is established that consists of representatives of the affected groups, including the agency issuing the rule. One member of the team is an objective outsider trained in the art of facilitating such discussions. The objective of negotiated rule making, of course, is to avoid disputes before they have a chance to blossom.

All representatives have the opportunity to present their point of view in relation to the proposed rule. Discussions follow, during which all of these issues are examined. Eventually, the team is expected to formulate a rule that reflects a consensus of the representatives. This consensus does not necessarily mean that all parts of the rule are enthusiastically embraced by all of the representatives. Rather, it means that all of the

Talking Points

The Framers and ADR: Rule by the Elite or Rule by the People?

Many Americans have a somewhat distorted view of the original Framers of the United States Constitution, envisioning all of them as sharing the same basic view of human nature, God, and good government. Moreover, this vision sees all of the Framers as sharing a dedicated and unwavering faith in a pure democratic state that gives all of the power to the people. As appealing and comforting as this view is, it is, nevertheless, essentially wrong.

John Adams, for example, favored establishing a government that would be ruled by a natural elite, as happens in a monarchy or an aristocracy. Apparently, Adams believed that because of their physical, intellectual, and moral genius, this elite group of citizens would be best suited to rule the rest of the people. Adams writes, "When superior genius gives greater influence in society than is possessed by inferior genius, or a mediocrity of genius, that is, than by the ordinary level of men, this superior influence I call natural aristocracy. . . . While I admit the existence of democracy, notwithstanding its instability, you [Taylor] must acknowledge the existence of natural aristocracy, notwithstanding its fluctuations." (p. 239)

John Taylor, a lawyer, scholar, senator, and one of the most vocal supporters of American representative democracy, countered this idea when he wrote, "Monarchy and aristocracy, have the strongest tendency of any conceivable human situation, to excite the evil moral quality, or propensity, of injuring others for our own benefit, both by the magnitude of the temptation, and the power of reaching it. . . . These forms of government are therefore founded in the evil moral qualities of man, and it is unnatural that evil moral qualities, should produce good moral effects." (p. 221)

Of the two positions, which would support the idea promoted by ADR that the people involved in disputes are best suited to determine the method for solving those disputes? Which would support the idea that jurists and litigators should be entrusted with the task of solving legal disputes through the traditional legal process of litigation? Which of the two positions do you prefer? Explain. For the sources referred to in this segment of Talking Points, see John Taylor, "An Inquiry into the Principles and Policy of the Government of the United States" (pp. 213–231) and John Adams, "Letters to John Taylor" (pp. 231–246), both in *Philosophy in America,* eds. Paul Russell Anderson and Max Harold Fisch (New York: Appleton-Century-Crofts, 1939).

parties agree that they have fashioned a rule that everyone on the rule-making team can live with. The text of the proposed rule is then submitted to the rule-making agency. The success of the process depends on the willingness of the members of the team to work in a cooperative fashion and the willingness of the agency to accept the results of the team's deliberations.

Despite its advantages, negotiated rule making cannot be used in all situations. Certain subject areas are more fitting than others. A suitable subject area for reg-neg would be one that will ultimately affect a wide range of individuals and institutions, is both complicated and controversial, and would meet with resistance if those individuals and institutions affected did not have a hand in shaping the rule. Reg-neg is also a wise course of action when the subject area affected involves nuances that fall outside the expertise of the agency representatives.

EXAMPLE 4-4:   Reg-Neg: The Great Lakes Initiative

The Ohio Environmental Protection Agency (OEPA) was charged with the task of drafting a series of rules to implement the Great Lakes Initiative. Rather than simply writing the rules and placing them before the affected parties, the OEPA decided to take a negotiated rule-making approach. Consequently, it created the Great Lakes Initiative External Advisory Group (EAG). The EAG was composed of representatives from the agency itself, from the regulated industry, and from environmental groups. The team engaged in eight months of intense negotiations. These negotiations followed a precisely planned series of steps carried out under the watchful eyes of professional facilitators. The EAG reached a firm consensus on most of the issues that arose during the negotiations. Consequently, the Joint Committee on Agency Rule Review of the Ohio General Assembly adopted a set of rules to implement the Great Lakes Initiative in a relatively harmonious atmosphere and with almost no conflict. This is an extremely successful example of reg-neg in action.

Post-Appellate Procedures

Post-appellate procedures involve taking a case that has been rejected or dismissed by a domestic court to an international organization such as the Inter-American Commission on Human Rights of the Organization of American States. In such a situation, a party that has exhausted all domestic remedies available, up to and including the United States Supreme Court, might ask such a non-governmental organization (NGO) to hear its case. The post-appellate case is brought against the government of the aggrieved party for allegedly failing to provide an appropriate legal remedy to redress the grievances of the victim. The claim generally involves the violation of some fundamental right, generally a due process or an equal protection right that is guaranteed by an international document such as the American Declaration of the Rights and Duties of Man or the United Nations Universal Declaration of Human Rights. The NGO then hears the case, considers the evidence, and determines whether the party's claim is justified. The NGO may demand that the government of the aggrieved party provide compensation for the injuries visited upon the victim. The NGO may also suggest actions beyond that compensation, including needed reforms in the governmental and/or judicial system to prevent such problems from occurring in the future. Whether the NGOs actually have jurisdiction over such claims is open to debate. Moreover, even if they have jurisdiction, whether their findings are actually enforceable against the government in question is problematic.

International Arbitration Agreements

An international arbitration agreement involves a pledge to use arbitration should the parties find themselves in disagreement as to the enforcement rights under the original contract. Generally, the agreement permits the parties to agree on a forum in which the arbitration will be held that is different from the home forum of either party. The parties also can agree to use the rules and procedures promulgated by an independent institution, such as the International Bar Association's Rules of International Commercial Arbitration.

There are several clear advantages to entering an international arbitration agreement. First, because the parties to the agreement are incorporated in different nation-states, they are free to specify whatever forum they can agree upon as the place to hold an arbitration hearing, should that become necessary. This agreement is in contrast with a litigation clause that might specify that the law of one or the other nation would apply to any legal dispute between the parties. Ultimately, such a clause can become very restrictive. The law of a particular nation-state might, for instance, specify that a dispute that arises within the borders of that nation-state would have to be tried within that nation-state. This rule can put one of the two corporations at a distinct disadvantage, one that may not become evident until the lawsuit has begun. Arbitration agreements can avoid this problem because the arbitration hearing can be held on neutral ground.

Second, when negotiating an arbitration agreement, the parties are also free to specify the identity of the arbitrators or leave open the option to choose the arbitrators at the time of the dispute from a large pool of potential experts. The arbitrators can thus reside in any location that satisfies all of the parties. Third, the same option is open to the parties in relation to their choice of legal representation. Rather than being limited to the forum in which the dispute is to be heard, the parties can bring in representation from any point on the globe. Fourth, using an international arbitration agreement avoids one of the most troublesome problems linked to international litigation: enforcement. Often a party that has won a favorable decree in one nation will find it challenging to execute that decree in any other nation. International arbitration eliminates this problem because the original arbitration contract will include the terms of enforcement.

Of course, as is often the case, the best laid plans of mice and CEOs can go astray. Thus, sometimes a corporation will find that the jurisdiction that it has chosen for an arbitration hearing has different ideas about whether certain arbitrators and/or attorneys will be permitted to practice within its borders. If a country decides that certain legal representatives and certain arbitrators are not welcome in its jurisdiction, then the parties may find themselves using local attorneys and/or arbitrators, something that not only defeats the objective of the international arbitration agreement but also places the validity and acceptability of the entire arbitration process at risk. This possibility also delays the process further because when an arbitrator is dismissed, the entire action usually must begin again.

Nor are these risks trivial. The danger is especially acute in Latin America, where some nation-states still apply a nineteenth century legal principle that says that foreign corporations doing business in a Latin American country or involved in an international legal dispute within the borders of such a country must apply the law of that country, regardless of any agreement made by the parties to the contrary. Sometimes this agreement means simply securing local legal assistance, but it can also mean that the foreign attorneys operating within that jurisdiction are subject to local law, which sometimes includes criminal penalties for not following the procedural rules of that jurisdiction. (Note: For a more detailed look at the problems associated with international arbitration agreements see: Lawrence W. Newman and David Zaslowsky, "International Litigation/International Arbitration—Pitfalls for Participants," *International Litigation and Arbitration Newsletter* November 2006, pp. 3–7 retrieved from http://www.bakernet.com. The article first appeared in *The New York Law Journal*, September 29, 2006).

The Science Court Proposal

A **science court** acts as a forum for disputes involving scientific and technological controversies. Individuals and institutions with concerns about certain scientific activities, such as genetic engineering, nuclear energy research, and so on, might ask the court to act as an impartial arbitrator in the evaluation of those concerns. The judges on the science court would be scientists educated in the areas under investigation, thus allowing them to use their expertise in deciding cases.

Supporters of the establishment of a science court argue that a panel of objective judges with scientific backgrounds provides a neutral body capable of making unbiased, well-informed decisions. Moreover, the science court would not necessarily provide the last word in any case held under its jurisdiction. An appeal stage would be a part of the process. Finally, the decision-making process involved in science-related controversies would be centralized by the science court, thus providing a forum that many individuals could take advantage of.

Critics of the science court proposal argue that a panel made up of objective judges with scientific backgrounds would be almost impossible to convene. Moreover, critics point out that the science court would represent an additional level of bureaucratic red tape. In addition, such a forum could rapidly become buried under an avalanche of claims, many of which would be a frivolous waste of the court's time. Finally, some critics argue that because the issues placed before a science court would be highly controversial, the entire process could be plagued with political considerations that would threaten the legitimacy of the entire process.

EXAMPLE 4-5:   The Science Court: A Powerful Lesson in Powerlessness

Two power co-ops, the Cooperative Power Association and the United Power Association, planned to construct a system of high-voltage power lines across farmland located in Minnesota. The farm owners objected to the way in which their land was appropriated for the project by the government and the co-ops. The farmers also objected to the planned location of the power lines because they would interfere with their ability to farm the land properly. The governor of Minnesota called for the creation of a science court to resolve the dispute. Unfortunately, the situation rapidly became politicized. The co-ops, which had received a green light for the project from conventional authorities, refused to cooperate with the science court unless they were allowed to continue building the power lines during the science court's deliberations. The farmers argued that the purpose for calling the science court in the first place would be undermined if the construction of the power lines was allowed to continue. Moreover, the farmers wanted an extended set of issues placed before the court, including the possible rerouting of the lines and the consideration of alternative power sources. The co-ops, in contrast, wanted the issues narrowed to an examination of any health problems associated with the power lines. Ultimately, the governor was compelled to withdraw his science court proposal because it caused more political problems than it had solved.

The Minnesota experience taught certain valuable lessons about the establishment of a science court. First, a science court will not succeed unless it has the power to compel the parties to submit to its authority. In the Minnesota case, for instance, the co-ops saw no reason to cooperate with a voluntary court because their project had already been approved by conventional authorities. Second, a successful science court must have the power to halt work done on any project that is the focus of the court's investigation. Otherwise, the court's entire process becomes an exercise in futility. Third, a successful science court will ensure that all sides have the opportunity to present their views on all issues facing the court. Permitting certain parties to speak on certain issues while denying the same right to others can destroy the credibility of the court and of those involved in its creation and operation.

Quick Quiz 4-3 True or False?

1. The partnering process begins with a meeting held after a contract has been finalized but before the project has begun.

2. In negotiated rule making, a government agency creates a new set of regulations without the troublesome, time-consuming, expensive, and difficult step of getting input from its constituency, thus streamlining the process, saving money, and eliminating controversy.

3. The proposed science court would act as a forum for disputes involving scientific and technological controversies.

Summary

4.1   Litigation has always been a part of the American legal system. Lately, however, things have begun to change. The extensive backlog in many court systems and the perceived injustice of many verdicts have led many people to seek other methods to redress their grievances. These other methods are often grouped under the heading of alternative dispute resolutions (ADR). Alternative dispute resolution occurs whenever individuals attempt to resolve a disagreement by stepping outside the usual adversarial system and applying certain creative settlement techniques, many of which have fact finding and the discovery of truth as their goal.

4.2   There are many different ADR techniques that can be invoked once a dispute has arisen between parties. These include but are not limited to mediation, arbitration, med-arb, early neutral evaluation, summary jury trials, and private civil trials.

4.3   Since ADR has become so popular in recent years, some business people are taking a proactive approach to the situation by agreeing in advance to submit to one of the alternative dispute resolution tools should a disagreement between the parties arise at a later date. These proactive ADR techniques include, but are not limited to, partnering, ADR contract clauses, settlement week, negotiated rule making, international arbitration agreements, the post-appellate option, and the science court proposal.

Key Terms

ADR contract clause, 80

alternative dispute resolution (ADR), 71

arbitration, 75

arbitrator, 75

early neutral evaluation (ENE), 77

international arbitration agreement, 84

med-arb, 77

mediation, 75

mediator, 75

negotiated rule making (reg-neg), 82

non-governmental organization (NGO), 84

partnering, 80

post-appellate procedures, 84

private civil trial, 79

science court, 85

settlement week, 82

summary jury trial, 77

Questions for Review and Discussion

1. What are the shortcomings of litigation?
2. What are the advantages and disadvantages of ADR?
3. What are the advantages of mediation?
4. What is the nature of an arbitration hearing?
5. What happens during the med-arb process?
6. What is the role of an early neutral evaluator?
7. What happens in the running of a summary judgment trial?
8. What are the advantages of a private civil trial?
9. What are the private options available under ADR?
10. What are the governmental options available under ADR?

Investigating the Internet

Access the Web site of International Chamber of Commerce (ICC) and write a short report about the ICC Dispute Resolution Services. Answer the following questions: (1) What is the International Chamber of Commerce? (2) When was the ICC formed, and what was its overriding goal at the time of its creation? (3) How does the ICC fight crime and/or evil? (4) Why should parties use ICC arbitration? (5) What are the advantages to the use of ICC arbitration?

Cases for Analysis

1. Turner Pte. Ltd. was the main contractor in the building of *Gateway,* a long-term project to be constructed in the heart of Singapore. One of Turner's subcontractors was a company called Builders Federal Ltd. (BFL). As part of the overall contract, the two companies signed an arbitration agreement, which was designated as Clause 22 in the main contract. When the two parties found themselves in the middle of several serious disputes, they invoked Clause 22 and began arbitration. Turner asked that Mr. David Gardam be appointed as the arbitrator, and BFL asked for Mr. Douglas Smith. The court appointed Smith. From the outset there was bad blood between Turner and Smith, which was revealed in a series of letters that went back and forth between the parties and Smith. At one point in the process, Turner realized that Clause 22 actually had no legal effect until each party activated it by giving their permission to proceed with arbitration. Smith denied that this was the case and ordered the arbitration process to continue. Turner objected, and Smith, who admitted that Turner had made a fairly convincing case, agreed to submit that argument to the High Court of Singapore. Nevertheless, Smith pushed the arbitration process forward. BFL was delighted, but Turner objected. Still the action went forward despite the precarious nature of Smith's position as arbitrator. Can the high court of Singapore dismiss Smith even though BFL is quite satisfied with his work as arbitrator? What grounds might be used to dismiss Smith? If Smith is dismissed, will the arbitration process continue or start over? *Turner (East Asia) Pte. Ltd. v. Builders Federal (Hong Kong) Ltd.* SLR 532 SGHC 47 (Singapore High Court).

2. Jessica Gonzales obtained an official restraining order from a Colorado court that prevented her estranged husband from approaching either her or her children any closer than 100 yards. The order, however, did not stop her husband, who kidnapped their three children. Mrs. Gonzales went to the police and asked for their help. The police did very little to help her, despite the restraining order. Early the next morning, Mr. Gonzales arrived at the police station and began shooting at police officers, who shot back and eventually killed him. After the shooting was over, the police found the bodies of the three young

daughters in Mr. Gonzales' truck. Mrs. Gonzales brought suit against the police department, arguing that her due process rights had been violated when the police did not enforce the restraining order. The case went from trial court to the appellate court to the United States Supreme Court, with no result other than a dismissal of the suit. Mrs. Gonzales, with the assistance of the American Civil Liberties Union, filed a post-appellate complaint against the United States with the Inter-American Commission on Human Rights. In her complaint, Mrs. Gonzales argued that she had been deprived of due process and equal protection under the American Declaration of the Rights and Duties of Man, an agreement that the United States was legally bound to follow. Mrs. Gonzales and her attorneys hoped that the commission would issue a judgment in her favor and against the United States. What two initial questions must be answered first before this post-appellate case can begin? Explain. *Jessica Ruth Gonzales v. The United States of America,* Petition No. P-1490-05, The Inter-American Commission on Human Rights of the Organization of American States.

3. In a case involving an ADR clause, the parties to a contract disagreed as to whether the clause required them to submit a dispute over a trade secret problem to arbitration. The clause required the parties to submit "any controversy or claim arising out of the agreement" to arbitration. Strictly speaking, the trade secret controversy did not arise "out of" the agreement. However, it was clear that the trade secret dispute was related to the agreement. The trial court held that the language of the ADR clause was too narrow and that because the trade secret dispute did not arise out of the controversy, the parties were not required to send it to arbitration. Should the appellate court overrule the trial court's decision rejecting the requirement that the parties arbitrate the trade secret dispute? Explain your response. *Tracer Research Corp. v. National Environmental Services, Co.,* 42 F. 3d 1292 (9th Cir.).

4. In the early 1990s, serious concerns about the dangers associated with genetic engineering arose after an incident pertaining to the use of certain genetically altered mice in experiments involving a highly infectious disease. In the wake of these concerns, the National Institute of Allergy and Infectious Diseases held a conference to discuss the level of safety that should be followed in laboratories involved in such research. Those involved in the conference included the researchers themselves, certain biosafety experts, representives from organizations involved in or planning to be involved in similar research, and governmental representatives from the Centers for Disease Control, the National Institutes of Health, and the Food and Drug Administration. Would this type of situation be appropriate for a reg-neg approach? Explain. Might a science court handle this type of situation even better than an agency's reg-neg procedure? Explain.

5. Andrei Kerensky, CEO of the Malenkov Electronic Surveillance Corporation, entered negotiations with Thomas John King, president and chair of the board for Beckett Industries, Inc., the purpose of which was to develop a new security system for Beckett. The system would use a newly designed security system based on a new laser electronic coding system developed by engineers at Malenkov. King and Kerensky finalized the deal, and the security system was installed at Beckett. After Malenkov's engineers installed the system, security personnel and engineering technicians at Beckett made some subtle alterations in the system's computerized control system. Shortly thereafter, the entire system crashed. When Malenkov's bill was not paid, Kerensky went to see King at Beckett's corporate headquarters. During a short encounter, King informed Kerensky that Beckett was not going to pay Kerensky and Malenkov because the system had crashed. King argued that Malenkov's engineers were responsible for the breakdown, while Kerensky insisted that the modifications made by the engineers at Beckett were at fault because of their unauthorized and incompetently rendered modifications to the system. Kerensky wants to sue King and Beckett but is hesitant to do so because the primary factual issues in the case focus on the engineering modifications. Consequently, he is apprehensive that a judge and jury will be lost by the technical jargon that may be used at trial. What alternatives are available to Kerensky?

Chapter 5   Criminal Law

The Opening Case

United States v. Sandoval-Mendoza

Marcos, a government informant, introduced Eduardo Sandoval-Mendoza to Tony, another government informant, for the purpose of enticing Sandoval-Mendoza into a government-sponsored drug-related sting operation. Sandoval-Mendoza did, in fact, sell 12 pounds of methamphetamines to the informants in three separate transactions. When he was arrested, Sandoval-Mendoza did not hide the fact that he had sold the drugs to Tony and Marcos. However, he argued that he had been entrapped by the two informants, who were clearly acting as government agents. The heart of Sandoval-Mendoza's case involved his unusual susceptability to suggestions made by the informants. He contended that he had a brain tumor, that the informants knew about his illness, that the illness weakened his ability to resist the temptation offered by the informants, and that they took advantage of this fact to invite him into a deal that they knew he would be unable to refuse. They were correct: Sandoval-Mendoza was unable to refuse, and as a result, he joined the deal and found himself on the receiving end of an arrest order by federal authorities for violating federal drug laws. Sandoval-Mendoza tried to support his entrapment argument by pre-senting expert testimony about his illness. The trial court refused to allow that evidence. As a result, the court heard only Sandoval-Mendoza, his sister, and his ex-wife testify about the effects of his illness, which was not enough to convince anyone that Sandoval-Mendoza had been entrapped. So he was convicted. However, on appeal, the Ninth Circuit Court decided that the trial court had made a serious mistake when it had refused to permit the expert testimony. To succeed in an entrap-ment defense, the defendant must demonstrate that he would not have committed the offense had he not been tricked into it by law enforce-ment officers or their duly appointed agents. The appeals court did not believe that Sandoval-Mendoza had been given a fair chance to pres-ent his case, and the judges sent the case back to the U.S. District Court. The Sandoval-Mendoza case demonstrates that whenever we study criminal law, we must focus not only on the crimes that have been committed but also on the rights of any defendants who might be accused of those crimes. In this chapter, we will look at all aspects of criminal law, including the elements of a crime, the definitions of specific crimes, and the defenses that can be presented by criminal defendants in a court of law. (See *United States v. Eduardo Sandoval-Mendoza,* No. 04-10118, 2006 D.C. No. Cr-01-40201-SBA-1 (27 Dec. 2006) (Corrected Reprint 19 Jan. 2007) and Laurie L. Levenson, "Criminal Law: Entrapment Defenses," *The National Law Journal,* February 5, 2007, p. 13.)

Opening Case Questions

1. What are the elements of criminal liability?

2. What is entrapment?

3. Which element of criminal liability would be eliminated by entrapment?

4. What error did the trial court make in this case?

5. What additional defenses might have been used by the defendant in this case?

LO Learning Objectives

1. Explain the purpose of criminal law.
2. Enumerate the various categories and classes of crimes.
3. Describe the nature of an act according to the meaning of criminal liability.
4. Identify the four mental states that can be found in the criminal code.
5. Distinguish motive from the required elements of criminal liability.
6. Explain the various theories of punishment within criminal law.
7. Enumerate and explain the elements of several key crimes.
8. Define and explain the nature of e-crime.
9. Explain the three standards for the insanity defense found in criminal law.
10. Outline the requirements of entrapment as a defense against criminal liability.

5-1 Definition and Classes of Crimes

Perhaps one of the most discussed and least understood areas of the law is criminal law. Most people think they know a lot about criminal law, because they read about it frequently in the newspaper and view programs about it on television. In fact, there is a lot of misinformation spread in the media about criminal law and procedure. This section of the chapter attempts to rectify some of these misconceptions by defining crime and explaining the various classes of crimes.

Definition of a Crime

A **crime** is an offense against the public at large. As such, a crime threatens the peace, safety, and well-being of the entire community. For this reason, crimes are punishable by the official governing body of a nation or state. Also for this reason, the state or federal government, representing the public at large, is the prosecution, that is, the one who brings the criminal action. The person accused of the crime is called the defendant. No act can be considered criminal unless it is prohibited by the law of the place where it is committed, and the law provides for the punishment of the offenders. These laws are created by the federal government and the governments of the 50 states.

The primary objectives of criminal law are to protect the public at large, to preserve harmony and stability within society, and to discourage future disruptive conduct. In contrast, tort law is concerned with private wrongs that have caused injury to an individual's physical health and well-being, property, business, or reputation. Because tort law pertains to private wrongs rather than public ones, it focuses on compensating the victim. Because criminal law protects the public, it seeks to eliminate crime by punishing the wrongdoers. When a tort is committed, the victim has a cause of action against the person who has committed the tort,

LO1

which may allow the victim to recover money as compensation for any injuries that he or she has suffered. In contrast, when a crime is committed, the government may prosecute the accused. A single act can be both a tort and a crime.

EXAMPLE 5-1:   Two Punishments for the Price of One

Marlowe Phillips invested $25,000 in a financial plan devised by his neighbor, Ted Franklin. Under the terms of the agreement between Phillips and Franklin, the former was to invest his money in prime real estate on Sanibel Island off the coast of Florida. After turning the money over to Franklin, Phillips discovered that the land was worthless. Phillips confronted Franklin several times and demanded a return of his money with no result. He then took his grievance to Chandler Raymond, the county prosecutor. After an extensive investigation, Raymond told Phillips that he did not have enough evidence to prosecute Franklin. Phillips confronted Franklin one last time. When Franklin still refused to pay, Phillips drove his SUV at top speed in Franklin's direction. Franklin jumped out of the way and saved himself at the last moment. Phillips's SUV continued on and hit Anne Turtledove, seriously injuring her. As a result, Phillips was prosecuted for criminal battery. However, battery is not only a crime, it is also a tort. Consequently, several months after Phillips was prosecuted for criminal battery, he was also sued by Turtledove in civil court for the tort of battery.

Criminal Law in the American System

The American legal structure consists of the federal and the state systems. Both make and enforce criminal law. However, because there are 50 states and the District of Columbia, it is actually more accurate to say that the American system is made up of 52 systems. Nevertheless, it is helpful to limit any discussion of the law to an examination of federal and state systems. We simply must remember that each state has its own code and its own procedures, which, though similar in most respects to all other states, may have its own peculiarities.

Federal Criminal Law   Another peculiarity about the American system is that the federal government has no express power in the Constitution that allows it to enact criminal law statutes or establish a national police force. Yet the federal government does enact criminal law and has set up the Federal Bureau of Investigation (FBI) as a national police force. The federal government also has a cabinet-level criminal law enforcement official called the attorney general who has the power to conduct federal criminal investigations. The existence of the federal criminal law system and the various national law enforcement agencies is made possible by the adaptive processes at work within the legal system itself.

Criminal Law as a Complex Adaptive System   The resourceful way in which Congress has assumed a set of powers never granted to it by the Framers of the Constitution demonstrates how the law acts as a complex adaptive system. The process works something like this: The Framers of the Constitution intended that Congress have only those powers enumerated in Article I, Section 8, of the Constitution. Because the term "police power" is not mentioned anywhere in the Constitution, the Framers did not give that power to the federal government but instead expected the states to exercise all police power. Consequently, Congress can create criminal law statutes only in those areas over which it has jurisdiction. For instance, Congress has the power to coin money, so it can set up laws against counterfeiting. Yet, as we've seen, Congress has created criminal law statutes in areas beyond counterfeiting. If there has been no constitutional amendment explicitly handing Congress police power, how did Congress get the power to create a set of criminal law statutes and a national police force?

The answer is that the law—as a complex adaptive system—did what such systems usually do; it adapted. The adaptation occurred when Congress extended its power through a generous interpretation of the Commerce Clause. The Commerce Clause, found in Article I, Section 8, Clause 3, of the U.S. Constitution, permits Congress to pass laws that regulate commerce "among the several States." Congress used this clause to regulate interstate criminal activities, which generally have an impact on "commerce." Although the ultimate results were a long time coming, eventually the courts, through a series of cases, culminating in the classic case of *Wickard v. Filburn* (63 S.Ct. 82), gave their "stamp of approval" to the legislature's interpretation of the Commerce Clause. In a sense then, Congress and the courts cooperated to give the federal governmnent police power, a power it did not have under the Constitution. That power includes the authority to create federal criminal law statutes and to establish a national police force.

Classes of Crimes

Under common law, crimes were dealt with in the order of their seriousness: treason, felonies, and misdemeanors. Most states now divide offenses into felonies and misdemeanors. A **felony** is a crime punishable by death or imprisonment in a federal or a state prison for a term exceeding one year. Some felonies are also punishable by fines. Some states define a felony as a crime subject to "punishment by hard labor," as an "infamous crime," or as a "crime subject to infamous punishment." Manslaughter, armed robbery, and arson are examples of felonies.

Some states also have separate categories for their most serious crimes. For instance, a state might classify premeditated murder and murder as *special felonies* or *capital felonies* if these are the only two offenses that might result in a death sentence or life imprisonment. States may also have a separate category for violent offenses. Sometimes these violent offenses are termed *aggravated felonies*. Assault with a deadly weapon might be an example of an aggravated felony.

A **misdemeanor** is a less serious crime, generally punishable by a prison sentence of not more than one year. Included in this category are offenses such as disorderly conduct. Some states also have a separate category for their least serious offenses. The label for these least serious offenses varies, but two of the most common are *petty offenses* and *minor misdemeanors*. Traffic violations and building code violations are usually within this classification.

Following her arrest for driving under the influence, Paris Hilton was charged with a misdemeanor and sentenced to 23 days in jail.

Quick Quiz 5-1 True or False?

1. A misdemeanor is a crime punishable by death or imprisonment in a federal or a state prison for a term exceeding one year.   *F*

2. The primary objective of criminal law is to protect victims.   *F*

3. It is impossible for a single act to be both a tort and a crime.   *F*

5-2 Elements of a Crime

The two elements necessary to create criminal liability are a criminal act and the required state of mind. Although it is difficult to generalize about both of these concepts, certain characteristics are common to each, regardless of jurisdiction. Nevertheless, keep in mind that criminal law is largely statutory in nature. Consequently, specific statutory definitions may vary from state to state.

A Criminal Act

Under American law, a crime cannot be committed unless some act has occurred. An individual cannot be accused of a crime for merely thinking of a criminal act. However, even a small act that appears by itself to be innocent can, in the proper context, become an illegal act. For example, even something as simple as inserting a key into the ignition of a vehicle can constitute an act under the law, if the driver is intoxicated at the time. The act is such an important element to criminal liability that convictions may be avoided or overturned if defendants can show that the statute under which they were prosecuted is ambiguous in its description of the act. Often, such ambiguity will occur when the legislature passes a statute that creates a new offense, when the statute outlaws an activity that may be protected by the U.S. Constitution, or when the statute seeks to outlaw statutes or behavior that cause no imminent negative effect but may eventually lead to great public harm. For instance, the courts have frequently held statutes that outlaw a status, such as drug addiction or vagrancy, to be void for vagueness. The courts have also struck down statutes that are overbroad. The language of a criminal statute is overbroad if the courts cannot determine what specific activity the legislature intended to outlaw.

Omissions and Refusals to Act   At times, the failure to act, an omission, or the outright refusal to act may be considered criminal. Generally, however, an omission must be coupled with a legally imposed duty. An air traffic controller who sees two planes on a collision course, yet fails to warn the pilots, would be held criminally liable for this omission. This liability exists even though the controller did not act but instead failed to act.

Involuntary Movement or Behavior   Many states specifically exclude involuntary movement and behavior from their general definition of a criminal act. Convulsions, reflexes, movements during sleep or unconsciousness, or behavior during a seizure are all considered involuntary movement or behavior falling outside the limits of criminal liability. However, the mere fact that someone is unconscious during a seizure may not absolve that individual of criminal liability if that person knew that he or she might suffer the seizure, yet took no precautions to avoid harming people or property. A person who decides to drive an automobile knowing that she or he is subject to sudden, unpredictable epileptic seizures may be criminally liable if a seizure causes that person to lose control of the vehicle and kill or injure someone.

The Required State of Mind

In general, a crime cannot be committed unless the criminal act named in the statute is performed with the required state of mind. Many state criminal codes include the following four states of mind:

- Purpose
- Knowledge
- Recklessness
- Negligence

Talking Points

Henry Kissinger, winner of the Nobel Peace Prize and a former Secretary of State, has certain ideas about the validity and effectiveness of the International Criminal Court (ICC), which differ from those proposed by Michael Byers of the University of British Columbia. After reading the following excerpts, evaluate each position in relation to what you've learned about criminal law in this chapter and to what you learned about criminal procedure in Chapter 3.

In his book, *War Law*, Byers writes, "[T]he International Criminal Court provides something dramatically new: a permanent court, largely immune to political interference, which can take over when countries are unable or unwilling to try alleged perpetrators, and to which the UN Security Council can assign jurisdiction over situations rather than having to create new tribunals each time from scratch. . . . Only the United States has actively endeavoured to undermine the court. With troops in 140 countries, a propensity to intervene under dubious legal circumstances, and interpretations of the laws of war that sometimes differ from those of other states, the single superpower feels vulnerable to international mechanisms for enforcing international criminal law."

Dr. Kissinger has a somewhat different perspective. In his book, *Does America Need a Foreign Policy?* Kissinger writes, "Distrusting national governments, many of the advocates of universal jurisdiction seek to place governments under the supervision of magistrates and the judicial system. But the prosecutor's discretion without accountability is precisely one of the flaws of the International Criminal Court. Definitions of the relevant crimes are vague and highly susceptible to politicized application. Defendants will not enjoy due process as understood in the United States. Any signatory state has the right to trigger an investigation. As the experience of the American special prosecutor shows, such a procedure is likely to develop its own momentum without time limits and can turn into an instrument of political warfare." (See H. Kissinger, *Does America Need a Foreign Policy? Toward a Diplomacy for the 21st Century* (New York: Simon and Schuster, 2001), 281; M. Byers, *War Law: Understanding International Law and Armed Conflict* (New York: Grove Press, 2005), 144–45.)

Purpose   Individuals act with **purpose** when they intend to cause the result that in fact occurs. For example, if a person were to point a loaded gun at another person with the intention of shooting that second person, and if shots are actually fired, the person with the gun would have acted with purpose. Some states choose to call this mental state *intent*. Intent or purpose should not be confused with *premeditation,* which is often an added condition in the case of aggravated or first-degree murder. Some states specifically define premeditation as an action that results from the criminal defendant's "prior calculation and design." If, in the previous example, the person with the gun had also planned to shoot the victim, and then actually carried out this plan, the shooting would have been premeditated.

Knowledge   When people act with an awareness that a particular result will probably occur, they act with **knowledge.** For instance, if the person with the gun in the preceding example took that loaded gun to a crowded shopping mall and began to fire at random, not aiming at anyone in particular, that person would be acting with the knowledge that a lot of people would be either wounded or killed. This awareness would be true even if the person with the gun were to yell, "I really don't want to shoot anyone. I hope I don't hit anybody!"

About the Law
The definition of many legal terms varies depending on the area of the law in which they are used. For example, in tort law, negligence is defined in relation to four elements: duty, breach of duty, proximate cause, and actual harm.

Recklessness Recklessness involves a perverse disregard of a known risk of negative consequences. People act recklessly when they are indifferent to a serious risk they know to exist. Two drivers who challenge each other to an illegal drag race on a public highway are acting recklessly. In other words, they have disregarded the possible serious consequences of their decision to engage in an illegal drag race.

Negligence People act with negligence when they fail to see the possible negative consequences of their actions. A person who cleans a hunting rifle without checking to see if it is loaded is acting with negligence, because that person has not bothered to look for any possible negative consequences that could result from those actions. Criminal negligence should not be confused with negligence in tort law. Negligence in tort law is concerned with the compensation of accident victims (see Chapter 6). In contrast, negligence in criminal law is concerned with punishing the wrongdoer and protecting the public at large.

The Matter of Motive

Motive in criminal law is the wrongdoer's reason for committing the crime. One common misconception about criminal law, which is perpetuated by countless television programs and films, is that motive is an element of criminal liability. Such is not the case. Establishing motive may help the prosecution persuade the jury that the accused is guilty, but proving an evil motive is not necessary for a criminal conviction.

The Matter of Punishment

The ultimate purpose of criminal law is to protect the public. This purpose means that criminal law must outline not only the offenses that are prohibited but also the negative consequences that result when an individual has committed one of those offenses. Many legal experts disagree however about what that punishment ought to be. Still, these experts have narrowed the debate to two approaches to the sentencing of convicted criminals: (1) consequences that are designed to protect the public at large and (2) those that are tailored to fit the individual offense or the individual offender.

Protecting the Public at Large Consequences that have been created to protect the public send a message not just to the convicted felon but also to all potential offenders. These techniques include deterrance, education, and retribution. Those experts who believe in *deterrence* advocate long and difficult prison sentences so that other people in society are dissuaded from committing similar offenses and thus suffering the same fate. Those who support the theory of *education* say that the criminal process should be presented in a public way so that the public will learn the difference between acceptable and unacceptable bevhavior. Finally, those who believe in *retribution* are convinced that it does society good to seek revenge against those who have disrupted the smooth running of the social system. This theory probably has the fewest supporters today. Still, some experts argue that obtaining retribution against those who seek to gratify themselves at the expense of others will prevent many potential offenders from committing similar misdeeds in the future.

Individual Offenses and Punishment Consequences that have been created to fit a particular offense or to punish a specific offender are designed to make certain that the individual offender will no longer engage in criminal activity in the future. The techniques for promoting this approach are prevention, restraint, and rehabilitation. Those experts who believe in *prevention* support long sentences in unpleasant prisons so that criminal defendants will abandon their criminal careers. Those who support *restraint* believe that criminal defendants should be incarcerated or even executed for capital offenses to prevent them from ever committing that crime—or any crime, for that matter—ever

BusinessWeek **Business Law in the News**

Prisons: Inmate Ed—With a Bus Ticket

Some Mexican citizens convicted of a crime in the U.S. are getting something beyond hard time: homework. Corrections Corp. of America has been running schools for the 5,000 plus Mexican nationals incarcerated at its private prisons in California, Colorado, New Mexico, and Texas.

The aim: getting inmates to stay in Mexico once they're released and deported. The curriculum, says Dennis Bradby, CCA's vice president for inmate programs, is one way to inject skilled workers into Mexico. "Therefore, there will not be a need [for the former inmates] to come back to this country," he says.

The Mexican government provides books, computers, and curriculum guidance for the classes—in math, reading, writing, and trade skills. (The course follows the requirements of Mexico's public education system.)

Running the program costs CCA about $230,000 a year for in-house teachers and inmate tutors. Some 3,700 Mexican inmates have graduated from the CCA elementary, junior high, and general equivalency diploma programs, including 500 in September. Since the classes were started by the prison corporation in 2003, the Mexican government has expanded the program, which is conducted in Spanish, to 29 other public and private prisons.

Mexican officials don't have statistics on how many graduates avoid criminal pursuits or find jobs back home after graduation. But, says Juan Solana, Mexican consul in Albuquerque, N.M., most Mexican immigrants say they would prefer to stay home, despite the high numbers who come to the U.S. illegally. Says graduate Francisco Sanz, 34, who will be deported next spring after doing time for acting as a drug courier: "When you have a job, you don't want to come back." Solana says more Mexican prisoners in the U.S. finish the program than U.S.-based Mexican civilians studying the same courses in community centers. "These people have a lot of time," he says.

Questions for Analysis

1. Which of the two approaches to the sentencing of convicted criminals does the CCA program support? Explain.

2. Which of the six punishment techniques does the CCA program promote? Explain.

3. Is the goal of helping inmates receive an education so that they do not have to have to pursue a criminal career practical? Explain.

4. What difficulties, if any, do you foresee for such a program? Explain.

5. Of what significance is the fact that the program has not tracked statistics on how many graduates avoid criminal pursuits or find jobs back home after graduation? Explain.

Source: Brian Grow, "Prisons: Inmate Ed—With a Bus Ticket," *BusinessWeek,* October 30, 2006, 14.

again. Finally, those who support the theory of *rehabilitation* say that convicted defendants ought to be given the opportunity to reform their conduct, restructure their lives, and start over.

Quick Quiz 5-2 True or False?

1. The two elements needed to create criminal liability are a criminal act and the requisite state of mind.   T

2. Individuals act with negligence when they act with the intention to cause the result that does in fact occur.   F

3. Motive is an element of criminal liability.   F

5-3 Specific Crimes

LO7

Statutory definitions and classifications of crimes vary from jurisdiction to jurisdiction. Nevertheless, several generalities can be drawn to simplify an examination of specific crimes. Crimes can be classified as crimes against people, crimes against property, and crimes involving business.

Crimes Against People

Crimes against people, most often referred to as *felonies*, include homicide, assault, battery, kidnapping, and hate speech.

Homicide Any killing of one human by another may be labeled as a **homicide**. Criminal homicide is either murder or manslaughter. When the unlawful killing is done with premeditation and deliberate intent, it is labeled as *aggravated murder*, *premeditated murder*, or *first-degree murder*. The definition of first-degree murder, or aggravated murder, differs from state to state. However, in general, first-degree murder involves one of the following circumstances: (1) killing someone with premeditation (thinking about it and planning the homicide in advance with "prior calculation and design"); (2) killing someone in a cruel way, such as with torture; or (3) killing someone while committing a major crime such as rape, robbery, or kidnapping.

If none of these conditions apply, the crime is known as *second-degree murder*. In most states, the distinction between first- and second-degree murder is important, because first-degree murder usually carries the death penalty, whereas second-degree murder does not. In contrast to murder, manslaughter is an unlawful killing without the intent to kill. A killing that results when a person acts in a state of extreme fright, terror, anger, or blind rage that destroys the ability to reason is known as *voluntary manslaughter*. When the unlawful killing results from negligence, the homicide is called *involuntary manslaughter*.

> **Did You Know?**
>
> In 1999, SabreTech, Inc., was indicted by a grand jury in Miami for the 110 deaths that resulted from the crash of ValuJet Flight 592. In the case, the corporation faced 110 counts of murder.

EXAMPLE 5-2: First Degree Murder and Voluntary Manslaughter

Brent Haywood entered a convenience store and robbed the clerk at gunpoint. As he was leaving the store, the clerk pulled a revolver from under the counter and ordered Haywood to stop. In response, Haywood fired his weapon at the clerk, who returned fire. In the exchange of gunshots, an innocent bystander, nine-year-old Teddy Newman, was shot and killed. Haywood was convicted of first-degree murder and sentenced to death by lethal injection. However, the judge, who opposed the death penalty, gave Haywood a life sentence. Teddy's father was in the courtroom when this sentence was announced. In a state of extreme rage, Teddy's father attacked and killed Haywood. Even though Teddy's father's actions were clearly intentional, they were performed in a state of extreme rage as a result of a reasonable provocation. Consequently, he was charged with voluntary manslaughter.

Assault and Battery **Battery** is the unlawful touching of another person. An accidental bumping of another person in a crowded hallway or in the school cafeteria line would not be battery, because the crime requires criminal intent or at least reckless behavior. Similarly, the touching that occurs between football players during a game would not be a battery, despite its violent nature, because all parties have consented to the contact, assuming that the contact is within the rules of the game. Battery usually involves the forceful use of a person's hand, knife, gun, or other weapon. However, a battery could also be committed by giving poison or drugs to an unsuspecting victim, spitting in someone's face, siccing a dog on someone, or even kissing someone who does not want to be kissed.

An **assault** is an attempt to commit a battery. The pointing or shooting of a gun at someone is the assault; the bullet striking the person is the battery. Some states no longer follow the common law distinction between assault and battery. Ohio, for example, has eliminated the term "battery" from its criminal code and substituted "assault" by itself.

Simple assault and battery are generally misdemeanors. *Aggravated battery* and *aggravated assault*, however, are felonies in most states. To qualify as an aggravated offense, the assault or battery must be committed with a deadly weapon, with the intent to murder, with the intent to commit rape, or with the intent to commit robbery. Some states call aggravated assault *felonious assault*.

Kidnapping The unlawful abduction of an individual against that person's will is known as **kidnapping**. It constitutes false imprisonment with the additional element of the removal of the victim to another place. Most state laws distinguish between simple kidnapping and the more serious offenses involving child stealing or demands for ransom.

Hate Speech In recent years, many legislative bodies have attempted to criminalize the use of certain symbols, writings, and speech intended to provoke outrage or fear on the basis of race, religion, color, or gender. These statutes and ordinances are frequently referred to as laws against *hate speech*. Such statutes are constitutional only if they are not content specific. Therefore, though it may be acceptable to draft a statute that outlaws any speech designed to rouse fear or outrage, regardless of the content of that speech, it would be impermissible to outlaw speech aimed at inciting outrage or fear based solely on race, religion, color, gender, or any similar category.

Has 9/11 increased hate speech focused on Muslim women?

Crimes Against Property

Burglary, arson, robbery, larceny, and extortion are the most common crimes against property committed in the United States today.

Burglary **Burglary** consists of a break-in of a dwelling or other building for the purpose of carrying out a felony. The slightest forced entry qualifies as a break-in. Inserting a stick through a window while remaining outside constitutes an entry. Entry through an open door or a window does not alone establish the act of burglary, but once the person is inside, the opening of an interior door would constitute a break-in.

Arson **Arson** is the willful and malicious act of causing the burning of another's property. Under rules established in the common law tradition, arson included only the burning of a person's home. Modern criminal statutes, however, have expanded the crime of arson to include the burning of other structures as well. In some states, arson also includes the burning of a house by its owner. The willful burning is often motivated by the intent to defraud an insurer of the property.

Robbery The act of taking personal property, including money, from the possession of another against that person's will, in that person's presence, and under threat to do great bodily harm or damage is **robbery**. When force is not used, robbery is committed when the victim is subjected to extreme fear.

BusinessWeek Business Law in the News

Media: Buying Clicks to a Tragedy

As news outlets deployed their teams to Blacksburg, Va., following the . . . shooting at Virginia Tech, the business operations of *The New York Times, The Washington Post,* CNN, and *Time* magazine were busy, too. Each bought ads on either Google or Yahoo! so that anytime someone searched the phrase "Virginia shooting," their links would pop up prominently on the right-hand side of the page. "Get info on the gunman and other breaking news from CNN.com," one . . . sponsored link read.

With an ever-growing chunk of total revenues coming from the Web, news outlets now scramble their online marketing staffers as quickly as they do reporters when a big story hits. These marketers employ a variety of tactics to take advantage of their audiences' piqued interest in times of crisis. "At the risk of sounding crass, these do become marketing events for these news sites," says Ben Crain, vice-president at Rapt Inc., which optimizes ad sales for Yahoo!, Dow Jones, CNET Networks, and others. Some argue that such self-promotion treads a dangerous line between being shrewd and exploitative. "It's a line of taste more than ethics," says Michael Hoyt, executive editor of the *Columbia Journalism Review*. "You push your newscast, of course, but do you do it on the back of a national tragedy?"

It's hard to gauge how many users go online for a story following a tragedy, but the impact on a news site is clear. Just two days after the shooting, abcnews.com said it had received 2.3 million unique visitors in one day, a 210% jump from the week before. CNN, meanwhile, saw its traffic spike . . . from its usual 7 million unique users to more than 19 million.

But in the world of Web news, success takes more than scooping the competition. A site's traffic can come from blogs such as The Huffington Post, news aggregator sites like Digg, or the major search engines. Maximizing traffic means courting all of them. Foremost, the story must be easy to find.

Even though most news operations are in a financial pinch these days, nearly all invest in technology, experts, or ads that help win prominent placement. CNN and *USA Today* both hired an outside search marketing firm, Reprise Media. In 2005, The New York Times Co. set up its own consultancy, Define Search Strategies, to help boost traffic from searches to just Web sites. (*BusinessWeek* does not currently buy search ads associated with breaking news but does buy them on general topics.)

Pricey Placements

Competition to be the top ad on the right-hand side of a search engine page is brisk. During the week . . . ads on terms like "Virginia tech massacre" cost as much as $5 per click, says Peter Hershberg of Reprise Media. A week later, the price tag was around a nickel per click.

For news sites, the advantages are threefold: Each additional viewer generates ad revenue on the day itself; the traffic for a high-impact story can build loyalty; and the surge in audience helps boost the monthly traffic numbers Web sites use to woo advertisers and impress Wall Street. (The *Times* does not run ads online next to stories it deems tragedies, such as the Virginia Tech shooting.)

Experts also employ such techniques as teaching editors how to present stories in a way that works online, with simple headlines, says Marshall Simmonds, CEO of Define. Simmonds recalls one artful turn of phrase when he first arrived. "The headline said: 'Pilgrims converge upon the Vatican, the passing of a papacy,'" says Simmonds. "It should have read, 'Pope John Paul II dies'" for online purposes. Traffic from search engines now accounts for 22% of *Times* traffic, vs. 14% two years ago.

A second step—one that both the *Times* and CNN used on the shooting story—is dividing up content into many specific topics. For example, each outlet created a set of special pages that commemorate those who died. In addition to serving as an online tribute, the pages were formatted to help the sites show up naturally in searches for a new set of keywords: the names of the individual victims.

Questions for Analysis

1. Is it ethically proper for news outlets to use horrendous crimes such as the tragedy at Virginia Tech to make money? Explain.

2. Michael Hoyt, executive editor of the *Columbia Journalism Review,* says, "It's a line of taste more than ethics." Do you agree with this assessment of the situation? Explain.

3. Does the sensational use of such stories encourage "copycat" killers? If so, should the media outlet that inspired the "copycat" be criminally responsible? Explain.

4. Is there any way that such stories might be categorized as a crime of hate speech? Explain.

5. Is there any way that a prosecutor might use such stories as a way to demonstrate that the copycat killer's crimes were premeditated? Explain.

Source: Burt Helm and Paula Lehman, "Media: Buying Clicks to a Tragedy: How News Outfits Boost Web Traffic when Stories like Virginia Tech Break," *BusinessWeek,* May 7, 2007, 42.

Larceny A person who takes and carries away the personal property of another without the right to do so is guilty of larceny. Generally, the victim need not be actually present for larceny to occur. The value of the property taken—$50 in many states, as high as $300 in others—determines whether the theft is *grand larceny,* a felony, or *petty larceny,* a misdemeanor. Shoplifting is a form of larceny.

Extortion Extortion is taking another's property with consent when such consent is coerced by threat to injure the victim's person, property, or reputation. Extortion is sometimes called *blackmail.*

Crimes Involving Business

Nonviolent in nature, business crimes are those carried out by a business or individual in the course of doing business to obtain a business-related advantage. Covering a wide range of illegal practices, business crimes are directed against individuals, other businesses, the government, or the public.

Larceny by False Pretenses The taking of someone's money or property by intentionally deceiving that person is known as larceny by false pretenses. The false statements made must be calculated to mislead and must induce the victim to rely on them.

Embezzlement Individuals who wrongfully take property entrusted to their care have committed the crime of embezzlement. In contrast to larceny, in which the offender takes the property without permission, the embezzler gains possession of the property or the money by legitimate means in the ordinary course of business. The embezzler then either keeps the property or puts it to personal use. It is no defense for the embezzler to argue that it was his or her intention to return the property after using it or when the rightful owner requested its return.

Bribery The crime of bribery involves a corrupt agreement induced by an *offer of* reward. Central to the offense is the offering, giving, receiving, or soliciting of something of value to influence official action or the discharge of a public duty. Whether the recipient accepts or rejects the bribe does not absolve the person who made the bribe. If the intended recipient accepts the bribe, then the recipient would be guilty of *bribery acceptance.*

Forgery Forgery is the false making or changing of a writing with the intent to defraud. The signing of another person's name to a check or other document without authority is forgery. Signing one's own name or pretending to be someone else of the same name is also forgery. Similarly, the creation of a fictitious identity and the signing of the name of that fictitious person with fraudulent purpose is considered forgery.

For there to be a crime in these circumstances, there must be an intent to defraud, and the item forged must have some legal effect. Thus, it would not be fraud to write someone else's signature on a will that was never witnessed, because an unwitnessed will has no legal effect. Uttering a forged instrument is also a crime. *Uttering* means to offer a forged instrument to another person, knowing that it is forged, and intending to defraud.

Racketeer Influenced and Corrupt Organizations Act   To prevent a criminal invasion of legitimate businesses, Congress enacted the Racketeer Influenced and Corrupt Organizations (RICO) Act. Under provisions of this statute, conducting a legitimate business with the funds acquired from a "pattern of racketeering activities" can give rise to criminal liability. Many of the offenses that fall within the scope of "racketeering activity"—such as arson and robbery—are serious crimes. Others, however, are less sinister. For example, both mail fraud and wire fraud fall within the definition of racketeering activities. The provisions of RICO can give rise not only to criminal charges but also to civil liability. Thus, it is not uncommon for individuals to seek damages in lawsuits filed against corporations that have violated RICO.

Quick Quiz 5-3   True or False?

1. In most states, the distinction between first- and second-degree murder is important because first-degree murder usually carries the death penalty while second-degree murder does not.   T

2. It is acceptable to draft a statute that outlaws speech aimed at inciting outrage or fear based solely on race, religion, color, gender, or any similar category.   F

3. Shoplifting is a form of larceny.   T

5-4 Electronic Crimes

As is true of most other crimes, statutory definitions and classifications of electronic crimes (e-crimes) or cybercrimes, as they are called in some jurisdictions, vary from state to state. Moreover, in the case of e-crimes, the definitions are even more varied because there is no agreement on what constitutes an e-crime (see Table 5-1). One approach to this task is to state that *e-crimes* involve any criminal act that includes a computer. This approach, which is often referred to as *computer trespass* or *e-trespass*, can solve many of the problems associated with *e-crime*, if only by an indirect treatment of such crimes. Another way to classify e-crimes is to distinguish between crimes committed with a computer and crimes committed against computers.

E-Trespass

A different type of problem arises when crimes that are already on the books are committed with a computer. As noted previously, one way to deal with this situation is to create a single, general offense called electronic trespass, e-trespass, or cybertrespass. *E-trespass* is the process of gaining access to a computer with the intent to commit a crime. In effect, in one single stroke, this technique incorporates the rest of a criminal code into this one crime, making it an offense to use a computer to commit any other crime in the code. In a state that takes this approach, all criminal statutes, but especially those pertaining to fraud, embezzlement, blackmail, and theft, become part of this one crime known as computer trespass.

> **Table 5-1** State Electronic Crimes
>
> **The General Approach**
>
> *Electronic Trespass*—Gaining access to a computer with the intent to commit a criminal act.
>
> **Crimes Committed with a Computer**
>
> *Electronic Extortion*—Gaining access to the computer records of a business or other institution and, in the process, uncovering the illegal, unethical, or negligent conduct of that organization and using that information to commit extortion.
>
> *Electronic Stalking*—Targeting an innocent victim for exploitation using that person's computer connections.
>
> *Electronic Spoofing*—Falsely adopting the identity of another computer user or creating a false identity on a computer Web site in order to commit fraud.
>
> **Crimes That Target Computers**
>
> *Electronic Terrorism*—Using a computer to disrupt or destroy one of the critical elements of the nation's electronic infrastructure.
>
> *Electronic Vandalism*—Attacking a computer system so that a Web site is completely destroyed or paralyzed.
>
> *Electronic Germ Warfare*—Using viruses to attack a computer system.
>
> *Identity Theft*—Using a computer to steal credit card information, financial data, access codes, passwords, and debit card information to clean out a person's bank accounts, to run up credit card debt, divert cash transfers, and disrupt the financial and personal life of the victim.

Crimes Committed with a Computer

Another approach to dealing with e-crime is to distinguish between using a computer to commit a crime and committing an offense against a computer or the owner of a computer. E-crimes that focus on the use of a computer include electronic extortion, electronic stalking, and electronic spoofing.

Electronic Extortion *Electronic extortion, e-extortion*, or *cyberblackmail*, as it is often called, can occur when an experienced hacker gains access to the computer records of a corporation or other institution and discovers some sort of illegal, negligent, or unethical conduct that might embarrass or otherwise damage the reputation or the financial health of the target organization. The hacker can then contact the company, also often using the computer, to threaten exposure unless he or she is handsomely compensated.

Electronic Stalking *Electronic stalking, e-stalking*, or *cyberstalking*, which is related to e-blackmail and often either precedes or follows it, involves targeting individuals for exploitation using their computer connections. Electronic stalkers usually target vulnerable individuals who may be searching for a genuine confidant. Minors are most often targeted by electronic stalkers. After gaining the trust of the minor or other innocent victim, the electronic stalker arranges a meeting so that he or she can take direct advantage of the innocent party.

Electronic Spoofing To commit *electronic spoofing, e-spoofing*, or *cyberspoofing*, an *electronic criminal* must falsely adopt the identity of another computer user or create a false identity on a computer Web site to commit fraud. A simple form of e-spoofing involves adopting the identity of an e-mailer to defraud the recipients of the original e-mail. Another type of e-spoofing involves creating phony Web sites or diverting users from legitimate Web sites to obtain credit card numbers, debit card numbers, passwords, or other confidential information to commit a wide variety of fraudulent activities. A third electronic spoofing method involves sending out phony e-mails that solicit buyers and, in the process, obtaining credit card information, account numbers, passwords, and so on. This last technique is known as *phishing*.

Crimes That Target Computers

Electronic crimes that target computers attempt to disable the computer itself, to disable the system that it operates, or to confiscate and use information stored on the computer, sometimes after erasing the original genuine data. Crimes that target computers include electronic terrorism, identity theft, electronic vandalism, and electronic germ warfare.

Electronic Terrorism   *Electronic terrorism*, *e-terrorism*, or *cyberterrorism* involves using a computer to disrupt or destroy one of the critical elements of the nation's electronic infrastructure, such as power systems, the air traffic control system, water and sanitation systems, ground transportation systems, the nation's stock exchanges, the banking system, or the national defense system. E-terrorists could send a virus into a critical computer system that causes the entire electronic infrastructure to collapse.

Identity Theft   Another cybercrime that targets computers and computer information is known as identity theft. In *identity theft*, a perpetrator using one of the techniques noted previously steals credit card information, financial data, access codes, passwords, or debit card information. The perpetrator then passes himself or herself off as the victim. Using this technique, the identity thief can clean out bank accounts, run up credit card transactions, divert cash transfers, and disrupt the financial and personal life of the victim.

Electronic Vandalism   Sometimes expert e-vandals can attack a computer system so that a Web site is completely destroyed or paralyzed to the extent that legitimate business can no longer be conducted on that site. This type of attack is known as *electronic vandalism, e-vandalism,* or *cybervandalism*. Often e-vandalism is used to cripple a business as a form of revenge for real or imagined wrongs, to exercise power over the business, or to hurt the owner of a business.

A Question of Ethics

Ronald King, who was recently elected mayor of a fairly large Midwestern city, has learned that an underground organization, named the Kesselmen Group, has infected the city's computer system with a virus that threatens to disrupt the city's safety forces' communication system and the city's water supply. If the virus is activated, it will prevent the police and the fire department from receiving emergency calls. The virus will also cause the city's sewer system to contaminate the city's main reservoir. The Kesselmen Group makes one demand: that Mayor King resign so that the deputy mayor, Diane Robertson, can become mayor. As the mayor's chief of staff, what would you advise him to do? Explain the reason for your response using one of the ethical theories identified in Chapter 1 of this textbook.

Electronic Germ Warfare When criminals use viruses to attack a computer system, they are engaged in *electronic germ warfare, e-germ warfare,* or *cybergerm warfare.* Clearly viruses can be used to attack computer systems for many of the e-crimes listed previously. Thus, an e-extortionist can threaten to unleash a virus into a company's computer system unless he or she is paid a certain amount of money. In effect, the e-extortionist is using the virus to extract ransom money from the business. Similarly, an e-terrorist or e-vandal can use a virus to disrupt a computer system for political or psychological reasons.

Federal E-Crimes

Many states have enacted legislation to combat these e-crimes and other electronic offenses. The federal government has also attempted to deal with the issue by passing a number of anti–e-crime statutes. The statutes of primary importance, as determined by the Computer Crime and Intellectual Property Section of the United States Department of Justice, include the Computer Fraud and Abuse Act, the Wiretap Act, the Unlawful Access to Stored Communications Act, the Identity Theft Act, the Access Device Fraud Act, and the CAN SPAM Act.

The Computer Fraud and Abuse Act Congress first specifically addressed the subject of computer crime more than two decades ago when, as a part of a comprehensive crime control statute, it created the Computer Fraud and Abuse Act. Currently, this act outlaws the following activities: obtaining national security information, compromising the confidentiality of a computer, trespassing in a government computer, accessing a computer to defraud, damaging a computer, damaging computer information, trafficking in passwords, and threatening to damage a computer.

The Wiretap Act Originally, the Wiretap Act covered only wire and oral communications. However, since the early days of this law, Congress has changed the statute to cover electronic communications. The purpose of this update was to protect the privacy of electronic communication in the same way that wire and oral communications are protected. To do this, the act prohibits the intentional interception of electronic communication.

The Unlawful Access to Stored Communications Act Congress enacted the Unlawful Access to Stored Communications Act to protect both voice mail and e-mail messages. The act expressly protects the confidentality, integrity, and availability of voice mail and e-mail transmissions when they are stored electronically. The act outlaws the intentional, unauthorized access to such messages and provides penalites that can climb as high as 10 years in prison and $250,000 in fines.

The Identity Theft Act The Identity Theft and Assumption Act, which was recently amended by the Identity Theft Penalty Enhancement Act, outlaws the unauthorized transfer, possession, or use of a means of identifying another person to violate federal law. The amendment adds a new crime, called aggravated identity theft, to the original statute. The section on aggravated identity theft makes it clear that identity theft is much worse when it involves certain very serious felonies, including terrorism.

The Access Device Fraud Act The objective of this federal statute is to make it unlawful to obtain money, property, or services through the fraudulent use of an access device that permits entry to a computer. Access devices are defined by the statute to include credit cards, debit cards, codes, PIN numbers, account numbers, and mobile identification numbers.

The CAN SPAM Act   Spam is the nickname for all of those pop-up advertisements that appear on computer screens while users are tapped into the Internet. The CAN SPAM Act is designed to deal with this problem, as well as the problem of unsolicited commercial e-mail.

Quick Quiz 5-4   True or False?

1.   Statutory definitions and classifications of e-crimes have become uniform within all jurisdictions in the United States.

2.   E-trespass is defined as gaining access to a computer with the intent to commit a crime.

3.   The federal government has passed several e-crime statutes.

5-5 Defenses to Criminal Liability

Because criminal liability lies within the elements of an act and the required mental state, a logical defense would be aimed at eliminating one or both of those elements. Most defenses attempt to do just that. The most common defenses are insanity, entrapment, justifiable force, and mistake. (See Table 5-2.)

The Insanity Defense

Although the insanity defense has been around for a long time, many people do not understand the nature of the defense. One of the key points of confusion is the difference between *competency to stand trial* and the *insanity defense* itself.

Competency to Stand Trial   Criminal defendants are generally presumed to be mentally competent to stand trial. However, the issue of competency to stand trial can be raised if the court, the defense attorney, or the prosecutor suspects that the defendant is not competent. If the issue of competency is raised, the defendant will undergo psychiatric examinations to determine his or her level of competency. Generally, defendants

---

Table 5-2   Criminal Liability and Defenses

Criminal Liability	Criminal Defenses

The act:
   Criminal behavior specifically
      outlined by statute
	Defenses to the act:
	   Act as defined is "status" only
	   Act as defined is ambiguous
	   Act as defined is overbroad

The mental state:
   Mental state specifically
      outlined by statute
   Purpose
   Knowledge
   Recklessness
   Negligence
	Defenses to the mental state:
	   Insanity
	   Entrapment
	   Justifiable force
	   Mistake

are considered competent to stand trial if they understand the nature and the purpose of the charges against them, and if they are capable of aiding their attorneys in their defense. When defendants are found to be incompetent, they are usually given treatment to improve their competency level so that they can understand what is going on and can assist in their case.

EXAMPLE 5-3: Competency and the Ability to Assist

The question of competency to stand trial was a key factor in a case in which Harold Gunther was prosecuted for the murder of one person and the attempted murder of two others. Listening at the door of an apartment, Gunther believed he heard three coworkers plotting against him. Convinced that he was about to be attacked, Gunther entered the apartment and assaulted his three coworkers, killing one and severely injuring the other two. Gunther consistently maintained that he was the intended target of a plot to destroy him. No evidence was ever presented that such a plot existed. In contrast, expert testimony indicated that Gunther was paranoid and delusional. Consequently, his defense attorney moved for a competency hearing. Despite the expert testimony, the judge in the case found Gunther competent to stand trial. The competency ruling was based on the fact that, despite Gunther's mental problems, he was capable of understanding the charges against him and was able to assist in his defense. Under state law, these were the only qualifications needed for a competency finding by the court. Gunther met these qualifications and was found competent to stand trial.

Not Guilty by Reason of Insanity (NGRI) American law recognizes that individuals cannot be held responsible for their actions if they do not know what they are doing. In addition, it serves no practical purpose to imprison someone who needs the care of mental health professionals. For these reasons, insanity is recognized as a valid defense to criminal conduct.

The oldest test of insanity is the **M'Naughten Rule**. Under this rule, a defendant can be found NGRI if, at the time the criminal act was committed, he or she was suffering from a mental disease that was so serious that the defendant did not know the nature of the act or did not know that act was wrong. Another test of insanity is the **irresistible impulse test**. This test holds that criminal defendants can be found NGRI if, at the time of the offense, they were stricken with a mental disease that prevented them from knowing right from wrong or that compelled them to commit the crime.

Under the **American Law Institute (ALI) test**, a person is not responsible if "as a result of mental disease or defect he lacks substantial capacity either to appreciate the criminality of his conduct or to conform his conduct to the requirements of law." The ALI test is plainly a relaxation of the usual insanity standard, as expressed in M'Naughten and the irresistible impulse test, because both of the older tests require "total" rather than "substantial" impairment. M'Naughten requires an inability to appreciate the wrongfulness of an action, and the irresistible impulse test requires a thorough loss of self-control.

It is important to understand that people found not guilty by reason of insanity do not automatically go free. Instead, they are committed to institutions and must undergo periodic psychiatric examinations. Once they are found to be sane, they may be released. Many people object to the fact that these individuals can look forward to release without serving any time in prison.

The Opening Case Revisited
United States v. Sandoval-Mendoza, Round 2

In The Opening Case at the beginning of this chapter, the criminal defendant, Eduardo Sandoval-Mendoza, was enticed into a drug deal by Marcos and Tony, two informants operating on behalf of the government. The fact that Tony and Marcos were not law enforcemant officers themselves but instead were informants did not eliminate Sandoval-Mendoza's right to use entrapment as a defense. The heart of the entrapment defense is that the defendant must demonstrate that he or she was tricked into committing the offense in question by law enforcement officers or *by their duly appointed agents*. In this case, Tony and Marcos were clearly duly appointed government agents who had been engaged solely for the purpose of enticing Sandoval-Mendoza into the government-sponsored sting operation.

Entrapment

If a law enforcement officer induces a law-abiding citizen to commit a crime, **entrapment may be used** as a defense. The person using the defense must show that the crime would not have been committed had it not been for the inducement of the officer. The defense of entrapment is not available to a defendant who would have committed the crime even without the involvement of the officer. This factor is referred to as the propensity to commit the crime. The entrapment defense can be used in many different types of criminal cases. However, it occurs most often when the police have engineered a sting operation designed to tempt individuals who already have the propensity to commit the crime in question. Often in a sting operation, the main players are undercover law enforcement officers. However, sometimes they can be informants or reformed crminals who are used by the police to tempt individuals who are known by the police to be presently involved in a pattern of criminal activity. The fact that the police have used informants rather than undercover agents will not negate the entrapment defense, as long as all of the other elements are present.

Justifiable Force

In general, the law will not condone the use of force to solve problems. Still, special circumstances may arise that justify the use of force. Three of these situations lead to the following defenses: self-defense, defense of others, and battered spouse syndrome.

Self-Defense When individuals have good reason to believe that they are in danger of death or serious injury, they can use force to protect themselves. This action is known as **self-defense**. In some states, the person claiming self-defense must retreat, if possible, before resorting to force. However, a person does not have a duty to retreat before using force if the attack occurs in his or her own home. When self-defense is used in a criminal case, the defendant must show that he or she was not the one who started the altercation in the first place. Moreover, in all cases, the person claiming self-defense must not have used more force than necessary to stop the unprovoked attack.

Defense of Others If a person uses force to rescue another person who is the victim of an apparent attack, most states will allow the rescuer to escape criminal liability. This exception is known as the **defense of others**. As in the case of self-defense, the rescuer must have good reason to believe that the victim was in danger of severe bodily injury or even death.

Battered Spouse Syndrome   The law also protects a married individual from being abused by his or her spouse. In most cases of spouse abuse, the wife is victimized by the violent outbursts of her husband. Many communities have established shelters where abused and battered wives can seek safety and receive counseling and legal services for themselves and their children. Wives who wish to protect themselves from the continual abuse caused by their husbands may seek legal help from the courts.

One such remedy is a *protective order*. Protective orders bar the abusing spouse from maintaining any contact with the victim. Such orders are enforced by the local police. Unfortunately, protective orders are not always effective. In some very severe cases, the victimized spouse has taken the law into her own hands and killed her tormentor. The set of circumstances that leads a woman to believe that the only way that she can escape death or severe bodily injury is to use force against her tormentor is called **battered spouse syndrome**. These circumstances are also known as *battered woman* or *battered wife syndrome*. Because the spouse had good reason to believe that she was in danger of death or severe bodily injury, battered spouse syndrome is considered a form of self-defense in some courts.

Mistake

Mistake is a defense to charges of criminal liability, as long as the mistake destroys one of the elements necessary to that crime. If the mistake does not destroy an element, it is not a valid defense. To be a successful defense, the mistake must be based on a reasonable belief. It would be no defense for a defendant to say that he shot his wife because he believed she was an invader from Mars. Note also that it is not a defense for an accused to say that she did not know that this particular conduct was prohibited by law. Nor is it a defense to a gambling charge for the defendant to argue that she did not know that the gambling law applied to her. Finally, the mistake must destroy the criminal nature of the act in the mind of the accused. It would be no defense, for example, if a defendant argued that he injured an individual by mistake when he was actually trying to injure someone else.

Quick Quiz 5-5 True or False?

1. Most defendants who are found NGRI are released immediately.   *F*

2. A person does not have to retreat to his or her own home before resorting to force to repel an attack.   *T*

3. Mistake is never a defense to a charge of criminal liability.   *F*

Summary

5.1   A crime is an offense against the public at large. As such, a crime threatens the peace, safety, and well-being of the entire community. For this reason, crimes are punishable by the official governing body of a nation or state. A felony is a crime punishable by death or imprisonment in a federal or a state prison for a term exceeding one year. Some felonies are also punishable by fines. A misdemeanor is a less serious crime that is generally punishable by a prison sentence of not more than one year.

5.2   The two elements necessary to create criminal liability are (a) an act and (b) the requisite state of mind. Generally speaking, a crime cannot be committed unless the criminal act named in the statute is performed with the requisite state of mind. Many state criminal codes include four possible states of mind: (a) purpose, (b) knowledge, (c) recklessness, and (d) negligence. Establishing motive may help investigators pinpoint the guilty party, but proving an evil motive is not necessary for a criminal conviction. Conversely, establishing the existence of a good motive will rarely absolve a defendant of criminal liability.

5.3   Crimes against people include homicide, assault, battery, kidnapping, and hate speech. Burglary, robbery, and arson are the most common crimes against property committed in the United States. Nonviolent in nature, business crimes are those carried out by a business or individual in the course of doing business to obtain a business-related advantage.

5.4   One approach to the task of defining e-crime or cybercrime is to state that e-crimes involve any criminal transgression that includes or impacts a computer. This approach is often referred to as computer trespass or e-trespass. Another way to classify e-crimes is to distinguish between crimes committed with a computer and crimes committed against computers. Crimes committed with a computer include e-extortion, e-stalking, and e-spoofing. Crimes committed against computers include e-terrorism, identity theft, e-vandalism, and e-germ warfare. Another way to fight e-crime is through the creation of federal anti–e-crime statutes.

5.5   Because criminal liability relies on the two essential elements of act and requisite mental state, a logical defense aims at eliminating one or both of those elements. Most defenses attempt to do just that. The most common defenses are insanity, entrapment, justifiable force, and mistake.

Key Terms

American Law Institute (ALI) test, 107

arson, 99

assault, 99

battered spouse syndrome, 109

battery, 98

bribery, 101

burglary, 99

crime, 91

defense of others, 108

embezzlement, 101

entrapment, 108

extortion, 101

felony, 93

forgery, 101

homicide, 98

irresistible impulse test, 107

kidnapping, 99

knowledge, 95

larceny, 101

larceny by false pretenses, 101

misdemeanor, 93

M'Naughten Rule, 107

negligence, 96

purpose, 95

recklessness, 96

robbery, 99

self-defense, 108

Questions for Review and Discussion

1. What is the purpose of criminal law?
2. What are the various categories and classes of crimes?
3. What is the nature of an act according to the meaning of criminal liability?
4. What are the four mental states that can be found in the criminal code?
5. What is motive, and how does it differ from the elements of criminal liability?
6. What are the various crimes against people?
7. What are the various theories involved in criminal punishment?
8. What are the various ways that the federal government has dealt with e-crime?
9. What are the three standards for the insanity defense found in criminal law?
10. What are the requirements of entrapment as a defense against criminal liability?

Investigating the Internet

The United States Justice Department maintains a Web site that includes a wide variety of information pertaining to federal criminal law statutes. Access the Web site and conduct a search for computer crimes. When you locate this section, find the department's manual devoted to Prosecuting Computer Crimes. Click on this site and answer the following questions: (1) When was the manual last updated? (2) What does the department recommend as the best practices for working with companies involved in a computer-related case? (3) What does the department recommend as a general principle for minimizing the effect on the operation of a company? (4) What specific examples does the department offer of this minimizing technique? (5) What does the department recommend as a way to rebuild a relationship with a business after an intrusion?

Cases for Analysis

1. Indy Sengchanthong was sleeping in his vehicle when he was found by a police officer. The vehicle was sitting motionless on the shoulder of the interstate, but the key was in the ignition, the ignition was placed in the "on" position, the wipers were moving, and the turn signal was flashing. When Sengchanthong's blood alcohol level was measured, it was found to be above the legal limit. He was therefore charged with being under the influence of alcohol while operating a motor vehicle. Sengchanthong argued that in his unconscious state, he could not possibly have been operating the vehicle. The prosecutor contended that the fact that Sengchanthong had placed the key in the ignition was enough. Placing the key in the ignition naturally leads to a sequence of events, the outcome of which would have been to operate the vehicle while under the influence. Was this enough to constitute an act in criminal law? Explain. *Sengchanthong v. Commissioner of Motor Vehicles*, No. SC17606 (Connecticut Supreme Court).

2. Michael Booth had not paid his child support, and so he found himself on the wrong side of a judge in Wabash, Ind. After finding Booth in contempt, Judge Robert McCallen III decided to use a special punishment on the defendant. Rather than sentence him to the county jail, Judge McCallen ordered Booth to sit beneath a sign that read, "I don't support my kids." The sign beneath which Booth sat was located in the lobby of the county building. Which theory of punishment in criminal law does this one fall under? Explain. "Deadbeat Dad Told to Wear Sign," *The National Law Journal*, October 16, 2006, p. 13.

3. McIver rented a room in his mobile home to Beal. One evening while McIver and Beal were drinking, they got into a heated argument, and McIver orderd Beal to vacate the premises immediately. When Beal refused, McIver called the police. Before the police arrived, Beal decided to leave but was prevented from doing so when McIver pulled out a pitchfork. To defend himself, Beal picked up a nearby machete, and he and McIver battled each other until McIver ended up on the floor. Beal then vacated the building. However, in the process, he fell over and was once more attacked by the pitchfork-wielding McIver. At that moment, the police arrived and took Beal away. Beal was charged with assault. Beal argued that he was simply defending himself from McIver's attack. Is Beal correct? *State V. Beal* (2007 WL 3431, Ct. App., N.C. 2007).

4. While at a party, Scott drank some punch that he did not know was laced with PCP. Subsequent to

this event, he exhibited bizarre behavior and began to hallucinate. Believing that his life and the life of the president were in danger, he attempted to commandeer several motor vehicles. He was charged, tried, and convicted of two counts of attempted theft. Will Scott's conviction be overturned? Explain. *People v. Scott,* 194 Cal. Rptr. 633 (CA).

5. Katie Roberts was wasting away from the effects of an incurable disease. She asked her husband Frank to help her commit suicide. In response to her request, Mr. Roberts mixed poison and water and placed the mixture on a chair within her reach. She took the poison and died several hours later. Mr. Roberts admitted placing the poison within her reach but denied having the required mental state for first-degree murder because he was responding to his wife's request and was motivated by love and mercy. Will he prevail? Explain. *People v. Roberts,* 178 N.W.690 (MI).

6. Several teenagers taped the broken legs of a chair together to create a cross, which they then ignited and placed on the lawn of an African-American family in the neighborhood. One of the teenagers, a minor, was charged with a misdemeanor under the St. Paul Bias-Motivated Crime Ordinance. The St. Paul ordinance criminalized the placing on private property of any "symbol, object, appellation, characterization or graffiti . . . which one knows or has reasonable grounds to know arouses anger, alarm, or resentment in others on the basis of race, color, creed, religion or gender." The defendant argued that the ordinance was an unconstitutional violation of the First Amendment. The city contended that the statute was constitutional because it was necessary for the preservation of a compelling state interest, namely, the right of group members who have been discriminated against in the past "to live in peace where they wish." Is the St. Paul ordinance constitutional? Explain. *R.A.V. v. St. Paul,* 505 U.S. 1992 (U.S. Sup. Ct.).

7. Tomas Reese entered a fast-food restaurant before the restaurant had opened for business through an unlocked rear entrance. The door had been left unlocked by an accomplice who was an employee of the restaurant. After entering the restaurant, Reese pushed one employee against

a soda machine and, while holding a gun to the neck of the manager, forced her to open the safe. Reese then locked the employees in a cooler and fled the scene with over $5,000. Has Reese committed burglary, robbery, or larceny? Explain. *State v. Reese,* 113 Ohio App. 3d. 642 (OH).

8. Cuttiford and Banks lived in the same duplex; Banks lived upstairs and Cuttiford lived downstairs. The two apartments shared a common internal stairway at the back of the duplex. A confrontation began between Banks and Cuttiford in the rear stairway of the duplex. Banks became rather violent and threatened Cuttiford and Cuttiford's wife. Cuttiford went to his apartment on the bottom floor and retrieved two guns from his bedroom. When he returned to the back door near the stairway, Banks told him, "You don't have the guts to use that, because you're going to have to use it because I'm going to kill you!" Banks then came at Cuttiford, lunging from the common stairway into the kitchen of the Cuttiford's apartment. Cuttiford then shot and killed Banks. At trial, Cuttiford argued that he shot Banks in self-defense. The trial court refused to instruct the jury that Cuttiford did not have to retreat into his own home before acting to repel an attacker. The court apparently believed the prosecution, which had argued that because Banks and Cuttiford occupied the same duplex, Cuttiford had the duty to retreat before repelling Banks's attack. Was the trial court judge correct in his instruction to the jury regarding self-defense? Explain. *State v. Cuttiford,* 639 N.E.2d 472 (OH).

9. Cowen had on many occasions operated as a paid drug informant for the FBI and the Ventura Police Department. The Ventura police asked Cowen to keep in touch with them, should he become involved in any deals. Subsequently, Cowen asked Busby to introduce him to any drug dealers he knew. Busby introduced Cowen to Mandell, who sold Cowen several samples of cocaine in anticipation of a $41,500 deal. Cowen then contacted the Ventura police. A police officer posed as Cowen's buyer, and both Busby and Mandell were arrested and eventually turned over to the federal authorities. Busby was convicted of possession of cocaine with the intent to distribute it. He appealed this conviction, claim-

ing that he had been entrapped by Cowen. Will Busby's entrapment defense succeed on appeal? Explain. *United States v. Busby,* 780 F.2d 804 (9th Cir.).

Quick Quiz Answers

5-1	5-2	5-3	5-4	5-5
1. F	1. T	1. T	1. F	1. F
2. F	2. F	2. F	2. T	2. T
3. F	3. F	3. T	3. T	3. F

Chapter 6 Tort Law

The Opening Case

Barnes v. Cohen Dry Wall, Inc. and Aelina Martin

Cohen Dry Wall, Inc., held a business-related party at which alcohol was served to one of the 19-year-old guests. While driving after the party, the guest caused a two-car accident that killed a passenger in the second vehicle, along with the guest himself. The representative of the deceased passenger brought a lawsuit against the driver's estate and against the host of the party. At trial, the jury found for the plaintiff and against the host, who appealed the case. The appeals court upheld the verdict. The case was then accepted by the Supreme Court of South Carolina. The issue before the court was whether a social host who transfers alcohol to a guest, who by law is under the legal age to receive alcohol, owes a duty to a third party who is injured or killed as a result of the underaged guest's intoxication. The host argued that under common law, social hosts do not owe a duty to third parties when an intoxicated adult leaves the premises and, while driving, injures a third party. The defendant concluded that because in this case, except for the alcohol prohibition, the guest was an adult, the court cannot extend liability beyond the intoxicated guest himself, who was driving the vehicle at the time of the accident. The court disagreed, pointing to numerous statutes demonstrating that the laws of South Carolina clearly promote the idea that people between the ages of 18 and 20 years lack the ability to make an informed choice about the consumption of alcohol. Nevertheless, the court also pointed out that the duty does not arise because of the statutes but is instead a common law duty that emerges from the public policy of the state of South Carolina. Thus, though the statutes are an expression of the state's policy, they are not the only source of expression. The court in its creation of common law can also affirm that same duty. (See *Marcum v. Bowden* and *Barnes v. Cohen Dry Wall, Inc. and Aelina Martin* Opinion No. 26259 (5 Feb. 2007) (S.C. Sup. Ct.); and "Social Host to be Liable for Underage Drinking," *The National Law Journal,* February 19, 2007, p. 15.)

Opening Case Questions

1. Does this case involve an intentional tort or negligence?

2. Why would the defendant in this case claim it owed no duty to the plaintiff?

3. Would the result in this case be different if the driver had been 21 years of age or older?

4. Does the case involve statutory law or common law?

5. What type of remedy would be appropriate in this case?

 Learning Objectives

1. Differentiate between the objectives of tort law and those of criminal law.
2. Outline the nature of vicarious liability.
3. Discuss the element of duty.
4. Identify the principal intentional torts and outline the elements of each.
5. Determine the four elements of negligence.
6. Contrast contributory negligence, comparative negligence, and assumption of the risk.
7. Judge in a particular case whether the doctrine of strict liability applies.
8. Discuss the emerging concept of e-tort law.
9. Outline the various remedies available in tort law.
10. Discuss the wrongful death and survival statutes.

6-1 Tort Law Defined

A **tort** is a private wrong that injures another person's physical well-being, emotional health, business, property, or reputation. The English word "tort" comes from the Latin word *tortus,* which can be translated as "twisted." A person who commits a tort and has thus engaged in "twisted" behavior is called a **tortfeasor**. The other party is alternately referred to as the injured party, the innocent party, the victim, or the plaintiff if a lawsuit has been filed. In the case of a lawsuit, the tortfeasor would be called a defendant.

Tort Law Versus Criminal Law

The primary purpose of tort law is to compensate for the injured party's loss. Another objective is to protect potential victims by deterring future tortious behavior. In contrast, criminal law involves a public wrong, that is, a wrong that affects the entire society. Because criminal law is concerned with protecting the public, its focus differs from that of tort law. When a crime is committed, government authorities begin legal actions designed to remove the offender from society. It is possible, however, for a single act to be both a tort and a crime. The U.S. Constitution protects people from being tried twice for the same crime. This rule is known as the principle of *double jeopardy*. Double jeopardy, however, does not protect a defendant from being sued under tort law for the consequences of an action, after that defendant has been tried in a criminal court for the same action.

Respondeat Superior

Business people must be especially aware of tort law because of the doctrine of *respondeat superior* ("let the master respond"). The doctrine of *respondeat superior*, which is also referred to as **vicarious liability**, may impose legal liability on employers and make them pay for the torts committed by their employees within the scope of the employer's business. The theory behind this doctrine is that the injuries to persons and property are the hazards of doing business, the cost of which the business should bear. The loss should not be borne by the innocent victim of the tort or by society as a whole (see Chapter 32).

EXAMPLE 6-1:   Yellow Cabs, Red Lights, and *Respondeat Superior*

Lori Roberts worked as a cab driver for the Barrows Cab Service in New York City. One afternoon, she picked up Ted Franklin at LaGuardia Airport. While driving up Fifth Avenue, Roberts was cut off by another driver at an intersection. Enraged, Roberts lost her concentration and ran a red light, then collided with a car driven by Jerry Lancaster. Lancaster can sue both Roberts and Barrows Cab under the doctrine of *respondeat superior*.

About the Law

The doctrine of *respondeat superior* is also known as vicarious liability.

The Element of Duty

LO3

One approach to the law is to think of legal liability in terms of elements. This approach emphasizes that no liability can be imposed against an individual unless all the elements are present. In tort law, the first element is duty. A **duty** is an obligation placed on individuals because of the law. The second element is a violation of that duty. A duty can be violated intentionally, through negligence, or under the theory of strict liability.

Quick Quiz 6-1 True or False?

1. A person who commits a tort is engaged in "twisted" behavior.
2. The purpose of tort law is to protect the public at large.
3. Employers are never liable for the torts of their employees because such a move would violate the constitutional prohibition against double jeopardy.

6-2 Intentional Torts

LO4

Intentional violations of duty include a vast variety of intentional torts, all of which have their own individual elements. Table 6-1 summarizes the primary intentional torts.

Assault and Battery

Under U.S. tort law, assault and battery, though often closely associated with each other, are separate torts. An **assault** occurs when the victim is placed in fear or apprehension of immediate bodily harm by a tortfeasor who has the present apparent ability to inflict that harm. No actual physical contact is needed for an assault. The essence of the tort lies in the fear or apprehension that is created in the victim.

EXAMPLE 6-2:   Assault with a Deadly Dart

Terry Kline and Patrick Fisher were playing a friendly game of darts at the Wood Street Tavern one evening when they invited Fred Feeney and David Ballentine to join them. Unknown to either Kline or Feeney, Ballentine was intoxicated. After losing several games, Ballentine became enraged and tried to hit Kline by throwing several darts at him. In his intoxicated state, Ballentine's aim was poor, and he did not hit Kline. Nevertheless, Ballentine has committed an assault.

Table 6-1 Intentional Torts

Tort	Definition
Assault	An assault occurs when the victim is placed in fear or apprehension of immediate bodily harm by tortfeasor who has the present apparent ability to inflict that harm.
Battery	A battery involves an offensive or harmful, unprivileged touching.
False imprisonment	When one party prevents another party from moving about freely, the first party has committed the intentional tort of false imprisonment.
Defamation	Any false statement communicated to others that harms a person's good name or reputation may constitute the tort of defamation.
Invasion of privacy	Invasion of privacy occurs when one person unreasonably denies another person the right to be left alone.
Misuse of legal procedure	Misuse of legal procedure occurs when one person brings a legal action with malice and without probable cause.
Intentional infliction of emotional distress	Intentional or reckless infliction of emotional distress occurs when an individual causes another to undergo emotional or mental suffering, even without an accompanying physical injury.
Disparagement	Disparagement involves any false statement communicated to others that somehow questions the quality of an item of property or that raises uncertainty as to who actually has legal ownership rights to the property in question.
Fraud	Fraud involves false statements or actions, or a combination thereof, that misrepresent facts so that an innocent party relies on those misrepresentations and suffers an injury or loss as a result.

A **battery** involves an offensive or harmful, unprivileged touching. Naturally, if in Example 6-2, Ballentine had actually managed to hit Kline, he would have committed a battery. However, as the definition points out, a touching need not be harmful to be a battery. Moreover, a battery does not always require the touching of the actual person of the victim, if the tortfeasor touches something closely associated with that victim. So, if a prankster pulls a chair out from under someone before that person sits down, and the person falls to the floor, the joker has committed a battery. Or if he or she knocks a cafeteria tray out of a diner's hands, again he or she has committed a battery, despite the fact that the actual person or the victim has not been contacted.

EXAMPLE 6-3:   Battery by Antibody

Lucy Pickett works as a nurse at Garner County Hospital. Because she knows that her patient, Jim Luger, is afraid of needles, she sneaked up behind him and injected him with an antibiotic that had been ordered by his primary physician. Despite her desire to help Luger, and her wish to save him from feeling unnecessary fear, Pickett has committed a battery.

False Imprisonment

When one party prevents another party from moving about freely, the first party has committed the intentional tort of **false imprisonment**. This tort is called false arrest in some states. The victim of false imprisonment need not be locked in a prison or a jail cell. All that is required is that the person's freedom of movement be restricted. For example, a physician who refuses to return a patient's clothing until a partial payment is received for a long overdue bill has committed false imprisonment.

Store owners must be very careful about detaining suspected shoplifters, because such a detention could result in a false imprisonment lawsuit if not handled properly. Still, because of the growing problem of shoplifting in society today, most states have laws that allow storekeepers to detain a suspected shoplifter if they have reasonable grounds to suspect that a shoplifting incident has occurred. However, the storekeeper must detain the suspect in a reasonable manner and for no longer than a reasonable length of time.

Defamation and Disparagement

Intentional torts such as battery, assault, and false imprisonment involve direct physical and psychological injury to an individual. These injuries are not the only type of harm, however, that can be imposed on individuals in tort law. Sometimes the injury results from words and hurts a reputation, which leads to monetary loss. Two of these word-oriented torts are defamation and disparagement.

Defamation   Any false statement communicated to others that harms a person's good name or reputation may constitute the tort of **defamation**. To be defamatory, the statement must hold the victim up to ridicule, contempt, or hatred. Defamation in a temporary form, such as speech, is **slander**; in a permanent form, such as writing, movies, videocassettes, or DVDs, it is **libel**.

People can usually bring a libel suit whenever the permanent statement is damaging to their reputation, is false, and is communicated to a third party. However, under common law, individuals can bring slander lawsuits even if they have suffered no actual loss if the false statements fall into one of the following categories:

1. An accusation that the victim of the slanderous statements has committed a very serious crime, such as murder or rape.
2. An accusation that the victim has a communicable disease, such as venereal disease.
3. An accusation that the victim has engaged in improprieties in a business, trade, or profession.
4. An accusation that an unmarried female victim has been unchaste.

Individuals may speak the truth without being sued successfully for defamation as long as it is done without spite or ill will. In addition, statements made by senators and representatives on the floor of Congress and statements made in a court of law are privileged. Privileged statements are not the proper subject of a defamation lawsuit. The idea behind creating these privileges is to promote the open debate of legislative and judicial matters.

The U.S. Supreme Court has given journalists the extra protection of the actual malice test when they write about public officials. Under the **actual malice test**, a public official must prove not only that the statement made or printed was false but also that it was made with actual malice. **Actual malice** means that the statement was made or printed either with the knowledge that it was false or with a reckless disregard for its truth or falsity. Later decisions expanded the actual malice test to cover public figures. Public figures are people like television actors, sports figures, and rock stars who seek out public fame and are readily recognizable by the public at large.

Temporary public figures are people who are placed against their will into the public view by some event beyond their control. Disaster victims, hostages, and rescuers are examples of temporary public figures. Generally, such people are held to the actual malice test as long as their notoriety lasts.

Disparagement

Disparagement involves any false statement communicated to others that somehow questions the quality of property or raises uncertainty as to who has legal ownership of that property. Generally, to recover for disparagement, the plaintiff must show monetary loss. Such losses may include the loss of sales, money spent to correct the public's image of a product, or expenses spent on litigation due to the disparagement. The difference between defamation and disparagement is that in defamation, the false charge is made about the victim's reputation, whereas with disparagement, the falsehood is made about a person's property or product. The falsehood usually casts doubt on the value of the product or on the property rights of the owner.

EXAMPLE 6-4:   Toys, Tots, and Tall Tales

Warren Barrington owned and operated Toys and Tots—From Two to Twelve, a toy store that specialized in educational toys for children between two and twelve years of age. Barrington and his wife, who operated the store as a partnership, did their best to market only original toys made of natural materials. Electronic toys, computers, and toys made of plastic were never sold in the store. During the National Toy and Model Association of America convention, Raymond Matthews, who owned a competitive shop, started several rumors, most of which suggested that many of the toys that were being shown by the Barringtons at the convention were not made of natural materials as advertised. He also suggested that those toys that were made of natural materials involved ideas stolen from him and that the Barringtons did not have the right to market them as they were doing at the convention. Matthews has clearly committed disparagement here. He has planted false reports about both the value of the Barrington's products and about the Barrington's property rights to the toys.

Fraudulent Misrepresentation

Another word-oriented tort is fraudulent misrepresentation. **Fraudulent misrepresentation**, or **fraud** as it is known in some states, occurs when false statements or actions, or a combination thereof, are made by one party in a way that causes another party to rely on those misrepresentations and then suffers an injury or loss as a result. Frequently, fraud involves a business relationship and works to destroy the mutual assent that ought to exist between the parties that are involved in a contract. For that reason, it is discussed at length in Chapter 9. However, fraud is also a tort and need not involve a contract.

Invasion of Privacy

The courts in the United States have consistently held that people have a right to privacy. Consequently, a violation of that right would involve the tort of **invasion of privacy**. The right to privacy can be violated in several ways:

1. Revelation of confidential records
2. Intrusion
3. Creating a false light
4. Exploitation

BusinessWeek ## Business Law in the News

TV Art Scam Bilked Buyers of Millions

A couple who sold art through televised auctions admitted selling bogus works and forging signatures of artists including Picasso, Chagall and Dali in a scam that bilked buyers out of millions of dollars, prosecutors said.

In court documents filed Monday, Kristine Eubanks, 49, and her husband, Gerald Sullivan, 51, were charged with conspiracy to commit mail fraud, wire fraud and interstate transportation of stolen property.

Eubanks also was charged with tax evasion, and Sullivan was charged with failure to file a tax return.

Prosecutors said the couple agreed to cooperate with investigators in an ongoing criminal probe to capture other scam artists. The two have not formally entered pleas.

"The defendants in this case have admitted to profiting by preying on the vulnerabilities of producers and consumers of art through an elaborate criminal enterprise," said J. Stephen Tidwell, assistant director of the FBI in Los Angeles.

The operation involved the couple's satellite television show, "Fine Arts Treasures Gallery."

The government estimated the show defrauded more than 10,000 people who paid more than $20 million for bogus art. Investigators seized nearly $4 million when Eubanks and Sullivan were arrested during a raid in September.

The couple told authorities they rigged the auctions of art and jewelry by creating inflated bids, and that they purchased fake art, forged art at a print shop and sold the bogus works on their show, according to court documents. Prosecutors said the couple also created false appraisals and certificates of authenticity.

Eubanks could face up to 10 years in federal prison; Sullivan up to six. Eubanks has been in custody since the September raid because she was on probation at the time. The two are from La Canada, about 15 miles northeast of Los Angeles.

Questions for Analysis

1. The article clearly involves a criminal prosecution. However, some crimes are also torts. What tort is involved in the scheme hatched by Eubanks and Sullivan?

2. What would a plaintiff have to prove to succeed in a tort claim against Eubanks and Sullivan? Explain.

3. Would a contract have to be involved to succeed in a lawsuit involving this case? Explain.

4. Why does the law permit a defendant to be prosecuted and sued for the same wrongful act? Explain.

5. Does the situation described in this article violate the doctrine of double jeopardy? Explain.

Source: "TV Art Scam Bilked Buyers of Millions," *BusinessWeek,* March 6, 2007, 1. www.businessweek.com.

Revelation of Confidential Records   Individuals who, because of their jobs, work with confidential records containing private information must ensure that those records remain private. A failure to protect such confidential matters could result in an invasion of privacy lawsuit. Although it is not a violation of privacy for individuals to discuss confidential matters for professional reasons, it could be an invasion of privacy to discuss those same records for non-professional reasons. The motive of the person who releases the information does not matter. Moreover, whether there has been an invasion of privacy depends on the level of privacy expected by that person in that situation. For instance, an employee would expect privacy involving his or her employment record but not concerning the information that is printed on his or her identification badge.

Intrusion   An individual's privacy can also be violated if there is an unwarranted intrusion into the person's expectation of privacy. Such an intrusion might occur if a person's photograph is taken and then published on the front page of a local newspaper. The issue at the heart of such case is the question of whether the plaintiff had a high expectation of privacy. Recall that the expectation of privacy depends on the situation. A person walking across a college campus has a very low expectation of privacy, whereas a person who is in his or her own home has a very high expectation of privacy. Thus, the publication of a photo of a person walking across campus would *not* be actionable as an invasion of privacy, but taking a similar photo while that person was in his or her home would be.

Creating a False Light   Creating a false light is closely akin to defamation because it involves the publication of information about a person that paints him or her in a way that the majority of the population would see as unfavorable. A fashion model who poses for photographs for a bathing suit catalog and finds her image printed in a sexually explicit magazine would have a cause of action for being placed in a false light.

Exploitation   The courts have held that an individual holds the rights to his or her own likeness to make money. An invasion of privacy can occur when one party uses an individual's photo, likeness, or name without permission for advertising, marketing, or publicity. Some courts treat the misappropriation of a person's likeness as a separate tort, calling it an invasion of the right to publicity.

Rock Hudson, an award winning veteran of over 60 major Hollywood films, began his career as a very successful and popular leading man starring in both romantic and macho roles. His acting career severely dwindled when news of his gay personal life surfaced.

Intentional Infliction of Emotional Distress

In recent years, the courts have recognized a tort called the **intentional or reckless infliction of emotional distress**. Before these more enlightened court decisions were handed down, victims who were injured emotionally by the wrongful acts of others could not recover damages without proving some sort of bodily injury. Today, in many states, someone who intentionally or recklessly causes another individual to undergo emotional or mental suffering will be responsible, even without an accompanying physical injury. The actions complained of must be extreme and outrageous and cause severe emotional suffering.

EXAMPLE 6-5:   Extreme and Outrageous Silence

Marc Christian, who gained notoriety as the live-in boyfriend of Rock Hudson, sued the estate of the late actor for the intentional infliction of emotional distress. Christian argued that he had been induced to continue having "high-risk" sexual relations with the late screen star because Hudson had remained silent and failed to inform him that he had contracted AIDS. As a result of Hudson's misrepresentations, Christian contended that he suffered extreme emotional distress when he learned that Hudson was ill. This was true, Christian argued, despite the fact that he was not HIV positive himself. Although Hudson did not attempt deliberately to transfer the virus to Christian and did not plan to cause Christian emotional distress, the inherent harmfulness of Hudson's actions could easily amount to extreme and outrageous conduct.

Misuse of Legal Procedure

The intentional tort known as the **misuse of legal procedure** occurs when one person brings a legal action with malice and without probable cause. When the misuse of the legal procedure involves the filing of a false civil lawsuit, it is called **wrongful civil proceedings**. In contrast, when the misuse involves bringing false criminal charges, it is labeled **malicious prosecution**. Some states use only the term "malicious prosecution" to refer to both forms of the tort. All of the following conditions must be present for a lawsuit based on misuse of legal procedure to succeed:

1. The defendant (the person against whom the misuse of legal procedure suit has been filed) must have brought civil or criminal charges against the plaintiff at an earlier time.

2. The earlier case must have been resolved favorably for the plaintiff.

3. The plaintiff must prove that the earlier case was brought by the defendant with malice and without probable cause.

When these conditions are present, an individual may be able to recover damages from the defendant for making the innocent party the target of a legal action without a good cause.

A related cause of action, which can easily be confused with malicious prosecution, is abuse of process. **Abuse of process** occurs when a legal procedure is used for a purpose other than that for which it is intended. It differs from malicious prosecution in that there is no requirement that the earlier case be brought without probable cause or be resolved favorably for the plaintiff. The tort can involve either a criminal or a civil case. Typically, abuse of process happens when a perfectly legal process is used as a pressure tactic to convince someone to do something he or she would not be inclined to do under ordinary circumstances.

EXAMPLE 6-6:   Misuse and Abuse: Crossing the Legal Line

Janice Franklin and Karen Yalta were involved in a very difficult dissolution of their partnership. As a result of this problematic dissolution, as well as many other factors, the two young women did not like each other. Accordingly, Franklin filed a lawsuit against Yalta for defamation. The lawsuit was resolved in Yalta's favor. Yalta then sued Franklin for wrongful civil proceedings. Yalta won the case because she was able to prove that the original defamation suit against her was fabricated by Franklin, who was motivated by hatred and ill will. This suit is an example of the misuse of legal proceedings. If Franklin had filed a defamation suit to force Yalta to agree to Franklin's terms in the dissolution, she would be involved in abuse of process. This involvement would be true even if Franklin had legitimate reasons for filing the defamation suit.

Quick Quiz 6-2 True or False?

1. Assault and battery never exist simultaneously.

2. To be defamatory, a statement need not be communicated to a third party.

3. The intentional infliction of emotional distress has yet to be recognized as a tort in any state jurisdiction.

6-3 Negligence

People and property are sometimes injured even when no one intends that the injury occur. Such an occurrence is usually labeled an accident. Although no one acted with intent, someone was injured. The victim has experienced pain and suffering, lost wages, or incurred medical or repair bills. Justice demands that the injured party be compensated. The part of tort law that is concerned with the compensation of accident victims is called **negligence**.

Elements of Negligence

The issue before the court in a negligence action is as follows: Under what circumstances can the actions of an alleged tortfeasor be labeled negligent so that the victim can be compensated? Four elements must be present to establish negligence: legal duty, breach of duty, proximate cause, and actual harm. Table 6-2 gives an overview of these four elements.

Legal Duty A determination that a legal duty exists between the parties must be made to establish liability through negligence. This issue is solely a question of whether the tortfeasor should have reasonably foreseen a risk of harm to the injured party. Often today, the element of duty is not at issue in a lawsuit. However, there are some instances, often when a novel case comes before a court, that the legal duty of the defendant may be placed at issue. The phrase "at issue" refers to a legal question that must be answered for the case to be decided.

Breach of Duty The judge or the jury must determine whether the person accused of negligence has breached the duty owed to the victim. A breach of duty occurs if the alleged tortfeasor has not met the appropriate standard of care. To determine if the alleged tortfeasor has met the appropriate standard of care, the court uses the reasonable person test. This test compares the actions of the tortfeasor with those of a reasonable person in a similar situation. If a reasonable person would not have done what the tortfeasor actually did, then the tortfeasor is liable. The reasonable person standard is an objective test. Circumstances may change, but the standard of care applied by a reasonable person does not. How a reasonable person would behave in one set of circumstances may not be the same in another set of circumstances.

Table 6-2 The Elements of Negligence

Element	Definition
Legal duty	A determination that a legal duty exists between the parties must be made to establish liability through negligence. This is solely a question of whether the tortfeasor should have reasonably foreseen a risk of harm to the injured party.
Breach of duty	The judge or the jury must determine whether the person accused of negligence has breached the duty owed to the victim. To determine if the alleged tortfeasor has met the appropriate standard of care, the court uses the reasonable person test.
Proximate cause	For the tortfeasor to be held liable, the unreasonable conduct must be the proximate cause of the victim's injuries. Proximate cause is the legal connection between the unreasonable conduct and the resulting harm.
Actual harm	The injured party in a lawsuit for negligence must show that actual harm was suffered.

The Opening Case Revisited

Barnes v. Cohen Dry Wall, Inc. and Aelina Martin, Round 2

In the case of *Barnes v. Cohen Dry Wall, Inc. and Aelina Martin,* the duty of the social hosts to an injured third party was at issue. Recall that the case involved a social gathering at which alcohol was served to an underaged guest. Later, while driving under the influence, the guest caused an accident that killed a passenger in another vehicle as well as himself. The representative of the estate of the passenger sued the host of the gathering. The social host argued that the business, as host, owed no duty to third parties who might have been injured or, as in this case, killed by the guest once the guest left the party. The host actually presented a fairly convincing case because, under common law, South Carolina courts had frequently ruled that social hosts did not owe a duty to third parties when intoxicated adults leave a party and, while driving, injure a third party. The Supreme Court of South Carolina, however, decided it was time to clarify the law further and therefore made it quite clear that when the guest is underaged, the social host does in fact owe a duty to third parties. Thus, in such cases in the future, the duty of social hosts in relation to underage drinkers will no longer be "at issue."

EXAMPLE 6-7:   The Case of the Unreasonable Limo Service

Luigi Tarentino hired a limousine from Highland Limo Service so that he and his wife, Maybeth, could attend their high school reunion in style. When the limousine arrived, Tarentino told the driver to take them to the Regency Hotel. Once they were on the freeway, it became clear that the driver did not know how to reach the hotel. Every time the driver took a wrong turn, Tarentino attempted to correct him. The driver continued to ignore Tarentino's instructions. Eventually, the driver, who later said he was aggravated by Tarentino's frequent interruptions, stopped the limousine and told Tarentino and his wife to walk to their reunion. He then drove off and left his passengers several miles from the hotel in the middle of an ice storm. While walking to the hotel, Tarentino slipped on a patch of ice and fell and broke his arm. Later the Tarentinos learned that the driver had a long history of similar conduct and that the limousine company had not done a proper search into the driver's work history before hiring him. The question to the jury was, "Would a reasonable person hire an employee who will be responsible for the safety of paying passengers without checking the work history of that potential employee?" The jury said no, and Highland was held liable for the injuries that befell Tarentino from this breach of duty to protect paying passengers from harm.

If the defendant in a particular case is a professional, such as a physician or an engineer, the circumstances—not the test—change. To determine whether the defendant acted reasonably, the jury would have to know how the reasonable professional would act under similar circumstances. Determining this point may require the use of expert witnesses to testify as to a reasonable professional's conduct under the circumstances.

Proximate Cause   It is not enough to simply show that the tortfeasor's actions were unreasonable. For the tortfeasor to be held liable, the unreasonable conduct must be the proximate cause of the victim's injuries. Proximate cause is the connection between the unreasonable conduct and the resulting harm. Proximate cause is sometimes referred to as legal cause. In determining proximate cause, the court asks whether the harm that resulted from the conduct was foreseeable at the time of the original action.

EXAMPLE 6-8:   The Limits of Foreseeability

Two Transglobal Airline mechanics failed to properly repair the landing gear of a TGA 747. As a result, the plane's landing gear collapsed on takeoff and the plane caught fire. Several passengers were injured. While racing to the scene of the crash, an airport fire truck blew a tire and hit a light pole. The pole fell onto Carbonari's car, smashing the trunk and damaging the new DVD player stored there. The injured passengers and Carbonari sued TGA and the mechanics. When the mechanics failed to properly prepare the landing gear, it would have been easy for them to foresee that their unreasonable conduct might cause the plane to crash on takeoff and injure some passengers. However, it would have been impossible for them to foresee that the fire truck would have a blowout and smash into a light pole that would hit Carbonari's car and damage both the car and the DVD player in the trunk. Therefore, the mechanics' conduct was the proximate cause of the injuries to the passengers but not of the damage to the car or the DVD player.

Note that in Example 6-8, the mechanics' actions were the actual cause of the damage to the car and the DVD player. In other words, had they repaired the landing gear properly, the fire truck would not have been on the runway; it would not have had the collision with the light pole; and the light pole would not have fallen on Carbonari's car. Actual cause must always be present. If the actions of the tortfeasor are not the actual cause of the accident, they cannot be the proximate cause.

Actual Harm   The injured party in a lawsuit for negligence must show that actual harm was suffered. In most cases, the harm suffered is a physical injury and is therefore visible. Harm suffered due to fright or humiliation is difficult to demonstrate. Courts often deny damages in actions for negligence unless they can see an actual physical injury. Actual harm can also come in the form of property damage.

A Question of Ethics

In Example 6-8, when the Transglobal mechanics failed to prepare the landing gear properly, they could not foresee that the fire truck would have a blowout, smash into a light pole that would hit Carbonari's car, and damage both the car and the DVD player in the trunk. Therefore, legally, their conduct was not the proximate cause of the damage to the car and the DVD player. However, would Transglobal owe an ethical duty to reimburse Carbonari for the damages that were inflicted on his car and his DVD player? Explain.

Defenses to Negligence

LO6

Several defenses can be used by the defendant in a negligence case. These defenses include contributory negligence, comparative negligence, and assumption of the risk.

Contributory Negligence

The defense of contributory negligence involves the failure of the injured party to be careful enough to ensure his or her personal safety. Contributory negligence completely prevents the injured party from recovering damages. In other words, if the injured party's negligence contributed to personal injury, the tortfeasor wins. Last clear chance is the injured party's defense to a charge of contributory negligence. Under this doctrine, a tortfeasor may be held liable if the injured party can show that the tortfeasor had the last clear chance to avoid injury.

Comparative Negligence

To soften the harsh effects of contributory negligence, many states have adopted comparative negligence statutes that require courts to assign damages according to the degree of fault of each party. Rather than deny all recovery, the court weighs the relative degree of wrongdoing in awarding damages. If the tortfeasor was 80 percent negligent, the injured party may be allowed to recover 80 percent of the losses suffered. Some states have adopted the "50 percent rule." Under this rule, an injured party who was found to be more than 50 percent negligent cannot recover any damages from the tortfeasor.

Assumption of the Risk

Another defense to negligence is assumption of the risk, which involves the voluntary exposure of the victim to a known risk. If the injured party was aware of the danger involved in a situation, and by his or her actions indicated a willingness to be exposed to the danger, then he or she has assumed that risk. An awareness of the extent

---

Did You Know?

Assumption of the risk can be raised as a defense in a case in which the plaintiff has been injured in a voluntary sports activity such as touch football. For a player in a touch football game to be found liable for injuries to another player, the first player would have to have caused the injuries intentionally or with a degree of recklessness beyond the usual action within such a sport.

Talking Points

The law of negligence has come under fire in recent years by legislators who seem not to understand the intricacies and the complexity associated with that area of torts. These legislators push for unnecessary reforms that threaten to undermine the effectiveness of the entire system. In his treatise, *Law's Empire,* the legal philosopher Ronald Dworkin argues that two very strong reasons exist for preserving laws that compensate people who have been involved in accidents. Dworkin explains it this way: "Our law as a whole recognizes two principles as pertinent to the loss people should be permitted to suffer through accidents. The first is the principle of collective sympathy. It holds that the state should try to protect people from being ruined by accidents even when the accident is their own fault. The principle is most apparent in regulative safety programs of different sorts, in workmen's compensation statutes and in state-subsidized schemes of insurance for risks to property and person not adequately covered in the private insurance market. The second is the principle of apportioning the costs of an accident among the private actors in the drama that produced it. It holds that accidental loss should be bourne by the person at fault, not the innocent victim. This principle is most evidently at work in negligence law, including legislative amendments or supplements to the common law of negligence." These two principles may at first seem contradictory. Explain why both principles can live together harmoniously as valid explanations to defend the practice of compensating people involved in accidents of all sorts. (See Ronald Dworkin, *Law's Empire*, Cambridge, MA: The Belknap Press of Harvard University, 1986, 269.)

of the danger is the court's primary consideration in awarding or denying damages. It is important that the victim's decision to enter the risky situation be voluntary. If he or she is forced to enter the risky situation because no other choice is available, it is not an assumption of the risk.

Quick Quiz 6-3 True or False?

1. Legal duty is never at issue in any lawsuit today. *f*

2. Proximate cause is sometimes referred to as legal cause. *T*

3. Under the defense of comparative negligence, the plaintiff always loses all the damages that he or she might have been awarded, absent the defense. *f*

6-4 Strict Liability

Under certain circumstances, the courts may judge a person liable for harm even though that person was not negligent and did not commit an intentional tort. This doctrine is known as **strict liability** or absolute liability. In recent years, strict liability has also been applied to product liability cases.

Grounds for Strict Liability

Under strict liability, the court will hold a tortfeasor liable for injuries to a victim even though the tortfeasor did not intend the harm and was not in any way negligent. Strict liability is generally applied when the harm results from an ultrahazardous or very dangerous activity. Such activities include using explosives and keeping wild animals. A number of dangerous activities, such as flying an airplane, operating X-ray equipment, and laying public gas lines, are not subject to liability without fault. These activities are recognized as essential to the economic health and welfare of the public.

Product Liability

Product liability is a legal theory that imposes liability on the manufacturer and seller of a product produced and sold in a defective condition. A product in **defective condition** is unreasonably dangerous to the user, to the consumer, or to property. Anyone who produces or sells a product in defective condition is subject to liability for the physical or emotional injury to the ultimate consumer and for any physical harm to the user's property. The courts have regularly held that liability for a defective product extends to the producer of the product, the wholesaler, and the retailer. The seller or producer must be engaged in the business of selling such products. In addition, the product manufactured or sold must be expected to reach the ultimate consumer without substantial change in the conditions under which it was originally manufactured or sold.

Product liability is not without its limits. In most states, product liability also is not available as a cause of action if the only property damaged is the defective property itself. In such a situation, the product owner must seek a remedy in sales law for breach of warranty. (Note: People who are injured by faulty products might also be able to bring a product liability lawsuit in negligence. This issue is discussed at length in Chapter 18.)

Counterfeit Colgate toothpaste was recently imported from China and sold in dollar stores across the U.S. How does this affect Colgate's reputation?

> **Quick Quiz 6-4** True or False?
>
> 1. Keeping wild animals is an ultrahazardous activity. T
>
> 2. Strict liability is also known as absolute liability. T
>
> 3. Product liability is completely unrelated to strict liability, and the two torts should never be confused with each other. F

6-5 Electronic Torts

Computers have provided unscrupulous individuals with new ways to commit crimes and torts. In the previous chapter, we examined electronic crimes or e-crimes. In this chapter, we focus on another group of legal problems, electronic torts. We look first at the nature of electronic tort law and then at the problems associated with defining, describing, and preventing electronic torts.

The Nature of Electronic Tort Law

An **electronic tort** or **e-tort** involves the invasion, distortion, theft, falsification, misuse, destruction, or financial exploitation of information stored in or related to an electronic device, including but not limited to desktop PCs, laptops, mobile phones, mainframes, phonecams, personal digital assistants (PDAs), and home computers that stand alone or are part of a network. E-torts rarely, if ever, involve any harm to a party's physical well-being. Instead, the victim's reputation has been hurt because a false statement has been posted on the Internet; the victim's emotional state has been disturbed because his or her privacy has been invaded; or the victim has suffered monetary harm because his or her identity has been stolen. We focus on the first two injuries, that is, those that are caused by defamation or disparagement and those that are caused by an invasion of privacy.

E-Defamation

E-defamation is the communication of false and destructive information about an individual through the use of an electronic device. Most legal moves in e-defamation have been designed to limit, rather than extend, liability for defamatory comments disseminated on the Internet. For example, when the courts were first involved in e-defamation, they easily extended liability for defamation from the party who posted a defamatory message on the Internet to the Internet service provider (ISP), such as America Online, that provided the vehicle for the posting. Thus, for instance, it was not difficult in one case for a court in New York to decide that the Prodigy Service Company was responsible when an investment banking firm sued for defamation after false statements were posted on an e-bulletin board that was under Prodigy's control.

After the Prodigy case, however, the Communications Decency Act was enacted by Congress to protect ISPs from future defamation suits for false statements that are posted by other individuals on the Net. Despite the passage of the law, many cases have been filed attempting to hold ISPs liable for defamatory postings. Few have succeeded. In one such case, AOL was found not liable for defamation even though the provider had been informed of the defamatory content of a posting and substantially delayed its removal. Moreover, the protection granted to ISPs has gone far beyond protection for defamatory postings. The courts also have found that ISPs are not liable when hackers place a virus into the system, when piracy is involved on the Net, or when an invasion of privacy takes place via a provider's link.

E-Disparagement

Disparagement involves any false statement communicated to others that in some way casts doubt on the quality of an item of property or a product offered for sale. E-disparagement involves the same activity on the Internet. The *YouTube* fad of recent years has opened an avenue for the new tort of e-disparagement. Businesses have begun to solicit videos from their consumers for postings on their own Web sites. These businesses often go so far as to run games and contests in which clients and customers can submit homemade advertisements or videos that will be added to the Web site of the business. Unfortunately, this process is filled with legal problems, not the least of which is the possibility of an e-disparagement lawsuit. Such homemade videos typically target the product of a company's competitor. Thus, a company that posts such videos must make certain that the competitor's product is not subject to false statements and descriptions. This assurance requires an enormous effort aimed at monitoring the content of such submissions. Legal activity in this area has not been heavy as of yet, but that is because the tort is so new. As time goes on and competitors find themselves injured by such postings, the activity will increase, and more e-disparagement lawsuits will be filed.

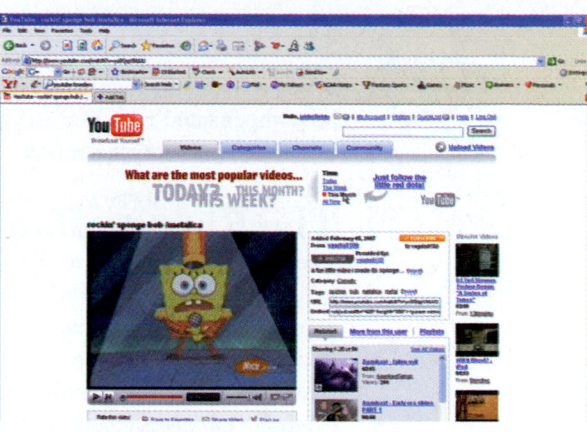

Sites such as YouTube make it easy for anyone to post derogatory or embarrassing videos online for the world to see. Disparagement can be obvious if the post is by a competing company but is more difficult to prove if done by a lone angry customer.

E-Invasion of Privacy

An e-invasion of privacy is the unwelcome intrusion into private matters initiated or maintained by an electronic device. Because the development of computer technology is in a constant state of flux, it is not surprising that the law is uncertain about just what constitutes an e-invasion of privacy. One area that has been expanded recently involves computer-related privacy in the workplace. As a result of at least one recent case at the federal appellate level, workers who are employed by businesses that keep a close eye on their workers' time on the Internet have no expectation of privacy, at least in relation to their Fourth Amendment rights, provided the employer has openly informed the workers about those surveillance procedures.

The low expectation of privacy has long been a part of the law in relation to governmental employees. Thus, it has been clear that the Fourth Amendment prohibition against unreasonable searches does not protect a government employee who knows that the government regularly monitors its employees' Internet use. The same standard now extends to employees within the private sector. How this ruling relates to the tortious invasion of privacy is problematic. However, because the standard for the invasion of privacy is based on the level of privacy expected, the fact that a worker knows that the company monitors computer use means that the expectation level is virtually nonexistent. The moral of the story is twofold: (1) Employers should routinely remind their workers that all computer use is monitored by the information technology department, and (2) workers should use computers for work-related tasks only—period.

Quick Quiz 6-5 True or False?

1. E-torts always involve information that has been invaded, distorted, stolen, falsified, or destroyed by an electronic device.

2. Most legal moves in e-defamation have been designed to extend liability.

3. The Communications Decency Act was enacted by Congress to protect ISPs.

6-6 Remedies for Torts

When a wrongdoer has injured another person by committing a tort, the victim can usually be compensated with monetary damages. However, at times, the equitable remedy of an injunction is more appropriate.

The Right to Damages

The compensation paid to the victims of a tort is known as **damages**. Damages can come in several forms. **Economic compensatory damages** are those that are directly quantifiable. These include damages awarded for lost wages, medical expenses, and expenses incurred in the repair or replacement of property. **Noneconomic compensatory damages** are those that result from injuries that are intangible and therefore not directly quantifiable. For example, damages resulting from pain and suffering, mental anguish, and loss of companionship are considered noneconomic. If the tortfeasor's acts are notoriously willful and malicious, a court may also impose punitive damages. These are damages above and beyond those needed to compensate the injured party. **Punitive damages** are designed to punish the tortfeasor so that similar malicious actions are avoided by others. For this reason, they are also referred to as exemplary damages. Some courts say that another purpose of punitive damages is to comfort the victim.

The Right to an Injunction

If a tort involves a continuing problem, such as the dumping of chemical waste into a river, the injured party may ask the court for an injunction. An **injunction** is a court order preventing someone from performing a particular act. If a tort involves some permanent fixture that harms the interests of the injured party, the court may order the wrongdoer to take positive steps to alleviate the problem. Thus, the court might order a company to clean up a landfill that has become a nuisance to neighborhood homes. If the company failed to complete the cleanup, it would be in contempt of court. Contempt of court is a deliberate violation of the order of a judge that can result in a fine or in jail time for the wrongdoer.

Quick Quiz 6-6 True or False?

1. Economic and noneconomic compensatory damages are essentially the same thing.

2. Punitive damages are designed to compensate the victim of a tort.

3. An injunction is never granted by the court in any kind of tort case.

6-7 Survival Statutes and Wrongful Death

Many of the common law rules regarding torts have become obsolete in the modern world. For instance, under common law, if someone died from another's wrongful act, then the right to bring a suit died also. This rule originated because the king would execute the wrongdoer and then take his or her property. As a result, there was no property left for the relatives of the wrongdoer's victim to recover in a tort suit. Modern statutes have, for the most part, eliminated this rule.

Survival Statutes

Many state legislatures have revised common law by passing survival statutes. Survival statutes allow a lawsuit to be brought even if both the plaintiff and the defendant are deceased. Many states also have survival statutes that preserve the right to bring a lawsuit for personal injuries, no matter what caused the death or deaths. Most states also allow such suits if the tort involves damage to personal or real property. However, there are some limitations placed on survival statutes. For instance, suits cannot be brought for libel or slander after the death of a defamed person, because such a suit is for injury to a live person's reputation. Survival suits are brought or defended by the lawful representative of the estate of the deceased.

Wrongful Death

Unlike survival statutes, wrongful death statutes preserve the right to bring a lawsuit only if the death is caused by the negligence or intentional conduct of the person who caused the death. Generally only family members who have lost the support of the deceased have the right to bring a wrongful death suit. The definition of family members generally includes husbands, wives, children, and parents. Under wrongful death statutes, creditors, business partners, and the like have no right to bring a lawsuit.

Quick Quiz 6-7 True or False?

1. Wrongful death is a cause of action that has been preserved from the days of common law.

2. Survival statutes allow a lawsuit to be brought even if both the plaintiff and the defendant are deceased.

3. Creditors, business partners, and the like have the right to bring wrongful death lawsuits.

Summary

6.1 A tort is a private wrong that injures another person's physical well-being, emotional health, property, or reputation. A person who commits a tort is called a tortfeasor. The other party is alternatively referred to as the injured party, the innocent party, or the victim. The primary purpose of tort law is to compensate the innocent party by making up for any loss suffered by that victim. The doctrine of *respondeat superior* may impose legal liability on employers and make them pay for the torts committed by their employees within the scope of the employer's business.

6.2 The principal intentional torts include assault, battery, false imprisonment, defamation, disparagement,

fraudulent misrepresentation, invasion of privacy, intentional infliction of emotional distress, and malicious prosecution.

6.3 Negligence is the failure to exercise the degree of care that a reasonable person would have exercised in the same circumstances. Negligence includes four elements: duty of care, breach of duty through a failure to exercise the appropriate standard of care, proximate cause, and actual harm. Three defenses to negligence are contributory negligence, comparative negligence, and assumption of risk.

6.4 Under the doctrine of strict liability, when people engage in ultrahazardous activities, they will be liable for any harm that occurs because of that activity, regardless of intent and regardless of care.

6.5   E-torts involve computer information that has been invaded, distorted, stolen, falsified, misused, destroyed, or exploited financially by an electronic device. Therefore, e-torts rarely involve any harm to a party's physical well-being. Instead, the victim's reputation has been hurt because a false statement has been posted on the Internet, the victim's emotional state has been disturbed because his or her privacy has been

invaded, or the victim has suffered monetary harm because his or her identity has been tampered with.

6.6   Tort remedies include monetary damages and injunctions.

6.7   Survival statutes allow a lawsuit to be brought even if both the plaintiff and the defendant are deceased. Wrongful death statutes preserve the rights of third parties affected by the death of the deceased to bring a lawsuit.

Key Terms

abuse of process, 122

actual malice, 118

actual malice test, 118

assault, 116

assumption of the risk, 126

battery, 117

comparative negligence, 126

contributory negligence, 126

damages, 130

defamation, 118

defective condition, 127

disparagement, 119

duty, 116

economic compensatory damages, 130

electronic tort or e-tort, 128

false imprisonment, 118

fraud, 119

fraudulent misrepresentation, 119

injunction, 130

intentional or reckless infliction of emotional distress, 121

invasion of privacy, 119

libel, 118

malicious prosecution, 122

misuse of legal procedure, 122

negligence, 123

noneconomic compensatory damages, 130

proximate cause, 125

punitive damages, 130

respondeat superior, 115

slander, 118

strict liability, 127

temporary public figures, 119

tort, 115

tortfeasor, 115

vicarious liability, 115

wrongful civil proceedings, 122

Questions for Review and Discussion

1. What is the difference between a tort and a crime?
2. What is vicarious liability?
3. What is meant by the legal term "duty"?
4. What are the principal intentional torts?
5. What are the elements of negligence?
6. What are the differences among contributory negligence, comparative negligence, and assumption of the risk?
7. When does strict liability apply?
8. What is an e-tort?
9. What remedies are available in tort law?
10. What innovations have been suggested for contemporary state tort reform?

Investigating the Internet

FindLaw maintains a Web site for legal professionals that includes several features for the layperson. One such feature is called *FindLaw for the Public*. Access *Find-Law*, locate *FindLaw for the Public*, and find the section labeled "Accident and Injury Center." Within the "Accident and Injury Center," locate a subtopic called Slip and Fall Accidents and answer the following questions: (1) What is the definition of a slip and fall accident? (2) What conditions are included within the list of causes of slip and fall accidents? (3) What must be proven to succeed in a slip and fall accident case? (4) What must a tenant show to prove a slip and fall case against a landlord? (5) What advice does the site give about slip and fall cases?

Cases for Analysis

1. Patrick Clawson was described by reporter Karen Branch-Brioso in a newspaper story as a "1970s era St. Louis journalist turned private eye turned FBI informant." The story was published in the *St. Louis Post-Dispatch*. The fact that he had been characterized as an "informant" bothered Clawson, who saw it as damaging to his reputation. Accordingly, he brought a libel case against the *Post-Dispatch*. Recall that to be libelous, a statement must be false and "hold the victim up to ridicule, contempt, or hatred." Clawson would have preferred the term "whistleblower" rather than " informant," because that term commands more respect. Why is the use of the term "informant" to describe Clawson not libelous? Explain. *Clawson v. St. Louis Post-Dispatch*, No. 04-CV-486; see also "Media Law: Label of 'Informer' Is Found Not Defamatory," *The National Law Journal*, September 11, 2006.

2. Curtis Ellison was riding as a passenger in his own vehicle when it was pulled over by the police for a parking violation. The vehicle had actually been targeted because the police had routinely checked the license plate through the department's database. This routine check had revealed that the owner of the vehicle had an outstanding warrant pending against him. When the police searched the van, they found two firearms hidden in the vehicle. As a result, Ellison was charged with felonious possession of a firearm. He argued that the search had violated his Fourth Amendment rights and that his right to

privacy had been infringed. The trial court agreed and dismissed the case. The case went to the appellate court. The issue before the appellate court was whether Ellison had a high expectation of privacy about the number on his license plate. Although this is a criminal case, it is still interesting to speculate on how the court would rule on the expectation of privacy in relation to a license plate. Why should the appeals court reverse the ruling by the trial court that there is a high expectation of privacy in relation to a license plate? Explain. *United States v. Ellison*, No. 04-1925; see also "Criminal Practice: No Privacy Expectation on License Plate Numbers," *The National Law Journal*, September 18, 2006, p. 16.

3. A St. Louis police officer was speeding the wrong way down a one-way street when he collided with a vehicle being driven by Ann Martin. Martin was seriously injured in the crash and brought a lawsuit against the police officer, the City of St. Louis, and the board of police commissioners. The board of commissioners is an agency of the state of Missouri. Martin passed away, and her daughter, Kimberly Hodges, took over as the plaintiff in the case. The case was settled in relation to the board and the officer but not the city. The City of St Louis argued that the officer could not be employed by both the board and the city at the same time. The city further argued that the officer's real employer was the board, so it, the city, could not be held liable under the doctrine of vicarious liability. Why should the

city be held liable under the doctrine of vicarious liability? Explain. *Hodges v. City of St. Louis,* No. SC87513; see also "Torts: Officer Is City Agent Even if Working for State Board," *The National Law Journal,* March 12, 2007, p. 15.

4. At the height of the modern civil rights movement, *The New York Times* ran a full-page advertisement entitled "Heed Their Rising Voices." The advertisement detailed police efforts in Montgomery, Ala., to suppress the nonviolent civil rights demonstrations being carried on there by thousands of college students. The police commissioner of Montgomery, L.B. Sullivan, filed a lawsuit against *The New York Times,* alleging that he had been libeled by information carried in the advertisement, even though he was never mentioned by name. Should the Court use the actual malice test in this case to determine whether the newspaper libeled the commissioner? Explain. *New York Times Co. v. Sullivan,* 376 U.S. 254 (U.S. Sup. Ct.).

5. Five Commerce City police officers were summoned to break up a disturbance at a local party of teenagers. At the party, Ralph Crowe, who had consumed eight cups of beer and three cups of alcoholic punch, became rowdy and had to be detained by the officers. The police released Ralph after receiving the assurances of his brother Eddie that he would drive Ralph home. After leaving the party, Eddie Crowe allowed Ralph to take the wheel. Instead of going home, Ralph drove to the site of another party, where he lost control of the car and ran down six people. The police officers were sued for negligence in releasing Ralph. Did the five officers owe a duty to the six victims of Ralph's drunk-driving accident? Explain. *Leake v. Cain,* 720 P.2d 152 (CO).

6. Seventy-four years of age at the time, Ramona Booker entered a drugstore by pushing her way through one door and then through a second. Both doors were extremely heavy, so Booker was compelled to use both hands, causing her cane to drag on the ground. As she entered the second door, the tip of her cane caught on the exposed coil of a security device, causing her to fall and injure herself. Booker brought a lawsuit against Revco DS, Inc., to recover for her injuries. Did the drugstore owe a duty to Booker and other customers to maintain a safe environment? Explain. Is Booker's lawsuit based on allegations that the store owners committed an intentional tort or that they were negligent? Explain. What test would be used to judge whether the drugstore owners should be held liable for

Booker's injuries? Explain. *Booker v. Revco DS, Inc.* 681 N.E.2d 499 (OH).

7. Queenway Tankers, Inc., Kingsway Tankers, Inc., the East River Steamship Corporation, and Richmond Tankers, Inc., all chartered supertankers designed by Transamerican Delaval, Inc. Under the terms of the charters, each shipping company was financially responsible for many repairs to the tankers. From the start, there were problems with the tankers' turbines, which needed extensive and costly repairs. The plaintiffs brought a product liability suit against Delaval. The suit alleged that the manufacturing defects caused the damage. Should the shipping companies have prevailed in product liability against the manufacturer? Explain. *East River Steamship Corporation v. Transamerican Delaval, Inc.,* 106 S. Ct. 2305 (U.S. Sup. Ct.).

8. Myers was injured when she slipped and fell on an ice patch on the front walkway of the Canton Centre Mall. The mall is owned and operated by Forest City Enterprises. Forest City had employees who were responsible for clearing the ice off of the mall walkways every morning. On this particular morning, they had cleared the ice from the walkway a short time before Myers took her tumble. Nevertheless, an ice patch had formed, and Myers did fall, sustaining injuries. Cooper, one of the employees charged with the ice-removal task, theorized that water may have been splashed up onto the sidewalk by passing cars where it froze sometime after their initial cleaning of the day. According to Cooper, "the vehicles could have splashed this back up on there . . . we're constantly moving around the building at all times, so anything can be going on in this half of the building while you're over here doing this half coming around." Was Forest City negligent in failing to keep the sidewalk clear of ice at all times that winter? What test would be used to judge Forest City's conduct? Explain. *Myers v. Forest City Enterprises, Inc.* 635 N.E.2d 1268 (OH).

9. Michelle Wightman was driving toward a railroad crossing at which the gates were down and the lights flashing. Wightman noted a stopped train a short distance from the gate. Believing the stopped train to be the cause of the closed gate, she drove around the gate and was struck and killed by a train that suddenly appeared from behind the stopped train. The stopped train had blocked her view of the oncoming train. Both trains were owned and operated by Consolidated Rail Corporation (CRC). Wightman's mother brought a wrongful death lawsuit and a survivorship action against CRC. In

response, CRC claimed that Wightman's action of driving around the gates, in violation of both state and city law regarding the operation of a motor vehicle at a railroad crossing, constituted negligence on her part. Furthermore, CRC argued that if Wightman had not crossed the tracks, she would not have been struck by the train. Therefore, her actions were the sole cause of the accident, and the railroad corporation should not be held liable for her death. The attorney for the plaintiff argued that the placement of the first train, blocking the view of the other track, contributed to the accident and that CRC should be held liable for Wightman's death. Should Wightman's own negligence be a complete bar to the plaintiff's recovery of damages in this case? Explain. *Wightman v. Consolidated Railroad Corporation,* 640 N.E.2d 1160 (OH).

Quick Quiz Answers

6-1	6-2	6-3	6-4	6-5	6-6	6-7
1. T	1. F	1. F	1. T	1. T	1. F	1. F
2. F	2. F	2. T	2. T	2. F	2. F	2. T
3. F	3. F	3. F	3. F	3. T	3. F	3. F

Part 1 Case Study

Kelo v. City of New London
United States Supreme Court
125 S.Ct. 2655

Summary

The case of Kelo v. City of New London is a fascinating exercise in case law for several reasons. First, it represents a landmark extension of the power of the government to intrude into the lives of private citizens. The Court's endorsement of this extension of power through eminent domain is unusual because the Supreme Court has, in recent years, demonstrated a tendency to reduce rather than extend government power. Second, the case is interesting because it represents another example of the Court's firm commitment to the use of precedent. The final opinion reveals that, while some members of the majority clearly sympathized with the homeowners, they suppressed these feelings because they realized the importance of following precedent, despite personal feelings. Finally, the case has stirred up an enormous amount of controversy because the Court suggests that the principle of eminent domain can be used to justify economic development created and financed by private corporations. Whether this stamp of approval will leal to an outpouring of such privately financed government "takings" remains to be seen.

The controversy that led to the case of Kelo v. City of New London began when the city fathers of New London decided to reactivate a long dormant private institution called the New London Development Corporation (NLDC) in order to take advantage of the one bright star on their economic horizon. That one bright star was a decision by the Pfizer Corporation to build a research and manufacturing center in the city. Members of the NLDC decided that the best thing to do was to redevelop the area in which the new center would be located. Accordingly, the NLDC began to buy up all of the land in that area of town. At this point, the city fathers hit a major league snag. Many of the people who owned land and homes in the Fort Trumbill neighborhood had no desire to move off the land or out of homes that they had lived in for years, and so they refused to deal with the NLDC. Not to be denied, the city invoked its power to confiscate land for public use under the principle of eminent domain which is found in the Fifth Amendment of the United States Constitution. Moreover, the power to exercise eminent domain in a situation like this was granted to the City by a Connecticut state statute that declares that taking land for economic development is considered to be public use.

Susette Kelo, along with several other land owners, filed a lawsuit to prevent what they called the unlawful, unconstitutional confiscation of their property. They contended, with a great deal of enthusiasm and public support, that the taking of their land for transfer to the NLDC for private development purposes did not qualify as public use as contemplated by the Framers of the Fifth Amendment. They also asserted rather convincingly that, even if the taking of their land did qualify as public use, the court had to demand that the city demonstrate with "reasonable certainty" that the taking of their land really would result in the public benefits so confidently predicted by the NLDC.

The lawsuit was filed in the state court of Connecticut and eventually reached the Supreme Court of Connecticut which, because it is an extension of the state, predictably sided with the NLDC. Ultimately, the dispute made its way up to the United States Supreme Court which granted a writ of certiorari indicating that it would consider the case. The court heard the arguments from both sides and after deliberating for about four months, in a close 5–4 ruling, held that the taking contemplated by the NLDC did, indeed, qualify as public use. The Court also rejected the plaintiffs' argument that the NLDC had to demonstrate with reasonable certainty that the benefits promised would actually be realized by the city and by the neighborhood directly affected by the changes.

Despite the fact that the Justices expressed sympathy for the soon-to-be-evicted property owners, they refused to endorse the strong test proposed by the plaintiffs. Instead, the Justices stated without reservation that the concept of public use was to be given the broadest possible interpretation. The Justices also held the real party responsible for such decisions ought to be the state legislature not the courts. Therefore, absent some sort of obvious abuse, which was not the case in New London's situation, the Court would uphold the legislature's definition of public use.

Applying this standard to the present case of Kelo v. New London, the Court determined that the city government and its surrogate, the NLDC, were acting under the legitimate authority of a state statute that gave the municipality the power to exercise eminent domain to take land for economic development and that such development qualified as public use. The Court ruled that the City and the NLDC had sufficiently demonstrated that there would be significant financial and economic benefits from the private development of this land. These benefits would include an increase in the rate of employment in the area and a significant jump in the amount of tax money collected by the local government. In addition, the Court believed that, given its limited ability to interfere in eminent domain determinations, the actions by the city government would stand. Simply put the Court will not invalidate decisions made by a city or actions taken by a municipal development corporation such as the NLDC when such actions are clearly in line with state law and are obviously a proper exercise of eminent domain as defined by that law.

Justice John Paul Stevens

Joined by Anthony Kennedy, David Souter, Ruth Bader Ginsburg, and Stephen Breyer

Those who govern the city were not confronted with the need to remove the blight in the Fort Trumbill area. But their determination that the area was sufficiently distressed to justify a program of economic rejuvenation is entitled to our deference. The City has carefully formulated an economic development plan that it believes will provide appreciable benefits to the community, including—but by no means limited to —new jobs and increased tax revenue. As with other exercises in urban planning and development, the City is endeavoring to coordinate a variety of commercial, residential, and recreational uses of land, with the hope that they will form a whole greater than the sum of its parts. To effectuate this plan, the City has invoked a state statute that specifically authorizes the use of eminent domain to promote economic development. Given the comprehensive character of the plan, the thorough deliberation that preceded its adoption, and the limited scope of our review, it is appropriate for us, as it was in *Berman,* to resolve the challenges of the individual owners, not on a piecemeal basis, but rather in light of the entire plan. Because that plan unquestionably serves the public purpose, the takings challenged here satisfy the public use requirements of the Fifth Amendment.

To avoid this result, petitioners urge us to adopt a new bright-line rule that economic development does not qualify as a public use. Putting aside the unpersuasive suggestion that the City's plan will provide only purely economic benefits, neither precedent nor logic supports petitioner's proposal. Promoting economic development is a traditional and long accepted function of the government. There is, moreover, no principled way of distinguishing economic development from other public purposes that we have recognized. . . . It would be incongruous to hold that the City's interest in economic benefits to be derived from the development of the Fort Trumbill area has less of a public character than any of those other interests. Clearly, there is no basis for exempting economic development from our traditionally broad understanding of public purpose.

Petitioners contend that using eminent domain for economic development impermissibly blurs the boundary between public and private takings. Again our cases foreclose this objection. Quite simply the government's pursuit of a public purpose will often benefit individual private parties. . . . Our rejection of that contention has particular relevance in the instant case: "The public end may be as well or better served through an agency of private enterprise than through a department of government—or so the Congress might conclude. We cannot say that public ownership is the sole method of promoting the public purposes of community redevelopment projects." *Id.*, at 34.

It is further argued that without a bright-line rule nothing would stop the city from transferring citizen A's property to citizen B for the sole reason that citizen B will put the property to more productive use and thus pay more taxes. Such a one-to-one transfer or property, executed outside the confines of an integrated development plan, is not presented in this case. While such an unusual exercise of government power would certainly raise a suspicion that a private purpose was afoot, the hypothetical cases posited by petitioners can be confronted if and when they arise. They do not warrant the crafting of an artificial restriction on the concept of public use.

Alternatively, petitioners maintain that for takings of this kind we should require a "reasonable certainty" that the expected public benefits will actually accrue. Such a rule, however, would represent an even greater departure from our precedent. "When the legislature's purpose is legitimate and its means are not irrational, our cases make clear that empirical debates over the wisdom of takings—no less than debates over the wisdom of other kinds of socioeconomic legislation—are not to be carried out in federal courts." *Midkiff*, 467 U.S. at 242. . .

Just as we decline to second-guess the City's considered judgments about the efficacy of its development plan, we also decline to second-guess the City's determinations as to what lands it needs to acquire in order to effectuate the project. "It is not for the courts to oversee the choice of the boundary line nor to sit in review on the size of a particular project area. Once the question of the public purpose has been decided, the amount and character of land to be taken for the project and the need for a particular tract to complete the integrated plan rests in the discretion of the legislative branch," *Berman*, 348 U. S. at 35-36.

In affirming the City's authority to take petitioners' properties, we do not minimize the hardship that condemnations may entail, notwithstanding the payment of just compensation. We emphasize that nothing in our opinion precludes any State from placing further restrictions on its exercise of the takings power. Indeed, many States already impose "public use" requirements that are stricter than the federal baseline. Some of these requirements have been established as a matter of state constitutional law, while others are expressed in state eminent domain statutes that carefully limit the grounds upon which takings may be exercised. As the submissions of the parties and their *amici* make clear, the necessity and wisdom of using eminent domain to promote economic development are certainly matters of legitimate public debate. This Court's authority, however, extends only to determining whether the City's proposed condemnations are for a "public use" within the meaning of the Fifth Amendment to the Federal Constitution. Because over a century of our case law interpreting that provision dictates an affirmative answer to that question, we may not grant petitioners the relief that they seek.

The judgment of the Supreme Court of Connecticut is affirmed.

It is so ordered.

Questions for Analysis

1. Why does the Fifth Amendment, which specifically applies to the federal government in Washington, affect a decision made by the state government? Explain.

2. What ethical character traits are the justices exemplifying by taking this stand? What ethical character traits are they violating? Explain.

3. Are the justices submitting to the pressure of ethical relativism by taking this stand, or are they seeking some sort of universal standard? Explain.

4. Why did Kelo and the other defendants bring this lawsuit to the state court of Connecticut? Explain.

5. In what way is the decision in this case an example of a strongly independent federal judiciary? Explain.

6. What factors might have motivated the justices of the United States Supreme Court to decide to hear this case? Explain.

7. What are the two considerations that a court should look at when determining whether to overturn a state's use of eminent domain? Explain.

8. In what way is this case a demonstration of the separation of powers? Explain. In what way is this case a demonstration of the system of checks and balances? Explain.

9. How well would this case be received by people who believe that the government that governs best governs least? Explain.

10. Is the decision by the Supreme Court in *Kelo* an example of the doctrine of devolution at work? Explain.

Part Two

Contract Law

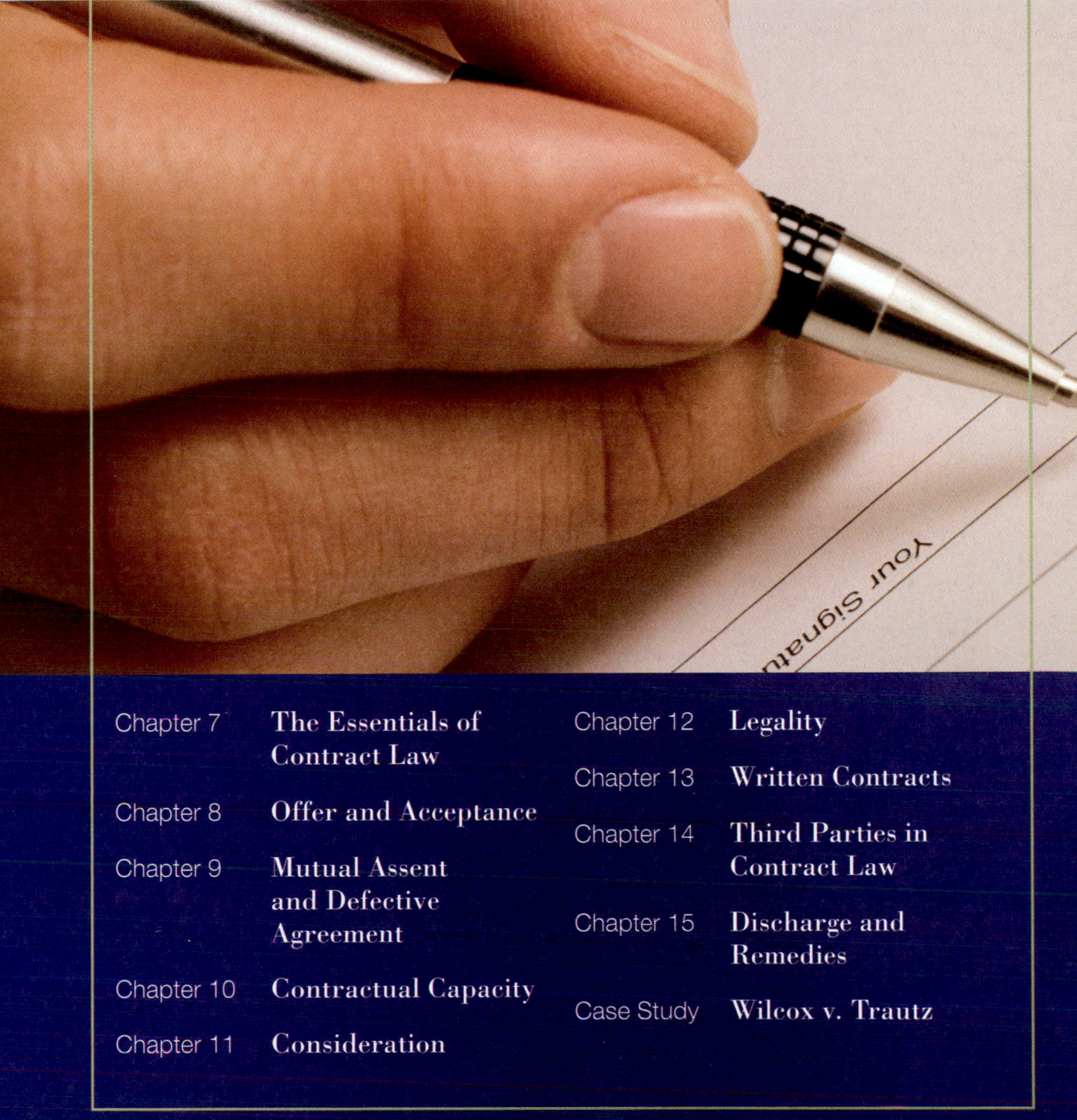

Chapter 7

The Essentials of Contract Law

The Opening Case
What a Difference a Verb Makes

A German company named MAN A.G. entered a complex and different contract with a Canadian company named Western Star Holdings, Ltd., to purchase a truck manufacturing firm called ERF. Western Star later was purchased by Freightliner LLC, which was actually owned by DaimlerChrysler (D/C). After the purchase went through, MAN began to suspect that somehow it had been tricked by Western Star into acquiring ERF, which now appeared vastly overvalued. In fact, MAN's investigation into the financial records of ERF revealed that Western Star had managed to alter the figures to hide heavy losses suffered by ERF. With few alternatives, MAN sued Western Star's new owners, Freightliner and D/C, for $500 million in damages. MAN won the case in the UK but found that it could not collect the money from Freightliner because Freightliner had depleted its entire bank account and was now without adequate funds. At that point, things looked rather bleak for MAN, which now owned ERF, an overvalued corporation, and could not collect a legitimate judgment from that company's former owner. Fortunately, the attorneys working for MAN noticed that Freightliner had altered a verb in one of the official papers filed in the lawsuit. Before the document in question had been filed, Freightliner had always claimed that the firm, "is" a heavy vehicle manufacturer. In the new document, the verb "is" had been changed to "was," so that the document read that Freightliner "was (but it is denied that it still is) a manufacturer of heavy vehicles." This small alteration led to a further investigation, which revealed that the funds in Freightliner's accounts had been redistributed by some very creative accounting so that the money that rightfully belonged to Freightliner, and therefore to MAN, had been transferred to several subsidiaries owned by Freightliner and D/C. MAN went to Freightliner's home state of Oregon and sued. The object of the lawsuit was to force Freightliner and D/C to reverse each of those transactions so that MAN could collect its money. In a final twist, MAN received not only the actual damages owed to it but also $350 million in punitive damages proving, once and for all, that this type of wrongdoing does not pay. (See Sandhya Bathija, "Business Fraud Case Was an International Affair: German Manufacturer Secures at Least $500M in Complex Litigation," *The National Law Journal*, February 26, 2007, pp. 52 and 54.)

Opening Case Questions

1. Was the contract between MAN and Western Star valid, void, or voidable? Explain.

2. Which theory, the will theory or the equity theory, was used to interpret this contract? Explain.

3. What are the six elements of a contract?

4. Which of the six elements was missing in the contract between MAN and Western Star?

5. Does a litigant usually receive punitive damages in a contract suit? Explain.

 Learning Objectives

1. Explain the three theories of contract law.
2. Identify the six elements of a contract.
3. Explain the place of the UCC in contract law.
4. Distinguish contracts from other agreements between different parties.
5. Explain the concept of privity and contract law.
6. Explain the nature of valid, void, voidable, and unenforceable contracts.
7. Contrast unilateral and bilateral contractual arrangements.
8. Outline the difference between express and implied contracts.
9. Discuss the difference between quasi-contracts and implied-in-fact contracts.
10. Differentiate between formal and informal contracts.
11. Explain how executory contracts differ from executed contracts.

7-1 The Basics of Contract Law

A **contract** is an agreement between two or more competent parties, based on mutual promises, to do or refrain from doing some particular thing that is neither illegal nor impossible. The agreement results in an obligation or a duty that can be enforced in a court of law.

EXAMPLE 7-1:   Deal or No Deal: Is Every Agreement a Contract?

Kristan Gregori was negotiating the sale of her restaurant, the Gregori Deli, to Tony Francisco. During the negotiation stage, Francisco asked Gregori to agree not to open a competing restaurant for five years anywhere in Jamestown. Gregori agreed. The sale of the restaurant was contingent upon Francisco selling his apartment building to Wellsian Real Estate Developers of Jamestown. That evening, Gregori told her cousin Betina that she would take her out to dinner if the deal with Francisco was finalized. There are several agreements within this scenario. The first is the sale of the restaurant. This contract will only go into effect if the second contract between Wellsian and Francisco is finalized. The third agreement between Gregori and her cousin Betina is only a social agreement and cannot be enforced as law. The non-competition agreement that Gregori has made with Francisco is a part of the overall agreement to sell the restaurant.

Contracts create binding legal obligations that each party may enforce against the other.

The contracting party who makes a promise is known as the **promisor**; the one to whom the promise is made is the **promisee**. The party who is obligated to deliver on a promise or undertake some act of performance is called the **obligor**. The contracting party to whom this party owes an obligation is called the **obligee**.

The Objectives of Contract Law

In Example 7-1, the contract between Gregori and Francisco is valid because it was entered into freely. Neither party was coerced into entering the agreement. Also, presumably, each side knew the terms of the contract and agreed to those terms without reservation. If for some reason in the future, Gregori believes that she did not receive enough for her restaurant, she will be unable to file a complaint against Francisco. Unless Francisco somehow defrauded or coerced her, the fact that Gregori did a poor job of negotiating and received too little for the deli will not matter to the court. The underlying objective of contract law is to determine whether the parties entered into the agreement freely. If the court determines that the parties willingly entered the agreement, then the contract is valid. If the court then determines that one of the parties violated this valid contract, that party will have to compensate the other party for any loss that results from the breach.

Usually, the courts will not make someone go through with a contract if they back out of the agreement. However, as noted previously, the courts will compel a party who has failed to live up to the agreement to compensate the innocent party for any loss that results from that breach. As a general rule, the court's goal in the remedy phase of a contract dispute is to place the injured party in as good a position as he or she would have been had the contract been carried out. There are built-in modifications to this theory however. For instance, the innocent party is not permitted to take advantage of the breach by deliberately raising the level of damages that the other party will have to pay as a consequence of the breach. This rule is known as the principle of **mitigation**. Another modification involves punitive damages. **Punitive damages** are damages that are designed to punish the offender. As a general rule, punitive damages are not permitted in contract law. However, in cases of fraud and other types of deceit, a court may approve punitive damages, because a party who engages in fraud has attempted to undermine the entire contract system, something the court will simply not abide.

Three Theories of Contract Law

It is always important to remember that contracts are based on the willful acts of the parties involved in the agreement, which is referred to as the will theory of contract law. The **will theory** is a general principle of law that states that a contract will exist once all of the parties with the legal capacity to contract have actually accepted all obligations and benefits under the contract and have exchanged, or promised to exchange, things of value. At times, to outsiders, the terms of a contract may seem disproportionate or unfair. However, as long as the parties freely enter a legal agreement with equal bargaining power and full contractual capacity, a valid contract will result.

The Opening Case Revisited, Part I

What a Difference a Verb Makes, Round 2

In The Opening Case, the Oregon court granted punitive damages to the plaintiff MAN in the amount of $350 million. The damages were divided between the two major defendants. Freightliner was assessed $70 million and DaimlerChrysler, the owner of Freightliner, was assessed $280 million. Although general principles of contract law do not normally permit punitive damages, in this case, the Oregon court did not hesitate to assess those damages against Freightliner and D/C because both corporations clearly committed fraud against MAN by hiding the assets of Freightliner to avoid paying the damages that had been awarded to MAN by a British court.

The will theory does, however, require that all the parties to a contract have the opportunity to know all of the facts that are important to that contract. This requirement exists because the will theory only works if there is a true "meeting of the minds" among the parties. The phrase "meeting of the minds" has long been used by the courts to describe a situation in which all of the parties to a contract know what is expected of them and what is expected of all the other parties to the contract. Without such a meeting of the minds, the parties cannot exercise their free will properly.

The will theory replaced an older theory of contract law that was referred to as the equity theory or the equal value theory. The **equal value theory** or **equity theory** insisted that a contract would be valid only if the things exchanged were of equal value. In an era when bartering was the primary way to create a contract, the equity theory worked very well. **Bartering** generally involves an exchange of services and/or goods that are equal in value, rather than a payment of money. In the nineteenth century, however, with the advent of industrial capitalism, the equity theory proved to be unworkable most of the time, because when an industrial capitalist invests money in a factory, a coal mine, or a railroad, that capitalist must make a profit to stay in business.

As a result, the courts introduced the will theory into contract law and said that the parties were free to add any terms to a contract, provided the terms were legal and that both parties agreed. Therefore, contracts freely entered into would be upheld by the court, even if the items exchanged were not equal in value. As a result, the industrial capitalists could charge enough money for products or services so that they could make a profit on those sales. Nevertheless, even with the will theory, principles of equity and justice still enter the question, but only if a party's free will has been thwarted by fraud, misrepresentation, mistake, duress, undue influence, something uncontrollable, or some event or circumstance that could not be reasonably foreseen.

However, because it is impossible for the courts to invade the consciousness of the parties, the courts must use the outward actions and the words of those parties as their standard of judgment. Over the years, this need to look at outward actions and words has led to a formalist theory of contract law. Under the **formalist theory** of contract law, the courts look to see if certain elements exist. Those elements are offer, acceptance, mutual assent, capacity, consideration, and legality. If each element is present, then a contract exists, regardless of what the parties may argue after the fact.

Talking Points

It is somewhat misleading to imply that capitalism did not begin until the nineteenth century. It is true that the word "capitalist" did not become popular until it was used by socialists in the 1800s as a negative label for the wealthy class of merchant-investors. However, the idea of investing wealth to make a profit dates back far into the Middle Ages. The shift from a barter system to a cash system actually began in the ninth century and had reached a high level of sophistication by the thirteenth century. This development led to some difficulty for the Catholic Church in Europe, which was restricted by Biblical warnings about the dangers of avarice. How was it possible for a church that could identify scriptural prohibitions against charging interest (see Deuteronomy 23:19–20 and Luke 6:34–35, for example) to condone making a profit? According to Rodney Stark in his book *The Victory of Reason,* one theologian with an answer to this question was Thomas Aquinas who, in the thirteenth century, called upon the work of St. Augustine, a fifth century theologian, to defend profit making. In interpreting Augustine, Aquinas proposed that it is logical for people to purchase something at a low cost to sell it at a higher cost. To this observation, Aquinas added his own thoughts, which dictated that the amount that someone will pay for something is based on how much he or she is willing to give up to obtain the item that is up for sale. Thus, except in cases of fraud or force, making a profit is justifiable. Do you agree with Thomas Aquinas and St. Augustine? Why or why not? (See Rodney Stark, *The Victory of Reason: How Christianity Led to Freedom, Capitalism, and Western Success,* New York: Random House, Inc., 2005, 54, 63—65.)

 **Offer** An offer is a proposal made by one party to another indicating a willingness to enter a contract. The person who makes an offer is called the offeror; the person to whom the offer is made is the offeree. (See Chapter 8.)

Acceptance In most cases, only a specifically identified offeree or his or her authorized agent has the right to accept an offer. Acceptance means that the offeree freely agrees to be bound by the terms of the offer at the exact time that the acceptance is communicated to the offeree. (See Chapter 8.)

Mutual Assent If a valid offer has been made by the offeror, and a valid acceptance has been made by the offeree, then mutual assent exists between them. Often the court will say that mutual assent exists only if there has been a "meeting of the minds" among the parties to the agreement. If mutual assent has been destroyed, the relationship that results is said to be a defective agreement. (See Chapter 9.)

Capacity The fourth element necessary to a make a contract complete is capacity. Capacity is the legal ability to make a contract. (See Chapter 10.)

Consideration The fifth element to any complete contract is the freely exercised mutual exchange of benefits and sacrifices. This willful exchange is called consideration. Consideration is the thing of value promised to the other party in exchange for something else of value promised by the other party. (See Chapter 11.)

Legality The final element of a binding contract is legality. Parties cannot be allowed to enforce a contract that involves doing something that is illegal. (See Chapter 12.)

> ### *The Opening Case Revisited, Part II*
> ### What a Difference a Verb Makes, Round 3
>
> In The Opening Case, the German corporation MAN entered a contract with Western Star, later owned by Freightliner and D/C, for the purchase of a corporation called ERF. For this contract to be competely valid, both sides had to know the terms of the agreement. Without that knowledge, there could be no true "meeting of the minds"—which is precisely what happened in this case; that is, Western Star had falsified the financial records of ERF. Given this situation, there could be no "meeting of the minds," between MAN and Western Star as required by the court.

Contracts and the UCC

As discussed in Chapter 2, the Uniform Commercial Code (UCC) is a unified set of statutes designed to govern almost all commercial transactions. Article 2 of the UCC sets down the rules that govern sale-of-goods contracts. All other types of contracts, including employment contracts and real property contracts, are governed by common law rules and certain special statutory provisions. Fortunately, in many cases, common law rules and UCC provisions are the same. Those differences that do exist are pointed out in the discussion of general contract law in Part II of this text. In Part III, both Article 2 of the UCC and sale-of-goods contracts are discussed. Property law contracts are analyzed in Part IV, and Part VII examines employment contracts.

Table 7-1 The Six Elements of a Contract

Element	Explanation
Offer	A proposal is made by one party (the offeror) to another party (the offeree), indicating a willingness to enter a contract.
Acceptance	The offeree agrees to be bound by the terms found in the offer.
Mutual assent	Offer and acceptance go together to create mutual assent or "a meeting of the minds." Assent can be destroyed by fraud, misrepresentation, mistake, duress, or undue influence.
Capacity	The law presumes that anyone entering a contract has the legal capacity to do so. However, minors are generally excused from contractual responsibility, as are mentally incompetent and drugged or intoxicated individuals.
Consideration	Consideration is the thing of value promised to the other party in a contract in exchange for something else of value promised by the other party. This mutual exchange binds the parties together.
Legality	Parties are not allowed to enforce contracts that involve doing something that is illegal. Some illegal contracts involve agreements to commit a crime or perform a tort. Others involve activities made illegal by statutory law.

During the lean years of the dot-com bust, computer networking consultant Robert B. Antia resorted to bartering with failing companies. He would offer his expertise in exchange for an arcane asset: their Internet Protocol addresses (such as 192.168.1.1.), which enable computers, cell phones, servers, and other devices to send packets of data to other devices across cyberspace. Someday, he figured, this finite resource might become valuable.

That day seems to be here. With millions of new computers, cell phones, and other devices going online every month, the supply of Internet Protocol (IP) addresses is growing scarce. With only 4 billion number combinations possible, an Internet registry group estimates that the 1 billion remaining unallocated addresses will run out by 2010. Familiar net addresses, such as www.businessweek.com, are just human-friendly names with numerical equivalents that enable one device to find another online. Migration to an upgraded version of the Internet, which would allow access for billions more devices, is moving too slowly to stem the looming address shortage.

Some believe this could add up to a gold mine for so-called legacy address holders, those who scooped up hundreds of millions of addresses at the dawn of cyberspace. They were doled out liberally by a handful of academics and government contractors before the commercial potential of the Internet—and the rules governing it—was clear. Those legacy holders range from little guys such as consultant Antia to a few huge corporations that hold many millions of addresses apiece. Because they were given control of IP addresses before the creation of Internet governing authorities in the 1990s, they aren't bound by the same contractual requirements as companies and individuals who lease their IP address from the Internet registries. That includes the obligation to make full use of any addresses.

What's not clear, though, is whether legacy holders can legally sell the addresses. The American Registry for Internet Numbers (ARIN), one of five nonprofits that were handed sterwardship of cyber-space, says holders should be obligated to turn over any unused addresses.

Today, the vast majority of Internet users—including most companies, Internet service providers, and universities—lease their address space from ARIN and the other registries. Leasing fees vary by region. ARIN, which governs Canada, the U.S., Latin America, and the Carribbean, charges from $1,300 per year for a small block of numbers to $18,000 for several million; the biggest users can pay tens of thousands of dollars a year for their space. Already, a market has sprung up for unauthorized sales of addresses issued through the registries. Some numbers have even shown up on eBay.

ARIN has begun a campaign to cajole legacy holders into depositing their unused addresses in the public pool. "There's a moral imperative here," argues ARIN General Counsel Stephen M. Ryan, a partner with the law firm McDermott Will & Emery in Washington, D.C. Legacy holders "have a duty to think about the community's interest as well as their own."

Questions for Analysis

1. In the sale of an Internet Protocol (IP) address, who would be the offeror and who would be the offeree? Explain.

2. Can the American Registry for Internet Numbers (ARIN) force IP holders to turn over or sell their unused addresses? Explain.

3. Was there a true "meeting of the minds" when the computer networking consultant bartered for the IP addresses that he now holds? Explain.

4. Do the IP address holders have an ethical obligation to turn over their unused addresses? Explain.

5. What ethical theory is the attorney using when he argues that there is a moral imperative to return the unused addresses? Explain.

Source: Lorraine Woellert, "A Coming Real Estate Crunch on the Net: With Online Addresses Getting Scarce, Holders of Unused Ones Could Be Sitting on a Treasure Trove," *BusinessWeek,* June 18, 2007, 65.

Contracts and Other Agreements

All contracts are agreements, but not all agreements are contracts. An agreement may or may not be legally enforceable. To be enforceable, an agreement must conform to the law of contracts. The courts have never been agreeable to the enforcement of social agreements: dates, dinner engagements, or the like. Many states have extended this concept to include agreements to marry and agreements to live together without the benefit of a marriage contract.

UCC 1-201(11) and (21) (see pages 955 and 956)

Contracts and Privity

The general rule of contract law is that the parties to a contract must stand in privity to one another. Privity means that both parties have a legally recognized interest in the subject of the contract if they are to be bound by it. Parties who do not have such an interest in the subject matter of the contract may not be bound by it. Their right to bring a lawsuit in the event of breach of contract would also be in question.

EXAMPLE 7-2:   Standing to Sue: What Are the Limits?

The Columbus Redbirds, a professional swim team, had a contract with the city to hold seven swim meets at the city's new nautorium in the downtown area. When the Redbirds corporation breached its contract and moved the team to Indianapolis, Columbus sued. In another development following the inauguration of the original lawsuit, a group of three downtown hotels and 15 restaurants joined together to bring a second lawsuit against the Redbirds for breach of contract. The city will have standing to bring its lawsuit because the city and the swim team were in privity. However, the hotels and the restaurants will not have standing to sue because they were not in privity under the terms of the original contract.

Despite this privity rule, it is possible for two or more parties to provide benefits to a third party. However, the law still makes a distinction between third parties who are intended beneficiaries and third parties who are incidental beneficiaries. In Example 7-2, the hotels and the restaurants are incidental rather than intended beneficiaries. In contrast, a life insurance contract generally involves intended beneficiaries. Thus, when an insurance company makes a payment on a life insurance contract, that payment is to an intended beneficiary. Moreover, an exception to the general rule of privity exists in cases involving warranties and product liability. (See Chapter 17.)

Quick Quiz 7-1 True or False?

1. A contract results in a duty that can be enforced in a court of law. T

2. A court's goal in the remedy phase of a contract case is to punish the party F
   who breached the contract.

3. The law makes no distinction between intended and incidental beneficiaries. F

7-2 Contractual Characteristics

Contractual characteristics fall into five different categories: valid, void, voidable, and unenforceable; unilateral and bilateral; express and implied; informal and formal; and executory and executed. Any given contract can be classifiable in all five ways. Thus, for example, a single contract could be said to be valid, bilateral, express, formal, and executed, or any other acceptable combination of characteristics.

Valid, Void, Voidable, and Unenforceable Contracts

A valid contract is one that is legally binding and fully enforceable by the court. In contrast, a void contract is one that has no legal effect whatsoever. For example, a contract to perform an illegal act would be void. A voidable contract is one that may be avoided or canceled by one of the parties. Contracts made by minors or induced by fraud or misrepresentation are examples of voidable contracts. An unenforceable contract is one that, because of some rule of law, cannot be upheld by a court of law. An unenforceable contract may have all the elements of a complete contract and still be unenforceable.

Unilateral and Bilateral Contracts

A unilateral contract is an agreement in which one party makes a promise to do something in return for an act of some sort. The classic example of a unilateral contract is a reward contract. A person who promises to pay $5 to the finder of a lost compact disk does not expect a promise in return. Rather, the person expects the return of the lost CD. When the CD is returned, the contract arises and the promisor owes the finder $5.

In contrast, a bilateral contract is one in which both parties make promises. Bilateral contracts come into existence at the moment the two promises are made. A breach of contract occurs when one of the two parties fails to keep the promise. When there is a breach of contract, the injured party has the right to ask a court of law to somehow remedy the situation. (Breach of contract and remedies are discussed in detail in Chapter 15.)

Express and Implied Contracts

A contract can be either express or implied. An express contract requires some sort of written or spoken expression indicating a desire to enter the contractual relationship. An implied contract is created by the actions or gestures of the parties involved in the transaction.

Express Contracts   When contracting parties accept mutual obligations, either through oral discussion or written communication, they have created an express contract. Oral negotiations in many cases will be reduced to writing, but this is not always necessary.

A written contract does not have to be a long, formal preprinted agreement. Although such lengthy, preprinted forms are common in some businesses, other, less

A Question of Ethics

Suppose you posted a reward notice that read, "Reward: $50 for the return of my lost college class ring." Suppose further that someone who did not know of the reward offer found your ring and returned it. Legally you would not have to pay the reward money to the person who found your ring because he or she did not know about your offer. However, would it be ethical not to pay the reward to the finder? Explain.

formal written documents are frequently used to show that a contract exists. For example, a written contract may take the form of a letter, sales slip and receipt, notation, or memorandum. A written contract may be typed, printed, keystroked, scrawled, or written in beautiful penmanship. In some situations, state laws require certain types of contracts to be in writing. (See Chapter 13.)

When a contract is placed in writing, it is essential that the content be as clear and unambiguous as possible. When faced with a dispute over an ambiguous clause, the court may be compelled to look at factual evidence to determine the actual intent of the parties. This review may mean that a case that could have been dismissed early will have to go to trial so that the court can make a factual determination of intent by looking at evidence beyond the terms in the writing.

When the law does not require a written agreement, an *oral contract* resulting from the spoken words of the parties will be enough. Parties to such an agreement, however, should anticipate the difficulty of proving the contractual relationship, should disputes arise later. Nevertheless, expressing every agreement in writing, in anticipation of a future need of proof, is impractical in the fast-paced modern world of business.

Implied Contracts One who knowingly accepts benefits from another person may be obligated for their payment, even though no express agreement has been made. An agreement of this type can be either implied-in-fact or implied-in-law. A contract implied by the direct or indirect acts of the parties is known as an **implied-in-fact contract**. Pumping gas into a car at a self-service gas station is an example of an implied-in-fact contract. Because the parties to a contract enter that contract by an exercise of free will, the court follows an objective rule in interpreting the acts and gestures of a party. Under this concept, the meaning of one's actions is determined by the impression those actions would make upon any reasonable person who might have witnessed them, not by a party's self-serving claim of what was meant or intended by the actions.

EXAMPLE 7-3: Implied-in-Fact Deals: Can Inaction Create a Contract?

Herbert Ward watched workers employed by the Rice Lawn and Garden Greenhouse as they chemically treated his front lawn. In fact, Ward had no contract with Rice and had not ordered any chemical treatments of his property. The treatment should have been performed on another house at 750 Maple Street, instead of at Ward's, which had an address of 570 Maple St. Ward never stopped the work crew, even though he knew that a mistake had been made. Rice would be within its rights to believe that the work was being done with Ward's consent. In assessing damages for the cost of the improvement, the court would apply the objective concept rule. A reasonable person who might have watched Rice treat the front lawn would conclude that Ward had freely consented to the work.

About the Law

The law that declares which contracts must be in writing is called the Statute of Frauds. In its original form when it was passed by Parliament in 1677, it was known as the Act for the Prevention of Fraud and Perjuries.

An **implied-in-law contract** is imposed by a court when someone is unjustly enriched. It is used when a contract cannot be enforced or there is no actual written, oral, or implied-in-fact agreement. Applying reasons of justice and fairness, a court may obligate one who has unfairly benefited at the innocent expense of another. An implied-in-law contract is also called a **quasi-contract**.

EXAMPLE 7-4:   Implied-in-Law Deals: Can Injustice Be Prevented?

Karl Rapp was found unconscious in his hotel room by Jan Stevens, the third-floor maid. She immediately called 911 and then notified Ken Kramer, the hotel manager. Kramer arranged to have Rapp placed in a hospital for emergency treatment. When Rapp regained consciousness, he refused to pay for the treatment, claiming that he was not aware of what was going on and had not agreed to what had been done to him. The case illustrates a quasi-contractual situation, wherein it would be unfair to allow the injured person to benefit at the expense of the hospital. In any suit that might arise over this expense, a court would require Rapp to pay the fair value of the services rendered.

The quasi-contract concept cannot apply, however, to obtain payment for an act that a party simply feels should be done. The concept also cannot be applied when one party bestows a benefit on another unnecessarily or through misconduct or negligence. A quasi-contract is not a contract in the true sense of the word, because it is created by the court. It does not result from the mutual assent of the parties, as do express or implied-in-fact contracts.

 ## Informal and Formal Contracts

The law sometimes requires that contracts follow formalities prescribed by statute or common law. These are called formal contracts. All others are classified as informal.

Informal Contracts   Any oral or written contract that is not under seal or is not a contract of record is considered an **informal contract**. An informal contract is also known as a *simple contract*. An informal contract generally has no requirements as to language, form, or construction. It comprises obligations entered into by parties whose promises are expressed in the simplest and usually most ordinary, nonlegal language.

UCC 2-203 (see page 961)

Formal Contracts   Under common law principles, a **formal contract** differs from other types of contracts in that it has to be (1) written; (2) signed, witnessed, and placed under the seal of the parties; and (3) delivered. A *seal* is a mark or an impression placed on a written contract indicating that the instrument was executed and accepted in a formal manner. The UCC removed the requirement for a seal in sale-of-goods contracts. Some states, however, still require the use of the seal in agreements related to the sale and transfer of real property.

Today, a person's seal may be any mark or sign placed after the signature intended to be the signer's seal. In states still requiring the seal or formal contract, it is sufficient to write the word *seal* after the signature.

EXAMPLE 7-5:   Formal Contracts: Is a Seal Still Needed?

Audrey Kimmel signed an agreement with Corey Baumberger to buy seven acres of farmland owned by Baumberger just outside Bellville. Later that day, Baumberger found another interested buyer who was willing to pay seven times as much as Kimmel had offered for the land. Kimmel had signed the sales agreement without including any representation of the seal. In any state that required such formality in all real property contracts, Kimmel would now be helpless in attempting to enforce the original contract that she had made with Baumberger.

Contracts of Record

A special type of formal contract is known as a **contract of record**. Often, such a contract is confirmed by the court with an accompanying judgment issued in favor of one of the parties. The judgment is recorded, giving the successful litigant the right to demand satisfaction of the judgment. A contract of record is not a contract in the true sense of the word, because it is court created. Although it does not have all of the elements of a valid contract, it is enforced for public policy reasons.

EXAMPLE 7-6:   Contracts of Record: When Can Litigants Demand Their Money?

Mortimer Byrne installed a new roof on Alexander Harper's house in Lakeside for the agreed-upon price of $7,500. Harper paid Byrne $4,000 so that he could secure materials. After the job was completed, Byrne sent Harper a bill for $3,500. Harper sent Byrne a check for $2,500, on which was written "in full payment of all money owed." These words were in very fine print and not seen by Byrne. Byrne sued Harper in the small claims division of the Ottawa County Court of Common Pleas for the amount still owed. The court ruled in favor of Byrne and entered a judgment against Harper for the money owed. Entry of the judgment created a contract of record, which was enforceable against Harper.

Executory and Executed Contracts

A contract that has not yet been fully performed by the parties is called an **executory contract**. Such a contract may be completely executory, in which case nothing has been done, or it may be partly executory, in which case the contract is partially complete. When a contract's terms have been completely and satisfactorily carried out by both parties, it is an **executed contract**. Such contracts are no longer active agreements and are valuable only if a dispute about the agreement occurs.

Quick Quiz 7-2 True or False?

1. A void contract is one that can be avoided by one or more of the parties. *F*

2. A formal contract is also known as a simple contract. *F*

3. A contract that has not yet been fully performed by the parties is called an executory contract. *T*

Summary

7.1 A contract is an agreement between two or more competent parties based on mutual promises to do or refrain from doing some particular thing that is neither illegal nor impossible. The six elements of a contract include offer, acceptance, mutual assent, capacity, consideration, and legality. Article II of the UCC covers sale-of-goods contracts; common law and special statutory provisions cover employment and real property contracts. To be enforceable, an agreement must conform to the law of contracts. The courts have never been agreeable to the enforcement of social contracts. Finally, the general rule of contract law is that the parties to a contract must stand in privity to one another.

7.2   Contractual characteristics fall into five different categories. These categories are valid, void, voidable, or unenforceable; unilateral or bilateral; express or implied; informal or formal; and executory or executed.

Key Terms

bartering, 143	formal contract, 150	promisee, 142
bilateral contract, 148	formalist theory, 143	promisor, 142
breach of contract, 148	implied contract, 148	punitive damages, 142
contract, 141	implied-in-fact contract, 149	quasi-contract, 149
contract of record, 151	implied-in-law contract, 149	unenforceable contract, 148
equal value theory, 143	informal contract, 150	unilateral contract, 148
equity theory, 143	mitigation, 142	valid contract, 148
executed contract, 151	obligee, 142	void contract, 148
executory contract, 151	obligor, 142	voidable contract, 148
express contract, 148	privity, 147	will theory, 142

Questions for Review and Discussion

1. How did the present theory of contracts evolve?
2. What are the six elements of a contract?
3. What is the place of the UCC in contract law?
4. What is the difference between contracts and other agreements?
5. What is the nature of privity and contract law?
6. What are the differences among valid, void, voidable, and unenforceable contracts?
7. What is the difference between a unilateral and bilateral contract?
8. What is the difference between an express and an implied contract?
9. What is the difference between quasi-contracts and implied-in-fact contracts?
10. What is the difference between an executory contract and an executed contract?

Investigating the Internet

The American Bar Association maintains a Web site that highlights various areas of the law. One part of the ABA Web site is entitled the "Section of Public Contract Law." Access the ABA Web site, find the section on Public Contract Law, and answer the following questions: (1) What are the two central themes that dominate the mission of the ABA Section on Public Contract Law? (2) What techniques are promoted by the section to achieve this mission? (3) What subcommittees are part of this ABA Section on Public Contract Law? (4) What is the latest news reported by this section? (5) What member services are available through this section?

Cases for Analysis

1. Several businesspeople secured a contract with the state of Massachusetts that permitted them to construct a bridge spanning the Charles River. The businesspeople intended to charge a toll for passage over the bridge to recover the expense of building the bridge and make a sizable profit off its operation. Later, another group of businesspeople made a similar contract. They too were permitted to build a bridge and charge a toll. There was, however, a six-year limit on the tolls that would be charged on the second bridge, transforming it into a free bridge after the end of the six-year period. The first group of businesspeople realized that the existence of a free bridge would make their bridge worthless. Accordingly, they sued to prevent the second bridge from being constructed. They argued that the original contract that they had negotiated with the state implied that no other bridge would be built. The second group argued that because there was no explicit agreement in the first contract preventing a second bridge from being built, the court, under the Contracts Clause of the Constitution, could not impair the rights they had freely negotiated under the new contract to build a second bridge. The case ended up in the United States Supreme Court. How did the Supreme Court decide the case? Explain. *Proprietors of the Charles River Bridge v. Proprietors of the Warren Bridge,* 11 Pet. 420 (USSCt. 1837). See also L. Friedman, "Economy and Law in the Nineteenth Century," *Law in America* (New York: The Modern Library, 2002), 49–54.

2. The Borg-Warner Protective Services Corporation and Burns International Security Services contracted to provide security for the Cleveland Institute of Art (CIA). Robert Adelman was struck by an object thrown by a CIA student from the roof of one of the Institute's buildings. Adelman sued both the CIA and the security corporations. The security corporations moved for summary judgment, arguing that they had contracted with CIA to protect the faculty and the students and that they therefore had no duty to protect pedestrians outside the buildings. Adelman argued that the contract specifically obligated the security corporations to control the activities of CIA students within the Institute's buildings. The disputed clause read that the security corporations agreed "to control the movement and activities of students

within the buildings at all hours." The trial court granted the summary judgment motion, and Adelman appealed. Should the appellate court reverse the decision of the lower court? Explain. If the case goes to trial, how will the court determine the meaning of the ambiguous clause? Explain. *Adelman v. Timman,* 690 N.E.2d 1332 (OH).

3. One of Stewart's clients gave him a check for $185.48. The check had been drawn up by the client's corporate employer and properly endorsed by the client. Nevertheless, the bank refused to cash the check for Stewart, even though there was enough money in the account to cover the $185.48. Could Stewart sue the bank for not cashing the check as he requested? Explain. *J.E.B. Stewart v. Citizens and Southern National Bank,* 225 S.E.2d 761 (GA).

4. Vokes was told that she would become a professional dancer if she took a very expensive dancing course offered by Arthur Murray, Inc. She was also continually told that she had great talent. The contract called for payments amounting to a total of $31,000. As it turned out, she never became a professional dancer and, in fact, had little or no talent. She sued Arthur Murray, claiming that the Arthur Murray people misrepresented the facts to entice her to enter the contract. The court agreed and found in her favor. Would Vokes have the right to void the contract? Explain. *Vokes v. Arthur Murray, Inc.,* 212 So.2d 906 (FL).

5. Anderson, a farmer, orally agreed to buy a used tractor from the Copeland Equipment Company for $475. Copeland delivered the tractor to Anderson, who used it for 11 days. During this period, Anderson could not borrow enough funds to cover the purchase price. Anderson therefore returned the tractor to Copeland. Both parties agreed that their sales contract was canceled when the tractor was returned. However, Copeland later claimed that under the doctrine of quasi-contract, Anderson was required to pay for the 11-days' use of the tractor. Do you agree with Copeland? Explain your answer. *Anderson v. Copeland,* 378 P.2d 1006 (OK).

6. B. L. Nelson & Associates, Inc., entered into a contract with the city of Argyle to design and construct a sanitary sewer collection and treatment facility for the city. The city attempted to get out of the contract

by citing certain provisions of the state constitution. These provisions made it illegal for the city to enter a contract for services if it did not have the money to pay for these services. Because the city did not have the funds to pay Nelson, it argued that the contract was illegal and therefore void. Was the city correct? Explain. *B. L. Nelson & Associates, Inc. v. City of Argyle,* 535 S.W.2d 906 (TX).

7. Peters entered into a contract to purchase Dowling's business. The following terms were agreed to: (a) Peters would take over all of Dowling's executory contracts, (b) Peters would purchase Dowling's tools at an agreed-to price, (c) Peters would accept full responsibility for all warranties made by Dowling on previous contracts, and (d) Dowling would remain as a consultant to the new firm for a period of five years. Analyze each part of this contract and classify each term according to whether it is executed or executory. *Wagstaff v. Peters,* 453 P.2d 120 (KS).

Quick Quiz Answers

7-1		7-2	
1.	T	1.	F
2.	F	2.	F
3.	F	3.	T

Chapter 8 | Offer and Acceptance

The Opening Case
When Is a Contract Case Not a Contract Case?

Traditionally, when one party refuses to pay another party for services rendered, the victimized party will—after some deliberation, much soul searching, and a brief preliminary investigation—decide to bring a breach of contract suit. This process was not the case when Terry Yates discovered that he had not been paid by Dynergy, Inc., after Yates had defended one of Dynergy's executives in a criminal fraud case. Yates pointed to a section of the corporation's bylaws that indicated a promise he would be paid for his work in defending the executive. Evidently, Dynergy had surrendered to a "suggestion" from the U.S. Attorney's Office in Houston that Dynergy might be indicted if it did not withhold Yates's payment. Rather than bring a breach of contract suit, as would have been expected, Yates brought civil suit against Dynergy alleging fraud. Apparently, Yates's attorney had realized that Dynergy had no fear of the contract case because, to a big company like Dynergy, the fees were not worth mentioning. Once the fees could be quadrupled under the fraud case however, Yates's attorney calculated that Dynergy would have had to sit up and take notice. That is exactly what happened. Yates won the case, and the jury awarded him his fees, which amounted to $500,000 and, in addition, $2 million in punitive damages, something that would not have happened had the lawsuit been filed as a breach of contract case. After the jury had rendered its verdict, the defendant, Dynergy, filed a motion asking the court to withhold its judgment. In a very unusual move, Dynergy argued that the suit was actually a contract case and that all that Dynergy had done was not perform its contractual duties. Put simply, Dynergy was saying, "Okay, okay, you caught us. We breached the contract. But fraud? No. No way." In effect, Dynergy was trying to escape that hefty $2 million award in punitive damages. The judge, however, did not take the bait. (See *Yates v. Dynergy Inc.* No. 2005-37892 (Harris Co., Texas Dist. Ct) and Marcia Coyle, "Attorney Wins Fees in Rare Civil Fraud Case: Pressure in Dynergy Case not to Pay Fees," *The National Law Journal*, June 4, 2007, p. 6.)

Opening Case Questions

1. If this case involves a contract, as Dynergy claims, who is the offeror and who is the offeree?

2. How was the offer communicated to the plaintiff in this case?

3. Were the terms of the offer clear and definite?

4. How did the offeree in this case express acceptance?

5. Was this contract unilateral or bilateral? Explain.

Learning Objectives

1. Explain how formalism guides the court in determining the elements of offer and acceptance.
2. Identify the three requirements of a valid offer.
3. Explain acceptance of an offer in the case of a unilateral contract and a bilateral contract.
4. Identify the role of the Uniform Commercial Code (UCC) in the law.
5. Define the mirror image rule.
6. Explain the UCC's concept of acceptance in contract law.
7. Relate the various means by which an offer can be revoked.
8. Explain what is meant by a firm offer in relation to the sale of goods and the UCC.
9. Explain what is meant by a lease option in relation to real property.
10. Identify those statutes that affect the formation of e-contracts.

8-1 Requirements of an Offer

The first element of a valid contract is the existence of an offer. As explained in the previous chapter, an **offer** is a proposal freely made by one party to another indicating a willingness to enter a contract. The **offeror** is the person who freely makes the offer, and the **offeree** is the person to whom the offer is made. As soon as the courts attempted to use the will theory of contract law, they could see how challenging it was to establish whether the offeror and offeree have actually agreed to the terms of a contract. Because the actual intent of each party was out of reach, the courts had to examine behavior to determine that intent. This problem led the courts to establish a formalist approach. According to formalism, if certain requirements are met, the court concludes that the parties intended to make and accept an offer. In the case of an offer, the courts established that there must exist: (1) serious intent, (2) clear and reasonably definite terms, (3) and communication to the offeree. It is to a discussion of these requirements that we now turn.

The Opening Case Revisited

When Is a Contract Case Not a Contract Case? Round 2

When Terry Yates defended one of Dynergy's executives in court, he fully expected to be paid for the legal services he had rendered. To demonstrate that he was correct, Yates pointed to a section of the corporation's bylaws that indicated a promise to pay for his work in defending the corporation's accounting executive. He was, in effect, the offeree who had by his actions in defending the corporate officer accepted the offer made by Dynergy, which was, in effect, the offeror. Later in the case, these facts became indisputable, especially when in filing a motion at the end of the trial, the attorney representing Dynergy all but admitted that a contract had been in effect all along.

Table 8-1 Requirements of an Offer	
Requirement	**Explanation**
Serious intent	The offeror's words must give the offeree assurance that a binding agreement is intended.
Clarity and reasonably definite terms	The terms of an offer must be sufficiently clear to remove any doubt about the contractual intentions of the offeror. Most courts require reasonable rather than absolute definiteness.
Communication to the offeree	The proposed offer must be communicated to the offeree by whatever means are convenient and desirable. The communication of the offer can be express or implied. Public offers are made through the media but are intended for one party whose identity or address is unknown. Invitations to trade are not offers.

Serious Intent

An offer is invalid if it is made as an obvious joke, during an emotional outburst of rage or anger, or under circumstances that might convey a lack of serious intent. The offeror's words or actions must give the offeree assurance that a binding agreement is intended. Serious intent is determined by the offeror's words and actions and by what the offeree had the right to believe was intended by those words and actions (see Table 8-1). It might be best to apply the following test to determine whether the offeror had serious intent: Ask whether the supposed offeror would, at the precise moment that the words are spoken or the actions taken, be prepared to be bound by those words or those actions. If the answer is "yes," a contract exists. If the alleged offeror says something like, "I'm looking for investors and I think you and your spouse fit the profile that I have in mind," no offer exists. The words appear to be inviting the other party to enter into a negotiation stage rather than presenting that party with a valid, enforceable offer.

Clear and Reasonably Definite Terms

The communicated terms of an offer must be sufficiently clear to remove any doubt about the contractual intentions of the offeror. No valid offer will exist when terms are indefinite, inadequate, vague, or confusing. Again, as in the case of serious intent, it might be best to apply a test to determine whether the terms in the alleged offer are clear and definite enough. Ask whether the terms are so clear that, if there were a breach, the court would know how to assess a remedy. If the answer is "yes," the terms are probably definite enough. If the answer is "no," then some crucial term in the alleged offer must be too unclear to create a contract.

EXAMPLE 8-1:   When Is it Possible to Assess a Remedy?

The Lindbergh-Sikorsky Aircraft Corporation e-mailed an offer to Kenneth Hiebel, the owner of the Triple R-Bar Ranch in Idaho. The e-mail stated, "Please consider this our offer to purchase 20,000 acres of your 61,200-acre ranch land near Harrington, Idaho. Our offering price is between $60,000 and $65,000 per acre. Please respond soon." If we apply the suggested test, we can easily see that this e-mail is not a legally effective offer. The terms are much too indefinite. The e-mail does not specify which of Triple R-Bar's acres Lindbergh-Sikorsky wants to purchase. Nor does it specify a set price per acre. If there were a breach of contract, the court would not know how to set damages. Would it use the $60,000 figure, the $65,000 figure, or something in between? If Lindbergh-Sikorsky asked for specific performance of the contract, the court would not know which acres to transfer to the aircraft company. All in all, the terms lack an appropriate level of clarity and definiteness to constitute an offer.

Degree of Definiteness   In general, an offer should include points similar to those covered in a newspaper story—who, what, when, where, and how much—if it is to be clear, definite, and certain. This requirement means that the offer should identify (1) the parties involved in the contract, (2) the goods or services that will be the subject matter of the contract, (3) the price the offeror is willing to pay or receive, and (4) the time required for the performance of the contract. Most courts require reasonable rather than absolute definiteness. Offers will be upheld as long as the language is reasonably definite enough to enable the court to establish what the parties intended the terms to be so that, should there be a breach, a remedy can be set.

EXAMPLE 8-2:   When Is a Proposal Not a Proposal?

Dr. Anita Hughes was developing a cold fusion reactor that would solve the energy problems of this country for decades to come. The Toledo Electric Illuminating Company sent a proposal to Hughes by fax, offering her a fair share of the profits if she would develop the fusion reactor for their exclusive use. On the next day, the National Atomic Research and Development Laboratories (NARDL) in Oakland also faxed Hughes a proposal offering not only to pay her $10,000,000 to develop the fusion reactor for them but also to reimburse her for all expenses related to the development of the reactor and give her 20 percent of the profits during the first 10 years of the sale of the fusion reactors to domestic, foreign, and alien power companies. Of the two proposals, the Toledo proposition is much too indefinite to be considered a real offer. The NARDL proposal, however, is definite enough, even though a final dollar amount has not been settled upon, because the court has a way to figure out what the parties intended and what the final amount should be. If there were a breach of contract, the court would know how to set a remedy for the innocent party.

Offers and the UCC   The UCC permits offers to omit certain information. It states that "even though one or more terms are left open, a contract for sale does not fail for indefiniteness if the parties have intended to make a contract and there is a reasonably certain basis for giving an appropriate remedy." Under this section of the UCC, cost-plus contracts, output contracts, requirement contracts, and current market price contracts are enforceable even though they are not complete in certain matters. A **cost-plus contract** does not include a final price; rather, the contract price is determined by the cost of labor and materials, plus an agreed-to percentage or dollar markup. A **requirements contract** is an agreement in which one party agrees to buy all of the goods it needs from the second party. The terms of a requirements contract must be carefully worded. If the agreement allows the buyer to purchase only those goods that the buyer desires or wishes, the agreement is unenforceable, because it is illusory in that the buyer is not really obligated to do anything. An **output contract** is an agreement in which one party consents to sell to a second party all of the goods that party makes in a given period of time. Finally, a **current market price contract** is one in which prices are determined by reference to the market price of the goods as of a specified date.

UCC 2-204 (3) (see page 961)

Communication to the Offeree

To be valid, an offer must be freely communicated to the offeree. The offeror's intentions may be communicated by whatever means are convenient and desirable. For example, the offer may be communicated orally, by mail, by fax machine, by e-mail, or by any other capable means. It may also be implied. The proposing party's acts and conduct in many cases are successful in communicating an intention to make an offer to another party that witnesses them. When acts and conduct are sufficient to convey an offeror's intentions, an implied offer results.

Public Offers   At times, an offer must be communicated to a party whose name, identity, or address is unknown. In such cases, the public offer is made. A **public offer** is one that is made through the public media but is intended for only one person whose identity or address is unknown to the offeror. A classic example of a public offer is an advertisement in a lost-and-found column in a newspaper. Although it is a public offer, it is legally no different from other types of offers.

Invitations to Trade   By contrast, invitations to trade are not offers. An **invitation to trade** is an announcement published to reach many persons for the purpose of creating interest and attracting responses. Newspaper and magazine advertisements, radio and television commercials, store window displays, price tags on merchandise, for sale signs on houses and businesses, for rent signs, and prices in catalogs fall within this definition. In the case of an invitation to trade, no binding agreement develops until a responding party makes an offer that the advertiser accepts. Nevertheless, in certain relatively rare circumstances, advertisements may be held to be offers. However, such advertisements would have to contain very particular promises, use phrases like "first-come, first-served," or limit the number of items to be sold. Because the number of people who can buy the product is very limited, the advertisement becomes an offer.

Auctions   An **auction** is a sale that is open to the public, during which potential buyers compete for the right to purchase certain items by placing higher and higher bids until the highest bid is reached and the auctioneer accepts on behalf of the seller. Many people have the mistaken belief that in an auction the original property owner, that is, the seller, is the offeror

BusinessWeek Business Law in the News

Liquidity Services: Sell It Again, Sam

Looking to unload 1,300 pounds of scrap titanium? Seeking top dollar for a truckload of new kitchen cabinets or hundreds of used laptops? EBay Inc. probably isn't your best choice for hawking such huge quantities of goods. But Liquidity Services Inc. might be. By drawing thousands of buyers to a single online marketplace to win higher sales, this dot-com is reinventing the resale and surplus industries the way that other Internet auctioneers transformed flea markets.

LSI is no garden-variety Net emporium. The company has auctioned off everything from cavalry horses to thousands of used iPods. And it's using data from millions of sales to change the way big retailers manage their reverse supply-chain headaches—returned items, refurbished goods, and other stuff they unload at fire sale prices. "We're turning nickels and dimes into quarters and dollars for our clients," says William Angrick, the 39-year-old founder and CEO.

The company is changing the game in the liquidation industry, which remains highly fragmented. Many retailers still rely on local cash buyers who haul away unwanted stock on quick notice. In comparison, LSI's centralized process brings huge efficiencies. The company determines the ideal lot size for a product, drums up would-be buyers, manages the bidding, and handles the final transaction. N.E.W. Customer Services Cos., an administrator of extended warranties based in Sterling, Va., credits LSI with sharply boosting proceeds from sales of mountains of broken or damaged goods. . . .

The auctioneer got its first break doing work for the U.S. government, landing the Defense Dept. as a client. Defense, which remains the company's biggest contract, had the equivalent of 1,500 full-time workers managing surplus sales from 200 warehouses. LSI landed its first contracts with Defense in June, 2001, and now handles all its public surplus sales.

These days, LSI runs three Internet auction sites, including one that hawks government surplus from Britain's Defense Ministry. The sites have more than 600,000 registered buyers. The company makes money by taking a commission on items that sell, not by charging for listings, as some other auction sites do. A fourth site, gowholesale.com, is a portal for small businesses looking for sources of inventory. . . .

Now Angrick is using his success in Defense surplus sales as a calling card with big-box retailers, manufacturers, and distributors. About 6% of everything that's bought at a brick-and-mortar store is subsequently returned. That number is almost double for online retailers. Analysts predict that this "reverse logistics" market will hit $63 billion in 2008. "The opportunity," says Angrick, "is incredible."

Questions for Analysis

1. When a local cash buyer hauls away unwanted stock from a retailer, is that cash buyer the offeree or the offeror? Explain.

2. When Liquidated Services Inc. places that unwanted stock on its auction Web site, are the bidders offerors or offerees? Explain.

3. How does Liquidated Services Inc. make a profit? Explain.

4. What is a reverse supply chain? Explain.

5. What role does Liquidated Services Inc. play in the online auction? Explain.

Source: Lorraine Woellert, "Liquidity Services: Sell It Again, Sam," *BusinessWeek*, June 4, 2007, 64.

and that the bidder is the offeree. These roles are true only if the auction has been expressly labeled as an **auction without reserve**. If the auction has not been so designated, it is considered an **auction with reserve**, which means that the bidders are the offerors and the seller is the offeree. Consequently, the seller can stop the bidding at any time that he or she wants, up to the time that the auctioneer declares a winner, generally by striking the podium with the gavel. A seller can also control the bidding somewhat if he or she establishes the lowest acceptable bid. In such a case, should the auctioneer *not* hear a bid that meets the least possible bid, he or she can reject all of those bids, and the seller retains the property.

Bait-and-Switch Confidence Games   Most of the time, an advertisement is not specific enough to constitute an offer, because it generally lacks certain key items. For one thing, the seller really does not promise to sell one, single, individual item to a named or easily identifiable buyer in an advertisement. The seller may decide not to deal with a particular customer because that customer's credit rating is in bad shape or because the seller has run out of the item that was advertised. Moreover, advertisements rarely contain all of the terms that will eventually become a part of the finished contract. However, sellers cannot engage in bait-and-switch tactics. The **bait-and-switch confidence game** is a deliberately deceptive practice that entices buyers into a place of business when the seller actually has no intention of selling the item at the price stated in the advertisment. The practice has been outlawed by the Federal Trade Commission. In addition, many, and perhaps most, states have similar laws prohibiting bait-and-switch confidence games.

Quick Quiz 8-1   True or False?

1. The person who freely makes an offer is called an offeree.

2. An offer is valid only if it has (a) serious intent, (b) clear and reasonably definite terms, and (c) communication to the offeree.

3. No valid offer will exist when terms are indefinite, inadequate, vague, or confusing.

8-2 Acceptance of an Offer

The second major element in a binding contract is acceptance of the offer. As previously stated, **acceptance** means that the offeree agrees to be bound by the terms set up by the offeror. Only the offeree, the one to whom the offer is made, has the right to accept the offer. If another party attempts to accept, that attempt would actually be a new and independent offer.

Did You Know?

Even though an auctioneer will say that the goods in an auction are being "offered for sale," the bidders at the auction are the parties who make the offer to buy those goods.

EXAMPLE 8-3:   When Do Two Wrongs Make a Right?

Friedman owned and operated Friedman Rare Books and Antiquities, a sole proprietorship that sold rare books, original manuscripts, and antiques to libraries, museums, galleries, and private collectors. Friedman met with Castillo and Bauer, the owners and operators of the Mather Rare Books Shoppe, and offered to sell them an original, first edition of Ezra Pound's *Cantos*. Hoffman, the owner of Seattle Rare Books and Antiquities, also learned that the edition was for sale. He called Friedman and, after inspecting the edition, bought it for $225,000. Friedman had mistakenly thought that Hoffman worked for the Mather shop. When he found out that Hoffman worked for the nearly bankrupt Seattle book store, he refused to deliver the edition of *Cantos*. Hoffman and the Seattle book store sued. The court held that no contract resulted. Only Castillo and Bauer, the parties to whom Friedman had made the offer to sell, could accept it.

Unilateral contracts do not usually require oral or written communication of an acceptance. When the offeror makes a promise in a unilateral contract, the offeror expects an action, not another promise in return. Performance of the action requested within the time allowed by the offeror and with the offeror's knowledge creates the contract.

Talking Points

In a landmark text entitled *The Stages of Economic Growth: A Non-Communist Manifesto,* the economist W.W. Rostow contends that societies go through five stages of economic growth: the traditional economy, the pre–take-off economy, the take-off economy, the mature economy, and the high-mass consumption economy. He further contends that only the United States, western Europe, and Japan have entered stage five. How has contract law contributed to this economic growth in the United States, western Europe, and Japan?

EXAMPLE 8-4:   When Is a Unilateral Offer Accepted?

Patrick Barnes and George Layton were employed by the Sailors' Maritime Service. When they expressed dissatisfaction with their jobs, their employer offered them a new contract whereby they would receive a 10 percent bonus on company profits if they remained with the firm. At times they discussed the terms of the new agreement with an official of Sailors' Maritime. Eventually, they decided that the offer was a good one, and they continued on the job as usual. Sailors' Maritime later refused to pay the 10 percent bonus, claiming that its offer had never been accepted. The court ruled this scenario to be a unilateral agreement and that their performance in remaining with Sailors' Maritime constituted acceptance.

In bilateral contracts, unlike unilateral ones, the offeree must communicate acceptance to the offeror. Bilateral contracts consist of a promise by one party in return for a promise by the other. Until the offeree communicates a willingness to be bound by a promise, there is no valid acceptance.

EXAMPLE 8-5:   When Does a Bilateral Agreement Go into Effect?

Suppose in the previous example, Sailors' Maritime had said to Barnes and Layton, "We will consider your written acceptance of this new proposal as binding us to the payment of the 10 percent bonus." There would have been the intention of creating a bilateral contract, supported by mutual promises by both Sailors' Maritime on the one hand and Barnes and Layton on the other.

Communication of Acceptance

Communication of acceptance of an offer may be either express or implied. In an express acceptance, the offeree chooses any method of acceptance, unless the offer states that the acceptance must be made in a particular manner. A stipulation such as "reply by fax" or "reply by e-mail" included in the offer must be carried out to achieve acceptance.

Face-to-Face and Telephone Communication   No special problem as to the timing of acceptance usually arises if the parties are dealing face-to-face. The acceptance becomes complete and effective as soon as the offeror hears the words of acceptance

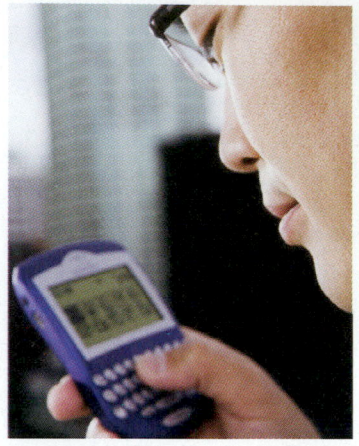

The offer can dictate the form of acceptance required. If using an e-mail or text message to accept an offer, always follow up with a written and signed correspondence to create a permanent record.

spoken by the offeree. In a similar vein, if the parties are negotiating over the telephone, the acceptance becomes effective when the offeree speaks the words of acceptance into the telephone receiver (see Table 8-2). When the parties negotiate by mail, telegram, private courier, e-mail, or fax, problems may arise, and the law provides certain rules as to when acceptance occurs.

Long-Distance Communication Under traditional common law principles, if a long-distance acceptance is made by an authorized method of communication, the acceptance is effective when it is sent. An authorized means of communication is one that has been endorsed by the offeror. The endorsement can be made either expressly or by implication. An acceptance is expressly endorsed by the offeror if he or she specifies the means of acceptance to be used by the offeror. Under traditional common law rules, an authorization of an acceptance is implied when the offeree accepts by the same means or by a means that is faster than that used to make the offer. Thus, an offer made through the mail is accepted when the acceptance is mailed or sent by a faster means such as a private courier (DHL, FedEx, or UPS), a fax, a phone call, an e-mail, or an in-person visit.

Text Messages Text-messages have become an integral, accepted method of communicating in many people's daily routine. It is quite common for people to "text" one another about informal, personal matters. However, texting business colleagues is another matter entirely. While text messages are efficient and fast, they are also, by nature and design, without detailed content. These shortcomings probably explain why texting is still not the usual way to communicate in the business world. Nevertheless, should an offeror ask for a text message acceptance, the offeree should not hesitate to respond as requested. An acceptance will be valid when sent if the offeree uses a technique requested or endorsed by the offeror. However, it is also good practice to follow up such an acceptance with something more detailed and more permanent, such as a confirmation letter.

The Uniform Commercial Code It is important to remember that contract law is affected by changes made by the Uniform Commercial Code. The UCC was written by a

---

Table 8-2 Communication of Acceptance

Method Used	Legal Effect
Face-to-face communication	Acceptance is complete and effective when offeror hears the words of acceptance.
Telephone communication	Acceptance is complete and effective when offeror hears the words of acceptance.
Text messages	Acceptance is complete when text message is sent, if offeror has asked for a text response. If not, the acceptance is complete when sent, only if a text message is faster than the requested method.
Authorized means of communication	Acceptance is complete and effective when given by that same medium (e.g., mailed offer is accepted when acceptance is dropped in the mail).
Acceptance improperly dispatched	Acceptance is complete and effective when it actually reaches offeror.

group of legal experts known as the National Conference of Commissioners on Uniform State Laws. The NCCUSL is made up of legal experts, including attorneys, judges, and law professors. These experts also review legal developments in all 50 states. These specialists then condense the law as it appears in the states into a series of precise model codes. The model codes are in a form that can be directly enacted into law by the various state legislatures. The model code that most concerns us in contract law is the Uniform Commercial Code, and the section of that code that is most crucial is Article 2, which covers the sales of goods.

The UCC asserts that a contract comes into existence if any reasonable means is used to communicate the acceptance. The UCC is quite explicit in noting that to establish a contract for the sale of goods, unless otherwise indicated by the offeror or by the circumstances, the offeree may accept the offer in any manner and by any medium that is reasonable. A contract for the sale of goods then comes into existence when the acceptance is sent, as long as the method used to send it is reasonable. The actual text of this rule is found in UCC 2-206 (1) (a).

Unequivocal Acceptance

To be effective, an acceptance must be *unequivocal,* which means that the acceptance must not change any of the terms stated in the offer. Under common law, this requirement is known as the mirror image rule.

The Mirror Image Rule Under the **mirror image rule,** the terms as stated in the acceptance must exactly "mirror" the terms in the offer. If the acceptance changes or qualifies the terms in the offer, it is not an acceptance. A qualified acceptance is actually a counteroffer. A **counteroffer** is a response to an offer in which the terms of the original offer are changed. No agreement is reached unless the counteroffer is accepted by the original offeror.

EXAMPLE 8-6:   When Must an Acceptance Mirror the Offer?

Susan Mowry, chairperson of the board of Oakcrest Properties, LLC, offered to purchase an apartment building on Parkview Avenue from Enduring Dreams Developers, Inc., for $42 million. The managers of Enduring Dreams said that the deal sounded good to them and they were ready to finalize the details immediately, but they needed at least $47 million for the property. Under the mirror image rule, despite all of the positive rhetoric offered by the management of Enduring Dreams, they really have not made an acceptance. What they have done under the mirror image rule is made a counteroffer. Mowry and Oakcrest are now free to accept or reject Enduring Dream's counteroffer or to make a new offer.

UCC 2-207 (see page 961)

Counteroffers Under the UCC The UCC has changed the mirror image rule for sale-of-goods contracts. Under the UCC, as long as there is a definite expression of acceptance, a contract will come into existence, even if an acceptance has different or additional terms. If the parties are not both merchants, the different or additional terms are treated as proposals for additions to the contract. If both parties are merchants however, the different or additional terms become part of the contract unless (1) they make an important difference to the contract, (2) the offeror objects, or (3) the offer limits acceptance to its terms. This exception is discussed further in Chapter 15.

Implied Acceptance

Acceptance may result from the conduct of the offeree. Actions and gestures may indicate the offeree's willingness to enter into a binding agreement.

Unordered merchandise delivered by mail can be treated as a gift by the recipient. If delivered by an agency other than the post office, individual state rules will differ.

Mailing of Unordered Merchandise Delivery of unordered merchandise through the mail is now considered nothing more than an offer to sell. In the past, unethical sellers attempted to treat the failure of the recipient to either return the goods or send money as an implied acceptance of the offer to sell goods. Complaints were made that this practice allowed unethical firms to use the mail to defraud consumers and saddle recipients with unwanted merchandise. These complaints led to corrective regulations that are now incorporated into the Postal Reorganization Act of 1970. According to this act, the recipient of unordered merchandise delivered through the mail may treat such goods as a gift. The receiver has no obligation to pay for or return the goods or to communicate with the sender in any way.

Unordered Goods Not Delivered by Mail When unordered goods are delivered by agencies other than the post office, the common law rule is usually followed. In general, the receiver is not obligated to contact the sender or pay for the goods. There is an implied obligation to retain the goods and give them reasonable care over a reasonable period of time. After that time, the receiver may consider that the sender no longer claims the goods and may use or dispose of them as desired. Some states, however, have laws similar to the postal law that allows recipients of unordered goods to consider them a gift no matter how they were delivered.

Silence as Acceptance

As a general rule, in most situations, the offeror cannot bind the offeree just by declaring that the offeree's silence will signal an acceptance. However, should both parties agree that silence on the part of the offeree will be regarded as an acceptance, then the offeree's silence would operate as a valid acceptance.

EXAMPLE 8-7:   When Will Silence Be Acceptance?

Sarah Jameson read an advertisement in *The Independent* inviting her to become a member of the New Era DVD Club. Jameson chose several DVDs that were listed in the advertisement. She paid only $1 for those DVDs and became a member of the DVD club. In doing so, she also agreed to purchase four more DVDs in a year's time. Under terms clearly specified in the advertisement, Jameson knew she would receive a brochure 12 times a year listing selections. The brochure would also identify the main selections, which would be sent to her automatically unless she sent a reply form to stop the shipment. In effect, Jameson agreed that whenever she did not return the reply card, her silence would amount to acceptance of the main selections.

Another exception to the general rule occurs when the offeree has allowed silence to act as an acceptance. The offeror cannot force the offeree into a contract by saying silence

A Question of Ethics

Suppose, after conducting a survey that revealed most people did not know about their rights under the Postal Reorganization Act, a company began a mailing campaign that sent unordered merchandise to certain targeted groups. Would such a move be ethical? Explain.

will mean acceptance. The offeree, however, can force the offeror into a contract if the offeror set up the silence condition.

EXAMPLE 8-8:   Who Can Make Silence Acceptance?

Jason Riley wanted to sell his 1962 Volkswagen. He wrote a letter to Rita Tenpenny offering to sell the Volkswagen to Tenpenny for $25,000. Riley ended the letter by stating, "If I don't hear from you by December 3 of this year, I will take your silence to mean you accept my offer." Tenpenny received the letter and did not reply. Although Riley could not bind Tenpenny to this contract, Tenpenny could hold Riley to his offer because Riley set up the silence condition himself.

Rejection of an Offer

A **rejection** comes about when an offeree expresses or implies a refusal to accept an offer. Rejection terminates an offer and all negotiations associated with it. Further negotiations could commence with a new offer by either party or a renewal of the original offer by the offeror. Rejection is usually achieved when communicated by the offeree.

Quick Quiz 8-2 True or False?

1. An authorized means of communication is one that has been endorsed by the offeror. *F*

2. Bilateral contracts consist of a promise by one party in return for a promise by the other. *T*

3. Delivery of unordered merchandise through the U.S. mail is an offer to sell. *F*

8-3 Revocation of an Offer

A **revocation** is the calling back of the offer by the offeror. With the exception of an option contract and a firm offer (discussed subsequently), an offer may be revoked any time before it has been accepted. The offeror has this right, despite what might appear to be a strong moral obligation to continue the offer. An offer may be revoked by the following methods and circumstances:

- Communication
- Death or insanity of the offeror
- Automatic revocation
- Destruction of the subject matter
- Passage of time
- Subsequent illegality of the contract

Revocation by Communication

An offer may be revoked by the offeror by communicating that intention to the offeree before the offer has been accepted. Revocation is ineffective if the acceptance has already been communicated, such as by mailing the acceptance in response to a mailed offer. Direct communication of revocation is not required if the offeree knows about the offer's withdrawal by other means.

EXAMPLE 8-9:   When Is a Revocation Not a Revocation?

Michael Sukarno offered to sell a painting entitled *The Pond at Ville d'Array* by the French artist Camille Corot to Arthur Kroeber for $987,000. It was mutually agreed that the offer would remain open for five days. Three days later, Kroeber read that Sukarno had sold the painting to the Rothman International Galleries for $1,200,000. Having learned of the sale, Kroeber would be aware that the offer had been withdrawn and at that point he could not accept. Suppose in this same case that the offer had been made in a letter received by Kroeber and, before any news of the sale to the Rothman International Galleries reached Kroeber, he had mailed a letter of acceptance to Sukarno. Although the acceptance may not reach Sukarno for another day, acceptance was complete upon the mailing of the letter, and revocation would not apply.

Automatic Revocation

When the terms of an offer include a definite time limit for acceptance, the offer is automatically revoked at the expiration of the time stated.

EXAMPLE 8-10:   When Can an Offer Be Revoked by Remote Control?

Uma Craig had just finished her new novel, *The Counterfeit Impostor*, when she offered to sell full publishing rights to Orascom Publishing for $25 million. Craig gave Orascom until May 20 to accept the offer. When Orascom did not accept Craig's offer by midnight on May 20, the offer was automatically revoked. Craig was not required to honor Orascom's acceptance on May 21. Instead, she was free to make a new offer to Orascom or to any other publisher.

Revocation by Passing of Time

When no time limit has been set, an offer will revoke automatically after the passing of a reasonable length of time. The time element is determined through a review of all facts and surrounding circumstances. Perishable characteristics of goods, price fluctuations, supply-and-demand factors, and other surrounding circumstances contribute to establish the reasonable time factor. For example, communicating an offer by fax or e-mail rather than by letter would ordinarily imply the need for haste in making acceptance.

Revocation by Death or Insanity

Death or insanity of an offeror automatically revokes an offer that has not yet been accepted. Both death and insanity preclude the possibility of a meeting of the minds. Revocation in both situations is immediate. Communication to the offeree is not required.

Revocation by Destruction

Destruction of subject matter related to an offer automatically revokes that offer. Destruction of the subject matter removes any possibility of performing an anticipated agreement.

Revocation by Subsequent Illegality

Restrictive legislation that would make performing an anticipated agreement illegal automatically revokes an existing offer. Any agreement resulting from an attempted acceptance of such offers would be unenforceable.

Quick Quiz 8-3 True or False?

1. A revocation is the calling back of the offer by the offeror. T

2. When the terms of an offer specify a time limit, the offer is automatically revoked by the expiration of that time limit. T

3. Destruction of the subject matter related to the offer never revokes that offer. F

8-4 Option Contracts

An **option contract** is an agreement that binds an offeror to a promise to hold open an offer for a predetermined or reasonable length of time. In return for this agreement to hold the offer open, the offeror receives money or something else of value from the offeree. Parties to an option contract often agree that the consideration may be credited toward any indebtedness incurred by the offeree in the event that the offer is accepted. Should the offeree fail to take up the option however, the offeror is under no legal obligation to return the consideration. An option contract removes the possibility of revocation through death or insanity of the offeror. The offeree who holds an option contract may demand acceptance by giving written notice of acceptance to the executor or administrator of the deceased offeror's estate or to the offeror's legally appointed guardian.

> **About the Law**
> Although the Ch'ing Dynasty, which ruled China from 1644 to 1911, codified the law of criminal offenses, it left civil law, for the most part, in the hands of the family and clan.

EXAMPLE 8-11:   Who Controls an Option Agreement?

Takashi Osaka offered to sell Andras Galai a collection of rare Japanese prints for $755,000. Galai requested time to consider the offer, and Osaka agreed to hold the collection for Galai for one week in return for Galai's payment of $755. Osaka died several days later. When Galai tendered the $755,000, the executor refused to deliver the collection, claiming that death had revoked the offer. The court ruled otherwise, with judgment given to the offeree based on the option agreement between Galai and the deceased.

Firm Offers and Sale of Goods Contracts

A special rule that involves the creation of a firm offer has been developed under the Uniform Commercial Code (UCC). A **firm offer** is created when a merchant agrees in writing to hold an offer open. Under this condition, no consideration is needed to hold that offer open. A firm offer may be made for a specified period of time. If no time limit is specified, then the offer may remain open for a reasonable amount of time. However, the upper limit for a firm offer is three months. Remember that a firm offer under the UCC involves only sale-of-goods contracts.

UCC 2-205 (see page 961)

Lease Options and Real Property Contracts

A **lease option** is a contract that permits a party to lease real property while at the same time holding an option to purchase that property. Generally, to hold open the option to purchase the leased property, the person leasing the property will make an additional deposit beyond the amount that an ordinary renter would make, so that he or she retains the opportunity to purchase that property at a later time. Because a lease option involves two separate contracts, the lease contract and the option contract, it is often divided into two documents. The lease contract will detail the terms of the lease, whereas the option contract will outline the terms under which the renter can exercise the option to purchase the property.

Quick Quiz 8-4 True or False?

1. An option contract is an agreement that binds an offeror to a promise to hold an offer open. T

2. Firm offers are outlawed by the Uniform Commercial Code. F

3. Option contracts do not remove the possibility of a revocation through the insanity of the offeror. F

8-5 Offer and Acceptance in Electronic Contract Law

As is true of most areas of the law, contract law, in general, and the law of offer and acceptance, in particular, have been affected by the use of computers in commercial settings. In many situations, the courts have taken orthodox laws that govern contracts and applied them to **electronic contracts** or **e-contracts**, that is, to contracts that are made using computers either via e-mail or the Internet or contracts that involve computer-related products such as databases and software. This application is true of the law as represented in the Uniform Commercial Code and the Restatement (Second) of Contracts. In addition, the courts must also be aware of several new approaches to e-contract law as represented by federal law and by the model codes written by the National Conference of Commissioners on Uniform State Laws. The new rules are found in the federal Electronic Signatures in Global and National Commerce Act (E-Sign Act), the Uniform Electronic Transactions Act, and the Uniform Computer Information Transactions Act.

The E-Sign Act

The E-Sign Act was passed by Congress several years ago and represents an effort by the national legislature to make certain that commercial e-documents are given the same credence as their paper counterparts. Simply stated, the act provides that e-contracts that are entered into over the Internet or via e-mail will be valid, provided that the parties to the e-contract have agreed that electronic signatures will be used. As long as the e-contract can be duplicated and stored, it will have the same validity as a paper contract. The act expressly applies to Article 2 (Sale of Goods Contracts) and Article 2A (Leases) of the UCC.

The Uniform Electronic Transactions Act

The Uniform Electronic Transactions Act (UETA) was written by the NCCUSL to ensure that e-contracts are given the same legal effect as their paper equivalents. The act does not create any new rules applying to offer, acceptance, assent, consideration, capacity, and legality but instead makes certain that the laws that govern these elements apply to e-contracts just as they apply to paper contracts. There are three basic elements under the UETA. First, the participants must concur on the use of an electronic medium to create their contractual relationship.

This agreement is usually not a problem, because the parties to an e-contract are generally aware of the nature of their relationship when they sit down at a computer. Second, once the first requirement is met, the act says that the electronic record generated by the computerized transaction will have the same weight that a paper document would have in a traditional transaction. Third, once the first requirement is met, the act acknowledges that an electronic signature is just as effective as a written signature on a paper document.

The Uniform Computer Information Transactions Act

The Uniform Computer Information Transactions Act (UCITA) arose when the NCCUSL and the ALI attempted to revise Article 2 (Sale of Goods Contracts) and Article 2A (Leases) of the UCC. Revising these articles to meet the demands of e-commerce and e-contractual relationships proved very difficult. In fact, the attempt was so difficult that the ALI dropped out of the process altogether, leaving the NCCUSL on its own. The NCCUSL then elected to write an entirely new act that came to be known as UCITA. One of the problems encountered by the NCCUSL in the writing of the new act was that many of the contracts that are entered into in cyberspace are more akin to licensing agreements than sale-of-goods contracts. The UCITA therefore covers such diverse areas as database contracts, software licensing agreements, customized software formulation, and the rights to multimedia commodities.

Many of the legal questions associated with Internet-made e-contracts are answered by the new act. For example, Section 102 of UCITA makes it clear that a license is to be considered "a contract that authorizes access to, or use, distribution, performance, modification, or reproduction of, information or information rights, but expressly limits the access or uses authorized or expressly grants fewer than all rights in the information, whether or not the transferee has title to a licensed copy." The UCITA has unified, streamlined, and refined the legal principles regarding such diverse areas as reverse engineering, consumer protection, shrinkwrap licenses, fair use, and consumer warranties. Despite all of this effort, the UCITA has been an extremely controversial act because many groups see it as increasing the rights and protections of software manufacturers rather than those of consumers.

Offer and Acceptance in Cyberspace

In addition to the terms included in most other offers, an electronic offeror should insert the following terms in his or her offer: (1) payment criteria, (2) remedies that can be used by the offeree, (3) refund policies, (4) return procedures, (5) dispute settlement instructions, (6) the applicability of cybersignatures, (7) liability disclaimers if needed, and (8) provisions relating to the offeree's manner of acceptance. In general, the offeree's acceptance in an e-contract is referred to as a "click-on" acceptance or a "click-on" agreement. A **click-on acceptance** or a **click-on agreement** is one that is created by having a party click on a box on the computer screen that states he or she agrees to be bound by the terms of the contract. Otherwise, it is important to recall that, as explained previously, when the agreement deals with goods, the provisions of Article 2 of the UCC will apply.

Quick Quiz 8-5 True or False?

1. The Uniform Electronic Transactions Act (UETA) was passed by Congress as a federal law.

2. The Electronic Signatures in Global and National Commerce Act was written by the National Conference of Commissioners on Uniform State Laws.

3. The process of accepting an online offer is often referred to as a "click-on" agreement.

Summary

8.1   As soon as the courts attempted to use the will theory to interpret contracts, they could see how challenging it was to establish whether the parties actually agreed to the terms of a contract. Because the actual intent of each party was out of reach, the courts established a formalist approach to the interpretation of contracts. According to formalism, if certain requirements are met, the court concludes that the parties intended to make and accept an offer. Agreement is reached when an offer made by one party is accepted by another party. An offer is valid if it has serious intent, clear and reasonably definite terms, and communication to the offeree.

8.2   The second major part of mutual assent is the acceptance of the offer. Only the offeree has the right to accept the offer. Communication of the acceptance may be either express or implied. Under common law principles, to be effective, an acceptance must not change any of the terms of the offer. This requirement is known as the mirror image rule. The UCC has altered the mirror image rule. Acceptance may result from the conduct or actions of the offeree. However, as a general rule, silence cannot be made an acceptance by the offeror.

8.3   At any time prior to acceptance, the offeror can withdraw the offer. Offers may be revoked by communication, by an automatic revocation, by the passage of time, by the death or insanity of the offeror, by the destruction of the subject matter, or by the subsequent illegality of the contract.

8.4   Some types of offers cannot be revoked by the offeror. These involve irrevocable or firm offers and option contracts. Lease option contracts involve an option to purchase real propery that is occupied by a tenant under a lease contract.

8.5   The principal rules concerning the interpretation and the enforcement of e-contracts are found in the federal E-Sign Act, the Uniform Electronic Transactions Act (UETA), and the Uniform Computer Information Transactions Act (UCITA).

Key Terms

acceptance, 162
auction, 160
auction with reserve, 161
auction without reserve, 161
bait-and-switch confidence
game, 162
click-on acceptance or
agreement, 171
cost-plus contract, 159

counteroffer, 165
current market price contract, 159
e-contracts, 170
electronic contracts, 170
firm offer, 169
invitation to trade, 160
lease option, 170
mirror image rule, 165
offer, 157

offeree, 157
offeror, 157
option contract, 169
output contract, 159
public offer, 160
rejection, 167
requirements contract, 159
revocation, 167

Questions for Review and Discussion

1. How does formalism guide the court in determining the elements of offer and acceptance?
2. What are the three requirements of a valid offer?
3. What is the difference between the acceptance of an offer in a unilateral contract and the acceptance of an offer in a bilateral contract?
4. What is the role of the Uniform Commercial Code (UCC) in the law?
5. What is the mirror image rule?
6. What is the UCC's position on acceptance in contract law?
7. What are the various means by which an offer can be revoked?
8. What is a firm offer?
9. What is a lease option contract?
10. What statutes affect the formation of e-contracts?

Investigating the Internet

One time that many people get involved in an option contract is when they rent a home with the option of later purchasing that same home. This arrangement is called a lease option. Lease option contracts are discussed at length on a Web site called *Your Lease Option: Home Ownership Made Simple*. Access this Web site, read about the nature of a lease option contract, and then answer the following questions: (1) What are the two parts of a lease option contract? (2) What terms should be included in a lease option contract? (3) What resources are available to help in the writing of a lease option contract? (4) What is the role of the "Good Faith Statement" in the closing process? (5) What is the role of the "Truth in Lending Document " in the closing process?

Cases for Analysis

1. An advertisement appeared in the *Chicago Sun-Times* for the sale of a Volvo station wagon at Lee Calan Imports, Inc., for $1,095. The advertisement had been misprinted by the *Sun-Times*. The actual price of the automobile was $1,795. O'Keefe showed up at Lee Calan and said he would buy the Volvo for $1,095. Lee Calan refused to sell the car for $1,095. O'Keefe sued, claiming that the advertisement was an offer that he accepted, creating a binding agreement. Was O'Keefe correct? Explain. *O'Keefe v. Lee Calan Imports,* 262 N.E.2d 758 (IL).

2. The Great Minneapolis Surplus Store published the following advertisement in a Minneapolis newspaper: "Saturday 9 A.M. 2 Brand New Pastel Mink 3-Skin Scarfs selling for $89.50—Out they go Saturday. Each . . . $1.00. 1 Black Lapin Stole. Beautiful, Worth $139.50 . . . $1.00. First Come First Served." Leftkowitz, the first customer admitted to the store on Saturday, tried to buy the Lapin stole. The store refused to sell, stating that the offer was for women only. Leftkowitz sued. Was the offer definite enough to allow Leftkowitz to tender a valid acceptance? Explain. *Leftkowitz v. Great Minneapolis Surplus Store,* 86 N.W.2d 689 (MN).

3. Morrison wanted to sell a certain parcel of land to Thoelke. He decided to make an offer by sending Thoelke a letter. When Thoelke received the letter, he decided to accept. He wrote a letter to Morrison saying that he would buy the land at the price quoted in the letter. Thoelke then mailed the letter. Before he received the letter from Thoelke, Morrison changed his mind and withdrew the offer to Thoelke. When Thoelke found out Morrison would not sell the land to him, he sued. Was Thoelke's letter a valid acceptance, binding Morrison to the sale? Explain. *Morrison v. Thoelke,* 155 So.2d 889 (FL).

4. Wholesale Coal Company ordered 25 carloads of coal from Guyan Coal and Coke Company. Guyan could not come up with 25 carloads. However, it did have 7 carloads available. Before shipping the coal, Guyan wrote back to Wholesale stating, "You can be sure that if it is possible to ship the entire twenty-five carloads, we will do so. But under the circumstances, this is the best we can promise you." When Guyan heard nothing from Wholesale, it shipped the 7 carloads. When Wholesale did not pay for the 7 carloads, Guyan brought suit to compel payment. Wholesale countersued, claiming Guyan had not yet delivered the remaining 18 carloads. Was Wholesale correct? Explain. *Guyan Coal and Coke Company v. Wholesale Coal Company,* 201 N.W. 194 (MI).

5. Tockstein wrote an offer to purchase a house owned by Rothenbeucher. Tockstein signed the offer and personally delivered it to Rothenbeucher. The offer included a condition that acceptance

must be made within 24 hours. At the end of that 24-hour period, the offer would be automatically revoked if Rothenbeucher had not accepted. Rothenbeucher signed the agreement within the 24-hour period. However, he did not deliver the acceptance to Tockstein personally, as Tockstein had done with the offer. Instead, Rothenbeucher delivered the acceptance to his own real estate agent, who delivered it to Tockstein after the automatic revocation time. Tockstein claimed that the offer was automatically revoked when Rothenbeucher did not deliver it within the specified time period. Was Tockstein correct? Explain. *Rothenbeucher v. Tockstein,* 411 N.E.2d 92 (IL).

6. Gina Greenhouse was a representative of the Dollar-or-Less chain of discount strores. In that capacity, she wrote to Louis Bolick and promised him that he would be granted a franchise agreement with Dollar-or-Less as long as he would

follow instructions and advice in preparing to open the store. Greenhouse wrote in the letter that Bolick did not have to reply if he agreed to these terms. Bolick received the letter and, according to Greenhouse's instructions, did not bother to reply. Instead, he began to make arrangements to open his store, part of which meant that he turned down a similar arrangement with Less-Than-A-Dollar, a chain of similar discount stores. Unfortunately, Greenhouse and Dollar-or-Less did not live up to the agreement. As a result, Bolick ended up without any contract, having turned down the arrangement offered by Less-Than-A-Dollar. Bolick sued Greenhouse and Dollar-or-Less. Greenhouse and Dollar-or-Less denied the existence of a contract, claiming that Bolick's silence in not answering Greenhouse's letter could not be construed as acceptance. Are they correct?

Quick Quiz Answers

8-1	8-2	8-3	8-4	8-5
1. F	1. T	1. T	1. T	1. F
2. T	2. T	2. T	2. F	2. F
3. T	3. T	3. F	3. F	3. T

Chapter 9

Mutual Assent and Defective Agreement

The Opening Case
Dunkelman v. Cincinnati Bengals

To raise funds for the construction of Paul Brown Stadium in Cincinnati, the Cincinnati Bengals offered a package deal to fans that would permit them to buy a permanent seat license, giving those fans the right to purchase season tickets each year for the same seats in certain premium seating locations. This arrangement, referred to as the Charter Ownership Agreement (COA), also included memberships in a sports restaurant and several lounges that were not offered to seat holders in other sections of the stadium. The language of the COA clause stated, "Once you have purchased your COAs and the new stadium opens, you must continue to purchase season tickets for your assigned seats on an annual basis to maintain your rights. Failure to purchase season tickets will forfeit your rights to the COA." In exchange for pledging to buy season tickets for six, eight, or ten years, fans received a guarantee that the COA ticket prices would increase only according to a set formula and that they could exit the contract at any time. The plaintiffs relied on this clause and purchased a COA. Years later, when the plaintiffs decided to cancel their COA before their term of years had expired, the Bengals tossed a penalty flag and pointed to the agreement, arguing that once the fans had agreed to purchase the COA, they were locked in to that agreement for the term of years to which they had agreed. Now, the Bengals continued, if the fans did not want the seats, fine, but they still had to pay the amount left over for the time remaining on their contract. The plaintiffs filed a class action lawsuit on behalf of all former COA holders who had been similarly treated by the Bengals' organization. The plaintiffs argued that they had been defrauded (or at least badly misinformed by a series of unintentionally misrepresented facts) by the Bengals, who had led them to believe that they could unilaterally cancel their COA simply by deciding not to pay for the next set of season tickets. The Bengals dismissed this assessment and argued that when the COA holders had agreed to hold on to their seats for a term of years, they had received, in return, a clear promise from the Bengals not to increase ticket prices for those years except according to a set formula. That was enough to bind the fans to whatever term of years they had originally signed on for. The Bengals now demanded payment for all of those years, even if the fans no longer wanted the seats. The court of appeals disagreed and upheld the plaintiffs' arguments, stating that the COA clause in the agreement clearly gave the plaintiffs the right to cancel their COA agreement simply by not paying for next season's tickets. Any other interpretation of such a straightforward clause would be, well, simply unbelievable. (See *Dunkelman v. Cincinnati Bengals,* 170 Ohio App. 3d 224, 2006.)

Opening Case Questions

1. Who is the offeror and who is the offeree in the COA contract? Explain.

2. What type of fraud is alleged by the plaintiffs in this case? Explain.

3. What is the difference between fraud and negligent misrepresentation? Explain.

4. What type of remedy is sought by the plaintiffs? Explain.

5. What other claims might have been put forth by the plaintiffs in this case? Explain.

 Learning Objectives

1. Explain the nature of mutual assent.
2. Identify the ways that mutual assent can be destroyed.
3. List the elements that must be proved to establish fraud.
4. Identify those situations that can give rise to claims of passive fraud.
5. Distinguish between fraud and misrepresentation, and contrast the remedies available for each.
6. Discuss the difference between unilateral and bilateral mistakes.
7. Judge which types of mistakes provide appropriate grounds for getting out of a contract.
8. Explain the nature of physical and emotional duress.
9. Explain the elements of economic duress.
10. Explain how the existence of a confidential relationship is a key factor in establishing undue influence.

9-1 Mutual Assent

As we have seen, the courts are interested in whether contracts have been negotiated and entered into freely. In Chapter 8, we focused on the fact that an offer is a proposal that is freely made by the offeror to the offeree. The proposal indicates the offeror's willingness to freely enter into a contract with the offeree. If the offer is seriously intended, clear and definite, and communicated to the offeree, the offeree may accept or reject it. The second element of a contract is the acceptance. If the offeree accepts the offer freely, then there is mutual assent between the parties. Mutual assent is the third element of a valid contract.

The Nature of Mutual Assent

Mutual assent means that the parties have had a "meeting of the minds." In other words, both parties know what the terms are, and both have willingly agreed to be bound by those terms. Mutual assent may be reached quickly, as in buying an iPhone on the Apple.com Web site, or it may result from weeks of negotiations related to a multimillion-dollar purchase of real estate. Whatever the case, mutual assent emerges from the communication of an offer and an acceptance between the contracting parties.

The Destruction of Mutual Assent

After mutual assent has been reached, the law protects the contracting parties in their contractual relationship. If one party or the other discovers that he or she has been cheated or finds out that a mutual mistake placed the party at a great disadvantage, that party is no longer bound to the terms of the agreement. Each party to a contract is protected from the tricks of the other party or from certain mistakes that may have affected their agreement

and destroyed mutual assent. If mutual assent has been destroyed, the contract is said to be a **defective agreement** (see Tables 9-1 to 9-3). A *defective agreement* can arise as a result of fraud, misrepresentation, mutual mistake, duress, or undue influence. The remainder of this chapter covers each of these potentially destructive forces.

Quick Quiz 9-1 True or False?

1. Mutual assent means that the parties have had a "meeting of the minds."

2. After mutual assent has been reached, the law protects the contracting parties in their contractual relationship.

3. If mutual assent has been destroyed, the contract is said to be a defective agreement.

9-2 Fraud and Misrepresentation

Fraud is a wrongful statement, action, or concealment pertinent to the subject matter of a contract knowingly made to damage the other party. Fraud, if proved, destroys any contract and makes the wrongdoer **liable** (i.e., legally responsible) to the injured party for all losses that result.

The Elements of Fraud

To destroy mutual assent through a claim of fraud, the complaining or innocent party must prove the existence of five elements.

1. The complaining party will have to prove that the other party made a false representation about some **material fact** (i.e., an important fact, a fact of substance) involved in the contract. A material fact is one that is very crucial to the terms of the contract.

2. The plaintiff must demonstrate convincingly that the other party made the representation knowing that it was false.

3. The plaintiff must show that the false representations were made with the intent that they be relied upon by the innocent party.

4. The complaining party must establish that there was a reasonable reliance on the false representations.

5. The plaintiff must verify that he or she actually suffered some loss by relying on the false representation after entering the contract.

A case involving either active or passive fraud must be based on these five elements.

EXAMPLE 9-1:   *Royal International Museum v. Rumbaugh International Galleries*

As director of acquisitions at the Royal International Museum, Sir Walter Osborne purchased two original paintings from Ms. Audrey Rumbaugh, owner and primary sales representative for Rumbaugh International Galleries, an Ohio corporation. The first painting was *Early Morning After a Storm at Sea* by Homer Winslow; the second was *Brittany Coast* by Charles-Francois Daubigny. Rumbaugh told Osborne that she had purchased the paintings from a private collector seven years before, that the paintings were genuine, and that they were in their original frames. As it turned out, most of what Rumbaugh told Osborne was false. The only thing that turned out to be true was that the two paintings were in their original frames. The paintings themselves were clever forgeries that Rumbaugh had purchased on the black market three weeks earlier. Both of the actual paintings were owned by the Cleveland Museum of Art. Osborne and the Royal Museum could sue Rumbaugh for a return of all the money paid to Rumbaugh and for any other damages that resulted from the falsely made statements, because the false statements made by Rumbaugh had been material to the contract. Moreover, Rumbaugh had intended that the false statement lead Osborne and the Royal Museum into the contract, and the false statements did, in fact, lead Osborne and the museum into the contract.

In the Royal International Museum example, all five elements of fraud are present. First, Rumbaugh made false representations about several material facts. In the Royal Museum example, the genuineness of the paintings was clearly material to the contract. Second, Rumbaugh made the representations knowing they were false. Third, the statements made by Rumbaugh were designed to lead the museum representative into relying on them. Fourth, the Royal Museum representative reasonably relied on the statements in the purchase of the paintings. Fifth, the museum actually suffered a financial loss because it paid a top price for two forgeries.

Types of Fraud

There is more than one way to commit fraud. The law distinguishes between fraud in the inception and fraud in the inducement. **Fraud in the inception** occurs when one party tricks another party into a contract by lying to the innocent party about the actual nature of the contract. In effect, because of false representations made by one party, the innocent party believes that he or she is doing "A" when he or she is actually doing "B." For example, if an insurance agent were to tell an accident victim that the paper she was signing was a privacy waiver, when it was actually an agreement releasing the insurance company from all liability, it would be fraud in the the inception. **Fraud in the inducement** occurs when one party tricks another party into a contract by lying about the terms of the agreement to get the innocent party to enter the contract under false pretenses. In this case, because of the false representations made by one party, the innocent party believes that he or she is doing "A," but "A" turns out to be actually "A–" or "A+" or "a" rather than simply "A." If, for instance, a loan officer at a bank were to tell a borrower that the interest rate on the loan would be 8% when it was actually 18%, that officer would have committed fraud in the inducement.

> ### About the Law
>
> While the common law courts of England were quite willing to acknowledge fraud in tort law, they were not as willing to see its application in contract law.

Active Fraud

Active fraud occurs when one party to a contract makes a false statement intended to deceive the other party and thus leads that party into a deceptively based agreement. The false statements made by Rumbaugh to the Royal Museum representative would fall into this category. Thus, Rumbaugh committed active fraud against the museum. False statements about material facts may also include illustrations and models that specifically relate to the description, condition, and characteristics of the subject matter of the contract. These "statements" need not be confined to oral or written representations. Actions designed to deceive, such as turning back a car's odometer or painting over rust spots, are considered statements about the condition of the subject matter of the contract.

The Opening Case Revisited, Part I
Dunkelman v. Cincinnati Bengals, Round 2

Recall that in the case of *Dunkelman v. Cincinnati Bengals,* in exchange for pledging to buy season tickets for six, eight, or ten years, fans received a guarantee that the COA ticket prices would increase only according to a set formula and a promise that they could exit the contract at any time. Or at least that is what they believed they had been assured in the COA clause. The plaintiffs relied on this clause and purchased the COA. When the plaintiffs decided to cancel their COA before their term of years had expired, the Bengals argued that they could not do so because, once the fans had agreed to enter the COA, they were locked into the contract for the term of years to which they had agreed. The plaintiffs argued that this claim was fraud in the inducement; that is, they had been lied to about the terms of the contract when they had agreed to enter the COA. It is fraud in the inducement because they knew they were agreeing to the COA for a set term of years but were misled about their ability to rescind the contract at will and about whether the Bengals would still expect them to pay for the all the tickets remaining, even though they no longer wanted to participate in the COA.

EXAMPLE 9-2: *Rhodes v. Hayden*

Gabriel Hayden owned a motorboat that was docked at the Butler Reservoir. Hayden, however, was about to move to the city and so was anxious to get rid of a boat for which he would have no use in the city. Kelly Rhodes, who was new in town, wanted to purchase a motorboat quickly so that she would have several weeks of summer weather left to enjoy the boat. Sensing that he could make a real killing on the deal, Hayden told Rhodes about the boat. Rhodes was impressed by Hayden's sales pitch, but she wanted to see the boat first and take it for a test run on the reservoir. Hayden agreed. Before Rhodes arrived the next day for the test run, Hayden patched up several obvious holes in the bottom of the boat with putty and poster board. Hayden knew the repairs would not make the boat seaworthy for longer than 15 minutes, but he figured that would be enough time to fool Rhodes into thinking that the boat was in good condition. Deceived by the apparently good condition of the boat, Rhodes purchased it. The next time she took it out on the reservoir, the boat quickly sank. Even though Hayden never actually told any verbal lies to Rhodes, he would still have committed fraud.

To be fraudulent, statements must involve facts. Opinions and **sales puffery** consist of the persuasive words and exaggerated claims made by salespeople to induce a customer to buy their product. As long as the comments are reserved to opinion and do not misstate facts, they cannot be considered fraud in a lawsuit, even if they turn out to be grossly wrong.

EXAMPLE 9-3: *Oldacker v. Kellog Formal Wear Shoppe*

Fran Holiday, a sales clerk representing the Kellog Formal Wear Shoppe, was trying to sell a tuxedo to Ken Oldacker. During the sales discussion, Holiday told Oldacker that the tux (1) came with two pairs of pants, (2) was made of 100 percent wool, (3) had a very rich texture, (4) looked very good on Oldacker, and (5) would make him look like a cross between Ted Turner and Donald Trump. The first two statements are statements of material fact and could be the basis of a lawsuit for fraud if they are proven false. The others are either opinions expressed by the seller or the persuasive puffery that might induce Oldacker to buy the tux and therefore could not be used as the basis of a lawsuit for fraud.

Passive Fraud

As noted previously, active fraud occurs when one party actually makes a false statement intended to deceive the other party in a contract. In contrast, **passive fraud**, which is generally called **concealment** or **nondisclosure**, occurs when one party does not say something about certain facts that he or she is under an obligation to reveal. If this passive conduct is intended to deceive and does in fact deceive the other party, fraud results. In general, a party is not required to reveal every known fact related to the subject matter of a contract. Certain facts may be confidential and personal. For instance, someone offering a DVD for sale need not disclose why it is being sold or how much profit will be realized. Hiding a fact becomes concealment, however, in certain circumstances. These circumstances include hidden problems and fiduciary relationships.

Fraud can occur in many ways. A consumer's best defense is to be knowledgeable, listen, and ask questions.

Hidden Problems As previously stated, in general a party is not under any duty to reveal everything about the subject matter of a contract. However, if the problem or defect is hidden and the other party cannot reasonably be expected to discover the defect, provided the problem involves some material fact, the offeror may be obliged to reveal it.

EXAMPLE 9-4: *Bernstein v. Crowley*

Franklin Bernstein had decided to purchase an apartment building in lower Manhattan near the World Financial Center, which he intended to convert into condominiums. Before finalizing the deal, he visited the building several times with the real estate agent representing the seller, Keyfitz Management, Inc. Each time, Bernstein examined a different aspect of the building, concentrating first on the plumbing, then on the electrical system, then on the heating and air conditioning system, and so on. He also hired Guftanson Contractors Ltd. to make a thorough inspection of the entire building. What Bernstein did not know and could not reasonably be expected to discover was that the foundation had been damaged when the World Trade Center collapsed in 2001. Max Crowley, the actual owner, knew of the damage. However, he did not reveal the problem to Bernstein. Crowley had committed passive fraud or concealment because he did not reveal a serious hidden problem that Bernstein could not reasonably be expected to discover on his own.

Business Law in the News

Is Federated as Flush as It Looks?
A Little Digging into the Numbers Tells a Very
Different Postmerger Story

Ever since Federated Department Stores Inc. acquired May Department Stores in August, 2005, Wall Street has cheered the creation of the retail colossus. Investors have taken heart in the company's rising free cash flow—the cash from operations left over after investments back into the business. Anticipation of large cost savings and increased market share has helped fuel a 43% rise in shares since the deal's announcement in February, 2005. Even a shortfall in first-quarter earnings, reported on May 16, and weak results from old May stores haven't dampened the enthusiasm. Says Federated CEO Terry J. Lundgren: "The merger is not just going well. It's going extremely well."

A hard look at same-store sales and cash-flow numbers, however, shows that it may be too soon for rejoicing. Much of Federated's cash flow stems from the $4.4 billion windfall it got when the retailer sold its credit-card portfolio to Citigroup in a series of transactions in 2005 and 2006. . . . While Federated's net income fell 29% last year, to $995 million, largely because of acquisition costs, cash flow from operations soared, more than doubling from 2004's $1.5 billion. But exclude the receivables sales to Citigroup and make adjustments for the May acquisition, and operating cash rose just $2.2 billion last year and $1.5 billion in 2005. That's much less than the $3.7 billion and the $4.1 billion, respectively, that a quick glance at Federated's cash-flow statement shows. "My concern is that cash flow is being driven by the liquidation of receivables that is not going to recur," says Jeremy Perler, a retail analyst at the Center for Financial Research & Analysis, a forensic accounting firm.

Federated's calculations show its free cash flow up slightly in both 2005 and 2006, even after stripping out the $4.4 billion. Says Chief Financial Officer Karen M. Hoguet: "The company has continued to produce very strong cash flow, and it has allowed us to return significant value to shareholders."

Same-store sales numbers, a vital metric of retail performance, are also murky. Since the completion of the $5.3 billion deal, Lundgren has remade the May chain, closing some outlets and converting others into Macy's stores. By the time the closures were done,

Federated had added 400 stores, bringing its total to 858. But the owner of Macy's and Bloomingdale's has offered little precise detail on the performance of former May stores. Until this February, it didn't include those locations in its calculation of sales at stores open at least a year—a critical measure of performance.

Edward Weller, an analysts at San Francisco-based ThinkEquity Partners, believes leaving out the weaker-performing May stores boosted Federated's same-store performance last year. Since it started including the May stores, Federated's results show monthly same-store sales rising an average 0.4% through April, down from a 7.2% average gain in the prior three months, when May stores were excluded. A Federated spokesman says: "We have provided an appropriate level of detail." CFO Hoguet says Federated didn't break out the earlier numbers because its same-store definition includes only stores it has operated for one fiscal year, and the first full year was 2006. The approach, while a legitimate choice, may not provide the most clarity for investors. It contrasts, for instance, with the approach of rival Bon-Ton Stores Inc., which broke out same-store results for its Carson's acquisition in the first quarter after its 2006 deal. Federated says it's not an apples-to-apples comparison, since Bon-Ton kept Carson's a separate company.

Underspending Troubles

The murky financials could be a concern for investors because Federated has recently boosted capital spending after lagging rivals for several years. From 2003 to 2005, *BusinessWeek*'s calculations show that it spent well below depreciation levels, the benchmark for simply maintaining assets. Macy's rivals J.C.Penney and Kohl's spent much more than depreciation. In 2005, Penney's depreciation was $372 million, and it spent $535 million in outlays. For Kohl's, depreciation was $340 million and expenditures were $828 million. Last year, Federated doubled capital spending, to $1.4 billion.

Federated counters that it is not underspending at all. It says that "marking to market" the stores it acquires—reassessing their value in light of current market conditions—raises the value of its assets and thus increases depreciation costs. Georgia Tech accounting professor Charles W. Mulford, who studies retailers, observes, however, that the new, higher-asset value is a more accurate reflection of replacement costs.

Federated prefers to calculate capital expenditures as a percentage of sales. By that measure, it spent 2.9% of sales on capital improvements in 2005, about the same as Penney. Sleepy rival Dillard's Inc. spent more, at 6%. In 2006, Federated's outlay was 5%.

Getting a true handle on Federated's performance is difficult. But one thing is certain: Federated can't count on more help from one-time events such as credit-card sales. Now it's up to the May acquisition to deliver.

Questions for Analysis

1. The article implies that the 43 percent increase in Federated shares was at least partially caused by the fact that Federated added a $4.4 billion "windfall" into its cash flow figures. Why would the addition of this $4.4 billion not qualify as fraud? Explain.

2. Federated reported an increase in cash flow of $3.7 billion in 2006 and $4.1 billion in 2005.

However, the article points out that when the $4.4 billion "windfall" and the value of the acquisition of the May Company stores are excluded from these cash flow totals, the figures drop to $2.2 billion in 2006 and $1.5 billion in 2005. Why would these bookkeeping discrepancies not qualify as fraud? Explain.

3. Federated does not include sales figures from a store until it has been with the parent corporation for a fiscal year. Apparently, this bookkeeping tactic makes its sales figures look better than they really are. Why is it not fraud to leave out these figures? Explain.

4. One of Federated's main rivals, Bon-Ton Stores Inc., does include new stores in these figures. Which of the two approaches is ethically correct? Explain.

5. Reports seem to show that Federated is spending less than it ought to just to maintain financial health. Yet spokespeople for Federated say the corporation is doing well financially despite this report. Are these spokespeople engaged in fraud or just "sales puffery" on a grand scale? Explain.

Source: Robert Berner, "Is Federated as Flush as It Looks? A Little Digging into the Numbers Tells a Very Different Postmerger Story," *BusinessWeek,* May 28, 2007, 71–72.

Some states have held that sellers are legally bound to reveal only problems so hidden that even an expert would not be able to uncover them. In these states, problems such as insect or rodent infestation would not be hidden problems because an expert could easily uncover them.

Fiduciary Relationships   A **fiduciary relationship** is a relationship based on trust. Such relationships exist, for example, between attorneys and clients, guardians and wards, trustees and beneficiaries, and boards of directors and corporations. If one party is in a fiduciary relationship with another party, then an obligation arises to reveal what otherwise might be withheld when the two parties enter an agreement.

A Question of Ethics

Suppose that you are showing your car to Tim Jorgenson, a potential buyer. You know that if Jorgenson takes your car out for a ride, he will notice that the front end rattles at speeds in excess of 35 miles per hour and that the brakes grind badly. Jorgenson, however, does not take the car on a test drive and therefore fails to detect any defects. Would you have an ethical duty to tell Jorgenson about the car's problems? Explain.

Table 9-1 Agreements Made Defective by Falsehood

Falsehood	Definition	Remedy
Active fraud	Active fraud occurs when one party to a contract makes a false statement intended to deceive the other party and thus leads that party into a deceptively based agreement.	Rescission and money damages
Passive fraud (concealment or nondisclosure)	Passive fraud occurs when one party does not say something about certain facts that he or she is obligated to reveal. Obligations arise in situations involving hidden problems and fiduciary relationships.	Rescission and money damages
Misrepresentation	Misrepresentation occurs when a false statement is innocently made with no intent to deceive.	Rescission only

EXAMPLE 9-5:   San Rafael Motor Corporation v. Groza

Otto Groza was vice president of business and finance for the San Rafael Motor Corporation when he learned that Toth Properties Ltd. wanted to buy 12,000 acres of ranch land owned by San Rafael. Groza was the only one at San Rafael who knew that a new extension of the interstate was going to be located on the acreage owned by the company. Moreover, Groza knew that Toth wanted the land for an outlet mall and an adjoining hotel and was willing to pay $19,000 per acre. Groza made a deal with Toth agreeing to sell the land at that price. He then went to the CEO and the board of San Rafael and offered to buy the farmland without revealing anything about the Toth deal. As a result, he purchased the acreage for $1,000 per acre and made an $18,000 profit on each acre he resold to Toth. Groza will be liable to San Rafael because he concealed a material fact that he was obligated to reveal because of his fiduciary relationship with the company.

The Opening Case Revisited, Part II

Dunkelman v. Cincinnati Bengals, Round 3

In The Opening Case of *Dunkelman v. Cincinnati Bengals,* fans received a guarantee that the COA ticket prices would not increase except according to a set formula in exchange for their promise to purchase season tickets for a set term of years. This promise was written into a contract clause that the plaintiffs relied on when they entered the COA. When the plaintiffs decided to cancel their COA before the term of years had expired, the Bengals said that the contract had locked them into that term. The plaintiffs argued that they had been defrauded by this clause. They also argued, however, that if the action by the Bengals did not amount to fraud, it at least amounted to misrepresentation. In cases like this, it is common for plaintiffs to plead alternative theories. The tactic was used here because though the plaintiffs may know that they were intentionally deceived, they may find it difficult to prove that the deception was deliberate.

Misrepresentation

Misrepresentation is a false statement made innocently with no intent to deceive. Innocent misrepresentation makes an existing agreement voidable, and the complaining party may demand rescission. **Rescission** means that both parties are returned to their original positions, before they entered into the contract. Unlike cases based on fraud, which allow rescission and damages, cases based on innocent misrepresentation allow only rescission, not monetary damages.

EXAMPLE 9-6: *Sanderson v. Straus*

Anthony Sanderson was browsing on eBay when he located what was labeled as a 1932 edition of *Brave New World* by Aldous Huxley, produced by Chatto and Windus, the London publisher that had printed the first edition of that landmark novel. The book was advertised as coming along with a companion book by Julian Huxley, entitled *If I Were Dictator,* published in 1934 by the London publishing house of Methuen. The seller was Juliette Straus, who set the minimum bid for the two volumes at GBP 8,700. Sanderson, who quickly bid on the two books, eventually won the auction with a successful bid of GBP 9,800. Later, after receiving the two books, Sanderson discovered that the copy of *If I Were Dictator* was actually a 1948 reprint of the original work. Without any indication of wrongdoing, Straus would be liable for nothing more than an innocent misrepresentation. In cases of this kind, the parties often renegotiate the purchase price if the agreement is affirmed.

If a party to an agreement makes an innocent misrepresentation and then later discovers that it is false, that party must reveal the truth. If the party does not reveal the truth, the innocent misrepresentation becomes fraud.

Talking Points

In his book, *Rights From Wrongs,* Alan Dershowitz quotes one of his own earlier works, an article that appeared in a 1971 issue of *The Nation,* when he writes, "(w)hen these strands are woven together, there emerges an approach to the limits of martial law that was encapsulated by Justice Holmes: martial law is not 'for punishment,' but rather 'by way of precaution, to prevent the exercise of hostile power.' This distinction between 'punitive' and 'preventative' law runs through the cases and has been echoed by many commentators. But no sharp line exists between punishment and prevention, as Blackstone recognized many years ago: 'If we consider all human punishment in a large and extended view, we shall find them all rather calculated to prevent future crimes than to expiate the past.'" People who commit fraud may be subject to punitive damages. Why are the courts willing to place punitive damages on someone who has committed fraud, but not on someone who has simply misrepresented the facts in a case? If the object of punitive damages is to prevent future wrongdoing, would it not be appropriate to use damages in both situations? Is there anything in the U.S. Constitution that would prevent this type of punishment? Is Dershowitz correct when he endorses Blackstone's belief that the purpose of punishment is to prevent future wrongdoing? Explain your answer to each question. (See Alan Dershowitz, *Right From Wrongs: A Secular Theory of the Origin of Rights,* New York: Basic Books, 2004, 214–215).

9-3 Mistake

When there has been no real meeting of the minds because of a mistake, mutual assent was never achieved, and the agreement may be rescinded. As in misrepresentation, mistake permits rescission.

Unilateral and Bilateral Mistakes

A mistake made by only one of the contracting parties is a **unilateral mistake** and does not offer sufficient grounds for rescission or renegotiation. When both parties are mistaken, it is a **bilateral mistake**. A bilateral mistake, which is also called a **mutual mistake**, may permit a rescission by either the offeror or the offeree.

The Nature of Mistakes

Mutual mistakes are of several kinds. Some are universally accepted as grounds for rescission. Others are not grounds for rescission. Still others can give rise to lawsuits, but not in all courts or in all states.

Mistakes as to Description   When both parties are mistaken in the identification and description of subject matter, there is a real mutual mistake, and rescission will be granted.

Mistakes as to Existence   Proof that the subject matter had been destroyed before the agreement was made gives grounds for rescission. Thus, if one party accepted an offer to purchase a boat that both parties mistakenly believed to be berthed at a specified marina, the agreement would be voidable if it were proved that moments before acceptance, the boat had been destroyed. Had the boat been destroyed after final acceptance, there would have been no mutual mistake, and an enforceable contract would have resulted.

Mistakes as to Value   When two parties agree on the value of the subject matter and later find they were both mistaken, it is a mutual mistake of opinion, not of fact. Mutual mistakes of opinion are not grounds for rescinding a contract.

Mistakes Through Failure to Read Document   Failure to read a document or the negligent reading of a document does not excuse performance on the grounds of a mistaken understanding of the document's contents. Exceptions may be made when conditions are printed on parking lot stubs, cleaner's tickets, hat check identifications, and the like. The law usually holds that these vouchers are given for identification purposes only. The courts generally are not favorable toward enforcing the fine-print conditions on the face or reverse side of such tickets.

Table 9-2   Agreements Made Defective by Mutual Mistake

Mistake	Legal Effect
Mistake as to description	Rescission will be granted.
Mistake as to existence	Proof that subject matter was destroyed *before* the agreement was made gives grounds for rescission.
Mistake as to value	Rescission will not be granted since value is a matter of opinion, not fact.

Mistakes of Law   Misunderstandings of existing laws do not give grounds for rescission. As often quoted, "Ignorance of the law is no excuse." Rescission may be allowed, however, when there have been mistakes related to the law of another state. In this way, the courts interpret mistakes of law of a different state as mistakes of fact, not of law. Some states have now adopted statutes that completely remove the so-called ignorance-of-law concept. In those states, any mutual mistake of law is sufficient to bring about a rescission.

Quick Quiz 9-3 True or False?

1. When both parties are mistaken in the identification and description of subject matter, there is no mutual assent.   T

2. Even if the subject matter has been destroyed before an agreement has been made, the courts will not permit rescission.   F

3. Mutual mistakes of opinion are grounds for rescinding a contract.   F

9-4 Duress and Undue Influence

Both duress and undue influence rob a person of the ability to make an independent, well-reasoned decision to enter a contractual relationship freely. Both of these conditions therefore strike at the heart of contract law. In general, **duress** may be viewed as an action by one party that forces another party to do what need not otherwise be done. Duress forces a person into a contract through the use of physical, emotional, or economic threats. In contrast, undue influence merely involves the use of excessive pressure. Moreover, undue influence requires the existence of a special relationship, generally of a confidential or fiduciary nature.

Age and infirmity can make the elderly vulnerable to duress and undue influence by caregivers.

Physical and Emotional Duress

Physical duress involves either violence or the threat of violence against an individual or against that person's family, household, or property. If only threats are used, they must be so intense and serious that a person of ordinary prudence would be forced into the contract without any real consent. Threats of physical duress are relatively rare today. Perhaps more common are threats that create emotional duress. **Emotional duress** arises from acts or threats that would create emotional distress in the one on whom they are inflicted. It is generally necessary that the action threatened be either illegal or illicit. Wrongful exposure to public ridicule, threatened false attacks on one's reputation, or unjust efforts to prevent employment might constitute emotional duress. It might also create duress to threaten a person with criminal charges or a civil lawsuit if there are no grounds for using such intimidating tactics. However, it is not duress to promise to exercise a legal right, such as bringing a justified lawsuit, should someone not comply with a reasonable request.

LO8

EXAMPLE 9-7:   *Douglas v. Grayson*

Lynn and Tony Grayson contracted with Max Douglas, who agreed to have aluminum siding placed on the Grayson house. As a part of the agreement, the Graysons stated that the house had to be completed by Memorial Day weekend because they planned to have their daughter's high school graduation party at the house at that time. One week before the planned party, Douglas still had not started the project. When Lynn Grayson discussed this delay with him, Douglas said that he was not certain that he could start that week and was relatively certain that even if he did start the project soon, he could no longer guarantee that the work would be done at the agreed time. Grayson stated that if he did not start that afternoon, she would find a contractor who would get the work done on time and would sue Douglas for whatever extra money it would cost her and her husband to get the house sided before the graduation party. This threat may cause Douglas distress, but because it is Grayson's legal right, there is no wrongful duress involved.

Economic Duress

Economic duress, also known as **business compulsion**, consists of threats of a business nature that force another party without real consent to enter a commercial agreement. To establish economic duress, the complaining party must demonstrate the existence of three elements:

1. The plaintiff must prove that the other party wrongfully placed the plaintiff in a precarious economic situation.

2. The plaintiff must show that he or she had no alternative other than to submit to the contractual demands of the wrongful party.

3. The plaintiff must demonstrate that he or she acted reasonably in entering the contract.

If the plaintiff can prove the existence of these three elements, the court will rule the contract voidable on grounds of economic duress.

EXAMPLE 9-8:   *National Air Races Inc. v. Macon City Airport Corporation*

The owners and operators of National Air Races negotiated a seven-year lease with the city of Macon for use of the Macon City Airport. Each summer, during the Fourth of July weekend celebration, the National Air Races were held at the Macon City Airport. One week before the first race of the fourth year under the contract, Macon City officials informed the owners and operators of the National Air Races that they would no longer be able to use the Macon City Airport for the Fourth of July races unless they paid a substantial rent increase. The owners and operators of the Air Races, who had already sold at least 5,000 tickets per race, accepted entry fees from 95 pilots, and had contracts with 20 concessionaires, could not find any other suitable airport within 120 miles of Macon. As a result, they agreed to the terms. Later, the owners of the Air Races sued Macon to have the rent increase rescinded. The court ruled that the rent increase was voidable due to economic duress.

Undue Influence

Undue influence occurs when the dominant party in a special relationship uses excessive pressure to convince the weaker party to enter a contract that greatly benefits the dominant party. A plaintiff who wants to demonstrate that he or she was enticed into a contract by undue influence must prove the existence of two elements.

First, the plaintiff must show that a special relationship existed between the parties. A special relationship can generally be characterized as one that is fiduciary in nature or one that involves domination. Examples of fiduciary relationships include the relationships of

Table 9-3 Agreements Made Defective by Force or Pressure

Type of Force or Pressure	Explanation	Legal Effect
Physical duress	Violence or threat of violence to person, family, household, or property	Contract voidable; rescission allowed
Emotional duress	Acts or threats that create emotional distress in the one on whom they are inflicted	Contract voidable; rescission allowed
Economic duress or business compulsion	Threats of a business nature that force another party without real consent to enter a commercial agreement	Contract voidable; rescission allowed
Undue influence	Dominant party in a special relationship uses excessive pressure to convince the weaker party to enter a contract to benefit the dominant one	Contract voidable; rescission allowed

Did You Know?

It is possible for a party to ratify a contract made under duress if, after the duress has ended, the party makes a new promise to abide by the terms of the original agreement. In such a situation, the party ratifying the contract need not supply any new consideration.

parent to child, guardian to ward, attorney to client, physician to patient, pastor to parishioner, and so forth. Relationships that involve dominance frequently occur when the stronger of the two parties is acting as a caretaker of the weaker party.

Second, the plaintiff must show that the other party used excessive pressure to take advantage of him or her to enter a contract that greatly benefits the party applying the pressure. In most cases involving undue influence, one party in the special relationship has enough strength and leadership to dominate the other party, who is obviously weaker and dependent.

EXAMPLE 9-9: *Armbruster v. McCann*

When Roger Armbruster was 10 years old, he was orphaned and inherited an enormous estate from his parents. Consequently, the court placed him under the guardianship of his aunt, Georgette McCann. Over the years, Armbruster came to depend on his aunt for a variety of things, including her educational and financial advice. After he reached maturity, Armbruster still maintained a close relationship with his aunt. The two of them lived together, and McCann handled all of Armbruster's financial affairs. At this time, McCann began to pressure Armbruster into signing over all his property to her in exchange for McCann's promise never to leave. McCann isolated Armbruster from relatives and friends and told him that everyone had abandoned him and that only she, McCann, cared about him. Convinced he had been completely abandoned by his family and friends, Armbruster signed over all his property. When Armbruster's half-sister found out what had happened, she took up her brother's cause and eventually convinced a court that in his weakened condition, Armbruster had submitted to McCann's excessive pressure in signing over all his property.

Undue influence should not be confused with persuasion or some subtle form of inducement. Although one might be induced to enter into agreements through the urging of someone such as an athletic coach, there is no undue influence if there is an absence of the required fiduciary or caretaker relationship. Persuasion and subtle inducement, while at times unethical, are not considered undue influence in the eyes of the law and do not, in and of themselves, provide a basis for rescinding agreements.

Quick Quiz 9-4 True or False?

1. Duress is an action by one party that forces another party to do what need not otherwise be done. T

2. Economic duress is also known as business compulsion. T

3. Undue influence should not be confused with persuasion or some subtle form of inducement. T

Summary

9.1   Offer and acceptance go together to create mutual assent. Mutual assent means that both parties know what the terms are and have agreed to be bound by those terms. If mutual assent has been destroyed, the contract is said to be a defective agreement. A defective agreement can arise as a result of fraud, misrepresentation, mutual mistake, duress, or undue influence.

9.2   Fraud involves a deliberate deception about some material fact that leads a party into an agreement that is damaging to that party. Fraud in the inception occurs when one party tricks another party into a contract by lying to the innocent party about the actual nature of the contract. Fraud in the inducement occurs when one party tricks another party into a contract by lying about the terms of the agreement to get the innocent party to enter the contract under false pretenses. Active fraud occurs when one party makes a false statement intended to deceive the other party and thus leads that party into a deceptively based contract. The deception can involve an oral statement or an action that misleads the other party about a crucial fact. Passive fraud, or concealment or nondisclosure, occurs when one

party does not say something that he or she is obligated to say. Misrepresentation is a false statement innocently made with no intent to deceive.

9.3   Unilateral mistakes, that is, mistakes made by one party, do not allow for rescission or renegotiation. When both parties are mistaken, it is a bilateral or a mutual mistake. A mutual mistake may allow for rescission by either party.

9.4   Duress and undue influence rob a person of the ability to make an independent, well-reasoned decision to enter freely into a contract. Physical duress involves violence or threats of violence. Emotional duress arises from acts or threats that would create emotional distress in the individual who is the object of the threats or acts. Economic duress consists of threats of a business nature that force another party without real consent to enter into a contract. Undue influence involves a special relationship. In most cases, undue influence involves the dominant party in the relationship applying excessive pressure to the weaker party, resulting in a contract that is of benefit to the dominant individual.

Key Terms

active fraud, 179
bilateral mistake, 186
business compulsion, 188
concealment, 181
defective agreement, 178
duress, 187
economic duress, 188
emotional duress, 187

fiduciary relationship, 183
fraud, 178
fraud in the inception, 179
fraud in the inducement, 179
liable, 178
material fact, 178
misrepresentation, 185
mutual assent, 177

mutual mistake, 186
nondisclosure, 181
passive fraud, 181
physical duress, 187
rescission, 185
sales puffery, 180
undue influence, 188
unilateral mistake, 186

Questions for Review and Discussion

1. What is mutual assent?
2. How can mutual assent be destroyed?
3. What five elements must be proved to establish that a contract is defective because of fraud?
4. What situations can give rise to claims of passive fraud?
5. What is the essential difference between fraud and misrepresentation? How do the remedies for each differ?
6. What is the difference between unilateral and bilateral (mutual) mistakes?
7. What types of mistakes provide appropriate grounds for getting out of a contract?
8. What is the nature of physical and emotional duress?
9. What are the elements of economic duress?
10. Why is the existence of a confidential relationship a key factor in establishing undue influence?

Investigating the Internet

The National Fraud Information Center/Internet Fraud Watch Program (NFIC/IFW) maintains a very active presence on the Web. Access the NFIC/IFW's Web site and answer the following questions: (1) What is the job of the NFIC/IFW? (2) How does someone file a complaint with the NFIC/IFW? (3) What process is followed once a complaint has been filed? (4) What pointers does the NFIC/IFW provide for people to avoid being victimized by fraud? (5) What are some of the resources provided by the NFIC/IFW?

Cases for Analysis

1. Walker and Cousineau were both in the gravel business. Walker placed an advertisement for a tract of land, claiming that he had an engineer's report that indicated the land held at least 80,000 cubic yards of gravel. In fact, Walker knew the land contained much less gravel. Cousineau purchased the land and began to excavate it. After 6,000 cubic yards of gravel had been removed, the supply ran out. Cousineau sued Walker, asking the court to rescind the contract. Did Cousineau win the case? Explain. *Cousineau v. Walker,* 613 P.2d 608 (AL).

2. Young sold a residential lot to Sorrell without revealing that the lot had been filled. The landfill was not obvious, and Sorrell could not have been reasonably expected to detect it. When Sorrell discovered the landfill, he sued Young and asked the court to rescind the agreement. Young claimed he was under no obligation to reveal the fill to Sorrell. Was Young correct? Explain. *Sorrell v. Young,* 491 P.2d 1312 (WA).

3. Boskett offered to sell a 1916 dime to Beachcomber Coins, Inc. Beachcomber examined the coin carefully and agreed to pay Boskett $500 for it. Later, Beachcomber asked a representative from the American Numismatic Society to examine the coin. The coin turned out to be counterfeit. No evidence existed to indicate fraud on Boskett's part. Beachcomber sued Boskett for rescission and a return of the $500. Beachcomber claimed this bilateral mistake of fact created grounds for a rescission. Was Beachcomber correct? Explain. *Beachcomber Coins, Inc. v. Boskett,* 400 A.2d 78 (NJ).

4. Prisoners rioted at the Iowa State Penitentiary and held prison staff members as hostages. The warden agreed in writing that no reprisals would be levied against the rioting inmates. In exchange, the prisoners released the hostages. After the hostages were released, several of the prisoners were punished for the riot. One prisoner, Wagner, was placed in solitary confinement for 30 days. He also received 180 days of administrative segregation and the loss of 1,283 days of goodtime earned. On what legal grounds could the warden refuse to keep his promise to the inmates? Explain. *Wagner v. State,* 364 N.W.2d 246 (IA).

5. Loral Corporation had a contract with the U.S. government to manufacture radar sets. Loral subcontracted with Austin Instrument for the production of precision parts to be used in the radar sets. In the middle of production, Austin told Loral that it would deliver no more parts unless Loral agreed to pay Austin a good deal more than originally agreed upon. Loral could not obtain the same parts in time from any other company. As a result, Loral agreed to the price increase. After delivering the radar sets, Loral sued Austin and asked the court to rescind the price increase. Did the court grant Loral's request? Explain. *Austin Instrument, Inc. v. Loral Corporation,* 272 N.E.2d 533 (NY).

6. Vargas, an artist, had been under contract with *Esquire* magazine for several years. When the time came for a new contract, Vargas met with the president of the company and signed the new contract without reading it. Later, Vargas found out that the contract did not say what he thought it said. He sued *Esquire,* arguing that he signed the agreement only because he had relied on the president of the company to look after his business affairs. Was this a case of undue influence? Explain. *Vargas v. Esquire, Inc.,* 166 F.2d 651 (7th Cir.).

Quick Quiz Answers

9-1	9-2	9-3	9-4
1. T	1. T	1. T	1. T
2. T	2. T	2. F	2. T
3. T	3. F	3. F	3. T

Chapter 10 Contractual Capacity

The Opening Case
Creative Writer or Clever Swindler?

During the spring of her junior year in high school, Jennifer Putnam took most of her life savings, an amount equal to about $1,800, out of the bank and used it to secure a place in the Young Creative Writers' Conference scheduled to be held at Bloomfield University in Westerville, Connecticut, that summer. When the forms arrived from the conference, she placed the number "19" in the box that asked for her age. The conference fee covered tuition, room, and board for 12 days, as well as a spending allowance at the campus bookstore for writing supplies. From the first, it became evident that Putnam was not satisfied with the conference. The classes were too large for her taste, and she did not receive the individual attention that she felt was her due. The online Web site that had advertised the conference had indicated that classes would consist of about 30 students, which turned out to be true, but it also promised private consultations, which Putnam decided were too few and too brief. Putnam never complained to anyone during the conference, other than a few of the other registrants. Instead, when she returned home, she sent an e-mail to the conference director indicating that she was a minor, and as a minor, she demanded her money back. The director of the conference refused to honor her request, and Putnam filed a suit in small claims court. The magistrate held that under common law, Putnam might have had the right to disaffirm the contract and Bloomfield University would have had supply a refund. However, a new state statute had declared that minors who misrepresent their age can disaffirm a contract only if they can return the consideration they received in the contract, which would place the other party back in the position it had been in before the contract took place. Had Putnam purchased a car from the university, there would be no problem. Putnam had not purchased a car, however. She had purchased services that had been rendered and could not now be returned. The magistrate also took judicial notice of the fact that the right to rescind contracts was given to minors as a protective device or "shield" against people who might try to take advantage of inexperienced minors. In the present case, Putnam had used the protection in a creative attempt to rescind a perfectly legitimate contract. In effect, she had used the shield of her minority as a sword to violate the rights of the university. Because the doctrine was not designed to allow minors to take advantage of innocent people, the magistrate had no problem denying Putnam's request. The magistrate also reminded Bloomfield University that it could countersue for punitive damages because Putnam had actually committed fraud against the university and the writer's program. The university wisely decided not to pursue that option.

Opening Case Questions

1. In the contract between Putnam and Bloomfield University, which party is the offeror and which is the offeree?

2. What common law rule did Putnam attempt to enforce in her argument before the magistrate?

3. What is the rationale behind that rule?

4. What initial error did Putnam make that may have cost her the case?

5. Why did Bloomfield University decide not to pursue punitive damages against Putnam?

 Learning Objectives

1. Describe the legal presumption regarding capacity.
2. Explain why the law allows minors to void contracts.
3. Differentiate between the age of minority and the age of majority.
4. Explain how the Constitution affects the age of majority.
5. Distinguish between emancipation and abandonment.
6. Assess the liability of a minor who lies about his or her age.
7. Describe the legal liability of minors in contracts involving necessaries.
8. Identify exceptions to the general rule about minors and contracts.
9. Explain the effects of mental impairment on contractual capacity.
10. Discuss the contractual capacity of drugged or intoxicated persons.

10-1 Minors' Rights and Obligations

The fourth element essential to a valid contract is the legal ability to enter into a contractual relationship. This legal ability is known as **capacity**. Because the will theory of contract law focuses on the free will of the parties, initially the law placed an enormous amount of emphasis on each party's contractual ability. Then when the law shifted from will theory to formalist theory, the law established a general presumption that anyone entering a contractual relationship has the legal capacity to do so. Therefore, someone enforcing an agreement does not have to prove that the other party had contractual capacity when the contract was negotiated and finalized.

However, this point is a **rebuttable presumption**; that is, a defending party has the right to attack the presumption to rescind a contract. Under the current state of the law, for example, contracts entered into by minors are voidable by the minor. The law allows minors the privilege to **disaffirm** (negate) a contract to protect them from adults who might take advantage of young people who do not fully understand their obligations. In effect, the privilege allows minors to get out of contracts they have entered before reaching adulthood. The law therefore protects minors by

LO1

Minors are able to rescind most contracts, however, adults that contract with minors generally cannot.

acknowledging that their immaturity and innocence may hinder their ability to choose freely in a wise and productive way. In effect, this move represents a step away from the purely formalist approach because it recognizes situations in which it would be unfair to hold a minor to an agreement that he or she did not understand as a direct result of his or her inexperience.

EXAMPLE 10-1:   Rebuttable Presumptions and Capacity

Terry Jacquet and Benjamin Olsen entered a contract that obligated Jacquet to sell her DVD player to Olsen. At the time, Jacquet was only 17 years old. Before the DVD player was delivered or any money exchanged, Jacquet changed her mind. Olsen brought suit in small claims court against Jacquet. It would not be necessary for Jacquet to prove she had contractual capacity, because the law presumes that such capacity exists. However, because the presumption is rebuttable, Jacquet could introduce evidence to show that, because she was a minor, she could rescind the contract.

About the Law

A rebuttable presumption is also known as a "disputable presumption."

When a minor indicates by a statement or act an intent not to live up to a contract, that minor is entitled to a return of everything given to the other party. This right exists even when the property transferred to the minor under the contract has been damaged or destroyed. A few states will deduct something from the amount due back to the minor if the goods are damaged. Most states, however, deduct nothing.

EXAMPLE 10-2:   The Case of DeNardo's Damaged Drew

Alex DeNardo was 16 years old when she purchased a set of 14 volumes of *The Adventures of Nancy Drew* from BuytheBook, Inc. The set cost $849. After having the volumes in her possession for three days, she decided to return the books to BuytheBook. On the way to the store, DeNardo dropped several volumes into a puddle of water, causing extensive damage to those volumes. Clyde Thistle, the store manager, said it would take $400 to repair the damaged volumes, and even then, they would no longer be in mint condition, which they had been when DeNardo purchased them. Most states would allow DeNardo a full refund of $849, despite the damaged condition of the volumes. A few states would deduct $400.

Definition of Minority

Minority, under common law, was a term that described persons who had not yet reached the age of 21 years. Upon reaching that age, a person was said to have reached **majority**. Ratification and adoption of the Twenty-Sixth Amendment to the U.S. Constitution in 1971 lowered the voting age in federal elections from 21 to 18 years. To avoid the confusion that would result from having two voting ages, the states started to enact new laws that enabled 18-year-olds to vote in state and local elections. Then states began to lower the age of majority to 18 years for certain types of contracts. Still, there are other age requirements that differ from state to state in relation to matters such as the legal ability to purchase alcoholic beverages, enter a marriage, buy tobacco products, and operate motor vehicles. Recently, for instance, in response to outside influences from a variety of social organizations and governmental institutions, many states have raised the legal age for purchasing and consuming alcohol to 21 years.

U.S. Const. Amendment 26 (see page 953).

Legal Age In some states, a person becomes an adult at the beginning of the day before his or her 18th (or in Nebraska his or her 19th) birthday. This strange quirk in the law occurs because the day on which a person is born is counted as the first day of life. Therefore, because the law does not consider fractions of days, on a person's 18th (or 19th) birthday, the person is really 18 (or 19) years and one day old.

EXAMPLE 10-3:   Limitations of the "Day Before Rule"

Simon Kodera was born on September 9. State law required people to be 21 years before they could purchase and consume alcoholic beverages. Because Kodera actually becomes 21 at any time on September 8, he would be legally allowed to celebrate at the local tavern on that date. Few bartenders and tavern owners know this rule though, and so from a practical, not a legal, point of view, Kodera would still probably have to wait until September 9 for his first (legal) drink.

Emancipation and Abandonment In some jurisdictions, minors who become emancipated, that is, no longer under the control of their parents, are responsible for their contracts. This responsibility means that they cannot void a contract, despite their apparent minority. Emancipated minors include those who are married, those in the armed forces, and those who leave home and, in the process, give up all right to parental support. In certain states, minors are even allowed to ask the court for a legally sanctioned emancipation. In any of these cases, an emancipated minor is said to have abandoned the usual protective shield given them. Although minors in these categories are no longer protected from liability on their contracts, merchants are still reluctant to deal with them on a credit basis, fearing that they may still attempt to disaffirm, or repudiate, their contracted debts. Again, for practical, not legal, reasons, merchants often require that minors get the signature of a responsible adult who will agree to guarantee payment of money owed.

Moreover, the hesitancy felt by some merchants in relation to emancipated minors is justified because a few states still hold to the opposite rule, that is, that emancipated minors do not give up the legal advantages associated with minority simply because they leave home or become married. To support this position, the courts in these jurisdictions note that the rule that allows minors to rescind contracts is based on the idea that minors are less experienced and less knowledgeable than adults about the consequences of their actions. It is therefore difficult to see why getting married or leaving home somehow bestows more

---

A Question of Ethics

As noted in Example 10-2, most states would allow DeNardo a full refund when she returns the books, even though they have been damaged. Consequently, there would be nothing illegal about DeNardo accepting the entire amount. However, ethically, should DeNardo accept the full $849, or should she acknowledge her culpability and volunteer to deduct the $400 needed to repair the books? Explain.

common sense on a minor who does so. In fact, one court remarked that getting married and leaving home may actually indicate that a minor has less good sense than another minor who does neither. Because this rule differs from state to state, it would be a good idea to check on the rule of law in your jurisdiction.

Misrepresentation of Age

Minors sometimes lie about their age when making a contract. Despite this misrepresentation of age, most states will allow the minor to disaffirm or get out of the contract. From one perspective, this allowance makes sense, because the theory that supports a minor's right to rescind a contract is based on the idea that the minor is immature and inexperienced. The fact that a minor lies about his or her age, in a strange but somehow logical way, actually confirms that the minor is both irresponsible and unworldly; otherwise, he or she would not have attempted to get away with such a lie in the first place. Nevertheless, some jurisdictions do not permit the minor to get away with the lie. Some states require the minor to place the adult party to the contract in the same situation that he or she was in before the contract. Others allow the adult to use tort law, rather than contract law, to sue the minor for fraud. Some states have also enacted statutes that allow recovery against a minor who is engaged in business and who misrepresents his or her age in a commercial contract. A number of states, for example, have statutes that deny disaffirmance if the minor has signed a written statement falsely asserting adult status. Without such a statute, the minor would be allowed to get out of the primary contract despite her or his signature on that primary contract or the contract asserting adult status.

Quick Quiz 10-1 True or False?

1. The law allows minors to disaffirm contracts.

2. Emancipated minors include those who are married and those in the armed forces, but not those who have simply left home.

3. No state will allow a minor to disaffirm a contract if he or she misrepresents his or her age.

10-2 Contractual Capacity of Minors

Executory contracts, those that have not been fully performed by both parties, may be repudiated by a minor at any time. A promise to deliver goods or render services at some future time need not be carried out by the minor who decides not to do so. This privilege is not available to an adult who contracts with a minor.

   If goods delivered to a repudiating minor are still in the minor's possession, it is the minor's duty to return them to the other party.

EXAMPLE 10-4:   Cancelling a Debt the Hard Way

Walt Andrews, who was 17 years old, purchased a new computer from the Alpha-Omega Computer Company. Andrews paid $250 down and agreed to pay the balance in 12 monthly installments. Four weeks later, after he had taken the computer home, Andrews decided he didn't want it any longer. When Alpha-Omega Computer Company refused to take back the computer, Andrews sued the company in small claims court for the return of his down payment and the cancellation of the balance he still owed. In most states, Alpha-Omega Computer Company would be required to make the refund and cancel the debt. Andrews would have to return the computer.

Contracts for Necessaries

Necessaries are those goods and services that are essential to a minor's health and welfare. Thus, necessaries can include clothing, food, shelter, medical and dental services, tools and equipment needed for the minor to carry out his or her business, and even, in some cases, educational expenses. If a minor makes a contract for necessaries, he or she will be liable for the fair value of those necessaries. Despite the general tenor of this principle, if the necessaries have already been provided to the minor by parents or others, the rule does not apply. In addition, not everything that a party claims as a necessary will actually be a necessary. To determine whether goods and services qualify as genuine necessaries, the court will inquire into the minor's family status, financial strength, and social standing or station in life. Necessaries, then, are not the same to all persons.

LO7

Did You Know?

Despite being designated as "necessaries," such things are not always needed to preserve or protect life. In fact, in one case the court held that funeral expenses were necessaries.

EXAMPLE 10-5:   November Necessaries in Newark

Angel Milavec had lived in Hawaii her entire life. Because she had started school one year before everyone else, she was only 17 when she graduated from high school and entered college. The college she attended was in Newark. She had never owned a winter coat, so she purchased one in November from the Hawthorne Brothers Department Store, while she was still 17. This coat would be a necessary, and any attempt to repudiate the purchase would probably fail.

Technically, a minor's contract covering necessaries is not enforceable against the minor in the truest sense of the term. Instead, the minor is required to pay the fair value of the necessaries that have been provided by the adult. The fair value is determined by the court. This approach to the law is an extension of the concept of quasi-contract. Remember that when applying the concept of quasi-contract, the court will require the parties to act as if there were a contract, even though a true contract does not exist. The point of requiring the minor to pay the fair value of the item is to play it straight with adults who carry the risk of dealing with minors in relation to necessaries. Allowing the minor to get away with completely rescinding such contracts would amount to unfair enrichment of the minor. The concept of quasi-contract is aimed at preventing this type of unjust enrichment.

There is an interesting corollary related to the concept of necessaries that many people, including minors and the adults who deal with them, overlook. This corollary is the standard that states that the rules related to necessaries apply only to executed contracts. An executed contract is one whose terms have been completely and satisfactorily carried out by both parties. In contrast, an executory contract is one that has not yet been fully performed by the parties. Wholly executory contracts calling for a future delivery or rendering of services may be repudiated by the minor. Thus, in the foregoing example, had Milavec's coat been ordered but not delivered or paid for, she could have repudiated her agreement with no damages or monetary loss being assessed against her.

Technically, parents are liable for a contract executed by a minor, even a contract for necessaries, *only* when they cosign the agreements. When a parent, or anyone else for that matter, cosigns for a loan or for a contract involving installment payments, the cosigner becomes a guarantor. A guarantor promises to pay the other party's debts if that party does not settle those debts personally. This promise is known as a guaranty of payment. In contrast, if parents do not cosign a contract, they are *not liable* for that contract, even though the contract was made by their minor child. As might be expected, there is an exception to this general rule. If a parent has neglected or deserted the minor, the parent may be held liable to a third person for the fair value of the necessaries supplied by the third party to the minor.

Other Contracts Not Voidable

LO8

By statute and court decision, certain other types of contracts have been excepted from the general rule that the contracts of minors are voidable at the minor's option. For public policy reasons, minors may not at their option disaffirm a valid marriage or repudiate an enlistment contract in the armed forces based on a claim of incapacity to contract. Neither may a minor repudiate a contract for goods and services required by law; for example, minors may not repudiate payments for inoculations and vaccinations required for attendance at a university or college or required in securing a visa for travel in certain foreign lands. They may also be prevented from terminating contracts with banks and other financial institutions for educational loans. Some states bar minors from repudiating agency contracts and insurance contracts. Others prevent them from voiding contracts for psychological care, pregnancy care, the transfer of stocks and bonds, and contracts involving child support. These exceptions are state-by-state issues, so it is wise to check your own state statutes to determine which of these contracts are not voidable by minors in your jurisdiction.

Shield or Sword Doctrine   If tempted to see the rescission rights of minors as unfair, we must keep in mind the original intent of the court in granting this power. As noted previously, the right to rescind contracts was given to minors as a protective device or "shield" against those unscrupulous adults who might try to take unfair advantage of the immaturity and inexperience of minors. This type of situation is precisely what the law envisioned when it granted minors the "shield" that allows them to rescind contracts.

The problem with this protective device is that it can be exploited by minors who use it to rescind legitimate contracts. In effect, an unprincipled minor can take this safeguard, which is meant as a protective shield, and transform it into a sword that violates the rights of the other party. Fortunately, the courts are not oblivious to this type of abuse. Because the doctrine was never meant to allow minors to take advantage of innocent people, the courts have no difficulty denying rescission rights to minors when they use it as a weapon against another contracting party.

About the Law

Under the Napoleonic Code, people under 30 years of age could not marry without their father's permission. In addition, a father could have his child incarcerated for as long as six months on his word alone.

EXAMPLE 10-6:   When a Shield Becomes a Sword

Rene Higgins, who was 17 years of age, purchased a round-trip airline ticket from Transglobal Airlines for a trip from Portland, Oregon, to Daytona Beach, Florida, for spring break. When spring break was over, Higgins returned to Portland and, on arrival, demanded the return of all the money that she had paid for the round-trip ticket.

Her demands were based on her rescission rights as a minor. Clearly, Higgins was using her right to rescind to take advantage of Transglobal Airlines. She was not using her rights as a minor as a protective shield, as the law intended. It is doubtful that Higgins will be permitted to recover money for her ticket.

Voidable Contracts and Innocent Third Parties   Another curb on a minor's right to rescind contracts appears in the provisions of the UCC. These provisions protect the rights of an innocent third party who purchases goods from an individual who originally purchased those same goods from a minor. Although individuals who buy goods from minors have voidable ownership rights, under the UCC, those same individuals can transfer valid ownership rights to an innocent third-party purchaser of those goods. Thus, rescission by a minor will not require the innocent purchaser to return the goods.

EXAMPLE 10-7:   Protecting the Innocent

Daniel Steiner, age 16 years, decided to sell his guitar to Vintage Instruments, Inc. Vintage then sold the guitar to Robert Cline, an innocent third-party buyer. Before Steiner became an adult, he decided to get back his guitar from Cline by disaffirming his contract with Vintage. Steiner would not be able to recover the guitar from Cline by disaffirming his contract with Vintage.

The UCC rule refers to the sale of personal property. In cases in which a minor has sold real estate to one who subsequently sells it to an innocent third party, the minor, on reaching adulthood, may disaffirm the sale and recover the real property.

The Opening Case Revisited

Creative Writer or Clever Swindler? Round 2

In *The Opening Case* at the beginning of the chapter, Putnam was tripped up because she lied about her age in her application. However, the magistrate in the small claims court also took judicial notice of the fact that Putnam had attempted to swindle the university by demanding her money back when she knew (a) that she had clearly taken advantage of the services supplied to her by the university, (b) that she had nothing of value to return to the university, and (c) that she had deliberately lied about her age. The magistrate noted that the right to rescind contracts was given to minors as a "shield" against people who might try to take advantage of the immaturity of those minors. In the this situation, however, Putnam had used the shield of her minority as a sword to violate the rights of the university. Because the doctrine was not designed to allow minors to take advantage of innocent people, the magistrate easily refused to honor Putnam's demands.

Talking Points

If minors can use their right to disaffirm a contract in a way that not only defeats the purpose of that right, but also does financial damage to the other party in the contract, why preserve that right at all? This question lies at the foundation of all rights. In his book, *Rights from Wrongs,* Alan Dershowitz addresses this very issue. Dershowitz asserts that though rights can always be twisted and abused, society is always better off with them than without, because the alternative is unthinkable. Dershowitz puts it this way: "Rights can indeed produce wrongs, because it is in the nature of rights that they serve as a check on the certainty of popular opinions. If rights are human inventions based on our experience with wrongs, then it is certainly possible for human beings to misunderstand the lessons of experience or to fail to recognize wrongs. It is also possible to misuse rights—to hijack them for narrow, temporary, partisan gain. Rights do not guarantee the right outcome. A world with rights is a world with risks, but experience teaches that a world without rights is a world with even greater risks." Can you identify other rights that have been misunderstood and abused in the areas that we've explored so far in this text, such as Constitutional law, criminal law, tort law, and contract law? Elaborate as best you can.

(See Alan Dershowitz, *Rights from Wrongs: A Secular Theory of the Origin of Rights,* New York: Basic Books, 2004, 143.)

Ratification of Minors' Contracts

People may ratify their contracts made during minority only after reaching their majority or within a reasonable time thereafter. **Ratification**, or **affirmance**, is the willingness to abide by contractual obligations. It may be implied by using the item purchased, making an installment payment, paying off the balance of money owed on a previously voidable contract, continuing to accept goods and services being provided under a contract, or just doing nothing about the contract after reaching majority. Affirmation may also result from the person's oral or written declaration to abide by the contract. These acts, as well as others, ratify an existing agreement and elevate it to the status of one that is enforceable against an adult.

Disaffirmance of Minors' Contracts

An individual may disaffirm an agreement made during minority before or within a reasonable time after reaching adulthood. The exact period of time will vary depending on the nature of the contract and on applicable state and local laws. Failure to disaffirm within a reasonable period of time would imply that the contract had been ratified. The method of disaffirmance is fundamentally the same as the method of ratification. Disaffirmance may be implied by the acts of the individual after achieving majority, such as by a failure to make an installment payment. Similarly, an oral or written declaration of disaffirmance would achieve the same end. In general, there are no particular protocols attached to the act of disaffirmance by a minor. However, it is generally a good idea to make the disaffirmance in writing so that there is a record of the transaction should questions arise at a later time. This recommendation is especially true if the contract is disaffirmed after the minor has reached the age of majority (see Figure 10-1).

```
                                17810 Windward Rd.
                                Terre Haute, IN  47811
                                September 9, 20 - -



Spectrum Electronics
433 East 310th Street
Willowick, IN  47812



    Please take notice that I, Andrew Heinzmann, of
    17810 Windward Road, Terre Haute, Indiana, hereby
    disaffirm the contract made on August 19 for the
    purchase of a Kurasaki MP3 player, model S-5293,
    from Spectrum Electronics, 433 East 310th Street
    in Willowick, Indiana.

    On August 19, the date the contract was entered, I was
    seventeen years of age, a minor under the laws of
    Indiana.

    I also demand a return of the $50.00 down payment that
    I gave you under the contract. I will return the
    MP3 player to your store at 1:00 p.m. on September 15.


    Thank you for your understanding in this matter.

                            Sincerely,

                            Andrew Heinzmann

                            Andrew Heinzmann
```

Figure 10-1 Sample letter indicating a minor's disaffirmance.

Quick Quiz 10-2 True or False?

1. Executory contracts, those which have not been fully performed by both parties, may be repudiated by a minor at any time.

2. Ratification is the willingness to abide by contractual obligations.

3. Necessaries are the same for all persons.

Business Law in the News

Barbie Goes from Vinyl to Virtual

Barbie has arrived in girls' bedrooms in coaches and convertibles, on party buses and dream boats, her friend Ken at her side. Now her latest vehicle is a data port, and her newest dream house is online. On Apr. 26, Mattel Inc. unveiled its newest Barbie: a $60 device that connects girls to a new Web site, BarbieGirls. com. Mattel is hoping that Barbie Girls will invigorate the brand and serve as a case study in how a 1950s-era business finds its place in the Digital Age.

At stake is Mattel's newfound momentum. The El Segundo (Calif.) toymaker's stock, a laggard for much of the past six years, has surged by 80% since July 14, in part because of a feeling on Wall Street that even though Barbie's U.S. sales are falling, Mattel overall is doing a better job connecting with tech-savvy kids. Top sellers last year included a $40 Elmo that wiggled across the floor and a $70 digital camera for tots. "Mattel watched products like iPods sell so well," says Sean P. McGowan of Wedbush Securities Inc. "They know parents will spend money if the toy is fun."

The combination of online and offline play is shaping up to be the hottest trend in toys. The most visible example is Webkinz, from privately held Canadian toymaker Ganz. The $11 stuffed animals come with distinctive pass codes that give kids one year of access to a site where they can play games and chat with friends. Ganz says it has sold more than 1.5 million of the critters since their introduction two years ago.

The latest Barbie isn't a doll but a 4½-inch-long gadget that attaches to a PC via a docking station and USB port. When the device goes on sale in July, it will be the only way kids can fully interact with BarbieGirls. com. In this virtual world, girls will create a character they can name, dress, and customize by skin tone, hair style, and expression. They'll shop for clothes and furniture in a virtual mall, using "B-bucks" earned by playing games and watching product promotion videos.

Girls will also be able to chat with friends on the site. Security software will monitor the exchanges and prevents them from giving out names, addresses, or phone numbers that could end up in the hands of predators. The Barbie device doubles as an MP3 player so kids can listen to music when not online. "We've had to redefine what a toy is," says Chuck Scothon, the Mattel senior vice-president in charge of the Barbie brand.

Clearly, Mattel hopes to borrow a page from the online video games, social networking sites, and instant messaging services that are so popular with today's kids. The company has run a Barbie. com site for a decade. Its mix of games, video clips, and product info makes it one of the most popular online destinations for girls, according to comStoreInc. The majority are 6 to 11 years old, many of them former doll buyers who are now likely to say they're embarrassed to play with a plastic princess. On the other hand, more than half of American 6- to 11-year-olds have gone online in the past 30 days, says Mediamark Research Inc.

Digital Duds

How to turn that into cold, hard cash? Mattel will sell snap-on accessories to dress up the Barbie Girls device, much the way people customize cell phones and iPods. But unlike some gaming companies, Mattel won't charge real money for virtual clothes and accessories; its goal is still to sell dolls, not run a Web business.

The competition will be close behind. Isaac Larian, CEO of MGA Entertainment Inc. and maker of trendy Bratz dolls, says he'll launch his own interactive doll and Web site, Be-Bratz.com, later this year. That's fine with retailers. "The more the child interacts with the brand, the more she'll go back and buy the traditional product," says Toys 'R' Us Inc. Chairman and Chief Executive Gerald L. Storch. At least that's the plan.

Questions for Analysis

1. The target market for the online Barbie Girl is six- to eleven-year-old girls. What problems might result for Mattel as it targets a market of individuals who have not reached the age of majority? Explain.

2. How can Mattel protect itself from the contractual dangers inherent in the decision to market the online Barbie Girl device? Explain.

3. What would happen if an 11-year-old girl, who had already purchased the online Barbie Girl device, later decided she would prefer to own the

much newer and more trendy interactive doll for the Be-Bratz.com Web site? Explain.

4. Considering the principle of minority and its possible negative effects, why might marketing a sports or military Web site for young boys be safer for toy manufacturers than the young girl doll market? Explain.

5. According to the article, 50 percent of American 6- to 11-year-olds went online in the last month. What possible negative effects might you predict given this statistic? Explain.

Source: Christopher Palmeri, "Barbie Goes from Vinyl to Virtual: Mattel Is Betting Its Online Barbie Girl Will Hold Kids Who've Outgrown Real Dolls," *BusinessWeek,* May 7, 2007, 68.

10-3 Other Capacity Problems

Persons deprived of the mental ability to comprehend contractual obligations have the right to disaffirm their contracts. Their rights are, in many respects, the same as the rights of minors. Agreements of mentally impaired persons are valid, voidable, or void, depending on the seriousness of their disability and whether they have been declared insane.

Persons Mentally Impaired

Under the orthodox rule of competency in contract law, a contract made by a person who is mentally infirm, has brain damage, is suffering from a physical illness such as Alzheimer's disease, or suffers from a psychological disorder may be voidable if the person's impairment is severe enough to rob that person of the ability to understand the nature, purpose, and effect of that contract. However, mental retardation, a psychological disorder, a physical illness that affects the operation of the brain, or brain damage by themselves do not necessarily reduce a person's ability to enter into contracts. The question will be whether the mental problem existed at the time the contract was made and was so serious that the person did not understand the nature of the contract. If that is the case, the mentally impaired person may disaffirm any contract made under the influence of that mental impairment.

The incompetent person must return all consideration received. Another way to say this is to note that the mentally impaired person must restore the other party to the same position that he or she was in before the contract was entered. This rule is true especially when the other party had no knowledge of the person's mental impairment. If, however, the other party knew about the person's mental impairment and took advantage of that knowledge, there is no requirement to return the other party to the identical place that he or she was in before the original agreement was established.

A second rule is also recognized by the Restatement of Contracts and by some states. That rule says that a person's contractual obligations may be voidable if that person suffers from a mental impairment that prevents him or her from acting in a reasonable manner. This rule goes beyond the orthodox rule, which requires that a person with an impairment must be unable to comprehend the nature of the agreement. Under this version of the rule, a person may understand the nature of the contract but, because of his or her impairment, be unable to stop himself or herself from entering the contract. In such a situation, as long as the contract has yet to be executed or, if executed, can be shown to be very unjust, the impaired person may void the contract. If the contract is executed or fair, the impaired party may still void the contract but also must return the other party to the place he or she was in before the contract was entered. If returning the other party to his or her precontract condition cannot be done, the court will decide on a fair alternative.

Persons Legally Insane

A person declared to be insane by competent legal authority is denied the right to enter contracts. Such persons will be under the care of a guardian who acts on behalf of the impaired person, who has in effect become a ward of the court. Any contractual relationship with others results is nothing more than a void agreement. In most states, persons who knowingly take advantage of one declared insane are subject to criminal indictment and prosecution.

Persons Drugged or Intoxicated

A contract agreed to by someone under the influence of alcohol or drugs may be voidable. Incompetence related to either alcohol or drugs must be of such a degree that a contracting party would have lost the ability to comprehend or be aware of obligations being accepted under the contract. A person who enters into a contract while in this condition may either affirm or disaffirm the agreement at a later time. Disaffirmance in such cases requires the return to the other party of all consideration that had been received. However, such a return may be refused when evidence indicates that the other party took advantage of the person's drunken or otherwise weakened condition.

EXAMPLE 10-8:   Involuntary Intoxication Invalidates the Agreement

Fred Santos attended a private dinner party at the home of David Lampton, an antique collector who lived in suburban Poplar Heights. Unknown to Santos, the punch at the dinner party had been laced with alcohol. After drinking several glasses, Santos became highly intoxicated. While intoxicated, he entered into a contract in which he sold his antique silver set to Lampton. When Santos recovered, he sought to disaffirm the contract. Because his involuntary state of intoxication had robbed Santos of his ability to comprehend the contract he was making with Lampton, he would be allowed to get out of the agreement.

Quick Quiz 10-3 True or False?

1. For a contract to be voidable by a person with a mental impairment, the mental problem must exist at the time the contract was made.

2. A person declared to be insane by competent legal authority cannot be denied the right to enter contracts.

3. A contract made by a person who is intoxicated is completely void.

Summary

10.1   The fourth element essential to a legally effective contract is the legal ability to enter into a contractual relationship. This legal ability is known as capacity. Under the law, there is a rebuttable presumption that anyone entering a contract has the legal capacity to do so. Because the presumption is rebuttable, a party can attack it. Minors are allowed this privilege. Minority means that an individual has not yet attained the age of majority.

10.2   An exception to the rule about minors and contracts involves necessaries. Necessaries are those goods and services that are essential to a minor's health and welfare. Thus, necessaries can include clothing, food, shelter, medical and dental services, tools and equipment needed for the minor to carry out his or her business, and even educational expenses. By statute and court decision, certain other types of contracts have been excepted from the general rule that the contracts of minors are voidable at the minor's option. Different states have different rules with regard to these exceptions.

10.3   Contracts of persons who are mentally infirm or mentally ill, but not legally declared insane, may be valid or voidable, depending on the seriousness of the mental problem. Persons declared to be insane by competent legal authority are denied the right to enter into contracts, and contracts entered into may be declared void. Incompetence related to alcohol or drugs must be of such a degree that the contracting party has lost the ability to comprehend or be aware of the obligations being accepted under the contract.

Key Terms

abandoned, 197

affirmance, 202

capacity, 195

disaffirm, 195

emancipated, 197

majority, 196

minority, 196

necessaries, 199

ratification, 202

rebuttable presumption, 195

Questions for Review and Discussion

1. What general presumption does the law make about a person's capacity to contract?
2. Why does the law allow minors to void contracts?
3. When does a person attain the age of majority?
4. How did Amendment 26 to the U.S. Constitution affect the age at which minors achieve majority?
5. What is the difference between emancipation and abandonment?
6. How do the states deal with minors who lie about their age when entering into contracts?
7. What is the legal liability of minors in relation to contracts for necessaries?
8. What are the other types of contracts that the law may except from the general rule that minors may void their contracts?
9. What is the legal effect of contracts made by persons who are mentally impaired?
10. What is the legal effect of contracts made by persons who are intoxicated or drugged?

Investigating the Internet

Minors frequently do not have a very complete understanding of either their rights or their responsibilities in contract law. One source of information on the Web about such things is the Federal Citizen Information Center (FCIC). Access the Web site for the FCIC and answer the following questions: (1) What are some of the free publications available through the FCIC that might interest young people? (2) What is featured on the Consumer Action Web site? (3) What are some of the recent happenings at the FCIC? (4) What are three of the most popular publications available through the FCIC? (5) What are some of the free online newsletters that a consumer can obtain through the FCIC?

Cases for Analysis

1. After she was married, Sherri Mitchell, a young woman of 17 years of age, was in an automobile accident in which she was hurt enough to require medical treatment. She was later approached by an insurance agent who offered her $2,500 as a settlement. All she had to do was sign a release that would absolve the insurance company of any complaint that she might have against it in regard to the accident. She agreed to accept the $2,500 and signed a release to that effect. However, she then changed her mind and decided to void the agreement. She argued that since she was 17 at the time she signed the release, she was a minor and could therefore void the contract. Is Mrs. Mitchell correct? Explain. *Mitchell v. State Farm Mutual Automobile Insurance Co.,* 963 S.W.2d (Ky. Ct. App.).

2. Ken Olsen, who was 17 and had a part-time job, was in the market for a new computer system. He found a new Macintosh system for $2900 at Macrotex, Inc. Beth Skidmore, an authorized sales representative for Macrotex, negotiated the deal with Olsen, knowing that he was only 17. Olsen paid $900 down and agreed to pay the balance over the next five years. Five days after he had purchased the computer system, Sarah Laurel, the owner of Macrotex, learned that Skidmore had sold the system to a minor. She told Skidmore to get the computer back and cancel the deal. Skidmore called Olsen and told him that she needed to have the computer back. She told Olsen that because he was a minor, she and Macrotex had the right to void the contract. Was Skidmore legally correct in this statement? What capacity, if any, does a minor have when entering a contract?

3. Anne Graham and Ted McCaslin entered into a contract that obligated Graham to sell her CD player to McCaslin. At the time, Graham was only 17. Graham turned the CD player over to McCaslin and received $450 from him in return as agreed. Two weeks later, Graham learned that McCaslin resold the CD player to Vaughn Winston for $550. Graham elected to rescind her contract with McCaslin and demanded that Winston return the CD player to her. Will Winston be obligated to honor Graham's rescission demand? Explain.

4. Sperry Ford sold a car to Bowling when Bowling was only 16 years old. Once Bowling had paid the full purchase price in cash, Sperry turned over the car and the certificate of title. After driving the car for only a week, Bowling discovered that the main bearing was burned out. When Bowling found out that repair costs would almost equal the price he'd paid for the car, he left the car on Sperry's lot and asked for his money back. Sperry Ford refused to give Bowling his money. Was Sperry justified in this refusal? Explain. *Bowling vs. Sperry,* 184 N.E.2d 901 (IN).

5. Quality Motors, Inc., refused to sell a car to Hays because he was only 16 years old. However, Quality told Hays that they would sell the car to an adult and then show Hays how to transfer the title to his name. Hays agreed with the scheme and came back with a friend who was 23. Quality sold the car to Hays's friend. Quality then gave Hays the name of a notary public who would transfer the title to Hays. After the transfer was accomplished, Hays's father found out about the deal and tried to get Quality Motors to take the car back. Quality replied that the car had been sold to an adult, so Hays could not disaffirm the contract. Is Quality correct? Explain. *Quality Motors v. Hays,* 225 S.W.2d 326 (AR).

6. The Bundy family entered a contract with Dalton to add vinyl siding to their house. Dalton assumed that the house belonged to the parents but later found out that it belonged to their daughter, who was a minor. Dalton argued that the siding was a necessary and that the daughter therefore should be liable to him for its reasonable value. Was the vinyl siding a necessary? Explain. *Dalton v. Bundy,* 666 S.W.2d 443 (MO).

7. Lonchyna enlisted in the U.S. Air Force while he was still a minor. Three times he applied for and received educational delays that put off the beginning of his tour of duty. The last time, he claimed he could void the contract, because he'd entered into it when he was a minor. Was Lonchyna correct? Explain. *Lonchyna v. Brown, Secretary of Defense,* 491 F. Supp. 1352 (N.D. IL).

8. Darwin Kruse was a construction worker. He was injured while working for the Coos Head Timber Company. Subsequent to the accident, Kruse signed an agreement with his employer that granted Kruse compensation in exchange for his promise not to sue. Kruse is now trying to have the agreement voided. Evidence introduced proved that

Kruse had an IQ of 83 and that he dropped out of school at age 18. When he dropped out of school, he was in the eighth grade but was doing less than sixth grade–level work. Will Kruse's "slowness" necessarily invalidate the contract? Explain. *Kruse v. Coos Head Timber Co.,* 432 P.2d 1009 (OR).

9. Krasner shared office space with Berk for many years. Periodically, they renegotiated a contract that stipulated how rental payments would be divided between them. Before the most recent agree-

ment was renegotiated, Krasner discovered that Berk was suffering from a serious case of senility that made him incapable of fully understanding the agreement. Nevertheless, Krasner negotiated with Berk, and they entered into the new contract. Sixty days later, Berk was forced to give up his business because of his mental problems. Berk then attempted to get out of the rental agreement based on his mental capacity. Would Berk succeed? *Krasner v. Berk,* 319 N.E.2d 897 (MA).

Quick Quiz Answers

10-1	10-2	10-3
1. T	1. T	1. T
2. F	2. T	2. F
3. F	3. F	3. F

Chapter 11   Consideration

The Opening Case

Pugh v. See's Candies, Inc.

As a young man, Wayne Pugh went to work for See's Candies, Inc., as a dishwasher. He was quickly promoted to candy maker, a job he maintained until he went into the military. After his discharge from the Army Air Corps, Pugh returned to work at the candy maker's plant in San Francisco. He worked his way up the corporate ladder through a series of positions, including assistant production manager and vice president in charge of production. Eventually, as vice president, he was put in charge of the See's northern subsidiary. Pugh's work record was absolutely spotless. He received all scheduled raises, bonuses, and promotions. He was never criticized for his work habits, either orally or in writing. Pugh also went above and beyond the call of duty by attending classes for three years in the evening to further his education in business, taking courses in law, economics, and plant layout. The president of See's repeatedly asserted that as long as Pugh was loyal to the corporation and performed his job well, his future was safe and sound with See's Candies. In addition, the president had a perfect history of never discharging a single administrative employee, except when it was justified. The president's successor continued this policy. At one point in his career, during negotiations with the union, Pugh opposed a plan by which the union and the corporation would agree to a payment process that paid temporary workers less than the competition's employees to gain a competitive advantage. Pugh objected to the plan, calling it a "sweatheart" deal that was unfair to the temporary workers. After a trip to Europe, that was part business and part vacation, Pugh returned to San Francisco, and was called into the president's office in Los Angels and, instead of receiving the promotion he expected, found out that he had been fired. The president offered no explanation whatsoever for Pugh's firing. He simply ordered Pugh to clean out his office and leave. Pugh complied but later brought a lawsuit against See's, arguing that the president's oral assurances to him that his future with See's was safe, the president's past practice of never firing any administrative employee except for good cause, and Pugh's absolutely perfect employment record had created an implied agreement that he would also not be discharged without good cause. The company argued that Pugh's contract was terminable at will and that, as a result, the president could fire him at any time. Pugh argured that the promises made by the president created an implied contract that Pugh would not be discharged without just cause. The trial court found for the company. The appeals court, however, clearly infuriated by the company's treatment of Pugh and convinced that promises that could not be denied had been made, reversed the decision and ruled in favor of Pugh. (See *Pugh v. See's Candies, Inc.,* 171 Cal.Rptr. 917, California Court of Appeals.)

Opening Case Questions

1. What is consideration?

2. Why is consideration so important to a contract?

3. What is *promissory estoppel*?

4. How is *promissory estoppel* similar to the implied contract created in this case?

5. What consideration did Pugh give to See's in return for the promises made by the president?

LO Learning Objectives

1. Explain the term consideration.
2. Describe the different types of detriment.
3. Identify the characteristics necessary for valid consideration.
4. Define the term unconscionable.
5. Explain whether a promise not to sue can be consideration.
6. Explain how a charitable pledge can be consideration.
7. Outline the procedure a debtor and creditor may use to settle a claim by means of accord and satisfaction.
8. Identify those agreements that may be enforceable by a court of law even though they lack consideration.
9. Explain the doctrine of *promissory estoppel.*
10. Relate agreements that on the surface appear to have consideration but that the courts refuse to enforce.

11-1 Requirements of Consideration

In the last three chapters, we have discussed four of the six elements of a contract: offer, acceptance, mutual assent, and capacity. A fifth element essential to any valid contract is the mutual promise to exchange benefits and sacrifices between the parties. This promise to exchange things of value is called **consideration**. If an agreement has no consideration, it is not a binding contract. For example, a promise to give someone a birthday present is not a contract. Instead, it is a promise to make a gift, because the giver receives nothing in exchange for the birthday present.

The Nature of Consideration

Consideration consists of a mutual exchange of gains and losses between contracting parties. In the exchange, a gain by the offeree is at the same time a loss to the offeror. Likewise, the gain bargained for by the offeror will result in a loss or sacrifice by the offeree. The legal term used to designate the gain that each party experiences is that party's legal benefit. Similarly, the legal term used to describe the sacrifice that each party must experience is that party's legal **detriment**. A legal detriment can be any of the following: (1) doing something (or promising to do something) that one has a legal right not to do; (2) giving up something (or promising to give up something) that one has a legal right to keep;

and (3) refraining from doing something (or promising not to do something) that one has a legal right to do. This last type of detriment is known as **forbearance**.

EXAMPLE 11-1:   The Ultimate Forbearance

Raymond Couch, a salesperson for the Taylor Hardware Distribution Company, was chosen as a contestant on a new reality show called *The Ultimate Scare Game*. Couch has planned to spend his four-week vacation on the show. Couch is perhaps the most effective salesperson on the sales force at Taylor. Consequently, Audrey Taylor, the CEO of Taylor Hardware, offered to pay Couch a bonus of $25,000 not to appear on the reality show, because to do so would put him at great risk. Couch agreed and gave up his place on the television program. Taylor would be legally bound to give Couch the $25,000. Because Couch had the legal right to go on the program, his sacrifice in giving up that opportunity is valid consideration. This detriment is known as forbearance.

Note in the previous example that the act of giving up *The Ultimate Scare Game* appearance may be highly beneficial to Couch's health and physical well-being, because he will not be subjected to the tricks, antics, and pranks that are the mainstay of the show. However, the medical and physical benefits do not change the fact that the sacrifice is a legal detriment, because Couch has every right to appear on the show. Each party has received a benefit and suffered a detriment, so the consideration has legal value.

The Characteristics of Consideration

Consideration has three characteristics: (1) The agreement must involve a bargained-for exchange; (2) the contract must involve adequate consideration; and (3) the benefits and detriments promised must themselves be legal.

Bargained-for Exchange
The law will not enforce an agreement that has not been bargained for. An agreement involves a **bargained-for exchange** when (1) a promise is made in exchange for another promise, (2) a promise is made in exchange for an act, or (3) a promise is made for forbearance of an act. The concept of bargaining means that each party will be hurt in some way if the other party fails to keep a promise. Conversely, each party gains something when the promises are kept and the exchange is made.

EXAMPLE 11-2:   Laptop Lending

Joanne Curtis agreed to loan Leo Fletcher her laptop so that Fletcher could give a PowerPoint presentation to a seminar with 15 students. There was no understanding that Fletcher would pay for the use of the laptop. Curtis then refused to allow Fletcher to use the miniature computer. Although Curtis might have an ethical duty to lend Fletcher the laptop, their agreement was not an enforceable one, in that it contained no bargained-for promise.

Adequacy of Consideration
The fact that a contract has legal value is not the same as saying that it has adequate consideration. However, there are no specific requirements, other than being legal, regarding what one party may promise the other party in return for a pledge to deliver goods and services. The promise itself is adequate consideration when it represents something of value. Thus, the promise to assist another to repair an automobile would be something of value promised. The value placed on goods and services need not be street or

The Opening Case Revisited, Part I
Pugh v. See's Candies, Inc., Round 2

When Pugh was fired by the president of See's Candies, he brought a lawsuit against See's arguing that the president could not deny that he, Pugh, had been promised that his job was safe and secure as long as he was loyal to the company and continued to do a good job. The company argued that Pugh would have to show that he had added consideration in exchange for this promise from the president. The court of appeals very explicitly stated that asking the court to make such a determination "is contrary to the general contract principle that courts should not inquire into the adequacy of consideration."

market value. It is important only that the parties freely agreed on the value and the price. In general, the courts do not look into the adequacy of consideration; that is, they do not look to see whether the value of the consideration was fair to both parties. As we've seen, in the wake of the Industrial Revolution, the courts no longer looked to see if the things exchanged in a contract are of equal value. Courts let people make their own agreements, placing their own values on the goods or services exchanged. The court then enforces those agreements.

There are, however, exceptions to this general rule. In one exception, the courts give a party relief when the consideration is so outrageous that it shocks the conscience of the court. A court may refuse to enforce a contract or any clause of a contract if it considers the contract or clause **unconscionable**, that is, the consideration is so ridiculously inadequate that it shocks the court's conscience. This designation usually happens when there is a great inequality in bargaining power between the two parties. In

The price and value of the goods exchanged need not be equal as long as the agreement is voluntary.

Talking Points

Although he does not necessarily endorse the position himself, in his book, *Public Goods, Private Goods*, Raymond Geuss of Cambridge University notes that some people have suggested that there ought to be two ways to determine the value of consideration, one for contracts made with private individuals and another for contracts made with the government. Geuss explains it this way: "What is judged to be 'good,' 'right,' 'valuable' (and alternatively, 'bad,' 'wrong,' 'nuisance') in the public sphere is to be evaluated by different standards from what is 'good' in the private sphere. The standards and procedures for justifying a particular course of action or choice, and the audience in whose eyes the justification must be convincing, are often thought to differ depending on whether what is at issue is a 'private' act (e.g., individual purchase of food for one's own consumption) or a public one (procurement of new trains for the municipal underground or new submarines for the navy)." Do you agree or disagree with the premise that two different rules should apply to consideration, based on whether the transaction is private or public? Regardless of your answer to the first question, which of the two realms, private or public, should be valued higher? Explain.

(See Raymond Geuss, *Public Goods, Private Goods* Princeton: Princeton University Press, 2001, 5.)

very specific matters, usually related to taxes, some states have adopted statutes dealing with adequacy. In general though, courts remain reluctant to disturb the promises made by parties to an enforceable contract.

Legality of Consideration   Consideration requires that the benefits and sacrifices promised between the parties be legal. Absence of legality renders the consideration invalid. Thus, a party cannot agree to do something that he or she does not have the legal right to do. Similarly, a party cannot promise not to do something that he or she has no legal right to do. Also, a party cannot make valid consideration out of a promise to stop doing something that was illegal to do in the first place.

Quick Quiz 11-1 True or False?

1. The fact that each party has received a benefit and suffered a detriment means that the consideration has legal value.

2. The legal term used to designate the gain that each party experiences is the party's legal benefit.

3. Consideration does not require that the benefits and sacrifices promised between the parties be legal.

11-2 Types of Consideration

Generally, consideration takes the form of money, property, or services. In certain special kinds of agreements and promises, however, the benefits and sacrifices are in some manner unique and not immediately obvious to the casual observer. Significant among these agreements are promises not to sue and charitable pledges.

Money as Consideration

Money is so closely connected with global commerce that we forget that it was not always part of the marketplace. The shift from a barter to a cash economy occurred when transporting goods to the market became difficult and hazardous. By the ninth century, the use of cash as a medium of exchange had become prevalent in medieval Europe. This shift to a cash economy was also accelerated by the need for credit. Because goods are perishable and the quality of goods can vary from transaction to transaction, contracts that required future payments were more attractive to merchants when coins rather than goods were involved. Thus, agreements based on credit backed up by coins had become commonplace throughout Europe by the eleventh century, as had the practice of lending coins in exchange for interest. By the thirteenth century, the use of mortgage agreements based on transferring the right to receive all of the cash income from a tract of land had become routine. Today, we are once again in an era of change as we move from a cash/credit economy to one based almost totally on electronic transfer. Nevertheless, when electronic transfers are involved, people still tend to think in terms of cash, even those who have not actually handled coins or currency for some time. For this reason, it is best to always remember that hidden at the foundation of all contracts is the idea of cash equivalency. (See Rodney Stark, *The Victory of Reason: How Christianity Led to Freedom, Capitalism, and Western Success,* New York: Random House, 2005, 60–61.)

Did You Know?

Common law judges would rarely entertain arguments regarding the adequacy of consideration, even in unconscionable situations. One exception involved the promise to repay immediately a greater sum of money than that originally transferred. This is what happened in the case of *Schnell v. Nell,* an 1861 case, in which a man promised to pay $600 in return for the loan of one penny.

BusinessWeek **Business Law in the News**

The Twisted Economics of Harry Potter: The Wizard Brings Both Profit and Pain to His Business Partners

Call it the curse of the Hogwarts. It turns out that—at least for some in the wizarding world—it's tough to make money out of magic. Harry Potter has fans clamoring in excitement as the seventh and last book in J.K. Rowling's hit series, *Harry Potter and the Deathly Hallows*, lands worldwide on July 21. With the fifth movie due out in weeks and the recent announcement of an Orlando theme-park attraction that could cost half a billion dollars, Pottermania is at an all-time high.

But what should be a pot of gold for Harry's business partners is turning into an empty cauldron for many of them. The most successful literary brand in recent history has made its author a billionaire, but others have not fared so well. Retailers, spellbound by the chance to reach millions of Potter-obsessed customers, are cost-cutting for market share to the point where many stand to lose money. For book publishers, the tsunami distorts results in Potter release years, creating wild share-price swings and a distraction from other parts of the business. Even Warner Bros. Entertainment Inc., which has made billions off the Harry Potter movies, saw sales and profits drop last year and in the first quarter without a fresh Potter offering in the mix.

For booksellers, the source of the pain is the mammoth retailers like Amazon.com, Wal-Mart, and Britain's ASDA chain, which have slashed prices by 50% to woo fans. "It's like being in the trenches with the bullets flying over you," says Sonia Benster, owner of The Children's Bookshop in Huddersfield, England. Amazon.com CEO Jeff Bezos concedes that the company won't make a profit from the new Potter book. But he told shareholders that it has racked up more than 1 million pre-orders so far—and, Amazon hopes, plenty of new customers who will buy other books. Because of such struggles for a piece of the Potter pie, notes Simon Fox of Britain's HMV Group, PLC, owner of the Waterstone's book chain, it's "hard to make money."

Independent booksellers can't even begin to compete on that scale. While many plan to fight back with special midnight parties—in the belief that it's no fun to wear a wizard hat in Wal-Mart—others are just opting out of the frenzy. "I won't be open at midnight," says Bonnie Stuppin of San Francisco's Alexander Book Co. Instead, she'll personally drop off copies to a few customers at no extra cost between midnight and 6 a.m. "It's sad that what little profit the industry can make off Harry Potter is being stripped away," says Stuppin. "If I ran my business that way, I wouldn't be here." Some booksellers who helped launch Potter in America, hosting signings with Rowling when she was starting out, are disillusioned. "In the beginning it was great for us, but the discount has become more important," says Valerie Lewis of Hicklebee's in San Jose, Calif. To Peter Glassman, owner of Manhattan's Books of Wonder, selling Potter below cost is "analogous to downloading music and the impact that has on music stores." . . .

Few face as gaping a hole with Harry's exit as its original publisher, Bloomsbury, which holds all rights to the titles outside the U.S. Last year, while the world waited as Rowling said she was working away on Book 7 in Scottish cafes instead of her multiple homes, the publisher's profits collapsed by three-quarters, to $10.3 million, as revenues fell almost a third, to $148.6 million. Spooked at the prospect of a one-trick pony, investors have sent Bloomsbury's share price down about 40% in the last year—even as a guaranteed hit is about to reach store shelves. . . .

Even if Harry Potter leaves a trail of profit-starved vendors and Potter-addicted producers in its wake as the series wraps up next month, the infatuation is unlikely to die. That's what Emerson Spartz, founder of the popular fan site MuggleNet.com, is betting on. Spartz, a University of Notre Dame sophomore who launched the site in 1999 at the age of 12, gets more than 1 million hits a day. He's pulling in "a six-figure income" from ads and his best seller, *MuggleNet.com's What Will Happen in Harry Potter 7*. He hopes to mimic the fan base that's grown around *The Lord of the Rings* and has no plans to close down the site. "There will always be people who get into Harry Potter fresh and want to meet other new Harry Potter fans," says Spartz.

Questions for Analysis

1. What happens in the marketplace that hurts a bookseller's profit margin when a popular character like Harry Potter appears in a new book? Explain.

2. Why would a bookseller like Amazon.com cut the consideration for a book like *Harry Potter and the Deathly Hallows* in half? Explain.

3. Who is hurt the most by these "consideration-slashing" efforts? Explain.

4. Why have investors begun to abandon Bloomsbury, the original Harry Potter publisher? Explain.

5. Is it unethical for booksellers to undercut others by selling the Harry Potter books at below the regular market level of consideration? Explain.

Source: Diane Brady with Kerry Capell and Joshua Vittor, "Juggernauts: The Twisted Economics of Harry Potter: The Wizard Brings Both Profit and Pain to his Business Partners," *BusinessWeek,* July 2, 2007, 38–39.

Property and Services as Consideration

Before money in the form of cash was accepted as a medium of exchange, consideration consisted of property and services. Sometimes, even today during recessionary or inflationary cycles, parties find it more beneficial to enter into barter agreements than to base their promises on cash payments. The courts have held that barter agreements contain valid consideration. For example, the exchange of services in return for the use of another's car or a promise to trade a DVD player for a cell phone represent benefits and sacrifices that constitute valid consideration to support a legally binding contract.

Promises Not to Sue

A promise not to sue, when there is the right, or at least the apparent right, to sue, is enforceable when it is supported by consideration. Promising not to sue is a forbearance. A promise not to sue in exchange for an amount of money is a customary way to settle or prevent a pending lawsuit. Settlements of this type often are preferred to expensive and time-consuming litigation. Such settlements are also better than submitting a claim to alternate dispute resolution procedures, such as arbitration or mediation.

EXAMPLE 11-3:   Releases and Promises Not to Sue

Patrick Sullivan was injured in midtown Manhattan during a confrontation between the NYPD and a trio of bank robbers who were attempting to escape after robbing a midtown branch of Chemical Bank. Sullivan discussed his legal rights with an attorney, who suggested that he might receive compensation from the NYPD if he brought suit against the city. When faced with the suit, the NYPD elected to offer Sullivan $250,000 if he would agree not to bring suit against the city. Sullivan agreed to these terms. The "thing of value" that Sullivan transferred to the city was his right to bring a lawsuit. A court would uphold this agreement on the basis of the promise between the parties.

Acceptance of an agreement not to sue, supported by consideration, terminates one's right to continue any lawsuit, presently or in the future, on grounds described in the agreement. A promise not to sue is commonly called a **release**. Agreements of this kind are usually negotiated and agreed upon before a suit is even filed. However, occasionally they are negotiated between attorneys after a lawsuit has been filed and sometimes even after a trial has begun. In such an event, the settlement is arranged in cooperation with the court and presiding judge. Interestingly enough, some states will uphold a promise not to sue exchanged for consideration, even if circumstances later indicate that the party granting the release did not have the right to sue in the first place, as long as at the time of the agreement, the exchange was made in good faith and fraud was not involved.

Charitable Pledges

Under traditional rules, charitable pledges are not enforceable as contractual obligations because they are not supported by consideration. The dependence of charitable institutions and nonprofit organizations on the solicitation of contributions has encouraged the courts to enforce charitable pledges as though they were contractual obligations. Basically, there are three ways that the courts can seek to uphold charitable pledges. The first way involves actual consideration, which occurs when charitable contributions are made on the condition that the promisor be remembered for the gift by having his or her name inscribed in some way on a memorial associated with the project. Some courts see this promise to install a memorial to the pledgor as consideration.

Courts today enforce charitable pledges by applying promissory estoppel and public policy.

A more contemporary approach is to use either *promissory estoppel* or public policy to support the claim. *Promissory estoppel* involves the detrimental reliance on a promise made by another party. If in reliance on a pledge or a series of pledges, a charity goes forward with a project, such as building an addition to the church hall or adding a wing to the synagogue, the courts will see the commencement of the project as evidence that the charity relied on the promises and will stop the promisors from denying the effects of the promise. At times pledges are used for the general operation and maintenance of a charitable or nonprofit organization rather than for a specific project.

When there is no promise to carry out a specific project, the courts have held that each pledge made is supported by the pledges of all others who have made similar pledges. This concept of consideration is used in support of all promises of money for undefined causes. The ultimate argument in this situation is that it would violate public policy to allow one pledgor to get away with denying his or her pledge when the other promisors relied on one another in making their individual pledges.

Quick Quiz 10-2 True or False?

1. Today contractual parties never find it beneficial to enter barter agreements.

2. If a party promises not to sue another party, and it is later discovered that the first party never really had the right to sue, the original promise not to sue is invalid in every state, and the consideration must be returned.

3. Even though charities depend on the solicitation of contributions, the courts have refused to enforce charitable pledges.

11-3 Problems with Consideration

Problems sometimes arise when the consideration involved in a contract is money and the parties disagree as to the amount of money that the debtor owes the creditor. How such problems are resolved depends on whether the transaction involves a genuine dispute as to the amount owed. One way such disputes can be settled is by an agreement known as accord and satisfaction.

Disputed Amounts

A **disputed amount** is one on which the parties never reached mutual agreement. It may be difficult at first to see how the amount due under a contract can end up as the focal point of a dispute, until we recall that the law permits a certain degree of incompleteness in the final terms of an agreement, provided there is a way to settle on the eventual amount owed. For instance, when a contractor is hired to do work on a home or an accountant is retained to figure out a client's taxes, the final amount owed is never laid out in absolute terms. Instead, the custom is to settle on an amount per hour, estimate the number of hours that will be spent on the job, and then settle on the final amount once the job is finished.

If a creditor accepts as full payment an amount that is less than the amount due, the dispute has been settled by an **accord and satisfaction**. **Accord** is the implied or expressed acceptance of less than what has been billed the debtor. **Satisfaction** is the agreed-to settlement contained in the accord. Only if the dispute is honest, and the offer to settle made in good faith, and not superficial or trivial will the courts entertain arguments based on accord and satisfaction.

EXAMPLE 11-4:   Lewis and Clarke's Learning Curve

Arthur C. Lewis hired C. S. Clarke to figure out his income tax for last year. During the initial consultation with Lewis, Clarke told him that his rate was $250 per hour. Clarke also estimated that the job appeared to be one that might take 10 to 20 hours of intensive work. (The fact that Lewis turned all of his records over to Clarke in a shoe box may have had something to do with this relatively high estimate, even though Clarke used a software package to do all his clients' returns.) When Clarke completed the work, he sent a bill to Lewis for 20 hours of work at $250 per hour for a total of $5,000. The number of hours included a five-hour seminar that Clarke took at the local college. When questioned about this, Clarke said that he had attended the seminar to learn how to deal with a problem that had cropped up in Lewis's return in relation to Lewis's limited liability company. Lewis did not believe that he should be charged with the time that Clarke spent at the seminar. Consequently, he deducted $1,250 from the bill and sent Clarke a check for $3,750. Lewis wrote the following notation on the check: "In full payment for all services involved in making out my tax return for last year." Clarke cashed the check and later sued Lewis's company in small claims court for the $1,250 balance. Clarke would not succeed in this lawsuit because he had already accepted a lesser amount, which had been offered by Lewis in good faith, in full payment of the amount in dispute.

Undisputed Amounts

An **undisputed amount** is one on which the parties have mutually agreed. Although a party may have second thoughts about the amount promised for goods or services rendered, the amount that was agreed to by the parties when they made their contract remains an undisputed amount. A part payment in lieu of full payment when accepted by a creditor will not cancel an undisputed debt.

EXAMPLE 11-5: Stewart's Home Improvement Plan

Bernice Stewart had new gutters and downspouts placed on her home, agreeing to pay the Hofstadter Home Improvement Company $2,625 for the parts and the labor charge for installation. A week later, before paying the $2,625, Stewart saw the same gutters and downspouts at the Port Clinton Home and Garden Show. She talked to the representative at the show, who told her he would have been able to sell her the gutters and downspouts and have them installed for only $2,125. Stewart sent a check to Hofstadter for $2,125 with the notation "In full payment for the gutters and downspouts applied to my home." Hofstadter deposited the check and demanded payment of the balance of $500. Stewart would still be obligated to pay that balance.

In this situation, there was no good faith dispute over what Stewart owed to Hofstadter for the gutters, the downspouts, or their installation. The buyer was simply trying to get the work done at the lower price that was quoted to her by the other installation company. The sum of $2,625 was an undisputed amount, and the balance of $500 is still owed to Hofstadter.

Quick Quiz 11-3 True or False?

1. A disputed amount is one on which the parties never reached mutual agreement.

2. If a creditor accepts as full payment an amount that is less than the amount due, the dispute has been settled by *promissory estoppel*.

3. An undisputed amount is one on which the parties have mutually agreed.

11-4 Agreements Without Consideration

As a general rule, an agreement without consideration will not be an enforceable contract, because consideration is so important as the binding element within a contractual relationship. Nevertheless, some states eliminate the requirement of consideration in specific types of agreements. In contrast, there are certain promises that the courts always refuse to enforce because they lack even the rudimentary qualities of valid consideration, even though on the surface they may appear to offer that much-needed element.

Enforceable Agreements

As noted previously, some states have chosen to eliminate the element of consideration in a few specifically named contracts. Unfortunately, as is frequently the case in such matters, there is no uniformity among jurisdictions as to the types of agreements subject to such laws. Still, some typical agreements falling into this category include promises under seal, promises after discharge in bankruptcy, debts barred by the statute of limitations, promises enforced by *promissory estoppel*, and options governed by the UCC (see Table 11-1).

LO8

Promises Under Seal A **seal** is a mark or an impression placed on a written contract indicating that the instrument was executed and accepted in a formal manner. Today a seal is usually indicated by the addition of the word "seal" or the letters "L.S."

Table 11-1 Agreements Without Consideration

Agreement	Legal Status
Promises under seal	Enforceable in some states for contracts not involving goods; unenforceable under the UCC for contracts involving goods
Promises after discharge in bankruptcy	Enforceable in most states
Promise to pay debts barred by statute of limitations	Enforceable
Promises enforced by promissory estoppel	Enforceable only if offeror knew that offeree would rely on the promise and offeree places himself or herself in a different and difficult position as a result of that promise
Option	Enforceable under the UCC if made by a merchant, in writing, stating the time period over which the offer will remain open
Illusory promises	Unenforceable
Promise of a gift	Unenforceable
Past considerations	Unenforceable
Preexisting duties	Unenforceable as a consideration in a new contract

UCC 2-203 (see page 961)

(*locus sigilli*, meaning "place of the seal") following a party's signature. Years ago, contracts under seal required no consideration. Some states still honor a promise under seal, but most have abolished this concept especially in relation to sale of goods contracts. In fact, the UCC has eliminated the use of the seal in all sale of goods contracts. However, a few states still require the use of the seal in real property and certain other types of transactions. Because there is no uniformity in this regard, it is advisable to research and consult the specific requirements in your jurisdiction.

Promises After Discharge in Bankruptcy

Persons discharged from indebtedness through bankruptcy may reaffirm their obligations, prompted perhaps by moral compulsion. In the past, reaffirmation has been the subject of abuse by creditors who used pressure against those whose debts have been excused. In response, Congress passed a bankruptcy reform act that makes it more difficult for creditors to extract such promises. The bankruptcy court must now hold a hearing when a reaffirmation is intended, informing the debtor that reaffirmation is optional, not required, and of the legal consequences of reactivating a debt. It is also up to the court to approve such reaffirmations. State laws, in most cases, provide that no new consideration need be provided in support of reaffirmation. Most states require that a reaffirmation be supported by contractual intent. Some states require the new promise to be in writing. However, when there is no such provision, an oral promise or reaffirmation is usually sufficient.

Debts Barred by Statutes of Limitations

State laws known as **statutes of limitations** limit the time within which a party is allowed to bring suit. The time allowed for the collection of a debt varies from state to state, usually from three to ten years. Some states allow more time for collection when the document of indebtedness is under seal, as in the case of a promissory note containing the seal of the maker. Debtors may revive and reaffirm debts barred by the statutes of limitations without the necessity of new consideration. Affirmation

The Opening Case Revisited, Part II

Pugh v. See's Candies, Inc., Round 3

After a trip to Europe, Pugh, the vice president of production at See's Candies and a 32-year employee with a perfect record, was called into the president's office and fired. Pugh brought a lawsuit against See's arguing that the president's oral assurances to him that his future with See's was safe, the president's past practice of never firing any administrative employee except for good cause, and Pugh's absolutely perfect employment record had created an implied agreement that he would not be discharged without good cause. The company argued that Pugh's contract was terminable at will. The court, convinced that the president's promises had created a contract, decided in Pugh's favor. Although Pugh did not use *promissory estoppel* in his case, he could have argued that the president had made definite promises that he, the president, could not now deny. Such an argument would have created a solid *promissory estoppel* case. This is correctly what happened in Example 11-6 below.

will result from the part payment of the debt. When a debt is revived, the creditor again is permitted the full term, provided by the statute of limitations, to make collection. Some states require a written reaffirmation when a debt made unenforceable by the statute of limitations is reactivated. Consequently, it would be best to check the rule in your jurisdiction.

Promises Enforced by *Promissory Estoppel*   The doctrine of *estoppel* denies rights to complaining parties that are shown to be the cause of their own injury. *Promissory estoppel* is a legal doctrine that restricts a party from denying that a promise was made under certain conditions, even though consideration has not been exchanged to bind an agreement. To be effective, *promissory estoppel* requires that the party making the promise know, or be presumed to know, that the other party might otherwise make a definite and decided change of position in contemplation of those promises. In reaching this doctrine, courts have accepted the principles of justice and fairness in protecting the party receiving the promise from otherwise unrecoverable losses.

LO9

EXAMPLE 11-6:   Radcliff and Rueters and *Promissory Estoppel*

Dale Radcliff was arrested for a crime she did not commit. Kevin Rueters, her supervisor at Yellowstone Enterprises, told her that he had to suspend her. However, he also told her that if she were later found not guilty and released, she would have her old job with the same seniority and pay grade that she had when she left. Two months later, the charges were dropped, and Radcliff tried to get her job back. Rueters refused to let her return to work. It took Radcliff four months to secure suitable employment. In a suit brought by Radcliff against Yellowstone to recover the pay she lost during those four months, the court ruled in her favor. Yellowstone and Rueters were stopped from denying the promise they'd made to Radcliff despite the absence of consideration from her because she had relied on that promise and had not looked for other work while suspended.

Although in Example 11-6, Yellowstone had received no consideration supporting the promise to hold open Radcliff's job for her while she was suspended, Radcliff had accepted the promise and placed herself in a very different and difficult position through her reliance upon the promise. Had Yellowstone not made such a promise, Radcliff would no doubt have looked for another job after Yellowstone had suspended her.

UCC 2-205 (see page 961)

Option   An **option** is the giving of consideration to support an offeror's promise to hold open an offer for a stated or a reasonable length of time. The UCC has made an exception to the rule requiring consideration when the offer is made by a merchant. In such cases, an offer in writing by a merchant, stating the time period during which the offer will remain open, is enforceable without consideration. The offer, which is called a **firm offer** or an **irrevocable offer**, must be signed by the offeror, and the time allowed for acceptance may not exceed three months. When the time allowed is more than three months, firm offers by merchants must be supported by consideration to be enforceable.

Unenforceable Agreements

The promises just described are exceptions to the general rule that consideration must support a valid contract. The exceptions are allowed by state statute or because the courts, in the interest of fairness or justice, find it inappropriate to require consideration. There are certain promises, however, that the courts will not enforce because they lack even the rudimentary qualities of valid consideration. Included in this category are promises based on preexisting duties, promises based on past consideration, illusory promises, and promises of future gifts and legacies.

Preexisting Duties   A promise to do something that one is already obligated to do by law or by some other promise or agreement cannot be made consideration in a new contract. Such obligations are called **preexisting duties**. The same rule of consideration applies to police officers, firefighters, and other public servants and officials who may pledge what appears to be some special service in exchange for a monetary reward, when all they have actually promised is to execute the duties they are already obligated to perform. Suppose, for instance, that the local fire chief, in exchange for a monetary reward, promises an apartment owner that he or she will provide protection should a fire break out in the owner's building. Neither the fire chief nor the apartment owner could enforce such an agreement in court. The promise is based on the chief's empty guarantee to do what is already his or her job.

Past Consideration   A promise to give another something of value in return for goods or services rendered and delivered in the past, without expectation or reward, is **past consideration**. Only when goods or services are provided as the result of bargained-for present or future promises is an agreement enforceable.

EXAMPLE 11-7:   Past Consideration Is No Consideration

Gale Hansen wanted to have her hair dyed before her college graduation party but could not afford to pay the $120 fee that was expected by the local hairdresser. Without any mention of payment, her friend Marianne Everett helped Hansen dye her hair. After seeing what a good job Everett did on her hair, Hansen told Everett that she'd give her $35 for helping. Hansen's promise to Everett is not enforceable because Everett has already completed the work. Her consideration is therefore in the past.

Illusory Promises An **illusory promise** is one that seems genuine but that on close examination actually fails to obligate the promissor to do anything. A party who makes an illusory promise is the only one with any right to determine whether the other party will benefit in any way. Illusory promises fail to provide the mutuality of promises required in establishing consideration.

EXAMPLE 11-8:   As Many Illusory Promises as You Might Desire

Pemberton Grocery agreed to buy such fruits and vegetables as it "might desire" for one summer season from Enchanted Farms, Inc. In return for this promise, Enchanted negotiated terms whereby it would give Pemberton a special schedule of discounts for the fruits and vegetables. The promise to buy as much as it "might desire" had actually obligated Pemberton to do nothing. Its promise was illusory because Pemberton might desire absolutely no fruits and vegetables and still keep its promise. The benefits that Pemberton were to derive from the schedule of discounts were not supported by a real or enforceable promise on Pemberton's part. A suit brought by either party to enforce this agreement would fail for want of consideration.

Future Gifts and Legacies The promise of a gift to be given at some future time or in a will is not enforceable if no consideration is given for the promise. Included here are promises to provide gratuitous services or to lend one's property without expectation of any benefits in return.

Quick Quiz 11-4 True or False?

1. An option is the giving of consideration to support an offeror's promise to hold an offer open for a stated length of time.

2. Although illusory promises provide the mutuality of promises required in establishing consideration, the courts will not enforce them due to the doctrine of unconscionability.

3. The promise of a gift to be given at some future time or in a will is completely enforceable even if no consideration is given for the promise.

Summary

11.1 The fifth element necessary to any valid contract is consideration. Consideration is the mutual exchange or promise to exchange benefits and sacrifices between contracting parties. Consideration has three requirements: (1) promises made during bargaining depend on the consideration to be received, (2) the consideration must involve something of value, and (3) the benefits and detriments promised must be legal.

11.2 Generally, consideration takes the form of money, property, or services. There are certain special kinds of agreements and promises to which the benefits and sacrifices are unique. Among these are promises not to sue and charitable pledges.

11.3 Problems sometimes arise when the consideration involved in a contract is money and the parties do not agree on the amount of money owed. If there is a genuine dispute, a creditor can accept an amount as full payment even though it is less than the amount claimed. Once the creditor has accepted the lesser amount, the dispute is settled by an act of accord and satisfaction. If the dispute is not genuine, accord and satisfaction do not apply.

11.4 As a general rule, contracts are not enforceable without consideration. However, some states eliminate the need for consideration in some agreements. These agreements include promises bearing a seal, promises after discharge in bankruptcy, debts barred by the statute of limitations, promises enforced by *promissory estoppel*, and options governed by the UCC. There are other agreements that seem to involve consideration but that the courts will not enforce. These agreements involve preexisting duties, past consideration, illusory promises, and gifts.

Key Terms

accord, 218
accord and satisfaction, 218
bargained-for exchange, 212
consideration, 211
detriment, 211
disputed amount, 218
estoppel, 221
firm offer, 222

forbearance, 212
illusory promise, 223
irrevocable offer, 222
locus sigilli, 220
option, 222
past consideration, 222
preexisting duties, 222
promissory estoppel, 221

release, 217
satisfaction, 218
seal, 219
statutes of limitations, 220
unconscionable, 213
undisputed amount, 218

Questions for Review and Discussion

1. What is consideration?
2. What are the different types of detriment?
3. What characteristics are necessary for consideration to be valid?
4. What is meant by the term "unconscionable"?
5. Can a promise not to sue be consideration?
6. How can a charitable pledge be consideration?
7. What is the procedure that a debtor and creditor may use to settle a claim by means of accord and satisfaction?
8. What agreements may be enforceable by a court of law even though they lack consideration?
9. What is the doctrine of *promissory estoppel*?
10. What agreements appear to have consideration but will not be enforced by the courts?

Investigating the Internet

Information about contract law can be found on a Web site called LegalTarget.com. As a research assignment, access the Web site and answer the following questions: (1) What are the three steps in the formation of a contract? (2) What definition does the Web site provide for the element of consideration? (3) According to this definition, what is the usual form of consideration? (4) What are the three ways that an offer can be accepted? (5) According to LegalTarget.com, when can mutual assent be disrupted?

Cases for Analysis

1. Twenty-two congressional representatives proposed a bill that would permit corporate shareholders to review the consideration packages that had been granted to key corporate executives of public corporations. The bill, which was named the Shareholder Vote on Executive Compensation Act, would empower the shareholders of public corporations to evaluate and vote on the appropriateness of the compensation packages that had been granted to the corporation's top five officers. The vote, however, would not obligate the corporation to change the compensation package if the shareholders disapproved of its terms. Would such a bill, if enacted into law, conflict with established contract law principles that permit parties to negotiate their own level of consideration? Explain. See Donna Block, "Proposal Seeks Shareholder OK on Executive Pay," *The National Law Journal,* March 12, 2007, p. 9.

2. Consideration can serve as a strong motivator. At least this is what a newly founded shareholder forum believes. The forum was formed to monitor the salaries of top corporate executives, especially CEOs, by matching those salaries with the executive's incentive package, which includes the corporation's latest list of objectives and the number or the percentage of those objectives that the executive must meet to receive incentive pay. The goal of incentive pay is to motivate top executives to do more than sit in the CEO's office from 9:00 to 5:00 each day. Is incentive pay a violation of the principle that says that preexisting duties cannot

be used as consideration in a new contract? Explain. See Gretchen Morgenson, "Hear Ye, Hear Ye: Coralling Executive Pay," *The New York Times,* June 17, 2007, sec 3, pp. 1 and 8.

3. General Motors decided to move a car producing operation to Arlington, Texas, from a plant located in Ypsilanti, Michigan. As a result, the township of Ypsilanti brought a lawsuit to stop General Motors from making the move. Ypsilanti argued that GM had promised to keep the plant in Ypsilanti in exchange for certain tax privileges. The township argued further that it had relied on those promises when it granted that tax abatement to the corporation. Therefore, GM should be forced to keep its promise to maintain the Ypsilanti plant. Should the court stop this move based on the doctrine of *promissory estoppel?* Explain. *Charter Township of Ypsilanti v. General Motors,* 508 N.W.2d 556 (Michigan Court of Appeals).

4. Aviation Electronics entered a contract with Sky Train Institute of Montana in which Aviation agreed to supply the institute with 17,000 component parts for the development of the institute's remote control bomber. The bomber had to be operational by December 3; otherwise, the institute would lose a research grant from the Department of Defense. After delivering 5,000 parts, Aviation told Sky Train that it wanted an additional $4 million beyond the original price agreed upon to deliver the remaining parts. Sky Train attempted to obtain the parts from other firms, none of which could fill the order in the

time limit required by the DOD contract specifications. To make the deadline stipulated in the government contract, Sky Train reluctantly agreed to the new price demanded by Aviation. What "thing of value," if any, has Aviation transferred to the institute that it did not already owe the institute under the original contract? Explain.

5. Savaretti offered to pay his niece, Wilma, $2,000 if she would agree to give up eating meat and pastries and drinking caffeinated beverages for six months. Wilma agreed and gave up these activities for six months. At the end of those six months, Savaretti refused to give Wilma the $2,000, arguing that because giving up caffeine, meat, and pastries was beneficial to her health, she suffered no detriment and was owed nothing. Wilma took Savaretti to small claims court and demanded payment of the $2,000. She argued that because she had the legal right to consume the caffeine, meat, and pastries, she suffered a legal detriment and was entitled to her money. How should the referee rule in this case? Explain.

6. Daniel Davidson told Velma Evans that he would hire her to work on an architectural job. He gave her a date to show up for work and told her to leave her present job. Relying on Davidson's statements, Evans left her job. Davidson never let Evans begin work, and as a result, she was out of work for six months. Evans sued Davidson for the wages she lost during those six months. Davidson argued that because they'd never decided on the final terms of employment, no contract ever existed between the two of them. Evans argued that the principle of *promissory estoppel* should apply here. Is Evans correct? Explain.

7. Mers was arrested and charged with a felony. Dispatch Printing, his employer, told him that he had to be suspended. However, Mers was also told that he could return to work if the case against him was resolved in his favor. Relying on this promise, Mers did not seek other employment. The case ended in a hung jury, and Mers reported back to work. Dispatch Printing, however, refused to let him work or pay him any back pay. In a suit against Dispatch Printing, what legal argument might Mers use to compel Dispatch Printing to pay him for any losses due to his reliance on the promise to let him return to work when the case ended in his favor? Explain. *Mers v. Dispatch Printing,* 483 N.E.2d 150 (OH).

8. The Mighty Fine Food Emporium agreed to buy such fruits and vegetables as it "might desire" for one summer season from Kennelsworth Farms and Vineyards. In return for this promise, Kennelsworth negotiated terms whereby it would give Mighty Fine a special schedule of discounts for the fruits and vegetables. Did the promise to buy as much as it "might desire" obligate Kennelsworth in any way? Are the benefits that Kennelsworth was to derive from the schedule of discounts supported by an enforceable promise on Kennelsworth's part? Would a suit brought by either party to enforce this agreement succeed? Explain each answer.

9. Graham O'Hanlon, without any mention of payment, helped his friend, Patricia Tippon, move from Westerville to Pepper Pike. The entire move took 48 hours to complete. At the end of the day, after she was in her new house, Tippon told O'Hanlon that she'd give him $200 for helping her move. Is Tippon's promise to O'Hanlon enforceable? Why or why not?

10. Vanoni Biological Supplies, Inc., contracted with the Hayden Institute to supply the Institute with 24,000 biological specimens for a series of experiments that the Institute has agreed to perform for the Maritime University of Columbia. The Institute must have the specimens by September 9 to meet the University's schedule. After delivering 12,000 of the specimens, Vanoni told the Institute that it wanted an additional $1,600 to deliver the remaining 12,000 specimens. Can Vanoni make the delivery of the remaining 12,000 specimens consideration in a new agreement with the Institute? Explain.

11. Seier agreed to pay $10,000 to Peek in exchange for all the stock in a corporation. The agreement was placed in writing. Nevertheless, when the time came for payment, Seier refused to live up to his end of the deal. His argument was that the stock was not worth the $10,000 that he had agreed to pay for it. Did the court listen to Seier's argument and attempt to determine the value of the consideration? Explain. *Seier v. Peek,* 456 So.2d 1079 (AL).

12. N. B. West Contracting Co., Inc., agreed to repave Koedding's parking lot. When the repaving work was done, Koedding was unsatisfied with the quality of the work. Consequently, he informed West of his intention to bring suit. West told Koedding that the lot would be resealed and that the job would be guaranteed for two years if Koedding agreed not to pursue the lawsuit, which had already commenced. Koedding agreed. After the repaving was completed a second time, Koedding was still not satisfied.

Would the agreement not to sue stop Koedding's lawsuit? Explain. *Koedding v. N. B. West Contracting Co., Inc.,* 596 S.W.2d 744 (MO).

13. Evans used his credit card to run up a $98.75 bill with the Rosen Department Store. When Rosen tried to collect, Evans wrote a check for $79.00. He wrote on the check that he meant it to be "full payment of all accounts to date." Rosen cashed the check. When Rosen sued Evans for $19.75 balance, Evans argued that under accord and satisfaction, the fact that Rosen cashed the $79.00 check meant that it had accepted that amount as full payment. Was Evans correct? Explain.

14. Jill Anderson agreed to purchase William and Teresa Dawson's flower shop for $75,000. Anderson paid the Dawsons $20,000 when the contract was signed. She also agreed to pay the balance of $55,000 at an interest rate of 8.5 percent per year for five years. This agreement meant that she would be making monthly installments of $1,128.41 to the Dawsons. During the negotiation stages of the contract, Anderson was told that all of the equipment in the store was in perfect condition. Moreover, the Dawsons told Anderson that she could expect a profit of $75,000 per year. Anderson discovered that the equipment needed extensive repairs and that the financial condition of the business had been misrepresented so that she made considerably less than the $75,000 that the Dawsons had cited. Accordingly, Anderson sent a check to the Dawsons for $6,560.21. On the reverse side of the check she wrote, "Payment in full for University Flower Shop." This final check would mean that after making installment payments for more than a year and a half, she had paid a total of $50,000 for the flower shop. In a letter that accompanied the check, Anderson indicated that because she had been misled by the Dawsons about the condition of the equipment and the financial state of the business, the store had actually been worth only $50,000 at the time she purchased it. The Dawsons disagreed but deposited the check and then brought suit against Anderson for breach of contract. Anderson argued that when the Dawsons negotiated her check, the debt was discharged under accord and satisfaction. Is Anderson correct here? Explain. *Dawson v. Anderson,* 698 N.E.2d 1014 (OH).

15. Tim W. Koerner and Associates, Inc., was a distributor for electrosurgical products for Aspen Labs, Inc. Zimmer U.S.A., Inc., purchased Aspen and replaced Aspen's distribution system with its own. Aspen remained in business as a subsidiary. Koerner sued Aspen and Zimmer, joined as defendants, trying to force them to honor a contract that Aspen and Zimmer had made compensating former Aspen dealers for their past efforts. Zimmer refused to honor the agreement. For whom did the court find and why? *Tim W. Koerner & Assocs., Inc. v. Aspen Labs, Inc.,* 492 F. Supp. 294 (S.W. TX).

16. Trisko purchased a loveseat from the Vignola Furniture Company. The loveseat arrived at Trisko's home in a damaged condition. Vignola agreed to repair the loveseat if Trisko agreed not to sue. Trisko agreed but then later brought suit. Vignola argued that Trisko could not bring suit because he had promised not to sue them in exchange for the repair of the loveseat. Trisko argued that Vignola had a preexisting duty to deliver an undamaged loveseat. This preexisting duty could not therefore be consideration in a new agreement. Was Trisko correct? Explain. *Trisko v. Vignola Furniture Company,* 299 N.E.2d 421 (IL).

Quick Quiz Answers

11-1	11-2	11-3	11-4
1. F	1. F	1. T	1. T
2. T	2. F	2. F	2. F
3. T	3. F	3. T	3. F

Chapter 12 Legality

The Opening Case

Snyder v. Snyder

When Snyder was released from prison, he used most of the money that was in his bank account to help his parents buy a neighborhood bar. At the time that the bar was purchased, Snyder and his parents agreed not to include his name on any written documents, because under state law at the time, a convicted felon could not hold a liquor license. Nevertheless, Snyder believed that he and his parents had entered an oral contract, under which he was made part owner of the bar. Subsequent to the purchase of the bar, Snyder made an additional payment of $10,000 to support its operation. During the 1980s and 1990s, Snyder continued to receive a share of the profits from the bar on a regular basis. In 1999, the deal was restructured so that he received $175 to $200 each week from the bar's income. This payment schedule continued until Snyder's mother died, after which his sister continued to pay him until his father put a stop to it. The bar was later sold for $200,000. Snyder received nothing at the time of the sale. As a result, he sued his father, arguing that he was a part owner of the bar due to the oral contract and that, as such, he was entitled to a fair share of the proceeds from the sale. At first, the argument sounded very good, and Snyder might have won the case—had it not been for a single but critical technicality. At the time of the oral contract, state law prohibited all convicted felons from having any interest in a liquor license. Therefore, any contract that Snyder entered that would connect him to a liquor license would be illegal. For that reason, the court turned down his request for a declaratory judgment. Ironically, the General Assembly later changed the law and gave the Division of Liquor Control the power to decide which convicted felons could obtain permits and which could not. Specifically, the new law reads, "[t]he division [of liquor control] may refuse to issue any [liquor] permit to or refuse to renew any permit of any person convicted of a felony that is reasonably related to the person's fitness to operate a liquor permit business in this state." Had it been up to the division to make the decision when Snyder made his original investment, he might have been declared fit, and none of these problems would have happened. (See *Snyder v. Snyder,* 170 Ohio App.3d 26, Court of Appeals of Ohio, Eleventh District, Ashtabula County.)

Opening Case Questions

1. Had the oral contract been legal, who would have been the offeror and who the offeree?

2. Is the contract in this case made illegal by common law, public policy, or statute?

3. Is the illegality in this case permanent or temporary?

4. What would have been the status of a contract made while the incapacity existed?

5. What would have been the fate of this contract under the new statute?

LO Learning Objectives

1. State the effect of illegality on a contract.
2. Identify those contracts made illegal by statutory law.
3. Explain the rationale behind usury laws.
4. Identify those wagering agreements that may not be illegal under state law.
5. Explain the rules regarding licenses and illegality.
6. Describe when an agreement might be considered unconscionable.
7. Identify those statutes that make Sunday agreement illegal.
8. Explain the legal principle of public policy.
9. Enumerate the contracts made illegal by public policy.
10. Explain the consequences of illegal agreements.

12-1 Agreements to Engage in Unlawful Activity

LO1

The sixth requirement of a complete contract is legality. A contract may include a valid offer, an effective acceptance, mutual assent, competent parties, and valid consideration and still be invalid because the agreement involves doing something illegal. An illegal agreement is void. It has no legal effect. In general, the law will not aid either party to an illegal agreement. Ordinarily, the court will leave the parties to an illegal agreement where they placed themselves. If an illegal agreement is still executory, the court will not order it performed or award damages for breach of contract. If the illegal agreement has been executed, the court will not award damages or assist in having it annulled. The most obvious type of illegal contract is one in which parties agree to perform some sort of unlawful activity. This activity could be a crime or a tort, depending on the circumstances. However, when we use the term "unlawful activity" in this context, we are referring to activities that are clearly wrong in and of themselves. These unlawful activities include crimes and torts that most people would recognize as wrong, even if there were no statute, regulation, or court decision to tell them it was wrong.

Agreements to Engage in Tortious Activity

The law will not uphold any contract that obligates one of the parties to commit a tort. For example, a newspaper reporter who agrees to defame several politicians in return for a position as their opponent's press secretary would find no remedy in the law should her benefactor fail to follow through after the libelous story were printed. The agreement to commit a tort would be void in the eyes of the law. This approach only makes good sense. The law cannot lend its approval to a contract that breaks the law, no matter how complete it is in relation to the other five elements.

Agreements to Engage in Criminal Activity

In like manner, the law cannot honor any agreement if the purpose of the agreement is to commit a crime. If, for example, a storekeeper would pay a known criminal to vandalize the shop of a competitor, that storekeeper would not be able to sue the criminal for breach of contract should the criminal take the money and run. As strange as it may seem, the nature of criminality is not always as clear as might be imagined. Because criminal law involves serious offenses that can result in the loss of a person's freedom or, more seriously, the loss of a person's life, all criminal statutes must be drawn as precisely and as clearly as possible. A statute that is obscure or outlines conduct that is ambiguous may be struck down by the court as void for vagueness. This ruling would mean that a contract that involves the conduct that is allegedly outlawed by a vague statute might not be void.

EXAMPLE 12-1: *United States v. Richardson*

Clark Richardson, a former adviser to the president, wrote a book entitled *The Lateness of the Hour*. Richardson entered a publishing agreement with Oakcrest Publications, Inc. Following the terms of a secrecy agreement signed by all government employees, Richardson submitted the manuscript to the government for its approval, then was arrested and prosecuted under a recently passed federal criminal statute that made it a crime to publish any material that "placed the present administration in a bad light." Accordingly, Oakcrest declared the publishing contract illegal and therefore void and demanded that Richardson return the advance that the publishing company had paid him. Richardson refused. At trial, the judge declared that the statute was void for vagueness and a violation of the First Amendment's guarantees of free speech and free press. Consequently, the publication of the book was legal; the contract itself was also legal and therefore binding on the publisher.

Agreements Made Illegal Under Statutory Law

Most people of good faith would know, even in the absence of any statute, regulation, ordinance, rule, or court decision, that the behavior outlined in the previous examples would be wrong. It is difficult to imagine, for instance, that the shopkeeper would be surprised to discover that it is wrong to hire someone to destroy his competitor's property. Similarly, it is not easy to believe that the reporter who agreed to lie in print thought that her behavior was in any way admirable. In contrast, some activities that do not seem wrong on the surface may have been made wrong by specific statutory enactments. Therefore, the fact that some of these activities are illegal may catch us by surprise. For example, the shopkeeper knows vandalism is illegal but may be confused to learn that he cannot hold a garage sale without a license. Or the reporter who knows that libel is wrong may be amazed to learn that her Wednesday-evening poker game is not legal. For this reason, we will examine those activities that are wrong because a statute says they are wrong. These activities include usurious agreements, wagering agreements, unlicensed agreements, unconscionable agreements, and Sunday (Sabbath) agreements.

Usurious Agreements   The illegal practice of charging more than the amount of interest allowed by law is called **usury**. To protect borrowers from excessive interest charges, each state has passed laws that specify the rate of interest that may be charged in lending money. These interest rates vary from state to state. Agreements to charge more than is allowed by law are illegal. Special statutes, however, allow small loan companies, pawn shops, and other lending agencies that accept high-risk applicants for credit to charge a higher rate of interest.

Payday Loan Regulations by State

States with regulations that exempt payday lenders:
California, Colorado, Florida, Iowa, Kansas, Kentucky, Louisiana, Minnesota, Mississippi, Missouri, Nebraska, Nevada, North Carolina, Ohio, Oklahoma, South Carolina, Tennessee, Washington, and Wyoming.

States with regulations that prohibit payday loans by setting maximum interest rates:
Alabama, Alaska, Arizona, Arkansas, Connecticut, Georgia, Hawaii, Maine, Maryland, Massachusetts, Michigan, New Hampshire, Pennsylvania, Rhode Island, Texas, Vermont, Virginia, West Virginia, and Puerto Rico, U.S. Virgin Islands.

States with regulations that permit payday loans and set no limits on small loan interest rates:
Delaware, Idaho, Illinois, Montana, New Jersey, New Mexico, New York, North Dakota, Oregon, South Dakota, Utah, and Wisconsin.

One state, Indiana, sets a maximum interest rate (36%), but allows payday loans by setting a minimum finance charge ($33).

Figure 12-1 State loan regulations.

EXAMPLE 12-2:   *Clapham v. Forest City Loan Company*

Derek Clapham had an outstanding balance of $70,000 on eight credit cards. Five of the companies were threatening legal action against Clapham. In a state of mild panic—if there really is such a thing as "mild panic"—Clapham decided to consolidate his loans by going to the Forest City Loan Company. Forest City agreed to loan Clapham the money but charged him 29 percent interest over a 48-month period. Although the usual maximum interest rate in the state was 21 percent, a state statute specifically authorized this higher maximum rate for high-risk applicants such as Clapham. Later Clapham tried to bring a lawsuit against Forest City, alleging that he had been charged more than the legal interest rate. The case was thrown out almost immediately on a motion to dismiss filed by Forest City on the grounds that the rate that Clapham was charged was within the rate authorized by the high-risk state statute.

So-called payday loans that come with a charge of more than 800 percent per annum have even become legal in some states. Payday loans are small loans that are given on a weekly basis for an extremely large fee. Many states provide for a different maximum interest rate when the loan goes to a business or involves a mortgage (see Chapter 31). Most states also have special usury statutes to monitor the interest charged by retailers and others when the contract involves an installment loan. Such statutes are often referred to as retail installment sales acts. Some transactions involve charges that appear to be interest but are actually legitimate expenses that can be collected without violating usury laws. The fees for a title search, an appraisal of land, or a credit report would fall into this category. Such fees must be genuine; any attempt to disguise usury as a special fee will not be tolerated by the courts. (See Figure 12-1 for state statutes.)

Payday loans provide high-interest rate credit for those who need quick cash and for those with credit problems.

EXAMPLE 12-3: *Bourne v. Emmet Financial Bank*

Matt Bourne decided to replace the siding on his house. To do so, he went to the Emmet Financial Bank and applied for a loan. Fay Defalco, the loan manager of Emmet, told Bourne that the company would need $2,500 upfront to process the loan. This processing, she told Bourne, would involve a credit check, an appraisal of the value of the house, and a title search. In fact, these things were not done, and the $2,500 fee was simply a way to charge extra interest above the maximum rate. Such a scheme is illegal. Once Bourne figured this out, he brought a lawsuit against Emmet for a refund of the phony processing fee.

The legal consequences associated with charging too much interest depend on the laws of the jurisdiction. Some states make the entire contract completely void. Other states allow the lender to collect only the principal with no interest at all. Others permit the lender to recover the principal and the interest up to what is actually allowed by law. Because these legal consequences vary from jurisdiction to jurisdiction, it would be wise to check the law in your state.

LO4   Wagering Agreements Any agreement or promise concerning a wager or some other form of gambling is invalid and may not be enforced. States make exceptions when bets are placed in accordance with laws that permit horse racing, state lotteries, church-related or charitable games of bingo, and gambling casinos regulated by state authority. However, even in states in which gambling is legal, it is frequently still illegal to borrow money to gamble.

LO5   Unlicensed Agreements Certain businesses and professions must be licensed before they are allowed to operate legally. One reason for requiring a license is to provide a source of revenue, part of which is used to supervise the business or profession being licensed. A city ordinance requiring all residents to obtain a license before holding a yard or garage sale would fall into this category. Another purpose that the government has in licensing individuals is to provide supervision and regulation of businesses and professions that might inflict harm on the public if they were allowed to operate without such controls. Physicians, nurses, dentists, attorneys, engineers, architects, public school teachers, and others in public service must be supervised for the protection of the public. Sometimes legislatures will enact laws that limit the ability of certain people to acquire special licenses. Thus, a state might pass a statute that limits the ability of convicted felons to obtain a license to own firearms or run an establishment that sells liquor. Courts distinguish between licenses purely for revenue and licenses for protection of the public. If a license is required simply to raise revenue, the lack of a license will not necessarily make a contract void. In contrast, if a licensing requirement is designed to protect the public, it is likely that unlicensed persons will not be able to enforce their contracts.

EXAMPLE 12-4: *Abernathy v. Catalina Steel Corporation*

Sandra Abernathy was hired by the Catalina Steel Corporation in Detroit to work on certain industrial engineering projects. But Abernathy had never obtained a license to become a registered engineer. A Michigan statute prohibited people from performing engineering services without having the appropriate license. When Catalina refused to pay Abernathy for a job they felt was poorly done, she sued them for breach of contract. The court found in favor of the steel company. The court felt that public welfare allowed the state to regulate and license engineers to provide for public safety.

Unconscionable Agreements   A court will not enforce a contract or any part of a contract that it regards as unconscionable. An agreement is considered unconscionable if its terms are so grossly unfair that they shock the court's conscience. When the court so desires, it will limit how the unconscionable clause in an agreement is carried out, provided it can do so without causing any unfair consequences.

EXAMPLE 12-5:   *Wynette Kitchen Supply Company v. Jenkins*

A telemarketer for the Wynette Kitchen Supply Company convinced Gina Jenkins, a 90-year-old widow who lived alone and did not hear very well, to purchase a set of pots and pans for $9,000. The actual value of the set was about $500. When Jenkins's niece found out that the telemarketer had pressured her aunt into this grossly unfair agreement, she told her not to pay the outrageous amount. When she failed to pay her bill and demanded that Wynette take the pots and pans back, the company sued her. Because of the difference in bargaining power and the incredibly unfair price, it is likely that the court would refuse to enforce the contract.

The Opening Case Revisited
Snyder v. Snyder, Round 2

Recall that in The Opening Case at the beginning of the chapter, when Snyder was released from prison, he used most of his savings to help his parents buy a bar. Snyder later made an additional payment of $10,000 to help run the bar. During the 1980s and 1990s, Snyder continued to receive a share of the profits from the bar on a regular basis. In 1999, the deal was restructured so that he received $175 to $200 each week from the bar's income, until Snyder's mother died, after which his sister continued to pay him until his father told her to stop. When the bar was sold for $200,000, Snyder asked for his share of the proceeds. When that share was not forthcoming, Snyder sued his father. Snyder might have won the case, had it not been for a very important detail. When the oral contract was made, state law prevented any convicted felon from having an interest in a liquor license. Therefore, even if circumstances might otherwise suggest that a contract had been created between Snyder and his parents, the fact that Snyder could not enter such a contract in the first place made the whole thing illegal from the start. For that reason, the court turned down his request for a declaratory judgment.

About the Law

Under the Napoleonic Code, it was illegal for a woman to enter a contract for the acquisition of property without her husband's written consent.

Of course, the party seeking to uphold the contract is allowed to present evidence that would show that the agreement is not as unfair as it may appear at first. The court would look at the commercial setting as well as the purpose and the effect of the agreement to determine its overall fairness.

Sunday Agreements   State statutes and local ordinances regulate the making and performing of contracts on Sunday. These laws are usually called **blue laws** because one of the first laws banning Sunday or Sabbath contracts was written on blue paper. Interestingly enough, the local legislative bodies had to act affirmatively to create statutes against Sunday contracts because, under common law, these contracts were perfectly legal. Today, the enforcement of restrictive blue laws varies in different geographical areas. Certain states have eliminated uniform statewide laws regulating Sunday activities but permit counties and incorporated cities, towns, and villages to adopt their own ordinances under a concept known as **local option**. Thus, adjoining counties may have opposing laws, with one opting by popular referendum to permit Sunday sales and the other opting to make such sales illegal. Other states have rolled back these laws almost entirely, permitting most contracts while prohibiting or limiting only a few select Sunday contracts, such as those involving the sale of alcohol.

Where laws do restrict Sunday business, two rules are usually observed. First, agreements made on Sunday or any other day requiring performance on Sunday may be ruled invalid. Exceptions to this rule are those agreements necessary to the health, welfare, and safety of the community and its residents. Second, agreements made on Sunday for work to be done or goods to be delivered on a business day are valid and enforceable. However, some states still require that there be an affirmation of such agreements on a day other than Sunday if such agreements are to be enforceable. The enforcement of blue laws varies widely from state to state, county to county, and village to village. Some localities have restrictive laws but prefer not to enforce them, permitting all types of commercial activity without interference. Religious influences have been of major importance where enforcement is strict. Highly populated urban areas have almost entirely succumbed to the pressures of commercialism and removed the Sunday blue laws from the books.

Did You Know?

Corbin on Contracts, one of the most respected treatises on contract law, begins its discussion of public policy by stating, "The loudest and most confident assertions as to what makes for the general welfare and happiness of mankind are made by the demagogue and the ignoramus."

Quick Quiz 12-1 True or False?

1. Special statutes sometimes permit small loan companies to charge a higher rate of interest for high-risk applicants.

2. A court will usually enforce an unconscionable contract if the immediate threshold test is met, at least in relation to that part of the agreement.

3. Wagering agreements are permitted in states with blue laws.

12-2 Agreements Contrary to Public Policy

The government has the power to regulate the health, safety, welfare, and morals of the public. This power emerges with the states simply because of their status as legitimate governing bodies. It has also become a part of the federal government's power under various interpretations of the U.S. Constitution. Any action that tends to harm the health, safety, welfare, or morals of the people is said to violate public policy. **Public policy** is the general legal principle that says no one should be allowed to do anything that tends to injure the public at large. Agreements most commonly invalidated as contrary to public policy are those to obstruct justice, interfere with public service, defraud creditors, escape liability, and restrain trade. Some of these agreements are prohibited by statute, such as those that suppress competition and those that interfere with public service. Consequently, they could have been listed and explained in the last section. Instead, these contracts are listed here with the other public policy–related contracts, because they share one thing in common, though such contracts are made between private individuals: They would hurt the entire social structure if the law enforced them in any way.

Agreements to Obstruct Justice

Agreements to obstruct justice include agreements to protect someone from arrest, to suppress evidence, to encourage lawsuits, to give false testimony, and to bribe a juror. The category also includes a promise not to prosecute someone or not to serve as a witness in a trial. Any agreement promising to perform any of these activities would be void.

EXAMPLE 12-6:   *Otterbacher Grocery Outlet v. Warner*

Sarah Jurgens was shopping at the Otterbacher Grocery Outlet when she slipped and fell, breaking her arm. Sam Warner, who witnessed the entire incident, was paid $700 by the owners of Otterbacher to forget everything he'd seen. Warner later changed his mind and testified truthfully about the facts concerning the incident. The agreement made with the owners of the Otterbacher Grocery Outlet is void because it is considered against public policy. Otterbacher filed a suit in small claims court against Warner asking for a return of the $700. However, after being informed that the entire contract was illegal from the outset, the owners immediately dropped the case and took an unscheduled vacation to Malaysia.

Agreements Interfering with Public Service

Agreements interfering with public service are illegal and void. Contracts in this group include agreements to bribe or interfere with public officials, to obtain political preference in appointments to office, to pay an officer for signing a pardon, or to illegally influence a legislature for personal gain.

A Question of Ethics

In March 2003, as Gulf War II was underway, a task force of attorneys working for the administration in Washington developed a set of legal arguments demonstrating that the President of the United States and his appointees should not be bound by prohibitions against torture as outlined in international law and federal statutory law. The legal memorandum produced at that time was only one of a series of legal memos written by administrative legal teams. Each memo was aimed at proving that American officials did not have to abide by the Geneva Conventions and other international agreements outlawing torture. What all of these memos seem to have overlooked is the basic premise that the overall public good is preserved only when the good of individuals is also preserved. In denying basic human rights to Iraqi detainees, the attorneys had forgotten (or ignored) a fundamental reason that the United States had agreed to be bound by such laws in the first place: To protect all soldiers, but especially our own, from such abuse.

BusinessWeek **Business Law in the News**

On the Brink of Artificial Life: Craig Venter says success is near, but critics blast efforts to patent synthetic organisms

First he succeeded in reading humanity's genetic code. Now gene pioneer J. Craig Venter believes he is within weeks or months of creating the world's first free-living artificial organism in his laboratory. It won't be much to look at—a tiny bacterium with only a few hundred genes. But if it's truly feasible, he says, "it will be one of the bright milestones in human history, changing our conceptual view of life."

It also could be lucrative. Venter's company, Synthetic Genomics Inc., has already filed controversial patents on synthetic bugs, which could make fuels such as ethanol or hydrogen. And on June 13 it announced a deal with energy giant BP PLC to find and modify naturally occurring microbes that can turn coal or oil below the earth's surface into cleaner fuel. Microorganisms "have the potential to provide all the transportation fuel we need in the U.S.," says Venter. "I joke that I'm going from the gene king to the oil king."

Swarm of Rivals

In this emerging field of synthetic biology, though, Venter has plenty of competitors. Amyris Biotechnologies adds suites of genes to yeast or bacteria to make an antimalaria drug and novel biofuels. Dozens of so-called gene foundries, including a Massachusetts Institute of Technology spin-off called Codon Devices Inc. in Cambridge, Mass., have sprung up to sell synthetic strands of DNA and other products. One company, EraGen Biosciences in Madison, Wis., even makes DNA from basic building blocks not found in nature, opening the door wider to new types of life. And many academics are trying to fashion free-living organisms from scratch. So far, they have synthesized such simpler microbes as the polio virus and the 1918 flu virus.

The benefits of such research could be enormous: not just drugs and fuels but also bugs that clean up pollution or flash when they detect explosives, plus a far deeper understanding of the basic mechanisms of biology. Venter imagines creating organisms worth billions or trillions of dollars.

But the pitfalls could be huge as well. What's to stop terrorists from buying pieces of DNA and fitting them together into a vicious pathogen, frets David C. Magnus, director of Stanford University's Center for Biomedical Ethics. "There are plenty of people lying awake worrying about this," he says.

Magnus and others have been working with DNA foundries, suggesting measures to reduce chances of dangerous organisms being unleashed, purposely or inadvertently. One idea: use software to spot purchases of DNA sequences that could be used as weapons. Another is to have "biosafety" officials oversee research to ensure that pathogens created in labs are kept under control. Such measures are still voluntary. "We've essentially made a gamble that the science will keep us one step ahead of any nefarious uses," Magnus says.

Even if synthetic biology can be kept out of the hands of terrorists, some scientists and activists worry that it could be locked up for commercial gain. In early June, the ETC Group, a watchdog organization based in Canada, launched a campaign against Venter's patent application. His synthetic organism will be a much bigger deal than Dolly, the cloned sheep, predicts ETC's Jim Thomas. He charges that Venter's company aims to be the "Microbesoft" of synthetic biology.

Less Special

Venter is not surprised by the attacks on his work. "Patents are a hot word," he says, "and people are afraid of synthetic organisms." He has won kudos for convening panels of bioethicists, religious leaders, and biowarfare experts to study the issues. They've concluded that the research shouldn't be stopped—though synthetic organisms must be controlled and contained. Environmental groups should be "ecstatic about what we are doing, since we provide one of the clear alternatives to burning oil and coal," Venter says.

Within weeks, his team expects to publish a paper showing how they have leapt many of the technical hurdles to creating synthetic life. But overcoming objections may not be as easy. While creating new life may not be playing God, says Arthur L. Caplan, director of the Center for Bioethics at the University of Pennsylvania, "it has revolutionary implications for how we see ourselves. When we can synthesize life, it makes the notion of a living being less special." And there's a perception that synthetic biologists may be "manipulating nature without knowing where they are going," he says. "There are arrogant scientists, and our friend Venter may be one of them."

Questions for Analysis

1. What public policy arguments might be used to outlaw contracts involving synthetic life? Explain.

2. Do any existing statutes that outlaw certain types of contracts apply to contracts involving artificial life? Explain.

3. What would be the status of a contract involving synthetic life if, after the contract had been entered and was being performed, synthetic life contracts were outlawed by the legislature? Explain.

4. What ethical arguments might be made against permitting contracts that buy and sell synthetic life? Explain.

5. What social and economic benefits suggest that it might not be a good idea to outlaw contracts involving synthetic life? Explain.

Source: John Carey, "Breakthroughs: On the Brink of Artificial Life: Craig Venter says success is near, but critics blast efforts to patent synthetic organisms," *BusinessWeek*, June 25, 2007, 40.

Agreements to Defraud Creditors

Agreements to defraud creditors, that is, agreements that tend to remove or weaken the rights of creditors, are void as contrary to public policy. Thus a debtor's agreement to sell and transfer personal and real property to a friend or relative for far less than actual value would be void if done for the purpose of hiding the debtor's assets from creditors with a legal claim to them.

Agreements to Escape Liability

A basic policy of the law is that all parties should be liable for their own wrongdoing. Consequently, the law looks with disfavor on any agreement that allows a party to escape this responsibility. One device frequently used in the attempt to escape legal responsibility is the **exculpatory agreement**. Such an agreement is usually found as a

Talking Points

In his landmark book *The Power Elite,* C. Wright Mills examines the amoral activities of people within every niche of the power network, including business, politics, and the military. At one point Mills makes the following observation: "A society that is in its higher circles and on its middle levels widely believed to be a network of smart rackets does not produce men with an inner moral sense; a society that is merely expedient does not produce men of conscience. A society that narrows the meaning of 'success' to the big money and its terms condemns failure as the chief vice, raising money to the plane of absolute value, will produce the sharp operator, and the shady deal. Blessed are the cynical, for only they have what it takes to succeed." Is Mills correct in his observation? Has America produced several generations of amoral leaders? Is Mills correct that this characteristic can be seen in business, politics, and the military, or might one of these levels of the power elite be more susceptible to this accusation than the others? Explain. Is this why the problems associated with illegal contracts have become more commonplace today? Explain.

clause in a longer, more complex contract or on the back of tickets and parking stubs. The exculpatory clause will state that one of the parties, generally the one who wrote the contract, will not be liable for any economic loss of physical injury even if that party caused the loss or injury.

EXAMPLE 12-7:   *Patterson v. McCarthy*

Ken Patterson, a truck driver who represented the Turtledove Trucking Company, was sent to a job that would involve transporting several canisters of toxic nerve gas. When Patterson arrived at the job, he was told he had to sign an additional contract with Benjamin McCarthy, the owner of the gas canisters. One of the clauses in the additional contract included an exculpatory clause that stated that Patterson and Turtledove Trucking would hold McCarthy blameless should Patterson be injured by the gas. During the trip, McCarthy and Richard Todd, a Hazmat engineer traveling with the team, were distracted by a problem with their travel schedule. While the two of them were focused on the difficulty with the schedule, the seals on one of the gas canisters leaked. Patterson, who was nearby, was overcome by the toxic fumes and had to be transported to a nearby hospital for treatment. Both Patterson and Turtledove Trucking sued McCarthy and Todd. McCarthy pointed to the exculpatory clause and said he was not liable. The court disagreed, saying that though the exculpatory clause might excuse him from events that were not his fault or were beyond his control, it could not protect him from his own negligence, which in this case the court decided had contributed directly to Patterson's injuries.

This exculpatory clause is an example of the type that the courts have found to be a violation of public policy. Such exculpatory clauses are not favored by the law because they permit behavior to fall below acceptable standards, which was what happened in the Patterson case. A clause simply disclaiming liability in general terms is often insufficient to release a party from his or her own negligence. Still, some courts will enforce exculpatory clauses if they do not offend public policy and there is no inequality of bargaining power between the parties. However, whenever an exculpatory provision is ambiguous, confusing, vague, incomplete, or can be interpreted in different ways, the court will construe the clause against the party it was designed to protect.

Agreements in Restraint of Trade

The law tries to be a constant protector of the rights of persons to make a living and to do business freely in a competitive market. If persons enter into contracts that take away these rights, the law will restore the rights to them by declaring such contracts void. A **restraint of trade** is a limitation on the full exercise of doing business with others. Agreements that have the effect of removing competition or denying to the public services they would otherwise have or that result in higher prices and resulting hardship are **agreements in restraint of trade** and can be declared void.

Agreements to Suppress Competition   Any agreement made with the intent of suppressing competition, fixing prices, and the like is void as an illegal restraint of trade. Such agreements are unenforceable because they deprive the public of the advantages guaranteed in an economy based on freedom to contract, laws of supply and demand, and fair and honest business dealing. However, agreements of this type may be legal and

enforceable if they do not violate the so-called **rule of reason standard** that is usually applied by the courts. The rule of reason is that such agreements are enforceable when they do not unreasonably restrict businesses from competing with one another.

To determine reasonableness, the courts consider such facts as the history of the restraint, the harm that results (if any), the reason for the practice, and the purpose attained. However, some standards are set by antimonopoly statutes such as the Sherman Antitrust Act, which name certain practices, such as price fixing, that are inherently anticompetitive by their very nature. Such practices are termed **per se violations** and prohibited whether or not anyone is actually harmed. (See the discussion of restraint of trade in Chapter 40. In addition to the Sherman Antitrust Act, Chapter 40 also covers the Clayton Act, the Robinson-Patman Act, and the Federal Trade Commission Act.)

Contracts Related to Copyright Infringement   A **copyright** is designed to protect the rights that attach to an artistic, literary, or musical work. A copyright holder is given the exclusive right to reproduce, publish, and sell a work that is set in a tangible medium of expression. Copyright owners also have the right to produce derivative works that come from the original copyrighted material. It would be illegal to enter a contract that would involve a promise to violate the rights of a copyright holder by agreeing to duplicate and sell copies of the original work. The Supreme Court has also declared it illegal for one party to provide a way for a second party to violate the copyright rights of a third party, even if the provider of the means does not itself violate the original copyright. This offense has been termed **contributory copyright infringement**.

Online music sites have cost the recording industry millions of dollars, forcing recording companies and performers, like rapper Ludacris, to vigorously defend their copyright protections.

The law also recognizes that there are exceptions to the rule that protects the holder of a copyright. The key exception is known as **fair use**. Copying items for such purposes as criticism, comment, news reporting, teaching, scholarship, and research is permissible. Libraries and archives may reproduce single copies of certain copyrighted materials for noncommercial purposes without obtaining permission from the copyright owners. Transforming a copyrighted work for purposes of parody and satire is also permissible.

Sale of Business   When a business is sold, it is common practice for the agreement to contain covenants that restrict the seller from entering the same type of business. Such **restrictive covenants** in a contract for the sale of a business will be upheld by the court if they are reasonable in time and geographical area. What is reasonable is determined by a careful examination of the business being sold. For example, an agreement by the seller of a barbershop not to open a similar shop in the same community for the next three years would undoubtedly be reasonable. In contrast, a wider geographical area or longer period of time might not be allowed by the court.

EXAMPLE 12-8:   *Holden v. Gerdel*

Vinnie Gerdel owned a neighborhood pizza and sub restaurant called the Pizza Pie Party Place, which he sold to Fran Holden. A condition to the sale was a clause in the contract that prohibited Gerdel from opening another pizza and sub restaurant anywhere in Indianapolis for a period of five years. Gerdel sought to have this condition invalidated as contrary to public policy. The court ruled that the provision covered such an extensive geographical area and such a long period of time that it was unreasonable. The court revised the agreement to allow Holden to restrain Gerdel from opening a pizza and sub restaurant within five miles of the Pizza Pie Party Place for two years.

Restrictive Employment Covenants   A restrictive employment covenant is an employment contract that limits a worker's employment options after leaving her or his present job. The objective of such a clause is to protect the present employer from an employee who might take trade secrets, customer lists, or other confidential material to a competitor. In a typical restrictive employment covenant (see Figure 12-2), an employee promises not to work for a competitor in the same field for a specified time period and within a specified geographical area after leaving the current job. Agreements like this are not favored by the law because they could deprive people of their livelihood, and they could severely limit competition. Consequently, restrictive employment covenants must be reasonable in the type of work they prohibit, the length of time involved in the prohibition, and the geographical area covered by the prohibition. Naturally, reasonableness as to work, time, and geography will vary from case to case, depending on the nature of the job involved in the prohibition.

```
                    RESTRICTIVE EMPLOYMENT COVENANT


        In consideration of my being employed by Hawthorne
    Savings and Loan, I, Vytataus Angelitis, the undersigned, hereby
    agree that when I leave the employment of Hawthorne, regardless of
    the reason I leave, I will not compete with Hawthorne, or its
    assigns or successors.

        The phrase "NOT COMPETE"  stated above means that I will not
    directly or indirectly work as a loan officer for a savings and
    loan association or any other financial institution that is in com-
    petition with Hawthorne.

        This restrictive employment covenant will extend for a radius
    of five miles from the present location of Hawthorne at 6802 East
    185th Street, Cleveland, Ohio. This covenant will be in effect for
    six months, beginning on the date of the termination of employment.

        Signed this second of March, 20 - -.



                             Vytataus Angelitis

                          Employee
```

Figure 12-2   A restrictive employment covenant. Note that the agreement is reasonable as to the type of work Angelitis is allowed to do (loan officer), the length of time involved (six months), and the geographical area covered by the prohibition (a five-mile radius from Hawthorne's location).

Nondisclosure Agreements   Some employers attempt to avoid the problems associated with restrictive employment covenants by using nondisclosure agreements. A **nondisclosure agreement** requires employees to promise that, should they leave their present place of employment, they will not reveal any confidential trade secrets that they might learn while on their current job. Because the limitation is placed on the use of confidential information rather than actual employment of the worker, such agreements do not deprive people of their employment and therefore do not constitute an extensive limit on competition.

Although helpful, nondisclosure agreements are often not needed to protect trade secrets. The court will generally issue an injunction to prevent the revelation or the utilization of trade secrets if the employer can convince the court that (1) the information revealed by the former employee was actually a trade secret, (2) the secret information was crucial to the running of the employer's business, (3) the employer had the right to use the trade secret, and (4) the former employee came into possession of the trade secret while in a position of trust and confidence and in such a way that it would be unfair for the former employee to disclose that trade secret in a way that would hurt his or her former employer. Of course, it is also necessary to show that the employee actually revealed the confidential information to a competitor.

EXAMPLE 12-9:   *Hawthorne v. Angelitis*

Hawthorne Savings and Loan Association attempted to prevent Vytataus Angelitis from working as a loan officer for any other savings and loan association in competition with Hawthorne and located within five miles of the present location of Hawthorne. This prohibition was to last for six months after Angelitis left Hawthorne. Five weeks after leaving Hawthorne, Angelitis took a job at the Lithuanian Savings and Loan Company as a loan officer. The Lithuanian Savings and Loan is located about three miles from Hawthorne. Hawthorne tried to stop Angelitis, claiming his knowledge of its customer lists would hurt its business. Hawthorne pointed to the restrictive employment covenant prohibiting Angelitis from taking such a job. The court held that the restrictions in the covenant were reasonable as to time, location, and type of job. (See Figure 12-2.)

Civil RICO Litigation   Another approach that employers can take to protect themselves against the theft of trade secrets by former employees is to file a civil action under the Racketeer Influenced and Corrupt Organizations (RICO) Act. Of course, this technique

A Question of Ethics

Suppose in Example 12-9 that the members of the board of directors of Hawthorne Savings and Loan Association knew the job Angelitis had taken with the Lithuanian Savings and Loan Company would not in any way realistically hurt their business. Suppose further that the Hawthorne board members knew Angelitis had been out of work for five weeks and that he and his family had many past due bills that they could not pay unless Angelitis remained at Lithuanian. Legally, the Hawthorne board members can prevent Angelitis from working for Lithuanian. However, would it be ethical for them to do so? Explain.

is unlike the use of restrictive employment covenants and nondisclosure agreements because it is a reactive approach that happens after the trade secret has been revealed. Nevertheless, the fact that such technique has been approved of by the courts has strengthened the effectiveness of the other two techniques. Former employees who contemplate breaching a restrictive employment covenant or a nondisclosure agreement might think twice about doing so if they know that their former employer could bring a RICO action against them. Under RICO, employers can, in addition to their other remedies, receive triple damages, attorney fees, and reasonable court costs should they prevail.

Quick Quiz 12-2 True or False?

1. Public policy says only the government should be allowed to do things that injure the public at large.

2. Per se violations of antitrust law are prohibited only if someone is actually harmed.

3. A nondisclosure agreement requires employees to promise that they will reveal trade secrets only when compensated properly.

12-3 Consequences of Illegality

Illegality of contract, as in promises to commit criminal acts, not only serves to void existing agreements but may lead to indictment and prosecution when sufficient evidence warrants such an action. Persons who agree to commit criminal acts for a promised consideration are involved in what criminal law defines as a **conspiracy**. Agreements that do not violate criminal laws may still be invalid. Thus, many agreements considered contrary to public policy have been declared invalid as against the public good but not illegal in terms of criminal liability. Both types of agreements fail to have the characteristics that permit legal enforcement.

In Pari Delicto Contracts

When both parties to an illegal agreement are equally wrong in the knowledge of the operation and effect of their contract, they are said to be *in pari delicto* (in equal fault). In such cases, the court will give no aid to either party in an action against the other and will award no damages to either. When the parties are not *in pari delicto*, relief will often be allowed if sought by the more innocent of the two. Although this rule is not applicable when one may be less guilty of premeditation (plotting or planning an illegal act) and intent to achieve a gain through known illegal acts, it may be applied when one party is not aware that a law is being broken and there is no intent to do a wrong.

EXAMPLE 12-10: *Kowalski v. International Shipping*

Gary Kowalski was an out-of-work snowmobile salesman who needed a job quickly. Following the advice of his neighbor, Larry Perdue, he tried to find employment on the Internet. Kowalski logged onto the Net and found an advertisement placed by International Shipping for a job entitled "product repackager." He applied for and was granted the position. As part of his training, Kowalski had to send International $500 for a starter kit that contained his repackaging instructions and supplies. When he received the supplies, they did not appear to be worth $5, let alone $500. Unfortunately, Kowalski was now committed to the job because of the cash outlay and so he did as he was told. Kowalski's job was to receive packages in the mail from American companies, unpack those packages, inspect them, and then repackage them for shipment to foreign addresses. After receiving and resending 12 packages, the shipments stopped. The very next day, Kowalski was surprised by a visit from federal agents who accused him of fencing goods purchased with stolen credit card numbers. Kowalski was not aware of this fact, and in an action against International, the court would rule that Kowalski might recover his $500 as the parties were not *in pari delicto*.

Illegality in Entire Agreement

Sometimes an agreement will be partly legal and partly illegal. If the legal part of a contract can be removed from the illegal part, without changing the essential nature of the contract, then the agreement is said to be divisible. The court will enforce the legal part but not the illegal part. As long as the main purpose of the agreement can be reached without enforcing the illegal part, the courts are likely to uphold the agreement.

EXAMPLE 12-11:   *Kavanaugh v. Fraser and Brambles, Inc.,* Part I

Fraser and Brambles Inc., a soap and cosmetics firm, entered a contract with Kavanaugh and Associates Advertising, Inc., a Dallas-based advertising agency. Under the terms of the agreement, Kavanaugh was supposed to fashion a national ad campaign for the marketing of 12 new cosmetic products produced by Fraser and Brambles. One of the products was a new sunscreen that was denied approval by the federal Food and Drug Administration (FDA). The part of the contract that involved the sunscreen now involved an illegal product. The part of the contract for that product, however, would be divisible from the overall contract, Kavanaugh would still be able to sue for the compensation promised, separating the illegal product from the main purpose of the agreement to advertise the new product line for Fraser and Brambles.

In contrast, if the legal part cannot be separated from the legal part, it is termed indivisible, and the entire agreement is void. Even though specific sections of the agreement may be legally enforceable, if standing alone, illegality of any part of the entire agreement renders it invalid.

EXAMPLE 12-12:   *Kavanaugh v. Fraser and Brambles, Inc.,* Part II

Suppose, in the previous example, all the new products that Fraser and Brambles intended to place on the national market were denied approval by the FDA. In such a situation, it is quite likely that the court would then declare the agreement to be illegal in its entirety. This determination would mean that the court would have to deny the Kavanaugh Advertising Agency any rights whatsoever under the contract, even if some of the clauses in the contract standing by themselves, such as time limits, the amount of consideration to be paid to the ad agency, the timing of the advertising campaign, or the types of media to be used, would be legal if the subject matter of the ad campaign itself had turned out to be legal.

Quick Quiz 12-3 True or False?

1. Persons who agree to commit criminal acts for a promised consideration are involved in what most state criminal codes define as piracy.

2. When neither party to an illegal agreement knows that the substance of the contract is illegal, each party is said to be *in pari delicto*.

3. If the legal part of the agreement can be separated from the illegal part, the agreement is said to be divisible.

Summary

12.1 An agreement might have offer, acceptance, mutual assent, competent parties, and consideration and still be invalid if the objective of the agreement is to do something that is illegal. One type of contract that fails in legality is one in which the parties agree to do some otherwise illegal act. This illegal act could be a crime or a tort. Some agreements are made illegal by statute even though the activities themselves are neither crimes nor torts. These agreements include usurious agreements, wagering agreements, unlicensed agreements, unconscionable agreements, and Sunday (Sabbath) agreements.

12.2 Public policy is a general legal principle that says no one should be allowed to do anything that tends to hurt the public at large. Agreements found void for a violation of public policy include agreements to obstruct justice, agreements interfering with public service, agreements to defraud creditors, exculpatory agreements, and agreements in restraint of trade.

12.3 Contracts that involve illegal agreements are invalid. Moreover, promises to commit illegal acts may lead to indictment and prosecution. If an entire agreement is illegal, no binding contract results. If only part of an agreement is illegal, the court may rescind only those parts found to be illegal. When both parties are equally at fault in creating an illegal agreement, the court will award no damages to either. When the parties are not in equal fault, relief will often be granted if sought by the innocent party.

Key Terms

Questions for Review and Discussion

1. What is the effect of illegality on a contract?
2. What contracts have been made illegal by statutory law?
3. What is the rationale behind usury laws?
4. What wagering agreements are not illegal under state law?
5. What are the rules regarding licenses and illegality?
6. When is an agreement considered unconscionable?
7. What statutes make Sunday agreement illegal?
8. What is the legal principle of public policy?
9. What are the contracts made illegal by public policy?
10. What are the consequences of an illegal agreement?

Investigating the Internet

A Web site known as the "Lectric Law Library" can be very helpul in explaining some of the basics of all areas of the law. Find the Web site of the Lectric Law Library, access contract law, and, in a short report, answer the following questions: (1) According to the Lectric Law Library, if a contract is illegal, what is its status under the law? (2) What standing do the parties to an illegal contract have in court? (3) Can a party to an illegal contract sue to recover any money that the party may have paid under the contract? (4) According to the Lectric Law Library, of the three types of illegal contracts, contracts to commit a crime, contracts to commit a tort, and contracts that violate public policy, which is the most difficult to define? (5) How does the Lectric Law Library describe violations of public policy?

Cases for Analysis

1. Clear Channel Broadcasting, Inc., required Diane Ignazio to sign a new contract that included an arbitration clause under which she agreed that all grievances that she might have with Clear Channel would be settled by arbitration. As part of the agreement, Ignazio gave up any right to bring a lawsuit against Clear Channel. When Ignazio was discharged, instead of moving to arbitration, she sued Clear Channel for discrimination and wrongful discharge. Clear Channel filed a motion to dismiss the case, arguing that Ignazio was bound by the arbitration agreement. Ignazio pointed to a clause in the agreement that rendered the entire agreement illegal. The clause allowed the arbitration award to be reviewed by a court based on the same broad standards used by an appeals court in reviewing a trial court's decision. This provision contradicts state law, which states that if an appeals court reviews an arbitration decision, it can only use a very limited approach to the appeal, including only such things as clerical error or misconduct. Clear Channel argued that even if the clause was illegal, it could be severed from the agreement, and the rest of the agreement could be enforced. In fact, the contract even included a clause that stated that any clause found illegal ought to be removed from the contract, so that the rest of the contract could be upheld. The question before the court was whether the illegal clause could be removed from the agreement without changing the essential nature of the contract. Is it legally permissible to remove the illegal part of a contract so that the court can uphold the legal part? Should the court sever the illegal clause in this case? Explain. *Ignazio v. Clear Channel*, 113 Ohio St.3d 276 (Ohio Supreme Court).

2. Cyberian Enterprises and BrandAid Marketing Corporation entered a deal under which Cyberian was supposed to purchase $21 million in Brand-Aid's stock. Cyberian, however, did not have the funds available to make the actual purchase, a fact that was concealed by Cyberian representatives. When BrandAid discovered the lie, it filed a lawsuit against Cyberian for fraud, breach of contract, and breaking federal securities law. Cyberian brought a countersuit against BrandAid for fraud because BrandAid had apparently failed to tell Cyberian about its own financial difficulties. However, BrandAid's financial problems were on file with the Securities and Exchange Commission (SEC). When the case went to District Court, the judge dismissed the case because, citing the doctrine of *in pari delicto*, he stated that both parties were at equal fault in concealing their financial difficulties. The case then went to the Second Circuit Court of Appeals, which decided that the trial court had made a mistake in dismissing the case. Why did the appeals court overturn the decision of the trial court? Explain. *BrandAid Marketing Corp. v. Biss*, 05-5243-cv (2d U.S. Cir. Ct. of App.). (See also Beth Bar, "Civil Practice: Finding of Equal Fault Is Overturned," *The National Law Journal,* September 11, 2006, p. 13.

3. Shannon Audley, a professional model, signed an agreement before starting work on a photo shoot at Bill Melton's studio. The agreement stated: "I, Shannon Audley, realize that working with wild and potentially dangerous animals (i.e., lion, white tiger, hawk) can create a hazardous situation resulting in loss of life or limb. I take all responsibility upon myself for any event as described above that may take place. I hold Bill Melton and T.I.G.E.R.S. or any of their agents free of any or all liability. I am signing this of my own free will." During the photo shoot, Audley was bitten on the head by the adult male lion with which she had been posing. Audley brought suit against Melton. Would the exculpatory clause be upheld by the courts? Explain. *Audley v. Melton*, 640 A.2d 777 (NH).

4. Judy Myers and the Terminix International Company entered a contract in which Terminix agreed to inspect Myers's home and eliminate any termite problem found there. The service cost Myers an initial payment of $1,300 plus annual renewal fees of $85. Terminix failed to eradicate the termite infestation, causing more than $41,000 in damage to Myers's home. The contract contained a clause that required the parties to submit any disputes to arbitration under the American Arbitration Association (AAA). What the contract did not disclose was that Myers would be required to pay a filing fee to submit a claim to AAA. In this case, the filing fee amounted to $7,000. In a lawsuit filed for breach of contract, Myers asserted that the undisclosed filing fee requirement was unconscionable. Is Myers correct? Explain. *Myers v. Terminix,* 697 N.E.2d 277 (OH).

5. When Donald Kennedy worked for Bridgestone/Firestone (B/F), he entered a nondisclosure agreement by which he promised that should he leave B/F's employ, he would not reveal any confidential trade secrets that he might learn while at B/F. When Kennedy left B/F, he went to work for the Hankook Tire Manufacturing Co., one of B/F's competitors. B/F elected to bring suit against both Hankook and Kennedy for breach of the nondisclosure agreement. Would this type of clause be upheld by the courts? Explain. *Bridgestone/Firestone, Inc. v. Hankook Tire Manufacturing Co., Inc.* 687 N.E.2d 502 (OH).

6. Asdourian obtained a contractor's license under the name "Artko Remodeling and Construction," which was the name under which he planned to incorporate his business. He signed the license application as the responsible managing party. Later, having not yet incorporated the business, Asdourian signed a contract under his own name to convert a garage into a restaurant for Mr. and Mrs. Araj. After completing the work and not being paid fully, Asdourian sued Mr. and Mrs. Araj for the money owed. They argued that they did not have to pay him because he did not have a contractor's license in his name. Do you agree? Why? *Asdourian v. Araj*, 696 P.2d 95 (CA).

7. A group of men known as the "last man's club" bought a hunting lodge in upstate New York for their headquarters. The men agreed that the land would belong to the last surviving member. The last surviving member was Crawford, who claimed exclusive title to the land. Crawford's claim was challenged by Quinn, the daughter of a deceased member of the club. Quinn argued that the agreement made by the club members was actually a wagering agreement and therefore was illegal. Was Quinn's claim correct? Explain. *Quinn v. Stuart Lakes Club, Inc.,* 439 N.Y.S.2d 30 (NY).

8. West was hired by the data processing department of the Alberto-Culver Company as a senior programmer. Because West had obtained the job through an employment agency, Alberto-Culver

was supposed to pay the agency a fee. However, Alberto-Culver found out that the employment agency was not licensed, as was required by Illinois law. Because the employment agency was not licensed, Alberto-Culver claimed it did not have a duty to pay the agency fee. Was Alberto-Culver correct? Explain. *T.E.C v. Alberto-Culver Company,* 476 N.E.2d 1212 (IL).

9. Williams, as a regular customer of Walker-Thomas Furniture, would buy household goods on time payments. A clause in each installment contract indicated that an unpaid balance would affect all items ever purchased. In effect, this clause meant that if Williams ever missed a payment, the store could repossess all the items that Williams had ever bought from Walker, regardless of how long ago they were purchased. Williams missed one monthly payment, and Walker attempted to repossess everything that Williams had purchased over the last five years. Williams claimed that the default clause was unconscionable. Was he correct? Explain. *Williams v. Walker-Thomas Furniture Company,* 350 F2d 445 (DC Cir.).

10. Peeples was seriously injured when he fell from a scaffold set up by Donar Systems, his employer. At the time of the fall, the work was being done for the city of Detroit. The city claimed that it was not liable because Donar's employment contract contained a clause that absolved the city of any liability for negligence regardless of who was at fault. Peeples claimed that this was an illegal exculpatory clause and asked the court not to uphold it. Did the court comply with Peeples' request?

Explain. *Peeples v. City of Detroit,* 297 N.W.2d 839 (MI).

11. The Topps Chewing Gum company and the Major League Baseball Players Association entered into exclusive five-year contracts for the services of the league's baseball players. Photographs of major league baseball players were to appear exclusively on baseball cards distributed by Topps with the sale of its chewing gum. The Fleer Corporation, a rival of Topps, brought suit for $16 million, alleging that the exclusive contracts would freeze out competition in this area and thus constituted "an illegal restraint on trade." Topps argued that Fleer could compete by seeking the agreements with players still in the minor leagues. Thus, Topps concluded, its competitive efforts were not unreasonable. Was Topps correct? Explain. *Fleer Corporation v. Topps Chewing Gum, Inc.,* 501 F. Supp. 485 (E.D. PA).

12. Trecher worked for Columbia Ribbon and Carbon Manufacturing Co., Inc., as a salesperson for several years. His employment agreement included a restrictive employment covenant that said he could not obtain a similar job anywhere in the United States for two years after he left Columbia. Trecher left Columbia and was hired as a salesperson by A-1-A Corporation, one of Columbia's competitors. Columbia filed a lawsuit to stop Trecher from working for A-1-A based on the restrictive employment covenant. Did the court stop Trecher from working for A-1-A? Explain. *Columbia Ribbon and Carbon Manufacturing v. A-1-A Corporation,* 369 N.E.2d 4 (NY).

Quick Quiz Answers

12-1	12-2	12-3
1. T	1. F	1. F
2. F	2. F	2. F
3. F	3. F	3. T

Chapter 13 Written Contracts

The Opening Case

Harry Rubin & Sons, Inc. v. Consolidated Pipe Company of America, Inc.

Carl Pearce, a salesman for Consolidated Pipe (Consolidated), met with representatives from Harry Rubin & Sons (Rubin) to negotiate Consolidated's sale of plastic hoops to Rubin. The negotiations resulted in three unwritten contracts. Each of these unwritten contracts involved products that were valued at more that $500. The agreements were never reduced to a formal written contract. When Consolidated failed to deliver the material, Rubin brought a lawsuit against Consolidated. Consolidated moved for a dismissal, arguing that because they were talking about a deal involving goods worth more than $500 and because there was no written contract, the agreements were unenforceable. For its part, Rubin pointed to a purchase order and a letter that covered the details of the agreement. The purchase order was for 30,000 hoops. The letter was a follow-up from Rubin to Consolidated stating that an additional 60,000 hoops were expected from Consolidated after the first delivery of 30,000. Rubin argued that the purchase order and the letter satisfied the requirements of Section 2-201 of the Uniform Commercial Code, which permits one party to an oral agreement between merchants to send a confirmation to the other party. This confirmation would then serve as the writing, unless that other party objected to its content. In this case, Consolidated never objected, and so *voila,* the written requirements were satisfied by the purchase order and the letter. Consolidated later objected, noting that the two documents in question never used the word "contract" or even "agreement" but instead referred to the entire arrangement as an "order." Therefore, Consolidated concluded, the two documents could not satisfy the statute. The court, in what amounted to a "you have got to be kidding" response, told Consolidated that it could not possibly be more wrong about the legal requirements established by the UCC. The purchase order and the letter were taken by the court to have clearly met the requirements of the statute. (See *Harry Rubin & Sons, Inc., v. Consolidated Pipe Company of America, Inc.,* 396 Pa. 506, Supreme Court of Pennsylvania.)

Opening Case Questions

1. In this contract, which party is the offeror and which is the offeree?

2. Why would the contract involving the sale of plastic hoops have to be in writing?

3. Why does the court refer to the Uniform Commercial Code in this case?

4. How could Consolidated have prevented the problem that arose in this case?

5. Why does the court rule in favor of Harry Rubin & Sons?

LO Learning Objectives

1. Point out the abuses that the Statute of Frauds was designed to eliminate.
2. Identify agreements that must be written under the Statute of Frauds.
3. List the information that must be in a written contract.
4. Explain the parol evidence rule.
5. Describe the exceptions under the parol evidence rule.
6. Explain the best evidence rule.
7. Explain the equal dignities rule.
8. Illustrate various methods of writing a signature.
9. Discuss the use of witnesses, acknowledgments, the seal, and recording.
10. Identify the most current e-commerce laws.

13-1 The Statute of Frauds

LO1

Often when people hear the word *contract,* they immediately think of a piece of paper. Instead, they should think of an agreement, which may or may not be in writing. Many contracts do not have to be in writing to be enforceable. Most oral contracts are valid and upheld by the court. Although it may be desirable to put a contract in writing so that its terms are clear, only certain kinds of contracts are required to be in writing. This chapter discusses the Statute of Frauds, which is the law that requires certain contracts to be in writing to be enforceable.

Early British law enforced oral contracts when they could be proven through the testimony of witnesses. Ironically, whereas witnesses were required to prove the existence of an oral agreement, the parties themselves were barred from testifying on their own behalf. As might have been expected, the parties began to pay off friends and associates to testify on their behalf. As a result, perjury became commonplace, and hundreds of phony contracts were enforced by a court system that knew better but had its hands tied. To correct these abuses, in 1677 Parliament passed the Act for the Prevention of Frauds and Perjuries, also called the Statute of Frauds. Some provisions of the Statute of Frauds were adopted into practice in the U.S. Courts after the colonies separated from England. Each state now has it own Statute of Frauds.

Contracts that Must Be in Writing

LO2

According to the Statute of Frauds, applicable in most states, six types of contracts must be in writing to be enforceable:

1. Contracts that cannot be completed within one year.
2. Contracts transferring real property rights.
3. Contracts for the sale of goods of $500 or more.
4. Certain contracts entered into by executors and administrators.
5. Contracts by one party to pay a debt of another party.
6. Contracts in consideration of marriage.

The third contract on the list, contracts for the sale of goods of $500 or more, is actually included in the Uniform Commercial Code rather than the Statute of Frauds. This point is covered in depth in Chapter 16.

Contracts that Cannot Be Completed Within One Year

If the terms of a contract make it impossible to complete the agreement within one year, the contract must be in writing.

EXAMPLE 13-1: *Strachan v. Wright Weber Construction*

Frank Strachan entered a contract with Wright Weber Construction for the building of an addition to his new home in Lakeside. The construction firm was to begin building the addition on April 2. Wright Weber agreed that the addition might be finished by March 1 of the following year, but also stipulated that May 1 of the following year was a more reasonable estimate. The details of the agreement were never reduced to writing. When Wright Weber ran into labor problems in August, it had to put the construction of the addition on hold. One month later, unable to resolve the labor dispute, Wright Weber shut the company down and abandoned the Strachan work site. As a result, Strachan had to negotiate a new contract with a new construction firm. The new contract cost $12,900 more than it would have had Weber completed the job as promised. In addition, because the lakeside house could not be used during construction, Strachan incurred storage costs for his furniture because he had to move out of the home he was living in to accommodate the new owners. He also had to live in a hotel for four months while the Lakeside addition was completed. Strachan sued Wright Weber. Wright Weber moved for a dismissal because the contract was not in writing. Strachan argued that the contract could have been completed within one year and was therefore outside of the statute. As a result, he correctly concluded that the writing was not needed.

In Example 13-1, Strachan is correct, and Wright Weber is wrong. Because Weber *could* have completed the contract within one year, or less for that matter, the contract *could have been* performed within one year, and the writing was not needed. This possibility is made clear by the fact that the first target date that Weber had agreed to was 11 months after the project began. Even though Weber indicated that the 13-month target date was more feasible, the firm stipulated that the 11-month target was feasible. This stipulation is all that is required by the statute. It is critical to understand that the operative words in the statute state that contracts "not to be performed" within one year must be in writing. If it is possible to perform a contract within one year, no matter how unlikely, then it falls outside the statute, and *no writing* is required. That was the case here.

Contracts Transferring Real Property Rights

Under the Statute of Frauds, conveyances of real property must be in writing to be enforceable. This provision covers the sale of land; however, it also covers trusts that are created by one party, the trustor, that permit a second party, the trustee, to possess and control the land for the advantage of a third party, the beneficiary. Whether the provision includes leases is problematic, because some jurisdictions permit short leases, generally those that last less than a year, to be oral. Most states, however, are relatively clear that leases that are designed to last longer than one year must be in writing to be enforceable. Moreover, it is not enough that the lease actually be in writing; the writing must also be presented to the court for it to be enforceable.

Although the marriage agreement itself does not have to be written, some contracts associated with marriage do.

EXAMPLE 13-2: *Nicklesworth v. Marblehead Properties*

Walt Nicklesworth entered a lease agreement with Marblehead Properties, under which Nicklesworth used the property located at 5293 Lake Shore Boulevard as a used bookstore. The terms of the lease included a right of first refusal, such that Nicklesworth could purchase the property if Marblehead ever decided to sell. Two years into the five-year lease, Marblehead sold the property to Daniel O'Donnell. Nicklesworth brought suit for breach of contract. At trial, no one could produce a written copy of the lease for the judge. The judge dismissed the case because the Statute of Frauds required a writing, and none could be produced at court.

It is also important to understand that when a party owns land, he or she owns a bundle of rights that can be distributed among various other parties. Thus, it is possible, for example, for the owner of a parcel of land to divide the rights to that land among several different parties. One party might hold a lease to a house on the land allowing her to live there, a second could have an easement that permits him to cross the land, a third might own the right to mine the land, and so on. The Statute of Frauds requires a writing for each of these different transactions. The object of this requirement is to make certain that there is a way to follow the trail of each of these rights to determine who owns them, should a dispute arise concerning them.

EXAMPLE 13-3: *Xavier v. Brookhaven*

In 1919, Pasha Patel owned several acres of land in the Upper Peninsula of the state of Michigan. Half a pond was located on Patel's land. The other half of the pond was located on land owned by Brooke Brookhaven. For a small consideration, Patel transferred the right to cut ice on her side of the pond each winter to Fred Xavier. The contract was oral and supposed to last for the next five winters. Each day from early October to late March, Xavier would cut the ice and remove it. He would carefully carve the ice into large cubes that fit perfectly into the ice boxes located in the rental cabins dotting the upper peninsula. (This was 1919, remember.) He then sold the ice to the cabin renters. One summer Brookhaven drained her part of the pond. In October, this action meant that ice was sparse, and what was available was sunk into the mud at the bottom of the lake and thus unusable for carving and sale. Xavier brought suit against Brookhaven, arguing that her action in draining the lake made his interest in the property worthless. The court asked for a copy of the written contract transferring the right to cut the ice to Xavier. When Xavier could not produce one, the judge dismissed the case.

An exception to the rule that contracts for the sale of land must be in writing is called **part performance** or **equitable estoppel**. The exception applies when a person relies on an owner's oral promise to sell real property and then makes improvements on the property or changes his or her position in an important way. The plaintiff in such a case must prove three elements to succeed in a lawsuit. First, the plaintiff must show that he or she made the improvement relying on the original promise and without suspecting that the other party intended to renege on the agreement. Second, the plaintiff must show that any other remedy, such as restitution for the amount spent, is not enough to satisfy his or her effort or outlay of funds. Third, the plaintiff must show that the part performance itself is evidence of the existence of the contract.

EXAMPLE 13-4:   *Zuer v. Iafigliola*

Jake Iafigliola agreed in an oral contract to sell Dwight Zuer a run-down parcel of storefront property for $50,000. The storefront was located across the street from the site of a new Target that was about to be established in the neighborhood. Relying on Iafigliola's agreement, Zuer spent $20,000 improving the premises so that he could move his DVD rental business into the storefront. Iafigliola then backed out of the deal. Zuer sued, asking the court to order Iafigliola to go through with the contract. Iafigliola argued this was a real property contract and it had to be in writing to be enforceable. Zuer asked the court to apply the part performance doctrine. Zuer made the following case: First, he had made the improvements relying on the original promise. Second, he pointed out that any other remedy, such as restitution for the amount spent, would not be enough, because he clearly wanted the storefront in the lot across from the new Target. Third, Zuer argued that the fact that he spent $20,000 to improve the storefront could not be explained in any other way other than his reliance on the contract. The court agreed and allowed the lawsuit even without the writing.

The courts do not require a writing for a contract in which the owner of land agrees to improve the land for the use of another party who has already received a partial interest in the land. In such a situation, the courts believe that once the real interest in the land has been transferred, the contract to improve the land does not create a new interest. Instead, the new contract is solely a promise to provide labor and make changes in the land. It therefore falls outside the statute, and no writing is required.

EXAMPLE 13-5:   *Dewey v. Collins*

Rene Collins owned a piece of land in rural Pennsylvania, just outside Streetsboro. Frederick Dewey received an easement across Collins's land. The easement, which was supposed to last for five years, was executed in a written document. After the first year, Dewey asked Collins to lay gravel on the small road that constituted the easement. Collins said that she would not lay the gravel herself but would permit Dewey to do so and reimburse him for the expense. Dewey laid the gravel and presented Collins with the bill. Collins refused to reimburse Dewey as agreed. Collins argued that because there was no writing, the contract, which involved land, was unenforceable. The referee disagreed, concluding that the agreement to lay gravel did not create a new interest. Instead, it simply involved a commitment to pay for improvements to land in which Dewey already owned an interest.

UCC 2-201 (see page 960)

Contracts for the Sale of Goods of $500 or More   Under the UCC, contracts for the sale of goods (moveable items) for $500 or more must be in writing to be enforceable. However, there are four exceptions to this rule. Oral contracts for the sale of goods of $500 or more will be enforced in situations involving the following:

1. Oral contracts between merchants when a written confirmation has been received by one party and not objected to by the other party.
2. Specially manufactured goods that cannot be resold easily.
3. Admissions in court.
4. Executed agreements.

These exceptions are discussed in more detail in Chapter 16. Under international law (the United Nations Convention on Contracts for the International Sale of Goods), contracts for the sale of goods need not be in writing.

Certain Contracts Entered by Executors and Administrators

An *executor* is a person who is named in a will to oversee the distribution of the estate of a deceased according to the provisions outlined in the will. An *administrator* is a person named by the court to do the work of an executor if none is named in the will or if the executor cannot or will not perform those duties. As a general principle of law, neither an executor nor an administrator is personally liable for the debts of the decedent's estate. Executors and administrators must pay the debts of the estate, to be sure, but out of the assets of the estate, not out of their own pockets. Thus, any promise to pay the debts of the estate using the executor's or the administrator's own funds is unenforceable without a writing.

EXAMPLE 13-6:   *Trautman v. Quinn*

Max Quinn was named the executor of his sister's estate. One of his sister's creditors, Nancy Trautman, demanded immediate payment of a debt of $6,600 owed by the deceased. To protect his sister's good name, Quinn promised Trautman that he would pay her the amount owed out of his own funds if the estate could not cover that amount. Trautman refused to agree unless Quinn placed the agreement in writing. Quinn agreed. After things calmed down, Trautman tried to collect the debt. Quinn refused to pay. Trautman was able to enforce the promise because she had written evidence of Quinn's agreement to pay the debt.

Contracts by One Party to Pay a Debt Incurred by Another Party

A promise made by one party to pay another person's debts, if that person fails to pay the debt, falls within the statute and must be in writing to be enforceable. Several terms have been used to describe these types of transactions. They are alternately referred to as a **guaranty of payment**, a **guaranty contract**, or a **collateral contract**. The promisor is usually called a **guarantor**. Often in a commercial setting, the guarantor is referred to as a **cosigner**. The person to whom the promise is made is the **obligee**, and the person who owes the original debt is referred to as the **obligor**. It is crucial to distinguish between guaranty contracts and original contracts.

An exception to this rule is known as the primary objective test. Under the **primary objective test** (also referred to as the **leading objective test** and the **main purpose test**), if the promise to pay another party's debt is actually made to obtain a gain for the guarantor, there is no need for a writing to enforce the promise. Suppose, for instance, that Hans McKnight, the owner of Scottish Inn, depends on the Hometown Bakery for the inn's sub buns for its lunch trade. Suppose further that McKnight knows that the Hometown Bakery has had some financial trouble and may have to shut down its operations if it cannot pay Jakub's Supply for its regular flour shipment. If McKnight promises Jakub's that, if it continues to supply Hometown with flour, he will pay the bill, that promise falls under the primary objective test and need not be in writing to be enforceable.

Contracts in Consideration of Marriage   Agreements made in consideration of marriage must be in writing to be enforceable. This part of the statute does not refer to the marriage contract itself or to engagement promises to marry, which are almost always oral. Rather, it refers to promises made by parties before marriage, in which they accept additional obligations not usually covered in the marriage vows. A **prenuptial agreement** (also referred to as a **premarriage agreement** and an **antenuptial agreement**) involves two people who are planning marriage and who agree to change the property rights they possess by law in a marriage (see Figure 13-1). Such promises are enforceable only if they are in writing and agreed upon prior to the marriage. Many state legislatures, as well as the District of Columbia, have enacted the Uniform Premarital Ageement Act (UPAA). The UPAA supports the use of prenuptial agreements and provides for their enforcement. Like most acts developed by the National Conference of Commissioners on Uniform State Laws, however, the provisions differ slightly from state to state. Accordingly, it is best to check the detailed provisions of the UPAA enacted in your home state.

EXAMPLE 13-7: *Forester v. Forester*

Griff Forester and Gina Chambers entered a prenuptial agreement in which Forester promised that he would have no claim on Chambers's property or business should they divorce. Chambers agreed to give Forester $90,000 each year for the remainder of his life in the event of their divorce. She also promised to transfer $200,000 into Forester's account the moment that he agreed to the contract. This contract falls within the statute and therefore would have to be in writing to be enforceable. Forester and Chambers did not consult an attorney however, but simply wrote up the agreement in long hand. When the couple divorced seven years later, Chambers refused to go along with the agreement because the prenuptial agreement was not executed as a preprinted notarized agreement. Forester argued that the only requirement was that the agreement be in writing, not that it be preprinted or notarized. He was correct.

Although this point is not directly related to the Statute of Frauds, it is good to know that a court is more likely to uphold a prenuptial agreement that includes a provision for consideration. The agreement in Example 13-7 contains the element of consideration and is therefore likely to be upheld in court, provided it was in writing in the first place.

```
                        Prenuptial Agreement


      Agreement made this 10th day of June, 20 - -, between Joseph Taft of 1273 Holly Lane,

Amesburgh, PA, and Susan Jacobs, of 299 Oak Lane, Amesburgh, PA.

      Whereas a marriage is shortly to be solemnized between the parties hereto:

      Whereas Susan Jacobs now owns a large amount of property and expects to

acquire from time to time additional property under a trust established by her uncle,

Henry Jacobs;

      Whereas Joseph Taft has agreed that all of the property now or in the future owned by

Susan Jacobs, or her estate, shall be free of all rights that he might acquire by reason

of his marriage to her.

      It is agreed as follows:

      1. Susan Jacobs shall have full right and authority, in all respects the same

as she would have if unmarried, to use, enjoy, manage, convey, mortgage, and

dispose of all of her present and future property and estate, of every kind and

character, including the right and power to dispose of same by last will and

testament.

      2. Joseph Taft releases to Susan Jacobs, her heirs, legal representatives, and

assigns, every  right, claim and estate that he might have in respect to said property by

reason of his marriage to Susan Jacobs.

      IN WITNESS WHEREOF the parties have hereunto set their hands and seals the day and

year first above written.
```

Joseph Taft
_____

Susan Jacobs
_____

Figure 13-1 Contracts made in consideration of marriage must be in writing to be enforceable.

Other Contracts

Other Contracts Each state has enacted special statutes outlining other agreements that must be in writing. Other contracts that are usually required by special statutes to be in writing include the release of a party from debt (general release) and the resumption of obligations after bankruptcy. In addition, some states require real estate listing contracts and insurance binders to be in writing. Other contracts that require a writing under the UCC are contracts for the sale of securities (stocks and bonds) and agreements creating security interests.

The Contents of a Writing

Just what is meant when the statute states that "the agreement must be in writing"? The statute requires only that the agreement be in writing—nothing more. The writing should be intelligible. It may be embodied in letters, memos, telegrams, invoices, and purchase orders sent between the parties. It may be written on any surface suitable for the purpose of recording the intention of the parties, as long as all the required elements are present.

Elements of a Writing   To be absolutely complete, a written agreement, or **memorandum**, as it is often called, should contain the following elements:

- Terms of the agreement
- Identification of the subject matter
- Statement of the consideration promised
- Names and identities of the persons to be obligated
- Signature of the party sought to be bound to the agreement

EXAMPLE 13-8:   *Shapiro v. Whitehall*

For several weeks, Mary Shapiro and Harry Whitehall discussed making an agreement under which Shapiro would lease from Whitehall several hundred acres of pasture land outside Mt. Vernon for grazing her horses. Shapiro said that she needed the agreement to last for five years, but Whitehall wanted to grant only a year-by-year lease that would be renewable at the end of each year. Eventually, they compromised on a three-year lease that would be renewable at the end of the second year. Because they had been squabbling about the terms for so long, once the agreement was reached, Shapiro wanted to reduce it to writing. The moment that they agreed to the compromise however, the two of them were standing in the parking lot at the local Super Wal-Mart. Shapiro pulled an envelope out of her back pocket and noted the conditions and terms of the agreement. She then handed the envelope to Whitehall, who signed it and returned it to Shapiro who, because it was starting to rain, quickly stuck it in her back pocket without adding her signature. The two of them then parted company. The deal went through without a hitch until the end of the second year, when Whitehall refused to allow Shapiro to use his land anymore, despite the terms of the original agreement. Shapiro had to find a replacement pasture that cost her twice as much. She sued Whitehall for the difference. In court, Whitehall claimed that the writing that Shapiro had produced was invalid because it was written on an old envelope and because Shapiro had not signed it. The court held that the envelope contract satisfied the requirements of the Statute of Frauds. The fact that the contract was handwritten on an envelope made absolutely no difference as long as all of the terms were present. Moreover, the fact that Shapiro's signature was missing made no difference, because Whitehall was the party sought to be bound.

It has been held that the words on a check given in payment for a purchase can often satisfy the requirements of a memorandum. A check identifies the parties and is signed by one party on the front and by the other party on the back. All that is necessary is to write some additional words on the memo line of the check to set forth the terms of the contract and identify the subject matter and the agreed price.

EXAMPLE 13-9: *Jameson v. Muldovan*

Frank Jameson and Gary Muldovan entered an agreement whereby Muldovan agreed to grant Jameson an easement across his land for five years. Jameson gave Muldovan a check for $4,000. Jameson wrote on the check that it was payment for the five-year easement granted by Muldovan for his land located at 433 East 310th Street in Willowick, Ohio. In a subsequent dispute, Muldovan did not deny the existence of the contract. However, he argued in a summary judgment motion that the contract was not enforceable because it involved real property rights and therefore had to be in writing. The court said that the check itself was evidence of a contract by one obligated to grant the easement rights, because it described the terms of the agreement, the subject matter, and the price to be paid.

Quick Quiz 13-1 True or False?

1. A contract is said to be outside the statute if it requires a writing to show that the two objectives of the Statute of Frauds have been met.

2. An administrator is a person who is named in a will to oversee the distribution of the estate of a deceased person according to the provisions outlined in the will.

3. Agreements made in consideration of marriage must be in writing to be enforceable.

13-2 Legal Rules for Written Contracts

Operating as a complex adaptive system, the legal system has developed certain basic criteria that make the construction and interpretation of written contracts as flawless as possible. These criteria act very much the way basic axioms or rules work in mathematics. Therefore, we could characterize these rules as unquestioned assumptions about the text of a writing that must be followed when an attorney, a magistrate, or a judge interprets a writing that claims to contain the terms of a contract. These four rules are: (1) the standard construction rule, (2) the parol evidence rule, (3) the best evidence rule, and (4) the equal dignities rule. The first two rules cover the interpretation of contracts, whereas the latter two govern their enforcement.

The Standard Construction Rule

Appropriately, the first of the interpretation rules is the most critical and the most fundamental of the four. The **standard construction rule** guides the entire interpretation process by directing the interpreter of a contract to determine the principal objective of the parties in the making of the contract. The *principal objective* is the primary or main goal that the parties hoped to accomplish by entering the agreement in the first place. Once this principal objective is stated, everything else must be interpreted to promote that principal objective. In line with this rule, the law also says that common words used in the contract are given their expected, everyday definition, and technical terms or professional slang will be given their technical or professional definitions. The standard construction rule also says that any standard operating procedures that are used in the parties' professions or trades should be followed whenever there is any doubt about what procedure should be used in the contract.

Because the standard construction rule is the most fundamental guideline involved in the interpretation of written contracts, it also guides the interpreter on matters of ambiguity and misinterpretation. The rule says that whenever an ambiguous term, clause, or line is found in a prewritten or preprinted contract, that ambiguity is interpreted against the party who wrote the contract. This approach should encourage those people who draft contracts to do so in clear and unambiguous terms, because if they draft a clause that is ambiguous, it will be interpreted against them. Thus, there is no profit in making things difficult to understand in any written contract.

The Parol Evidence Rule

Under the **parol evidence rule**, evidence of oral statements made before signing a written agreement is usually not admissible in court to change or contradict the terms of a written agreement. Following oral discussion and negotiation, parties may reduce their agreements to some written form. When this is done, only the terms, conditions, and promises included in the writing will be allowed as evidence in court. This provision is enforced because the court presumes that the parties will have put everything they agreed to in the writing.

EXAMPLE 13-10:   *Twaine v. Krell, Inc.*

Emily Twaine purchased a $1,250 desktop computer from Krell, Inc. Before all of the documents of sale were signed, the salesperson promised that she would get round-the-clock tech support from Krell technicians whenever she had a problem with her computer or any of the software associated with the computer. Krell subsequently refused to take care of any problems that Twaine had with the computer. The court ruled that the salesperson's oral warranty statements were not admissible in court because they were not contained with the other conditions in the written sales agreement.

Exceptions to the Parol Evidence Rule   The parol evidence rule will not

apply when unfair and unjust decisions might result from its application. In cases in which a written agreement is incomplete, oral evidence may be used to supply the missing terms. Similarly, when a written contract is obscure or indistinct in certain of its terms, oral evidence may be used to clarify those terms. Also, if a written agreement contains a typographical or clerical error of some sort, the court will allow oral evidence as to the true intent of the parties.

EXAMPLE 13-11:   *Bulwark v. Greene*

Edgar Bulwark was hired as an independent contractor to produce a series of magazine and journal articles that would appear under the name of a famous, and very busy, newspaper columnist named Arnold Greene. The written agreement had an error that indicated that Bulwark would receive $500 per article. The actual amount of consideration was supposed to be $5,000. The court would likely allow oral evidence to correct this obvious error.

In general, the courts allow a party to a written agreement to introduce oral testimony to show that the contract is void or voidable due to a lack of mutual assent or contractual capacity. The courts are willing to allow such testimony because it does not affect the terms of the agreement. Rather, it seeks to discredit the entire transaction. Thus, it is permissible to introduce oral evidence as to fraud, duress, misrepresentation, mistake, and undue influence. Similarly, it is appropriate to offer oral testimony as to a party's minority or mental incompetence.

EXAMPLE 13-12:   *Staniland v. Morris*

James Staniland contracted with Richard Morris to purchase an original painting by Henrietta Stein, an artist who was part of the Dadaist movement in Paris during the 1920s. After signing the written contract, Staniland took the painting and had it placed in the lobby of his business office. After one week, a customer spotted the painting and told Staniland that it was a forgery and that he had been defrauded by Morris. When Staniland took the witness stand during the trial, he was permitted to introduce evidence of the oral statements made by Morris that led him to the fraudulent conclusion that the painting was a genuine work by Stein. The court allowed the testimony because it did not affect the terms of the agreement. Rather, it sought to discredit the entire transaction.

If a written agreement depends on some event before it becomes enforceable, oral evidence may be offered regarding that condition precedent. A **condition precedent** is an act or promise that must take place or be fulfilled before the other party is obligated to perform his or her part of the agreement. The courts allow this type of oral evidence because, like the oral evidence involving assent and capacity, it does not have an impact on the terms of the agreement, but it does affect the enforceability of the entire contract.

EXAMPLE 13-13:   *Lauretig v. Pierce*

Asa Pierce agreed to lease Jay Lauretig's warehouse. The terms of the lease were laid out in a lengthy, detailed written agreement. However, as a condition precedent, a credit history and background check by Lauretig on Pierce would have to come back flawless; otherwise, the deal would be canceled. When the Search and Discover Detective Agency reported that Pierce had both a bad credit rating and two criminal convictions on drug charges, Lauretig refused to go through with the contract. At court, the judge permitted oral testimony about the credit check and the criminal background search because they were precedent conditions that had to be met before the contract went into effect.

Oral evidence may be used to prove that the parties orally agreed to rescind or modify the terms of a written contract after entering into it. Subsequent negotiations to change or rescind the agreement are permitted, and evidence to that effect does not undermine the spirit of the parol evidence rule. However, if the change in the contract involves an agreement that would have to be in writing under the Statute of Frauds, then a writing would be required. Similarly, if the original written contract requires later modifications to be in writing, then that written requirement will rule.

EXAMPLE 13-14:   *George Laurie Construction v. Popson*

George Laurie Construction entered into a contract with Terry and Sherrie Popson, the terms of which indicated that Laurie Construction was to place aluminum siding, downspouts, and gutters on the Popson vacation house on Kelley's Island. The agreement was written out in a long, preprinted contract with blanks for the pertinent individual information. All of the appropriate blanks were filled in, the contract was signed by all the parties, and the job began on schedule. Once Laurie was on the job for three days, Sherrie Popson decided that she wanted a window placed on the house. She discussed the cost of the additional work with George Laurie, who agreed to make the change indicated. The additional terms were not put in writing. After the job was completed, the Popsons paid the original amount but did not pay the added cost of the new window. The small claims court allowed testimony as to the terms involving the window because those terms represented negotiations subsequent to the original agreement to change the original terms.

UCC 1-205, 2-202, 2-208 (see pages 958 and 961)

As a final exception to the parol evidence rule, the UCC allows oral testimony about how the parties have done business together over a long time period. The UCC makes allowance for this type of testimony because, from a practical point of view, parties often get so used to dealing with each other in a particular way that they neglect to include certain terms in their written agreements. Similarly, some practices are so universal in a particular trade, business, or industry that the parties feel no need to include such universal practices in their written contracts. Accordingly, the UCC allows oral testimony to supplement a written agreement as to these practices.

EXAMPLE 13-15:   *Commonwealth Chemical Company
v. St. Clair Printing, Inc.*

St. Clair Printing, Inc., and the Commonwealth Chemical Company have been doing business for 20 years. St. Clair prints all labels, business cards, letterheads, invoices, and purchase orders for Commonwealth. During their long time working together, St. Clair has always delivered orders to Commonwealth. When a new foreman took over the bindery and delivery operation for St. Clair, he decided that there would be no deliveries to any customers outside a five-mile radius of the print shop. As a result, Commonwealth did not receive an important order of labels and lost several big orders. When Commonwealth sued St. Clair for breach of contract, St. Clair pointed out that there was nothing mentioned in the written contract about delivery responsibilities falling to St. Clair. However, because of their 20-year history of consistently dealing with each other, the court allowed oral testimony about past practices to supplement the written contract.

The Best Evidence Rule

Under the **best evidence rule**, the courts generally accept into evidence only the original of a writing, not a copy. Under this rule, a written instrument is regarded as the primary or best possible evidence. Thus, the best evidence rule concurs with and supports the parol evidence rule.

BusinessWeek Business Law in the News
Homeowners: Sweetening the Sale

Real estate agent Chris Elizabeth Griffith tells her clients they need to be creative to lure buyers. In Bonita Springs, Fla., a Gulf Coast community crowded with vacation homes and newly built condos, she suggests her sellers offer to pay a year's worth of association fees, annual property taxes, or closing costs. Her favorite tease to put in home listings: "Call for the latest juicy incentives."

The practice, which popped up last year as a way for builders to move unsold inventory, has now spread aggressively to the existing-home market, which accounts for 85% of all sales. And it's not just furniture being used to sweeten the deal. The latest trend is cash enticements to the tune of tens of thousands of dollars. There are no national numbers, but in the Washington area, deals with some form of seller subsidy jumped from 35% to 58% in two years, according to Lisa Fowler, a researcher at George Mason University's Center for Regional Analysis. The average home sold there for $470,000 in April with a subsidy of $9,700.

Such a rise has serious implications. The incentives, which don't figure into the national home-price data reported by industry groups, may be masking a steeper downturn. Fowler found that prices in D.C. fell by 0.2% over the past year if incentives were included, compared with a 0.7% rise if they weren't.

Subsidies aren't new. But the latest surge, fueled by the huge run in prices in recent years, may have legs. Given all the equity that sellers have built up—some $10.9 trillion, according to the Federal Reserve, vs. $7.8 trillion in 2002—they usually don't mind forking over some of their gains to get the deal done. Buyers often find a subsidy more appealing than a lower price, since it means they don't have to put up as much cash. "Part of it's psychological, but part of it is financial," says Fowler.

The most aggressive deals may be downright fraudulent. Lenders scrutinize transactions to make sure any cash subsidies go toward legitimate home expenses and aren't a way for the buyer to avoid a required down payment. Generally, if the incentives top 6% of the purchase price, it's a red flag. "These days you cannot get into a home unless you're putting some money down, at least 10% for those with less-than-stellar credit," says Frank McKenna, chief fraud strategist at Base Point Analytics, which analyzes mortgage data. "If borrowers are subverting that by getting cash back from sellers, that's when lenders consider it a misrepresentation or fraud."

Questions for Analysis

1. In the real estate transactions discussed in this article, who is the offeror and who is the offeree?

2. Why is the equal dignities rule important to the transactions discussed in the article?

3. Would the seller's agreement to pay the buyer's association fees, annual property taxes, or closing costs have to be in writing? Why or why not?

4. What other rule or rules would require the real estate contracts to be in writing?

5. Is there anything unethical about the seller's agreement to pay the buyer's association fees, annual property taxes, or closing costs? Explain.

Source: Christopher Palmeri and Peter Coy, "Homeowners: Sweetening the Sale," *BusinessWeek,* May 21, 2007, 38.

The Equal Dignities Rule

The **equal dignities rule**, which is followed in some states, provides that when a party appoints an agent to negotiate an agreement that must be in writing, the appointment of the agent must also be in writing. In contrast, the appointment of an agent to negotiate an agreement that the law does not require to be in writing may be accomplished through an oral agreement.

Quick Quiz 13-2 True or False?

1. Whenever an ambiguous term is found in a preprinted contract, that ambiguity is interpreted in favor of the party who wrote the contract.

2. The principal objective is the main goal that the parties hope to accomplish by entering an agreement.

3. Parol evidence is another term for written evidence.

13-3 Formalities of Construction

Certain formalities are usually followed in the formation of anything other than the simplest kinds of written agreements. Although the Statute of Frauds may necessitate nothing more than the briefest written disclosure of promises, conditions, and terms, plus the signature(s) of the obligated party or parties, usually contracts in general commercial and consumer use are carefully written, researched for legal compliance, and signed. Furthermore, leases and contracts for the sale of real property may have additional requirements of content and formality that extend beyond these demands.

Signature Requirements

Written agreements should be, but need not be, signed by both parties. If signed by only one party, any obligation in the agreement would be limited to that party alone. Parties should use their usual signatures, that is, the signatures used in other matters in the regular course of business. However, any mark that the signer intends to be a signature will be the legal signature of that person. Although it is unusual, a party may adopt any name desired in creating a contractual obligation, as long as the party intends to be bound by that signature. Thus, a well-known actress may sign a hotel register using a name other than her real name as a means of protecting her privacy. A signature may be a full name or initials, and it may be printed, typewritten, or stamped, as with a rubber stamp. However made, a signature must be provided with the intent to be bound thereby.

Facsimile Signatures With the increased use of facsimile (fax) machines, methods have been adopted to bypass the best evidence rule by giving authentication to signatures sent by way of facsimile machines. A facsimile signature will be acceptable on a contract if the contract states that facsimile signatures are valid. More commonly, however, people fax copies of signed documents to other parties, and follow it up by sending the original signed documents by overnight mail or express delivery. Some states have enacted statutes allowing certain facsimile signatures.

EXAMPLE 13-16:   Massachusetts General Laws
Chapter 92

Massachusetts has enacted the following statute relative to residence insurance agents: "A facsimile of a signature of any such resident agent imprinted on any property or casualty insurance policy issued by mail, computer modem or facsimile machine, so-called, shall have the same validity as a written signature." (Mass. Gen. Laws Chapter 92, s. 43.)

In addition, some states have adopted the **Uniform Facsimile Signatures of Public Officials Act**. This law allows the use of facsimile signatures of public officials when certain requirements are followed.

In cases in which a party cannot sign the written agreement due to illness, physical disability, or some other physical reason, another person may sign for that person. The signature should be followed by a statement indicating that the contracting party was physically unable to sign the document and that a signature was placed on the document by another person in the contracting party's presence and at the request of the contracting party. The person who has signed for the contracting party then signs the document (see Figure 13-2). Persons who lack the ability to read or write are often obliged to sign contracts. In such situations, the law accepts the person's mark, usually an X, properly witnessed, as a valid signature (see Figure 13-3).

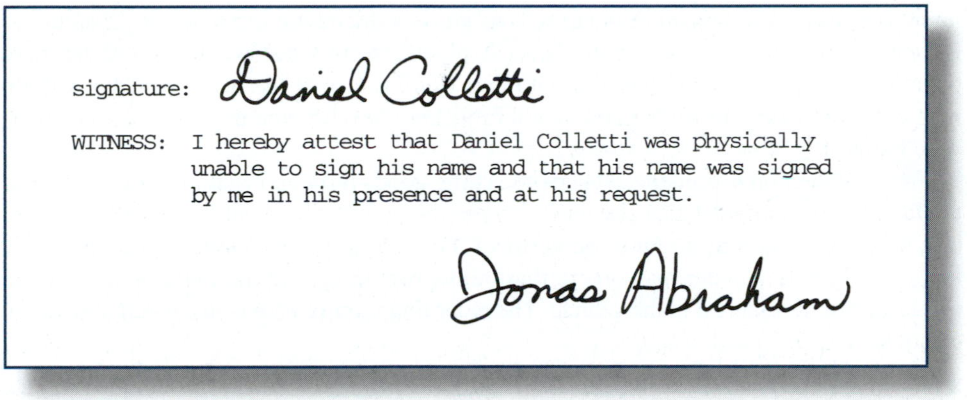

signature: *Daniel Colletti*

WITNESS: I hereby attest that Daniel Colletti was physically
unable to sign his name and that his name was signed
by me in his presence and at his request.

Jonas Abraham

Figure 13-2   The signature for an incapacitated person bears a witness's name.

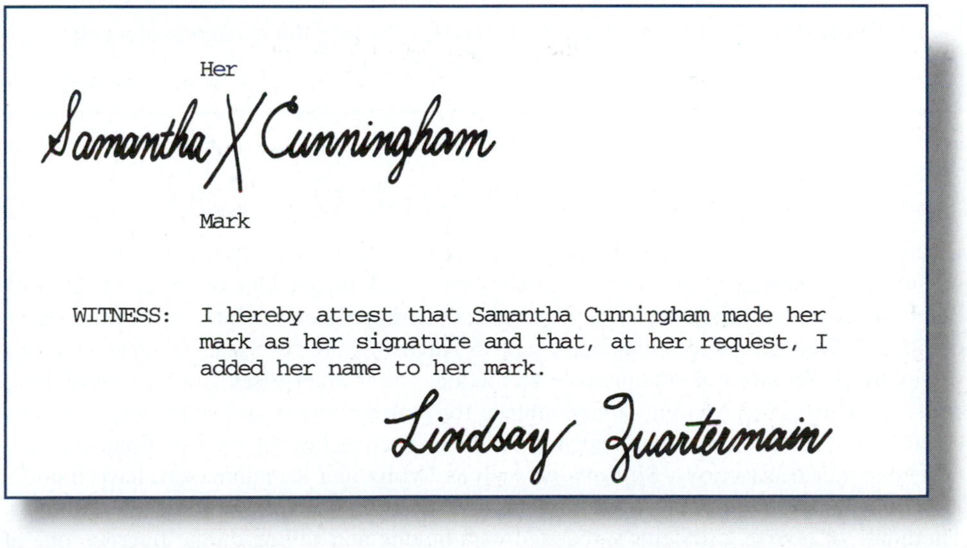

Her
Samantha X Cunningham
Mark

WITNESS: I hereby attest that Samantha Cunningham made her
mark as her signature and that, at her request, I
added her name to her mark.

Lindsay Quartermain

Figure 13-3   The signature (*X*) of a person who does not know how to write has been witnessed.

Witnesses and Acknowledgments

Witnesses are required in the signing of a will and sometimes a deed, but in most other documents, their signatures are at the option of the contracting parties. To ensure that no misunderstanding will arise as to the acceptance and signing of a written agreement, the use of witnesses is advised. Certain official documents, such as a certificate of title to a motor vehicle and a deed to real property, require the owner's signature and an **acknowl-edgment** by a notary public that the signature was the person's free act and deed. The notary witnesses the signing of the document and then acknowledges this act by signing the document and adding the official seal to it. A notary is not authorized to read the document being signed and may be prevented from doing so.

The Seal and the Recording of Contracts

Some states still make use of a seal when a formal contract is signed. Contracts for the sale and transfer of real estate sometimes fall within this category. Historically, the seal was a carefully designed coat of arms, or other suitable design, mounted in a ring and used to impress markings in melted sealing wax placed on a document. As noted in Chapter 11, modern practice has dispensed with this custom, and today's seal is usually nothing more than the word *seal* or the initials *L.S.* for *locus sigilli* (place of the seal) printed or written next to the signature. In some states, a seal furnishes consideration in a contract that otherwise has none.

As a protection to lenders and persons selling goods through installment contracts and the like, the law provides that certain documents be recorded in a public office for inspection by anyone wishing to know about them. For example, when money is loaned on a motor vehicle, the lender may record that transaction in the appropriate public office to protect his or her interest in the vehicle. The recording requirement is discussed in detail in Chapter 31.

Quick Quiz 13-3 True or False?

1. Written agreements must always be signed by both parties to the contract.

2. Facsimile signatures are not acceptable in any state.

3. The seal has become an outmoded means of proving the existence of a contract and, as a result, is no longer used in any state.

13-4 E-Commerce and the Law

Electronic commerce, or e-commerce as it is often called, involves transacting business by one of a wide variety of electronic communication techniques. One of the most common e-commerce techniques involves buying and selling directly on the Internet by accessing a company's Web site. Some companies, such as Amazon.com, have made a name for themselves by perfecting this e-commerce technique. Other enterprises, such as eBay, have made a business of providing a marketplace for putting buyers and sellers together in a electronic auction setting (see Chapter 16). Others, such as PayPal, provide financing support for other transactions. Still others, such as Orbitz and Priceline.com, have found a niche in the marketplace by providing access to bargain services on airlines and hotels. There are, of course, problems associated with buying and selling on the Internet, one of which involves the difficulty of authenticating the identity of the person on the other side of an Internet connection. Another involves the question of how to deal with the fact that electronic transactions do not produce paper documents the same way that traditional transactions do. In both cases, the law has done what any complex adaptive system does; it has reacted and provided some solutions to these difficulties.

Verification Problems

Many e-consumers are attracted to the Internet because they can shop for a wide variety of products that might not be available from stores and businesses in their own hometowns. Buyers also have the additional advantage of being able to do all of this shopping from the comfort and security of their home or office. In addition, sellers enjoy many advantages when they do business on the Internet, including that through its Web site, a business can reach an enormous number of potential customers in a relatively short period of time. However, these advantages can also give rise to problems, because firms that transact business on the Internet often deal with customers who are strangers to them. This issue is also a problem on auction sites such as eBay, because the buyers and sellers do not know one another. Questions therefore can arise as to the identity of a stranger and his or her authority to enter a contract.

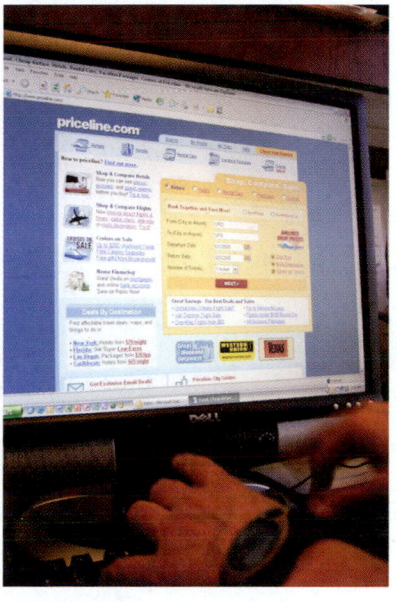

Online shopping is fast, easy, and convenient. Utilizing digital signatures is an effective method used by businesses to verify the legitimacy of the transaction.

These problems can be solved in a number of ways. For example, the parties can avoid the problem altogether by adding a term that delays the creation of the contract until the identities of the parties can be verified by some means other than computers. Or a business might elect to use its Web site only as an advertisement site. These solutions are unsatisfactory to most businesspeople, however, because they eliminate the advantages of doing business on the Internet. Another technique is for the parties to an Internet transaction to customize the verification process for each contract individually. However, in the interests of efficiency and cost, it would be preferable to have a process that applies to all contracts.

A possible solution to this problem is the use of digital signatures. A **digital signature** is an encoded message that appears at the end of a contract that is created online. The receiver of the encoded message can use that encryption to authenticate both the identity of the sender and the content of the message. The digital signature is provided by a party known as a **certification authority**. It is the job of the certification authority to provide businesses with digital signatures and make certain that those signatures are kept current. Those businesses and legal practitioners who promote the use of digital signatures hope that the courts and/or the legislatures will institute a principle that states the use of a digital signature creates a rebuttable presumption that the signature is authentic and that the terms of the transaction have not been altered in transmission.

Offer and Acceptance Online   An electronic party should always ensure that the following terms appear in his or her online agreement package: (1) payment procedure, (2) remedies that can be used by the offeree, (3) refund policies, (4) the return process, (5) dispute settlement instructions, (6) the applicability of e-signatures, (7) liability disclaimers, and (8) provisions relating to the offeree's manner of acceptance. In general, the other party's manner of acceptance in an e-contract is manifested by having that party click on a box on the computer screen that states he or she agrees to be bound by the terms of the contract. Sometimes this process of acceptance is referred to as a "click-on" acceptance or "click-on" agreement. In a sense then, this "click" amounts to the party's signature. It is also critical to remember that when an e-agreement deals with goods, the provisions of Article 2 of the Uniform Commercial Code apply.

Online Advertisement "Click" Fraud   One problem that arises in this area is verifying the identity of the "clicker." When companies are actually creating contracts, they police the process of verification rather closely. However, the click-on process functions not only in online contracts but also for online advertisements. Companies that advertise on the Internet often make contracts with search engines like Google, Yahoo, America Online, or Ask Jeeves. The terms of these contracts generally include a provision that states the company that places the advertisement will pay the search engine on the basis of the number of clicks detected on that advertisement. The clicks are supposed to be a foolproof way to gauge interest in the advertiser's service or product. However, policing the nature of exactly who clicks and when has proven difficult. Thus, hundreds of thousands of unverifiable, and likely phony, clicks have occurred on advertisements, often inflating the bills of the advertisers, which still must pay per click. The problem arises because the search engines often farm out the actual posting of the ads to intermediary companies, called domain parkers, that get paid on the basis of the number of clicks on the ads for which they are responsible. The domain parkers then transfer the ads to subsidiary Web sites. Some of these Web sites display advertisements and nothing more. This scenario provides a fertile ground in which the phony click campaigns grow. Some owners of these subsidiary Web sites double as con artists who pay fraudulent clickers a small amount to click on the ads, thus driving up the cost for the advertisers and increasing the Web site owner's split of the proceeds. Some even use "clickbot" software, capable of mechanically clicking on certain advertisements at programmed intervals. All of the major search engines have found themselves in litigation because of this new *e-confidence game.* (See Brian Grow and Ben Elgin, "Click Fraud: The Dark Side of Online Advertising," *BusinessWeek,* October 2, 2006, 46–57.)

Electronic Commerce Legislation

Electronic commerce legislation has taken many forms over the past decade. However, the three most influential acts have been the E-Sign Act, the Uniform Electronic Transactions

Talking Points

The electronic revolution is not something that can be ignored nor even underplayed by entrepreneurs who want to succeed in a globalized economy. The problem of electronic verification is only one small piece of an enormous puzzle that confounds and simultaneously challenges the modern businessperson. Businesspeople, however, are not the only segment of the population who have captured the resources of the Internet. Political activists can use those resources to attack all aspects of corporate culture. In his book *The Lexus and the Olive Tree,* Thomas L. Friedman identifies this tactic when he writes, "In such a world, activists have to learn how to use globalization to their advantage. They have to learn how to compel companies to behave better by mobilizing global consumers through the Internet. I call this the 'network solution for human rights,' and it's the future of social advocacy. It is bottom up regulation, or side by side regulation—not top-down regulation. You empower the bottom, instead of waiting for the top, by shaping a coalition that produces better governance without global government." Sounds good, but can you spot any flaws in Friedman's "network solution for human rights" or in his idea of global governance via the Internet? If we are not always positive who is on the other side of the screen when we are buying a DVD on eBay, are we not also susceptible to manipulation by governmental agents or corporate directors masquerading as activists? Think about it. (*Source:* Thomas L. Friedman, *The Lexus and The Olive Tree. New York:* Random House, 2000, 207.)

Act (UETA), and the Uniform Computer Information Transactions Act (UCITA). A fourth new law that deals with a slightly different but no less serious problem, that of credit cards and identity theft, is the Fair and Accurate Credit Transactions Act (FACT).

The E-Sign Act   The E-Sign Act is a federal act designed to deal with problems associated with e-commerce, especially those related to the recognition of electronic contracts and electronic signatures. Basically the act states that if the parties to a contract have voluntarily agreed to transact business electronically, the electronic contract that results will be just as legally acceptable as a paper contract. The act also notes that the parties must be able to store and reproduce the electronic record of the contract; otherwise, the e-record will not be legally sufficient under the act. The final word here is that under the provisions of the E-Sign Act, e-contracts and e-signatures are just as legitimate as their ink counterparts. There are a few documents that are not covered by this statute, including court records, eviction notices, health insurance cancellations, wills, foreclosure notices, prenuptial contracts, and divorce papers. However, sale and lease of goods contracts as covered by the Uniform Commercial Code are included in the E-Sign Act.

The Uniform Electronic Transactions Act (UETA)   The Uniform Electronic Transactions Act establishes the same type of legal parity between electronic records and paper records as does the E-Sign Act. It does not establish any new guidelines governing contracts just because they are entered electronically. The approach therefore is not to establish the differences between electronic contracts and paper agreements but instead to focus on the similarities. As a result, once the parties to a contract have voluntarily agreed to enter a transaction using an electronic medium, the agreement that results in electronic form, including the electronic signatures, will be just as valid as a paper agreement. The UETA applies only to transactions that involve some sort of commercial, business, or governmental matter. The law also states that if an act, such as the Statute of Frauds, requires a writing and a signature, an electronic record and an electronic signature will fulfill that requirement. The UETA defines an electronic signature as "an electronic sound, symbol, or process attached to or logically associated with a record and executed or adopted by a person with the intent to sign the record."

The Uniform Computer Information Transactions Act (UCITA)
The Uniform Computer Information Transactions Act (UCITA) focuses on contracts that involve the sale or lease of computer software, computer databases, interactive products, multimedia products, and any other type of computer information. The UCITA is in line with the basic provisions of the E-Sign Act and the UETA, in that it also declares that any transaction entered into using an electronic medium is just as valid as a paper agreement. Not all states have adopted the UCITA, so it is important to check on the applicability of the statute in your jurisdiction.

The Fair and Accurate Credit Transactions Act (FACT)   The Fair and Accurate Credit Transactions Act (FACT) is Congress's antidote to one manifestation of the identity theft epidemic. The new law, which is actually an amendment to the Fair Credit Reporting Act (FCRA), is designed to cut down on identity theft related to the use of credit cards. The act prohibits merchants from using credit card receipts that show anything other than the last five credit card numbers. Receipts also cannot display credit card expiration dates. In effect, because the act outlaws such numerical displays, identity thieves will no longer be able to assume the identity of a consumer by obtaining a copy of a credit card receipt and using the credit card number and expiration date on the receipt to "verify their identity" over the phone or online.

> ## Quick Quiz 13-4 True or False?
>
> 1. The E-Sign Act is a model act designed to deal with problems associated with e-commerce.
>
> 2. The Uniform Electronic Transactions Act was passed by Congress to deal with the legality of electronic transactions.
>
> 3. The UCITA is not in line with any of the provisions of the E-Sign Act or the UETA.

Summary

13.1   The Statutes of Frauds outlines six types of contracts that must be in writing to be enforceable. These include contracts that cannot be completed within one year; contracts transferring real property rights; contracts for the sale of goods of $500 or more; certain contracts entered by executors and administrators; contracts by one party to pay a debt incurred by another party; and contracts in consideration of marriage.

13.2   The legal system has developed certain basic criteria that make the construction and interpretation of written contracts consistent. These four criteria are (1) the standard construction rule, (2) the parol evidence rule, (3) the best evidence rule, and (4) the equal dignities rule.

13.3   Certain formalities are followed in the formation of contracts. Written agreements need not be signed by both parties. However, any agreement signed by only one party would obligate only that party. Facsimile signatures are allowed on a contract if the contract states that such signatures are valid. Some states have statutes allowing facsimile signatures. Persons who are illiterate usually sign written contracts with an X. Such signatures should be witnessed. Witnesses are not required when parties enter written agreements.

However, to avoid misunderstandings, the use of witnesses is advisable. Some states still make use of the seal when a party enters a contract, though most have disposed of the custom. The law provides that some documents must be recorded in a public office for inspection by the public.

13.4   Electronic commerce involves transacting business by one of a wide variety of electronic communication techniques. One of the most common e-commerce techniques involves buying and selling directly on the Internet by accessing a company's Web site. There are problems associated with buying and selling on the Internet. One of these problems involves the difficulty of verifying the identity of the person on the other side of an Internet connection. Another involves the question of how to deal with the fact that electronic transactions do not produce paper documents. In both cases, the law has provided some solutions to these difficulties. Three laws that address these problems include the E-Sign Act, the Uniform Electronic Transactions Act (UETA), and the Uniform Computer Information Transactions Act (UCITA). A fourth act that deals with the problem of identity theft is the Fair and Accurate Credit Transactions Act (FACT).

Key Terms

acknowledgment, 264

antenuptial agreement, 254

best evidence rule, 260

certification authority, 265

collateral contract, 254

condition precedent, 259

cosigner, 254

digital signature, 265

equal dignities rule, 261

Questions for Review and Discussion

1. What abuses did the Statute of Frauds attempt to eliminate?
2. What agreements must be written under the Statute of Frauds?
3. What information must be in a written contract?
4. What is the parol evidence axiom?
5. What are the exceptions under the parol evidence axiom?
6. What is the best evidence axiom?
7. What is the equal dignities axiom?
8. What are the various methods of writing a signature?
9. How are witnesses, acknowledgments, the seal, and recordings used today?
10. What are the most current e-commerce laws?

Investigating the Internet

Access the Equality in Marriage Web site and report on prenuptial agreements. In writing the report, answer the following questions: (1) What is the definition of a prenuptial agreement offered on the Web site? (2) What are the three basic rules that a couple should follow in writing a prenuptial agreement? (3) How many states recognize the validity of prenuptial agreements? (4) Which states have enacted the Uniform Prenuptial Agreement Act (UPAA)? (5) What should be included in a prenuptial agreement?

Cases for Analysis

1. Several identity theft victims filed a series of class action lawsuits against firms that had not made the changes required by the Fair and Accurate Credit Transactions Act (FACT) by the statutory deadline. One of the issues before the court was whether the victims had to demonstrate that the offending company deliberately refused to comply or did so with reckless disregard for the new requirements. Which standard would be the appropriate one in this situation? Explain. Amanda Bronstad, "Suits Multiply over Credit Card Exposure: Cash Registers Displaying Too Many Digits Spark Dozens of Class Actions," *The National Law Journal*, February 19, 2007, p. 4.

2. Harold Perdue entered an individually negotiated employment contract with Nicholas Paynter. Under terms of the contract, Perdue was to work for Paynter as a private investigator in Paynter's newly established firm, known as Eye-Spy Investigations. The employment contract was on a trial basis and was to last for nine months. That nine-month period was set to begin one month after Paynter had set up shop. However, Paynter could not begin his operation until the contractors finished remodeling his office. Johnson Contractors, Ltd., had promised to have the office completed within one to three months. One month after the contract had been finalized, Paynter notified Perdue that he had hired someone else and that his services were no longer needed. Perdue, who had relied on the contract, had turned down several other lucrative offers that had since been filled by other operatives. Moreover, Perdue was now having trouble getting a similar job. Perdue threatened to bring suit against Paynter. Paynter told Perdue to go ahead and sue. Privately, Paynter believes that he is immune to a lawsuit because, since Johnson Construction had three months to finish remodeling the office, the contract could not have been performed within one year. Perdue argued that, because Johnson could have finished in less than one month, the contract could be performed within a year, and it did not have to be in writing to be enforceable. Who is correct here? Explain.

3. Meng, a vice-president at Boston University, resigned his position to protest what he regarded as the unethical and unprofessional behavior of the university's president, John Silber, in terminating a recently renewed contract with Linkage Corporation. Silber orally promised Meng, as a severance package when he resigned, 14 months of salary and benefits and free tuition for two of his children if either should attend the university. Was the oral promise enforceable? Explain. *Meng v. Trustees of Boston University,* 96-9776 Appeals Court (MA).

4. As part of an employment agreement, Bazzy orally promised to give Hall an option to buy 1,000 shares of company stock at $20 per share. Hall brought suit against the company when it refused to sell the stock to him. What legal argument may Bazzy's company use to refuse to sell the stock to Hall as agreed? *Hall v. Horizon House Microwave, Inc.,* 506 N.E.2d 178 (MA).

5. Anna Wilson was assistant manager of a Montgomery Ward store. When Montgomery Ward announced that it would be closing the store, the manager quit, leaving Wilson in charge. A district manager orally promised Wilson that if she stayed on and assisted in the closing of the store, she would receive a sum of money calculated according to a certain formula. Wilson stayed on and managed the closing of the store (which took two months) in addition to her regular duties. Montgomery Ward refused to pay her the money, claiming that the oral promise was unenforceable. Was the store correct? Why or why not? *Wilson v. Montgomery Ward,* 610 F. Supp. 1035 (DC IN).

6. Curtis Hendrix orally agreed to compensate Beverly Spertell for services rendered in connection with their living together out of wedlock. Later, when suit was brought to collect the money, Hendrix argued that the oral contract was unenforceable under the Statute of Frauds. Do you agree with Hendrix? Explain. *Spertell v. Hendrix,* 461 N.Y.S.2d 823 (NY).

7. Lawson hired Konves to conduct extensive audits of her 87 boutiques, located throughout the United States. As part of the agreement, Lawson required Konves to spend one week at each boutique. Konves demanded a written agreement before she would agree to Lawson's terms. Why was Konves correct in making this demand?

8. Butler leased a certain piece of property from Wheeler with an option to purchase it at a later date. The agreement was handwritten and consisted of two separate documents, each listing part of the transaction. Butler later attempted to purchase the property but Wheeler refused to sell, claiming that the agreement was unenforceable because it was contained in two documents. Was Wheeler correct? Explain. *Butler v. Lovoll,* 620 P.2d 1251 (NV).

9. Ray's Motor Sales sold a mobile home to Hathaway. Before the written contract was signed, the salesperson told Hathaway that Ray's would take care of any problems that Hathaway might have with the mobile home. This promise was not included in the written document. When Hathaway had problems with the mobile home, he asked Ray's to take care of them. Ray's refused to be of any assistance. Could Hathaway enforce Ray's promise? Explain. *Hathaway v. Ray's Motor Sales,* 247 A.2d 512 (VT).

10. Madden sued the president and board of directors of Georgetown College over several different issues involving breach of contract and negligence. One question before the court was whether the

contract was under seal. The question was crucial because it affected the statute of limitations. In this case, the word *seal* was printed on the page. However, it was not next to the signatures but an inch above and to the left, over the word *attest*. Was this a sealed contract? Explain. *President of Georgetown College v. Madden,* 505 F. Supp. 557, (D. MD).

Quick Quiz Answers

13-1 1. F	13-2 1. F	13-3 1. F	13-4 1. F
2. F	2. T	2. F	2. F
3. T	3. F	3. F	3. F

Chapter 14

Third Parties in Contract Law

The Opening Case

Alternatives Unlimited-Special, Inc. v. Ohio Department of Education

The Cleveland Alternative Learning Academy (CALA) was formed by Alternatives Unlimited-Special, Inc. (AU). In the original contract creating the school, AU designated the Ohio Department of Education (ODE) as the school's sponsor, thus complying with the requirements of state law. However, the contract was unclear about the identity of the governing authority of the school. The ambiguity arose because the documents used two contradictory terms at various points in the contract when they referred to governance issues. Thus, at times, it appeared as if the school would be run by a board of directors, whereas at other times, a separate governing authority seemed in charge. In addition, the actual contract was signed by two different persons, who both stated that they were the governing authority of CALA, adding a third layer of ambiguity to the problem. None of these details would have mattered had CALA run smoothly. Unfortunately, that was not the case. In fact, immediately after its formation, CALA began to suffer operational and financial problems. The primary cause of the problems was that CALA added three grades to its elementary school program without getting approval from the ODE. When CALA asked the state to ratify this de facto expansion, the state refused. Therefore, the school received no government funding for the added grades. In addition, the school had not reached predicted enrollment levels and was therefore forced to repay the state all of the extra money that it had received on the basis of its prediction. Despite these financial setbacks, the school opened its doors for another term. As the academic year progressed however, it became clear that CALA would never recover from the enormous shortfall, and as a result, it was forced to close. Then, AU sued the ODE for breach of contract. The ODE took one look at the confusing language of the original contract and hollered "foul." As the ODE argued, AU was not the governing authority of CALA and therefore could not bring the lawsuit. Adding insult to injury, the ODE argued that AU was not even an intended third party beneficiary and therefore even under that argument could not claim standing to sue. Accordingly, the ODE filed a motion to dismiss the case. This tactic might have worked too, had it not been for one small, but ultimately fatal, technicality. The court took special notice that the state of Ohio, in an earlier lawsuit involving CALA, had successfully argued that AU was the proper governing authority of CALA. Not to be fooled twice, the court of appeals ruled that the state could not have it both ways. It then kicked the case back down to the Court of

Claims for further deliberations. (*See Alternatives Unlimited-Special, Inc. v. Ohio Department of Education,* 168 Ohio App.3d 592, Tenth District Court of Appeals of Ohio.)

Opening Case Questions

1. What is a third party?

2. What is a third party beneficiary to a contract?

3. What is the difference between an intended and an incidental third party beneficiary?

4. What are the three types of intended third party beneficiaries?

5. Why would it profit AU to be labeled as an intended third party beneficiary?

LO Learning Objectives

1. Explain the legal rights given to intended beneficiaries.
2. Identify the legal rights given to incidental beneficiaries.
3. Explain the assignment of rights.
4. Explain the delegation of duties.
5. Identify the three parties in an assignment.
6. Indicate who is responsible for giving notice of an assignment.
7. Explain the obligations of the parties to an assignment.
8. Identify contracts that cannot be assigned.
9. Explain the nature of a novation.
10. Distinguish between a novation and an assignment.

14-1 Contracts and Third Parties

A **third party** is a person who may in some way be affected by a contract but who is not one of the contracting parties. A third party, also known as an **outside party**, is at times given benefits from a contract made between two or more other parties. A third party receiving benefits from a contract made by others is known as a **third party beneficiary** or sometimes simply as a **beneficiary** to the contract. Although not obligated by the agreement made between those in privity, third parties may have the legal right to enforce the benefits given them by such agreements.

Intended Beneficiaries

A beneficiary in whose favor a contract is made is an **intended beneficiary**. With exceptions in some states, an intended beneficiary can enforce the contract made by those in privity of contract. Those who are most frequently recognized to be intended beneficiaries and have the right to demand and enforce the benefits promised are creditor beneficiaries, donee beneficiaries, and insurance beneficiaries.

Creditor Beneficiaries   A **creditor beneficiary** is an outside third party to whom one or both contracting parties owe a continuing debt of obligation arising from a contract. Frequently, the obligation results from the failure of the contracting party or parties to pay for goods delivered or services rendered by the third party at some time in the past.

EXAMPLE 14-1: *Hodges v. Castele*

Annette Marquard owed Floyd Hodges a balance of $1,236 for the vinyl siding that Hodges put on her house. On another contract, Marquard agreed to resolve some problems that Vince Castele was having with his computer on the condition that Castele would give Marquard's $250 fee to Hodges toward payment of the $1,236 debt. The second contract made Hodges a creditor beneficiary with the right to demand payment from Castele if the $250 were not paid. When Castele did not pay the amount due, Hodges brought suit against Castele in small claims court. When Castele argued that Hodges was not even a party to the original contract, the referee ruled that as an intended third party beneficiary to the Castele–Marquard contract, Hodges did indeed have standing to sue.

Donee Beneficiaries A third party who provides no consideration for the benefits received and who owes the contracting parties no legal duty is known as a **donee beneficiary**. However, the contracting parties owe the donee beneficiary the act promised; if it is not forthcoming, the donee beneficiary may bring suit. The consideration that supports this type of agreement is the consideration exchanged by the parties in privity of contract.

EXAMPLE 14-2: *Carpenter v. Shepherd*

Carl Carpenter agreed to landscape Wade Shepherd's property for $600. Carpenter, however, wanted Shepherd to pay the $600 fee to Carpenter's daughter. The daughter would be the donee beneficiary. When Shepherd failed to pay her the $600, Carpenter's daughter had the right to bring suit to collect the money.

Insurance Beneficiaries An individual named as the beneficiary of an insurance policy is usually considered a donee beneficiary. The beneficiary does not have to furnish the insured with consideration to enforce payment of the policy. In some cases, an insurance beneficiary may also be a creditor beneficiary. This situation occurs in consumer or mortgage loans when the creditor requires the debtor to furnish a life-term insurance policy naming the creditor as the beneficiary. The policy will pay the debt if the debtor dies before the loan has been repaid (see Chapter 30).

Incidental Beneficiaries

An **incidental beneficiary** is an outside party for whose benefit a contract was not made but who would substantially benefit if the agreement were performed according to its terms and conditions. An incidental beneficiary, in contrast to an intended beneficiary, has no legal grounds for enforcing the contract made by those in privity of contract.

EXAMPLE 14-3: *Faber v. The Brotherhood of Aerospace Workers*

Mark Faber owned a hotel and restaurant in downtown Indianapolis. The Brotherhood of Aerospace Workers (BAW) had a contract with the city for the use of the municipal auditorium for the union's annual convention. One week before the convention, the

union announced that it was canceling the meeting. The move was a clear violation of BAW's contract with the city. Faber brought suit against the BAW for damages due to lost business caused by the breach. The court dismissed the case on a motion for summary judgment. The court ruled that Faber was an incidental beneficiary and therefore had no grounds on which to bring the suit against the union.

Quick Quiz 14-1 True or False?

1. A third party who provides no consideration and owes no legal duty to the contracting parties is a donee beneficiary.

2. The principle of privity stopped many judges from establishing third party rights.

3. Incidental and intended beneficiaries have the same rights.

14-2 The Law of Assignment

When people enter contracts, they receive certain rights and incur particular duties. It is completely accepted today that, with some exceptions noted subsequently and unless the contract itself provides otherwise, these rights and duties can be transferred to others. An **assignment** is a transfer of a contract right, and a **delegation** is a transfer of a contract duty.

The Opening Case Revisited

Alternatives Unlimited-Special, Inc. v. Ohio Department of Education, Round 2

The Cleveland Alternative Learning Acadamy (CALA) was formed by Alternatives Unlimited-Special, Inc. (AU) in a contract with the Ohio Department of Education (ODE). Unfortunately, CALA had extensive financial difficulties when it failed to get support from the ODE for its expanded coverage of grades two, seven, and eight. To make matters worse, ODE demanded repayment for funds that had been spent on the academy on the basis of inaccurate enrollment predictions. Eventually, the academy's financial problems became too much to handle, and it had to shut down. Alternatives Unlimited-Special then sued the ODE for breach of contract. The department filed a motion to dismiss, arguing that AU had no standing to sue because it was not really a party to the contract. In addition, the ODE claimed that AU failed to qualify as an intended third party beneficiary. This move was absolutely necessary for the ODE because, under contract law, an intended third party beneficiary has standing to sue on such a contract. However, had AU been merely an incidental beneficiary, the ODE would not have had to file the additional claim. An incidental beneficiary, in contrast to an intended third party beneficiary, has no legal grounds for enforcing a contract made by the actual contracting parties.

EXAMPLE 14-4:   *Fisher v. Ruppert*

Fred Fisher wanted to purchase Steve Ruppert's dry cleaning business. Ruppert, however, refused to sell to Fisher because of a long-standing dispute between the two businesspeople. Instead, Ruppert entered a written agreement to sell the business to Hazel Harding. Nothing in the contract said the contract could not be assigned to another party. Before the deal was carried out, Harding assigned her rights under the contract to Fisher. Ruppert was now contractually bound to sell the business to Fisher, even though he did not want to. When Ruppert refused to sell the business to Fisher, he was in breach of contract and would suffer legal consequences, undoubtedly intensifying the bad blood that already existed between Fisher and him.

Assignment and Delegation Distinguished

In general, rights are *assigned,* and duties are *delegated.* In most cases, both are governed by the same rules. If A is owed money by B, A may assign to C the right to collect the money. However, if A has agreed to pay B to harvest 200 acres of wheat for a price, B may delegate the duty of harvesting to C. Restrictions against the delegation of duties are presented later in this chapter.

EXAMPLE 14-5:   *Wesley, et al. v. Lerro*

Lee Wesley agreed to lay cement on the driveway leading up to Walter Lerro's house for $24,000. Plans and specifications were provided by Lerro. Wesley delegated the duties involved in laying the asphalt to Hanover Construction, Inc., another contractor. Hanover then assigned the right to collect the $24,000 from Lerro to Olsen Construction Supplies, Ltd. Lerro, who did not like the way his job and his money were being bounced all over the tri-county area, refused to pay Olsen. Lerro then called Wesley and ordered him to tear out the driveway because he was insulted by the fact that Wesley thought so little of his job that he had assigned it to Hanover. In hindsight, this choice was probably a poorly thought out decision, because everyone involved in the situation, from Wesley to Hanover to Olsen, sued Lerro, who still ended up paying the original $24,000—and then some.

Parties to Assignment

Three parties are associated with any assignment. Two of the parties are the ones who entered the original agreement. The party who assigns rights or delegates duties is the **assignor**. The outside third party to whom the assignment is made is the **assignee**. The remaining party to the original agreement is the **obligor**.

EXAMPLE 14-6:   *From King to Gomez to Walker*

Lisa Gomez owed Roger King $500 for some photography work that King had done for her. At the same time, King owed Ted Walker $500 back rent. King assigned Walker the right to receive the money from Gomez. In this situation, King was the assignor, Walker the assignee, and Gomez the obligor. The following flowchart clearly illustrates these points.

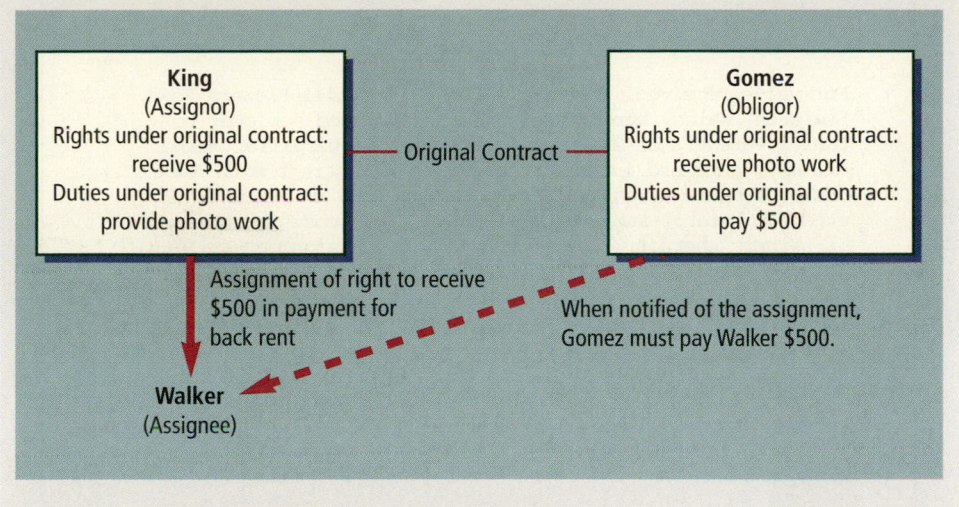

Consideration in Assignment

Consideration is not required in the assignment of a contract. When there is no supporting consideration, however, the assignor may repudiate the assignment at any time prior to its execution. In the previous example, the consideration supporting King's assignment is found in the rental agreement between King and Walker.

In addition, when no consideration is given for an assignment, creditors of the assignor may have the assignment rescinded on the grounds that it is a fraudulent conveyance. A **fraudulent conveyance** is a transfer of property with the intent to defraud creditors. If the $500 assignment to Walker in Example 14-6 had been a gift instead of payment for back rent, King's creditors could have had the assignment rescinded, because they could rightfully anticipate the money coming from Gomez.

Assignment Methods

To be valid, an assignment must follow certain accepted procedures designed to protect all of the parties. Form of assignment, notice of assignment, and the rights of parties in successive or subsequent assignments must conform to practices established by case law and state statutes.

Form of Assignment   Assignment may be accomplished through written, oral, or implied agreements between the assignor and the assignee. Parties to an assignment must observe the requirement provided by the equal dignities rule discussed in Chapter 13. Under that rule, the law requires that if the agreement by the original parties must be in writing, the assignment also must be in writing.

EXAMPLE 14-7:   *Parenti v. Joliet*

Alexis Amenott agreed in writing to sell his collection of antique glassware to Francis Joliet for $1,600. The written contract was executed properly, following the requirements of the Statute of Frauds. Joliet then made an oral assignment of the contract to Daniel Parenti. Sometime later, Joliet had second thoughts and decided to renege on the assignment. When Parenti tried to enforce the assignment, he discovered, much to his dismay, that because the assignment had not been in writing, the court could refuse to enforce it.

Assignment

For value received, I, Francis Joliet, of 4444 Flowers Road,
Lewiston, Maine, hereby assign, transfer, and set over to
Daniel Parenti, of 2441 Kenwood Circle, Bainesville, Maine,
all my rights and interests in and to a contract with Alexis
Amenott, dated March 2 of this year, a copy of which is
attached hereto, subject to all terms and conditions thereof.
In witness whereof, I have executed this assignment at 97
Erieview Plaza, Mercedes, Maine, on May 4, 20 - -.

_____
Francis Joliet, Assignor

Acceptance of Assignment

Daniel Parenti hereby accepts the foregoing assignment, subject to all terms and conditions therefore.

May 4, 20 - -   _____
                        Daniel Parenti, Assignee

Figure 14-1 The type of assignment that Joliet should have made to Parenti in Example 14-7. Why was the contract between Joliet and Amenott required to be in writing?

Some state and federal laws require certain types of assignments to be in writing (Figure 14-1).

Notice of Assignment   An assignment is valid at the time it is made. As a measure of protection against subsequent assignments, the assignee should give notice of the assignment to the obligor. Although this obligation falls to the assignee, either party may give notice. Once notice is received, the obligor should deal with the assignee. If notice is not given, it would be normal practice for the obligor to render performance to the original contracting party, the assignor. If due notice has been given and the obligor makes payment to the assignor, the obligor is not excused from making payment to the assignee.

A Question of Ethics

Joliet's oral agreement in Example 14-7 to assign the contract to Parenti was unenforceable because of the equal dignities rule. Is the equal dignities rule just and fair? How do you feel about the legality of someone breaking an oral promise? Why does the law have such a provision? Is it ethical? What has happened to the old-fashioned saying that a person's word is his or her bond?

Bryant, Inc.
6225 St. Clair Avenue
Cleveland, OH 44103

June 15, 20 - -

Mr. Carl Newfield
750 Maple Street, Apt. 4-C
Lakewood, Ohio 44117

Dear Mr. Newfield:

You are hereby notified that Pendleton Architects Limited of Euclid, Ohio, has assigned to Bryant, Inc., all rights to its claim against you in the amount of $750.

You are further notified to direct all payments to Bryant, Inc., at the above address to ensure credit for payment.

Sincerely yours,

Norbert Bryant

Norbert Bryant
Vice-President

Figure 14-2   The format used by Bryant, Inc., in the case described in Example 14-8, to notify Newfield of the assignment from Pendleton.

EXAMPLE 14-8:   *Bryant, Inc. v. Newfield*

Carl Newfield owed Pendleton Architects Limited $750 as a final payment for architectural work. Pendleton in turn owed Bryant, Inc., a substantial sum. As partial payment of that amount, Pendleton assigned Newfield's debt to Bryant. As the assignee in this case, Bryant sent a letter to Newfield indicating that the debt that Newfield owed to Pendleton should now be paid to Bryant, Inc. Figure 14-2 presents a copy of the letter that Bryant sent to Newfield informing him of the assignment. Newfield would now be legally required to adhere to the assignment. When Newfield refused to honor the assignment, Bryant could bring suit against him.

Subsequent Assignments   Should the assignor make a subsequent assignment of the same right, the courts must decide which of the two assignees has a superior right and claim against the obligor. A majority of the states hold that the first assignee has a superior right, even if a later assignee was the first to give notice of the assignment to the obligor. A minority of courts hold that whichever assignee was first to give notice of assignment has a superior right and claim to any assigned benefits.

Quick Quiz 14-2   True or False?

1. A delegation is the transfer of a contractual right.

2. The equal dignities axiom has no application in the law of assignment.

3. It is the responsibility of the assignor to give notice of the assignment to the obligor.

About the Law

An assignment, rather than a negotiation, occurs when a check is transferred to a third party without a required endorsement.

14-3 Assignment Rights, Duties, and Restrictions

Rights can be assigned, and duties can be delegated. Although this rule seems simple enough, disputes still arise regarding both assignment and delegation. What is generally in dispute is whether a particular right or duty can be transferred and, if so, what legal effects arise from that transfer.

Rights and Duties of the Assignee

The rights and duties of the assignee are the same as those previously held by the assignor under the original contract. It is fair to say that the assignee "steps into the shoes" of the assignor. Claims the assignor may have had against the obligor now belong to the assignee. Also, defenses the obligor may have had against the assignor's claims may now be used against the assignee.

The assignee's duty in an assignment is to give notice of the assignment to the obligor. The obligor is allowed a reasonable time to seek assurance that an assignment has been truly made. Making the assignment in writing reduces the possibility of fraudulent representation as an assignee.

EXAMPLE 14-9:   The Quitter–Stalker Assignment, Part I

Quitter appeared at the payroll department of the Meadville Delivery Company and told the paymaster that one of Meadville's drivers, Stalker, had made an assignment of part of his paycheck to her. Under terms of the assignment, Quitter was to receive

Talking Points

In the opening paragraph of the first chapter of their book, *Empire,* Michael Hardt and Antonio Negri make it clear that if a world order exists, it is not because it emerged automatically from the dealings of diverse influences or because it was orchestrated by an independent, extremely powerful center of authority. In fact, Hardt and Negri are so certain that this premise is correct that they demand that the reader eliminate these "two common conceptions . . . the notion that the present order somehow rose up *spontaneously* out of the interactions of radically heterogeneous global forces, as if this order were a harmonious concert orchestrated by the natural and neutral hidden hand of the world market; and second, the idea that order is dictated by a single power and a single center of rationality *transcendent* to global forces, guiding the various phases of historical development according to its conscious and all-seeing plan, something like a conspiracy theory of globalization." What is your reaction to these statements? If world order did not emerge from the dealings of different influences or under the direction of a single authority, how did it emerge? Think about the logical legal principles of assignment and delegation. Or consider the consistent rules related to third party beneficiaries. These principles and rules arose from different people dealing with one another and attempting to reach a fair and acceptable conclusion to genuine disputes about ownership rights, payment duties, and so on. Does this contradict or support the Hardt–Negri thesis? Explain. (Source: Michael Hardt and Antonio Negri, *Empire,* Cambridge, MA: Harvard University Press, 2001, 3.)

$150 of the money that Meadville owed Stalker. Meadville, the obligor, would not have to pay Quitter the $150 until the paymaster had a reasonable amount of time to verify the assignment.

Liabilities and Warranties of the Assignor

The assignor is obligated to any express and implied warranties that serve to protect either the assignee or the obligor. A **warranty** is a promise, statement, or other representation that a thing has certain qualities.

Warranties to the Assignee   The assignor is bound by an implied warranty that the obligor will respect the assignment and make the performance, as required by the original agreement between the assignor and the obligor.

EXAMPLE 14-10:   The Quitter–Stalker Assignment, Part II

Suppose, in the Quitter–Stalker assignment, that the Meadville Trucking Company had been either unwilling or unable to pay Quitter the $150. Stalker would be bound by an implied warranty to Quitter that the $150 would be paid. If the assignment were a gift to Quitter, there would be no enforceable warranty in the absence of consideration between the assignor and the assignee.

Warranties to the Obligor   If the assignor delegates to an assignee duties owed the obligor, there is an implied warranty that the duties delegated will be carried out in a complete and satisfactory manner.

EXAMPLE 14-11: *Donohue v. Heinecken*

Heinecken delegated the duties under a contract for the remodeling of Donohue's kitchen to Edberg. Edberg's work was unsatisfactory. After careful investigation, Donohue discovered that the work done by Edberg was far below what was considered satisfactory in the home remodeling profession. Donohue sued Heinecken for the amount of money Donohue subsequently spent to have the kitchen done properly. The court awarded that money to Donohue, stating that Heinecken had breached the implied warranty that duties delegated would be carried out in a complete and satisfactory manner.

Restrictions on Assignments

LO8

Although most contracts may be assigned, those for personal and professional services may not. The right of assignment may also be restricted by agreement of the original parties to the contract and, in certain cases, by law.

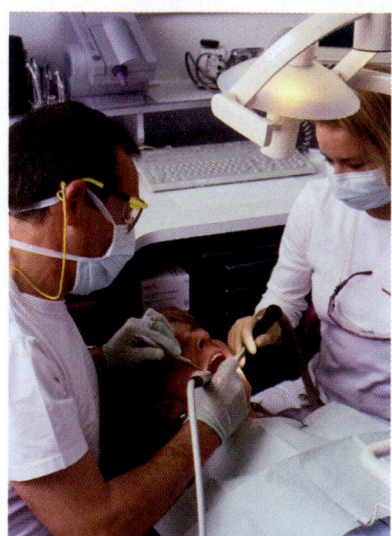

Professionals, like the dentist above, are chosen based on their particular skills and abilities and may not delegate their professional duties to another.

Restrictions on Personal and Professional Service Contracts
A party may not delegate duties that are of a personal or professional nature. *Personal,* in this context, means "other than routine." Musicians or artists, for example, could not delegate their services to someone else. They are chosen for their ability or artistic talent. Professional services are those rendered by physicians, lawyers, certified public accountants, ministers, and others. People in these occupations are selected because of their special abilities, and their services could not be delegated to someone else. In contrast, routine services may usually be delegated. These are services performed by electricians, mechanics, woodworkers, plumbers, waitstaff, bankers, publishers, and others whose skills and abilities are judged according to the usual customs and standards of the marketplace.

Restrictions Imposed by Original Contract
Parties to a contract may include a condition that will not allow its assignment. Some courts have held that a restriction against the assignment of a debt owed by the obligor robs the assignor of a property right guaranteed by law and would be contrary to public policy. Other courts have permitted this restrictive condition. If, in Example 14-11, Donohue had included a condition against assignment, the assignment to Edberg would have been void.

Restrictions Imposed by Law
Assignment, in special situations, may be restricted by law or declared void because it is contrary to public policy. Thus, members of the armed services may not assign any part of their pay except to a spouse or family member. Police officers, persons elected or appointed to public office, and others are likewise restricted from making assignment of their pay or of duties that they have been especially chosen to perform.

Novation and Assignment

LO9

LO10

Sometimes a party to a contract will assign all rights and delegate all duties to a third party (the assignee). Once this happens, the assignee will work directly with the obligor, performing the duties and receiving the benefits. Nevertheless, the assignor will remain in privity of contract with the obligor and be liable to the obligor if the assignee does not perform or performs improperly.

BusinessWeek Business Law in the News

EADS' Unlikely American Ascent

In recent months nothing but bad news has emanated from European Aeronautic Defence & Space Co. The epic production delays plaguing the vaunted Airbus A380 superjumbo jet have saddled the company with a $3.3 billion cost overrun. They've also triggered the departure of several top officers, including two CEOs.

But there's one surprising bright spot for EADS—in the U.S., of all places, where the European aerospace giant has never been particularly well liked. Defying the skeptics, its U.S. defense arm, EADS North America Inc., is thriving. The unit's sales have steadily ballooned to more than $1 billion—up from just $400 million in 2004. And now, under the leadership of CEO Ralph D. Crosby Jr., 59, a former senior Northrop Grumman Corp. executive, the European–American company is actually contending (with partner Northrop) for one of the richest Pentagon prizes in decades: the $100 billion contract to replace aerial refueling tankers. "Everybody thought the penetration of the North American market by anyone other than the British was near impossible—certainly not by a company with a heavy French accent," says Joseph F. Campbell Jr., aerospace analyst for Lehman Brothers Inc.

Crosby's strategy has been simple: "Crawl, walk, run," as he puts it. He has been careful to bid only on U.S. defense contracts where EADS clearly brought something unique to the table. A good example is the light-utility helicopters built by Eurocopter. It offered a noncombat chopper that cost less and could be delivered more quickly than the ones offered by U.S. competitors, the U.S. Army concluded. What's more, EADS boasted clearly superior technology. The U.S. Army purchased 322 helicopters last year, the single biggest Eurocopter order. "We were quite prudent about the expectations we had established and claims we made," Crosby said.

His experience in the domestic defense industry has given him discerning political antennae. One of Crosby's first moves was establishing stateside final production factories, which brought 645 high-paying assembly jobs, in Texas, Mississippi, and Alabama. Another 210 people are expected to be hired in Mississippi as the helicopter factory there shifts into high

gear. That has helped win the support of high-powered senators such as Richard C. Shelby (R-Ala.) and Jeffrey Sessions (R-Ala.), who sit on influential Appropriations and Armed Services committees, respectively. Another key friend in Washington is Senate Commerce Committee member Trent Lott (R-Miss.).

Crosby has also been savvy about partnering with big U.S. contractors. EADS North America, for example, is joining with Raytheon Co. and engine maker Pratt & Whitney in the bid to win the U.S. Army Joint Cargo Aircraft contract. The initial competition is for 33 small, off-the-shelf cargo aircraft worth $1.3 billion. But it could ultimately run as high as $6 billion for 145 planes.

For Crosby and his staff of U.S. defense executives, the acid test is tankers. The initial contract is for 180 planes worth about $30 billion, and the Pentagon will announce the winner in October. But battling for the lucrative tanker will put his European company in the glaring political spotlight for a contract that doubters say will never go to a company backed by the French government. Beyond tankers, the real staying power of EADS North America will be tested during the decline in defense spending, which is expected to start in two years. "What happens when the budgets start going down is the small guys and the foreigners get squeezed out," says Loren B. Thompson, a defense analyst for Lexington Institute, a Washington think tank. "The system only welcomes foreigners when the budgets are flush."

Crosby brushes off the criticism. "This is the largest defense acquisition for the next 20 years," he says. "We came here to win."

Questions for Analysis

1. Who might be considered third party beneficiaries in EADS's contract for Army helicopters? Explain.

2. Are these third party beneficiaries intended beneficiaries or incidental beneficiaries? Explain.

3. If EADS breaks the Army helicopter contract, what legal rights would these third party beneficiaries have, if any? Explain.

(Continued)

Business Law in the News *(Continued)*

4. Do EADS's stateside final production plants in Texas, Mississippi, and Alabama constitute a delegation of duties? Explain.

5. Does EADS's arrangement with Raytheon Co. and Pratt & Whitney constitute a delegation of duties? Explain.

Source: Stanley Holmes, "EADS' Unlikely American Ascent: Despite Setbacks for Airbus, the European Aerospace Giant Is Scoring U.S. Defense Deals," *BusinessWeek,* April 9, 2007, 68.

EXAMPLE 14-12:   *Superfine Market v. Allgood Canning Company*

Allgood Canning Company entered into a contract to sell 1,000 cases of baked beans to Superfine Market for a specific price. Shortly thereafter, Allgood delegated its duty to ship the beans and assigned its rights to receive the money to Fastway Canning Company. The beans Fastway shipped turned out to be bad. If Superfine were to bring suit for damages, it would have to be brought against Allgood, because that was the company with which it had contracted. There was no privity between Superfine and Fastway.

In contrast, if all three parties agree, the assignor can be released from liability at the time of the assignment, and privity of contract can exist between the assignee and the obligor. Such an arrangement is called a **novation**, which is a substitution, by mutual agreement, of a new party for one of the original parties to a contract. If, in Example 14-12, Superfine and Fastway had agreed to release Allgood from responsibility under the original contract, a novation would have occurred. Privity of contract then would have been between Superfine and Fastway. Superfine's only recourse upon receiving the bad beans would have been to bring suit against Fastway because, by mutual consent, Allgood had been discharged.

Quick Quiz 14-3 True or False?

1. The phrase "assignment of a contract" means the same thing as the phrase "assignment of rights."

2. Personal and professional duties are just as transferable as all other duties.

3. Novations have been outlawed under the Restatement of Contracts.

Summary

14.1 Third parties are at times given benefits through a contract made between two other parties. Some contracts are made specifically to benefit a third party. Such a third party is known as a third party beneficiary. Three types of intended beneficiaries include creditor beneficiaries, donee beneficiaries, and insurance beneficiaries. Some third parties benefit from a contract even though the contract was not made for their benefit. These parties are known as incidental beneficiaries.

14.2   The transfer of contract rights to a third party outside of the original agreement is an assignment. In general, rights are assigned, and duties are delegated. However, the rules apply to both transfers in the same way. The party who assigns rights or delegates duties is the assignor. The outside third party to whom the assignment is made is the assignee. The remaining party to the original agreement is the obligor. The assignee must give notice of assignment to the obligor.

14.3   The rights and duties of the assignee are the same as those held by the assignor under the original agreement. Contracts for personal or professional services cannot be assigned. Assignments also can be limited by agreement. A novation occurs when two contracting parties agree to replace one of the parties with a new party. The new party (the assignee) agrees to enter the contract with the remaining original party (the obligor), causing a privity of contract between them.

Key Terms

assignee, 276	donee beneficiary, 274	outside party, 273
assignment, 275	fraudulent conveyance, 277	third party, 273
assignor, 276	incidental beneficiary, 274	third party beneficiary, 273
beneficiary, 273	intended beneficiary, 273	warranty, 281
creditor beneficiary, 273	novation, 284	
delegation, 275	obligor, 276	

Questions for Review and Discussion

1. What are the legal rights given to intended beneficiaries?
2. What are the legal rights given to incidental beneficiaries?
3. What is an assignment of rights?
4. What is a delegation of duties?
5. Who are the three parties in an assignment?
6. Who is responsible for giving notice of an assignment?
7. What are the obligations of the parties to an assignment?
8. What contracts cannot be assigned?
9. What is the nature of a novation?
10. How does a novation differ from an assignment?

Investigating the Internet

Access the Web site for the National Conference of Commissioners on Uniform State Laws and conduct a search for the Uniform Fraudulent Transfer Act. Answer the following questions with regard to the act: (1) Under Section 1–Definitions, how does the Uniform Fraudulent Transfer Act define a "transfer"? (2) Also under Section 1, what law is the primary legal source of this definition? (3) Under Section 1, how does the act define the term "asset"? (4) In Section 2–Insolvency, when is a debtor considered insolvent? (5) In Section 3–Value, according to the act, under what circumstances is value given for a transfer of obligation?

Cases for Analysis

1. Lyla Prendergast hired Rene Jolas to paint portraits of the Prendergast family. The commission was to consist of one portrait that involved the entire family, to include Mr. and Mrs. Prendergast; their three children, Brittany, Bryce, and Stephen; Stephen's wife, Gwenyth; and Bryce's husband, Peter. Jolas was also to do an individual portrait of each family member. Jolas did the family portrait himself and the individual portraits of Mr. and Mrs. Prendergast. However, because he had other commitments, Jolas delegated the duty to do the other portraits to Jack Fleming. This delegation was unknown to Mrs. Prendergast. When the portraits were unveiled, Mrs. Prendergast was satisfied with the portraits of herself and her husband and that of the family, but she did not believe that the other portraits were up to the talent of Jolas. Nevertheless, she took the portraits and paid Jolas. Several months later, while at dinner, the Prendergast family was discussing the portraits, and Mrs. Prendergast finally figured out that the other portraits had been done by Fleming. When she protested to Jolas, he argued that because there was no clause in their contract forbidding the delegation, it was his right to make such a transfer. Mrs. Prendergast argued that he had no such right. Who is correct here? Explain.

2. The Louisville Thoroughbreds, a professional soccer team, entered a seven-year agreement with the city to hold 26 soccer matches each year at the city's outdoor stadium in the downtown area. The Thoroughbreds lived up to their end of the agreement for the first four years. However, by the end of the fourth year, the owner of the Thoroughbreds threatened to move the team to Tampa because the city had not made the agreed-to repairs and improvements to the stadium. The city argued that the improvements had to be made only if the overall attendance for five years running passed the 1 million mark. The Thoroughbreds argued that the team had reached the million mark each year and that the five-year rule was therefore inoperative. When the city continued to avoid making the repairs and improvements, the Thoroughbreds corporation moved the team to Tampa, as promised. The city sued the team. In a parallel development following the filing of the original lawsuit, a group of seven downtown hotels and twelve restaurants joined together to bring a second lawsuit against the Thoroughbreds for breach of contract. The Thoroughbreds filed a summary judgment motion to dismiss the second lawsuit, arguing that the hotels and restaurants did not have standing to sue because they were not in privity under the terms of the original contract and were therefore only incidental beneficiaries under the contract with the city. The hotels and restaurants argued that they were in fact intended beneficiaries, because the whole idea of having a professional soccer team in the downtown area was to stimulate business in that part of town. Who will prevail in the summary judgment motion? Explain.

3. Leslie and Roland lived together without being married and had one child. In addition, Leslie had two children from an earlier marriage. After a four-year relationship, Roland brought court proceedings to evict Leslie and obtain custody of their child. Leslie hired a lawyer who brought a breach of contract action on her behalf against Roland. Shortly thereafter, Leslie and Roland settled both lawsuits by themselves without the attorney's participation. They agreed that Leslie and the three children would return to live with Roland and that he would support them. Roland also agreed to pay Leslie's legal fees. Can the attorney recover his legal fees from Roland under the agreement between Leslie and Roland? Why or why not? *Margolies v. Hopkins,* 514 N.E.2d 1079 (MA).

4. Under a divorce decree, Blackston was ordered to pay $600 a month in child support to his former wife. The decree provided that the payments were to be paid to the clerk of the court's office. The clerk of the court assigned the right to receive the payments to the Department of Human Resources. Who was obligated to notify Blackston of the assignment? *Blackston v. State Ex Rel. Blackston,* 585 So.2d 58 (AL).

5. Gary Jones retained the law firm of Irace and Lowry after being injured in a motorcycle accident. Later, Jones required surgery after dislocating his shoulder in an unrelated incident. Having no money to pay the surgeon, Jones signed a letter requesting that the money from the accident

settlement be assigned to Dr. Herzog for treatment of a shoulder injury that occurred at a different time. The law firm was notified of the assignment. When the settlement was received by the law firm, Jones instructed the firm to pay the money to him rather than to the surgeon. It did, and the surgeon was never paid. Could Dr. Herzog recover the money owed him from the law firm? Why or why not? *Herzog v. Irace,* 594 A.2d 1106 (ME).

6. The Chicago Tribune Syndicate and Press Service, Inc., had a contract to furnish the old Washington Post Company with four comic strips. These strips included *The Gumps, Gasoline Alley, Winnie Winkle,* and *Dick Tracy.* The *Washington Post* went bankrupt, and the bankruptcy trustee assigned the right to receive these comic strips to the reorganized company owned by Meyer. The Tribune Syndicate claimed that the contract could not be assigned. Accordingly, it canceled it and sold the rights of those strips to the *Washington Times.* Was the contract to furnish the comics assignable? Explain. *Meyers v. Washington Times Co.,* 76 F.2d 988 (DC Cir.).

7. Powder Power Tool Corporation negotiated a collective bargaining agreement with the International Association of Machinists. The agreement went into effect on August 24. Employees, however, were to receive a wage increase retroactive to April 1. Several workers who had been employed on April 1 at the old wage scale were not working on August 24. These workers assigned their rights to the retroactive wage increase to Springer. The corporation refused to pay Springer, claiming that the former employees were not parties to the contract, and, as incidental beneficiaries, could not bring suit to enforce the contract. Was the corporation correct? Explain. *Springer v. Powder Power Tool Corporation,* 348 P.2d 1112 (OR).

8. Copeland contracted with McDonald's Systems, Inc., for a franchise. Copeland was granted the fast-food outlet franchise for Omaha. McDonald's also gave Copeland first refusal rights for any plans to open other franchise outlets in Omaha. Copeland exercised the right several times, opening several additional outlets. He then sold the franchise to Schupack and assigned to Schupack the right to open new McDonald's outlets in Omaha. When Schupack tried to exercise the first refusal right, McDonald's objected, claiming its relationship with Copeland developed through a special confidence in Copeland's ability to manage and promote its new franchise outlets. Was McDonald's correct? Explain. *Schupack v. McDonald's Systems, Inc.,* 264 N.W.2d 827 (NE).

9. Timbercrest built a house for the Murphys. After occupying the house for a while, the Murphys complained of several problems. Timbercrest fixed the problems, and the Murphys had no further complaints. The Litwins bought the house from the Murphys three years later. When the house was sold, neither the Litwins nor the Murphys were aware of any problems. After living in the house for two years, the Litwins became aware of several problems. The Litwins then contacted the Murphys and had the Murphys assign them their rights under the original construction agreement with Timbercrest. The Litwins then sued Timbercrest, claiming Timbercrest had breached its contract with the Murphys by not providing them with a house free of defects. Were the Litwins correct? *Litwins v. Timbercrest Estates, Inc.,* 347 N.E.2d 378 (IL).

10. Nolan wrote the song "Tumbling Tumbleweeds" and, in an agreement with Sam Fox Publishing Company, transferred all rights to the song to the company. In return, Nolan was to receive royalties according to terms laid out in the agreement. Sam Fox later assigned all rights and interests in "Tumbling Tumbleweeds" to Williamson Music, Inc. Was it necessary for Sam Fox to obtain Nolan's consent before making the assignment to Williamson? Explain. *Nolan v. Williamson Music, Inc.,* 300 F. Supp. 1311 (S.D. NY).

Quick Quiz Answers

14-1	14-2	14-3
1. T	1. F	1. F
2. T	2. F	2. F
3. F	3. F	3. F

Chapter 15   Discharge and Remedies

The Opening Case
Saewitz v. Epstein

Epstein owned a house on a 93-acre parcel of land in Woodstock, New York. Mr. and Mrs. Saewitz negotiated an option contract for the purchase of the Woodstock property, agreeing to pay a nonrefundable option fee of $30,000. In addition to the option contract, the Saewitzes entered a second agreement with Epstein under which they would lease the property for one year at a rate of $4,000 per month. As part of this second contract, they paid a security deposit of $4,000. At the end of the year, they could exercise the option and purchase the property. Later that year, a winter storm did extensive damage to the property, including the electrical system, leaving the house without power. The Saewitzes paid for repairs to the exterior of the house and then, after talking to Epstein, hired an electrician to repair the electrical system. Unfortunately, in the course of his repair work, the electrician damaged a gas line on the property, leading to additional repairs. In the spring, when they were having the land surveyed, the Saewitzes discovered that Eva Rose, a neighbor, held an easement allowing her to cross the property. Further investigation revealed that the easement could not be severed from the property. Because they had never been told about the permanent easement, something that completely destroyed their enjoyment of the property, the Saewitzes vacated the house and sued Epstein for breach of contract. Here is what they asked for in damages: (1) a return of six months' worth of rental payments totaling $24,000; (2) $4,511.43 for the money that they paid to repair the property after the storm; (3) a return of their $4,000 security deposit; (4) a return of their $30,000 option payment; (5) $7,600 for the survey of the property; (6) reimbursement for the $1,200 spent on a title search; and (7) payment of their legal costs amounting to $5,000. Epstein filed a counterclaim. Here is what he asked for: (1) payment of the remaining rent amounting to $23,006; (2) payment of maintenance and utility expenses of $5,214.52; (3) $114.59 for repairs to the damaged gas line; (4) repayment of $265.71 for carpet cleaning; and (5) an unspecified amount for repairs to a pump on the Woodstock property. The general rule of damages in contract law is that the court must place the parties in as good a position as they would have been had the contract been performed. As this case illustrates, the rule is easy to articulate but difficult to implement. After all was said and done, the Saewitzes left the courthouse victorious but with only $12,655.17 in their pockets rather than the $76,311.43 they had demanded from Epstein. (See *Saewitz v. Epstein*, 6 F. Supp. 151, Northern District of New York.)

Opening Case Questions

1. What is the general rule of damages in contract law?

2. Would the maintenance fees requested by Epstein be compensatory damages? Explain.

3. Why did the court refuse to give the Saewitzes attorney's fees? Explain.

4. Why did the Saewitzes not ask for specific performance of the contract? Explain.

5. Could the Saewitzes use anticipatory repudiation in this case? Explain.

LO Learning Objectives

1. Explain the concept of reasonable time in the performance of a contract.
2. Relate what constitutes satisfactory performance of a contract.
3. Outline the difference between complete and substantial performance.
4. Distinguish among conditions precedent, concurrent, and subsequent.
5. Define tender of performance.
6. List the ways that a contract can be discharged by nonperformance.
7. Clarify the concept of anticipatory repudiation.
8. Enumerate the types of damages available in the event of a breach of contract.
9. Describe mitigation of damages.
10. Contrast specific performance with injunctive relief.

15-1 Discharge by Performance

Most contracts are discharged by **performance**, which means that the parties do what they agreed to do under the terms of the contract. When performance occurs, the obligations of the parties end. Sometimes, however, the parties do not perform in a timely or satisfactory manner. At other times, they perform partially but not completely. At still other times, they do not perform at all.

Time for Performance

When the time for performance is not stated in the contract, the contract must be performed within a reasonable time. A **reasonable time** is the time that may fairly, properly, and conveniently be required to do the task that is to be done, considering attending circumstances. Whether a task is performed within a reasonable time is a question of fact to be decided by the jury in a jury trial or the judge in a nonjury trial.

EXAMPLE 15-1:   *Rostow Aviation, Ltd. v. Futuregraphics, Inc.*

Rostow Aviation, Ltd., entered a contract with Futuregraphics, Inc., for the design and implementation of a new Web site for Rostow. The Web site was supposed to be up and operational within 60 days of the making of the contract. Futuregraphics was one week late in the completion of the Web site. Rostow attempted to rescind the agreement, claiming that time was of special importance. The court ruled that it had

A Question of Ethics

The court held Rostow to the contract in Example 15-1 even though Futuregraphics was one week late in fulfilling its part of the agreement. Because time really was not essential to the agreement, and because Rostow presumably knew that, was it ethical for Rostow to raise the issue of Futuregraphics' lateness in the first place? If time had been important to the completion of the Web site, did Rostow have a responsibility to raise the issue of time before the contract was finalized? If Futuregraphics knew it was running behind schedule, did it have a duty to notify Rostow and offer some sort of compensation for the breach? Explain your answers.

not been clearly established that time was essential for the completion of the Web site. Because time was not essential to the satisfactory performance of the agreement, Rostow was held to the contract.

When the time for performance is stated in the contract but there is nothing to indicate that time is of particular importance, the court will usually allow additional time to perform. When the time for performance is stated in the contract and there is something special about the contract that indicates time is essential, the time for performance will be strictly enforced.

EXAMPLE 15-2:   *Carter City School System v. Spectrum Images, Inc.*

Spectrum Images, Inc., entered a contract with the entire Carter City school system for the design, production, and distribution of the yearbooks for each of the system's three high schools. A very strict schedule was developed for each high school yearbook staff, specifying when the manuscript, art, and photos had to be delivered to Spectrum; when the material had to be read and returned; and when the page proofs had to be read, corrected, and returned to Spectrum. The yearbooks were to be delivered to each high school 90 days after Spectrum had received all page proofs so that they would be ready for distribution on the graduation day for each of the high schools. In such a situation, it is clear that time is an important factor in this agreement. Unfortunately, the students at two of the three schools did not return the proofs on time, and the yearbooks were late. This missed deadline caused an extra expense for the city school system, which had to send the yearbooks to students by FedEx because they were no longer on campus to pick up their books personally. When Carter City sued Spectrum, the court ruled that because the students knew that time was of the essence and had not made the scheduled deadline, the city could not complain when Spectrum failed to meet the delivery date.

Similarly, when the phrase "time is of the essence" is included among the terms of a written contract, the time period will be enforced. The phrase makes it clear that the time element is of the utmost importance to the parties.

Some contracts use a "best efforts" clause to avoid committing parties to a date but instead committing them to do their best to perform by a certain date. A *force majeure*

clause provides for the intervention of unforeseen circumstances. Such a clause usually limits those circumstances to extreme or unusual events, such as acts of God, strikes, and government regulations.

Satisfaction of Performance

Satisfactory performance exists when either personal taste or objective standards have determined that the contracting parties have performed their contractual duties according to the agreement. Satisfactory performance is either an express or implied condition of every contract. Sales agreements for consumer goods often note this condition by including the words: "money back if not entirely satisfied." In other contracts, satisfaction may be carefully defined according to the expectations of the parties. When there is no express agreement, the law implies that work will be done in a skillful manner and the materials or goods will be free of defects. Ordinarily, the parties may be discharged from a contract only if there has been satisfactory performance.

Sometimes, one person will agree to do something to another person's satisfaction. Services rendered in a beauty salon or barbershop, photographs taken at a studio, and portraits painted by an artist fall within this classification. Regardless of the skill and application of the person doing the work, dissatisfied customers may, on the basis of their personal judgment and satisfaction, refuse to make payment.

EXAMPLE 15-3:   *Droulliard v. Velliquette*

Christine Droulliard commissioned Jean Luc Velliquette to sculpt a marble statuette for the front lawn of her summer residence and paid him an advance of $25,000. Velliquette, who was quite confident in his skills and talent as an artist, told Droulliard that unless she was satisfied with his work, she would not have to pay for the statuette. Droulliard's personal taste and judgment would be the determining factor of satisfaction in this situation. When the statuette was unveiled, Droulliard was shocked to see what Velliquette had produced. Consequently, she refused to pay him anything and demanded that he start over. Velliquette rejected her demand, saying that he had already completed what was clearly a masterpiece, and if Droulliard could not see that, she was to blame. Droulliard sued for the return of her advance. The court ruled in her favor because performance of the contract was to be determined by her personal taste and judgment.

Velliquette was a victim of his own vanity. Had he not agreed to allow Droulliard's personal taste and judgment determine his performance, he would have won the case. Satisfactory performance of contracts that do not involve personal taste is determined by an objective standard. Contracts for mechanical devices and services offered by tradespeople, for instance, are of this type.

EXAMPLE 15-4:   *Hutchinson Construction, Ltd. v. Baymount Beach Entertainment, Inc.*

Hutchinson Construction, Ltd., contracted with Baymount Beach Entertainment, Inc., to construct a new high-speed roller coaster for the summer opening of Baymount's amusement park in Idlewild, New Jersey. Because of a serious defect in the construction plans, the scaffolding for the roller coaster would not support the weight of the cars. As a result, Baymount would not accept the roller coaster in its unsafe condition, and the company refused to pay Hutchinson. When Hutchinson sued for nonpayment, Baymount countersued, demanding that Hutchinson remove the structure so that the entertainment company could hire a new construction firm to build a different roller coaster for next season. The court used an objective standard and concluded that the construction of an unsafe roller coaster could not possibly qualify as satisfactory performance. The decision went to Baymount.

Complete and Substantial Performance

Complete performance occurs when all the parties fully accomplish every term, condition, and promise to which they agreed. **Substantial performance** occurs when a party, in good faith, executes all promised terms and conditions with the exception of minor details that do not affect the real intent of their agreement. Complete performance terminates an agreement, freeing the parties of any further obligation. Ordinarily, substantial performance also serves to discharge the agreement but with one difference: A party who correctly complains that the other party's performance has been substantial but not complete has the right to demand reimbursement from the offending party to correct those details that were not performed.

EXAMPLE 15-5:   *South Central State College v. McLaughlin Construction, Inc.*

McLaughlin Construction, Inc., was the primary contractor for the construction of a new engineering center for South Central State College. The construction of the center was supposed to be completed within one year, and the doors were to open in time for the fall term. The building was completed by fall, but the architect for McLaughlin had committed an error. Apparently, he had failed to take into consideration the stress that would be placed on the floor-to-ceiling windows in the building's lobby. As a result, several of those floor-to-ceiling windows developed cracks. An inspection by the state engineers demonstrated that the cracks posed no danger to anyone in or near the building. Nevertheless, the cracked windows were quite unsightly, and they leaked heavily when it rained, flooding the lobby. Consequently, the college demanded that the construction company make repairs at its own expense. The company refused, and the college threatened to rescind the entire contract. Instead, cooler heads prevailed, and the college hired another construction firm to make adjustments to the stress so that the floor-to-ceiling windows would be the showpieces they were supposed to be. When the college asked for and was refused reimbursement for the additional expense, it sued McLaughlin. The court held that there had been substantial performance of the original contract. However, because the cracked windows were caused by an error on the part of the McLaughlin architect, the court awarded reimbursement costs to the college.

Contractual Conditions

Some contracts have conditions or terms that determine the rights and duties of the parties prior to performance, during performance, and following performance. These conditions may be classified as conditions precedent, conditions concurrent, or conditions subsequent.

Condition Precedent

A **condition precedent** is a condition that requires the performance of certain acts or promises before the other party is obligated to pay money or provide any other agreed to consideration. In a *unilateral contract*, the performance of a condition precedent serves as the offeree's acceptance of the offer. In a *bilateral contract,* it is a promise that if not performed leads to either rescission or termination of the entire agreement.

Compliance with a contract is complete only when the parties satisfy all of the conditions in the contract.

EXAMPLE 15-6:   The Pressler Case

Pressler, a third-year law student, signed an agreement to accept a position with a law firm. The members of the firm agreed to hire Pressler on the condition that she receive her law degree and pass the bar examination in their state. Earning the law degree and passing the bar examination are conditions precedent to the performance of the obligation of the law firm in giving Pressler the position.

Condition Concurrent

A condition that requires both parties to perform at the same time is a **condition concurrent**. A promise to deliver goods supported by the buyer's promise to pay on delivery is a very common condition concurrent. Real estate sales agreements, by custom, usually state that the owner–seller will deliver a good and complete deed to the real property on the buyer's presentation of either cash or a certified check for the amount of the purchase price. Failure of either to do as promised concurrently would be a breach of the express contract condition.

Condition Subsequent

A **condition subsequent** is one in which the parties agree that the contract will be terminated when a prescribed event occurs or does not occur. An agreement between a builder and a client stating that contract performance would terminate if a required building permit were not obtained from the issuing public authority within 60 days after the contract is signed is a condition subsequent. Some warranties included in contracts also illustrate these conditions.

EXAMPLE 15-7:   *Graham v. Metcalf*

Luben Metcalf agreed to remodel Trisha Graham's back porch for $15,000. Both parties signed a written agreement. One clause in the agreement stated that Metcalf guaranteed the improvements would be free of defects for 12 months after the work was completed. Graham agreed to pay for the improvements upon completion. Metcalf's guarantee constituted a condition subsequent, that is, a condition that applies after both parties have performed their primary obligations under the contract. When, after only 1 month, the roof of the porch roof leaked, Graham demanded that Metaclf return and fix the problem. Metcalf repeatedly refused to do anything about the leaky roof. Graham was forced to hire another contractor to correct Metcalf's errors. Graham then successfully sued Metcalf and recovered the cost of the repairs.

A condition subsequent is commonly contained in a fire insurance policy, for example. The insured typically agrees in the policy that the report of a fire loss must be made within 30 days of the loss or the insurer will be free of the obligation to reimburse for loss.

Tender of Performance

Tender of performance means to offer to do what one has agreed to do under the terms of the contract. If someone has agreed to sell a parcel of land for $40,000, for example, tender of performance would be offering to give a signed deed to the buyer at the agreed time. Similarly, **tender of payment** would be presenting the $40,000 to the seller at the agreed time.

It is important to make tender even if one knows that the other party is not going to perform the contract. This provision is necessary in some states to test the other party's willingness and ability to perform. If neither party has made tender, the court would hold that a breach of contract has not been established. Thus, neither party would be in a position to bring suit against the other.

People who must perform acts (e.g., selling goods, performing services) are excused from performing if they make proper tender and it is rejected. However, people who must pay money are not excused from paying if their tender of payment is rejected. They are merely excused from paying further interest on their obligation.

Quick Quiz 15-1 True or False?

1. Very few contracts are discharged by performance.

2. A condition precedent is a condition that requires the performance of certain actions before the other party to the contract is obligated.

3. Tender of performance means to offer to do what one has agreed to do under the terms of the contract.

15-2 Discharge by Nonperformance

Nonperformance may be defined as failing to fulfill or accomplish a promise, contract, or obligation according to its terms. Sometimes the failure to perform makes a party vulnerable to legal action. However, not every instance of nonperformance results in a legal action. Sometimes, nonperformance results from mutual agreement between the parties. At other times, nonperformance is excused because of conditions that make performance impossible or by operation of law. Nevertheless, under certain circumstances, nonperformance will result in a breach of contract. Discharge by nonperformance often comes about in the following ways:

- Discharge by agreement
- Discharge by operation of law
- Discharge by impossibility
- Discharge by breach of contract

Discharge by Agreement

Parties to a contract may stipulate the time and conditions for termination and discharge as part of their agreement. They also may subsequently agree not to do what they had originally promised. The latter is the case when there is a mutual rescission of the contract, a waiver of performance by one or more of the parties, a novation, or an accord and satisfaction to liquidate an outstanding debt or obligation.

Termination by Terms of the Contract   During contract negotiations, parties may agree to certain terms that provide for automatic termination of the contract. For example, a professional athlete may contract with management that their agreement will be terminated if for any reason the player becomes either physically or mentally incapable of rendering full performance.

Mutual Rescission   Contracting parties may, either before or after performance commences, rescind their contract as a result of further negotiation and by their mutual assent. **Mutual rescission**, in the majority of cases, requires both parties to return to the other any consideration already received or pay for any services or materials already rendered.

Termination by Waiver   When a party with the right to complain of the other party's unsatisfactory performance or nonperformance fails to complain, **termination by waiver** occurs. It is a voluntary relinquishing (waiver) of one's rights to demand performance. A waiver differs from a discharge by mutual rescission in that a waiver entails no obligation by the parties to return any consideration that may have been exchanged up to the moment of rescission. Discharge by waiver, when made, is complete in itself.

Novation   By novation, the parties to a contract mutually agree to replace one of the parties with a new party. The former, original party is released from liability under the contract. Novation is discussed in detail in Chapter 14.

Talking Points

Have students read and discuss the following quotations representing different points of view about how the law operates in relation to private property, contracts, and labor law:

Law is needed to make sure that agreements are by and large respected and that those who do not respect them can be forced to make good the loss.
— Tony Honore, About Law: An Introduction, Oxford: Clarendon Press, 1995, 47.

[In the nineteenth century,] government and law had a critical role in the economy. Some aspects of that role were basic, so basic that people tended to take them for granted. They took for granted, for example, the idea of private property—in land, in commodities of all sorts. They took for granted the institutions of *contract*: the right to buy and sell, to make agreements, with the understanding that the force of law stood behind these agreements.
— Lawrence M. Friedman, Law in America: A Short History. New York: The Modern Library, 2002, 38.

The Court has fulfilled two principal functions since the New Deal era: (1) legitimating the transformation of property that has occurred in the modern capitalist economy; and (2) managing social conflict by ensuring formal, but limited, representation for select groups, primarily before the administrative agencies of the modern state.
— Carl Swidorski, "Constituting the Modern State: The Supreme Court, Labor Law, and the Contradictions of Legitimation," in Radical Philosophy of Law: Contemporary Challenges to Mainstream Legal Theory and Practice. David Candill and Steven Jay Gold, Atlantic Highlands, NJ: Humanities Press, 1995, 163.

Accord and Satisfaction   An accord and satisfaction is a new agreement resulting from a bona fide dispute between the parties as to the terms of their original agreement. The mutual agreement to the new terms is the accord; performance of the accord is the satisfaction—thus, accord and satisfaction. The accord, though agreed to, is not a binding agreement until the satisfaction has been made. The original agreement therefore is not discharged until the performance or satisfaction has been provided as promised. Accord and satisfaction is discussed in Chapter 10.

General Release   A **general release** is a document expressing the intent of a creditor to release a debtor from obligations on an existing and valid debt. A general release terminates a debt and excuses the debtor of any future payment, without the usual requirement that consideration be given in return.

Discharge by Impossibility

Occasionally, it becomes impossible to perform a contract. For example, when the subject matter of a contract, without the knowledge of the parties, had been destroyed before the contract was entered into, the contract would be discharged.

EXAMPLE 15-8:   *McFadden v. Sterkel*

While working in Seattle, Nancy McFadden agreed to purchase a condominium in Tampa belonging to Walter and Wilma Sterkel for $580,000. The contract was drawn up and signed, and McFadden gave the Sterkels a certified check. Neither party knew that a hurricane had destroyed the condo the night before at its Florida location. Although no one realized it at the time the parties entered the contract, performance was impossible. Both parties were discharged of any promise of performance. The Sterkels, however, refused to return the check. McFadden had to take them to court to get her money back.

Conditions that arise subsequent to the making of a contract may either void the agreement or make it voidable by one of the parties. Discharge through impossibility of performance may, in some situations, be allowed only if the specific and anticipated impossibility has been made a condition to the agreement.

When the exact subject matter of an executory contract has been selected by the parties and later is destroyed, the performance obligation is discharged. In contrast, when the contract is not specific in the description or the location of the subject matter, a promisor is not discharged if the subject matter intended for delivery is destroyed. In this case, the promisor is obligated to locate and deliver subject matter of the same kind and quantity that could be secured elsewhere. Any financial losses due to the misfortune must be borne by the promisor.

When the performance of a contract promise requires execution of acts declared illegal because of existing common law, statute, or public policy, the contract is void from its inception. When the performance of a contract is made illegal through the passing of laws subsequent to the formation of the contract, the contract is likewise declared void, and the parties are discharged.

The death, insanity, or disability of a party obligated to perform an act that requires a special talent or skill terminates and discharges an agreement, including promises to perform by musicians, artists, writers, skilled craftspeople, and certain professionals. When promised services are to be performed for the personal benefit of a promisee, the death of the promisee will also terminate the agreement. When the contract relates to services that may be performed by others and do not demand the personal services of the contracting party, performance is not excused through death, insanity, or disability. The guardian of the party involved or the estate of the deceased may be held liable for performance.

Frustration-of-Purpose Doctrine   The **frustration-of-purpose doctrine** releases a party from a contractual obligation when performing the obligations would be thoroughly impractical and senseless. The doctrine is applied only in those cases in which a party recognizes and understands possible risks and accepts them in contemplation of performance.

EXAMPLE 15-9:   *Stewart v. Gaverick*

George Gaverick rented a 50th-floor apartment from Thomas Stewart for the night of December 31. The apartment had a balcony overlooking Times Square in midtown Manhattan. The rental period was for only 24 hours, and the landlord knew that the purpose of the contract was to allow Gaverick an unrestricted view of Times Square for the city's New Year's Eve celebration. Unfortunately, a terrorist alert canceled the entire Times Square celebration that year. Stewart still demanded payment from Gaverick and brought a suit in small claims court to recover the amount due. The referee refused to force Gaverick to pay for the apartment. The referee concluded that, because the apartment was of no use to Gaverick, the purpose of the agreement was frustrated, and Gaverick would not have to pay the rent.

Commercial Impracticability   Although not identical to the frustration-of-purpose doctrine, a related concept is known as **commercial impracticability**. Under this doctrine, the courts may excuse the nonperformance of one party to a contract because an unforeseen and very severe hardship has arisen that would place an enormous hardship on that party. Commercial impracticability is not the same as impossibility, because the party still can perform the contract. It is just that the performance itself would cause a great deal of adversity. Also with commercial impracticability, the purpose of the contract is not undermined by the unforeseen event, so the frustration-of-purpose doctrine does not apply. Nevertheless, under this relatively modern doctrine, some parties may escape performance if the unforeseen event was truly unforeseen and not in any way the fault of the party seeking an escape from performance.

Discharge by Operation of Law

The performance of a promised act may be discharged by operation of law. Some law that causes the parties to be discharged from their obligations, such as bankruptcy or the statute of limitations, comes into play in this case.

Bankruptcy   Through the provisions of the Bankruptcy Reform Act (see Chapter 31), a discharge in bankruptcy from a court will be allowed as a defense against the collection of most, but not all, debts of the bankrupt. Therefore, most contractual obligations to pay money come to an end when a party files for bankruptcy.

Statute of Limitations   State statutes providing time limits within which suits may be brought are known as statutes of limitations. Each state sets its own time limits. In general, actions for collection of open accounts (charge accounts) must be brought within

About the Law

State laws protect minors by providing that statutes of limitations do not begin running until plaintiffs who are minors attain their majority, which is the day before their eighteenth birthday.

three to five years, written agreements within ten years, and judgments from ten to twenty years. Those states requiring a seal on certain contracts have still other limitations and requirements that are much broader than those applied to simple contracts. The time limit for bringing suit for breach of a sales contract is four years under the Uniform Commercial Code. The statute of limitations does not technically void the debt, but it gives the debtor a defense against any demand for collection.

Discharge by Breach of Contract

When there is a breach of contract, the injured party has the right to remedy in court. There are several ways in which a breach may occur.

Deliberate Breach of Contract

A breach of contract results when one of the parties fails to do what was agreed to under the terms of the contract. When time is of the essence, there is a breach if performance is not completed within the time limits agreed to by the parties. A breach also results if the performance has been negligent or unskillful. The services rendered must adhere to the standards of skill, as determined by the custom of the marketplace. Wrongful performance or nonperformance discharges the other party from further obligation and permits that party to bring suit to rescind the contract or recover money to compensate it for any loss sustained. Such compensation is known as *damages.*

EXAMPLE 15-10:   *Carnegie Hall Musical Association, Inc. v. Newel Yurchak*

Newel Yurchak, an internationally renowned violinist, contracted to perform at Carnegie Hall on January 19. Carnegie Hall and the Carnegie Foundation had brochures and posters printed and posted notice of the performance on their Web site. Carnegie also aired advertisements on NPR and public television. On the day before the performance, Yurchak informed Carnegie that he was not going to perform. Through Yurchak's nonperformance, the contract between him and Carnegie was discharged. Carnegie could seek damages from Yurchak on the grounds of breach of contract.

Repudiation and Anticipatory Breach

An **anticipatory breach** occurs when a party to a contract either expresses or clearly implies an intention not to perform the contract, even before being required to act. The repudiation must indicate a deliberate refusal to perform according to the terms of the contract. Breaches of this kind are also called *constructive breaches.* The injured party may either commence suit at the time of the anticipatory breach or await the date agreed to for performance, thus giving the breaching party time to reconsider and begin performance. To succeed in a case based on anticipatory repudiation, the injured party must demonstrate that he or she was ready, willing, and able to comply with the contract but could not do so because of the other party's material breach. Anticipatory breach cannot be used if the only action repudiated was the promise to pay money to another party.

Abandonment of Contractual Obligations

Stopping performance once it has begun is called **abandonment of contractual obligations**. Leaving or deserting a party's obligations discharges the other party from any promises made and permits a suit for damages. A temporary, or short-lived, interruption of performance is not deemed abandonment. To constitute abandonment, the promisor must have inexcusably interrupted performance with the obvious intention of not returning to complete the obligations promised.

The Opening Case Revisited, Part I
Saewitz v. Epstein, Round 2

In The Opening Case at the beginning of the chapter, the Saewitzes were un-
nerved, disappointed, and dismayed when they discovered that their neighbor,
Eva Rose, had a permanent easement on the Epstein property. An easement is a
legal right to cross another person's property. The fact that Rose could cross the
property destroyed their privacy and eliminated their enjoyment of the land. Still,
they might have been able to live with this inconvenience, had they not learned
that Epstein had known about the easement all along but failed to tell them
about it. Even then they might have gone along with the deal, had they not discovered that there was absolutely no way to remove the Rose easement from
Epstein's land. Epstein's failure to deliver a tract of land that was free from any
and all legal encumbrances was an anticipatory repudiation that the Saewitzes
felt released them from the contract. They decided that they would not wait six
more months to see if Epstein would do something about the Rose easement.
However, they also did not approach Epstein and offer to exercise the option if
he removed the easement. Instead, without saying anything to Epstein, they
simply moved out. They then labeled Epstein's action as anticipatory repudiation
and sued. The court, however, did not buy that argument. The court stated that
to defend nonperformance because of breach of contract based on anticipatory
repudiation, the Saewitzes would have to show that they had been ready, willing,
and able to uphold their part of the deal. Because, upon learning about the
easement, they did not attempt to exercise the option but instead moved out,
they had not demonstrated the level of willingness that the court demanded.

Quick Quiz 15-2 True or False?

1. A general release is a document expressing the intent of a creditor to release a
   debtor from the obligations of an existing and valid debt.

2. With commercial impracticability, the purpose of a contract is undermined by
   an unforeseen event.

3. Stopping a performance once it has begun is called abandonment of contractual obligations.

15-3 Damages and Equitable Remedies

A breach of contract releases the injured party from any obligations under the contract and
gives that party the right to ask a court of law for a remedy. The usual remedy for breach of
contract is the payment of damages in the form of money. At times, however, the payment
of monetary damages is not enough to satisfy the injured party. In such situations, the injured party will ask the court for rescission, specific performance, or an injunction.

Standard Damages in Contract Law

Damages describe money awarded to parties who have been victimized or suffered injury to their legal rights by others. Damages are of different kinds, and the nature of a claim usually determines what type of damages will apply. In some states, by statute or judicial rule, juries are charged with two decisions: They must decide which party is to be given favorable judgment and determine how much is to be awarded in damages. Appeals to a higher court are allowed when the amount of damages awarded appears to be unreasonably low or excessively high.

Actual or Compensatory Damages

Actual damages are the sum of money equal to the real financial loss suffered by the injured party. Because they are intended to compensate the injured party, actual damages are also called **compensatory damages**. Thus, damages awarded for nondelivery of promised goods or services would be an amount equal to the difference between the price stated in the contract and what the promisee would have to pay elsewhere. Should the same goods or services be conveniently available elsewhere at the same or at a lower price, no actual loss could be claimed.

EXAMPLE 15-11:   *Conte v. Sedgard*

Zach Sedgard entered a contract with Will Conte in which Sedgard promised to construct a fence around Conte's property for $4,890, including materials and labor. Sedgard then refused to honor his promise, arguing that the prices for his materials had gone up so much that it was impossible for him to construct the fence without losing a great deal of money. Conte hired Fred Winchester to complete the job for him. Winchester charged Conte $5,890. When Conte sued Sedgard for breach of contract, the actual damages would be $1,000, the difference between the $4,890 that Sedgard agreed to and the $5,890 that Conte was charged by Winchester, another equally competent and reputable builder.

Incidental and Consequential Damages

Incidental damages and consequential damages are awarded for losses indirectly but closely attributable to a breach. **Incidental damages** cover any expenses paid out by the innocent party to prevent further loss. **Consequential damages** result indirectly from the breach because of special circumstances that exist with a particular contract. To recover consequential damages, the injured party must show that such losses were foreseeable when the contract was made.

Punitive or Exemplary Damages

Damages in excess of actual losses suffered by the plaintiff awarded as a measure of punishment for the defendant's wrongful acts are **punitive damages**, also called *exemplary damages*. They are of the nature of court-ordered punishment rather than compensation for a known loss. Punitive damages are awarded when a defendant is responsible for abusive and dishonest practices in consumer transactions that are unconscionable and contrary to the public good. Often such abusive and dishonest practices are associated with certain business-related torts, including fraudulent misrepresentation, disparagement, the violation of an implied covenant of fairness and honesty, and intentional interference with an existing contract.

Fraudulent Misrepresentation

Previously in the text, we examined fraudulent misrepresentation, or fraud as it is referred to in many jurisdictions, in tort law and in relation to the disruption of mutual assent in contract law. As we learned, fraud occurs when one

The Opening Case Revisited, Part II
Saewitz v. Epstein, Round 3

Recall that in The Opening Case at the beginning of the chapter, once the Saewit-zes learned that the Woodstock property could not be disentangled from the Rose easement, they packed their furniture and personal property into two trucks and a car and left the house to return to Florida. Unfortunately, at the time that they va-cated the house, they still had the better part of six months to go on their lease. Therefore, the Woodstock property was suddenly vacant. Consequently, Epstein had to pay Rose to come over to the property and make regular inspections to en-sure that everything was in proper order. Eventually, the payments to Rose sur-passed $2,000. The court ruled that these payments were consequential damages to which Epstein was entitled. The damages in this case were consequential be-cause they resulted indirectly from the breach; once the Saewitzes were no longer on the property, Epstein had to do something to protect his investment.

party makes false statements or commits some sort of false action that causes another party to rely on those falsehoods, who then experiences an injury or loss as a result. Because fraud is a deliberate attempt to subvert proper business relationships, the court views it as espe-cially reprehensible, and those that commit fraud will find themselves paying not only com-pensatory damages, if applicable, but also punitive damages. The idea of punitive damages is to punish the defrauding party to such an extent that he or she will be dissuaded from any future fraudulent conduct. Punitive damages are also supposed to serve as a deterrent so that other people do not even think about commiting fraud. For this reason, punitive damages are also called exemplary damages. Exemplary damages are used as an example for other "would-be con artists" who ought to know better than to subvert the law through fraud.

Disparagement   Previously, we learned that disparagement involves any false state-ment communicated to others that somehow questions the quality of property or raises uncer-tainty as to who has legal ownership of that property. Disparagement can involve business if the "disparager" is unjustly attacking the quality of a businessperson's product. Generally, to recover damages for disparagement, the plaintiff must show monetary loss. These losses may include the loss of sales and money spent to correct consumers' impressions of a product.

EXAMPLE 15-12:   *Armstrong v. Dent*

Frieda Armstrong owned and operated The Victorious Vegan, a vegetarian restaurant that boasted a totally meat-, fish-, and dairy-free menu. Several times when big conven-tions were in town, Lex Dent, who owned a competitive restaurant, spread rumors, most of which suggested that many of the specialty vegetarian soups that Armstrong had on her menu used beef and chicken stock in their recipes. He also suggested that several other items on the menu were based on recipes stolen from him and that Armstrong did not have the right to serve them in her restaurant. Dent has clearly committed disparage-ment here. He has planted false reports about both the purity of Armstrong's vegetarian soups and Armstrong's property rights to certain items on the menu. Armstrong, how-ever, will have to show that any lost sales are due to Dent's behavior and/or that she had to spend money to undo Dent's campaign of disparagement.

Business Law in the News

The Supreme Court: Open for Business

With controversial rulings on abortion and campaign finance, the current U.S. Supreme Court has waded into some of the most explosive issues in American politics. Under the leadership of new Chief Justice John G. Roberts, the high court appears to be on the verge of rewriting vast tracts of settled Constitutional law. But there's another important emerging feature of the Roberts Court that has not drawn nearly as much attention: its sympathy to business.

Consider this: Out of 15 cases in which the U.S. Chamber of Commerce filed friend-of-the-court briefs, presenting the views of its corporate members, the chamber won 13—the chamber's highest winning percentage in its 30-year history. Indeed, the court's 2006-07 term, drawing to a close this month, has been a banner year for business, with important victories in areas ranging from antitrust and banking to shareholder suits and punitive damages.

The true sea change brought about by the Roberts court stems from its willingness to take business cases for review. The group presided over by his predecessor, William H. Rehnquist, simply wasn't interested, instead favoring cases involving criminal law, school prayer, or other matters involving fundamental constitutional rights. "There was a period there toward the end of the Rehnquist years when you couldn't buy an antitrust or securities case onto the docket to save your life," says Carter G. Phillips, an appellate specialist with Sidley Austin in Washington who has argued before the Supreme Court dozens of times.

That's changed dramatically. Of 73 cases heard by the court in the current term, 29 (40%) involved or were significant to business, according to statistics compiled by Akin Gump Strauss Hauer & Feld, a law firm with an active practice before the court. That's up from around 30% during the previous two terms. Already, nearly 50% of cases for the session beginning next October involve business. A big one slated for next term involves the degree to which shareholders may seek compensation from bankers, accountants, and lawyers who may have helped executives commit securities fraud.

Another promises to resolve whether federal approval of medical devices shields their makers from injury lawsuits. . . .

One of the court's most liberal members, Ruth Bader Ginsburg, authored the court's 8-1 opinion in *Tellabs v. Makor,* which raised the hurdle for plaintiffs to move forward with securities fraud lawsuits. That's part of what leads academics and practitioners to see the Roberts court as more pragmatic than political in the business arena. "These are not expansive cases with a lot of ideological jargon in them," says Herb Hovenkamp at the University of Iowa College of Law about the court's business rulings. "They are fairly technical, fairly narrowly written."

Shrinking Damages

Still, even rulings that were measured and lacking in explicit ideological pronouncements may have the potential for broad impact. In throwing out a $79.5 million punitive damage award against Altria Group Inc.'s Philip Morris in a smoking lawsuit, for example, the court said that jurors may consider harm only to parties in the case, not to the public at large. In theory that will dramatically shrink the size of any punitive damages award. While Conrad of the chamber considers the case a win, she says she wished the court had gone further and set forth a formula to cap punitive damages. But David R. Stras, a law professor at the University of Minnesota and former clerk for Justice Thomas, calls the case "a sleeper in terms of its import" and thinks it will drastically curtail awards in other cases.

Similarly, Hovenkamp thinks the court's ruling in the Credit Suisse case could have widespread impact. In a June 18 decision, the court nixed efforts by plaintiffs to sue securities underwriters for anticompetitive conduct in the market for initial public offerings. Heavy regulation of this area by the Securities & Exchange Commission, the justices ruled, precludes private antitrust claims. While the court's decision could be read as applying narrowly to Wall Street firms subject to SEC oversight, Hovenkamp says it may well be extended to other areas, such as telecommunications, where companies are also subject to close federal monitoring for anticompetitive activity.

Advocacy groups for consumers and plaintiffs are maintaining hope by clinging to the notion that rulings made by the Roberts court are evolutionary, not revolutionary. Bonnie I. Robin-Vergeer, a senior attorney at Public Citizen Litigation Group in Washington, acknowledges "it's probably fair to say that the court is friendlier to business than in past years." But she, too, observes that many of the court's rulings have been crafted in a narrow way. "There's some saving grace in that," she says.

Questions for Review

1. The article states that the U.S. Chamber of Commerce "won 13" out of 15 business-related cases heard recently by the Supreme Court, "the chamber's highest winning percentage in its 30-year history." What false impression has the writer created about the relationship between the Chamber of Commerce and these cases?

2. Why was the $79.5 million punitive damage award overturned by the Supreme Court in the Philip Morris case?

3. Was the Philip Morris case a contract or a tort case? Explain.

4. Why did the Chamber of Commerce consider the court's ruling in the Philip Morris case a benefit for business?

5. What is a damage cap? Why would the business community prefer to have the court approve damage caps? Explain.

Source: Michael Orey, "Justice: The Supreme Court: Open for Business: The Roberts Court Is Showing a Willingness to Referee Corporate Concerns," *BusinessWeek,* July 9 & 16, 2007, 30–31.

Violating an Implied Covenant of Fairness and Honesty   Some courts have ruled that there exists an implied covenant in certain contracts, especially employment-related contracts. This implied covenant binds each party to a relationship based on honesty and fairness. In short, it means that neither party will unfairly or dishonestly cheat the other out of anything that should be honored because of their contractual relationship. Interestingly enough, the existence of an implied covenant has absolutely nothing to do with anything that the parties actually communicate to each other. The implied covenant exists simply because the contract exists. The courts that recognize this type of covenant have no difficulty assessing punitive damages against a party who violates this valued agreement. Implied covenant is covered at length in Chapter 35 on Employment Law.

Talking Points

The covenant of honesty and fairness is based on a very basic principle first articulated by Immanuel Kant and later developed by the American philosopher John Rawls. Rawls calls this principle the Veil of Ignorance. He explains the principle in his work, *A Theory of Justice,* in which he writes that the veil of ignorance assumes that an individual has no knowledge about "his place in society, his class position or social status; nor does he know his fortune in the distribution of natural assets and abilities, his intelligence and strength, and the like." In this state of ignorance, decisions will always be honest and fair. If I do not know my place in society, I do not know how or if I will gain by any decision, and so I fashion all decisions so that, no matter where I end up, I will find that decision to be fair. Why do you suppose that such a commonsense principle does not receive more attention in the law? Explain.

Source: John Rawls. *A Theory of Justice.* Cambridge, MA: Harvard University Press, 1999, p. 118.

Intentional Interference with an Existing Contract It is perfectly permissible for businesspeople to compete for the same customer. However, once one of those competitors has entered a contract with a customer, the other competitors must honor that contract and cannot tempt the customer into a breach. To do so would be the tort of intentional interference with an existing contract. To be found liable for this tort, the offending party's innocent target must actually be involved in an existing contract, the offending party must know about that contract, and he or she must then cause the innocent target to violate the terms of that agreement. As in the case of fraud, the courts consider the tort of intentional interference to be so reprehensible that an offending party found liable will often be compelled to pay punitive damages.

Special Types of Damages

In addition to standard damages, the court will consider assessing other types of damages whenever a situation calls for them. The special types of damages that are available to the court include nominal damages, present and future damages, liquidated damages, and damages under *quantum meruit*. The court will not, however, grant speculative damages.

Nominal Damages Token damages awarded to parties who have experienced an injury to their legal rights but no actual loss are **nominal damages**. Common law usually awarded six cents to the successful plaintiff when no actual losses were shown. In today's practice, the award is usually one dollar.

EXAMPLE 15-13:   *The United States Football League*
v. The National Football League

The United States Football League (USFL) sued the National Football League (NFL), alleging that the NFL had engaged in unfair competitive practices that violated federal statutory law. The USFL also claimed that the NFL had intentionally interfered with certain USFL contractual relationships and even with some potential contracts. The jury decided that the NFL had been involved in some unfair competitive practices but that its actions had not hurt the USFL. As a result, the USFL was awarded $1 in nominal damages. This figure then was raised to $3, because the statute that was violated allowed for three times the damages awarded.

Present and Future Damages Damages may be awarded for present injuries and for others that might reasonably be anticipated in the future. Thus, a party charged with fraud in the sale of a building infested with termites may be held liable for all damages revealed at the time of the suit and for damages that would reasonably be forthcoming as a result of the undisclosed and concealed infestation of the property.

Liquidated Damages Parties may stipulate (agree) as a condition of their contract to the amount of damages that might be assessed if there is a breach. Damages agreed to in the initial contract are called **liquidated damages**. Liquidated damages must be realistic and in proportion to the losses that might be reasonably anticipated should there be a breach. When liquidated damages are found to be excessive or unreasonable, a court will disregard them and leave the matter of setting damages to the discretion of a jury.

Damages Under *Quantum Meruit*   The doctrine of *quantum meruit* (i.e., as much as one had earned) is important in assessing damages in cases founded on contracts implied in law, or quasi-contracts. Thus, when there has been no express or implied mutual agreement, a court will at times impose an obligation against a party who has been unjustly rewarded at the innocent expense of another. Damages awarded are in an amount considered reasonable in return for the benefits the one party derived through the quasi-contract relationship.

Speculative Damages   Courts do not allow **speculative damages**. These damages are computed on losses that have not actually been suffered and that cannot be proved; they are damages based entirely on an expectation of losses that might be suffered from a breach. They differ from future damages in that speculative damages are not founded on fact but only on hope or expectation. Their basis is nothing more than a calculated guess as to the gains a party might have received had there not been a breach.

Mitigation of Damages

The injured party has an obligation to do what is reasonably possible to mitigate the damages, that is, to keep damages to a minimum. A party who has been wronged by another's breach must exercise reasonable precautions to prevent the damages from becoming unfairly and unreasonably burdensome to the other party.

Equitable Remedies

When money in the form of damages is not enough to provide a fair and just award to the injured party, the court may grant an equitable remedy. Rather than simply order the breaching party to pay damages, a court issuing an equitable remedy compels the breaching party to perform an act or refrain from performing an act. The two most common equitable remedies are specific performance and injunctive relief.

Specific Performance   A decree of **specific performance** is a court order calling for the breaching party to do what he or she promised to do under the original contract. The courts order specific performance only when the subject matter of a contract is unique or rare. The classic example of unique subject matter calling for specific performance is a contract for the sale and transfer of title to land, because each piece of land is unique. However, unique or rare subject matter could also include such items as antiques, family heirlooms, original works of art, and special animals, such as a particular race horse. Obviously, an award of monetary damages would not provide the injured party satisfaction in any of these situations.

Contracts for personal services are rarely enforced through specific performance. Demanding that an unwilling party perform promised personal services would be contrary to Amendment 13 of the U.S. Constitution, which prohibits human servitude. A remedy in cases of this kind, however, may be found through injunctive relief.

Injunctive Relief   An **injunction** is an order issued by a court directing that a party do or refrain from doing something. An injunction may be either temporary or permanent. A temporary injunction is issued as a means of delaying further activity in any contested matter until the court determines whether a permanent injunction should be entered or the injunction should be removed entirely. One who disobeys an injunction does so under threat of penalty of contempt of court.

Litigation Costs

Litigation is not free. Someone must pay attorney's fees, filing costs, expert witness fees, research expenses, subpoena costs, photocopying bills, deposition costs, and so on. These costs are usually divided into attorney's fees, on the one hand, and all other expenses, on the other. The general rule of law in relation to attorney's fees has always been that each party will pay his or her own attorney. There are exceptions to this rule, but all such exceptions are authorized by statutory law. Other expenses, such as those involved in filing the case and issuing subpoenas, are referred to as **taxable expenses** or **taxable costs**. These expenses can be charged against the *losing party*. There are also taxable costs incurred in appealing a case, such as the cost of filing the appeal, the costs incurred when the clerk must prepare a record of the case, and so on. These are also chargeable against the losing party.

Quick Quiz 15-3 True or False?

1. Actual damages are also called compensatory damages.

2. Punitive damages cover any expenses paid out by the innocent party to prevent further loss.

3. The courts order specific performance only when the subject matter of a contract is unique or rare.

Summary

15.1   Most contracts are discharged by performance, which means that the parties do what they agreed to do. When the time for performance is not stated in a contract, it must be performed within a reasonable time. When the time is stated, the court will allow additional time to perform unless something indicates that time is of the essence; then, time for performance will be strictly enforced. Unless the parties agree otherwise, satisfactory performance will be determined by objective standards. Substantial performance will discharge the agreement with the right to reimbursement for correcting details that were not completed. Conditions may determine the rights and duties of the parties prior to performance, during performance, and following performance. It is important to make tender of performance to test the other party's willingness and ability to perform. If neither party makes tender, a breach of contract is not established.

15.2   Nonperformance can discharge contractual obligations. Not every instance of nonperformance results in a breach of contract. Parties can agree to discharge a contractual obligation by terms in the contract,

mutual rescission, waiver, novation, accord and satisfaction, or general release. Contractual obligations can also be discharged when it becomes impossible to perform a contract. The frustration-of-purpose doctrine releases a party from a contractual obligation when performing the obligation would be impractical and senseless. These obligations can also be discharged by operation of law under principles of bankruptcy and the statute of limitations. When contractual obligations terminate by agreement or by operation of law, no liability falls to either party. However, when breach of contract comes from a deliberate breach, a repudiation of contractual obligation, or an abandonment of performance, liability will result.

15.3   A breach of contract relieves the injured party from any obligation under the contract. Breach of contract also gives the injured party the right to ask a court of law for a remedy, usually in the form of damages. Injured parties are required to mitigate their damages. When money will not be sufficient relief, the injured party may ask for specific performance or injunctive relief.

Key Terms

abandonment of contractual obligations, 298

actual damages, 300

anticipatory breach, 298

commercial impracticability, 297

compensatory damages, 300

complete performance, 292

condition concurrent, 293

condition precedent, 293

condition subsequent, 293

consequential damages, 300

frustration-of-purpose doctrine, 297

general release, 296

incidental damages, 300

injunction, 305

liquidated damages, 304

mutual rescission, 295

nominal damages, 304

performance, 289

punitive damages, 300

reasonable time, 289

satisfactory performance, 291

specific performance, 305

speculative damages, 305

substantial performance, 292

taxable costs, 306

taxable expenses, 306

tender of payment, 294

tender of performance, 294

termination by waiver, 295

Questions for Review and Discussion

1. What does the term "reasonable time" mean in the performance of a contract?
2. What constitutes satisfactory performance of a contract?
3. What is the difference between complete and substantial performance?
4. What are the differences among conditions precedent, concurrent, and subsequent?
5. What is tender of performance?
6. What are the ways that a contract can be discharged by nonperformance?
7. What is the concept of anticipatory repudiation?
8. What are the types of damages available in the event of a breach of contract?
9. What is mitigation of damages?
10. What is the difference between specific performance and injunctive relief?

Investigating the Internet

The 'Lectric Law Library Web site can answer many basic questions about virtually every area of the law. Locate the Web site, access "Contract Law—Nonperformance and Breach of Contract," and in a short report, answer the following questions: (1) According to the 'Lectric Law Library, what is the basic rule in relation to the performance of a contract? (2) What behavior is required from the aggrieved party if that party wants to support a claim that the other party has breached a contract? (3) What is the ordinary remedy for a breach of contract? (4) According to the 'Lectric Law Library, should a party expect to receive punitive damages in a contract suit? (5) According to the 'Lectric Law Library, when might a party expect to receive punitive damages?

Cases for Analysis

1. Teri Fischer was the owner of the Anchorage Fish and Game Building. Fischer prevailed upon Kennedy Associates, Inc., to help finance the construction of an addition to the Fish and Game Building. Kennedy agreed to provide a loan to cover 90 percent of the cost of the addition. The loan was to run for 25 years at an interest rate of 13.125 percent. Final approval of the loan, however, was conditional upon a requirement that the *completed* building pass an inspection by Kennedy. The main objective of the inspection was to make certain the addition would supply sufficient collateral for the 25-year loan. Accordingly, once the addition was substantially completed, Kennedy hired an independent inspector, Cherrier, who, after inspecting the building, rated it in poor condition. As a result of the inspection report, Kennedy decided not to go through with the loan agreement. Fischer then sued Kennedy for breach of contract, arguing that the Cherrier report had been premature, because the addition was not totally completed at the time of the inspection. Kennedy therefore had breached the contract before the condition precedent had been met. Kennedy argued that at the time of the inspection, the only things left incomplete were the unfinished concrete stoops and the absence of paint in some areas, so the building was ready for inspection. The trial court agreed with Fischer. Kennedy appealed. Was the inspection performed in a timely manner so that Kennedy could cancel the contract for failure to meet a condition precedent? Explain. *Kennedy Associates, Inc. v. Fischer,* 667 P.2d 174 (Alaska Supreme Court).

2. When Kent contracted to have his new house constructed, he specifically noted that the plumbing must be made by Reading manufacturers. After the house had been completed, Kent did an inspection tour during which he discovered that, though much of the plumbing had come from Reading, there were some parts that did not. After making his discovery, Kent demanded that the non-Reading plumbing fixtures be ripped out and replaced with the supplies he had specified in the contract. In addition, Kent refused to pay the contractor until the proper plumbing supplies were added to the house. The contractor brought suit against Kent, arguing that though there were minor deviations from certain specified parts of the contract concerning the plumbing fixtures, he had nevertheless substantially performed his end of the deal. Kent stuck to his strict construction of the contract and labeled the contractor's performance unsatisfactory. He thus claimed to be released from the agreement unless the contractor lived up to every term in the original agreement. Who should prevail in this case? Explain. *Jacob and Young v. Kent,* 129 N.E. 889.

3. The Morin Building Products Company was commissioned by Baystone Construction to install aluminum siding on the walls of Baystone's factory. Once the project was finished, Baystone inspected the job and expressed dissatisfaction primarily because the siding lacked an appropriately uniform finish. Morin argued that, based on an objective judgment of the work, the siding that the company had installed fit quite well with the utilitarian function of the business. Baystone argued that a standard of satisfactory performance should be used to judge the results of the siding job and that because Baystone was not satisfied, the court should rule that Morin had not properly performed. Who will prevail in this case? Explain. *Morin Building Products Company v. Baystone Construction,* 717 F2d 413.

4. Sai Grafio agreed to paint Gerald Weaver's and Katherine Brewer's house for $5,650. Weaver and Brewer paid for the paint job in installments but stopped payment on the final $1,845 check, claiming that Grafio had breached the contract by doing a poor job. The lower court judge found that the only defect in the paint job was a footprint left on the roof that would cost $50 to repair. How much money, if any, and under what legal theory, did the court allow Grafio to recover for the paint job? *Weaver v. Grafio,* 595 A.2d 983 (DC).

5. Kvassay contracted in writing to sell 24,000 cases of baklava at $19 per case to Great American Foods, Inc., over a one-year period. Great American breached the contract after Kvassay had deliv-

ered 3,000 cases. The contract contained the following clause: "If Buyer refuses to accept or repudiates delivery of the goods sold to him, under this Agreement, Seller shall be entitled to damages, at the rate of $5.00 per case, for each remaining to be delivered under this contract." Kvassay used the $5 figure, after calculating that he would earn a net profit of $3.55 per case if the contract were fully performed. When the contract was breached by Great American, Kvassay sued for $105,000 ($5 × 21,000 cases not delivered). What is the legal name for the clause in the contract? What argument might Great American use to have the clause declared void? *Kvassay v. Murray, 808 P.2d 896 (KS).*

6. Arthur Murray, Inc., and Parker entered a series of contracts under which Arthur Murray agreed to teach Parker how to dance. Under the terms of each agreement, refunds were impossible, and the lessons could not be canceled. After the contracts were entered, Parker suffered a permanent disability that made it physically impossible for him to dance. When Arthur Murray refused to refund any part of Parker's money, he sued to rescind the contracts on grounds of impossibility. Arthur Murray claimed that the nonrefund clause must be upheld by the court. Was Arthur Murray correct? Explain. *Parker v. Arthur Murray, Inc., 295 N.E.2d 487 (IL).*

7. Shaw leased a service station from Mobil Oil. Shaw's monthly rent was based on his purchase of gasoline from Mobil. He was to pay 1.4 cents per gallon or a $470 minimum monthly rent. Each month Shaw would have to purchase 33,572 gallons to meet this minimum. In July, Shaw ordered 34,000 gallons, which would have allowed him to meet more than the minimum rent. Mobil, however, could deliver only 25,678 gallons. Nevertheless, Mobil attempted to collect the $470 minimum monthly rent. Shaw brought suit against Mobil, claiming that his payment of the $470 minimum and Mobil's delivery of at least 33,572 gallons were conditions concurrent. Shaw argued that because Mobil had not met its part of the bargain, he was not obligated to meet his because Mobil's failure was a breach of contract. Was Shaw correct? Explain. *Shaw v. Mobil Oil Corporation, 535 P.2d 756 (OR).*

8. Bob Pagan Ford, Inc., hired Smith to work as a car salesperson in Galveston County. As part of his contract, Smith agreed not to work as an auto salesperson in Galveston County for three years after leaving his employment with Bob Pagan Ford. Smith worked for Bob Pagan for only a few months. He then left and took a sales job with another dealership in Galveston County. Was injunctive relief an appropriate remedy in this case? Explain. *Bob Pagan Ford, Inc., v. Smith, 638 S.W.2d 176 (TX).*

9. Kucha sold a house to Pilder for $75,293. The agreement was in writing, as required by the Statute of Frauds. As part of the contract, Kucha agreed to pay for the remodeling of the sunporch. However, when Kucha found out that it would cost $12,728 to do the remodeling, he refused to sell the property. Pilder sued to compel Kucha to go through with the deal. Kucha argued that under the circumstances the court could not force him to sell under any equitable remedy. Was Kucha correct? Why or why not?

10. The Congress-Kenilworth Corporation hired Erickson Construction to build its new concrete waterslide, Thunder Mountain Rapids. The project was completed and opened to the public. When Congress-Kenilworth discovered extensive cracking of the concrete flumes within the water slide, the corporation refused to pay the amount due under the contract. The operation of the structure as a waterslide was not affected by the cracking. Erickson sued to recover the amount due under the contract. Erickson claimed that under the doctrine of substantial performance, Congress-Kenilworth should pay for the amount due under the contract, less an amount needed to offset the defects. Was Erickson correct? Explain. *W. E. Erickson Construction, Inc., v. Congress-Kenilworth Corporation, 477 N.E.2d 513 (IL).*

11. The Commonwealth of Massachusetts entered into a contract with John J. Paonessa Company, Inc., for resurfacing and improvements on Route 128. Part of the contract called for replacing the grass median strip with bituminous concrete surfacing and precast, concrete barriers. The contracts had provisions that allowed the Commonwealth to make modifications for items found to be unnecessary. Paonessa subcontracted with Chase Precast Corporation to supply 25,800 linear feet of double-face median barrier. However, the Commonwealth deleted the median barriers from the contract after a

group of angry residents complained about using concrete barriers instead of the grass median strip. At the time, Chase had produced about half of the required barriers and stopped producing any more. The company was paid for all of the barriers it had produced but sued Paonessa for the amount of profits it had lost from the cancellation of the contract. Under what legal theory may Paonessa be excused from completing the contract with Chase? Explain. *Chase Precast v. John J. Paonessa Co.*, 554 N.E.2d 868 (MA).

Quick Quiz Answers

15-1 1. F	15-2 1. T	15-3 1. T
2. T	2. F	2. F
3. T	3. T	3. T

Part 2 Case Study

Wilcox v. Trautz

Supreme Judicial Court of Massachusetts

693 N.E.2d 141 (MA)

Summary

Carol Wilcox and John Trautz lived together as an unmarried couple for 25 years, beginning when they were both in their twenties. During that period, Wilcox contributed $25 a week toward general household expenses. She performed household duties, including all the food and clothes shopping, which she paid for solely from her earnings. When Wilcox became involved in another relationship, Trautz sought legal advice regarding his rights with respect to the assets acquired during their relationship. The parties signed an agreement providing, among other things, that "each party's earnings and property is his or hers alone, and the other party shall have no interest in the property of the other." The assets, all in Trautz's name, included a house, valued at $180,000; an amphibious airplane, valued at $55,000; various bank accounts totaling $1,300; individual retirements accounts; and a one-half share of real estate in Maine, valued at $15,000. Wilcox had no assets other than a small bank account, the other one-half share of the Maine real estate, household furniture, clothing, and jewelry. The lower court judge held that the agreement was invalid and that to prevent unjust enrichment, Wilcox was entitled to damages of approximately $30,000. Trautz appealed.

The Court's Opinion

Justice Greaney

We have not previously passed on the validity of written agreements between two unmarried cohabitants that attempt to define the rights of the parties as to services rendered and property acquired during their relationship. Our early decisions precluded the enforcement of an agreement between unmarried parties if the agreement was made in consideration that the parties should cohabit. More recently, we have held valid oral promises between unmarried cohabitants so long as "illicit sexual relations were [not] an inherent aspect of the agreement or a 'serious and not merely an incidental part of the performance of the agreement.'" *Margolies v. Hopkins,* 514 N.E.2d 1079 (1987).

Social mores regarding cohabitation between unmarried parties have changed dramatically in recent years and living arrangements that were once criticized are now relatively common and accepted. "As an alternative to marriage, more couples are choosing to cohabit. These relationships may be of extended duration, sometimes lasting as long as many marriages. In many respects, these cohabitation relationships may be quite similar to conventional marriages; they may involve commingling of funds, joint purchases of property, and even the birth of children." With the prevalence of nonmarital relationships today, a considerable number of persons live together without benefit of the rules of law that govern property, financial, and other matters in a marital relationship. Thus, we do well to recognize the benefits to be gained by encouraging unmarried cohabitants to enter into written agreements respecting these matters, as the consequences for each partner may be considerable on termination of the relationship or, in particular, in the event of the death of one of the partners. "In recent years, increased attention has focused on the advisability of unmarried couples entering into cohabitation contracts in which they . . . detail the financial consequences of dissolution." This may be especially important in a jurisdiction like Massachusetts where we do not recognize common law marriage, do not extend to unmarried couples the rights possessed by married couples who divorce, and reject equitable remedies that might have the effect of dividing property between unmarried parties.

Courts in other jurisdictions have concluded, as we did in *Margolies v. Hopkins*, supra, that an express agreement between adult unmarried persons living together is unenforceable only to the extent that it explicitly and inseparably is founded on sexual relations. . . . Furthermore, such agreements are not invalid merely because the parties may have contemplated the creation or continuation of a nonmarital relationship when they entered into the agreement. As the New York Court of Appeals stated in *Morone v. Morone,* 413 N.E.2d 1154, "[t]he theory of these cases is that while cohabitation without marriage does not give rise to the property and financial rights which normally attend the marital relation, neither does cohabitation disable the parties from making an agreement within the normal rules of contract law." Although none of these cases specifically concerns a written agreement between unmarried cohabitants attempting to resolve issues such as the parties' rights as to property, earnings, and services rendered, the principles they announce also apply to such an agreement. Implicit in these principles is tacit acknowledgement that unmarried cohabitants may agree to hold real property jointly or in common, agree to create joint bank and other accounts, do the same for investments, and, of course, make testamentary dispositions. These financial and property arrangements stem from a relationship that involves sexual cohabitation, but, in creating them, the parties are principally motivated by an intention to hold, or dispose of, property in a mutually acceptable way in order to manage day-to-day matters and to avoid litigation when the relationship ends. Such financial planning is enforceable according to the usual rules of contract. It makes no sense to uphold these arrangements between unmarried cohabitants, but to withhold enforcement of written agreements between the same parties when they attempt to settle the financial and other consequences if they should separate.

To the extent we have not previously done so, we adopt the view that unmarried cohabitants may lawfully contract concerning property, financial, and other matters relevant to their relationship. Such a contract is subject to the rules of contract law and is valid even if expressly made in contemplation of a common living arrangement, except to the extent that sexual services constitute the only, or dominant, consideration for the agreement, or that enforcement should be denied on some other public policy ground. We shall no longer follow cases in this Commonwealth to the contrary.

Nothing we say here today is intended to derogate from the clear distinction we have made in our cases between the legal rights of married and unmarried cohabitants. . . . Nor should anything we have said be taken as a suggestion or intimation that we are retreating from our prior expressions regarding the importance of the institution of marriage and the strong public interest in ensuring that its integrity is not threatened. We have never recognized common law marriage in this Commonwealth, nor have we "permitted the incidents of the marital relationship to attach to an arrangement of cohabitation without marriage." We do not do so now. . . .

We conclude that the plaintiff and the defendant were free to contract with respect to property, financial, and other matters relevant to their relationship, and that the specific agreement at issue is valid and enforceable. It is undisputed that the parties, both adults, had the capacity to contract and understood each other's financial worth prior to the execution of the agreement. Moreover, the plaintiff was advised to seek counsel regarding the agreement and chose not to do so. There was no claim of fraud, overreaching, or unconscionability. The plaintiff is employed and makes no assertion that as a result of the agreement, she will be unable to support herself. The judge found that the plaintiff was not forced or coerced to sign the agreement.

Finally, we note that the plaintiff voluntarily entered into a relationship with the defendant, and continued to live with him for many years despite her knowledge that he was unlikely to marry her. The agreement she signed essentially tracked the living arrangement she had shared with the defendant for twenty-five years, in which they maintained separate legal and financial identities, and did not merge their financial affairs. There is no evidence that during the course of their relationship, the plaintiff was the "weaker" of the two cohabitants, or that she had been dissatisfied with the way they managed their affairs.

The judgment is vacated, and a new judgment is to be entered declaring the agreement to be valid and enforceable and disposing of the damages claim in the defendant's favor.

So ordered.

Questions for Analysis

1. On what occasion would the court's early decision preclude the enforcement of any agreement between unmarried parties?

2. What was required in more recent decisions for oral promises between unmarried cohabitants to be valid?

3. Why does the court believe it should recognize the benefits to be gained by encouraging unmarried cohabitants to enter into written agreements?

4. What is the theory of the cases holding that express agreements between adult unmarried persons living together are enforceable?

5. What view does the court adopt regarding contracts of unmarried cohabitants?

Part Three

Sales and Consumer Protection

Chapter 16   Sale and Lease of Goods

The Opening Case
"An Eventful Day"

Phil Sturges's day began with him going online and buying a high-definition DVD camcorder. Next, he had an interview for a job as manager for a new KMart store that would be opening soon in his community. That afternoon, just as he was about to leave to go to an antique auction, Sturges received word that he had received the job as store manager. Elated, he attended the auction and bid an exceptionally high amount for an antique table. The auctioneer refused to sell the table at that price however, believing that it was worth even more money. Sturges felt that because nothing had been said about the auctioneer's right to refuse the highest bid, it should have been sold to him for the amount he bid. Things improved that evening, however, when a private party agreed to buy Sturges's second-hand car, which he had advertised for sale in the newspaper.

Opening Case Questions

1. What law governs the online purchase of the camcorder?

2. Does the Uniform Commercial Code govern Sturges's employment agreement?

3. Did the auctioneer have the legal right to refuse to sell the antique table to Sturges?

4. Does the Uniform Commercial Code govern Sturges's agreement to sell the car to the private party?

 Learning Objectives

1. Determine when to apply the law of sales under the UCC.
2. Describe the special rules for sales contracts.
3. Explain the four exceptions to the rule requiring that contracts for the sale of goods costing $500 or more must be in writing.
4. Judge, in a given situation, whether a writing satisfies the requirements of the UCC.
5. Contrast an auction with reserve with an auction without reserve.

16-1 The Sale and Lease of Goods

In the previous nine chapters, you have studied general contract law, which governs contracts for such things as real estate, employment, and personal services. Now, in Chapters 16 through 19, you will study a different type of law—the law of sales—that governs the sale and lease of goods. It is a very old law that grew from the customs and practices of businesspeople, merchants, and mariners in early English times. The law of sales has gone through many changes over the years and is now part of the Uniform Commercial Code (UCC), which has been adopted, either in whole or in part, by every state in the United States.

Sales of Goods

Goods are defined as all things (other than money, stocks, and bonds) that are movable. They include the unborn young of animals, growing crops, timber, and minerals if they are to be sold separately from the real property. Office furniture, mobile homes, human blood, milk, numismatics, wedding pictures, electricity, waste paper, kerosene, Christmas trees, ships, airplanes, horses, soybeans, polyethylene film, a printing press, and a book of recipes have all been held to be goods by the courts.

UCC 2-105(1) (see pages 959–960)

Goods that are not yet in existence or under the control of people are called **future goods**. They include fish in the sea, minerals in the ground, goods not yet manufactured, and commodities futures.

UCC 2-105(2) (see page 960)

> **EXAMPLE 16-1:**   Contract for Future Goods
>
> Byron, Ltd., contracted to sell its cotton crop to Deep Southfield, Inc., before the crop had been planted. This agreement to sell a commodity at a certain time in the future for a certain price is legally enforceable. Under the UCC, it is called a contract to sell future goods.

A **sale** is a contract that transfers ownership of goods by the seller to the buyer for a price. Thus, every time you buy goods and receive ownership of them, a sale occurs. A **contract for sale** includes both a present sale of goods and a contract to sell goods at a future time.

Whenever anyone buys food in a supermarket, gasoline at a gas station, clothing at a shopping mall, a meal at a restaurant, or even a daily newspaper, a sale of goods occurs. In fact, several sales contracts usually occur for a particular item before the item reaches the consumer and sometimes even after it reaches the consumer.

UCC 2-106(1) (see page 960)

> **EXAMPLE 16-2:**   Sales Contracts at Different Levels
>
> The Steven Andrew Corporation manufactures lawn mowers. The company enters into sales contracts with its suppliers every time it purchases parts and materials to make the mowers. In addition, the company enters into sales contracts with wholesalers when it sells the mowers. Similarly, wholesalers enter into sales contracts when they sell the mowers to retailers. In the same manner, retailers enter into sales contracts when they sell the mowers to consumers. Going even further, consumers enter into sales contracts when they sell their second-hand lawn mowers to other private parties. All of these contracts are governed by the UCC.

The Opening Case Revisited, Part I
"An Eventful Day"

Sturges's employment agreement was not governed by the UCC because it was not a contract for the sale of goods. Rather, it was a contract for services, which is governed by the common law of contracts. His agreement to sell the car to the private party was governed by the UCC because it was a contract for the sale of goods.

A gift is not considered a sale because, though title passes, it is not given for a price. Similarly, a bailment (e.g., when an item is left at a store to be sold on consignment) does not meet the definition of a sale because title does not pass between the parties. Bailments are discussed in Chapter 22.

Article 2 of the UCC applies whenever people buy or sell goods, whether in person, online, over the telephone, or in any other manner. This law applies to sales of goods between private parties and sales of goods by businesspeople or merchants. To determine whether the UCC applies, ask if the contract is a contract for the sale of goods. If the answer is yes, apply the law under the UCC. If the answer is no, apply the common law of contracts discussed in Chapters 7–15 (see Table 16-1).

UCC Article 2 (see page 959)

Table 16-1   Different Laws Apply to Different Transactions

Transaction	Applicable Law
Contract for the sale of real estate	General contract law (sometimes referred to as common law) and real property law
Contract for employment	General contract law and employment law
Sale of goods between two private parties	UCC (Article 2)
Sale of goods by a merchant to a consumer	UCC (Article 2) and state consumer protection laws
Sale of goods between two merchants	UCC (Article 2)
Contract for a mixture of goods and services—consisting mostly of goods	UCC (Article 2)
Contract for a mixture of goods and services—consisting mostly of services	General contract law
Sale of goods over the Internet	UCC (Article 2)
Sale of goods at an auction	UCC (Article 2)
The leasing of goods	UCC (Article 2A)
International sales of goods	United Nations convention on Contracts for the International Sale of Goods (CISG)
Sale of stock on the stock market	UCC (Article 8)
The writing of a check, promissory note, or draft	UCC (Article 3)

The Opening Case Revisited, Part II
"An Eventful Day"

Article 2 of the UCC governs Sturges's online purchase of the camcorder because it was a sale of a good.

Leases of Goods

The leasing of goods is governed by Article 2A of the Uniform Commercial Code. This article includes leasing of such things as automobiles, trucks, machinery, computers, furniture, electronic equipment, and all types of tools. Many of the rules that are found in the UCC relating to the sale of goods (discussed in the following chapters) also apply to the leasing of goods under Article 2A of the UCC.

UCC 2A-101-531 (see page 979)

Contracts for Both Goods and Services

When a contract includes both goods and services, the dominant element of the contract determines whether it is a contract for goods or a contract for services. If the sale of goods

BusinessWeek Business Law in the News
E-Commerce: Cash Registers Are Ringing Online

When it comes to analyses of consumer spending, online sales are often overlooked. But retail e-commerce sales growth far outpaces that of overall consumer spending and shows no sign of letting up. That means online sales will only grow in importance when it comes to gauging the health of consumer spending.

Fourth-quarter retail e-commerce sales surged 24.6% from the previous year, according to the U.S. Census Dept. That rapid growth is a reason why fourth-quarter non-auto and non-gasoline retail sales looked much better than the widely followed chain-store sales figures.

The quarterly e-commerce figures also far exceeded the government's strong monthly figures for nonstore retailers, which includes catalog and other forms of direct sales. Fourth quarter nonstore sales grew 7.6% from the year before, beating most other retail categories.

As more consumers buy online, e-commerce sales account for a larger chunk of overall retail spending. Sales of $108 billion in 2006 topped those at electronics and appliance stores. And in the final quarter of

2006, online shopping accounted for 3% of total retail sales, nearly double the share at the end of 2002.

The torrid growth of online retail sales should continue through 2007. According to the research firm Cowen & Co., e-commerce retail sales will climb another 20%, to $129 billion, in 2007. One apparent reason for the ongoing strength is that e-commerce retailers are doing a good job. The fourth-quarter American Customer Satisfaction Index from the Stephen M. Ross School of Business at the University of Michigan showed an improved score for e-commerce businesses. In particular, online retailers are one of the highest-rated among the 43 different industries covered by the survey.

While the law of large numbers means growth of more than 20% per year will be hard to sustain, e-commerce sales are expected to climb at a double-digit pace for the rest of the decade, reaching 4.3% of total sales by 2010.

Source: James Mehring, "Cash Registers Are Ringing Online," *BusinessWeek*, March 5, 2007, 24.

is dominant, as when someone purchases a furnace and has it installed, the law under the UCC applies. In contrast, if the performance of services is dominant, as when someone has a furnace repaired and a few new parts are installed, the common law of contracts applies instead.

Quick Quiz 16-1 True or False?

1. A gift is considered a sale.

2. Money, stocks, and bonds are movable items that are not goods.

3. The dominant element of a contract determines whether it is a sales contract or a services contract.

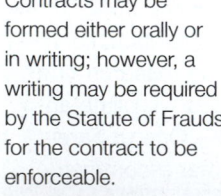

LO2

UCC 1-203 (see page 958).

UCC 1-205 (see page 958).

UCC 2-204(1)(2) (see page 961).

16-2 Special Rules for Sales Contracts

The fundamental rules of contract law, discussed in the previous nine chapters, serve as a base in the UCC, but the UCC is often more flexible. Some special rules for sales contracts follow.

Good Faith

Under the UCC, every contract or duty imposes an obligation of good faith. In other words, the parties to a sales contract must act and deal fairly with each other.

Course of Dealings and Usage of Trade

Contracts may be formed either orally or in writing; however, a writing may be required by the Statute of Frauds for the contract to be enforceable.

When the parties have dealt with each other before, their prior dealings give special meaning to sales contracts. Similarly, **usage of trade**, that is, any method of dealing that is commonly used in the particular field, is given special meaning. Unless the parties express otherwise, a course of dealings or usage of trade may be used to supplement or qualify the terms of a sales contract.

Formation of a Sales Contract

A contract may be made in any manner that shows that the parties reached an agreement. It may be oral (with some exceptions) or in writing, or it may be established by the conduct of the parties. An enforceable sales contract may come about even if the exact moment of its making cannot be determined and even though some terms are not completely agreed upon.

EXAMPLE 16-3:   Oral Terms Enforceable

Cargill, Inc., entered into a written contract with Fickbohm for the purchase of a certain amount of corn at $1.26 a bushel. The parties had orally agreed that the corn would be delivered sometime between June 1 and July 31, but the delivery date was omitted from the writing. Fickbohm failed to deliver the corn and argued that the contract was unenforceable because the delivery date had been omitted from the writing. The court disagreed, saying that the contract was enforceable even though all the terms were not set forth in the writing.

A Question of Ethics
Five Easy Principles? It's Not Enough to Know What to Do. Understanding Why Is Important Too

The five fundamental ethical principles that are the foundation of right conduct in any arena of your life are:

- Do no harm
- Make things better
- Respect others
- Be fair
- Be compassionate

These principles reveal the secrets to living a rich, satisfying, and happy life, and we have known about them for more than 5,000 years. Every religious tradition in the world teaches them, as do parents in every country. Without them civilization would be impossible because there would be nothing but chaos everywhere. These principles have a transforming effect on who we are and where we go in life, and for that reason, we can rightly refer to them as "life principles."

VALUES WE'RE TEMPTED TO IGNORE

You might wonder, "If these principles are so commonplace, why should I waste my time reading a column about them?" It's true that they're commonplace, but it's also true that in our hectic, overcommitted lives, we get so caught up in the details of getting through the day that it's easy to forget how important these principles are in everything we do. We're also tempted every day to ignore them and to place value on things that ultimately aren't that important. So taking a few steps back to consider these principles is a helpful thing to do.

Yes, they are simple, but too often we let fear, anger, or other negative emotions get us off track from following these principles, and it's sometimes difficult to get back to where we want to be. For example, how often do we really keep "Do no harm" in mind during out daily interactions with people? If a co-worker is nasty to us, aren't we tempted to return the nastiness and tell ourselves, "Serves them right"?

Do we always keep the principle of fairness front and center in our thinking? If so, how do we explain our choice at work to surf the Internet, make personal phone calls, and take a sick day when we're feeling fine?

On the face of it, the principles are about making a difference in the lives of other people. To this extent, taking them seriously seems like something we have to do, something we ought to do, something that, quite frankly, we'd rather not do.

CENTRAL TO HAPPINESS

What we'll discover, however, is that making ethics our central concern is actually the best way to lead a richer, more fulfilled life. A life that helps us get the things we want: a job we love, the right partner, and a comfortable place to live. By taking ethics seriously, we serve as role models to our children and increase the chances that they will go into the world and make us proud.

Recent scandals in the news show the risks we take when we neglect these principles: public humiliation, shame, and in some cases a lengthy visit to prison. But the main reason for taking ethics seriously is not the dangers of failing to do so, but rather because it's the right thing to do.

The path to a happier, more fulfilled life lies in becoming reacquainted with the principles of ethics, which tell us how we should treat one another. When we act with integrity, we feel better about ourselves, and we then create the conditions for making many wonderful choices in our own lives.

Just as a house needs a strong foundation so that it can do what it was meant to do, society needs a strong moral foundation to function effectively. The most fundamental building block of any society is Principle No. 1: Do no harm. This is both the most important because we would live in constant fear if we could not trust others to take the principle seriously. It is the easiest of the five principles to apply to out lives because in most cases, all we have to do is . . . nothing.

THE ETHICS OF GETTING INVOLVED

Requires that we take action so that harm will not occur to someone else, and thus a corollary of "Do no harm" is "Prevent harm." When we're at a cocktail party and we see an obviously inebriated person about to leave and drive away, the right thing to do is to prevent a foreseeable accident, which can mean taking the person's keys away or arranging for someone to take him or her home.

Edmund Burke once said, "All that is necessary for evil to flourish is for good [people] to do nothing." When we witness someone else doing something they shouldn't be doing, it may be easier to do nothing, but the easiest thing to do isn't always the right thing to do.

When we take the high road, we give a gift to others—and ourselves. It's the greatest gift of all.

Source: Bruce Weinstein, "Five Easy Principles?" *BusinessWeek.com,* January 10, 2007.

UCC 2-206(1)(a) (see page 961)

Offer and Acceptance

To establish a contract for the sale of goods, unless otherwise indicated by the offeror or the circumstances, the offeree may accept the offer in any manner and by any medium that is reasonable. A contract for the sale of goods comes into existence when the acceptance is sent, as long as the method used to send it is reasonable.

EXAMPLE 16-4: Reasonable Acceptance

Goodwin sent a letter by the U.S. Postal Service to Callaghan, offering to buy 10 file cabinets for $700 if Callaghan would ship them promptly. Callaghan accepted the offer by e-mail. The contract came into existence when the e-mail was sent.

Unless the buyer indicates otherwise, an order or other offer to buy goods for prompt shipment may be accepted by either a prompt shipment or a prompt promise to ship. In Example 16-4, Callaghan could have accepted the offer by promptly shipping the file cabinets instead of promising to ship them. Under this rule, the goods that are shipped may be either conforming or nonconforming goods. **Conforming goods** are those that are in accordance with the obligations under the contract. **Nonconforming goods** are those that are not the same as those called for under the contract or that are in some way defective.

UCC 2-206(1)(b) (see page 961)

UCC 2-106(2) (see page 960)

Firm Offer

The UCC holds merchants to a higher standard than nonmerchants. A **merchant** is a person who deals in goods of the kind sold in the ordinary course of business or who otherwise claims to have knowledge or skills peculiar to those goods. Although most rules under the UCC apply to both merchants and nonmerchants alike, some rules apply only to merchants. One such rule involves a firm offer.

UCC 2-104(1) (see page 959)

No consideration is necessary when a merchant promises in writing to hold an offer open for the sale or lease of goods. Known as a **firm offer**, the writing must be signed by the merchant, and the time period for holding the offer open may not exceed three months. This rule differs from the general rule of contract law (discussed in Chapter 7), which requires consideration in an option contract.

UCC 2-205 (see page 961)

EXAMPLE 16-5:   Firm Offer

Sunrise Supply Co. offered to sell Jones a pool filter for $250. This price was especially good for that product. Although he wanted the filter, Jones thought that he might be transferred to another location. He needed four weeks to decide whether to buy the filter. Sunrise agreed in writing to hold the offer open to Jones for four weeks. Although Jones provided no consideration for holding the offer open, it was a firm offer and could not be revoked by Sunrise. Sunrise's firm offer also came within the UCC's three-month limit.

Open-Price Terms

Another change that the UCC has made is that a contract for the sale of goods may be established even though the price is not settled. Such **open-price terms** may occur when the parties intend to be bound by a contract but fail to mention the price or decide to set the price later. Under non-UCC law, no contract would come about because the terms are not definite. The UCC allows such a contract to come into existence. If the parties cannot agree on the price at the later date, the UCC requires that the price will be reasonable at the time the goods are delivered.

UCC 2-305(1) (see page 962)

EXAMPLE 16-6:   Price-Less

Ayers contracted to buy chicken feed from Sparton Grain & Mill Co. As part of the contract, Sparton agreed to buy and market all of Ayers's eggs. The price that Ayers was to pay for the feed was not mentioned. The court held that the UCC requires the price to be a reasonable one when no price is quoted.

Output and Requirements Terms

Sometimes, a seller will agree to sell "all the goods we manufacture" or "all the crops we produce" to a particular buyer. This agreement is known as an **output contract**. At other times, a buyer will agree to buy "all the oil we need to heat our building" (or some similar requirement) from a particular seller. This agreement is called a **requirements contract**. Such contracts often were not allowed under common law because the quantity of the goods to be bought or sold was not definite. The UCC allows output and requirements contracts for the sale of goods, as long as the parties deal in good faith and according to reasonable expectations.

UCC 2-306 (see page 963)

EXAMPLE 16-7:   Unreasonable Expectations

Spencer Oil Co. agreed to sell to Lopaz Manufacturing Co. all the heating oil Lopaz would need during the next year. Spencer knew that Lopaz used about 5,000 gallons of oil each year. During the summer, Lopaz enlarged its building to an extent that it would require 25,000 gallons of heating oil during the next year. Spencer would not be bound to supply that amount of oil to Lopaz because it was far beyond the amount it expected to supply.

Additional Terms in Acceptance

UCC 2-207 (see page 961)

Under the general rules of contract law, an acceptance of an offer must be an absolute, unqualified, unconditional assent to the offer. If the acceptance differs in the slightest from the offer, it is considered a rejection. The UCC changes this rule somewhat. A contract for the sale of goods occurs even though the acceptance states terms that are additional to or different from those offered or agreed upon (unless acceptance is made conditional on assent to the additional terms). The additional terms are treated as proposals for additions to the contract if the parties are not both merchants. If both parties are merchants, the additional terms become part of the contract unless they materially alter it, the other party objects within a reasonable time, or the offer limits acceptance to its terms.

This rule is intended to deal with two typical situations. The first is when an agreement has been reached either orally or by informal correspondence between the parties and is followed by one or both of the parties sending formal acknowledgments or memos that contain additional terms not discussed earlier.

EXAMPLE 16-8:   Additional Terms in Acceptance

Cobb and Sons, Inc., reached an oral agreement with Valley Theatres, Inc., for the sale of an air conditioning system. Later, Cobb put the agreement in writing, signed it, and sent it to Valley for its signature. Valley signed the writing but added additional terms relative to the date of completion of the contract. Because both parties were merchants, the additional terms would become part of the contract unless Cobb objected to them within a reasonable time. Had one of them not been a merchant, the contract would have to come into existence without the additional terms, and the added terms would have been treated as proposals for additions to the contract.

The second situation in which this rule applies is one in which a fax or letter intended to be the closing or confirmation of an agreement adds further minor suggestions or proposals, such as "ship by Thursday" or "rush."

EXAMPLE 16-9:   Different Terms in Acceptance

Cal-Cut Pipe and Supply, Inc., offered in writing to sell used pipe to Southern Idaho Pipe and Steel Co., specifying a delivery date. Southern Idaho accepted by sending a check but changed the delivery date. Cal-Cut mailed a confirmation containing the original delivery date with the postscript, "We will work it out." The court held that there was a binding contract between them despite the conflicting delivery terms.

Modification

Under the general rules of contract law, if the parties have already entered into a binding contract, a later agreement to change that contract needs consideration to be binding. The UCC has done away with this rule in contracts for the sale of goods. An agreement modifying a contract for the sale of goods needs no consideration to be binding. Any such modification may be oral unless the original agreement is in writing and provides that it may not be modified except by a signed writing. Any such clause in a form supplied by a merchant to a nonmerchant, however, must be separately signed (such as in the margin) by the nonmerchant to be effective.

UCC 2-209(1) (see page 962)

UCC 2-209(2) (see page 962)

Quick Quiz 16-2 True or False?

1. Under the UCC, a contract comes into existence when the acceptance is sent if the method used is reasonable.

2. No consideration is necessary to establish a firm offer when a consumer promises in writing to hold an offer open for the sale or lease of goods.

3. Under the UCC, a contract for the sale of goods may be established even though the price is not settled.

16-3 Form of Sales Contracts

Many sales contracts are oral rather than written. They are often made by telephone, at a store counter, face-to-face between private parties or businesspeople, or both. As long as the price is under $500, an oral contract for the sale of goods is enforceable. Millions of such contracts are made daily by people in our society.

UCC 2-201(1) (see page 960)

If the price is $500 or more, a sales contract must be in writing to be enforceable. This rule, however, has four exceptions.

EXAMPLE 16-10:   Unenforceable Oral Agreement

Deena Sampson agreed to buy a car from Ted Words for $2,500. The agreement was oral and called for payment of the full amount in cash upon delivery of the car the next day. Unless one of the exceptions in the discussion to follow applies, the oral contract cannot be enforced by either party because it was over $500 and not evidenced by a writing of any kind.

A lease of goods, under the UCC, must be in writing if the total payments to be made under the lease are $1,000 or more.

Exceptions to the General Rule

There are four exceptions to the requirement that contracts for the sale of goods for $500 or more and the lease of goods for $1,000 or more must be in writing to be enforceable. These exceptions involve the following:

UCC 2A-201 (see page 000)

1. Oral contracts between merchants in which a confirmation has been received by one party and not objected to by the other party.
2. Specially manufactured goods.
3. Admissions in court.
4. Executed contracts.

Oral Contracts Between Merchants   An exception to the general rule occurs when there is an oral contract between two merchants. If either merchant receives a written confirmation of the oral contract from the other merchant within a reasonable time and does not object to it in writing within 10 days, the oral contract is enforceable.

UCC 2-201(2) (see page 960)

EXAMPLE 16-11:   Both Parties Are Merchants

David Brown, the owner of Tom Shea's Restaurant, telephoned Northeast Supply Co. and placed an order for $760 worth of merchandise. Later that day, he mailed a written confirmation of the order. Northeast Supply Co. received the confirmation and made no objection to it, making the oral contract enforceable.

Specially Manufactured Goods   Another exception occurs when goods are to be specially manufactured for the buyer and are not suitable for sale to others in the ordinary course of the seller's business. If the seller has made either a substantial beginning in manufacturing the goods or commitments to buy them, the oral agreement will be enforceable.

UCC 2-201(3) (see page 960)

EXAMPLE 16-12:   Specially Manufactured Goods

Lifetime Windows, Inc., entered into an oral agreement to manufacture 15 oversized windows for Harold Cohen for the price of $6,000. The windows were such an odd shape that no one else would have a need for them. When the windows were manufactured, Cohen refused to take them on the ground that the oral contract was unenforceable. The court held against Cohen, however, and enforced the oral agreement. The windows were specially manufactured and were not suitable for sale to others.

Admissions in Court   If the party against whom enforcement is sought admits in court that an oral contract for the sale of goods was made, the contract will be enforceable. The contract is not enforceable under this exception, however, beyond the quantity of goods admitted.

UCC 2-201(3)(b) (see page 961)

Executed Contracts   When the parties carry out their agreement in a satisfactory manner, the law will not render the transaction unenforceable for want of an agreement in writing. Executed contracts (those that have been carried out) need not be in writing; the writing requirements apply only to contracts that are executory, that is, not yet performed.

UCC 2-201(3)(c) (see page 961)

This provision means that contracts for goods that have been received and accepted need not be in writing.

If there has been a part payment or a part delivery, the court will enforce only that portion of the agreement that has been performed.

> ## EXAMPLE 16-13:   Executed Contract
>
> Gilmore orally agreed to sell Nash three electric guitars and a powerful amplification system for $1,900. Delivery was to be made in 10 days, at which time Nash agreed to have the money ready for payment. If Gilmore had delivered one of the three guitars to Nash, the court would enforce payment for that one instrument.

Requirements of Writing

The writing that is required to satisfy the UCC must indicate that a contract for sale has been made between the parties and mention the quantity of goods being sold. It must also be signed by the party against whom enforcement is sought (the defendant). A writing is acceptable even though it omits or incorrectly states an agreed-upon term. However, a contract will not be enforceable beyond the quantity of goods shown in such writing. For that reason, it is necessary to put the quantity of goods to be bought and sold in the written agreement. Although a paper similar to the one shown in Figure 16-1 may be used, an informal note, memorandum, fax, or sales slip will satisfy the writing requirements.

LO4

UCC 2-201(1) (see page 960)

Signature Requirements Under the UCC, a signature includes any symbol made with the intent to authenticate a writing. Thus, in addition to a handwritten signature, the courts have held various kinds of marks, including an X and a typewritten name, qualify as a signature as long as they were written with the intent to be signatures.

UCC 1-201(39) (see page 957)

In the present age of fax machines and electronic communication, the law regulating electronic signatures is in a developing stage and varies from state to state. Some states' laws say that any form of electronic symbol can qualify as a signature as long as it includes a security procedure. Other states are more particular, saying that an electronic signature is effective only if it is:

- Unique to the person using it;
- Capable of verification;
- Under the sole control of the person using it; and
- Linked to the data in such a manner that if the data are changed, the signature becomes invalid.

The federal government has addressed this issue by enacting the E-Sign Act, which takes the approach that electronic signatures are acceptable if the parties agree to use them. Also, the instrument on which the signature is used must be capable of being duplicated and stored on a computer. The E-Sign Act is discussed further in Chapters 8 and 42.

International Law

Interestingly, the trend in other countries is to eliminate the requirement that a sales contract be in writing. Great Britain, for example, after having such a requirement for 277 years, did away with it in 1954. International sales law also has no writing requirements for a sales contract; instead, a sales contract may be proved by any means.

CONTRACT FOR SALE OF GOODS

AGREEMENT made by and between Ozzie Caldwell (Seller) and Geordi Hasenzahl (Buyer).

It has been agreed between the two parties that:

1. Seller agrees to sell, and Buyer agrees to buy, the following described property: one regulation-size pool table now located at the residence of Ozzie Caldwell, RD #1, Box 118, Ashberry, Kentucky.

2. Buyer agrees to pay Seller the total price of $850.00;

   payable as follows:

   $600.00 deposit herewith

   $250.00 balance by cash or certified check at time of transfer

3. Seller warrants he has full legal title to said property, authority to sell said property, and that said property shall be sold free and clear of all claims by other parties.

4. Said property is sold in "as is" condition. SELLER HEREBY EXCLUDES THE WARRANTY OF MERCHANTABILITY AND FITNESS FOR A PARTICULAR PURPOSE.

5. Parties agree to transfer title on February 7, 20 - -, at RD #1, Box 118, Ashberry, Kentucky, the address of the Seller.

6. This agreement shall be binding on the parties, their successors, assigns, and personal representatives.

7. This writing is intended to represent the entire agreement between the parties.

Signed under seal this nineteenth day of January, 20 - -.

Geordi Hasenzahl
Buyer

Ozzie Caldwell
Seller

Figure 16-1   With four exceptions, contracts for the sale of goods of $500 or more must be in writing to be enforceable. A formal writing such as this is not necessary to satisfy the writing requirements of the UCC, however.

BusinessWeek # Business Law in the News

J.C. Penney Gets the Net

Which brick-and-mortar retailer attracts the most shoppers to its Internet store? The answer may surprise you: J.C. Penney Corp., the century-old, moderate-priced department store chain so troubled six years ago that many were predicting its imminent demise.

In recent years, Penney's has consistently ranked among the top five Web sites in terms of the number of paying customers it attracts, according to Nielsen//NetRatings. In the first quarter, jcp.com drew 926,000 such shoppers, which put it in the company of eBay, Amazon.com, Ticketmaster, and Bertelsmann's online music business. The achievement has gone largely unnoticed, with most of the talk about Penney's turnaround centering on the re-vitaliztion of its merchandise. "The perception out there is the we are an old store doing well," says CEO Myron "Mike" Ullman III. "Most don't think of Penney and the Internet in the same sentence."

Penney's online success reflects a broader trend among traditional retailers: using the Net not only as a place to make a sale but also as a tool to lure shoppers to stores. Penney led the way, though in encouraging cooperation between its Web site and its stores. "Most retailers fought territorial battles as the Internet started to eat into store sales," says Jim Okamura, senior partner at J.C. Williams Group. "Penney embraced the Internet from the outset."

Necessity can foster innovation. Penney's catalog revenues peaked at about $4 billion in the late 1990s and have fallen every year since, though at a slower rate recently. Last year they were $1.7 billion. Online sales, meanwhile, totaled 1.3 billion in 2006.

When Penney launched its Web site in 1994, it sold one product: Power Rangers. It was a modest start, but the company—long comfortable selling directly to consumers through its catalog—had the right mind-set to make a smooth transition to the Internet.

Local Pickup

Since then, Penney's Internet, store, and catalog businesses have become far more intertwined. Like Sears Holdings Corp., it sells a wider variety of goods on the Internet: nearly three times the number of products available in its 1,000 stores. That has proved to be a cost-effective way to sell slow-moving items, says Bernie Feiwus, senior vice president of Penney Direct, who has experience in the dot-com world as well as at Neiman Marcus. Shoppers have responded. Candy Washington, a Cochranville (Pa.) nurse, says she often shops at jcp.com with her 9-year-old daughter because it has more items in the larger size her child wears.

Feiwus says that mailing specialty catalogs, such as for baby furniture, spurs sales online as well. In August, Penney became one of the few retailers to make Internet access available at its 35,000 check-out registers. And it was one of the first to allow on-line shoppers to pick up and return orders at stores. Now they can check which clothes are in stock at local stores, too, a feature no other major apparel retailer offers.

As a result, Penney has one of the most productive Web sites among mainstream retailers, says Heather Daugherty, a Nielsen analyst. Internet sales accounted for 6% of Penney's $20 billion in total sales in 2006. That compares with 4% at Sears and less than 1% at Wal-Mart Stores Inc., according to Internet Retailer. Even more promising for Penney: The average age of its online shoppers is 25 to 35, considerably younger than those in its stores.

Questions for Analysis

1. What broader trend is being used by retailers when they use the Internet?

2. How did J.C. Penney lead the way in the use of the Internet?

3. How did Penney's catalog sales compare with its online sales in 2006?

4. Why did Penney have the right mind set to make a smooth transition to the Internet?

5. How does the variety of products sold on the Internet compare with the retailer's store sales?

6. In what ways does Penney combine its online sales with its store sales?

Source: Robert Berner, "J.C.Penney Gets the Net: Its Quiet Mastery of e-Biz Has Helped Turn the Department Store Around," *BusinessWeek*, May 7, 2007, 70.

CISG Articles 1 and 2
(page 1018)

CISG Articles 4 and 5
(page 1018)

International sales law, called the United Nations **Convention on Contracts for the International Sale of Goods (CISG)**, applies only to sales between businesses whose places of business are in different countries that have adopted the law. It does not apply to sales of goods that are bought for personal, family, or household purposes. Also, the international law does not apply to auction sales; sales of stock, securities, negotiable instruments, or money; sales of ships or aircraft; or sales of electricity. The United States adopted the international sales law in 1988, and by 2007, 70 countries had made it part of their law.

The CISG is similar in many ways to the UCC. It also contains some differences. The CISG governs only the formation of a sales contract and the rights and duties of the parties that arise from it. The CISG is not concerned with the validity of a contract regarding, for example, the sale of illegal drugs, which would be governed by other laws. In addition, the CISG does not apply to the liability of the seller for death or personal injury caused by the goods to any person. In such a case, people would have to look to other laws for a remedy.

Quick Quiz 16-3 True or False?

1. A lease of goods must be in writing if the total payments to be made under the lease are $500 or more.

2. Contracts for goods that have been received and accepted for $500 or more need not be in writing.

3. A required writing under the UCC must indicate the quantity of goods being sold.

16-4 Auction Sales

UCC 2-328(2) (see
page 967)

UCC 2-328(3) (see
page 967)

UCC 2-328(4) (see
page 968)

Auctions are frequently used to dispose of unwanted property, satisfy judgments, and to liquidate foreclosed property.

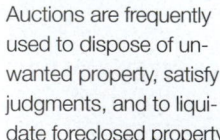

In an auction sale, the auctioneer presents goods for sale and invites the audience to make offers, which are known as bids. This process is similar to an invitation to trade. Bidders in the crowd respond with their offers. The highest bid (offer) is accepted by the auctioneer, usually by the drop of the gavel, together with the auctioneer's calling out the word *sold*. If, while the gavel is falling, a higher bid comes from those in the crowd, the auctioneer has two options: declare the goods sold or reopen the bidding.

An auction sale is "with reserve" unless the goods are expressly put up without reserve. In an **auction with reserve**, the auctioneer may withdraw the goods at any time before announcing completion of the sale if the highest bid is not high enough. In an **auction without reserve**, after the auctioneer calls for bids on an article or lot, that article or lot cannot be withdrawn unless no bid is made within a reasonable time. In either case, a bidder may retract a bid until the auctioneer's announcement of completion of the sale. A bidder's retraction does not revive any previous bid.

The practice of planting persons in the crowd for the purpose of raising bids by innocent purchasers is not allowed. Except in a forced sale, such as by a sheriff, if a seller (or the seller's agent) makes a bid at an auction without notifying other bidders, a buyer has two options. Under the UCC, a buyer may either avoid the sale or take the goods at the price of the last good-faith bid prior to the completion of the sale. In a forced sale, as when a sheriff auctions property on foreclosure or to satisfy a lien creditor, the owner is allowed to bid on the property being sold.

Auctions on the Internet provide the opportunity to buy and sell goods worldwide as well as locally. An Internet auction can be either person-to-person or business-to-person. In person-to-person auctions, sellers offer

The Opening Case Revisited, Part III

"An Eventful Day"

The auctioneer had the right to refuse to sell the antique table to Sturges for the amount of Sturges's bid. Because the terms of the auction were not announced, it was an auction with reserve, allowing the auctioneer to withdraw the goods if the highest bid is not high enough.

items directly to consumers. The highest bidder must deal directly with the seller to arrange for payment and delivery. In contrast, operators of business-to-person auctions have control of the items being offered and take charge of payment and delivery of goods bought and sold.

Internet auction fraud is alarming. Sometimes sellers don't deliver the goods or deliver something less valuable than they advertised. At other times, sellers don't disclose everything about a product or fail to deliver it when they say they will. The Federal Trade Commission (FTC) provides helpful information about Internet auctions in its free brochures and on its Web site.

Quick Quiz 16-4 True or False?

1. In an auction sale, the auctioneer makes offers to sell goods to members of the audience.

2. In an auction sale without reserve, the auctioneer may withdraw the goods at any time before announcing completion of the sale.

3. The practice of planting persons in the crowd for the purpose of raising bids by innocent purchasers is allowed.

Summary

16.1 The Uniform Commercial Code (UCC), which contains the law of sales, has been adopted, either in whole or in part, by every state in the United States. Article 2 of the UCC applies whenever people buy or sell goods. It applies to transactions between private parties as well as transactions by businesspeople or merchants. Article 2A applies to leases of goods. When a contract includes both goods and services, the dominant element of the contract governs whether it is a contract for goods or a contract for services. A contract for sale includes both a present sale of goods and a contract to sell goods at a future time.

16.2 The following special rules that are different from general contract law apply to sales contracts:

- Every contract or duty imposes an obligation of good faith.
- Prior dealings and usage of trade may be used to supplement or qualify the terms of a sales contract.
- A sales contract may be made in any manner that shows that the parties reached an agreement.
- Unless otherwise specified, an offeree may accept an offer in any way that is reasonable, including a prompt shipment of the goods.

- A written promise by a merchant to hold an offer open needs no consideration to be binding.
- A sales contract may be made even though the price is not settled. If the parties cannot agree on a price, it will be a reasonable price at the time of delivery.
- Output and requirements contracts are allowed in sales contracts as long as the parties deal in good faith and according to reasonable expectations.
- A sales contract may result even when an offeree adds different or additional terms from those offered or agreed upon. The different terms do not become part of the contract unless both parties are merchants and no objection is made to them within a reasonable time.
- No consideration is necessary to modify a contract for the sale of goods.

16.3   With four exceptions, a contract for the sale of goods for $500 or more and the lease of goods for $1,000 or more must be in writing. The exceptions are oral contracts between merchants in which a confirmation has been received by one party and not objected to by the other party, specially manufactured goods, admissions in court, and executed contracts. A required writing must indicate that a contract for sale has been made between the parties and mention the quantity of goods sold. The writing must be signed by the party against whom enforcement is sought. The United Nations Convention on Contracts for the International Sale of Goods (CISG) applies to sales between U.S. businesses and foreign businesses. The law is similar in many ways to the UCC.

16.4   In an auction sale, offers are made by the people in the audience. The acceptance takes place when the auctioneer bangs the gavel. In an auction with reserve, the auctioneer need not accept the highest bid. In an auction without reserve, the auctioneer must accept the highest bid.

Key Terms

auction with reserve, 330

auction without reserve, 330

conforming goods, 323

contract for sale, 317

Convention on Contracts for the International Sale of Goods (CISG), 330

firm offer, 323

future goods, 317

goods, 317

merchant, 323

nonconforming goods, 323

open-price terms, 323

output contract, 324

requirements contract, 324

sale, 317

usage of trade, 320

Questions for Review and Discussion

1. The law of sales applies to what types of contracts?
2. Name three items that are considered goods. Name one item that is a future good.
3. When a contract includes both goods and services, what determines whether it is a contract for goods or a contract for services?
4. What does a contract for sale include?
5. Describe three special rules that apply to sales contracts.
6. Compare an option contract with a firm offer. How do they differ?
7. When must a sales contract be in writing? When must a lease of goods be in writing?
8. What four exceptions apply to Question 7?
9. What are the requirements of a writing, when one is required, under the UCC?
10. Compare an auction with reserve with an auction without reserve. At what point is the reserve status established?

Investigating the Internet

Look up the requirements for writing a valid electronic signature under the laws of your state. Go to www.findlaw.com and click "For Legal Professionals." Then click "States" under "Cases and Codes." Select your state from the list that follows. When your state's statute or code appears, examine it for a table of contents or other way to find an Electronic Signature or Digital Signature Act. If this action draws a blank, try Googling any combination of these words.

Cases for Analysis

1. Brenda Brandt had a medical device implanted as part of her treatment for a serious medical condition. A charge for the device was included in the hospital bill. Later, the device was recalled by its manufacturer as substandard. Brandt had suffered serious complications, and the device was removed. She brought suit against the hospital for, among other things, breach of warranty under the Uniform Commercial Code. Was the purchase of the medical device from the hospital covered under the Uniform Commercial Code? Explain. *Brandt v. Boston Scientific Corporation,* Docket No. 93982, Illinois Supreme Court (IL).

2. Alberto Parreira, a lobsterman, contracted in writing to sell Sam Adams 1,000 pounds of fresh lobsters at a particular price during the following season. A few months later, when lobsters became plentiful and the price went down, Adams tried to get out of the contract. He argued that the contract was not enforceable because the lobsters had not yet been caught when the contract was made. Do you agree with Adams? Why or why not?

3. Harnois entered into an oral contract with Neverson to lease a compact computer and a printer for three months for $600. In an attempt to rescind the contract, Harnois claimed that the contract was unenforceable because it was not in writing. Do you agree with Harnois? Why or why not?

4. The Missouri Farmers Association (MFA) entered into a contract to spray all but a 14-foot strip of McBee's 51-acre soybean field. The field was to be sprayed for cockleburr, and MFA was to select the chemical and method to be used for spraying. The evening before the beans were sprayed, they were a good color and height. The evening after they were sprayed, they were brown, crumbly, and dry. Except for the 14-foot unsprayed strip, the beans died within two or three days after the spraying was done. Did the UCC cover this transaction? Why or why not? *Missouri Farmers Assoc. v. McBee,* 787 S.W.2d 756 (MO).

5. Curry entered into a contract to sell four wheel bearings to Litman for $300. Before the contract was carried out, Curry told Litman that the cost of bearings had increased and that he would have to change the price to $400. Litman agreed to pay $400 for the bearings. Later, Litman refused to pay the additional $100, claiming that Curry gave no consideration for Litman's promise to pay the extra money. Was Litman correct? Why or why not?

6. Coleman bid $2,050 for a D-7 tractor at a public auction. Nothing was stated that the auction was with reserve. The auctioneer yelled "sold," accepting Coleman's bid. Later, the owner of the tractor refused to sell it for $2,050, saying that the auction was with reserve and that he could refuse to accept the bid. Did the owner have to sell the tractor to Coleman for $2,050? Why or why not? *Coleman v. Duncan,* 540 S.W.2d 935 (MO).

7. Ferguson agreed to sell to R. L. Kimsey Cotton Co., Inc., all the cotton produced by Ferguson on a specified parcel of land at an agreed price. The agreement was in writing and contained other terms. Later, Ferguson argued that the agreement was invalid because the quantity and subject matter were vague and indefinite. Was Ferguson correct? Why or why not? *R. L. Kimsey Cotton Co., Inc., v. Ferguson,* 214 S.E.2d 360 (GA).

8. Carolina Transformer Co., Inc., brought suit against Anderson for several thousand dollars owed it for the purchase of transformers. Anderson testified in court that he had orally negotiated the contract and reached a final agreement with Carolina for the purchase of the transformers. Anderson argued, however, that he was not responsible because under the UCC, a contract for the sale of goods of $500 or more is not enforceable unless it is in writing. Do you agree with Anderson? *Carolina Transformer Co. v. Anderson,* 341 So.2d 1327 (MS).

9. O'Brien placed a telephone order for 20 shipments of lettuce from Soroka Farms. Soroka Farms shipped the lettuce to a cooler, where it was held under cold storage. It was later shipped, on O'Brien's orders, directly to O'Brien's customers. O'Brien refused to pay for the lettuce, arguing that the contract was not enforceable because it was over $500 and not in writing. Do you believe that the oral contract was enforceable in this case? Why? See also *O'Day v. George Arakelian Farms, Inc.,* 540 P.2d 197 (AZ).

10. Representatives of a fish marketing association (AIFMA) and a fish company (NEFCO) met at Bristol Bay, Alaska, to negotiate a marketing agreement for the forthcoming fishing season. At this meeting, NEFCO's agent, Gage, signed an agreement that contained the price that was to be paid for the fish and other details about the transaction. It omitted the quantity of fish to be purchased. Later, when suit was brought on the agreement, NEFCO argued that it was unenforceable because the written agreement failed to mention the quantity. Do you agree with NEFCO? Explain. *Alaska Indus Fish Mktg. Assoc. v. New England Fish Co.,* 548 P.2d 348 (WA).

Quick Quiz Answers

16-1	16-2	16-3	16-4
1. F	1. T	1. F	1. F
2. T	2. F	2. T	2. F
3. T	3. T	3. T	3. F

Chapter 17

Title and Risk of Loss in Sales of Goods

The Opening Case
"The Wandering Cockapoo"

Bruce Fields, who operated an alligator farm near Everglades City, Florida, paid cash for a cockapoo puppy that he purchased from his 17-year-old neighbor, Jenna, who was going off to a boarding school that didn't allow pets. In its new environment, the puppy strayed dangerously close to the alligators, so Fields sold it to his friend, Charlie Jones, for the same price he paid for it. Jones fell in love with the puppy and named it Indiana. When the time arrived for Jones to go on a cross-country camping trip, he dropped off his beloved cockapoo at a kennel to be cared for while he was away. The kennel was part of a reputable pet supply store in the community that also sold kittens, dogs, hamsters, and other small animals as part of its routine business. When Jones returned from his trip, he went to the kennel to pick up Indiana and was told that a salesperson had mistakenly sold the dog to a woman named Claudia Crocker, who was unaware that the dog belonged to Jones. During the six weeks that Jones was away, Crocker became very attached to the cockapoo and refused to give it up. To complicate matters, Jenna, living at home for the summer, requested the return of her cockapoo from Bruce Fields, saying that she was a minor when she sold it to him.

Opening Case Questions

1. What kind of title did Fields receive when he bought the cockapoo from Jenna?

2. What kind of title did Jones receive when he bought the cockapoo from Fields?

3. What kind of title did Crocker receive when she bought the cockapoo from the pet supply store?

4. Does Jones have a cause of action against Crocker for the animal's return?

LO Learning Objectives

1. Contrast voidable title with void title.
2. Discuss the rights of the parties when goods that are entrusted to merchants are sold to others in the ordinary course of business.
3. Determine, in a given case, when title to goods passes from the seller to the buyer.

4. Decide, in different situations, whether the buyer or the seller of goods must bear the risk of loss.
5. Compare a sale on approval with a sale or return.
6. Describe when buyers and sellers of goods have insurable interests in those goods.

A Question of Ethics
Principle No. 2: Make Things Better

Ethics asks us to use our knowledge and skills to positively affect others. But we also must be judicious in how we use our resources to do so.

> "Fredo, you're nothing to me now. You're not a brother, you're not a friend. I don't want to know you or what you do. I don't want to see you at the hotels. I don't want you near my house. When you see our mother, I want to know a day in advance, so I won't be there. You understand?"
>
> —*Michael Corleone*, in The Godfather: Part II,
> *after learning that his brother Fredo played a role in an attempt on his life.*

Life Principle No. 2: Make Things Better is where ethics splits off from the law. After all, there are legal as well as ethical implications of intentionally harming others. However, no law requires that we help others or make the world a better place. If, at the end of our lives, we look back and see that we devoted ourselves primarily or exclusively to satisfying our own needs and desires, and we haven't done anything illegal, that's fine. But is a life devoted strictly to "me" a fully rich and satisfying life? Is it an ethical one? Is it the best life we can live?

Of course not. If you're reading this though, chances are you already buy into the "make things better" principle. In fact, I suspect that the reason you went into the line of work you did is because you recognize that this is one way, perhaps the best way, for you to use your knowledge and talents to make a positive difference in the lives of others. There are lots of ways—some of them much easier—for you to simply make a buck.

But you took this job because—dare I use such flowery language?—you saw this occupation as a calling. I feel comfortable making this statement, because if you took this job simply to acquire wealth, with no immediate or long-range concern for helping others, you probably aren't interested in reading about ethics.

DON'T RANK THE LIFE PRINCIPLES

Now don't get me wrong. I'm not knocking the acquisition of wealth. Ethics does not require us to be completely self-sacrificing. The question is, though, does focusing simply on gratifying one's own desires lead to happiness? Does this bring out the best in us?

You might say that Life Principle No. 2, Make Things Better, is not as vital as Life Principle No. 1, Do No Harm. That is, it is more important to avoid harming people than it is to help them. Although it is easier to apply Life Principle No. 1 than No. 2, since Do No Harm requires either avoiding action or taking only minimal action, it is a mistake to rank these principles. Both are part of a checklist we should consider when deciding how to act.

One of the main differences, though, between Life Principle Nos. 1 and 2 is that Do No Harm applies to everyone who could be affected by our actions, while No. 2 has to, of necessity, be applied selectively. Even Mother Teresa could not possibly have benefited everyone in the world, though she went much further than most of us.

WHOM SHOULD WE BENEFIT?

There is only so much of ourselves we can give without becoming emotionally and financially bankrupt. How should we decide who has a rightful claim on the goods or actions we can bestow upon them?

All things being equal, the closer someone is to us, the stronger our duties are toward him or her. Imagine a series of nine concentric circles, with "A" being the innermost circle, radiating outward:

A) Self
B) Spouse or partner
C) Immediate family (mother, father, children)
D) Distant family (grandparents, aunts and uncles, nephews and nieces, cousins)
E) Oldest and best friends
F) Boss, co-workers, assistants
G) Members of the immediate community
H) Fellow citizens
I) Everyone else

It's unfortunate to miss a friend's birthday, but it is unconscionable to forget our spouse's. It's kind to listen compassionately to a co-worker's complaints about her deadbeat husband over lunch, but it is obligatory to alleviate our children's anxiety about going to school for the first time.

IN AND OUT OF CIRCLES

This imaginary diagram is only a guideline for ranking who in our lives deserves our help. It doesn't always hold. Think about how Michael Corleone ultimately responded to being betrayed by his brother: He authorized Fredo's murder. (Of course, Fredo had not exactly ordered his circles appropriately.) While Michael's response was extreme and revealed how much he had deteriorated morally, it also shows how through their actions, people—even blood relatives—can move closer or further away from us.

Ethics asks—even requires—that we use our knowledge and skills to benefit others. In so doing, we enrich our own lives. As we'll see later, however, getting something back isn't the reason to take ethics seriously; it's just a nice consequence of doing so.

Source: Bruce Weinstein, "Principal No. 2: Make Things Better," *BusinessWeek.com*, January 18, 2007.

17-1 Void and Voidable Title

Title is the right of ownership to goods. People who own goods have title to them. Sellers sometimes give a bill of sale to a buyer as evidence that the sale took place. A **bill of sale** is a written statement evidencing the transfer of personal property from one person to another. It does not prove, however, that the seller had perfect title to the goods. The goods may have been stolen, obtained by fraud, purchased from a minor or incompetent person, or entrusted with the seller by the true owner and sold by mistake. The question that arises in such cases is whether an innocent purchaser for value receives good title to the goods. The answer to this question depends on whether the seller's title to the goods was void or voidable and whether the goods had been entrusted to a merchant.

The Opening Case Revisited, Part I
"The Wandering Cockapoo"

Fields received voidable title when he purchased the cockapoo from Jenna because she was a minor. However, because anyone with voidable title can transfer good title to a good faith purchaser for value, Jones received good title when he purchased the puppy from Fields, and Jenna lost her right to disaffirm the contract on the ground of minority.

Void Title

With the exception of voidable title, buyers of goods acquire whatever title their sellers had to the property. If a seller has **void title** (no title at all), a buyer of the goods obtains no title to them.

EXAMPLE 17-1:   Purchase of Stolen Goods

A thief entered Rodriguez's apartment and stole her brand new, 42-inch, plasma TV set, which had just been purchased that day and had not yet been removed from its carton. The thief sold the set to Guthrie, an innocent purchaser, who believed that the thief was the real owner of the set. Rodriguez would have the legal right to the return of the television set from Guthrie if its whereabouts were located. Guthrie's only right of recourse would be against the thief for the money paid for the set. Anyone who buys stolen goods receives no title to them.

The continued sale of the stolen property through several innocent buyers would not in any way defeat the real owner's right to the property. The rights of possession and title of successive buyers of stolen property can never be any better than the rights of the thief, who had no title to them.

Innocent purchasers may bring suit against the person from whom stolen goods were purchased for breach of warranty of title. This remedy is explained in Chapter 19.

Voidable Title

Anyone who obtains property as a result of another's fraud, misrepresentation, mutual mistake, undue influence, or duress holds only voidable title to the goods. **Voidable title** means title that may be voided if the injured party elects to do so. This kind of title is also received when goods are bought from a minor or a person who is mentally impaired. Some people refer to voidable title as title that is valid until voided.

Anyone with voidable title to goods is able to transfer good title to others. According to the UCC, "A person with voidable title has power to transfer a good title to a good faith purchaser for value."

EXAMPLE 17-2:   Fraudulent Purchase

Dayton bought an expensive surround speaker system from Merchandise Mart on a 30-day charge account. In making the purchase, Dayton made several fraudulent statements to the store's credit department. Although the set was bought by fraudulent

---

Did You Know?

A multimillion-dollar masterpiece painted by Monet entitled *Nympheas, 1904* that had been plundered by the Nazis during World War II was identified by the granddaughter of its owner when it was displayed at the Boston Museum of Fine Arts in 1998. The museum had borrowed the painting from a French museum. Upon learning that it was stolen, the French government returned the painting to the heirs of its rightful owner.

UCC 2-403(1) (see page 968)

The Opening Case Revisited, Part II
"The Wandering Cockapoo"

Crocker received good title to the cockapoo when she bought it in the ordinary course of the pet supply store's business. Jones's cause of action would be against the pet supply store that owned the kennel for money damages that he suffered from the loss.

means, a resale by Dayton to an innocent purchaser for value would cut off the right of Merchandise Mart to demand the return of its former property. Although the store cannot recover the goods, it may bring an action against Dayton for any loss suffered due to the fraud.

Entrusting Goods to a Merchant

UCC 2-403(2) (see page 969)

People often entrust goods that belong to them to merchants. For example, they leave their watches with jewelers and their television sets with stores to be repaired. When this occurs, if the merchant sells the goods in the ordinary course of business to a third party who has no knowledge of the real owner's rights, the third party receives good title to them. The original owner who entrusted them to the merchant loses title to the goods altogether but may bring an action against the merchant for money damages caused by the loss.

The reason for this rule of law is to give confidence to people who buy in the marketplace. People can be assured that they will receive good title to property (except stolen property) that they buy from a merchant who deals in goods of that kind in the ordinary course of business.

Quick Quiz 17-1 True or False?

1. *Void title* means title that may be voided if the injured party elects to do so.

2. *Voidable title* means no title at all.

3. The reason for the law giving good title to people who buy entrusted goods from merchants is to give confidence to people who buy in the marketplace.

17-2 The Passage of Title and Risk of Loss

UCC 2-509 (see page 970)

It is not unusual for goods to be stolen, damaged, or destroyed while they are awaiting shipment, are being shipped, or are awaiting pickup after a sales contract has been entered. When something happens to the goods, it becomes necessary to determine who must suffer the loss: the seller or the buyer. The rules for determining the risk of loss are contained in the UCC. Except when goods are to be picked up by the buyer and in a few other cases, whoever has title to the goods bears the risk of loss.

Goods must be identified in the contract before title can be transferred to the buyer. **Identified goods** are specific goods that have been selected as the subject matter of the contract. Once goods are identified, title passes to the buyer when the seller does whatever is required under the contract to deliver the goods. Contracts calling for the seller to deliver the goods are either *shipment contracts* or *destination contracts*.

Shipment Contracts

A **shipment contract** is one in which the seller turns the goods over to a carrier for delivery to the buyer. The seller has no responsibility for seeing that the goods reach their destination. In a shipment contract, both title and risk of loss pass to the buyer when the goods are given to the carrier.

When goods are purchased and identified to the contract, the buyer frequently assumes title and risk of loss even before the delivery is made.

UCC 2-501 (1) (see page 969)

UCC 2-401 (2) (see page 968)

EXAMPLE 17-3:   Shipment Contract that Went Sour

Underwood was employed by Kentucky Cardinal Dairies to pick up milk from various farmers and deliver it, in the farmers' cans, to the dairy. When no one was looking, he poured some of the milk from the farmers' cans into his own cans and sold it to another dairy. He was charged with unlawfully taking milk "which was the property of Kentucky Cardinal Dairies." In his defense, he argued that the milk was still the property of the farmers because it had not yet reached the dairy. The court disagreed, holding that title to the milk passed to the dairy the moment it was picked up by Underwood because that was the time and place of shipment.

Shipment contracts are often designated by the term *f.o.b. [the place of shipment]* (such as f.o.b. Chicago). The abbreviation **f.o.b.** means "free on board." When goods are sent **f.o.b. the place of shipment**, they will be delivered free to the place of shipment. The buyer must pay all shipping charges from there to the place of destination. The terms indicate that title to the goods and the risk of loss pass at the point of origin. Delivery to the carrier by the seller and acceptance by the carrier complete the transfer of both title and risk of loss. Thus, the buyer accepts full responsibility during the transit of the goods. (See Table 17-1.)

EXAMPLE 17-4:   Monkeying With a Shipment Contract

Joshua Nichols of Hartland, Maine, shipped a pair of live chimpanzees to Osgood, a zoologist in Ellensburg, Washington. Terms of the shipment were f.o.b. Hartland, Maine. During the shipment, the carrier was involved in an accident, and the chimpanzees escaped. Osgood would suffer the loss because title and risk of loss passed to her in Hartland, Maine. Undoubtedly, Osgood would place a claim against the carrier in its obligation as the insurer of goods accepted for shipment.

Table 17-1 Abbreviations	
Abbreviation	**Meaning**
f.o.b. New York	Free on board to New York (This would be a *shipment contract* if shipped from New York.)
f.o.b. Los Angeles	Free on board to Los Angeles (This would be a *destination contract* if shipped from New York.)
c.o.d.	Collect on delivery
c.i.f.	Cost of goods shipped, insurance, and freight
c.f.	Cost of goods shipped and freight
f.a.s.	Free alongside vessel or at a dock

Destination Contracts

LO3

LO4

UCC 2-401(2) (see page 968)

UCC 2-319 (see page 965)

If the contract requires the seller to deliver goods to a destination, it is called a **destination contract**. Both title and risk of loss pass to the buyer when the seller tenders the goods at the place of destination. **Tender** means to offer to turn the goods over to the buyer.

Destination contracts are often designated by **f.o.b. the place of destination** (such as f.o.b. Tampa); goods shipped under such terms belong to the seller until they have been delivered to the destination shown on the contract. Similarly, the risk of loss remains with the seller until the goods are tendered at destination. Tender at destination requires that the goods arrive at the place named in the contract, the buyer is given notice of their arrival, and a reasonable time is allowed for the buyer to pick up the goods from the carrier.

EXAMPLE 17-5:   Destination Contract

Suppose, in Example 17-4, the shipment to Osgood had been made under terms of f.o.b. Ellensburg, Washington. Title and risk would not have passed at the shipping point. Nichols would have had to suffer the loss, and Osgood would have had no obligation for payment.

UCC 2-320 (see page 966)

UCC 2-319(2) (see page 965)

When terms of shipment do not specify shipping point or destination, it is assumed to be a shipment contract. Adding the term **c.o.d.** (collect on delivery) instructs the carrier to retain possession until the carrier has collected the cost of the goods.

The term **c.i.f.** (cost, insurance, and freight) instructs the carrier to collect all charges and fees in one lump sum. This sum includes the cost of goods shipped, insurance, and freight charges to the point of destination. The term **c.f.** means that insurance is not included in the sum.

The term **f.a.s. vessel** (free alongside vessel) at a named port requires sellers to deliver the goods, at their own risk, alongside the vessel or at a dock designated by the buyer.

LO3

LO4

No Delivery Required

When the contract calls for the buyer to pick up the goods, title passes to the buyer when the contract is made. Risk of loss, however, passes at different times depending on whether the seller is a merchant. If the seller is a merchant, the risk of loss passes when the buyer

Table 17-2 Passage of Title and Risk of Loss

Terms of Contract	Title Passes	Risk of Loss Passes
Shipment contract	When goods are delivered to carrier	When goods are delivered to carrier
Destination contract	When goods are tendered at destination	When goods are tendered at destination
No delivery required	When contract is made	*Merchant seller:* When buyer receives goods; *Nonmerchant seller:* When seller tenders goods to buyer
Document of title	When document of title is given to buyer	When document of title is given to buyer
Agreement of the parties	At time and place agreed upon	At time and place agreed upon

receives the goods. If the seller is not a merchant, the risk of loss passes to the buyer when the seller tenders the goods to the buyer (see Table 17-2).

UCC 2-401(3)(b) (see page 968)

UCC 2-509(3) (see page 971)

EXAMPLE 17-6: Tender of Goods

Rivera agreed to sell her Aurora fiberglass kayak to Gray for $2,500. Gray paid for the kayak and said that he would pick it up from Rivera's yard the next evening. Gray was called out of town, however, and did not pick up the kayak, which had been made ready for him. The kayak was stolen a week later from Rivera's yard. Gray must suffer the loss because the kayak had been tendered to him. Had Rivera been a merchant, she would have had to assume the loss because Gray had not yet received possession of the kayak.

Fungible Goods

The UCC defines **fungible goods** as "goods of which any unit is, by nature or usage of trade, the equivalent of any like unit." Wheat, flour, sugar, and liquids of various kinds are examples of fungible goods. They have no important characteristics that identify them as coming from a particular supplier, and they are usually sold by weight or measure. Title to fungible goods may pass without the necessity of separating goods sold from the bulk. Under the UCC, "an undivided share of an identified bulk of fungible goods is sufficiently identified to be sold although the quantity of the bulk is not determined."

UCC 2-105(4) (see page 960)

EXAMPLE 17-7: Fungible Goods

Logan Trucking Co. owned a large fuel storage tank that was partially filled with diesel fuel. The exact quantity of fuel in the tank was not known. The company was going out of business. Interstate Trucking Co. contracted to buy half of the fuel in the tank, and Union Trucking Co. contracted to buy the other half. Both buyers agreed to send their own trucks to pick up the fuel. Title passed to the buyers when the contract was made even though the exact quantity of each sale was unknown and neither buyer had taken a share of the fuel from the entire lot.

Documents of Title

Sometimes, when people buy goods, they receive a document of title to the goods rather than the goods themselves. They then give the document of title to the warehouse or carrier that is holding the goods and receive possession of them. A **document of title** is a paper giving the person who possesses it the right to receive the goods named in the document. Bills of lading and warehouse receipts, as explained in Chapter 22, are examples of documents of title. However, an automobile title certificate has not been given the legal status of a document of title, as the term is used in the UCC.

When a document of title is used in a sales transaction, both title and risk of loss pass to the buyer when the document is delivered to the buyer.

UCC 2-401(3)(a) (see page 968)

EXAMPLE 17-8:   Document of Title

Manchez stored a large quantity of wheat in a grain elevator and, in return, was given a warehouse receipt. Later, Manchez sold the wheat to Rodney. Upon receipt of the money for the wheat, Manchez signed and delivered the warehouse receipt to Rodney. Rodney received title to the wheat when the document was delivered to her.

Agreement of the Parties

The parties may, if they wish, enter into an agreement setting forth the time that title and risk of loss pass from the seller to the buyer. With one exception, title and risk of loss will pass at the time and place agreed upon. If the agreement allows the seller to retain title after the goods are shipped, title will pass to the buyer at the time of shipment, regardless of the agreement, and the seller will have a security interest in the goods rather than title. A security interest gives the seller a right to have the property sold in the event that the buyer fails to pay money owed to the seller (see Chapter 31).

UCC 2-401(1) (see page 968)

EXAMPLE 17-9:   Security Interest

Raymond agreed to sell Glover her John Deere tractor for $12,000. The agreement called for Glover to pay $3,000 down and the balance in monthly installments for two years. Under the terms of the agreement, title to the tractor would not pass to Glover until the $12,000 was paid in full. Because Raymond delivered the tractor to Glover on the day that the agreement was signed, title passed to Glover at that time, regardless of the terms in the contract. The effect of those terms was to give Raymond a security interest in the tractor for the balance of the money owed to her.

Revesting of Title in Seller

Buyers, after entering into sales contracts, sometimes refuse to accept the goods that are delivered or are otherwise made available to them. In all such cases, title to the goods returns to the seller. This reversion is true whether or not the buyer's rejection of the goods is justified. Similarly, title to goods returns to the seller when the buyer accepts the goods and then for a justifiable reason decides to revoke the acceptance. A justifiable reason for revoking an acceptance would be the discovery of a defect in the goods after having inspected them.

When the seller sends goods to the buyer that do not meet the contract requirements and are therefore unacceptable, the risk of loss remains with the seller. For situations in which the buyer accepts the goods but later discovers some defect and rightfully revokes

UCC 2-401(4) (see page 968)

UCC 2-510 (see page 971)

UCC 2-510(3) (see page 971)

the acceptance, the passage of risk of loss depends on whether the buyer is insured. If the buyer has insurance, that insurance will cover the loss. If there is no insurance, the risk of loss remains with the seller from the beginning.

When the buyer breaches the contract with regard to goods that have been identified to the contract, the seller may, to the extent of having no insurance coverage, treat the risk of loss as resting with the buyer.

International Sales

The rules governing international sales are given in the United Nations Convention on Contracts for the International Sale of Goods (CISG). The international law does not address questions dealing with the passage of title because the laws of each country vary considerably. Instead, it leaves such questions to be decided by domestic law. This determination exists because third parties are usually involved in claiming title for themselves, and the laws of each country vary considerably.

In contrast, the rules governing the passage of risk of loss are addressed in international law and are quite similar to those found in the UCC. The risk of loss passes to the buyer when the goods are handed over to the first carrier for transmission to the buyer unless the seller agrees to hand them over at a particular place. In that case, the risk of loss passes to the buyer at that time. Sometimes, goods are sold when they are in transit. When this kind of sale occurs (with some exceptions), the risk of loss passes to the buyer when the contract is made. In all other situations, the risk of loss, in general, passes when the buyer takes over the goods.

CISG Article 4 (see page 1018)

CISG Articles 67-69 (see page 1025)

Quick Quiz 17-2 True or False?

1. With a few exceptions, whoever has title to goods also bears the risk of loss.

2. When a contract calls for a non-merchant buyer to pick up the goods so that no delivery is required, the risk of loss passes to the buyer when the contract is made.

3. Fungible goods must be separated from the bulk before title to them can pass to a buyer.

17-3 Sales with Right of Return

Because of competition and a desire to give satisfaction, goods are sometimes sold with the understanding that they may be returned even though they conform to the contract. Determination of ownership and risk of loss while such goods are in the buyer's possession is sometimes necessary. Sales with the right of return are of two kinds: sale on approval and sale or return.

Sale on Approval

A sale that allows goods to be returned even though they conform to the contract is called a **sale on approval** when the goods are primarily for the buyer's use. When goods are sold on approval, they remain the property of the seller until the buyer's approval has been expressed. The approval may be indicated by the oral or written consent of the buyer or by the buyer's act of retaining the goods for more than a reasonable time. Using the goods in a reasonable and expected manner on a trial basis does not imply an acceptance. Grossly careless use and a failure to inform the seller of the buyer's intent to return, however, could constitute an acceptance.

UCC 2-326 (see page 967)

BusinessWeek   # Business Law in the News

Easy to Buy. Easy to Return?

As online shopping grows, consumers find that the ease—or difficulty—of returning items differs greatly by retailer.

Wendy Slaney, a career counselor and avid shopper, is joining millions of Americans in a post-holiday ritual: returning merchandise. And like an increasing number of Americans, she won't be heading to the mall but to the UPS (UPS) store, where she expects to wait in line to spend about $12 to return a pair of Harley Davidson (HOG) riding boots she bought for her boyfriend. She's not thrilled about the extra trip—or forking over the shipping cost—nor was she pleased that the boots' box had no packing slip or contact information from Van's Fine Men's Shoe Shop, the Milwaukee retailer where she bought them.

"I went online for the cheaper prices and the convenience of not having to spend my nights and weekends shopping in the crowds," says Slaney of Worcester, Mass. "So returns can be a nuisance. I'm hoping this one goes smoothly."

Work in Progress

Online sales surged this holiday season—up 26% from last year, at a growth rate four times faster than traditional stores. And along with the surge in sales comes the commensurate surge in holiday gift returns. But while the experience of buying online has become more popular for its ease and deep discounting, returning merchandise remains a hassle for many consumers. Trips to jam-packed post offices, costly shipping fees, and weeks of waiting for an exchange or refund stand in sharp contrast to the ease of a click and quick delivery of a gift, often with free shipping. Retail experts say that while all-e-tailers are keen to sell merchandise, only some have yet realized the need to treat customers well when they return purchases.

"Some companies figure they don't have a relationship with the person getting the gift, so there is less emphasis on making the return process smooth," says George Whalin, president of Retail Management Consultants in San Marcos, Calif. "But the smart ones know it's worth investing the time or money to please a potential customer."

Online returns policies for many companies are still a work in progress, and customers' experiences vary by store. The range of return policies ranges from the uber customer-friendly to the more basic. Consumers like Slaney praise shoe retailer Zappos, which pays shipping costs in both directions, and L.L. Bean, which accepts returned items years after they're purchased and even offers exchanges and credits without a receipt. Such generosity could incur steep costs or leave stores vulnerable to fraud, but these retailers' focus is on long-term loyalty rather than short-term cash flow.

"It's an honor system," says Dave Teufel, a spokesman for L.L. Bean of Freeport, ME. "We've been in business for 95 years and we've not found abuse an issue. Our focus is to ensure customers are completely satisfied." Teufel says online sales surpassed catalog sales this fall for the first time.

Buy Online, Return at Store

Larger stores don't take risks with such liberal policies, although many have sought to simplify the online return process. An increasing number of retailers such as BestBuy Stores (BBY) allow online customers to return items to brick-and-mortar stores, though BestBuy allows each customer only one return without a receipt. Retailers like Target.com (TGT) and Amazon.com (AMZN) offer gift receipts with the package and do not list the price of enclosed items—though such receipts aren't available for every item on Amazon, which can be awkward for gift-giving. Like many retailers, Wal-Mart (WMT) has customers pay for shipping costs on return items if the item isn't defective or the result of a company error. And the wait can be as long as three weeks for an online return to Wal-Mart.

A Wal-Mart spokesperson said the company's online return policy has not changed in response to an increase in online purchases, and that the system works well because there are so many brick-and-mortar stores to accept merchandise returns from online sales.

Overall, consumers were happy shopping online this season. A survey released Dec. 19 by Shop.org and Shopzilla showed that more than two-thirds, or

71.2%, of online shoppers surveyed said they were "very satisfied" with their online holiday buying. But it remains to be seen how cheerful these buyers will be as they pack up items and ship them back for returns.

Naughty or Nice?

"I don't like having to pay return shipping if something doesn't fit—it gets expensive," says Jim McGrath, 51, also of Worcester, Mass. Frequent online shoppers like Slaney are developing lists of companies they'll continue patronizing online and those they'll skip.

Slaney said that after a series of problems with Victoria's Secret, for example, she'll never buy from them online again. She said the company, a unit of Limited Brands (LTD), claimed that a package of items she returned had never arrived. After seven weeks of disputes, she ended up with a $50 credit for $79 of merchandise. A Victoria's Secret representative did not immediately return a phone message.

"I'm done with them now," says Slaney. But she says the experience won't stop her shopping online; it'll just make her choosier about who gets her business—and from now on, she'll insure all returns and request a return receipt.

Questions for Analysis

1. Why did Wendy Slaney shop online?

2. Why does returning merchandise from online purchases remain a hassle for many consumers?

3. Why do some companies put less emphasis on making the return process smooth?

4. Why do some consumers praise the return policies of Zappos and L.L. Bean?

5. How do some larger retailers such as BestBuy handle returns on online sales?

Source: Moira Herbst, "Easy to Buy. Easy to Return?" Business-Week.com, December 29, 2006.

Goods held by the buyer on approval are not subject to the claims of the buyer's creditors until the buyer decides to accept them. In addition, the risk of loss remains with the seller until the buyer has accepted the goods.

UCC 2-327 (see page 967)

UCC 2-326 (see page 967)

Sale or Return

A sale that allows goods to be returned even though they conform to the contract is called a **sale or return** when the goods are delivered primarily for resale. When such a sale occurs, the buyer takes title to the goods with the right to revest (reinstate) title in the seller after a specified period or reasonable time. In such cases, the buyer must accept all of the obligations of ownership while retaining possession of the goods. Goods held on sale or return are subject to the claims of the buyer's creditors.

While in the buyer's possession, the goods must be cared for and used in a reasonable manner, anticipating their possible return in the same condition as when received, after making allowance for ordinary wear and tear. Also, the goods must be returned at the buyer's risk and expense.

EXAMPLE 17-10:   Consignment Contract

Butcher owned a gift shop in which she sold other people's goods on consignment. Hanson delivered a dozen handmade braided rugs to Butcher with the understanding that she would be paid for any that were sold. Any rugs that did not sell after three months would be returned to Hanson. This agreement was a sale or return because the rugs were delivered primarily for resale. Butcher would be required to pay Hanson for any rugs that were damaged, lost, or stolen while in Butcher's possession.

About the Law

Unless a product is defective, the right to return it is not automatic. Stores generally offer the right to return merchandise for goodwill purposes, and it has become so common in our society that customers incorrectly believe it is their legal right to return goods. Such right, if any, is created by statute, contract, or store policy. If no statute, contract, or store policy creates that right, then a buyer cannot legally return the merchandise to the seller for a refund unless it is defective. Some states' consumer protection laws requre stores to notify cusomers, either with a sign or orally before the purchase, that an item cannot be returned.

UCC 2-501(1) (see page 969)

Quick Quiz 17-3 True or False?

1. Goods that are sold on approval are subject to the claims of the buyer's creditors until the buyer decides to accept them.

2. Goods that are sold on approval remain the property of the seller until the buyer's approval has been expressed.

3. Goods that are sold on sale or return are not subject to the claims of the buyer's creditors.

17-4 Insurable Interest

People must have an insurable interest in property to be able to place insurance on it. An **insurable interest** is the financial interest that an insured party has in the insured property. Buyers may place insurance on goods the moment a contract is made and the goods are identified to the contract. At this point, buyers receive an insurable interest in the goods they buy. They obtain an insurable interest even though they might later reject or return the goods to the seller. Notwithstanding the buyer's right to insure the goods, sellers retain an insurable interest in the goods as long as they have title to them. Insurable interests are discussed in more detail in Chapter 30.

EXAMPLE 17-11:   Dual Insurable Interests

While shopping on vacation in an antique store in Connecticut, Maniff, who lived in Nevada, came upon a Native American totem pole she liked. She decided to buy the totem pole on the condition that the antique dealer would ship it f.o.b. Winnemucca, Nevada. The dealer agreed. Maniff received an insurable interest in the totem pole when it was identified to the contract. At the same time, the dealer retained an insurable interest in it until it was tendered at its destination in Winnemucca. Both Maniff and the antique dealer could insure the totem pole.

Summary

17.1 Anyone with void title to goods, such as a thief, can never give good title to another person. Anyone with voidable title, such as someone who buys goods from a minor, may transfer good title to a good faith purchaser for value. When goods are entrusted to a merchant that sells them without authority to someone in the ordinary course of business, the purchaser obtains good title.

17.2 With few exceptions, such as when goods are to be picked up by the buyer, whoever has title to the goods bears the risk of loss. Goods must be identified to the contract before title can be transferred to the buyer. Once goods are identified, title passes to the buyer when the seller does whatever is required under the contract to deliver the goods. In a shipment contract, both title and risk of loss pass to the buyer when the goods are given to the carrier. In a destination contract, both title and risk of loss pass to the buyer when the seller tenders the goods at the place of destination. When the contract calls for the buyer to pick up the goods, title passes to the buyer when the contract is made. If the seller is a merchant, the risk of loss passes when the buyer receives the goods. If the seller is not a merchant, the risk of loss passes to the buyer when the seller tenders the goods to the buyer. Title to fungible goods may pass without the necessity of separating goods sold from the bulk. When a document of title is used, both title and risk of loss pass to the buyer when the document is delivered to the buyer. In general, the parties may establish by agreement the time and place for the passage of both title and risk of loss. Title returns to the seller when the buyer refuses to accept the goods. Similarly, the risk of loss remains with the seller when the goods that are shipped do not meet the contract requirements.

17.3 Goods sold on approval remain the property of the seller until the buyer's approval is expressed. In addition, the seller retains the risk of loss. In contrast, in a sale or return, the buyer takes title to the goods but is given the right to return the goods to the seller at a later time. The buyer must care for the goods in a reasonable manner and suffer the risk of loss.

17.4 Buyers have an insurable interest in goods the moment a contract is made and the goods are identified to the contract. In addition, sellers retain an insurable interest in goods as long as they still have title to them.

Key Terms

bill of sale, 338	f.o.b., 341	sale or return, 347
c.f., 342	f.o.b. the place of destination, 342	shipment contract, 341
c.i.f., 342	f.o.b. the place of shipment, 341	tender, 342
c.o.d., 342	fungible goods, 343	title, 338
destination contract, 342	identified goods, 341	void title, 339
document of title, 344	insurable interest, 348	voidable title, 339
f.a.s. vessel, 342	sale on approval, 345	

Questions for Review and Discussion

1. What is the difference between void title and voidable title? Explain.
2. What are the rights of an innocent purchaser of stolen goods?
3. What are some examples of people who have voidable title to goods?
4. What are the rights of the owner of goods who entrusts the goods to a merchant who sells them in the ordinary course of business?
5. When do title and risk of loss pass to the buyer in a shipment contract?
6. When do title and risk of loss pass to the buyer in a destination contract?
7. When do title and risk of loss pass to the buyer when the contract calls for the buyer to pick up the goods?
8. When do title and risk of loss pass to the buyer when a document of title is used?
9. What is the difference between a sale on approval and a sale or return?
10. When may buyers place insurance on goods they purchase?

Investigating the Internet

Trade between China and the United States has skyrocketed in recent years. At the beginning of 2007, 70 countries had adopted as part of their law the U.N. Convention on Contracts for the International Sale of Goods (CISG). This international law applies only to sales between businesses whose places of business are in different countries that have adopted the law. Check the Internet to see if China has adopted it. A good place to start is at a search engine such as Google, keying in "states adopting CISG."

Cases for Analysis

1. Circuit City allowed customers to purchase items in Massachusetts and pick them up at a New Hampshire store, enabling them to avoid the 5 percent Massachusetts sales tax. Circuit City credited the sales to its Massachusetts stores and gave employees in those stores commissions for them. The Massachusetts Commissioner of Revenue asserted that title passed at the cash register in Massachusetts when Circuit City received payment and the receipt was handed to the customer. Circuit City took the position that title did not pass until the purchased merchandise was physically placed in the customer's hands in New Hampshire. With whom do you agree? Explain. *Circuit City Stores, Inc. v. Commission of Revenue,* 439 Mass 629 (MA).

2. Wheel Sports Center entered into a sales contract agreeing to deliver a motorcycle to Ramos for the price of $893. Ramos paid the full price for the motorcycle and immediately had it insured and registered in his name. However, before it was delivered to Ramos, the motorcycle was stolen from Wheel Sports Center. Who must suffer the loss, Wheel Sports Center or Ramos? Why? *Ramos v. Wheel Sports Center,* 409 N.Y.S.2d 505 (NY).

3. Estes purchased a late-model Chevrolet Caprice sports coupe from Howard, an automobile dealer in Mississippi. Later, it was discovered that the vehicle had been stolen from a Chevrolet dealership in Florida and, after a circuitous route, eventually had come to rest in Mississippi. The bill of sale to the vehicle had been forged. Estes contended that he has good title to the vehicle because he bought the auto from a dealer. Was Estes correct? *Allstate Ins. Co. v. Estes,* 345 So.2d 265 (MS).

4. Brown, who operated Jack's Skelly Service Station, was sued by his former wife for child support payments. During the trial, the question arose as to who owned the gasoline in the service station tanks, Brown or Brown's supplier, Martin. Brown had entered into a "special Keep-Full motor fuel sales agreement" under which Martin agreed to deliver to Brown's place of business Skelly motor fuel. The agreement stated that title to the fuel "shall be and remain with Martin until removed from the tanks through and by means of computing pumps." Who owned the gas in the tanks, Brown or Martin? Why? *Stewart v. Brown,* 546 S.W.2d 204 (MO).

5. Fanning, who was 17 years old, sold her bicycle to Gerard, an adult, for $75. The next day, Gerard advertised the bicycle for sale in the classified section of a local newspaper and sold it for $150. The person who bought the bicycle was unaware that it had belonged to Fanning. When Fanning discovered what Gerard had done, she attempted to get the bicycle back from the person who bought it, claiming that Gerard had voidable title to the bicycle. Does Fanning have the legal right to the return of the bicycle? Why or why not?

6. Harold Marcus entered into a contract with Corrigan's Yacht Yard & Marine Sales, Inc., to trade in his 34-foot Silverton power boat toward a later-model Mainship boat. He delivered his Silverton boat to the yacht yard at the time of the contract in

November. The new boat was not to be delivered until the following April. The yacht yard sold the Silverton boat to William Heiselman soon after receiving it. When the yacht yard was unable to deliver the Mainship boat to Marcus in April, Marcus took back his Silverton boat. Who had title to the boat, Marcus or Heiselman? Explain. *Heiselman v. Marcus,* 488 N.Y.S.2d 571 (NY).

7. Gallo entered into a contract in October to deliver 3,500 heifers to Weisbart's ranch between May 1 and October 1 of the next year. Gallo experienced difficulty in raising the heifers due to rising costs and a severe winter, and his bank foreclosed on the cattle before they could be delivered to Weisbart. Weisbart claimed that sale of the cattle occurred in October when the contract was made and that title passed to him at that time. Do you agree with Weisbart? Why or why not? *Weisbart & Co. v. First Nat'l. Bank,* 568 F.2d 391 (5th Cir.).

8. Mann bought a Lincoln Continental Mark IV automobile from Kilbourn American Leasing, Inc., for $6,500 cash. He received by mistake from Kilbourn a title certificate for a similar but different vehicle. Kilbourn later borrowed money from a bank and gave the correct title certificate for Mann's car to the bank as security for the loan.

The bank claims that Mann does not have title to the car because he did not receive the title certificate. Was the bank correct? Why or why not? *National Exch. Bank v. Mann,* 260 N.W.2d 716 (WI).

9. Eberhard Manufacturing Company sold goods to Brown Industrial Sales Company without agreeing on who would bear the risk of loss. The contract contained no f.o.b. terms. Eberhard placed the goods on board a common carrier with instructions to deliver them to Brown. The goods were lost in transit. Who suffered the loss, Eberhard or Brown? Why? *Eberhard Mfg. Co. v. Brown,* 232 N.W.2d 378 (MI).

10. Henry Heide, Inc., received a warehouse receipt for 3,200 100-pound bags of sugar that it bought from Olavarria. The corporation withdrew 800 bags of the sugar from the warehouse (where thousands of pounds were stored), but when it returned for the balance, it discovered that the warehouse was padlocked and empty. Some 200,000 pounds of sugar had mysteriously disappeared from it. Henry Heide, Inc., carried insurance for such a loss, but its insurance company refused to pay, claiming that the corporation had no insurable interest in the sugar. Do you agree with the insurance company? Why or why not? *Henry Heide, Inc., v. Atlantic Mut. Ins. Co.,* 363 N.Y.S.2d 515 (NY).

Quick Quiz Answers

17-1	1. F	17-2	1. T	17-3	1. F
	2. F		2. F		2. T
	3. T		3. F		3. F

Chapter 18

Performance and Breach of the Sales Contract

The Opening Case

"Mango Mania"

Moonlight Wholesalers of Gambier, Ohio, ordered a shipment of fresh mangos from José Garcia Frutas of Veracruz, Mexico, to be delivered on July 15. Having a full stock of fresh mangos, José Garcia Frutas shipped the goods to Moonlight two weeks early. Without opening the boxes, Moonlight sent the entire shipment c.o.d. to its retailer, Garden-Fresh Produce Co. When it arrived, the shipper would not allow the boxes to be inspected until they had been paid for. Garden-Fresh paid for the shipment, opened the boxes, and discovered that they contained lemons, not mangos. When told of the mistake, Moonlight notified José Garcia Frutas. It also told Garden-Fresh to sell the lemons and that it would send a replacement shipment as soon as possible. Garden-Fresh, however, threw away the lemons and refused to reimburse Moonlight for them. José Garcia Frutas then shipped the correct order of mangos to Moonlight, which arrived on July 14.

Opening Case Questions

1. Must Moonlight pay José Garcia for the mangos?

2. Did Garden-Fresh have the right to inspect the shipment before paying for it?

3. Could Garden-Fresh rightfully throw away the lemons?

4. Who can be held responsible for the loss of the lemons?

LO Learning Objectives

1. Discuss, in general, the obligations of the parties to a sales contract.
2. Determine whether the requirements for tender of delivery and tender of payment have been met in given cases.
3. Explain the buyer's right to inspect goods.
4. Describe the buyer's rights and duties when improper goods are delivered.
5. Judge, in given cases, whether the seller has the right to correct an improper tender of delivery.
6. Compare the remedies that are available to the seller with those available to the buyer when sales contracts are breached.

18-1 Obligations of the Parties

The obligations of the parties to a sales contract are simple and straightforward: The seller is obligated to turn the goods over to the buyer, and the buyer is obligated to accept and pay for them, both acting in accordance with the terms of the contract. In addition, all parties must act in **good faith**, which means that they must act honestly.

The court need not enforce a contract or part of a contract that it finds to be unconscionable. An **unconscionable contract** is one that is so one-sided that it is oppressive and gives unfair advantage to one of the parties. Unequal bargaining power, the absence of a meaningful choice by one party, and unreasonably one-sided terms, when put together, indicate unconscionability.

When disputes arise between parties who have dealt together in the past, the court often looks to their past dealings to give meaning to the disputed transaction. When interpreting the meaning of contracts, the court may also consider any usage of trade, that is, any particular methods of doing business, that are commonly used in that field. Although terms that are expressly stated in a contract will usually control the contract's meaning, the parties' past dealings and usage of trade are often considered to supplement or qualify the express terms.

EXAMPLE 18-1:   Course of Dealings

Associated Hardware Supply Company negotiated with Big Wheel Distributing Company for the purchase of merchandise. The parties could not agree on the pricing of the goods. Associated Hardware wanted to pay cost plus 10 percent, whereas Big Wheel insisted on the dealers' catalog price less 11 percent. Although the parties exchanged letters, there was never any formal agreement on pricing. Over a two-year period, Associated Hardware ordered goods from Big Wheel amounting to more than $850,000, paying for them on a catalog-less-11-percent basis. Later, when an additional $40,000 was owed for merchandise purchased, Associated Hardware refused to pay, claiming that no agreement had been reached as to the pricing of the goods. Finding in favor of Big Wheel, the court attached great weight to the way the parties had dealt in the past. It held that the parties' course of dealing for the two-year period governed the sale of the remaining merchandise.

UCC 1-205 (see page 958)

International Law   The GISC has similar provisions for international sales. Under that law, the parties are bound by practices they have established between themselves. In addition, unless they agree otherwise, the parties must follow the methods of dealing in international trade that are widely known and regularly observed by parties in the same type of trade.

CISG Article 9 (see page 1019)

Quick Quiz 18-1 True or False?

1. According to the law of sales contracts, all parties must act in good faith, which means they must act honestly.

2. Fraud and duress are indications of unconscionability.

3. The parties' past dealings are never considered to supplement the terms of an express contract.

BusinessWeek Business Law in the News
Why the Gap Won't Stop Growing

Can anything stop the Chinese export machine? In August the mainland's trade surplus hit $18.8 billion—the fourth straight month with a record-setting gap. For the year to date, the surplus stands at $94.7 billion, 57% ahead of a year ago. Although China's imports jumped to a record $72 billion, exports surged nearly a third to—yes, another record—$90.8 billion. And much of that gap can be attributed to the vast quantities of goods shipped to eager American consumers. For the year, China's exports to the U.S.

look set to approach $300 billion, up from $243 billion in 2005.

Just what are Americans buying? Numbers won't be available until 2007, but it's a safe bet that gizmos such as TVs and iPods were popular. U.S. Commerce Dept. data show that electronic gear was the largest category of imports from China last year. That's a big change from a decade ago, when low-tech manufactured goods dominated. Below, the true scope of America's imports from China.

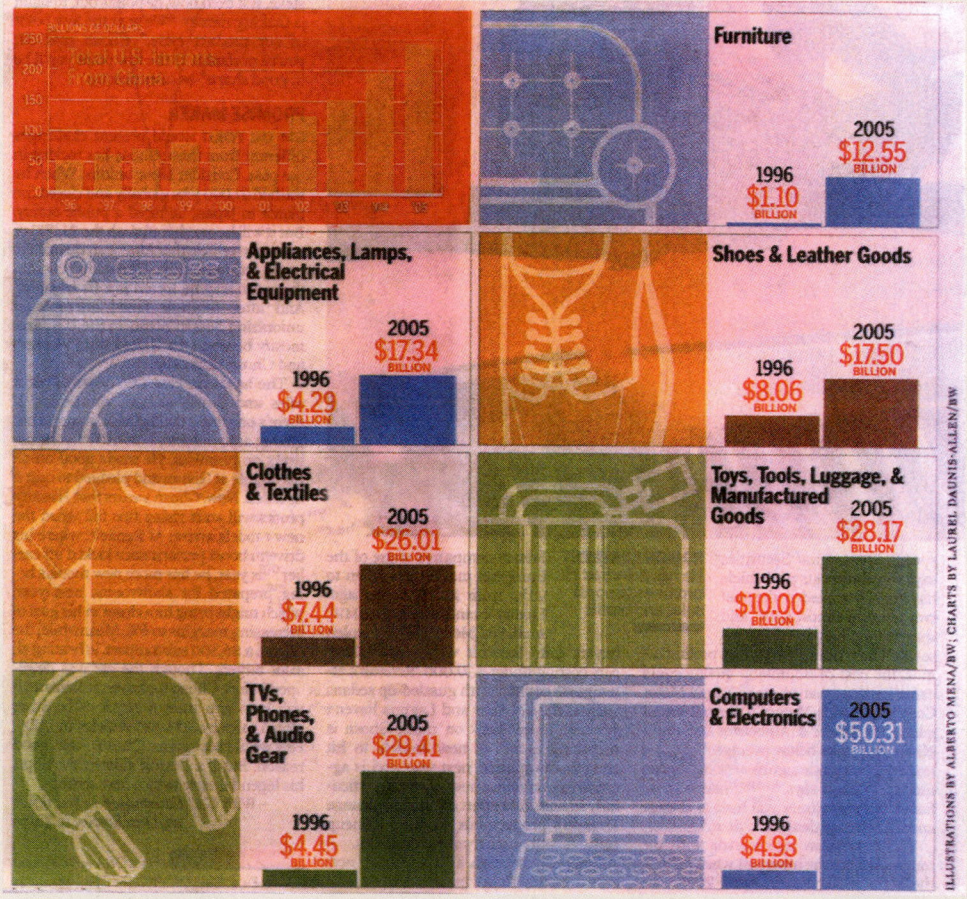

BILLIONS OF DOLLARS
Total U.S. Imports from China
Total $243.5

Furniture
2005 $12.55 BILLION
1996 $1.10 BILLION

Appliances, Lamps, & Electrical Equipment
2005 $17.34 BILLION
1996 $4.29 BILLION

Shoes & Leather Goods
2005 $17.50 BILLION
1996 $8.06 BILLION

Clothes & Textiles
2005 $26.01 BILLION
1996 $7.44 BILLION

Toys, Tools, Luggage, & Manufactured Goods
2005 $28.17 BILLION
1996 $10.00 BILLION

TVs, Phones, & Audio Gear
2005 $29.41 BILLION
1996 $4.45 BILLION

Computers & Electronics
2005 $50.31 BILLION
1996 $4.93 BILLION

ILLUSTRATIONS BY ALBERTO MENA/BW; CHARTS BY LAUREL DAUNIS-ALLEN/BW

Questions for Analysis

1. How much was the gap in billions of dollars between China's imports and exports as of the date of this article?

2. To what is the gap attributed?

3. What was the expected amount of China's exports to the U.S. in 2006, the year of this article?

4. What are Americans buying in greatest numbers from China compared with a decade ago?

Source: Nicholas Saminather, "Why the Gap Won't Stop Growing," *BusinessWeek*, September 25, 2006.

18-2 Tender of Performance

When the seller offers to turn the goods over to the buyer and when the buyer offers to pay for them, **tender of performance** occurs. It is the offering by the parties to do what they have agreed to do under the terms of the contract. Tender is necessary to test the party's ability and willingness to perform his or her part of the bargain. The seller must make tender of delivery, and the buyer must make tender of payment. If one party fails to make tender and the other breaches the contract, the one not making tender cannot bring suit.

Tender of Delivery by Seller

To be in a position to bring suit on a sales contract, the seller of goods must make **tender of delivery**, that is, offer to turn the goods over to the buyer. Failure to make this offer is an excuse for buyers not to perform their part of the bargain.

Manner of Seller's Tender   To make proper tender, the seller must put and hold conforming goods at the buyer's disposition during a reasonable hour of the day.

UCC 2-507 (see page 970)

UCC 2-503(1)(b) (see page 969)

EXAMPLE 18-2:   Unreasonable Tender

Gipsum Canning Co. agreed to sell 1,000 cases of canned beets to Green Grocers for $8.40 a case. Before shipping the goods, however, Gipsum was offered $9.60 a case from another company. Gipsum delivered the 1,000 cases of beets to Green Grocers's loading platform at 3:00 in the morning. Finding no one there, Gipsum took the goods and sold them to the other company at the higher price. When sued, Gipsum claimed that Green Grocers had breached the contract by not accepting the goods when they were tendered at the loading platform. The court disagreed, saying that Gipsum did not put and hold the goods at the buyer's disposition during a reasonable hour of the day.

In addition, the seller must notify the buyer that the goods are being tendered. It is the responsibility of the buyer, however, to furnish facilities that are suitable for receiving the goods.

Shipment Contract   In a shipment contract, the seller must put the goods in the possession of a carrier and contract with that carrier for their transportation. Any necessary documents must be sent to the buyer, who must be promptly notified of the shipment.

UCC 2-504 (see page 970)

Goods in Possession of Warehouse   Sometimes, goods are in the possession of a warehouse and are to be turned over to the buyer without being moved. When this situation occurs, tender requires that the seller either tender a document of title covering the goods or obtain an acknowledgment by the warehouse of the buyer's right to their possession.

UCC 2-503(4) (see page 969)

EXAMPLE 18-3:   Tender of Warehouse Goods

Spiegel purchased 5,000 cases of canned onions from Ingalls at a price that was much lower than the wholesale market price of the same product. The cases of onions had been stored by Ingalls at the East Side Storage Warehouse. Spiegel

> wished to continue storing the onions at the same warehouse, as she had no immediate use for them. Ingalls notified East Side Storage Warehouse that the onions had been sold to Spiegel. Tender occurred when the warehouse acknowledged to Spiegel that it was now holding the cases of onions for her instead of for Ingalls.

CISG Articles 30–34
(see pages 1020–1021)

International Law   For international sales, the seller must deliver the goods and hand over any documents relating to them and any ownership rights as required by the contract. If the seller is not bound to deliver the goods to a particular place, the seller must hand the goods over to the first carrier for transmission to the buyer. If there is no carrier involved, the seller must place the goods at the buyer's disposal.

Tender of Payment by Buyer

Although the seller is obligated to deliver the goods to the buyer, this obligation stands on the condition that the buyer make tender of payment, unless otherwise agreed. **Tender of payment** means offering to turn the necessary money over to the seller. Such tender may be made by any means or in any manner that is commonly used in the ordinary course of business. The seller has the right to demand payment in legal tender but must give the buyer a reasonable time to obtain it. **Legal tender** is money that may be offered legally in satisfaction of a debt and that must be accepted by a creditor when offered.

UCC 2-511(1) (see
page 971)

EXAMPLE 18-4:   Tender of Payment

Thompson Computer Sales agreed to sell a computer to Rubin for $4,500 c.o.d. When the equipment was delivered, Rubin offered to pay Thompson with a check. This offer was a sufficient tender of payment, because checks are commonly used in the ordinary course of business. Thompson did not have to accept Rubin's check if it did not wish to do so though. If the company refused to take the check, however, it would have to give Rubin a reasonable amount of time to obtain legal tender.

UCC 2-511(3) (see
page 971)

UCC 2-512 (see page
971)

Payment by check is conditional under the UCC. If the check clears, the debt is discharged. If the check is dishonored, the debt is revived.

When a contract requires payment before inspection, as when goods are shipped c.o.d., the buyer must pay for them first, even if they turn out to be defective when they are inspected. Of course, if the defect is obvious, the buyer would not have to accept or pay for the goods. Payment by the buyer before inspecting the goods does not constitute an acceptance of them. Upon discovering a defect and notifying the seller, the buyer may use any of the remedies that are mentioned later in this chapter against the seller for breach of contract.

CISG Articles 53–59
(see pages 1023–1024)

International Law   Under international law, the buyer must pay the price for the goods and take delivery of them as required by the contract and the law. The price must be paid on the date fixed by the contract, without the need for a request or compliance with any formality on the part of the seller.

Quick Quiz 18-2 True or False?

1. Tender of performance is the offering by the parties to do what they have agreed to do under the terms of the contract.

2. A party who fails to make tender cannot bring suit if the other party breaches the contract.

3. Tender of payment is money that may be offered legally in satisfaction of a debt and that must be accepted by a creditor when offered.

18-3 Buyer's Rights and Duties upon Delivery of Improper Goods

Except when goods are shipped c.o.d. or when the contract provides for payment against a document of title, the buyer has the right to inspect the goods before accepting or paying for them. The inspection may take place after the goods arrive at their destination. Expenses of inspection must be borne by the buyer but may be recovered from the seller if the goods do not conform to the contract and are rejected by the buyer. Goods conform to a contract when they are in accordance with the obligations under the contract.

UCC 2-513 (see page 971)

UCC 2-106(2) (see page 960)

When defective goods or goods not of the kind specified in the contract are delivered, the buyer may elect to reject them all, accept them all, or accept any commercial unit or units and reject the rest. A **commercial unit** is a single whole for the purpose of sale, the division of which impairs its character or value on the market. For example, a commercial unit may be a single article (e.g., a machine) or a set of articles (e.g., suite of furniture, assortment of sizes). It may be a quantity (e.g., bale, gross, carload) or any other unit treated in the marketplace as a single whole item.

International Law In the case of international law, the buyer must examine the goods within as short a period as is practicable in the circumstances. This inspection may be done after the goods arrive at their destination when the goods are shipped by carrier.

Failure of the buyer to inspect goods upon delivery results in an acceptance of the goods, even if nonconforming.

UCC 2-601 (see page 971)

CISG Article 38 (see page 1021)

The Opening Case Revisited, Part I
"Mango Mania"

Because Moonlight did not examine the goods when they arrived before sending them on to Garden-Fresh, it may be liable to José Garcia Frutas for the loss of the lemons that were wrongfully thrown away by Garden-Fresh.

Rejection

UCC 2-602 (see page 972)

A rejection occurs when a buyer refuses to accept delivery of goods tendered. A rejection must be done within a reasonable time after delivery or tender to the buyer. After a rejection, the buyer may not claim ownership of the goods. In addition, the buyer must notify the seller of the particular defect in the goods so as to give the seller an opportunity to correct the defect. If the goods are in the buyer's possession, the buyer must hold them with reasonable care long enough for the seller to remove them. A buyer who is not a merchant has no other obligation regarding goods that are rightfully rejected.

UCC 2-604 (see page 972)

Buyer's Duties in General

If the seller gives no instructions within a reasonable time after being notified of the rejection, the buyer may store the goods for the seller, reship them to the seller, or resell them for the seller. In all cases, the buyer is entitled to be reimbursed for expenses.

Merchant Buyer's Duties

A special duty comes into existence when a buyer who is a merchant rejects goods. Merchant buyers have a duty after the rejection of goods in their possession or control to follow any reasonable instructions received from the seller with respect to the goods. If there are no such instructions, they must make reasonable efforts to sell the goods for the seller if they are perishable or threaten to decline speedily in value.

Merchants who sell rejected goods are entitled to be reimbursed either by the seller or from the proceeds of the sale for reasonable expenses of caring for and selling the goods. They are also entitled to such commission as is usual in the trade or, if none, a reasonable sum not exceeding 10 percent of the proceeds of the sale.

UCC 2-603(1) (see page 972)

UCC 2-603(2) (see page 972)

UCC 2-606 (see page 972)

Acceptance

Once goods have been accepted, they cannot be rejected. Acceptance of goods takes place when the buyer, after a reasonable opportunity to inspect them, does any of the following:

- Signifies to the seller that the goods are conforming, that is, that they are in accordance with the obligations under the contract.
- Signifies to the seller a willingness to take them even though they are not conforming.
- Fails to reject them.
- Performs any act that is inconsistent with the seller's ownership.

The Opening Case Revisited, Part III
"Mango Mania"

Garden-Fresh should not have thrown away the lemons. The company had a special duty to follow Moonlight's instructions to sell the lemons, and it would have been entitled to receive its usual commission.

EXAMPLE 18-5:   Buyer's Use of Goods

Kandy Corp. bought concrete-forming equipment from Economy Forms Corp. Kandy used the equipment for six months before notifying Economy that it was inadequate. The court held that the use of the forms in construction was an act inconsistent with the seller's ownership and constituted an acceptance of the goods by Kandy.

When the buyer accepts goods and later discovers something wrong with them, the buyer must notify the seller within a reasonable time after the discovery. The failure to give proper notice will prevent the buyer from having recourse against the seller.

UCC 2-607(3) (see page 972)

Revocation of Acceptance

If a buyer has accepted goods on the assumption that their nonconformity would be corrected by the seller and the seller does not do so, the buyer may revoke the acceptance. This revocation must be made within a reasonable time after the buyer discovers the nonconformity. A revocation of an acceptance is not effective until the buyer notifies the seller of it. Buyers who revoke an acceptance have the same rights and duties with regard to the goods involved as if they had rejected them.

UCC 2-608 (see page 973)

International Law   Under international law, the buyer must notify the seller within a reasonable time after discovering a lack of conformity of the goods. If such notice is not given, the buyer loses the right to claim that the goods did not conform to the contract. Even then, any such notice must be given to the seller no later than two years after the goods were actually handed over to the buyer.

CISG Article 39 (see page 1022)

Quick Quiz 18-3 True or False?

1. Buyers have no right to inspect goods before paying for them when they are shipped c.o.d.

2. After a rejection of goods, the buyer must notify the seller of the particular defect in the goods so as to give the seller an opportunity to correct the defect.

3. Merchant buyers have a duty after the rejection of goods in their possession to follow any reasonable instructions received from the seller with respect to the goods.

A Question of Ethics
Principal No. 3: Respect Others (Part 1)

Keeping secrets and telling the truth are two basics when it comes to being a good friend and associate, but they're not always easy to do.

There are three important ways to fulfill our ethical obligation to treat others with respect:

• Protecting Confidentiality
• Telling the Truth
• Keeping Our Promises

There's a lot to be said about each, so this week we'll focus on the first two.

PROTECTING CONFIDENTIALITY

What keeps a relationship alive? Why do your customers remain your customers? How do you explain the fact that your dearest friends have stayed by your side over the years? There are many possible answers to these questions, but they are all rooted in a simple moral concept: trust. When others trust you, they are more likely to continue being your customer, employer, or friend. Without trust, there isn't much possibility of having a meaningful relationship—or any relationship at all.

For example, if your clients couldn't trust you to protect the information contained on their credit cards, they surely wouldn't remain your customers for long. If a friend discovers that you have blabbed a secret he shared with you about a sensitive personal matter, he will question what kind of friend you are. If you muster the courage to disclose to your therapist, minister, or rabbi a deeply held anxiety you have, and you find out that your confidante jokingly shared this information at a cocktail party, your faith in this person would be shattered.

The information that's most important to us (including but not limited to, financial, psychological, or medical information) is an extension of who we are and what we value. When we share that information with someone, we rightly expect him or her to disclose it only to others who have a genuine need to know. Your family physician appropriately tells a specialist about the result of your latest examination, but she shouldn't go home and discuss it with her spouse.

Of course, the duty to protect confidentiality is not absolute. If you tell your therapist that you plan to kill your ex-girlfriend, and you're serious about it, your therapist has a duty to disclose this information to relevant third parties, such as law enforcement. In this case, the duty to protect another's life outweighs the duty to protect confidentiality. These situations are rare, however, and we violate the rule of confidentiality at our peril.

TELLING THE TRUTH

Another way that we show respect for others is by telling them the truth. There are several caveats here: We have a duty to tell the truth only to those who have a right to it; and the duty to tell the truth, like the duty to keep confidences, is extremely important—but it is not absolute.

With regard to the first proviso, imagine your boss asking you, "So how is your sex life?" You not only have a right not to provide a truthful response, but you would be entirely justified in telling him that it's none of his business, in whatever colorful or poetic way you wish. On the other hand, if your boss asks you why you botched a certain client's account, then you ought to tell him what happened, even if doing so reveals something about yourself about which you're not particularly proud (e.g., you didn't follow up with the client in the way you should have, or at all).

Regarding caveat No. 2, imagine that a friend asks you if you like the new dress she has just bought, and you think it looks horrible. Telling her the truth would not only hurt her feelings, it would give her information that she probably doesn't want in the first place. (After all, since she has already bought the dress, does she want to know exactly what you think, or does she want what Oprah might call "validation"? The smart money is on the latter.)

The challenge to living an ethical life is finding ways to honor both the duties to do no harm and to be truthful. Regarding your friend, you could, for example, find something about the dress that you do like, and mention only that ("I really like you in bright colors," or "I love that fabric").

On a more serious note, the courageous people in World War II who lied to the Nazis to protect Jews in hiding were doing the right thing, because they rightly valued protecting human life over the duty to be truthful. As we saw with exceptions to the duty to protect confidentiality, however, this situation is both extreme and rare, and thus in most circumstances, our instinct should be to tell the truth, at least to those who have a rightful claim to it, and to the extent that we can do so without violating the other ethical principles at stake.

Source: Bruce Weinstein, "Principle No. 3: Respect Others (Part 1)," *BusinessWeek.com,* January 25, 2007.

18-4 Seller's Right to Cure Improper Tender

Sellers may sometimes **cure** an improper tender or delivery of goods; that is, they may correct the defect that caused the goods to be rejected by the buyer. When the time for performance has not yet expired, the seller has the right to cure the defect and make a proper tender within the contract time. If the time for performance has expired, the seller is allowed to have an additional amount of time to substitute a conforming tender if the seller has reasonable grounds to believe that the goods that were delivered were acceptable. In all cases, sellers must notify buyers that they are going to cure the improper tender or delivery.

UCC 2-508 (see page 970)

EXAMPLE 18-6:   Cure of Improper Tender

Caravan Motel ordered 10 dozen bath towels from samples shown by Fleming Towel Company's representative. The representative made a mistake in writing up the order. As a result, the towels that were delivered were inferior to those shown to Caravan at the time the order was given. Caravan rejected them. Because the Fleming Towel Company had reasonable grounds to believe that Caravan Motel would accept the towels that were delivered, it was allowed additional time to substitute correct towels for the ones that were delivered. When it learned of the rejection, Fleming Towel Company was required to notify the motel that it intended to cure the nonconforming delivery.

The Opening Case Revisited, Part IV
"Mango Mania"

Because the mangos were delivered to Moonlight before the date of delivery, Moonlight was not in breach of contract and would be responsible for paying José Garcia for them.

The seller does not have the right to cure improper tender when a buyer accepts nonconforming goods, even though the buyer may later sue the seller for breach of contract. The seller has this right only when the buyer either rejects the goods tendered or revokes an acceptance of the goods.

CISG Article 37 (see page 1021)

International Law   Under international law, the seller may cure any defect in the goods if the goods were delivered before the date of delivery. Up to that date, the seller may deliver any missing part, make up any deficiency in the quantity of goods delivered, or replace any defective goods without being in breach of contract. However, the seller may exercise this right only if it does not cause the buyer unreasonable inconvenience or expense.

Quick Quiz 18-4 True or False?

1. When time for performance has not yet expired, the seller may cure a defect and make proper tender within the contract time.

2. If the time for performance has expired, the seller is never allowed time to cure a defect.

3. The seller has the right to cure improper tender even when the buyer accepts nonconforming goods.

18-5 Breach of Contract

Breach of contract occurs when one of the parties fails to do what was agreed upon in the contract. When this happens, the other party to the contract has specific remedies available under the UCC. All parties must attempt to mitigate the damages, that is, to keep them as low as possible.

Anticipatory Breach

UCC 2-610 (see page 973)

Sometimes, one of the parties will notify the other party before the time for performance that he or she is not going to conform. This notification is known as *anticipatory breach* (see Chapter 15). It is a breach committed before there is a present duty to perform the contract. Under older contractual law, the injured party in such a case had to wait until the actual time for performance before bringing suit or taking some other action. It was necessary to wait for the actual time for performance to know for sure that the other party was indeed not going to perform. Under the UCC, when either party repudiates the contract before the time for performance, the injured party may take action immediately if waiting would be unjust or cause a material inconvenience. Any of the remedies for breach of contract are available to the aggrieved party, in addition to the right to suspend his or her own performance.

EXAMPLE 18-7:   Anticipatory Breach

Baily ordered 10 steel I-beams to be made to order from Midwest Steel Co. for use in a building that Baily was going to begin building in six months. Midwest Steel agreed to deliver the I-beams on or before that date. Two months before the delivery date, Midwest Steel notified Baily that it would not be able to fill the order. Baily could treat the contract as having been breached and use any of the buyer's remedies that are available to him under the UCC.

Seller's Remedies When Buyer Breaches

When a buyer breaches a sales contract, the seller may select from a number of remedies. Table 18-1 lists remedies sellers may employ when the buyer breaches.

UCC 2-703(a) (see page 975)

Withhold Delivery of Goods If the goods have not been delivered, the seller has a right to keep them upon learning of the buyer's breach.

Stop Delivery of the Goods If, after shipping the goods, the seller discovers that the buyer is **insolvent** (unable to pay debts), the seller may have the delivery stopped. This right is known as **stoppage in transit** and is permitted after goods have been shipped but before they have reached their destination.

The seller must give information to the **carrier** (the transportation company) to satisfy the latter that the buyer is insolvent. In addition, the seller must accept responsibility for any damage suffered by the carrier for not completing the shipment. If the insolvency information is incorrect, both the seller and the carrier could be sued for damages.

UCC 2-705 (see page 975)

The seller may also stop delivery of a carload, truckload, planeload, or larger shipments of express or freight when the buyer repudiates or fails to make a payment that is due before delivery or otherwise breaches the contract. If the seller has issued a

---

Table 18-1   Seller's Remedies When the Buyer Breaches

1. Withhold delivery of any goods not yet delivered.

2. If the buyer is insolvent, stop delivery of any goods that are still in the possession of a carrier.

3. Resell any goods that have been rightfully withheld, and then sue the buyer for the difference between the agreed price and the resale price.

4. If the goods cannot be resold, sue the buyer for the difference between the agreed price and the market price.

5. Sue the buyer for the price of any goods that were accepted by the buyer.

6. Cancel the contract.

document of title, the seller can stop delivery only by surrendering the document to the carrier. If the buyer has received the document, delivery of the goods cannot be stopped in transit.

UCC 2-706(1) (see page 975)

UCC 2-704(2) (see page 975)

Resell the Goods

The seller may resell the goods or the undelivered balance of them. In the case of unfinished manufactured goods, a seller may either complete the manufacture and resell the finished goods or cease manufacture and resell the unfinished goods for scrap or salvage value. In such cases, the seller must use reasonable commercial judgment to avoid losses. After the sale, the injured party may sue the other for the difference between what the property brought on resale and the price the buyer had agreed to pay in the contract.

UCC 2-706(4)(b) (see page 976)

Resale may be a public or private sale. If it is a private sale, the seller must give the buyer reasonable notice of its intention to resell the goods. If it is a public sale, it must be made at a place that is normally used for public sales, if such a place is available. In addition, if the goods are perishable or threaten to decline in value speedily, the seller must give the buyer reasonable notice of the time and place of resale.

UCC 2-706(4)(d) (see page 976)

A purchaser who buys in good faith at a resale takes the goods free of any rights of the original buyer. Furthermore, the seller is not accountable to the buyer for any profit made on the resale. The seller who chooses to do so may buy the goods at resale.

UCC 2-708 (see page 976)

UCC 2-710 (see page 976)

Recover Damages

The seller may retain the merchandise and sue the buyer for either the difference between the contract price and the market price at the time the buyer breached the agreement or the profit (including overhead) that the seller would have made had the contract been performed. In either case, the seller is also entitled to *incidental damages*. These damages are reasonable expenses that indirectly result from the breach, such as expenses incurred in stopping delivery of goods, transporting goods, and caring for goods after the buyer's breach.

UCC 2-709 (see page 976)

Sue for Price

The seller may sue for the price of any goods that the buyer has accepted. Similarly, upon the buyer's breach, the seller may bring suit for the price of goods that cannot be resold at a reasonable price. In addition, the seller may sue the buyer for the price of any lost or damaged goods after the risk of their loss has passed to the buyer. The seller who sues the buyer for the price must hold for the buyer any goods that are under the seller's control. The goods may be sold, however, at any time resale is possible before the collection of a judgment in the case. The net proceeds of any resale must be credited to the buyer. Any goods that are not resold become the property of the buyer if the buyer pays for them as a result of a court judgment.

UCC 2-106 (see page 960)

Cancel the Contract

The seller can cancel the contract. This cancellation occurs when the seller puts an end to the contract because the other party breached. When cancellation takes place in this manner, the seller may use any of the remedies mentioned for breach of contract.

Buyer's Remedies When Seller Breaches

When the seller breaches the contract by failing to deliver goods or delivering improper goods, the buyer may cancel the contract and recover any money paid out. The buyer may also choose any of the remedies outlined in Table 18-2.

UCC 2-711 (see page 976)

UCC 2-712 (see page 977)

Cover the Sale

The buyer may **cover** the sale, that is, buy similar goods from someone else. The buyer may then sue the seller for the difference between the agreed price and the cost of the purchase. Cover must be made without unreasonable delay.

Table 18-2   Buyer's Remedies When the Seller Breaches

1. Cancel the contract.

2. Sue the seller for the return of any money that has been paid.

3. Cover the sale—that is, buy similar goods from someone else and sue the seller for the difference between the agreed price and the cost of the purchase.

4. Sue the seller for the difference between the agreed price and the market price at the time the buyer learned of the breach.

5. If nonconforming goods have been accepted, notify the seller that they do not conform to the contract. Then, if no adjustment is made, sue the seller either for breach of contract or for breach of warranty.

6. When goods are unique or rare, sue for specific performance.

EXAMPLE 18-8:   Cover of a Sales Contract

Flamme Bros. contracted to deliver a specific quantity of corn to Farmers' Union Co-op Co., a cooperative grain elevator. When Flamme Bros. failed to deliver the corn, Farmers' Union bought corn from its members over a two-week period. The court held that this purchase was cover of the contract without unreasonable delay. Farmers' Union recovered the difference between the agreed price of the corn from Flamme Bros. and the price it paid to the farmers for the corn it bought.

Sue for Breach   When a seller breaches a contract by not delivering the goods, the buyer may sue for damages if any were suffered. The measure of damages is the difference between the price that the parties agreed upon and the price of the same goods in the marketplace on the date the buyer learned of the breach. In addition, the buyer may sue for incidental and consequential damages.

UCC 2-713 (see page 977)

UCC 2-715 (see page 977)

UCC 2-718(1) (see page 977)

Damages for breach of contract may be liquidated, that is, agreed upon by the parties when they first enter into the contract. Liquidated damages will be allowed by the court if they are reasonable. These damages are discussed in more detail in Chapter 15.

Keep Goods and Seek Adjustment   When improper goods are delivered, the buyer may keep them and ask the seller for an adjustment. If no adjustment is made, the buyer may sue the seller for either breach of contract or breach of warranty, whichever applies. The amount of the suit would be the difference between the value of the goods contracted for and the value of the goods received. Warranties are discussed in Chapter 19.

UCC 2-714(2) (see page 977)

EXAMPLE 18-9:   Swimsuit Adjustment

Bare Essentials, Inc., ordered 20 dozen swimsuits from a swimsuit manufacturer. The suits that were delivered were different from the samples shown by the manufacturer's representative. Because the store needed swimsuits for its spring trade, it decided to keep them. If no adjustment is made by the manufacturer, Bare Essentials, Inc., can sue the manufacturer for damages (including loss of profits) that were suffered because of the breach of the express warranty that the goods would be the same as the sample.

UCC 2-716(1) (see page 977)

Sue for Specific Performance   When the goods are unique or rare, the buyer may ask the court to order the seller to do what he or she agreed to do under the contract terms. This request is known as an action for specific performance of the contract. A decree of specific performance, if granted by the court, would require the seller to deliver to the buyer the goods described in the sales agreement. This type of action is permitted only when an award of money will not give the buyer sufficient relief. Contracts for *objets d'art*, rare gems, antiques, and goods described as one-of-a-kind come within the scope of this type of action. Under the UCC, the decree of specific performance may include the payment of the price, damages, or other relief as the court may deem just. Specific performance is discussed in more detail in Chapter 15.

UCC 2-716(3) (see page 977)

Buyers have a right of replevin for goods that have been identified to the contract if, after a reasonable effort, they are unable to buy the goods elsewhere. A **writ of replevin** is a court action that allows a person entitled to goods to recover them from someone who has them wrongfully.

UCC 2-725 (see page 979)

Statute of Limitations

Nearly all lawsuits have a time limit within which suit must be brought. If the time limit is exceeded, the action is forever barred. In general, an action for breach of a sales contract must be brought within four years after the date of the breach. The parties may, if they wish to do so, provide for a shorter time period, not less than one year, in their sales agreement. They may not, however, agree to a period longer than four years.

CISG Article 49 (see page 1023)

International Sales   Under international law, the buyer may declare the contract avoided if there is a fundamental breach of contract by the seller. In such a case, if the seller has delivered the goods, the buyer must declare the contract avoided within a reasonable time after learning of the breach. If the delivery is late however, the buyer must declare the contract avoided within a reasonable time after learning that delivery has been made or lose the right to avoid the contract. If the goods do not conform to the contract, the buyer may reduce the price proportionately. This action may not be taken, however, if the seller remedies the defect or the buyer refuses to allow the seller to remedy the defect.

CISG Articles 61–64 (see page 1024)

If the buyer fails to perform any obligations, the seller may require the buyer to pay the price, take delivery, or perform any other obligations. In addition, the seller may fix an additional period of time for performance by the buyer. The seller may also declare the contract voided if there is a breach of contract by the buyer. However, if the buyer has paid the price, the seller must declare the contract voided within a reasonable time after learning of the breach. Also, if the buyer pays late, the seller cannot declare the contract voided after becoming aware that the buyer has paid.

CISG Articles 74–77 (see page 1025)

Damages for breach of contract by one party consist of a sum equal to the loss, including lost profits, suffered by the other party as a consequence of the breach. The damages may not exceed the loss that the breaching party ought to have foreseen. As with the UCC, if there has been a breach and the buyer has bought goods in replacement or the seller has resold the goods, the party claiming damages may recover the difference between the contract price and the price in the substitute transaction. Likewise, if there has not been a purchase or resale, the party claiming damages may recover the difference between the contract price and the market price of the goods. Anyone who relies on a breach of contract must take reasonable measures to mitigate those damages.

A party is not liable for the failure to perform an obligation if the failure was due to an unforeseen impediment that was beyond the party's control.

CISG Articles 79 (see page 1026)

Avoidance of a contract releases both parties from their obligations, subject to any damages that may be due. A party who has performed the contract either in whole or in part may claim restitution from the other party. If both parties are bound to make restitution, they must do so at the same time.

CISG Articles 81 (see page 1026)

Both sellers and buyers are required to take steps to preserve the goods when there is a breach of contract. The goods may be deposited in a warehouse for safekeeping. In appropriate cases, such as when there could be rapid deterioration, goods may be sold after notice is given to the other party.

CISG Articles 85–88 (see page 1027)

Quick Quiz 18-5 True or False?

1. When a buyer breaches a sales contract, the seller may, among other things, resell any goods that have been rightfully withheld, and then sue the buyer for the difference between the agreed price and the resale price.

2. When a seller breaches a sales contract, the buyer may always sue the seller for specific performance of the contract.

3. In general, a lawsuit for breach of a sales contract must be brought within six years after the date of the breach.

Summary

18.1 Sellers and buyers must follow the terms of their contract and act in good faith.

18.2 Tender of performance is necessary to test the other party's ability and willingness to perform. Tender of delivery requires the seller to make conforming goods available to the buyer at a reasonable hour of the day. Tender of payment may be made by any means that is commonly used in the ordinary course of business. The seller may demand legal tender if he or she gives the buyer a reasonable time to obtain it.

18.3 Except when goods are shipped c.o.d. or when the contract provides for payment against a document of title, the buyer has the right to inspect goods before accepting or paying for them. When improper goods are delivered, the buyer may elect to reject all of them, accept all of them, or accept any commercial unit or units and reject the rest. Rejection of goods must be done within a reasonable time, and the buyer must notify the seller of the reason for the rejection. Even after accepting goods, buyers may revoke an acceptance if the goods were accepted on the assumption that their nonconformity would be corrected or if their nonconformity could not be easily detected.

18.4 Sellers may cure defects or nonconformities that caused the goods to be rejected by the buyer.

18.5 When a buyer breaches a sales contract, the seller may withhold delivery of any goods not yet delivered, stop goods that are in transit, resell the goods or the undelivered balance of them, retain the goods and bring suit for damages, bring suit for the price of any goods that the buyer has accepted, or cancel the contract. When a seller breaches a sales contract, the buyer may cancel the contract and recover any money paid out, buy similar goods from someone else and sue the seller for the difference in price, sue the seller for damages for nondelivery, keep the goods and deduct the cost of damages from any price still due, or sue for specific performance if the goods are rare or unique.

Key Terms

carrier, 363	insolvent, 363	tender of performance, 355
commercial unit, 357	legal tender, 356	unconscionable contract, 353
cover, 364	stoppage in transit, 363	writ of replevin, 366
cure, 361	tender of delivery, 355	
good faith, 353	tender of payment, 356	

Questions for Review and Discussion

1. What are the obligations of parties to a sales contract? Describe them in general terms.
2. Why is tender of performance necessary?
3. What is required of the seller in making tender of delivery? What form of payment may be used by the buyer in making tender of payment? When may the seller demand legal tender?
4. What is the right of the buyer to inspect goods that are received under a sales contract? Explain.
5. What three choices does a buyer have when defective or nonconforming goods are delivered?
6. Describe the manner in which buyers must reject goods if they decide to do so. After a rejection, what may buyers do with goods in their possession? What special duty applies to a merchant buyer?
7. When can a seller correct an improper tender of delivery?
8. How does older contractual law compare with the UCC as it applies to anticipatory breach?
9. What remedies are available to a seller when a buyer breaches a sales contract? Explain.
10. What remedies are available to a buyer when a seller breaches a sales contract? Explain.

Investigating the Internet

Log onto the 'Lectric Law Library's Law Practice Forms by going to **http://www.lectlaw.com/forms.htm.** Click "Our Main Forms Room." Then scroll down to "Business & General Forms" and look for forms that are of interest to you.

Cases for Analysis

1. Kathleen Liarkos purchased a used Jaguar XJS automobile from Pine Grove Auto Sales. After experiencing various mechanical problems, she discovered that the vehicle's odometer had been turned back. Liarkos notified the seller that she revoked her acceptance of the vehicle. When is this

remedy available to a buyer? *Liarkos v. Mello,* 639 N.E.2d 716 (MA).

2. P&F Construction Corporation ordered 338 door units for an apartment condominium project from Friend Lumber Corporation. The doors were delivered to the job site three weeks after they were ordered. Each door unit came wrapped in clear plastic. Three and one-half months after receiving the door units, P&F Construction notified Friend Lumber that the doors were one-quarter inch off size. P&F refused to pay Friend Lumber the balance due. What rule of law may Friend Lumber use to recover the money owed? *P&F Const. v. Friend Lumber Corp.,* 575 N.E.2d 61 (MA).

3. William Young had cut evergreen boughs and sold them exclusively to Frank's Nursery & Crafts, Inc., for 10 years. Upon receiving a $238,000 order for 360 tons of boughs from Frank's, Young obtained cutting rights from many farmers, repaired his machinery, and made 75 new hand tyers to tie the evergreen bundles. Several months later, Frank's reduced its order to less than $60,000 for about 70 tons of boughs. Young delivered the 70 tons of boughs and sued Frank's for breach of contract. How were Young's damages computed? *Young v. Frank's Nursery & Crafts, Inc.,* 569 N.E.2d 1034 (OH).

4. Herman Googe agreed to buy an automobile from Irene Schleimer. Later, Googe changed his mind and refused to buy the car. Schleimer, without making tender of delivery, brought suit against Googe for breach of contract. Did Schleimer recover damages? Explain. *Schleimer v. Googe,* 377 N.Y.S.2d 591 (NY).

5. Mr. and Mrs. Aldridge bought a motor home from Sportsman Travel Trailer Sales, located in Texas. Two years later, after traveling more than 14,000 miles on trips to Louisiana, Colorado, and California, they attempted to reject the motor home, claiming that it was defective. Could they return the vehicle and recover damages? Explain. *Explorer Motor Home Corp. v. Aldridge,* 541 S.W.2d 851 (TX).

6. Dehahn agreed to sell and Innes agreed to buy for the price of $35,000 a 35-acre gravel pit, a back hoe, a bulldozer, a loader, two dump trucks, and a low-bed trailer. Dehahn had recently lost his bid for reelection as road commissioner in the town, so he was required to remove the equipment from town property. He moved the equipment to a field owned by Innes, across from the driveway to Innes's home, and left the keys in the vehicles.

Later, Innes canceled the contract and refused to make any payments. When sued, Innes argued that Dehahn failed to make tender of delivery of the equipment. Do you agree with Innes? State why or why not. *Dehahn v. Innes,* 356 A.2d 711 (ME).

7. Formetal Engineering Co. placed an order with Presto Manufacturing Co., Inc., for 250,000 polyurethane pads to be used in making air-conditioning units. The pads were to be made according to samples and specifications supplied by Formetal. When the pads arrived, Formetal discovered that they did not conform to the sample and specifications, in that there were incomplete cuts, color variances, and faulty adherence to the pads' paper backing. Formetal notified Presto of the defects and said that it was rejecting the goods and returning them to Presto. The goods, however, were never returned. Was the rejection proper? Explain. *Presto Mfg. Co. v. Formetal Eng'g. Co.,* 360 N.E.2d 510 (IL).

8. City National Bank of Crete agreed to sell and deliver to Goosic Construction Company a set of concrete forms for the sum of $200, which Goosic paid. The forms had been repossessed at an earlier time by the bank and were stored at another location. When Goosic arrived at the storage location to pick up the forms, a Mr. Roberts claimed a storage lien and refused to allow Goosic to take possession of the goods. Goosic never received the forms, which had a fair market value of $1,500. Did the City National Bank make proper tender of delivery? If Goosic Construction Company won the case, how much would it recover? Give reasons for your answers. *Goosic Const. Co. v. City Natl. Bank,* 241 N.W.2d 521 (NE).

9. Sagebrush Sales Co. sold building materials to Pace, a retail lumber dealer. As the goods were unloaded at Pace's lumberyard, Pace noticed that two of the truckloads contained materials that he had not ordered. He nevertheless permitted the unordered goods to be unloaded without objection and wrote on his copy of the invoice "not ordered." Pace then telephoned Sagebrush's office and asked why they were sending him extra lumber. The employee replied that he did not know but that he would have the salesperson call Pace. No further complaint was made by Pace to Sagebrush. The goods were placed into Pace's inventory and offered for sale to the public. Pace made a partial payment for the goods but refused to pay the full amount, claiming that he had not accepted the unordered goods. Do you agree with Pace? Why or

why not? *Pace v. Sagebrush Sales Co.,* 560 P.2d 789 (AZ).

10. Carolyn McQueen bought a new Fiat Spider from American Imports, Inc. The deal included a $500 trade-in allowance on McQueen's Oldsmobile, and McQueen borrowed the money to buy the car from a credit union. She paid for the Fiat by check and promised to deliver an Oldsmobile for trade-in the next week. Two days later, the Fiat overheated. McQueen had also discovered that neither the speedometer nor the odometer functioned properly. American Imports, Inc., towed the car to its garage, replaced a broken fan belt, and tightened a nut on the speedometer that also controlled the odometer. After the repairs were made, McQueen refused to take the car, saying that she wanted a new one. She stopped payment on the check. When sued for the purchase price, McQueen claimed that she had revoked her acceptance of the Fiat and could therefore cancel the contract. Was McQueen within her rights? Why or why not? *American Imports, Inc., v. G.E. Emp. West. Region Fed. Credit Union,* 245 S.E.2d 798 (NC).

Quick Quiz Answers

18-1	18-2	18-3	18-4	18-5
1. T	1. T	1. T	1. T	1. T
2. F	2. T	2. T	2. F	2. F
3. F	3. F	3. T	3. F	3. F

Chapter 19

Warranties and Product Liability

The Opening Case
"The Jewel"

While browsing through a used car lot, Ortega was approached by a fast-talking salesperson who said, "I've got a beauty that just came in. Take a look at that baby," pointing to a shiny, red Mustang. "It's a jewel, and I can let it go at a good price. You won't find a better car for the money anywhere."

"What'll it get for mileage?" Ortega asked.

"I guarantee you'll get 35 miles per gallon driving in the city with that beauty," the salesperson quickly replied.

Ortega bought the Mustang and discovered, after a few weeks, that the car's mileage averaged 19 miles per gallon in city driving instead of the 35 miles the salesperson had guaranteed.

Four months later, Ortega returned to the used car lot and reminded the salesperson of the guarantee. The salesperson responded, "Oh, we don't make guarantees. Take a look at your sales slip." Ortega then saw that the salesperson had written the words "as is" on the sales slip.

Opening Case Questions

1. Are the comments, "It's a jewel," and "You won't find a better car for the money anywhere," considered warranties?

2. Is the salesperson's oral guarantee of 35 miles per gallon a warranty?

3. Do the words "as is" written on the sales slip assist the dealer in this case?

4. Can Ortega win a lawsuit against the dealer for damages?

LO Learning Objectives

1. Describe the three ways in which an express warranty may be created.
2. State the requirements of the Magnuson-Moss Warranty Act.
3. Compare the meaning of a "limited" warranty with that of a "full" warranty.
4. Differentiate among the implied warranties of fitness for a particular purpose, merchantability, and usage of trade.
5. Explain the warranty of title.
6. Describe the duty to notify sellers of a defective product.

7. Recognize the ways in which warranties may be excluded.
8. Determine the persons to whom warranties are made under the laws of your state.
9. State why it is often difficult for a consumer to win a product liability case on the theory of negligence.
10. Explain what an injured party must prove under the strict liability theory to recover from the manufacturer of a dangerous and defective product.

19-1 Warranty Protection

Have you ever bought something that did not work when you took it home? Have you ever purchased an item that turned out to be damaged or broken when you opened the box? Have you ever paid for something that you wanted for a particular purpose, only to find that it would not do the job? Has a salesperson ever made a statement or a promise about a product that did not come true? Have you ever found an impurity or a foreign substance in food that you bought in a store or ate in a restaurant? The UCC gives you protection in all of these types of situations under its law of warranties. A warranty is another name for a guarantee.

UCC 2-313 (see page 964)

Express Warranties

An **express warranty** is an oral or written statement, promise, or other representation about the quality of a product. Express warranties arise in three different ways: by a statement of fact or promise, by a description of the goods, or by a sample or model.

In states that have adopted Article 2A of the UCC, express warranties arise when goods are leased in exactly the same way that they arise when goods are sold.

UCC 2A-210 (see page 983)

UCC 2-313(1)(2) (see page 964)

Statement of Fact or Promise   Whenever a seller of goods makes a statement of fact about the goods to a buyer as part of the transaction, an express warranty is created. The seller's statement is treated legally as a guarantee that the goods will be as they were stated to be. This guarantee exists whether the seller is a merchant or not. If the goods are not as they were stated to be, the seller has breached an express warranty.

> ### EXAMPLE 19-1:   Statement of Fact
>
> Wambach went into a furniture store and told the clerk that he wanted a mahogany table. The clerk showed Wambach a table and said that it was made of solid mahogany. Soon after buying it, Wambach learned that the table was made of pressed wood covered by a mahogany veneer. The statement by the clerk was an express warranty that the table was made of solid mahogany. Wambach would be able to sue the store for breach of express warranty if the store refused to remedy the situation.

An express warranty also occurs when a seller makes a promise about the goods to a buyer. The promise must relate to the goods and be part of the transaction.

Manufacturers often include express warranties with the products they sell. They are usually found inside the package containing the product and are sometimes referred to as guarantees.

Formal words such as *warranty* or *guarantee* do not have to be used to create an express warranty. A seller may not intend to make a warranty, but if the language used by the seller is a statement of fact or a promise about the goods and is part of the transaction, an express warranty is created. Advertisements often contain statements and promises about goods that are express warranties.

The Opening Case Revisited, Part I
"The Jewel"

The salesperson's statement that Ortega will get 35 miles per gallon driving in the city is an express warranty. The fact that it is oral makes no difference, other than that it may be difficult for Ortega to prove.

EXAMPLE 19-2:   Advertisement Creates Warranty

Tuffco Auto Polish was advertised as a safe, noncorrosive polish, manufactured to the highest standards required of finishes. Myron bought a can of the polish, and it ruined the finish of her new car. Myron could have sought damages against the seller, claiming that the advertised statements were warranties made to any prospective purchaser.

Warranties are based on statements of fact. Opinions of salespersons and exaggerated and persuasive statements are not included. Courts have long recognized the temptation of salespersons to indulge in sales puffery or to extol their wares beyond the point of fact. Buyers must use good judgment in separating a seller's statements of fact from statements that are opinion or puffery. Such statements as "this is the best television set on the market" or "this VCR is a good buy" are examples of sales talk or puffery. They are not express warranties.

Description of the Goods   Any description of the goods that is made part of the basis of the bargain creates an express warranty that the goods will be as described.

UCC 2-313(1)(b) (see page 964)

EXAMPLE 19-3:   Catalog Description Creates Warranty

Kiley ordered a gas grill from a catalog. The catalog description said that the grill contained a swing-away warming rack. The grill that was delivered, however, had a fixed warming rack. Kiley could have had a cause of action against the seller for breach of express warranty if the seller refused to remedy the situation.

The Opening Case Revisited, Part II
"The Jewel"

The salesperson's statements to Ortega that "It's a jewel" and "You won't find a better car for the money anywhere" are examples of puffery and would not be considered express warranties.

Sample or Model   It is a common practice of salespeople to show samples of their products to prospective buyers. When a sample or model becomes part of the basis of the bargain, an express warranty is created. The seller warrants that the goods that will be delivered are the same as the sample or model.

UCC 2-313(1)(c) (see page 964)

CISG Articles 35 and 36 (see page 1021)

International Law   Under the CISG, sellers must deliver goods that are of the quantity, quality, and description required by the contract. Except when agreed otherwise, the goods do not conform with the contract unless they are fit for the purpose for which goods of the same description would ordinarily be used and for any particular purpose made known to the seller and relied on by the buyer. Also, the goods must be of the quality of goods that the seller has held out to the buyer as a sample or model and contained or packaged in the manner usual for such goods.

Advertising Express Warranties   The Federal Trade Commission has established specific rules for advertising express warranties on goods that are sold in interstate commerce:

- An advertisement stating that a product is warranted must tell you how to get a copy of the warranty before you buy the product.

- Advertisers who use expressions such as "Satisfaction Guaranteed," "Money-Back Guarantee," and "Free Trial Offer" must refund the full purchase price of their product at the purchaser's request. Any conditions, such as those limiting the return of the product, must be stated in the ad.

- Advertisers who warrant products for a lifetime must fully explain the terms of their promises, such as "Good for as long as you own the car."

Always read the agreement fully. A full refund often doesn't include shipping and handling costs and may require that the items be returned in their original packaging.

Magnuson-Moss Warranty Act   The federal Magnuson-Moss Warranty Act is designed to prevent deceptive warranty practices and provide consumers with more information about warranties that are made on products they buy. The act applies only when written warranties are made voluntarily for purchases of **consumer products**. These products are defined as tangible personal property normally used for personal, family, or household purposes. Because it is a federal law, the act affects only warranties on products that are sold in interstate commerce.

Under the act, when a written warranty is given to a consumer on goods costing more than $10, the warranty must disclose whether it is a full or a limited warranty. When goods cost more than $15, the written warranty must be made available before the consumer decides to buy the product. The writing must express the terms and conditions of the warranty in simple and readily understood language.

A **full warranty** is one in which a defective product will be repaired without charge within a reasonable time after a complaint has been made about it. If it cannot be repaired within a reasonable time, the consumer may have either a replacement of the product or a refund of the purchase price. The consumer will not have to do anything unreasonable to get warranty service, such as ship a heavy product to the factory. A full warranty applies to anyone who owns the product during the warranty period, not only the original buyer. A full warranty must also state its duration, for example, a "full one-year warranty."

> ## EXAMPLE 19-4:   Full Warranty
>
> Kienitz bought an electric range manufactured by a well-known firm. Attached to the box containing the range were several papers, one of which read as follows: "Full one-year warranty. If your range fails because of a manufacturing defect within one-year from the date of original purchase, we will repair the product without charge to you. Parts and service labor are included. Service will be provided in your home in the forty-eight contiguous states, the state of Hawaii, or in the District of Columbia." This paper was a full warranty.

A **limited warranty** is any written warranty that does not meet all of the requirements for a full warranty. The consumer is not given the absolute, free-of-charge repair or replacement of a defective product, as in the full warranty. Something less than a complete remedy is given to the consumer.

Examples of limited warranties are those that cover only parts, not labor; allow only a pro rata (divided proportionately) refund or credit in the case of a defect rather than a full refund; require the buyer to return a heavy product to the store for service; or cover only the first purchaser.

UCC 2-314(1) (see page 964)

Implied Warranties

Under the UCC, an **implied warranty** is a warranty that is imposed by law rather than by statements, descriptions, or samples given by the seller. It arises independently and outside the contract. The law annexes it, by implication, into the contract that the parties have made. Implied warranties are designed to promote high standards in business and to discourage harsh dealings. There are three types of implied warranties: the implied warranty of merchantability, the implied warranty of fitness for a particular purpose, and the implied warranty that is derived from a course of dealing or usage of trade.

Merchantability One of the most beneficial warranties, from the point of view of a buyer, is the implied **warranty of merchantability**. This warranty provides that, unless excluded in one of the ways discussed, whenever a merchant sells goods, the merchant warrants that the goods are merchantable. This warranty is given when the seller is a merchant with respect to goods of that kind. It is given by manufacturers, wholesalers, and retailers whenever they sell goods to give assurance that products sold by them are fit for the purpose for which the goods are to be used. The warranty of merchantability is not given by someone who is not a merchant.

A warranty of merchantability is a valuable protection for consumers.

> ## EXAMPLE 19-5:   Private Party
>
> Perez bought a second-hand car for $3,500 from Osgood, a private party. Perez drove the car home, parked it in her driveway, and turned off the engine. The next morning, the car would not start. The automobile mechanic who was called to try to start the car informed Perez that it would cost $1,200 to repair the car so that it would start properly. Perez cannot recover from Osgood for breach of warranty of merchantability because Osgood is not a merchant.

To be merchantable, goods must at least pass without objection in the trade under the contract description; if fungible goods, be of fair average quality; be fit for the ordinary purposes for which such goods are used; be of the same kind, quality, and quantity; be adequately contained, packaged, and labeled as the agreement may require; and be in conformance with any promises or statements of fact made on the container or label.

UCC 2-314(2) (see page 964)

EXAMPLE 19-6:   Warranty of Merchantability

If Osgood had been a merchant in Example 19-5, Perez could have recovered from Osgood for breach of warranty of merchantability. An automobile that will not start is not fit for the ordinary purposes for which automobiles are used and is therefore not merchantable.

A claim for breach of warranty of merchantability can be made only when a defect exists at the time the goods are purchased.

EXAMPLE 19-7:   No Defect at Time of Purchase

Haven Hills Farm purchased a truck tire from Sears, Roebuck. On a trip from Mississippi to Alabama, the tire blew out, causing the truck to turn on its side, destroying 11,862 dozen eggs. At the time of the blowout, the tire was four and one-half months old and had been driven 30,000 miles. Haven Hills claimed that Sears was liable for breach of the implied warranty of merchantability. It argued that Sears sold the tire in a defective condition. In finding in favor of Sears, Roebuck, the court held that there was no evidence of a defect in the tire at the time it left the control of the manufacturer or seller.

Day-old chickens with bird cancer, contaminated blood received in a blood transfusion, applesauce that was inedible because of poor taste and smell, contaminated cheese, and food containing impurities are a few examples of goods that the courts have held to be non-merchantable.

Fitness for a Particular Purpose   Sometimes buyers will have the seller select goods for them rather than select them themselves. They rely on the seller's knowledge and experience to choose the product after telling the seller of the particular use they have for the goods. This arrangement creates an implied **warranty of fitness for a particular purpose**. When the buyer relies on the seller's skill and judgment to select the goods, the seller implicitly warrants that the goods will be fit for the purpose for which they are to be used.

UCC 2-315 (see page 964)

EXAMPLE 19-8:   Reliance on Seller's Judgment

McGuire purchased a television set in a store that had a sign on the wall declaring, "No refunds!! All sales final!!" McGuire told the clerk that she needed a cable to connect the new set to her VCR. The clerk went to the shelf, selected a cable, and

The Opening Case Revisited, Part III
"The Jewel"

The four-month delay by Ortega to inform the car dealer of the breach of warranty would probably be found by a court to exceed the reasonable time period within which the dealer must be notified.

told McGuire that the cable would do the job. That evening, McGuire discovered that the cable would not fit the VCR. Even though the sign said that all sales were final, McGuire would be able to return the cable. McGuire relied on the store clerk's judgment in selecting the cable, which created an implied warranty that the cable would connect to the VCR.

Usage of Trade   Other implied warranties may arise from the ways in which the parties have dealt in the past or by usage of trade. For example, when a person sells a pedigreed dog, there is an implied warranty that the seller will provide pedigree papers to demonstrate the conformity of the animal to the contract. The reason this implied warranty arises is that providing such papers has become a well-established custom or practice of the trade.

UCC 2-314(3) (see page 964)

Warranty of Title

UCC 2-312(1) (see page 964)

Whenever goods are sold, either by a merchant or a private party, the seller warrants that the title being conveyed is good and that the transfer is rightful. This warranty is known as the **warranty of title**. It includes an implied promise that the goods will be delivered free of any liens (claims of others) about which the buyer has no knowledge. When anyone buys goods that turn out to be stolen, the rightful owner will be entitled to the return of those goods. The innocent purchaser may sue the seller for breach of warranty of title.

EXAMPLE 19-9:   Warranty of Title

Lopez bought a racing bicycle from Perkins at a yard sale for $125. Shortly thereafter, Lopez learned that the bicycle had been stolen from Garcia. Garcia, the true owner, would be entitled to the return of the bicycle. Lopez's rights would be against Perkins for breach of warranty of title.

When the buyer is aware that the person selling the goods does not personally claim title to them, the warranty of title is not made by the seller. Such is the case, for example, in sheriff's sales and sales by personal representatives of estates.

International Law   Under international law, which applies only to sales between businesses whose places of business are in different countries that have adopted the law, the seller must deliver goods that are free from any right or claim of a third party. This rule does not apply, however, when the buyer enters into a contract knowing that others have rights or claims to the goods. Similarly, the rule does not apply when the buyer agrees to take the goods subject to the rights or claims of others. In addition, buyers must notify sellers within a resonable time after becoming aware of any rights or claims of others to the goods.

CISG Articles 41-44 (see page 1022)

Duty to Notify Seller of Defective Product

To recover money damages for breach of warranty, buyers of defective goods must notify the seller of the defect within a reasonable time either after the discovery or after the defect should have been discovered. Failure to do so will prevent them from recovering damages for breach of warranty.

International Law   Under the CISG, buyers must notify sellers within a reasonable time after discovering any lack of conformity of the goods. Recall that the seller must deliver goods that are of the quantity, quality, and description required by the contract. The goods also must be contained or packaged in the manner that is required by the contract. Unless the parties agree otherwise, the goods must be fit for the purposes for which goods of the same description would ordinarily be used; be fit for any particular purpose expressly or implied and made known to the seller, unless the buyer did not rely on the seller's skill and judgment; possess the qualities of goods that the seller has held out to the buyer as samples or models; and be contained or packaged in the manner usual for such goods or, if none exists, in a manner adequate to preserve and protect the goods.

LO6

UCC 2-607(3)(a) (see page 972)

CISG Article 39 (see page 1022)

CISG Article 35 (see page 1021)

Quick Quiz 19-1 True or False?

1. No warranty of title is given when goods are sold by a private party.

2. An implied warranty occurs when a seller makes a promise about the goods to a buyer.

3. Whenever a merchant sells goods, unless it is excluded, the merchant warrants that the goods are merchantable.

19-2 Exclusion of Warranties

To exclude the implied warranty of merchantability in states that allow it, the word *merchantability* must be used in the disclaimer. If the exclusion is in writing, it must be in large, bold type so that it is conspicuous. To exclude the implied warranty of fitness for a particular purpose, the exclusion must be in writing and also be conspicuous.

LO7

UCC 2-316(2) (see page 964)

EXAMPLE 19-10:   Warranty Exclusion

Valdez bought a used car from Kinkaid Motors, Inc., for $2,095. Printed on the sales slip, which Valdez signed, were the following words in large, bold, capital letters: "THE SELLER HEREBY EXCLUDES THE WARRANTY OF MERCHANTABILITY AND FITNESS FOR A PARTICULAR PURPOSE." Two days later, when the car broke down, Valdez had no recourse against the car dealer for breach of either implied warranty.

A Question of Ethics
Principle No. 3: Respect Others (Part 2)

Keeping promises is a cornerstone of respect—for others and ourselves. What would our word be worth if we constantly broke it?

PROMISES AND TRUSTWORTHINESS

You have just made plans to have dinner with a friend you have not seen in a while. Then another friend invites you to a party you would really love to attend, but to do so, you would have to break the engagement with your first friend. What should you do?

The obvious thing is to ask if you can bring your dinner date to the party. Let's assume for the sake of argument that for some reason you can't. It would not only be rude to cancel the dinner date, it would be unethical, because it would involve breaking a promise simply to indulge your own desires.

There are always extenuating circumstances that justify breaking a rule. If, for example, a parent is rushed to the emergency room an hour before the dinner date, we not only have a right to reschedule the dinner, but we have a moral obligation to do so. Our duty to our parent outweighs the duty to our friend. The example we're considering, however, doesn't involve a life-or-death decision

One of the rules that keeps relationships in working order is the rule of keeping our promises. After all, our word would be meaningless if we broke it on a regular basis. At the heart of this moral obligation is the concept of trust. We maintain the trust that people place in us by, among other things, keeping our promises. By keeping the date, you maintain your integrity, and you'll feel better about yourself, even if you end up sacrificing what seems to be the more appealing opportunity. And who knows? You may end up enjoying the dinner after all.

NOT FOR PROFESSIONALS ONLY

Closely related to the concept of promise-keeping is fidelity, or loyalty. We get not only "fidelity," but "confidentiality" (as well as "Fido," the standard nickname for dogs, the most faithful of pets) from the Latin root *fide*. When we speak of a professional having a fiduciary responsibility to a client, we mean that the professional has an ethical obligation to be loyal to his or her client. This duty is tied to the very notion of professionalism.

In fact, the word "professional" comes from another Latin word that means "to make a public declaration." The professional publicly declares to devote his or her knowledge or skills to the benefit of others. This does not mean that physicians or attorneys, for example, have to be self-sacrificing. Rather, professionalism means that in choosing to become a doctor or lawyer, one's primary mission is not to enrich oneself. We go to our physician or lawyer rightly expecting that the recommendations we get will be based on our best interests, not theirs. We trust them to do what is right for us, since they have pledged to do so.

Professionals aren't the only ones who have a duty to keep promises, however; all of us do. Sometimes we create that duty ourselves, such as when we declare, "I promise to call you." Sometimes the duty is created for us, such as when we are hired to do a job. Signing a contract for employment is a legal act, but it is also a form of promise-making and is therefore an ethical act as well. We pledge to our employer that we will do the job that is asked of us. Our employer, in return, promises to create a work environment that allows us to do our job and, every two weeks or so, to pay us.

If we routinely spend our time at work surfing the Internet for shopping bargains or yakking on the phone with friends, we have not only violated our contract; we have broken our promise to our employer and are no longer entitled to remain an employee in good standing. Similarly, if we do our job well but our employer fails to pay us, or turns a blind eye to reports of sexual or racial harassment in the workplace, the company has broken its promise to us, and we are entitled to redress. (Whether it is in our interest to file a lawsuit is another matter.)

PROMISE-KEEPING IN EVERYDAY LIFE

Now that we know the "why" of keeping promises, here are some simple ways we can apply this aspect of Life Principle No. 3 in our business and personal relationships:

1. Don't make promises you can't keep.

2. Keep the promises you make.

3. If you can't keep a promise for a legitimate reason (which does not necessarily include something better coming along), be honest with the person to whom you made the pledge.

Source: Bruce Weinstein, "Principle No. 3: Respect Others (Part 2)," *BusinessWeek.com,* January 31, 2007.

A common practice in the sale of used cars, lawnmowers, electrical appliances, and similar merchandise is for the seller to stipulate that the goods are being sold as is. The use of expressions such as *as is*, *with all faults*, and others is another way to exclude implied warranties. However, those words do not exclude express warranties or the warranty of title.

Implied warranties may also be excluded under the UCC by having buyers examine the goods. When buyers have examined the goods, the sample, or the model as fully as they desire (or have refused to examine them when given the opportunity), there is no implied warranty as to defects that an examination would have revealed.

Under the Magnuson-Moss Warranty Act, any clause purporting to exclude or limit consequential damages for breach of warranty must appear conspicuously on the face of the warranty. **Consequential damages** are losses that do not flow directly and immediately from an act but only from some of the consequences or results of the act.

UCC 2-316(3)(a) (see page 965)

UCC 2-316(3)(b) (see page 965)

Did You Know?

The purchase of automobiles has been the major consumer complaint for many years. To help remedy these problems, individual states have enacted "lemon laws." These are laws that are designed to protect consumers when they buy defective automobiles.

EXAMPLE 19-11:   Consequential Damages

Souci bought a freezer made by a reputable manufacturer. The freezer carried a full one-year warranty. The following sentence appeared in boldface type on the face of the warranty: "In no event shall this company be liable for consequential damages." Shortly after buying the freezer, Souci filled it with $1,500 worth of meat. Several days later, the freezer stopped working owing to a defect in its manufacture. Under the warranty, the company would have to repair or replace the freezer, but it would not be responsible for the loss of the meat. This loss would be considered consequential damage, which the company had effectively disclaimed.

The Opening Case Revisited, Part IV
"The Jewel"

The words *as is* written on the sales slip would not operate to exclude the express warranty made by the dealer, because such language excludes only implied warranties.

Consumer Protection

The Magnuson-Moss Warranty Act places limits on the exclusion of implied warranties to consumers. Under the act, if either a full or limited express warranty is made to a consumer, the implied warranties of merchantability and fitness for a particular purpose may not be excluded during the warranty period. This law also applies if the seller gives the buyer a service contract.

In addition, many states have protected consumers even further by saying that implied warranties cannot be excluded when goods are sold to consumers. If the sale of the car to Valdez in Example 19-10 had taken place in Connecticut or Massachusetts, Valdez would have had legal recourse against Kinkaid Motors. Those states and 11 others do not allow sellers to exclude implied warranties when goods are sold to consumers.

Human Blood and Tissue

In some states, including Florida and Massachusetts, a statute provides that the procurement, processing, storage, and distribution of human blood are considered services rather than a sale, and warranties do not apply. The Massachusetts statute reads as follows:

> The implied warranties of merchantability and fitness shall not be applicable to a contract for the sale of human blood, blood plasma, or other human tissue or organs from a blood bank or reservoir of such other tissues or organs. Such blood, blood plasma, or tissue or organs shall not for the purposes of this Article be considered commodities subject to sale or barter, but shall be considered as medical services [MASS. GEN. L. ch. 106 §2-316(5)].

Quick Quiz 19-2 True or False?

1. The word *merchantability* must be used to disclaim the warranty of merchantability, and it must be written in large, bold type.

2. If a buyer examines the goods, no implied warranty of merchantability is made as to defects that an examination would have revealed.

3. Implied warranties may not be excluded when a seller gives either a full or limited express warranty to a consumer.

19-3 Privity Not Required

Under earlier law, warranties extended only to the actual buyer of the product, that is, the one with whom the seller had dealt or was in privity of contract. People who were injured by defective products had no remedy against the seller for breach of warranty unless they themselves had purchased the goods. Thus, if children were injured by foreign objects in food that had been bought by their parents, the children could not recover for injuries because they had not purchased the goods. The UCC has abolished the requirement of privity. Instead, it provides three alternatives from which a state may choose. In all of the alternatives, warranties extend to people who would normally be expected to use the goods as well as to those who actually buy them.

UCC 2-318 (see page 965)

> *Alternative A*   A seller's warranty, whether express or implied, extends to any natural person who is in the family or household of his buyer or who is a guest in his home if it is reasonable to expect that such person may use, consume, or be affected by the goods and who is injured in person by breach of the warranty. A seller may not exclude or limit the operation of this section.
>
> *Alternative B*   A seller's warranty, whether express or implied, extends to any natural person who may reasonably be expected to use, consume, or be affected by the goods and who is injured in person by breach of the warranty. A seller may not exclude or limit the operation of this section.
>
> *Alternative C*   A seller's warranty, whether express or implied, extends to any person who may reasonably be expected to use, consume, or be affected by the goods and who is injured by breach of the warranty. A seller may not exclude or limit the operation of this section with respect to injury to the person of an individual to whom the warranty extends.

Most states have adopted one of the alternatives provided in the UCC. A few states, however, have written their own version of the law. Table 19-1 (page 384) indicates the alternative that has been adopted by each state.

Quick Quiz 19-3 True or False?

1. Today, warranties extend only to the actual buyer of a product.

2. The UCC has retained the requirement of privity of contract.

3. Under the UCC, warranties extend to people who would normally be expected to use the goods as well as to those who actually buy them.

19-4 Product Liability

One of the most important areas of law for consumers today is known as **product liability**. Under this law, which is a tort rather than a breach of contract, a buyer or user of a product who is injured because of the product's unsafe or defective condition may recover damages from the manufacturer, the seller, or the supplier of the goods. Injuries to persons or damage to property caused by defects in design and manufacture give consumers the right to seek recovery under the law of product liability. This law does not apply to international sales. Article 5 of the CISG states that it does not apply to the liability of the seller for death or personal injury caused by the goods to any person.

CISG Article 5 (see page 1018)

Product liability suits are usually based on one of two legal theories, negligence or strict liability, both of which are tort actions.

Negligence

One legal theory that is available to people who are injured by faulty products is negligence. This tort, which is explained more fully in Chapter 5, may be defined as the failure to exercise that degree of care that a reasonably prudent person would have exercised under the same circumstances and conditions. To recover for negligence in a product liability

Table 19-1 UCC Alternatives to Privity

State	Alternative	State	Alternative	State	Alternative
Alabama	B	Kentucky	A	North Dakota	C
Alaska	A	Louisiana	NA	Ohio	A
Arizona	A	Maine	OV	Oklahoma	A
Arkansas	A	Maryland	A	Oregon	A
California	NA	Massachusetts	OV	Pennsylvania	A
Colorado	B	Michigan	A	Rhode Island	OV
Connecticut	A	Minnesota	C	South Carolina	A
Delaware	B	Mississippi	A	South Dakota	B
District of Columbia	A	Missouri	A	Tennessee	A
Florida	A	Montana	A	Texas	OV
Georgia	A	Nebraska	A	Utah	C
Hawaii	C	Nevada	A	Vermont	B
Idaho	A	New Hampshire	OV	Virginia	OV
Illinois	A	New Jersey	A	Washington	A
Indiana	A	New Mexico	A	West Virginia	A
Iowa	C	New York	OV	Wisconsin	A
Kansas	B	North Carolina	A	Wyoming	B

Notes: NA = Not applicable; OV = Own version.

case, it is necessary to prove all of the following: There was a negligent act on the part of the manufacturer or supplier of the goods; injuries were suffered by someone who used the goods; and the injuries were caused by the negligent act.

EXAMPLE 19-12: Negligent Distribution

Lee Boyd Malvo and John Allen Muhammad were convicted of murder in the Washington, DC/Virginia–area sniper shootings in which 10 people were killed. It was alleged that 17-year-old Malvo strolled into Bull's Eye Shooter Supply and walked out with a 3-foot, .223-caliber Bushmaster rifle, a civilian version of the military M-16. Suit was brought by the victims' families for the negligent distribution of weapons against the gun dealer as well as against the gun's manufacturer, Bushmaster Firearms. In a settlement, Bull's Eye Shooter Supply agreed to pay $2 million to eight plaintiffs, and Bushmaster Firearms agreed to pay $550,000.

It is not easy for an injured consumer to win a case on the theory of negligence, because injured parties usually have no evidence of the negligent act by the manufacturer. They were not present when the goods were made and normally have very little information about the manufacturing process. Injured parties are often more successful in bringing suit for breach of warranty of merchantability rather than negligence.

Strict Liability

Under the doctrine of strict liability, it is not necessary to prove a negligent act on the part of the manufacturer or seller when someone is injured by a defective product. **Strict liability** is a legal theory, adopted by two-thirds of the states, that imposes liability on manu-

facturers or suppliers for selling goods that are unreasonably dangerous, without regard to fault or negligence. The principal consideration under the doctrine of strict liability is the safety of the product, not the conduct of the manufacturer or supplier of the goods. Under this rule of law, manufacturers have the duty to design reasonably safe products. They must also give proper instructions for the product's use and provide warnings of possible danger.

How many potential liability/strict liability issues can you identify in the photo?

People who are injured or suffer property damage from a defective product may recover from the manufacturer or seller only if they can prove all of the following:

1. The manufacturer or seller sold the product in a defective condition.
2. The manufacturer or seller was engaged in the business of selling the product.
3. The product was unreasonably dangerous to the user or consumer.
4. The defective condition was the proximate cause of the injury or damage.
5. The defective condition existed at the time it left the hands of the manufacturer or seller.
6. The consumer sustained physical harm or property damage by use or consumption of the product.

The defective condition may arise through faulty product design, faulty manufacturing, inadequate warning of danger, or improper instructions for the product's use.

EXAMPLE 19-13: Design Defect

Stewart stood on the lifting platform of a forklift and caused it to raise him to a rack 16 feet above the floor level so that he could inventory some ball bearings. Suddenly, the lift apparatus failed. The platform fell to the floor, and Stewart was seriously injured. The cause of the failure was attributed to negligent repair work performed a few days earlier by Scott-Kitz Miller Co., a company responsible for the maintenance of the equipment. Scott employees had removed some bolts holding the lift guide and reinserted them backward. In this position, the bolts protruded in such a way that when an attempt was made to lower the raised platform, the lift assembly would hang at the top of the mast, then fall to the floor. The court held that the forklift was defectively designed. It would have required very little effort or expense to design the bolts so that they could not accidentally be inserted backward.

BusinessWeek Business Law in the News

Made in China. Sued Here

America's product liability attorneys have begun rolling out the lawsuits as stories about unsafe and counterfeit imports from China continue to make headlines. The defendants: U.S. companies that distribute the products to American consumers. The cases might prove to be the vanguard in a march of litigation, with plenty of deep-pocketed American companies targeted.

On June 26 such a lawsuit prompted regulators to demand a recall of nearly a half-million Chinese-made tires. Foreign Tire Sales, a Union (N.J.) distributor of tires made by Hangzhou Zhongce Rubber, was named in a wrongful death case filed in a New Jersey federal court after one of its made-in-China tires allegedly caused an accident that killed two people. In turn, Foreign Tire Sales has sued its Chinese supplier. Both companies say they're not at fault.

Lawyers have also gone after U.S. companies such as Del Monte, which sold pet treats made with tainted Chinese ingredients. Del Monte, which issued a voluntary recall, hasn't yet responded to the suit. "We're just as interested in getting answers as some of the other folks," says John McDonough III, head of litigation at the New York office of Cozen O'Connor, which is representing the company.

Meanwhile, the Washington (D.C.) firm of Cohen, Milstein, Hausfeld & Toll is weighing litigation against Western distributors of Chinese-made counterfeit glycerin that found its way into cold medicine, killing hundreds of children in Panama and elsewhere. "Do people along the chain have responsibility for knowing where key ingredients are coming from? The answer

you're going to find in an era of globalization is 'Yes'," says Cohen Milstein's Michael Hausfeld.

Despite a wave of business-friendly legal reforms in recent years, companies can be held liable in most states in the U.S. even if they unwittingly sell a dangerous product. "All you have to show is that the product was defective," says William Ruskin, a defense litigator with Epstein, Becker & Green in New York. "It's no defense to say, 'We didn't know'." Under product-liability law, one company often can be held 100% liable for all damages awarded to all consumers, regardless of its market share or the amount of tainted product it might have sold.

Don't expect plaintiffs' lawyers to make their way to China. They aren't likely to bother with small, far-flung producers that can't afford to pay big judgments.

Questions for Analysis

1. Who are the defendants in cases involving unsafe and counterfeit products from China?

2. How did Foreign Tire Sales respond to a wrongful death case after one of its made-in-China tires allegedly caused an accident that killed two people?

3. Do people along the supply chain have the responsibility to know where key ingredients are coming from in international trade?

4. What must be shown before companies can be held liable for selling a dangerous product?

Source: Lorraine Woellert, "Made in China. Sued Here," *BusinessWeek,* July 9 & 16, 2007, 9.

The manufacturer's and seller's liability extends to all persons who may be injured by the product. Injured bystanders, guests, or others who have no relationship to the product, the seller, or the manufacturer may seek damages caused by defects in the offending product.

EXAMPLE 19-14:   Dangerous Product Design

Ryder Truck Rental rented a truck to Jackson. While Jackson was waiting for a light to change, the truck moved forward because of its faulty brake system. Martin, in another car, was injured when the truck hit her car. The Delaware Supreme Court ruled, on appeal, that Ryder could be held liable even without proof of its negligence. It was only necessary for the injured party to prove that the truck had an unreasonably dangerous product design that caused personal injury or property damage to the plaintiff.

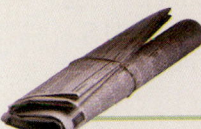

How to Put the Right Cap on Punitive Damages

In an important but split decision, *State Farm v. Campbell,* the U.S. Supreme Court in 2003 held that "the Due Process Clause [of the 14th Amendment] prohibits the imposition of grossly excessive or arbitrary punishments on defendants in tort cases." This was the second High Court ruling in the past few years that rightly objected to steep punitive damage awards.

Punitive damages are often added to compensatory damages awarded to victims of drunk drivers, medical malpractice, defective goods, and others who suffer because of careless or irresponsible behavior. There is no controversy about the fact that incompetent doctors, intoxicated or reckless drivers, and companies that produce dangerous and shoddy products should have to pay for the harm they cause.

But compensatory damages alone may not be enough to deter harmful actions. It is not always possible for victims to detect careless medical practices, dangerous goods, and other behavior. Moreover, some victims may be unwilling to file lawsuits because of the sizable expense in time and money, the discomfort of having to testify in court, and the uncertainty that they will win even legitimate cases. So punitive damages are often valuable; they help encourage such lawsuits and deter dangerous behavior.

Given that punitive damages are desirable, how big should they be? In his dissent in the *State Farm* case, Justice Antonin Scalia argued that the determination of punitive damages should continue to be left to individual judges and juries because the Supreme Court cannot devise a "principled application" that determines what these damages should be in different circumstances.

Unfortunately, under the present system, the principle that juries sometimes use is the depth of defendants' pockets. The Utah jury in the *State Farm* case awarded the Campbells $2.6 million in compensatory damages and $145 million in punitive damages. On appeal, the Utah Supreme Court reduced compensatory damages to $1 million but allowed the punitive ones. Punitive damages, therefore, amounted to 145 times compensatory—a ratio that is far too high.

State Farm may have misled the Campbells, but its behavior was not especially reprehensible. It assured the Campbells they had no liability and no need to hire counsel to defend Curtis Campbell against charges he caused a serious auto accident. When the jury returned a large judgment against him, State Farm at first refused to pay but eventually relented and paid.

Excessive punitive damage awards are not harmless transfers of wealth: They damage the functioning of the U.S. economy and judicial system. Companies pass these costs on to consumers via higher prices. In addition, large punitive damages encourage expensive class-action law firms, driven by the prospect of big contingency fees, to pursue unwarranted suits.

The challenge is to find rules to set punitive damages that are neither too weak nor clearly excessive. The Supreme Court indicated in the *State Farm* case that the ratio of punitive to compensatory damages should generally be in the single digits. Antitrust laws have established this ratio at 3 to 1 in private suits against companies engaged in monopolistic business practices. Although trebling damages is a rigid rule, it can be administered consistently and is a reasonable standard to apply in tort cases as well.

Strict limits on the ratio of punitive to compensatory damages would elevate the importance of accurate measurement of compensatory harm. For example, loss of life in automobile accidents caused by drunk drivers, or wrong statements by producers of drugs that cause severe harm or death to inappropriate users, damage victims and their heirs in ways that go far beyond the loss of future earnings. Although economists have developed techniques to gauge the monetary value to individuals of the loss of future activities due to wrongful deaths, juries have been reluctant to rely on them.

One might agree either with the majority of justices in the *State Farm* case that the 14th Amendment implies restrictions on punitive damages, or with Justice Ruth Bader Ginsburg, who argued in her dissent that federal courts should defer to state legislators in the setting of punitive damages. But unless more is done at the judiciary or legislative levels to limit these damages, the American tort system will continue to be costly and arbitrary.

Questions for Analysis

1. What was the holding of the U.S. Supreme Court in *State Farm v. Campbell*?

2. For what reasons may compensatory damages not be enough to deter harmful actions?

3. What did Justice Scalia argue in his dissent in the *State Farm* case?

4. What was the ratio of compensatory damages to punitive damages in the case?

5. In what ways do excessive punitive damage awards damage the functioning of the U.S. economy and judicial system, from the viewpoint of this article?

6. What examples illustrate how strict limits on the ratio of punitive damages to compensatory damages would elevate the importance of accurate measurement of compensatory harm?

Source: Gary S. Becker, "How to Put the Right Cap on Punitive Damages," *BusinessWeek*, September 15, 2003, 28.

Duty to Warn   Sometimes a duty is placed upon manufacturers to warn consumers that harm may result from a product. Unavoidably unsafe products may require a warning to inform the consumer of possible harm. If the warning is adequate, consumers may be required to use the product at their own risk. A warning must specify the risk presented by the product and give a reason for the warning. When the danger that is presented by a product is obvious, however, no duty to warn exists because a warning will not reduce the likelihood of injury.

Punitive Damages   In addition to recovering damages to compensate them for their losses, injured parties in strict liability cases sometimes recover punitive damages. These are monetary penalties imposed as a punishment for a wrongdoing.

Quick Quiz 19-4 True or False?

1. Strict liability laws impose liability on manufacturers or suppliers for selling goods that are unreasonably dangerous.

2. Only people who are in privity of contract may seek damages for injuries caused by defects in products.

3. Manufacturers sometimes have a duty to warn consumers of possible harm that may result from the use of a product.

Summary

19.1   Express warranties arise by a statement of fact or promise, by a description of the goods, and by a sample or model. Federal law requires that written warranties on consumer products be labeled as either full or limited warranties. When merchants sell goods, they warrant that the goods are merchantable. In addition, when a buyer relies on the seller's skill and judgment in selecting the goods, the seller warrants that the goods will be fit for the purpose for which they are to be used. Other warranties may arise from the ways in which

parties have dealt in the past. When goods are sold, either by a merchant or a private party, the seller warrants that the title is good and that there are no liens on the goods. To be able to sue for breach of warranty, a buyer of defective goods must notify the seller of the defect within a reasonable time after discovering the defect.

19.2   Except when express warranties are made, sellers may exclude the warranties of merchantability and fitness for a particular purpose. Such an exclusion must be in writing and conspicuous. The words *as is* and *with all faults* serve to disclaim implied warranties but not the warranty of title. However, many states protect consumers by saying that implied warranties cannot be excluded when goods are sold to consumers. In addition, the distribution of human blood and tissue is considered a service rather than a sale in some states, making warranties under the UCC inapplicable.

19.3 Warranties extend to people who would normally be expected to use the goods as well as to those who actually buy them.

19.4 Buyers who are injured by unsafe or defective products may sometimes recover damages from the manufacturer, seller, or supplier of the goods under product liability laws. Lawsuits are brought under either of two theories, negligence or strict liability.

Key Terms

consequential damages, 381

consumer products, 375

express warranty, 373

full warranty, 375

implied warranty, 376

limited warranty, 376

product liability, 383

strict liability, 385

warranty of fitness for a particular purpose, 377

warranty of merchantability, 376

warranty of title, 378

Questions for Review and Discussion

1. In what three ways may express warranties be created?
2. Under the Magnuson-Moss Warranty Act, what must be done when a written warranty is given to a consumer?
3. What is the difference between a full warranty and a limited warranty?
4. When does the implied warranty of fitness for a particular purpose arise? When and by whom is the warranty of merchantability given?
5. What is the warranty of title that is made by a seller of goods? Explain.
6. What special rules must be followed to exclude the warranties of merchantability and fitness for a particular purpose? In what other ways may warranties be excluded?
7. What notice must buyers of defective goods give to recover damages for breach of warranty?
8. What provision does the UCC make relative to privity of contract under the law of warranties?
9. Why is it often difficult for a consumer to win a product liability case on the theory of negligence?
10. What must an injured party prove to recover from a manufacturer for strict liability?

Investigating the Internet

Have you ever owned a motor vehicle that you thought was a lemon and wondered what you could do about it? You have studied about warranties in this chapter, and warranty law can help you with the purchase of motor vehicles (and other goods), especially if your vehicle turns out to be a lemon. However, because the purchase of lemons (not the yellow kind) has brought so many complaints from buyers, most states have passed their own lemon laws—each different from the others. Log on to a search engine and key in "State Lemon Laws." You may be pleased to learn how your state law can help you.

Cases for Analysis

1. DiCintio leased from Adzan Auto Sales a Jeep Grand Cherokee Laredo sport utility vehicle manufacured by DaimlerChrysler for a three-year period. Soon after accepting delivery, the automatic transmission failed to shift gears properly, and then the vehicle started to pull to the left while being driven, after which it began to "idle rough" and stall while stopped at traffic lights. DiCintio took the vehicle to authorized dealers for repairs on six or seven occasions, but the defects persisted. When Adzan Auto Sales refused to terminate the lease or give him another car, DiContio brought suit against DaimlerChrysler for breach of the Magnuson-Moss Warranty Act. Does DiCintio have a cause of action under this law? Explain. *Mark DiCintio v. DaimlerChrysler Corporation, et al,* 768 NE2d 1121 (NY).

2. Lohr bought a mobile home from Larry's Homes. The home was damaged during delivery and never fully set up on Lohr's property. Larry's Homes attempted some repairs, but they were insufficient. An arbitrator found that the intended repairs would not have been enough even if they had been carried out. Lohr took the case to arbitration on the grounds of a breach of the warranty of merchantability under the UCC. Does the UCC apply to this case? Why or why not? *Lohr v. Larry's Homes of Virginia.* Arbitrated by McCammon Group referred out of Cumberland County Circuit Court (VA).

3. Caswell bought a gas grill to give to his friend, Kile, as a birthday present. The grill exploded the first time it was used due to a factory defect, and Kile was injured. The manufacturer of the grill argued that it was not responsible for Kile's injuries because Kile had not purchased the grill. There was no privity of contract between Kile and the manufacturer. How would you decide?

4. Shaffer ordered a glass of rosé wine at the Victoria Station Restaurant. As he took his first sip of wine, the glass broke in his hand, causing permanent injuries. Shaffer brought suit against the restaurant for breach of warranty of merchantability. The restaurant's position was that because it did not sell the wine glass to Shaffer (only its contents), it was not a merchant with respect to the glass and therefore made no warranty. Do you agree with the res-

taurant? Why or why not? *Shaffer v. Victoria Station, Inc.,* 588 P.2d 233 (WA).

5. McCoy bought an antique pistol from the Old Fort Trading Post for $1,000. Later, the gun was taken from McCoy by the police when they learned that it was stolen property. The police turned the gun over to the rightful owner. McCoy notified the Old Fort Trading Post of what had happened and asked for the return of his money, but the owner of the business refused to give him a refund. What remedy, if any, did McCoy have against the owner of the trading post? Explain. *Trial v. McCoy,* 553 S. W.2d 199 (TX).

6. Werner purchased a sloop from Montana for $13,250. During the negotiations before the sale, Montana had told Werner that the sloop would "make up" when placed in the water and would become watertight. Werner placed the sloop in the water and allowed sufficient time for the planking to swell to form a watertight hull, but it still leaked and could not be sailed. He then discovered extensive dry rot in the hull and learned that the cost of repairs would be substantial. Montana refused to take the sloop back and refund Werner's purchase price. Did Werner have a cause of action against Montana? If so, on what grounds? Explain. *Werner v. Montana,* 378 A.2d 1130 (NH).

7. Romedy bought a car from Willett Lincoln-Mercury, Inc. He did not inspect it until four or five days after it was delivered to him. Three weeks later, he notified the dealer that the car did not contain the equipment that the dealer had said it would contain. He did, however, continue to make payments on the car. Later, he brought suit against the dealer for breach of warranty. Did he recover damages? Explain. *Romedy v. Willett Lincoln-Mercury, Inc.,* 220 S.E.2d 74 (GA).

8. Mr. and Mrs. Benfer bought a mobile home from Thomas, a mobile home retailer. Prior to the purchase, Thomas had told them that the type of mobile home he carried had a one-quarter-inch sheathing on the siding that made it better than cheaper units. Thomas showed them a model of the mobile home that he carried and pointed out to them the grade of plywood sheathing that was on the model. When the mobile home was delivered to them, they were given several written warranties

signed by the manufacturer, Town & Country Mobile Homes, Inc., including one that specifically warranted that the mobile home was sheathed with one-quarter-inch plywood beneath the prefinished aluminum exterior wall surface. Later, the Benfers discovered that their mobile home did not contain this sheathing. Did they have a cause of action against the retailer, Thomas? Why or why not? *Town & Country Mobile Homes, Inc., v. Benfer,* 527 S.W.2d 523 (TX).

9. Hensley bought a used Plymouth automobile from Colonial Dodge, Inc. The following language was written in small print on the back of the purchase agreement: "No warranties, expressed or implied, are made by the dealer with respect to used motor vehicles or motor vehicle chassis furnished hereunder except as may be expressed in writing by the dealer." After driving only three or four blocks, Hensley noticed that the windshield wipers and the brake lights were not working properly. He returned the car to the dealer to correct the problems. When he next received the car, it started to lose compression and slowed down to 20 or 25 miles per hour before he got halfway home. The engine sounded as if it were "missing quite badly." After arriving home, which was about six miles from the dealer's place of business, Hensley was unable to get the car started again. An investigation revealed that the car needed a new engine, which the dealer refused to provide. Did Hensley recover damages from the dealer for breach of warranty? Why or why not? *Hensley v. Colonial Dodge, Inc.,* 245 N.W.2d 142 (MI).

10. Paul and Cynthia Vance invited Carl and Jeanne Leichtamer to go for a ride in the Vances's four wheel drive jeep at an "off the road" recreation facility called the Hall of Fame Four-Wheel Club. The club had been organized by a jeep dealer who showed films to club members of jeeps traveling in hilly country. This activity was coupled with a national advertising program of American Motor Sales Corporation encouraging people to buy jeeps that could drive up and down steep hills. As the jeep went up a 33-degree sloped, double-terraced hill, it pitched over from front to back and landed upside-down. The Vances were killed, and the Leichtamers were severely injured. The jeep was equipped with a factory-installed roll bar attached to the sheet metal that housed the rear wheels. When the vehicle landed upside down, the flat sheet metal gave way, causing the roll bar to move forward and downward 14 inches. The Leichtamers argued that the weakness of the sheet metal housing upon which the roll bar had been attached was the cause of their injuries. The manufacturer claimed that the roll bar was provided solely for side-roll protection, not pitchover, as occurred in this case. Did the Leichtamers recover against the manufacturer on a theory of strict liability? Why or why not? *Leichtamer v. American Motors Corp.,* 424 N.E.2d 568 (OH).

11. Michael P. Babine was injured when he was thrown from an "El Toro" mechanical bull that he rode at a nightclub. The club had placed mattresses around the bull to cushion the fall of riders, but the mattresses were not adequately pushed together. Babine was thrown off during his ride and hit his head on the floor where there was a gap between the mattresses. Before riding the bull, Babine had signed a form releasing the nightclub from liability for injuries sustained from the activity. The mechanical bull had been manufactured for the purpose of being a training device for rodeo cowboys, and it was purchased second-hand by the nightclub. Babine sought to recover damages from the manufacturer under the theory of product liability. Did he succeed? Why or why not? *Babine v. Gilley's Bronco Shop, Inc.,* 488 So.2d 176 (FL).

Quick Quiz Answers

19-1	19-2	19-3	19-4
1. F	1. T	1. F	1. T
2. F	2. T	2. F	2. F
3. T	3. T	3. T	3. T

Chapter 20 | Consumer Protection

The Opening Case
"Triple Trouble"

While browsing through a large used car lot, Frank Avila saw a sharp-looking, four-year-old Toyota Tundra double-cab pickup that he liked. A large sign on the vehicle gave the price, but nothing indicated the kind of warranty, if any, that went with it. When Avila took the truck out for a test drive, the salesperson pointed out that the odometer read only 30,000 miles and said that the vehicle was fully warranted but gave no details. Avila decided that he would think it over and left. Later that day, he discovered that his wallet was missing. He returned to the used car lot and, much to his relief, found the wallet on the ground next to the vehicle he had driven. Still interested in the pickup, he opened the door and noticed a folded paper under the seat. Looking at it, he saw that it was a receipt for service on the vehicle three months earlier. The mileage written on the receipt was 57,000. Later that evening, Avila discovered that his VISA card was missing from the wallet. He notified VISA of the loss by telephone. Despite his prompt notice, a thief had been able to charge purchases totaling $1,600.

Opening Case Questions

1. What warranty law did the used car lot violate?

2. How does the law protect against odometer tampering?

3. Will Avila be legally responsible for paying the full $1,600 back to the credit card company?

LO Learning Objectives

1. Discuss the Federal Trade Commission (FTC) Act and explain how the act is enforced.
2. Describe four federal laws designed to prevent unfair or deceptive acts.
3. Identify several FTC rules designed to protect the consumer.
4. State the purpose of the Consumer Product Safety Act.
5. Explain how consumers can benefit from the Consumer Leasing Act.
6. Identify and state the purpose of six consumer credit laws.

20-1 Federal and State Consumer Protection Laws

Consumer protection laws apply to transactions between someone conducting a business and a consumer. A **consumer** is someone who buys or leases real estate, goods, or services for personal, family, or household purposes. Thus, people who buy or rent things for personal use from a business are protected by consumer protection laws. However, if they buy the same things from another consumer or for business use, they are not, with some exceptions, protected by consumer protection law.

State consumer protection offices provide information and help enforce state consumer protection laws. They sometimes assist consumers with individual problems. Consumer protection offices are located in state and county offices and, in some cities, the mayor's office.

Federal consumer protection law stems from the Federal Trade Commission (FTC) Act, which states that "unfair or deceptive acts or practices in . . . or affecting commerce are hereby declared unlawful." The act defines **commerce** as "commerce among the several states or with foreign nations or the District of Columbia." Thus, the act applies to businesses that sell real estate, goods, or services in interstate commerce or that somehow affect interstate commerce. **Interstate commerce** is business activity that touches more than one state. Purely local business activity, which has no out-of-state connections, called **intrastate commerce**, is not governed by the FTC Act.

LO1

EXAMPLE 20-1: Intrastate Commerce

Ortega owned a farm on which he grew a variety of vegetables. He sold the vegetables to a local store and to consumers who stopped at his roadside stand. Because his business was purely local, it would not be governed by the FTC Act. Instead, his business would be regulated by the consumer protection laws, as well as other laws, of his own state.

The FTC investigates violations of the FTC Act. If the FTC believes a violation of the law occurred, it may attempt to obtain voluntary compliance by entering into a consent order with the violating company. A **consent order** is an order under which the company agrees to stop the disputed practice without necessarily admitting that it violated the law. If an agreement cannot be reached, the FTC may issue a complaint. This action begins a formal hearing before an administrative law judge. If a violation of law is found, a cease-and-desist order or other appropriate relief may be issued.

EXAMPLE 20-2: Cease-and-Desist Order

Jay Norris, Inc., made false claims about a number of products listed in its mail-order catalogs and advertisements. It described a "flame gun" that would dissolve the heaviest snowdrifts and whip through the thickest ice; the product did neither. A roach powder was described as completely safe to use and as never losing its killing power, even after years; the powder was neither safe to use nor very deadly to roaches. Cars were listed as carefully maintained and thoroughly serviced; they were former New York taxicabs, many in poor condition. The FTC issued a cease-and-desist order prohibiting Jay Norris, Inc., from representing the safety or performance characteristics of any product unless such claims were fully and completely substantiated by competent and objective material available in written form.

Consumers may bring individual or class-action lawsuits against businesses for violating FTC rules. A **class-action lawsuit** is one that is brought by one or more plaintiffs on behalf of a class of persons. Usually, suit must be brought within one year after the violation. Alternate dispute resolutions are also available for resolving this type of problem (see Chapter 4).

Quick Quiz 20-1 True or False?

1. Consumer protection laws apply to transactions between someone conducting a business and a consumer.

2. A consumer is someone who buys or leases real estate, goods, or services for personal, family, or household purposes.

3. Intrastate commerce is business activity that touches more than one state.

20-2 Unfair or Deceptive Acts or Practices

The FTC Act prohibits unfair or deceptive acts or practices. The FTC and the courts have determined that certain activities are unfair or deceptive. They include fraudulent misrepresentations, sending unordered merchandise, bait-and-switch schemes, and odometer tampering.

Fraudulent Misrepresentations

It is unfair or deceptive for a seller to make a *fraudulent misrepresentation,* that is, a statement that has the effect of deceiving the buyer. A misrepresentation usually occurs when the seller misstates facts important to the consumer.

Making false statements about the construction, durability, reliability, safety, strength, condition, or life expectancy of a product is a deceptive practice. It is also deceptive to fail to disclose to a buyer any fact that would cause the buyer not to enter into the contract.

You may see ads like the following in newspapers and magazines: "Would you like to earn hundreds of dollars a week at home in your leisure time? Many people are supplementing their income in a very easy way. Let us tell you how. . . ." An offer like this may sound very attractive, particularly if you are unable to leave your home to work. But be cautious about work-at-home ads, especially ones that promise large profits in a short period of time. Although some work-at-home plans are legitimate, many are not. Home employment schemes are some of the oldest kinds of classified advertising fraud.

Unordered Merchandise

Except for free samples clearly and conspicuously marked as such and merchandise mailed by charitable organizations soliciting contributions, it is a violation of the postal law and the FTC Act to send merchandise through the mail to people who did not order it.

Similarly, it is illegal to send a bill for such unordered merchandise or to send **dunning letters**, that is, letters requesting payments.

People who receive unordered merchandise through the mail may treat it as a gift. They may keep the merchandise or dispose of it in any manner they see fit without any obligation whatsoever to the sender. In addition, senders of unordered merchandise must attach a statement to the package informing recipients of their right to keep and use the goods.

Bait-and-Switch Schemes

A **bait-and-switch scheme** is an alluring but insincere offer to sell a product or service that the advertiser in truth does not intend or want to sell. Its purpose is to switch customers from buying the advertised merchandise to buying something else, usually at a higher price or on a basis more advantageous to the advertiser.

The FTC law prohibiting bait-and-switch activity states: "No advertisement containing an offer to sell a product shall be made when the offer is not a *bona fide* effort to sell the advertised product." Any of the following activities could indicate a bait-and-switch scheme:

- Refusal to show, demonstrate, or sell the product offered in accordance with the terms of the offer.
- "Put down" of the product by acts or words of the seller.
- Failing to have available at all outlets listed in the advertisement a sufficient quantity of the advertised product to meet reasonably anticipated demands.
- Refusing to take orders for the advertised product to be delivered within a reasonable period of time.
- Showing a product that is defective, unusable, or impractical for the purpose represented in the advertisement.

Odometer Tampering

The federal Odometer Law prohibits people from disconnecting, resetting, or altering the odometer of a motor vehicle to register any mileage other than the true mileage driven. Anyone who sells a car or even gives it away, unless it is older than 25 years, must provide the new owner with a written statement disclosing the odometer reading at the time of the transfer. If the seller has reason to believe that the mileage reading on the odometer is incorrect, the disclosure statement must indicate that the actual mileage traveled is unknown.

An odometer must be set at zero if it is repaired and cannot be adjusted to show the true mileage. In addition, the car owner must attach to the left doorframe a written notice showing the true mileage before the repair or replacement and the date that the odometer was set at zero. It is illegal for anyone to alter or remove any such notice attached to the doorframe of a car.

Quick Quiz 20-2 True or False?

1. A misrepresentation usually occurs when the seller misstates facts important to the consumer.

2. People who receive unordered merchandise through the mail must either return the merchandise or pay for it.

3. An odometer must be set at zero if it is repaired and cannot be adjusted to show the true mileage, and a written notice of the date of repair and the true mileage must be attached to the left doorframe of the car.

A Question of Ethics
Principle No. 4: Be Fair (Part 1)

We can learn everything we need to know about the concept of fairness by looking at how some children behave at birthday parties.

Imagine you have a son, Larry, for whom you throw a birthday party one afternoon. Your sister brings her two boys, Curly and Moe, to the celebration. When Moe gets a bigger piece of birthday cake, Curly cries, "That's not fair." Seeing someone who appears no different than him get more cake strikes Curly as wrong, unjust, unfair.

If there's a good reason to give Curly a smaller piece (say, for example, he is overweight), it's justifiable and fair to cut different sized pieces of cake for the two boys. In fact, it's not only fair, it would be wrong to do otherwise, since one boy deserves a smaller piece (hence the term "dessert," or that which is deserved).

Now suppose that your sister explains to Curly why he's getting a smaller piece, but this reason doesn't placate the lad and he throws a temper tantrum. "All right, young man, now you won't get any," your sister tells him. "I'm taking you home, where you won't get any cake. And because you're acting so childishly, you won't be allowed to watch TV for the rest of the weekend."

THREE BRANCHES OF FAIRNESS

This response, of course, makes Curly even more upset, and his ratcheted-up tantrum is now justified. After all, he has been on the receiving end of a true injustice: Banishing him from the party and taking away his television privileges for so long seems, by any reasonable standard, an excessive punishment. It is, in short, unfair.

You feel so bad about the turn of events for Larry's special day that you decide to make up for the interruption by having your spouse run out to get the latest child-friendly video game that all the kids will enjoy.

This story introduces us to three branches of the concept of fairness. Imagine a pie chart that represents justice, divided into three equal wedges. They represent, in no particular order:

- Distributive justice, which refers to how scarce resources are made available to a group of people with varying degrees of needs, desires, and other factors. Think of this in terms of who deserves a raise, and how much.
- Retributive justice, which refers to how we punish those who violate standards of behavior. What is fair punishment if an employee does something wrong? Should the fact that the employee happens to be the son or daughter of a close friend matter in deciding this?
- Rectificatory justice, which refers to how we rectify a situation in which a person or group of persons has been treated unfairly. When coming aboard as a new manager, how should you deal with an unjust situation created or ignored by your predecessor?

Let's examine each in turn.

DISTRIBUTIVE JUSTICE

"You can't always get what you want," Mick Jagger sang in one of the Rolling Stones' most famous songs, but many of us would beg to differ with his next assertion: "If you try sometime, you just might find you get what you need." How many people do you know who are satisfied with their lot in life? Do your colleagues, friends, and family members believe that their needs are being adequately met? Since we live in a world of scarcity, it is natural to want to know how we are to divide what there is among those who want or need it. Tom Beauchamp and James Childress identify the following as standards we might use to make such a decision:

1. To each person an equal share
2. To each person according to need
3. To each person according to effort
4. To each person according to contribution
5. To each person according to merit
6. To each person according to free-market exchange

One standard isn't necessarily better than another, as Beauchamp and Childress note. Context is everything. For a birthday party in which some children are on a restricted diet because of their weight, it would be wrong to employ standard No. 1. It would be just as wrong to use standard No. 5, because children have equal merit when it comes to getting cake (as opposed to advancing in a spelling bee or musical contest). In the context of a party, "To each according to need" seems like a better criterion to use in distributing cake and ice cream.

When it comes to giving out raises, it would seem that No. 4 or No. 5—contribution and merit—should be considered. But what about the person who puts out more effort than anyone else, yet accomplishes less? How much should effort count?

Even when it seems that a standard is apt, you may have to think again. Let's say the resource in question is something far more scarce than ice cream or money, such as organs for transplant. No. 2—need—might seem obvious. Yet some argue that lifestyle choices that adversely affect one's health—deciding to smoke or failing to seek treatment for alcoholism, for example—should play a role in determining who should be given a transplant.

Obviously this is a complex issue and beyond the scope here to address thoroughly. The point is simply that of the six standards listed above for deciding who gets what (and there are other standards one can think of), no one standard applies to every situation. "One size fits all" might apply to baseball hats or mood rings but certainly not to how we realize the life principle of fairness.

Source: Bruce Weinstein, "Principle No. 4: Be Fair (Part 1)," *BusinessWeek.com*, February 8, 2007.

The Opening Case Revisited, Part I
"Triple Trouble"

The old receipt that Avila found under the seat of the four-year-old pickup was evidence that the vehicle's mileage had been turned back and possibly that the salesperson had committed a fraudulent misrepresentaiton. If Avila were to proceed further with the purchase of the vehicle, the seller would have to provide him with an accurate odometer disclosure statement.

20-3 The FTC Trade Regulation Rules

To correct wrongdoings in the marketplace, the FTC has established trade regulation rules that must be followed by companies that transact business in interstate commerce. Some of these rules are discussed here.

Used Car Rule

Many consumer complaints involve the purchase of a used car. To remedy this situation, the FTC established the **Used Car Rule**. The rule requires used car dealers that sell more than five used vehicles in a 12-month period to place a window sticker, called a **Buyer's Guide**, in the window of each used car they offer for sale. The Buyer's Guide provides the following information:

- A statement that the car is sold *as is* if it is sold with no warranties. (Some states do not allow used cars to be sold as is by car dealers.)

The buyers guide this dealer must place in the window of each car for sale becomes part of the contract automatically.

- A statement that the car is sold with implied warranties only if that is the case (see Chapter 19).

- A statement telling whether the warranty is "full" or "limited" (see Chapter 19) and citing the length of the warranty period if the car is sold with an express warranty. In addition, the guide must list the specific systems that are covered by the warranty and state the percentage of the repair costs the buyer will be required to pay.

- A statement that tells consumers not to rely on spoken promises.

- A suggestion that consumers ask whether they may have the vehicle inspected by their own mechanic either on or off the premises.

- A list of the 14 major systems of an automobile and some of the principal defects that may occur in these systems.

Dealers are required to put a Buyer's Guide on all used vehicles they offer for sale, including automobiles, light-duty vans, and light-duty trucks. The guide becomes part of the sales contract and overrides any contrary provision that may be in the contract.

Cooling-Off Rule

The FTC has established the **Cooling-Off Rule** to give consumers an opportunity to change their minds after signing contracts with people who come to their houses. Under this rule, sales of consumer goods or services over $25 made away from the seller's regular place of business, such as at a customer's home, may be canceled within three business days after the sale occurs. This rule requires the seller to give the buyer two copies of a cancellation form, one of which the buyer may send to the seller any time before midnight of the third business day after the contract was signed. The law also applies to consumer product parties given in private homes and to sales made in rented hotel rooms or restaurants.

EXAMPLE 20-3:   Cooling-Off Rule

Nesbit saw an advertisement in a local newspaper advertising Oriental rugs for sale at a local motel. She went to the motel, purchased an Oriental rug, and was given a sales slip saying that all sales were final. The company violated the FTC rule. It did

The Opening Case Revisited, Part II
"Triple Trouble"

The used car lot violated the FTC's Used Car Rule by not placing a buyer's guide on the window of the truck and failing to provide information about the warranties that went with the vehicle.

not provide her with a cancellation form that she could use to cancel the contract within three days. Although the FTC cannot resolve individual complaints, it does want to know about them. Nesbit should have notified her state consumer protection office and sent a copy of her complaint to the Enforcement Division, Federal Trade Commission, Washington, DC 20580.

Under the laws of some states, such as New York, the three-day right to cancel does not begin until the seller gives the buyer a written notice of the right to cancel. Until such notice is given, the buyer may use any means to notify the seller of the cancellation of the contract.

The Cooling-Off Rule does not apply to sales made at the seller's regular place of business, sales made totally by mail or phone, or sales under $25. In addition, it does not apply to sales for real estate, insurance, securities, emergency home repairs, or arts and crafts sold at fairs or other locations.

Negative Option Rule

When consumers subscribe to a magazine, CD club, or other plan that sends products on an ongoing basis, the Negative Option Rule applies. Under such plans, sellers regularly send announcements describing the current selection. If the subscriber does nothing, the seller will ship the selection automatically. If the subscriber does not want the selection, he or she must tell the seller not to send it, and there is a deadline for notification. Under the Negative Option Rule, sellers must tell subscribers:

- How many selections they must buy, if any.
- How and when they can cancel the membership.
- How to notify the seller when they do not want the selection.
- When to return the "negative option" form to cancel shipment of a selection.
- When they can get credit for the return of a selection.
- How postage and handling costs are charged.
- How often they will receive announcements and forms.

Identity Theft

Identity theft has become a serious problem for consumers in recent years. This crime occurs when someone uses another's identifying information, such as a name, Social Security number, or credit card number, without their permission, to commit fraud or other crimes. Identity thieves might rent an apartment, obtain a credit card, or establish a telephone account in another person's name. That person may not find out about the theft until he or she reviews the credit report or credit card statement and notices charges he or she didn't make—or until he or she is contacted by a debt collector.

Although some identity theft victims can resolve their problems quickly, others spend hundreds of dollars and many days repairing damage to their good name and credit record. Some consumers victimized by identity theft may lose out on job opportunities or be denied loans for their education, housing, or cars because of negative information on their credit reports.

Although the Federal Trade Commission does not resolve individual consumer problems, it does serve as a clearinghouse for complaints from victims of identity theft. To learn more about this subject, log on to the FTC's identity theft site. If you believe you are a victim of identity theft, go online and fill out the FTC's identity theft consumer complaint form. This form will help the FTC investigate fraud and may lead to law enforcement action.

Online Transactions Involving Foreign Countries

Online transactions are skyrocketing both domestically and internationally, and many times people are not even aware they are dealing with someone in a foreign country. When there is a problem involving an online transaction with someone in a foreign country, consumers may, if they wish, file a complaint at www.econsumer.gov. Although no action will be taken on an individual's behalf, information contained in the complaint may be entered into a consumer complaint database maintained by the FTC. The complaints are made available to government law enforcement agencies in participating countries. This database allows the agencies to spot new trends, uncover new scams, and target suspect companies and individuals for law enforcement actions.

Antispam Law

The **Can Spam Act** is an attempt by the federal government to reduce the use of unsolicited commercial e-mail, commonly known as **spam**, on the Internet. Under the law, unsolicited commercial e-mail messages must be truthful and cannot use misleading subject lines or incorrect return addresses. E-mail containing pornography must be specifically labeled in the subject line. In addition, spammers cannot harvest e-mail addresses from chat rooms and other sites without permission. The law authorizes the FTC to establish a "do-not-e-mail registry" and provides for fines of $250 for each e-mail violation.

If you have a specific complaint about spam, look online for "FTC consumer complaint forms" and use the form provided there to contact the FTC. You can also forward spam directly to the Commission at spam@uce.gov without using the complaint form.

Antislamming Law

Slamming is the illegal practice of changing a consumer's telephone service without permission. New consumer protection rules created by the Federal Communications Commission (FCC) provide a remedy if you've been slammed.

If you have been slammed and have not paid the bill of the carrier who slammed, you do not have to pay anyone for service for up to 30 days after being slammed. This rule means you do not have to pay either your authorized telephone company (the company you actually chose to provide service) or the slamming company. You must pay any charges for service beyond 30 days to your authorized company, but at that company's rates, not the slammer's.

If you have been slammed, have paid your phone bill, and only then discover that you have been slammed, the slamming company must pay your authorized company 150 percent of the charges it received from you. Out of this amount, your authorized company will then reimburse you 50 percent of the charges you paid to the slammer. For example, if you were charged $100 by the slamming company, that company will have to give your authorized company $150, and you will receive $50 as a reimbursement.

With these rules, the FCC has taken the profit out of slamming and protected consumers from illegal charges.

Figure 20-1   Once your number is registered, how long will it remain in the
National Do Not Call Registry?

**NATIONAL
DO NOT CALL
REGISTRY**

Place your telephone number on the National Do Not Call Registry by calling toll-free
1-888-382-1222 (TTY: 1-866-290-4236) or going online to donotcall.gov. Registration is free.
   Placing your telephone number on the Do Not Call Registry will stop all telemarketing
calls except those from political organizations, charities, and people making surveys. You
can expect fewer calls within three months of the date you sign up for the registry. Your number will stay in the registry for five years, until it is disconnected, or until you delete it from
the registry. You may renew your registration after five years.
   Telemarketers are required to search the registry every three months and avoid calling
any phone numbers that are on the registry.
   If you receive telemarketing calls after you have registered your telephone number and it
has been in the registry for three months, you can file a complaint at donotcall.gov or by calling toll-free 1-888-382-1222 (TTY: 1-866-290-4236). You will need to provide the date of the
call and the name or phone number of the company that called you. Telemarketers who disregard this law can be fined up to $11,000 for each call they make.

Mail, Telephone, Internet, or Fax Rule

The FTC has established a rule to protect consumers who order goods by mail, telephone, Internet, or fax machine. Under the rule, sellers must ship orders within the time promised in
their advertisements. If no time period is promised, sellers must either ship the order within 30
days after they receive it or send the consumer an option notice. The option notice tells the
consumer of a shipping delay and gives the consumer the option of agreeing to the delay or
canceling the order and receiving a prompt refund. Instructions on how to cancel the order
must be included in the notice. In addition, the seller must provide a free means for consumers
to reply.

Telemarketing Sales Rule

The FTC's Telemarketing Sales Rule is designed to protect consumers from abusive and unscrupulous telemarketers. The rule has established the *Do Not Call Registry* (see Figure 20-1)
that makes it easier for consumers to reduce the number of unwanted sales calls they get. The
rule also requires telemarketing firms to identify themselves on Caller ID technology. The
name displayed by a telemarketer on a Caller ID must either be the business trying to make a
sale or the company making the call. The display must also include a phone number that consumers can call and ask that the company no longer call them.
   Under the Telemarketing Sales Rule:

- It is illegal for a telemarketer to call a consumer if the consumer has asked not to be
  called.

- Calling times are restricted to the hours between 8:00 AM and 9:00 PM.

- Telemarketers must tell the consumer that it is a sales call, the name of the seller, and
  what they are selling before they make their pitch. If it is a prize promotion, they must
  tell the consumer that no purchase or payment is necessary to enter or win.

- It is illegal for telemarketers to misrepresent any information, including facts about their
  goods or services, earnings potential, profitability, the risk or liquidity of an investment,
  or the nature of a prize in a prize-promotion scheme.

- Before consumers pay, telemarketers must tell them the total cost of the products or services offered and any restrictions on getting or using them or that a sale is final or nonrefundable.

- It is illegal for telemarketers to withdraw money from a consumer's checking account without the consumer's express, verifiable authorization.

- Telemarketers cannot lie to get consumers to pay, no matter what method of payment is used.

- Until the services are delivered, consumers do not have to pay for (1) *credit repair* (promises to change or erase accurate negative information from a consumer's credit report); (2) *recovery room* (promises to recover previously lost money to telemarketing scams); or (3) *advance-fee loans* (promises to guarantee a loan for a fee paid in advance).

Consumers who have the slightest doubt about a telephone offer should ask for written information about the product, service, investment opportunity, or charity that is the subject of the call. They should resist high-pressure sales tactics and talk to a family member or friend before responding to the call. Consumers should never give out their bank account or credit card number to anyone who calls them. Similarly, they should never send money by courier, overnight delivery, or wire to anyone who insists on immediate payment.

900-Telephone Number Rules

The 900 telephone number is used sometimes in telemarketing because the consumer, rather than the seller, pays the phone charge. Some consumers have been charged excessively for 900-number services or have not received the services advertised. Some 900-number scams disclose a cost per minute but do not reveal that you must listen for many minutes to hear all of the information. Other 900 services use announcers who speak so quickly that you need to call back to understand the message.

Some scams promote 900-prefix numbers for job or housing information. Once you place—and pay for—the call, you are told that the job or house is already taken. Some television promotions encourage children to call 900 numbers for "free" gifts or stories. Teenagers may call 900-number talklines to chat with other teens—usually at a cost-per-minute charge. They sometimes make these calls without telling their parents or fail to understand that the phone calls cost money. Parents have received phone bills of thousands of dollars.

In addition, FTC regulations require that people who dial 900-prefix numbers be warned of the cost of the calls and given a chance to hang up before being charged. Telephone companies must block service to 900-prefix numbers if so requested by the customer. Telephone customers must be sent pay-per-call disclosure statements annually, and any prefix other than 900 is prohibited for use as a pay-per-call service. Telephone companies cannot disconnect phone service to customers who refuse to pay for 900-number calls, and rules have been established for resolving billing disputes.

Telephone psychic Ms. Cleo, claiming to be a Jamaican shaman, was the paid spokeswoman for the Spirit Psychic Network which received millions of 900-number calls. Born Youree Cleomili Harris in Los Angeles, CA, she and the network were shut down after numerous law suits and investigations.

20-4 Consumer Product Safety Act

To protect consumers from dangerous products, Congress passed the Consumer Product Safety Act. The act established the Consumer Product Safety Commission (CPSC) to protect consumers from unreasonable risk or injury from hazardous products. The act covers products or component parts, American-made or imported, that are manufactured or distributed for sale to a consumer for personal use, consumption, or enjoyment.

EXAMPLE 20-4:   Unsafe Vehicles Banned

Hundreds of people were being killed and thousands were being injured while riding on three-wheel, all-terrain vehicles (ATVs). The vehicles, which have large, soft tires, were designed for off-road use. Because of the many deaths and injuries, the commission banned the sale of new three-wheel ATVs in the United States in 1987. In addition, the commission required manufacturers of ATVs to spend more than $8 million advertising to the public the safety problems with three-wheel vehicles.

The commission can order the recall of products found to be inherently unsafe and dangerous. It has the authority to impose civil fines for violations of its standards and cease-and-desist orders. Private citizens, acting in their own behalf, may bring suit to establish or enforce a safety rule if the commission fails to act. Information may be obtained from the commission, and unsafe products may be reported by telephoning its hotline: 1-800-638-CPSC.

20-5 Consumer Leasing Act

The Consumer Leasing Act is a federal law requiring leasing companies to inform consumers of all of the terms of a lease of personal property. Consumers can use the information to compare one lease with another or the cost of leasing with the cost of buying the same property.

The law applies only to personal property leased by an individual for a period of more than four months for personal, family, or household use. It does not cover daily or weekly rentals, leases for apartments or houses, or leases to anyone for business purposes.

Did You Know?

Gift certificates often expire before they are used, and only a few states have laws that protect consumers when their certificates expire. In New Hampshire, gift certificates under $100 cannot have expiration dates, and in Rhode Island and California, it's against the law to put an expiration date on any gift certificate. In Hawaii, sellers must honor gift certificates for a period of at least two years. In Massachusetts, gift certificates must be honored for seven years. After that period, businesses may keep the money if the dates of issuance and expiration are marked on them. If not, they must be honored forever.

EXAMPLE 20-5:   Businesses Not Protected

Guzman decided that her business could be managed much more efficiently if it had a computer. The cost of buying a computer, however, was more than Guzman could afford. She considered leasing one. The Consumer Leasing Act would not apply to Guzman's lease, because the computer was for business rather than personal use. She would be able to make a better decision, however, if she asked the leasing company for the same information the company would be required to provide to a consumer.

The law requires that consumers be given a written statement informing them of the full cost of the lease, including the cost of any necessary licenses, taxes, or other fees. Consumers must be informed of any insurance requirements and penalties for late payment. They must also be told who is responsible for maintaining and servicing the property. In addition, they must be told whether they can buy the property and, if so, when and at what price. The law also places a limit on the amount of a **balloon payment** (a very large final payment) to no more than three times the average monthly payments.

Advertisements of leases are also regulated by law. If an advertisement mentions the amount or number of payments, specifies a particular down payment, or states that no down payment is required, it must also disclose the total of regular payments, the consumer's responsibility at the end of the lease, and whether the consumer may purchase the property.

Quick Quiz 20-4 & 20-5 True or False?

1. The requirements of the Consumer Leasing Act apply to overnight rentals of videos from a video store.

2. The Consumer Leasing Act applies to the leasing of a copy machine to a business.

3. Consumers must be told, when they lease property, whether or not they can buy it and, if so, when and at what price.

20-6 Consumer Credit Laws

People buy more on credit today than ever before. They borrow money from banks, credit unions, finance companies, and automobile manufacturers. They have charge accounts with stores, restaurants, and major oil companies. They often have more than one nationally recognized credit card. Due to this extensive use of credit, Congress has found it necessary to pass federal laws to protect the consumer.

Truth in Lending

Because lending institutions and businesses charge different rates of interest to consumers, it often pays to shop around before borrowing money or buying on credit. To help consumers know the truth about the cost of borrowing money, Congress passed the Truth-in-Lending Act. Under this act, lenders must disclose two important things to borrowers: the **finance charge** (the actual cost of the loan in dollars and cents) and the **annual percentage rate (APR)** (the true rate of interest of the loan). With this information, consumers can compare the cost of loans from different lenders before deciding from which to borrow. Surprisingly, the APR sometimes turns out to be greater than it would appear at first glance.

> ## EXAMPLE 20-6:   True Rate of Interest
>
> Hana borrowed $100 for one year and agreed to pay a finance charge of $10. If she kept the $100 for the year and at the end of the year paid back the full amount, together with the $10 finance charge, the APR would be 10 percent. If, however, she paid the $110 in 12 monthly installments of $9.17 each, the APR would be 18 percent. The latter rate is higher because during the course of the year, she would have the use, on the average, of only about half of the $100.

The APR is computed with the use of a complicated mathematical formula. Tables provided by the Federal Reserve Banks are helpful in determining the exact APR on any loan.

The Truth-in-Lending Act regulates the advertising of credit terms. If an advertisement mentions one feature of credit, such as the amount of a down payment, it must mention all other important terms, such as the terms of repaying the loan. Whenever an advertisement mentions a finance rate, it must be stated as an APR, and that term must be used.

Equal Credit Opportunity

The Equal Credit Opportunity Act was passed by Congress to ensure that all consumers are given an equal chance to receive credit. The law makes it illegal for banks and businesses to discriminate against credit applicants because of their sex, race, marital status, national origin, religion, or age or because they get public assistance income. The law must be followed by anyone who regularly extends credit, including banks, credit unions, finance companies, credit card issuers, and retail stores. Some of the rights to consumers under the act are as follows:

1. People who apply for credit may not be asked to reveal their sex, race, national origin, or religion; whether they are divorced or widowed; their marital status, unless they are applying for a joint account or a secured loan (marital status may, however, be asked in the states of Arizona, California, Idaho, Louisiana, Nevada, New Mexico, Texas, Washington, and Wisconsin—all of which are community property states [see Chapter 20]); information about their spouse, except in community property states, unless the spouse is also applying for credit or will use the account; their plans for having or raising children; and whether they receive alimony, child support, or separate maintenance payments if they will not be relying on that income.

2. When deciding to extend credit, creditors must not consider the applicant's sex, marital status, race, national origin, or religion; consider the applicant's age, unless the applicant is a minor or is considered favorably for being over 62; refuse to consider public assistance income in the same manner as other income; and refuse to consider income from part-time employment, pensions, or retirement programs.

3. Applicants may apply for credit under the name given to them at birth, their married name, or a combination of both. They may receive credit without a cosigner if they meet the creditor's standards. In addition, applicants have a right to know within 30 days whether their application for credit has been accepted or rejected. If rejected, they have a right to know the reasons for the rejection within 60 days.

4. People may bring suit in a federal district court either individually or with others against creditors that violate this law. If they win, they may be awarded their actual losses plus attorney's fees, court costs, and punitive damages (damages designed to punish the wrongdoer).

BusinessWeek Business Law in the News
Cap One's Credit Trap

When Brad Kehn received his first credit card from Capital One Financial Corp. in 2004, it took him only three months to exceed its $300 credit limit and get socked with a $35 over-limit fee. But what surprised the Plankinton (S.D.) resident more was that Cap One then offered him another card even though he was over the limit—and another and another. By early 2006, he and his wife had six Cap One Visa and MasterCards. They were in over their heads.

The couple was late and over the limit on all six cards, despite occasionally borrowing from one to pay the other. Every month they chalked up $70 in late and over-limit fees on each card, for a total of $420, in addition to paying penalty interest rates. The couple fell further behind as their Cap One balances soared. Even so, they still received mail offers for more Cap One cards until they sought relief at a credit counseling agency this May. "I didn't open them," says Kehn, 33, who manages a truck stop and runs a carpet-cleaning business on the side. "I owe these people that much damn money and they are willing to give me another credit card? This is nuts."

Credit card experts and counselors who help overextended debtors say there's nothing crazy about it. Cap One, they contend, is simply aiming to maximize fee income from debtors who may be less sophisticated and who may not have many options because of their credit history. By offering several cards with low limits, instead of one with a larger limit, the odds are increased that cardholders will exceed their limits, garnering over-limit fees. Juggling several cards also increases the chance consumers may be late on a payment, incurring an additional fee. And if cardholders fall behind, they pile up over-limit and late fees on several cards instead of just one. "How many more ways can I fool you?" says Elizabeth Warren, a Harvard Law School professor who has written extensively on the card industry. "That is all this is about."

Consumers may not be the only ones who are unaware of Cap One's ways. Its practice of issuing multiple cards to some borrowers with low credit ratings doesn't appear well-known in the investment community. And just how much Cap One relies on fee income, vs. interest, is a mystery, since, like most lenders, it doesn't disclose that. All credit card companies have become more reliant on fee income in recent years, but in a report issued in 2002, William Ryan, an invest-

ment analyst at Portales Partners, warned that Cap One's earnings could be "devastated" if regulators cracked down on multiple cards or fees.

That hasn't happened. For now, Cap One's approach looks pretty savvy, however onerous it may be for some customers. Ronald Mann, card-industry expert, says that by generating so much revenue from late and over-limit fees, as well as interest, Cap One likely more than offsets for the risk of card holders filing for bankruptcy. "The premise is to make money even if [Cap One] never gets fully repaid," says Mann, a law professor at the University of Texas in Austin. (Mann has been retained by a party suing Cap One in a business dispute.)

In a written response to questions, Cap One acknowledges that it offers multiple cards. "Our goal is to offer products that meet our customers' needs and appropriately reflect their ability to pay," it says. The company also stated: "Within our current U.S. portfolio, the vast majority of Capital One credit card customers hold one with a very small percentage choosing to have three or more cards." Spokeswoman Tatiana Stead declined to offer precise numbers or to say whether households with three or more cards were concentrated among "subprime" borrowers, who have low credit ratings.

Under the Radar

THE NATION'S fifth-largest credit card issuer, with $49 billion in U.S. credit card receivables as of the end of June, McLean (Va.)-based Cap One is a major lender to the subprime market. According to Cap One's regulatory filings, 30% of its credit card loans are subprime. Representatives of 32 credit counseling agencies contacted by *BusinessWeek* say that Cap One has long stood out for the number of cards it's willing to give to subprime borrowers. "In the higher-risk market, no lender is more aggressive in offering multiple cards," says Kathryn Crumpton, manager of Consumer Credit Counseling Service of Greater Milwaukee. Other big card-industry players that do subprime lending include Bank of America, Chase, and Citigroup. Representatives for Chase and Citigroup say they do not offer multiple cards to subprime customers. (BofA did not respond to inquires.)

Last year, West Virginia Attorney General Darrel V. McGraw Jr. filed an action in state court seeking documents from Cap One related to its issuance of multiple cards, as well as other credit practices. Other than that, however, Cap One's practices do not appear to have drawn regultory scrutiny. A spokesman for the Federal Reserve, Cap One's primary federal overseer, declined to comment about Cap One, but said that in general the regulator doesn't object to multiple cards. Still, Fed guidelines warn multiple-card lenders to analyze the credit risk tied to all the cards before offering additional ones.

If consumers were using one Cap One card to make payments on another, it could artificially hold down the company's delinquency and charge-off rates, metrics investors closely watch because they affect earnings, says Allen Puwalski, senior financial analyst at the Center for Financial Research & Analysis in Rockville, Md. In filings with U.S. Securities and Exchange Commission, Cap One says its delinquency and charge-off rates as of Sept. 30 were 3.6% and 2.5%, respectively, about middle of the pack for major card lenders.

In an e-mail, Cap One's Stead says: "It is not our practice—nor our intention—to offer an additional card to customers who are curently delinquent or over limit on a Capital One card." But Daniel Carvajal believes that's just what Cap One tried to get him to do. Carvajal, 38, who is confined to a wheelchair with cerebral palsy and lives with his mother in Miami, says he exceeded his $1,500 Cap One credit limit last Christmas by several hundred dollars and was late on payments in January and February. In March, he says, a Cap One representative offered him a second card, which he refused. Using the new card to catch up with his first, he suspects, "is what they wanted me to do."

Some overextended Cap One customers admit using one card to pay another. In mid-2005, Kehn, the South Dakota truck-stop manager, already over the limit on three Cap One cards with $300 to $500 limits, received an offer from Cap One for another card with a $500 limit. He transferred part of the balances from the first three cards to get them under the credit limit. When his wife got a second card in early 2006 with a $1,500 cap, the couple took expensive cash advances on it to try to help make payments on the five other Cap One cards. "I robbed Peter to pay Paul," Kehn says.

Christine Garcia, 41, of Orange, Calif., said she and her husband did the same when stretched with five Cap One cards between them. So did Bernice Thompson, 46, of Fort Smith, Ark., who, along with her husband, had seven Cap One cards. "We got caught in a circle, and couldn't get out," says Thompson.

These examples bring into question Cap One's public stance on its subprime lending. Analysts, including Carl Neff, ratings director on card securitizations for Standard & Poor's, say Cap One tells investors that it carefully controls risk by giving such borrowers only small lines of credit. Indeed, the largest percentage of Cap One's 28 million credit-card accounts, 43%, have balances of $1,500 or less, according to its SEC filings. But if many borrowers had larger aggregate balances because they have multiple accounts, that percentage would be lower, and Cap One's "underwriting wouldn't appear as conservative as it looks," says the Financial Research Center's Puwalski.

Like other big card companies, Cap One securitizes most of its card receivables as bonds, which are rated by credit agencies such as Standard & Poor's (S&P is a unit of The McGraw-Hill Companies, publisher of *BusinessWeek*). Cap One's ratings are strong, allowing it to command a higher price for the bonds. But Neff of S&P says he is surprised Cap One would offer riskier borrowers multiple, low-limit accounts given what it has told the market. "If it was a very prevalent practice, that would lower [Cap One's credit] quality in our eyes," Neff says. A sampling of credit counseling agencies across the country indicates that about a third of the troubled debtors they see with Cap One cards have two or more Cap One accounts.

Ron Nesbitt, 37, a Macon (Ga.) truck driver, and his wife sought credit counseling last year. By the second half of 2004, Nesbitt says, the couple had become consistently late and over limit on six Cap One cards, generating $348 in fees alone each month. "It was out of control," he says.

Questions for Analysis

1. What surprised Brad Kehn after he had exceeded his credit limit and was charged with an over-limit fee?

2. What did Cap One do after the couple was late and over the limit on all six of their cards?

3. What do credit card experts and counselors mean when they say there's "nothing crazy about it"?

4. What does Cap One tell investors about how it controls risk?

5. What does a sampling of credit counseling agencies across the country indicate about Cap One debtors?

Source: Robert Berner, "Cap One's Credit Trap," *BusinessWeek,* November 6, 2006, 35.

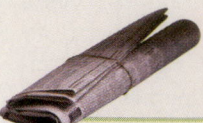

BusinessWeek Business Law in the News

Study Now—And Pay And Pay And Pay Later

Thousands of low-income adults borrow at high interest rates to go back to school to learn new skills. Many end up falling into a debt spiral.

John Liles of Cleveland, Ga., dreamed of becoming a sports coach. He had lost his $9-an-hour job as a machine operator in 2005 as a result of a lengthy bout with diabetes. His illness hadn't stopped him from coaching his children's sports teams, however, and he hoped to turn the hobby into a career. He needed an associate's degree, so he signed up to study online with American InterContinental University (AIU).

To obtain loans, the school guided him to SLM Corp., better known as Sallie Mae. Liles, now 47, says he explained to AIU that he couldn't afford interest of more than 9%, and the school encouraged him to move ahead with the loan application. Several months into his courses, he says he was shocked to discover in a form Sallie Mae sent him that one of his loans, for $6,000, was growing at 18.1%. It would require monthly payments of $110 for the next 15 years, totaling $19,924. "I can't afford it," he says.

Cases like Liles' are proliferating as the cost of education has far outpaced the availability of low-interest loans whose repayment the federal government guarantees. With enrollment rising in trade schools, more lower-income students are relying on high-interest private loans, such as the one Liles received. "For hundreds of thousands of citizens, the worst mistake they ever made was to go back to school," says Alan Collinge, founder of advocacy group Student Loan Justice.

Many borrowers describe the loan process as opaque, saying schools and lenders don't explain interest rates or postgraduation payments. Some borrowers say they were unaware that private loans are different from less expensive federally guaranteed loans. "When you hear 'Sallie Mae,' you think of somebody's favorite aunt baking them a pie," says borrower Molly Cosgrove of Portland, Ore. "You don't think of high-interest loans." Once a federally sponsored organization, Sallie Mae became a fully independent corporation in 2004. It offers both private and federally backed loans.

After losing her $20,000-a-year job at a call center, Cosgrove enrolled in Western Culinary Institute in Portland in 2004, planning to become a chef. She says the school lined up student loans for her with assurances that the terms would be reasonable and her diploma would attract appealing job offers. She asked few questions. Today, Cosgrove, 33, has her degree—and $43,000 in debt, most of it accruing interest at 18.5%. Unable to get a job as a chef for more than $8.50 an hour, she went back to answering phones for $13 an hour. She owes Sallie Mae $553 a month but doesn't have anything close to that to spare. "I can't see a way out of the mess I inadvertently created," she says.

Career Education Corp. (CECO), which owns both AIU and Western Culinary Institute, says it is not responsible for, and often not aware of, loan terms, which are agreed to by the student and lender. It adds that its schools inform students that private loans carry higher interest rates.

Sallie Mae says the terms of its private student loans are made clear in writing to would-be borrowers before any money is disbursed. "These are college students. At some point you have to read what you're signing," says Barry Feierstein, Sallie Mae's senior vice-president for private credit loans.

The lender says it recently capped rates on new private loans and is exploring ways to relieve the high rates facing some recent graduates. "We want people to have a fighting chance," says Feierstein.

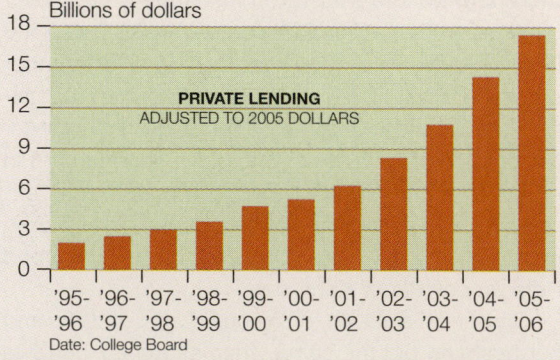

EXPENSIVE DEBT

As private lending for education proliferates, more students are carrying debt with higher interest rates

Billions of dollars

PRIVATE LENDING
ADJUSTED TO 2005 DOLLARS

Date: College Board

Source: Ben Elgin, "Study Now—And Pay And Pay And Pay Later," *BusinessWeek*, May 2, 2007, 66.

The Opening Case Revisited, Part III
"Triple Trouble"

If the charges occurred before VISA received notice of the theft, Avila would be
liable for $50 of the unauthorized charges. If the charges occurred after VISA had
received notice, Avila would have no liability.

Unauthorized Use of Credit Cards

Sometimes credit cards are lost, stolen, or used by people who have no authority to use
them. Under the Truth-in-Lending Act, credit cardholders are not responsible for any unauthorized charges made after the card issuer has been notified of the loss, theft, or possible
unauthorized use of the card. Such notice may be given to the card issuer by telephone,
letter, or any other means. Even then, credit cardholders are responsible only for the first
$50 of any unauthorized charges. Debit cards do not have this built-in protection (see
Chapter 28).

The credit cardholder can avoid the $50 liability if the credit card issuer has not in-
cluded on the card a method to identify the user of the card, such as a signature, a photograph, or other means of identification. Card issuers must notify cardholders in advance of
the potential $50 liability.

Credit card issuers are not allowed to send out unsolicited credit cards unless they are
a renewal or substitute for a card already in use.

Fair Credit Reporting

The Fair Credit Reporting Act was passed by Congress to ensure that consumers are treated
fairly by credit bureaus and consumer reporting agencies. A consumer has the right to
know all information (other than medical information) that is in his or her files. A consumer also has the right to know, in most cases, the source of the information on file. In
addition, a consumer has the right to be told the name of anyone who received a credit report in the past year (or two years if the credit report relates to a job application).

Consumers who wish to know what information a credit bureau has on file about them
can order a credit report on the Internet or from the following sources:

- Equifax, P.O. Box 740256, Atlanta, GA 30374 (800) 685-1111
- Trans Union, P.O. Box 1000, Chester, PA 19022 (800) 916-8800
- Experian, P.O. Box 949, Allen TX 75013 (888) 322-5583

There may be a fee of up to $9 for the report. If errors are found, credit bureaus must inves-
tigate and then correct or delete information that is inaccurate, incomplete, or obsolete. If
the credit bureau retains information that the consumer believes to be incorrect, the consumer's version of the facts must be inserted in the file. Also, creditors are required to tell
consumers the specific reasons for the denial of credit.

Fair Credit Billing

Errors are sometimes made in bills sent out by retail stores, credit card companies, and
other businesses that extend credit. To make it easier for billing errors to be corrected,
Congress has passed the Fair Credit Billing Act (FCBA). The law establishes a procedure
for the prompt handling of billing disputes.

Under the act, when consumers believe an error has been made in a bill, they must notify the creditor within 60 days after the bill was mailed. The notice must identify the consumer and give the account number, the suspected amount of error, and an explanation of why the consumer believes there is an error. The creditor must acknowledge the consumer's notice within 30 days. Then, within 90 days, the creditor must conduct an investigation and either correct the mistake or explain why the bill is believed to be correct.

Another provision of the act gives consumers protection when they buy unsatisfactory goods or services with credit cards. If you have a dispute with a credit card purchase, do not pay the bill for the disputed item. Instead, notify the credit card issuer by telephone immediately. The credit card issuer will put the disputed amount on hold and send you a form to fill out explaining the dispute. The credit card issuer will attempt to resolve the dispute and inform you of the results. Then, if the problem is not corrected and suit is brought by the credit card issuer, the consumer may use as a defense the fact that unsatisfactory goods or services were received. For this law to apply, the initial transaction must have taken place in the consumer's state or within 100 miles of the consumer's mailing address. Creditors may not give cardholders a poor credit rating for exercising their rights under this act.

Fair Debt Collection Practices

Under the Fair Debt Collection Practices Act, specific rules must be followed by companies that are in the business of collecting debts for others. Some of these rules are as follows:

1. When trying to locate someone, a debt collector may not communicate by postcard or tell others that the consumer owes money.

2. When the debt collector knows that the consumer is represented by an attorney, the debt collector may communicate only with the attorney.

3. A debt collector may not communicate with the consumer at any unusual or inconvenient time or place. Unless there are circumstances to the contrary, the convenient time for communicating with a consumer is between the hours of 8:00 AM and 9:00 PM.

4. A debt collector may not communicate with the consumer at the consumer's place of employment if the debt collector knows that the employer prohibits such communication.

5. A debt collector may not communicate, in connection with the collection of a debt, with any person other than the consumer, the consumer's attorney, the creditor's attorney, or a consumer reporting agency.

6. If a consumer notifies a debt collector in writing that the consumer refuses to pay the debt or wishes the debt collector to cease further communication, the debt collector must cease communication, except to notify the consumer of a specific action.

7. Debt collectors may not harass consumers or use abusive techniques to collect debts. The use or threatened use of violence or other criminal means to harm the person, property, or reputation of consumers is not allowed. In addition, debt collectors may not use obscene or profane language or publish a list of those who allegedly refuse to pay debts. It is also illegal for a debt collector to cause a telephone to ring or to engage in repeated telephone conversations with the intent to annoy the consumer.

Debt collectors who violate this law may be sued for actual damages, punitive damages, and attorneys' fees.

Quick Quiz 20-6 True or False?

1. Lenders must disclose the finance charge and the annual percentage rate of loans to borrowers to help borrowers compare the cost of loans from different lenders.

2. It is illegal for banks and businesses to discriminate against credit applicants because of their sex, race, marital status, national origin, religion, age, or because they get public assistance income.

3. Credit cardholders are responsible for all unauthorized charges made before the card issuer has been notified of the loss, theft, or unauthorized use of the card.

Summary

20.1 Consumer protection laws apply in transactions between a business and a consumer. State consumer protection offices help enforce state consumer protection laws and sometimes assist consumers with individual problems. The FTC Act makes unfair or deceptive acts or practices in or affecting commerce unlawful. The federal law applies to businesses that deal with interstate commerce or that affect interstate commerce.

20.2 Unfair or deceptive acts or practices are prohibited by the FTC Act. Consumers need to be alert for telemarketing fraud and work-at-home schemes. Only free samples and items sent by charities may be mailed to people who did not request them. People who receive unordered merchandise through the mail may treat the merchandise as a gift. Bait-and-switch schemes are prohibited. True odometer readings on cars must be disclosed to buyers.

20.3 The FTC has established rules to help correct wrongdoings in the marketplace. The Used Car Rule requires dealers to inform buyers of the warranties that go with the car by placing a Buyer's Guide in the window of each used car offered for sale. The Cooling-Off Rule gives consumers three days to change their minds when they enter into contracts away from the place of business of the seller. The Negative Option Rule protects consumers when they subscribe to magazines, CD clubs, or other plans that send products on an ongoing basis. The Can Spam Act is designed to reduce the use of unsolicited e-mail on the Internet. The FTC's anti-slamming law provides a remedy for consumers whose telephone service is changed without their permission.

The Mail, Telephone, Internet, or Fax Rule requires sellers to ship orders within the time promised in their advertisements. If no time period is promised, they must ship orders within 30 days. If they cannot do so, they must give consumers the option to cancel the order and receive a refund. The Telemarketing Sales Rule helps protect consumers from abusive and deceptive telemarketers. Consumers can place their telephone numbers on the national Do Not Call Registry to stop most telemarketing calls. The FTC requires people who dial 900-prefix numbers to be warned of the cost of the call. The FTC also allows customers to block such services if requested.

20.4 The Consumer Product Safety Commission establishes safety standards for consumer products. The commission has the power to recall unsafe products and impose fines on violators.

20.5 The Consumer Leasing Act requires companies that lease personal property to consumers for longer than four-month periods to disclose the full cost of the lease as well as other details of the transaction.

20.6 Many laws protect consumers who apply for or obtain credit. Lenders must make certain disclosures before lending money. It is illegal for creditors to discriminate against credit applicants because of their sex, race, marital status, national origin, religion, or age or because they get public assistance income. Credit cardholders are not responsible for any unauthorized charges made after the card issuer has been notified of the loss, theft, or possible unauthorized use of the card. Even then, cardholders are responsible only for the first $50 of any unauthorized charges. Consumers have the right to know all information about themselves (other than medical information) that is on file with a credit bureau. They also have a right to know the name of anyone who received a credit report in the past year. A procedure has been established for the prompt handling of billing disputes dealing with charge accounts. Debt collectors are prohibited from harassing or abusing debtors when they attempt to collect debts.

Key Terms

annual percentage rate (APR), 404

bait-and-switch scheme, 395

balloon payment, 404

Buyer's Guide, 398

Can Spam Act, 400

class-action lawsuit, 394

commerce, 393

consent order, 393

consumer, 393

Cooling-Off Rule, 398

dunning letters, 395

finance charge, 404

interstate commerce, 393

intrastate commerce, 393

slamming, 400

spam, 400

Used Car Rule, 398

Questions for Review and Discussion

1. To what transactions do consumer protection laws apply?
2. What acts are declared unlawful by the Federal Trade Commission Act?
3. Name and describe four unfair or deceptive acts.
4. Describe the Used Car Rule, the Cooling-Off Rule, and the Mail, Telephone, Internet, or Fax Rule.
5. Highlight the main features of the Telemarketing Sales Rule, the 900-Telephone-Number Rules, the Negative Option Rule, antispam law, and antislam law.
6. Explain the purpose of the Consumer Product Safety Act and describe the powers of the Consumer Product Safety Commission.

7. What benefits do consumers receive from the Consumer Leasing Act?
8. What two important things must lenders disclose to borrowers under the Truth-in-Lending Act, and what does the Equal Credit Opportunity Act prohibit?
9. How are credit cardholders protected under the Truth-in-Lending Act? What protection are credit cardholders given under the Fair Credit Billing Act?
10. List three rules that must be followed by debt collecting companies under the Fair Debt Collecting Practices Act.

Investigating the Internet

After looking back over The Opening Case at the beginning of this chapter, go online to the *Consumer Action* Web site. Following the sample complaint letter you find at that site, write a letter that Frank Avila could send to the used car lot owner regarding his disappointing experiences with the company. Then, while still online, look for the *FTC Consumer Complaint Form* that Avila could use if he wishes to notifiy the Federal Trade Commision of his experience.

Cases for Analysis

1. Emerson told a store clerk that she needed some furniture right away to furnish her empty condo. The clerk showed Emerson a leather couch and chair and said that they were in stock and could be delivered the following Friday. Emerson bought the items, paying for them with her credit card. The furniture was not delivered Friday as promised, and Emerson was told by the store that it could not be delivered for a month. What would you suggest that Emerson do to remedy the situation?

2. Barrett owned some apartment buildings that he operated for business purposes. He did not live in any of the apartments. The Adirondack Bottled Gas Corp. supplied the apartment buildings with a propane-tank storage system. A dispute arose, and in a suit against Adirondack, Barrett claimed that the consumer protection law applied to the transaction. Do you agree with Barrett? Why or why not? *Barrett v. Adirondack Bottled Gas Corp.,* 487 A.2d 1074 (VT).

3. Harriet Glantz lost her job. She was unable to find work for several months and fell behind in the payment of her debts. A debt collector telephoned her at 11:45 PM, used profanity, and threatened to "take care of her" if she didn't pay the amount owed. Were Glantz's rights violated? Explain.

4. Ingram went to a used car lot in a large city and bought a used car. On his way home from the lot, the car that he had purchased broke down. The engine stopped running altogether. The used car lot refused to fix the car because the salesperson had written "as is" on the sales slip. Ingram had not been informed that the car was sold to him as is. Was a consumer protection law violated? Explain.

5. Prior to his marriage, Edward Garber had been in financial difficulty and had a poor credit rating. His wife, Natalie, applied for a credit card in her family name, fearing that she would be turned down if she used her married name of Garber. She was told that she must use her married name on a credit application. Could Natalie have used her family name when she applied for credit? Explain.

6. Horack bought a used Mustang from a used car lot. The odometer showed that the car had been driven only 30,000 miles. Later, while cleaning her car, Horack found a service receipt showing that the actual mileage on the car a year earlier was 45,000 miles. Was a law violated? Explain.

7. Carboni's MasterCard bill contained several charges that she had not made. Upon investigation, she discovered that her credit card was missing from her wallet. She immediately notified the bank of the lost credit card. The unauthorized charges on the bill that she received amounted to $375. Did Carboni have to pay the full amount of the bill? Explain.

8. Delores Bierlein paid a $200 deposit toward the rental of the Silver Room at Alex's Continental Inn for her wedding reception. Later, Bierlein canceled the reception because her fiancé was transferred from Ohio to New York. The inn refused to refund Bierlein's deposit. The consumer protection law of that state requires suppliers to furnish receipts when they receive deposits. Bierlein was not given a receipt for her $200 deposit. When she sued for the return of the $200, the question arose as to whether this transaction fell within the consumer protection law. Do you think it does? Explain. *Bierlein v. Alex's Continental Inn, Inc.,* 475 N.E.2d 1273 (OH).

9. In response to a radio advertisement, Mr. and Mrs. Lancet telephoned Hollywood Decorators, Inc., and arranged for Mr. Wolff, a company representative, to visit their home. During Wolff's visit, the Lancets signed a contract for interior decoration and paid a $1,000 deposit. Two days later, the Lancets canceled the contract by telephone and asked for the return of their deposit. Twelve days after that, the Lancet's attorney wrote a letter to the company renewing the cancellation. Were they bound by the contract they signed? Why or why not? *Hollywood Decorators, Inc., v. Lancet,* 461 N.Y.S.2d 955 (NY).

10. After receiving an unsuccessful surgical procedure designed to facilitate weight loss, Gatten brought suit against the physician for violation

of the state consumer protection law. That law read in part, "unfair methods of competition and deceptive practices in the conduct of any trade or commerce are unlawful." Gatten based her case on statements made to her about her course of treatment and the probable results of that treatment. Does the unsuccessful treatment by a physician fall within the consumer protection law? Explain. *Gatten v. Merzi,* 579 A.2d 974 (PA).

Quick Quiz Answers

20-1	20-2	20-3	20-4 & 20-5	20-6
1. T	1. T	1. F	1. F	1. T
2. T	2. F	2. T	2. F	2. T
3. F	3. T	3. F	3. T	3. F

Part 3 Case Study

Atkinson v. Elk Corp. of Texas
California Appellate Court, Sixth District
No. H028933

Summary

James Atkinson contracted with Pacific Coast Roofing to re-roof his family home. Atkinson chose shingles manufactured by Elk as the roofing material. The brochure in which the shingles were advertised contained the following language: "When you upgrade to Prestique I *High Definition,* you get the protection and durability to match the beauty. Elk's 30-year limited warranty covers both labor and shingles, plus you get a 5-year limited wind warranty." When Atkinson went to the building supply facility from which the shingles were purchased, there was no other limited warranty on display, nor was he given one. Based on the written warranty he saw in the brochure, Atkinson instructed Pacific to use Elk Prestique I shingles to re-roof his home. Atkinson paid Pacific $7,400 for the re-roofing work. Included in that price was the cost of the shingles.

Five and one-half years later, while cleaning the gutters in his roof, Atkinson noticed cracks in many of shingles. Immediately, he contacted Pacific. Pacific contacted Elk, which examined the shingles and found them to be defective. Elk sent Atkinson a check for $2,949.79, saying it was the prorated amount for materials and labor for the shingles. Atkinson returned the check and brought suit for breach of warranty under the Magnuson-Moss Warranty Act.

The trial court found against Atkinson, saying that because the contract was for a "lump sum" with no separate charge for materials, and the shingles were incorporated into a dwelling, the shingles were not consumer goods under Magnuson-Moss.

The Court's Opinion

Elia J., with Rushing P.J. and Premo, J. concurring

The Magnuson-Moss Warranty Act applies to written warranties on tangible personal property which is normally used for personal, family, or household purposes. This definition includes property which is intended to be attached to or installed in any real property without regard to whether it is so attached or installed. This means that a product is a 'consumer product' if the use of that type of product is not uncommon. The percentage of sales or the use to which a product is put by any individual buyer is not determinative. For example, products such as automobiles and typewriters which are used for both personal and commercial purposes come within the definition of consumer product. Where it is unclear whether a particular product is covered under the definition of consumer product, *any ambiguity will be resolved in favor of coverage.* . . .

The definition of 'Consumer product' limits the applicability of the Act to personal property, 'including any such property intended to be attached to or installed in any real property without regard to whether it is so attached or installed.' This provision brings under the Act separate items of equipment attached to real property, such as air conditioners, furnaces, and water heaters.

The coverage of separate items of equipment attached to real property includes, but is not limited to, appliances and other thermal, mechanical, and electrical equipment. (It does not extend to the wiring, plumbing, ducts, and other items which are integral component parts of the structure.) State law would classify many such products as fixtures to, and therefore a part of, realty. The statutory definition is designed to bring such products under the Act regardless of whether they may be considered fixtures under state law.

The coverage of building materials which are not separate items of equipment is based on the nature of the purchase transaction. An analysis of the transaction will determine whether the goods are real or personal property. The numerous products which go into the construction of a consumer dwelling are all consumer products when sold 'over the counter,' as by hardware and building supply retailers. This is also true where a consumer contracts for the purchase of such materials in connection with the improvement, repair, or modification of a home (for example, paneling, dropped ceilings, siding, roofing, storm windows, remodeling). However, where such products are at the time of sale integrated into the structure of a dwelling they are not consumer products as they cannot be practically distinguished from realty. Thus, for example, the beams, wallboard, wiring, plumbing, windows, roofing, and other structural components of a dwelling are not consumer products when they are sold as part of real estate covered by a written warranty.

In the case where a consumer contracts with a builder to construct a home, a substantial addition to a home, or other realty (such as a garage or an in-ground swimming pool) the building materials to be used are not consumer products. Although the materials are separately identifiable at the time the contract is made, it is the intention of the parties to contract for the construction of realty which will integrate the component materials. Of course, as noted above, any separate items of equipment to be attached to such realty are consumer products under the Act." (Italics added.)

Elk contends that Atkinson did not purchase the shingles over the counter or specifically contract for the purchase of the shingles in connection with the improvement or repair of the roof. Instead, he contracted to have his house completely re-roofed. Elk argues that this distinction is dispositive because Pacific purchased the shingles from the supplier, and installed the shingles on the roof along with the other roofing materials in completing the re-roofing contract. Thus, Pacific provided an integrated roofing system. According to Elk, this means that Atkinson did not purchase the shingles or any other consumer product when he contracted for the new roof. Therefore pursuant to 16 Code of Federal Regulations part 700.1, subdivisions (e) and (f) the roofing shingles are not consumer products under Magnuson-Moss.

A close examination of this section reveals that some items that normally or usually become a part of realty when incorporated into a structure are still considered consumer products when their incorporation is part of an improvement, modification or repair of a home. (16 C.F.R. § 700.1(e) (2006), ["The numerous products which go into the construction of a consumer dwelling are all consumer products when sold 'over the counter,' as by hardware and building supply retailers. This is also true where a consumer contracts for the purchase of such materials in connection with the improvement, repair, or modification of a home (for example, paneling, dropped ceilings, siding, *roofing,* storm windows, remodeling")].)

With respect to products that are incorporated into realty, we find that the crucial distinction is the *time of sale*. If the products are purchased in order to add them to an existing dwelling, then the products are consumer products. If, on the other hand, the products are purchased as part of a larger real estate sales contract, or contract for a *substantial* addition to a home, they are not. (16 C.F.R. § 700.1(e) and (f) (2006), italics added.)

As the *Muchisky* court explained, "It appears that as to products which are becoming a part of realty the distinction drawn is whether the product is being added to an already existing structure or whether it is being utilized to create the structure." (*Muchisky, supra,* 838 S.W.2d at p. 78.)

Here Pacific purchased the roof shingles at Atkinson's behest, in order that Pacific would add them to Atkinson's existing home. Although the intent was to incorporate the shingles into the realty, they were not purchased "as part of real estate covered by a written warranty."

Consequently, we conclude that under the facts of this case, roofing shingles are consumer products under Magnuson-Moss. Accordingly, we reverse the trial court's summary adjudication on this point.

Questions for Analysis

1. Why did the trial court find against Atkinson?
2. To what does the Magnuson-Moss Warranty Act apply?
3. What property does the definition of the Act include?
4. What was Elk's contention in this case?
5. What is the crucial distinction in determining whether an item that is incorporated into realty is a consumer product?
6. In whose favor did the court rule relative to the Magnuson-Moss Warranty Act?

Part Four

Property

Chapter 21   Personal Property

The Opening Case

"A Memorable Day"

Emily had a wonderful twenty-first birthday celebration. Her boyfriend gave her a mini-DVD camcorder, and her sister gave her a $50 gift certificate to Tom Shea's, a popular seafood restaurant. Emily's grandfather telephoned her from Florida to say his present to her was his convertible sports car. She could pick it up at his winter home in Florida any time. The next day, she received news that her grandfather had passed away in Florida before she had had time to pick up the car. She let a year go by before going to the restaurant to use the gift certificate and was told that the certificate had expired. She and her boyfriend ate there anyway, but after leaving the restaurant, Emily realized that she had left her camcorder at their table. She learned from the waitress that another party had found the camcorder and was supposed to have returned it to her. Later, the police found the camcorder at a pawn shop and identified it as hers.

Opening Case Questions

1. Is Emily entitled to her grandfather's car?

2. Could the restaurant keep the money that had been paid for the gift certificate?

3. What duty did the restaurant owe to Emily concerning her camcorder?

4. Can Emily recover the camcorder from the pawn shop?

LO   Learning Objectives

1. Give examples of tangible and intangible personal property.
2. Describe the methods of owning property with others.
3. Differentiate among lost property, misplaced property, and abandoned property.
4. Identify the requirements of a completed gift.
5. Explain the law that applies to stolen property.
6. Discuss the law of patents, copyrights, trademarks, and trade secrets.

21-1 Personal Property

Broadly defined, **personal property** is everything that can be owned other than real estate. It is divided into two kinds, tangible and intangible.

Tangible personal property is property that has substance and that can be touched, such as a book, a pair of jeans, or a television set. Also called goods, or **chattels**, tangible personal property is movable and includes animals and crops.

Intangible personal property, in contrast, is property that is not perceptible to the senses and cannot be touched. Accounts receivables and stock certificates are examples of intangible personal property. Another name for this type of property is **chose in action**, which means evidence of the right to property but not the property itself. In addition to the items mentioned, chose in action includes money due on a note or contract, damages due for breach of contract or tort, and rights under insurance policies.

Ownership of Personal Property

When personal property is owned solely by one person, it is said to be owned in **severalty**. When it is owned by more than one person, it is said to be held in **cotenancy**. The types of cotenancies discussed here are tenancy in common, joint tenancy, and community property. Other forms of cotenancies are examined under the heading of real property in Chapter 23.

When two or more people own personal property as **tenants in common**, each cotenant's share of the property passes to his or her heirs upon death. In contrast, when two or more people own personal property as **joint tenants** (sometimes referred to as **joint tenants with the right of survivorship**), each cotenant's share of the property passes to the surviving joint tenants upon death. Nine states recognize **community property**, which is property (except a gift or inheritance) that is acquired by the personal efforts of either spouse during marriage and that, by law, belongs to both spouses equally. The states that recognize community property are the following: Arizona, California, Idaho, Louisiana, Nevada, New Mexico, Texas, Washington, and Wisconsin. Spouses can leave their half of the community property by will to whomever they choose. If they die without a will, their share passes to their surviving spouse.

Lost, Misplaced, and Abandoned Property

The finder of lost property has a legal responsibility, usually fixed by statute, to make an effort to learn the identity of the owner and return the property to that person. Advertising the property in a general circulation newspaper is usually evidence of the finder's honest effort to locate the owner. Statutes in many states provide that if the finder of lost property has made an effort to locate the owner and has not been successful within a period specified by law, the property belongs to the finder.

The Opening Case Revisited, Part 1

"A Memorable Day"

Misplaced Property Emily's camcorder was misplaced rather than lost and should have been retained by the restaurant for Emily to pick up.

If lost property is found on the counter of a store, on a table in a restaurant or hotel, on a chair in a washroom, or in some similar public or semipublic place, it is considered not to be *lost* but to have been *misplaced*. It is reasonable to suppose that the owner will remember leaving it there and return for it. For this reason, the finder may not keep possession of the article but must leave it with the proprietor or manager to hold for the owner. If the property is found on the floor or in the corridor or any other place that would indicate it was not placed there intentionally, the finder may retain possession of the article while looking for the true owner. In this case, it is not likely that the owner would recall where it was lost.

EXAMPLE 21-1:   Misplaced Property

While walking along a beach one morning, Carlow noticed a plastic bag near the edge of the water. She opened the bag and discovered that it contained a large sum of money. In the bag with the money was a bank deposit slip made out in the name of a nearby seafood restaurant. Carlow had a legal duty to return the money to the restaurant.

Suppose the bank deposit slip had not been in the bag and Carlow was unsuccessful in an attempt to find the rightful owner. After making a sincere effort to locate the real owner, and after the period of time set by state statute, Carlow would become the owner of the money.

When property is found and turned over to officials of a state, without any claim registered by the finder, the property becomes the property of the state after a period of time set by statute. The same rule applies to bank deposits and other claims that have been abandoned by persons in whose names such claims were registered. In these latter instances, a period of up to 20 years may be required to establish the right of the state to take title. In some states, gift certificate money that is unclaimed after a certain number of years is supposed to be transferred to the state under the abandoned property law. When property reverts to the state, it is said to **escheat**. Some states have statutes that remove gift certificates from their abandoned property law, treating them in different ways.

Abandoned property is property that has been discarded by the owner without the intent to reclaim ownership of it. Courts require clear and convincing evidence of both the desertion of the property by the owner as well as the owner's intent not to return to it before determining that property was indeed abandoned. With some exceptions, anyone who finds abandoned property has the right to keep it and obtains good title to it, even against the original owner.

Old shipwrecks are often the subject of abandoned property cases. If an abandoned shipwreck is found outside the boundaries of a state, either the law of finds or the law of salvage applies under admiralty law. The *law of finds* gives ownership to the finder if all of

The Opening Case Revisited, Part II

"A Memorable Day"

Abandoned Property In states that treat unclaimed gift certificates as abandoned property, Emily would be entitled to the value of the gift certificate if she claimed it before it became the property of the state.

the following apply: (a) the property is abandoned, (b) the finder intends to acquire the property, and (c) the finder has possession of the property. The *law of salvage* gives a **salvor** (one who salvages) the right to compensation for assisting a foundering vessel. **Salvage** is the reward given to persons who voluntarily assist a sinking ship or recover its cargo from peril or loss. In addition, the United States Convention on the Law of the Sea (UNCLOSIII) requires salvors to protect the historical character of shipwrecks.

If an abandoned shipwreck is found in the submerged land of any state of the United States, the Abandoned Shipwreck Act of 1987 applies rather than the *law of finds* or the *law of salvage.* This Act gives states the right of ownership to shipwrecks found beneath their waters.

EXAMPLE 21-2:   Law of Finds

In 2004, the federal court awarded full ownership of a Civil War–era shipwreck to Odyssey Marine Exploration. The salvage company agreed to pay $1.6 million to an insurance company that had paid claims when the ship sank. The *SS Republic* was a side-wheel steamer that went down in 1865 while en route from New York to New Orleans after fighting a hurricane for two days. The salvage company discovered the shipwreck 1,700 feet below the surface of the Atlantic Ocean approximately 100 miles off the Georgia coast. Among other relics, the ship contained $400,000 (face value) of gold and silver coins, which may now be worth up to $180 million.

In 2007, the salvage company mentioned in Example 21-2 salvaged about 17 tons of silver and gold colonial-era coins estimated to be valued at $500 million from a different spot on the floor of the Atlantic. This discovery is expected to be shared with the British government, and the government of Spain has filed a claim to the treasure in a U.S. district court.

Gifts of Personal Property

People often make gifts of personal property. There are three requirements for a gift to be completed: the **donor** (the one giving the gift) must intend to make a gift, the gift must be delivered to the **donee** (the one receiving it), and the donee must accept the gift. Once all three requirements are met, the gift cannot be taken back by the donor. It is known as an absolute gift, or **gift** *inter vivos* (between the living).

The gift of an engagement ring is a conditional gift, given in contemplation of marriage. Most courts hold that the donor of an engagement ring is entitled to its return if the engagement is broken by mutual agreement or by the donee. A few courts allow the return of the ring even when the donor breaks the engagement. These courts theorize that it is better to break the engagement without penalty than to have an unhappy marriage.

The Opening Case Revisited, Part III

"A Memorable Day"

No Car for Emily Emily would not be entitled to her grandfather's car because it had not been delivered to her before he passed away.

Uniform Transfers to Minors Act Problems can easily arise when gifts are given to minors. Sometimes, parents or guardians use such gifts for themselves rather than for the minor. At other times, donors make gifts to minors and then change their minds and take the gifts back. Gifts to minors are often used as tax shelters. Formerly, wealthy parents in high tax brackets often made gifts to their minor children as a way to shift unearned income to lower-bracket taxpayers. The IRS has changed this practice with the so-called kiddie tax. Effective January 1, 2008, unearned income (dividends and interest) of a child under the age of 19 up to $1,700 is taxed at the child's income tax rate and, above that, at the parent's income tax rate. This rule also applies to college students under the age of 24 unless they provide over half of their own support from earned income (wages and salaries).

The Uniform Transfer to Minors Act (UTMA), which has been adopted by most states, also prevents some of these problems. The act establishes a procedure for gifts to be made to minors. Under the procedure, minors are assured that gifts to them will either be used for their benefit or made available to them when they become adults. The income from gifts that are given to minors is taxable according to the kiddie tax rules mentioned previously. The UTMA allows money, securities, real property, and tangible and intangible personal property to be transferred to a custodian for the minor's benefit. The age of 21 rather than 18 years is used as the age when the custodianship terminates, because the IRS uses that age to terminate certain trusts.

Gift *in Causa Mortis* A gift given during one's lifetime, in contemplation of death from a known cause, is a **gift *in causa mortis***. A gift *in causa mortis* is conditional, and it is ineffective if the donor does not die as expected or if death is caused by circumstances other than those feared.

EXAMPLE 21-3: Void Gift *in Causa Mortis*

Rossano was seriously ill following an abdominal operation. Realizing that death might be near, Rossano signed over a savings account to Hall, giving Hall the savings book with necessary notations of assignment. Rossano did die three weeks later, not because of the surgery but because of an automobile accident. Rossano's executor may declare the gift *in causa mortis* void and demand the return of Rossano's savings for the benefit of the estate.

Anatomical Gifts With so many medical advancements in recent years, there is an increased need in society for gifts of human bodies, tissues, and organs for medical education, research, and transplantation. The Uniform Anatomical Gift Act was revised in 2006 to help meet present-day needs.

The Opening Case Revisited, Part IV
"A Memorable Day"

Emily Is the Owner Emily can recover her camcorder from the pawn shop because it was stolen from her, and she is the true owner.

Stolen Personal Property

Although a presumption of title to goods usually follows possession of them, it is possible for a person to have possession of goods without having title, just as it is possible for a person to have title without having possession. Thus, a thief acquires no title to goods that are stolen and therefore cannot convey a good title. The true owner never relinquished title to the goods, and even an innocent purchaser who acquired the goods in good faith and for value would be obliged to return the goods to the owner. Title to stolen goods never left the true owner, and possession can always be regained by that owner if the goods can be found, no matter in whose possession they may be at the time.

A Question of Ethics
Principle No. 4: Be Fair (Part 2)

In order to determine fairness, including just punishment, we need to start by asking the right questions.

RETRIBUTIVE JUSTICE AND FAIRNESS

Deciding who gets what of a limited amount of goods or services is one aspect of fairness. Judging whether someone should be punished and, if so, in what way, is another. This second dimension of fairness is retributive justice.

A good manager asks, "What's the right way to punish an employee who has done something he or she shouldn't have?" The concerned parent wonders, "How should I deal with my misbehaving child?" Both questions are fundamentally ethical ones, and the most straightforward standard for meting out justice is this: The punishment should fit the crime. Whether a proposed punishment is fitting requires a thorough accounting of the facts, an understanding of the relevant law (if the infraction involves a breach of civil or criminal law), and a commitment to disregarding everything about the situation that isn't relevant.

When a person accused of wrongdoing is punished in a way that seems unfair to him or her, that person is likely to claim discrimination. But is discrimination inherently unfair? No, it isn't, and to this issue we now turn.

FAIRNESS AND DISCRIMINATION

Universities legitimately discriminate against students whose grade-point averages and SAT scores are below a certain level. Employers discriminate against applicants who lack the requisite knowledge or skill, and that's perfectly acceptable. Single people discriminate against suitors to whom they aren't attracted or with whom they don't share fundamental values, and rightly so. To discriminate is simply to make a judgment based on certain standards or criteria. Discrimination is unfair only when it's based on irrelevant criteria.

What constitutes irrelevant criteria? The answer is, as we saw in last week's column about distributive justice, context-dependent. That is, the standards that are acceptable in one area amount to prejudice in another. It's wrong, for instance, to use the ability to play Scrabble well as a factor in determining who's entitled to rent an apartment, but if you want to compete in Scrabble tournaments, that skill is (and should be) the primary, or sole, determinant of acceptance.

Title VII of the 1964 Civil Rights Act prohibits basing employment decisions on such factors as race, religion, gender, veteran status, and age. Each of these personal characteristics, however, may be a legitimate basis for screening some people in and others out of a group beyond the workplace. Is it wrong to exclude non-Catholics from a Catholic singles mixer? It's hard to see why. If you never served in the armed forces, could you reasonably be denied membership in the local Veterans of Foreign Wars club? Of course. If a personal quality is relevant to the position to which someone aspires, it's acceptable to use that quality as the basis of discrimination. If a quality is irrelevant, it's wrong to use it.

In grappling with what kind of punishment is fitting for a child who misbehaves, an employee who uses a client's account for personal expenses, or a student who cheats on an exam, we must exclude all those considerations that shouldn't play a role in our decision-making. The following questions are right to consider in our efforts to come up with a fair response:

- What was the nature of the offense?
- How many times has the person committed the offense before?
- What's the magnitude of the harm that resulted from the infraction?
- Were the consequences of the offense reasonably foreseeable?
- If the misconduct occurred in an institution, is there a policy that specifies what the punishment is to be? If so, is it fair?
- If the misconduct involves a violation of the law, what does the law specify as a punishment? If so, is it fair? (Granted, the latter question applies only to those in the judicial system, but the men and women entrusted with the responsibility of applying the law should still take the notion of fairness into account.)

On the other hand:

- The college president who responds to a student's violation of the honor code with merely a stern warning because that student's parents donate a lot of money to the school;
- The CEO who responds to an employee's harassment of a coworker with indifference "because the guy is a friend of mine;" and
- The parent who ignores her child's pot smoking "because it would be hypocritical of me to punish him for something I did myself as a teen"

are all guilty of using irrelevant criteria in meting out justice, which results in unfair outcomes—and the failure to honor Life Principle No. 4.

FAIRNESS AND RECTIFICATORY JUSTICE

Rectificatory justice is just a fancy way of saying "making things right again." When a person or a group of people have been the victim of injustice, he, she, or they are entitled to some sort of compensation. This might involve money, or goods and services, or a simple apology.

Where retributive justice is concerned with responding fairly to the perpetrator of wrongdoing, rectificatory justice focuses on how the good parent, employer, or society should care for the victim of another's wrongful conduct. As is the case with distributive and retributive justice, our efforts to "make things right again" don't come from a rigid formula or set-in-stone criteria. Rather, one seeks to combine knowledge of the facts with an application of the relevant rules (e.g., "give to others their due—no more, and no less") along with the wisdom that can come only from experience.

Source: Bruce Weinstein, "Principle No. 4: Be Fair (Part 2)," *BusinessWeek.com,* February 15, 2007.

21-2 Intellectual Property

An original work fixed in a tangible medium of expression is **intellectual property**. It includes patents, copyrights, trademarks, and trade secrets. To encourage innovation and creativity, the government has enacted patent, copyright, trademark, and trade secret laws. These laws give special rights to the owners of intellectual property.

Patents

A **patent** is a grant from the government that gives an inventor the exclusive right to make, use, and sell an invention for a period set by Congress, generally 20 years from the date the patent application was filed. When the period expires, the subject matter of the patent becomes **public domain**, that is, owned by the public and not protected by copyright. A patent may not be obtained if the subject matter of the patent would be obvious to a person having ordinary skill in the field.

> **EXAMPLE 21-4:**   Too Obvious
>
> In 2007, the U.S. Supreme Court invalidated a patent that had been issued for a gas pedal electronic sensor that could be adjusted according to the driver's height. In *KSR International Co. v. Teleflex Inc.*, the court said that designing a gas pedal in such a way was obvious to the average gas pedal designer and therefore not an invention that could be patented.

To be patentable, a device must be useful and consist of some new idea or principle not known before. It must be a discovery, as distinguished from mere mechanical skill or knowledge. There are three types of patents:

- Utility patents
- Design patents
- Plant patents

A **utility patent** is a patent granted to someone who invents or discovers any new and useful process, machine, article of manufacture, or composition of matter, or any new and useful improvement thereof.

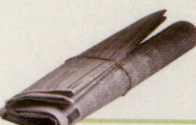

Companies should focus on better ideas and work with Congress and the U.S. Patent & Trademark Office to fix the system.

The U.S. Supreme Court has ruled in a case that's likely to have big implications for everyone affected by patents. At issue in the case is whether an idea is too obvious to be patented. This may seem esoteric, but intellectual-property issues are striking closer to home for many people and point to the need for patent reform.

For instance, Research In Motion's (RIMM) Black-Berry service was in jeopardy of being shuttered last year until a patent dispute was settled out of court. A case involving Apple (AAPL) iPods was similarly settled. And with a record-setting award in a patent case involving MP3 files, it's safe to say that intellectual property now has the attention of many.

These types of issues and crises are finally being addressed by the Supreme Court, Congress, the U.S. Patent & Trademark Office (USPTO)—even the private sector.

Overprotection

To be successful, we need to restore a balanced approach that doesn't over- or under-protect the rights of patent holders. For instance, we currently overprotect by allowing patents on business methodologies that have no technical underpinnings. We publish patent applications, but then limit feedback that can be provided to the USPTO by experts from the public. This feedback could be invaluable in identifying cases where a patent may not be warranted.

The threat of lavish patent infringement awards can have a chilling effect, too. For example, patent award damages are often ratcheted up if the courts find the infringer to have intentionally ignored existing patent protections. So the system actually rewards those who haven't checked to see whether a patent already exists.

Rules that lead companies to place blinders on their developers is a startling sign that patent law has lost touch with the concept of teaching the public about new inventions, which is, after all, the reason for granting patents.

Innovation Stifled

Then there's the matter of under-protecting patents. Even as the threat of penalty prompts some companies to rush the application process, some inventors may be slow to seek legal protection for ideas. That's because unlike other countries, the U.S. gives precedence to those who are first to invent, but not necessarily the first to file a patent application. That opens the door to disputes between a patent holder and a party that can argue it came up with the idea first—even if it hasn't yet applied for a patent.

Also, the sheer volume of patent filings makes it impossible for the USPTO to review patent applications in a timely fashion. All of this creates uncertainty, which is harmful to innovation and the economy.

And intellectual property is a big contributor to the economy: U.S. intellectual property is worth $5 trillion to $5.5 trillion, say economists Kevin Hassett and Robert Shapiro. That's more than the gross domestic product of any other country.

Congress Must Get Involved

Ned Davis Research found that 80% of the value of Standard & Poor's 500-stock index companies now comes from intangible assets. And according to the U.S. Commerce Dept., American intellectual property comprises more than half of all U.S. exports, driving approximately 40% of the country's growth.

Given the stakes, it should be no surprise that the Supreme Court has accepted seven patent cases in the past two years—far more than in recent memory. The cases focus on issues involving shutting down suspected patent infringers, extending U.S. patent law overseas, and determining what kinds, and combinations, of ideas can be protected by patents.

But the courts merely interpret the legal equivalent of radiological charts; it is Congress that actually performs the surgery. And Congress does appear ready to operate, contemplating the most sweeping patent reforms in 50 years. Among other improvements, these reforms would require a systematic approach for assigning realistic values to infringed patents and provide a new way for parties to reassess a granted patent's validity without a lawsuit.

A Classic Arbitrage

While the USPTO is dependent on Congress to establish the patent laws, it has already started making internal improvements. This spring it is experimenting with a program that will enable expert volunteers, including those from IBM (IBM), to provide feedback to patent examiners on selected patent applications. Better and more efficient patent examination will improve patent quality by reducing the issuance of overbroad patents.

By bringing 21st-century knowhow to a 200-year-old institution, the USPTO is performing a classic arbitrage: pairing those who have expertise, motivation, and access to information with those who need it but lack the resources to generate it.

The private sector is beginning to voluntarily help in other ways, too. For example, when IBM, the top holder of U.S. patents, seeks patents for business methods, it aims to do so only for those methods underpinned by deep technical content. Pure business methods can be difficult to examine and tempt some to seek patents of questionable merit.

A Role For Small Biz

IBM also is encouraging other patent practitioners to follow its lead with a sort of voluntary, corporate Hippocratic Oath that would institutionalize innovation-friendly patenting behavior. For instance, if more companies focused on ideas of higher technical quality, were transparent about which patents they owned or were applying for, helped review public patent filings, and permitted others to comment on their own pending patents, the likelihood of legal controversy would be reduced.

Small businesses also can play a role. There is a sense that for them, especially, the system has become too complex and expensive. Some smaller businesses have fallen prone to patent pawn shops, which buy patents cheap, only to resell or license those patents at disproportionate profits. If we are going to have meaningful patent reform, we need to give small businesses a voice. An online brainstorming forum this spring for small businesses might be a step in the right direction.

Consensus must underpin action. For while the Supreme Court can adjudicate, Congress legislate, and the USPTO and private sector innovate, we won't have broad progress until all parties work with one another, with the right balance, moderation, and the greater good at heart.

Questions for Analysis

1. In what ways do we currently overprotect patent holders?

2. How does the system reward those who haven't checked to see whether a patent already exists?

3. How are some patents underprotected?

4. In what way has the U.S. Patent Office started making internal improvements?

5. What might help bring about innovation-friendly patenting behavior?

6. How might small businesses play a role?

Source: David Kappos, "It's Time for Patent Reform," *BusinessWeek.com,* March 28, 2007.

EXAMPLE 21-5:   Article of Manufacture

A microbiologist invented a bacterium capable of breaking down crude oil. The U.S. Patent and Trademark Office denied a patent on the bacterium, claiming that it was alive and therefore not patentable. On appeal, the U.S. Supreme Court held that the live, human-made bacterium is patentable. The court said that such a microorganism is a "manufacture" or "composition of matter" within the meaning of the patent law.

Did You Know?

Thomas Edison obtained a total of 1,093 personal patents during his lifetime!

A **design patent** is a patent granted to someone who invents a new, original, and ornamental design for an article of manufacture. In contrast to a utility patent, which protects the way an article is used and works, a design patent protects the way an article looks. Both design and utility patents may be obtained on the same invention if it has ornamental as well as functional characteristics. Design patents are granted for 14 years instead of the 20-year period given for other types of patents.

A **plant patent** is a patent granted to someone who invents or discovers and asexually reproduces any distinct and new variety of plant. Asexually grown plants are those that are reproduced by means other than from seeds, such as by the rooting of cuttings, layering, budding, grafting, inarching, and so forth.

To obtain a patent, an inventor must file an application with the U.S. Patent and Trademark Office. The application is examined by the office, and a search is made for a similar device that has already been patented. Inventors may avoid disappointments by conducting preliminary searches themselves before filing patent applications. A search room is located in the Patent and Trademark Office in Arlington, Virginia, where the public may search and examine all U.S. patents granted since 1836. In addition, patent depository libraries are located in almost every state in the United States (at large public or university libraries) and available for public use. For search purposes, patents are arranged according to a classification system of over 400 classes and more than 120,000 subclasses.

To be legally protected, a patented item must be marked with the word *patent* followed by the patent number. If this is not done, anyone making the same item without knowledge of the patent cannot be sued for damages. Some inventors put the words *patent pending* or *patent applied for* on their products. These words have no legal effect, however, other than informing others that an application for a patent has been filed. Patent protection does not begin until the patent is actually granted.

Any unauthorized making, using, or selling of a patented invention during the term of the patent is known as a **patent infringement**. A federal court can issue an injunction ordering an infringing party to discontinue the infringement. In addition, the court can order the infringing party to pay monetary damages to the owner of the patent.

EXAMPLE 21-6:   Patent Infringement

In 1991, a federal court ordered Eastman Kodak Company to pay Polaroid Corporation $925 million in damages for infringing on seven of Polaroid's patents on instant cameras and film. Previously, in 1985, the court ruled that there was an infringement and ordered Kodak to discontinue manufacturing and selling its instant camera products.

Some new products, such as drugs, must go through a governmental review period before they can be marketed. Because the products cannot be sold while they are being reviewed, the review period is not counted as part of the 20-year term of the patent.

Universities, small companies, and nonprofit organizations are allowed to retain ownership of patents gained as a result of federal grants and contracts. The law does not provide this benefit to large corporations, however.

Transfers of Patent Rights   Like other personal property, a patent may be sold, given away, or passed on to others through inheritance. The transfer of a patent is accomplished by the use of an assignment (see Chapter 14), which must be in writing. An assignment may transfer the entire interest in the patent to another or assign part interest, such as a one-half or a one-sixteenth interest. To be effective by subsequent assignees of a patent, an assignment must be recorded at the Patent and Trademark Office within three months from its date.

In addition to being owned by individuals (including corporations), patents may be owned jointly by two or more people. Any joint owner of a patent interest, no matter how small a share, may make and use the invention without regard to the other owners unless they have agreed otherwise. Similarly, unless they have agreed otherwise, any joint owner may sell his or her interest in the patent without regard to the other owners.

International Law   Most foreign countries have their own patent laws, which differ from U.S. laws. Anyone wishing to obtain a patent in a foreign country must file an application with that country's patent office. A treaty, called the Paris Convention for the Protection of Industrial Property, is adhered to by 93 countries, including the United States. Under the treaty, each country guarantees to citizens of the other countries the same rights in patent and trademark matters that it gives to its own citizens. In addition, the treaty gives priority rights to people who apply for patents. This priority right means that when a patent application is first filed in a member country, the applicant may, within one year (six months in the case of a trademark), apply for protection in all other member countries. The latter applications are regarded as having been filed on the same date as the first application was filed.

Another treaty, called the Patent Cooperation Treaty, adhered to by 41 countries including the United States, provides for centralized filing procedures and a standardized application form.

Copyrights

A **copyright** is a right granted to an author, composer, photographer, or artist to exclusively publish and sell an artistic or literary work for the life of the author plus 70 years. In addition to books, magazines, and newspapers, works that may be copyrighted include such things as computer software, graphic arts, architectural designs, motion pictures, and sound recordings.

EXAMPLE 21-7:   Copyright Infringement

A music-swapping service, Napster, Inc., allowed Internet users to search one another's hard drives for music files and download the songs in a compressed digital file format. Napster was forced to discontinue its online file-swapping business, however. The federal court held that the company infringed on at least two of the copyright holders' exclusive rights: the rights of reproduction and distribution.

Originality is a requirement for something to be copyrighted. Mere facts, standing alone, cannot be copyrighted because they are not original. If, however, facts are selected, coordinated, and arranged in an original manner, the presentation of them may be copyrighted.

Piracy   Piracy is a form of copyright infringement. It includes the duplication, forgery, or direct distribution of software in a manner that violates the author's copyright. Video piracy—the camcording of films in a movie theatre—has become a major national problem. It is estimated that video piracy costs the city of New York $637 million in retail sales and $50 million in annual city and state sales taxes. Some states are increasing penalties to try to stop this crime.

EXAMPLE 21-8:   Increased Penalties for Piracy

Claiming that video piracy is not a victimless crime, in 2007, New York City Mayor Michael Bloomberg upped the penalty for illegal camcording. Until then, secret tapers faced just a summons, up to a $250 fine, and the remote possibility of a 15-day jail sentence. Now, they could be hit with a misdemeanor charge that could mean as much as six months in jail and a $5,000 fine. (*Source:* Elizabeth Woyke, "NYC Does Not Love Video Pirates," *BusinessWeek*, May 21, 2007, p. 14.)

The law allows some copying to be done without permission under the **fair use doctrine**. This doctrine provides that copyrighted material may be reproduced without permission if the use of the material is reasonable and not harmful to the rights of the copyright owner. The duplication of copyrighted materials for profit by a copyshop would not be a fair use because it would adversely affect the potential market for the copyrighted work. Copying items for such purposes as criticism, comment, news reporting, teaching, scholarship, and research is permissible. Libraries and archives may reproduce single copies of certain copyrighted materials for noncommercial purposes without obtaining permission of the copyright owner.

EXAMPLE 21-9:   Fair Use

Universal City Studios, Inc., and Walt Disney Productions, Inc., brought suit against Sony Corporation of America, manufacturers of Betamax. Universal and Disney claimed that Sony infringed on their copyrights by manufacturing and selling Betamax videotape recorders, allowing people to tape record their copyrighted films at home. The U.S. Supreme Court held in favor of Sony. The court said that noncommercial recording of material broadcast over the public airwaves that is intended for home use only is a fair use of copyrighted works and does not constitute copyright infringement.

The Computer Software Copyright Act includes computer programs among "writings" to which exclusive rights can be granted. The act defines a computer program as "a set of statements or instructions to be used directly or indirectly in a computer in order to bring about a certain result." Under the act, it is not an infringement for the owner of a copy of a computer program to make another copy provided that its duplication is essential in the use of a particular machine.

In the case of *Lotus Development Corp. v. Paperback Software International,* the federal court held that the copyright on the Lotus 1-2-3 spreadsheet program was infringed by the spreadsheet program VP-Planner. The court held that the organization, sequence, and structure of Lotus 1-2-3's menu commands were protected by its copyright. However, in a 1995 case, *Lotus Development Corp. v. Borland International Inc.,* the court held that Lotus's drop-down menu lists on computer screens could not be copyrighted. The court said that the Lotus menu command hierarchy is an uncopyrightable method of operation.

Original material appearing on a Web site may be protected by copyright; however, a domain name may not be copyrighted. The Internet Corporation for Assigned Names and Numbers (ICANN), a nonprofit organization, administers the assignment of domain names through accredited registers. Procedures for registering the contents of a Web site can be found in Circular 66, *Copyright Registration for Online Works,* put out by the U.S. Copyright Office.

Copyright registration is accomplished by completing a simple form (see Table 21-1 and Figure 21-1) and sending it, with a small fee and a copy of the work, to the U.S. Copyright Office in Washington, DC. In the past, it was necessary to put the following notice on the work: © or the word *copyright* followed by the date and the name of the owner. This requirement became optional in 1989, however, when the United States adhered to the Berne Convention for the Protection of Literary and Artistic Works. Authors' and artists' works now have worldwide copyright protection as a result of the United States's adherence to three treaties: the Pan American Convention, the Universal Copyright Convention, and the Berne Convention.

Table 21-1 Commonly Used Copyright Forms	
Use This Form	**To Obtain a Copyright For**
TX	Published or unpublished nondramatic literary works
PA	Published or unpublished works of the performing arts
SR	Published or unpublished sound recordings
VA	Published or unpublished works of visual arts
SE	Serials (newspapers, magazines, newsletters, annuals, journals, etc.)
RE	Renewal of copyright

The Digital Millennium Copyright Act was enacted by Congress in 1998, bringing copyright law into the digital age. The Act implements the provisions of two international treaties, which give writers, artists, and other creators of copyrighted material global protection from piracy in the new millennium. Among other things, the Act:

- Makes it a crime to circumvent antipiracy measures built into commercial software.
- Outlaws the manufacture, sale, or distribution of code-cracking devices used to illegally copy software.
- Exempts nonprofit libraries, archives, and educational institutions under certain circumstances.
- Limits Internet service providers from copyright infringement liability for simply transmitting information over the Internet.
- Limits liability of nonprofit institutions of higher education when they serve as online service providers for copyright infringement by faculty members or graduate students.
- Requires that licensing fees be paid to record companies for the use of musical recordings.

Trademarks

A **trademark** is any word, name, symbol, or device adopted and used by a manufacturer or merchant to identify goods and distinguish them from those manufactured or sold by others. (See Figure 21-2.) It is different from a patent in that it does not apply to an invention or manufacturing process. Rather, it applies to the name or mark used to identify a product. The function of a trademark is to identify the source of a product, that is, the one who makes it. Coke, for example, is made only by the Coca-Cola Company, and Wheaties are made only by General Mills. In a 1995 case involving green-gold SUN GLOW pads, the U.S. Supreme Court held that color alone can fit a definition of a trademark as a symbol to distinguish one brand from a competitor.

The term **trade dress** refers to the total image or appearance of a product rather than something that is functional. Trade dress includes such things as size, shape, color, texture, and design. It also includes advertising and marketing techniques used to promote a product's sale. Injured parties can bring suit for trade dress infringement as long as they can prove that the matter sought to be protected is not functional.

Owners of trademarks have the exclusive right to use the particular word, name, or symbol that they have adopted as their trademark. Trademarks can be established in three different ways: under common law, under state statute, or under the Federal Trademark Act of 1946.

Copyright Office fees are subject to change. For current fees, check the Copyright Office website at *www.copyright.gov*, write the Copyright Office, or call (202) 707-3000.

Short Form TX
For a Nondramatic Literary Work
UNITED STATES COPYRIGHT OFFICE

REGISTRATION NUMBER

TX _____   TXU _____

Effective Date of Registration

Application Received

Deposit Received
One _____   Two _____

Fee Received

Examined By

Correspondence ☐

TYPE OR PRINT IN BLACK INK. DO NOT WRITE ABOVE THIS LINE.

1 | **Title of This Work:**

Alternative title or title of larger work in which this work was published:

2 | **Name and Address of Author and Owner of the Copyright:**

Nationality or domicile:
Phone, fax, and email:

Phone ( )   Fax ( )
Email

3 | **Year of Creation:**

4 | **If work has been published, Date and Nation of Publication:**

a. Date _____ Month _____ Day _____ Year   *(Month, day, and year all required)*

b. Nation

5 | **Type of Authorship in This Work:**

Check all that this author created.

☐ Text (includes fiction, nonfiction, poetry, computer programs, etc.)
☐ Illustrations
☐ Photographs
☐ Compilation of terms or data

6 | **Signature:**

Registration cannot be completed without a signature.

*I certify that the statements made by me in this application are correct to the best of my knowledge.** Check one:

☐ Author   ☐ Authorized agent

X _____

7 | OPTIONAL | **Name and Address of Person to Contact for Rights and Permissions:**

Phone, fax, and email:

☐ Check here if same as #2 above.

Phone ( )   Fax ( )
Email

8 | **Certificate will be mailed in window envelope to this address:**

Name ▼
Number/Street/Apt ▼
City/State/ZIP ▼

Complete this space only if you currently hold a Deposit Account in the Copyright Office.

9 | Deposit Account # _____
Name _____

DO NOT WRITE HERE   Page 1 of _____ page

*17 U.S.C. § 506(e): Any person who knowingly makes a false representation of a material fact in the application for copyright registration provided for by section 409, or in any written statement filed in connection with the application, shall be fined not more than $2,500.

Rev: August 2003—30,000   Web Rev: August 2003   ♻ Printed on recycled paper

U.S. Government Printing Office: 2003-496-605/60

Figure 21-1 *Copyright Application.* Copyright forms with instructions and current fees can be found on the Internet.

The Underwood devil is thought to be the oldest registered food trademark still in use in the United States. William Underwood started a small condiment business in Boston in 1822, which mushroomed into a lucrative canned-food venture during the Civil War. Underwood's canned foods were among the staples that pioneers took with them on their way west. In 1867, Underwood's sons developed a process they called "deviling," in which they mixed ground ham with special seasonings to make a uniquely tasting food product. In 1870, the company obtained a patent on its world-famous trademark. The trademarks for Samson's (a man and a lion), Nabisco's Cream of Wheat, General Electric's GE Medalion, Carnation brand condensed milk, and Pabst Milwaukee Blue Ribbon Beer are all over 100 years old.

Figure 21-2 Trademarks identify the source of a product. Others may make deviled ham but when you see the logo with the red devil, you know that this deviled ham is from Underwood.

Common Law Trademarks

Under common law, trademarks may be established by usage rather than by registration with the state or federal government. To claim such a mark, the party must demonstrate that use of the mark has been of such quality and for such a duration that it has come to identify goods bearing it as originating from that party. The mark must have developed a secondary meaning—not merely identification of the product but rather identification of its producer.

EXAMPLE 21-10: Common Law Trademark

Powers, who published a small newspaper, decided to name the paper the *Daily Planet*. D. C. Comics, Inc., publishers of the Superman comic book, brought suit to stop Powers from using that name. Evidence was introduced to show that the *Daily Planet* first appeared in the Superman story in 1940. Since then it has played a key role not only in the Superman story but also in the development of the Superman character. In addition, D. C. Comics, Inc., has used the Superman character in connection with many products born of the Superman story. These products have included school supplies, toys, costumes, games, and clothes. The court enjoined Powers from using the name *Daily Planet*. It held that D. C. Comics, Inc., had demonstrated an association of such duration and consistency with the *Daily Planet* that it had established a common law trademark in that name. The *Daily Planet* has, over the years, become inextricably woven into the fabric of the Superman story.

State Trademark Statutes Although the U.S. Constitution gives exclusive control to the federal government over patents and copyrights, it is silent about trademarks. Therefore, federal laws apply only to trademarks that are used in interstate commerce.

Each of the 50 states has statutes that regulate the use of trademarks in intrastate commerce, that is, within the boundaries of the state. Although there has been an attempt to make the trademark laws of each state uniform, they differ substantially.

The Federal Trademark Act of 1946

The Federal Trademark Act of 1946, called the Lanham Act, provides for registration of trademarks with the U.S. Patent and Trademark Office. To be eligible for registration, the goods or services must be sold or used in more than one state or in one state and a foreign country. A trademark cannot be registered if it consists of immoral, deceptive, or scandalous matter; matter that may disparage or falsely suggest a connection with persons, living or dead, institutions, beliefs, or national symbols, or which may bring them into contempt, or disrepute; the flag or coat of arms or other insignia of the United States or of any state or municipality, any foreign nation, or any simulation thereof; the name, signature, or portrait of any living individual, except with that person's written consent; the name, signature, or portrait of a deceased President of the United States during the life of a surviving spouse, if any, except by the written consent of the spouse; or a mark that so resembles a mark registered in the Patent and Trademark Office or a mark or trade name previously used in the United States by another and not abandoned, as to be likely to cause confusion when applied to the goods of the applicant, cause mistake, or deceive.

An application to register a trademark may be filed six months before the mark is used in commerce. This application reserves the mark so that no one else can use it during the reservation period. No registration will be issued, however, until the mark is actually used in commerce, which means "the bona fide use of a mark in the ordinary course of trade." One automatic extension of the six-month reservation period is allowed, and other extensions are available upon a showing of good cause. The reservation period before the actual use of the mark in commerce may not exceed three years, however. In addition, to prevent trafficking in trademarks, the reservation of a trademark may not be sold or assigned to anyone other than a successor to the business of the applicant. A trademark registration remains in force for 10 years and may be renewed for additional 10-year periods, unless it is canceled or surrendered by nonuse.

Anyone who registers a trademark may give notice that the mark is registered by displaying the following with the mark: "Registered in U.S. Patent and Trademark Office" or "Reg. U.S. Pat. & Tm. Off." or the letter R enclosed within a circle, as ®.

Companies can lose their trademark protection if the marks are used as a generic term by a large segment of the public for a long period of time.

EXAMPLE 21-11:   Generic Term

In the 1980s, the Murphy Door Bed Co. was refused a trademark registration for its Murphy bed. The court held that the name Murphy bed had been appropriated by the public to designate a type of bed that folds into a wall or closet.

Former trademarks that have been lost by becoming generic terms by a large segment of the public include cornflakes, cube steak, dry ice, escalator, high octane, kerosene, lanolin, linoleum, nylon, raisin bran, shredded wheat, trampoline, and yo yo.

Companies often use a word such as *brand* after the name of their product in their advertisements to remind people that the product name is a registered trademark. They also place advertisements in writers' magazines and other journals (such as the one shown in Figure 21-3) pointing out that fact.

Figure 21-3   For many, the name Xerox is synonymous with document copying. How can this be bad for the Xerox Corporation? (Reprinted with permission of the Xerox Corporation.)

Trade Secrets

A **trade secret** is a plan, process, or device that is used in business and is known only to employees who need to know the secret to carry out their work. Examples of trade secrets are customer lists, chemical formulas, manufacturing processes, food recipes, marketing techniques, and pricing methods.

Businesses often protect trade secrets by having employees sign nondisclosure agreements in which they agree not to disclose trade secrets to others. Even without such an agreement, however, the law forbids employees to disclose their employer's trade secrets both while they are employed and after they leave the employment. When this employee duty is violated, courts will often not allow the use of the trade secret by others to whom the secret has been given. The U.S. Supreme Court has held that state trade secret laws do not conflict with federal patent laws, saying they both are incentives to encouraging invention. The subject of trade secrets is discussed in more detail in Chapters 12 and 42.

Quick Quiz 21-2 True or False?

1. A patent gives an inventor the exclusive right to make, use, and sell an invention for a period set by Congress, generally 20 years from the date the patent was granted.

2. A copyright gives the exclusive legal right to reproduce, publish, and sell a work for the life of the author plus 70 years.

3. A federally registered trademark remains in force for 10 years but may be renewed for additional 10-year periods.

Summary

21.1 Personal property is everything that can be owned except real estate. Anyone who finds lost property must make a reasonable effort to find the owner. Misplaced property must be turned over to the manager of the place where it is found. Abandoned property is property that has been intentionally discarded by the owner and may be kept by a finder. The Abandoned Shipwreck Act gives states the right to shipwrecks beneath their waters. For a gift to be completed, the donor must intend to make a gift, it must be delivered to the donee, and the donee must accept the gift. A thief acquires no title to goods that are stolen and therefore cannot convey a good title to others.

21.2 A patent gives the owner the exclusive right to make, use, or sell an invention for a term set by Congress, generally 20 years from the date the patent application was filed. Copyrights give their owners the exclusive right to publish their work for the life of the author plus 70 years. Trademarks, which protect product names and marks, may be established either by usage or by registration. Registered trademarks remain in force for 10 years and may be renewed. Trade secrets, known only to employees who need to know the secret to carry out their work, are protected by employer–employee agreements as well as by law.

Key Terms

abandoned property, 422

chattels, 421

chose in action, 421

community property, 421

copyright, 431

cotenancy, 421

design patent, 429

donee, 423

donor, 423

escheat, 422

fair use doctrine, 432

gift *in causa mortis*, 424

gift *inter vivos*, 423

intellectual property, 427

joint tenants, 421

joint tenants with the right of survivorship, 421

patent, 427

patent infringement, 430

personal property, 421

plant patent, 430

public domain, 427

salvage, 423

salvor, 423

severalty, 421

tenants in common, 421

trade dress, 433

trademark, 433

trade secret, 437

utility patent, 427

Questions for Review and Discussion

1. What is community property, and how many states recognize it?
2. When may someone who finds lost property claim ownership of it?
3. How has the Abandoned Shipwreck Act of 1987 affected the law of finds and the law of salvage?
4. What are the requirements for a gift to be completed?
5. What assurances are minors and donors given by following the procedures of the Uniform Transfers to Minors Act?
6. What kind of title is given by a thief who sells stolen goods to an innocent person? Explain.
7. What do patents protect?
8. What do copyrights protect?
9. What is the protection given by the registration of a trademark?
10. How can companies lose their trademark protection? Name some products that have lost trademark protection in this way.

Investigating the Internet

When Peter Lucia died, his widow decided to donate both of his kidneys to his long-time friend, Robert Colavito, who was suffering from end-stage renal disease. Peter's left kidney was airlifted to a Miami hospital where Colavito was waiting for its implantation. Peter's right kidney remained in New York.

Before the operation, Colavito's surgeon discovered that Peter's left kidney was irreparably damaged by aneurysms and therefore unfit for implantation. His staff called the New York Organ Donor Network to ask for delivery of the second kidney and learned that it had already been implanted in another patient. As the intended donee, Colavito brought suit against the organ donor network and others for damages.

The U.S. Court of Appeals for the 2nd Circuit (*Colavito v. New York Organ Donor Network, Inc.,* Docket No. 05-1395-cv, 2006) sent questions to the New York Court of Appeals before making its final decision. Look on the Internet for the answers given by the New York Court of Appeals as well as the final decision of this case by the U.S. Court of Appeals. Look for the case at **Findlaw.com** or key in the words *anatomical gift* or the parties' names in any search engine.

Cases for Analysis

1. Susan Lacroix's Yerf-Dog go-kart was stolen from her driveway one evening when she went inside to have dinner. The thief placed an advertisement in the newspaper and sold it to Ronald Casey for half what it was worth. Later, Lacroix recognized the kart in Casey's yard and identified it as hers through its serial number. In a suit brought by Lacroix for the return of the go-kart, Casey argued

that he now had title to the kart because he paid for it without knowledge that it had been stolen. Is Casey's argument sound? Explain.

2. Rural Telephone Service Company published a telephone directory consisting of white and yellow pages. Rural obtained data for the directory from its telephone customers, who provided their names and addresses when they applied for telephone service. Feist Publications, Inc., specialized in publishing more extensive telephone directories covering a much larger area than Rural's coverage. When Rural refused to license its white pages listings to Feist for a directory covering 11 different telephone service areas, Feist extracted the listings it needed from Rural's directory and published them without Rural's consent. Is Feist liable for copyright infringement? Why or why not? *Feist Publications, Inc. v. Rural Tel. Service Co.,* 499 U.S. 340 (U.S. Sup. Ct).

3. Michigan Document Services, Inc., a commercial copyshop, reproduced without permission substantial segments of copyrighted works of scholarship, bound the copies into "course packs," and sold them to students for use in fulfilling reading assignments given by professors at the University of Michigan. The company argued that it could legally do this under the "fair use" doctrine of the copyright law. Do you agree? Explain. *Princeton University Press v. Michigan Document Services, Inc.,* 99 F.3d 1381 (6th Cir.).

4. Pollard found a valuable first edition that someone had dropped on the street. She took the book home, placing it with others in a collection of first editions. The owner's name could not be found in the lost book, and Pollard made no effort to locate the owner. Did she thus have title to the book? Explain. See also *Doe v. Oceola,* 270 N.W.2d 254 (MI).

5. Vincent Hartwell admired a valuable book collection on his uncle's bookshelf. To Hartwell's surprise, his uncle said that he planned to give the books to Hartwell as a gift and that he could have them at that moment. Hartwell replied that he was living in a dormitory and had no place to keep the collection. His uncle said, "Consider the books yours. I'll keep them here, and when you're ready for them, come and get them." Hartwell thanked his uncle and left for school. His uncle died a week later. Hartwell's cousin, Kathleen Lane, inherited the uncle's entire estate. She claimed that the valuable book collection belonged to her. Who was the legal owner, Hartwell or Lane? Explain.

6. In the course of writing a research paper for one of her classes, Kirby copied a number of pages from several books at the library. She took the copies home to continue her research in a more relaxed atmosphere. A friend in her law class told Kirby that she had violated the copyright laws by copying the pages from the various books. Was the friend correct? Why or why not?

7. In his will, Gavegnano left all his tangible personal property to his daughter, Caroline. At the time of his death, he owned 19 thoroughbred horses. In addition, a cashier's check made payable to him for $33,000 was found among his belongings. The lower court judge held that the horses and the check were tangible personal property and should be given to Caroline under the terms of the will. Caroline's brothers appealed the decision, claiming that neither the horses nor the check were tangible personal property. Were Caroline's brothers correct? Explain. *Pagiarulo v. National Shawmut Bank,* 233 N.E.2d 213 (MA).

8. As a condition of their employment, Kewanee Oil Co. employees signed agreements not to disclose confidential information or trade secrets they obtained as employees. One of the projects they worked on was a novel 17-inch crystal that was useful in the detection of ionizing radiation. Several employees left Kewanee and started their own business manufacturing the same crystal. When sued by Kewanee, the employees argued that state trade secret laws were in conflict with federal patent laws and therefore invalid. Do you agree with the employees' argument? Explain. *Kewanee Oil Co. v. Bicron,* 416 U.S. 470 (U.S. Sup. Ct).

Quick Quiz Answers

21-1		21-2	
1.	T	1.	F
2.	T	2.	T
3.	F	3.	T

Chapter 22   Bailments

The Opening Case
"A Rough Night's Sleep"

The Rosiers were guests at the Gainesville Holiday Inn. Before retiring for the night, they locked their outside door but did not secure the chain latch. At about 1:30 AM, they awoke to find a ski-masked burglar in the room at the foot of their bed. Mr. Rosier jumped from the bed and tackled the intruder. A struggle ensued. Mr. Rosier was stabbed twice, and Mrs. Rosier was also injured. In a suit brought by the Rosiers against the inn, a security expert testified that the type of lock used on the door was a low-grade, residential lock. The expert said that the industrywide standard was a mortise lock, which when locked from the inside would secure the door with a deadbolt and could not be opened by a maid's passkey or a duplicate room key.

Opening Case Questions

1. Was the Holiday Inn responsible to the Rosiers for their injuries?

2. What duty of care do innkeepers have toward their guests' property?

LO Learning Objectives

1. Determine when a bailment occurs.
2. Name and describe the principal types of bailments.
3. Discuss the burden of proof as it relates to bailments.
4. Make clear an innkeeper's duty to accept all guests.
5. Explain innkeepers' duties of care to their guests and their guests' property.
6. Give reasons for the use of credit card blocking by innkeepers.
7. Describe the liability imposed on common carriers for damages to goods transported by them.
8. Discuss the duties and obligations of carriers toward passengers and their baggage.
9. Identify the classes of warehouses and describe their rights and duties.
10. Explain a warehouser's lien.

22-1 Bailments of Personal Property

A **bailment** is the transfer of possession and control of personal property to another with the intent that the same property will be returned later. Renting a movie from a video shop, borrowing a friend's car, and leaving clothes at the cleaners are examples of bailments. The person who transfers the property is the **bailor**. The person to whom the property is transferred is the **bailee**. In a bailment, neither the bailor nor the bailee intends that title to the property should pass. The bailee has an obligation to return the same property to the bailor, or to someone the bailor designates, at a later time. A bailment does not occur when the person in possession of the property has no control over it. For example, it is not a bailment when someone parks a car in an unattended parking area. (See Figure 22-1.)

When you rent a DVD, you are the bailee in a mutual benefit bailment and use ordinary care in the protection of the bailment.

EXAMPLE 22-1:   Not a Bailment

Sewall parked his car in the same parking lot he used each day. He paid the attendant, locked the car, and took the keys with him. The attendant remained on duty only in the morning and left the lot unattended for the rest of the day. There were several entrances and exits to the lot. When Sewall returned for his car, he discovered that it had been stolen. The court held that this scenario was not a bailment. The attendant had exercised no control over the vehicle whatsoever. Instead, it was simply a rental of a parking space. Sewall lost the case against the parking lot owner because he could not prove that the employees had committed a negligent act.

In contrast, courts have held it to be a bailment when someone parks a car in a garage or lot that has an attendant present at all times to check cars going in and out.

EXAMPLE 22-2:   Bailment

Eduardo drove his car to the entrance of the public parking garage at Logan International Airport in Boston. He entered the garage through a gate by taking a ticket from a machine, drove into the garage, parked and locked his car, and took the keys with him. The exit from the garage was attended at all times. When Eduardo returned four days later, he discovered that his car had been stolen. The court held that this situation was a bailment because the parking garage had possession and control of the vehicle. Eduardo recovered the value of the car from the parking garage because the garage could not prove that it had used reasonable care to prevent the theft of the car.

THIS IS A SELF-PARKING FACULTY CLAIM CHECK. PLEASE BE CAREFUL in parking your car so that you do not damage your own car or those of your fellow parkers. PARK AT YOUR OWN RISK. THIS IS NOT A BAILMENT. EMPLOYEES NOT AUTHORIZED TO ACCEPT DELIVERY OF YOUR CAR.

This check is a Contract of Lease between Middletown Parking Authority, Lessor, and you as Tenant, for a parking space. By renting the space, you agree that there is no Bailor-Bailee relationship between you and the Lessor. Term of lease from hour to hour, rental as payable.

1.   Lessor is not responsible for personal property; and Lessor assumes no liability for fire, theft, or casualty except from its own negligence.

2.   Any suits or actions against Lessor for any claim arising out of this lease shall be filed within ninety (90) days of date of occupancy of the leased premises.

MIDDLETOWN PARKING AUTHORITY
FIRST & MAIN STREETS

PLEASE PAY CASHIER
BEFORE GETTING IN YOUR CAR

Figure 22-1   The small print on this parking-garage ticket states that it is not a bailment. Some states, including Massachusetts, have statutes making disclaimers on signs and tickets in parking lots and garages void as against public policy.

When an individual loans goods to another with the intention that the goods may be used and later replaced with an equal amount of different goods, it is not a bailment. Instead, it is known as *mutuum*.

EXAMPLE 22-3:   *Mutuum*

Susan Chin borrowed a cup of flour from her neighbor. She used the flour in a cake that she made that evening. She returned a cup of flour to her neighbor the next day after shopping at a grocery store. The loan of the flour was a *mutuum* rather than a bailment because the parties did not intend that the identical particles of flour that were borrowed would be returned.

Quick Quiz 22-1 True or False?

1.   It is a bailment when someone parks a car in an unattended parking lot.

2.   In a bailment, the bailor intends to pass title to the bailee.

3.   A *mutuum* is the transfer of possession and control of personal property to another with the intent that the same property will be returned later.

22-2 Principal Types of Bailments

There are three principal types of bailments: bailments for the sole benefit of the bailor, bailments for the sole benefit of the bailee, and mutual-benefit bailments. In the first two types, called **gratuitous bailments**, property is transferred to another person without either party's giving or asking for payment of any kind. Such bailments lack consideration; therefore, they may be rescinded at any time by either party. Parties to such agreements usually consider them only as favors. In reality, however, definite legal responsibilities are placed upon both the bailor and the bailee.

Bailments for Sole Benefit of Bailor

When possession of personal property is transferred to another for purposes that will benefit only the bailor, **bailments for the sole benefit of the bailor** result.

EXAMPLE 22-4:   Bailment for Sole Benefit of Bailor

Conte agreed to deliver Higgins's watch to a jewelry shop, which she would pass on the way to work. Higgins gave her the watch, and she placed it in a briefcase with other valuables. Conte was promised no payment for this act. It was a favor. It was also a bailment for the sole benefit of the bailor.

In a bailment for the sole benefit of the bailor, the bailee owes a duty to use only *slight care*, because the bailee is receiving no benefit from the arrangement. The bailee is required only to refrain from **gross negligence**, or very great negligence—much more serious than ordinary negligence.

EXAMPLE 22-5:   Merely Ordinary Negligence

The Martins asked two girls, Bell and Christian, to live in their home during the Martins' vacation. The contents of the house were badly damaged by fire when one of the girls left a pan of grease unattended on a range burner. This situation was a gratuitous bailment for the sole benefit of the bailor. Bell and Christian were not liable for damage to the Martins' property because they were not grossly negligent.

The bailee has no implied right to use the bailor's property in a bailment for the sole benefit of the bailor. Use without permission is technically a tort of conversion on the part of the bailee; it would make the bailee liable for any damages that might result, even if the bailee had used great care and was not guilty of negligence. (Conversion is the civil wrong that arises when one unlawfully treats another's property as one's own.)

EXAMPLE 22-6:   Unauthorized Use

Lindstrom agreed to care for Holbart's car while Holbart was absent from the city. Although permission to use the car had not been given, Lindstrom drove the car many times to save having to walk.

In Example 22-6, if Lindstrom had become involved in an accident as a result of the unauthorized use of Holbart's car, he would have been liable to Holbart for damages. In a case like this, it would not even be necessary for the bailor to prove lack of care by the bailee.

In a bailment for the sole benefit of the bailor, the bailor has a duty to reimburse the bailee for any expenses the bailee might have in the care of the property.

Bailments for Sole Benefit of Bailee

Transactions in which the possession of personal property is transferred for purposes that will benefit only the bailee are gratuitous **bailments for the sole benefit of the bailee**.

EXAMPLE 22-7:   Bailment for Sole Benefit of Bailee

Martin asked Kahn if she might use the latter's car for a trip she planned to make to Kansas City. Kahn agreed to lend the car, asking nothing in return for this favor. The bailment was created for the sole benefit of the bailee, Martin.

In a bailment for the sole benefit of the bailee, the bailee is required to use *great care* because possession of the goods is solely for the bailee's benefit. The bailee is responsible for **slight negligence**, which is the failure to use that degree of care that persons of extraordinary prudence and foresight are accustomed to use.

EXAMPLE 22-8:   Great Care Required

Perez borrowed her aunt's car and used it to drive 9,000 miles on a cross-country trip. At no time during the entire trip did she check the oil in the engine. This negligence resulted in damage to the motor. Because Perez did not exercise great care, she will be responsible for any repairs resulting from her negligence.

In this type of bailment, the bailee has the right to use the property for the purposes for which the bailment was created. Use for other purposes or over a longer period of time than provided for in the agreement will make the bailee responsible for any damages that may result to the property, regardless of the amount of care exercised.

EXAMPLE 22-9:   Unpermitted Use

Robbins used Castro's chainsaw to cut up a small tree that fell during a storm. The cutting of the tree was all that Castro had agreed to allow Robbins to do with the saw. Robbins decided to cut up another piece of timber awaiting the fireplace. Through no fault of Robbins's, the saw's engine caught fire. Even though Robbins was not responsible for the fire, he was obligated to reimburse Castro for the damage because he used the saw for a purpose other than that to which was agreed.

Any *ordinary* and *expected expense* incurred in the use of another's property must be borne by the bailee. For example, gas and oil for the operation of the chainsaw in Example 22-9

A Question of Ethics
The Fifth Life Principle: Be Loving

Treating ourselves with respect is one of the most important ways we can express love and compassion in our lives

The fifth and final Life Principle is rarely found in traditional books on ethics. In those, you will see plenty of discussion of rights and responsibilities, of justice and fairness, of duties to keep one's promises and avoiding harming others. Indeed, the Life Principles of Do No Harm, Make Things Better, Respect Others, and Be Fair are the foundation of any and all moral systems, and they are found in every religion and culture that has ever existed or is likely to exist. We cannot imagine a society that did not place these notions front and center, whether codified in the law or taught by parents and in Sunday school. But if the moral life were made up only of allegiance to these principles, it would be a pretty barren one indeed.

Where Life Principles 1-4 are obligatory, Life Principle No. 5, Be Loving, might best be considered "above and beyond the call of duty." To be loving to one's neighbor is an ideal to which we should aspire, yet if we fail to act lovingly to those with whom we come into contact, we can hardly be considered unethical (unless your job is to love people, which raises ethical and legal questions of its own, at least outside of the state of Nevada).

Can we be faulted by failing to prevent harm to others when doing so would take little effort? Yes; Life Principle No. 1 requires this of us. If a friend of yours has just lost her mother, Life Principle No. 2 asks that you console your friend, even if it is uncomfortable for you to do so. If you pass along a rumor you have heard about a neighbor, you have violated Life Principle No. 3. If you fire an employee for not doing her job well but give another employee a pass for the same behavior just because the second employee happens to be the daughter of a close friend, you are compromising Life Principle No. 4.

But it seems a stretch to suggest that we err by not loving the annoying co-worker, the crazy driver who cuts us off on the highway, or the lazy clerk at the grocery store. That is, we might choose to take the high road here, but can we rightly say that it is our ethical obligation to do so? Whether it is our duty to be loving to all with whom we come into contact, or whether love is above and beyond the call of duty, I will hereby make a case for a fifth Life Principle that asks us to treat others with kindness, care, and compassion—that is, with love.

WHAT'S LOVE GOT TO DO WITH IT?

Popular songs largely concern love, but that's love of a very specific kind: that between romantic partners. We see a similar obsession in popular movies, magazines, books, and television shows. What's more, American popular culture has become one of our most widely exported commodities. Travel anywhere in the world and you will hear many of the same songs, see many of the same movies and TV programs, and read many of the same romance novels that you find at home. It is difficult to grow up anywhere in the world and not believe that "love" means "a burning desire to be linked forever with another person."

It was not always this way.

Source: Bruce Weinstein, "The Fifth Life Principle: Be Loving," *BusinessWeek.com*, February 22, 2007.

should be paid for by Robbins. However, repairs and adjustments not caused by ordinary use or damages not attributed to the bailee's negligence become the responsibility of the bailor. The bailee is not obligated to replace parts that break down because of the gradual use and depreciation of the other's property over an extended period. If the chainsaw had simply worn out through no fault of Robbins, he would not have been responsible.

EXAMPLE 22-10: Unusual and Unexpected Expense

Swanson, with Oberly's permission, took Oberly's motorcycle on a trial ride. Every precaution was taken to avoid damage. Nevertheless, on the way home, the front tire blew, and Swanson found it necessary to buy a new tire. The old tire had been badly worn in many places. The blowout was not caused by Swanson's negligent use. Oberly, the bailor, would be responsible for any *unusual* and *unexpected* expenses resulting from the tire blowout, including the obligation of reimbursing Swanson for the tire.

Mutual-Benefit Bailments

When personal property is transferred to a bailee with the intent that both parties will benefit, a **mutual-benefit bailment** results. Ordinary bailments involving business transactions are usually mutual-benefit bailments in which the businessperson is paid for his or her services.

Renting an item such as a car or a videotape, leaving a car at a garage to be repaired or a suit to be cleaned at a cleaners, placing one's property in storage, and leaving a diamond ring at a pawn shop (a *pledge*) in exchange for a loan of money are examples of mutual-benefit bailments.

EXAMPLE 22-11: Pledge

Cohen borrowed $7,400 from the American Arlington Bank. As security for the loan, the parties signed a bailment agreement making the bank the bailee of Cohen's valuable painting of King George III of England, allegedly one of three portraits of the king by the eighteenth-century painter George Ramsey. The painting was hung in the office of the bank's vice president. This agreement was a pledge because the bank had possession and complete control over the painting while the loan was outstanding. The UCC governs the subject of pledges, discussed in more detail in Chapter 31.

A **consignment contract** is a type of mutual benefit bailment in which the **consignor** entrusts goods to the **consignee** for the purpose of selling them. If the goods are sold, the consignee, known as the *factor*, will forward the proceeds, less a fee, to the consignor. If they are not sold, they will be returned.

In a mutual-benefit bailment, the bailee owes a duty to use *reasonable care*. **Reasonable care** means the degree of care that a reasonably prudent person would use under the same circumstances and conditions. The bailee is responsible for **ordinary negligence**, which is the failure to use the care that a reasonable person would use under the same circumstances.

EXAMPLE 22-12: Reasonable Care Required

Champine stored his boat, motor, and trailer in Field's building for the winter for $10. Champine expressed some doubts about the soundness of the building, particularly concerning the structure of the roof. Field assured him that the building was safe. The roof collapsed after a winter snowstorm, damaging Champine's boat. In allowing Champine to recover from Field, the court said that the relationship imposed a duty on the bailee to use reasonable care, which he failed to do.

Pawn shop agreements may start out as bailments, however, failure of the bailor to retrieve the goods in a specified time may cause the bailor to forfeit ownership.

Many courts today apply the reasonable care standard to all types of bailments, including bailments for the sole benefit of the bailor and bailments for the sole benefit of the bailee.

In a mutual-benefit bailment, the bailee must use the property only for the express purposes permitted by the bailor, as provided for in the contract of bailment. The rental of a car, tools, or formal wear, for example, implies the right of reasonable use. Failing to use the property as agreed makes the bailee responsible for any damages that might result, regardless of the degree of care exercised.

EXAMPLE 22-13: Duty to Use Reasonable Care

Smith rented a tuxedo from the Valet Shop. While wearing it, he crawled under a friend's car to make an adjustment to the brakes. Smith was liable to the Valet Shop for the resulting damage to the suit. The bailed property had not been used for the purposes permitted by the bailor. A reasonably prudent person would know that one does not crawl under a car while wearing a rented tuxedo.

Quick Quiz 22-2 True or False?

1. A bailment for the sole benefit of the bailee is a gratuitous bailment.

2. In a bailment for the sole benefit of the bailor, the bailee has an implied right to use the bailor's property.

3. In a mutual-benefit bailment, the bailee owes a duty to use reasonable care.

22-3 Burden of Proof

Sometimes items are damaged, lost, or stolen when they are in the possession of a bailee. In the past, the bailor had to prove that the bailee was negligent to recover against the bailee for damages. This proof was very difficult to obtain because the bailor was not in a

position to know what caused the loss, because the bailee had possession of the property at the time. Most courts today shift the burden of proof in bailment cases to the one who is in the best position to know what happened—that is, to the bailee. Today, when items in the possession of a bailee are damaged, lost, or stolen, the burden is on the bailee to prove that it was not negligent.

> ### EXAMPLE 22-14:   Failure to Use Reasonable Care
>
> Edwards took her Cadillac automobile to the Crestmont Cadillac garage to have a tire changed and the wheels aligned. When she returned later to pick up the car, she learned that it had been stolen from the garage. The court held Crestmont responsible. It had not used reasonable care in preventing the car from being stolen. The court said that a bailee is presumed to be negligent when it fails to redeliver the bailed property, unless it can prove that it was not negligent.

Refer again to Examples 22-1 and 22-2. In the former example, which was not a bailment, the burden was on Sewall to prove that the parking lot owner was negligent. In contrast, Example 22-2 involved a bailment, placing the burden on the parking garage (the bailee), to prove that it was not negligent.

22-4 Special Bailments

Certain types of bailees, including innkeepers, common carriers, and warehousers, have extraordinary obligations in addition to the duties imposed on all bailees.

Innkeepers

An **innkeeper** is the operator of a hotel, motel, or inn that holds itself out to the public as being ready to entertain travelers, strangers, and transient guests. A **transient** is a guest whose length of stay is variable. A lodger is discussed in Chapter 24.

To assist travelers in obtaining accommodations, common law imposed the duty upon innkeepers to accept all people who requested a room if one was available. In addition, innkeepers were considered insurers of their guests' property. With some exceptions, these standards are still the law today.

> ### EXAMPLE 22-15:   Duty to Accept All Transients
>
> Section 7, Chapter 140, of the Massachusetts General Law reads, "An innholder who, upon request, refuses to receive and make suitable provision for a stranger or traveler shall be punished by a fine of not more than fifty dollars."

The Civil Rights Act of 1964 prohibits discrimination in the selection of guests for reasons of race, creed, color, sex, or ethnic background. People may be turned away when all rooms are occupied or reserved. In addition, innkeepers may refuse to accommodate people whose presence might endanger the health, welfare, or safety of other guests or the safety of the establishment itself.

The Opening Case Revisited, Part I

"A Rough Night's Sleep"

The lower court held that because the Rosiers failed to secure the chain latch to the outside door, the inn was not responsible. The court of appeals reversed the lower court's decision, holding that a jury should decide whether the motel used reasonable care in protecting its guests.

Innkeeper's Duty of Care   Innkeepers must use reasonable care in protecting their guests from harm. They are responsible for injuries to their guests caused by the inn's negligence or the negligence of employees.

Innkeepers must respect their guests' rights of privacy. Guests are guaranteed exclusive and undisturbed privacy of rooms assigned by the hotel. Interruption of the guests' privacy through unpermitted entry by hotel employees or other guests creates a liability in tort for invasion of privacy.

EXAMPLE 22-16:   Invasion of Privacy

Nash stopped at the Riverside Motel for the night. After taking a shower, she opened the bathroom door and discovered a couple bringing suitcases into her room. The motel clerk had assigned the room to another couple by mistake. Nash may seek damages against the motel for invasion of privacy.

Innkeepers have a greater duty of care toward their guests' property than is imposed in a usual mutual-benefit bailment. With exceptions (as described subsequently), innkeepers are held by law to be insurers of their guests' property. The insured property includes all personal property brought into the hotel for the convenience and purpose of the guests' stay. In the event of loss, the hotelkeeper may be held liable, regardless of the amount of care exercised in the protection of the guests' property.

EXAMPLE 22-17:   Insurer of Guest's Property

Upon checking into the Concord Hotel, Mr. and Mrs. Modell placed two diamond rings in the hotel's safe deposit vault. Later, Mrs. Modell withdrew the rings from the vault to wear that evening. When she went to return them later that night, she was told by the desk clerk that the vault was closed until the next morning. That night, the Modells' room was broken into, and the rings were stolen. The hotel was held liable for the loss of the rings because it did not provide a place for their safekeeping.

Innkeepers are not liable as insurers in four cases:

1. Losses caused by a guest's own negligence.
2. Losses to the guest's property due to acts of God or acts of the public enemy.
3. Losses of property due to accidental fire in which no negligence may be attributed to the hotelkeeper. This exception also includes fires caused by other guests staying at the hotel at the same time. Such persons, even though on other floors, are called fellow guests.
4. Losses arising out of characteristics of the property that cause its own deterioration.

Hotels, inns, and motels must use ordinary care in the protection of their guests, but are held to be insurers of the guest's property, with four exceptions.

EXAMPLE 22-18:   Guest's Own Negligence

At the Village Hotel, guests were advised to lock their doors whenever leaving their rooms, and bellhops instructed guests in the use of the locks. Hamlin left the hotel without locking the room door, and property was stolen from his room. The hotel was not liable for this loss.

In most states, innkeepers are further protected by laws limiting the amount of claim any guest may make for a single loss. The limit is usually $500 or less, depending on the state in which the hotel is located. These laws also give the innkeeper the right to provide a safe or vault for the better protection of the guests' valuables. A guest who does not use the safe provided for valuables will be personally responsible for losses and may not seek recovery from the innkeeper.

Innkeeper's Lien and Credit Card Blocking Innkeepers have a lien on their guests' property. A **lien** is a claim that one has against the property of another. If a guest cannot pay the bill, the innkeeper is permitted to take possession of the guest's property as security for payment at some later date. Payment of the bill releases the property and terminates the right of lien.

Credit card blocking is a common method used by hotels to secure payment for a room. Under this system, guests are asked for a credit card when they register. The hotel then contacts the card issuer electronically with the estimated cost of the bill. If the card issuer approves the transaction, the guest's available line of credit is reduced by the esti-

The Opening Case Revisited, Part II
"A Rough Night's Sleep"

With exceptions, innkeepers are held by law to be insurers of their guests' property. If any of the Rosiers' property were lost or damaged in this case and the jury found that the Rosiers' were not negligent, the hotel could be held responsible up to any limit set by state statute.

mated amount. This procedure is known as a block (or authorization). The final actual charge for the room will replace the block within a day or two after the guest checks out. If the guest pays the final charge with cash, check, or a different credit card however, the block can remain on the original credit card for as long as 15 days.

Carriers

The events of September 11, 2001, changed the lives of Americans in many ways, most notably in the field of transportation. Two months after 9/11, President Bush signed into law the Aviation and Transportation Security Act (ATSA), which among other things established a new Transportation Security Administration (TSA) within the Department of Transportation. The TSA protects the nation's transportation systems to ensure freedom of movement for people and commerce. Soon thereafter, Congress established the Department of Homeland Security, which oversees the Coast Guard, Customs Service, Immigration and Naturalization Service, and TSA. Collectively, these organizations are responsible for protecting the nation's transportation system and supervising the entry of people and goods into the United States.

LO7

   Carriers are businesses that undertake to transport persons, goods, or both. If a carrier holds itself out to the general public to provide transportation for compensation, it is called a **common carrier**. Like hotels, common carriers cannot turn away people who ask for their services, with exceptions for security reasons.

   Common carriers of goods are insurers of all goods accepted for shipment. They are liable as insurers regardless of whether they have been negligent. The Carmack Amendment to the Interstate Commerce Act states that a carrier is liable for damages to goods transported by it unless there is proof that the damage occurs because of one of the following exceptions:

- Acts of God (e.g., floods, tornadoes, cyclones, earthquakes)
- Acts of the public enemy (wartime enemies, terrorists, and the like)
- Acts of public authorities
- Acts of the shipper
- The inherent nature of the goods (e.g., perishable goods, evaporating and fermenting liquids, diseased animals)

EXAMPLE 22-19:   Insurer of Goods

Whitehall Packing Co. engaged Amway Truck Lines to transport 40 barrels of fresh meat from its plant in Wisconsin to Howard Johnson's in New York. The federal government required plastic liners in the barrels, and Howard Johnson's would not allow dry ice in them. The refrigerator unit in Amway's truck operated properly. The truck experienced delays and took longer than its normal running time for the trip. When it arrived in New York, the meat in the barrels had an off, or gassy, odor and was not considered acceptable by the U.S. government inspector. An expert meat inspector testified that the barreled meat was smothered because of the use of the plastic liners and the absence of dry ice. Some hanging meat in the same truck was found to be in perfect condition. Although there was no evidence that Amway was negligent, the court held it responsible, saying that it was an insurer of the meat.

   In addition to being insurers, common carriers of goods must accept *without discrimination* all goods offered to them for shipment. Under the Interstate Commerce Act, discrimination through either the selection of customers or the use of preferential rates is illegal. Exceptions to the rule against discrimination are as follows:

1. A common carrier is not required to accept goods of a type that it is not equipped to carry.

2. The carrier may refuse goods that are inherently dangerous and that would create hazards beyond the control of the carrier's usual safety facilities.

3. The common carrier may refuse goods that it does not represent itself as hauling.

4. The carrier may refuse goods that are improperly packed. Proper packaging is determined by the type of goods being shipped, the length of the haul, and the usual custom of the trade.

5. The carrier may refuse goods that are not delivered at the proper place and time.

Common carriers will not be excused from liability for losses due to strikes, mob violence, fire, and similar causes. Labor unions are required to give notice of impending strikes weeks in advance of the strike dates to allow carriers to reject shipments that might be damaged by delays caused by strikes. The carrier is required to ship goods by the proper route, protect them during shipment, and deliver them to the proper person.

UCC 7-309(2)   Carriers may limit the amount of their liability to the value stated on the **bill of lading**, which is the written contract between a common carrier and a shipper.

EXAMPLE 22-20:   Failure to Read Contract

Bratton hired Allied Van Lines, Inc., to transport her household goods from Ohio to Florida. When the goods were picked up, Bratton signed a bill of lading that contained a provision limiting the carrier's liability to $1.25 per pound (which amounted to $4,500) or the actual value of the goods as written on the bill of lading. There was a place on the bill of lading for Bratton to fill in the actual value of the goods ($10,630). She failed to do so. The shipment was destroyed in transit. Bratton argued that because she did not read the document and was unaware of any provision affecting the carrier's liability, she was not bound by the words in the bill of lading. The court held that a bill of lading containing a limitation of the carrier's liability is binding, even though the shipper had not read it.

UCC 7-307   A common carrier has the right to the payment of fees agreed upon for the shipment of the goods and a lien on all goods shipped for the amount of the shipping charges due. Should the shipper or the party receiving the goods fail to pay the charges, the carrier has the right to sell the goods at public sale.

EXAMPLE 22-21:   Carrier's Lien on Goods Shipped

The Hanlon Book Company ordered paper from the Maine Paper Company. The paper was shipped from Bangor, Maine, under terms that transferred title to the paper when delivered to the carrier. Hanlon Book Company refused to pay shipping costs when informed of the arrival of the shipment. Notice was finally given to both firms of the carrier's intention to sell the paper to recover shipping charges. At a public sale, the paper brought a high bid of $2,237. The carrier deducted shipping costs and turned over the balance to the Hanlon Book Company.

Common Carriers of Passengers   A **passenger** is defined as a person who enters the premises of a carrier with the intention of buying a ticket for a trip. One continues to be a passenger as long as one continues the trip. This relationship is terminated after the person has reached the destination printed on the ticket and left the premises of the carrier.

Prior to 9/11, common carriers had an obligation to accept all passengers who sought passage over their lines. This rule has changed. By order of the U.S. Congress, the Federal Aviation Administration (FAA) has established regulations that require the screening of passengers and property before they enter an aircraft to search for dangerous weapons, explosives, and other destructive substances. Passengers who do not consent to the screening must be refused transportation.

49 U.S. Code 44901(a)

49 U.S. Code 44902

Functioning under the Department of Homeland Security, the TSA's mission is to prevent terrorist attacks and protect the U.S. transportation network. Its work encompasses all sectors of transportation, from container ships in harbors to trucks on highways to commuter trains in subways.

The approach to security on aircraft includes thorough screening of baggage and passengers by highly trained screeners, fortified cockpit doors in all airliners, thousands of federal air marshals aboard a record number of flights, and armed federal flight deck officers. A list of items that cannot be taken on board an aircraft can be found on the Internet.

Here are some travel tips suggested by the TSA, as also summarized in Figure 22-2:

Before you go . . .

- Visit www.tsa.gov for all the latest security policies.
- Pack liquids/gels/aerosols in your checked baggage. For a short trip you are permitted to carry on 1 quart-size, clear plastic, zip-top bag holding 3 ounces or less containers of liquids, gels or aerosols. Limited to one bag per traveler.
- Exceptions include: baby formula/breast milk/baby food while traveling with a small child, medications, and liquids (to include water, juice or liquid nutrients) or gels for

Figure 22-2 The Transportation Security Administration provides these rules for carrying on an aircraft small quantities of liquids, gels, and aerosols.

diabetics or other medical needs. All exceptions must be declared to the Security Officer for screening.

- All footwear must be removed for X-ray screening. Wearing footwear that can be easily removed helps.

- Pack valuables such as jewelry, cash, and electronics, as well as fragile items, in your carry-on. This will speed the screening process.

- Avoid wearing accessories that contain metal, which will set off the metal detector.

- Put all undeveloped film in your carry-on bag, because checked baggage screening equipment may damage film.

- If carrying a firearm, please check with your airline for appropriate procedures.

- Leave lighters at home. TSA collects thousands of lighters a day.

  When you arrive. . .

- Take your quart-size, plastic, zip-top bag out of your carry-on and place separately in bin.

- Declare all permitted liquid exceptions to the Security Officer in front of the checkpoint.

- Take your laptop and video cameras with cassettes out of their cases for screening.

- Remove your outer coat, suit coat, jacket, or blazer to place in bin for X-ray.

- Place the following items in your carry-on before entering the screening checkpoint: cell phones and personal data assistants, keys, loose change, jewelry, and large metal items.

49 U.S. Code 44902(b)

Common carriers may not discriminate in the selection of passengers on the basis of race, color, national origin, religion, sex, or ancestry. Carriers may refuse passengers (1) when all available space is occupied or reserved; (2) if they are disorderly, intoxicated, insane, or infected with a contagious disease; or (3) since 9/11, when the carrier decides a passenger "is or might be inimical to safety."

Racial profiling, the act of targeting a person for criminal investigation primarily because of racial or ethnic characteristics, may not be a motivating factor in a carrier's decision to refuse transportation. A passenger who has boarded a plane that has not taken off must leave the plane if told to do so by an authorized airline representative.

A carrier must exercise reasonable care in the protection of passengers. Injuries that are reasonably foreseeable or preventable and that result from the carrier's negligence give the passenger a right to sue for damages. However, if injuries are not reasonably foreseeable or preventable, the carrier is not responsible.

EXAMPLE 22-22:   Carrier's Duty to Protect Passengers

Three men who were intoxicated boarded a commuter train around midnight. They were talking loudly and making a lot of noise. A conductor saw them and told them not to bother passengers. At the next stop, while the conductor let passengers on and off the train, the men went to another car. There, they assaulted, hit, and kicked a passenger. As soon as the conductor reboarded the train, he sought out the three men, discovered what they had done, and had them arrested. In a suit brought by the injured passenger against the carrier, the court held in favor of the carrier. The court said that the incident occurred so quickly and unexpectedly that the conductor, acting with the highest degree of care under the circumstances, could not have averted it.

Bumped Airline Passengers   When an airline flight is overbooked, the airline must first find volunteers willing to give up their seats for ones on the next available flight. If there are not enough volunteers, other passengers may be denied a seat in accordance with the airline's priority rules. Airlines are required to establish and publish priority rules for determining which passengers holding confirmed reservation space will be denied boarding on an oversold flight.

Passengers who are denied boarding involuntarily, that is, bumped, may be entitled to compensation. If the airline can arrange alternate transportation that is scheduled to arrive at the passenger's destination within one hour of the original arrival time, there is no compensation. However, if the alternate flight gets to the destination between one and two hours late, the passenger is entitled to a cash payment equal to the price of one fare, up to $200. This amount doubles if the passenger is more than two hours late.

Passengers may refuse all compensation and bring private legal action. Federal regulations state: "The passenger may decline the payment and seek to recover damages in a court of law or in some other manner." In 1994, the U.S. Supreme Court confirmed that passengers who are bumped from a scheduled flight may sue the carrier for damages.

Passengers' Baggage   Since 9/11, dangerous weapons, explosives, destructive items, and items that may be deemed to present a potential threat cannot be carried on board an aircraft. Many items that cannot be hand-carried may, however, be carried in the luggage compartment of planes. The law has no requirement for returning banned items that are left at airport security checkpoints. In addition, those who attempt to bring banned items through airport

---

BusinessWeek Business Law in the News

Travelers, Prepare to Be Smelled

It greets travelers with discreet puffs of air, just enough to dislodge a trace of explosives from skin, hair, or clothing. And it can detect them right through shoes. It's the latest bomb-sniffing technology, and it may be coming to a train station or airport near you.

On May 3, the U.S. Transportation Security Administration announced a 30-day trial at Amtrak's New Carrollton (Md.) station, testing a system made by General Electric. It's also looking at the Sentinel II, the system built by British security company Smiths Group. The devices, which cost up to $150,000, are used in nuclear power plants in the U.S. and Canada. Britain's Heathrow and Manchester Airports are testing them.

Travelers walk through a gate similar to a metal detector where currents of air circulate, then get sucked back into the machine for analysis, which takes eight seconds. It's sensitive enough, says Bill

Mawer, president of Smiths Detection North America, a unit of the British company, to foil a would-be shoe bomber whose sneakers are still on and laced.

The TSA already uses 3,500 desktop baggage detectors at the nation's airports. But they depend on security guards taking swipes off suspicious passengers' bags to test for explosives. The Sentinel does the job on everyone, no muss, no fuss.

Questions for Analysis

1. Would discreet puffs of air blown against your skin be disturbing as you proceed through a security checkpoint?

2. What kind of security measures, if any, do you currently find most disturbing?

Source: Catherine Yang, "Travelers, Prepare to Be Smelled," *BusinessWeek*, May 24, 2004, 16.

Common carriers must protect passengers and their carry-on luggage with at least ordinary care. Ordinary care today is much different than ordinary care was in the past.

checkpoints are subject to civil penalties of up to $1,100 per violation, as well as criminal penalties. Passengers must declare any hazardous materials that they are carrying. Violators of federal hazardous materials regulations may be subject to a civil penalty of up to $27,000 for each violation and, in appropriate cases, criminal penalties.

In conjunction with the carrying of passengers, a carrier is obliged to accept a reasonable amount of baggage. Excess baggage may be shipped by a passenger or through payment of additional fees. Baggage limits vary with different airlines. Personal luggage carried aboard an airline and kept at one's seat does not generally fall within the baggage weight limits permitted each passenger.

When a baggage car or baggage compartment is available for checking luggage, the carrier is considered an insurer of the luggage checked by the passengers and left in these places. Property kept by passengers at their seats or in overhead compartments places upon the carrier the obligation of exercising ordinary care for its safety.

Federal rules place limits on the liability of airlines for lost luggage. For travel wholly within the United States, the maximum liability of an airline for lost luggage is $3,000 per passenger. Excess valuation may be declared on certain types of articles. However, some carriers assume no liability for fragile, valuable, or perishable articles.

Warehousers

When goods are stored in a warehouse, the relationship of bailor and bailee is created between the owner of the goods and the warehouser. The UCC defines a **warehouser** as a person engaged in the business of storing goods for hire. A **warehouse** is a building or structure in which any goods, but particularly wares or merchandise, are stored. A **warehouse receipt** is a receipt issued by a person engaged in the business of storing goods for hire.

UCC 7-102(h)

UCC 1-201(45)

Although both common carriers and warehousers are mutual-benefit bailees, they perform different functions. Common carriers are engaged in moving goods. Warehousers keep goods in storage. At times, however, one or the other will perform both functions.

LO9

Warehousers may be classified as public or private. A **public warehouser** is one that owns a warehouse in which any member of the public who is willing to pay the regular charge may store goods. Grain elevators in the Midwest, used to store farmers' grain, are sometimes established as public warehouses. A warehouser whose warehouse is not for general public use is a **private warehouser**. Most warehousers fall into this latter category.

Sometimes, businesspeople will borrow money using goods that they have stored in a warehouse as security for the loan. The one who lends the money is given the warehouse receipt. If the debt is not paid, the holder of the receipt may obtain possession of the goods in storage. This practice is called **field warehousing**.

UCC 7-204(1)

A warehouser must use the amount of care that a reasonably careful person would use under similar circumstances. Failure to use such care is negligence and makes the warehouser liable for losses or damages to the goods.

EXAMPLE 22-23:   Reasonable Care Required

Bekins Warehouse stored Keefe's household goods in its warehouse beneath some sprinkler system pipes. It did not inspect the area before placing the goods there. One of the pipes was unconnected, and water from the pipes leaked onto Keefe's goods, damaging them. Bekins's failure to inspect the area of storage was a negligent act that made Bekins responsible for the loss.

The parties may limit the amount of liability of the warehouser by including terms to that effect in the storage agreement or warehouse receipt.

UCC 7-204(2)

EXAMPLE 22-24:   Contract Limitation

The warehouse receipt given by Bekins to Keefe in Example 22-23 limited Bekins's liability to 10 cents per pound per article. The limitation was enforceable even though it was not specifically called to Keefe's attention when the warehouse receipt was signed.

If goods are not removed from a warehouse at the end of a storage period, the warehouser may sell them. Before doing so, however, the warehouser must notify the owner that they are going to be sold and give that person the right to redeem them. If no time for storage is fixed in the agreement, the warehouser must give at least 30 days' notice to the owner before selling the goods.

UCC 7-206

LO10

A warehouser has a lien on the goods that are in the warehouser's possession. A **warehouser's lien** is the right to retain possession of the goods until the satisfaction of the charges imposed on them. The lien is for the amount of money owed for storage charges, transportation charges, insurance, and expenses necessary for the preservation of the goods. The lien is a possessory one. It is lost when the warehouser voluntarily delivers the goods or unjustifiably refuses to deliver them. If the owner of the goods owes the warehouser money for the storage of other goods, the warehouser has a lien for the other debt only if it is so stated in the warehouse receipt.

UCC 7-209

If the person who stored the goods is a merchant in the course of business, the warehousers's lien may be enforced by a public or private sale at any time or place and on any terms that are commercially reasonable. Notice must be given to all persons known to claim an interest in the goods. The notice must include a statement of the amount due, the nature of the proposed sale, and the time and place of any public sale (see Figure 22-3).

UCC 7-210(1)

If the person who stored the goods is not a merchant, more complicated rules must be followed to enforce the warehouser's lien. In addition to giving notice to all persons known to claim an interest in the goods, the nonmerchant must advertise the pending sale in a local newspaper. Notices and advertisements must contain specific information set forth in the UCC.

UCC 7-210(2)
UCC 7-210(3)

PUBLIC AUCTION
Warehouser's Lien Sale
To be held at
The Carriage House
NORTH BROADWAY, ELMWOOD, N.H.

Wednesday, July 1 at 6:30 p.m.

Preview at 5 p.m.
We have moved the sale for the convenience of the sale
12 containers with inventory of the following merchandise; living room sets, kitchen sets, bedroom sets, chests of drawers & more; Washer, dryers & refrigerators. Also, a large assort. of TV's, stereos, lamps, mirrors, shelves, glass, a lg. number of box lots, dishes, bric-a-brac & much, much more.
Terms: cash or check w/ preapproval
E.B. MAPLE, Auctioneers N.H. Lic. 112
34 Main St., Elmwood, N.H. 555-1200

Figure 22-3   Before this warehouser's lien sale is held, notice must be given to all persons known to have an interest in the goods.

> ### Quick Quiz 22-4 True or False?
>
> 1. Innkeepers may turn away strangers and travelers if they desire, even when they have rooms available.
>
> 2. Common carriers are insurers of goods accepted for shipment only when they are negligent.
>
> 3. With a few exceptions, bumped airline passengers must be offered alternate transportation plus the money back for their tickets.

Summary

22.1 A bailment occurs whenever someone transfers possession and control of personal property to another with the intent that the same property will be returned later.

22.2 The principal types of bailments are: bailments for the sole benefit of the bailor, bailments for the sole benefit of the bailee, and mutual-benefit bailments. Under modern law, bailees owe a duty to use reasonable care with the goods in their possession. Former law, still followed in some states, required the bailee to use great care in a bailment for the sole benefit of the bailee, slight care in a bailment for the sole benefit of the bailor, and ordinary care in a mutual-benefit bailment.

22.3 When goods are lost or damaged while in the possession of a bailee, the burden is on the bailee to prove that no negligence was involved; if this proof cannot be made, the bailee will be held responsible for the loss.

22.4 Innkeepers are required to accept all guests unless there are no vacancies. They must respect their guests' right of privacy. With some exceptions, innkeepers are insurers of their guests' property. In most states, however, they are protected by laws limiting their liability to a specific dollar amount. Innkeepers have a lien on guests' property for the amount of any unpaid bills.

The Transportation Security Administration (TSA), under the Department of Homeland Security, is responsible for protecting the United States' transportation system. The TSA's approach to security includes thorough screening of baggage and passengers, fortified cockpit doors, and the use of air marshals.

Common carriers of goods are liable as insurers of the goods they ship regardless of whether they have been negligent. They are not responsible for damages caused by acts of God, acts of the public enemy, acts of public authorities, acts of the shipper, and the inherent nature of the goods. With some exceptions, bumped airline passengers are entitled to a payment of denied boarding compensation.

Public warehousers must accept goods for storage by any member of the public willing to pay for the service. Private warehouses are not for general public use. Warehousers must use reasonable care in storing goods. They have a lien on goods until storage charges are paid.

Key Terms

bailee, 443
bailment, 443

bailments for the sole benefit of the bailee, 446

bailments for the sole benefit of the bailor, 445

Questions for Review and Discussion

1. What are the principal types of bailments? Give an example of each.
2. How does the standard of care imposed on a bailee today differ from the degrees of care recognized in former years?
3. How has the burden of proof shifted, under today's law, when items in the possession of a bailee are damaged?
4. What obligation does an innkeeper have to accept guests?
5. What is a common carrier's liability for damage to goods it transports?
6. What does the Transportation Security Administration's approach to security include?
7. What are the rules for carrying small amounts of liquids, gels, and aerosols on an aircraft?
8. What are the two classes of warehousers? Explain their differences.
9. What duty of care is owed by a warehouser to the owner of stored goods?
10. Explain the warehouser's lien. What amount of money does it involve? When is it lost?

Investigating the Internet

A friend who has never flown before is going with you on a trip. Your friend, who will have both checked and carry-on baggage, asks you what can and cannot be brought on the flight. The answer to this question is located on the Internet. Can you help your friend find the answer?

Cases for Analysis

1. David Bess rented three outdoor booth spaces at the Traders World flea market to display his inventory of Beanie Babies for sale. He stored his inventory in a locked trailer, which he left parked at the flea market overnight. When he returned the next morning, he discovered that the padlock on his trailer had been changed. Upon forcing the trailer open, he found that his entire inventory of Beanie Babies, which he estimated had a value of $60,000 to $75,000, was missing. In a suit against Traders World, Bess argued that the transaction was a bailment. Do you agree with Bess? Why or

why not? *Bess v. Traders World, Inc.*, CA2001-06-063 (OH)

2. Schaeffer boarded a 30-passenger, single-aisle turboprop airplane carrying two pieces of baggage. When asked by a flight attendant to surrender one carry-on for proper storage, he refused and became verbally abusive. The captain of the plane decided not to depart with the disruptive passenger on board because he was concerned about the safety of the flight. When asked to leave the plane, Schaeffer refused, and the Port Authority police were called to remove him. Must a passenger who has boarded a plane that has not taken off leave the plane when told to do so by an authorized representative? Explain. *Schaeffer v. Cavallero*, 54 F. Supp.2d 350 (S.D.N.Y.).

3. Torczyner, a diamond salesman, registered as a guest at the Hilton Hotel in Denver, Colorado. He placed his diamonds in the hotel safe when he did not need them for business purposes. On the last day of his visit, he removed the gems from the safe, left the hotel to make some business calls, and returned for the purpose of packing and checking out. Instead of placing the diamonds in the hotel safe, Torczyner carried them to his room. There, he was assaulted by two men who beat him and robbed him of the diamonds. Is the hotel responsible for the loss of the diamonds? Explain. *Pacific Diamond Co. v. Superior Ct.*, 85 Cal. App. 3rd 871 (CA).

4. Joe Scott left his automobile with Purser Truck Sales, Inc., to be repaired. Purser Truck Sales turned the automobile over to Lonz Radford to make the repairs. The car was demolished while in the possession of Radford. In a suit brought by Scott against Purser, the trial court held in favor of Purser, because Scott presented no evidence indicating that Purser was negligent. Was the trial court correct? Why or why not? *Scott v. Purser Truck Sales, Inc.*, 402 S.E.2d 354 (GA).

5. Grabert stored his Cessna 175A aircraft in Noel's hangar for $30 a month. The Cessna required a key to be started, and the key was either left in the plane's ignition or hung on a knob on the instrument panel. At night, the hangar was locked. A key to the hangar door was left outside on the top of a meter box so that aircraft owners could get to their planes at any hour of the day or night. Cameron, a part-time employee of the airport, stole the plane one night when he was off duty. He did not have a pilot's license. The plane crashed, and Cameron was killed. Was the owner of the airport liable for the destruction of the plane? Explain. *Grabert v. James C. Noel Flying Service, Inc.*, 360 So.2d 1363 (LA).

6. Donovan, who was 17 years of age, was hired by Schlesner as a gas station attendant. This job included pumping gas, keeping the station clean, washing windows, and taking care of customers. Donovan was also required to keep the books to reflect the sale of such items as gas, milk, and candy. Schlesner deducted money from Donovan's pay each week for shortages that appeared in the books. In a suit that Donovan brought to recover the money so deducted, Schlesner claimed that Donovan was a bailee of the goods that were sold in the gas station. Do you agree with Schlesner? Why or why not? *Donovan v. Schlesner*, 240 N.W.2d 135 (WI).

7. F-M Potatoes, Inc., stored potatoes for Suda. The oral agreement provided for a storage rental price of 40 cents per hundredweight to February 1 and an additional 10 cents per hundredweight to April 1. F-M Potatoes controlled the temperature and atmospheric conditions of the warehouse. Suda stored 13,000 hundredweight of potatoes in the warehouse. The potatoes spoiled because F-M Potatoes failed to maintain the proper temperature and atmospheric conditions. F-M Potatoes argued that the arrangement was a lease rather than a bailment, and hence, it was not liable for the spoilage. Do you agree? Explain. *F-M Potatoes, Inc., v. Suda*, 259 N.W.2d 487 (ND).

8. James Reed and Deborah Addis, husband and wife, were the only guests at the Red Inn in Provincetown, Massachusetts. An owner of the inn checked the building at 12:30 AM, found the windows closed and the doors locked, and left. Shortly thereafter, the guests were awakened by a fire alarm. They ran down the stairs and found the premises dark and full of smoke. The dining room was afire. The guests tried to leave by the door they had entered earlier, but it was locked. Other efforts to escape from the first floor were unsuccessful. Ultimately, they returned to the second floor, forced open a window, and jumped out, causing both to be injured. An investigation showed that the fire had been set by an arsonist. Did the inn have a duty to protect the guests from a fire set by an arsonist? Why or why not? *Addis v. Steele*, 648 N.E.2d 773 (MA).

9. Poroznoff was living in a room at the YMCA on a week-to-week basis. It was his only residence.

While there, he became drunk and disorderly and was arrested by the police. On his return to the YMCA, he found that his room was locked. He was told by the management not to reenter the building. Poroznoff argued that since the room at the YMCA was his only residence, he was not a transient guest. He claimed that he had rights of a tenant. Do you agree with Poroznoff? Why or why not? *Poroznoff v. Alberti,* 401 A.2d 1124 (NJ).

10. A state agency attempted to inspect Blair Academy's dormitories as hotels under the state's hotel and multiple-dwelling law. The law of that state defined a hotel as any building "which contains 10 or more units of dwelling space or has sleeping facilities for 25 or more persons and is kept, used, maintained, advertised as, or held out to be, a place where sleeping or dwelling accommodations are available to transient or permanent guests." Did Blair Academy's dormitories come within that state's definition of a hotel? Explain. *Blair Academy v. Sheehan,* 373 A.2d 418 (NJ).

11. A storage company stored Conrad's household furniture for $25 a month. Conrad made the first payment, left town, and paid nothing for five months. The storage company sold Conrad's furniture at an auction without notifying Conrad or advertising the sale in the newspaper. Conrad claims that his rights were violated by the storage company's sale of the goods. Do you agree with Conrad? Why or why not? See also *Poole v. Christian,* 411 N.E.2d 513 (OH).

12. Fairchild made plane reservations for a flight to Chicago. She arrived at the airport one hour before the scheduled departure time and was told that her flight had been overbooked and that there were no remaining seats on the plane. The airline asked for volunteers to give up their seats but no one volunteered. What are Fairchild's rights?

Quick Quiz Answers

22-1		22-2		22-4	
1. F		1. T		1. F	
2. F		2. F		2. F	
3. F		3. T		3. T	

Chapter 23   Real Property

The Opening Case
"The Dream House"

Tim and Celeste were excited. They were about to make the largest purchase of their lives—their first home. It was a pretty house, beautifully landscaped with newly planted trees. Inside, the floors were covered with wall-to-wall carpeting, and the windows had new curtains. One side of the property formed the bank of a stream. Another side was bordered by a fence covered with roses. Many questions came to mind as they entered into this important transaction.

Opening Case Questions

1. Did the curtains and wall-to-wall carpeting go with the house?

2. Were the rose bushes and newly planted trees included in the purchase?

3. What rights would they have to the stream and the water flowing through it, and at what point in the stream was the property line?

4. What kind of deed would they receive? Who would own the property if one of them died?

LO   Learning Objectives

1. Explain what constitutes real property.
2. Discuss air rights, subterranean rights, and water rights.
3. Decide whether an item is a fixture or personal property.
4. Identify three ways of creating an easement.
5. Differentiate between freehold and leasehold estates.
6. Describe the different types of co-ownership of real property.
7. Identify the methods of acquiring title to real property.
8. Differentiate among the various types of deeds.
9. Explain adverse possession.
10. Discuss zoning laws.
11. Explain eminent domain.

23-1 The Nature of Real Property

Real property is defined as the ground and everything permanently attached to it. It includes building, fences, and trees on the surface; earth, rocks, and minerals under the surface; and the airspace above the surface.

Trees and Vegetation

Trees, flowers, shrubs, vineyards, and field crops that grow each year without replanting (perennials) are considered real property. These plants have been planted and cultivated with the intention that they remain as a part of the real estate. Once planted and growing, such improvements to the land are called *fructus naturales* (fruit of nature).

In contrast, crops or garden plantings that produce flowers, vegetables, or other harvest only for the year in which they are planted (annuals) are called *fructus industriales* (fruit of industry). These are treated as personal property rather than real property.

EXAMPLE 23-1:   Fruit of Industry

When the Freeman farm was sold early in the spring, the new owner was deeded "all the real property consisting of what is known as the Freeman farm." A 25-acre section of winter wheat had been planted the fall prior to the sale and would be ready for harvest the following July. Unless the parties agreed otherwise, the wheat crop would not be part of the sale of the farm, because it is an annual plant and would be treated as personal property. The wheat crop would still belong to whoever planted it.

A tree belongs to the person on whose land the trunk is located. People who own adjoining land have the right to cut off trespassing tree branches in their airspace and trespassing roots at the boundary line of their property. Whenever property owners dig down at the very edge of their own property, however, they must provide support to their neighbor's land so that it does not cave in.

Air Rights

In early England, landowners owned the airspace above their property to "as high as the heavens." This law changed with the increased use of the airplane. Modern court decisions have held that landowners own the airspace above their land to as high as they can effectively possess or reasonably control. This height usually extends as high as the highest tree or structure on their property. It is a trespass for anyone to run wires through someone else's airspace or to use another's airspace in any way without permission. Electric and telephone companies must obtain easements for the right to run wires through the airspace of property owners (see page 469).

The Opening Case Revisited, Part I
"The Dream House"

The newly planted trees and the rose bushes on the property that Tim and Celeste were about to purchase were included in the purchase. Because they both are perennials (*fructus naturales*), they are part of the real property.

Congress has enacted legislation that gives the public the right of freedom of transit through the navigable airspace of the United States. The **navigable airspace**, subject to FAA regulations, is the space above 1,000 feet over populated areas and above 500 feet over water and unpopulated areas. In airport cases involving planes landing and taking off, the courts try to strike a balance between the landowners' rights to the exclusive possession of their airspace, free from noise and exhaust fumes, and the public need for air travel.

Air rights are valuable and often sold to interested buyers, particularly in land-depleted metropolitan areas. For example, in New York City, developers bought air rights over the access to the George Washington Bridge and constructed multistory buildings. Two privately owned buildings have been constructed in the airspace over the Massachusetts Turnpike near Boston. Use of air rights becomes important when land is no longer available for new buildings. The private use of airspace also becomes a tax source for otherwise untaxable land owned by a city or state government.

Subterranean Rights

Unless excluded in the deed, the owner of land has exclusive title to material below the surface of the land. The right extends to the point determined to be the exact center of the earth. These subterranean rights are often sold to corporations exploring for coal, oil, or other mineral deposits. Taking out oil or minerals from below the surface would constitute trespass if such rights were not obtained from their owners.

EXAMPLE 23-2:   Subterranean Trespass

McGee's house and lot were adjacent to land on which a small industrial plant had been built. McGee discovered that the plant owners had driven drainage pipes underground from the plant into her land. She may charge the plant owners with trespass. She can also sell this right to the plant or demand that the practice be stopped and the pipes be removed.

A landowner must not dig a cellar or other excavation so close to the boundary of a neighbor as to cause the neighbor's land to cave in or the neighbor's building to be damaged. A person excavating who fails to shore up the adjoining land is liable to the neighbor for damages.

Water Rights

People who own land along the bank of a river or stream are called **riparian owners**. They have certain rights and duties with respect to the water that flows over, under, and beside their land. Owners of land through which a stream flows own the soil beneath the water. If a nonnavigable stream is a boundary line between two parcels of land, the owner on each side owns to the center of the stream. If the stream is navigable, however, each owner owns only to the bank of the stream, and the bed is owned by the state. A navigable stream in some states is defined as one that ebbs and flows with the tide. In other states, it is defined as a stream that is capable of being navigated by commercial vessels.

Although property owners may own the land under a stream, they do not own the water itself. Their right to the use of the water depends on the doctrine followed in their state. Most states east of the Mississippi River follow the riparian rights doctrine. Under this doctrine, owners of land bordering a stream have equal rights to use the water passing by or through their property. Each riparian owner may make reasonable use of the water for domestic purposes such as drinking, cooking, and bathing. In addition, they may use the water for irrigation purposes if it does not interfere unreasonably with the use being made by other riparian owners downstream. Owners may not sell the water from the stream to outside third parties.

The Opening Case Revisited, Part II
"The Dream House"

The rights that Tim and Celeste would have to the bed of the stream would depend on whether the stream is navigable, as defined by their state's law. If it were navigable, they would own to the bank of the stream. However, if it were nonnavigable, they would own to the center of the stream. Tim and Celeste's legal use of the water flowing through the stream depends on whether their state follows the *riparian rights* doctrine or the *prior appropriation* doctrine.

Some states west of the Mississippi, where water is less plentiful, follow the prior appropriation doctrine. This doctrine follows a seniority system. The first person to make beneficial use of the water has the right to take all he or she is able to use before anyone else has any rights to it. If there is water left over, the next person in seniority may use all the water that can be put to beneficial use.

Other states west of the Mississippi follow a combination of the riparian rights doctrine and the prior appropriation doctrine.

In New England states, a small pond (less than 10 acres) is owned by the person who owns the ground underneath. In contrast, a great pond (10 acres or more) is owned by the state, and private abutters own the land only to the lower water mark. Great ponds are usually accessible to the public for swimming, boating, and fishing.

Percolating water is water that passes through the ground beneath the surface of the earth without any definite channel. It consists of rainwater that slowly oozes and seeps through the soil or water that infiltrates the banks or bed of a stream. Subterranean water is water that lies wholly beneath the surface of the ground. It may be either percolating water or water that flows in underground channels or lies still in underground lakes. Common law gave property owners the absolute right to percolating water below their land. Under modern statutes, however, property owners may draw only the water that is reasonably required to satisfy their needs. Other property owners damaged by unreasonable use may seek an injunction against such use in a court of equity.

Rainwater on the surface of the earth may not be artificially channeled to an abutter's property without permission of the abutter. Unless a drainage easement is obtained to drain water onto another's land, surface water must be left to its natural watercourse.

Fixtures

When personal property is attached to real property, it is known as a **fixture** and becomes part of the real property. Built-in stoves and dishwashers, kitchen cabinets, and ceiling light fixtures are examples of fixtures. Disagreements sometimes occur over whether an item is a fixture.

EXAMPLE 23-3:   Real or Personal Property?

The Rodriguezes bought a house from the Smiths. After the closing, when they moved in, the Rodriguezes discovered that the Smiths had taken with them the wall-to-wall carpeting in the living room. The Rodriguezes had expected the carpeting to go with the sale of the house as part of the real property. The Smiths treated the carpeting as personal property and took it with them.

In deciding whether an item is a fixture, the courts ask the following questions: Has there been a temporary or permanent installation of the personal property? Can it be removed without damaging the real property? Another question asked is whether the personal property has been adapted to the intended use of the real property.

EXAMPLE 23-4:   Indications of a Fixture

In Example 23-3, if the carpeting were tightly nailed to the floor, there is a good chance that it would be held by the court to be a fixture. The same would be true if the carpeting covered plywood flooring. In both cases, the carpeting would be considered part of the real property and belong to the new buyers. If the living room were oddly shaped and the carpeting were cut to fit that shape, it would be further evidence that the carpeting was a fixture. It had been adapted to be used in that odd-shaped room.

Also, the court would ask, what was the intent of the party at the time the personal property was attached to the real property?

EXAMPLE 23-5:   Intent of Parties

Franklin complained to her landlord that the kitchen in her apartment needed to be modernized. The landlord gave her permission to improve the kitchen as long as it could be done without cost to him. Franklin installed cabinets, a built-in stove, and an under-the-counter dishwasher. She also bought a new refrigerator. Even though Franklin paid for them, the cabinets, stove, and dishwasher would be fixtures and belong to the landlord. The refrigerator, which was not built in, would remain the personal property of the tenant.

Trade fixtures are those items of personal property brought upon the premises by the tenant that are necessary to carry on the trade or business to which the premises will be devoted. Contrary to the general rule, trade fixtures remain the personal property of the tenant or occupier of the property and are removable at the expiration of the term of occupancy. Trade fixtures are not treated as part of the real property.

Quick Quiz 23-1 True or False?

1. Landowners do not own the airspace above their land.

2. Unless excluded in the deed, landowners own the land under their property to the center of the earth.

3. Fixtures are considered part of real property unless they are trade fixtures.

The Opening Case Revisited, Part III
"The Dream House"

The best way for Tim and Celeste to handle the question of whether the curtains and wall-to-wall carpeting go with the house is to write specifically in the purchase and sale agreement, before they sign it, that the items are or are not included in the sale. If it is not written in the agreement and the matter goes to court, a judge or jury will seek answers to the following questions:

- Has there been a temporary or permanent installation of the curtains and carpeting? Temporary items would not be fixtures.
- Can they be removed without damage to the real property? If so, they may not be fixtures.
- Have they been adapted to the intended use of the property?
- What was the intent of the owner when the curtains and carpeting were placed in the house?

23-2 Easements

An **easement** (also called a **right of way**) is the right to use another's land for a particular purpose. Easements are used to give people the right to pass over another's land, to run wires through another's airspace, to drain water onto another's property, or to run pipes underneath someone else's ground. The one who enjoys the easement and to whom it attaches is called the **dominant tenement**. In contrast, the one on whom the easement is imposed is called the **servient tenement**.

EXAMPLE 23-6:   Parties to an Easement

Hatfield owned a long, narrow strip of land that ran between a lake and a highway. She decided to sell the front half of the lot that bordered the highway to McCoy and keep the back half that bordered the lake for her own use. To give McCoy the ability to reach the lake, an easement was placed in the deed granting McCoy the right to "pass and repass" over Hatfield's property to reach the lake. In this easement, McCoy is the dominant tenement and Hatfield is the servient tenement. Also, to give Hatfield the ability to reach the highway, an easement was placed in the deed, reserving to Hatfield the right to "pass and repass" over McCoy's property to reach the highway. In this easement, Hatfield is the dominant tenement and McCoy is the servient tenement.

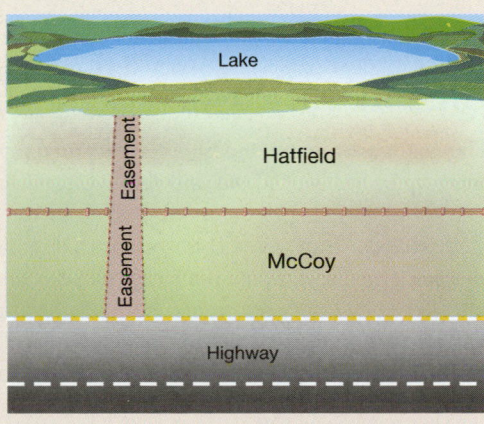

An easement may be created in three ways: by grant, by reservation, and by prescription. To create an easement by grant, the owner of the land signs a deed, giving the easement to the dominant tenement, and keeps the remainder of the land. To create an easement by reservation, the owner of the land grants to another person the entire parcel of land except for the easement that he or she keeps. An **easement by prescription** is an easement that is obtained by passing over another's property without permission, openly and continuously for a period of time set by state statute (20 years in many states). People claiming easements by prescription must show that they used (but did not possess) part of another's property openly, notoriously, and in a hostile manner for the prescribed period. This proof is similar to that used in adverse possession, discussed later in this chapter.

A legal easement may exist even if it isn't in writing. For example, the law allows people access to their homes so, if the only access is by crossing through another land owner's property, the court may grant permission through an "easement by necessity."

Once an easement is created, it runs with the land. This condition means that future owners will have the right to use the easement unless one of them gives it up by a deed or by not using it for a long period of time.

Utility companies will sometimes need to go on private land to replace or repair their equipment. Therefore, residential landowners all have easements permitting such companies to enter the land for the sole purpose of doing their work.

EXAMPLE 23-7: Easement Runs With Land

By warranty deed in 1907, Jesse Horney conveyed the northern portion of his real estate to Wayne County Lumber Company. That deed included the following provision: "Said Jesse Horney hereby conveys to Wayne County Lumber Company the right of ingress and egress for teams and wagons in conducting their business through an open driveway along the South line to South Main Street." The property was conveyed to a different lumber company in 1930 and to a third lumber company in 1943. Later, in a dispute over the easement, the court held that the easement ran with the land and belonged to the third lumber company. In this case, Horney's property was the servient tenement. The lumber company's property was the dominant tenement. A profit *à prendre* is a special type of easement with the added privilege of removing something of value from the servient property. For example, the right to enter another's property and remove sand, gravel, soil, or the like is called a profit *à prendre*. This right may be created by deed, will, or adverse use.

EXAMPLE 23-8: Profit *à Prendre*

The Bates Company and Sawyer executed an agreement that provided Bates could enter upon Sawyer's land and remove sand, gravel, and stone. Bates agreed to pay Sawyer a set rate per cubic yard or short ton for all the sand removed. The agreement stated, "Sawyer will not grant to anyone else the privilege of removing sand and stone from said parcel during the period hereof . . . but Sawyer reserves to herself, her successors and assigns, the right during said period . . . to go on and use said tract of land for any purpose they may desire, but without unreasonable interference with the rights of said Bates." The court held that Bates possessed a profit *à prendre* under the agreement.

23-3 Estates in Real Property

An estate is the interest or right that a person has in real property. A leasehold estate comes from a lease and is an interest in real estate. In a freehold estate, the holder owns the land for life or forever. Anyone with a freehold estate may transfer that interest to another by sale, gift, will, or by dying without a will. Freehold estates are either estates in fee simple or life estates.

Estates in Fee Simple

Anyone owning real property outright—that is, forever—is said to have an **estate in fee simple**. The estate descends, on the death of the owner, to the owner's heirs. The owner of an estate in fee simple has absolute ownership in the real estate, with the right to use or dispose of it as desired, so long as the use of it does not interfere with others' rights.

EXAMPLE 23-9:   Fee Simple Estate

When the Landers bought the land on which to build their house, they received an estate in fee simple from the former owners. They thus received full rights to the property. They may sell it, give it away, or use it as they wish. The only restrictions are those contained in the deed or required of them by law.

Life Estates

A person who owns real property for life or for the life of another owns an interest in real property called a **life estate**. Such an estate may be created by deed, by will, or by law. When the terms of a deed or will state that the property is to pass at the end of a life estate to someone other than the grantor or the grantor's heirs, the future interest is a **remainder estate**.

EXAMPLE 23-10:   Life Estate

Rosengard deeded her farm to Kinkaid for life. The deed stated that upon Kinkaid's death, the property was to pass to Honig in fee simple. Kinkaid owns a life estate in the farm. Honig owns a remainder estate until Kinkaid's death, then an estate in fee simple.

The owner of a life estate may convey that interest to another. Thus, in Example 23-10, if Kinkaid conveys his interest to Jenkins, Jenkins will own a life estate for the duration of Kinkaid's life, after which the property will belong to Honig. When the terms of a deed or a will state that property is to return to the grantor or the grantor's heirs at the expiration of a life estate, the future interest is a **reversion estate**.

Life estates are sometimes created by operation of law. Dower and curtesy are examples. Years ago, in England, **dower** was the right that a widow had to a life estate in one-third of the real property owned by the husband during the marriage. **Curtesy** was the right that a widower had, if children of the marriage were born alive, to a life estate in all real property owned by the wife during the marriage. The rights of dower and curtesy were in addition to rights given to spouses under the law of wills.

EXAMPLE 23-11:   Common Law Curtesy

Before her marriage, Clark received title to an old house through a will left by her grandfather. Although her husband had no rights in this property at the time of their marriage, such rights arose with the birth of their first child. Her husband thereafter had the right of curtesy should Clark die while she was still married to him.

Many states have either done away with common law dower and curtesy altogether or modified them to reflect modern-day needs.

Quick Quiz 23-3 True or False?

1. An estate in fee simple descends, on the death of the owner, to the owner's heirs.

2. The owner of a life estate may not convey that interest to another.

3. Dower and curtesy are examples of life estates created by operation of law.

23-4 Co-Ownership of Real Property

Real property may be owned individually or by two or more persons known as **cotenants**. Cotenant relationships include:

- Tenancy in common
- Tenancy by the entirety
- Joint tenancy
- Tenancy in partnership
- Community property

Tenancy in Common

When two or more persons own real property as **tenants in common**, each person owns an undivided share of the whole property. A cotenant's share of the property transfers to that cotenant's heirs upon his or her death rather than to the surviving cotenants. Each cotenant is entitled to possession of the entire premises. This rule is known as unity of possession. Tenants in common have the right to sell or deed away as a gift their share in the property without the permission of the other cotenants. When this action occurs, any new owner becomes a tenant in common with the remaining cotenants. One cotenant's interest is not necessarily the same as another cotenant's interest.

EXAMPLE 23-12:   Tenants in Common

Ingalls and Carpenter owned a parcel of real property as tenants in common. When Ingalls died, his three children inherited his estate equally. The children became tenants in common (each owning a one-sixth interest) with Carpenter, who owned a one-half interest in the property.

Tenants in common may separate their interests in the property by petitioning the court for a partition of the property. If the court allows the petition, either it will divide the property into separate parcels so that each cotenant will own a particular part outright, or it will order the property sold and divide the proceeds of the sale among the cotenants. Creditors may reach the interest of a tenant in common by bringing a lawsuit against that particular cotenant and, if successful, having that cotenant's interest sold to pay the debt.

By statute in most states, co-ownership of property by two or more persons is considered a tenancy in common unless the relationship is expressly indicated as a joint tenancy or a tenancy by the entirety.

Joint Tenancy

When two or more persons own real property as **joint tenants**, the estate created is a single estate with multiple ownership. Each tenant owns the entire estate, subject to the equal rights of the other joint tenants. Four unities must be present to create a joint tenancy: time, title, interest, and possession:

1. The unity of time means that all owners must take title at the same time.
2. The unity of title means that all owners must derive title from the same source.
3. The unity of interest means that all owners must have equal interests in the property.
4. The unity of possession means that all owners must have the equal right to possess the property.

Upon the death of one joint tenant, the entire ownership remains with the other joint tenants and does not pass to the heirs or devisees of the deceased cotenant. For this reason, joint tenants are often identified as joint tenants with the right of survivorship.

EXAMPLE 23-13:   Joint Tenants

If Ingalls and Carpenter, in Example 23-12, had owned the parcel of real property as joint tenants instead of as tenants in common, Carpenter would have owned the entire property outright when Ingalls died. Ingalls's three children would not have been entitled to any interest in the real property whatsoever.

A joint tenant may deed away his or her interest to a new owner without permission of the other joint tenants. The new owner, in such a case, becomes a tenant in common with the remaining joint tenants. As in the case of a tenant in common, a joint tenant may petition the court for a partition of the estate, which would end the joint tenancy. Creditors may levy upon the interests of a joint tenant on execution and take over that particular joint tenant's interest as a tenant in common with the remaining joint tenants. To levy on execution means to collect a sum of money by putting into effect the judgment of a court.

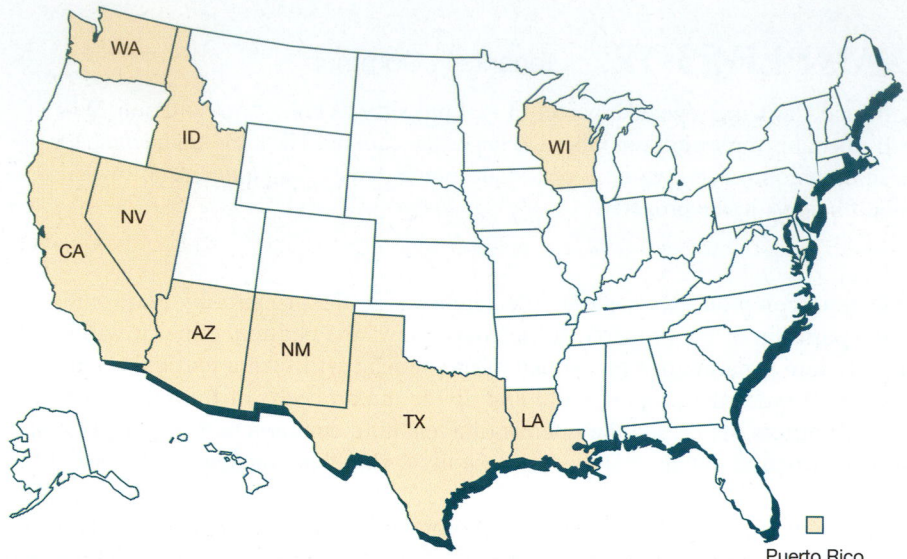

Puerto Rico

Figure 23-1 Community property jurisdictions.

Community Property

Community property is property (except a gift or inheritance) that is acquired by the personal efforts of either spouse during marriage and that, by law, belongs to both spouses equally. The law originated in Spain, was embraced by Mexico, and is presently followed in Puerto Rico and nine U.S. states (see Figure 23-1). Although state laws differ, they all operate on the theory that both spouses contribute equally to the marriage—that all property acquired during the marriage is the result of the combined efforts of both of them. Although one spouse may earn all the money to acquire the property, all the property acquired is considered community property.

With differences among the community property jurisdictions, couples may enter into agreements that declare property that would otherwise be community property to be the separate property of either the husband or the wife. Similarly, they may do the opposite and declare their separate property to be community property. Even though Alaska is not a community property state, Title 34, Chapter 77, of the Alaska Statutes allows married couples to enter into a community property agreement.

In community property jurisdictions, each spouse can make a will leaving half the community property to whomever he or she chooses. If a spouse dies without a will, the deceased's half will pass according to intestate law discussed in Chapter 25. Upon divorce, community property is divided equally and becomes owned by the couple as tenants in common.

Tenancy by the Entirety

A **tenancy by the entirety** may be held only by a husband and wife and is based upon the common law doctrine known as unity of person. Under this very old doctrine, a husband and wife were regarded, under the law, as one. In theory, each spouse owned the entire estate, and neither could destroy it by any separate act. The husband, however, had the entire control over the estate, including the exclusive right to possession and the right to all rents and profits. Upon the death of either spouse, the surviving spouse owned the entire estate outright. Although an individual creditor of the husband could levy and sell on execution the husband's interest in the tenancy, the property always remained subject to the wife's survivorship right, and if the husband died before the wife, the creditor lost that interest. The wife's right of survivorship was not attachable by her individual creditors.

EXAMPLE 23-14:   Tenants by the Entirety

The DeVoes owned their home together as tenants by the entirety in a state that still followed the old common law rules. While driving a car titled in his name alone, Mr. DeVoe caused an accident that resulted in serious injury to another person. The injured person obtained a judgment against Mr. DeVoe that far exceeded his insurance coverage. The DeVoes' house was sold by the sheriff to satisfy the judgment, and they had to move out. Five years later, however, when Mr. DeVoe died, Mrs. DeVoe became the outright owner of the property because she survived Mr. DeVoe. Her right of survivorship in the property could not be taken from her. The person who bought the property at the sheriff's sale lost all ownership interest in it when Mr. DeVoe died.

Had the judgment in Example 23-14 been against Mrs. DeVoe instead of Mr. DeVoe, the property could not even have been attached by the injured person. Thus, from a practical point of view, ownership as tenants by the entirety protected both spouses from losing their real property when a judgment was obtained against either spouse individually.

Although the husband, acting alone, could not convey or encumber the *entire estate*, he could convey or encumber his interest in the property held as tenants by the entirety. Because the husband had the exclusive right to possession, he could sell the property or give a mortgage on it without the wife's consent. However, as in the DeVoe case, anyone buying the property or receiving a mortgage on it would lose all ownership interest should the wife survive the husband.

In the event that the husband and wife divorced, the tenancy by the entirety no longer existed, and they became tenants in common, with separate and equal rights in the property.

Some states have done away with the statute of tenancy by the entirety. Other states have enacted statutes giving equal rights to husbands and wives who own property as tenants by the entirety. Still other states require both spouses to consent to a valid mortgage on property owned as tenants by the entirety.

Tenancy in Partnership

Ownership of real property by partners is called a tenancy in partnership and is governed by the Uniform Partnership Act in those states that have adopted it. This type of co-ownership of real property is discussed in Chapter 37.

Table 23-1 summarizes the differences among the various cotenant relationships.

Quick Quiz 23-4 True or False?

1. When three people own property as tenants in common and one of them dies, the deceased's share of the property passes to the surviving tenants in common.

2. When three people own property as joint tenants and one of them dies, the deceased's share of the property passes to his or her heirs.

3. Three people cannot own property as tenants by the entirety.

Table 23-1 Cotenant Relationships

	Tenants in Common	Joint Tenants	Tenants by Entirety	Tenants in Partnership	Community Property
1. Who can be cotenants	Any number of people	Any number of people	Only husband and wife	Only partners	Only husband and wife
2. At death, deceased's share goes	To deceased's heirs*	To surviving cotenants	To surviving spouse	To surviving partners	To deceased's heirs*
3. Title	Separate title for each cotenant	One title to the entire property	Husband has title (under the doctrine of unity)†	Title is in the partnership	Title is in the community
4. Division of ownership interests	Cotenants can have equal or unequal interests	All interests must be equal	Interests equal; husband has the right to control and manage†	Interest same as partnership interest	Both interests equal
5. Right to possession of entire premises	Equal with all cotenants	Equal with all cotenants	Husband only†	Equal with all partners for partnership business only	Equal with both spouses
6. Right to convey ownership interest	May convey to another without permission of cotenant	May convey to another but will end joint tenancy relationship	Husband may convey to anyone; wife's interest is protected†	May convey only with consent of copartners	May convey personal property without spouse's permission; must have written permission to convey real property
7. Right to partition the property	Yes	Yes	No	No	No
8. Owner's separate interest reachable by creditors	Yes	Yes	Husband's only†	No	No. Whole community only, depending on state law

*Either by will or the law of intestate succession if the deceased had no will.

†At common law. States have either abolished this type of tenancy or amended it to give equal rights to men and women.

The Opening Case Revisited, Part IV
"The Dream House"

The answer to the question of who would own the property if either Tim or Celeste died depends on how they took title as cotenants. If they took title as tenants in common, the deceased person's heirs would become the owners of the property, either through a will or the law of intestate succession. In contrast, if they took title as joint tenants or tenants by the entirety, the surviving spouse would automatically own the property outright. If it was community property, the deceased person's heirs would own half and the surviving spouse would own the other half.

23-5 Methods of Acquiring Title to Real Property

Title to real property may be acquired by sale or gift, will or descent, or occupancy.

LO7

Title by Sale or Gift

Ownership and title to real property are most frequently transferred from one owner to another by sale or by gift. This action is done by transferring a written instrument called a deed. The person transferring title is the **grantor**. The person to whom the title is transferred is the **grantee**. A deed becomes effective when it is delivered to the grantee. A deed to real property may be bestowed as a gift from the owner or through a sale. In the case of a gift, consideration is not given by the grantee for the deed. There are four types of deeds:

LO8

- General warranty deed
- Special warranty deed

Foreigners spent a record $37.7 billion on U.S. commercial property in 2006, says a report by real estate firm Jones Lang LaSalle. All major metro markets except San Francisco and L.A. had gains in foreign investment. Why the Left Coast snub? Asian investors are buying closer to home, and California is too long a plane ride for Europeans, says JLI. – Michael Arndt, *BusinessWeek,* March 12, 2007.

Top 5 U.S. markets for foreign investment

Foreign investment '06	Washington	San Francisco	Chicago	Boston	Manhattan
	$1.6 Billion	$1.8	$2.1	$2.4	$5.7
Percent change from '05	49.6%	−14.5%	80.4%	450.2%	60.4%

Figure 23-2 Real property investment by foreigners in the United States.

- Bargain-and-sale deed
- Quitclaim deed

General Warranty Deed A **general warranty deed**, sometimes called a full covenant and warranty deed, contains express warranties under which the grantor guarantees the property to be free of encumbrances created by the grantor or by others who had title previously. It is the most desirable form of deed from the point of view of the grantee because it warrants (gives assurances) that title is good.

Special Warranty Deed A **special warranty deed** contains express warranties under which the grantor guarantees that no title defect arose during the time that the grantor owned the property, but not otherwise. No warranties are made as to defects that arose before the grantor owned the property.

EXAMPLE 23-15:   Special Warranty Deed

Grant sold a vacant lot to Tuttle. The lot had been left to Grant through the will of a distant relative. Grant had never had the title searched, but she could guarantee Tuttle that no liens or claims against the property had been created since she inherited the property. Grant would be safe in granting title under a special warranty deed. The buyer would be protected only by making a title search that would disclose claims not covered by the seller's warranty.

Bargain-and-Sale Deed A **bargain-and-sale deed** is one that transfers title to property but contains no warranties. The form of the deed is the same as that of a warranty deed except that the warranties are omitted. Because a bargain and sale necessarily involves the idea of a valuable consideration, this type of deed is not valid without consideration. It could not be used to convey a gift of real property.

Quitclaim Deed A **quitclaim deed** (also called a deed without covenants) is one that transfers to the buyer only the interest that the seller may have in a property. This type of deed merely releases a party's rights to the property. It contains no warranties. It is used when one gives up some right in the property, such as an easement or dower and curtesy, or to cure a defect in the chain of title.

The Opening Case Revisited, Part V
"The Dream House"

The kind of deed that Tim and Celeste will receive depends upon the kind that is commonly used in that state and the kind that the grantor is willing or able to give. The general warranty deed gives the most protection, followed in descending order by the special warranty deed, the bargain-and-sale deed, and the quitclaim deed.

Title by Will or Descent

When people die owning real property solely in their own name or with others as tenants in common, title passes to their heirs at the moment of death. If they die with a will, title passes to the people named in the will. If they die without a will, title passes to the heirs, as tenants in common, according to the laws of intestacy discussed in Chapter 25. A deed is not used when title passes to heirs in this manner. Instead, the records of the probate court establish title to the property. A deed may be used, however, by the personal representative of an estate to transfer title to real property to another. This transfer may be done in many states by authority granted in a will or by a license issued by the court.

Title by Adverse Possession

Title to real property may be obtained by taking actual possession of the property openly, notoriously, exclusively, under a claim of right, and continuously for a period of time set by state statute. This method of obtaining title to real property is called **adverse possession**. To establish such ownership rights, claimants must prove the following:

- They have had continuous use of the property for 20 years (or a period set by state statute).
- This use has been without interruption by the owner.
- It was without the owner's permission.
- It was with the owner's knowledge.

Proof of these facts in court will give a person superior rights over the one in whose name a deed is recorded. A court of equity has the power to declare the one claiming under adverse possession to be the new owner.

EXAMPLE 23-16:   Adverse Possession

Wilhelm and Kupersmith were next-door neighbors. Not realizing where the true property line was, Wilhelm built a garage and driveway two feet onto Kupersmith's land. He used the garage and driveway continuously, with Kupersmith's knowledge, for the next 22 years. The error was discovered when Kupersmith sold her property to a new owner, who had it surveyed. Wilhelm, through court action, was able to obtain title to the land on which the garage and driveway were located by adverse possession.

Quick Quiz 23-5 True or False?

1. A general warranty deed is the most desirable form of deed for a grantee to receive.

2. If a person dies without a will, title passes to the heirs as tenants in common without the use of a deed.

3. A quitclaim deed releases a party's rights to property and contains no warranties.

A Question of Ethics
The Trouble With Business Ethics

Companies are increasingly emphasizing ethics, but a recent case at Wal-Mart shows how problematic such policies can be for employees

In the post-Enron, post-WorldCom, post-Tyco era, ethics has become one of the hottest topics in the business world. Business schools have entire courses dedicated to the topic. Companies have instituted more rigorous ethics policies and set up global ethics offices. One of the fastest-growing employment categories is chief ethics officer, as evidenced by the creation of that post at the New York Stock Exchange (NYX), Nortel Networks (NT), Marsh & McLennan (MMC), and Hewlett-Packard (HPQ).

But a recent case at Wal-Mart Stores (WMT) shows how difficult it can be to push "ethics" in the corporate world. A few months after going through a new employee training session with a heavy emphasis on ethics, Chalace Epiey Lowry acted on the guidance to report any activity that seemed the least bit suspicious. Lowry told the company's ethics office about what she thought could be a case of insider trading by one of her supervisors, Mona Williams, vice-president of corporate communications.

The company determined that Williams had done nothing wrong. But Lowry's identity was revealed to Williams, leading Lowry to conclude that she could no longer work in the department. Now she's looking for another job, but there's no guarantee she'll get one at Wal-Mart. "I acted in good faith, just pointing out that there might have been some wrongdoing," says Lowry. "But it was really disheartening to see how it was handled." (See *BusinessWeek.com,* 6/12/07, "Wal-Mart's Latest Ethics Controversy.")

THE DANGERS OF WHISTLEBLOWING

Lowry's case, unfortunately, is representative of exactly how ethics complaints and whistleblowers are handled at many corporations. "Most employees are reluctant to make any complaints for fear that they will either lose their job or get redirected into another position," says Jim Fisher, Shaughnessy fellow at the Emerson Center for Business Ethics at St. Louis University. "People who go into a situation naively thinking that they are taking care of a problem often find that it doesn't turn out that way. In fact, 95% of the time, whistleblowers lose their jobs."

The emphasis on ethics is hard to miss. Many of the companies leading the way are those that have been embroiled in scandals in the past. For instance, CA (CA), the former scandal-tainted Computer Associates, two years ago had hired Patrick Gnazzo, a former chief trial attorney for the U.S. Navy. And former Securities & Exchange Commission Chairman Richard Breeden, who was first hired to be an outside monitor of accounting firm KPMG moved into a similar role at Hollinger International (HLR), where Conrad Black stirred up trouble and ultimately a lawsuit.

Eric Dinallo and Beth Golden, alumni of former New York Attorney General Eliot Spitzer's office, were hired at Morgan Stanley (MS) and Bear Stearns (BSC), respectively (see *BusinessWeek.com,* 2/13/06, "The New Ethics Enforcers"). Wal-Mart itself set up its global ethics office in 2004 and prides itself on having one of the strictest ethics codes in the industry.

Its employees aren't allowed to accept even a drink from their suppliers.

Source: Pallavi Gogoi, "The Trouble with Business Ethics," *BusinessWeek.com,* June 22, 2007.

23-6 Zoning Laws

Zoning laws regulate the uses that may be made of properties within specified geographical areas or districts. Residential zoning prohibits properties from being used for commercial purposes within a given area. Multifamily zoning permits construction of apartment buildings. Limited-commercial zoning allows the construction of small stores but restricts the building of large shopping malls and commercial centers. Industrial zoning allows the building of factories, and agricultural zoning allows farming in a particular area. Zoning laws help keep property values from declining and protect against the undesirable use of neighboring property.

Newly passed zoning laws do not apply to existing uses of the land. Such uses are called **nonconforming uses** if they are not allowed under the new zoning law. They may continue in existence but may not be enlarged or changed in kind.

By appeal to the local zoning board, variances may be given to individuals or businesses when justified and reasonable. A **variance** is an exemption or exception that permits a use that differs from those allowed under the existing ordinance. Variances are granted in special circumstances to protect property owners who might otherwise suffer a hardship if zoning laws were applied and enforced arbitrarily.

Decisions of a local zoning commission may be appealed to county commissioners, a county court, or the highest court in the state.

23-7 Eminent Domain

All ownership of private property is subject to the government's superior rights if property is needed for a public purpose. **Eminent domain**, also called **condemnation**, is the right of federal, state, and local governments, or other public bodies, to take private lands, with compensation to their owners, for a public purpose. The right is exercised for such purposes as new highway construction, public parks, and state hospitals, as well as to reinvigorate depressed areas.

In 2005, the U.S. Supreme Court held in *Kelo v. City of New London* that the government could take private property to promote private economic development. The Court said that an increased tax base, higher-paying jobs, and other benefits fulfilled a public purpose. In its decision, the Court further noted, "nothing in our opinion precludes any State from placing further restrictions on its exercise of the takings power." Within two years after that unpopular decision, more than 80 percent of U.S. states changed their laws on the subject, making it more difficult to take private property by eminent domain. Some states, including Florida, have taken a broad approach, such as forbidding the use of eminent domain for any kind of private development. Others, including Missouri, have made guarded changes, such as not allowing farmland to be classified as "blighted." In 2007, the New Jersey high court held that before invoking eminent domain, a municipality must prove a site is truly "blighted," not simply "not fully productive."

Except as mentioned, the right of eminent domain is not available to persons or businesses when taken for private profit. In such situations, property may be acquired only through mutual agreement and for consideration acceptable to the owner. Eminent domain is at times extended to public utilities when it can be shown that denial of a right-of-way for electric, telephone, gas, or other lines may interrupt construction of installations that provide needed services to an entire community.

In Chicago, residents of the suburbs surrounding O'Hare International Airport are actively protesting airport expansion that threatens homes, cemeteries, and other private property.

Business Law in the News
How to Make a Deal Bloom

The housing market is in turmoil. For buyers, this is a time to negotiate. If you're a seller, you may need to adjust your expectations. Here are timely tips for those on both sides of the contract.

For Sellers

GET ON THE NET More than 80% of shoppers check out home listing sites such as Realtor.com before they buy. Make sure your sales agent has at least six good photos of your home and a video tour online. "Listings with six photos get almost 300% more viewers than those with single photos," says Errol Samuelson, president of Realtor.com.

DRESS UP THE HOUSE Everybody's watching the home makeover shows these days. Hiring a designer to spruce up your home can cost as little as $150 for a consultation, says Denver home stager Lynn Hodges. For a few hundred more, she'll bring plants, modern art, and furniture. Your sales agent will often pick up the tab.

DON'T OVERPRICE Developer Robert Sheridan tried everything from free kitchen upgrades to financing incentives to move condos at his Lakeshore at Andersen Springs complex in suburban Phoenix. What worked: slashing prices by 10%. "People are looking over their shoulder at what their neighbor sold for a year ago," he says. "That's not the market today."

BE GREEN Environmentally friendly features are in, especially if buyers don't have to pay for them. You can give your home a green sheen inexpensively by replacing incandescent bulbs in light fixtures with energy-saving compact fluorescent ones. Put filters on the faucets and a compost bin in the backyard.

FORGET ABOUT AS IS Do some fixing on your fixer-upper. Replace old kitchen and bathroom fixtures, wallpaper, mirrored walls, paneling, and other accoutrements of bygone design with more contemporary looks. Paint walls taupe, not white.

For Buyers

SELL YOUR HOME FIRST Put your current house on the market before you go looking for a new one. Properties are taking longer to sell, notes Phyllis Haber, an agent with Prudential Douglas Elliman in Huntington, N.Y. If you find your dream house before you unload your old one, "unless you can carry two mortgages, you may lose a deal."

RESEARCH COMPARABLE PRICES To get the latest sale prices for similar properties in the neighborhood you're looking in, ask your real estate agent for recent sales data from the multiple listing service. Home appraisal sites such as Zillow.com that rely on deed or mortgage filings can be a few months behind.

BE REALISTIC ABOUT PRICE Lowball offers turn off sellers, and negotiating from there could get contentious. Make an offer of no more than 10% below the asking price if the home is already fairly priced, says Mark Nash, author of 1001 Tips for Buying and Selling a Home. Then ask for concessions, such as having the seller pay closing costs.

DON'T WALK AWAY IF THE SIGN SAYS "SOLD" New-home builders are experiencing cancellations, so it pays to keep in touch with the salespeople. Jim Widner, a general manager at builder KB Home, says a buyer in Las Vegas recently snagged a model that was in short supply after receiving a text message from a salesperson saying it was available again.

PUT YOUR FINANCIAL HOUSE IN ORDER Before shopping for a mortgage, order free copies of your credit reports at annualcreditreport.com. Don't rush to cancel old credit cards. Having a long history can improve your credit score.

Questions for Analysis

1. Why is it important for sellers to have at least six good photos and a video tour on line?

2. What does it mean to "be green"?

3. How much should an offer be, according to this article?

Source: Christopher Palmeri, "How to Make a Deal Bloom," *BusinessWeek,* March 26, 2007, 131.

When private property is taken by eminent domain proceedings, the owner must be paid the fair value of what has been taken. The owner is not required to accept an amount offered by those assessing the value of the property. But if the offer is refused, the owner must then seek greater compensation through action in the state or federal courts.

EXAMPLE 23-17:   Eminent Domain

Interstate 95 was designed to cut a swath through a residential section of Chester. Hundreds of homes, businesses, and churches lay in the path of the new highway. Kovach refused to accept the $89,500 offered by assessors for his property. An appeal was made through the county court, with Kovach claiming a fair value of $115,000; this amount would provide the family with a similar home in a comparable neighborhood of the same city. The court might accept the assessors' figure as final; increase the amount offered; or, in some instances, reduce the $89,500 if it were considered excessive when reviewed.

In 1987, the U.S. Supreme Court held that property owners must be compensated by the government when regulations that are unduly burdensome deprive them of the use of their land.

EXAMPLE 23-18:   Just Compensation

The First English Evangelical Lutheran Church of Glendale sought compensation from the County of Los Angeles, claiming that a flood control ordinance deprived the church of the use of a 21-acre parcel of land in a canyon alongside a creek. The ordinance had been passed after a forest fire denuded the hills upstream from the property and a flood had killed several people and destroyed some buildings on the land. The church had previously used the land as a campground and recreational area for handicapped children. The Supreme Court held that the church was entitled to compensation if it could prove that the regulation preventing the use of the land was unduly burdensome. The court's decision was based on the Fifth Amendment to the U.S. Constitution, which states that private property may not "be taken for public use, without just compensation."

Quick Quiz 23-6 and 23-7 True or False?

1. Newly passed zoning laws do not apply to nonconforming uses, that is, existing uses of the land.

2. Exceptions to zoning laws are unfair and therefore not allowed.

3. Eminent domain is the right of federal, state, and local governments to take private lands, without compensation to their owners, for public use.

Summary

23.1 Real property is the ground and everything permanently attached to it. It includes the airspace above the surface to as high as the owner can use and the ground under the surface. Although property owners may own the land under a stream, they do not own the water itself. Their rights to use of the water vary, depending on the doctrine of law followed in their state. Property owners may use only that amount of subterranean water that is reasonably required to satisfy their needs. Rainwater may not be artificially channeled to an abutter's property without permission of the abutter. Fixtures are personal property that are so permanently attached to real property that they become part of the real property.

23.2 Easements give people the right to pass over another's land, to run wires through another's airspace, to drain water onto another's property, and to run pipes underneath another's ground. Easements run with the land.

23.3 An estate in fee simple is the greatest interest that one can have in real property. It descends to one's heirs upon death and can be disposed of in any manner during one's lifetime. In contrast, a life estate lasts only for someone's life. At the owner's death, the estate either reverts to the former owner or passes on to someone else.

23.4 People may own real property individually or with others. When two or more people own real property as tenants in common, the interest of a deceased owner's share passes to the heirs upon death. In contrast, when two or more people own real property as joint tenants or tenants by the entirety, the interest of the deceased owner's share passes to any other cotenants upon death. Only a husband and wife can own property as tenants by the entirety, and the property is protected from creditors unless both the husband and the wife are debtors.

23.5 A deed is used to transfer real property by sale or gift. The records of the probate court, instead of a deed, establish title to property when an owner dies. Title to real property may be gained by adverse possession. This action requires possession of another's property openly, notoriously, exclusively, under a claim of right, and continuously for a period of time set by state statute.

23.6 Zoning laws regulate the uses that may be made of properties within specified geographical areas. Newly passed zoning laws do not apply to nonconforming uses, which are uses that were in existence before the zoning law was passed. Nonconforming uses may not be enlarged or expanded. Variances may be issued by boards of appeals to people who suffer undue hardship from zoning laws.

23.7 Eminent domain is the right of federal, state, and local governments, or other public bodies, to take private lands for a public purpose. Owners must be paid the fair value of the property taken.

Key Terms

adverse possession, 479

bargain-and-sale deed, 478

community property, 474

condemnation, 481

cotenants, 472

curtesy, 472

dominant tenement, 469

dower, 472

easement, 469

easement by prescription, 470

eminent domain, 481

estate in fee simple, 471

fixture, 467

general warranty deed, 478

grantee, 477

grantor, 477

joint tenants, 473

life estate, 471

navigable airspace, 466

nonconforming uses, 481

quitclaim deed, 478

real property, 465

remainder estate, 471

reversion estate, 472

right of way, 469

riparian owners, 466

servient tenement, 469

Questions for Review and Discussion

1. What type of vegetation is considered real property? What type is considered personal property?
2. Under modern court decisions, to what extent do landowners own the airspace above their land?
3. What questions are asked in deciding whether an item is a fixture?
4. In what three ways may an easement be created?
5. How does a freehold estate differ from a leasehold estate?
6. What is the difference between common law dower and common law curtesy?
7. In each of the following tenancies, who owns the property when a cotenant dies: a tenancy in common, a joint tenancy, and a tenancy by the entirety?
8. In what three ways may title to real property be acquired?
9. Describe a nonconforming use of real property. When might a variance be given?
10. What is eminent domain?

Investigating the Internet

Following the 2005 U.S. Supreme Court decision in *Kelo v. City of New London*, more than 80 percent of U.S. states changed their laws on the subject of eminent domain, either by court decisions or by amending their statutes. Look online for changes your state has made since 2005 in its eminent domain law.

Cases for Analysis

1. Aloi sold a section of her land to Bell, including in the deed an easement allowing Bell to cross Aloi's property to reach the newly acquired parcel. Three years later, Aloi sold his property to Cadd. Shortly thereafter, following an argument, Cadd put a chain across Bell's right of way, saying that he had not given permission for Bell to cross his land. How should the court rule on this case and why?

2. Alfonso DiFilippo and his brother, Pasquale, owned a parcel of real property as tenants in common. Pasquale died in 1961 leaving a life estate in the property to his widow, Annie, with the remainder estate when Annie dies to Alfonso. Annie died in 1985. Alfonso died in 1969, leaving his interest in the property to his wife, Maria. What interest did Maria own in the property when she died in 1981? *DiFilippo v. DiFilippo,* 640 N.E.2d 1120 (MA).

3. When its lease expired, Kingston Frameworks made plans to move to another building. Preparations were made to remove shelving, mat and glass cutters, display boards, benches, and other fixtures that had been built into the store when the lease first started. All the shelves and fixtures were specially designed for the picture-framing business. The landlord told the owners of Kingston Frameworks to stop removing the items from the property. Could they remove the shelves and other fixtures that were paid for and installed by them during their tenancy? Why or why not? See also *George v. Town of Calais,* 373 A.2d 553 (VT).

4. Smith and Dudley are next-door neighbors. The branches of a large maple tree on Smith's property hang over Dudley's driveway, dripping sap onto Dudley's car. Smith refuses to trim the branches overhanging Dudley's driveway, saying that she does not want to spoil the beauty of the tree. What are Dudley's legal rights in this situation?

5. The Eisenmanns purchased a 90-acre tract of land on which they drilled a 179-foot-deep irrigation well. When the well was completed, they began pumping water at the rate of 650 gallons per minute. Two of the surrounding landowners, the Prathers (whose well was 121 feet, 10 inches deep) and the Furleys, lost the use of their wells the next day. A third neighbor, the Zessins, lost the use of their well three days later. The surrounding landowners sought money damages for the loss of the use of their wells from the Eisenmanns. Did they recover these damages? If so, how much? Explain. *Prather v. Eisenmann,* 261 N.W.2d 766 (NE).

6. Two years after Jean Russell was divorced from Billy Russell, Jean signed a quitclaim deed conveying her interest in their jointly owned real property to Billy. Later, she tried to have the deed set aside on the ground that Billy gave her no consideration. Was she successful? Why or why not? *Russell v. Russell,* 361 So.2d 1053 (AL).

7. Soon after Walter and Elsie Wienke were married, Walter conveyed property that he owned on Ridgewood Drive to himself and Elsie as tenants by the entirety. At the same time, Elsie conveyed property that she owned on Harlan Street to herself and Walter as tenants by the entirety. Twelve years later, Elsie conveyed the Harlan Street property by warranty deed to Colonial Discount Corporation. Walter objected to this sale and did not sign the deed. Colonial Discount Corporation sold the property to Danny and Glenda Lynch. Walter Wienke contended that a conveyance by one tenant by the entirety was inoperative. Do you agree with

Walter? Why or why not? *Wienke v. Lynch,* 407 N.E.2d 280 (IN).

8. Richard and Olive Misner began to develop a campground on land that they owned on Olive Lake. The zoning law in existence at the time allowed campgrounds to be built in that area. A year later, however, the county rezoned the area to "agricultural and lake resort" use, which did not permit campgrounds. At the time the new law went into effect, the Misners had built ten campsites with facilities and three primitive campsites on their property. When they continued to use and expand the campground after the new zoning law was passed, neighbors complained that they were violating the law. Could the Misners continue to use and expand the property as a campground? Explain. *Misner v. Presdorf,* 421 N.E.2d 684 (IN).

9. The Lowell Five Cents Savings Bank took a second mortgage from Stephen Coraccio on property owned by Stephen and his wife, Nancy, as tenants by the entirety. Stephen defaulted on the mortgage, and the bank began foreclosure proceedings against him. Nancy did not know of the mortgage and did not assent to it. She learned of the mortgage only after reading the foreclosure notice in the newspaper. Can a husband give a mortgage on property owned with his wife as tenants by the entirety without the wife's consent? Explain. *Coraccio v. Lowell Five Cents Sav. Bank,* 612 N.E.2d 650 (MA).

10. Walter and Emma Barrett jointly executed a warranty deed conveying three lots of land to Chandler and Jean Clements as joint tenants with the right of survivorship. Six years later, Jean Clements conveyed her one-half undivided interest in the property to Wheeler. Chandler claimed that Jean could not sell her interest to another person without his approval. Was he correct? *Clements v. Wheeler,* 314 So.2d 64 (AL).

Quick Quiz Answers

23-1	23-2	23-3	23-4	23-5	23-6 & 23-7
1. F	1. F	1. T	1. F	1. T	1. T
2. T	2. T	2. F	2. F	2. T	2. F
3. T	3. T	3. T	3. T	3. T	3. F

Chapter 24 | Landlord and Tenant

The Opening Case
"The Apartment"

In their junior year of college, Sheryl Gant and Bethany Silk decided to rent an apartment rather than continue living in the dormitory. They knew two students who were leaving college with six months remaining on their lease and decided to take over their apartment. After the first month, things started going wrong. Gant came home from school late one afternoon to find the landlord in the apartment. When she rejected the landlord's improper advances, he demanded the rental payment that was due and declared that the rent would be double after that. Gant paid the rent that was due. When the girls returned home the next day, they found that the electricity had been shut off. This time, the landlord told them that they had been evicted. He said that he had leased the apartment to the prior occupants and had not given his permission for Gant and Silk to live there.

Opening Case Questions

1. Can two students take over another student's apartment without the landlord's permission?

2. Can a landlord legally enter a tenant's apartment without permission?

3. Can a landlord raise the rent without giving notice?

4. Can a landlord disconnect an apartment's electricity?

LO Learning Objectives

1. List the five elements necessary to create a landlord–tenant relationship.
2. Compare a landlord–tenant relationship with licenses and lodging.
3. Define the four types of leasehold interests.
4. Identify the essential requirements of a lease.
5. Clarify rent control and security deposits.
6. Discuss the law regarding options to renew, options to purchase, assignments, and subletting.
7. Distinguish between assignment and subletting of a leased premise.
8. Make clear the duties of landlords and tenants.
9. Discuss tort liability as it applies to landlords and tenants.
10. Describe the methods used to evict tenants.

24-1 The Landlord–Tenant Relationship

LO1

The landlord–tenant relationship is a contractual arrangement in which the owner of real property allows another to have temporary possession and control of the premises in exchange for consideration. The agreement that gives rise to the landlord–tenant relationship is called a **lease**. The property owner who gives the lease is the **lessor** or **landlord**, and the person to whom the lease is given is the **lessee** or **tenant**. There are five elements necessary for the creation of a landlord–tenant relationship:

1. Consent of the landlord to the occupancy by the tenant.
2. Transfer of possession and control of the property to the tenant in an inferior position (in subordination) to the rights of the landlord.
3. The right by the landlord to the return of the property, called the right of reversion.
4. The creation of an ownership interest in the tenant known as a leasehold estate.
5. Either an express or implied contract between the parties that satisfies all the essentials of a valid contract (mutual assent, competent parties, consideration, lawful purpose).

Although rent is usually paid by the tenant to the landlord for the arrangement, it is not essential to the creation of the landlord–tenant relationship.

24-2 Leasing Versus Other Relationships

LO2

Other relationships that may be compared with the landlord–tenant relationship are licensing and lodging.

Leasing Compared with Licensing

A lease differs from a license in that a lease gives an interest in real property and transfers possession, whereas a **license** gives no property right or ownership interest in the property but merely allows the licensee to do certain acts that would otherwise be a trespass.

EXAMPLE 24-1:   License Rather than Lease

The city of Topeka was given a gift of 80 acres of land for use as a public park by the heirs of Guilford G. Gage. The deed signed by the heirs contained a condition that the property would revert to them if the property were ever deeded or leased to a third party. After the park was established, the city granted the exclusive right to McCall to construct and operate, for a period of five years, a miniature train on the premises. Under the agreement, McCall was subject in virtually all respects to the control of the city, and either party could terminate the arrangement by giving 30 days' notice. The heirs of Gage claimed that the transaction was a lease and that the property should be returned to them. In holding that McCall had a license rather than a lease, the court said that all McCall had was "the exclusive right to operate as the City may dictate."

Because a license confers a personal privilege to act and not a present possessory estate, it does not run with the land and is usually not transferable. It may be made orally or in writing and may be given without consideration. In addition, a license need not delineate the specific space to be occupied.

In contrast, a lease gives the tenant exclusive possession of the premises as against all the world, including the owner. It describes the exact property leased and states the term of the tenancy and the rent to be paid. In addition, in some states, a lease must be in writing.

Permission to sell Christmas trees at a gas station, to hold dance parties in a hall, and to place a sign on the outside of a building have all been held to be licenses rather than leases.

Leasing Compared with Lodging

A **lodger** is one who has the use of property without actual or exclusive possession of it. A lodger is a type of licensee, with a mere right to use the property. The landlord retains control of the premises and is responsible for its care and upkeep. Unlike a tenant, a lodger has no right to bring suit for trespass or to eject an intruder from the premises. One who lives in a spare room of a house, for example, whose owner retains direct control and supervision of the entire house, is a lodger.

Quick Quiz 24-1 & 24-2 True or False?

1. In a landlord–tenant relationship, the tenant has an ownership interest in the property.

2. A license gives no ownership interest in the property to the licensee.

3. A lodger is a type of licensee, with a mere right to use the property.

24-3 Types of Leasehold Interests

The interest conveyed by a lease is called a **leasehold estate** or a **tenancy**. There are four kinds of leasehold estates:

1. Tenancy at will
2. Tenancy for years
3. Periodic tenancy
4. Tenancy at sufferance

Tenancy at Will

A **tenancy at will** is an ownership interest (estate) in real property for an indefinite period of time. No writing is required to create this tenancy, and it may be terminated at the will of either party by giving proper notice. The notice requirement to terminate a tenancy at will varies from state to state. It ranges from the time between rent periods to 30 days' written notice from the next day that rent is due.

The rule generally followed in this country is that a tenancy at will comes to an end when the property is sold by the landlord to a third party. The notice required by state law must be given to the tenant in any event.

Tenancy for Years

A **tenancy for years** is an ownership interest (estate) in real property for a definite or fixed period of time. It may be for one week, six months, one year, five years, ninety-nine years, or any period of time, as long as it is definite. Such a tenancy automatically terminates on the expiration of the stated term. A tenancy for 100 years or more creates an estate in fee simple, transferring absolute ownership to the tenant. For this reason, leases are sometimes written for 99-year periods.

In some states, a tenancy for years may be oral if the term is shorter than one year; otherwise, it must be in writing. Other states require all tenancies for years to be in writing. A tenant who remains in possession of the premises at the expiration of the term with permission of the landlord, but without a new lease, is a tenant at will in some states. In other states, such a tenant is known as a periodic tenant.

Periodic Tenancy

A **periodic tenancy**, which is also known as a **tenancy from year to year** (or month to month or week to week), is a fixed-period tenancy that continues for successive periods until one of the parties terminates it by giving notice to the other party.

Unless the landlord or tenant gives advance notice of an intention to terminate the lease, it will be automatically renewed at the end of each fixed period for the same term. Advance notice varies from state to state, but it generally is defined as a period of three months for periodic tenancies of one year or longer and "one period" for periodic terms of less than a year.

EXAMPLE 24-2:   Inadequate Notice

Pasco's year-to-year lease expired on December 31. On November 15, she gave her landlord notice of her intention to terminate the lease. In her state, three months' notice is necessary to terminate a year-to-year tenancy. Pasco's landlord therefore could hold her to an additional year.

The death of a tenant who holds a periodic tenancy does not terminate the tenancy. Rather, the interest of the tenant passes to the personal representative of the deceased's estate.

EXAMPLE 24-3:   Death Does Not End Period Tenancy

Wilson was in possession of rental property originally leased to his father on a month-to-month basis. After the father's death, the landlord notified Wilson to vacate the premises on the grounds that the tenancy had ceased automatically. When Wilson refused to leave, criminal trespass charges were filed against him. He was found not guilty. The court held that his father's interest in the premises passed to him and that he was entitled to proper notice to end the month-to-month tenancy.

A periodic tenancy may be created impliedly by a landlord accepting rent from a tenant for years whose lease has expired or who is wrongfully in possession. Some states treat the latter situation as a tenancy at will.

Tenancy at Sufferance

A **tenancy at sufferance** arises when tenants wrongfully remain in possession of the premises after their tenancy has expired. It often comes about at the expiration of the term of a tenancy for years or when a tenancy at will has been properly terminated and the tenant remains in possession. Such a tenant is a wrongdoer, having no estate or other interest in the property. A tenant at sufferance is not entitled to notice to vacate and is liable to pay rent for the period of occupancy. A periodic tenancy or a tenancy at will may come about, however, instead of a tenancy at sufferance if a landlord accepts rent from a tenant whose tenancy has expired.

EXAMPLE 24-4:   Accepting Rent Creates Tenancy

Sutherland, an attorney, rented a suite of rooms in the Metropolitan Building in Chicago that she used for law offices. When her two-year lease expired, she negotiated with the owner of the building for a new lease. The negotiations extended over a period of several months, and the parties could not reach agreement. The landlord accepted rent each month from Sutherland during the period of negotiations. Sutherland was not a tenant at sufferance during the negotiation period because the landlord accepted rent from her during that time. A month-to-month tenancy was created. The landlord was required to give Sutherland a month's notice to end the tenancy.

Quick Quiz 24-3 True or False?

1. A tenancy at will is an ownership interest in real property for a definite period of time.

2. A lease for 100 years or more transfers absolute ownership of the property to the tenant.

3. A periodic tenancy automatically renews at the end of each period unless the landlord or tenant gives advance notice to terminate it.

24-4 The Lease Agreement

The agreement between a lessor and a lessee, called a lease, creates the landlord–tenant relationship. It provides the tenant with exclusive possession and control of the real property of the landlord. Because the lease is a contract, the general rules of contract law apply to it.

EXAMPLE 24-5:   Counteroffer Not Acceptance

Piccarelli, a representative of Mister Donut, expressed interest in leasing Tull's property. He sent a letter to Tull describing the "rudiments of our deal" and concluding with an expression of hope "that in the very near future preliminaries will be completed." This letter was followed by a form of lease sent by Piccarelli to Tull for the latter's approval. Tull signed the lease, after changing it materially, and returned it to Mister Donut for a countersignature. Nothing further was done, and the transaction never materialized. Tull's building was vandalized and burned after his tenants were evicted in anticipation of leasing the property to Mister Donut. When Tull sued Mister Donut, the court held that no contract and thus no lease came about. The initial letter was no more than an agenda for further discussion. The first draft of the lease sent by Piccarelli to Tull was an offer, and the revised document was a counteroffer that was never accepted by Mister Donut.

LEASE

This lease made the 20th day of August, 2005, between ROBERT VICKERS, herein called Landlord, and ETHEL LOPAZ, herein called Tenant, witnesseth:

The Landlord leases to the Tenant the following described premises: Four rooms and a bath on the first floor of the premises located at 17 Rosebud Terrace, Ashmont, New Hampshire, for the term of one year commencing at noon on the first day of September 2005 and ending at noon on the 31st day of August, 2006.

The Tenant agrees to pay to the Landlord the sum of $6,000 for the said term, in eleven (11) monthly payments as follows: The first and last months' rent of $1,000, plus a security deposit of $500, payable on September 1, 2005, and $500 on the first day of each month thereafter.

The Landlord agrees that the Tenant on paying the said rent and performing the covenants herein contained shall peaceably and quietly have, hold, and enjoy the premises for said term.

The Tenant agrees that at the expiration of the time mentioned in this lease she will give peaceable possession of the said premises to the Landlord in as good a condition as they now are, the usual wear, unavoidable accidents, and loss by fire excepted, and will not make or suffer any waste thereof, nor assign this lease, nor sublet, nor permit any person to occupy the same, nor make or suffer to be made any alteration therein, without the consent of the Landlord in writing having first been obtained, and that the Landlord may enter to view and make improvements, and to show the premises to prospective tenants or purchasers.

The covenants herein shall extend to and be binding upon heirs, executors, and administrators of the parties to this lease.

IN WITNESS WHEREOF, the parties have hereunto set their hands and seals the day and year first above written.

Robert Vickers
_____
Robert Vickers

Ethel Lopaz
_____
Ethel Lopaz

Figure 24-1 This is an example of a lease.

The essential requirements of a lease are: (1) a definite agreement as to the extent and bounds of the leased property, (2) a definite and agreed term, and (3) a definite and agreed price of rental and manner of payment (see Figure 24-1).

EXAMPLE 24-6:   Rent Uncertain

Schumacher leased a retail store to a tenant for a five-year term. The renewal clause stated that "the Tenant may renew this lease for an additional period of five years at annual rentals *to be agreed upon*; Tenant shall give Landlord thirty (30) days written notice, to be mailed certified mail, return receipt requested, of the intention to exercise such right." The tenant gave timely notice to renew the lease, but the parties could not agree on the rent for the new term. The court held that the agreement to renew the lease was unenforceable because the amount of rent was uncertain.

Rent Control

LO5

Some large communities have passed rent control laws to keep rents within an affordable range. These laws limit what landlords can charge for rental property and often contain procedures that must be followed before tenants may be evicted. In a number of areas, rent control laws have caused landlords to turn their apartments into condominiums, leading to shortages in rental apartments. Such laws differ from place to place. Some states, including Massachusetts, have done away with rent control laws altogether.

Security Deposits

In addition to the first month's rent, landlords often require either a security deposit or the last month's rent, or both, to be paid at the beginning of a tenancy. The deposit protects landlords against damages to their property as well as nonpayment of rent. Due to abuses of such deposits by landlords, state legislatures have passed laws regulating security deposits on residential property. Such laws spell out the rights of tenants and make it easier for tenants to prevail in court. Although these laws differ from state to state, the following characteristics are commonly found: Most states limit security deposits to one, one and one-half, two, or two and one-half months' rent, and most states require that security deposits be placed in interest-bearing accounts. The interest is either paid to tenants on an annual basis or accrued in their favor. Security deposits may not be commingled with other money belonging to the landlord. Also, the landlord is given a specific period, usually 30 days after the lease ends, to account for the security deposit and return the balance due to a tenant. Many states have now "put teeth" into the law, providing for double or triple damages, court costs, and attorney's fees for tenants whose security deposits are wrongfully withheld.

Read the lease before you sign it. It defines the rights and obligations due by the landlord and tenant.

LO5

EXAMPLE 24-7:   Double Damages

Santos rented a $450-per-month apartment from Hollis for a term of two years. When Santos's tenancy ended, Hollis refused to return any of the $450 security deposit to Santos, claiming that the damages to the apartment fully offset the amount of the deposit. Santos hired a lawyer, who brought suit against Hollis. The landlord was able to demonstrate only $70 in damages to Santos's apartment. The court found that Hollis had wrongfully withheld $380 of Santos's security deposit. The court awarded Santos a judgment for double damages of $760 plus attorney's fees of $200. With court costs, the landlord was forced to pay over $1,000.

Landlords of commercial property may also require security deposits, but the consumer protection statutes do not usually cover commercial leases.

Option to Renew or to Purchase

Many leases contain a provision allowing the lessee to have the option to renew the lease for one or more additional periods. An option to renew gives the lessee the right, at the end of the lease, to a new lease for an additional period. The new lease is on the same terms as the old one, with the possible exception of an increase in the rent. To exercise the option, the lessee must notify the lessor on or before the date set forth in the lease to do so.

A lessee may, if the lease so provides, be given an option to purchase the property. This option is an agreement by the lessor to sell the property to the lessee for a stated price. To exercise the option, the lessee must notify the lessor, within the time period stated in the lease, of the decision to purchase the property.

EXAMPLE 24-8:   Option to Purchase

Larson purchased a parcel of real property for $19,140 and leased it to the Panhandle Rehabilitation Center. The lease was for ten years and contained an option to buy for $19,000. After leasing the premises for five years and spending $5,000 to improve it, Panhandle notified Larson of its intention to exercise its option. By this time, the property was worth $38,000. Larson refused to sell the property to Panhandle for $19,000. The court ordered her to do so.

Assignment and Subletting

An assignment of a lease occurs when the interest in the leased premises is transferred by the lessee to another person for the balance of the term of the lease. The new party, called the assignee, steps into the shoes of the tenant, or assignor, and is liable for all of the original tenant's obligations and entitled to all the original tenant's rights under the lease. In contrast, it is called a **sublease** or **underlease** if the transfer is for a part of the term but not for the remainder of it.

A lease may be assigned or sublet unless the lease states otherwise. Many leases are written so that they require landlord approval for an assignment or a sublease. However, in some states, the landlord cannot withhold such approval unreasonably. An assignment or sublease will be held valid if the landlord accepts rent over a period of time from either an assignee or a subtenant.

The Opening Case Revisited, Part I
"The Apartment"

In *The Opening Case,* the lease could be assigned or sublet to Gant and Silk unless there was a clause in the lease that stated otherwise. In any event, the acceptance of rent from the students amounted to an implied acceptance of their tenancy.

Steve Hogan was in a bind. The executive director of Colorado's Northwest Parkway Public Highway Authority had run up $416 million in debt to build the 10-mile toll road between north Denver and the Boulder Turnpike, and he was starting to worry about the high payments. So he tried to refinance, asking bankers in late 2005 to pitch investors on new, lower-interest-rate bonds. But none of the hundreds of investors canvassed was interested.

Then, one day last spring, Hogan got a letter from Morgan Stanley that promised to solve all of his problems. The bank suggested Hogan could lease the road to a private investor and raise enough money to pay off the whole chunk of debt. Now Hogan, after being inundated with proposals, is in hot-and-heavy negotiations with a team of bidders from Portugal and Brazil. "We literally got responses from around the world," he says.

With state and local leaders scrambling for cash to solve short-term fiscal problems, the conditions are ripe for an unprecedented burst of buying and selling. All told, some $100 billion worth of public property could change hands in the next two years, up from less than $7 billion over the past two years; a lease for the Pennsylvania Turnpike could go for more than $30 billion all by itself. "There's a lot of value trapped in these assets," says Mark Florian, head of North American infrastructure banking at Goldman, Sachs & Co.

There are some advantages to private control of roads, utilities, lotteries, parking garages, water systems, airports, and other properties. To pay for upkeep, private firms can raise rates at the tollbooth without fear of being penalized in the voting booth. Privateers are also freer to experiment with ideas like peak pricing, a market-based approach to relieving traffic jams. And governments are making use of the cash they're pulling in—balancing budgets, retiring debt, investing in social programs, and on and on.

But are investors getting an even better deal? It's a question with major policy implications as governments relinquish control of major public assets for years to come. The aggressive toll hikes embedded in deals all but guarantee pain for lower-income citizens—and enormous profits for the buyers. For example, the investors in the $3.8 billion deal for the Indiana Toll Road, struck in 2006, could break even in year 15 of the 75-year lease, on the way to reaping as much as $21 billion in profits, estimates Merrill Lynch & Co. What's more, some public interest groups complain that the revenue from the higher tolls inflicted on all citizens will benefit only a handful of private investors, not the commonweal.

There's also reason to worry about the quality of service on deals that can span 100 years. The newly private toll roads are being managed well now, but owners could sell them to other parties that might not operate them as capably in the future. Already, the experience outside of toll roads has been mixed: The Atlanta city water system, for example, was so poorly managed by private owners that the government reclaimed it.

Such concerns weigh on the minds of public officials like Hogan. He intends to negotiate aggressively with corporate suitors and has decreed that the buyer must share future toll-hike revenues with the local governments that built the highway. But with the market for infrastructure still in its infancy, every deal is different. The ideal blend of up-front payment, toll hikes, and revenue sharing hasn't been found.

Flood of Money

Many investors think of infrastructure investing as a natural extension of the private equity model, which is based on rich cash flows and lots of debt. But there are important differences. Private equity deals typically play out over 5 to 10 years; infrastructure deals run for decades. And the risk levels are vastly different. Infrastructure is ultra-low-risk because competition is limited by a host of forces that make it difficult to build, say, a rival toll road. With captive customers, the cash flows are virtually guaranteed. The only major variables are the initial prices paid, the amount of debt used for financing, and the pace and magnitude of toll hikes—easy things for Wall Street to model.

Investors can't get in fast enough. They recently deluged Goldman Sachs with $6.5 billion for its new infrastructure fund, more than twice the $3 billion it was seeking. Pension funds in particular like the long-term investment horizons, which match their funding needs well. Infrastructure "delivers similar yield expectations to high-yield bonds and real estate, with less risk," says Cynthia F. Steer, chief research strategist at pension consulting firm Rogerscasey.

On the other side of the bargaining table from the investment firms sit struggling governments suddenly amenable to the idea of selling control of assets to solve short-term problems. The burden of maintaining roads, bridges, and other facilities, many built during the 1950s, is becoming difficult to bear. Federal, state, and local governments need to spend an estimated $155.5 billion improving highways and bridges in 2007, according to transportation officials, up 50% over the past 10 years. And that's hardly the only obstacle they face. In 2006 alone, states increased their Medicaid spending by an estimated 7.7%, to $132 billion. And state and local governments could be on the hook for up to $1.5 trillion in retiree liabilities, estimates Credit Suisse.

The combination of eager sellers and hungry buyers is shaking loose public assets across the country. The 99-year lease of the Chicago Skyway that went for $1.8 billion in 2005 was the first major transaction. Last year came the Indiana deal. Now states and cities are exploring the sale of leases for the turnpikes in New Jersey and Pennsylvania, a toll road in Texas, Chicago Midway Airport, and several state lotteries. Suddenly politicians around the country are wondering how much cash they might be sitting on. Based on the going rate of about 40 times toll revenues, the iconic Golden Gate Bridge could probably fetch $3.4 billion were California interested in selling. The Brooklyn Bridge? If permission were granted by New York City to charge the same tolls as the George Washington Bridge, a private owner might shell out as much as $3.5 billion for it.

Pavement Pricing

But there's a downside to the quick cash: planned toll hikes that are usually quite aggressive. Chicago's Skyway could see car tolls rise from $2 in 2005 to $5 by 2017. For some perspective, if a similar scheme were applied to the Pennsylvania Turnpike during its 67 years of existence, the toll for traveling from the Delaware River to the Ohio border would be as much as $553 now instead of $22.75.

Indiana legislators became so alarmed by promised hikes that they changed the terms before the toll road lease was completed. The state set aside $60 million to pay the difference in tolls for up to two years or until the buyers install electronic tolling equipment. After that, the fee for cars with electronic toll cards will rise to $4.80 over the full 157 miles, while the fee for cars without the cards will soar to $8. After 2010, both rates will rise each year by 2%, the pace of inflation, or the rate of economic growth, whichever is highest.

The certainty of future toll hikes doesn't jibe with the uncertainty of service quality. Assets sold now could change hands many times over the next 50 years, with each new buyer feeling increasing pressure to make the deal work financially. It's hardly a stretch to imagine service suffering in such a scenario; already, the record in the U.S. has been spotty. In 2003 the city of Atlanta ended a lease of its water system after receiving complaints about everything from billing disputes to water-main breaks. The city wrestled with the owner, United Water Inc., over basics like the percentage of water meters it should monitor. Both parties acknowledge that the contract lacked specifics. In the end, "we didn't believe we were getting performance," says Robert Hunter, commissioner for Atlanta's Dept. of Watershed Management. "I don't believe the city will ever look at privatizing essential services again." United Water says the contract wasn't financially feasible because Atlanta's water system was in worse shape than the city had represented.

A Champion's Perspective

States are wrestling with other public policy issues, too. Bankers say New York could reap a combined $70 billion for long-term leases on a bunch of assets, including the state's lottery, the Tappan Zee Bridge, and the New York State Thruway. New York state officials have looked into the option of leasing the lottery, which itself might command $35 billion—a sum that could substantially upgrade, say, New York's higher education system. The downside? The state would probably have to remove constraints on the lottery's marketing designed to discourage people from gambling more than they can afford. If the state insists on keeping the constraints in place, it could reduce the value of selling it.

Chicago's experience shows the possibilities and the pitfalls of privatization. Former CFO Levenson has been one of the movement's biggest champions. He was an architect of the Skyway deal, which kicked off the market. Then he sold control of

(Continued)

Business Law in the News (*Continued*)

parking garages to Morgan Stanley for $563 million. Next, he started shopping around a lease for Midway Airport that could fetch as much as $3 billion. And soon the city hopes to auction off rights to operate some recycling plants. Levenson dismisses critics who argue that he has dumped prized assets. "This is not like where a person goes in and buys a loaf of bread from a store and walks out with that loaf of bread," he says. "Some entity, we expect, will make an offer to lease the Midway Airport for 75 to 99 years, and the following day I'm pretty sure it will still be there."

Levenson doesn't understand how local governments can afford not to put public works up for sale. Thanks to the 99-year lease for the Skyway, Chicago has paid off its debt and handed over $100 million to social programs like Meals on Wheels. Plus, says Levenson, it's earning as much in annual interest on the $500 million it has banked from the transaction as it used to earn from running the Skyway ($25 million).

In some ways, Levenson argues, the city still has control over the highway. The agreement with the new owners spells out guidelines in mind-numbing detail, dictating everything from how quickly potholes must be filled (24 hours) to how rapidly squirrel carcasses must be removed (8 hours). If Macquarie and Cintra violate those conditions, the city can take back the road.

A Smooth Ride?

It's all encouraging, except that Chicago "probably could have gotten more without privatizing," according to Dennis J. Enright, a principal and founder of NW Financial. His firm's analysis shows that Chicago could have done a lot better by handling the whole deal itself. It could have raised tolls and sold tax-exempt municipal bonds backed by the scheduled hikes. That would have given the city the up-front cash it needed while preserving some of the income from the toll hikes. Instead, that money will go to Macquarie and Cintra.

Meanwhile, the higher tolls will take a big bite out of lower-income people's wallets. "You have to ask yourself if you want roads that used to be considered a public service to be rationed by income class," says Princeton University economics professor Uwe E. Reinhardt. Chicago says it hasn't received any formal complaints from citizens, though two different drivers recently went to extremes to avoid tolls, says Skyway maintenance manager Michael S. Lowrey. When the new owners introduced free towing for broken-down vehicles, the drivers called the Skyway for help, claiming to be stranded. After workers hauled the vehicles past the tollbooths, they hopped in their cars and sped away.

Pushback against private investors is now playing out in different ways elsewhere. In Pennsylvania, the state turnpike commission is going head-to-head with private bidders for the right to operate the state's 537-mile toll road. Pennsylvania desperately needs cash to repair its nearly 6,000 structurally deficient bridges. Some pundits expected Pennsylvania Governor Edward G. Rendell to propose hikes in gas taxes and other fees to fund the projects. But in December, Rendell unexpectedly announced plans to privatize the turnpike. Timothy J. Carson, vice-chairman of the commission, scrambled to submit an expression of interest for the turnpike to continue to run itself. His proposal is being judged against many others, including those from big Wall Street firms.

Carson isn't dissuaded by arguments that investors are better qualified to run turnpikes profitably. "There's no magic here," he says. "These [deals] are largely driven by one factor: the permitted toll increases." Carson says the state doesn't need to hand over the turnpike to private owners. Historically, he says, the state wanted the turnpike to collect only enough money to break even. But it could just as easily adopt its own toll-hike schedule. The state could also charge tolls on more roads. In other words, the public could remain in control simply by changing the turnpike's mission. That would ensure that the benefits of the toll hikes were spread throughout the populace, says Carson.

Pennsylvania's isn't the only turnpike authority exploring the possibility of bidding for roads. The North Texas Tollway Authority calculated in March that it would have valued a partially constructed 25-mile stretch of highway near Dallas 26% more than a private investor had bid. Now it's considering making a formal bid. And on Apr. 11, the Texas House of Representatives passed an amendment by a vote of 134 to 5 to impose a two-year moratorium on privatizing state toll roads. "We need to put the brakes on these private toll contracts before we sign away half a century of future revenues," said representative Lois W. Kolkhorst, who proposed the bill. A similar bill was passed in the state senate on Apr. 19.

With so much money at stake and so many options available to states, it's impossible to know how the great infrastructure craze may play out. But this much is certain, says Pennsylvania's Carson: "People are willing to pay more than they are currently being charged. The only question is to what extent you're willing to take advantage of that."

Questions for Analysis

1. What did Morgan Stanley suggest that would promise to solve all of Hogan's problems?

2. For how much could the Pennsylvania Turnpike be leased?

3. What are some advantages to the private control of roads, utilities, lotteries, water systems, and airports?

4. How are lower-income citizens adversely affected by the selling of leasing rights?

5. How do private equity deals compare with infrastructure investing?

6. List some recent activities pertaining to leasing public infrastructure throughout the country.

7. What is a downside to obtaining quick cash in return for leasing infrastructure?

8. Why did Atlanta end its lease of its water system?

9. What are some possible assets the City of New York could lease out?

10. According to Dennis J. Enright's firm's analysis, how could Chicago have gotten more from privatization?

11. Whom will the higher tolls harm?

12. Why isn't Carson dissuaded by arguments that investors are better qualified to run turnpikes profitably?

Source: Emily Thornton, "Roads to Riches: Why Investors Are Clamoring to Take Over America's Highways, Bridges, and Airports—And Why the Public Should Be Nervous," *BusinessWeek,* May 7, 2007, 50–57.

Quick Quiz 24-4 True or False?

1. Most states require that security deposits be placed in interest-bearing accounts with the interest belonging to the tenant.

2. A lessee may be given either an option to renew the lease or an option to purchase the property but not both.

3. A sublease occurs when the interest in the leased premises is transferred by the lessee to another person for the balance of the term of the lease.

24-5 Landlord's Duties

A good lease agreement will carefully spell out the respective rights and duties of the landlord and the tenant. However, state and local laws may restrict or expand upon what is set forth in the lease.

Duty to Refrain from Discrimination

A landlord may not discriminate in selecting tenants on the grounds of race, creed, color, or sex. In most states, a landlord may restrict rentals to persons without children but may not restrict a married couple's freedom to bear children during the leasehold.

EXAMPLE 24-9:   Unenforceable Terms

The Stimsons, a married couple, rented a luxury apartment from Chester Realty Associates. A condition inserted in the lease read, "The lessee agrees that if a child or children are born to the tenants during the period of the lease, the lease will be automatically terminated without the necessity of notice from the landlord." This condition is not enforceable against the Stimsons. Persons may not be denied the freedom of bearing children through contracts made with a landlord or others.

Duty to Maintain the Premises

When real property is rented for dwelling purposes, there is an implied warranty, called the **warranty of habitability**, that the premises are fit for human habitation. This provision means that the landlord warrants there are no defects vital to the use of the premises for residential purposes. Examples of defects are unsafe electrical wiring, a malfunctioning heating or cooling system, broken windows, a leaking roof, and infestation of insects.

EXAMPLE 24-10:   Warranty of Habitability

Jefferson leased an apartment for one year from Berman. A series of breaks in underground heating pipes caused the tenant to receive intermittent heat for two months. Finally, in early October, the pipe burst completely, and the tenant was without heat and hot water for two weeks. The court held that even though the landlord was not at fault, the warranty of habitability had been breached. Jefferson was not required to pay rent during the period that the apartment had no heat.

Many municipalities have adopted ordinances to protect tenants from unsafe or unhealthy conditions created by a landlord's refusal to make necessary repairs. Building inspectors, health authorities, and other public officials are empowered to make inspections and demand improvements when they are contacted by dissatisfied tenants. In many cases, ordinances permit the tenant to cease payment of rent for the period during which the landlord fails to make the repairs or improvements needed.

The majority of states hold that a landlord has a duty to clear common entryways of natural accumulations of snow and ice. Some states, nevertheless, still follow the older rule that the landlord owes no duty to tenants to clean common entryways of ice and snow unless there is an agreement on the part of the landlord to do so.

Duty to Deliver Peaceful Possession

The tenant is entitled to the exclusive peaceful possession and quiet enjoyment of the rental premises. **Quiet enjoyment** is the right of a tenant to the undisturbed possession of the property. The landlord may not interfere with the tenant's rights of possession as long as the tenant abides by the conditions of the lease and those imposed by law.

A Question of Ethics
Cheating—or Postmodern Learning?

On Apr. 27, the dean of Duke's business school had the unfortunate task of announcing that nearly 10% of the Class of 2008 had been caught cheating on a take-home final exam. The scandal, which has cast yet another pall over the leafy, Gothic campus, is already going down as the biggest episode of alleged student deception in the B-school's history.

Almost immediately, the questions started swirling. The accused MBAs were, on average, 29 years old. They were the cut-and-paste generation, the champions of Linux. Before going to B-school, they worked in corporations for an average of six years. They did so at a time when their bosses were trumpeting the brave new world of open source, where one's ability to aggregate (or rip off) other people's intellectual property was touted as a crucial competitive advantage.

It's easy to imagine the explanations these MBAs, who are mulling an appeal, might come up with. Teaming up on a take-home exam: That's not academic fraud, it's postmodern learning, wiki style. Text-messaging exam answers or downloading essays onto iPods: That's simply a wise use of technology.

One can understand the confusion. This is a generation that came of age nabbing music off Napster and watching bootlegged Hollywood blockbusters in their dorm rooms. "What do you mean?" you can almost hear them saying. "We're not supposed to share?"

GO ALONG OR GO SOLO

That's not to say that university administrators should ignore unethical behavior, if it in fact occurred. But in this wired world, maybe the very notion of what constitutes cheating has to be reevaluated. The scandal at Duke points to how much the world has changed, and how academia and corporations are confused about it all, sending split messages.

We're told it's all about teamwork and shared information. But then we're graded and ranked as individuals. We assess everybody as single entities. But then we plop them into an interdependent world and tell them their success hinges on creative collaboration.

The new culture of shared information is vastly different from the old, where hoarding information was power. But professors—and bosses, for that matter—need to be able to test individual ability. For all the talk about workforce teamwork, there are plenty of times when a person is on his or her own, arguing a case, preparing a profit and loss statement, or writing a research report.

Still, many believe that a rethinking of the assessment process is in store. The Stanford University Design School, for example, is so collaborative that "it would be impossible to cheat," says D-school professor Robert I. Sutton. "If you found somebody to help you write an exam, in our view that's a sign of an inventive person who gets stuff done. If you found someone to do work for free who was committed to open source, we'd say, 'Wow, that was smart.' One group of students got the police to help them with a school project to build a roundabout where there were a lot of bike accidents. Is that cheating?"

That's food for thought at a time when learning is becoming more and more of a social process embedded in a larger network. This is in no way a pass on those who consciously break the rules. With countries aping American business practices, a backlash against an ethically rudderless culture can't happen soon enough. But the saga at Duke raises an interesting question: In the age of Twitter, a social network that keeps users in constant streaming contact with one another, what is cheating?

Source: M. Conlin, "Cheating—Or Postmodern Learning? Duke's B-School Scandal Points Up the Fuzzy Ethics of a Collaborative World," *BusinessWeek,* May 14, 2007, 42.

EXAMPLE 24-11:   Breach of Quiet Enjoyment

Smith Grocery & Variety, Inc., leased one store in a two-store mall from Northern Terminals, Inc. The lease entitled Smith to the use of the parking areas (between 14 and 20 spaces) abutting the leased premises. Five months after Smith opened for business, Northern Terminals added an additional store to the mall without increasing the mall's parking facilities. Smith's business declined due to the severe parking shortage caused by the opening of a Triple-S Blue Stamp Redemption Center in the new addition. The court held that Northern Terminals, Inc., breached the covenant of quiet enjoyment. There was a substantial interference with the lessee's use of the premises, which was caused by the lessor's taking away of the parking spaces.

The right to exclusive possession by the tenant makes the landlord a trespasser should there be any unauthorized entry by the landlord into the rented premises.

EXAMPLE 24-12:   Trespass

Benson & Childs rented a skylight suite for their architecture offices. The lease gave the owner permission to enter only when a request had been made or in the event of extreme emergency. The landlord entered the offices late one evening for what he termed was his regular safety and fire inspection. Benson & Childs may treat the landlord's trespass as a breach of their right to sole possession, giving them the right to terminate the lease and charge the landlord in either a civil or a criminal complaint.

A tenant who is wrongfully evicted is not required to return and may consider the lease as ended. An **eviction** is an act of the landlord that deprives the tenant of the enjoyment of the premises. It is called an **actual eviction** when the tenant is physically deprived of the leasehold. When the tenant is deprived of something of a substantial nature that was called for under the lease, it is termed a **constructive eviction**. The tenant is justified in abandoning the premises without paying rent when a wrongful eviction occurs. The tenant must mitigate (lessen) any damages, however, if possible.

The Opening Case Revisited, Part II
"The Apartment"

In The Opening Case, the landlord violated Gant's right to exclusive, undisturbed possession of the premises by going into the apartment without permission. The landlord also committed a constructive eviction by shutting off the electricity.

EXAMPLE 24-13:   Constructive Eviction

Sound City, U.S.A., was interested in renting space in a shopping center. An inspection of the premises disclosed portions of the ceiling tile missing or hanging loose, water marks on the ceiling, and bare fluorescent light fixtures. As a result, Sound City included in its one-year lease an addendum (addition), whereby the landlord agreed to repair and paint the ceiling tile, cover the light bulb fixtures, panel the south wall, and erect a partition. Sound City moved into the shopping center, but after three months and many complaints, the repairs were never completed. It then moved out. The landlord brought suit for the remaining nine months' rent. The court held against the landlord, saying that there had been a constructive eviction. The physical appearance of the store was an important factor in the successful operation of Sound City's business. The failure to repair the premises properly in accordance with the lease rendered the premises unsuitable for the purpose for which they were rented.

Quick Quiz 24-5 True or False?

1. When real property is rented for dwelling purposes, there is an implied warranty of habitability, which means that snow will be cleared from common entryways.

2. A tenant is entitled to quiet enjoyment of the property, which means that walls between adjoining apartments must be soundproof.

3. A landlord is never considered a trespasser on the leased property.

24-6 Tenant's Duties

The tenant has the duty to pay rent to the landlord. In addition, the landlord has the right to remove, through court procedures, a tenant for nonpayment of rent, disorderliness, or illegal or unpermitted use of the premises.

A tenant has the duty to observe the valid restrictions contained in the lease. Leases may impose duties of all kinds as long as they are legal and do not deny a tenant's constitutional rights. Failure to abide by the restrictions agreed to at the time of the signing of the lease gives the landlord the right to seek the eviction of the tenant.

EXAMPLE 24-14:   Lease Violation

Bogg's lease states that he cannot paint any exterior woodwork or walls without first getting written permission from the landlord. Painting these surfaces, even though doing so improves the property, gives the landlord the right to terminate Bogg's lease.

Unless agreed otherwise, the tenant must turn over to the landlord all fixtures (except trade fixtures belonging to a business) that have been made a permanent part of the real property by the tenant during the leasehold.

EXAMPLE 24-15:   Fixtures Become Real Property

Dr. Hembly installed partitions in a rented house, dividing the living room into consultation offices. New lighting fixtures were installed, as well as a built-in air conditioning system. Hembly would be barred from removing the additions at the expiration of her lease or upon her eviction, as they had become real property.

Tenants also have a duty to avoid damaging or destroying the property, that is, commit waste. **Waste** is defined as substantial damage to premises that significantly decreases the value of the property.

Quick Quiz 24-6 True or False?

1. A landlord has the right to remove by force a tenant for nonpayment of rent.

2. Tenants must comply with valid restrictions contained in the lease.

3. Tenants cannot commit waste, that is, damage the premises in such a way that its value is decreased significantly.

24-7 Tort Liability

When a person is injured on leased property, the one who is in control of the part of the premises where the injury occurs usually is responsible if the injury was caused by that person's negligence. The landlord, for example, is responsible for injury to others that may be caused by a defect in the common areas, such as hallways and stairways.

EXAMPLE 24-16:   Common Area Defect

Wilson sustained serious injuries when she fell on a defective step while descending the front stairway of her apartment building. The landlord was held liable for Wilson's injuries because she was negligent in failing to keep the steps in a reasonably safe condition.

Although landlords are not guarantors of the safety of persons in a building's common area, they are not free to ignore reasonably foreseeable risks of harm to tenants and others lawfully on the premises. Landlords must take reasonable steps to guard against foreseeable criminal acts of third parties.

EXAMPLE 24-17:   Unforeseeable Violence

Whittaker was an editorial assistant for a publishing company that leased space in an office park building. One Sunday, she drove to the office park and let herself into the building with a key that she was entitled to have. While attempting to unlock a door to the publishing company's office, she was attacked from behind by an unknown person. The assailant threatened Whittaker, blindfolded her, and took her to an adjoining area where he raped her. In a suit brought by Whittaker against the owner of the building, the court held that the landlord had no duty to Whittaker to provide protection because the random act of violence was not foreseeable.

Tenants are responsible, in most cases, for reasonably foreseeable injuries to persons caused by defects in the portion of the premises over which they have control.

EXAMPLE 24-18:   Tenant's Responsibility

While visiting a friend's second-floor apartment, Ward fell down a single step leading to the bathroom. In a suit brought against the landlord for her injuries, Ward lost the case. The court said that the tenant was the responsible occupier of the premises. Any duty owed to the tenant's guest relative to the step was owed by the tenant, not the landlord.

24-8 Eviction Proceedings

LO10

States today do not allow landlords to use force to evict tenants. Instead, they must make use of statutory remedies that are available to them. Some states do, however, recognize the right of landlords to enter wrongfully held premises and take over possession if it can be done peacefully.

Ejectment is the common law name given to the lawsuit brought by the landlord to have the tenant evicted from the premises. This older remedy is still available in many states; however, it is time consuming, expensive, and subject to long delays.

Unlawful detainer is a legal proceeding that provides landlords with a quick method of evicting a tenant. The proceeding is referred to by different names in different states, including the following: summary process, summary ejectment, forcible entry and detainer, and dispossessory warrant proceedings. The remedy provides landlords with a quick method of regaining possession of their property and protects tenants from being ousted by force and violence. Strict notice requirements must be followed by the landlord, after which both parties are given their day in court. If a forcible eviction becomes necessary, it is done by the sheriff under the supervision of the court.

The Opening Case Revisited, Part III
"The Apartment"

In The Opening Case, the landlord could not raise the rent until the expiration of the lease and could not evict Gant and Silk without having the grounds to do so and without following proper procedures under state law.

EXAMPLE 24-19:   Improper Execution

Several months after Koonce fell behind in her rent payments, her landlord brought summary process proceedings against her. The court issued an execution (an order to carry out its judgment) giving the landlord possession, rent arrearages, and costs. Armed with the execution, a sheriff went to the premises and removed three fans, a stereo system, a record collection, a digital clock radio, a double-bed quilt, an iron, and a portable tape recorder. He also left a note saying that execution would be carried out if the rent were not paid. The court held that this was an improper procedure. It was the duty of the sheriff, once the execution was placed in his hands, to remove all Koonce's possessions, sell such of them as were necessary to satisfy the execution, and make the rest of her possessions available to her. Piecemeal exercise of an execution was not permissible.

Quick Quiz 24-7 & 24-8 True or False?

1. Tenants are responsible, in most cases, for reasonably foreseeable injuries to persons caused by defects in the portion of the premises over which they have control.

2. Landlords may usually use force to evict tenants.

3. Strict notice requirements must be followed by a landlord to evict a tenant.

Summary

24.1 The landlord–tenant relationship is a contractual arrangement whereby the owner of real property allows another to have temporary possession and control of the premises in exchange for consideration.

24.2 A lease differs from a license in that a lease conveys an interest in real property and transfers possession, whereas a license conveys no property right or interest but merely allows the licensee to do certain acts that would otherwise be a trespass. A lodger, a type of licensee, has the use of property without the actual or exclusive possession of it.

24.3 A tenancy at will is an ownership interest (estate) in real property for an indefinite period of time. A tenancy for years is an estate for a definite period of time, no matter how long or how short. A periodic tenancy is a tenancy that continues for successive periods until one of the parties terminates it by giving notice to the other party. A tenancy at sufferance arises when tenants wrongfully remain in possession of the premises after their tenancy has expired.

24.4 A lease creates the landlord–tenant relationship. Because it is a contract, the general rules of contract law apply to it. State laws often regulate security deposits on residential property. A lease may be assigned or sublet unless the lease states otherwise.

24.5 A landlord may not discriminate in selecting tenants on the grounds of race, creed, color, or sex. Premises that are rented for residential purposes must be fit for human habitation. Tenants are entitled to peaceful possession and quiet enjoyment.

24.6 Landlords have the right to evict tenants for nonpayment of rent, disorderliness, and unpermitted use of the premises. Tenants must observe the valid restrictions in a lease and not commit waste.

24.7 When someone is injured, the person in control of that part of the premises where the injury occurs is responsible if negligent.

24.8 Peaceable entry, ejectment, and unlawful detainer are the principal methods available to landlords to regain possession of their premises. Of these, unlawful detainer (called by different names in different states) is the most commonly used method. This remedy provides landlords with a quick method of regaining possession of their property and protects tenants from being ousted by force and violence.

Key Terms

actual eviction, 502

constructive eviction, 502

ejectment, 505

eviction, 502

landlord, 489

lease, 489

leasehold estate, 490

lessee, 489

lessor, 489

license, 489

lodger, 490

periodic tenancy, 491

quiet enjoyment, 500

sublease, 495

tenancy, 490

tenancy at sufferance, 491

tenancy at will, 490

tenancy for years, 490

tenancy from year to year, 491

tenant, 489

underlease, 495

unlawful detainer, 505

warranty of habitability, 500

waste, 504

Questions for Review and Discussion

1. What five elements are necessary for the creation of the landlord–tenant relationship?
2. How does a lease compare with a license and with lodging?
3. In what ways do the following tenancies differ: tenancy for years, periodic tenancy, tenancy at will, and tenancy at sufferance? Explain.
4. What are the three essential requirements of a lease?
5. How does the assignment of a lease compare with the subletting of a lease?
6. When and by whom is the implied warranty of habitability made?
7. What duties do landlords have under a lease?
8. What duties do tenants have under a lease?
9. What are the obligations of the tenant and the landlord when someone is injured on leased property?
10. What are the three principal methods available to landlords to regain possession of premises when tenants fail to leave at the end of a tenancy? Describe each method.

Investigating the Internet

At the time the manuscript for this book was written, several cities and states in the United States were considering the idea of entering into long-term leases of their infrastructure (e.g., toll roads, bridges, lotteries) to private groups to obtain immediate, much needed cash. Some of these measures appear in the Business Law in the News feature on page 496. Research on the Internet to determine how far this type of initiative has progressed and whether it has occurred close to where you live or travel.

Cases for Analysis

1. Bech owned a building in which Cuevas resided as a tenant at will. Alleging that Cuevas had committed waste, Bech delivered a letter to Cuevas ordering her to vacate the premises in two days. The law of that state required 30-day notice to evict a tenant at will. Must Cuevas vacate the premises? Explain. *Bech v. Cuevas,* 534 N.E.2d 1163 (MA).

2. The following language was in a handwritten agreement signed by Harold and Saul and their respective wives: "Saul & Zelda get the option to rent the lower level of the Hope Chest store when their lease expires. If they do take it, they will pay the same rate of rent per square foot that Harold is paying for his store. Saul & Zelda will do all the fixing up at their expense. Entrance to upper level has to be maintained from Newbury Street—similar to how it is now. Saul and Zelda have to let Harold know six months ahead of time: (lease expires by May 31, 1987, so that Saul and Zelda have to let Harold know by Nov. 31, 1986). Saul and Zelda cannot use the name Simon or Simon's or anything with the Simon name as a name for their store. Too confusing." Does the language contain the essential elements of a lease? Explain. *Simon v. Simon,* 625 N.E.2d 564 (MA).

3. Goldstein rented an apartment from Dunbar as a tenant at will. She paid her rent on time and took good care of the premises; she was never disorderly. Dunbar decided to evict Goldstein and rent the apartment to a college friend who was moving to the area. He sent Goldstein a proper notice to quit. Goldstein claimed that she could not be asked to leave because she had done nothing wrong. Do you agree with Goldstein? Explain. See also *Ralo, Inc., v. Jack Graham, Inc.,* 362 So.2d 310 (FL).

4. Sarah H. Brown and Sandy F. Soverow agreed to rent separate apartments from Osborn, the owner of an apartment complex called Nob Hill Apartments, which was being constructed. Because their single apartments were not yet completed, Brown and Soverow agreed to rent one larger apartment in the complex and live in that until their separate apartments were finished. A fire occurred in the apartment shortly after Brown put some leftover liver and gizzards for her dogs on the electric stove and left the apartment. In the lawsuit that followed, the contention was made that Brown and Soverow were lodgers rather than tenants. Do you

agree with the contention? Explain. *Osborn v. Brown,* 361 So.2d 82 (AL).

5. Alabama Outdoor Advertising Co., Inc., leased part of a lot from All State Linen Service Co. to erect a commercial advertising sign. The term of the lease was for "indefinite years, beginning 1st day of January, 1973, and ending year to year thereafter." When All State sold the lot, it was argued that Alabama's lease was a tenancy at will and therefore came to an end when the lot was sold. Do you agree with this argument? Why or why not? *Industrial Mach., Inc., v. Creative Displays, Inc.,* 344 So.2d 743 (AL).

6. Nash rented an apartment from Short for $500 a month. Nash always paid his rent on time. He fell behind, however, when his company went out of business and he lost his job. At a point when the amount in arrears reached $1,000, Short pushed Nash out of the apartment and padlocked the door. Nash claimed that Short violated the law by using force to evict him. Short claimed that he had a right to do so. For whom would you decide? Why? See also *Sempek v. Minarik,* 264 N.W.2d 426 (NE).

7. Friedman's tenancy came to an end on June 30. His landlord did not return or account for any portion of Friedman's security deposit until the following September 1. A statute in that state requires landlords to either return or account for security deposits within 30 days after the termination of a tenancy. Failure to do so entitles the tenant to an award of damages equal to three times the amount of the security deposit plus 5 percent interest from the date when the payment became due, together with court costs and reasonable attorney's fees. Was Friedman entitled to recover from the landlord? *Friedman v. Costello,* 412 N.E.2d 1285 (MA).

8. Elmer and Bonnie Cummings, as lessors, entered into a lease with Leo and Glen Ward for the rental of a building from March 16, 1966, to July 31, 1974. The lease provided that there could be no assignment without the written consent of the lessors. In October 1966, the Wards assigned the lease to Robert and Alice Smith with no written consent from the Cummingses. The Cummingses accepted rent from the Smiths for five years without objection. Was the assignment valid? Why or why not? *Smith v. Hegg,* 214 N.W.2d 789 (SD).

9. Sorrells rented a single-family dwelling house from Pole Realty Company. When eviction proceedings were brought against her for nonpayment of rent, Sorrells claimed that there had been a breach of the implied warranty of habitability. Pole Realty Company argued that the warranty of habitability did not apply to the rental of single-family residences. Do you agree? Explain. *Pole Realty Co. v. Sorrells,* 417 N.E.2d 1297 (IL).

10. The Kings leased a residential dwelling from a partnership called JA-SIN. The lease agreement provided that the tenants were to "take good care of the house" and "make, at their own expense, the necessary repairs caused by their own neglect or misuse." A guest of the Kings, Sharon Ford, tripped on a loose tread on one step while descending an outside stairway and sustained personal injuries. Who was responsible, the landlord or the tenant? Give the reason for your answer. *Ford v. JA-SIN,* 420 A.2d 184 (DE).

Quick Quiz Answers

24-1 & 24-2	24-3	24-4	24-5	24-6	24-7 & 24-8
1. T	1. F	1. T	1. F	1. F	1. T
2. T	2. T	2. F	2. F	2. T	2. F
3. T	3. T	3. F	3. F	3. T	3. T

Chapter 25 · Wills, Trusts, and Estates

The Opening Case
"Unexpected Happenings"

When Brad and Cindy Puentes were married, Cindy had a baby boy from a prior marriage and knew she would be unable to have another child. The couple, who lived in Massachusetts, adopted a baby girl from China. Three years later, Brad won the state lottery. When the $735,000 check arrived, Brad put it in his desk drawer and took Cindy out to dinner to celebrate. On their way home that evening, they were both killed instantly by a drunk driver. Cynthia still had a will, made during her first marriage following the birth of her son. Brad had a living will that he had signed during a brief stay in the hospital. They owned their home jointly.

Opening Case Questions

1. Will Cindy's will be used to settle her estate?

2. Does a living will dispose of one's property at death?

3. What law comes into play in this case to determine inheritance?

4. What effect does the adoption have on the inheritance?

5. Will Brad's stepson inherit from Brad?

6. Will the children inherit equal amounts?

LO Learning Objectives

1. Give details about the sources of probate law and its relevance to business entities.
2. Discuss the types and purposes of advance directives.
3. Determine whether a person who makes a will has the capacity to do so.
4. Explain the formal requirements for executing a will.
5. Compare the protection of children with the protection of spouses under the law of wills.
6. Identify the different methods of revoking or changing a will.
7. Explain the three grounds for contesting a will.
8. Decide, in different situations, who will inherit the property of someone who dies without a will.
9. Ascertain the lawful heirs when an inheritance depends upon the exact time of death.
10. Describe the steps to be taken by an executor or administrator in settling an estate.
11. Differentiate among the various types of trusts and determine when they might be used.

25-1 Sources and Relevance of Probate Law

The term **probate** refers to the process of handling the will and the estate of a deceased person. Each state has its own laws passed by its legislature, different from other states, governing the writing of wills and the settling of estates. For this reason, it is necessary to check one's own state law to ascertain the rules for writing a will and to determine how property passes when someone dies. In an attempt to standardize and modernize the different state laws on this subject, the Uniform Probate Code has been set up, but only 16 states have made it part of their law at this time (see Figure 25-1).

Relevance of Probate to Business

Because probate matters deal with the handling of people's estates, and because all businesses are owned by people in one way or another, the subject of probate law is relevant to all forms of business entities. When sole proprietors die, for example, the assets of their businesses pass to their heirs according to their states' probate laws. When owners of a corporation—that is, stockholders—die, their solely owned shares of stock pass to their heirs in a similar fashion. The death of a partner in a partnership form of business automatically dissolves the partnership. In such event, the deceased partner's estate has the right to either be paid the value of the partner's share or have the partnership ended.

Quick Quiz 25-1 True or False?

1. Each state has its own laws passed by its legislature, different from other states, governing the writing of wills.

2. The subject of probate law is relevant to all forms of business entities.

3. When sole proprietors die, the assets of their businesses pass to their heirs, according to their states' probate laws.

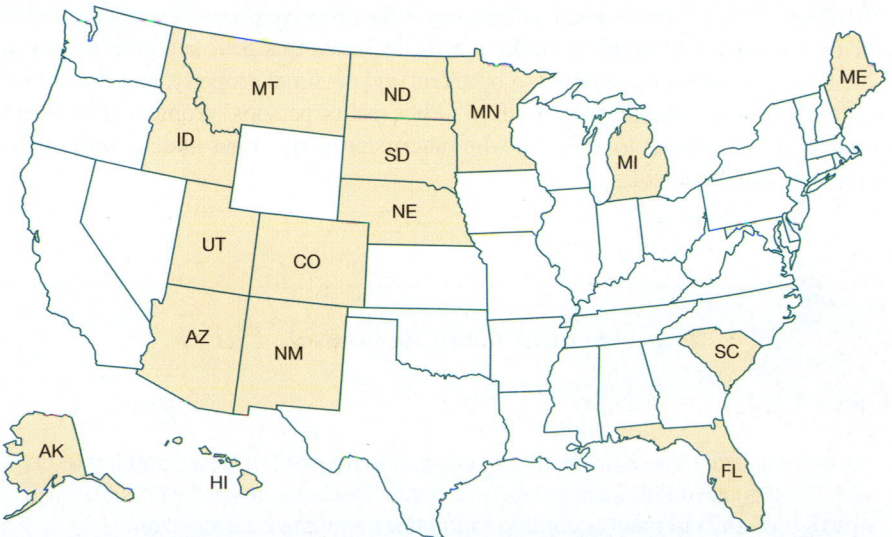

Figure 25-1   States that have made the Uniform Probate Code part of their state law.

25-2 Preliminary Matters and Probate Terminology

It is not uncommon for people to prepare for possible future misfortune by making advance arrangements to handle them while they are still mentally and physically able to do so. A good time to do this is when a will is executed, because all the necessary documents can be prepared, signed, and witnessed simultaneously.

Advance Directives

Advance directives are written statements in which people give instructions for their future medical care if they become unable to do so themselves. The most common type of advance directive is the **living will**, which is a written expression of a person's wishes to be allowed to die a natural death and not kept alive by heroic or artificial methods. Another vehicle that is used for this purpose is the **health care proxy**—a written statement authorizing an agent to make medical treatment decisions for another in the event of incapacity.

A **durable power of attorney** (discussed in Chapter 34) is a document authorizing another person to act on one's behalf with words stating that it is to either survive one's incapacity or become effective when one becomes debilitated. This authorization is not the same as an ordinary *power of attorney,* discussed in Chapter 33, which would have questionable effect upon one's incapacity.

Probate Terminology

A **will**, also called a **last will and testament**, is a formal document that governs the transfer of property at death. A person who dies with a will is said to die **testate**. A person who dies without a will is said to die **intestate**. The giving away of one's property by will is known as testamentary disposition.

A person who makes a will is called a **testator** if a man or a **testatrix** if a woman. (The masculine forms of terms like *testator* are used for purposes of discussion here. They refer to people of either sex.) Personal property that is left by will is called a **bequest** or legacy, except in states that have adopted the Uniform Probate Code. Real property that is left by will is known as a **devise**. Those who receive property by will are referred to as beneficiaries. They are also known as **legatees** if they receive personal property and **devisees** if they receive real property under a will. In states that have adopted the Uniform Probate Code, the term *devise* refers to both real and personal property, and the term *devisee* refers to a person who receives a gift of either real or personal property. The term **heir** is a broader term referring to a person who inherits property either under a will or from a person dying without a will.

The Opening Case Revisited, Part I
"Unexpected Happenings"

A living will is not the same as a "last will and testament" and has nothing to do with the disposition of one's property at death. Because he died without a will, Brad's property will pass according to the law of intestate succession.

25-3 Dying with a Will

LO3

Any person who has reached the age of adulthood (18 years) and is of sound mind may make a will. The issue of soundness of mind is raised only when someone contests a will on that ground. In determining whether a testator was of sound mind when making a will, the court asks the following questions: When making the will, did the testator know, in a general way, the nature and extent of the property he or she owned? Did the testator know who would be the natural recipients of the estate? Was the testator free from delusions that might influence the disposition of the property? Did the testator know that he or she was making a will? If all of these questions are answered in the affirmative, the court will find that the testator was of sound mind when making a will.

EXAMPLE 25-1:   Soundness of Mind

At the time of the execution of his will, Stein was suffering from loss of memory. His son observed his father's failing health and mental illness over a period of time. He once observed his father's failure to recognize his own wife. Stein's daughter once observed her father's failure to recognize her and another relative, both of whom he saw frequently. The court disallowed the will, saying, "The testator did not have mind and memory sound enough to know and understand the businesses upon which he was engaged at the time of execution."

Requirements for Executing a Will

The laws governing the making and signing of wills are not uniform throughout the United States because they are a product of state statutes. Nevertheless, a will that is properly executed according to the laws of one state will be given full faith and credit in another state. The laws are highly technical and require strict adherence to detailed formalities. Many lawsuits have occurred over the years because people have attempted to make their own wills without consulting a lawyer. Often, in such cases, a technicality causes the will to be disallowed by the court, and the true wishes of the deceased are not carried out.

LO4

Formal Requirements   With the exception of a nuncupative will, discussed later, a will must be in writing, signed by the testator, and attested to in the testator's presence by the number of witnesses established by state law (see Figure 25-2). Each of the particular statutory requirements of the state where the will is made must be met for a will to be valid.

Did You Know?

It can be risky to draft one's own will or even to use a pre-printed generic will found in a stationery store. The law of wills is very technical, and unique language is often used in the drafting of wills that may not be fully understood by laypeople. In addition, the law of wills varies considerably from state to state, making a generic will unreliable in many cases.

LAST WILL AND TESTAMENT
OF
JUDITH M. DORE

I, JUDITH M. DORE, of Salem, County of Essex, Commonwealth of Massachusetts, make this my Last Will and Testament, hereby revoking all earlier wills and codicils.

ARTICLE I

I give, devise, and bequeath all my estate, real, personal, and mixed and wherever situated to my husband, PETER DORE, if he is living on the thirtieth day after my death.

ARTICLE II

If my husband, PETER DORE, is not living on the thirtieth day after my death, I give and devise all of my property of every kind and wherever located which I own at the time of my death or to which I am then in any way entitled in equal shares to my children, ALAINA DORE and DAVID DORE, but if either of them shall not be living, his or her share thereof shall pass to his or her issue then living by right of representation, and in default of such issue then his or her share shall pass to the survivor of them.

I, the undersigned testator, do hereby declare that I sign and execute this instrument as my last will, that I sign it willingly in the presence of each of said witnesses, and that I execute it as my free and voluntary act for the purposes herein expressed, this 15th day of January, 2005.

_____
Judith M. Dore

We, the undersigned witnesses, each do hereby declare in the presence of the aforesaid testator that the testator signed and executed this instrument as her last will in the presence of each of us, that she signed it willingly, that each of us hereby signs this will as witness in the presence of the testator, and that to the best of our knowledge the testator is eighteen (18) years of age or over, of sound mind, and under no constraint or undue influence.

_____   _____
(Witness)   (address)

_____   _____
(Witness)   (address)

COMMONWEALTH OF MASSACHUSETTS
COUNTY OF ESSEX

On this 15th day of January, 2005, before me, the undersigned notary public, personally appeared JUDITH M. DORE, proved to me through satisfactory evidence of identification, which was a current Massachusetts driver's license, to be the person whose name is signed on this instrument, and acknowledged to me that she signed it voluntarily for its stated purpose.

_____
Charles E. Jones, Notary Public

Figure 25-2 These are sample portions of a formal will drafted according to Massachusetts law. The laws of each state are not the same on the subject of wills.

EXAMPLE 25-2:   Improperly Signed and Witnessed

Dugan's will contained the following clause: "All United States Savings Bonds in safety deposit box #559 Farmers Bank 10th and Market Sts., Wilmington, Del., to be given to the people and places as marked." When Dugan died, a number of U.S. Savings Bonds were found in his safe deposit box. There was also a handwritten list of the names of various individuals and organizations and, next to each name, serial numbers, dates, and face amounts corresponding to specific bonds. Further specific notations were written on small slips of paper and attached to each bond with a rubber band. The court held that there was no effective testamentary transfer of the bonds. Neither the list nor the envelopes nor the small slips of paper satisfied the statutory requirements for executing a will. They were not properly signed and witnessed. Dugan's wishes as stated in the will were never carried out.

A will may be typewritten or handwritten, or it may consist of a filled-in form. It need not be under seal. The will offered for probate must be the original and not a copy. In a case in which a testator executed both an original and a carbon copy of a will and later canceled only the carbon, the court has held that it could be presumed that the testator also intended to cancel the original. Problems of this nature can be avoided by executing only an original will.

A will must be signed by the testator. The place of the signature on the will and the requirement as to who must be present at the signing vary from state to state. In some states, a will must be signed at the end of the instrument; in other states, the signature may be placed anywhere on the paper. Similarly, some states require a will to be signed in the presence of witnesses, whereas others allow a will to be signed privately if the testator acknowledges to the witnesses when they sign that it is his or her signature. Testators who are not able to write may make a mark, such as an X, attested to by the required number of witnesses. If the testator's condition makes movement impossible, as in paralysis, another person may sign for the testator. This signing must be done at the request of the testator, in the testator's presence, and in the presence of witnesses.

With the exception of some wills that are handwritten, wills must be witnessed by the number of witnesses prescribed by state law. Almost every state today requires that a will be witnessed by two witnesses. Witnesses must sign in the presence of the testator and, in some states, each other's presence. Because the witnesses may be called upon to attest to the genuineness of the testator's signature and soundness of mind, it is advisable that witnesses be younger than the testator. In some states, no age requirements are given for witnesses. Instead, minors may witness a will as long as they are of sufficient understanding and competent to testify in court as to the facts relating to the execution of the will. In other states, witnesses must have reached a certain age, such as 14, 16, or 18 years, to qualify as a witness.

In many states, persons and their spouses who witness a will may not receive gifts under the will unless there are still other witnesses. The failure to observe this provision may result in their being disinherited.

EXAMPLE 25-3:   Witnesses and Their Spouses Cannot Benefit from Will

Delbert executed a will leaving all of his property to his three stepdaughters, Jane, Noreen, and Frances, who had been very close to him during his lifetime. Jane's husband was one of the subscribing witnesses to the will. When Delbert died, Jane received nothing from her stepfather's estate. A statute in that state makes void any testamentary gift to a subscribing witness or spouse of such a witness.

Some states protect beneficiaries who witness a will by allowing them to inherit up to the amount that they would have inherited had the deceased died without a will. In Example 25-3, had Delbert died in such a state, Jane would have inherited up to the amount she would have inherited had Delbert died without a will.

A Question of Ethics

Contrary to her stepfather's wishes, Jane, in Example 25-3, received nothing under her stepfather's will when he died. Would Noreen and Frances have an ethical duty to share their inheritance with Jane?

Need for Accuracy   Certain words often used in wills may have a legal interpretation that is different from their everyday meaning. Care must be taken to describe each bequest and devise in a manner that will satisfy the legal definition. For instance, a testator may use the word *heirs* when really meaning *children*. The differences in the meanings of the two words could result in much dispute and expensive litigation. It is also important to avoid ambiguous language.

EXAMPLE 25-4:   Ambiguous Language

Sparacio made a will leaving his property to his daughter, Mary, and his friend, Eileen, "as in their mutual agreement they decide." The court held that the will was invalid. It was impossible to determine under the terms of the will how much to give Mary and how much to give Eileen.

Informal Wills   A *holographic will* is one that is not witnessed but is written entirely in the handwriting of the testator. About half the sates in the United States treat holographic wills as valid. The other half do not recognize them because of the lack of witnesses.

EXAMPLE 25-5:   Holographic Will

Sedmak resided in Pennsylvania. The following handwritten document was found among his papers when he died:

My Brother Mil   Oct 6, 72

Please see that Zella Portenar receives $5,000 from my savings account it is in the Western Savings Bank.

George A. Sedmak
or Alexander Sedmak

The Pennsylvania court held the unwitnessed document to be a valid holographic will.

Oral wills made by persons in their last illness or by soldiers and sailors in actual combat are nuncupative wills. *Nuncupative wills* are valid only in some states and are restricted to the giving of personal property only. Testators must indicate their bequests and state that those hearing the statements are to be considered witnesses to the oral will.

Protection of Spouses

Most state laws contain various devices that are designed to give protection to surviving family members when a spouse dies. Some states provide for a **family allowance**, sometimes called a **widow's allowance**, which is an amount of money taken from the decedent's estate and given to the family to meet its immediate needs while the estate is being probated. The amount of the allowance is either a fixed, statutory amount or discretionary with the court and is not chargeable against other benefits given to the family members. Another family protection is the **homestead exemption**, which puts the family home beyond the reach of creditors up to a certain limit. Still another protective device provided by some states is known as **exempt property**, which is certain property of a decedent that passes to the surviving spouse or children and is beyond the reach of creditors. In some states, for example, $3,500 worth of personal property passes automatically to the surviving spouse or, if none, to surviving children equally. The rights of dower (for a widow) and curtesy (for a widower) are also available in some states, providing the surviving spouse with certain property rights in real property owned by the deceased spouse.

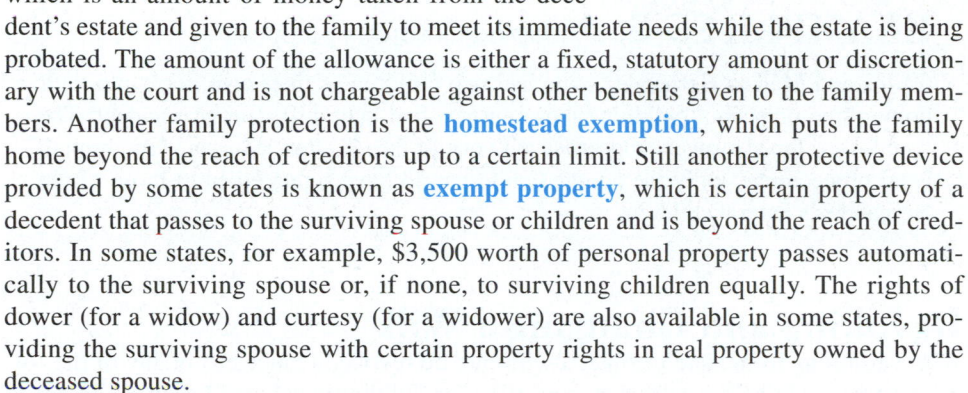

Wills provide for the smooth transfer of property and assure the rights of the heirs and beneficiaries.

In addition to the rights mentioned, surviving spouses are assured a share of a deceased spouse's estate. A surviving spouse who does not like the provisions of a deceased spouse's will may choose to take a portion of the estate set by state statute rather than accept the amount provided in the will. In some states, this sum is referred to as a spouse's **forced share**. In other states, it is called a spouse's **elective share**. The amount the surviving spouse will receive varies from state to state. In some states, it is the amount the spouse would have received had the deceased spouse died without a will. In other states, the amount is computed by the use of a different formula.

Protection of Children

Children who can prove that they were mistakenly (rather than intentionally) left out of a parent's will are protected by the laws of most states. Forgotten children will receive the same share that they would have received had their parent died without a will. This situation does not mean that a parent may not disinherit a child. Parents are not obligated to leave children anything, but, to avoid litigation, such an intention should be shown in the will. A testator who wishes to disinherit a child should name the child in the will and make the statement that the child was intentionally omitted. By doing so, the omitted child cannot claim to have been mistakenly omitted from the will.

Adopted children, under modern laws, are given the same legal rights as natural children. They inherit from their adopting parents. In contrast, stepchildren, unless they have been adopted by a stepfather or stepmother, do not inherit from a stepparent. Children who have been taken into the family for one reason or another but never legally adopted have no right of inheritance.

The Opening Case Revisited, Part II
"Unexpected Happenings"

The fact that Cindy and Brad's daughter was adopted makes no difference. She will have the same legal rights as a natural child and will inherit from her adopting parents. Because Brad did not adopt his stepson, the boy will not receive an inheritance from Brad.

EXAMPLE 25-6:   Adopted Children Protected

Carlos and Malana Hernandez, who had two children of their own, took into their home three preschool children whose parents had been killed in an accident. The couple developed a special closeness with one of the children, adopting him through legal proceedings. Only the adopted child would have rights equal to those of the Hernandez's natural children.

Revoking and Changing a Will

With variations from state to state, a will may be revoked (canceled) in any of the following ways: (1) burning, tearing, canceling, or obliterating the will with the intent to revoke it; (2) executing a new will; and (3) in 11 states, the subsequent marriage of the testator. The 11 states are Connecticut, Georgia, Kansas, Kentucky, Massachusetts, Nevada, Oregon, Rhode Island, South Dakota, West Virginia, and Wisconsin. In most states, the divorce or annulment of a marriage revokes all gifts made under a will to the former spouse and revokes the appointment of the former spouse as executor of the will.

Sometimes testators wish to make slight changes in a will. They may do so by executing a new will or executing a **codicil**, which is a formal document used to supplement or change an existing will. A codicil must be executed with the same formalities as a will. It must be signed by the testator and properly witnessed. In addition, it must refer to the existing will to which it applies.

The Opening Case Revisited, Part III
"Unexpected Happenings"

Cindy's will will not be used to settle her estate because, under Massachusetts law, her subsequent marriage had the effect of revoking her will. Cindy's estate will pass under the law of intestate succession, because she died without a will.

EXAMPLE 25-7:   Properly Executed Codicil

Rueda made a will giving her entire estate to her husband. Later, Rueda enjoyed unusual financial success and felt inclined to leave $100,000 toward a new church building under construction in her parish. Rueda's attorney prepared a codicil, which Rueda formally executed in the presence of two witnesses. The bequest to the church contained in the codicil became an integral part of the will itself.

A properly executed codicil has the effect of republishing a will. It is said that a codicil breathes new life into a will, which means that the codicil will reestablish a will that had been formerly revoked or improperly executed. If, for example, a will is witnessed by only one person in a state that requires two witnesses, the will is invalid. However, if a properly signed and witnessed codicil is added at a later date, the will becomes valid.

Contesting a Will

LO7

Only persons who would inherit under an earlier made will or under the law of intestacy (described later in this chapter) are allowed to contest a will. A will may be contested on any of three grounds: improper execution, unsound mind, and undue influence.

When the formal requirements for executing a will are not followed precisely, a will may be contested on the grounds that it was executed improperly. Because laypeople are not usually aware of the formal requirements for executing a will, it can be risky for them to make their own.

Another grounds to contest a will is to allege that the testator was of unsound mind. When such an allegation is made, the burden is on the person presenting the will to the court to prove that the testator was of sound mind. This proof may occur by testimony and affidavits of witnesses and by testimony of the deceased's physician.

A will may also be attacked and held invalid if a probate court finds that the testator made the will under circumstances of undue influence. When persons come under the influence of another to the degree that they are unable to express their real intentions in a will, the will may be declared invalid. The court must distinguish between undue influence and the kindness, attention, advice, guidance, and friendliness shown toward the testator by the one named in the will.

EXAMPLE 25-8:   Undue Influence

Smolak executed a will prepared by a lawyer whom he had selected and with whom he had conferred several times before the date on which the will was signed. His niece, Sandra, was the major beneficiary under that will. A week later, he executed another will under which his nephew Michael and Michael's brother were named principal beneficiaries. This will was executed at the same time that Smolak executed a deed conveying his farm to Michael and Michael's brother (which conveyance he later sought to rescind, claiming that it was procured by fraud). The second will was executed at the office of a lawyer employed by Michael. Michael had made arrangements for a conference between his lawyer and Smolak. Michael attended that conference and also attended the execution of the resulting will. Smolak never conferred privately with Michael's lawyer concerning the second will and therefore never had an opportunity to express his true intentions out of earshot of his nephew. The court held that the second will was procured through undue influence and was therefore void.

25-4 Dying Without a Will

When people die without a will, their property passes to others according to the various state laws of **intestate succession**. These state laws, which are not the same, contain the rules governing the allocation of intestate property. Personal property is treated differently from real property. *Personal property* is dispersed according to the law of the state where the deceased permanently resided (his or her domicile) at the time of death and passes to the personal representative to be distributed to the heirs. In contrast, *real property* passes according to the law where the property is located and passes directly to the heirs upon the death of the owner. The personal representative receives title to real property only when it must be sold to pay debts of the estate.

The following steps are taken to ascertain who will inherit from someone who dies without a will:

- Determine the rights of the surviving spouse, if any.
- Determine the rights of the other heirs.

Rights of the Surviving Spouse

Under a typical state statute, if a person dies intestate, the rights of the surviving spouse are as follows: If the deceased is survived by **issue** (children, grandchildren, great-grandchildren), the surviving spouse is entitled to one-half of the estate. If the deceased is survived by no issue but by blood relatives, the surviving spouse is entitled to $200,000 plus one-half of the remainder of the estate. If the deceased is survived by no issue and no blood relatives, the surviving spouse is entitled to the entire estate. Keep in mind that this particular formula will differ from state to state.

Rights of Other Heirs

Under the same typical state statute, if a person dies intestate, the property will pass, subject to the rights of the surviving spouse, as follows: If the deceased is survived by issue, the property passes in equal shares to the deceased's children, with the issue of any deceased child taking that child's share. If the deceased is survived by no issue, the property passes in equal shares to the deceased's father and mother or the survivor of them. If the deceased is survived by no issue and no father or mother, the property passes to the deceased's brothers and sisters, with the issue of any deceased brother or sister taking that brother's or sister's share. If the deceased is survived by no issue and no father, mother, brother, or sister, or issue of any deceased brother or sister, the property passes to the deceased's **next of kin** (those who are most nearly related by blood).

The Opening Case Revisited, Part IV

"Unexpected Happenings"

Because both Cindy and Brad were survived by issue, their son and daughter will be their only heirs. The children will not inherit equally, however, because a stepchild does not inherit by intestate succession.

If the deceased is survived by no blood relatives and no surviving spouse, the estate **escheats** to (becomes the property of) the state. In all states, the property of a person who dies without a will goes to the state only when there is no surviving spouse, issue, or kindred (see Figure 25-3).

If the Deceased Is Survived by:	*A Surviving Spouse (if any) Receives:*	*Any Remainder Is Distributed:*
Issue (lineal descendants such as children, grandchildren, great-grandchildren)	One-half of the estate	Equally to the deceased's children. If any children are also deceased, their children divide their deceased parents' share equally.
No issue but by kindred (blood relatives)	$200,000 plus one-half of the remainder of the estate	Equally between the deceased's father and mother or to the survivor of them. *However, if both parents are deceased, then:* Equally among the deceased's brothers and sisters. If any brothers or sisters are also deceased, their children divide their deceased parents' share equally. *However, if there are no living brothers or sisters or nieces or nephews, then:* Equally among the deceased's *next of kin* (those who are most nearly related by blood, including aunts, uncles, and cousins).
No issue and no kindred	The entire estate *However, if there is no surviving spouse, issue, or kindred, then:* The entire estate *escheats* to (becomes the property of) the state.	

Figure 25-3   This is an example of the way intestate property is distributed under a typical state statute (Massachusetts).

EXAMPLE 25-9:   Intestate Succession

Henrietta Johnson, whose domicile was Massachusetts, died intestate. She was survived by her husband, Arnold, a daughter, Bertha, and two grandchildren, Candice and Daniel, who were the children of her deceased son. Under state statute, Arnold will inherit 50 percent of the estate, Bertha will inherit 25 percent, and Candice and Daniel will each inherit 12.5 percent.

Quick Quiz 25-4 True or False?

1. Under a typical state statute, if a person dies intestate survived by no issue and no blood relatives, the surviving spouse is entitled to the entire estate.

2. Under the same typical state statute, if the deceased is survived by issue, the property passes, subject to the rights of the surviving spouse, in equal shares to the deceased's children, with the issue of any deceased child taking that child's share.

3. Under the same typical state statute, if the deceased is survived by no issue, and no father or mother, the property passes, subject to the rights of the surviving spouse, to the deceased's grandchildren.

 **25-5 Simultaneous Death**

When two people die in a common disaster so that it is impossible to determine who died first, the Uniform Simultaneous Death Act often comes into play. This law contains rules that are followed when the inheritance of property depends upon the time of death, and there is nothing to indicate that the parties died other than at the same time. The following rules are followed:

1. The separately owned property of each person passes as if he or she had survived unless a will or trust provides otherwise. For example, if a husband and wife die together in a plane crash, the husband's individually owned property passes to his heirs as though his wife were not living at the time of his death. Similarly, the wife's individually owned property passes to her heirs as though her husband were not living at the time of her death.

2. Property owned jointly by both of the deceased is distributed equally. In this example, half of the couple's jointly owned property passes to the husband's heirs; the other half passes to the wife's heirs.

3. When the beneficiary of an insurance policy dies at the same time as the deceased, the proceeds of the insurance policy are payable as if the insured had survived the beneficiary. Suppose, in the example, the wife was the beneficiary on the husband's life insurance policy. The wife would be regarded as deceased at the time of the husband's death. The proceeds of the policy go to the husband's estate unless an alternate beneficiary is named in the policy.

The Opening Case Revisited, Part V
"Unexpected Happenings"

The Uniform Simultaneous Death Act comes into play in this case because there is nothing to indicate that the parties died other than at the same time. Half of all joint property the couple owned will pass to Cindy's heirs—her son and daughter. The other half will pass to Brad's heir—his daughter. The lottery winnings, which were owned by Brad, will pass to his heir alone—his daughter.

EXAMPLE 25-10:   Simultaneous Death Act Not Applicable

John F. Kennedy, Jr., and his wife, Carolyn Bessette Kennedy, were killed in 1999 when their plane crashed into the ocean off the coast of Martha's Vineyard. The Uniform Simultaneous Death Act did not apply because the gifts to the spouses in each will were prefaced by the phrase "if she (or he) is living on the thirtieth day after my death."

Quick Quiz 25-5 True or False?

Under the simultaneous death act,

1. If a husband owns a house in his own name and he and his wife die at the same time in an accident, one-half the value of the house will pass to his wife's heirs.

2. If a husband and wife own a house jointly, and he and his wife die at the same time in an accident, one-half of the value of the house will pass to his wife's heirs.

3. If a husband names his wife as the only beneficiary of a life insurance policy, and he and his wife die at the same time in an accident, the proceeds of the policy will go to the wife's estate.

25-6 Settling an Estate

LO10

When people die owning assets, their estates must be **probated**, that is, settled under the supervision of the court. The court that supervises the procedure is called a probate court in some states and a surrogate court, or orphan's court, in others.

The first step in probating an estate is to determine whether the deceased left a will. If a will exists, it usually names a personal representative called an **executor** (male) or **executrix** (female) who is the person named in the will to carry out its terms. If there is no will, or if the executor named in the will fails to perform, someone must petition the court to settle the estate. That person, if appointed, is called an **administrator** (male) or

administratrix (female). In states that have adopted the Uniform Probate Code (see Figure 25-1), executors and administrators are called **personal representatives**.

Before an executor or administrator is appointed, notice of the petition for appointment is published in a newspaper and sent to all heirs, legatees, and devisees. Anyone with grounds to object may do so. Witnesses are sometimes asked to testify or sign affidavits about their knowledge of the execution of the will. Testimony is not necessary when all heirs and next of kin assent to the allowance of the will and no one contests it.

To ensure faithful performance, the executor or administrator is required to post a bond. A **bond** is a promise by the executor or administrator (and the sureties, if any) to pay the amount of the bond to the probate court if the duties of the position are not faithfully performed. **Sureties** are persons or insurance companies that stand behind executors or administrators and become responsible for their wrongdoing. In some states, a bond is not required if the will indicates that the executor or administrator need not post bond. In other states, a bond is always necessary, but sureties are not required if the will so dictates.

When a satisfactory bond has been filed, the court issues a certificate of appointment, called letters testamentary, to an executor or letters of administration to an administrator. The executor or administrator, called a **fiduciary** (one in a position of trust), is then authorized to proceed. The fiduciary's job consists of gathering the assets, paying the debts and taxes, and distributing the remaining assets in accordance with the will or the law of intestate succession.

Quick Quiz 25-6 True or False?

1. If a husband and wife die at the same time in an automobile accident, the separately owned property of each spouse passes as if he or she had died first unless a will or trust provides otherwise.

2. Testimony of witnesses is not necessary when all heirs and next of kin assent to the allowance of the will and no one contests it.

3. In the context of settling an estate, a *bond* is a certificate of indebtedness obligating the issuer to pay the bondholder interest plus the principal on the maturity date.

25-7 Trusts

A **trust** is a legal device by which property is held by one person (the **trustee**) for the benefit of another (the beneficiary). The person who sets up the trust is called the *settlor*. The property that is held in trust is the *corpus,* or *trust fund.*

When a trust is established, title is split between the trustee, who holds legal title, and the beneficiary, who holds equitable or beneficial title. This separation allows the trustee to manage the trust property for the benefit of the beneficiary. Trusts are established to save taxes, provide for the needs of young children, and prevent money from being squandered, among other reasons.

Property is often placed in trust so that it will be preserved for future generations. In such cases, only the income is given out during the life of the trust, with the principal held in relatively safe investments. The rule against perpetuities prevents trusts (except charitable trusts) from lasting indefinitely. This rule in many states requires trust property to become owned by the beneficiary outright not later than 21 years after the death of some person alive at the creation of the trust.

LO11

BusinessWeek Business Law in the News

Can You Trust Your Trustee?

For one Pennsylvania woman, the familial attachment to Wachovia Bank is strong. Her husband's grandfather helped found it over a century ago in North Carolina in a space once occupied by a Chinese laundry. But that connection to the institution doesn't stop the woman, who asked not to be identified, from expressing dissatisfaction over Wachovia's management of a family trust. Her beef? The portfolio has generated annual returns of less than 3% since the couple began receiving payments three years ago. "It's awkward, I've got to tell you," she acknowledges. "But I really think we should be achieving better results."

While the bank can't comment on the case, Bernard Destafney, a Wachovia managing director who oversees personal trusts in Philadelphia, says beneficiaries don't always understand that trusts must be managed for more than one generation. The aggressive risks that an individual could take with personal funds wouldn't be acceptable in the trust world, and 3% could be a fair return if the trust is trying to preserve its capital. "Generally trusts are very long term so risks and rewards are balanced very carefully," Destafney says.

Unhappy with what you're getting from a trust? Rid yourself of the idea that you're going to take the account to the bank down the street. If you try to dislodge a trust company through the legal system, the institution can typically use the trust's cash to fight you. Besides, case law traditionally backs the banks.

Still, you are not powerless. Your best bet is to arm yourself with tough questions while remaining gracious. "Sitting down and talking is the only way," says Standish Smith, the founder of Heirs, a nonprofit advocacy group for trust beneficiaries in Villanova, Pa. "When people get confrontational, the trustees just turn off."

Experts say tensions are increasing between trustees and beneficiaries these days. That's partly because they are strangers. A trust established in a small-town bank decades ago could now be parked in an institution thousands of miles away, says Eugene F. Maloney, corporate counsel at Federated Investors and a professor of trust law at Boston University School of Law. "Twenty-two mergers later," he says, "the beneficiary gets handed off to a call center, and all of a sudden you have a recipe for problems."

Trust companies aren't required to operate in the same locale where the account was opened. But in nearly all states, they must follow a weighty document called the Uniform Prudent Investor Act, which dictates the considerable fiduciary responsibilities institutions must assume when overseeing trust accounts.

Fiduciary auditors say, however, that bank trust departments aren't always following the rules that demand they act in the beneficiary's best interests. Common violations include forcing trust accounts to pay high commissions or taking payments from outside mutual fund vendors without sharing it with the trusts. "We have conducted fiduciary audits of bank trust departments, and their adherence to fiduciary standards are as woeful as we find in corporate boardrooms," says Ronald Hagan, chief executive officer at Roland/Criss Fiduciary Services in Dallas, which advises the retirement planning industry.

If you want to be a savvier beneficiary, here's what you need to do:

Know the Questions

Get a copy of the free checklist developed by Fiduciary360 (fi360.com), a fiduciary practices firm in Sewickley, Pa. The list of 68 questions will give you a good idea of what to ask. Don Trone, Fiduciary360's chief executive officer, says the most important thing is to ask for the trust's investment policy statement, which is the blueprint for how the assets are to be managed. Then make sure the trust officers are following it. For instance, if granddad wanted the portfolio to be split evenly between government bonds and stock funds, check to see if that is what's tucked inside the account.

Scrutinize the Costs

One sure way to boost income is to reduce the fees. For trusts of $1 million, a ball park figure is 0.75% a year, and the rate comes down as the trust grows. The fee may drop to 0.20% to 0.30% at $10 million,

(continued)

Business Law in the News *(continued)*

but don't expect them to drop anymore. If you think your trust's fees are too high, take that up with the bank. That's what Smith did for his wife's $8.5 million trust. He got a reduction.

Watch out, too, for the bank's proprietary mutual funds. If the account is paying both fund expenses and an annual trust fee, that's too much, says Roger Krasnicki, a St. Louis attorney and principal of Fiduciary Solutions, a litigation support and trust consulting firm. To compensate for the extra layer of fees, some banks provide a rebate to their trust accounts. If your trust isn't getting one, ask for it.

Get a Second Opinion

Fiduciary sleuths—specially trained accountants, attorneys, and investment consultants—can be especially valuable when a bank is preparing to close out a trust and distribute the money once heirs sign release forms. In some of these cases, Stewart Frank, a managing director of the Tillit Group, a fiduciary consulting firm in Bingham Farms, Mich., has been asked to poke around before anybody signs anything. The results can be shocking. "In the first case we looked at it, we found what looked like a couple of million dollars worth of problems that had accumulated over a long period of time," Frank recalls.

What happens if a fiduciary uncovers mistakes? A lawyer can lean on the bank for damages. Since banks abhor publicity, they will often agree to a confidential settlement. Frank says he often sees errant banks reimbursing beneficiaries for 66% to 75% of the lost assets.

Look for an Escape Route

Some trust documents include a removal clause that permits a beneficiary to move a trust to another financial institution. That's the option that Nancy Pietrafesa, an artist and writer in Berkeley, Calif., chose after she discovered that she was a co-beneficiary of a trust that her grandfather had established decades earlier. Pietrafesa was stunned to learn that the bank had never changed the original investments in 30 years. "We were able to move the trust and get someone who is much more in line with what my grandfather had wanted," she says.

Few trusts set up years ago have such clauses. But it's a good feature to include if you're establishing one today. That way, your heirs will have some leverage with the bank long after you're gone.

Questions for Analysis

1. Why was the beneficiary dissatisfied with Wachovia's management of the trust funds?

2. What do beneficiaries sometimes fail to understand about trusts?

3. What would be a fair return if a trust were trying to preserve capital?

4. What might happen if you were to try to dislodge a trust company through the legal system?

5. What is the best way to deal with a trustee bank?

6. Why are tensions increasing between trustees and beneficiaries these days?

7. In nearly all states, what must trust companies follow as a guide for trustees?

8. What four suggestions may help a beneficiary in dealing with a trustee?

Source: Lynn O'Shaughnessy, "Can You Trust Your Trustee?" *BusinessWeek,* November 6, 2006, 12.

Types of Trusts

The two principal types of trusts are testamentary trusts and living trusts. A **testamentary trust** is a trust that is created by a will. It comes into existence only upon the death of the testator. The terms of the trust, together with the names of the trustee and beneficiaries, are set out in the body of the will itself.

EXAMPLE 25-11:   Spendthrift Trust

Emile Hanson died, leaving four grown sons and daughters. His children had never demonstrated any real ambition and had depended heavily on their prospects of receiving large legacies from the estate. Hanson feared that his heirs would quickly spend their inheritances and have nothing to support themselves in the years ahead. He therefore provided for this possibility in his will by placing all assets in trust. The assets would remain intact, safely invested, and a small income would be paid from the trust income to the children. Hanson's purpose was realized in that the estate would be preserved and the surviving children would not squander their inheritance.

In a trust, such as the one illustrated in Example 25-11, provision must be made for final distribution of the trust's assets when the purpose of the trust has been served. For example, Hanson could have the trust property go to a church, college, or some other worthy nonprofit organization on the death of the last surviving child. He also could have designated a grandchild or grandchildren as the ultimate beneficiaries.

A **living trust**, also called an *inter vivos* trust, comes into existence while the settlor is alive. It is established by either a conveyance in trust or a declaration of trust. In a **conveyance in trust**, the settlor conveys away the legal title to a trustee to hold for the benefit of either the settlor or another as a beneficiary. In a **declaration of trust**, the settlor holds the legal title to the property as trustee for the benefit of some other person (the beneficiary) to whom the settlor now conveys the equitable title. A living trust may be either irrevocable or revocable. If it is *irrevocable,* the settlor loses complete control over the trust and cannot change it. The advantage of an irrevocable trust is that the income from the trust is not taxable to the settlor, and estate and inheritance taxes are avoided. The disadvantage of such a trust is that it can never be rescinded. The settlor can never get back that which has been put in an irrevocable trust, regardless of the circumstances. A *revocable* living trust may be taken back or changed at any time during the settlor's lifetime. It has neither estate tax nor income tax advantages; however, it can serve the purpose of relieving the cares of management of money or property, as well as other purposes.

A spendthrift is one who spends money profusely and improvidently. A *spendthrift trust* is designed to provide a fund for the maintenance of a beneficiary and, at the same time, secure the fund against that person's improvidence or incapacity. In some states, all trusts are considered to be of this type. In others, a clause must be placed in the trust instrument to the effect that the beneficiary cannot assign either the income or the principal of the trust and neither the income nor the principal can be reached by the beneficiary's creditors. Spendthrift trusts are not permitted in some states.

A charitable, or public, trust is one established for charitable purposes, such as the advancement of education; relief to the aged, ill, or poor; or the promotion of religion. For the trust to be valid, the identity of the person to be benefited must be uncertain. The rule against perpetuities does not apply to a charitable trust.

A *sprinkling trust,* or *spray trust,* allows the trustee to decide how much will be given to each beneficiary rather than have the settlor make the decision. The advantage of this type is that the trustee can compare the tax brackets of the beneficiaries long after the settlor is dead and cause a smaller tax liability to occur by giving more money to those beneficiaries in the lowest tax brackets. It also has built-in spendthrift provisions. The chief objection to this type of trust is that it gives the trustee too much control.

Obligations of the Trustee

The trustee is obligated by law to use a high standard of care and prudence in the investment of funds held by the trust. If real property is held in trust, it is the trustee's obligation to supervise and care for the property. When economic and other reasons indicate the need to shift trust assets to safer areas of investment, it becomes the duty of the trustee to make such changes. If investments selected by the trustee fail, the trustee is held liable unless a court rules that the action was taken with prudence and caution.

The trustee relationship is one of great and continuing responsibility. Appointment as a trustee should not be accepted by those without the knowledge and background that would afford prudent and good management. Banks, trust companies, and other kinds of fiduciary corporations offer professional services in the administration of trusts. They provide professional investment services and generally give maximum security and benefit for the fees charged.

Quick Quiz 25-7 True or False?

1. When a trust is established, title to the trust property is held completely by the trustee.

2. A *spendthrift* is one who is frugal and careful about spending money.

3. Trustees are obligated by law to use an average standard of care when investing funds for the trust.

Summary

25.1 Because each state's law is different on the subject of probate law, it is necessary to check one's own state law when dealing with probate matters. Furthermore, the subject of probate law is relevant to all forms of business entities.

25.2 Living wills and health care proxies are used to provide instructions for future medical care when one is no longer capable of doing so. A durable power of attorney authorizes another person to act on one's behalf even after one's incapacity. The terms *will, last will and testament, testate, intestate, testator, testatrix, bequest, devise, legatees, devisees,* and *heir* are frequently used in the field of probate law.

25.3 Any person who has reached adulthood and is of sound mind may make a will. Wills must be in writing, signed by the testator, and attested to in the testator's presence by two witnesses in most states. In some states, no formalities are necessary when a holographic will is made. Oral wills by soldiers and sailors in com-

bat may be used to bequeath personal property. Probate laws of each state are not the same.

Surviving spouses are given protection through such provisions as a family allowance, a homestead exemption, exempt property, and the rights of dower and curtesy. They are also assured of a share of a deceased spouse's estate by taking an elective share instead of the amount provided by the will. Children who can prove that they were mistakenly (rather than intentionally) omitted from a parent's will may be able to receive an intestate share of their parent's estate. Adopted children, under modern laws, are given the same legal rights as natural children.

A will may be revoked by burning, tearing, canceling, or obliterating the will with the intent to revoke it; by executing a new will; and in some states, by the subsequent marriage of the testator. The divorce or annulment of a marriage revokes all gifts made under a will to the former spouse. A codicil must be executed with the same formalities as a will. It has the effect of republishing a will that was formerly revoked or improperly executed. A will may be contested on the grounds of improper execution, unsound mind, and undue influence.

25.4   When people die without a will, their property passes to others according to the law of intestate succession, which varies from state to state. Personal property is dispersed according to the law of the state where the deceased was domiciled and passes to the personal representative for distribution. Real property passes according to the law where the property is located and goes directly to the heirs.

In finding out who will inherit, courts determine the rights of the surviving spouse, if any, followed by the rights of other heirs.

25.5   Special rules apply when people die simultaneously. Separately owned property passes as if its owner had survived the other person. Property owned jointly by both decedents is distributed equally. Insurance proceeds are payable as if the insured survived the beneficiary when they both die at the same time.

25.6   When people die owning assets, their estates must be probated. Heirs are notified, and an executor or administrator is appointed by the probate court. This fiduciary then gathers the assets, pays the debts and taxes, and distributes the remainder in accordance with the will or the law of intestate succession.

25.7   Trusts are used, among other reasons, to save taxes, provide for the needs of young children, and prevent money from being squandered easily. They may be created to take effect while a person is alive or after a person dies. When a trust is established, title is split between the trustee, who holds legal title, and the beneficiary, who holds equitable or beneficial title. The trustee manages the trust fund for the beneficiary.

Key Terms

administrator, 523

administratrix, 524

advance directives, 512

bequest, 512

bond, 524

codicil, 518

conveyance in trust, 527

declaration of trust, 527

devise, 512

devisees, 512

durable power of attorney, 512

elective share, 517

escheats, 521

executor, 523

executrix, 523

exempt property, 517

family allowance, 517

fiduciary, 524

forced share, 517

health care proxy, 512

heir, 512

homestead exemption, 517

intestate, 512

intestate succession, 520

issue, 520

last will and testament, 512

legatees, 512

living trust, 527

living will, 512

next of kin, 520

personal representatives, 524

probate, 511

probated, 523

sureties, 524

testamentary trust, 526

testate, 512

testator, 512

testatrix, 512

trust, 524

trustee, 524

widow's allowance, 517

will, 512

Questions for Review and Discussion

1. Why is it necessary to check one's own state laws before writing a will or determining how property passes when someone dies?

2. In what way is the subject of probate law relevant to a sole proprietorship? A corporation? A partnership?

3. What is the difference between a living will and a health care proxy, and how do they differ from a durable power of attorney?

4. Who may make a valid will?

5. What questions does the court ask in determining whether a testator was of sound mind when making a will?

6. In general, what are the formal requirements for executing a will?

7. What are some devices that are designed to give protection to family members when a spouse dies?

8. What must omitted children prove in order to inherit under a parent's will? What provisions should be made in a will by a testator who wishes to disinherit a child?

9. How are adopted children protected under modern inheritance laws?

10. In what ways may a will be revoked?

11. Following the statute shown in Figure 25-2, who will inherit from, and in what amount, the estate of a person who dies intestate survived by a spouse and two children ($60,000 estate); a spouse and a father and mother ($400,000 estate); a spouse and no blood relatives ($90,000 estate); three children ($90,000 estate); a brother and two children of a deceased sister ($90,000 estate); no blood relatives and no surviving spouse ($90,000 estate); and a spouse and a 90-year-old aunt ($500,000 estate)?

12. What three special rules apply when people die simultaneously?

13. What are the steps that must be taken to settle an estate? Explain.

14. How and for what reason is title to property split when a trust is established? Explain.

Investigating the Internet

State laws of intestate succession are not the same. Look up the law of intestate succession for your state. Then select a member of your family who you think should have a will but may not and determine who would inherit if that person should die without a will. Without giving names of actual people, share this information with the class.

Cases for Analysis

1. Miguel Ruiz, who had a wife and two small children, did not have a will. A friend told Miguel that he should have a will because if he died without one, everything he owned would go to the state. Was the friend correct? Explain.

2. Ling Lee, who had two children, made a will leaving $1 to her husband, Seung, and the balance in equal shares to her two children. When Ling died, her husband, Seung, claimed that he was legally entitled to more than $1. Do you agree with Seung? Explain.

3. D. W. Elmer, a hospital patient, was seriously ill and unable to write his name. He executed his will, however, by making a belabored X on the paper in the presence of witnesses. Can a signature on a will made by an X be valid? Explain. *In re Estate of Elmer,* 210 N.W.2d 815 (ND).

4. James and Wanda Barns, husband and wife, were killed in a head-on automobile collision. It was impossible to determine who died first, and neither one had a will. The couple owned the following items as joint tenants: the house in which they resided and its furnishings, a savings account, and a checking account. James owned a car and some Lucent stock separately in his name. Wanda owned a car and a certificate of deposit separately in her name. James was survived by two children of another marriage; Wanda was survived by one child of another marriage. Who will inherit their property?

5. Julia Dejmal executed her will while a patient in St. Joseph's Hospital. The will was witnessed by Lucille and Catherine Pechacek. Catherine was 19 years old and employed as an assistant X-ray technician at the hospital. The age of majority at the time in that state was 21. It was contended that the will was not valid because one of the witnesses to it was a minor. Do you agree with the contention? Why or why not? *Matter of Estate of Dejmal,* 289 N.W.2d 813 (WI).

6. Lazer, a wealthy 17-year-old, learned that he was suffering from AIDS. He wrote a will leaving everything he owned to a friend he had met in school. Two years later, when Lazer died, his parents claimed that the will was not valid. Do you agree with Lazer's parents? Explain.

7. Santiago, a widower, made a will leaving $1 to his son, Carlos, and the balance in equal shares to his other children, Benito and Angelita. The estate, after deducting debts, taxes, and expenses, amounted to $90,000. When Santiago died, Carlos claimed that he was legally entitled to $30,000 from his father's estate. Was Carlos correct? Why or why not?

8. Evidence was introduced in court to show that, at the time she executed her will, Blanch Robinson suffered from schizophrenia. She had delusions about having had a love affair with Nelson Eddy and was suspicious, mistrustful, and perhaps deluded about her friends and acquaintances. Dixon, who had been left out of the will, contended that Robinson lacked the mental capacity to make a will. Do you agree with Dixon? Explain. *Dixon v. Fillmore Cemetery,* 608 S.W.2d 84 (MO).

9. Walsh, as settlor, executed a declaration of trust, naming himself as trustee and giving himself the income from the trust during his lifetime. After his death, the income was to be paid to his second wife for her life, and upon her death, to his two children, Edward and Margot. Upon their deaths, the income was to be paid to the children of Edward and Margot, after which it terminated. The trust expressly provided that the settlor had not made any provisions for his third child, Patricia, because "previous provisions had been made in her behalf." After executing the instrument, Walsh transferred to the trust the family residence, three farms, and a checking account. Patricia argued that the trust was testamentary and therefore invalid because it failed to comply with the statute of wills. Was this a testamentary or an *inter vivos* trust? Explain. *First Nat'l Bank v. Hampson,* 410 N.E.2d 1109 (IL).

10. Whitman Winsor's will read in part: "I give, devise, and bequeath all my property, real and personal, to my daughter Lucy T. Winsor. . . . I deem it only right and just that my said daughter Lucy T. Winsor shall have all my property . . . because she has lived with me and cared for me for many years, and it is my will that all shall be hers." Winsor had another daughter, Caroline, who was not provided for in the will. Is Caroline entitled to an intestate share of her father's estate? Why or why not? *Hauptman v. Conant,* 400 N.E.2d 272 (MA).

Quick Quiz Answers

25-1	25-2	25-3	25-4	25-5	25-6	25-7
1. T	1. F	1. F	1. T	1. F	1. F	1. F
2. T	2. F	2. F	2. T	2. T	2. T	2. F
3. T	3. T	3. T	3. F	3. F	3. F	3. F

Part 4 Case Study

Estate of Saueressig v. Goff
Supreme Court of California
136 P3rd 201 (CA)

Summary

Timothy Saueressig typed his will, which left his property to his friends, Scott Smith, Harry Ernst, and Cliff Thomas, and named Smith as his executor. Saueressig had no brothers or sisters, and his parents were deceased. He never married and had no children. To his beneficiaries' knowledge, he had "no known next of kin."

Saueressig took the will to his friends Joongok Shin and her husband Theodore Boody at the Mail Boxes Etc. franchise that Shin owned to have Shin notarize his will. Saueressig explained to them that he had drafted his will to eliminate one of the beneficiaries under a previous will. Boody watched as Saueressig signed the will, and Shin notarized his signature.

The lower court disallowed the will, finding that it did not qualify as a holographic will because its material terms were typed, and it did not qualify as a formal will because it was signed by only one witness, the notary Shin, rather than two witnesses as required by the Probate Code.

One week later, the Court of Appeals decided a different case (*Estate of Eugene,* 104 Cal.App.4th 907) in which it held that a witness may sign the will after the death of the testator. In light of this new authority, Saueressig's will was resubmitted to probate with a declaration from Boody that both he and Shin had watched Saueressig sign the will and that he was prepared to sign the will as the necessary second witness. The lower court again disallowed the will, but the Court of Appeals reversed, stating: "We find nothing in the language of the statute to preclude an otherwise qualified witness from signing a will after the death of the testator." This case is an appeal from that decision.

The Court's Opinion

Corrigan, J.

A will that meets statutory requirements is effective upon the testator's death. Probate Code section 6110 requires a will be signed by two witnesses. The question here is whether the signature of a witness affixed after the testator's death satisfies the statute. We conclude that such postdeath subscription is not permitted, and reverse the contrary Court of Appeal judgment.

Before 1985, a formal will required attestation by two witnesses in the presence of the testator. The required presence of the testator foreclosed any argument that a witness's signature affixed after the testator's death would satisfy the statute.

That year the Legislature substantially revised the Probate Code [to read] a will "shall be witnessed by being signed by at least two persons each of whom (1) being present at the same time, witnessed either the signing of the will or the testator's acknowledgment of the signature or of the will and (2) understand that the instrument they sign is the testator's will."

The issue here is the scope of the legislative intent in eliminating the requirement that the witnesses sign the will in the testator's presence. Plainly, [the statute] contains no express temporal limitation on when the witnesses must sign the will in order for the document to be valid. Thus, it is ambiguous as to whether it permits postdeath attestation.

A number of states have construed statutes similar to [this] as prohibiting postdeath attestation. In *re Estate of Flicker* (1983) 215 Neb. 495 [339 N.W.2d 914], construed Nebraska's statute "to require that the witnesses to a will must sign it before the testator's death. A line must be drawn, and we believe that it is unreasonable to follow the alternative of permitting witnesses to sign a will at any time after the testator's death and prior to the 3-year statute of limitations for probate or testacy proceedings. . . . As a practical matter, we can think of no good reason for a delay in signing by witnesses until after the testator's death. Permitting witnesses to sign a will after the death of a testator would erode the efficacy of the witnessing requirement as a safeguard against fraud or mistake. We must bear in mind that we are dealing with an instrument allegedly signed or acknowledged by a man who is now dead. He is not present to confirm or reject it. Requiring completion of formalities of execution prior to death is likely to minimize miscarriages of justice." Other states have made similar observations. "[I]f the will speaks as of the date of the testator's death, it follows that the document should be complete at that time. Consequently, we adopt the bright line rule that witnesses' signatures should be affixed to the document at least by the time it becomes operative, the death of the testator." (*Matter of Estate of Royal* (Colo. 1992) 826 P.2d 1236; *Matter of Estate of Mikeska* (1985) 362 N.W.2d 906; *Rogers v. Rogers* (1984) 691 P.2d 114)

We find *Crook*, 95 Cal.App.4th 1194, and the cases from other states following a similar rule, to be persuasive. Such an interpretation is consistent with the critical principle that a will is operative following the death of the testator. It is not effective a week or a year later, or whenever purported witnesses manage to comply with the statutory requirement. While the dissent superficially acknowledges this rule, it nonetheless maintains that postdeath attestation is permitted.

The dissent relies on the fact that the Uniform Probate Code, through a comment regarding the actual statutory language, allows postdeath attestation. However, we are governed by section 6110(c) of [our statute], not the Uniform Probate Code.

In addition, while the Legislature did not expressly address the question of whether section 6110(c) permitted postdeath attestation, comments in the legislative history regarding a related area are instructive. As originally introduced, section 6110(c) required "at least two persons" be "present at the same time" to witness "either the signing of the will or the testator's acknowledgement of the signature or of the will." The section was amended to delete the requirement that the witnesses be "present at the same time."

Our conclusion regarding the legislative intent is consistent with sound public policy. As the Cal. Law Commission observed, "The formalities for execution of an attested will are to ensure that the testator intended the instrument to be a will, to minimize the opportunity for fraudulent alteration of the will or substitution of another instrument for it, and to provide witnesses who can testify that the testator appeared to be of sound mind and free from duress at the time the testator signed or acknowledged the will." The opportunity for fraud is obviously greater once the testator is dead. The lack of any requirement that the testator be living when the witness signs the will would deprive the testator of the chance to dispute the attestation and the consequent validity of the will. Only if he is still alive can the testator say, "This will is not mine," or "I did not ask this person to witness my will." Interpreting section 6110(c) to allow postdeath attestation would, for example, permit a witness to validate a will that the deceased testator executed, but deliberately did not have signed because of changed intent.

. . . A rule allowing postdeath attestation would essentially substitute oral testimony for the Legislature's requirement of a written signature. It would encourage will contests and put witnesses, not the testator, in control of the disposition of an estate. As one court observed decades ago, if witnesses could sign after the testator's death, " '[t]he final disposition of the estate would thereby be made to depend, not solely upon the intention of the testator, but upon the will or caprice of one who had been requested to perform the very simple act of becoming a witness. The legislature never intended to give to subscribing witnesses such power.... A will must be a valid, perfect instrument at the time of the death of the testator. It takes effect at the instant the testator dies. If invalid then, life cannot be given to it by the act of a third party.'"

…The dissent expresses the concern that by concluding postdeath attestation is not permitted by the statute, we are "supplying language the Legislature omitted." Similarly, the dissent states, "The majority apparently concludes that the Legislature must have made a mistake in removing the requirement that a witness sign a will in the presence of the testator without inserting a requirement that the witness sign the will before the testator's death."

In fact, the opposite is true. Section 6110(c) requires that the will "be witnessed by being signed by at least two persons." If we were to conclude that postdeath attestation is available, we would be adding the language "before or after the testator's death" to the current statutory requirement. We agree that it is not for us to draft statutes in the Legislature's stead. Rather, the task here is to discern what the Legislature meant by the language it has chosen. The Legislature may at some point conclude that postdeath attestation offers sufficient safeguards against fraud to allow it. That is its prerogative. However, in the absence of any evidence the Legislature has added this option to the Probate Code, it is not up to this court to do so. Given the history and context of section 6110(c), the most reasonable interpretation of the statutory language is that postdeath attestation is not an act the Legislature has authorized.

The Court of Appeal's judgment is reversed. The matter is remanded to that court with instructions to direct the trial court to reinstate its previous order denying probate of Saueressig's will.
George, C. J., Kennard, J., Baxter, J., and Chin, J., concurred.

Dissenting Opinion

Moreno, J.

I agree with the Court of Appeal. If Boody is permitted to sign the will as the second witness, which he is prepared to do, the requirements of section 6110, subdivision (c) will be satisfied. The statute requires that the will be signed by two persons who were present at the same time to witness the signing or acknowledgment of the will, but the statute places no restrictions on when the witnesses must sign the will. Boody and Shin were "present at the same time" and "witnessed ... the signing of the will." Nothing in the statute requires that Boody must have signed the will before Saueressig died.

In interpreting a statute, we are guided first and foremost by its language. "We begin by examining the statutory language, giving the words their usual and ordinary meaning." [citation omitted] "If the plain, commonsense meaning of a statute's words is unambiguous, the plain meaning controls." Nothing in the language of section 6110, subdivision (c) states or even suggests that there is a limit upon when the witnesses may sign the will.

...I fail to see how the circumstance that the statute does not limit when a witness may sign a will renders the statute ambiguous with respect to postdeath

attestation. But even if we assume for purposes of argument that section 6110, subdivision (c) is ambiguous, the majority's review of the legislative history of the statute does not support its conclusion that the Legislature meant to require witnesses to sign a will before the testator dies.

The majority concludes that "nothing in the language or legislative history of section 6110 indicates that by modifying the execution requirements, the Legislature intended to permit postdeath attestation." I disagree. The Legislature's repeal of the only provision in the former statute that required, as a practical matter, that the witnesses sign the will while the testator was alive is a strong indication that the Legislature intended to permit a witness who was present when the testator signed the will to sign the will at any time, even after the testator has died. This conclusion is supported by the fact that section 6110, subdivision (c) was patterned in large part upon the Uniform Probate Code, which since has been interpreted to permit a witness to sign a will after the death of the testator.

In 1990, the Uniform Probate Code was amended to provide that a witness to a will must sign the will "within a reasonable time" after witnessing the signing or acknowledgement of the will. The comment to the amended provision states: "The witnesses must ... sign within a reasonable time after having witnessed the signing or acknowledgment. There is, however, no requirement that the witnesses sign before the testator's death; in a given case, the reasonable-time requirement could be satisfied even if the witnesses sign after the testator's death."

The Arizona Court of Appeals relied upon the above quoted comment in *In re Estate of Jung* 109 P.3d 97, to hold that an Arizona statute that codified this provision of the Uniform Probate Code did not require that a witness sign the will prior to the death of the testator, noting that the statute required only that the witness sign the will "within a reasonable time" and adding: "The language of the statute does not limit that reasonable time to a time before the decedent's death and the comment to the [Uniform Probate Code] provision on which it is based expressly notes that a witness signing after the testator's death is not prohibited."

The majority's conclusion that this court should read into section 6110, subdivision (c) an unstated requirement that the witnesses must sign the will while the testator is alive also is based upon the fact that "a will is operative following the death of the testator."

But another of our sister states reached the opposite conclusion based upon reasoning that I find more convincing. *In Matter of Estate of Peters* (1987) 107 N.J.

263 [526 A.2d 1005], the testator signed his will in the presence of several witnesses, including two persons who had come for the express purpose of witnessing the signing of the will, but the witnesses inadvertently failed to sign the will. The testator died 15 months later. Eighteen months after the testator died, the trial court ruled that the witnesses who were present when the testator signed the will could sign the will at that time, because the governing statute, like section 6110, did not restrict when a witness could sign the will. The Supreme Court of New Jersey disagreed, ruling that a witness must sign the will "within a reasonable period of time from the execution of the will," and concluding that, under the circumstance, 18 months was not a reasonable time. (*Estate of Peters,* supra, 107 N.J. at pp. 275) In so holding, however, the court expressly declined to adopt a "bright-line rule" that a witness could not sign a will after the death of the testator, observing: "There may indeed be cases in which the affixation of witnesses' signatures after the testator's death would be reasonable, particularly if the witnesses were somehow precluded from signing before the testator died."

I agree with the Supreme Court of New Jersey that there is no bright-line rule prohibiting a witness from signing a will after the death of the testator. It is within the power of the Legislature to adopt such a rule, but it has not done so. And there is nothing inherent in the common law governing wills that requires such a rule, as is demonstrated by the fact that the Uniform Probate Code permits a witness to sign a will after the death of the testator.

The majority understandably is concerned that "[t]he opportunity for fraud is obviously greater once the testator is dead," but the same is true when the testator falls into a coma or becomes mentally incompetent. Thus, a requirement that a witness must sign the will within a reasonable time after witnessing the testator's signature, as required by the Uniform Probate Code, would be a far more effective deterrent against fraud than a bright-line rule prohibiting a witness from signing a will even a few minutes after the testator has died but not years after the testator has become mentally incompetent. But the wisdom of such provisions is for the Legislature to debate, not this court. We must apply the law as the Legislature has written it, and section 6110, subdivision (c) does not prohibit a witness from signing a will after the death of the testator.

The majority apparently concludes that the Legislature must have made a mistake in removing the requirement that a witness sign a will in the presence of the testator without inserting a requirement that the witness sign the will before the testator's death. If this is so, it is a mistake that is beyond the authority of this court to correct. This court cannot correct a statute by supplying language the Legislature omitted, except to avoid an anomalous result that is at odds with the statutory language. That is not the case here. The result that would follow if we applied the statute according to its terms is hardly anomalous. Rather, this result would be consistent with the Uniform Probate Code and would be fair in the circumstances of this case by giving effect to the clearly expressed wishes of the decedent. Werdegar, J. concurred.

Questions for Analysis

1. What makes the California statute ambiguous as to whether it permits postdeath attestation?

2. What does the court believe would happen if witnesses were permitted to sign a will after the death of a testator?

3. What did the Colorado court say about the issue in the *Estate of Royal* case?

4. What does the court believe a rule allowing postdeath attestation would do?

5. What is the main thrust of the dissenting judge's argument that the second witness be permitted to sign the will and the will be allowed?

6. Do you agree with the dissenting opinion? Why or why not?

Part Five

Negotiable Instruments

Chapter 26

Purpose and Types of Negotiable Instruments

The Opening Case
"The Student Loan"

Kennith Nardone loaned a friend he had met in class $125 to buy a textbook, knowing that she was expecting an income tax refund check very shortly. Thankful for the loan, the friend wrote on a piece of paper "IOU $125" and signed it. Nardone showed the IOU to another classmate, who told him that it wasn't legal and wrote the following note to use instead: "Thirty days after date, I promise to pay to the order of Kennith Nardone $125 out of the proceeds of my income tax refund." A month after signing the replacement note, Nardone's friend still had not received the refund check from the IRS, so she asked her parents to give her a check payable to Kennith Nardone for $125. The friend's parents mailed her a cashier's check payable to Nardone, but before it arrived, her refund check came in the mail, and she paid Nardone from the proceeds. She suggested that her parents stop payment on the cashier's check.

Opening Case Questions

1. Was the IOU a negotiable instrument?

2. Was the replacement note negotiable?

3. Can payment on a cashier's check be stopped?

LO Learning Objectives

1. State the purpose of negotiable instruments.
2. Identify the two kinds of negotiable instruments that contain a promise to pay money.
3. Identify the two kinds of negotiable instruments that contain an order to pay money.
4. Differentiate among certified checks, bank drafts, cashier's checks, traveler's checks, and money orders.
5. Name the parties to each kind of negotiable instrument.
6. Judge whether specific instruments contain the requirements of a negotiable instrument.

26-1 Purpose of Negotiable Instruments

LO1

Throughout history, people have had a need to transact business without carrying around large sums of money. In the Middle Ages, for example, merchants carried gold and silver with them as they traveled from one fair to another buying goods. They were in constant danger of being robbed and needed a safer and more convenient method of exchanging their gold and silver for the goods they bought. A system was developed by which merchants could deposit their precious metals with goldsmiths or silversmiths for safekeeping. When the merchants bought goods, instead of paying for them with gold or silver, they simply filled in a piece of paper, called a bill of exchange (now known as a draft). The bill of exchange ordered the goldsmith or silversmith to give a certain amount of the precious metal to the person who sold the goods. That person would then take the bill of exchange to the goldsmith or silversmith and receive payment. In a similar fashion throughout history, people have borrowed money from one another, necessitating an orderly system of procedures and laws to govern credit transactions.

The law of negotiable instruments has developed to meet these needs. Checks, drafts, and notes are used conveniently and safely as a substitute for money and to obtain credit in today's society. With the rapid development of e-commerce and electronic banking, computer and electronic technology is now being used as a substitute for checks and other paper transactions, as well as for actual check processing through the banking system. As a result, it is estimated that the number of checks written in the United States will decline greatly during the next decade.

The law of negotiable instruments is found in Article 3 of the UCC. This article was originally drafted in 1952. Since that time, many new developments have occurred in the commercial field. To adapt to modern technology and practices, Article 3 of the UCC was revised in 1990. All states except New York and South Carolina have adopted the revised article.

Under the UCC, a **negotiable instrument** is a written document signed by the maker or drawer that contains an unconditional promise or order to pay a fixed amount of money on demand or at a definite time to the bearer or to order. There are two basic kinds of negotiable instruments: promise instruments (including notes and certificates of deposit) and order instruments (including drafts and checks).

UCC Revised (1990)
3-104(e)-(j) (see
page 000)

Quick Quiz 26-1 True or False?

1. In the Middle Ages, a bill of exchange was a paper that ordered a goldsmith or silversmith to give a certain amount of gold or silver to a person who sold goods.

2. A bill of exchange is now known as a note.

3. The vast majority of states have adopted the 1990 revised Article 3 of the UCC.

26-2 Promise Instruments

LO2

Two types of negotiable instruments contain a *promise* to pay money. They are *notes* and *certificates of deposit*.

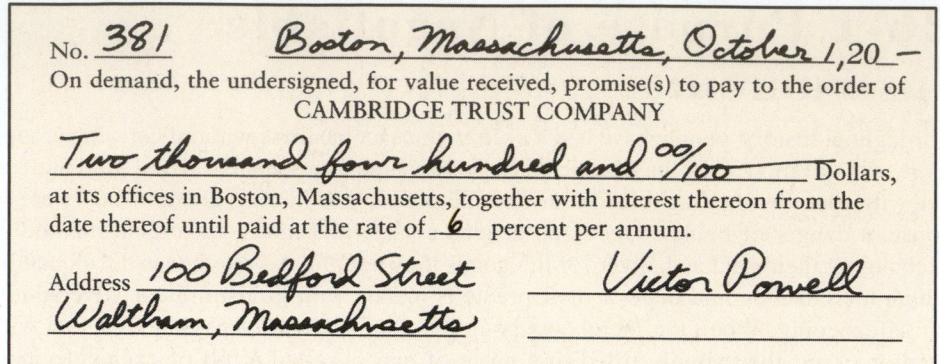

Figure 26-1 A demand note is payable whenever the payee demands payment.

Notes

A **note** (often called a promissory note) is a written promise by one party, called the *maker,* to pay money to the order of another party, called the *payee*. People who loan money or extend credit as evidence of debt use notes. When two or more parties sign a note, they are called *comakers*.

UCC Revised (1990)
3-104(e) (see page 000)

A **demand note**, as its name implies, is payable whenever the payee demands payment (Figure 26-1). A holder of a demand note may decide to collect the balance due at any time and for any reason. A time note, in contrast, is payable at some future time, on a date named in the instrument. Unless a note is payable in installments, the principal (face value) of the note plus interest must be paid on the date that it is due. In an **installment note**, the principal together with the interest on the unpaid balance is payable in installments (series of payments) at specified times.

UCC Revised (1990)
3-108(a) (see page 000)

Certificates of Deposit

UCC Revised (1990)
3-104(j) (see page 000)

A **certificate of deposit (CD)** is an instrument containing an acknowledgment that a bank has received a sum of money and a promise by the bank to repay the sum of money. A CD is a note of the bank, and CDs are written for a specific time period, such as six months, one year, two years, or five years. Banks pay higher interest for longer-term CDs and more interest than regular savings accounts because the depositor cannot withdraw the money before the due date without penalty. Some banks allow a one-time early withdrawal from a CD without penalty.

Quick Quiz 26-2 True or False?

1. People who loan money or extend credit as evidence of debt use notes.

2. A time note is payable whenever the payee demands payment.

3. A CD is a note of the bank.

26-3 Order Instruments

Two other types of negotiable instruments contain an *order* to pay money. They are *drafts* and *checks*.

Drafts

UCC Revised (1990) 3-104(e) (see page 000)

In contrast to notes, which are *promises* to pay money, drafts are *orders* to pay money. They are more complicated than notes because they involve three parties rather than two. The most common type of draft in use today is the check, but this was not always the case. For example, in Ernest Hemingway's *A Farewell to Arms*, a novel set in Italy during World War I, one of the characters, an American major, discusses with his friend Rinaldi the possibility of going to Milan:

> The tickets are very expensive. I will draw a sight draft on my grandfather, I said. A what? A sight draft he has to pay or I go to jail. Mr. Cunningham at the bank does it. I live by sight drafts. Can a grandfather jail a patriotic grandson who is dying that Italy may live? Live the American Garibaldi, said Rinaldi. Viva the sight drafts, I said.

A **draft** (also called a **bill of exchange**) is an instrument in which one party writes an instrument ordering a second party to pay money to a third party. The one who draws the draft (that is, the one who orders money to be paid) is called the *drawer*. The one who is ordered to pay the money is called the *drawee*. The one who is to receive the money is known as the *payee*.

EXAMPLE 26-1:   Sight Draft

In Hemingway's novel, the major would be the drawer of the draft, and his grandfather would be the drawee. The story does not name the payee of the draft, but it could be the railroad ticket office or a bank in Italy—whomever is to receive the money. If this situation involved a check, the person who signed the check would be the drawer, the bank would be the drawee, and the one to whom the check were written would be the payee.

A draft may be presented by the holder to the drawee for payment or for acceptance. When a draft is presented for payment, the drawee may decline to pay it unless it has been accepted. If the drawee refuses to pay an unaccepted draft, the draft is dishonored, and the drawee has no liability for refusing to pay it. In contrast, when a draft is presented for acceptance, the drawee is asked to become liable on the instrument. **Acceptance** is the drawee's signed agreement to pay the draft as presented. If the drawee refuses to accept the draft, it is dishonored, and again, the drawee has no liability. Drawees are liable on drafts only when they accept them, that is, agree to become liable on them.

To accept a draft, the drawee need only sign the draft across the face of the instrument. It is customary, however, when accepting a draft, for the drawee to write "accepted" across the face of the instrument, followed by the date and signature. An acceptance must be written on the draft itself; it may not be written on a separate piece of paper. By accepting a draft, the drawee agrees to pay the instrument at a later date when it becomes due.

Sight and Time Drafts
A **sight draft** (Figure 26-2) is payable as soon as it is presented to the drawee for payment. A **time draft** (Figure 26-3) is not payable until the lapse of a particular time period stated on the draft. Drafts that are payable "thirty days after sight" and "sixty days after date" are examples of time drafts.

Domestic and International Bills of Exchange
A **domestic bill of exchange** is a draft that is drawn and payable in the United States. A draft that is drawn in one country but payable in another is called an **international bill of exchange** or **foreign draft**.

About the Law

A **trade acceptance** is a draft used by a seller of goods to receive payment and extend credit. Drafts are often used in combination with bills of lading, which are receipts given by freight companies to people who ship goods. A seller will ship goods to a buyer and send a bill of lading, with a trade acceptance attached, to a bank in the buyer's city. The trade acceptance orders the buyer to pay money to the seller or another party. The buyer must either pay the money or accept the draft to receive the bill of lading from the bank. The freight company will not release the goods to the buyer unless the buyer has possession of the bill of lading.

UCC Revised (1990) 3-409 (see page 000)

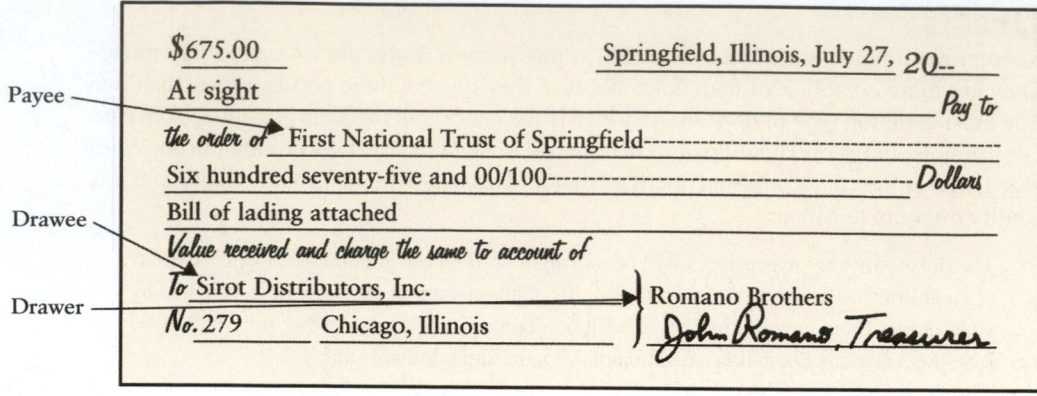

Figure 26-2 A sight draft is payable as soon as it is presented to the drawee for payment. How do you know that this draft has not been accepted by the drawee?

Checks

UCC Revised (1990)
3-104(f) (see page 000)

A **check** is a draft drawn on a bank and payable on demand. It is the most common form of a draft. It is drawn on a bank by a drawer who has an account with the bank and is made to the order of a specified person or business named on the check or to the bearer. A check is a safe means of transferring money, and it serves as a receipt after it has been paid and canceled by the bank.

In the check shown in Figure 26-4, Evans is the drawer; she has an account with the Western National Bank. Alicia Adams Fashions, Inc., is the payee. Western National Bank, on which the check is drawn, is the drawee.

Ownership of a check may be transferred to another person by indorsement by the payee. In this manner, a check may circulate among several parties, taking the place of money. A bank must honor a check when it is properly drawn against a credit balance of the drawer. Failure to do so would make the bank liable to the drawer for resulting damages.

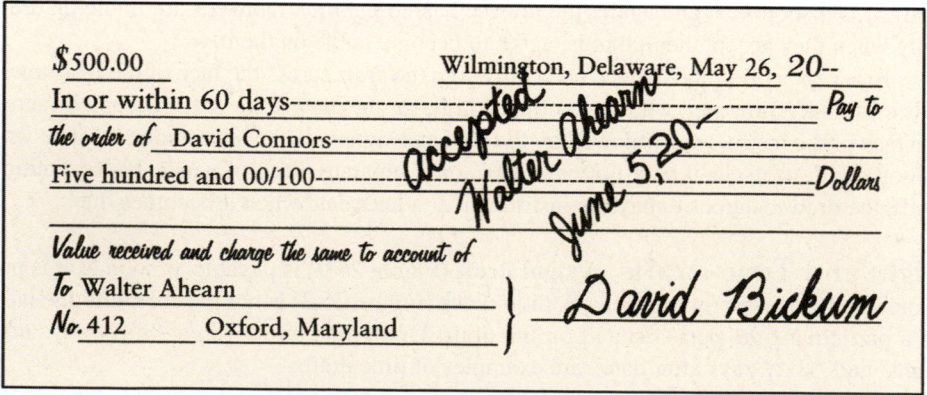

Figure 26-3 A time draft is not payable until the lapse of a particular time period stated on the draft. How do you know that this draft has been accepted by the drawee?

Stub (record of checks drawn)   Payee   Amount of check   Check number
                                                                  (written in words and figures)

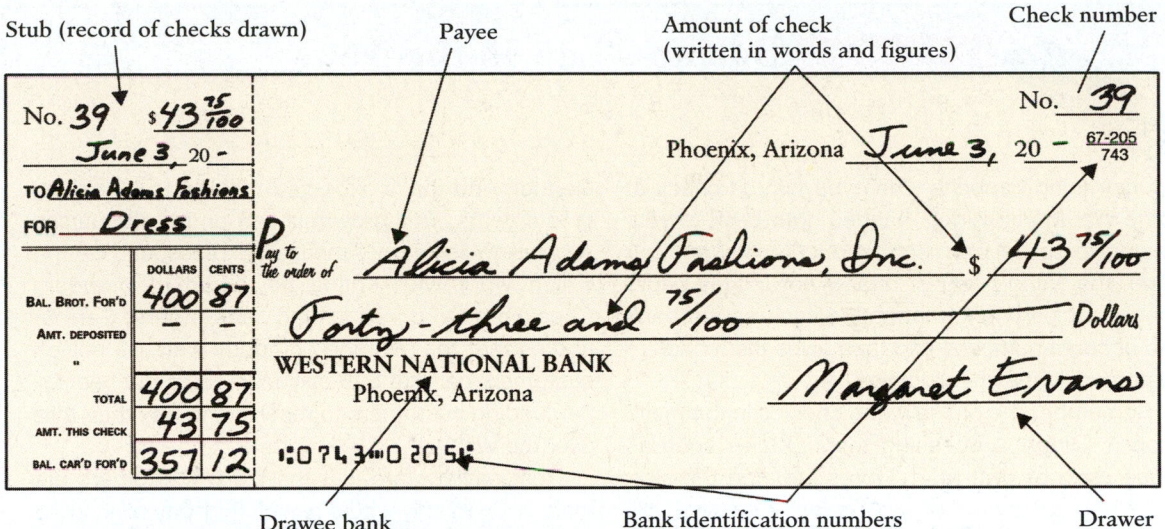

Drawee bank   Bank identification numbers   Drawer

Figure 26-4 All elements of a sample check are identified.

Form for Checks Banks provide regular and special printed check forms. These check forms display a series of numbers printed in magnetic ink, which make it possible to process checks speedily and accurately by computer. The first set of figures is the bank's Federal Reserve number. This number is followed by the bank's own number. The second set of numbers is the depositor's account number. The use of printed forms is not required however. Any writing, no matter how crude, may be used as a check if it is a draft drawn on a bank and payable on demand.

EXAMPLE 26-2: Unusual Check

While on a fishing trip in the Maine woods, Nichols lost his belongings when his canoe tipped over. A camper sold Nichols a jacket, some camping equipment, and enough food to make it to the nearest town. Because Nichols had lost his money, he wrote out a check on a piece of notebook paper ordering his bank to pay to the order of the camper $80. Although unusual, this writing amounted to a valid check that would have to be honored by Nichols's bank.

UCC Revised (1990)
3-409(d) (see page 000)

Certified Checks A **certified check** is a check that is guaranteed by the bank. At the request of either the depositor or the holder, the bank acknowledges and guarantees that

A funny thing happens when you write a check at some Wal-Marts: It gets handed right back to you. Hoping to speed payments, reduce costs, and cut fraud, the world's largest retailer now scans paper checks for pertinent information such as the bank and account number—and then gives them back to customers in the checkout line.

Remember the old saw, the check's in the mail? Drop it. Digital processing technologies such as those used by Wal-Mart Stores Inc. and the sky-rocketing adoption of online bill payment are reshaping the $30 billion business of printing, transporting, and processing checks. Driving the transformation are banks, credit-card companies, and merchants eager to simplify an antiquated system that involves as many as 28 middlemen. They have plenty of motivation: Handling an on-line payment costs only 10¢, roughly one-third that of processing a paper check, according to Atlanta consultant Global Concepts. The result: The number of checks written annually should decline by about one quarter by 2007, to 30 billion, estimates researcher Celent Communications LLC. "This is a transformational moment," says Jonathan Wilk, senior vice-president at Bank of America Corp.

The age-old practice of printing checks and shuttling them around the country in armored cars is in upheaval. No. 1 check printer Deluxe Corp. is closing three of its 13 printing plants and fighting for its margins by pushing higher-priced check designs and fraud-prevention services. One of the Web's unlikeliest victims is AirNet Systems Inc., in Columbus, Ohio, which gets nearly 70% of its $140 million in revenues from flying checks between cities on Learjets. AirNet is shifting its focus to passenger charters and express shipments of donor organs. "We've seen this bogeyman coming," says Wynn D. Peterson, AirNet's vice-president for corporate development.

Fostering Loyalty

And he's coming fast. This year, 65 million U.S. consumers are paying some of their bills online, almost twice as many as last year, according to Gartner. And that's expected to jump to 73 million in four years. This growth is a boon for companies such as Wells Fargo, American Express, and Sprint, which work with online bill payment pioneers CheckFree Corp., edocs Inc., and others. Gartner figures that the average company with 1.9 million customers can cut $26 million in costs per year by persuading customers to receive and pay their bills over the Web.

Cost savings are just the start. Customers are more likely to stay with a bank if they pay bills online there. At Wells Fargo & Co., customers who pay bills online are 75% less likely to leave the bank than other customers. "No doubt, the benefits far outweigh the expenses," says Jim Smith, executive vice-president for consumer Internet products at Wells Fargo.

Even when payments are not made online, paper checks are going digital. Behind this modernization is the Check Clearing for the 21st Century Act, known as Check 21. This law, which goes into effect in October, is expected to kick off a mass adoption of check imaging by putting electronic images of checks on equal legal footing with paper originals for the first time. Even banks that aren't equipped to handle digital checks have to accept printouts of them, known as "substitute checks," as payment. During the past three years, startups Viewpointe Archive Services, Endpoint Exchange, and NetDeposit have rolled out software and services that convert checks into digital files so they can be stored and swapped electronically. Banks could reap big savings. The cost of upgrading to digital check handling will reach $1.9 billion next year, but the industry could save $2.1 billion annually from the shift, estimates Celent.

The changes will allow the banking behemoths to compete more fiercely with community banks. The corner florist and local Wal-Mart typically do business with a nearby bank because they want to get credit for their daily deposits as quickly as possible. With digital check processing, proximity no longer matters. Merchants can choose banks that offer quick and secure processing for the lowest price—wherever they happen to be located.

Shuttered printing plants. Grounded Learjets. Struggling community banks. They're all signs of how the business of checks is changing in the Digital Age.

Questions for Analysis

1. What does Wal-Mart do with checks that customers give the company at checkout registers?

2. What is the cost of handling an online payment compared with that of processing a paper check?

3. What company is an unforeseen victim of the rapid change in the processing of paper checks?

4. In addition to cost savings, what is another advantage for banks when bills are paid online?

5. Why may small, local community banks find it more difficult to compete with large, nationwide banks?

Source: Andrew Park, with Ben Elgin and Timothy J. Mullaney, "Checks Check Out," *BusinessWeek*, May 10, 2004, 83.

---

sufficient funds will be withheld from the drawer's account to pay the amount stated on the check. A prudent person will request a certified check when involved in a business transaction with a stranger rather than accept a personal check.

A certified check, under the UCC, is "a check accepted by the bank on which it is drawn." The UCC places no obligation on a bank to certify a check if it does not want to do so, and the refusal to certify is not a dishonor of the check. When a check is certified, the drawer is discharged regardless of when it was done or who obtained the acceptance. Figure 26-5 illustrates a certified check.

UCC Revised (1990) 3-414(c) (see page 000)

UCC Revised (1990) 3-104(g)(h) (see page 000)

Bank Drafts and Cashier's Checks   A **bank draft**, sometimes called a **teller's check** or *treasurer's check*, is a check drawn by one bank on another bank in which it has funds on deposit in favor of a third person, the payee. Many banks deposit money in banks in other areas for the convenience of depositors who depend upon the transfer of funds when transacting business in distant places. When the buyer is unknown to the seller, such checks are more acceptable than personal checks.

A **cashier's check** is a check drawn by a bank upon itself. The bank, in effect, lends its credit to the purchaser of the check. It is the equivalent of a promissory note of the bank. Courts have held that payment cannot be stopped on a cashier's check because the bank, by issuing it, accepts the check in advance. People who will not accept personal checks will often accept cashier's checks. Such a check may be made payable either to

Figure 26-5   The State Street Bank became primarily liable when it certified this check.

Online banking and bill paying has replaced the need for paper transactions for many customers.

the depositor, who purchases it from the bank, or to the person who is to cash it. If the check is made payable to the depositor, it must be indorsed to the person to whom it is transferred.

Traveler's Checks   A **traveler's check** is similar to a cashier's check, in that the issuing financial institution is both the drawer and the drawee. The purchaser signs the checks in the presence of the issuer when they are purchased. To cash a check, the purchaser writes the name of the payee in the space provided and countersigns it in the payee's presence. Only the purchaser can negotiate traveler's checks, and they are easily replaced by the issuing bank if they are stolen. Traveler's checks are issued in denominations of $10 and up, and the purchaser of the checks ordinarily pays a fixed fee to the issuer.

Money Orders   A **money order** is a type of draft that may be purchased from banks, post offices, telegraph companies, and express companies as a substitute for a check. Instead of being drawn on an individual's account as is a check, however, a money order is drawn on the funds of the organization that issues it. That organization promises payment from its own funds. Purchasers of money orders fill in their name and address and the name of the payee on the instrument. They are given a receipt along with the money order. If the money order is lost and the purchaser has the receipt, it will be replaced if it has not already been cashed. U.S. Postal Service money orders can be purchased for amounts up to $1,000. U.S. International Postal Service Money Orders are often used to send money to foreign countries. Telegraphic money orders may be used to send money quickly. Under the UCC, a *bank* money order is a check, even though it is described on its face as a money order, and payment can be stopped on it like an ordinary check.

Quick Quiz 26-3 True or False?

1. A drawee is required to pay an unaccepted draft when it is presented for payment.

2. A cashier's check is a check drawn by a bank upon itself.

3. A stop-payment order can be placed on a money order.

UCC Revised (1990) 3-104(i) (see page 000)

UCC Revised (1990) 3-104(f) (see page 000)

The Opening Case Revisited, Part I
"The Student Loan"

Payment cannot be stopped on the cashier's check. The girl should have Nardone indorse the check either to her or to her parents. Nardone would not legally be entitled to the proceeds of the cashier's check, because he had already been paid.

26-4 Parties to Negotiable Instruments

The following are parties to negotiable instruments:

LO5

- Maker or comaker
- Drawer
- Issuer
- Drawee
- Payee
- Bearer
- Holder
- Holder in due course
- Indorser
- Indorsee
- Acceptor

A **maker** is a person who signs a note, that is, a person who promises to pay. **Comakers** are two or more people who sign the same note promising to pay. A **drawer** is a person who signs a draft, that is, the one who orders payment. An **issuer** is either a maker or a drawer of an instrument. A **drawee** is a person ordered in a draft to make payment. A **payee** is a person to whom a note or draft is payable.

UCC Revised (1990) 3-103 (see page 000)

A **bearer** is a person who is in possession of a negotiable instrument that is payable to the bearer or to cash. A person who is in possession of an instrument that has been indorsed in blank (by the payee's signature alone) is also a bearer. A **holder** is a person who is in possession of a negotiable instrument that is issued or indorsed to that person's order or to bearer. A *holder in due course* is a holder of a negotiable instrument who is treated as favored and given immunity from certain defenses. A detailed discussion of holders in due course can be found in Chapter 28.

UCC 1-201(5) (see page 000)

UCC Revised (1990) 3-109(a) (see page 000)

UCC 1-201(20) (see page 000)

An **indorser** is a person who indorses a negotiable instrument, in most cases by signing one's name on the back of the paper. The different kinds of indorsements are discussed in Chapter 27.

An **indorsee** is a person to whom a draft, note, or other negotiable instrument is transferred by indorsement. An **acceptor** is a drawee of a draft who has promised to honor the draft as presented by signing it on its face. (See Figure 26-6.)

UCC Revised (1990) 3-204 (see page 000)

Quick Quiz 26-4 True or False?

1. A maker is a person who signs a draft.

2. A holder is a person who is in possession of a negotiable instrument that is issued or indorsed to that person's order or to bearer.

3. A bearer is a person who is in possession of a negotiable instrument that is payable to bearer or to cash.

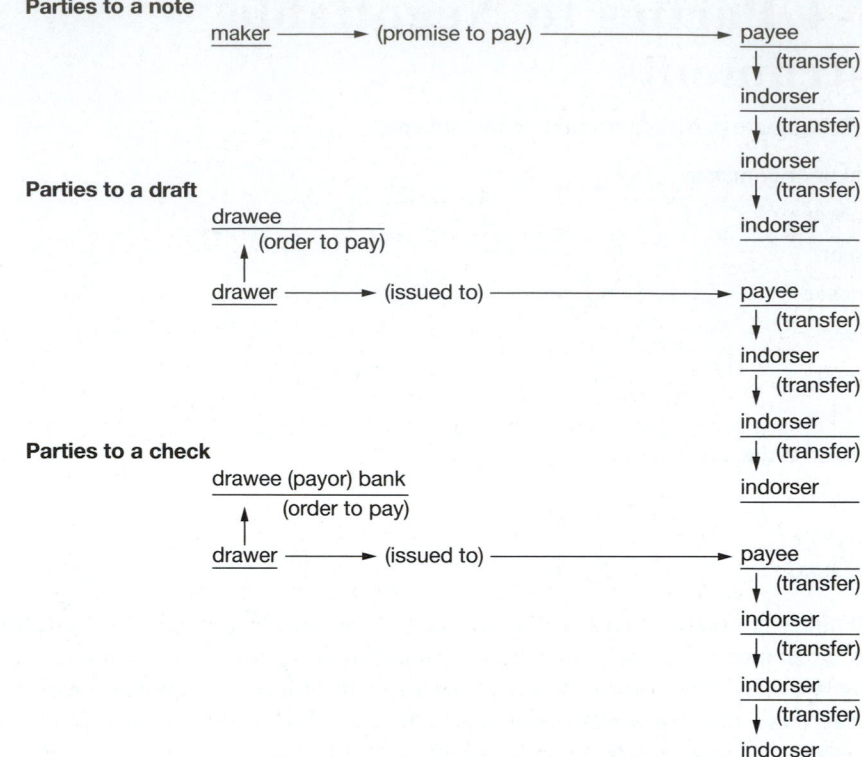

Figure 26-6 This diagram illustrates the relationship of the principal parties to negotiable instruments.

26-5 Requirements of Negotiable Instruments

To be negotiable, instruments must:

- Be in writing
- Be signed by the maker or drawer
- Contain an unconditional promise or order to pay
- Be made out for a fixed amount of money
- Be payable on demand or at a definite time
- Except for checks, be payable to order or to bearer

UCC Revised (1990) 3-104(a) (see page 000)

As will be discussed in Chapter 27, instruments that do not meet all of these requirements can be transferred to others by assignment. They cannot, however, be transferred by negotiation.

Written Instrument

A negotiable instrument must be in writing (see Figure 26-7), which includes printing, typewriting, pen or pencil writing, or any other tangible form of writing. A negotiable instrument written in pencil is, however, an invitation to alteration by forgery. If forgery should happen, the person who drew the instrument would be responsible for any loss caused by the negligent drawing of the instrument.

UCC 1-201(46) (see page 000)

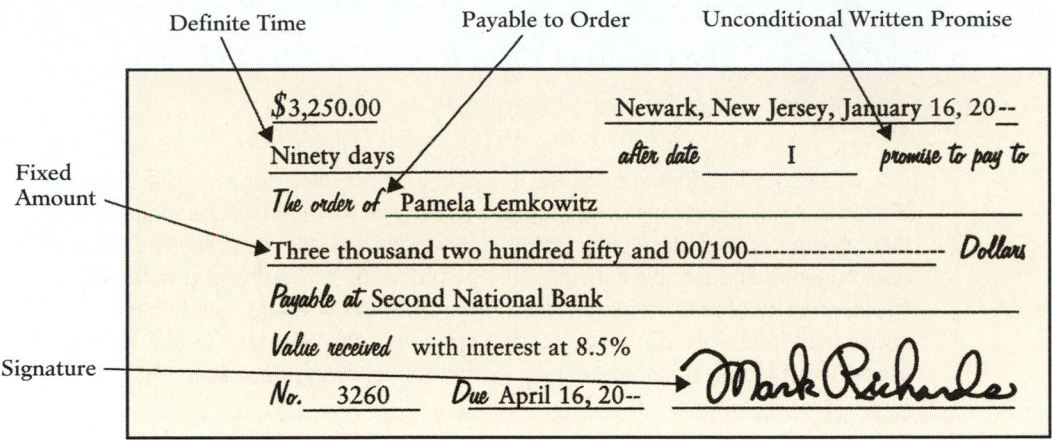

Figure 26-7 The requirements of negotiability are indicated on this ninety-day note.

Signature of Maker or Drawer

To be negotiable, an instrument must be signed by the maker or drawer. Any writing, mark, or symbol is accepted as a signature as long as it is the writer's intent to be a signature. It may be handwritten, typewritten, printed, or produced by a machine.

A signature may be made by an agent (one who represents and acts for another) or other representative. No particular form of appointment is necessary to establish such authority. Agents who sign their own names to an instrument are personally obligated if the instrument neither names the person represented nor shows that the agent signed in a representative capacity. The signature may appear in the body of the instrument as well as at the end.

UCC Revised (1990) 3-401(a)(b) (see page 000)

UCC Revised (1990) 3-402 (see page 000)

Unconditional Promise or Order to Pay

To be negotiable, an instrument must contain no conditions that might in any way affect its payment. Statements requiring that certain things be done or that specific events take place prior to payment make the instrument a simple contract rather than negotiable paper.

UCC Revised (1990) 3-104(a) (see page 909)

> ## EXAMPLE 26-3:   Conditional Note
>
> Chung signed the following note to the Chu-Tai Appliance Co.: "I promise to pay to the order of Chu-Tai Appliance Co. $550 sixty days after the delivery of my new refrigerator." This instrument is not negotiable because it is conditional upon the delivery of the refrigerator.

An instrument is conditional, and thus not negotiable, if it states that it is subject to any other agreement. The same is true if an instrument states that it is to be paid only out of a particular fund. This latter rule does not apply to instruments issued by government agencies. An instrument may state that it "arises out of" another agreement without being conditional. Similarly, a negotiable instrument may indicate a particular account that is to be charged.

In addition to being unconditional, a negotiable instrument must contain a promise to pay (as in a note) or an order to pay (as in a draft). A writing that says "Due Karen Osgood $600" or "IOU $600" is not negotiable because it is neither a promise nor an order to pay.

UCC Revised (1990) 3-106(b) (see page 000)

UCC Revised (1990) 3-104(a) (see page 000)

The Opening Case Revisited, Part II
"The Student Loan"

The IOU is not negotiable because it is neither a promise nor an order to pay. The note is not negotiable because it is conditional. Payment will be made only if the income tax refund is a sufficient amount and is actually received. The note could be made negotiable if it were changed to read, "to be charged to the proceeds of an income tax refund." This wording would not affect negotiability, because the friend's general credit is relied upon, and the reference to the income tax refund is simply a record-keeping instruction following payment.

Fixed Amount of Money

UCC 1-201(24) (see page 000)

UCC Revised (1990) 3-107 (see page 000)

A negotiable instrument must be payable in a fixed amount or sum certain of money. This stipulation means an amount of money that is clearly known. *Money* is defined as a medium of exchange adopted by a domestic or foreign government as part of its currency. Thus, a fixed amount of money need not be money of the United States.

EXAMPLE 26-4:   Foreign Money

In exchange for a commissioned painting, Emil Hauser of Stuttgart, Germany, sent a note to Ann Maggio, of New York City, which read, "Ninety days after date, I promise to pay to the order of Ann Maggio 5,000 euros (signed) Emil Hauser." The note was negotiable. On the due date, it would probably be paid in American dollars, according to the exchange rate of euros and dollars as of the date of payment.

Payable on Demand or at a Definite Time

Negotiable instruments must be made payable on demand or at a definite time. This requirement makes it possible to determine when the debtor or promisor can be compelled to pay. Without this information, the present value of an instrument cannot be determined.

Demand Paper   An instrument is payable *on demand* when it so states or when it is payable "on sight" or "on presentation." The key characteristic of demand instruments is that the holder can require payment at any time by making the demand upon the person who is obligated to pay.

UCC Revised (1990) 3-108(a) (see page 000)

UCC Revised (1990) 3-108(b) (see page 000)

Definite-Time Paper   Certainty as to the time of payment of an instrument is satisfied if it is payable on or before a stated date. Instruments payable at a fixed period after a stated date or at a fixed period after sight are also considered payable at a definite time. In each instance, a simple mathematical calculation makes the maturity date certain. The expressions "one year after date" and "thirty days after sight" are definite as to time. An undated instrument payable sixty days after date is negotiable as a demand paper.

A promise to pay only upon an act or event, the time of whose occurrence is uncertain, is not payable at a definite time. Thus, an instrument payable when a person marries, reaches a certain age, or graduates from college or one payable within a specific period of time after a named person's death is not negotiable.

Payable to Order or to Bearer

Negotiable instruments, except for checks, must be payable to order or to bearer. The terms *to the order of* and *to bearer* are called words of negotiability. Article 3 of the UCC was revised in 1990 to allow checks (but not other instruments) that are not payable to order or to bearer to be negotiable. Thus, a check, but no other instrument, payable "to Mary Harris" is negotiable in all states except New York and South Carolina, which have not adopted the revised Article 3.

Payable to Order An instrument is payable to order when it states that it is payable to the order of any person with reasonable certainty. The maker or drawer may state "Pay to the order of Mary Doe," "Pay to Mary Doe or order," or "Pay to Mary Doe or her assigns." An instrument may be payable to the order of the maker or drawer; the drawee; a payee who is not the maker, drawer, or drawee; two or more payees; an estate, trust, or fund; an office or officer by title; or a partnership or an unincorporated association.

Payable to Bearer An instrument is payable to bearer when it states that it is payable to bearer or the order of bearer, a specified person or bearer, cash or the order of cash, or any other indication that does not designate a specific payee. An instrument is payable to bearer when it does not state a payee. An instrument made payable to both, such as "Pay to the order of Anthony Andrews or bearer," is payable to order unless the word "bearer" is handwritten or typewritten.

UCC Revised (1990) 3-104(c) (see page 000)

UCC Revised (1990) 3-109(b) (see page 000)

UCC Revised (1990) 3-109(a) (see page 000)

EXAMPLE 26-5:   Not Payable to Order or Bearer

Joseph Andrews signed a promissory note that stated, "I promise to pay Ray Brown" a certain amount of money. The note was not negotiable because it was not payable to order or to bearer. The person to whom the note was transferred by Brown was not entitled to the special protection that would have been available had the note been negotiable.

Dates and Controlling Words

The omission of the date does not affect the negotiability of an instrument. When the date is omitted, the date on which the instrument is received is considered to be the date of issue. An instrument may be predated or postdated without affecting its negotiability. Handwritten terms control typewritten and printed terms, and typewritten terms control printed terms. Words control figures, except when words are ambiguous (capable of being understood in more than one way). The numbering of, or the failure to number, an instrument does not affect its negotiability.

UCC Revised (1990) 3-113 (see page 000)

Quick Quiz 26-5 True or False?

1. Instruments that do not meet all of the requirements of negotiability are void.

2. A signed writing that reads "I promise to pay to John Gore $500" is negotiable.

3. A signed writing that reads "Pay to the order of Janet Giron $2,000 when she graduates from college" is negotiable.

Summary

26.1 The purpose of negotiable instruments is to allow people to transact business without carrying around large sums of money and to allow them to borrow money more easily. Computer and electronic technology is now being used as a substitute for checks and other paper transactions.

26.2 A note is a written promise by one party to pay money to another party. A certificate of deposit is the acknowledgment by a bank of the receipt of money and a promise to pay the money back on the due date, usually with interest.

26.3 A draft is an instrument by which the party creating it orders another party to pay money to a third party. A check is a draft drawn on a bank and payable on demand.

26.4 The parties to a draft are the drawer, drawee, and payee. The parties to a note are the maker and payee.

A bearer is a person who is in possession of a negotiable instrument that is payable to the bearer or to cash. A holder is a person who is in possession of an instrument that is issued or indorsed to that person's order or to the bearer. A holder in due course is a holder of a negotiable instrument who is treated as favored and given immunity from certain defenses. An indorser is a person who indorses a negotiable instrument. An indorsee is a person to whom an instrument is transferred by indorsement. An acceptor is a drawee of a draft who has promised to honor the draft by signing it on its face.

26.5 To be negotiable, an instrument must be in writing and have the signature of the maker or drawer, an unconditional promise or order to pay, for a fixed amount of money, payable on demand or at a definite time, and payable to order (except checks) or to bearer. Predating, postdating, or the omission of the date do not affect the negotiability of an instrument. Words control figures, except when words are ambiguous.

Key Terms

acceptance, 541
acceptor, 547
bank draft, 545
bearer, 547
bill of exchange, 541
cashier's check, 545
certificate of deposit (CD), 540
certified check, 543
check, 542
comakers, 547
demand note, 540

domestic bill of exchange, 541
draft, 541
drawee, 547
drawer, 547
foreign draft, 541
holder, 547
indorsee, 547
indorser, 547
installment note, 540
international bill of exchange, 541

issuer, 547
maker, 547
money order, 546
negotiable instrument, 539
note, 540
payee, 547
sight draft, 541
teller's check, 545
time draft, 541
trade acceptance, 541
traveler's check, 546

Questions for Review and Discussion

1. What is the purpose of negotiable instruments?
2. What are the two kinds of negotiable instruments that contain a promise to pay money?
3. What are the two kinds of negotiable instruments that contain an order to pay money?
4. Who are the parties to a note? Who are the parties to a draft?
5. How do the following notes differ from one another: demand note, time note, and installment note?
6. When is a drawee liable on a draft?

7. What form must be used to write a check?

8. How does a bank draft differ from a cashier's check?

9. What is the obligation of a bank to certify a check?

10. What is the difference between a bearer of a negotiable instrument and a holder?

Investigating the Internet

Reread the Business Law in the News article "Checks Check Out." Then go on the Internet, search for "Online Banking" or "Internet Banking," and look for tips about safe banking on the Internet. Write a report on your findings.

Cases for Analysis

1. Haas deposited two checks totaling $42,000 into his account at the Meridian Bank and, at the same time, purchased a $35,000 money order. He then went to the Trump Plaza and Casino, where he received cash for the money order for gambling purposes. The next day, the two checks were returned to Meridian Bank unpaid with a notation "account closed." The bank put a stop-payment order on the money order and refused to pay it when it was presented by Trump Plaza for payment. Trump argued that payment could not be stopped on a money order. Do you agree with Trump? Why or why not? *Trump Plaza Associates v. Haas,* 692 A. 2d 86 (NJ).

2. Gail Sak wanted to give her niece, Kim Ryan, a gift of money for her twenty-first birthday, which was two weeks away. Because she was leaving for a trip to Europe the next day, Sak gave Ryan a check dated that day reading, "Pay to the order of Kim Ryan when she reaches the age of twenty-one (signed) Gail Sak." Was the check negotiable? Why or why not?

3. In exchange for legal services rendered to her by the law firm of Westmoreland, Hall, and Bryan, Barbara Hall wrote the following letter: "I agree to pay to your firm as attorney's fees for representing me in obtaining property settlement agreement and tax advice, the sum of $2,760, payable at the rate of $230 per month for twelve (12) months beginning January 1, 1970. Very truly yours, Barbara Hall Hodge." Was the letter a negotiable instrument? Give the reason for your answer. *Hall v. Westmoreland, Hall & Bryan,* 182 S.E.2d 539 (GA).

4. Barton signed a promissory note promising to pay to the order of Scott Hudgens Realty & Mortgage, Inc., the sum of $3,000. The note stated, "This amount is due and payable upon evidence of an acceptable permanent loan … and upon acceptance of the loan commitment." Was the note negotiable? Why or why not? *Barton v. Scott Hudgens Realty & Mortg.,* 222 S.E.2d 126 (GA).

5. Melanie E. Regan wrote the following words on a sheet of notebook paper in her own handwriting: "Twenty years from date, I, Melanie E. Regan promise to pay to the order of Ryan M. Brown $10,000 without interest." She did not sign the paper at the end. Is the instrument negotiable? Why or why not?

6. In 1969, Gentilotti wrote a check payable to the order of his five-year-old son for $20,000. The check was postdated to 1984. It was delivered to the child's mother, who kept it for the child. The check was indorsed by the father, as follows: "For Edward Joseph Smith Gentilotti / My Son / If I should pass away / The amount of $20,000.00 dollars / Shall be taken from / My Estate at death. / S. Gentilotti 11-25-69." Gentilotti died in 1973. Was the check negotiable? Explain. *Smith v. Gentilotti* 359 N.E.2d 953 (MA).

7. Joshua Nichols drew the following draft on his Uncle David Nichols and gave it to Natalie Brown in payment for a used car: "To David Nichols: On demand, pay to the order of Natalie Brown $7,000 (signed) Joshua Nichols." When Brown presented the draft to David Nichols for payment, the latter refused to pay it, arguing that the UCC did not require him to do so. Is Nichols correct? Why or why not?

8. James Ahmed gave William Cooper a draft that read, "To Esther Blum: Ninety days from date, pay to the order of William Cooper $5,000 (signed) James Ahmed." Cooper telephoned Blum to see if she would honor the draft. Blum said that she would and, to show her good faith, wrote Cooper a letter saying that she would honor the draft. Was the draft accepted by Blum? Explain.

9. Norek reported to his insurance company that his car had been stolen. The insurance company delivered to Norek a draft drawn on itself and payable through the First Pennsylvania Bank in the amount of $5,878.63. The draft was payable to Norek and to General Motors Acceptance Corporation (GMAC), which held a security interest on the car. Upon receiving the draft, GMAC released its lien on the vehicle and gave Norek the title certificate. Soon thereafter, it was discovered that the automobile had not been stolen and that Norek's claim was fraudulent. The insurance company stopped payment on the draft. GMAC claims that the draft was a check. Do you agree with GMAC? Why or why not? *Gen. Motors Accept. v. Gen. Acc. Fire & Life,* 415 N.Y.S.2d 536 (NY).

10. Duester bought a combine and grain platform on credit. He could not pay the amount owed when it became due. To avoid having the combine repossessed, Duester went to the bank for a cashier's check. An authorized teller made out a check payable to John Deere Company in the amount of $8,455.84 and signed it. Because the bank had recently established a policy requiring two signatures on a cashier's check, the teller excused herself to request a loan officer to come to the counter to sign the check. When the teller returned with the loan officer, Duester and the check were not there. Outside the bank, Duester gave the check to an agent of the John Deere Company who had come to repossess the equipment. When the check was presented for payment, however, the bank refused to pay it. Must the bank pay the cashier's check? Explain. *John Deere Co. v. Boelus State Bank,* 448 N.W.2d 163 (NE).

Quick Quiz Answers

26-1	26-2	26-3	26-4	26-5
1. T	1. T	1. F	1. F	1. F
2. F	2. F	2. T	2. T	2. F
3. T	3. T	3. T	3. T	3. F

Chapter 27

Transferring Negotiable Instruments

The Opening Case
"A Watertight Case"

Manzi, who was 17 years old, bought a second-hand boat from Lucas for $550, paying for it by personal check. The transaction took place late on Friday afternoon, so Lucas kept the check over the weekend. Meanwhile, the boat had developed a leak and sunk while Manzi was trying it out. Fortunately, Manzi swam safely to shore. He telephoned his bank early Monday morning and stopped payment on the check. That afternoon, Lucas indorsed the instrument and cashed it at her bank, which was not the bank on which it was drawn. The check was returned to the bank that had cashed it, marked "payment stopped."

Opening Case Questions

1. Can that bank recover its money from Manzi?

2. Can that bank recover its money from Lucas?

LO Learning Objectives

1. Differentiate between an assignment and a negotiation of an instrument.
2. Explain why the concept of negotiability is one of the most important features of negotiable instruments.
3. Name and describe four kinds of indorsements.
4. Identify the implied warranties that are made when people indorse negotiable instruments.
5. Explain the contract that is made when people indorse negotiable instruments.
6. Determine the indorsement required on instruments with more than one payee.
7. Describe the legal effect of a forged or unauthorized indorsement, and recognize three exceptions to the unauthorized indorsement rule.

27-1 Transferring Instruments

When an instrument is first delivered by the maker or drawer for the purpose of giving rights to any person, it is said to be *issued*. When the person to whom it is issued delivers it to a third party, it is *transferred*. Instruments can be transferred by assignment or by negotiation.

Assignment

An **assignment** is the transfer of a contract right from one person to another. Negotiable instruments are assigned either when a person whose indorsement is required on an instrument transfers it without indorsing it or when it is transferred to another person and does not meet the requirements of negotiability. In all such transfers, the transferee has only the rights of an assignee and is subject to all defenses existing against the assignor (see Chapter 14).

UCC Revised (1990) 3-105 (see page 1000) and 3-203 (see page 1004)

An assignment of negotiable instruments also occurs by operation of law when the holder of an instrument dies or becomes bankrupt. In such cases, title to the instrument vests in the personal representative of the estate or the trustee in bankruptcy.

Negotiation

A **negotiation** is the transfer of an instrument in such form that the transferee becomes a *holder* (a person in possession of an instrument issued or indorsed to that person, to that person's order, to bearer, or in blank). In contrast to an assignment, a negotiation gives greater rights to transferees.

UCC Revised (1990) 3-201 (see page 1003)

If an instrument is payable to order, such as "pay to the order of," it is known as **order paper**. To be negotiated, order paper must be indorsed by the payee and delivered to the party to whom it is transferred. If an instrument is payable to bearer or cash, it is called **bearer paper** and may be negotiated by delivery alone, without an indorsement. When order paper is indorsed with a blank indorsement, it is turned into bearer paper and may be further negotiated by delivery alone.

EXAMPLE 27-1:   Assignment

Albright sold 100 cases of beans to Brodie for $12 a case. In exchange, Brodie gave Albright a promissory note, promising to pay the $1,200 in six months at 6 percent per annum interest. The note was not negotiable, however, because it read, "I promise to pay to Albright" instead of "I promise to pay to the order of Albright." To obtain needed cash, Albright transferred the note to her bank. This transfer was an assignment rather than a negotiation, because the note did not contain the proper words of negotiability discussed in Chapter 26. Brodie refused to pay the bank the amount due on maturity because the beans he had received from Albright were defective. They were not merchantable. Because the transfer of the note was an assignment rather than a negotiation, the bank was subject to the same defense as Albright and could not enforce payment of the note. Its only recourse was against Albright. Had the note been negotiable, the bank could have received greater rights than its transferor had. It could have forced Brodie to pay the note, even though Brodie received bad beans.

Quick Quiz 27-1 True or False?

1. Instruments can be transferred only by negotiation.

2. A negotiation of an instrument gives greater rights to transferees than an assignment.

3. Osgood gave Rowe a check that read "Pay to the order of bearer $100." Rowe could negotiate the check without indorsing it.

27-2 The Concept of Negotiability

The concept of negotiability is one of the most important features of negotiable instruments. Largely because of this feature, negotiable instruments are highly trusted and used daily by millions of people. When an instrument is transferred by negotiation, the person receiving the instrument is provided with more protection than was available to the person from whom it was received. The person receiving the instrument is able, in many instances, to recover money on the instrument even when the person from whom the instrument was received could not have done so.

Instruments that do not meet all of the requirements of negotiability cannot be negotiated. However, they can be transferred by assignment, which is governed by the ordinary principles of contract law. People who receive instruments by assignment are not given the special protection provided those who receive instruments by negotiation, because they cannot be *holders in due course*, as explained in Chapter 28.

BusinessWeek Business Law in the News

There Goes the Cheap Money

Eastman Chemical Co. may not be a household name, but as the credit flowed freely on Wall Street, the Kingsport (Tenn.) maker of specialty chemicals was able to borrow for a song. Last May, when the Eastman Kodak Co. spin-off acquired a rival's resins business, the company covered the $244 million purchase mostly by issuing commercial paper—30-day, renewable notes with a mere 2.5% interest rate. And although Eastman originally planned to replace the paper with longer-term debt, management became loath to give up that great rate. Instead, it just rolled the notes over every month.

But with the spate of big-name bankruptcies and accounting scandals sending tremors through the credit markets, Eastman's chief financial officer, Albert J. Wargo, moved recently to change that. He traded in $400 million of Eastman's short-term borrowing for longer-term notes costing 7%. While the move will cut a hefty $18 million out of Eastman's

pretax profits this year, Wargo takes solace that rates remain historically low. "The short-term markets are not as stable as they used to be," he sighs. "I'm willing to suffer a little pain right now because at some point in the future, rates will be higher."

Wargo has plenty of company. Since the fall, Moody's Investors Service, Standard & Poor's, and other rating agencies have applied tougher scrutiny to corporate balance sheets—effectively pushing many borrowers out of the volatile short-term lending market. At the same time, the prospect of economic recovery has convinced most execs that a rise in interest rates is inevitable. The combination has sent chief financial officers throughout Corporate America scrambling to shore up balance sheets with more stable debt and lock in today's low rates while they can. The latest to go long: AOL Time Warner Inc., which on Apr. 3 sold $6 billion in bonds, largely to reduce its short-term obligations.

The massive shift has sent the value of outstanding commercial paper of nonfinancial companies in the U.S. falling sharply: From a peak of $315 billion in November, 2000, it has dropped to some $172 billion today. Analysts expect it could contract further in coming months. And another corporate blowup could cause the commercial paper market to dry up even more. "If the commercial paper market were to shut down, AOL and lots of other companies could have real problems," says Philip Olesen, a fixed-income analyst at UBS Warburg.

The trouble is, bolstering the balance sheet with more stable debt comes at a considerable expense. With the equity markets largely closed to issuers and with bankers tightening credit as well, many borrowers are issuing long-term bonds at rates that are double, or even triple, what they were paying on the short end. Louise Purtle, head of U.S. credit strategy at Credit-Sights, a New York research firm, estimates that General Electric Capital Corp.'s recent sale of $11 billion of longer-term bonds in order to begin scaling back its massive $100 billion exposure to the commercial paper market will raise its borrowing costs by as much as $100 million this year alone. Analysts estimate that similar shifts on the part of AOL and Verizon Communications could raise those companies' borrowing costs by $300 million and $100 million, respectively. That could trim about 3% off of AOL's earnings this year and trim Verizon's by 1%.

Add that up for every company making the switch, and the collective toll on corporate profits—and the U.S. economy—could be huge. David Wyss, chief economist at S&P, estimates that the shift out of commercial paper and into bonds could raise Corporate America's borrowing costs overall by as much as $30 billion this year.

While that's just a fraction of the $752 billion in pretax profits that Corporate America earned last year, it's still enough to shave as much as two-tenths of a percentage point off of gross domestic product this year. And that means plenty of money that might otherwise have gone into capital spending, new product development, or marketing will be diverted to debt payments. "It's just one more nick against the recovery," says Wyss.

Of course, the sudden rush into bonds illustrates just how many companies let their balance sheets get out of whack in the 1990s. Many companies quietly used commercial paper to slash borrowing costs and bolster sagging profits. Indeed, new commercial paper borrowing equaled roughly 18% of nonfinancial corporate long-term borrowing in 2000, about twice the level of 1995.

There's a simple reason why. With short maturities—from 1 to 270 days—commercial paper was originally intended to help cover short-term funding needs such as payrolls. But when the annualized interest cost for commercial paper fell as low as 1.75% in the late 1990s, many companies began using it to finance longer-term projects such as constructing new factories.

But while it's cheap, commercial paper is an inherently risky form of borrowing. If questions of financial health arise, a company may find itself unable to roll over short-term notes. The reason: Securities & Exchange Commission regulations require that money-market funds—the main buyers of commercial paper—keep at least 95% of their assets in the highest-grade commercial paper. As a result, companies such as Tyco International Ltd. and Kmart Corp. were suddenly shut out of the commercial paper market when they were downgraded by the rating agencies. The ensuing liquidity squeeze was a big reason the latter was forced to file for Chapter 11 on Jan. 22. "Investors in commercial paper have zero tolerance for credit risk," says Jack Malvey, chief global fixed-income strategist at Lehman Brothers Inc.

Despite the higher costs, many managements say that there is a bright side to debt rejiggering. Thanks to 11 Federal Reserve rate cuts last year, investment-grade companies can still borrow at just above 6%—a fraction of the 11% rate those same borrowers would have paid coming out of the 1991 recession. To every debt cloud, a silver lining.

Questions for Analysis

1. Where did Eastman Chemical Co. get the $244 million to buy a rival's resin business?

2. Why do you think that Eastman's chief financial officer traded $400 million of Eastman's short-term borrowing for longer-term notes?

3. What did the sudden rush to bonds illustrate?

4. Why did new commercial borrowing increase so much between 1995 and 2000?

5. Why is commercial paper an inherently risky form of borrowing?

Source: Dean Foust and Margaret Popper, with Amy Barrett, Peter Elstrom, and bureau reports, "There Goes Cheap Money," *BusinessWeek*, April 15, 2002, 44.

The payee is never guaranteed to receive payment on a check, so some small businesses choose not to accept personal checks.

27-3 Negotiation by Indorsement

An instrument is indorsed when the holder signs it, thereby indicating the intent to transfer ownership to another. Indorsements may be written in ink, typewritten, or stamped with a rubber stamp. They may be written on a separate paper (rider, or *allonge*), as long as the separate paper is so firmly affixed to the instrument that it becomes part of it. Although the UCC does not require indorsements to be on any particular side of the paper, for convenience, they are usually placed on the back of the instrument. Anyone who gives value for an instrument has the right to have the unqualified indorsement of the person who transferred it, unless it is payable to bearer.

Regulation CC, issued by the Federal Reserve Board under the Competitive Banking Act, has established standards for check indorsements (Figure 27-1). Under the regulation, the back of a check is divided into specific sections designed to protect the indorsement of the depository

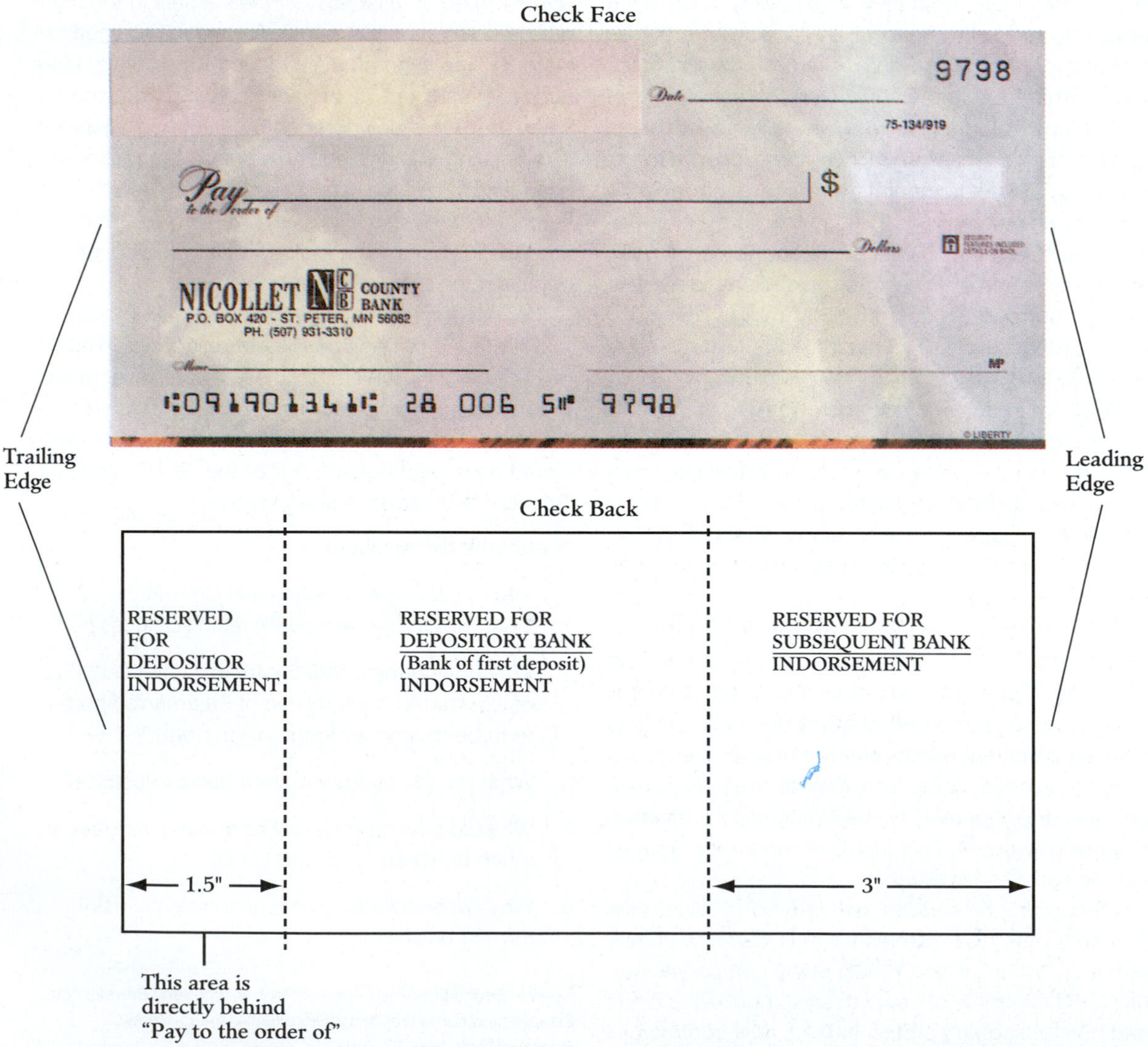

Figure 27-1 Regulation CC has issued check indorsement standards.

bank (the bank of first deposit). The first one-and-one-half inches from the trailing edge of the check is reserved for the payee's indorsement.

UCC Revised (1990) 3-204(a) (see page 1004)

Negotiation is effective to transfer an instrument, even when it is transferred by a minor, a corporation exceeding its powers, or any other person without capacity; obtained by fraud, duress, or mistake of any kind; part of an illegal transaction; or made in breach of duty. Any such negotiations, however, may be rescinded except as against a holder in due course (defined and explained in Chapter 28), who is given special protection.

UCC Revised (1990) 3-202(a) (see page 1003)

There are four commonly used types of indorsements: blank indorsements, special indorsements, restrictive indorsements, and qualified indorsements.

Blank Indorsements

A **blank indorsement** consists of the signature alone written on the instrument. No particular indorsee (person to whom an instrument is indorsed) is named. When an instrument is indorsed in blank, it becomes payable to the bearer and may be transferred by delivery alone. If the instrument is lost or stolen and gets into the hands of another holder, the new holder can recover its face value by delivery alone. For this reason, a blank indorsement should be used only in limited situations, such as at a bank teller's window. A blank indorsement turns order paper into bearer paper and may be transferred by delivery alone.

UCC Revised (1990) 3-205(b) (see page 1004)

EXAMPLE 27-2:   Blank Indorsement

Carol Barcley received her first paycheck from the restaurant where she worked as a part-time hostess. She took the check to the bank, where she indorsed it in blank at the teller's window. This was a proper time and place to use a blank indorsement, because there was no likelihood that the check would get lost or stolen.

When an instrument is made payable to a person under a misspelled name or a name other than that person's own, the payee may indorse in the incorrect name, in the correct name, or in both. Signatures in both names may be required by a person paying or giving value for the instrument.

UCC Revised (1990) 3-204(d) (see page 1004)

Special Indorsements

A **special indorsement** (also called an **indorsement in full**) is made by writing the words *pay to the order of* or *pay to*, followed by the name of the person to whom it is to be transferred (the indorsee) and the signature of the indorser. When indorsed in this manner, the instrument remains an order instrument and must be indorsed by the indorsee before it can be negotiated further.

UCC Revised (1990) 3-205(a) (see page 1004)

A Question of Ethics

As part of its direct-mail advertising, a company included a $100 check payable to the recipient. Printed on the back of the check were these words: "By indorsing this check, the indorsee agrees to purchase. . . ." Is this marketing practice ethical?

EXAMPLE 27-3:   Special Indorsement

Frank Cully withdrew $3,500 from his savings account to buy a car from Glendale Motors, Inc. When he made the withdrawal, Cully received a check from the bank payable to him for $3,500. He took the check to Glendale Motors, indorsed it with a special indorsement, and received title to the car. A special indorsement (indorsement in full) creates order paper, which requires the signature of the indorsee. Because the check could not be legally transferred or negotiated further until Glendale indorsed it, all parties were protected.

INDORSE HERE

Pay to the order of Glendale Motors Frank Culley

DO NOT WRITE, STAMP OR SIGN BELOW THIS LINE
RESERVED FOR FINANCIAL INSTITUTION USE*

UCC Revised (1990)
3-205(c) (see page 1004)

UCC Revised (1990)
3-206(a) (see page 1004)

The holder of an instrument may convert a blank indorsement into a special indorsement by writing the words *pay to the order of a person* or *pay to a person* above the indorser's signature.

Restrictive Indorsements

A **restrictive indorsement** limits the rights of the indorsee in some manner to protect the rights of the indorser. Indorsements for deposit or collection are restrictive indorsements designed to get an instrument into the banking system for the purpose of deposit or collection. When a check is indorsed "for deposit only," as in Figure 27-2, the amount of the instrument is credited to the indorser's account before it is negotiated further. Retail stores often stamp each check "for deposit only" when it is received. This wording provides protection in the event the check is stolen. Checks mailed to the bank for deposit should always be indorsed in this way.

An indorsement that purports to prohibit further transfer, such as "pay Olga Peterson only," may be further negotiated after the directions in the indorsement are carried out. Thus, after Olga Peterson is paid, any holder of the instrument may continue to negotiate it. A restrictive indorsement does not prevent further transfer or negotiation of the instrument.

Figure 27-2 A restrictive indorsement limits the subsequent use of the instrument.

A **conditional indorsement**, a type of restrictive indorsement, purports to make the rights of the indorsee subject to the happening of a certain event or condition. A person paying the instrument or taking it for value, however, may disregard the condition.

UCC Revised (1990) 3-206(b) (see page 1004)

EXAMPLE 27-4:   Conditional Indorsement

Gallo wished to transfer a dividend check that he received to his grandson, James Ingram, as a birthday gift (see the indorsement in the illustration). Because Gallo did not want Ingram to cash the check before his eighteenth birthday, he issued a conditional indorsement. However, under the UCC, a bank or anyone else who gives Ingram money or value for the check will not be affected by the condition.

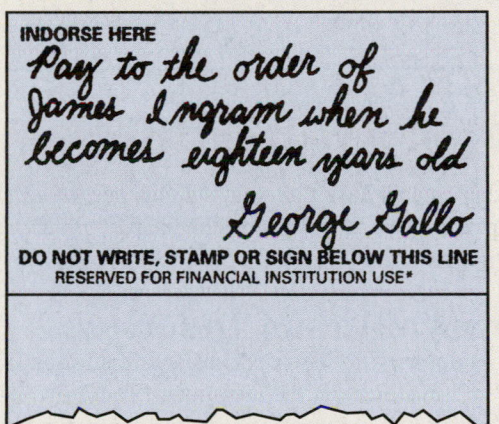

Qualified Indorsements

A **qualified indorsement** is one in which words have been added to the signature that limit the liability of the indorser. By adding the words *without recourse* to the indorsement, the indorser is not liable in the event the instrument is dishonored, that is, not paid by the maker or drawer.

UCC Revised (1990) 3-415(b) (see page 1012)

EXAMPLE 27-5:   Qualified Indorsement

A $25,000 check was made payable to Attorney Samuel Brock in payment of a client's claim. Brock indorsed the check to the client, George Rose, "without recourse." By using this indorsement, Brock would not be responsible for payment if the check failed to clear, because a qualified indorsement limits the contractual liability of the indorser.

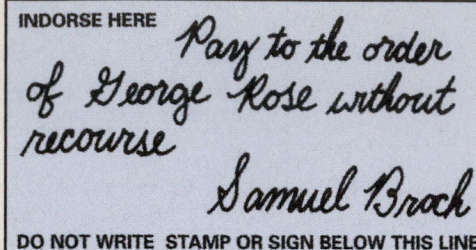

INDORSE HERE

Pay to the order of George Rose without recourse

Samuel Brock

DO NOT WRITE STAMP OR SIGN BELOW THIS LINE
RESERVED FOR FINANCIAL INSTITUTION USE*

Quick Quiz 27-2 and 27-3 True or False?

1. A blank indorsement should be used only in limited situations, such as a bank teller's window.

2. A special indorsement creates bearer paper and can be negotiated without further indorsement.

3. Checks mailed to the bank for deposit should always be indorsed with a blank indorsement.

27-4 Obligations of Indorsers

Indorsements have threefold significance. In addition to being necessary to negotiate order paper, they create obligations on the part of the indorser. These obligations come in the form of implied warranties and a contractual promise to pay subsequent holders of the instrument.

LO4

UCC Revised (1990)
3-416 (see page 1013)

Warranties of Indorsers

An indorser who receives consideration for an instrument makes five warranties to subsequent transferees of the instrument. These five warranties are as follows.

First, the indorser is entitled to enforce the instrument. This warranty gives assurances to subsequent holders that the person indorsing it did not steal it or come into possession of it in an unlawful manner.

EXAMPLE 27-6:   Indorser's Warranty

State National Bank accepted a check from Lawless for deposit to her account. The check contained a blank indorsement by Anthony Fiore, in addition to Lawless's indorsement. The bank later discovered that Lawless had found the check in a supermarket. A stop payment order had been issued by the real owner, Anthony Fiore. Lawless, by her indorsement, had warranted that she was the true owner of the check. She would be held liable on this warranty for any loss suffered by the bank.

Second, the indorser warrants that all signatures are authentic and authorized.

EXAMPLE 27-7:   Forged Indorsement

A check made payable to Jones was indorsed by his stepmother, who forged his signature and cashed the check at the Commonwealth Bank & Trust Co. The bank had a cause of action for the recovery of the money from Jones's stepmother on the grounds of breach of the warranty that all signatures are authentic and authorized.

Third, the next warranty is that the instrument has not been altered. The indorser warrants that there has been no alteration or other irregularity.

EXAMPLE 27-8:   Check Alteration

Cushing wrote a check payable to the order of Daly for $5 and delivered it to Daly. Daly altered the check to read $500, indorsed it, and cashed it at a bank. Cushing would have to pay only the original amount of the check ($5), unless it could be shown that she was negligent in writing it so that it could be easily altered. The bank's recourse would be against Daly for breach of this warranty.

Fourth, the instrument is not subject to a defense of any party that can be asserted against the indorser.

EXAMPLE 27-9:   Not Subject to Defenses

In *The Opening Case* of this chapter, Manzi cannot be held responsible for paying the check because he was a minor when he issued the check. Lucas, however, by indorsing the check, warranted that she is not subject to Manzi's defense of minority.

A qualified indorser (one who uses the words *without recourse,* as in Example 27-5) does not make this warranty. Such an indorsement warrants only that the indorser has no knowledge of a defense that may be used.

Fifth, the last warranty provides that the indorser has no knowledge of the bankruptcy of the maker, acceptor, or drawer.

The Opening Case Revisited
"A Watertight Case"

The bank cannot recover the $650 from Manzi because he was a minor when he entered into the contract. He could have used the defense of minority against anyone who sued him on the contract. The bank, however, can recover the $650 from Lucas. By indorsing the check, she impliedly warranted that there were no defenses that she could have used to defend herself, including Manzi's defense of minority.

EXAMPLE 27-10:   No Knowledge of Bankruptcy

Julien Rodriguez indorsed his paycheck and deposited it in his account at a local bank. Unbeknownst to Rodriguez, his company had filed for Chapter 11 bankruptcy on the day the paychecks were issued. Had Rodriguez been aware of the bankruptcy, he would have breached the warranty that he made when he indorsed the check and could have been held liable for any losses suffered by the bank because of it.

Contract of Indorsers

Unless an indorsement states otherwise (e.g., by words such as *without recourse*), every indorser agrees to pay any subsequent holder the face amount of the instrument if it is **dishonored** (not paid by the maker or drawee). To enforce this obligation, it is necessary for the holder to do two things. The holder of an instrument must first present it for payment to the maker or drawee when it is due. If that person refuses to pay the instrument, it is said to be dishonored. The holder then must notify the indorser or indorsers of the dishonor. If the holder is a bank, notice must be given by midnight of the next banking day. Holders other than banks must give notice within 30 days after the dishonor. Failure by the holder to make presentment and give timely notice of dishonor to an indorser has the effect of discharging that indorser from liability on the contract to pay subsequent holders of the instrument.

UCC Revised (1990) 3-415(a) (see page 1012)

UCC Revised (1990) 3-503(c) (see page 1016)

UCC 415(a) (see page 1012)

EXAMPLE 27-11:   Indorser's Obligation

When Ralph Brownlee received his paycheck, he indorsed it in blank and gave it to his mother, Sandra Jones, in payment for room and board. Jones, in turn, indorsed the check and gave it to Robert Allen for work done on her house. Allen indorsed it and asked his sister, Diana Sklar, to drop it off at the Security Loan Company for him on her way to work. Security required Sklar to indorse the check, even though it was applied to her brother's loan. The check bounced, and a substitute check was returned to Security Loan marked "insufficient funds."

INDORSE HERE

Ralph Brownlee
Sandra Jones
Robert Allen

Diana Sklar

DO NOT WRITE STAMP OR SIGN BELOW THIS LINE
RESERVED FOR FINANCIAL INSTITUTION USE*

Security Loan had the right to demand payment from any of the indorsers shown on the back of the check if it gave them proper notice. The obligation of an indorser is owed to a person entitled to enforce the instrument or to a subsequent indorser who paid the instrument.

Quick Quiz 27-4 True or False?

1. Indorsers of negotiable instruments warrant that the maker or drawer is still alive.

2. Indorsers of negotiable instruments warrant that the maker or drawer is a reputable person.

3. Indorsers of negotiable instruments agree to pay any subsequent holder the face amount of the instrument if it is not paid by the maker or drawer.

27-5 Multiple Payees, Missing and Forged Indorsements

If an instrument is payable to either of two payees, as in "pay to the order of Eric Foss *or* Betty Foss," the indorsement of only one of the payees in necessary to negotiate it. However, if an instrument is payable to both of two payees, as in "pay to the order of Eric Foss *and* Betty Foss," the indorsement of both payees is necessary for a proper negotiation.

UCC Revised (1990)
3-110(d) (see page 1002)

UCC 3-116 page 1002

EXAMPLE 27-12: Payee's Indorsement Required

Middle States Leasing Corporation drew a check payable to the order of two payees, Interpace Corporation and United Leasing Services, Inc., in the sum of $150,000. United Leasing Services, Inc., indorsed the check and received the entire proceeds from the drawee bank without the indorsement of Interpace Corporation on the instrument. Because the instrument was not indorsed by both payees, the bank was held responsible to Middle States Leasing Corporation for the entire amount of the check.

A bank that has taken an instrument from a customer to send through the bank collection process may supply any indorsement of the customer that is necessary to title. This rule is designed to speed up bank collections by eliminating the necessity to return to a depositor any items that were not indorsed. Such an indorsement may not be supplied by a bank, however, if the instrument contains the words *payee's indorsement required.*

UCC 4-205

Unauthorized or Forged Indorsements

An unauthorized signature or indorsement is one made without actual, implied, or apparent authority. With three exceptions and unless ratified (approved afterward), an unauthorized or forged signature does not serve as the signature of the person whose name is signed. It has no effect. In addition, when an instrument is paid on a forged indorsement, the tort of

UCC Revised (1990)
3-403(a) (see page 999)

conversion takes place. For example, when a bank pays proceeds to a forger and the payee's wishes are not carried out, the bank is held liable for converting the payee's funds. **Conversion** is the wrongful exercise of dominion and control over another's personal property.

EXAMPLE 27-13:   Unauthorized Indorsement

Seventeen checks payable to the Mott Grain Company, totaling $40,520.93, were deposited to the personal bank account of Baszler, the company's manager. Baszler disappeared with the money but was later found and convicted of embezzlement. Nine of the checks contained restrictive indorsements, requiring them to be deposited in the company's bank account. The remainder of the checks bore blank indorsements, such as "Mott Grain Co./Verson Baszler." Baszler's only authority was to deposit the checks in the Mott Grain Co.'s account. The bank was held liable to the grain company, in conversion, for the amount of all of the checks.

There are three exceptions to the general rule that an unauthorized indorsement has no effect. The exceptions are designed primarily to promote negotiability of negotiable instruments. They are as follows.

UCC Revised (1990)
3-404(a) (see page 1010)

Imposters   An imposter is someone who impersonates another. When an instrument is issued to an imposter on the false belief that the imposter is the payee, the indorsement by any person in the name of the payee is treated as an effective indorsement. This rule places the loss, in such a case, on the one who is in the best position to prevent it—the maker or drawer of the instrument.

EXAMPLE 27-14:   Imposter Rule

Covington was induced in a fraudulent oil-land scheme to issue a cashier's check to an imposter under the false belief that the imposter was a person named Baird. The imposter's indorsement of the name Baird on the check was held by the court to be effective to negotiate the instrument. The bank that paid the check was not held liable in conversion, and the check was considered to be properly negotiated. The indorsement by the imposter was treated as an effective indorsement.

No Interest Intended; Fictitious Payee   When the maker or drawer of an instrument intends the payee to have no interest in the instrument or the payee is a fictitious person, an indorsement by any person in the name of the payee is effective.

UCC Revised (1990)
3-404(b) (see page 1010)

EXAMPLE 27-15:   No Interest Intended

Gordon loaned $5,000 to Wolf, intending Wolf to have the entire interest in the money. He made the check payable jointly, however, to Wolf and Wolf's wife, Norma. When the check was cashed, Norma's indorsement was forged. The court held that the forged indorsement was valid because Gordon did not intend Norma to have any interest in the instrument.

Padded Payrolls   When an agent or employee of the maker or drawer pads the payroll by supplying the employer with fictitious names, an indorsement by any person in the name of each fictitious payee is effective. This rule places the burden of preventing this type of fraud on the party who is in the best position to prevent it—either the drawer (if a draft) or the maker (if a note).

UCC Revised (1990) 3-405 (see page 1010)

EXAMPLE 27-16:   Padded Payroll

Harrison, the payroll clerk for Industries, Inc., made out payroll checks for 10 employees who did not exist and had her employer sign them. She negotiated the 10 checks by indorsing them in the names of the fictitious payees. The indorsements by Harrison were effective. Industries, Inc., not the bank, had the burden of preventing this type of fraud, which it was in a position to avoid. Industries, Inc., would be liable for any losses suffered as a result of the padding of the payroll.

Quick Quiz 27-5   True or False?

1. A check that is payable to "Thomas Scanlon and Jo Dee Scanlon" must be indorsed by both Thomas and Jo Dee to be negotiated.

2. A bank that has taken an instrument from a customer to send through the bank collection process may supply any indorsement of the customer.

3. Without exception, a forged signature does not serve as the signature of the person whose name is signed.

Summary

27.1   Negotiable instruments that do not meet all of the requirements of negotiability cannot be negotiated. They can only be transferred by assignment. People who receive instruments by assignment are not given the special protection provided those who receive instruments by negotiation. To be negotiated, order paper must be indorsed by the payee and delivered. In contrast, bearer paper may be negotiated by delivery alone.

27.2   When an instrument is transferred by negotiation, the person receiving the instrument may obtain more protection than was given to the person from whom it was received.

27.3   When an instrument is indorsed in blank, it becomes bearer paper. When an instrument is indorsed in full, it becomes order paper. A restrictive indorsement limits the subsequent use of an instrument. A qualified indorsement limits the liability of the indorser.

27.4   An indorser who receives consideration for an instrument warrants that he or she has good title to the instrument, all signatures are genuine or authorized, the instrument has not been materially altered, no defense of any party is good against the indorser, and he or she has no knowledge of any insolvency proceedings of the maker, acceptor, or drawer. Unqualified indorsers agree to pay subsequent holders the amount of an instrument if timely presentment is made, if the instrument is dishonored, and if they are given proper notice.

27.5   Instruments payable to one payee *or* another payee require the indorsement of only one of the payees. In contrast, instruments payable to one payee *and* another payee must be indorsed by both payees. A bank taking an instrument for deposit may supply a customer's missing indorsement. With three exceptions and unless ratified, an unauthorized or forged signature does not serve as the signature of the person whose name is signed. A bank commits the tort of conversion when it pays money to a forger. Exceptions occur when an instrument is issued to an imposter, a payee is not intended to have an interest in an instrument, or a payroll is padded with fictitious names.

Key Terms

allonge, 560
assignment, 557
bearer paper, 557
blank indorsement, 561
conditional indorsement, 563

conversion, 568
dishonored, 566
indorsement in full, 561
negotiation, 557
order paper, 557

qualified indorsement, 563
restrictive indorsement, 562
special indorsement, 561

Questions for Review and Discussion

1. What is the difference between an assignment and a negotiation of an instrument?
2. Describe the concept of negotiability. What protection is available in many instances to a transferee of an instrument that has been negotiated?
3. What is the difference between a blank indorsement and a special indorsement?
4. Why should a blank indorsement be used only in limited situations, such as at a bank teller's window?
5. How does a restrictive indorsement differ from a qualified indorsement?

6. What warranties are made by an indorser who receives consideration for an instrument?
7. What contract does an indorser make with subsequent holders of a negotiable instrument?
8. What indorsements are necessary to negotiate an instrument that is payable to one person *and* another person and an instrument that is payable to one person *or* another person?
9. What are the legal consequences that arise when an instrument is paid on a forged indorsement?
10. What are the three exceptions to the general rule that any unauthorized indorsement is not effective?

Investigating the Internet

You have learned from this chapter that, with three exceptions, a forged indorsement, unless ratified, does not serve as the signature of the person whose name is signed. What should you do if your signature on a check were forged? For suggestions, go to www.google.com and key in the words "indorsement of negotiable instruments." Also, key in the alternative spelling "endorsement," because the term is often misspelled.

Cases for Analysis

1. David Shin, a silver collector, ran short of cash. He borrowed $1,500 from Vinnie Gaff, giving Gaff the following note: "Thirty days from date, I promise to pay to the order of Vinnie Gaff $1,500 worth of silver (signed) David Shin." Gaff indorsed the note and gave it to Kia Lai in exchange for services

rendered by Lai. What legal term describes the transfer of the note from Gaff to Lai? Explain your answer.

2. Powell, intending to write a check to Thompson Electric, Inc., instead made it payable to the order of "Tompson Electric." Thompson Electric, Inc., indorsed the check with its name correctly spelled. Was the indorsement valid? Why or why not? *State v. Powell,* 551 P.2d 902 (KS).

3. Tufi forged the payee's name on the front of a U.S. Treasurer's check. When convicted of a forgery, he appealed, contending that a signature on the front of a check cannot be an indorsement. May an indorsement be written on the front of an instrument? Explain. *United States v. Tufi,* 536 F.2d 855 (9th Cir.).

4. Morse wrote a check for $2,500 payable to Reynolds for services rendered. Reynolds fraudulently raised the check to $5,500, indorsed it "without recourse," and deposited it in her bank account. Later, when the alteration was discovered, Reynolds argued that she was not responsible because her indorsement was qualified. Do you agree with Reynolds? Why or why not? See also *Wolfram v. Halloway,* 361 N.E.2d 587 (IL).

5. Sanders borrowed $5,000 from Waskow, giving Waskow a promissory note that read, "One year from date, I promise to pay to the order of James Waskow $5,000, without interest (signed) Mary Sanders." Six months later, Waskow died. The unindorsed note was in the possession of Waskow's landlord, who claimed that Waskow had given him the note in payment of back rent. Was the landlord a holder of the note? Why or why not? See also *Smathers v. Smathers,* 239 S.E.2d 637 (NC).

6. When checks were received by Palmer & Ray Dental Supply, Wilson, a company employee, indorsed them with a rubber stamp reading: "Palmer & Ray Dental Supply" (followed by the company's address). Wilson deposited some of the checks in the company's account but cashed the rest, keeping the money for herself. The company contended that the indorsements were restrictive and therefore that the bank should not have cashed them. Were the indorsements

restrictive? Explain. *Palmer & Ray Dental Supply, Inc., v. First Nat'l Bank,* 477 S.W.2d 954 (TX).

7. Commercial Credit Corporation issued a check payable to Rauch Motor Company. Rauch indorsed the check in blank and delivered it to a bank. The bank typed a very long special indorsement, payable to Lamson, on two legal-size sheets of paper and stapled them to the checks. May an indorsement be written on a separate paper and stapled to the checks? Explain. *Lamson v. Commercial Credit Corp.,* 531 P.2d 966 (CO).

8. The indorsement of the payee of a check drawn by Funding Systems Leasing Corporation was forged. Below the forged indorsement was added the signature of another person that was not forged. The check was deposited with the Sumiton Bank, which claimed to be a holder. Was the bank a holder? Why or why not? *Sumiton Bank v. Funding Sys. Leasing Corp.,* 512 F.2d 774 (5th Cir.).

9. The United States of America issued a check of the U.S. Treasury in the amount of $49,314.47 payable to two companies: Floors, Inc., and American Fidelity Fire Insurance Company. Floors, Inc., indorsed the check with a rubber stamp indorsement, "For Deposit Only, Floors, Inc.," deposited it in its account in the Peoples National Bank, and later withdrew the money. Was the check properly negotiated? Why or why not? What tort, if any, did the Peoples National Bank commit? Explain. *Peoples Nat'l. Bank v. American Fidelity Fire Ins.,* 386 A.2d 1254 (MD).

10. Darrell Davis was in possession of a promissory note signed by his deceased father which read: "1 year after date for value received, the undersigned maker promises to pay to the order of _____ $12,000. (signed) Aubrey Davis." The name of the payee was left blank. Darrell alleges that his grandmother was the holder of the note and that she transferred it to him prior to her death so that he could collect it for her. Although the note was not indorsed, Darrell argues that bearer paper may be negotiated by delivery alone and need not be indorsed. Is the note bearer paper? Explain. *Davis v. Davis,* 838 S.W.2d 415 (KY).

Quick Quiz Answers

27-1	27-2 & 27-3	27-4	27-5
1. F	1. T	1. F	1. T
2. T	2. F	2. F	2. T
3. T	3. F	3. T	3. F

Holders in Due Course, Defenses, and Liabilities

The Opening Case

"A Flat Screen Fiasco"

"Look honey!" Ralph said to his wife June, as he looked closely at the classified section of the local newspaper. "This is too good to be true! Somebody's selling their 50-inch Plasma HDTV for $1,000."

"Really? Let me see," she replied, reaching for the paper. "You're right! That's an awfully low price. It's even got a built-in HD tuner. I'll call the number."

Later that evening, Ralph and June decided to buy the set and gave the seller a $1,000 check, who accepted it, saying, "It'll take a few days for your check to clear. I'll call you when it does, and you can come and get the set. It's pretty heavy. You'll need a pickup truck and someone to help you carry it."

Four days later, after not hearing from the seller, Ralph and June went to the seller's apartment and found it empty. Later, they learned that their check had been raised to $2,000, cashed at a check-cashing business, and $2,000 had been withdrawn from their bank account before they could stop payment on it.

Opening Case Questions

1. Do Ralph and June have any recourse against the bank for the increased amount of the check?

2. Can the couple recover their loss from the check cashing business?

LO Learning Objectives

1. State the requirements of being a holder in due course and describe the special protection given to a holder in due course.
2. Define a holder.
3. Explain the protection given to a holder through a holder in due course.
4. Name six personal defenses.
5. Discuss the protection given to people who sign consumer credit contracts.
6. Name six real defenses and explain the significance of a real defense.
7. Differentiate between primary liability and secondary liability and list the parties who are primarily liable and secondarily liable.
8. Describe the conditions that must be met to hold a secondary party liable.

28-1 Holder in Due Course

A basic principle of contract law is that people cannot transfer greater rights than they have themselves. This rule, however, does not apply to the law of negotiable instruments. People who are *holders in due course* of negotiable instruments can receive even more rights than those who held the instruments before them. Largely for this reason, negotiable instruments are used frequently and passed liberally from one person to another.

EXAMPLE 28-1:   Holder in Due Course Protected

Alan Andrews sold his sports car to Elizabeth Barlow for $2,500. To make the sale, Andrews told Barlow that the radiator was brand new and that the brakes had been relined two weeks earlier; however, neither of these claims was true. Barlow gave Andrews a check for $2,500. While driving the car home, Barlow became aware of the fraud and stopped payment on the check. Andrews, however, had indorsed the check and given it to Catherine Cain, a holder in due course. Cain could collect the full $2,500 from Barlow. Even though Barlow was defrauded, she cannot use that defense against a holder in due course, because such holders are protected against this kind of fraud. Her cause of action would have to be against Andrews, who committed the fraud.

A **holder in due course** is a *holder* who takes an instrument:

- For value
- In good faith
- Without notice that anything is wrong with the underlying transaction

Holder

To be a holder in due course, the person in possession of the instrument must first be a **holder**. To be a holder means that the instrument must have been issued or indorsed to that person, to that person's order, or to bearer.

UCC Revised (1990) 3-302(a)(2) (see page 1005)

UCC Revised (1990) 1-201(20) (see page 958)

EXAMPLE 28-2:   Not a Holder

John and Nancy Augustine contracted with Hanover Homes Corporation for the construction of a house. They obtained a commitment for a mortgage loan from a lending company, which issued checks periodically as the construction progressed. The checks were made payable to John, Nancy, and Hanover Homes Corporation. The last check that was issued by the lending company was deposited in Hanover's bank account without Nancy's indorsement on it. The bank that received the check for deposit was not a holder because, without Nancy's indorsement, the check was not issued or indorsed to it, to bearer, or in blank. Because the bank was not a holder, it could not be a holder in due course.

Value

A person must give value for an instrument to qualify as a holder in due course. Thus, if an instrument is transferred to a person as a gift, that person would not qualify as a holder in

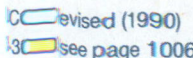

UCC Revised (1990)
3-30(see page 1006)

due course. People give value for instruments when they give the consideration that was agreed upon or accept instruments in payment of debts.

EXAMPLE 28-3: Value

Musial received his paycheck from his employer on Friday. The value Musial gave for the check was his services as an employee.

UCC 201 (19) (see page 5)

UCC Revised (1990)
3103(4) (see page 99)

Good Faith

To be a holder in due course, the holder must take the instrument in good faith. Good faith means *honesty in fact* and fair dealing. It requires that the taker of a commercial instrument act honestly. If the taker is negligent in not discovering that something was wrong with the paper, it does not establish lack of good faith.

EXAMPLE 28-4: Good Faith

Leo's Used Car Exchange purchased three cars at a car auction from Villa, paying for them with two checks totaling $15,150. Villa presented the checks to a bank and asked the teller to give him cash, because he was going to another auction and needed it. The teller did so without obtaining the bank manager's approval, which was against the bank's policy. Shortly thereafter, Leo's Used Car Exchange stopped payment on the checks because title to the three cars was not clear. The lower court held that the bank that cashed them was not a holder in due course because of the teller's negligence in failing to obtain the manager's approval before cashing the checks. The appellate court reversed the lower court's decision, holding that good faith means honesty in fact. The court said, "Nothing in the definition suggests that, in addition to being honest, the holder must exercise due care to be in good faith." Because the bank was a holder in due course, it was able to recover the $15,150 from the drawer of the checks, Leo's Used Car Exchange.

Without Notice

To be a holder in due course, a holder must not have notice of any claim or defense to an instrument or notice that an instrument is overdue or has been dishonored. A holder has notice of a claim or defense if the instrument bears visible evidence of forgery or alteration. The same is true if the instrument is so incomplete or irregular as to make its legal acceptance doubtful. Notice of a claim or defense is also considered given if the holder knows that the obligation of any party is voidable.

EXAMPLE 28-5: Notice of a Defense

Susan Luft, who was 17 years old, borrowed $350 from Henry Minkus. She gave Minkus a promissory note, promising to pay the money back in 90 days. Minkus indorsed the note and sold it at a discount to Applebee, telling Applebee that it came from a minor. Applebee was not a holder in due course because she knew that Luft was a minor and could disaffirm the contract to pay back the money.

UCC Revised (1990)
3-302(a)(2) (see page 1005)

A holder has notice that a demand instrument is overdue when more than a reasonable length of time has elapsed since it was issued. A check is overdue 90 days after its date. For other instruments, such as a note or draft, a reasonable time depends on the circumstances of each case.

UCC Revised (1990) 3-304 (see page 1006)

EXAMPLE 28-6:   Notice of Overdue Instrument

Genaro misplaced a check that he had received for cleaning out a neighbor's attic. He found the check four months later and cashed it at a nearby video shop. The video shop was not a holder in due course because it took the instrument when it was more than 90 days old.

Knowledge of some facts does not in itself give the holder notice of a defense or claim. For example, the fact that an instrument is postdated or antedated does not prevent someone from being a holder in due course; neither does completing an incomplete instrument constitute having such notice, unless the holder has notice of any improper completion.

Holder Through a Holder in Due Course

A holder who receives an instrument from a holder in due course acquires the rights of the holder in due course, even though he or she does not qualify as a holder in due course. This stipulation is called a **shelter provision**. It is designed to permit holders in due course to transfer all of the rights they have in the paper to others.

UCC Revised (1990) 3-203(b) (see page 1004)

EXAMPLE 28-7:   Holder Through a Holder in Due Course

Irwin gave Hill a $150 check in payment for an antique chair. Hill indorsed the check and gave it to McGraw in payment for a debt. Because McGraw took the check for value, in good faith, and without notice, he was a holder in due course of the instrument. McGraw indorsed the instrument with a special indorsement and gave it to his niece as a graduation present. McGraw's niece was not a holder in due course because she did not give value for the instrument. However, she had the rights of a holder in due course, because she received the check from a holder in due course.

The shelter provision does not apply to a holder who has committed fraud or an illegal act.

A Question of Ethics

As part of their direct mail advertising, companies sometimes include what appears to be a check but, when examined carefully, lacks one of the requirements of negotiability, such as the words, "Good only when applied to the purchase of . . . ." Is this marketing practice ethical?

Quick Quiz 28-1 True or False?

1. A holder is a person who is in possession of a negotiable instrument that is issued or indorsed to that person's order or to bearer.

2. Able bought a book from Baker and gave Baker a $25 check. Baker indorsed the check and gave it to Charlie in payment of a debt. Charlie was not a holder in due course of the check.

3. Charlie indorsed the check he received in Question 2 from Baker and gave it to David as a birthday gift. David had the rights of a holder in due course of the check.

28-2 Personal Defenses

UCC Revised (1990)
3-305(b) (see page 1006)

The favorable treatment that holders in due course receive ensures that they take instruments free from all claims to them on the part of any person and free from all personal defenses of any party *with whom they have not dealt*. **Personal defenses** (also called **limited defenses**) are defenses that can be used against a holder but not a holder in due course of a negotiable instrument. (The terms *personal defense* and *limited defense* come from common law and are not used in the UCC.) The most common personal defenses are breach of contract, failure or lack of consideration, fraud in the inducement, lack of delivery, and payment (see Table 28-1).

Breach of Contract

Negotiable instruments are often issued in exchange for property, services, or some other obligation as part of an underlying contract. Sometimes, the party to whom the instrument was issued breaches the contract by failing to perform or by performing in an unsatisfactory manner. If suit is brought on the instrument by a holder against the maker or drawer,

Table 28-1 Most Common Personal Defenses

Defense	Description
Breach of contract	One of the parties to a contract has failed to do what he or she has previously agreed to do.
Failure of consideration	One of the parties to a contract has failed to furnish the agreed consideration.
Lack of consideration	No consideration existed in the underlying contract for which the instrument was issued.
Fraud in the inducement	The drawer or maker of an instrument is persuaded to enter negotiable instrument into a contract because of a misrepresentation of some fact regarding the item purchased.
Lack of delivery of a negotiable instrument	A payee forcibly, unlawfully, or conditionally takes an instrument from a maker or drawer. The maker or drawer did not intend to deliver the instrument.
Payment of a negotiable instrument	The drawer or maker of an instrument has paid the amount of the instrument.

The Opening Case Revisited

"A Flat Screen Fiasco"

Ralph and June cannot recover the $1,000 from the check-cashing business, because that business was a holder in due course of the instrument. It took the check for value (the $1,000), in good faith, and without notice that anything was wrong with the underlying transaction. The defense of failure of consideration (not receiving the plasma HDTV) cannot be used against a holder in due course.

the latter may use breach of contract as a defense. Because breach of contract is a personal defense however, it may not be used if the holder of the instrument is a holder in due course unless the parties dealt with each other.

Lack or Failure of Consideration

Lack of consideration is a defense that may be used by a maker or drawer of an instrument when no consideration existed in the underlying contract for which the instrument was issued. The ordinary rules of contract law, discussed in Chapter 11, are followed to determine the presence or absence of consideration in such a case.

EXAMPLE 28-8:   Lack of Consideration

Lowell, without any mention of payment, helped his friend Ransom move from Cambridge to Gambier. At the end of the day, after he was in his new apartment, Ransom told Lowell that he'd give him some money for helping him move. The next day, Ransom gave Lowell a $200 check. Lowell cashed the check at a local bar and promptly left town. Ransom then stopped payment on the check. Ransom's promise to pay Lowell was not enforceable because Lowell had completed the work when the promise was made—it was past consideration. The local bar could recover the $200 from Ransom, however, because it was a holder in due course and was not subject to the personal defense of lack of consideration.

Failure of consideration is different. It is a defense that the maker or drawer may use when the other party breaches the contract by not furnishing the agreed consideration.

Both lack of consideration and failure of consideration are personal defenses. They may not be used against a holder in due course.

Fraud in the Inducement

There are two kinds of fraud: fraud in the inducement and fraud as to the essential nature of the transaction. The first is a personal defense; the second is a real defense, discussed on page 579. The five elements of fraud are explained in depth in Chapter 9. When someone is induced by a fraudulent statement to enter into a contract, that person may have the contract rescinded. However, he or she may not use that defense against a holder in due course. A holder in due course can cut through the defense of fraud in the inducement and collect from the person who was defrauded. In Example 28-1 on page 573, Barlow had to pay Cain, a holder in due course of the check, even though she had been induced by fraud to write the check to Andrews.

Lack of Delivery

Every commercial instrument may be revoked by its maker or drawer until it has been delivered to the payee. *Delivery* is the voluntary transfer of possession of an instrument from one person to another. If the transfer of possession is not voluntary, the instrument has not been "issued." Thus, in the event a payee forcibly, unlawfully, or conditionally takes an instrument from a drawer, the drawer has the defense of lack of delivery. The payee therefore may be denied the right to collect on the instrument. If the payee negotiates the instrument to a holder in due course however, this defense is removed.

EXAMPLE 28-9: Lack of Delivery

Morse wrote out a check payable to the order of Smith, intending to give it to Smith after Smith had completed a certain amount of work. Smith discovered the check on Morse's desk and took it without doing any work at all. Smith was not entitled to the check; however, if she negotiated the check to a bank, store, or private party for value, in good faith, and without notice (a holder in due course), Morse would have to honor the check even though Smith failed to do the required work.

Payment

Payment of an instrument by a maker or drawee usually ends the obligations of the parties. However, if a negotiable instrument is negotiated to a holder in due course after it has been paid, it will have to be paid again. This rule exists because payment is a personal defense, which cannot be used against a holder in due course. Because of this rule, anyone who pays a demand instrument should have it marked "paid" and take possession of it. This requirement is not as important with a time instrument, unless it is paid before its due date, because no one can be a holder in due course of a past due instrument.

Consumer Protection

The protection that is given to holders in due course was not always fair to consumers who bought on credit in the past.

EXAMPLE 28-10: Former Law

In 1975, Ruby Merlin bought a car from a used car dealer. She paid a small amount down and signed a consumer sales contract agreeing to pay the balance in 24 monthly installments. The used car dealer negotiated the contract (which was actually a promissory note) to a finance company and received payment immediately. The next day, the car's transmission stopped working, and the dealer refused to fix it. Merlin would still have to pay the finance company the full amount due on the note because the finance company was a holder in due course and was not subject to personal defenses.

In 1976, the FTC adopted the **holder in due course rule**. Under this rule, holders of consumer credit contracts who are holders in due course are subject to all claims and defenses that the buyer could use against the seller, including personal defenses. Thus, if the situation described in Example 28-10 were to occur today, Merlin's defense that the car's transmission did not work could be used against the finance company, even though it was a holder in due course. When sellers of consumer products have arrangements with financial institutions to finance their customer's purchases, the financial institutions are subject to the customer's personal defenses. They lose their protection as holders in due course.

Quick Quiz 28-2 True or False?

1. Personal defenses are defenses that can be used against a holder in due course but not a holder of a negotiable instrument.

2. The most common personal defenses are infancy and illegality.

3. If a negotiable instrument is negotiated to a holder in due course after it has been paid, it will have to be paid again.

28-3 Real Defenses

Some defenses can be used against everyone, including holders in due course. These defenses are known as **real defenses** or **universal defenses**. The terms *real* and *universal defense* come from the common law and are not used in the UCC. No one is required to pay an instrument when they have a real defense. Real defenses include infancy and mental incompetence, illegality and duress, fraud as to the essential nature of the transaction, bankruptcy, unauthorized signature, and alteration (see Table 28-2).

UCC Revised (1990) 3-305(a)(1) (see page 1006)

Infancy and Mental Incompetence

A minor (person under the age of 18 years) or mental incompetent need not honor a negotiable instrument if it was given in payment for a contract that the minor or mental incompetent may

---

Table 28-2   Most Common Real Defenses

Defense	Description
Infancy and mental incompetence	The maker or drawer of the instrument was a minor or mentally incompetent.
Illegality	The underlying contract for which the instrument was issued was illegal.
Duress	The instrument was drawn against the will of the maker or drawer because of threats of force or bodily harm.
Fraud as to the essential nature of the transaction	A false statement was made to the maker or drawer about the nature of the instrument being signed.
Bankruptcy	An order for relief was issued by the federal court that ended all the debtor's outstanding contractual obligations.
Unauthorized signature	Someone wrongfully signed another's name on an instrument without authority to do so.
Material alteration	The amount of the instrument or the payee's name was changed wrongfully after it was originally drawn by the maker or drawer.

disaffirm on the grounds of minority or incompetency. This rule is true even if the instrument comes into the hands of a holder in due course. Similarly, persons who have been found insane by a court are not liable on a negotiable instrument, because their contracts are void.

Illegality and Duress

An instrument that is associated with duress or an illegal act, such as twisting one's arm or drug trafficking, would be void and uncollectible by anyone, even a holder in due course. This provision is true even if the holder in due course is unaware of the illegal acts or conditions.

EXAMPLE 28-11:   Illegality—a Real Defense

The Condado Aruba Caribbean Hotel loaned Tickel, who resided in Colorado, $20,000. The money was loaned for the purpose of gambling at the hotel's casino in Aruba, Netherlands Antilles, where gambling is legal. Tickel wrote two checks to repay the debt, each of which was returned for insufficient funds. When suit was brought on the checks, the Colorado court held that gambling debts are unenforceable in that state even against a holder in due course. Tickel was not liable on the checks that he had written to the hotel.

Fraud as to the Essential Nature of the Transaction

Fraud as to the essential nature of the transaction is more serious than fraud in the inducement. When this type of fraud occurs, the defrauded party has no knowledge or opportunity to learn of the true character or terms of the matter. Because of its seriousness, it is a real defense and may be used against anyone, even a holder in due course.

EXAMPLE 28-12:   Fraud as to the Essential Nature of the Transaction

Duffy, who was almost blind, was asked by Ingram to sign a receipt. Duffy signed the paper without having had it read to him. The paper was actually a note promising to pay Ingram $2,500. Duffy would not be required to pay the note, even to a holder in due course, because this kind of fraud is more critical than fraud in the inducement.

Bankruptcy

Bankruptcy may be used as a defense to all negotiable instruments, even those in the hands of a holder in due course. Holders of such instruments will receive treatment equal to that of other similar creditors when the debtor's assets are collected and divided according to the bankruptcy law. This law is explained in more detail in Chapter 32.

Unauthorized Signatures

Whenever someone signs another's name on an instrument without authority, it is a forgery. Unless ratified, it does not operate as the signature of the person whose name is signed. Instead, it operates as the signature of the person who signed it, that is, of the wrongdoer.

UCC Revised (1990)
3-403(a) (see page 1010)

The Opening Case Revisited

"A Flat Screen Fiasco"

Unless the check was written negligently so that it could have been easily altered, Ralph and June can recover the difference between the original and the altered amount from the bank, because the bank must pay only the amount for which the instrument was originally written.

EXAMPLE 28-13:   Forgery—a Real Defense

With no authority to do so, Parks signed Brown's name on a note, promising to pay Rivera $3,000 in 90 days. The note was negotiated by Rivera to a holder in due course. Brown would not have to pay the money to the holder in due course because the unauthorized signature is a real defense. Parks had committed a crime. The holder in due course could recover from Rivera who, in turn, could recover from the wrongdoer, Parks.

Alteration

Sometimes negotiable instruments are altered after they leave the hands of the maker or drawer. Usually, the alteration involves changing the payee's name or increasing the amount of an instrument. The alteration of an instrument may be used as a real defense. Unless an instrument is written negligently so that it can be easily altered, makers and drawers are not required to pay altered amounts. They must pay only the amount for which the instrument was originally written.

Writing a check in pencil is legal, but not a good idea. It leaves the check vulnerable to alteration by a dishonest person.

UCC Revised (1990) 3-407 (see page 1011)

EXAMPLE 28-14:   Alteration—a Real Defense

Martinez wrote out a check in a proper manner for $315 and gave it to Video Sales in payment for a DVD player. Video Sales raised the check to read $815. Martinez's bank honored the altered check. Martinez could seek reimbursement from his bank for $500, the difference between the original and the altered amount.

Any person who negligently contributes to a material alteration of an instrument or an unauthorized signature may not exercise the defense of alteration or lack of authority against a holder in due course, a drawee, or other payor who pays the instrument in good faith. For example, using a pencil to write a check or not being careful to keep the figures compact and clear gives a dishonest holder an opportunity to alter the amount. The careless writer would be without defense.

UCC Revised (1990) 3-406 (see page 1011)

28-4 Liability of the Parties

UCC Revised (1990)
3-401 (see page 1009)

No person is liable on an instrument unless that person's signature or the signature of an authorized agent appears on the instrument. Parties to negotiable instruments have different liability depending on their function.

Makers, Acceptors, and Certain Drawers

UCC Revised (1990)
3-412, 3-413 (see page 1012)

The following are obligated to pay an instrument without reservations of any kind. They are said to be primarily liable:

*   The maker of a note.

*   The issuer of a cashier's check or other draft in which the drawer and the drawee are the same person.

*   The acceptor of a draft.

Other Drawers and Indorsers

UCC Revised (1990)
3-414, 3-415 (a)(c) (see page 1012)

Other drawers and indorsers have limitations on their obligation to pay an instrument. They are said to be secondarily, or conditionally, liable. The drawer of a draft that has not been accepted is obligated to pay the draft to anyone who is entitled to enforce it; however, if a bank accepts a draft, the drawer is discharged. If a drawee other than a bank accepts a draft and it is later dishonored, the obligation of the drawer is the same as an indorser stated here.

UCC Revised (1990)
3-501 (see page 1014)

Indorsers are obligated to pay an instrument only when the following conditions are met: (1) The instrument must be properly presented to the drawee or party obliged to pay the instrument, and payment must be demanded; (2) the instrument must be dishonored, that is, payment refused; and (3) notice of the dishonor must be given to the secondary party within the time and in the manner prescribed by the UCC. If all three of these conditions are not met, drawers of drafts and indorsers are discharged from their obligations.

Presentment   **Presentment** means a demand made by a holder to pay or accept an instrument. Presentment may be made by any commercially reasonable means, including oral, written, or electronic communication. If requested by the person to whom presentment is made, the person making presentment must exhibit the instrument and provide identification.

UCC Revised (1990)
3-502 (see page 1015)

Dishonor   *Dishonor* means to refuse to pay a negotiable instrument when it is due or to refuse to accept it when asked to do so. An instrument is dishonored when proper presentment is made and acceptance or payment is refused. Dishonor also occurs when presentment is excused and the instrument is past due and unpaid. The presenting party has recourse against indorsers or other secondary parties after notice of dishonor has been given.

EXAMPLE 28-15:   Dishonor

A note was presented to Baker for payment on the date specified. Baker refused to honor it, claiming the note was a forgery. The holder would have to proceed against the indorsers to obtain payment. The note was dishonored when Baker refused to pay it.

Notice of Dishonor Obligations of indorsers and drawers of instruments may not be enforced unless they are given notice of the dishonor or notice is excused. Notice of dishonor may be given by any reasonable means, including oral, written, or electronic communication, and is sufficient if it reasonably identifies the instrument and indicates that the instrument has been dishonored or has not been paid or accepted. The return of an instrument given to a bank for collection is sufficient notice of dishonor.

Nonbank holders must give notice of the dishonor to the drawer and indorsers within 30 days following the day of dishonor. Banks taking instruments for collection must give notice before midnight of the banking day following the day the bank was notified of the dishonor. Delay in giving notice of dishonor is excused when the holder has acted carefully and the delay is due to circumstances beyond the holder's control. Presentment and notice of dishonor are also excused when the party waived either presentment or notice of dishonor.

Quick Quiz 28-4 True or False?

1. Indorsers never have liability to pay.

2. Presentment can be made by oral, written, or electronic communication.

3. Notice of dishonor must be given by nonbank holders to indorsers within 30 days following the day of dishonor.

About the Law

Formerly, it was necessary to send a protest to drawers and indorsers when a draft payable outside the United States was dishonored. A *protest* is a certificate of dishonor that states that a draft was presented for acceptance or payment and was dishonored, together with the reasons given for refusal to accept or pay, made under the hand and seal of a United States consul or notary public. Today, under the revised (1990) UCC, a protest is no longer required but may still be used.

UCC Revised (1990) 3-503 and 3-504 (see pages 1015–1016)

Summary

28.1   A holder in due course is a holder who takes the instrument for value, in good faith, without notice that it is overdue or has been dishonored, and without notice of any defenses against it or claim to it. Good faith means honesty in fact. A holder who receives an instrument from a holder in due course receives all the rights of the holder in due course.

28.2   Personal defenses can be used against a holder but not a holder in due course. The most common personal defenses are breach of contract, lack or failure of consideration, fraud in the inducement, lack of delivery, and payment. Holders of consumer credit contracts who are holders in due course are subject to all claims and defenses that the buyer could use against the seller, including personal defenses.

28.3   Real defenses can be used against anyone, including a holder in due course. Real defenses are infancy and mental incompetence, illegality and duress, fraud as to the essential nature of the transaction, bankruptcy, unauthorized signature, and alteration.

28.4   Makers of notes and acceptors of drafts have an absolute liability to pay. Indorsers have a liability to pay only if an instrument is presented properly for payment, the instrument is dishonored, and proper notice of dishonor is given to the secondary party.

Key Terms

failure of consideration, 577

holder, 573

holder in due course, 573

holder in due course rule, 578

lack of consideration, 577

limited defenses, 576

personal defenses, 576

presentment, 582

real defenses, 579

shelter provision, 575

universal defenses, 579

Questions for Review and Discussion

1. What are the requirements for being a holder in due course?
2. What is the purpose of the shelter provision, and when will it not apply?
3. Why are personal defenses sometimes called limited defenses? Identify the most common personal defenses.
4. What protection is given to consumers who sign consumer credit contracts?
5. What is the significance of real defenses? Explain.
6. Name the parties to an instrument who are obligated to pay without reservation. When are indorsers obligated to pay instruments?
7. How may presentment be made?
8. When is an instrument dishonored?
9. In what way may notice of dishonor be given?
10. When must nonbank holders give notice of dishonor to the drawer and indorsers?

Investigating the Internet

Many people who took out subprime mortgages (see Chapter 31) during the past several years have found that they cannot afford to keep up the mortgage payments, and their mortgages have foreclosed. One of the incentives for giving subprime mortgages was a federal law called the Home Ownership and Equity Protection Act (HOEPA). This law has a built-in provision similar to the holder in due course rule described in this chapter. The provision eliminates holder in due course protection for purchasers and assignees of HOEPA mortgages. Look online to determine whether the rule has helped homeowners with their struggles with subprime mortgages. Key in "HOEPA" and "holder in due course rule" on any of the following search engines: Google, Yahoo!, Alta Vista, Lycos, Netscape, MSN, AOL, Ask Jeeves, All the Web, Homepage Hotbot Web Search, LookSmart, or any others that you may find helpful.

Cases for Analysis

1. Without authority to do so, Allen signed Baker's name on a note, promising to pay Cohen $5,000 in 30 days. The note was negotiated to Davidson who was a holder in due course. Will Davidson be successful in recovering the $5,000 from Baker in court? Why or why not?

2. Refrigerated Transport Co., Inc., employed a collection agency to collect some of its overdue accounts. The collection agency indorsed, without authority, checks made payable to Refrigerated Transport and deposited them in the agency's own checking account. Was the bank that accepted the checks for deposit a holder in due course? Why or why not? *Nat'l Bank v. Refrigerated Transp.,* 248 S.E.2d 496 (GA).

3. Andersen entered into a franchise agreement with Great Lake Nursery, under which Andersen was to grow and sell nursery stock and Christmas trees. Great Lake was to provide trees, chemicals, and other items. Andersen signed an installment note that read in part, "For value received, Robert Andersen promises to pay to Great Lake Nursery Corp. $6,412." Great Lake indorsed the note and transferred it to First Investment Company. Later, Andersen stopped making payments because Great Lake filed bankruptcy and failed to perform its part of the franchise agreement. May Andersen use failure of consideration as a defense when sued by First Investment Company on the note? Why or why not? *First Inv. Co. v. Andersen,* 621 P.2d 683 (UT).

4. In exchange for an asphalt paving job, Paulick gave Bucci a note promising to pay to the order of Bucci $7,593 in six months with 10 percent per annum interest. Payment was not made on the due date, and Bucci brought suit. Paulick used failure of consideration as a defense, claiming that the paving job was improperly done. The court held that Bucci was a holder in due course because he had taken the instrument for value, in good faith, and without notice of any claims or defenses of Paulick's. Could Paulick use the defense of failure of consideration against Bucci? Why or why not? *Bucci v. Paulick,* 149 A.2d 1255 (PA).

5. Carolyn Brazil wrote a check to a contractor who agreed to make certain improvements on her home. She wrote the check in reliance on the contractor's false representation that the materials for the job had been purchased, when in fact, they had not. Brazil had the bank on which the check was drawn stop payment on it. Another bank, which cashed the check and became a holder in due course of the instrument, attempted to recover the amount of the check from Brazil. Could it do so? Explain. *Citizens Nat'l Bank v. Brazil,* 233 S.E.2d 482 (GA).

6. As part of the purchase price for a 9,040-acre ranch, Kirby gave Bergfield a $20,000 check drawn on the Bank of Bellevue. Bergfield had her banker telephone the Bank of Bellevue to inquire about Kirby's account balance to be sure that the check was good. It was learned that there was not enough money in Kirby's account to cover the check. Bergfield continued to hold the check and did not present it to the Bank of Bellevue for payment. Later, Bergfield argued that the telephone call to the bank was a presentment and demand for payment of the check. Do you agree? Why or why not? *Kirby v. Bergfield,* 182 N.W.2d 205 (NE).

7. Haik transferred his stock in Petrocomp, an oil exploration company, to Rowley in exchange for five $10,000 promissory notes. The notes were signed by Rowley and indorsed by Rowley's son, Stephen. Rowley failed to pay the notes when they became due. No presentment for payment was made by Haik on the due date, nor was a timely notice of dishonor given to Rowley's son, Stephen. Could Haik hold Stephen liable on the notes as an indorser? Explain. *Haik v. Rowley,* 377 So.2d 391 (LA).

8. David and Nettie Weiner signed seven promissory notes, totaling $89,000, in their capacity as president and secretary of NMD Realty Co. In addition, they indorsed each note on the reverse side with their individual signatures. Each note contained the following provision: "The Maker and indorser or indorsers each hereby waives presentment, demand, and notice of dishonor." The Weiners claimed that, because they are secondarily liable, the bank may not proceed against them individually until after presentment, notice of dishonor, and protest have occurred. Do you agree with the Weiners? Explain. *Bank of Delaware v. NMD Realty Co.,* 325 A.2d 108 (DE).

9. Rutherford purchased real property from Ethel Stokes for $35,000. He paid $5,000 down and signed

a promissory note for the balance. The note was secured by a deed of trust (a type of security interest, discussed in detail in Chapter 31). When payments on the note were overdue, Stokes considered foreclosing on the property. Prior to doing so, however, she negotiated the note to Craig, who purchased it at a discount with notice that it was in default. Was Craig a holder in due course of the note? Why or why not? *Matter of Marriage of Rutherford*, 573 S.W.2d 299 (TX).

10. Bolton wrote a check for $20,000 to his daughter, Joyce, intending to make a gift. The check was drawn on the State Bank of Wapello and mailed to Joyce in Maryland, where she was living. Joyce received the check, indorsed it, and mailed it to her bank in Baltimore with instructions to use it to establish a certificate of deposit in joint tenancy with her father. Was Joyce a holder in due course of the check? Explain. *Matter of Estate of Bolton*, 444 N.W.2d 482 (IA).

Quick Quiz Answers

28-1	1. T	28-2	1. F	28-3	1. T	28-4	1. F
	2. F		2. F		2. F		2. T
	3. T		3. T		3. F		3. T

Chapter 29

Bank–Depositor Relationships, Deposits, and Collections

The Opening Case
"Off on a Taxing Vacation"

It was Friday the 13th, Dominic Belchick's lucky day. That morning while shaving, he noticed a piece of paper at the bottom of his bathroom laundry basket and discovered it was a $250 state income tax refund check he had received a year earlier that he had forgotten about. When he returned home from work that afternoon at 5:35, he found that his $2,500 federal income tax refund check had arrived in the mail. It was perfect timing. Belchick had the following week off and needed the money for a vacation he had planned for that week. He raced out the door, hopped into his car, and sped to the bank, getting there just before it closed (the bank's cut-off hour was 2:00 p.m.) and deposited the two checks into his account. He spent the weekend leisurely packing for the trip, then stopped by the bank to withdraw the needed funds as he left for vacation on Monday. To his dismay, he heard the teller say, "I'm sorry, Mr. Belchick, that $250 check you gave us was too old for us to take so we're returning it, and we can't give you the money for the larger check until tomorrow."

Opening Case Questions

1. Was the bank obligated to take the small check and pay $250 to Belchick?

2. Was the bank within its rights to hold Belchick's money another day?

LO Learning Objectives

1. Clarify the bank–depositor relationship.
2. Explain the duties of a bank relative to honoring orders, death of a customer, forged and altered checks, availability of funds, and the midnight deadline.
3. Explain the duties of a depositor relative to bad checks and examining accounts.
4. Compare an oral stop-payment order with a written stop-payment order.
5. Describe the insurance coverage that protects bank accounts.
6. Discuss the protection given to consumers by the Electronic Fund Transfer Act.
7. Name the different terms used to describe banks during the bank collection process.
8. Outline a check's life cycle.
9. Describe the principal features of the Check 21 Act.

29-1 The Bank–Depositor Relationship

LO1

The relationship between the drawee bank and its customer is that of both debtor and creditor and agent and principal. The relationship arises out of the express or implied contract that occurs when the customer opens a checking account with the bank. The bank becomes a debtor when money is deposited in the bank by the customer. At this time, the customer is owed money by the bank and is therefore a creditor. When an **overdraft** occurs, that is, when the bank pays out more than the customer has on deposit, the debtor–creditor role reverses, and the bank becomes the creditor.

UCC 4-201

UCC 4-212

The bank acts as the customer's agent when it collects or attempts to collect checks or other negotiable instruments made payable to the customer. If the items are deposited in the customer's account, any settlement made by the bank with the customer is provisional. A provisional settlement may be revoked by the bank if an item that the bank is attempting to collect is dishonored. The bank may charge back the amount of any credit given for the item to its customer's account or obtain a refund from its customer.

EXAMPLE 29-1:   Provisional Settlement

Baker Company deposited in its checking account a check it had received in the mail from a customer. Baker Company's bank credited its account for the amount of the check and sent it through the clearinghouse for collection. The check was returned to the bank because of insufficient funds. Baker Company's bank charged back (debited) the amount it had credited to Baker Company's account.

The Bank's Duties

LO2

The bank owes a duty to its depositors to honor orders and to protect funds. However, these duties carry strict limitations.

UCC 4-401

UCC 4-402

Duty to Honor Orders   The drawee bank is under a duty to honor all checks drawn by its customers when there are sufficient funds on deposit in the customer's account. If there are insufficient funds on deposit, the bank may charge the customer's account even if it creates an overdraft. If a bank fails to honor a check because of a mistake on its part, the bank is liable to the customer for any actual damages the customer suffers. The drawee bank has no liability to the holder of the check, however, unless it is certified.

EXAMPLE 29-2:   Bank's Liability Extends to Actual Damages Only

Rougier, who had $178 in her checking account, wrote out a check for $78.42 and mailed it to the telephone company in payment of a telephone bill. Due to a mistake on its part, Rougier's bank dishonored the check and returned it to the telephone company marked "insufficient funds." As soon as the error was discovered, the telephone company was notified, and the check was redeposited and honored by the bank. Because Rougier suffered no loss, the bank was not liable for dishonoring the check. Had Rougier's telephone been disconnected because of the dishonored check, the bank would have been liable to her for the cost of restoring service. The bank was not liable to the telephone company.

The Opening Case Revisited, Part I

"Off on a Taxing Vacation"

The bank was not obligated to take the small check and pay $250 to Belchick because it was a stale check—more than six months old.

A bank is under no obligation to a customer to pay a stale check unless it is certified. A **stale check** is a check that is presented for payment more than six months after its date. A bank, however, may honor a stale check without liability to its customer if it acts in good faith.

UCC 4-404

EXAMPLE 29-3:   Bank Must Act in Good Faith

The Chemical Bank paid a check that had been written by New York Flameproofing Co. ten years earlier on a check form no longer used by that company. The account on which the check was drawn had been closed for seven years, and the company's address written on the check had changed seven years earlier. In holding against the bank for paying the check, the court said that such payment was a reckless disregard of due care, so much as to constitute bad faith. The bank was liable for the amount paid.

The drawee bank is not liable to a holder of a check for dishonoring the instrument unless it is certified. The holder's recourse is against the drawer or indorsers on their secondary liability.

UCC 4-405

Death or Incompetence of Customer   The drawee bank is not liable for the payment of a check before it has notice of the death or incompetence of the drawer. In any event, a bank may pay or certify checks for 10 days after the date of death of the drawer. This rule permits holders of checks that are drawn shortly before the drawer's death to cash them without the necessity of filing a claim with the court handling the deceased's estate.

Forged and Altered Checks   A **forgery** is the fraudulent making or alteration of a writing. A forgery is committed when a person fraudulently writes or alters a check or other form of negotiable instrument to the injury of another. The commission of forgery is a crime, subject to a fine and imprisonment. The offering of a forged instrument to another person when the offeror knows it to be forged is also a crime, known as **uttering**. If a bank, in good faith, pays the altered amount of a check to a holder, it may deduct from the drawer's account only the amount of the check as it was originally written.

EXAMPLE 29-4:   Bank Responsible for Paying an Altered Check

Lane wrote out a $400 check, in a nonnegligent fashion, to the order of Robinson in payment for repairs to Lane's house. Robinson raised the check to $4,000. If Lane's bank pays the full $4,000 to Robinson, it can deduct $400 from Lane's account, but no more. The bank must either get the money back from the wrongdoer, Robinson, or suffer the loss. The bank would be able to deduct the full $4,000 from Lane's account if the alteration was facilitated by Lane's carelessness in writing the check.

The depositor is also protected against a signature being forged. When a checking account is opened, the depositor must fill out a signature card, which is permanently filed at the bank. Thereafter, the bank is held to know the depositor's signature. The bank is liable to the depositor if it pays any check on which the depositor's signature has been forged.

Availability of Funds In the past, banks were not uniform in the amount of time they required before they would make funds available to their depositors. Some banks held funds longer than others, and many banks did not disclose their holding policy to their customers.

EXAMPLE 29-5: Earlier Law

Remez received a check from her father, who lived in a distant city. She deposited it in her checking account and was told by the teller that she would not be able to draw a check on the funds for ten days. Remez's friend inquired at her own bank about its holding policy and was told that it would have made the funds available in five days.

To address the issue, Congress passed the Competitive Banking Act. Under the act, the Federal Reserve Board of Governors issued Regulation CC, which requires banks to make funds available to depositors according to a prescribed schedule (Table 29-1). With exceptions, funds from checks drawn on the U.S. Treasury or any state or local government and any bank draft, cashier's check, or postal money order must be made available on the next business day following the banking day of deposit; funds from checks drawn on banks within the same Federal Reserve district must be made available within two business days following the banking day of deposit; and funds from checks drawn on banks outside the bank's Federal Reserve district must be made available within five business days following the banking day of deposit. A *business day* is defined under Regulation CC as Monday through Friday, except for most federal holidays. A *banking day* is any business day (up to the bank's cut-off hour) when the bank is open for substantially all of its banking activities.

EXAMPLE 29-6: Fund Availability

Edna Chase deposited a $500 local check that was payable to her in her bank at 3:00 p.m. on Monday. The bank's cut-off hour for the day's transactions was 2:00 p.m. Because the deposit was made after the bank's cut-off hour, it was considered received on Tuesday. The first $100 must be made available to Chase by Wednesday, and the remaining $400 must be made available by Thursday, the second business day after the banking day of deposit.

Table 29-1 Availability of Funds (Under $5,000) You Deposit in Your Bank	
Type of Check	**Funds Must Be Made Available for Withdrawal**
"On us" check [drawn on your bank]	1st business day* after the banking day† of deposit
Local check (except $100‡) [drawn on a bank in same check-processing region]	2nd business day* after the banking day† of deposit
Nonlocal (except $100‡) [drawn on a bank in a different check-processing region]	5th business day* after the banking day† of deposit
Electronic payment	1st business day* after the banking day† of deposit
Cashier's check	1st business day* after the banking day† of deposit
Certified check	1st business day* after the banking day† of deposit
Government check	1st business day* after the banking day† of deposit
U.S. Postal Service money order	1st business day* after the banking day† of deposit

*Monday through Friday except most federal holidays.

†Any business day (up to the bank's cut-off hour) when the bank is open for substantially all of its banking activities.

‡The first $100 (or the total amount of the deposit if less than $100) must be made available on the 1st business day after the banking day of deposit.

Exceptions are made for new accounts, deposits greater than $5,000, accounts that are repeatedly overdrawn, deposits of a suspicious nature, and emergency conditions. In addition, some state laws require even shorter time periods for banks to make funds available.

Regulation CC also requires banks to disclose in advance their policy for making funds available to depositors. Such disclosures must be made when the account is initially opened and on conspicuously visible notices at teller stations in the bank.

UCC 4-302

Midnight Deadline   Payor banks are required to either settle or return checks quickly. If they do not do so, they are responsible for paying them. If the payor bank is not the depositary bank, it must settle for an item by midnight of the banking day of receipt.

The Opening Case Revisited, Part II
"Off on a Taxing Vacation"

The bank was within its rights, because the deposit was made after the bank's cut-off hour on Friday, and Saturday and Sunday are not business days, so the deposit is considered to have been made on Monday—the next banking day. Because the funds are from a U.S. Treasury check, they must be made available by the first business day following the banking day of deposit, which is Tuesday.

UCC 4-104(h)

EXAMPLE 29-7:   Bank's Midnight Deadline

LaPierre wrote a check to Kimberly Motors for $2,500 in payment for a secondhand car. The payor of the check (the bank on which it was drawn) was the National Bank & Trust Co. Kimberly Motors deposited the check into its account in the Southwest Mutual Bank (the depositary bank), which sent it on for collection. LaPierre's car broke down before she reached home that evening. She immediately stopped payment on the check. The National Bank & Trust Company must return the check to the Southwest Mutual Bank, with a notation that payment has been stopped, before midnight of the day that it received the check. If it keeps the check longer than that, it will be liable for payment.

If the payor bank is also the depositary bank, it must either pay or return the check or send notice of its dishonor on or before its midnight deadline. In this case, the bank's **midnight deadline** is midnight of the next banking day following the banking day on which it receives the relevant item.

EXAMPLE 29-8:   Longer Deadline for Depository Bank

If the National Bank & Trust Company in Example 29-7 had also been the depositary bank, it would have had an extra day to handle the check. The bank would have had until midnight of the next banking day to return the check to Kimberly Motors with the notation that payment had been stopped.

The Depositor's Duties

Depositors, in general, owe a duty to the banks in which they have checking accounts to have sufficient funds on deposit to cover checks that they write. They must also examine their bank statements and canceled checks promptly and with reasonable care and notify the bank quickly of any discrepancies.

Bad Checks   Most states have statutes making it larceny or attempted larceny for a person to issue a check drawn on a bank in which the person has insufficient funds. Such statutes usually have the following provisions that must be observed in the prosecution of anyone issuing a *bad check,* sometimes called an *NSF check:* The payee has the obligation of informing the drawer of the nonpayment of the check, together with notice of the provisions of the bad-check law and of the party's legal rights and obligations. After receiving notice of nonpayment, or dishonor, the drawer is given a specified number of days, usually five or ten, in which to make the check good, without fear of prosecution. Failure to make full payment of the check within the number of days allowed by statute serves as presumption of guilt that the drawer issued the check with full knowledge of the facts and with intent to defraud.

Banks and their customers must both perform their responsibilities properly for the system to function effectively.

EXAMPLE 29-9:   Bad Check Notice

State National Bank received Yoder's check for $120 due on an installment note it held. After it was deposited, the check was returned to State National with the notification "insufficient funds." The bank's collection department sent a certified letter to Yoder, which explained his responsibility under the bad-check statute. Failure on the part of Yoder to make the check good within the period of time indicated would result in a criminal complaint being lodged against Yoder through the office of the state's prosecuting attorney.

Bad-check statutes are effectively used as a means of collection. Most bad-check writers make an effort to make full payment of the check when advised that they are subject to prosecution. (See Figure 29-1.)

Many banks offer overdraft protection service to their depositors, which covers small overdrafts that are usually caused by the mistake of the drawer in balancing the checkbook. This service is important under the Check 21 Act, because checks may have a shorter float time than in the past. With this service, the bank honors small

Date:_____

Check Maker's name

Address

Dear Check Maker:

    You are hereby notified that your

        check number_____,

        dated _____,

        and drawn on _____(bank)_____,

        in the amount of $ _____,

        made payable to _____,

has been returned unpaid.

    You should be advised that the check deception law, I.C. § 35-43-5-5, provides that:

        "A person who knowingly or intentionally issues or delivers a check for the payment of or to acquire money or other property, knowing that it will not be paid or honored by the credit institution upon presentment in the usual course of business, commits check deception, a Class A misdemeanor."

        The maximum penalty for a class A misdemeanor is one year in prison and a fine of $5,000.00.

        Please be advised that if you do not make arrangements to pay this check within the next ten (10) days, this case will be sent to the Marshall County Prosecuting Attorney's Office for the preparation of criminal check deception charges.

Sincerely,

(your name and address)

Marshall County Prosecutor's Office—revised 8/99

Figure 29-1   This is a sample letter used in the State of Indiana notifying the drawer of a bad check that criminal charges will be brought if the check is not paid.

overdrafts and charges the depositor's account. This service saves the drawer the inconvenience and embarrassment of having a check returned to a holder marked "insufficient funds."

UCC 4-406

Duty to Examine Accounts   The UCC imposes a duty on depositors to examine their bank statements and canceled checks promptly and with reasonable care when they are received from the bank. They must report promptly to the bank any forged or altered checks. If they do not do so, depositors cannot hold the bank responsible for losses due to the bank's payment of a forged or altered instrument.

The exact time within which a depositor must notify a bank is not established except in the case of the same wrongdoer forging or altering more than one check. In that case, the bank must be notified of the wrongdoing within 30 days after the depositor receives the bank statement.

EXAMPLE 29-10:   Must Notify Bank of Forgery

Applegard's checkbook was stolen from her desk without her knowledge. The thief filled out three of the stolen checks, forged Applegard's signature, and cashed them. Applegard must notify the bank of the forgery within 30 days after she receives the bank statement. If she does not do so and her bank suffers a loss, her bank will not be liable for paying the forged checks.

The absolute limit for notifying a bank of a forged or altered check is one year from the time the depositor receives the bank statement. The limit is three years, however, in the case of a forged indorsement on a check.

Antedated and Postdated Checks   A check may be antedated or postdated. It is antedated when it is written and dated on one day and delivered at a later time. A check is postdated when the drawer delivers it before its stated date. However, a bank may charge a postdated check against a customer's account unless the customer has notified the bank of the postdated check within a reasonable time for the bank to act on it. Any such notice by a customer to a bank is effective for the same time periods allowed for stop-payment orders, discussed subsequently. If a check is undated, its date is the date that it was first given to someone.

UCC 4-401(c)

Stop-Payment Rights

LO4

Drawers may order a bank to stop payment on any item payable on their account. The stop-payment order must be received in time and in such a manner as to afford the bank a reasonable opportunity to act on it. An oral order is binding upon the bank for 14 calendar days only, unless confirmed in writing within that period. A written order is binding for only six months, unless renewed in writing. The burden of establishing the fact and amount of loss resulting from the payment of an item contrary to a binding order to stop payment is on the customer.

UCC 4-403
UCC 4-403(3)

Bank's Right of Subrogation   If a bank fails to stop payment on a check, it is responsible for any loss suffered by the drawer who ordered the payment stopped. The bank, however, may take the place of any holder, holder in due course, payee, or drawer who has rights against others on the underlying obligation. This right to be substituted for another is known as the bank's right of subrogation. It is designed to prevent loss to the bank and unjust enrichment to other parties.

UCC 4-407

Table 29-2	How a Husband, Wife, and One Child May Have Insured Accounts Totaling $1,000,000
Individual Accounts:	
Husband	$ 100,000
Wife	$ 100,000
Child	$ 100,000
Joint Accounts:	
Husband and Wife	$ 100,000
Husband and Child	$ 100,000
Wife and Child	$ 100,000
Revocable Trust Accounts:	
Husband as Trustee for Wife	$ 100,000
Husband as Trustee for Child	$ 100,000
Wife as Trustee for Child	$ 100,000
Wife as Trustee for Husband	$ 100,000
	$1,000,000

EXAMPLE 29-11:   Bank's Right of Subrogation

Jervey was induced by fraud to enter into a contract with Glidden. As part of the transaction, Jervey wrote and delivered a check to Glidden for $1,500. When Jervey discovered the fraud, she immediately ordered her bank to stop payment on the check. The bank, by mistake, ignored the stop-payment order and paid the $1,500 to Glidden. The bank must return the $1,500 to Jervey but may sue Glidden for fraud under its right of subrogation.

Insured Accounts

The Federal Deposit Insurance Corporation (FDIC) insures deposits in banks as well as in savings and loan associations. The basic insurance coverage protects individual bank accounts for up to $100,000 and joint accounts for up to an additional $100,000. Revocable trust and payable-on-death bank accounts are protected for up to $100,000 for each beneficiary who is a close relative and named in the account records. (See Table 29-2.)

Quick Quiz 29-1 True or False?

1. The bank acts as the customer's principal when it collects checks or other negotiable instruments made payable to the customer.

2. The drawee bank has no liability to the holder of a check unless it is certified.

3. The commission of forgery is a crime, subject to a fine and imprisonment.

A Question of Ethics

Is there ever a situation in which it would be ethical to write a check when you knew there were insufficient funds in the bank to cover it?

29-2 Electronic Banking

Electronic banking (also called **electronic fund transfers** or **EFTs**) uses computers and electronic technology as a substitute for checks and other banking methods. People can go to automatic teller machines (ATMs) 24 hours a day to make bank deposits and withdrawals. They can pay bills by phone, have deposits made directly to their bank accounts, and pay for retail purchases directly from their bank accounts.

Some banks have arrangements for payment by **e-check** (sometimes called *electronic check conversion*), which is a system in which funds are electronically transferred from a customer's checking account, eliminating the need to process a paper check. Under one system, the customer writes out an ordinary check and gives it to a merchant when making a purchase. After obtaining the customer's written authorization, the merchant passes the check through an instrument that reads the information on the check and converts the payment from a paper check to an electronic funds transfer. The merchant then voids the check and returns it to the customer with a receipt. Payment by e-check is cheaper to process and usually is accomplished sooner.

An **ATM card** is used together with a personal identification number (PIN) to gain access to an automatic teller machine either on or off the bank premises. In contrast, a **debit card** (also called a *check card* or *cash card*) is used to subtract money electronically from a bank account to pay for goods or services. Debit cards are used at stores rather than at ATM machines and usually require the use of the customer's signature rather than a PIN. Many banks now use a combination ATM–debit card that performs both functions.

Some banks prefer that customers use ATMs for their regular banking transactions, even featuring accounts that charge a fee for the use of live tellers.

There are two kinds of debit cards: online and offline. *On*line debit cards make an immediate transfer of money from the customer's bank account to the merchant's bank account. *Off*line debit cards record a debit against the customer's bank account, which is processed later.

A debit card offers less protection than a credit card. Unlike a credit card, a debit card payment cannot be stopped if a purchase is defective or an order is not delivered. In addition, your liability for the unauthorized use of your ATM or debit card is limited to $50 only if you notify the issuer within two business days of the loss or theft of the card. Your liability increases to $500 if notice is delayed beyond that time, and it becomes unlimited when notice is not given within 60 days. The unauthorized use of an ATM card is a criminal offense punishable by a $10,000 fine and/or 10 years in prison.

EXAMPLE 29-12: Stolen ATM Card

A thief stole Hockmeyer's purse from a grocery store shopping cart. Three days later, Hockmeyer notified the bank that her ATM card was missing. By then, however, the thief had found the card along with Hockmeyer's secret identification number and withdrawn $800 from her account. Because the bank was notified within three days of the theft, Hockmeyer lost $500. Had she notified the bank within two business days of the theft, she would have lost only $50.

Regulation E, issued by the Federal Reserve Board under the Electronic Fund Transfer Act, establishes the basic rights, liabilities, and responsibilities of consumers who use electronic fund transfer services and financial institutions that offer these services. Transactions covered under the regulation include:

• Point-of-sale purchases
• Automated teller machine transfers

BusinessWeek Business Law in the News

Japanese Banks: Reading Your Palm for Cash

When Japanese consumers need lots of cash in a hurry, they go to their banks and raise their right hands—their palms or their index fingers, more precisely.

ATMs at many banks in Japan now have scanners that take a snapshot of the veins in a customer's finger or palm, then compare that picture against a digital image stored on the account holder's bank card. The extra high-tech step allows customers to withdraw the equivalent of tens of thousands of dollars at a time from accounts.

Over the past two years, dozens of financial houses have added the biometric security systems to their ATMs in response to legislation passed in 2006 that holds banks liable for ATM withdrawals made with stolen or counterfeit bank cards. Customers have a few complaints: The scanners can't get a reading in bright light, they say, or when one's forefinger is even slightly curled away from the screen. But for most, the extra cash overshadows the extra hassle.

By now, some 20,000 of Japan's 110,000 ATMs have vein scanners, with sales of the technology at $70 million, according to the Japan Automatic Identification Systems Assn., an industry trade group. Not bad for a business that practically didn't exist three years ago.

Will high-tech palm reading come to American banks? Some bankers and ATM makers have looked into the idea, but there are problems. The systems are expensive to install. And security consultants like Chris McGoey of Los Angeles-based McGoey Security Consulting worry that higher withdrawal limits would make ATM robberies more attractive. Perhaps more important, a format war is shaping up in Japan between two versions of the security technology—one that is likely to slow its adoption abroad.

The two incompatible technologies are Fujitsu's (which scans palm veins) and Hitachi's (which reads finger veins). Because most bank cards still have a magnetic strip that works at any ATM for lower withdrawal limits, the format rivalry has had few casualties. But with banks considering phasing out the strips, that may change. "We're hoping the one we chose will become the standard," say Teisuke Kitayama, financial president of Sumitomo Mitsui, which uses Hitachi's system. So far, Hitachi appears to have the lead. Besides Sumitomo Mitsui, its customers include Mizuho Financial Group and Japan's soon-to-be-privatized postal system, which also runs a bank with 117 million customers.

Chinese Takeout: Counting Cash, Not Votes

Given the bad publicity plaguing Diebold's electronic voting machines in the U.S., the $2.6 billion company may feel it's a relief to do business in China, which won't be holding elections anytime soon. Diebold is hitching its fortunes to the rapid growth of self-service banking on the mainland, selling thousands of its ATMs to Chinese banks. "China is the most important market for us as we look into the future," says President and CEO Thomas W. Swidarski, who predicts 20% to 30% growth for those ATM sales in the next few years. The goal: a $1 billion Chinese sales operation in 7 to 10 years.

Key to reaching that goal, the company says, is maintaining a solid reputation for ATM service and security in China, where it has a 63-city service team. Diebold says its safety features (including a sensor to detect whether a device for information skimming, a common scam in China, is attached to

an ATM's card slot) make its machines safer than those of competitors. Will concerns about Diebold's voting machines in the runup to American elections raise questions among China's avid netizens about ATM security? "Our technology speaks for itself," says Swidarski, who adds that "never" has a Chinese banker asked about the voting machine flap in the U.S.

Questions for Analysis

1. What do ATMs at many banks in Japan now have?

2. What motivated financial houses to take this approach?

3. Why is this biometric security system not likely to come to American banks soon?

4. What company makes the electronic voting machines now selling in China?

5. What is this American company's goal?

6. What is key to reaching that goal?

7. What is one of the machine's safety features?

Sources: Kenji Hall, "Japanese Banks: Reading Your Palm for Cash," *BusinessWeek,* February 19, 2007, 16; Dexter Roberts, "Chinese Takeout: Counting Cash, Not Votes," *BusinessWeek*, October 6, 2006, 14.

- Telephone-initiated transfers requiring an entry password (PIN)

- Transfers resulting from debit card transactions requiring an entry password (PIN)

- Internet banking

UCC 4A-103-505

UCC 4A-104

UCC 4A-103

Under the act, consumers are entitled to receive a written receipt whenever they use an ATM. In addition, the transaction must appear on the periodic statement sent to the consumer. The consumer has 60 days to notify the bank of any error on the periodic statement or terminal receipt. After being notified, the bank has 10 business days to investigate the error. If the bank needs more time, it may take up to 45 days to complete the investigation, but only if the money in dispute is returned to the consumer's account.

Because the Electronic Fund Transfer Act is a consumer protection law, it does not apply to transactions between banks and other businesses. A different law, Article 4A of the UCC, has been adopted by many states to govern EFTs made by banks and businesses. Under the UCC, a business that orders money to be sent electronically is called the *originator*. The business that is to receive the money is called the *beneficiary*.

EXAMPLE 29-13: Electronic Transfers by Banks

Data Control, Inc., sold a computer system to Western Sales, Inc., for $2 million. When the system was installed, Western Sales ordered its bank to pay $2 million to Data Control. Because both companies had accounts in the First National Bank, the bank simply debited Western Sales' account and credited Data Control's account for $2 million. Western Sales was the originator; Data Control was the beneficiary. If Data Control had used a different bank, the First National Bank would have ordered that bank, called the beneficiary's bank, to credit Data Control's account for $2 million.

Businesses that deal with large sums of money need to be able to make quick transfers to avoid a loss of interest, among other reasons; EFTs help meet this need.

Quick Quiz 29-2 True or False?

1. Consumers have 30 days to notify the bank of any error on the periodic statement received for the use of an ATM.

2. A consumer's liability for the unauthorized use of an ATM card is limited to $500 if notice of the loss or theft of a card is given the issuer within two business days.

3. The unauthorized use of an ATM card is a criminal offense punishable by a $500 fine and/or five years in prison.

Did You Know?

- A *credit* card is like a loan. You agree to pay the money back later at a high interest rate unless you pay the full amount when the bill arrives. A *debit* card, in contrast, means "subtract"—when you use it, you subtract the money from your own bank account.

- If your *credit* card is lost or stolen, you can't lose more than $50. In contrast, if someone uses your *ATM* or *debit* card without permission, you can lose much more unless you notify your bank quickly.

- A *debit* card is often easier to obtain than a credit card and allows you to spend what is in your bank account.

- A *debit* card gives you less protection than a credit card when you purchase items that are defective or never delivered.

- Using a *debit* card instead of writing

Continued

checks saves you from showing identification or giving out personal identification at the time of a transaction.

29-3 Bank Deposits and Collections

The tremendous number of checks handled by banks and the countrywide nature of the bank collection process require uniformity in the law of bank collections. For this reason, Article 4 of the UCC contains rules and regulations for handling bank deposits and collections.

Bank Descriptions

During the bank collection process, banks are described by different terms, depending on their particular function in a transaction. Sometimes a bank takes a check for deposit. At other times, it pays a check as a drawee. At still other times, it takes a check for collection only. The different terms that are used to describe banks and their meanings are as follows: A **depositary bank** is the first bank to which an item is transferred for collection, even if it is also the payor bank. The term **payor bank** describes a bank by which an item is payable as drawn or accepted. It includes a drawee bank. **Intermediary bank** defines any bank to which an item is transferred in the course of collection, except the depositary or payor bank. The **collecting bank** is any bank handling the item for collection, except the payor bank, and the **presenting bank** is any bank presenting an item, except a payor bank. **Remitting bank** describes any payor or intermediary bank remitting for an item.

UCC 4-105

A Check's Life Cycle

The life cycle of a check begins when the drawer writes a check and delivers it to the payee. The payee may take the check directly to the payor bank (the bank on which it was drawn) for payment. If that bank pays the check in cash, its payment is final, and the check is returned to the drawer with the next bank statement. However, it is more likely that the check will be deposited in the payee's own account in another bank. That bank, known as the depositary bank, acts as its customer's agent to collect the money from the payor bank. Any settlement given by the depositary bank in this case is **provisional** (not final). It may be revoked if the check is later dishonored. The check is sent (sometimes through an intermediary bank) to a collecting bank, which presents the check to the payor bank for payment. If it is honored by the payor bank, the amount will be deducted from the drawer's account, and a substitute check will be returned to the drawer with the next bank statement. If the check is dishonored for any reason, a substitute check will be returned to the payee via the same route that it was sent, and all credits given for the item will be revoked (see Figure 29-2).

UCC 4-213
UCC 4-201

The Check 21 Act

Named for the twenty-first century, the **Check 21 Act** brings the check-clearing method into the modern age by the use of electronic check processing. Such processing could not be done prior to this 2004 law, because of the legal requirement that original checks be presented to the drawee bank for payment. Under this law, a new negotiable instrument called a substitute check is used. A **substitute check** (also called an image replacement document or IRD) is a paper reproduction of both sides of an original check that can be processed just like the original check. Under the new law, banks are not required to use substitute checks, but when they do so for consideration, they make the following warranties:

- The substitute check contains an accurate image of the front and back of the original check.
- It is the legal equivalent of the original check.
- No drawer, drawee, indorser, or depositary bank will be asked to pay a check that it already has paid.

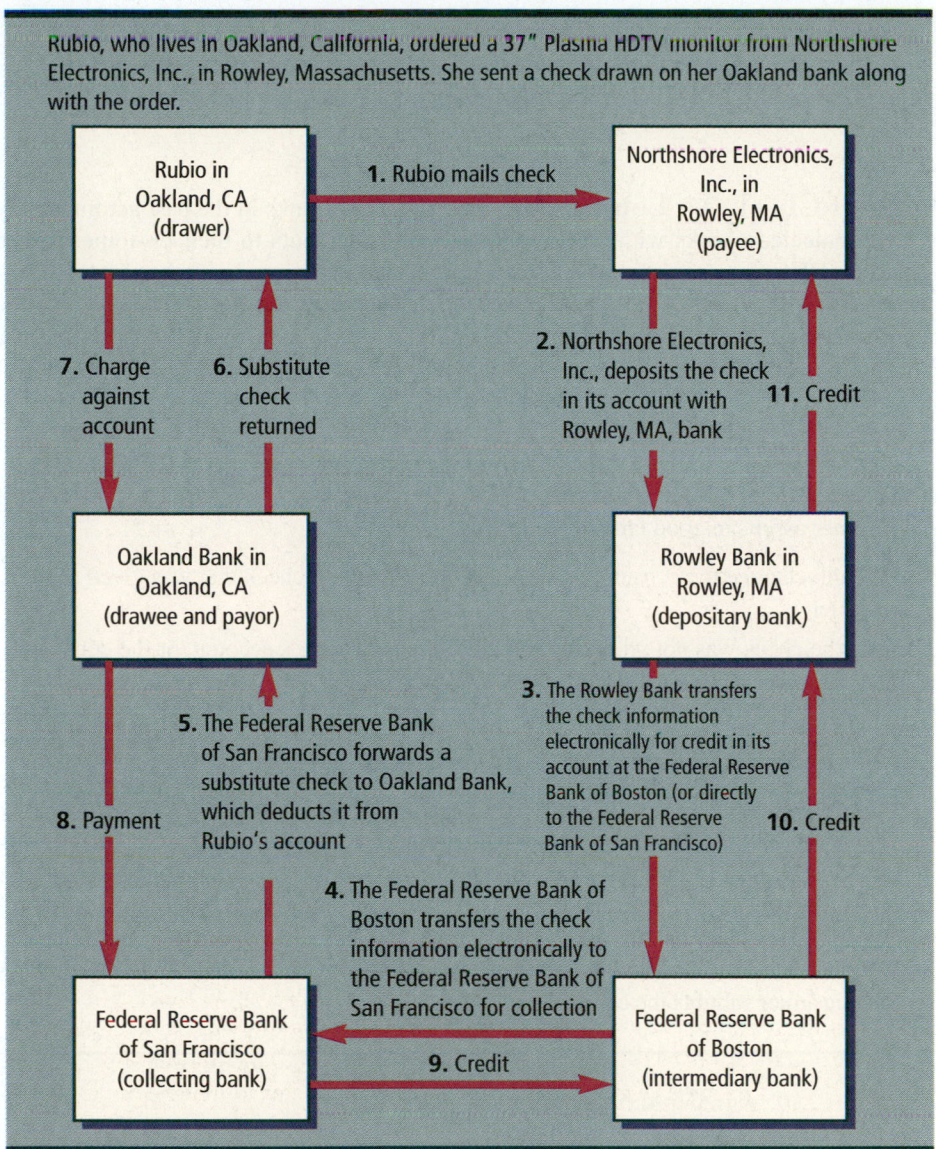

Rubio, who lives in Oakland, California, ordered a 37″ Plasma HDTV monitor from Northshore Electronics, Inc., in Rowley, Massachusetts. She sent a check drawn on her Oakland bank along with the order.

Rubio in Oakland, CA (drawer)

1. Rubio mails check

Northshore Electronics, Inc., in Rowley, MA (payee)

7. Charge against account

6. Substitute check returned

2. Northshore Electronics, Inc., deposits the check in its account with Rowley, MA, bank

11. Credit

Oakland Bank in Oakland, CA (drawee and payor)

Rowley Bank in Rowley, MA (depositary bank)

5. The Federal Reserve Bank of San Francisco forwards a substitute check to Oakland Bank, which deducts it from Rubio's account

8. Payment

3. The Rowley Bank transfers the check information electronically for credit in its account at the Federal Reserve Bank of Boston (or directly to the Federal Reserve Bank of San Francisco)

10. Credit

4. The Federal Reserve Bank of Boston transfers the check information electronically to the Federal Reserve Bank of San Francisco for collection

Federal Reserve Bank of San Francisco (collecting bank)

9. Credit

Federal Reserve Bank of Boston (intermediary bank)

Figure 29-2   The life cycle of Rubio's check is traced through its collection and clearinghouse routes. Before the Check 21 Act became effective in October 2004, the check in this example would have had to be physically transported by plane or truck around its entire route.

EXAMPLE 29-14:   Electronic Check Clearing

Suppose that the Rowley bank, in the example given in Figure 29-2 illustrating the life cycle of a check, has elected to use electronic check processing, including substitute checks as a method of clearing checks. When it receives the original check deposited by Rubio, it can transfer the check information electronically to the Federal Reserve Bank of San Francisco. That bank can create a substitute check to present to the Oakland Bank, where it is deducted from Rubio's account. Under the law, the Oakland Bank is

> required to accept the substitute check. As a result, instead of transporting the original check across the country by plane or truck, the Rowley, Massachusetts, bank can collect the substitute check at a much faster pace, using only local California transportation.

UCC 4-406 (a)(b)

Original Check No Longer Returned   Many banks in the past automatically returned canceled checks with their monthly bank statements to their customers, even though the UCC does not require that original checks be returned unless a customer requests them. The Check 21 Act, which takes precedence over the UCC, changes this rule. Under the Check 21 Act, the customer has a right only to a paper substitute check that is a reproduction of the front and back of the original. Bank customers no longer have an absolute right to see their original canceled checks.

Consumer Protection   To protect consumers from losses related to substitute checks, the Check 21 Act includes a consumer's right to claim an *expedited credit*. This right exists if the consumer asserts in good faith the following four facts:

- The bank charged the consumer's account for a substitute check that was given to the consumer.
- Either the check was not properly charged to the consumer's account, or the consumer has a warranty claim with respect to the substitute check.
- The consumer suffered a resulting loss.
- The production of the original check or a better copy of the original check is necessary to determine the validity of any claim.

If the consumer makes a claim within 45 days after receiving the bank statement or substitute check, the bank must investigate it and make any necessary recredit to the consumer's account. If the bank needs more than 10 days to investigate and resolve the complaint, it must recredit the consumer's account for an amount up to $2,500 while it completes its investigation. The bank must recredit any remaining balance greater than $2,500 no later than 45 days after the consumer submits the claim.

Quick Quiz 29-3 True or False?

1. A collecting bank is any bank to which an item is transferred in the course of collection, except the depositary or payor bank.

2. If the payor bank pays a check in cash, its payment is final.

3. Under the Check 21 Act, bank customers no longer have an absolute right to see their original canceled check.

Summary

29.1   The drawee bank must honor all checks (except stale checks) drawn by its customers when there are sufficient funds on deposit. Failure to do so makes the bank liable to the customer for any actual damages the customer suffers. The drawee bank has no liability to the holder of a check unless it is certified. Banks may pay checks for 10 days after the death of a drawer. Banks are responsible for paying altered or forged checks. Banks must make funds available to depositors according to a specific schedule. In addition, banks must pay or return checks on or before their midnight deadline. Depositors must examine their bank statements and canceled checks promptly. It is a crime to write a check with insufficient funds in the bank. Oral stop-payment orders are binding upon the bank for 14 days; written orders to stop payment are binding for six months. Bank accounts are insured by the FDIC for up to $100,000 for individual accounts and up to an additional $100,000 for joint accounts.

29.2   Consumers who use EFTs have 60 days to notify the bank of an error; thereafter, the bank must investigate. A consumer's liability for the unauthorized use of an ATM card is limited to $50 if notice of the loss or theft of a card is given the issuer within 2 business days. The consumer's liability increases to $500 when notice is withheld beyond 2 business days and becomes unlimited when notice is not given within 60 days. Article 4A of the UCC governs EFTs made by banks and businesses.

29.3   If a payee cashes a check at a payor (drawee) bank, the payment is final. If, instead, the payee deposits a check in his or her bank, which sends it to the payor bank for collection, any payment is provisional. The Check 21 Act establishes *substitute checks*, which may be returned to bank customers in place of the canceled original check and thus make check clearing much quicker through the use of electronic processing.

Key Terms

ATM card, 597	forgery, 590	remitting bank, 600
Check 21 Act, 600	intermediary bank, 600	stale check, 590
collecting bank, 600	midnight deadline, 593	subrogation, 595
debit card, 597	overdraft, 589	substitute check, 600
depositary bank, 600	payor bank, 600	uttering, 590
e-check, 597	presenting bank, 600	
electronic fund transfers (EFTs), 597	provisional, 600	

Questions for Review and Discussion

1. What is the liability of a bank for dishonoring an uncertified check due to a mistake on its part to its customer? To a holder of the check? In the case of a stale check?
2. What is the bank's responsibility as to the payment of checks after the death of the drawer? The payment of forged and altered checks?
3. When must banks make funds available to depositors for checks drawn on the U.S. Treasury? A bank draft? A cashier's check? Checks drawn on banks within the same Federal Reserve district? Checks drawn on banks outside the bank's Federal Reserve district?
4. What crimes may occur when someone writes a check with insufficient funds? Why is it important for depositors to examine their bank statements promptly?
5. How does an oral stop-payment order compare with a written stop-payment order as it affects the bank's obligations?
6. How may a husband, wife, and one child have insured accounts totaling $600,000 in a bank?
7. In what way are consumers protected by the Electronic Fund Transfer Act?
8. How do EFTs help meet the needs of businesses that deal with large sums of money?
9. What is the difference between a *depositary bank* and a *payor bank*?
10. What is the life cycle of a check that is deposited in a payee's bank?
11. What is the principal feature of the Check 21 Act?

Investigating the Internet

Every three years, the Board of Governors of the Federal Reserve System conducts a survey of consumer finances to gain a better understanding of the financial condition of families in the United States and the effects of changes in the economy. The data collected in the survey also support a wide variety of research on topics including saving, investment, debt payments, pension coverage, business ownership, the use of financial institutions, credit discrimination, and financial markets. The most recent survey will be completed in December 2007, after the manuscript for this book is written.

Log onto the Internet and key in the words "Federal Reserve System" to find information uncovered by the latest survey. Of particular interest is information about the dramatic decrease in recent years of the use of cash and checks and the increase in the use of electronic payments by the American public.

Cases for Analysis

1. Arthur Woods died holding an annuity payable on his death to his wife, Dorothy. In payment of the annuity, a checking account for $24,900 was established in Dorothy Woods's name. The bank sent the checkbook and account statements to Woods's attorney, who had requested that the account be established for Woods. Six unauthorized checks bearing Dorothy Woods's forged signature were drawn on her checking account. Woods discovered the forgeries a year later when she received the checkbook and bank statements from her attorney. She notified the bank of the forgeries 15 months after they had been written. Was the bank responsible for paying the forged checks? Why or why not? *Woods v. MONY Legacy Life Insurance Company,* 84 N.Y.2d 290 (NY).

2. Kelco bought a truck from Felton, paying for it with a cashier's check she had obtained from her bank. On her way home, the truck broke down. Kelco immediately telephoned her bank and told it to stop payment on the cashier's check. Later, Kelco discovered that her bank had not stopped payment on the cashier's check and instead had paid it. Did Kelco have a claim against the bank? Explain. See also *Taboada v. Bank of Babylon,* 408 N.Y.S.2d 734 (NY).

3. Granite Corp. sent a check to Overseas Equipment Co. When the check was reported lost, Granite wrote to its bank telling it to stop payment on the check. Granite then sent the money to Overseas Equipment Co. by wire. Thirteen months later, the check turned up, and Granite's bank paid it. Did the bank violate its duty to stop payment on the check? Explain. *Granite Equip. Leasing Corp. v. Hempstead Bank,* 326 N.Y.S.2d 881 (NY).

4. While in the hospital during his final illness, Norris wrote out a check and gave it to his sister. She deposited it in her bank account. Norris died before the check cleared, and his bank refused to pay it. May a bank honor a check when it knows of the death of the drawer? Explain. *In re Estate of Norris,* 532 P.2d 981 (CO).

5. On June 18, Templeton deposited in his bank account a $5,000 check that was payable to his order. The check reached the drawee bank through normal banking channels on June 22. That bank had received a stop-payment order on the check on May 15 and, therefore, refused to honor it. It kept the check until June 28, when it returned it to Templeton with the notification that payment had been stopped. Did the drawee bank violate a duty it owed to Templeton? Explain. *Templeton v. First Nat'l Bank,* 362 N.E.2d 33 (IL).

6. In payment for services rendered, one of Stewart's clients gave him a check for $185.48 that had been drawn by the client's corporate employer and had been made payable to the order of the client.

Although properly indorsed by the client, the drawee bank flatly refused to cash the check for Stewart. The bank acknowledged that the check was good, that is, that there were sufficient funds in the account. Could Stewart sue the bank for refusing to honor the check? Why or why not? *Stewart v. Citizens & Nat'l Bank,* 225 S.E.2d 761 (GA).

7. Fitting wrote an $800 check on her account with Continental Bank. A bank employee had mistakenly placed a hold on the account, causing the bank to dishonor the check when it was presented for pay-

ment. Fitting was unable to prove that she suffered damages because of the dishonor. Could she recover damages from the bank? Explain. *Continental Bank v. Fitting,* 559 P.2d 218 (AZ).

8. Roberta Lunt deposited a $625 nonlocal check payable to her with a teller at her bank at 10:30 a.m. on Monday. The next day, Tuesday, she went to the bank to withdraw $300 and was told by the teller that she could have only $100 from the check she had deposited the day before. When must the funds be made available to Roberta? Explain why.

Quick Quiz Answers

29-1	29-2	29-3
1. F	1. F	1. F
2. T	2. F	2. T
3. T	3. F	3. T

Part 5 Case Study

Triffin v. Dillabough and American Express
Supreme Court of Pennsylvania
670 A.2d 684; 716 A.2d 605

Summary

Three American Express money orders were stolen from one of its agents, and 100 others were stolen while being shipped to a different agent. When stolen, all of the money orders contained the preprinted signature of the chairman of American Express, but they were blank as to the amount, sender, and date.

Stacy Anne Dillabough presented two of the stolen money orders for payment at Chuckie Enterprises, Inc. (Chuckie's), a check-cashing operation in Philadelphia. The money orders were in the amounts of $550 and $650 and listed Dillabough as the payee and David W. (last name undecipherable) as the sender. Two months later, Robert Lynn presented another one of the stolen money orders for payment at Chuckie's in the amount of $200, which listed himself as payee and Michael C. Pepe as the sender.

After being cashed at Chuckie's, the money orders traveled the regular bank collection routes and were returned to Chuckie's bearing the stamp "REPORTED LOST OR STOLEN—DO NOT REDEPOSIT." American Express refused to pay Chuckie's the face amounts of the money orders. Chuckie's then sold them to Triffin, a commercial discounter. By written agreements, Chuckie's assigned all of its right, title, and interest in the money orders to Triffin.

In court, Triffin obtained judgments by default against Dillabough and Lynn. In a trial with American Express, the court found that the money orders were not negotiable instruments and entered a judgment in favor of American Express. On appeal, the Superior Court reversed the trial court and held that the money orders were negotiable instruments and that Triffin had the status of a holder in due course, entitling him to recover the face amount of the money orders from American Express.

The Court's Opinion

Madame Justice Newman

The Superior Court has described the purpose of negotiable instruments and the Commercial Code as follows:

> A negotiable instrument is an instrument capable of transfer by indorsement or delivery. Negotiability provides a means of passing on to the transferee the rights of the holder, including the right to sue in his or her own name, and the right to take free of equities as against the assignor/payee. [Citations omitted.] The purpose of the Commercial Code is to enhance the marketability of negotiable instruments and to allow bankers, brokers, and the general public to trade in confidence. [Citations omitted.] As a matter of sound economic policy, the Commercial Code encourages the free transfer and negotiability of commercial paper to stimulate financial interdependence.

Manor Bldg. Corp. v. Manor Complex Assocs., 645 A.2d 843. With these principles in mind, we turn to a discussion of the American Express money orders at issue here.

The threshold question is whether the money orders qualify as negotiable instruments under Division Three of the Commercial Code, 3101, et seq., which governs negotiability.[1] Both parties agree that if the money orders are not negotiable instruments then Triffin's claims against American Express must fail. Initially, we note that the Commercial Code does not specifically define the term "money order," nor does it provide a descriptive list of financial documents that automatically qualify as negotiable instruments. Instead, 3104(a) sets forth the following four-part test to determine if a particular document qualifies as a negotiable instrument:

A. Requisites to negotiability. Any writing to be a negotiable instrument within this division must:

  1. be signed by the maker or drawer;

  2. contain an unconditional promise or order to pay a sum certain in money and no other promise, order, obligation or power given by the maker or drawer except as authorized by this division;

  3. be payable on demand or at a definite time; and

  4. be payable to order or to bearer.

The Superior Court described the face of the money orders in question as follows:

> Prior to being stolen[,] the American Express money orders read: "AMERICAN EXPRESS MONEY ORDER . . . CHASE SAVINGS BANK . . . DATE (blank). PAY THE SUM OF (blank), NOT GOOD OVER $1,000, TO THE ORDER OF (blank). Louis V. Gerstner, Chairman. SENDER'S NAME AND ADDRESS (blank). Issued by American Express Travel Related Services Company, Inc., Englewood, Colorado. Payable at United Bank of Grand Junction, Downtown, Grand Junction, Colorado.

The first requisite of negotiability, a signature by the drawer or maker, "includes any symbol executed or adopted by a party with present intention to authenticate a writing." § 1201. "Authentication may be printed, stamped or written; it may be by initials or by thumbprint. . . . The question always is whether the symbol was executed or adopted by the party with

present intention to authenticate the writing." Additionally, section 3307(a)(2) states that when the effectiveness of a signature is challenged, it is presumed to be genuine or authorized unless the signer has died or become incompetent. Here, the drawer, American Express, affixed the pre-printed signature of Louis Gerstner, its then Chairman, to the money orders in question before forwarding them to its agents. American Express does not argue that Gerstner's signature was affixed to the money orders for any reason other than to authenticate them. Accordingly, the money orders satisfy the first requisite for negotiability.

The second requisite, American Express argues, is lacking because the money orders do not contain an unconditional promise or order to pay. Specifically, American Express claims that a legend it placed on the back of the money orders qualifies an otherwise unconditional order on the front directing the drawee to "PAY THE SUM OF" a specified amount "TO THE ORDER OF" the payee. The legend provides as follows:

IMPORTANT
DO NOT CASH FOR STRANGERS

THIS MONEY ORDER WILL NOT BE PAID IF IT HAS BEEN ALTERED OR STOLEN OR IF AN INDORSEMENT IS MISSING OR FORGED. BE SURE YOU HAVE EFFECTIVE RECOURSE AGAINST YOUR CUSTOMER.

PAYEE'S INDORSEMENT

According to American Express, this legend renders the order to pay conditional on the money order not being altered, stolen, unindorsed or forged and destroys the negotiability of the instrument.

We disagree. In a factually similar case, the Louisiana Court of Appeal construed a legend on the back of an American Express money order similar to the one at issue here. *Hong Kong Importers, Inc. v. American Express Co.*, 301 So.2d 707. The legend there stated "CASH ONLY IF RECOURSE FROM INDORSER IS AVAILABLE. IF THIS MONEY ORDER HAS NOT BEEN VALIDLY ISSUED OR HAS BEEN FRAUDULENTLY NEGOTIATED, IT WILL BE RETURNED." The money order also had the following language printed on its face: "KNOW YOUR INDORSER CASH ONLY IF RECOURSE IS AVAILABLE." The Louisiana Court held that the legend on the back and the language on the front did not convert the money order into a conditional promise to pay, but merely operated as a warning to the party cashing the money order to protect himself against fraud. Although *Hong Kong* was decided before Louisiana

---

[1] Although the Commercial Code has been revised since the transactions in this case occurred, its basic provisions survived the 1992 amendments. We expect that this Opinion will provide guidance for transactions conducted pursuant to the Commercial Code as amended in 1992.

adopted the Uniform Commercial Code, we find its rationale to be persuasive and applicable to § 3104.

American Express attempts to distinguish *Hong Kong* by asserting that the legend in this case is more specific because it explicitly conditions payment on the money orders not being altered, stolen, unindorsed or forged. This argument misses the point. "Any writing which meets the requirements of subsection [(a)] and is not excluded under Section [3103] is a negotiable instrument, and all sections of this [Division] apply to it, *even though it may contain additional language beyond that contemplated by this section.*" § 3104, Comment 4 (emphasis added). An otherwise unconditional order to pay that meets the section 3104 requirements is not made conditional by including implied or constructive conditions in the instrument. § 3105(a)(1). Moreover, purported conditions on an otherwise negotiable instrument, that merely reflect other provisions of the law, do not vitiate negotiability. *State v. Phelps*, 608 P.2d 51 (Ariz. Ct. App. 1979). Here, the alleged conditions on the back of the money orders are nothing more than a restatement of American Express' statutory defenses against payment because of alteration, absence of signature, and forgery. Contrary to American Express' claims, expressing those statutory defenses in a legend with the conditional phrase "THIS MONEY ORDER WILL NOT BE PAID IF . . ." does not elevate the legend to a condition for the purposes of 3104(a) because it is merely a restatement of the defenses present in the Commercial Code. The legend is simply a warning that American Express has reserved its statutory defenses. Whether these defenses are effective against Triffin is a separate question to be answered after resolving the issue of negotiability. We hold, therefore, that the money orders contain an unconditional order to pay, and satisfy the second requisite of negotiability.

The third requisite, that the writing be payable on demand or at a definite time, and the fourth requisite, that the writing be payable to order or bearer, are clear from the face of the money orders and are not disputed by the parties. Thus, the American Express money orders qualify as negotiable instruments pursuant to § 3104.

American Express contends that even if the money orders are facially negotiable, they should not be viewed as negotiable instruments because they were never issued or otherwise "placed in the stream of commerce." Issue is defined as "[t]he first delivery of an instrument to a holder or a remitter." § 3102. Delivery is defined as the "voluntary transfer of possession." § 1201. American Express argues that because the money orders were incomplete when stolen and subsequently completed without authorization, the money orders were never delivered and it should have no liability for them.

Authorized completion and delivery, however, are not listed as requisites to negotiability in section 3104. Moreover, section 3115 specifically permits the enforcement of incomplete and undelivered instruments and provides as follows:

A. General rule. When a paper whose contents at the time of signing show that it is intended to become an instrument is signed while still incomplete in any necessary respect it cannot be enforced until completed, but when it is completed in accordance with authority given it is effective as completed.

B. Unauthorized completion. *If the completion is unauthorized the rules as to material alteration apply (section 3407), even though the paper was not delivered by the maker or drawer,* but the burden of establishing that any completion is unauthorized is on the party so asserting [emphasis added].

Section 3407 provides that the defense of unauthorized completion discharges a party from liability to any person *other than a holder in due course.* § 3407(a)(2); § 3407(b). "A subsequent holder in due course may in all cases enforce the [negotiable] instrument according to its original tenor, and when an incomplete instrument has been completed, he may enforce it as completed." 3407(c). Additionally, section 3305 provides that a holder in due course takes a negotiable instrument free from the defense of non-delivery. § 3305, Comment 3.

When read together, sections 3115, 3407 and 3305 demonstrate that unauthorized completion and non-delivery do not prevent enforcement of an otherwise negotiable instrument. Instead, the three sections permit a holder in due course to enforce the undelivered instrument as completed. . . .

The next question then, is whether Triffin has the rights of a holder in due course who can enforce the negotiable money orders.

Section 3302(a) describes a holder in due course as follows:

A. General rule. A holder in due course is a holder who takes the instrument:

1. for value;

2. in good faith; and

3. without notice that it is overdue or has been dishonored or of any defense against or claim to it on the part of any person. § 3302(a).

Because the trial court held that the money orders were not negotiable instruments, it never answered the question of Triffin's status as a holder in due course. . . .

Triffin obtained the money orders from Chuckie's pursuant to a written agreement by which Chuckie's assigned all of its right, title and interest in the money orders to Triffin. Triffin could not become a holder in due course in his own name because he had notice of American Express' defenses when he took the money orders from Chuckie's. § 3302(a)(3). However, Triffin could acquire the status of a holder in due course from Chuckie's through the assignment if Chuckie's was a holder in due course because a transferee acquires whatever rights the transferor had, even if the transferee is aware of the defenses to enforcement. § 3201. Therefore, the focus of our inquiry is whether Chuckie's was a holder in due course.

The parties do not dispute that Chuckie's took the money orders for value. Paul Giunta, the owner of Chuckie's, testified that he paid Dillabough and Lynn the face value of the money orders, minus a two percent fee. Thus, section 3302(a)(1) is satisfied. The second element of section 3302(a), good faith, is defined as "honesty in fact in the conduct or transaction concerned." § 1201. The evidence established that Giunta recognized Dillabough and Lynn from previous transactions and required them to present photographic identification. Additionally, although the trial court did not discuss each element of Chuckie's holder in due course status, it did opine in a discussion of its legal conclusions on the record that Chuckie's acted in good faith. Moreover, American Express does not argue that Chuckie's failed to act in good faith. Based on Giunta's actions, we cannot say that the trial court erred in concluding that Chuckie's acted in good faith. Therefore, section 3302(a)(2) is satisfied. Regarding section 3302(a)(3), there was no evidence presented that Chuckie's had any notice that the Dillabough and Lynn money orders were stolen when he cashed them. Accordingly, the record demonstrates as a matter of law that Chuckie's was a holder in due course. Because Triffin stands in Chuckie's shoes as its assignee, Triffin has attained the status of a holder in due course. §3201.

American Express further contends that even if Triffin qualifies as a holder in due course, the money orders are still not enforceable because the legend on their backs limits the "tenor" of the instruments. Pursuant to § 3413(a), American Express claims that it is only obligated to pay an instrument "according to its tenor." The 1979 Commercial Code does not define "tenor." The 1992 amendments to section 3413(a), however, substitute the word "terms" for the word "tenor." § 3413(a). Therefore, it appears that no substantive change was intended by the substitution of the word "terms" for the word "tenor" and we will treat these words synonymously. Thus, American Express is essentially arguing that each money order should be enforced according to its terms, which state that the money order "WILL NOT BE PAID IF IT HAS BEEN ALTERED OR STOLEN OR IF AN INDORSEMENT IS MISSING OR FORGED."

As previously discussed, the legend on the back of the money orders is merely a warning that restates American Express' defenses against persons other than holders in due course in the event of alteration, theft, lack of indorsement or forgery. These defenses are ineffective against a holder in due course. § 3305; § 3407(c). Because Triffin has attained holder in due course status through the assignment of the money orders from Chuckie's, American Express cannot enforce the defenses against him. Accordingly, American Express is liable to Triffin for the face value of the money orders.

The Order of the Superior Court is affirmed.

Dissenting Opinion

Mr. Justice Castille

The majority concludes that appellee Robert J. Triffin ("appellee") is entitled to recover the value of the money orders at issue because the money orders were negotiable instruments and because appellee was a holder in due course of those negotiable instruments. However, since the money orders at issue contained express conditional language which precluded negotiability under the relevant statute, I must respectfully dissent from the majority's conclusion....

At issue here is the second of the four statutory prerequisites to negotiability, the requirement of an "unconditional" promise or order. Regarding this prerequisite, section 3105 provides:

A. Unconditional promise or order. A promise or order otherwise unconditional is not made conditional by the fact that the instrument:

1. is subject to implied or constructive conditions;

   ...The comment to section 3105 states:

   1. Nothing in [paragraph (a) subsection (1)] is intended to imply that language may not be fairly construed to mean what it says, but implications, whether of law or fact, are not to be considered in determining negotiability.

Thus, the statute clearly distinguishes between language which creates an implied condition and language which creates an express condition. The latter renders a promise or order non-negotiable while the former does not.

This conclusion derives further support from the revised § 3106(a), which provides that

> . . .a promise or order is unconditional unless it states (1) an express condition to payment. . . .

Here, the operative language in the money orders at issue clearly created an "express" condition and thereby rendered the money orders non-negotiable. The language at issue . . . explicitly conditions payments on the money orders' not being altered or stolen and the indorsements' not being missing or forged. The use of the word "if" renders the condition an express one, since "if" by definition means "on *condition* that; in case that; supposing that." Webster's New World Dict., 2d College ed. (emphasis added).

Furthermore, the official comment to revised section 3106 explains what the code intends by drawing the distinction between implied and express conditions:

> If the promise or order states an express condition to payment, the promise or order is not an instrument. For example, A states, "I promise to pay $100,000 to the order of John Doe if he conveys title to Blackacre to me." The promise is not an instrument because there is an express condition to payment. However, suppose a promise states, "In consideration of John Doe's promise to convey title of Blackacre I promise to pay $100,000 to the order of John Doe. That promise can be an instrument if [section 3104] is otherwise satisfied.

Accordingly, the use of the word "if" creates an express condition which otherwise might be lacking, and thereby precludes a money order from being a negotiable instrument under the statute. The language at issue in this case created the same type of express condition which is embodied in the Comment; consequently, the language precludes the money orders from being negotiable instruments.

The reasons proffered by the majority to justify its departure from this seemingly inescapable statutory logic are strained. First, the majority cites a case, decided by the Louisiana Court of Appeal in 1974, in which a condition incorporating the word "if" was construed not to bar negotiability. In that case, the Louisiana Court did not evaluate the significance of the word "if" or the significance of the condition which that word introduced. Moreover, in 1974, Louisiana had not yet adopted Article III of the Uniform Commercial Code ("UCC"). Hence, it appears that the Louisiana decision was decided against the backdrop of the Code of Napoleon. See *9 to 5 Fashions, Inc. v. Petr L. Spurney*, 538 So.2d 228, 233 (La. 1989) (discussing roots of Louisiana's civil code in the Napoleonic code). Pennsylvania, on the other hand, has adopted Article III of the UCC, which speaks directly to the issue presented in this case, as explained supra. A decision by an intermediate Louisiana appellate court interpreting French legal principles should not override the explicit statutory guidance furnished by the Pennsylvania legislature on an issue of Pennsylvania law.

The majority also seizes on Comment 4 to § 3104, which states that "any writing which meets the requirements of subsection [(a)] and is not excluded under Section [3103] is a negotiable instrument, and all sections of this [Division] apply to it, *even though it may contain additional language beyond that contemplated by this section*" (emphasis added by majority). Since, as explained supra, the money orders contained language which precluded them from satisfying subsection (a), the quoted language from Comment 4 does not further the majority's argument.

Finally, the majority attempts to support its conclusion by referring to the principle that "purported conditions on an otherwise negotiable instrument, that merely reflect other provisions of the law, do not vitiate negotiability." The majority contends that the language at issue amounts merely to a restatement of appellant's statutory defenses against payment where there has been alteration (§ 3407), theft (§ 3306(4)), absence of signature (§ 3401) and forgery (§ 3404). The majority overlooks the fact that all of these statutory defenses are, by their own terms, ineffective against holders in due course. On the other hand, the language at issue here—which categorically states that the money order will not be paid if it was stolen—is operative even against holders who have taken in due course. As noted in the Comment to section 3105(a)(1), conditional language may be fairly construed to mean what it says. By its plain terms, the language at issue here sweeps beyond the scope of appellant's statutory defenses, and therefore does more than simply "reflect other provisions of the law."

In sum, the statute at issue in this case is devoid of ambiguity, and the application of that statute to these facts compels a conclusion contrary to that reached by the majority. Consequently, I respectfully dissent.

Mr. Justice Cappy joins this dissenting opinion.

Questions for Analysis

1. What did the court say is the four-part test to determine whether a particular document qualifies as a negotiable instrument? Were these basic requirements changed by the 1990 UCC revision?

2. What does the definition of a signature on a negotiable instrument include?

3. How did the court respond to American Express's argument that the following words created a condition: "this money order will not be paid if it has been altered or stolen or if an indorsement is missing or forged"?

4. Why does the fact that the money orders were completed without authorization and not delivered have no effect on negotiation of an instrument?

5. Why could Triffin not become a holder in due course?

6. Why could Triffin acquire the status of a holder in due course?

7. In his dissenting opinion, what argument did Mr. Justice Castille use to try to persuade the other justices that the money orders were not negotiable?

8. Do you agree with the dissenting opinion? Why or why not?

Part Six

Insurance, Secured Transactions, and Bankruptcy

Chapter 30 | Insurance

The Opening Case
"Triple Indemnity"

Sarah and Joseph Nastasia were married in 2004 and bought their dream house on the shore in Pas Christian, Mississippi. Sarah took out a life insurance policy on Joseph's life, naming herself as beneficiary. She continued to pay the premiums even after they were divorced in 2006. The divorce judgment contained an order that the couple's late-model Infinity that was registered and insured in their names jointly "shall belong to Joseph outright." Their "dream house" was completely washed away in Hurricane Katrina. The couple had homeowner's insurance but no flood insurance. Joseph was killed in 2007 while driving the Infinity at a high rate of speed on Interstate 70 without wearing a seat belt. The Infinity was totaled. The couple had not gotten around to removing Sarah's name from the insurance policy as a co-owner of the Infinity.

Opening Case Questions

1. Could Sarah collect on the life insurance policy?

2. Could she collect on the automobile insurance policy?

3. Will they collect on their homeowner's policy for the loss of their home?

LO Learning Objectives

1. Define risk management and explain the purpose of insurance.
2. Identify the contractual elements that are necessary to make an insurance agreement binding.
3. Make clear the importance of insurable interest.
4. Differentiate among straight life, limited-payment life, term, and endowment insurance.
5. Identify exemptions from risk and optional provisions that may be part of a life insurance policy.
6. Explain how insurable interest differs with life insurance and property insurance.
7. Explain the coinsurance clause in most property insurance policies.
8. Describe the kinds of losses that are covered by fire insurance, marine insurance, homeowner's and renter's insurance, and flood insurance.
9. Differentiate among the principal kinds of automobile insurance and determine which insurance covers a particular loss.
10. Describe the benefits that are often included in health insurance policies.

11. List the steps to be followed in applying for, obtaining, and maintaining an insurance policy.
12. Judge, in given situations, whether an insurance policy can be canceled.

30-1 Risk Management

Although life has always been full of risks and uncertainties, it has become even more so since 9/11. A process called risk management is used by many businesses to identify, analyze, control, and communicate risks of all kinds, from the making of an accounting error to having the company's security compromised. Hazards such as accidents, fire, and illness pose a constant threat to our well-being. The principal protection against losses from such hazards is insurance. The purpose of insurance is to spread the losses among a greater number of people. (See Table 30-1.) **Insurance** is a transfer of the risk of economic loss from the insured to the insurance company. Small contributions made by a large number of individuals can provide sufficient money to cover the losses suffered by a few as they occur each year. The function of insurance is to distribute each person's risk among all others who may or may not experience losses.

Parties to an Insurance Contract

The parties to an insurance contract are the insurer (sometimes called *underwriter*), the insured, and the beneficiary. The **insurer** accepts the risk of loss in return for a **premium** (the consideration paid for a policy) and agrees to **indemnify**, or compensate, the insured against the loss specified in the contract. The **insured** is the party (or parties) protected by the insurance contract. The contract of insurance is called the **policy**. The period of time during which the insurer assumes the risk of loss is known as the life of the policy. A third party, to whom payment of compensation is sometimes provided by the contract, is called the **beneficiary**.

Table 30-1 Examples of Risk Management Strategies		
Risks		**Strategies for Reducing**
Personal Event	**Financial Impact**	**Financial Impact**
Disability	• Loss of income • Increased expenses	• Savings and investments • Disability insurance
Death	• Loss of income	• Life insurance • Estate planning
Property loss	• Catastrophic storm damage to property • Repair or replacement • Cost of theft	• Property repair and upkeep • Auto insurance • Homeowner's insurance • Flood or earthquake insurance
Liability	• Claims and settlement costs • Lawsuits and legal expenses • Loss of personal assets and income	• Maintaining property • Homeowner's insurance • Auto insurance

Source: Gordon W. Brown, *Understanding Business and Personal Law,* 11th ed. Woodland Hills, CA: Glencoe/McGraw-Hill, p. 752.

Contractual Elements

Insurance policies, like other contracts, require an offer, an acceptance, mutual assent, capable parties, consideration, and a legally valid subject matter. The application filled in by an applicant is an offer to the insurer, which may then accept or reject the offer. To have mutual assent, the parties must have reached agreement on the terms of the contract. A party to a contract must also be capable of understanding the terms of the agreement. Consideration arises from the premiums paid by the insured and the promise of the insurer to pay money to the beneficiary if a certain event happens. Finally, the subject matter must not be tainted with illegality. For example, a fire insurance policy written on a building in which the owners permitted the illegal manufacture of fireworks would be void in the event of a fire.

Insurable Interest

A person or business applying for insurance must have an insurable interest in the subject matter of the policy to be insured. An **insurable interest** is the financial interest that a policyholder has in the person or property that is insured. In the case of life insurance, all people have an insurable interest in their own lives as well as the lives of their spouses and dependents. Business partners have an insurable interest in each other because they could suffer a financial loss if a partner dies. A corporation can have a financial interest in its key employees for the same reason. In the case of property insurance, anyone who would suffer a financial loss from damage to property would have an insurable interest in that property. For life insurance, the insurable interest must exist at the time the insurance is purchased. In contrast, for property insurance, the insurable interest must exist at the time of loss.

Subrogation

Insurance companies have the right to step into the shoes of the party they compensate and sue any party whom the compensated party could have sued. This substitution of one person in place of another relative to a lawful claim is known as **subrogation**.

Quick Quiz 30-1 True or False?

1. The purpose of insurance is to spread losses among people who can most afford it.

2. An application filled in by an insurance applicant is a binding contract on the insurer.

3. Anyone can obtain insurance on another person or property, regardless of their relationship.

30-2 Types of Insurance

It is possible to obtain insurance against almost any risk if an individual or business is willing to pay the price. The premium charged will depend on the risk involved. Life insurance, property insurance, and health insurance are discussed here.

Life Insurance

Life insurance is an insurance contract that provides monetary compensation for losses suffered by another's death. Anyone has an insurable interest in the life of another if a financial loss will occur if the insured dies. For example, an insurable interest exists if the

The Opening Case Revisited, Part I
"Triple Indemnity"

Sarah was able to collect on the life insurance policy. Because of the divorce, she no longer had an insurable interest in Joseph's life when he died; however, she did have an insurable interest at the time the policy was originally issued.

person who buys the insurance is dependent on the insured for education, support, business (partners), or debt collection. A life insurance policy will remain valid and enforceable even if the insurable interest terminates. It is necessary only that the insurable interest exists at the time the policy was issued.

Premiums for life insurance are based on several factors, including the age and health of the insured, the coverage, and the type of policy. It is less expensive to buy life insurance at a young age because the death rate for young people is very low, and their health is usually at its peak.

If an individual takes out insurance on him- or herself, it is not necessary for the beneficiary to have an insurable interest in the insured's life. However, if a person takes out life insurance on someone else, that person must have an insurable interest in the insured's life.

The principal types of life insurance are straight life, limited-payment life, term, and endowment insurance.

Straight Life Insurance   **Straight life insurance**, which is also known as **ordinary life insurance** or **whole life insurance**, requires the payment of premiums throughout the life of the insured and pays the beneficiary the face value of the policy upon the insured's death. The amount of the premium is determined by the age of the insured at the time of purchase and normally stays the same throughout the life of the policy. The younger the insured, the lower the premium, because the company expects to collect many years' worth of premiums.

Straight life insurance contains an investment feature known as the *cash surrender value*. The cash surrender value usually builds up slowly at first but in later years approaches the face amount of the policy. At some stated point (usually at the age of 95 or 100 years), it equals the face value of the policy. An insured can cancel a straight life policy at any time and receive its cash surrender value. Straight life insurance also contains a feature called a *loan value*, which is an amount of money that may be borrowed against the cash surrender value of the policy, usually at a relatively favorable rate of interest. During inflationary times, when bank interest rates are high, insurance policies are often excellent sources of loans at low interest rates.

LO4

EXAMPLE 30-1:   Straight Life Insurance

At age 18 years, LaPlume purchased a straight life insurance policy with a face value of $20,000. The premiums were quite modest. At some later time, LaPlume could borrow on the policy or trade it in for its cash surrender value. Or, LaPlume could continue premium payments until death. If LaPlume died while a loan was outstanding, the insurance company would deduct the amount of the loan from the amount it paid to LaPlume's beneficiary.

A form of straight life insurance, called **universal life insurance,** allows the policy owner flexibility in choosing and changing terms of the policy. Within certain guidelines, the policy owner can modify the face value of the policy as well as the premiums in response to changing needs and circumstances in the policy owner's life. Under a typical universal life policy:

- Premiums may be increased or decreased within policy limits.
- The amount of insurance may be increased, subject to evidence of insurability, or decreased, subject to set minimums.
- The owner may borrow up to the maximum loan value at a prearranged interest rate. Policy loans reduce the cash surrender value and death benefit.
- Withdrawals may be made from the cash surrender value.

Limited-Payment Life Insurance

Limited-payment life insurance provides that the payment of premiums will stop after a stated length of time—usually 10, 20, or 30 years. The amount of the policy will be paid to the beneficiary upon the death of the insured, whether the death occurs during the payment period or after. Because of the limited number of payments made by the insured, the premiums are proportionately higher than those for straight life; however, the cash surrender value grows faster than that of straight life insurance.

Term Insurance

Term insurance is issued for a particular period, usually five or ten years. The time period is known as the term. Term insurance is the least expensive kind of life insurance because term policies have no cash or loan value, as others do. Term insurance offers protection alone, in contrast to straight life, which combines protection with a savings plan. Premiums for term insurance, unlike those for straight life, commonly go up at the end of each term. It costs a 25-year-old relatively little to buy term insurance. By the age of 60, however, the insured must pay much higher premiums for this same coverage. But by that time, ordinarily, the insured's overall financial responsibility to others has lessened and thus less coverage may be needed.

Term insurance is often renewable at the end of each period simply by paying the increased premium, without need for a new medical examination. In addition, many term insurance policies are *convertible*; that is, they can be converted to straight life policies without taking a new medical examination—allowing protection throughout the insured's lifetime.

A modified form of term insurance is *decreasing term insurance*. The premium stays constant from year to year, but the amount of protection (death benefit) decreases over the years. This type of insurance is widely used to cover the outstanding balance of a home mortgage.

Endowment Insurance

Endowment insurance is a type of protection that combines life insurance and investment so that if the insured outlives the time period of the policy, the face value is paid to the insured. If the insured does not outlive the time period of the policy, the face value is paid to the beneficiary. Because this type of policy builds up a cash value more rapidly than other policies, the premium is higher.

EXAMPLE 30-2:   20-Year Endowment

Swenson, aged 18 years, purchased a $20,000 face value, 20-year endowment policy. His beneficiary will get $20,000 if Swenson dies before age 41. If he survives, Swenson will get a check for $20,000 at age 41.

Annuity   An **annuity** is guaranteed retirement income purchased by paying either a lump-sum premium or making periodic payments to an insurer. The insured may choose either (a) to receive an income for a certain fixed number of years, with a beneficiary receiving whatever is left of the annuity when the insured dies, or (b) to receive payments as long as the insured lives and, upon death, lose whatever is left of the annuity.

Exemptions from Risk   Many life insurance policies contain clauses that exempt the insurance company from liability in certain situations. For example, policies often do not cover the insured when riding in an airplane, violating the law, or working in certain dangerous occupations.

A number of jurisdictions have held that beneficiaries cannot receive the benefits from a life insurance policy when the insured is legally executed. These courts base their reasoning on the theory that it would be against public policy for beneficiaries to receive insurance proceeds in such cases. They also note that death by legal execution is not one of the risks assumed by the insurance company. In contrast, other courts allow beneficiaries to receive life insurance benefits in cases of execution because denial of recovery is not a deterrent to crime.

In most cases, the courts allow a beneficiary to receive benefits under a life insurance policy when the insured is murdered, except when the murderer is also the beneficiary. A beneficiary who murders the insured forfeits all rights under the life insurance policy.

Most policies provide that beneficiaries can recover for a death caused by suicide if the suicide occurs more than two years after the policy was taken out. They may not recover, however, when the policy contains a provision preventing such recovery or when the life insurance was purchased by someone planning suicide or who was insane. One example of a named beneficiary who could recover would be a creditor of the insured.

Life insurance policies usually include an exemption from liability in times of war. The exemption states that the insurer will not be liable on the policy if the insured is killed while a member of the armed forces, generally outside the continental United States, or by service-connected causes.

Optional Provisions   Life insurance policies have many optional provisions that may be purchased by the insured. Three popular options are double indemnity, waiver of premium, and guaranteed insurability.

For an additional premium, the insured may purchase a benefit known as **double indemnity**, or accidental death benefit. This option provides that if the insured dies from accidental causes, the insurer will pay double the amount of the policy to the beneficiary. Death must occur within 90 days of the accident for this benefit to apply.

The *waiver of premium* option excuses the insured from paying premiums if he or she becomes disabled. Some insurance policies automatically include the waiver in their provisions; others offer it as an extra-cost option.

A *guaranteed insurability* option allows the insured to pay an extra premium initially in exchange for a guaranteed option to buy more insurance at certain specified times later. The additional insurance can be purchased with no questions asked; thus, no new medical examination is required even if the insured develops a serious illness before exercising the option.

Did You Know?

Young families with large financial obligations are usually better off with term life insurance rather than whole life. The substantially lower premiums may enable them to purchase needed coverage to protect against loss of income at a time when they most need it.

Insurance protects you and your family providing security for unexpected occurences.

The Opening Case Revisited, Part II

"Triple Indemnity"

Sarah was not able to collect on the automobile insurance policy. Her insurable interest in the Infinity came to an end when the court ordered that the Infinity belonged to Joseph outright.

Property Insurance

Property insurance can be purchased to protect both real and personal property. To establish the existence of an insurable interest in property, the insured must demonstrate a monetary interest in the property. This monetary interest means that the insured will suffer a financial loss if the property is damaged or destroyed. Unlike life insurance, this insurable interest must exist when the loss occurs.

Property insurance can be made less expensive by the use of a **deductible**, which is an amount of any loss that is to be paid by the insured. It can be a specified dollar amount, a percentage of the claim amount, or a specified amount of time that must elapse before benefits are paid. The bigger the deductible, the lower is the premium charged for the same coverage.

Coinsurance Clauses   **Coinsurance** is an insurance policy provision under which the insurer and the insured share costs, after the deductible is met, according to a specific formula. Most property and inland marine policies have a coinsurance clause, which limits the insurance company's liability for a loss if the property is not insured for its full replacement value. For example, if a homeowner's insurance policy has an 80 percent coinsurance clause, the building must be insured for 80 percent of its replacement value to receive full reimbursement for a loss (see Figure 30-1).

Fire Insurance   A fire insurance policy is a contract in which the fire insurance company promises to pay the insured if some real or personal property is damaged or

---

TYPICAL COINSURANCE CLAUSE

"The insurance company will pay that part of a loss that the insurance carried bears to 80 percent of the replacement cost of the building."

It would cost $100,000 to replace Felipe Garcia's house. If he insured it for $60,000, the insurance company would pay only three-fourths of any loss, computed as follows:

$$\frac{\text{Amount of insurance carried}}{\text{Percent of replacement cost}} \quad \frac{\$60,000}{80\% \text{ of } \$100,000} \quad = \quad \frac{\$60,000}{\$80,000} \quad = \quad \frac{3}{4}$$

A fire partially destroys the building, causing $40,000 worth of damage. Because of the co-insurance clause, Garcia would recover $30,000 (¾ of the loss) from the insurance company.

Figure 30-1   Here is a typical coinsurance clause found in an insurance policy. It limits the insurer's liability for a loss if the property is not insured for its full replacement value.

destroyed by fire. A fire insurance policy is effective on delivery to the insured, even before the premium is paid. Even an oral agreement will make fire insurance effective.

The insurer's liability under a fire policy usually covers losses other than those directly attributed to fire. Under most policies, claims may also be made for losses from water used to fight the fire; scorching; smoke damage to goods; deliberate destruction of property as a means of controlling a spreading fire; lightning, even if there is no resultant fire; riot or explosion, if a fire does result; and losses through theft or exposure of goods removed from a burning building.

Marine Insurance Marine insurance is one of the oldest types of insurance coverage, dating back to Venetian traders who sailed the Mediterranean Sea. **Ocean marine insurance** covers ships at sea. **Inland marine insurance** covers goods that are moved by land carriers such as rail, truck, and airplane. Inland marine insurance also covers such items as jewelry, fine arts, musical instruments, and wedding presents. Customers' goods in the possession of bailees, such as fur-storage houses and dry cleaners, are also covered by inland marine insurance.

A *floater policy* is one that insures property that cannot be covered by specific insurance because the property is constantly changing in either value or location. A personal property floater, for example, covers personal property in general, wherever it is located.

Homeowner's and Renter's Insurance Many of the leading insurance companies offer a combination policy known as the **homeowner's policy**. This insurance gives protection for all types of losses and liabilities related to home ownership. Among the items covered are losses from fire, windstorms, burglary, vandalism, and injuries suffered by other persons while on the property. Losses from flooding generally are not covered under a homeowner's policy. **Renter's insurance** protects tenants against the loss of personal property, liability for a visitor's personal injury, and liability for negligent destruction of the rented premises.

Flood Insurance Flooding can be caused by heavy rains, melting snow, inadequate drainage systems, failed protective devices such as levees and dams, and tropical storms and hurricanes. Nevertheless, most commercial, homeowner's, and renter's insurance policies do not cover flood damage. To obtain such coverage, special flood insurance must be obtained from an insurance agent.

Most flood insurance is backed by the National Flood Insurance Program (NFIP), established by Congress in response to the high cost of taxpayer-funded disaster relief for flood victims and the amount of damage caused by floods. Communities that agree to manage flood hazard areas by adopting minimum standards can participate in the NFIP. However, communities that do not participate in the program cannot receive flood insurance, federal grants and loans, federal disaster assistance, or federal mortgage insurance for the acquisition or construction of structures located in flood hazard areas of their community. Most lending institutions require borrowers to obtain flood insurance when they buy, build, or improve structures in Special Flood Hazard Areas (SFHAs). Lending institutions that are federally regulated or federally insured must determine if the structure is located in an SFHA and provide written notice requiring flood insurance.

Following hurricane Katrina, the nation's costliest storm, which devastated the Gulf Coast in 2005, many insurance claims were delayed, and others

Without adequate insurance, most people would be unable to even approach status quo after suffering a catastrophic event.

The Opening Case Revisited, Part III
"Triple Indemnity"

It is unlikely that Sarah and Joseph would be able to recover much, if any, of their hurricane losses because they did not have flood insurance. Much of the damage to homes along Mississippi's Gulf Coast was caused by the storm surge of water rather than by wind. Their case would be reopened and reviewed, however, under the insurers' agreement with the state attorney general.

were not paid on the grounds that damages were caused by water rather than by wind, though most homeowners had little or no flood insurance. Hundreds of lawsuits were brought by disgruntled homeowners against insurance companies, and some million-dollar jury verdicts against the companies were settled out of court. Some of the jury awards were for punitive damages because the companies failed to pay the claims quickly enough. A federal appeals court found that many insurance policies covering property in New Orleans contained flood exclusions. The court said, "Regardless of what caused the failure of the flood-control structures that were put in place to prevent such catastrophe, their failure resulted in a widespread flood that damaged the plaintiffs' property. Their policies clearly excluded water damage caused by floods." One lower federal court case upheld the insurance company's view that homeowner policies cover damage from a hurricane's wind but not the rising water that ensues, including wind-driven surge. Several major insurers in Mississippi, which does not allow punitive damages in these cases, entered into an agreement with the Mississippi Attorney General to pay about $80 million to 639 policyholders whose claims were denied following Katrina. As part of the agreement, insurers were required to reopen and review claims filed by policyholders who live in that state.

Automobile Insurance

Automobile insurance provides for indemnity against losses resulting from fire, theft, or collision with another vehicle and damages arising out of injury by motor vehicles to the person or property of another. The following are the most common types of automobile insurance:

- Bodily injury to others
- No-fault insurance
- Bodily injury caused by an uninsured auto
- Bodily injury caused by an underinsured auto
- Medical payments
- Property damage to someone else's property
- Collision insurance
- Comprehensive coverage
- Substitute transportation insurance
- Towing and labor insurance

Bodily injury to others (**bodily injury liability insurance**) covers the risk of bodily injury or death to pedestrians and the occupants of other cars arising from the negligent

BusinessWeek **Business Law in the News**

In Tough Hands at Allstate

It's fighting accusations that its methods deny policyholders legitimate benefits

David Berardinelli is something of a bon vivant. The Santa Fe (N.M.) plaintiffs' lawyer collects fine wine, has chefs from local restaurants over to cook in his home, and restores classic Porsches. He's also about to become a published author.

His book, *From Good Hands to Boxing Gloves,* won't burn up the best-seller lists. But it's already making waves. It tells the story of the key role played by management consultant McKinsey & Co. in reengineering auto insurance claims operations at Allstate Corp.—and it's a story Allstate doesn't want told.

In February, a New Mexico state court rejected Allstate's efforts to keep Berardinelli from publishing his book, which will be marketed to trial lawyers nationwide later this year. Since 2004, Allstate has been defying an order by the same court to make available public copies of some 12,500 PowerPoint slides McKinsey prepared for the insurer, which form the basis of the book. That's quite unusual—big companies almost never ignore judicial orders. In a court filing, Allstate has characterized its actions as "respectful civil disobedience."

What is it that Allstate so badly wants to keep under wraps? In a written response to *BusinessWeek,* the insurer says the McKinsey material contains proprietary business secrets. The documents also present a clear risk to the company's reputation. The title of Berardinelli's book is drawn from a McKinsey slide that suggests that Allstate should treat some of its claimants with "boxing gloves," rather than with its trademark "good hands." Collectively, the documents present a portrait of business strategies that are at odds with the insurer's carefully cultivated public image. Rather than simply rushing to the scene of an accident and doling out cash, Allstate deploys a variety of systems set in place by McKinsey to make sure it pays the minimum necessary—and it plays hardball with those who seek more.

Berardinelli, 57, has provided *BusinessWeek* an exclusive copy of a draft of the book, as well as more than 200 typed pages of notes he took on the McKinsey slides. His tale illuminates the largely hidden role McKinsey has played as a key architect of claims practices in use across the insurance industry today. In addition to advising Allstate, McKinsey has also done work for Farmers Insurance Group, USAA, State Farm, and Fireman's Fund (AZ). While many of the cost-reduction strategies McKinsey recommended at Allstate remain in place, some have been reined in following legal and regulatory challenges in several states.

Epic War

Berardinelli's book is certainly a partisan one, written to support "bad faith" lawsuits that he and other attorneys have filed against Allstate alleging mistreatment of policyholders. He says that the McKinsey project, which lasted from 1992 until at least 1997, institutionalized aggressive practices aimed at enriching investors at the expense of customers. "When you strip away all the fancy jargon, all this is a plan for switching money from the policyholders' pockets to the shareholders' pockets," he maintains. In the decade after Allstate instituted the McKinsey program in 1995, the amount of money it paid out per premium dollar in car accident cases declined from about 63 cents to 47 cents, according to A.M. Best.

McKinsey declined to comment, citing client confidentiality. But Allstate says Berardinelli's allegations are "unfounded and unproven." Rather than trying to cheat customers, the company says, its claims revamp was just good management: an effort to "become the premier claim organization in the industry." A major goal, it says, was to benefit policyholders by identifying "exaggerated and fraudulent claims." In its written response, Allstate further said its "processes are absolutely sound" and that its goal is "to investigate, evaluate, and promptly resolve each claim fairly, based on the merits."

The battle over the McKinsey documents is just the latest round in an epic, decades-long war between insurers and the plaintiffs' bar over access to one of the biggest treasure troves of cash ever created: the billions of dollars in premiums held by insurers to pay claims. For years, each side has cast the other as evil incarnate. In the early 1990s, when Allstate retained McKinsey, there was a widespread sense among insurers that they were paying too many illegitimate

(Continued)

Business Law in the News (Continued)

automobile-accident claims and that an aggressive plaintiffs' bar, fueled by a wave of newly allowed attorney advertising, bore much of the blame. One focus of the program McKinsey introduced at Allstate, called Claim Core Process Redesign (CCPR), was aimed at striking a blow at that trend.

But plaintiffs' attorneys around the country allege that various elements of CCPR go beyond eliminating fraudulent claims and operate in a systematic way to deny policyholders legitimate benefits. Copies of Allstate's massively thick CCPR manuals have been circulating among trial lawyers for years. Although plaintiffs have had piecemeal success in bad-faith cases against Allstate, the insurer points to seven court rulings that have rejected attacks on CCPR. Last December a Montana state court noted that while CCPR practices may be illegal "if misapplied in a particular case, they nevertheless are neutral with no manifestly illegal purpose."

Berardinelli is convinced that the McKinsey material could turn the tide. The documents "explain why McKinsey built CCPR," he says. In his book he compares Allstate to a vendor of canned peas and argues that the documents "show how McKinsey . . . deliberately designed Allstate's claim factory to arbitrarily 'underfill' every can of Allstate insurance."

Dry Spigot

Another major focus was on "subjective" injuries, meaning claims for such things as emotional distress and pain and suffering, as opposed to "objective" injuries, such as broken limbs. To get a handle on these claims, the notes on the slides show, McKinsey worked with Allstate to install Colossus, a computerized claim-evaluation system sold by Computer Sciences Corp. (CSC). Colossus compares a claimant's injuries with a database of similar cases and recommends a settlement range. Plaintiffs' attorneys have alleged that insurers can "tune" Colossus to consistently spit out lowball offers.

Berardinelli's notes show one McKinsey slide stating that the system has been "extremely successful in reducing severities with reductions in the range of 20% for Colossus-evaluated claims." ("Severities" is insurance industry jargon referring to the size of claim payments.) In its written response to *BusinessWeek,* Allstate says that "Colossus is merely a tool used to assist in the valuation" of some bodily injury claims and that adjusters use

their expertise to come up with appropriate settlements "on each individual claim."

One of the key elements of McKinsey's plan was reducing the number of claimants who turn to attorneys after an accident for help in collecting on their insurance. The consultants even forecast what the potential gains in this area would mean for Allstate's stock. A 25% drop in attorneys appearing in several categories of cases could add $1.60 to Allstate's share price, one slide states, according to Berardinelli's notes.

The boxing gloves slide was displayed in open court in a case against Allstate in Kentucky last year. It states that by "holding the line" on cases where accident victims hire lawyers, Allstate could achieve "a new distribution of settlement times" on subjective-injury claims. "By increasing the number of early unrepresented settlements," the slide says, Allstate could give 90% of these claims the "good hands" treatment, resolving them within about 200 days. But the slide shows the remaining 10% getting "boxing gloves" treatment, and a graph shows resolution of their claims taking as much as four years or longer.

It took two years for an interim appellate court, and then the New Mexico Supreme Court, to rule that Allstate's appeal failed because it had filed it one day too late. With the Supreme Court ruling in hand in March 2004, Berardinelli returned the McKinsey material he had to Allstate and demanded a clean copy, free of the restrictive printing. Allstate refused, prompting the trial court judge to hit it with the most extreme civil sanction a court can order, a default judgment—finding it liable without trial in the underlying bad-faith case.

Allstate is appealing that ruling. In a court filing, Allstate argues that Berardinelli's aim is not to have the McKinsey documents for use in a particular case but to be able to disseminate their contents to lawyers around the country. As he puts the finishing touches on his book manuscript, Berardinelli would be hard-pressed to disagree.

Questions for Analysis

1. How did a New Mexico court rule on Allstate's efforts to stop the publication of Berardinelli's book?

2. In what way has Allstate been defying a court order?

3. What does Allstate wants to keep under wraps?

4. What business strategies do the documents collectively present?

5. According to A.M. Best, how did things change in the decade after Allstate instituted the McKinsey program?

6. How does Allstate respond to the charges against it?

7. What is "Claim Core Process Redesign (CCPR)"?

8. What are "subjective" injury claims?

9. What does the boxing glove slide, shown in open court, state?

Source: Michael Orey, "In Tough Hands at Allstate: It's Fighting Accusations that Its Methods Deny Policyholders Legitimate Benefits," *BusinessWeek,* May 1, 2006, http://www.business-week.com.

operation of the insured's motor vehicle. Under liability insurance, the insurer is liable for damages up to the limit of the insurance purchased. The insurance company must also provide attorneys for the insured's defense in any civil court action.

No-fault insurance, currently required in 12 states[1] and the District of Columbia, places limitations on the insured's ability to sue other drivers but allows drivers to collect damages and medical expenses from their own insurance carriers, regardless of who is at fault in an accident. This coverage helps cut down on fraudulent and excessively high claims. It also eliminates costly litigation needed to determine the negligence or lack of negligence of people involved in automobile accidents.

Bodily injury caused by an uninsured auto (**uninsured-motorist insurance**) provides protection against the risk of being injured by an uninsured motorist. The coverage applies when the person who caused the accident was at fault and had no bodily injury liability insurance to cover the loss. It protects the insured, the insured's spouse, relatives in the same household, and any other person occupying an insured automobile. It also protects people who are injured by hit-and-run drivers. No coverage is provided to persons injured in an automobile used without the permission of the insured or the insured's spouse. Uninsured-motorist insurance provides no reimbursement for damages to the insured's property.

Bodily injury caused by an underinsured auto (**underinsured-motorist insurance**) provides protection against the risk of being injured by an underinsured motorist. For an insured to collect this insurance, someone without enough bodily injury coverage must have caused the accident.

Medical payments insurance pays for medical (and sometimes funeral) expenses resulting from bodily injuries to anyone occupying the policyholder's car at the time of an accident. In some states, it pays for the medical bills of all family members who are struck by a car or who are riding in someone else's car when it is involved in an accident.

Property damage to someone else's property (**property damage liability insurance**) provides protection when other people bring claims or lawsuits against the insured for damaging property such as a car, fence, or tree. The person bringing the claim or suit must prove that the driver of the motor vehicle was at fault.

Collision insurance provides against any loss arising from damage to the insured's automobile caused by accidental collision with another object or with any part of the road-bed. Liability under collision insurance is limited to the insured's car.

Comprehensive coverage provides protection against loss when the insured's car is damaged or destroyed by fire, lightning, flood, hail, windstorm, riot, vandalism, or theft. The insurance company's liability is limited to the actual cash value of the vehicle at the time of the loss.

[1]Florida, Hawaii, Kansas, Kentucky, Massachusetts, Michigan, Minnesota, New Jersey, New York, North Dakota, Pennsylvania, and Utah.

Substitute transportation insurance reimburses up to specified limits for car rental or transportation costs, including taxi, bus, and train fare, while the insured's car is undergoing covered repairs.

Towing and labor insurance reimburses up to specified limits for towing and labor charges whenever the insured's car breaks down, whether or not an accident is involved.

Health Insurance

With the increasingly high costs of prescriptions, other medical products, and services, affordable health insurance is a foremost need in today's society. Many people obtain health insurance through a group insurance plan from the company for which they work. Others have individual plans that they purchase directly from an insurer. Still others have government health insurance plans through government employment, Medicare, and Medicaid (see Figure 30-2). Health insurance policies often include the following benefits:

- Physician care
- Prescription drugs
- Inpatient and outpatient hospital care
- Surgery
- Dental and vision care
- Long-term care for the elderly

Major medical coverage pays for expenses beyond those covered by a basic plan, including long-term hospitalization and catastrophic illness.

Year of birth	Full retirement age
1937 or earlier	65
1938	65 and 2 months
1939	65 and 4 months
1940	65 and 6 months
1941	65 and 8 months
1942	65 and 10 months
1943–1954	66
1955	66 and 2 months
1956	66 and 4 months
1957	66 and 6 months
1958	66 and 8 months
1959	66 and 10 months
1960 and later	67

Note: People who were born on January 1 of any year should refer to the previous year.

Figure 30-2 Age to Receive Social Security Benefits.
Source: Social Security Administration, SSA Publication No. 05-10035.

HMOs and PPOs   Health Maintenance Organizations (HMOs) contract with doctors and other health care professionals to provide health care services for their members. Members pay monthly premiums and must choose from a list of doctors provided by the HMO. HMOs encourage their members to have regular checkups, immunizations, and other forms of early treatment. In this way, it is hoped that people will be less likely to require more expensive kinds of treatment. Many different kinds of organizations sponsor HMOs, including doctors, community groups, insurance companies, labor unions, and corporations.

A Preferred Provider Organization (PPO) is a group of health care providers, such as doctors or hospitals, that provide care for groups of employees at reduced rates. PPOs are usually sponsored as part of an employer's group health plan. Employees choose among the health care providers on the PPO list when they need treatment. Choosing a non-PPO provider reduces the benefits paid to the insured under the plan.

Medicare and Medicaid   People 65 years of age and older who are covered by Social Security are eligible for **Medicare**, a federally funded health insurance program. The age for eligibility began increasing in 2003 at two-month intervals over at 12-year period (see Figure 30-2). Medicare Part A helps pay for inpatient hospital care. Medicare Part B pays for 80 percent of doctors' and other medical services. Many people buy their own medigap insurance to cover the 20 percent not covered by Medicare.

Medicaid is a health care plan for low-income people. State governments administer Medicaid, which is funded by both state and federal funds.

Disability Insurance   Disability insurance pays benefits when a person cannot work because of a disability. Total, or long-term, disability pays if the insured cannot perform normal job duties for a year or longer; partial, or short-term, disability pays for a few months of being disabled.

Long-Term Care Insurance   Long-term care insurance helps pay for home care, whether provided by family and friends or through professional home care organizations, when an insured becomes chronically ill. It also helps cover care received in adult day care, assisted-living facilities, and nursing homes. Benefits are usually payable when an insured is unable to perform certain daily living activities without assistance, such as eating, bathing, dressing, or using the bathroom.

Legal Protection   A variety of state and federal laws help make it easier for people with preexisting conditions to obtain and keep health insurance. A federal law known as HIPAA (Health Insurance Portability and Accountability Act) sets national standards for all health plans. Among its specific protections, HIPAA:

1. Limits the use of preexisting condition exclusions.

2. Prohibits group health plans from discriminating by denying coverage or charging extra for coverage based on a person's or family member's past or present poor health.

3. Guarantees certain small employers, and certain individuals who lose job-related coverage, the right to purchase health insurance.

4. Guarantees, in most cases, that employers or individuals who purchase health insurance can renew the coverage regardless of any health conditions of individuals covered under the insurance policy.

Another federal law known as COBRA (Consolidated Omnibus Budget Reconciliation Act) allows employees to keep their group insurance for a specific period of time after being laid off. Under COBRA, employees who have been laid off pay their own premiums but can shift to another group plan upon starting a new job.

30-3 The Insurance Policy

In most states, the insurance policy (which is the insurance contract) comes in a standard form. These forms are carefully drafted by insurance commissioners with help from the states' legal advisers. In this way, the consumer-buyer is protected from deception or fraud. As an additional protection to consumers, some states now require that insurance contracts must be written in clear, understandable language and printed in a readable typeface. Insurance policies, nevertheless, are **adhesion contracts**—that is, contracts drawn by one party that must be accepted as is on a take-it-or-leave-it basis.

Application

The first step in obtaining an insurance policy is to fill in an application. The application is an offer made by the applicant to the insurance company. As with any offer, the offeree, in this case the insurance company, may accept or reject the offer.

Binders

The waiting period between the offer and the acceptance opens the insured to potential risk. To avoid this risk, the insured can arrange to have the insurer issue a binder. A **binder**, or binding slip, will provide temporary insurance coverage until the policy is formally accepted. The binder will include all of the usual terms that would be included in the actual policy to be issued.

Premiums

An insurance contract differs from most other contracts in that it requires the payment of premiums. The amount of the premium is determined by the nature and character of the risk and by how likely the risk is to occur. The premium increases as the chance of loss increases. Thus, a premium on a fireproof building in a city with a fire department will be much lower than the premium on a barn located where firefighting equipment is not available.

Lapse

When the insured stops paying premiums, an insurance contract is said to lapse. This feature may not mean, however, that the contract will terminate automatically on the date that the last premium is paid. It may also not lapse automatically if the insured makes a delayed payment. Although state laws differ, most states allow for a grace period in which the insured may make payments to keep life and health insurance policies in force. Beyond this period, however, the insurance contract will lapse, and the policy will terminate. Automobile and property insurance policies usually have no grace periods and will terminate when a premium is not paid when due.

30-4 Cancellation of Insurance by Insurer

Under certain conditions, the insurer is given a legal right to forfeit, or cancel, an insurance policy. Proof of a forfeiture permits cancellation either before a loss or at the time the claim is made on a policy. Among the grounds permitting forfeiture are a breach of warranty and a concealment or misrepresentation of a material fact by the insured (Table 30-2). Neither the insured nor the insurer may deny statements or acts previously made or committed that might affect the validity of the policy.

Warranties

A *warranty* is an insured's promise to abide by restrictions, especially those written into a policy that are intended to be conditions precedent to the existence of coverage. By statute in many states, an insurance company has the burden of proof in establishing that a warranty has been breached (broken) by the insured. If this breach is proved, the insurer may cancel the contract or refuse payment of loss to the insured or to a beneficiary.

EXAMPLE 30-3:   Breach of Warranty

Nicole Duffy, a well-known NASCAR driver, applied for life insurance after being involved in several racing accidents. Community Life was aware of these accidents, and Duffy agreed not to race while the policy remained in force. Duffy was killed while racing in an important race. Community Life could rescind any obligation to pay Duffy's beneficiaries.

Table 30-2 Cancellation of Insurance Policies

Grounds for Cancellation	Explanation
Warranty violation	Insured fails to abide by restrictions especially written into the policy
Concealment	Insured deliberately withholds fact of material importance to insurer's decision to issue a policy
Misrepresentation	Insured gives false answers to questions in the insurance application that materially affect the insurer's risk

Concealment

Fraudulent concealment is any intentional withholding of a fact that would be of material importance to the insurer's decision to issue a policy. The applicant need only give answers to questions asked. However, the insured may not conceal facts that would be material in acceptance of a risk.

EXAMPLE 30-4:　Concealment

VanDorn, an insurance agent for Canadian Life, inspected Kalintor's building before issuing a fire insurance policy. Kalintor did not show VanDorn the basement, which was filled with flammable chemicals. After the policy was issued, Kalintor's building burned to the ground. Canadian Life later learned of the secret lab and was permitted to cancel Kalintor's policy.

Misrepresentation

If an insured party gives false answers, or *misrepresentations,* to questions in an insurance application that materially affect the risk undertaken by the insurer, the contract is voidable by the insurer. A representation is material if the facts represented influence the insurer's decision to issue the policy or the rate of premium to charge.

EXAMPLE 30-5:　Misrepresentation

The Clark family applied for fire insurance from the Alabama Farm Bureau Mutual Casualty Insurance Company. The Clarks answered no when asked whether they had ever been arrested. When their house was destroyed by fire and they attempted to collect under the policy, an investigation revealed that the Clarks had both been arrested on previous occasions. The court upheld the Farm Bureau's denial of benefits due to this deliberate material misrepresentation.

Although all jurisdictions agree on the effects of a deliberate deception, there is disagreement as to the effects of an innocent misrepresentation. A majority of the states hold that the intent of the insured is irrelevant. Even an innocent misrepresentation would make the policy voidable by the insurer. A minority of states would not allow the insurer to deny coverage to an insured whose misrepresentation was unintentional.

EXAMPLE 30-6:　Innocent Misrepresentation

Folk took out an insurance policy with Countryside Casualty. When asked if he had any physical impairments, Folk, who suffered from epilepsy, said no. When Folk was killed in an automobile accident, his estate attempted to collect the insurance. Countryside, which had discovered Folk's epilepsy, refused to pay, claiming he had misrepresented his physical health. Evidence indicated that Folk genuinely did not consider his epilepsy, which was controlled by drugs, to be a physical impairment. In a majority of states, Folk's belief would make no difference. The policy would still be voidable by Countryside. In a minority of states, Folk's innocent misrepresentation would not allow Countryside to deny recovery under the policy.

Estoppel

An insurer may not deny acts, statements, or promises that are relevant and material to the validity of an insurance contract. This bar to denial is called an *estoppel*. When an insurer has given up the right to cancel a policy under certain circumstances by granting the insured a special dispensation, the insurer cannot deny that dispensation when the chance to cancel or deny liability arises.

EXAMPLE 30-7:   Estopped from Denying Liability

Maxwell, an insurance agent for Fidelity, called on MacLaine, who wanted fire insurance to cover her new cabin. The cabin was heated by a woodburning stove that, according to Fidelity's specifications, was located too close to a wooden wall. Maxwell told MacLaine not to worry about those specifications. He then falsified the measurements on the application. Two weeks later, MacLaine's cabin burned to the ground. Due to Maxwell's behavior, Fidelity would be estopped from denying its liability to MacLaine under the policy.

When the insurance company gives up one of its rights to help the insured, the company has made a *waiver*. A waiver, which is actually a form of estoppel, can be implied from the conduct of the insurance company. For example, when an insurance company cashes the check of a lapsed policy, it has, in effect, given up or waived its right to cancel that policy. Once a right has been waived, the insurer may not later deny its waiver.

Quick Quiz 30-4 True or False?

1. An insurance company may refuse to pay for a loss if it can prove that the insured breached a warranty to abide by certain restrictions.

2. If an insured gives false answers to questions in an insurance application, the insurance company can do nothing about it unless it discovers the fraud before any loss.

3. An insurer may not deny acts, statements, or promises that are relevant and material to the validity of an insurance contract.

Summary

30.1   Insurance is a transfer of the risk of economic loss from the insured to the insurer. Insurance policies require the elements of a contract: offer, acceptance, mutual assent, capable parties, consideration, and legality. To be insured, one must have an insurable interest in the subject matter of the policy. The parties to an insurance contract include the insurer, the insured, and the beneficiary.

30.2　It is possible to obtain insurance for a variety of risks. Life insurance provides funds to a beneficiary on the death of the insured. A beneficiary must have an insurable interest when the policy is issued but need not have that interest when the insured dies. The principal types of life insurance are straight life, limited-payment life, term, and endowment insurance. Principal types of property insurance include fire, marine, homeowner's, flood, and automobile insurance. In the case of property insurance, the insured must have an insurable interest when the loss occurs. Health insurance helps pay for such things as physician care, prescription drugs, inpatient and outpatient hospital care, surgery, dental and vision care, and long-term care for the elderly. Federal laws include HIPAA, which sets national standards for all health plans, and COBRA, which allows employees to keep group insurance for a specific period after being laid off.

30.3　The first step in obtaining an insurance policy is to fill in an application. A binder provides temporary insurance coverage between the time the application is made and the time the policy becomes effective. Premiums are the consideration or payment an insured gives the insurer for its acceptance of risk. A lapse occurs when the insured stops paying premiums.

30.4　Under certain conditions, the insurer is given a legal right to cancel an insurance policy. Grounds permitting cancellation include breach of warranty, concealment of material facts, and misrepresentation on an application. Under the estoppel rule, an insurer is not allowed to deny certain statements, activities, or waivers.

Key Terms

adhesion contracts, 628

annuity, 619

beneficiary, 615

binder, 628

bodily injury liability insurance, 622

coinsurance, 620

collision insurance, 625

comprehensive coverage, 625

deductible, 620

double indemnity, 619

endowment insurance, 618

homeowner's policy, 621

indemnify, 615

inland marine insurance, 621

insurable interest, 616

insurance, 615

insured, 615

insurer, 615

life insurance, 616

limited-payment life insurance, 618

Medicaid, 627

medical payments insurance, 625

Medicare, 627

no-fault insurance, 625

ocean marine insurance, 621

ordinary life insurance, 617

policy, 615

premium, 615

property damage liability insurance, 625

renter's insurance, 621

straight life insurance, 617

subrogation, 616

substitute transportation insurance, 626

term insurance, 618

towing and labor insurance, 626

underinsured-motorist insurance, 625

uninsured-motorist insurance, 625

universal life insurance, 618

whole life insurance, 617

Questions for Review and Discussion

1. What contractual elements are found in an insurance policy?
2. Name and describe the principal types of life insurance.
3. What are four situations that might permit the insurer to deny paying life insurance claims?
4. Why are the waiver of premium option and the guaranteed insurability option popular optional provisions of life insurance policies?
5. In what ways do requirements of insurable interests differ for property insurance and life insurance?

6. What are the seven situations in which an insurer's liability under a fire insurance policy may extend beyond the damage caused directly by the fire? List the five examples of the losses that might be covered by a homeowner's policy.

7. Name seven kinds of automobile insurance. What are the risks covered by each of these policies?

8. What benefits are often included in health insurance policies? How does Medicare differ from Medicaid?

9. What is the first step in obtaining an insurance policy? Describe the device used to protect the insured between the time of this first step and the time the policy is actually obtained by the insured.

10. Why do insurance premiums differ from one insured to another? What happens when an insured fails to maintain a policy by missing a premium payment?

11. How might breach of warranty, concealment, and misrepresentation be used by an insurance company to cancel a policy?

Investigating the Internet

Flooding is the most common natural disaster in this country. Until 2005, when Hurricane Katrina took the lives of more than 1,800 people along the Gulf Coast and flooded 80 percent of New Orleans, many homeowners were unaware that they were not covered by flood insurance. To make matters worse, some insurance companies claimed that hurricane insurance covered wind damage but not water damage. Look online at "The Hurricane Information Insurance Center" and **www.floodsmart.gov** to determine whether your community is protected from flooding and what you can do to safeguard yourself, your family, and your property during a hurricane.

Cases for Analysis

1. Juan Ramos's wife, Maria, became concerned after a violent storm caused disastrous flooding in a community not too far down the river from where their house was located. She felt comforted when her husband told her that they were fully protected against flooding by their homeowner's insurance policy. The following spring, a flood caused serious damage to their home, and Juan's insurance agent told him that his homeowner's policy did not cover flood damage. What recourse do the Ramoses have against the insurance company?

2. Al Zuni Trading, Inc., purchased a $1 million life insurance policy on the life of one of its officers, Thomas McKee. Three months later, McKee resigned from the company. Two years later, McKee died. Did Al Zuni Trading, Inc., have an insurable interest in the life of McKee,

and thus, was it entitled to the million dollars? Explain. *In re Al Zuni Trading, Inc.,* 947 F.2d 1403 (9th Cir.).

3. U.S. Aviation Underwriters issued an aircraft insurance policy to Cash Air, Inc., covering its employees. The policy stated that to be covered under the policy, the aircraft must be "flown only by a pilot or pilots described on the Coverage Summary page." Each policy coverage page stated that a pilot not named in the policy must be one who holds "an AA commercial pilot certificate with AA multi-engine and instrument ratings who has flown a minimum of 2,500 hours as pilot in command, at least 1,000 hours of which shall have been in multi-engine aircraft and at least 25 hours of which shall have been in Piper PA 31-350 aircraft." Peter Covich, an

employee of Cash Air, Inc., did not meet the pilot experience requirements when the Piper Seneca airplane he was piloting crashed, causing personal injuries and property damage. Must the insurance company pay for the loss? Explain. *U.S. Aviation Underwriters v. Cash Air,* 568 N.E.2d 1150 (MA).

4. Victory Container Corporation was owned by the three Radin brothers. Two of those brothers also owned the Warrensburg Paper and Board Corporation. Victory had no direct ownership of the Warrensburg plant however. Nevertheless, Victory took out a fire insurance policy on the Warrensburg plant. When the Warrensburg property was damaged, Victory attempted to collect under the policy. Did Victory have an insurable interest in the Warrensburg property? Explain. *Victory Container Corporation v. Calvert Fire Insurance Company,* 486 N.Y.S.2d 211 (NY).

5. Avrit and Schuring entered an agreement to purchase a certain property. Each paid $1,000 as a down payment. They were later to pay an additional $25,000. The seller of the property was to maintain insurance until the deal was finalized. Avrit and Schuring also obtained an insurance policy on the property. Before the deal was finalized, fire damaged the property. Avrit and Schuring attempted to collect on their policy, but the insurance company claimed that Avrit and Schuring had no insurable interest at the time of the fire. Did Avrit and Schuring have an insurable interest between the time of the down payment and the time the deal was finalized? Explain. *Avrit v. Forest Industries Insurance Exchange,* 696 P.2d 583 (OR).

6. Martin Searle's life insurance policy contained a standard suicide clause. Under the clause, Allstate would not be liable to the beneficiary, Alice Searle, should Martin commit suicide within the first two years of the policy even if Martin were insane at the time of his death. Martin committed suicide ten months after the policy went into effect. Allstate refused to pay Alice any benefits under the policy. Alice sued the company, claiming that her husband had been mentally deranged at the time of the suicide and did not realize the consequences of his action. Allstate argued that the sanity clause removed the issue of mental incapacity from the case. Who would prevail in a majority of states? Explain. *Searle v. Allstate Life Insurance Company,* 212 Cal. Rptr. 466 (CA).

7. Bayer took his car to Whitaker's auto repair shop for repairs. Whitaker took the car for a test drive, with Bayer seated in the passenger seat. During the test drive, a car operated by another person drove on the wrong side of the road and collided with Bayer's vehicle, injuring Bayer. Neither Bayer's vehicle nor the vehicle owned by the wrongdoer was insured. Whitaker carried insurance on his own vehicles, including uninsured-motorist insurance. Could Bayer recover from Whitaker's insurance company under the uninsured-motorist provision of the policy? Why or why not? *Bayer v. Travelers Indemnity* Co., 267 S.E.2d 91 (VA).

8. Riggins contacted the Hartford Insurance Company and asked for an all-risk policy for his truck. An underwriter for Hartford agreed to the policy and issued a binder on March 28. On April 2, before the full policy had been executed, Riggins left on a trip, hauling liquor. Sometime during the trip, the liquor was stolen. Hartford refused to pay, arguing that the final policy that would have been issued would not have covered the hauling of liquor. Riggins argued that the all-risk binder was in effect at the time of the theft and that he was therefore covered, even though the final policy would not have covered him. Was Riggins correct? Explain. *Hilt Truck Lanes, Inc., v. Riggins,* 756 F.2d 676 (8th Cir).

9. When Sidney Henry applied for insurance with State Farm, he was asked whether he had ever had recurrent indigestion or a hernia. Henry answered no to each question. In fact, he had experienced recurring indigestion, and it had been diagnosed as either an ulcer or a hernia. The policy was issued. Eight months later, Henry died of cancer of the esophagus. When Eula Henry applied for benefits, State Farm denied her request. Eula argued that the misrepresentations were not material because her husband died from cancer, not the illnesses he was questioned about. Was Mrs. Henry correct? Explain. *Henry v. State Farm,* 465 So.2d 276 (LA).

10. On January 13, Lax made out a check to State Farm Insurance to pay for her automobile insurance, which had lapsed 62 days earlier. Unfortunately, she forgot to mail the check. On January 22, Lax was killed when trying to pass a truck. The check was found in the wreckage and taken to a State Farm agent who mailed it to the main office. The main office, with knowledge of the accident, cashed the check. The beneficiaries argued

that State Farm's conduct in cashing the check with knowledge of the accident constituted a waiver of its right to cancel the policy due to her failure to pay by the due date. Were the beneficiaries correct? Explain. *VanHulle v. State Farm,* 254 N.E.2d 457 (IL).

Quick Quiz Answers

30-1	30-2	30-3	30-4
1. F	1. T	1. F	1. T
2. F	2. F	2. T	2. F
3. F	3. T	3. F	3. T

Chapter 31 Mortgages and Security Interests

The Opening Case
"Security Blanket"

Avery, a retail appliance dealer, borrowed money from a bank, which took a security interest in all of Avery's present and after-acquired inventory and equipment. The bank perfected its security interest by filing. Later, still short of cash, Avery bought some inventory from a wholesaler that also took and perfected a security interest in the inventory that was purchased. Still later, Avery bought a computer on credit from a computer store, which also took and perfected a security interest in the computer. Finally, Avery sold a stove and a microwave oven on credit to Sweeney, a customer, and took a purchase-money security interest in both items. Sweeney sold the microwave to a friend and paid nothing to Avery for either item.

Opening Case Questions

1. Whose security interest will prevail between the bank and the wholesaler?

2. Whose security interest will prevail between the bank and the computer store?

3. Whose security interest will prevail between the bank and Sweeney?

4. Whose security interest will prevail between Avery and Sweeney's friend?

LO Learning Objectives

1. Differentiate between a secured and an unsecured loan and explain why a creditor needs a security interest when lending money or extending credit.
2. Identify six types of mortgages and decide which will best suit a particular situation.
3. Explain the legal effect of recording a mortgage and the priorities involved when more than one mortgage is held and recorded on the same property.
4. Discuss junior mortgages.
5. Describe and distinguish between the rights and duties of the mortgagor and the rights and duties of the mortgagee.
6. Explain how a security interest is created for personal property, and distinguish between the attachment and the perfection of a security interest.

7. List the requirements of a security agreement.
8. Describe the events that must occur for a security interest to attach.
9. Decide whether security interests are perfected in cases involving various kinds of collateral.
10. Determine who will have priority when several parties claim a security interest in the same property.
11. Discuss what rights a secured party has when a debtor defaults by failing to make payments when due.

31-1 Necessity of Security Devices

Security is the assurance that a creditor will be paid back for any money loaned or for credit extended to a debtor. Debts are said to be secured when creditors know that somehow they will be able to recover their money. Lenders of money and people who extend credit often require a security device to protect their financial interests. A security device is a way for creditors to get their money back in case the borrower or debtor does not pay. A **secured loan** is one in which creditors have something of value, usually called *collateral,* from which they can be paid if the debtor does not pay. In general, if creditors are not paid the debt owed to them, they can legally gain possession of the collateral. The collateral is then sold, and the money is used to pay the debt. The right to use the collateral to recover a debt is called the creditor's **security interest**. If creditors lend money but do not require collateral, they have made an unsecured loan. An **unsecured loan** is one in which creditors have nothing of value that they can repossess and sell to recover the money owed to them by the debtor. Both real property and personal property can be used to secure a debt.

31-2 Real Property as Security

When real property is used as security for a loan, a device known as a mortgage is used to establish collateral for the loan. A **mortgage** is a transfer of an interest in property for the purpose of creating a security for a debt. The one who borrows the money (the **mortgagor**) conveys his or her interest in the property to the lender (the **mortgagee**) while at the same time retaining possession of the property. The borrower signs a promissory note (explained in Chapter 26) as evidence of the loan in addition to a mortgage instrument. The mortgage creates a legal claim to the property. This legal claim, also called a lien, gives the lender the right to have the property sold if the debt is not paid. Once the land is sold and the debt is paid, the mortgagor's obligation to the mortgagee is over. However, if the sale of the property does not satisfy the whole debt, the mortgagor will still owe the balance.

EXAMPLE 31-1:   Mortgage Foreclosure

Mayo bought a house for $144,000. Of this sum, she put up $50,000 in cash. Mayo then took out a $95,000 loan from the Unicorp Bank to cover the rest of her purchase. When Mayo could not meet the mortgage payments, Unicorp foreclosed and sold the house for $6,593 less than what was owed. Mayo would be personally liable for the $6,593, plus interest, until the debt was paid.

Mortgage Costs

There are many costs connected with obtaining a mortgage. Initially, a potential borrower must pay a mortgage application fee, an appraisal fee, a credit report fee, and an inspection fee. If the loan is approved, the borrower often pays an origination fee, which is a charge for issuing the loan. Sometimes, the borrower pays interest in a lump sum upfront, called points, to get a lower rate of interest. A point is a one-time charge equal to 1 percent of the principal amount borrowed. Thus, if three points are charged on an $80,000 mortgage, the borrower will be required to pay a one-time fee of 3 percent of $80,000, which amounts to $2,400. If all IRS requirements are met, points are tax deductible.

Other items charged to the borrower include charges for document preparation, attorney's fees, title insurance, surveyor fees, termite inspections, mortgage insurance, and homeowner's insurance.

Types of Mortgages

There are many different types of real property mortgages (Table 31-1). Some of the most common mortgages are the conventional, the variable-rate, the graduated-payment, the balloon-payment, the Federal Housing Administration (FHA) and Veterans Administration (VA), and deeds of trust.

Table 31-1   Some Methods of Financing a House

Type	Description
Fixed-Rate Mortgage	Fixed interest rate, usually long-term; equal monthly payments; including principal and interest, until debt is paid in full
Variable- or Flexible-Rate Mortgage	Interest rate changes based on a financial index, resulting in possible changes in monthly payments, loan term, and/or principal; some plans have rate or payment caps
Balloon-Payment Mortgage	Monthly payments based on fixed interest rate, usually short-term; payments may cover interest only with principal due in full at term's end
Graduated-Payment Mortgage	Lower monthly payments rise gradually then level off for duration of term; with flexible interest rate, additional payment changes possible, if index changes
Shared-Appreciation Mortgage	Below-market interest rate and lower monthly payments in exchange for a share of profits when property is sold or on a specified date; many variations
Assumable Mortgage	Buyer takes over seller's original, below-market rate mortgage
Seller Take-Back	Seller provides all or part of financing with a first or second mortgage
Wraparound Mortgage	Seller keeps original low-rate mortgage; buyer makes payments to seller who forwards a portion to the lender holding original mortgage; offers lower effective interest rate on total transaction

Conventional Mortgage

A **conventional mortgage** involves no government backing by either insurance or guarantee. The loan is made by private lenders, and the risks of loss are borne exclusively by them. In the past, conventional mortgages had fixed interest rates that stayed the same during the life of the mortgage, regardless of fluctuations in the economy. Changes in recent years, however, have resulted in the creation of variations to the fixed-interest rate mortgage.

Variable-Rate Mortgage

A **variable-** or **flexible-rate mortgage** has a rate of interest that changes according to fluctuations in the index to which it is tied. The index rate may be the bank's prime rate or the Federal Reserve Board discount rate. As the index rate goes up and down, so does the rate of interest charged on the loan. This rate may be more or less than the index rate but always varies with it.

The obvious advantage of the variable-rate mortgage is the drop in the amount of the mortgage payment when the rate drops. However, mortgage payments can also rise when the rate rises. In general, a change in payments, either up or down, does not occur without some advance warning. Also, variable-rate mortgage agreements must include a maximum rate that cannot be exceeded. In addition, the frequency of these changes in the rate is usually restricted by the terms of the mortgage agreement.

Graduated-Payment Mortgage

A **graduated-payment mortgage** has a fixed interest rate during the life of the mortgage; however, the monthly payments made by the mortgagor increase over the term of the loan. In the first years of the mortgage, the payments are low. The payments gradually increase over time, usually reaching a plateau at which the payments remain fixed. This type of mortgage is advantageous for young people, whose income may be expected to increase as their mortgage payments increase.

Balloon-Payment Mortgage

A **balloon-payment mortgage** has relatively low fixed payments during the life of the mortgage, followed by one large final (balloon) payment. The mortgage has a fixed interest rate, but it is written for a short time period, such as five years. At the end of the time period, the mortgagor usually must find new financing, either with the same or with a different lender, at the current interest rate.

Reverse Mortgage

A **reverse mortgage** is a type of loan that allows home owners, over the age of 62 years, to convert some of the equity in their home into cash while retaining ownership of their home. The loan is repaid when the borrower dies or the property is sold.

FHA and VA Mortgages

Some mortgages, though given by private lenders, are backed by federal agencies. The FHA and the VA are responsible to the lending institution in the event of a mortgagor's default and foreclosure on an FHA or VA mortgage. The U.S. government, through these agencies, reimburses the mortgagee for any loss and takes over the property. Such properties are then offered for sale to interested buyers to recover the government's loss. The Government National Mortgage Association (Ginnie Mae), through its *mortgage-backed securities* program, guarantees the money provided by investors will be paid back.

There are many different types of mortgages. Knowing which type fits your needs, both in the present and for the future, makes home-ownership easier and more enjoyable.

Another way the federal government is involved with home mortgages is through two government agencies: the Federal Home Loan Mortgage Corp. (Freddie Mac) and the Federal National Mortgage Association (Fannie Mae). These agencies are federally chartered corporations with publicly traded stock that are designed to encourage investment in home

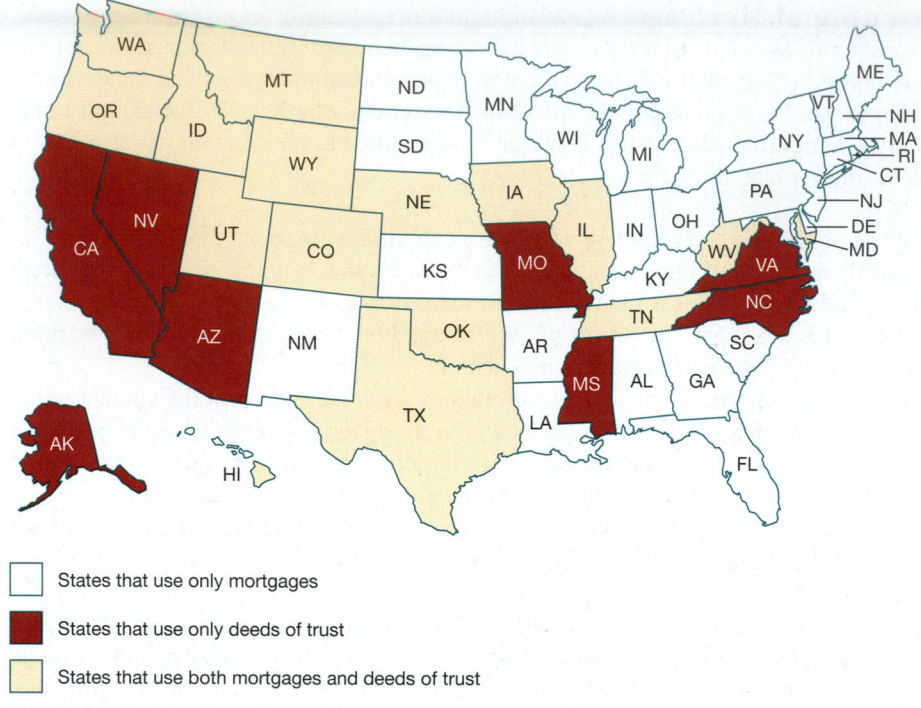

States that use only mortgages

States that use only deeds of trust

States that use both mortgages and deeds of trust

Figure 31-1 Use of Mortgages and Deeds of Trust.

mortgages. Many banks and mortgage companies make their profits on points and then sell their mortgages to Freddie Mac or Fannie Mae. The banks and mortgage companies that originate the loans are also paid to service them—that is, collect the monthly payments and foreclose when necessary.

Deed of Trust In some states, a deed of trust is used instead of a mortgage. In a conventional mortgage, the mortgagor conveys all or part of his or her interest in the property directly to the mortgagee. Under a **deed of trust**, the mortgagor conveys his or her interest in the property to a disinterested third party, known as a trustee. The mortgagor remains on the property, but the trustee holds certain rights to that property as security for the mortgagor's creditors. If the debtor defaults, the trustee can sell the property for the benefit of those creditors. The provisions of many deeds of trust allow the trustee to sell the property without going to court. For this reason, some legal authorities do not consider a deed of trust a true mortgage, because true mortgages require a foreclosure action for the sale of the property. Figure 31-1 indicates the states that use either mortgages or deeds of trusts, and states that use both mortgages and deeds of trusts.

Federal Protection

The Real Estate Settlement Procedures Act (RESPA), a federal law, gives consumers protection when they apply for a loan. Under this law, the lender must give the consumer a copy of a booklet that explains the real estate settlement procedure. The lender must also give the consumer an estimate of the costs that will be incurred in obtaining the loan. Later, a uniform settlement statement must be filled out, which shows the exact cost of the settlement. Consumers have the right to see the completed form on the day before the closing if they wish. Finally, the lender must give the consumer a truth-in-lending statement showing the true costs of the interest and finance charges on the mortgage loan.

Another federal law, the Private Mortgage Insurance (PMI) Act, requires homeowners to purchase private mortgage insurance when they take out a mortgage with less than a 20 percent down payment. This insurance protects the lender from default losses in the event a loan becomes delinquent. The law provides for two situations in which borrower-paid PMI may be canceled: automatically or by request.

- *Automatically.* In general, when the homeowner's equity position reaches 22 percent of the original value of the property, the lender must automatically cancel the PMI. The borrower must be current in making payments for automatic cancellation to apply. Different requirements exist for high-risk mortgage loans.

- *By request.* Homeowners can request cancellation of the PMI when their equity position reaches 20 percent of the original value of the property, if they meet certain criteria.

Recording the Mortgage

Like a deed, a mortgage must be in writing and delivered to the recorder's office in the county where the property is located. Recording a mortgage notifies any third party who may be interested in purchasing the property or in lending money to the owner that the mortgagee has an interest in the real property covered by the mortgage. If the mortgage is not recorded and a later mortgage is given on the same property, the new mortgage is superior to the first. The second mortgagee must not know about the first mortgage and must record the mortgage properly. A failure to record the first mortgage, however, would not remove the obligation of the mortgagor to the first mortgagee. The debt would simply be unsecured.

LO3

EXAMPLE 31-2:   Unsecured Loan

Klein needed $20,000 to cover several bad investments. She obtained the money from the Newman Financial Bank by giving the bank a first mortgage on her house. The bank failed to have the mortgage properly recorded. Silver later bought the house from Klein. Because Silver found no mortgage against the property recorded in the county recorder's office, he took the house free of the mortgage. Klein, however, still owed the bank $20,000 plus interest.

Junior Mortgages

Sometimes an owner of real property may execute a junior mortgage on the property. A **junior mortgage**, also called a **second** (or subsequent) **mortgage**, is a mortgage subject to a prior mortgage. For example, if a homeowner wants to improve the mortgaged property and needs another loan to do so, he or she may use the property as security for another loan. If this transaction occurs, the mortgagor is said to have executed a second mortgage on the property. Some people have three or more mortgages on one parcel of property. If all the mortgages are recorded, the holders of second and subsequent mortgages may exercise their rights against the property only after prior mortgages have been paid off. Thus, if the first mortgagee causes the property to be sold and is paid off in full, the second and subsequent mortgages are paid out of the proceeds that remain. The first mortgagee acts as a trustee of the surplus funds for the benefit of the junior mortgagees.

EXAMPLE 31-3: Second Mortgage

Zelentz wanted to add a new bedroom onto his house but did not have the ready cash. His house was already mortgaged to Mercedes Savings and Loan for $80,000. Nevertheless, he decided to take out a second mortgage with Cuyahoga Savings. Cuyahoga loaned Zelentz $10,000 because he pledged his home as security should he fail to repay the loan. When Zelentz defaulted on the mortgage to Mercedes and the loan from Cuyahoga, Mercedes caused the house to be sold for $90,000. Because Mercedes held the first mortgage, it was paid first. After Mercedes had its $80,000, Cuyahoga would collect its $10,000.

Holders of first mortgages sometimes enter into a **subordination agreement** in which they agree to allow their mortgage to be reduced in priority to a person holding a second mortgage. Their mortgage is **subordinated**, that is, placed in a lower order than the second mortgage. The agreement is recorded at the Registry of Deeds and has the effect of turning a second mortgage into a first mortgage and turning a first mortgage into a second mortgage.

A **home equity loan** is an example of a junior mortgage. It is either an outright loan or a line of credit made available to homeowners based on the value of the property over and above any existing mortgages. Such a loan takes advantage of the equity that has built up in a home over a period of time. Home equity loans are often used to consolidate credit card balances or other debts that have higher interest rates. Unlike interest paid on a credit card balance, interest paid on a home equity loan is tax deductible.

Rights and Duties of the Mortgagor

By law and by agreement, the mortgagor has certain rights and duties in conjunction with the mortgage. First, the mortgagor has the right to possess the property. Second, the mortgagor has the right to any income produced by the property. For instance, the mortgagor would be entitled to any rent proceeds gained from leasing all or part of the property. The mortgagor could, however, assign this right to the mortgagee, which is sometimes done as a condition of executing the original mortgage agreement.

Third, the mortgagor has the right to use the property for a second or third mortgage. Fourth, the mortgagor has the **equity of redemption**, that is, the right to pay off the mortgage in full, including interest, and thus discharge the debt in total.

In addition to these rights, the mortgagor has certain duties. Chief among these duties is to make payments on time. Mortgagors must preserve and maintain the mortgaged property for the benefit of the mortgagee's interest and security. Similarly, the mortgagor is often required to insure the property to the benefit of the mortgagee for the amount of the mortgaged debt.

The mortgagor also must pay all taxes and assessments that may be levied against the property. Frequently, the mortgagor will ease the burden of these obligations by paying a percentage of the insurance premium and taxes each month along with the mortgage payment. The mortgagee holds the money in an escrow account. An escrow account is a special account into which money is deposited before the payment of the insurance or taxes is due. The money stays in the account until the time comes to pay the insurance or tax. The mortgagee then takes the money out of the account and makes the payments.

Rights and Duties of the Mortgagee

The mortgagee has the unrestricted right to sell, assign, or transfer the mortgage to a third party. Whatever rights the mortgagee had in the mortgage are then the rights of the assignee. The only way the mortgagor could stop the mortgagee from assigning the mortgage is to pay the mortgagee everything owed on the mortgage. Sometimes an assignment by the mortgagee to another mortgagee can cause unforeseen problems for the mortgagor.

EXAMPLE 31-4:   Mortgage Assignment

The Chamberlins financed the purchase of their house through the Midway Savings Bank, a local bank with only four branches, all in the city of Bromfield. The Chamberlins made their mortgage payments faithfully each month, in person, at the branch on their street. Without warning, they received notice that Midway had assigned their mortgage to the Unicorp Mortgage Corporation, a multimillion-dollar financial institution headquartered in New York. Although the Chamberlins had no desire to deal with Unicorp, they had no choice in the matter. The only way they could avoid dealing with Unicorp would be to make full payment of the mortgage debt.

Mortgagees have the right to receive each installment payment as it falls due. Frequently, mortgagees will include a term in the mortgage agreement allowing an **acceleration** of the debt if the mortgagor fails to meet an installment payment. This term means that a default on one installment payment will make the entire balance due immediately, giving the mortgagee the right to collect the full amount. In general, a clause allowing acceleration must be executed in good faith. In other words, before invoking the acceleration clause, the mortgagee must genuinely believe that the mortgagor will not be able to make good on the debt and that the mortgagee's security interest is therefore threatened. If the matter ends up in court, the mortgagor will have the burden of proving that the mortgagee did not act in good faith.

If the mortgagor has defaulted or has failed to perform some other agreement in the mortgage, the mortgagee has the right to apply to a court to have the property sold. This right is called **foreclosure**. It takes priority even when the mortgagor files for bankruptcy. Because, in a majority of jurisdictions, a mortgage is a lien on the land, a foreclosure is an equitable action. The mortgagor does not have a right to a jury trial in a foreclosure action.

A mortgage is foreclosed when the mortgagee proves the amount of the unpaid debt (including interest and other charges) and the property is sold by and under the direction of a court. The proceeds from the sale are then applied to the payment of the debt. Any money remaining after the claims of the mortgagee have been satisfied goes to the mortgagor or to the second and subsequent mortgagees.

The mortgagee's financial interest in mortgaged property gives rise to certain constitutional rights. Under Amendment 14 to the U.S. Constitution, mortgagees cannot lose their interest in property without due process of law.

EXAMPLE 31-5:   Loss of Due Process

Northmore Bank and Trust made a $456,000 loan to Perez. It secured that loan with a mortgage on a warehouse owned by Perez. The county commissioners wanted the Perez property for an expansion of the county airport. The county paid Perez a nominal amount for the warehouse and then had it demolished. Northmore received no notice of the demolition until after the building had been torn down. Northmore sued the county, claiming that its constitutional due process rights had been violated. The court agreed with Northmore's claim.

U.S. Const. Amendment 14 (page 950)

How to Avoid Foreclosure

Has the American dream of homeownership turned into a personal nightmare? To hold onto your house, consider these tips and traps.

If you suddenly find yourself faced with the possibility of losing your home because of economic disaster or your own negligence, don't panic—there are steps you can take to avoid becoming another foreclosure statistic.

Others have not been so lucky. According to foreclosure listing database RealtyTrac, 1.26 million foreclosure filings were reported in 2006, up 42% from 2005, with an average rate of one filing for every 92 households.

"While foreclosures are not at historically high levels, a 42% year-over-year increase is certainly noteworthy," says James J. Saccacio, chief executive officer of RealtyTrac. The increase in foreclosures last year, Saccacio explains, was driven both by a general deceleration in home sales across the country and the impact of increases in monthly payments on adjustable rate mortgages (ARMs).

ARMs are set at a lower initial rate that resets to reflect current rates more closely after a fixed period of time, usually one, three, five, seven, or 10 years. Some $407 billion in ARMs reset in 2006, according to Fannie Mae (FMN). As monthly rates shot up, many unsuspecting homeowners became unable to afford their payments, forcing them into foreclosure.

Other homeowners needed to foreclose because they were hit with economic tragedies such as natural disasters, divorce, illness, or layoffs. Detroit documented the highest annual foreclosure rate among the nation's largest metropolitan areas, with foreclosure filings representing 4.9% of all households, or one filing for every 21 homes. It's no coincidence that the Motor City's unemployment rate is 7.2%, the highest among metro areas with populations of 1 million or more.

Don't Rule Out Refinancing

With auto sales off to a weak start this year in Detroit and more than $1 trillion in ARMs eligible to reset in 2007, high-risk homeowners have even more reason to boost their immunity against foreclosures this year.

At the first sign of danger, get in touch with your lender to see if there are alternative loan products available. This is especially important if you know the payment on your ARM is about go up and you have even the slightest doubt about being able to afford the higher rate. Because of embarrassment or false hope that financial difficulties will blow over, many people do not act quickly enough.

"By addressing the problem as early in the process as possible, you can avoid the trouble before it happens," says Rick Sharga, vice-president for marketing at RealtyTrac.

Foreclosure laws vary by state, so make sure you know exactly how much time you can buy. New Yorkers, consider yourselves lucky—you have 455 days from the time you are delinquent on your loan payments before a lender can take possession of the house. Texans, you better hustle, because the pre-foreclosure period is just 27 days, shortest in the U.S.

Rework It or Sell It

If refinancing isn't an option, ask your lender about loan modification. Remember, Sharga says, banks want to avoid foreclosure, too. They lose money every time they foreclose on a house, and a high rate of default could even lead to the loss of a license.

Forbearance is an agreement that allows you to pay less than the full amount of your loan payment, or sometimes nothing at all, during a certain period of time. Mortgage companies may consider you for this option if you can prove that funds from a tax refund, bonus, or elsewhere will bring an end to your tight financial situation at a specific time in the near future.

You may also be able to reinstate by paying the amount you are behind in a lump sum by a certain date. Or you may be eligible for a repayment plan that gives you a fixed amount of time to repay the total amount you owe by combining a portion of past dues with your regular monthly payment.

You can also contact a Realtor to find out what options you may have for selling your home before it is repossessed. "Selling the property below full market value is a lot better than losing everything," Sharga notes. In a market like California or New York, a soon-to-be foreclosed home can fetch up to 90% of its market value if it's moved early enough, he says, though 60% is closer to the national average. However, remember that pre-foreclosure selling is a time-vs.-cost decision—the more quickly you need to sell your home, the bigger the discount at which you need to price it.

Don't Make Another Mistake

"Foreclosure is a time when people are economically and emotionally vulnerable," Sharga says. So be wary of anybody who says they are a foreclosure rescue service, and don't sign anything without having a lawyer look at it. If something sounds too good to be true, it usually is.

"Equity skimming" is one common scam in which someone posing as a buyer approaches you and offers to pay off your mortgage. This "buyer" may suggest that you move out quickly and deed the property to him or her. The buyer then collects rent for a while, does not make any mortgage payments, and eventually allows the mortgage company to foreclose.

Phony counseling agencies may also offer to perform certain services for a fee that you can do yourself for free, such as negotiating a new payment plan with your mortgage company. If you are seeking counseling, make sure the organization with which you're dealing is certified by the U.S. Housing & Urban Development (HUD) Dept.

One legitimate organization is the Home Ownership Preservation Foundation (HPF), a Minneapolis nonprofit that receives funding from the government and lending institutions. HPF has a hotline, (888) 995-HOPE, to help homeowners who are struggling financially. The organization, which sets up financial budgets and creates tailored plans to avoid foreclosure, recently launched a nationwide campaign for foreclosure prevention.

Ultimately, homeowners may need professional consulting to get their finances in order. Sixty percent of Americans live paycheck-to-paycheck, according to HPF. While a lot of people end up in foreclosure because of economic disaster, many others had eyes bigger than their stomachs when taking out a mortgage and later found their payments difficult to digest. Your lender is required to tell you how much your monthly payment, at most, may adjust to, and you need to be sure you can afford it when that happens.

"Take a hard look at your personal finances," Sharga cautions. "Your home is probably the single biggest financial investment you are going to make."

Questions for Analysis

1. What drove the increase in foreclosures in the prior year?

2. What should homeowners do at the first sign of danger that they cannot pay their mortgage?

3. What should borrowers ask for if refinancing is not an option?

4. What is the meaning of "forbearance"?

5. When may mortgage companies consider forbearance?

6. Why should a borrower contact a Realtor when paying the mortgage is a problem?

7. What is equity skimming?

8. Name a legitimate organization that helps homeowners who are struggling financially.

Source: Maya Roney, "How to Avoid Foreclosure," *BusinessWeek,* February 5, 2007, http://www.businessweek.com.

Mortgagees also have certain duties imposed by law. Both state and federal legislation prohibits lenders from discriminating against borrowers because of race, creed, color, sex, or ethnic background. Such legislation imposes a duty to use nondiscriminatory criteria in approving and disapproving mortgage applications. For example, a lender may not refuse a mortgage to a prospective borrower simply because that borrower is a woman. Similarly, a lender could not refuse a mortgage to a borrower because that borrower is Hispanic. The mortgagee also has the duty to respect all rights properly claimed by the mortgagor.

Purchase by Mortgage Takeover

Mortgages often contain a clause providing that if the property is sold, the mortgage becomes due and payable. If the mortgage does not contain such a clause, the property may be sold with the mortgage remaining on it. In such takeovers, the transfer of title to a new buyer is subject to the buyer's payment of the seller's mortgage at the existing rate of interest.

A Question of Ethics

The Chamberlins' mortgage, in Example 31-4, was assigned by their local bank to a multimillion-dollar financial institution headquartered in New York. The assignment was done without the Chamberlins' consent, and they had no desire to deal with the distant bank. The assignment of the mortgage by the bank was legal; however, was it ethical? Explain your response.

In purchasing a property already mortgaged, the buyer will either **assume the mortgage** or take the property **subject to the mortgage**. When buyers decide to assume the mortgage, they agree to pay it. When they take the property subject to a mortgage, the seller agrees to continue paying the debt.

Quick Quiz 31-1 & 31-2 True or False?

1. A security device is a way for creditors to get their money back in case the borrower or debtor does not pay.

2. A home equity loan is an example of a junior mortgage.

3. The mortgagor has the right to possess the mortgaged property and to any income produced by the property unless otherwise assigned.

31-3 Personal Property as Security

Article 9 of the UCC brings all personal property security devices, or security interests, together under one law. The property that is subject to the security interest is called **collateral**. A security interest is created by a written agreement, called a **security agreement**, which identifies the goods and is signed by the debtor. The lender or seller who holds the security interest is known as the **secured party**. A security interest is said to attach when the secured party has a legally enforceable right to take that property and sell it to satisfy the debt. It is said to be **perfected** when the secured party has done everything that the law requires to give the secured party greater rights to the goods than others have.

The following definitions apply to secured transactions:

- **Consumer goods** are goods that are used or bought for use primarily for personal, family, or household purposes.

- **Equipment** are goods other than inventory, farm products, or consumer goods.

- **Farm products** are crops or livestock or supplies used or produced in farming operations.

- **Inventory** are goods other than farm products held for sale or lease or raw materials used or consumed in a business.

- **Fixtures** are goods that are so related to real estate that an interest arises in them under real estate law.

- **Purchase money security interest** is a security interest taken by a lender or a seller of an item to secure its price.

- **Buyer in the ordinary course of business** is a person who in good faith and without knowledge that the sale is in violation of ownership rights or security interest of a third party buys goods in ordinary course from a person in the business of selling goods of that kind, not including a pawnbroker.

UCC 9-102(23)

UCC 9-102(33)

UCC 9-102(34)

UCC 9-102(48)

UCC 9-102(41)

UCC 9-103

UCC 1-201(9) (see page 955)

Security Agreement

A security agreement is an agreement that creates a security interest. It must be in writing, be signed by the debtor, and contain a description of the collateral that is used for security.

UCC 9-105(l)

EXAMPLE 31-6:   Security Agreement Must Describe Collateral

Moody Industries contracted to purchase certain robotics equipment from Universal. Moody's president signed a promissory note identifying Universal as a secured party. When Moody filed for bankruptcy, Universal claimed to have a security interest in the robotics equipment. Because the promissory note did not describe the collateral, Universal did not hold a valid security interest in the equipment.

If Universal had provided enough information about the collateral to allow the court to identify it without a detailed description, the result would have been different. Had Universal made reference to the equipment by including purchase order or invoice numbers, the court could have identified the equipment and would have upheld the validity of the security agreement.

Attachment of a Security Interest

To be effective, a security interest must be legally enforceable against the debtor. This enforceability is known as **attachment**. Attachment occurs when three conditions are met. First, the debtor has some ownership or possessive rights in the collateral. Second, the secured party (or creditor) transfers something of value, such as money, to the debtor. Third, the secured party takes possession of the collateral or signs a security agreement that describes the collateral.

UCC 9-203

EXAMPLE 31-7:   Attachment of Security Interest

Conroy loaned Lightfoot $5,000 for six months at 8 percent interest. Lightfoot secured the debt by giving Conroy several uncut diamonds that Lightfoot owned. Conroy agreed to return the diamonds when Lightfoot paid the debt. The security interest was legally enforceable because all three conditions were met. First, Lightfoot had ownership rights in the diamonds. Second, Conroy gave Lightfoot something of value (the $5,000). Third, Conroy took possession of the diamonds. The security interest would also have attached if Lightfoot had kept the diamonds but signed a security agreement describing them.

Creditors may obtain security interests in property acquired by the debtor after the original agreement is entered. The creditor does so by placing a provision in the security agreement that the security interest of the creditor also applies to goods the debtor acquires at a later time. It is known as a **floating lien**. This lien is important to creditors who take security interests in goods, such as food items, that are sold and replaced within short periods of time. The lien is lost when the goods are sold but regained as soon as the debtor takes possession of the new property.

UCC 9-204

Perfection of a Security Interest

When a security interest attaches, it is effective only between debtor and creditor. Such creditors, however, want to make certain that no one else can claim that collateral before they do if the debtors fail to pay them back. To preserve the right to first claim on the collateral, creditors must perfect their interest. A security interest can be perfected in one of three ways: by filing a financing statement in the appropriate government office, by attachment alone, or by possession of the collateral.

Perfection by Filing   Security interests in most kinds of personal property are perfected by filing a financing statement in a public office. The office may be a central one (secretary of state's office) or a local one (county recorder or city clerk) where the debtor resides or has a place of business. The proper office for filing depends on the type of collateral and varies from state to state.

UCC 9-302

A financing statement must give the names of the debtor and the secured party. It must be signed by the debtor and give the address of a secured party from which information regarding the security interest may be obtained. It must also give a mailing address of the debtor and contain a statement indicating the types, or describing the items, of collateral. When the financing statement covers such things as fixtures, crops, timber, minerals, oil, and gas, the statement must also contain a description of the real estate concerned.

EXAMPLE 31-8:   UCC Financial Statement

Dig Big Excavator, Inc., was the low bidder on a job to clear a 50-acre wood lot on which a shopping center was to be built. The company borrowed $40,000 from the Second National Bank to purchase some equipment it needed for the job. To secure the loan, the bank required Dig Big's president to sign a security agreement that described the purchased equipment. The security agreement was perfected when the bank filed this UCC financing statement with the secretary of state's office and the city hall of the town where the business was located.

UCC FINANCING STATEMENT
FOLLOW INSTRUCTIONS (front and back) CAREFULLY

A. NAME & PHONE OF CONTACT AT FILER [optional]
Cary Havitall, (603) 907-1234

B. SEND ACKNOWLEDGMENT TO: (Name and Address)
Second National Bank
42 Main Street
E. Hampstead, NH 03826

THE ABOVE SPACE IS FOR FILING OFFICE USE ONLY

1. DEBTOR'S EXACT FULL LEGAL NAME-insert only one debtor name (1a or 1b)-do not abbreviate or combine names

1a. ORGANIZATION'S NAME				
Dig Big Excavator, Inc.				
1b. INDIVIDUAL'S LAST NAME	FIRST NAME	MIDDLE NAME		SUFFIX

1c. MAILING ADDRESS	CITY	STATE	POSTAL CODE	COUNTRY
205 Hunt Pond Rd.	Sandown	NH	03873	USA

1d. SEE INSTRUCTIONS	ADD'L INFO RE ORGANIZATION DEBTOR	1e. TYPE OF ORGANIZATION	1f. JURISDICTION OF ORGANIZATION	1g. ORGANIZATIONAL ID #, if any [X] NONE

2. ADDITIONAL DEBTOR'S EXACT FULL LEGAL NAME-insert only one debtor name (2a or 2b)-do not abbreviate or combine names

2a. ORGANIZATION'S NAME				
2b. INDIVIDUAL'S LAST NAME	FIRST NAME	MIDDLE NAME		SUFFIX

2c. MAILING ADDRESS	CITY	STATE	POSTAL CODE	COUNTRY

2d. SEE INSTRUCTIONS	ADD'L INFO RE ORGANIZATION DEBTOR	2e. TYPE OF ORGANIZATION	2f. JURISDICTION OF ORGANIZATION	2g. ORGANIZATIONAL ID #, if any [ ] NONE

3. SECURED PARTY'S NAME (or NAME of TOTAL ASSIGNEE of ASSIGNOR S/P) - insert only one secured party name (3a or 3b)

3a. ORGANIZATION'S NAME				
Second National Bank				
3b. INDIVIDUAL'S LAST NAME	FIRST NAME	MIDDLE NAME		SUFFIX

3c. MAILING ADDRESS	CITY	STATE	POSTAL CODE	COUNTRY
42 Main Street	E. Hampstead	NH	03826	USA

4. This FINANCING STATEMENT covers the following collateral:
North Star Hydraulic 20-ton log splitter
30 HP Nortrac tractor #N644L3
18 HP 1.5 ton Mini Excavator #EX77304
30 HP Nortrac Bulldozer #721H35

5. ALTERNATIVE DESIGNATION [if applicable]:	LESSEE/LESSOR	CONSIGNEE/CONSIGNOR	BAILEE/BAILOR	SELLER/BUYER	AG. LIEN	NON-UCC FILING

6.	This FINANCING STATEMENT is to be filed [for record] (or recorded) in the REAL ESTATE RECORDS. Attach Addendum [if applicable]	7. Check to REQUEST SEARCH REPORT(S) on Debtor(s) [ADDITIONAL FEE] [optional]	All Debtors	Debtor 1	Debtor 2

8. OPTIONAL FILER REFERENCE DATA

FILING OFFICE COPY — UCC FINANCING STATEMENT (FORM UCC1) (REV. 05/22/02)

Perfection by Attachment Alone   A purchase money security interest in con- UCC 9-302(1)(d)
sumer goods is perfected the moment it attaches, with the exception of motor vehicles UCC 9-302(3)(b)
and fixtures. Security interests on motor vehicles are perfected by making a note of the
lien on the certificate of title issued by the state government. Security interests on fixtures are perfected by filing a financing statement with the registry of deeds where the
land is located.

EXAMPLE 31-9:   Perfection of Purchase Money Security Interest

Sabatini purchased a new 34" widescreen HDTV for $1,999.99 from Steinbeck's
TV Outlet. To pay for the TV, she borrowed money from the Atlantic Finance Company, which took a security interest in the TV by entering into a security agreement
with Sabatini. Because this interest was a purchase money security interest and the
TV set was a consumer good, the security interest would become perfected the moment it attached, that is, when Sabatini signed the agreement and received the TV
set, and Steinbeck received payment from the finance company.

UCC 9-313

Perfection by Possession   A security interest may be perfected when the secured
party (creditor) takes possession of the collateral. This possession is called a pledge. The
borrower, or debtor, who gives up the property, is the pledgor. The secured party, or creditor, is the pledgee. A secured party who has possession of the collateral must take reasonable care of the property. The debtor must reimburse the secured party for any money spent
to take care of the property.

EXAMPLE 31-10:   Pledge of Personal Property

After Sabatini paid off the debt to the Atlantic Finance Corporation, she decided to
buy a CD player. This time, she borrowed the money from her cousin, Colter, who
agreed to lend Sabatini the money only if he could have her CD player as security
until she repaid him. Colter's security interest in the CD player became perfected
when he took possession of it.

Priorities and Claims

LO10

Sometimes, two or more parties claim a security interest in the same collateral. At other
times, unsecured parties claim that they have better rights than secured parties. The UCC
helps resolve these conflicts. The following are some of the provisions, stating who prevails over whom in particular situations:

1. A perfected purchase money security interest in inventory has priority over a conflict- UCC 9-312(3)
    ing security interest in the same inventory.

2. A purchase money security interest in collateral other than inventory has priority over UCC 9-312(4)
    a conflicting security interest in the same collateral if it is perfected when the debtor UCC 9-307(1)
    receives the collateral or within 10 days thereafter.
    UCC 9-301(1)(c)
3. Buyers of goods in the ordinary course of business (except farm products) prevail over
    security interests in the seller's inventory.

The Opening Case Revisited
"Security Blanket"

1. Between the bank and the wholesaler, the wholesaler will prevail because a perfected purchase money security interest in inventory has priority over a conflicting security interest in the same inventory (rule 1).
2. Between the bank and the computer store, the computer store will prevail because the purchase money security interest was in collateral other than inventory (a computer) but was perfected when the collateral was received (rule 2).
3. Between the bank and Sweeney, Sweeney will prevail because buyers of goods in the ordinary course of business prevail over security interests in the seller's inventory (rule 3).
4. Between Avery and Sweeney's friend, Sweeney's friend will prevail because buyers of consumer goods are not affected by perfected security interests of which they have no knowledge (rule 5). Collateral may be repossessed by the lender if a borrower defaults on a loan.

UCC 9-307(2)

UCC 9-301

UCC 9-312(5)(a)

UCC 9-312(5)(b)

UCC 9-601

Collateral may be repossessed if the debtor defaults, but the repossession may not breach the peace.

4. Buyers of farm products in the ordinary course of business, to the extent that they pay for and receive collateral without knowledge of the security interest, take precedence over nonperfected security interests.
5. Buyers of consumer goods are not affected by perfected security interests of which they have no knowledge.
6. In all other cases, a perfected security interest prevails over an unperfected security interest.
7. Conflicting security interests rank according to priority in time of filing or perfection.
8. When two or more parties have unperfected security interests in the same collateral, the first to attach prevails over the other parties.

Default of the Debtor

If a debtor defaults by failing to make payments when due, the secured party may satisfy the debt by taking possession of the collateral. Because of the difficulties of doing this, the perfection of a security interest by possession, as in a pledge, is better than other types of perfection. Collateral may be repossessed without going through the court if it can be done without causing a disturbance; otherwise, the creditor must use legal processes.

LO11

After repossessing the goods, the secured party (the creditor) may sell them at a public auction or private sale. The terms of the sale must be reasonable, and the debtor must be given notice of the time and place of any public auction so that he or she may bid on them personally. If the goods are consumer goods and the debtor has paid 60 percent or more of the cash price of a purchase money security interest, the secured party cannot keep the goods. They must be sold.

Quick Quiz 31-3 True or False?

1. A security interest is perfected when the secured party has a legally enforceable right to take that property and sell it to satisfy the debt.

2. Security interests in most kinds of personal property are perfected by filing a financial statement in a public office.

3. Buyers of goods in the ordinary course of business (except farm products) prevail over security interests in the seller's inventory.

Summary

31.1 Individuals and institutions that lend money need some assurance that they will have their money returned to them. Security devices serve as this means of assurance.

31.2 Purchases of real property are generally secured by a mortgage. A mortgage is a transfer of an interest in property for the purpose of creating a security for a debt. Some common types of mortgages include the conventional mortgage, the variable-rate mortgage, the graduated-payment mortgage, the balloon-payment mortgage, FHA and VA mortgages, and deeds of trust.

31.3 When personal property is purchased on credit, the seller frequently retains a security interest in the property. Property that is subject to a security interest is called collateral. A security interest is created by a written agreement called a security agreement, which identifies the goods and is signed by the debtor. To be effective between debtor and creditor, a security interest must be made legally enforceable. This legality is known as attachment. To be effective against third parties who might also claim the secured property, the creditor must perfect the security interest. Perfection is accomplished by filing a financing statement, by attachment alone in certain cases, or by taking possession of the collateral.

Key Terms

acceleration, 643

assume the mortgage, 646

attachment, 647

balloon-payment mortgage, 639

buyer in the ordinary course of business, 646

collateral, 646

consumer goods, 646

conventional mortgage, 639

deed of trust, 640

equipment, 646

equity of redemption, 642

farm products, 646

fixtures, 646

flexible-rate mortgage, 639

floating lien, 647

foreclosure, 643

graduated-payment mortgage, 639

home equity loan, 642

inventory, 646

junior mortgage, 641

mortgage, 637

mortgagee, 637

mortgagor, 637

perfected, 646

purchase money security interest, 646

reverse mortgage, 639

second mortgage, 641

secured loan, 637

secured party, 646

security agreement, 646

security interest, 637

subject to the mortgage, 646

subordinated mortgage, 642

subordination agreement, 642

unsecured loan, 637

variable-rate mortgage, 639

Questions for Review and Discussion

1. Why do creditors frequently require security devices when lending money or extending credit?
2. In what principal way does a conventional mortgage differ from an FHA or a VA mortgage?
3. What are the differences among a variable-rate mortgage, a graduated-payment mortgage, and a balloon-payment mortgage?
4. Why is it important to record a mortgage in a public office in the county where the property is located?
5. What are four rights that belong to a mortgagor? What are four rights that belong to a mortgagee?
6. In the purchase of real property, what is the difference between assuming a mortgage and taking property subject to a mortgage?
7. What elements must be included in a security agreement?
8. Explain the reasons for perfecting a security interest. What are the different ways this may be done?
9. What rules are found in the UCC for determining who prevails over whom when secured and unsecured parties lay claim to the same collateral?
10. What rights and responsibilities does a secured party have if a debtor defaults by failing to make payments when due?

Investigating the Internet

According to RealtyTracMortgage of Irvine, California, foreclosures in the United States increased to a record level in the first half of 2007. Almost 926,000 foreclosure notices were filed during that six-month period, 56 percent more than a year earlier. Go online and key in the phrase "The Mortgage Professor's Website." This site will lead you to an enormous amount of helpful, practical, and up-to-date information about mortgages. Known as "The Mortgage Professor" by his nationally syndicated newspaper column readers, Wharton School of Business professor emeritus Jack Guttentag presents the latest mortgage information. You will find online calculators to help you determine such things as what price you can afford to pay for real property according to your personal financial situation.

Cases for Analysis

1. Sanchez bought a house for $100,000, paying $10,000 down and financing the balance through a local bank. As part of the closing costs, Sanchez was required to take out private mortgage insurance to protect the bank in case she defaulted on the mortgage. She had an excellent credit rating and always paid her mortgage payments when they were due. Two years after buying the property, she received an inheritance and used the money to pay an additional amount of $10,000 to the bank toward the principal of the loan. Hoping to cut down on her monthly payments, she asked the bank to cancel the mortgage insurance, but the bank refused. Does Sanchez have any rights in this situation? Explain.

2. Robert and Sherrell Bergeron gave a first mortgage on their property to First Colonial Bank and a second mortgage to Ford Motor Credit Company. When the Bergerons were unable to pay the mortgage, the bank foreclosed. The property was sold at a foreclosure sale for more money than the Bergerons owed the bank. The Bergerons claim

that they are entitled to the surplus funds from the sale. Do you agree? Explain. *First Colonial Bank for Savings v. Bergeron,* 646 N.E.2d 758 (MA).

3. When the Prestons took out a variable mortgage with the First Bank of Marietta, their interest rate was 9 percent. The agreement allowed First Bank to raise or lower the interest rate at any time, provided that the Prestons received 30 days' advance notice. When the bank raised the interest rate to 11 percent, the Prestons refused to pay, arguing that the agreement was unenforceable, because it set no limit on what interest rate they might be forced to pay. Were the Prestons correct? Explain. *Preston v. First Bank of Marietta,* 473 N.E.2d 1210 (OH).

4. The Woolseys ran a mink farm that was mortgaged to the State Bank of Lehi. The agreement included provisions that allowed acceleration and foreclosure if the Woolseys failed to pay their obligations under the contract. The Woolseys defaulted on several payments, and the bank foreclosed. The couple demanded a jury trial on the foreclosure action. They also argued that the bank had not acted in good faith in its acceleration and foreclosure. Were the Woolseys entitled to a jury trial? Explain. Who had the burden of proof in demonstrating the bank's good faith in accelerating payments and demanding foreclosure? *State Bank of Lehi v. Woolsey,* 565 P.2d 413 (UT).

5. Bloom executed a real estate mortgage in favor of Lakeshore Commercial Finance Corporation on September 16. On October 4, Bloom executed another mortgage on the same described real estate in favor of Northridge Bank. Northridge, without notice of the mortgage to Lakeshore, recorded its mortgage at 9:28 a.m. on October 25. On that same date, at 3:07 p.m., the prior mortgage executed in favor of Lakeshore was recorded. Bloom defaulted on the mortgages. The value of the real estate was insufficient to satisfy both mortgages fully. Which party had first rights to the property, Lakeshore or Northridge? Why? *Northridge Bank v. Lakeshore Com. Fin. Corp.,* 365 N.E.2d 382 (IL).

6. Cramer's mortgage contained a provision requiring her to pay monthly tax and insurance payments into an escrow account held by the bank in addition to principal and interest. Cramer paid the principal and interest regularly but refused to pay the tax and insurance escrow payments. The bank brought foreclosure proceedings. Did it have the right to foreclose on Cramer's mortgage? Explain. *Cramer v. Metro. Sav. & Loan Ass'n.,* 258 N.W.2d 20 (MI).

7. Matthews Motors sold a Buick Riviera to Jenkins for $11,500. Matthews then borrowed money from Averysboro National Bank, using the Buick as collateral. When Matthews defaulted on the loan, the bank attempted to repossess the Buick from Jenkins. Jenkins refused to surrender the automobile, claiming that he and not Matthews owned it. The bank brought suit, asking the court to force Jenkins to turn over the Buick. Should the court grant the bank's request? Why or why not? *Averysboro National Bank v. Jenkins,* 328 S.E.2d 399 (GA).

8. Giant Wholesale agreed to supply Hendersonville Food Center with groceries if the owner, William Page, would guarantee all debts incurred by Hendersonville. Page agreed, and a security agreement was drawn up. The security agreement gave Giant a security interest in Hendersonville's groceries and equipment. Giant failed to file a financing statement properly. When Hendersonville ran into financial difficulty, Page turned over the checking account to Giant. When this maneuver did not work, Giant repossessed all of Hendersonville's inventory. Page later went bankrupt. Gray, the bankruptcy trustee, brought a suit against Giant, claiming that the inventory was part of Page's property and thus subject to the bankruptcy proceeding. Gray argued that because the financing statement had not been filed, Giant's security interest had not been perfected. Was Gray correct? Explain. *Gray v. Giant Wholesale,* 758 F.2d 1000 (4th Cir.).

9. U.S. Electronics, a Missouri corporation with a place of business in DeKalb County, Georgia, borrowed money from a Missouri bank. The corporation gave the bank a security interest in all of its machinery and equipment. The bank filed a financing statement in Fulton County rather than in DeKalb County, as required by law. U.S. Electronics defaulted on the loan and fell behind on its rent. The corporation's landlord obtained a judgment against it for past due rent, becoming a lien creditor. The landlord claimed priority over the bank for the proceeds of a sheriff's sale of the machinery and equipment, arguing that the bank's security interest was not perfected. Do you agree? Why or why not? *United States v. Waterford No. 2 Office Center,* 271 S.E. 2d 790 (GA).

10. Lallana bought a car on credit from a dealer who assigned the contract and the security agreement to Bank of America. When Lallana failed to make several payments, the bank repossessed the car. The bank notified Lallana that if she did not redeem the car or reinstate the contract within 15

days, it would sell the car. The bank then sold the car at a public auction for $5,000 and sued Lallana for $11,249, the balance due on her loan. The Kelly Blue Book's estimated retail value of the car at the time of the auction was $14,820. Did the bank give Lallana proper notice of the sale? Why or why not? *Bank of America v. Lallana,* 960 P.2d 1133 (CA).

Quick Quiz Answers

31-1 & 31-2	31-3
1. T	1. F
2. T	2. T
3. T	3. T

Chapter 32 — Bankruptcy

The Opening Case

"Musical Chairs"

Alfredo Martinez, a talented musician who graduated from Othmer Music Academy, became deeply in debt after spending beyond his means. He and his wife Ingrid, who did not work outside the home, had purchased a new house in Texas three years earlier with no money down. Among other things, they purchased their household furnishings, a new car, and three musical instruments on credit. Although Alfredo earned $60,000 a year as a musician, it was not enough to make the monthly payments for the house, car, furniture, musical instruments, credit cards, a large student loan, insurance, and other bills. The couple met with a credit counselor and learned that their monthly disposable income amounted to $110. The counselor also determined that $110 was not enough to pay 25 percent of their outstanding, unsecured debts over a five-year period.

Opening Case Questions

1. Do the Martinezes qualify for Chapter 7 bankruptcy? If so, in what way do they satisfy the means test?

2. What other options, if any, would the Martinezes have to file for bankruptcy if they do not qualify under Chapter 7?

3. What choice, if any, do the Martinezes have in selecting which exemptions to use?

4. To what cap, if any, will the homestead exemption be subject?

5. How will a discharge in bankruptcy affect Alfredo Martinez's student loan?

6. In what special way, if any, will Alfredo Martinez's musical instruments be treated?

LO Learning Objectives

1. Summarize the history of bankruptcy law in the United States.
2. Discuss restoring credit following bankruptcy.
3. State the criteria necessary to be eligible to file voluntarily for Chapter 7 bankruptcy.
4. Explain the "means test" that is required for filing Chapter 7 bankruptcy.
5. State the criteria necessary for creditors to force debtors into involuntary bankruptcy.

6. Distinguish between an *order for relief* and *automatic stay* in the bankruptcy process.
7. List the federal exemptions that debtors are allowed to exclude from the bankruptcy process.
8. Clarify the requirements for selecting federal or state exemptions when filing for bankruptcy.
9. Recognize those debts that have priority payment status under the Bankruptcy Code.
10. List debts that cannot be discharged by a bankruptcy debtor.
11. Explain Chapter 11 bankruptcy, emphasizing the reorganization process.
12. Discuss Chapter 12 bankruptcy and explain its requirements for eligibility.
13. Describe Chapter 13 bankruptcy and explain its requirements for eligibility.

32-1 Bankruptcy's History

Bankruptcy is the legal process by which the assets of a debtor are sold to pay off creditors so that the debtor can make a fresh start financially. This definition pinpoints the two most crucial objectives of bankruptcy law. First, the law protects the creditors who have lent money or extended credit to the debtor by making certain that the debtor's money is divided fairly. Second, the law gives debtors an escape from their financial burdens and allows them to build new lives.

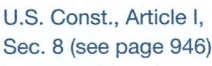

These objectives have not always been the priority in the history of bankruptcy law. Early laws favored creditors. In addition to losing all of their property, debtors were often put in debtor's prison and sometimes, though not in the United States, put to death. The first federal bankruptcy law in the United States was enacted in 1800. Under that law, only creditors could begin a bankruptcy proceeding, and only merchants could qualify as debtors. That law lasted only three years before Congress repealed it. In 1840, debtor's prisons were abolished in the United States, and a year later, Congress passed a bankruptcy law that lasted only two years. Following the turmoil of the Civil War, Congress enacted a third bankruptcy law in 1867 that lasted eleven years. It wasn't until 1898 that permanent bankruptcy legislation came about in the United States, with a law that gave businesses protection from creditors and lasted, with modifications during the Great Depression, for eighty years. The Bankruptcy Reform Act of 1978 again brought major changes, making it easier for businesses and individuals to obtain bankruptcy relief. It was in 1978 that Chapters 11 and 13 of the Bankruptcy Code (discussed subsequently) were created, allowing businesses and individuals to reorganize and keep going. In addition, debtors were allowed to keep more of their assets, giving them a better chance to make a fresh start with their activities. The 1994 Bankruptcy Reform Act continued honing the law and created the National Bankruptcy Commission to study the subject and make recommendations. In 2005, following a period of easy credit with many people spending far above their means, Congress made it more difficult to declare bankruptcy by enacting far-reaching changes to the Bankruptcy Code. The current law is explained in this chapter.

Constitutional Authority

The U.S. Constitution gives the federal government jurisdiction over bankruptcy proceedings by stating that "Congress shall have the Power . . . To establish . . . uniform laws on the subject of Bankruptcies throughout the United States." Congress exercised this power when it enacted the Bankruptcy Code, which is found in Title 11 of the United States Code (USC).

U.S. Const., Article I, Sec. 8 (see page 946)

Restoring Credit Following Bankruptcy

A personal bankruptcy filing remains on a debtor's credit report for 10 years and has a detrimental effect on the ability to establish a line of credit. However, most debtors who file bankruptcy have already established a poor credit rating anyway, and filing bankruptcy gives them an opportunity to begin anew. A good number of their debts become discharged, which improves their debt-to-income ratio—a factor that potential creditors look at carefully. The more time that elapses after the bankruptcy filing, the easier it is to reestablish credit.

Many people in this situation switch from credit cards to debit cards, which is like paying cash because instead of initiating a charge, debit cards withdraw money instantly from a bank account (see Chapter 29). Some banks offer *secured credit cards* in which customers deposit money in the bank to guarantee that their credit card charges will be paid. Until their credit is reestablished, their credit limit is the same as the amount of their bank deposit. Credit card issuers sometimes allow debtors to continue using their credit cards if they agree in writing, after the bankruptcy filing, to pay off the old debt. Often, this allowance also requires an agreement by the debtor to pay the credit card balance each month without carrying a balance.

People who are able to make a down payment and have steady income may be eligible for a mortgage loan as soon as two years following a discharge in bankruptcy.

32-2 Liquidation—Chapter 7, Bankruptcy Code

Chapter 7 of the Bankruptcy Code, sometimes referred to as ordinary bankruptcy, provides a system in which debtors are forced to sell much of their property and use the cash to pay their creditors a portion of the amount owed each one. This process is also called **liquidation**. See Table 32-1 for a summary of different types of bankruptcy procedures.

Commencing the Action

Under Chapter 7 bankruptcy, the debtor may be an individual, partnership, corporation, or other type of business. The process may be either voluntary or involuntary. With voluntary bankruptcy, the debtor files the bankruptcy petition. With involuntary bankruptcy, creditors file the papers to force the debtor into bankruptcy and pay them off.

 **Voluntary Proceedings**   Debtors sometimes realize that their financial position can never improve without some drastic action and decide to file a bankruptcy petition on their own. Under the 2005 Bankruptcy Act, however, not everyone is allowed to file for Chapter 7 bankruptcy. To qualify, debtors must do all of the following:

- Satisfy the **means test**, discussed next.

- Meet with an approved nonprofit credit counselor before filing for bankruptcy.

- Provide a federal income tax return for the most recent tax year.

- Take a course in financial management after filing for bankruptcy.

 **The Means Test**   The means test consists of three steps, the passing of any one of which allows the debtor to file for Chapter 7 bankruptcy. The first step is to compare the debtor's average income during the previous six months with the median income for a family of that size in the debtor's state. If the debtor's income is less than the state's median income, the debtor is eligible to file for Chapter 7 bankruptcy. Every state's medium income is provided by the U.S. Census Bureau and can be found at www.census.gov.

Table 32-1 Types of Bankruptcy Procedures

Chapter	Who Can File?	When Used?	Special Features
Chapter 7: Ordinary Bankruptcy	Only those who (a) have income below the state's average family income for families of that size, (b) meet with an approved nonprofit credit counselor before filing, (c) provide a federal income tax return for the most recent tax year, and (d) take a course in financial management after filing.	Used when debtor wants to discharge most debts and begin with a clean slate	Debtor's property is liquidated; some property is exempt; some debts cannot be discharged
Chapter 11: Reorganization	Individuals, partnerships, and corporations can file; railroads can file; only commodity brokers and stockbrokers cannot; filing can be voluntary or involuntary	Used when debtor, usually a business, wants to continue operating but needs to reorganize and liquidate debts	Debtor-in-possession feature; debtor files plan within 120 days; plan must be fair, equitable, and feasible; creditors can also file plans; confirmation needed
Chapter 12: Family Farmer or Fishing Business Debt Adjustment	Family farmer or fishing businesses that receive 50 percent of income from farming or fishing can file, including partnerships and corporations; debt ceiling of $3,275,000 for farming and $1,500,000 for fishing.	Used when debtor has a family farming or fishing business and needs a debt adjustment plan to keep running	Debtor-in-possession feature; debtor files plan within 90 days; plan lasts three years (with two-year possible extension); plan must be confirmed
Chapter 13: Individual Debt Adjustment	Individuals who meet with a credit counselor and have steady income only; no corporations or partnerships; no involuntary filings allowed; debt ceiling of $307,675 for unsecured and $922,975 for secured.	Used when an individual debtor with a steady income voluntarily decides to adopt a debt adjustment plan	Only the debtor can file a plan; payments must start 30 days after plan submitted; a few debts cannot be discharged; plan lasts three years (with two-year possible extension)

EXAMPLE 32-1:   The Means Test—Step One

Raymond and Jessica Mattik lived with their two children in a house they owned in North Carolina. They were very much in debt. Not only were they behind in their payments for their late-model car and household furnishings, but they also owed the maximum amount on five different credit cards. When the interest on their adjustable-rate mortgage increased dramatically, they considered filing for bankruptcy. Together, they earned $58,200 annually. They would be eligible to file for Chapter 7 bankruptcy because their income was less than $59,481—the median income for a family of four in North Carolina. Because they qualified under this first step, they are finished with the means test.

Suppose Raymond and Jessica, in Example 32-1, had income that exceeded their state's median income for a family of four. Then, they would have to go to step two of the means test, which is more complicated. Step two requires debtors to determine whether they have enough income to pay off some of their unsecured debts. This determination requires subtracting certain deductions, which vary according to where they live, and arriving at a figure called their **disposable income**. If their disposable income is less then $100 a month, they pass the means test and will be allowed to file for Chapter 7 bankruptcy. If it is more than $167 a month, however, they fail the means test and cannot file for Chapter 7. They may, however, be able to convert the case to Chapters 11, 12, or 13 of the Bankruptcy Code discussed subsequently.

EXAMPLE 32-2:   The Means Test—Step Two

Robert and Carol Kling lived with their two children in Texas, where the median income for a family of four is $57,511. Because their combined income of $57,800 is greater than this median, they did not pass step one of the means test and had to go to step two. After deducting certain amounts prescribed for their geographical area, their disposable income was $110 a month—again, too high to pass the means test because it was over $100. They now must go to step three of the test.

The third step in the means test is taken only by debtors who do not qualify for Chapter 7 bankruptcy under the first two steps. Under this final step, a determination is made as to whether the debtor has the ability to pay unsecured debts over a five-year period. If a debtor's monthly disposable income is between $100 and $167 but not enough to pay more than 25 percent of outstanding unsecured debts over a five-year period, the debtor passes the means test and will be allowed to file for Chapter 7 bankruptcy. In contrast, if the disposable income is enough to pay those debts over five years, the debtor does not pass the means test and will be required to switch over to another bankruptcy chapter, such as Chapter 13, discussed later.

To petition for bankruptcy, debtors file official forms with the nearest U.S. Bankruptcy Court. These courts are attached to district courts within the federal court structure (see Chapter 3). Official forms for filing bankruptcy can be obtained at legal stationery stores as well as www.uscourts.gov. The form asks debtors to name all of their creditors and indicate how much money they owe those creditors. The form also requires a listing of their property

The Opening Case Revisited, Part I
"Musical Chairs"

The Means Test—Step Three The Martinezes did not pass step one of the means test because Alfredo's annual income was $60,000—more than the median income for a family of four in the state of Texas. Similarly, they failed to pass step two of the test because their monthly disposable income was between $100 and $167. The couple did, however, pass step three of the means test, because their monthly disposable income was not enough to pay more than 25 percent of outstanding unsecured debts over a five-year period. The couple therefore qualified for Chapter 7 bankruptcy. Had they not qualified for Chapter 7, they might have satisfied the requirements to file under Chapter 13 of the Bankruptcy Code.

and a statement of income and expenses. Finally, the form asks debtors to list all of the property that they feel should be exempt from the sale when it comes time later in the bankruptcy proceeding to sell what they own.

Involuntary Proceedings   Under Chapter 7 of the Bankruptcy Code, creditors may be able to force debtors, other than farmers, into involuntary bankruptcy if the debtor fails to pay bills generally as they become due. Creditors must prove that the outstanding debts are not subject to a bona fide dispute. A single creditor who is owed a debt of more than $13,475 can file if the debtor has fewer than 12 creditors. If the debtor has 12 or more creditors, 3 of them must file the petition. The combined debt owed the 3 must exceed $13,475. This dollar amount, instituted in 2007, is adjustable every three years to reflect changes in the consumer price index.

> ## EXAMPLE 32-3:   Involuntary Bankruptcy
>
> Goodell had an excellent job with a high salary and a promise of continued advance-ment. However, he made several miscalculations in the stock market that severely damaged his financial picture. Consequently, though he owned a lot of property, he had little cash on hand. This situation caused him to fall behind on his payments to most of his 14 creditors. Three of those creditors, the Bromfield Department Store, the Mariano Oil Company, and the Financial Bank, filed an involuntary bankruptcy petition against Strasser in federal court. Because Strasser owed them more than $13,475, the petition was accepted.

Debtors must file an objection within 20 days of the petition if they wish to contest it. Involuntary petitions cannot be filed against farmers, charities, or cities.

Order for Relief

An **order for relief** is the court's command that the liquidation begin. In a voluntary filing, the bankruptcy petition itself becomes the order for relief and is effective the moment it is filed with the court. In an involuntary case, the court does not issue the order immediately because the debtor is allowed 20 days to contest the filing, after which a hearing is held to determine whether an order for relief will be issued. When an order for relief is issued, a **case trustee** is named by the court. The trustee schedules a meeting of creditors, which the debtor is required to attend to answer questions about financial matters. Following the meeting, the trustee reports to the court as to whether the case should proceed.

The trustee is charged with the responsibility of liquidating the assets of the debtor for the benefit of all interested parties. Bank accounts, including debit cards, can no longer be used because they become the property of the bankruptcy trustee.

> ## A Question of Ethics
>
> A limited partnership that had been established solely to buy, develop, and sell a certain parcel of Florida real estate filed a voluntary petition for bankruptcy. The court appointed Marvin J. Bloom as trustee to the debtor's bankruptcy estate. Bloom sought to employ his own real estate firm as a consultant to assist in the sale of the debtor's property. What ethical question arises in this case?

Automatic Stay

The moment the order for relief occurs, an **automatic stay** goes into effect. This stay is a self-operating postponement of collection proceedings against the debtor. Further efforts by creditors against the debtor to collect debts must stop immediately, except for debts caused by fraud, amounts owed for back taxes, family support, and student loans that do not impose a hardship on the debtor. Among other things, the stay prohibits creditors from beginning or continuing:

- Lawsuits
- Foreclosure sales
- Collection proceedings
- Repossession activities

Automatic stay applies to both voluntary and involuntary petitions. Creditors who ignore the stay can be held in contempt of court.

EXAMPLE 32-4:   Order for Relief and Automatic Stay

Hilenbrand found herself so deeply in debt that she could pay very little on her bills. One of her creditors, Linden Musical Supplies, told her that it was about to file a lawsuit against her. At that point, being able to pass the means test, Hilenbrand filed a bankruptcy petition in federal court. Because she filed voluntarily, the petition was considered the order for relief. At this time, the automatic stay provision of the Bankruptcy Code went into effect. If Linden Musical Supplies carried out its planned action, it could be held in contempt of court.

Federal Exemptions

As part of the fresh start approach under the Bankruptcy Code, debtors are permitted to exempt or exclude certain items of property from the bankruptcy process, which means that the property is kept by the debtor and cannot be sold to pay the debtor's outstanding bills. Exemptions can be doubled for married couples who file jointly.

The following federal exemption amounts were in effect in 2007 and are subject to adjustment at three-year intervals after that to reflect the change in the Consumer Price Index, rounded to the nearest $25.

Federal Homestead and Household Exemptions   The Bankruptcy Code allows debtors to keep a maximum of $18,450 in equity in the debtor's place of residence and in property used as a burial ground. This allowance is known as the federal **homestead exemption**.

EXAMPLE 32-5:   Federal Homestead Exemption

Carlson purchased a home for $120,000 by placing $15,000 down and borrowing the balance from the East Savings and Loan Association. East held a first mortgage on the property. Carlson was later forced to file for bankruptcy. Using the federal homestead exemption, she would be allowed to exempt up to $18,450 in equity in her home. Because she only has a little over $15,000 in equity, this amount would be safe from her creditors.

The Opening Case Revisited, Part II
"Musical Chairs"

Professional Instruments If Martinez chooses the federal exemptions, he may retain an amount up to $1,850 in musical instruments to help give him a fresh start after bankruptcy. This amount could be different under the state exemption.

Debtors can also keep a maximum of $475 for any single item of furniture, household goods, clothes, appliances, books, crops, animals, or musical instruments. The total of all exemptions taken in this category cannot exceed $9,850. Debtors are also allowed to exempt $1,225 in jewelry beyond the $9,850 set aside for the other household items mentioned previously. In addition, they may keep any other property not exceeding the value of $975, plus up to $9,250 of any unused amount of the $18,450 homestead exemption.

Necessities   Congress allows debtors to maintain a minimum standard of living by exempting certain necessary items of property. For example, debtors are allowed to exclude a maximum of $1,850 in professional tools, instruments, and books. In addition, they can exempt up to $2,950 in a motor vehicle. Finally, medical supplies that have been prescribed for the health of the debtor can be excluded.

Benefits and Support Payments   Again, to allow debtors to maintain a minimum standard of living, Congress allows the exclusion of certain benefits and support payments. For instance, alimony and child support payments can be excluded. Benefits received under Social Security or a disability program are also exempt. Profits that are due under profit-sharing, pension, and annuity plans may be excluded. Furthermore, debtors are allowed to protect payments due to them under certain court orders. For example, if someone owes a debtor damages resulting from a personal injury tort case, those damages are exempt up to $18,450. Life insurance contracts carried for the benefit of a relative or approved beneficiary that have yet to mature are also protected. Finally, tax-deferred retirement funds are exempt under the 2005 bankruptcy act.

State Exemptions

The Bankruptcy Code allows states to use exemptions created by the state legislature rather than the federal exemptions (see Figure 32-1). Often, the dollar amounts included in the state statutes will be a more accurate assessment of property values within each state, because the state legislators are more flexible in such matters than members of Congress, who must consider property values across the entire country. Every state has its own set of bankruptcy exemptions. Fifteen states, plus the District of Columbia and Puerto Rico, allow their residents to choose either their own state's exemptions or the federal exemptions. All other states require their residents to use only their own state's exemptions and not the federal, unless the debtor has not lived in the state long enough.

To use a state's exemption, the debtor must have lived in that state for the two years (730 days) prior to filing bankruptcy. If a debtor has not lived in a specific state for the previous two years, the debtor must use the state where he or she lived during the majority of the 180 days preceding the two-year period. If neither of the two options apply, the debtor may use the federal exemptions.

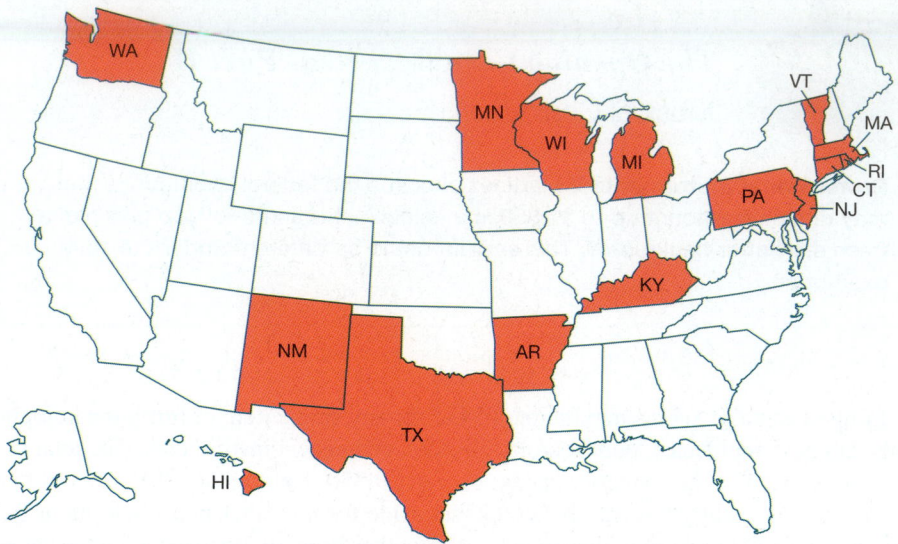

Figure 32-1 These states allow their residents who experience bankruptcy to choose either their own state's exemptions or the federal exemptions in determining what may be excluded from the bankruptcy process. All other states require their residents to use their own state's exemptions exclusively.

The use of a state's homestead exemption has even stricter requirements. A state's homestead exemption is capped at $125,000 (regardless of any state law providing for a larger amount) unless the debtor acquired the homestead within three years and four months before filing for bankruptcy. The cap also applies to debtors who owe debts arising from fiduciary fraud, racketeering, violation of security laws, crimes, or intentional torts that caused serious bodily injury or death within the preceding five years.

Trustee's Duties

After the order for relief is granted, a trustee will be appointed to take control of the debtor's property. One of the first things the trustee does is set aside, under the trustee's avoiding powers, any payments or other transfers made by the debtor within 90 days before the filing of the petition. If the debtor is a business, the bankruptcy court may authorize the trustee to operate the business for a limited period of time. In addition, the trustee sells the debtor's property to obtain cash. The trustee then distributes the cash among the creditors according to set priorities.

The Opening Case Revisited, Part III
"Musical Chairs"

Residency Requirement Because the state of Texas allows its residents to choose either the state or federal exemptions, and because the Martinezes had lived in that state for more than two years, they could select either the state or federal exemptions.

The Opening Case Revisited, Part IV
"Musical Chairs"

If the Martinezes file for bankruptcy now—three years after buying their home—they would be four months short of the required time to own the house without being subject to the $125,000 cap on the homestead exemption.

Property Distribution   The Bankruptcy Code provides a priority list that indicates which categories of debts are paid first (Table 32-2). Each category must be paid in full before moving on to the next category. As explained in Chapter 31, secured creditors have the right to take their collateral to satisfy the debt, and that collateral is not sold by the trustee. Although there are some narrow exceptions to this rule, most secured creditors are protected.

Table 32-2 Payment Priorities	
Debt	**Explanation**
Secured debts	Creditors with security interests take their collateral first.
Domestic obligations	Support obligations owed to a spouse or child.
Administrative expenses	Bankruptcy trustee and others involved in bankruptcy process are paid next.
Certain unsecured debts	All unsecured debts after an involuntary petition has been filed, but before order for relief has been granted, are paid next.
Wages	Employees are paid next; maximum, $4,300 per employee.
Benefit plans	Contributions owed on employee benefit plans are paid next; maximum, $4,300 per employee.
Workers in the fishing and farming industries	Owner-operators of fish storage processing plants pay worker creditors next; owner-operators of grain storage plants pay farmer creditors next.
Deposits and advances	Deposits made for purchase or lease of property are paid next, as are advances made for personal, family, and household services.
Taxes	Certain taxes are paid next.
Bank commitments	Unsecured commitments to maintain the capital of a bank.
Death or injury claims	Claims for death or injury caused by debtor's intoxication from alcohol or drugs.
Remaining unsecured creditors	All other unsecured creditors are paid from any balance remaining.
Debtor	If anything is left, it goes back to the debtor.

> ## EXAMPLE 32-6:   Secured Creditor Protected
>
> Perez purchased a digital camera from Digicam Corp. Perez financed the deal by signing a security agreement with the company. Under the agreement, Digicam retained a security interest in the property, allowing it to repossess the camera if Perez defaulted on the loan. Digicam was a secured creditor. The digital camera was the collateral.

Exceptions to Discharge

LO10

Once the trustee has run through all the aforementioned creditors, the debtor's debts are said to be discharged, which means that the debts are wiped away, and the debtor is allowed to begin again. If the bankruptcy debtor does not have enough money to cover the debts, they are nevertheless considered discharged. However, there are some exceptions to this general rule. Some debts cannot be discharged. In other words, even though the debtor has gone through the entire bankruptcy proceeding, money may still be owed to certain creditors.

Debts Created by Misconduct   Certain debts that have fallen into the debtor's lap because of misconduct cannot be charged in bankruptcy. For example, any debts that arose because of the debtor's fraudulent behavior cannot be discharged. Similarly, the debtor cannot escape legal liability for any debt that arose from willful and malicious misconduct. Finally, if the debtor knew about a debt that was not on the original list of debts, that unlisted debt cannot be discharged.

Debts Enforced by the Government   Certain debts that the debtor owes the government remain on the books even after the bankruptcy proceeding has ended. These include certain back taxes, student loans that do not impose a hardship on the debtor, and many government fines and penalties. Similarly, several types of court-enforced debts cannot be discharged, including alimony and child support or any legal liability that resulted from a court-ordered judgment for driving while intoxicated. Finally, any debts that were not discharged under a previous bankruptcy cannot be discharged under the new bankruptcy proceeding.

Debts Created by Excessive Spending   Congress also refuses to allow bankruptcy debtors to discharge any excessive expenditures that occur around the time of the bankruptcy filing. This measure prevents people from running up big bills unnecessarily because they think they will not have to pay the full amount due on these bills when their assets are finally distributed. Thus, debts for luxury items that exceed $500 in value cannot be discharged if those items were purchased within 90 days before the order for relief was granted. Likewise, the debtor cannot discharge any cash advances paid to a creditor under

> ### *The Opening Case Revisited, Part V*
> ### "Musical Chairs"
>
> **Student Loans** Student loans that do not impose a hardship on the debtor are not discharged in bankruptcy proceedings.

an open-ended credit plan that total more than $750 if those advances were made within 70 days of the relief order.

EXAMPLE 32-7: Nondischargeable Debt

Caswell finally realized that his financial problems were out of control. Consequently, he decided to file for bankruptcy on the following Monday. That weekend, he charged $7,000 on his credit card on a weekend trip to Atlantic City before filing for bankruptcy on Monday. Caswell would not be allowed to discharge the $7,000 debt in bankruptcy.

Quick Quiz 32-1 & 32-2 True or False?

1. The U.S. Constitution gives state courts jurisdiction over bankruptcy proceedings.

2. Under Chapter 7 bankruptcy, debtors are forced to sell most of their property and use the cash to pay their creditors a portion of the amount owed each one.

3. The Bankruptcy Code allows states to use a list of exemptions created by the state legislature rather than the federal exemptions.

32-3 Reorganization—Chapter 11, Bankruptcy Code

LO11

Chapter 11 of the Bankruptcy Code provides a method for businesses to reorganize their financial affairs and still remain in business. If allowed to continue in operation, companies may be able to overcome their difficulties without having to sell most of their property. In a **reorganization**, a qualified debtor creates a plan that alters the repayment schedule. A Chapter 11 filing is available to sole proprietors, partnerships, and corporations and may be either voluntary or involuntary. Individuals who file must receive credit counseling from an approved credit counseling agency before doing so. Unlike Chapter 7, Chapter 11 also allows railroads to file. The only individuals specifically excluded from filing under Chapter 11 are commodity brokers and stockbrokers, who must use Chapter 7.

In June of 2007, Tweeter announced that it was filing for Chapter 11 bankruptcy protection. They plan to rework their business model for a more efficient and profitable future.

Special Features of Chapter 11

One of the most attractive features of Chapter 11 for business debtors is that the business continues to operate after the filing. A debtor is referred to as a **debtor in possession** under Chapter 11 because the debtor keeps possession and control of the assets, continues to run the firm, and performs most of the functions that a trustee performs in other types of bankruptcy. However, if the problems of the business have been caused by poor judgment, mismanagement, or dishonesty, a case trustee may have to step in to examine the debtor's financial position and provide the court, creditors, and tax authorities with financial information as necessary.

 **BusinessWeek** **Business Law in the News**

Securing a Loan After Bankruptcy

Small business hopefuls with shaky credit histories must be prepared to explain what happened in the past—and why their future businesses will be profitable.

I'm a cosmetologist and would like to open my own salon and spa. I need to borrow $30,000, but I declared personal bankruptcy a couple years ago, following a divorce. I have rebuilt my personal credit score to 630, gotten a secured and an unsecured credit card, and five months ago got a car loan. Is there any hope that I'll qualify for a small business loan? If not, do I have other options?

—*J.L., Lansing, Ill.*

Getting a lender to make you a business loan after a recent bankruptcy will be a tough sell. Lenders evaluate many factors when they decide whether or not to make a loan, and a bankruptcy on your record from less than 10 years ago is going to start you off with a major strike against you.

"You always need to sell a new-business loan," says J. Scott Bovitz, a bankruptcy attorney with the Los Angeles law firm of Bovitz and Spitzer. Nonetheless, it certainly can't hurt to try. Talk to a bank that specializes in small-business lending, and ask them what their criteria are for making loans to people with recent bankruptcies. If they turn you down, go to a local credit union and talk to them. Also, check in with the economic development department in the city where you want to locate your salon. The city personnel may be able to refer you to a regional nonprofit investment fund or a community development agency that makes loans to micro-business owners in low-income areas.

If you own a home, you may have less trouble getting the loan if you're willing to put that home up as collateral and pay higher interest rates, experts say. If the loan is for equipment that can be repossessed by the lender if you default on the loan, that may also make your challenge less daunting. Finding a business partner with good credit, or a relative who's willing to co-sign on the loan with you, could also increase your chances of success.

At any rate, be prepared to thoroughly explain the circumstances that led to your bankruptcy, why

it happened, and why you can make this business a profitable enterprise. Do you have the experience necessary to market your shop, bring in customers, effectively manage personnel, and handle finances? "Most new businesses fail, and banks know it," Spitzer says. You'll need to change their minds about your chances of beating the odds. Remember: Running a business is a very different thing than working for someone else. What is special about you? What should lenders take into account when making their decision? Does your neighborhood really need another salon and spa? Do the demographics support your belief that you'll have an ample customer base?

You'll need to answer all these, and plenty of other tough questions from lenders, before you can "sell" yourself as a reasonable risk for a new business loan. If you're not able to find one, you might consider asking friends or family members to invest some seed money in your venture. But before you try, get some entrepreneurial education. Free and low-cost business training and counseling are available at organizations such as SCORE (http://www.score.org), your local Small Business Development Center (http://www.sba.gov/sbdc), or through an online course such as My Own Business (http://www.myownbusiness.org). The American Bankruptcy Institute has a consumer education center that may help answer additional questions: http://www.abiworld.org/Template.cfm?Section=Consumer_Education_Center. Good luck!

Karen E. Klein is a Los Angeles-based writer who covers entrepreneurship and small-business issues.

Questions for Analysis

1. What should you ask when you talk to a bank that specializes in small business lending?

2. What should you do if the bank turns you down?

3. What does the author suggest about collateral and other help?

4. What should you be ready to explain?

Source: Karen E. Klein, "Securing a Loan After Bankruptcy," *BusinessWeek,* August 9, 2006. www.businessweek.com.

As with a Chapter 7 voluntary case, the bankruptcy petition itself becomes the order for relief. The moment it is filed, the debtor assumes the position of "debtor in possession." At the same time, an automatic stay goes into effect, stopping collection proceedings against the debtor. In an involuntary case, the order for relief comes later, because the debtor is allowed time to contest the filing.

The Reorganization Plan

When a Chapter 11 petition is filed, the debtor has 120 days, during which it has the exclusive right to file a reorganization plan. The 120-day period may be shortened or lengthened by the court.

When the exclusive period ends, creditors (and the case trustee, if any) can file competing plans. The debtor also files a disclosure statement containing information about the debtor's assets, liabilities, and business affairs to allow creditors to make informed decisions about the reorganization plan. The disclosure statement must be approved by the court before there can be a vote by creditors on the reorganization plan.

Creditors' Committee
A creditors' committee is appointed to investigate the operation of the business and assist the debtor in possession in developing and administering a reorganization plan. Membership on the committee normally consists of the creditors who hold the seven largest unsecured claims against the debtor.

Plan Qualifications
The Bankruptcy Code requires fairness, equity, and feasibility in the creation of a reorganization plan. The plan will group claims against the debtor into the following classes:

- Secured creditors
- Unsecured creditors entitled to priority (for such things as taxes and bankruptcy costs)
- General unsecured creditors
- Equity security holders, such as shareholders and limited partners

The law requires equal treatment for all creditors grouped in a class. In addition, the plan must be feasible; that is, there must be a good chance that the plan will actually work. The law does not require an absolute guarantee of success. A plan may be difficult to implement because of labor or supply problems and still be feasible within the meaning of the law.

Plan Approval
If the plan has not changed the legal rights of the members of a class, then no approval is required from that class. However, **impaired classes**—those whose creditors receive less than full value of their claims—have the right to vote on the plan by ballot. More than one-half of the creditors who hold at least two-thirds of the amount of allowed claims in each class must accept the plan before it is approved. If there are impaired classes of claims, the plan must be approved by at least one impaired class. In addition, in the case of individual debtors, the plan cannot be confirmed over a creditor's objection without committing all of the debtor's disposable income over the next five years.

EXAMPLE 32-8:　Plan Approval

The Miller Chemical Company filed for reorganization under Chapter 11 of the Bankruptcy Code. One class of creditors included unsecured creditors who were owed $2,000 or less. A second class included unsecured creditors who were owed more

Did You Know?

According to a plan approved by the federal bankruptcy court, Enron's creditors, who are owed $66 billion, will receive approximately 20 cents on the dollar.

than $2,000. The plan called for a complete repayment of all Class 1 creditors, according to the terms of their original contracts. This provision made Class 1 an unimpaired class. The Class 2 creditors would have a choice: They could receive either a 60 percent repayment on the date of confirmation or 100 percent repayment extended over four years. The extended repayment plan called for a 30 percent repayment on the date of confirmation and seven 10 percent payments at six-month intervals. More than one-half of the Class 2 creditors would have to approve the plan. In contrast, the Class 1 creditors had no approval rights, because Class 1 was unimpaired.

Plan Confirmation The court will hold a hearing on the confirmation of the reorganization plan. A **confirmation** officially places a plan in operation. After confirmation, all property dealt with in the plan is free and clear of claims of creditors and equity security holders. The debtor is discharged from any debts that arose before the date of confirmation.

EXAMPLE 32-9: Citation Corp.'s Reorganization Plan

In 2007, Citation Corp. filed for Chapter 11 bankruptcy protection. In less than one month, the bankruptcy court confirmed the auto parts maker's reorganization plan. Under the plan, the company's lenders agreed to exchange $191 million in debt for a new $30 million loan and all of the company's stock. Claims by the company's unsecured creditors would be paid in full in the course of ongoing business, and stockholders were given warrants to buy new classes of stock.

Quick Quiz 32-3 True or False?

1. Chapter 11 of the Bankruptcy Code provides a method for businesses to reorganize their financial affairs and still remain in business.

2. The automatic stay provision found in Chapter 7 of the Bankruptcy Code is not used in Chapter 11 proceedings.

3. A trustee is appointed to run the firm when a business files a Chapter 11 bankruptcy petition.

32-4 Family Farmer or Fishing Business Debt Adjustment— Chapter 12, Bankruptcy Code

LO12

The Family Farmer or Fishing Business Debt Adjustment Act is designed to help farming and fishing proprietors, with regular income, create a plan for debt repayment that will allow them to keep their family businesses running. Thus, Chapter 12 is an alternative to the ordinary bankruptcy procedure provided for by Chapter 7. To be eligible, the operation must receive 50 percent of its total income from farming or fishing. Also, 50 percent of a farmer's debt must result from farm expenses, and 80 percent of a fishing business's debt must relate to either farming or fishing. Chapter 12 is voluntary—only the debtor may file a petition for this type of bankruptcy.

The family farm, a vanishing breed in the United States.

Chapter 12 has some important characteristics that allow individuals to file debt adjustment plans. First, Chapter 12 sets a $3,275,000 debt ceiling for farming and $1,500,000 for fishing. Second, in addition to individuals, Chapter 12 is open to partnerships and corporations as long as one-half of the outstanding stock or equity in the business is owned by one family or by one family and its relatives. Also, the family or the family and its relatives must conduct the farming or fishing undertaking.

Chapter 12 Procedures

Like a filing under Chapters 7 and 11, a filing under Chapter 12 creates an automatic stay of the collection of most debts. It is possible for creditors to ask the court to exempt them from the stay. However, a hearing on such a motion would have to be held, and the creditors would have to show why the court should grant exemptions.

As is the case in Chapter 7 and 11, the court will appoint a trustee to handle the farm's and fishing business's finances. The Chapter 12's trustee evaluates the case and serves as disbursing agent, collecting payments from the debtor and making disbursements to creditors.

The Chapter 12 Plan

Unlike the Chapter 11 debtor, who has a 120-day deadline to devise a reorganization plan, the Chapter 12 farming or fishing debtor is limited to 90 days. The clock starts running toward that 90-day deadline when the bankruptcy petition is filed. Debtors, however, can file for an extension.

Contents of the Plan   The Chapter 12 plan must include several provisions. First, the plan must provide for payment of fixed amounts to the trustee on a regular basis over a three-year period. The trustee then distributes the funds to the creditors according to the terms of the plan, which usually offers creditors less than the amount owed. Second, the plan must make certain that all priority claims, such as taxes and bankruptcy costs, are paid in full. Secured creditors must be paid at least the value of their collateral. Unsecured creditors must receive at least as much as they would if the debtor's nonexempt assets were liquidated under Chapter 7. The plan must not take longer than three years to complete, unless the time is extended by the court. The maximum extension is for two years.

Confirmation Hearing   Within 45 days after the plan's filing, the bankruptcy judge holds a confirmation hearing to decide whether the plan is feasible and follows the standards of the Bankruptcy Code. Creditors are notified and may appear to voice their approval or objections to the confirmation. If the judge confirms the plan, the trustee will begin disbursing funds according to the plan. If the judge does not confirm the plan, the debtor may file a modified plan, change to Chapter 7 bankruptcy, or allow the case to be dismissed and take some other course.

EXAMPLE 32-10:   Court Approves Payment Plan

Bemis, who owned a dairy farm, filed for debt adjustment under Chapter 12. Bemis filed a payment plan with her bankruptcy petition. Under the plan, unsecured creditors owed more than $500 would receive 60 percent of the amount owed to them, payable monthly over a three-year period. Kimble Supply Co. objected to the plan, arguing that it would receive more if Bemis's assets were liquidated under Chapter 7 bankruptcy. Because Bemis was turning over 100 percent of her disposable income to the trustee for debt repayment however, the court did not support Kimble's objection.

The debtor will receive a discharge after completing all payments agreed to and certifying that all domestic support obligations up to that time, if any, have been paid. The discharge releases the debtor from all debts listed in the plan.

LO13   32-5 Individual Debt Adjustment— Chapter 13, Bankruptcy Code

Sometimes debtors overextend their credit. They have regular income, but they cannot pay all their bills. If given time, they may eventually be able to pay at least part of the amount they owe to each creditor. Rather than selling the debtor's property, Chapter 13 of the Bankruptcy Code permits an individual debtor to put in place a repayment plan. Upon completion of payments under the plan, they receive a discharge from most remaining debt.

Excessive credit card debt is often a major contributory cause to consumer bankruptcy.

Only individual debtors, including sole proprietors and self-employed people, can take advantage of Chapter 13 provisions. Neither corporations nor partnerships can file. The petition will not be allowed if the debtor received a bankruptcy discharge under Chapters 7, 11, or 12 within the previous four years or a discharge under Chapter 13 within the previous two years.

To be eligible for Chapter 13, debtors must first meet with an approved nonprofit credit counselor. Their unsecured debts, such as credit cards and student loans, cannot exceed $307,675, and their secured loans, such as mortgages and car loans, cannot be more than $922,975. Also, the debtor must have an already established steady income. Only voluntary filings are permitted under Chapter 13.

The automatic stay provision clicks into place under Chapter 13 when the relief order is issued. A trustee oversees the Chapter 13 process. If Chapter 13 does not work out under certain circumstances, the individual may be allowed to convert to a Chapter 7 bankruptcy, which changes the repayment plan to a liquidation.

The Chapter 13 Plan

The debtor must file a repayment plan with the court, along with the Chapter 13 bankruptcy petition. Shortly thereafter, a trustee will be appointed and a meeting will be scheduled allowing the debtor to present the plan and be questioned by the trustee and creditors.

The plan must provide for payments of fixed amounts to the trustee on a regular biweekly or monthly basis. The trustee, in turn, distributes the money to creditors according to the terms of the plan. The payments must either satisfy all debts or consist of all the debtor's disposable income during the plan's period. The plan must make certain that priority debtors receive full payment.

Also, like Chapter 12, if the plan sets up groups of creditors, all group members must be treated equally. Finally, Chapter 13 debtors must abide by the rule requiring that the payment plan be completed within three to five years.

Plan Confirmation

Chapter 13 creditors have no prior input while the plan is being created. Secured creditors have approval powers, but unsecured creditors do not. Unsecured creditors may of course object to the plan at the hearing. However, similar to Chapter 12, Chapter 13 will not allow the court to go along with an objection if the debtor plans to turn over 100 percent of all disposable income to the trustee for debt repayment.

Payments The debtor must start payments within 30 days of submitting the plan to the court. If the court has yet to hold its hearing, the debtor pays the trustee. The trustee holds the money until the court upholds or rejects the plan.

Discharge Once the amounts agreed to under the plan are paid, all remaining debts are discharged. The list of debts that cannot be discharged under Chapter 13 is much shorter than those included under Chapter 7. Only alimony, child support, and priority claims must be satisfied in full under Chapter 13. Every other debt may be discharged one way or another.

Quick Quiz 32-4 & 32-5 True or False?

1. Chapter 12 of the Bankruptcy Code provides a method for individual debtors to develop a repayment plan and, upon completion of payments under the plan, be discharged from most remaining debt.

2. Sole proprietors can file bankruptcy under Chapter 13 of the Bankruptcy Code, but corporations and partnerships cannot.

3. Under Chapter 13 of the Bankruptcy Code, secured creditors have approval powers of a repayment plan, but unsecured creditors do not.

Summary

32.1 Bankruptcy is the legal process that allows a debtor to get a fresh start by selling personal property to pay off creditors. The U.S. Constitution gives the federal government jurisdiction over bankruptcy proceedings. The Bankruptcy Code enacted by Congress is found in various chapters of Title 11 of the USC. In 2005, Congress made it more difficult to file for bankruptcy.

32.2 Chapter 7 of the Bankruptcy Code covers ordinary bankruptcy, which is also called liquidation. To qualify, debtors must pass a means test, undergo counseling, provide a federal income tax return, and take a course in financial management. A case trustee sells the debtor's property and uses the cash to pay creditors a portion of the amount owed to each one. The process can be either voluntary or involuntary.

32.3 Reorganization under Chapter 11 of the Bankruptcy Code allows businesses to overcome financial difficulties without selling *all* their property. Instead, a reorganization plan is drawn up that changes the debtor's payment schedule. The new schedule allows the debtor to keep the business going while paying creditors.

32.4 Chapter 12 of the Bankruptcy Code applies to family farmer and fishing businesses in financial difficulty. Under Chapter 12, a family farmer or fishing business can maintain the activity while following a debt adjustment plan to satisfy creditors.

32.5 Chapter 13 of the Bankruptcy Code applies only to individual debtors with established steady incomes. Such debtors can prepare a debt-adjustment plan that will provide for repayment of outstanding debts.

Key Terms

automatic stay, 662

bankruptcy, 657

case trustee, 661

confirmation, 670

debtor in possession, 667

disposable income, 660

homestead exemption, 662

impaired classes, 669

liquidation, 658

means test, 658

order for relief, 661

reorganization, 667

Questions for Review and Discussion

1. What is the source of power that enables Congress to create federal statutory law dealing with bankruptcy and other debt-adjustment procedures?
2. What four requirements must debtors meet to file for Chapter 7 bankruptcy?
3. Explain the means test required for filing Chapter 7 bankruptcy.
4. How does a debtor voluntarily institute a bankruptcy proceeding? Under what conditions can the debtor's creditors institute an involuntary proceeding?
5. Explain the automatic stay process. How does it fulfill the objectives of the Bankruptcy Code?
6. What are the classes of property that can be exempted from sale when a debtor files for bankruptcy?
7. What are the priority of claims on a debtor's assets once the debtor's property has been sold and reduced to cash?
8. Which debts cannot be discharged under a bankruptcy proceeding?
9. What is the purpose of Chapter 11 bankruptcy?
10. What approvals are required for a Chapter 11 reorganization plan to go into effect?
11. Who may file for Chapter 12 bankruptcy, and what are the eligibility requirements?
12. What is the purpose of Chapter 13 bankruptcy, who can file, and what is necessary to be eligible?

Investigating the Internet

States have different bankruptcy exemptions. Find out what your state's exemptions are by going online. First, determine whether your state gives you a choice to use either federal or your state's exemptions or requires you to use only your state's exemptions. Second, compare your state's exemptions with the federal exemptions. If you have a choice, which might you use? One source for this information is **www.bankruptcyaction.com**.

Cases for Analysis

1. Robert Marrama filed for Chapter 7 bankruptcy. In his petition, he did not disclose a vacation home that he had placed in trust. When Marrama discovered that the case trustee was going to take the vacation property as an estate asset, Marrama decided to convert his case to Chapter 13, which would allow him to keep the property and pay his debts over time. The bankruptcy court held that the failure to disclose the vacation home demonstrated bad faith by the debtor and refused to allow the conversion to Chapter 13. Do you agree with the bankruptcy court? Why or why not? *Marrama v. Citizens Bank,* 05-996 U.S. Supreme Court.

2. Soon after the birth of their second child, misfortune fell on the lives of Kurt and Leah Lyons. Kurt got laid off, the landlord raised their rent, they received notice that their car was about to be repossessed, and dunning letters arrived daily from credit card companies. Reluctantly, the couple filed for personal bankruptcy. Their disappointed parents told them that the bankruptcy would remain on their credit rating for the rest of their lives and that they would never again be able to establish a line of credit or obtain a mortgage to buy a house. Were Kurt and Leah's parents correct? Explain.

3. Lisa and William Leeper filed a Chapter 13 bankruptcy petition. One of the unsecured debts they listed on their bankruptcy petition was an amount owed to the Pennsylvania Higher Education Assistance Authority to attend college under a guaranteed student loan program. Will the loan to attend college be discharged by the bankruptcy court?

Explain. *Leeper v. Pennsylvania Higher Education Assistance Agency,* 94-3372 & 94-3373, U.S. Court of Appeals (3rd Cir.).

4. When a Florida court dismissed Nellie Cortez's voluntary bankruptcy petition, it ordered her not to file another petition "under any chapter of the Bankruptcy Code for a period of twelve months." Two months later, an involuntary bankruptcy petition was filed in California by Cortez's stepfather, Thomas Bronkovic. The California court dismissed that case, finding that Cortez had colluded with her stepfather and that the case was, in fact, her own "voluntary" petition rather than her stepfather's "involuntary" petition. While the California case was pending, the FDIC brought suit against Cortez to enforce certain promissory notes. Did FDIC violate the automatic stay provision of the Bankruptcy Code? Why or why not? *Federal Deposit Insurance Corporation v. Cortez,* 96-6047, U.S. Court of Appeals (2nd. Cir.).

5. Dyana Landrin was convicted of grand larceny after she admitted she took nearly $19,000 from the Community Mutual Savings Bank while she was employed as a teller. The county court ordered her to pay restitution to the bank—that is, return the money. Before paying restitution, Landrin filed a petition for relief under Chapter 7 of the Bankruptcy Code. Is the money owed to the bank discharged by the bankruptcy petition? Explain. *In re Landrin,* 93-B-20920 (Bankr. S.D. NY).

6. Three creditors filed an involuntary bankruptcy petition against the Manchester Lakes Association, alleging that the association was not paying its bills

when they came due. Manchester fought the petition, arguing that its general partner, Dominion Federal Savings and Loan, had enough money to pay these bills as they came due, even though it was not doing so. Should the court refuse to grant the order for relief if the debtor could prove it had the ability to pay its bills? Explain. *In re Manchester Lakes Association, 47 B.R. 798 (Bankr. E.D. VA).*

7. Finding itself in great financial difficulty, Fidelity Mortgage Investors filed a voluntary bankruptcy petition in a New York bankruptcy court. When the petition was filed, the automatic suspension went into effect. Ignoring the suspension, Camelia and Farnale, two of FMI's creditors, filed suit against FMI in a Mississippi federal court. As a result, FMI was forced to pay out enormous sums of money in its own defense on the Mississippi case. FMI then returned to the bankruptcy court in New York and asked that both Camelia and Farnale be held in contempt of court for ignoring the suspension. Should the New York bankruptcy court hold Camelia and Farnale in contempt? Explain. *Fidelity Mortgage Investors v. Camelia Builders, Inc.,* 550 F.2d 47 (2nd Cir.).

8. When the Rahls filed for bankruptcy, they attempted to exclude their entire silverware set from the bankruptcy sale by listing each piece at a value far under the $200 maximum allowed for each item of individual household goods at that time. Had they listed the silverware as one item, it would have been worth more than $6,000. Thus, the entire set would not have been exempt. By listing each piece of silverware separately, the total

value did not exceed $4,000, and the entire set could be saved. Should the court force the Rahls to list the silverware set as one item, thus limiting the exemption to $200? Explain. *In the Matter of Rahl,* 14 B.R. 153 (Bankr. E.D. WI).

9. Dubuque stole more than $4,000 from his employer, U-Haul. He later pled guilty to "theft by unauthorized taking or transfer." The court sentenced him to pay back the stolen money. When Dubuque filed for bankruptcy, U-Haul claimed that this debt would qualify as an exception to discharge. Was U-Haul correct? Explain. *In re Dubuque,* 46 B.R. 156 (NH).

10. U.S. Truck Company, Inc., filed for a reorganization under Chapter 11 of the Bankruptcy Code. When the reorganization plan was presented for confirmation, one creditor objected to the plan. The creditor argued that the debtor was facing a possible strike and a new labor contract, both of which could place an additional strain on the debtor's finances. These potential labor problems, the creditor concluded, made the plan unfeasible. U.S. Truck admitted that the labor problems existed but noted that the company had recently rebounded from its financial problems to become very successful. Moreover, the labor union had just ratified two previous labor contracts by a 95 percent majority vote. U.S. Truck concluded that these factors made the plan workable, which was enough under the code, because the code did not require a guarantee of success. Was the conclusion correct? *In the Matter of U.S. Truck Co., Inc.,* 47 B.R. 932 (Bankr. E.D. MI).

Quick Quiz Answers

32-1 & 32-2	32-3	32-4 & 32-5
1. F	1. T	1. F
2. T	2. F	2. T
3. T	3. F	3. T

Part 6 Case Study

In re: Lisa A. Bloch, Debtor Plaintiff v. Windham Professionals, et al., Defendants

United States Bankruptcy Court for the District of Massachusetts, 257 B.R. 374

Summary

Lisa A. Bloch filed for bankruptcy relief, seeking a discharge of her student loan obligations. A 41-year-old woman with no dependents, Bloch attended a number of prestigious universities and colleges including Radcliffe, Cornell, Harvard, and Princeton. Her graduate education, a master's degree in public administration from Suffolk University in Boston, was financed through five promissory notes totaling $41,863, which had been assigned to the defendant, Educational Credit Management Corp. (ECMC).

While in Boston, she established a pattern of sporadic, full-time employment supplemented by part-time clerical assignments arranged by temporary employment agencies. The evidence at trial suggested that Bloch has an impressive educational résumé and an abundance of marketable skills, including considerable computer background and some management experience. After obtaining her master's degree, she moved to Seattle, Washington, without a job and incurred moving expenses of approximately $5,000. Her employment woes continued in Seattle, where she failed to obtain permanent work. Her testimony revealed that she survived for the last year by living with friends and paying expenses by accepting a gratuitous $4,000 loan. Bloch admitted she had no physical or mental disabilities that would hinder her from working full time, but for some unexplained reason, either a personality issue or perhaps wanderlust, she had not been employed in any one full-time position for longer than a year since attaining her master's degree.

At the time of the trial, Bloch worked less than 30 hours per week at $20 per hour, earning approximately $2,350 per month gross pay. She testified that she was reluctant to seek additional evening or weekend employment because it would impede her search for a permanent full-time position. She presented evidence showing her current monthly living expenses to be approximately $2,200.

At trial, Bloch expressed optimism about an improvement in her job prospects, a desire to repay her outstanding loans, and an acknowledgment that she only brought this action as a result of her frustration in dealing with the various student loan agencies.

The Court's Opinion

Joel B. Rosenthal, United States Bankruptcy Judge

Section 523(a) (8) of the Bankruptcy Code states:

> A discharge under sections 727, 1141, 1228(a), 1228(b), or 1328(b) of this title does not discharge an individual debtor from any debt for an educational benefit, overpayment or loan made, insured or guaranteed by a governmental unit, or made under any program funded in whole or in part by a governmental unit or nonprofit institution, or for an obligation to repay funds received as an educational

benefit, scholarship or stipend unless excepting such debt from discharge under this paragraph will impose an undue hardship on the debtor and the debtor's dependents. . . .

(T)he issue . . . is whether the Debtor has met her burden of proving that excepting her student loan obligations from discharge will cause her "undue hardship."

This Court has adopted the "totality of the circumstances" test. . . . In *Dolan v. American Student Assistance, et al.*, 256 B.R. 230, this Court stated that a debtor seeking discharge of student loans under §523(a)(8) "must prove by a preponderance of the evidence, that (1) his past, present, and reasonably reliable future financial resources; (2) his and his dependents' reasonably necessary living expenses, and; (3) other relevant facts or circumstances particular to the debtor's case are such that excepting the student loans from discharge will prevent the debtor from maintaining a minimal standard of living, even with the advantage of a discharge of his other pre-petition debts." By making specific findings as to each of these matters, the Court must then determine if excepting a debtor's student loans from discharge will impose an "undue hardship" on that debtor and the debtor's dependents. Having stated the applicable analysis for "undue hardship" in this Court, I now turn to this Debtor's request for relief.

A. The Debtor's Past, Present and Reasonably Reliable Future Financial Resources

While it may be true the Debtor's past and present income are insufficient to pay her student loans and still maintain a minimal standard of living, the Debtor has nonetheless not proven to the Court's satisfaction that her prospects for increasing her future income are so bleak as to warrant a discharge of her student loans.... The Debtor currently makes $2,350 per month, and the Debtor's current living expenses suggest her past and present income have not been enough to service her student loans. The Court believes, though, that the Debtor could significantly enhance her future income by exploiting her educational credentials and the job skills she has acquired in past employment. Although highly educated, the Debtor's résumé and testimony indicate a presently unstable and uninspiring employment history, but the Court is convinced this will change, particularly in light of the favorable economic conditions present in Boston and Seattle, as well as the Debtor's portable credentials and job skills.

Furthermore, the Court believes the Debtor could do more to maximize her income by increasing the length of her work week. The Debtor admitted she works an average of only 29.5 hours per week. The Debtor has failed to show that this is reasonable given her economic circumstances and abilities. A 29.5 hour work week is a personal choice she has made and is not linked to any physical or mental disability, nor is it motivated by a need to care for any dependents. The Debtor stated her unwillingness to take part-time evening or weekend work because she says this would interfere with her job search. The Court finds this explanation unconvincing. It is not at all unreasonable to expect this Debtor to supplement her income by taking part-time weekend or evening work in order to meet her student loan obligations. . . . An increase in the Debtor's work hours, either at a part-time job or at her present temporary position, would raise her monthly income, possibly allowing her to make some effort at repayment of her student loans. The Debtor's strong educational background, coupled with her transferable skills and talents should assist her in her search for employment. Based on her education, and her articulate pro se presentation in this adversary proceeding, the Court is confident that the Debtor will bounce back by finding employment commensurate with her education. Therefore, the Court concludes the Debtor's past, present, and reasonably reliable future financial resources will allow her to pay her student loan obligations and still maintain a minimal standard of living.

B. The Debtor's Reasonably Necessary Living Expenses

In addition to the Court's conclusion that the Debtor's future income prospects will allow her to repay her student loans without undue hardship, the Court likewise finds the Debtor has not done all she can to minimize her reasonably necessary living expenses, and as such the Court denies her the relief requested. . . . The Court's review of the Debtor's living expenses leads to the conclusion that her living expenses are, for the most part, modest. The Debtor could however reduce her substantial rent expense in some manner with a resultant monthly savings of perhaps hundreds of dollars. For example, the Debtor could reduce her rent expense by taking a more affordable apartment, or perhaps by taking in a roommate in her present home. Either of these options would help ease her present financial burdens. Thus, the Court finds the Debtor has not done all she can to minimize her reasonably necessary living expenses such that she is entitled to a discharge of her student loans for "undue hardship" under §523(a)(8).

C. The Debtor's Other Relevant Facts or Circumstances

While the Court has already concluded the Debtor has not taken steps to maximize her current income and minimize her expenses, the Court also looks to see if there are facts or circumstances unique to the Debtor's case that warrant granting a discharge of her student loans, notwithstanding the Court's conclusions above. In this case, the Debtor has failed to present evidence of any facts or circumstances that would lead this Court to conclude that excepting her student loans from discharge would impose an undue hardship. On the contrary, the Debtor's facts and circumstances militate against granting a discharge. For example, the Debtor has no dependents that might place a burden upon her monthly income or expenses. . . . Also, the Debtor is fortunately not burdened with any handicap or disability that precludes her from any of the vocational fields the Debtor is qualified to enter. Additionally, the Debtor has continually professed a willingness to repay her outstanding student loans, and but for the purported inflexibility of the lenders' policies would enter into a payment arrangement to meet those obligations.

As the Court can find no compelling reason to grant this Debtor a discharge of her student loans, the Court must find for the defendant, ECMC, and leave the prevailing party with the suggestion that it work with this Debtor to reach a transitional agreement until the Debtor's employment situation changes.

Questions for Analysis

1. What must a debtor prove to be excepted from the rule that a student loan obligation cannot be discharged in bankruptcy?

2. What is the name of the test that the court has adopted to determine whether an exception exists?

3. What three points must a debtor prove to meet the test?

4. Summarize the court's opinion on each point.

5. What was the decision of the court?

Part Seven

Chapter 33

The Principal and Agent Relationship

The Opening Case
Cramer v. Auglaize Acres

When Rex Cramer learned that his father, Frank Cramer, had been severely injured while living at Auglaize Acres County Home, he brought a lawsuit against the home, which was operated by the county commissioners of Auglaize County. As an extension of the county government, the county home was considered a subdivision of the state, and the nurses who had cared for Frank at the time of his accident were, as a result, government employees. Therefore, using the doctrine of *respondeat superior*, Cramer sued not only the two nurses whose negligent conduct led directly to Frank's death but also the county home and Auglaize County. The doctrine of *respondeat superior* extends the liability of employees to their employer. In this case, the doctrine would extend liability from the nurses to the county home and from the home to the county itself. The county reacted immediately by filing a motion to dismiss under a state statute that established sovereign immunity for all political subdivisions of the state, including the county and the county home. Cramer replied that though the statute did establish sovereign immunity for all state subdivisions, it also created several exceptions to the rule. One such exception occurs when an employee is accused of negligent conduct while working for a state subdivision which is performing a proprietary function, such as owning and operating a nursing home. The county addressed this argument by noting that even if the exception were valid, the county had a statutory defense. That defense stated that a political subdivision of the state would keep its immunity if "the injury death, or loss to a person or property resulted from the exercise of judgment or discretion . . . unless (that) judgment or discretion was exercised with malicious purpose, in bad faith, or in a wanton and a reckless manner." The state Supreme Court agreed that the defense *might* be valid. However, the question of whether the employees had actually exercised discretion and judgment or had acted with recklessness, malice, wantonness, or in bad faith was a matter for the jury to decide. For that reason, the court kicked the entire matter back down to the trial court and said, in essence, "It's all yours. Try again." (See *Cramer v. Auglaize Acres*, 113 Ohio St.3d 266, Ohio Supreme Court.)

Opening Case Questions

1. What is the doctrine of *respondeat superior*?

2. Are the nurses in this case employees or independent contractors? Explain.

3. Were the nurses acting within the scope of their employment?

4. What is the doctrine of sovereign immunity?

5. Why does sovereign immunity apply to the county home?

Learning Objectives

1. Describe the nature of the agency relationship.
2. Outline the doctrine of vicarious liability.
3. Distinguish among the different types of principals.
4. Differentiate among the different type of agents.
5. Explain the liability of agents.
6. Clarify the liability of principals.
7. Illustrate how agents relate to business associations.
8. Disclose how agency relationships are created.
9. Explain the purpose of the Uniform Computer Transactions Act.
10. Describe the goal of the Uniform Electronic Transactions Act.

33-1 The Law of Agency

In an essay entitled, "How Culture Changes," the anthropologist George Peter Murdock of Yale University, explains, "It is a fundamental characteristic of culture that, despite its essentially conservative nature, it does change over time and from place to place." The fact that the law is a part of this process of change has been a recurring theme throughout this book. The emergence of the law of agency within our culture is another prime example of this tendency toward change within the legal complex adaptive system. Many of the changes that we have seen throughout the book emerge because the law must adapt to deal with shifts in culture and social norms caused by technology, political conflict, economic problems, and interpersonal relationships. The emergence of the law of agency, in contrast, was precipitated by a different set of circumstances. The law of agency emerged because people are limited in the amount of work they can handle, in the knowledge they can retain, and in their physical ability to travel from one place to another.

LO1

LO2

The Nature of Agency

Because the law of agency developed in response to human limitations, it was forced to borrow many of its principles from other, older, and more well-developed areas of the law. Thus, in agency law, concepts that are found in tort law, contract law, trust law, and remedies can also be found in agency. However, the law of agency also has been around long enough to have developed its own rules. Thus, the concept of vicarious liability, for example, though it involves tort law, nevertheless arose because of agency. The same is true of concepts such as inherent agency power, undisclosed principals, and the ratification of agency authority. Because the law of agency has its own principles, rules, doctrines, and concepts, all of which emerged independently and belong only to agency, it is said to be *sui generis*, that is, a law unto itself.

Agency is a legal relationship in which one party, the **agent**, is authorized to act for and under the control of the second, the **principal**, in negotiating and making contracts with a third party. The **third party** is that individual with whom the agent deals for the principal. The principal must indicate in some manner that the agent is to act for and under the control of the principal. An agency relationship is always **consensual** because the agent must agree to act for the principal. The agency relationship is *fiduciary* because the agent and principal trust each other. The relationship may or may not arise because of a contract; however, it is always consensual. If an agency relationship does not result from a contract, it a **gratuitous agency**, and the agent is a **gratuitous agent**. Once an agency relationship has been created, certain obligations, rights, and liabilities arise that relate to the principal, the agent, and the third party. Except for the obligation to compensate the agent in a contractual relationship, the obligations, rights, and liabilities remain the same, regardless of whether the agent is contractual or gratuitous.

> ## EXAMPLE 33-1:   Superheroes and Agency Law
>
> Several individuals were hired by Taylor Toys, Inc., to serve as sales representatives to introduce Taylor's new line of action figures based on comic book superheroes, just in time for the summer release of several new superhero films. These representatives visited toy stores at malls, interviewed store managers, and, in many cases, obtained orders for the new action figures. This arrangement constituted an agency relationship in which Taylor Toys (the principal) is liable for the actions of its sales representatives (the agents) in their dealings with its many customers (the third parties).

Principal–Agent Relationship

In an agency relationship, the agent has the authority to represent the principal (see Figure 33-1). Therefore, the principal is liable for the agent's acts when the agent deals with third parties for the principal. In the principal–agent relationship, the agent performs duties for the principal that require the exercise of judgment and discretion and that result in a contract. Any person legally capable of entering into a contract may be a principal. Anyone appointed by the principal may be an agent. Even a minor or one who is mentally limited may be an agent, inasmuch as the acts of such persons are considered to be those of the principal.

Employer–Employee Relationship

The legal principles governing the relationship of principal and agent and of employer and employee are basically the same. The main distinction between the two relationships is the agent's

Figure 33-1   The agent has the authority to represent the principal in an agency relationship.

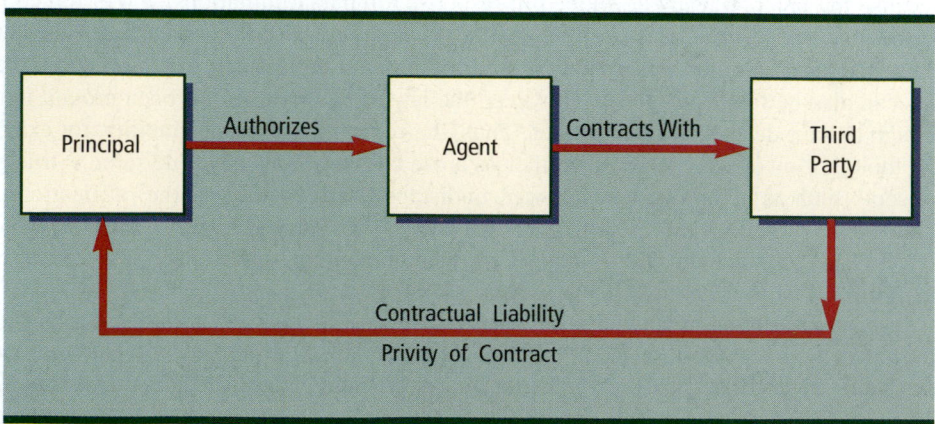

authority to contract. Whereas an agent always has some sort of power to enter contracts on behalf of a principal, an employee does not always have this power. An employee who merely performs mechanical acts for the employer under the employer's direction is not an agent. In contrast, a person who is an employee and who does have the power to enter contracts for the employer would have the status of an agent, even without a formally executed contract of agency. Not all agents are employees of their respective principals, however. A real estate broker who is appointed by a homeowner to sell a house is an agent but not an employee.

Master–Servant Relationship

The terms *master* (employer) and *servant* (employee) are not outdated but continue to be used in some legal circumstances. A **master** is a person who has the right to control the activities of another person. The person whose activities are controlled is called the **servant**. A servant who has the right to conduct the business of the master is also an agent. In common usage, the terms *employer* and *employee* refer to the master–servant relationship. The terms *master* and *servant* are used instead of *employer* and *employee* in a legal setting when questions of tort liability arise.

Proprietor–Independent Contractor Relationship

An **independent contractor** is a party who contracts to do a job and retains complete control over the methods employed to obtain final completion. The party for which an independent contractor works is often referred to as a **proprietor**. Independent contractors are not subject to the control of the proprietor. They maintain all required business licenses and permits and pay all job-related expenses; they are obligated only to get the job done. The proprietor has the right to specify the results of the job in question. Moreover, he or she has the right to inspect and approve, or disapprove, the results of the independent contractor's performance. Independent contractors are not employees; however, they may be agents. The distinction depends on whether the independent contractor has the right to enter a contract on behalf of the proprietor. For instance, an individual might hire a financial expert to buy and sell stocks in his or her name. The financial expert would be an independent contractor as well as an agent. However, the expert would not be an employee.

> ### About the Law
> The definition of many legal terms varies depending on the area of the law in which they are used. *Principal* is one such term. In criminal law, a principal is defined as the chief perpetrator of a crime.

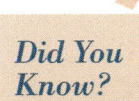

> ### *Did You Know?*
> In the early development of agency law, the principal was also known as the "constituent" and the "chief."

Talking Points

In his book, *The Ethical Imperative*, the philosopher Richard L. Means makes the following observation: "There are those who seem to believe that society does not exist in any real sense. Ayn Rand and her followers broadcast that it is only the individual who truly exists, and that the true nature of the individual is to maximize his or her own self-interest, economic profit, and personal satisfaction. This is called 'objectivism' by the true believer in 'Randian philosophy.' Such a view seems widespread in American culture, as almost any contact with the luncheon circuit of service clubs, chambers of commerce, and trade associations will readily verify." In contrast, the American philosopher Thomas Dewey, in his book *Individualism: Old and New*, points out, "Our material culture, as anthropologists would call it, is verging on the collective and corporate." In light of these two quotations, and the study of agency in this chapter, explore the following two questions: Does the law of agency promote collective behavior by allowing persons, including corporate, governmental, and institutional organizations, to operate on a massive scale through its agents? Or does it promote individualism by allowing individuals to extend their own influence beyond their immediate physical restraints?

The highest-paid player in major league baseball, Alex Rodriguez, with his agent Scott Boras.

Why the Distinctions Are Significant

The distinctions among these relationships frequently can be crucial in determining the nature and the extent of legal liability. It is important to note, however, that the names themselves are not controlling. Instead, it is the true nature of the relationship that is critical. Calling a servant an independent contractor does not transform the nature of the relationship if the master still controls the servant's conduct.

Contractual Liability   An agent is appointed by a principal to negotiate and enter into contracts on behalf of the principal. Therefore, the principal is bound to the terms of those contracts. Unless an employee is also an agent, he or she has no power to negotiate and enter contracts for the employer. Moreover, an independent contractor has no power to bind the proprietor to a contract, unless expressly authorized to do so.

Tort Liability   The distinction between master–servant and proprietor–independent contractor relationships is especially critical in determining the nature and the extent of tort liability. Even though everyone is responsible for his or her own tortious conduct, there are times when the law will hold not only the tortfeasor but also the person who engaged the tortfeasor liable for the tort. This type of liability is called **vicarious liability**. Vicarious liability is based on the principle of *respondeat superior* (let the master, or the superior, respond). In most cases, a court will apply this principle when faced with a master–servant relationship, because the master has the right to control the physical conduct of the servant (see Figure 33-2).

Figure 33-2   This chart shows the flow of principal/employer tort liability under the *respondeat superior* doctrine.

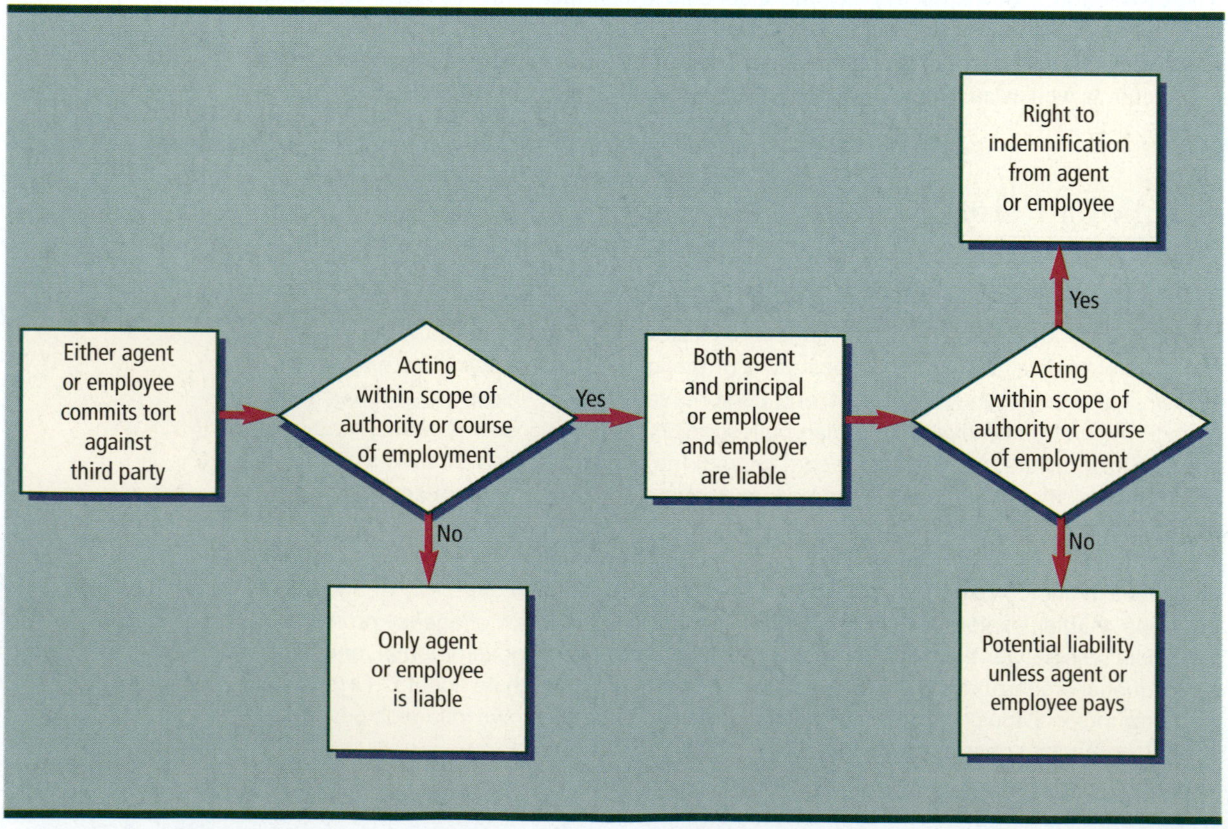

Either agent or employee commits tort against third party	→ Acting within scope of authority or course of employment

Acting within scope of authority or course of employment — Yes → Both agent and principal or employee and employer are liable → Acting within scope of authority or course of employment — Yes → Right to indemnification from agent or employee

Acting within scope of authority or course of employment — No → Only agent or employee is liable

Acting within scope of authority or course of employment — No → Potential liability unless agent or employee pays

The concept of master–servant liability—in fact, the entire concept of agency law itself—from a historical perspective arose from Roman laws that dealt with masters and slaves. Under traditional Roman law, if a slave committed an offense against an innocent party, the slave owner was required to surrender the slave to the victim. Eventually, however, the law allowed the slave owner to pay the victim a sum of money so that the owner could retain the services of a valuable slave. Soon the custom became to sue the owner directly because, in most cases, the owner would prefer to keep the slave and pay the victim. Later, the Roman courts also began to hold innkeepers and ship owners directly liable for torts committed by those who worked for them, on the basis of the idea that both ship owners and innkeepers held a high duty to those who traveled on their ships or who stayed at their inns. Often, a case was brought directly against the ship owner or the innkeeper, on the basis of the idea that they had a responsibility to make sure they had the best workers in their employ. As we shall see shortly, these two doctrines are still part of the law today in the form of nondelegable duties and the ideas of negligent hiring and negligent retention. Moreover, because ship owners and innkeepers were just as likely to have free people working for them as slaves, the courts saw vicarious liability in terms of all workers, not just slaves. Nevertheless, the terms master and servant remain with us still today.

EXAMPLE 33-2: The Right to Control Is Control

Quentin Carraway was employed as a delivery driver for the St. Clair Printing Co. His supervisor, Ken Popson, was one of the owners of the company. Popson was responsible for setting the driving schedules. Every morning, Popson would post a list of the companies that were to receive deliveries from St. Clair. The posted list would include both the contents of the delivery and the order in which the packages were to be delivered. Popson also had all of the paperwork compiled so that all the drivers had to do was pick up the packing slips and invoices, load the packages, and get on the road for the day. Popson, however, never checked to see whether the drivers actually followed his suggested order, and so some of the drivers, including Carraway, would decide on their own routes and change the order of the deliveries to fit the route, rather than the other way around. When Carraway had an accident that injured several individuals and damaged several vehicles, the victims sued St. Clair on the basis of vicarious liability. Because Popson had the *right* to control the delivery drivers, the fact that Carraway had changed the suggested order of the deliveries would not absolve the company of liability.

To apply the doctrine of *respondeat superior* in a tort case, two questions must be answered. First, is the alleged tortfeasor a servant or an independent contractor? This first question often can be answered simply by looking at the degree of control that the hiring person has over the hired person. A master has the right to control the activities of a servant. A proprietor does not have the right to control independent contractors.

If the degree of control is unclear or in dispute, the court can apply other guidelines to determine whether the hired person is a servant or an independent contractor. For example, independent contractors usually have the power to choose their own workers and discharge them on the job. They usually provide their own equipment and tools and are responsible for performing the entire job, including cleaning up. Workers paid by the hour are usually considered servants. Those who are paid by the job are usually independent contractors. Most of the time, if working hours are set by the hiring person, the worker is a servant. A worker who determines his or her own hours is most often an independent contractor.

Painters, physicians, and plumbers are examples of independent contractors when they are in business for themselves. They can lose this status and become employees, however, if they are hired as members of an employer's staff.

Second, if the court determines that a master–servant relationship exists, it will turn to the next question, that is, the scope of employment. The **scope of employment** involves the range of activities for which the servant is engaged. For the doctrine of *respondeat superior* to apply, a tort must be committed while the worker was performing a task for which he or she was hired, or at least one that he or she was authorized to perform by his or her employer. To determine whether a servant was operating within the scope of employment, ask the following questions:

1. Was the action committed by the employee authorized by the employer?
2. Where did the action take place?
3. Were the employer's interests promoted by the action?
4. Did the employer supply the instrumentality used in the action?
5. Was this action performed by other employees on a regular basis?
6. Was the action committed by the employee criminal?

EXAMPLE 33-3:   From LaGuardia to the Marquis

Anne Rutgers works as a cab driver for the Starshine Cab Company. While on a routine run transporting a passenger from New York's La Guardia Airport to the Marriott Marquis Hotel in Times Square, she collided with a car driven by Ian Harrington. Harrington wanted to sue both Rutgers and the Starshine Cab Company. He did so under the doctrine of vicarious liability because Rutgers was (a) an employee under the control of the cab company and (b) operating within the scope of her employment.

If we apply these six factors, the outcome of Example 33-3 becomes obvious. First, Rutgers's activity of driving a cab was authorized by her employer. Second, the incident took place in midtown Manhattan, where Rutgers is authorized to drive. Third, the business of her employer was advanced by transporting a passenger from the airport to a hotel. Fourth, she was using a cab owned by the company. Fifth, she was driving a cab, which was something that she did on a regular basis. Sixth, there was nothing criminal about her action. If several of the questions listed led to the opposite answers, a different decision might result. Consider, for instance, the following example.

EXAMPLE 33-4:   From the Marquis to Jersey

Suppose in Example 33-3, after the accident in midtown, Rutgers got off work and instead of returning the cab to the company garage, as she was supposed to, she drove the cab to New Jersey to visit some friends and to have a drink or two in a neighborhood bar to calm her nerves. If in that situation she were to leave the bar and collide with a pedestrian, or anyone else for that matter, she would be operating outside the scope of her employment, and the cab company would not be liable for her negligence. In these two examples, the result is clear. Not all cases, however, offer this type of clarity. Consider, for instance, the following example.

EXAMPLE 33-5:   The Case of the Racing Golf Carts

Raymond Meyers was employed as an accountant for the Enson-McKnight Aeronautics Company. He worked in the tax department of the manufacturer, determining how to handle taxation problems for the company's branches in Europe and South America. In July at the company's Independence Day picnic held on company grounds, Tony Enson, the president and CEO of the company, tried to convince Meyers to drive one of the company-owned golf carts in a golf cart race. Meyers did not want to get into the race and argued that he had no experience driving a golf cart. Nevertheless, the president insisted. Again Meyers refused. Finally, when it was clear that the president was about to get very angry with Meyers, he agreed to enter the race. Meyers lost control of the golf cart and drove into a group of passers-by, injuring several of them. The victims sued both Meyers and Enson-McKnight on the basis of vicarious liability. The company argued that it should not be held liable because operating a golf cart was outside the scope of Meyers's employment as a tax accountant. The plaintiffs argued that because Meyers was essentially ordered by the president to drive the company-rented golf cart at the company-sponsored picnic in a company-controlled race, the doctrine of vicarious liability applies.

No definitive answer exists in this case. Both sides have valid arguments. The defendants can argue quite convincingly that the employee, who was a tax accountant at the company, was not acting within the scope of his employment when he drove a golf cart into the group of passers-by. Moreover, the company can argue that driving a golf cart does not further the business of the aeronautics company. However, the plaintiffs can argue, with equal conviction, that because the accountant was ordered by the president of the company to drive a company-rented golf cart at a company-sponsored picnic on company-owned property, he was essentially operating within the scope of his employment.

Most of the time, vicarious liability is applied to negligence cases, because workers are not usually hired to commit intentional torts. There are, of course, exceptions to this rule. If, for example, a servant commits a tort intending to further the master's business, as when a bouncer at a casino uses force to eject an unruly patron, the master may be liable for battery. Or if a security guard at a department store detains an innocent shopper by locking him or her in a room for several hours, the owner of the store might be liable for false imprisonment. Moreover, if the master could reasonably foresee that the servant might commit the intentional tort, as might be the case with a bouncer in a casino or a security guard in a department store, the master may be liable for that tort.

The law also makes a distinction between intentional torts that cause actual physical harm and those that do not result in such harm. In the case of a physical tort, the master will always be liable, assuming all of the other tests are met. However, in nonphysical torts, the master is liable only if the servant possesses actual or apparent authority. Actual authority, as we shall detail later, is real authority that exists because of some communication between the principal and the agent. Apparent authority exists when the principal has led a third party to the reasonable belief that a nonagent has certain agency powers.

When a master loans a servant to another master, the servant is referred to as a **borrowed servant**. In such a situation, a question may arise as to which master should bear the loss caused by the servant's tort. The answer to this question depends on which master had control of the servant when the tort occurred. Other circumstances, such as whose work is being performed

Independent contractors are not employees of the homeowner.

and who supplies the tools and the place of work, are relevant in answering this question. The skill of the worker, the length of time the worker has been aiding in the other's business, and the manner in which the worker is paid may also be relevant to show the ease with which control over a worker is shifted from one master to another.

EXAMPLE 33-6:   The Blundering Borrowed Bulldozer

Fred Anderson was regularly employed by Georgetown Construction as a bulldozer driver. Georgetown subcontracted the building of several airfields throughout the south to Riverdell Construction. Riverdell was so impressed with Anderson's work that the company requested that he be permitted to join them on six more jobs. Georgetown agreed. Anderson showed up to work at sites completely controlled by Riverdell every day for 18 months. Whenever special training was needed, he received it from Riverdell. He used Riverdell's equipment and tools, and when the Riverdell crew was on the road, he stayed with them at their hotel at Riverdell's expense. While Georgetown continued to pay Anderson's wages Riverdell later reimbursed them for the payments. Anderson rarely contacted or was contacted by Georgetown for that entire 18-month period. During the nineteenth month, Anderson lost control of a bulldozer, which smashed into a truck driven by Victor Lazlo. Lazlo wants to sue both Anderson and Riverdell, but Riverdell claims that Anderson is not its employee. Under these circumstances, it is likely that the court would rule that Anderson is the borrowed employee of Riverdell. The key factor is that Riverdell had complete control over the activities of Anderson and had exercised that control extensively for 18 months.

In some situations, the court may hold the proprietor liable for the torts of the independent contractor. For instance, in some jurisdictions, if a proprietor is negligent in checking an independent contractor's qualifications and consequently hires someone who is incompetent, the proprietor may be held liable should an innocent third party be injured by the negligence of the incompetent independent contractor. In this case, the court may hold the proprietor liable for the **negligent hiring** of the incompetent independent contractor. Similarly, a proprietor may be liable for the **negligent retention** of an incompetent independent contractor if, after hiring the independent contractor, the proprietor learns that the contractor is incompetent and does not dismiss the contractor. A proprietor may also be open to liability when the independent contractor has been hired to perform a nondelegable duty. A **nondelegable duty** is one that the proprietor cannot delegate, or pass off, to another party.

EXAMPLE 33-7:   The Question of Nondelegable Duties

Because it was suffering from a fiscal shortfall, Airflight Airlines Inc. had elected to hire an independent maintenance firm to service its entire fleet of jet aircraft. The independent firm, Jackson Maintenance, Inc., made several serious errors that caused one of Airflight's planes to lose a wheel on a landing. The crash landing injured several passengers. Both Airflight and Jackson Maintenance were sued by the injured passengers. Even though Airflight could show that Jackson Maintenance was an independent contractor, the airline company could not escape liability for the accident because a common carrier, such as an airline company, cannot delegate its duty to protect its passengers.

BusinessWeek **Business Law in the News**
Japan's Lost Generation

By just about any measure, Japan is back. The economy is growing at 2% a year, company profits are soaring, and land prices are rising. Unemployment, meanwhile, is down to 4% as Japan Inc. has started hiring again, with many college grads receiving multiple job offers. Suddenly, the future looks bright for a new generation of Japanese.

Try telling that to Sadaaki Nehashi. The 31-year-old contract worker at delivery company Yamato Transport makes just $1,100 a month sorting packages—about a third of the average income for full-time employees in Japan. That's a step up from when he landed the job six years ago, though not enough for Nehashi to afford a place of his own, so he lives at his parents' modest home in central Tokyo. "I've had to lower my expectations a bit," says Nehashi, who graduated from university with a degree in marine biology in 2000. "But if I waited around for a full-time job, I might have been waiting forever."

If a rising tide lifts all boats, then why are millions of Japanese like Nehashi treading water? There's an entire generation of people in their late 20s and early 30s who came of age during Japan's so-called lost decade, a stretch of economic stagnation that started to ease in 2003. Through that period, with Japanese companies in retrenchment mode, young people faced what came to be known as a "hiring ice age." Many settled for odd jobs or part-time work to make ends meet but hoped eventually to find their way into regular employment with the stars of corporate Japan. Instead, they're being passed over in favor of new graduates—a serious problem in a country that still values lifetime employment and frowns on midcareer job-hopping.

This group is called the "lost" or "suffering" generation. Some 3.3 million Japanese aged 25 to 34 work as temps or contract employees—up from 1.5 million 10 years ago, according to the Ministry of Internal Affairs. These young people have various less-than-desirable classifications in hierarchy-conscious Japan. They might be *keiyakushain*, or contract workers, typically lower-paid than full-time staff, with fewer benefits and minimal job security. Or they're *hakenshain* (people employed by temp agencies); *freeters* (those who flit from one menial job to

the next); or, at the bottom, *NEETS* (an acronym coined in Britain that stands for not employed, in education, or in training). The plight of such folks was the subject of a recent television drama called *Haken no Hinkaku*, or *Dignity of the Agency Worker*, the saga of a twentysomething temp who must put up with the snobbery of full-time colleagues despite her long list of qualifications. . . .

These millions of young people face a life that's vastly different from that of their parents. For Japan's postwar baby boomers, jobs provided certainty, spurring them to partner and procreate. Faced with insecurity, many of Japan's twenty- and thirtysomethings are doing neither. The number of marriages fell to 714,000 in 2005 from 1 million-plus in the 1970s. That could exacerbate a drop in Japan's birthrate, already among the lowest in the developed world. "You don't get maternity pay, and you have no job to return to—that makes it hard," says Masako Ikeda, a 30-year-old who works at a video game company in Tokyo but is employed by a job agency. . . .

Meanwhile, some disgruntled Japanese contract workers are pressing for change the old-fashioned way. Electronics giant Canon Inc. is in the spotlight after Hideyuki Ohno, a 32-year-old temporary worker at the company's Utsunomiya factory, near Tokyo, organized 17 other temps into a union. His beef: After seven years on the job, he's still employed by an agency, not Canon. Ohno, who earns $2,200 a month polishing glass lenses for steppers, the complex machines used to make semiconductors, says he hasn't had a raise in five years. "I heard my salary was nearly half of a regular staffer of the same age, but I tried not to care about it too much," says the father of two. Then Ohno read in a newspaper that Canon may have violated employment law in not offering him a permanent position after his many years with the company. That spurred him to file a complaint with the Labor Standards Office.

Despite growing profits, Canon still relies heavily on outside help. In 2006, it increased its ranks of contract employees by 19%, to 37,000; permanent staff rose 4%, to 50,753. Canon declined to comment on Ohno's case but says it treats temporary workers fairly and follows all labor laws.

(Continued)

Business Law in the News *(Continued)*

Ohno says the dispute has opened a rift between temps and full-timers at the plant where he works. After he launched his lawsuit, tape was put on the floor to demarcate the line between permanent employees and temps. "We used to all work together," says Ohno. "But now they don't even say, 'Good morning.'"

Questions for Analysis

1. Would Japanese workers classified as *keiyakus-hain* be considered employees or independent contractors in the United States? Explain.

2. Would the workers classified as *hakenshain* be considered employees or independent contractors in the United States? Explain.

3. Would Masako Ikeda be considered an employee or an independent contractor in the United States? Explain.

4. Would Hideyuki Ohno be considered an employee or an independent contractor in the United States? Explain.

5. In addition to the obvious advantage of paying out lower wages, what other advantage would a company have for continuing to employ contract workers? Explain.

Source: Ian Rowley and Kenji Hall with Hiroko Tashiro in Tokyo, "Global Business Workplace: Japan's Lost Generation: Japan Inc. Is Back, But Millions of Young Workers Have Been Left Behind," *BusinessWeek*, May 28, 2007, 40–41.

Criminal Liability   The principal or employer ordinarily is not liable for an agent's or employee's crimes, unless the principal or employer actually aids or participates in their commission. The commission of a crime usually requires a state of mind that is specified in the criminal statute. Thus, if the principal or employer had not authorized the crime, the courts would conclude that the requisite mental state has not been shown. A principal or employer will be held criminally liable for acts done by an agent or employee to further an illegal business. In addition, most states have enacted statutes that hold a principal or employer liable for certain crimes committed by their agents or employees, even though they acted disobediently. Examples of such statutes are those that penalize the sale of impure foods or alcoholic beverages. Principals or employers may also be penalized for the acts of managerial or advisory persons who are acting in the scope of authority or employment, unless they act in disobedience of instructions and not for the purpose of serving the principal or employer. Although principals can, in some cases, be held liable for the criminal activity of their subordinates, they will generally be fined but not imprisoned, because most states have enacted laws that prevent imprisonment for vicarious crimes.

Sovereign Immunity and the Federal Government   **Sovereign immunity** is a doctrine preventing a lawsuit against a government authority without the government's consent. The doctrine is no longer as important a defense for government torts as it once was. The Federal Tort Claims Act of 1946 limits the federal government's sovereign immunity. Whenever a federal employee harms a third party or private property while driving a motor vehicle in the course of employment, the federal government is liable. However, the 1946 law explicitly preserves governmental immunity for a vaguely defined category of "discretionary" actions by officials.

EXAMPLE 33-8:   Above-Ground Radioactive Fallout

In 1982, a federal district court judge held that radioactive fallout from above-ground nuclear tests had caused at least nine people and perhaps dozens of others to die of cancer. The judge ruled that the federal government must pay damages under the Federal Tort Claims Act, explaining that while the high-level decision to conduct the tests had been discretionary, and thus was immune from liability, officials had conducted the tests in a negligent manner by failing to monitor radiation adequately or warn residents of neighboring areas in Nevada, southern Utah, and northern Arizona who lived downwind from the test site about radiation hazards and how to reduce them. A federal appeals court, however, held that all aspects of the testing program were conducted in accordance with discretionary decisions of the Atomic Energy Commission and were thus immune from liability. The U.S. Supreme Court in 1988 refused to hear an appeal from the appellate decision.

Sovereign Immunity, *Respondeat Superior,* and the States

The doctrine of sovereign immunity has been abolished or at least modified in some states by judicial decision and in others by legislation. However, the formula for determining when the government is liable for its own torts and for the torts of its employees, and when it retains its immunity, is often difficult to unravel. Generally, the starting point is to determine whether the state has a statute for preserving or eliminating sovereign immunity. If a statute exists that preserves immunity, the next step would be to determine whether the state has established any exceptions to the elimination of sovereign immunity. These exceptions would override sovereign immunity and permit a plaintiff to sue the state. For instance, even if immunity has been preserved in most cases, it might be forfeited if the action complained about involves a government employee's negligence while working for a state agency involved in the state's proprietary activities or its governmental functions.

The final step would be to determine if any defenses are available to the state that would permit the state to escape liability, even though its sovereign immunity has been removed. Many states have special statutes that list the defenses that can be used by the state to reassert its sovereign immunity. Because a state government can only act through its employees, some of these defenses focus on the actions of those employees and echo the doctrine of *respondeat superior.* Generally, this criterion begins by establishing that in most situations, the employees of the state government or of a political subdivision of the state government are immune from litigation under the doctrine of sovereign immunity. Thus, the statute will generally preserve sovereign immunity if the actions of the employee were discretionary in nature but will impose liability if the actions were performed outside the scope of their employment or outside of their official duties, or if their actions were reckless, malicious, wanton, or in bad faith. Sometimes the legislature will also create special statutes that impose liability for certain specifically named activities. Thus, a state might make school bus drivers liable automatically for not stopping at railroad crossings. Or it might make school nurses liable for not reporting a case of suspected child abuse to the proper authorities, and so on.

A Question of Ethics

In Example 33-8, a federal appeals court decided that the discretionary nature of the atomic tests conducted by the U.S. government made the federal government immune from liability. This ruling meant that legally, the government did not have to compensate anyone injured as a result of those tests. However, was it ethical for the government to ignore the claims of the injured parties? Explain.

The Opening Case Revisited, Part I
Cramer v. Auglaize Acres, Round 2

The *Cramer* case at the beginning of this chapter is a classic example of how the doctrines of *respondeat superior* and sovereign immunity play out in a lawsuit. When Rex Cramer brought his lawsuit against Auglaize Acres, he had to establish that the home was operated by the county commissioners of Auglaize County. He did so because, as an extension of the county government, the county home was considered a subdivision of the state, and the nurses who had cared for Cramer's father, Frank, at the time of his accident therefore were government employees. Using the doctrine of *respondeat superior*, Cramer could sue both the nurses whose conduct led directly to Frank's death and Auglaize County, which ran the home. In response, the county filed a motion to dismiss under a state statute that established sovereign immunity for all political subdivisions of the state. Cramer's attorney had anticipated this move and argued that though the statute established sovereign immunity for state subdivisions, it also created several exceptions to the rule. One such exception occurs when an employee is accused of negligent conduct while working for a state subdivision which is performing a proprietary function, such as owning and operating a nursing home. The burden then shifted back to the county, which had to raise a defense to Cramer's exception. The county defended itself by noting that even if the exception were valid, the county would not lose its immunity unless the injury to Frank had been caused by malice, bad faith, reckless behavior, or wanton conduct.

Quick Quiz 33-1 True or False?

1. Agency is an area of the law that arose because of the physical restraints imposed on people by the natural rules of the universe.

2. When a master loans a servant to another master, the servant is known as an independent contractor.

3. Most states have enacted laws that will prevent imprisonment for vicarious crimes.

33-2 Principles of Agency

Now that the different types of relationships involved in business have been discussed, the focus of the chapter can return to the principal–agent relationship. Several key guidelines help the courts distinguish among different types of principals and the different types of agents. Other principles help explain how agency law relates to minors and how it relates to business organizations.

Types of Principals and Agents

There are three types of principals. A **disclosed principal** is one whose identity is known by third parties dealing with that principal's agent. When an agent does not reveal the existence of an agency relationship but appears to act on his or her own behalf rather than for another, an **undisclosed principal** exists. A **partially disclosed principal** exists when the agent, in dealing with third parties, reveals the existence of an agency relationship but does not identify the principal. Agents are generally classified according to the scope of their responsibility. A **general agent** is a person who is given broad authority to act on behalf of the principal in conducting the bulk of the principal's business activity on a daily basis.

EXAMPLE 33-9: The General Duties of a General Manager

Jay Crockett, manager of the Inverness New and Used Car Shop, hired Thompson Decorators, Inc., to redecorate the showroom at Inverness. Crockett also employed two new used car salespeople to work the showroom on the weekends. As a general agent, Crockett has the authority to take these independent actions, which protect and promote the interests of the dealership.

A **special agent** is a person who is authorized to conduct only a particular transaction, conduct a series of related transactions, or perform only a specified act for the principal. Examples are real estate brokers, lawyers, and accountants who are retained to do a specific job and whose authority is restricted to those acts necessary to accomplish it. A **factor**, or common merchant, is a special agent who is employed to sell merchandise consigned for that purpose. The factor has possession of the goods and sells them for and on behalf of a principal. A factor who guarantees the credit of a third party to a principal and guarantees the solvency of the purchaser and performance of the contract is known as a *del credere* **agent**. In the event of default, the *del credere* agent is liable to the principal.

EXAMPLE 33-10: The Antique Agent

Edna Freeman hired Leonard Tenpenny to act as her agent in the sale of several antiques. The contract of agency included a promise by Tenpenny that Freeman would not suffer any loss because of any sales on credit that Tenpenny made with third parties. Shortly after, Tenpenny sold a rare first edition of one of Louis Bromfield's novels, valued at $50,000, to Robert Fisher on credit. Fisher later declared bankruptcy. As a *del credere* agent, Tenpenny had guaranteed the credit of Fisher and is liable to Freeman for the value of the book.

Liability of Principals and Agents

The principal is liable for all contracts that a general or special agent may enter into with third parties, as long as the agent acts within the authority conferred by the principal. An undisclosed principal can be held liable for the acts of the agent once the identity of the principal is disclosed. Once the principal's identity is revealed, a third party may sue either the principal or the agent. Following this election however, the third party cannot later decide to sue the other, unless the principal was undisclosed at the time the choice was made.

When an agent is not known to be an agent and is acting as a principal, the agent can be held liable as a principal. When a person is known to be an agent, but it is not known for whom the agent acts, the third party can also hold the agent liable. In addition, when an agent exceeds the authority conferred by the principal, the agent can be made personally liable.

Minors and Business Associations

The law of agency frequently interacts with the laws related to *minors*. For example, a principal may not use the infancy of an agent as a reason for avoiding a contract made by that agent. The principal who is a minor may generally avoid or accept a contract made by an agent to the same extent that he or she could have, had the principal dealt directly with the third party. However, state statutes are not universal in the way they treat the business contracts of minors. Some state courts have held that a minor who is sufficiently mature to run a business may not avoid business-related contracts made while running the business.

EXAMPLE 33-11:   Minors, Business, and Agency Liability

Lew Shaver, a minor who owned a sports card shop, hired Quilla Henderson, an adult, as shop manager. Henderson contracted with a supply house to purchase six new display cases for the shop. Shaver refused to accept delivery or pay for the cases. In the event the court interprets this transaction to be reasonably related to the carrying on of Shaver's business, it could hold that the purchase agreement was binding on Shaver.

The activities of all *business associations*, from partnerships to corporations, also interact with agency law. Almost every executive of a business firm acts as the firm's agent in some capacity. For example, a purchasing agent is authorized to make agreements to buy equipment and supplies. A salesperson may be authorized to complete sales agreements. The treasurer can dispense the firm's money. The operation of partnerships and corporations illustrates the application of agency law.

Partnerships   The Uniform Partnership Act and the partners' agreement govern partnership operations. Every partner in a partnership is an agent of that partnership for the purpose of its business. Thus, partners as agents are liable for the contracts that each makes on behalf of the business. The appointment of an agent by one partner is binding on all other partners.

EXAMPLE 33-12:   Partners, Business, and Agency Liability

Yuri Korolyov and Sergei Leonov operated the Russian Space Collectibles Shop as partners. During Leonov's vacation, Korolyov ordered a large selection of cosmonaut hats. Although Leonov was not present and might disagree with the selection of merchandise, he will be liable for his share of the expense. Korolyov was acting as agent for the partnership, representing both himself and Leonov.

Corporations   A corporation is an artificial person created by state statute, which authorizes it to provide and deliver products and/or services by means of the agents acting on its behalf (see Chapter 38). All aspects of agency law pertaining to wrongful acts committed by agents against third parties or their property also apply to corporations. A corporation, being a legal entity only, cannot act for itself. All officers and employees are either agents or servants of the corporation, the principal.

Quick Quiz 33-2 True or False?

1. A partially disclosed principal exists when the agent, in dealing with third parties, reveals only the existence of the agency but not the identity of the principal.

2. A principal may not use the minority of an agent to avoid a contract made by that minor agent.

3. Corporations never need to deal through agents.

33-3 Creation of the Agency Relationship

An agency is created by some action or conduct on the part of the principal. A would-be agent cannot by conduct alone or by any statement establish an agency relationship. It is therefore wise for a third party, when dealing with an agent, to determine the nature and extent of the agent's authority. An agency relationship is generally created by the following methods:

LO8
LO9
LO10

- By appointment and implication
- By necessity and operation of law
- By estoppel and ratification

Agency by Appointment and Implication

The usual agency relationship is created by *appointment*. In an agency by appointment, the principal expressly hires or otherwise engages the agent to act for and on behalf of the principal. The agreement may be oral or written in the form of a power of attorney. A **power of attorney** is an instrument in writing by which one person, a principal, appoints another as agent and confers the authority to perform certain specified acts on behalf of the principal. It establishes the authority of the agent to third parties with whom the agent may deal.

EXAMPLE 33-13:   Limitations on the Power of Attorney

Olga Stepford employed Samuel Benson as an agent to develop a recently purchased tract of land in Texas. Specifically, she wanted to drill for oil on the land. She executed a power of attorney authorizing Benson to contract for the purchase or sale of any property and to execute any necessary leases affecting Stepford's interest in the Texas property. Benson also had the power to hire drillers to search for the oil. Benson hired The Tornado Drilling Company to commence drilling operations. Two weeks into the drilling, Eddie Krebs, the owner of Tornado, came to Benson and asked for a loan so that he could make some outstanding late payments on his drilling equipment. If he failed to make the payments, his equipment would be repossessed and the drilling would stop. Benson made the loan using Stepford's funds.

Krebs later defaulted on the loan and left the country, vanishing without a trace. When Stepford attempted to hold Benson liable for the lost funds loaned to Krebs, the agent argued that the power of attorney granted him by Stepford empowered him to make the loan. In an interpretation of the terms of the power of attorney, the court reasoned that Benson's power to purchase, sell, lease, and hire drillers did not include the power to make a loan.

An agency by *implication* may be created voluntarily by any conduct or actions of the principal and agent that reflect the intent to create an agency relationship, even though such intent is not expressed orally or in writing. Any conduct or words of the principal that give another cause to believe that the principal approves of that person acting as agent is sufficient to create an agency. Allowing a person to act as an agent knowingly and without objection is also viewed as permission to act as an agent. Often when an agency relationship is created by appointment, the words used to make the appointment and spell out the agent's powers and abilities may not include everything that the agent is permitted to do. Thus, when a principal appoints an agent to handle the sale of her house, she might not say directly to the agent that he has the power to permit a prospective buyer to inspect the basement and the garage of the house. Such powers, however, would be created by implication.

Equal-Dignities Rule   In most states, the equal-dignities rule provides that when a principal authorizes an agent to enter into a written contract on behalf of the principal, the agent's authority to do so must also be in writing. The rule generally applies when the type of contract that the authorized person is to negotiate for another is required by the Statute of Frauds to be in writing.

Agency by Necessity and by Law

An agency by *necessity* is created lawfully when circumstances make such an agency necessary. If, for example, a real estate agent contracts for the repair of burst water pipes in the absence of the owner whose property the agent has been employed to sell, the court would hold that an agency of necessity had been created to prevent loss to the owner (principal). The courts may create or find an agency by *law* when there is none if it appears from the facts that a necessity or desired social policy is involved. A child to whom a parent has failed to provide the necessities of life may be declared by the court an agent of the parent for the purpose of purchasing necessities the parent failed to provide. Under such an agency relationship, the parent would be bound by such contracts as long as they are reasonable.

EXAMPLE 33-14:   The Need for Agency by Necessity

Andy Farmington, the father of six children, placed an advertisement in the classified section of the local newspaper stating that he would no longer be responsible for any bills unless contracted by him. He then abandoned his family. His wife, Emily Farmington, bought food and clothing for the children and herself. She also took the two youngest children to the doctor and purchased the antibiotics ordered by the doctor for the children. Mrs. Farmington charged everything to her husband. Under these circumstances, Mrs. Farmington had become an agent by necessity, and her husband would be responsible for contracts made by her for all reasonable necessaries of life.

The Opening Case Revisited, Part II

Cramer v. Auglaize Acres, Round 3

In the *Cramer* case at the beginning of the chapter, Rex Cramer, the plaintiff, argued that Auglaize County, which operated Auglaize Acres, was liable for the tortuous conduct of two nursing employees. In his attempt to extend liability from the nurses to the home, Cramer used two alternative legal theories: *respondeat superior* and agency by estoppel. We have examined *respondeat superior* at length, but the second theory, agency by estoppel, could use a bit more attention. Cramer raised the agency by estoppel argument on the off chance that Auglaize Acres might argue that the nurses were not employees but were instead independent contractors. As independent contractors, *respondeat superior* would not apply, and Auglaize Acres would not be liable. Agency by estoppel would remedy this situation for Cramer. In essence, Cramer could argue that even though the nurses were not really employees, Auglaize Acres made it appear as if they were. Auglaize might have done so by issuing name tags and uniforms to the nurses and giving them responsibilities that would lead a resident like Frank to believe that they were actually employees. Thus, Cramer could argue, the administrators who run Auglaize Acres cannot now ignore or deny that their actions created the impression that the nurses were employees. Agency by estoppel is also known as apparent authority because, as in this case, Auglaize Acres made it *appear* as if the nurses had *authority* that they did not really have. Under apparent authority, it is the appearance, not the reality, that matters.

Agency by Estoppel and by Ratification

An agency by *estoppel* is created when one person is falsely represented to be an agent when no such agency relationship exists, or when an agent is falsely represented to possess authority outside the scope of his or her actual authority. Agency by estoppel is also known as apparent authority. Although apparent authority is often thought of within the context of contract law, it is also used in tort law. In hospitals, for example, physicians and other health care professionals, who are actually independent contractors, may appear to the patient to be agents of the hospital. Under these circumstances, a hospital might be held liable for the negligence of the health care practitioner. This holding would occur if the hospital presents itself to the public as a dispenser of health care assistance and if the patient believes that the hospital, rather than a particular professional, is providing that assistance. Apparent authority is covered in more detail in Chapter 34.

Agents sometimes perform acts on behalf of the principal that exceed their authority. In such cases, the principal for whom the agent claimed to act may either ignore the transaction or affirm it by *ratification*. **Ratification** occurs when the principal approves the unauthorized act performed by an agent or by one who has no authority to act as an agent. Although an agent generally is personally liable to third parties for actions in excess of the agent's authority, this liability is not true when the third party knows that the agent has exceeded the proper level of authority.

In addition to an intent to ratify, certain other conditions must be fulfilled for ratification to be valid: The principal must have the capacity to ratify and have knowledge of all the material facts. The act to be ratified must be legal and been done on behalf of the principal. Moreover, the ratification must apply to the entire act of the agent, and ratification must occur before the third party withdraws. The principal cannot accept the benefits of an unauthorized act and then refuse to accept the obligations that are part of it. The principal becomes bound as though the agent had authority to act.

Agency by Electronics

The Uniform Computer Information Transactions Act (UCITA) is valuable because it clearly establishes the nature of an electronic agent. According to UCITA, an *electronic agent* (also referred to as a *cyber agent* or *e-agent*) can be characterized as a computer program that acts without human intervention to begin an activity, answer cybermessages, deliver or accept *electronic mail*, or enter electronic contracts as a representative of an individual who does not intervene in the action taken by the electronic agent at the actual time of the electronic agent's activity. It is clear then that a *bot* (*robot*, *shopping bot*, *cyberbot*, or *e-bot*) that searches cyberspace for the lowest price in a contract, sifts through the Internet for the best accommodations, hunts cyberspace for the most economical plan, or spontaneously responds to a bidding process during an electronic auction is an electronic agent. The UCITA makes it clear that a principal, now termed an *electronic principal*, who places authority in the "hands" of an electronic agent will be liable for the electronic contracts entered by that electronic agent, even if the electronic principal remains ignorant of what the electronic agent has done because the electronic principal either ignores or forgets about the automated process.

Another model act, the Uniform Electronic Transactions Act (UETA), has legitimized the use of electronic agents by certifying that contracts made by electronic agents have the same binding effect as contracts created by human agents. The net effect of these provisions is to guarantee that a company that has used an electronic agent to receive and process an order sent by an electronic agent will not be able to deny the effectiveness of that electronic contract. The provisions also state that once an individual has received an e-mail, he or she is considered to have received notice of an e-contract, even if that person ignores or trashes the e-mail without opening or reading it. The UETA also says that e-agents must be programmed to give the other party a confirmation that the electronic contract has been entered. Otherwise, the e-contract is voidable by that party.

Quick Quiz 32-3 True or False?

1. The equal dignities rule has been outlawed in most states.

2. An agency by estoppel is created when one person is falsely represented to be an agent when no such agency relationship exists.

3. Ratification occurs when the principal approves the unauthorized act performed by an agent.

Summary

33.1   Agency is the legal fiduciary relationship that exists when the principal authorizes the agent to create, modify, or end contractual relations involving the principal and third parties. The contracts that the agent negotiates are between the principal and third parties, and the principal is bound to perform them as if the principal had personally executed the agreement. The courts are often called upon to distinguish among relationships between principal and agent, employer and employee, master and servant, and proprietor and independent contractor. The main difference between the principal–agent and employer–employee relationships is the agent's authority to contract. The terms master (employer) and servant (employee) are used when questions of tort liability arise. Even though all people are responsible for their own tortuous conduct, there are times when the law will hold not only the actual tortfeasor but also the person who engaged the tortfeasor liable for the tort. The name given to this type of liability is vicarious liability.

32.2   Any person legally capable of entering into a contract may be a principal. There are three kinds of principals—disclosed, undisclosed, or partially disclosed. Anyone may be appointed an agent. Agents are commonly classified as general agents, special agents,

factor, and *del credere* agents. A principal is liable on all contracts that a general or special agent enters into, as long as the agent acts with the authority of the principal. An agent acting as a principal can be held liable as a principal. Partnerships, corporations, and other businesses all act through agents.

33.3   An agency relationship generally may be created by appointment, implication, necessity, or operation of law. Under certain circumstances, the principal may be legally prevented (estopped) from asserting that the agent's act was unauthorized. Ratification by the principal of an unauthorized act by another person does not create agency, but it has the effect of agency. When the principal does not ratify another's unauthorized act, the person who acted without authority is personally liable for the contract.

Key Terms

agency, 683	independent contractor, 685	scope of employment, 688
agent, 683	master, 685	servant, 685
borrowed servant, 689	negligent hiring, 690	sovereign immunity, 692
consensual, 684	negligent retention, 690	special agent, 695
del credere agent, 695	nondelegable duty, 690	*sui generis*, 683
disclosed principal, 694	partially disclosed principal, 695	third party, 683
factor, 695	power of attorney, 697	undisclosed principal, 695
general agent, 695	principal, 683	vicarious liability, 686
gratuitous agency, 684	proprietor, 685	
gratuitous agent, 684	ratification, 699	

Questions for Review and Discussion

1. What is the nature of the agency relationship?
2. What is vicarious liability?
3. What are the different types of principals?
4. What are the different types of agents?
5. How does liability flow to agents?
6. How are principals liable?
7. How do agents relate to business associations?
8. How are agency relationships created?
9. What is the purpose of the Uniform Computer Information Transactions Act?
10. What is the purpose of the Uniform Electronic Transactions Act?

Cases for Analysis

1. During batting practice in the batting cages at Howland High School, while under the supervision of baseball coach Thomas Eschman, Jeffrey Elston was injured when a ball hit a protective screen, ricocheted, and struck him in the head. Elston was life-flighted to Cleveland by helicopter, where he was treated for head injuries at Rainbow Babies and Children's Hospital. Later Elston's parents brought suit against the high school. The school pointed to a state statute that granted state subdivisions, such as the school district, sovereign immunity. Elston's parents argued that the actions under scrutiny involved a school-related activity located on government-owned property, which clearly made it one of the exceptions to the sovereign immunity rule. The school district defended itself by arguing that the coach's actions not only represented a legitimate exercise of his professional discretion but were also carried out in good faith and were free from wanton, reckless, or malicious conduct. Should the school district escape liability here? Explain. *Elston v. Howland Local Schools,* 113 Ohio St.3d 314 (Ohio Supreme Court).

2. A delivery truck driver who worked for the *Evening Star* in Washington, D.C., was on his route when he was commanded by a police officer to follow a traffic violator to apprehend him. The police officer then jumped onto the side of the truck and held on for the duration of the chase. During the high-speed pursuit, Balinovic was injured when the truck collided with his car. Balinovic wanted to sue both the driver and the *Evening Star* under the theory of vicarious liability. Would vicarious liability apply here? Was the driver a servant of the *Evening Star?* Was the driver operating within the scope of employment? Explain. *Balinovic v. Evening Star Newspaper Co.,* 113 F.2d 505 (D.C. Cir.).

3. Janet Young worked in an administrative capacity for the International Brotherhood of Locomotive Engineers. She was given a 10-year contract by John Sytsma, the president of the union. The president regularly engaged in hiring union employees without consulting with either the executive committee or the advisory board of the union. In addition, the president entered into other contracts on behalf of the union. Although these powers were not specified in the constitution, the union knew that he dealt with the hiring of employees and that he routinely entered nonemployment contracts on behalf of the union. Sometime after Sytsma was defeated in a reelection bid, Larry McFather, the new president, discharged Young. McFather argued that Sytsma did not have the capacity to enter a 10-year employment contract with Young because the authority to do so was not specified in the union's constitution. In addition, McFather pointed out that the contract had been entered during the union's convention, during which the power to govern the union falls to the delegates at the convention. In response, Young argued that the past practices of the union led her to the reason-

able belief that the president had the power to grant her the employment contract. She also argued that even though the power to hire employees was not in the union constitution, the power to do so was implied by the powers of the president to preside over the union's administrative matters. Is Young correct on either of these points? Explain. *Young v. International Brotherhood of Locomotive Engineers,* 683 N.E.2d 420 (OH).

4. Mularchuk was employed as a part-time reserve police officer for the borough of Keansburg, New Jersey. He was never given any training, and he was not required to submit to any training with respect to the revolver he carried. A quarrel arose between McAndrew, who had car trouble, and a towtruck driver whom McAndrew had called for assistance. Mularchuk proceeded to make arrests and, in the course of events, shot and seriously injured McAndrew. Was the borough of Keansburg liable to McAndrew under the doctrine of *respondeat superior?* Explain. *McAndrew v. Mularchuk,* 162 A.2d 820 (NJ).

5. Food Caterers, Inc., had a franchise agreement with Chicken Delight, Inc. Carfiro was employed by Food Caterers to deliver hot chicken bearing the trademark "Chicken Delight." While making a delivery, Carfiro was involved in an accident that killed McLaughlin. In a suit naming Chicken Delight, the franchiser, as defendant, the McLaughlin estate argued that Carfiro was an agent of Chicken Delight, because Carfiro was acting for the benefit of the company. There was no evidence, however, that Carfiro was hired, paid, instructed by, or even known by Chicken Delight. The decision was for whom, and why? *Estate of McLaughlin v. Chicken Delight, Inc.,* 321 A.2d 456 (CT).

6. While Elliot was an inmate at the state-run Chillicothe Correctional Institution, he was hit in the face by Turner, a corrections officer at the institution and therefore a state employee. Elliot brought a lawsuit against the state under the doctrine of *re-spondeat superior.* The state argued that because Turner had acted recklessly in striking Elliot, his actions were outside the scope of his employment. Therefore, the state concluded, the court should dismiss Elliot's claim against it. Were Turner's actions outside the scope of his employment as a prison guard? Explain. *Elliot v. Ohio Department of Rehabilitation and Correction,* 637 N.E.2d 106 (OH).

7. Nielson had limited authority to purchase cattle for his principal, Hauser Packing Company. Christensen, who knew of Nielson's limited authority and also knew that Nielson was exceeding that authority, nevertheless contracted with Nielson to sell cattle to the packing company. When the packing company refused to accept the cattle, Christensen brought suit against Nielson for damages, showing that Hauser Packing Company refused to ratify the unauthorized act of its agent. The judgment was for whom, and why? *Christensen v. Nielson,* 276 P. 645 (UT).

8. Hoddeson entered the showroom of the Koos Brothers Furniture Store, along with her aunt and four young children. She was met by a man dressed in a suit. He asked if he could help her, and she consented. He showed her several pieces of bedroom furniture, including a mirror that she liked very much. She eventually decided on several pieces of furniture and gave the man cash in the amount of the purchases. He then told her that the items that she had requested were out of stock but that they would be shipped very soon. The furniture items were never shipped to the Hoddesons, who eventually found out that there was no record of either the transaction or the alleged sales clerk. The Hoddesons brought suit against Koos Brothers. What argument can the Hoddesons use that might persuade the court that Koos Brothers should be held liable for their loss? Explain your response. *Hoddeson v. Koos Brothers,* 135 A.2d 702 (NJ).

Quick Quiz Answers

33-1	33-2	33-3
1. T	1. T	1. F
2. F	2. T	2. T
3. T	3. F	3. T

Chapter 34 — Agency Operation

The Opening Case

Scott v. Ross, Workman, Simpson, and the Cult Awareness Network

Kathy Tonkin and her six children were members of an organization known as the Life Tabernacle Church (Tabernacle). After 12 months within the Tabernacle, Tonkin left the church because she was convinced that it was a harmful cult. When she left the Tabernacle, she took her three youngest children with her, but the three oldest children, Scott, Thysen, and Matthew, decided not to leave. Tonkin called the Seattle Community Service hotline, which referred her to Shirley Landa, a high-profile anti-cult activist associated with a group called the Cult Awareness Network (CAN). Landa was one of the organizers of a group called the Citizens Freedom Foundation, the forerunner of CAN. She was also on CAN's list of contacts in Washington, received about five referrals from CAN every year, and formerly had been a member of the CAN board. The Cult Awareness Network relies primarily on contact people like Landa to act as their field agents; CAN expressly asks contact people to say that they are "assisting on behalf of CAN." In this case, after being contacted by Tonkin and reviewing the case, Landa recommended that Tonkin contact Rick Ross, a professional deprogrammer who frequently worked on behalf of CAN. Ross successfully deprogrammed Thysen and Matthew, the two younger Tonkin children, but did not succeed in deprogramming Scott. Ross, along with two of his associates, Mark Workman and Charles Simpson, took custody of Scott and detained him for five days, in an effort to deprogram him. After pretending to be won over, Scott got away from his captors and eventually brought this lawsuit against Ross and CAN. Attorneys for CAN argued that the case against the network should be dismissed because Ross was not its agent. In turn, Scott argued that Ross was referred by Landa, who was an agent of CAN, and that she had both express and implied authority to make such referrals. Scott pointed out that CAN had many such contact agents, that it operated mostly through those contact agents, that those contact agents had the express authority to say that they assisted CAN, that CAN itself had a long history of using deprogrammers like Ross, and that CAN knew about the activities of Ross. Therefore, Scott concluded, Ross was working as an agent of CAN. Both the trial court and the appellate court agreed. (See *Scott v. Ross, Workman, Simpson, and the Cult Awareness Network,* Case No. 96-35050, U.S. Court of Appeals for the Ninth Circuit.)

Opening Case Questions

1. What is express and implied authority?

2. Does it make any difference to Scott's argument that Landon is a gratuitous agent? Explain.

3. Could Scott have argued that Landon's authority was apparent rather than express or implied? Explain.

4. If the case had been based on apparent authority, would the outcome have changed? Explain.

5. Why did CAN choose to disavow its relationship with Ross and Landon? Explain.

 Learning Objectives

1. Distinguish between express and implied agency authority.
2. Define apparent authority.
3. Explain the consequences of an unauthorized delegation of agency authority.
4. Indicate when an agent can legally appoint a subagent.
5. Enumerate the duties of an agent to the principal.
6. List the remedies available to a principal.
7. Clarify the duties that a principal has in relation to an agent.
8. Disclose the remedies of an agent.
9. Name the ways that an agency relationship can be terminated.
10. Identify who is entitled to a notice that an agency has ended.

34-1 Scope of an Agent's Authority

Agents may perform only acts that have been authorized by the principal. Agents who exceed their delegated authority become personally liable. Unauthorized actions do not bind the principal unless those actions can be reasonably assumed by a third party to be within the scope of the agent's authority. Authority granted to an agent may be express, implied, or apparent.

Express, Implied, and Apparent Authority

The agent's **express authority** is the authority that the principal voluntarily and specifically sets forth as oral or written instructions in the agency agreement. Sometimes referred to as *actual authority,* express authority may also be indicated by conduct, as when a sales representative informs the principal of travel plans, and no objection to them is expressed. **Implied authority** is the agent's authority to perform acts that are necessary or customary to carry out expressly authorized duties. It stems from the reasonable effort of an agent to understand the meaning of the principal's words describing what the agent is to do. Implied authority can be described as *incidental authority* when the acts performed are reasonably necessary to carry out an express authority. For example, an agent might have incidental authority to contract for the repair of the principal's van that broke down while being used to deliver perishable products that the agent had express authority to sell and deliver. Implied authority may be described as *customary authority* when the agent acts in conformity with the general trade or professional practices of the business.

Talking Points

Oliver Wendell Holmes Jr., one of the most powerful and influential legal minds of the nineteenth century, and his twenty-first-century counterpart, Richard Posner, have some very interesting ideas on the nature of agency. After reading the following quotations, consider the underlying implications that these ideas have for human nature, in general, and the concept of freedom, in particular, especially as these ideas relate to agency and employment.

"This is the progress of ideas as shown us by history; and that is what is meant by saying that the characteristic feature which justifies agency as a title of the law is the absorption *pro hac vice* of the agent's individuality in that of his principal."—Oliver Wendell Holmes Jr., *The Common Law* (New York: Barnes and Noble Books, 2004), 143.

"The natural state of human beings is one not of equality but of dependence on more powerful human beings. Economic freedom, including freedom of contract, in the classical liberal sense is one of the luxuries established by social organization."—Richard Posner, *Overcoming Law* (Cambridge: Harvard University Press, 1995), 300–301.

Consider the following questions: Is Holmes correct that the underlying concept of agency is based on the disappearance of the agent's individuality into the principal, so that the agent, from a legal standpoint at least, ceases to exist? If so, is this concept explained by Posner's declaration that the basic human state is one of dependence on more powerful beings? In the agency relationship, is the principal always the more powerful of the two members? Consider the following agency relationships and explore the question of whether the agent in fact disappears into the principal. Also consider whether the agent or the principal holds more power in these relationships: (1) attorney–client; (2) stock broker–investor; (3) seller–real estate agent; (4) trustor–trustee; (5) CEO–corporation; (6) department store–sales clerk; (7) manager–hotel owner; (8) partner–partner; (9) president–college; and (10) ward–guardian.

Apparent authority is an accountability doctrine whereby a principal, by virtue of words or actions, leads a third party to believe that an agent has authority, even though no such authority was intended. Apparent authority is sometimes referred to as *agency by estoppel, apparent agency*, and *ostensible agency*. The principal may make known to the third party in a variety of ways that such authority exists. For instance, it may be generated by making a direct statement to the third party, permitting someone to have a meaningful business title, enabling someone to occupy a position of authority, or allowing someone to perform duties that give a third party reason to believe that the person has the authority to act for the principal. Sometimes apparent authority can even arise because the principal fails to act in some way. For example, apparent authority may be created if the principal terminates an agent's actual authority but fails to give proper notice of that termination to those who are entitled to receive such notice. Such apparent authority is sometimes referred to as **lingering apparent authority**.

EXAMPLE 34-1:   Limiting Lingering Authority

Sabastian Sandoval worked as a purchasing agent for BiblioBuyers, Inc., a used-book company that recycled used textbooks, purchased primarily from college professors. Sandoval generally visited professors in their offices and paid them in cash for their used books. Occasionally, he would take the books and promise a cash payment on his next visit. When he did this, he would give each professor a credit receipt, written out on BiblioBuyers letterhead, indicating the title of the books he'd purchased and the total amount the company owed to each individual. Sometimes this debt amounted only to a few dollars per instructor. However, in some cases, it amounted to hundreds of dollars. Later, when Sandoval was discharged by BiblioBuyers, the company did not notify any of the professors on his regular route. Sandoval took advantage of this oversight by visiting those professors on his route, taking their books, and giving them credit receipts on BiblioBuyers letterheads. He then took the books and sold them to Alpha-Best-Bet Book Buyers, BiblioBuyers' fiercest competitor. When the professors demanded their money, BiblioBuyers discovered Sandoval's deceit. Because the company had not notified the professors, the company had clothed Sandoval with lingering apparent authority. The company could have limited its liability by informing the professors about Sandoval's termination.

The party with whom the agent is dealing must reasonably believe that the agent has authority to so act, have had no notice of a lack of such authority, and act or rely on the agent's appearance of authority. Once the principal clothes an agent with the semblance of

The Opening Case Revisited, Part I
Scott v. Ross, Workman, Simpson, and the Cult Awareness Network, Round 2

In The Opening Case at the beginning of the chapter, Kathy Tonkin contacted Shirley Landa to help rescue her oldest son Jason Scott from the influence of the Life Tabernacle Church (Tabernacle). Landa was a gratuitous agent who was connected to a group known as the Cult Awareness Network (CAN), an organization that formed to combat cults. Landa recommended that Tonkin contact Rick Ross, a deprogramming expert, who could rehabilitate Scott. Tonkin contacted Ross, who then took custody of Scott to begin the deprogramming procedure. Something went wrong however, and Scott got away from Ross. Scott then brought this lawsuit against Ross and CAN. In turn, CAN attempted to distance itself from Ross by claiming that Ross was not its agent. The court, however, did not buy this argument. Instead, it took notice of the fact that Ross had been recommended by Landa, who had the implied, if not the express, authority to make such referrals in the name of CAN. To prove this authority, the plaintiff had produced evidence demonstrating that CAN expressly told all of its contact agents, including Landa, to tell their clients that they assisted CAN in its work. The plaintiff had also verified that CAN was aware of Ross and his work and had on occasion used Ross directly. Finally, the plaintiff had established that CAN was aware that Landa recommended Ross for other deprogramming sessions. From all of this evidence, the court concluded that Landa had the express power to represent CAN and carry out its mission, part of which was to rescue young people who had been misled by cults. Within this express authority was the implied authority to do what was necessary to carry out that express authority. The express authority to assist CAN thus included the implied authority to recommend deprogramming agents such as Ross whom CAN had itself directly used in the past to carry out its anti-cult mission.

Did You Know?

In seventeenth century Europe, most monarchs appointed a favorite who acted like an agent in carrying out the monarch's private and public affairs. The favorite acted as the monarch's confidant, companion, proxy, and envoy. One famous example is Cardinal Richelieu (1585–1642), who acted as the royal favorite of King Louis XIII of France.

The Opening Case Revisited, Part II

Scott v. Ross, Workman, Simpson, and the Cult Awareness Network, Round 3

In The Opening Case at the beginning of the chapter, it was quite clear to the court that Landa had the actual authority to recommend deprogrammers like Ross to concerned parents like Tonkin. However, even if this had not been the case, there was enough evidence to hold CAN liable under the doctrine of apparent authority. Recall that apparent authority is created by something that the principal, in this case CAN, communicates to a third party, like Tonkin. Because CAN was in the habit of referring concerned parents to deprogrammers like Ross and because CAN had actually recommended Ross for deprogramming purposes in the past, it would not be unreasonable for Tonkin and others to assume that Landa, an actual agent of CAN, had that same authority. Thus, even if Landa had not had the actual authority to recommend Ross, she did have the apparent authority to do so.

authority, the principal cannot deny that the authority exists when another person has relied on that appearance. The doctrine of apparent authority protects innocent third parties who rely on the impression created by the principal's words, acts, or conduct that appropriate authority has been conferred on the agent.

In some states, apparent agency in hospitals has become the focus of tort reform. In such states, hospitals can avoid clothing independent health care practitioners, such as staff physicians, with apparent authority by posting notices that announce that the practitioners who render care in the hospital are independent contractors rather than hospital employees. The hospital may protect itself further by adding a sentence that specifically states that the hospital is not liable for the actions of such independent contractors, unless those actions are directly controlled by the hospital.

Appointment of Subagents

Agents are appointed by principals because of their assumed fitness to perform some particular job. Because principals rely on the agent's personal skill and integrity, they do not ordinarily give agents the power to delegate someone else to do the job they have agreed to do. Should an agent delegate authority without authorization, the acts of the subagent do not impose any obligation or liability on the principal to third parties. In some instances, the agent is permitted to delegate authority, even if the agency agreement does not contain an express power of delegation. Such an intention may be implied from the nature of the

A Question of Ethics

Suppose the director of a hospital knows that a physician is incompetent but allows the physician to continue to treat patients at that hospital. Suppose further that only the director knows of the problem and that there is no evidence to prove that the director knew of the physician's incompetence. Would it be ethical for the director to allow the hospital to escape liability in a malpractice suit based on the tort reform provision discussed here? Why or why not?

employment or custom and usage. A real estate broker, for example, has the implied authority to delegate authority to salespersons. The nature of the business is such that it is presumed that the principal (seller) contemplates that the authority given to the agent (broker) would be exercised through the broker's agents (subagents).

Exceptions to the Delegation of Authority

The purpose of agency cannot be criminal or contrary to public policy. In addition, some acts must be performed in person, not delegated to an agent. Nondelegable acts include, but are not limited to, voting, serving on juries, testifying in court, making a will, and holding public office. However, forms required by law, such as tax returns and license applications, may be executed by an agent provided that the identity of the principal, as well as the identity and capacity of the agent, are clearly shown.

Quick Quiz 34-1 True or False?

1. Apparent authority is the agent's authority to perform acts that are needed or customary in the performance of the principal's business.

2. Implied authority is generally referred to as agency by estoppel.

3. Apparent authority is never used in tort law.

34-2 The Agent's Obligations to a Principal

LO5

The agency relationship between agent and principal establishes rights and obligations that may be expressed in the agreement or merely implied. As noted in Chapter 33, an individual who acts as agent for another has a fiduciary relationship with the principal. This relationship implies the placement of trust and confidence in the agent that the agent will serve the principal's interests before all others. Thus, an agent may not enter any agency transaction in which the agent has a personal interest. An agent must also not take a position in conflict with the interest of the principal.

In compliance with the agency contract and the fiduciary relationship, various obligations are imposed on the agent. These obligations generally involve the following duties:

- To obey all instructions and be loyal to the principal.
- To exercise reasonable judgment, prudence, and skill and account for all property.
- To perform work personally and communicate fully with the principal.

Obedience and Loyalty

The agent, whether being paid or acting gratuitously, must obey all reasonable and legal instructions issued by the principal that relate to the agency agreement. In obeying the instructions of the principal, the agent is duty-bound to remain within the **scope of authority** (i.e., the range of acts authorized by the principal). For example, if the agent were to sell equipment to a third party in violation of the principal's instructions, the agent would be liable for any injury suffered by the principal.

An agent may not engage in any activity that would result in a conflict of interest with the business of the principal. This duty of loyalty implies strict and continuing faithfulness to the principal's best interests at all times. Hence, the agent must resist any temptation to use acquired confidential information to advance the agent's own interest at the expense of the principal's.

EXAMPLE 34-2:   The Dangers of Disloyalty

Carl Vermeer worked as the chief financial officer for Filodyne Electronics, Inc. In a meeting with Hannah Garrison, the CEO and president of Filodyne, Vermeer learned that Filodyne was about to patent a new nanomachine that would be capable of performing microsurgery on certain individuals to repair arterial blockages. Vermeer took this information and offered it to Kenneth Pierce, the president of Global Electronics, Inc., in exchange for a position with Global. In this scenario, there is no doubt that Vermeer violated his duty of loyalty to Filodyne and Garrison.

Real estate agents can work with both the buyer and the seller on the same transaction but must make full disclosure when they do.

Judgment, Prudence, Skill, and the Duty to Account

Agents imply that they possess the required knowledge, training, and skill to perform and carry out their agency obligations properly with reasonable care and diligence. Unless an agent claims to be an expert, the principal is entitled to expect that the agent has the degree of skill commonly displayed by others employed in similar work. An expert, such as a person in a profession requiring specific education and a special license, must use the expert judgment, prudence, and skill possessed by others who have been admitted to those professions. Whether an expert or not, the agent may be liable to the principal for losses resulting from personal neglect or incompetence.

The agent has a duty to keep a separate account of the principal's funds. Whatever money the agent receives during and as a result of the agency relationship is held in trust for the principal. An accounting must be given to the principal within a reasonable period of time after money or property is received or disbursed. Money collected by the agent must be held separate from funds belonging to the agent. If deposited in a bank, the money must be deposited in a separate account and so identified that a trust is apparent. Failure to keep such funds separate is known as *commingling*, and the agent may be held personally liable for any resulting losses.

EXAMPLE 34-3:   The Consequences of Commingling

In Example 34-1, we learned that Sandoval visited college professors and, whenever he found suitable used textbooks, paid the professors in cash for those books. Occasionally, Sandoval would also resell some of the books he bought from students. Whenever he made a cash collection from such sales, Sandoval would mix the money with his own cash. Unfortunately, when BiblioBuyers asked for an accounting, Sandoval could not remember which part of the cash belonged to him and which part was rightfully the property of BiblioBuyers. When BiblioBuyers asked for all of the cash, which was its right under agency law, Sandoval refused to turn over the cash. This problem with the cash turned out to be the precipitating event that led to his ultimate discharge.

Personal Service and Communication

The agency relationship is usually one involving an agreement for personal services. In the absence of the authority to do so, an agent may not delegate duties to others unless such duties are purely mechanical in nature and require no particular knowledge, training, skill, or responsibility.

The agent is duty-bound to keep the principal fully informed of all facts that materially affect the subject matter of the agency and that come to the agent's attention when acting within the agent's scope of authority. The law assumes that if an agent receives either notice or information, it was also communicated to the principal. Therefore, the rights and liabilities of the principal to any third party are the same as if the principal had personally received the notice or information.

> ## EXAMPLE 34-4:   A Commitment to Communicate
>
> Marcy Magliozzi instructed Barbara Harrison to purchase a particular furnished house on Catawba Island for her. While examining the final contract, Harrison discovered that several thousand books that were in the house would not be considered as part of the "furnishings" that went along with the sale. Despite this exception, Harrison completed the purchase for Magliozzi. A little later, Magliozzi discovered that the books did not come with the "furnished" house. Magliozzi demanded that the contract be voided. Because in the course of carrying out her duties and before buying the house, Harrison learned that the books were not part of the deal, the law assumes that Magliozzi had the same information. She cannot use the loss of the books as the basis for voiding the contract.

Remedies Available to the Principal

Remedies are always available when an agent fails to observe a duty owed to a principal. For instance, the principal may do one or more of the following:

- Terminate the agent's contract of employment.
- Withhold compensation otherwise due the agent.
- Recover profit the agent made in violation of agency obligations.
- Recover money or property gained or held by the agent to which the principal is entitled.
- Restrain the agent from continuing to breach the agency obligations.
- Recover damages from the agent for breach of the contract of employment or assessed against the principal for the agent's wrongdoing.
- Rescind a contract entered into by the agent based on an improper relationship between the agent and the third party.

Quick Quiz 34-2 True or False?

1. In obeying the orders of a principal, the agent has a duty to stay within the scope of authority granted by the principal.

2. The law assumes that information communicated to the principal is known by the agent.

3. The agent has a duty to keep a separate account of the principal's funds.

34-3 The Principal's Obligations to the Agent

The agreement between a principal and an agent creates the duties the principal owes to the agent. Even when the agency agreement is silent, there are implied obligations owed to the agent. Among the principal's actual and implied duties are the following obligations:

- To compensate, reimburse, and indemnify the agent
- To cooperate with the performance of the agent's duties

Compensation, Reimbursement, and Indemnification

The principal is under a duty to pay an agent an agreed amount or the fair value for work or services that the agent performs within the scope of authority or employment, unless the agent agrees to perform gratuitously. In addition, the principal must make salary deductions and payments to the government as are required by law. All states have statutes that provide for the enforcement of the payment of wages and that place penalties on delinquent employers. The agent may not recover compensation for illegal services, even though they were rendered at the request of the principal. The agent may also forfeit rights to compensation when the agent breaches his or her duties to the principal.

The principal is obligated to reimburse the agent for any reasonable expenses incurred while working on the principal's behalf and within the scope of the agent's authority or employment. The agent cannot recover for expenses due to the agent's own negligence. Recovery is also barred when expenses incurred by an agent are unnecessary or unreasonable in the discharge of the agency.

Agents are also entitled to **indemnification** (i.e., payment for loss or damage suffered) if they incur a loss or are damaged as a result of a request made by the principal. The obligation to pay for the agent's personal loss or damage, which may occur in the future or

---

Talking Points

The question of how human rights arise has been a perennial problem among legal philosophers. Two such philosophers, Jeffrie Murphy and Jules Coleman, suggest one answer, whereas Robert Paul Wolff proposes another. In their book *Philosophy of Law,* Murphy and Coleman state: "Rights protected by inalienability rules are not transferable. The right to one's freedom from servitude and the right to vote are examples of rights protected by inalienability rules." In contrast, Wolff writes in his essay "Beyond Tolerance" that "Those philosophers are therefore deeply mistaken who suppose that the social inheritance is a burden to be cast off, a spell from which we must be awakened. Without that inheritance the individual is exactly nothing—he has no organized core of personality into which his culture has not penetrated." Murphy and Coleman propose that certain human rights are inalienable; that is, they exist regardless of the social context. Wolff suggests that the human individual is nothing outside the social context. Which view is correct? How would these approaches to human nature affect agency rules? Agency appears to preserve individual integrity by permitting individuals to expand the scope of their activities, yet, it also evolves from the idea that the servant is absorbed into the master and therefore ceases to exist separate from the master. Which side of the dichotomy does agency law promote today? Explain.

BusinessWeek

Business Law in the News

An eBay for the Arts and Crafts Set

At the Brooklyn headquarters of online marketplace Etsy, which proclaims itself "your place to buy and sell all things handmade," there isn't an Aeron chair in sight. Instead, in keeping with the site's artisanal ethos, nearly everything is made or scavenged by a staff member. The computers are assembled from spare parts; the office halfpipe (for skateboarding) and stage (for bands) are built from salvaged wood. Except for the odd Ikea item, most of the furniture was found on the street.

With its casual offices, user-generated content, and snowballing word of mouth, Etsy fits the mold for a second-wave dot-com success story almost perfectly. Armed with $1 million in funding, the 35-person, two-year-old Etsy boasts more than 300,000 registered members. Some 50,000 are sellers, moving more than $12 million in goods and netting the company just over $1 million.

Etsy is the brainchild of 27-year-old co-founder Rob Kalin, who went to six colleges in five years before graduating from New York University. While working as a designer for getcrafty.com in 2005, he noticed the community site was conspicuously lacking an e-commerce component. Kalin and two friends set about building their own, hoping to create not just a cozier version of eBay for artisans but a company they would want to work for. That means employees are grouped into teams based on functions and everyone gets decent health insurance. Even though Kalin's grandfather, a veteran of IBM and General Electric, peppered him with questions about target audiences and market share, Kalin skipped the business plan. "There's so much you can't plan for, so instead of trying to fudge the numbers," he decided, "we'll just launch it and see."

"Don't Be Greedy"

Kalin isn't completely winging it. He has learned tons from the dot-comers before him. Although Etsy items are sold, not auctioned, its business model is similar to eBay's: Etsy collects a 20¢ listing fee and a 3.5% commission on each item sold. Etsy also sells slots in a showcase of featured items for $7 a day.

Kalin has stacked Etsy's board with high-profile Web startup veterans Caterina Fake, co-founder of Flickr, and Albert Wenger, former president of del.icio.us, both of which were acquired by Yahoo! Kalin says much of what he has taken away from them boils down to "don't be greedy." His board has advised him not to spend money he doesn't have, not to take in more investment than he needs, and to keep in mind that the Etsy community has high expectations.

So Kalin has turned down offers to sell banner ads. Meanwhile, he stages virtual town hall meetings and is tweaking the site to give sellers more visibility and keep them happy. "I now sell much better on Etsy than I do on eBay," says Kimberly Smith, who started selling hand-printed baby duds on Etsy two years ago. "People go to Etsy looking for something handmade, something unique," she says, while eBay attracts brand-name bargain-hunters.

Kalin chooses site improvements carefully, not wanting to alter Etsy's homegrown feel. A new payment system will allow buyers to purchase from multiple sellers in one transaction. Since Etsy sellers already hail from 84 different countries, adding currency conversion and foreign-language support is in the works for 2008. German publisher Hubert Burda Media has signed on as a partner and investor, and Kalin's team is scouting for offices in Berlin and London.

Kalin also hopes to expand Etsy's offline ventures. Etsy runs workshops open to local crafters and would like to provide support services, such as business advice and small loans. "The big goal is to enable people around the world to make a living making things," Kalin says, and that includes the man himself.

Questions for Analysis

1. Is Etsy the principal or the agent in its relationship with the artisans who sell on its site? Explain.

2. How is Etsy compensated for the work that it does for its artisan customers?

3. If Etsy does eventually allow buyers to buy from multiple sellers in one transaction, will it have violated its duty of loyalty? Explain.

(Continued)

is already suffered, is avoidable if the loss or damage results from an action the agent knew to be illegal or from the agent's negligence. Public policy also requires employers to indemnify employees for personal injury sustained in the course of employment, except for self-inflicted injury or intoxication. State worker's compensation laws hold that the cost of paying for such injury should be a part of the operating expense of the business.

Cooperation with the Agent

The principal, having granted the agent the duty to perform certain tasks, must not interfere with the performance of those tasks. Should the principal make the agent's job difficult or impossible, the principal has breached the duty of cooperation.

Remedies Available to the Agent

The remedies of an agent against a principal are based on the principal's breach of express or implied contract obligations. Where appropriate, the agent has the option of exerting one or more of the agent's rights:

- Leave the principal's employ.
- Recover damages for the principal's breach of contract.
- Recover the value of services rendered.
- Obtain reimbursement for payments made for the principal.
- Secure indemnity for personal liability sustained while performing an authorized act for the principal.

Quick Quiz 34-3 True or False?

1. An agent may forfeit rights to compensation when the agent breaches his or her duties to the principal.

2. An agent cannot recover expenses from the principal if those expenses are a result of the agent's own negligence.

3. If a principal makes an agent's job difficult or impossible, that principal has breached the duty of cooperation.

34-4 Termination of Agency

The agency agreement may be terminated by the acts of one or both parties to the agreement or by operation of the law. When the authority of the agent is terminated, the agent loses the right to act for the principal.

Termination by the Actions of the Parties and by Law

Both principal and agent may terminate an agency relationship by their acts. Most agency relationships are terminated when the parties have satisfied their contractual obligations. The relationship also may be discharged by mutual consent, as well as when either the agent or the principal breaches the agency contract.

Fulfillment of Purpose   When the purpose for which the agency was created is achieved, the agency is terminated. If an agent is appointed for a specific period of time, the arrival of that time terminates the agency. In short, when the contract is performed, the agency is at an end.

Mutual Agreement   The parties to an agency relationship may terminate it at any time by agreement, even before the contract is fully performed.

Revocation or Renunciation   The principal or the agent usually has the power (if not necessarily the right) at any time to terminate the agency relationship. Acting with or without cause, the principal may terminate the agreement by simply recalling the agent's authority to act (i.e., **revocation**). Even though the principal's act of revocation may be a violation of contract, the agent's authority is terminated. Agents may terminate by simply giving notice to principals that they are quitting (i.e., **renunciation**). Unless the terms of the agency agreement permit termination "at will," agents and principals who end their relationship may be liable for damages resulting from the violation of the contractual promise (see Figure 34-1). Nevertheless, one cannot be forced to work against one's will.

The termination of the agency agreement by operation of the law results when significant events make the continuance of the agency impossible or impractical. Termination by operation of the law occurs in instances of death, insanity, bankruptcy, or impossibility of performance.

Death   The death of the principal or agent ordinarily terminates the agency relationship automatically, even without notice. Hence, any agreement made between the agent

Figure 34-1 This chart indicates how liability is determined after the termination of an agency relationship.

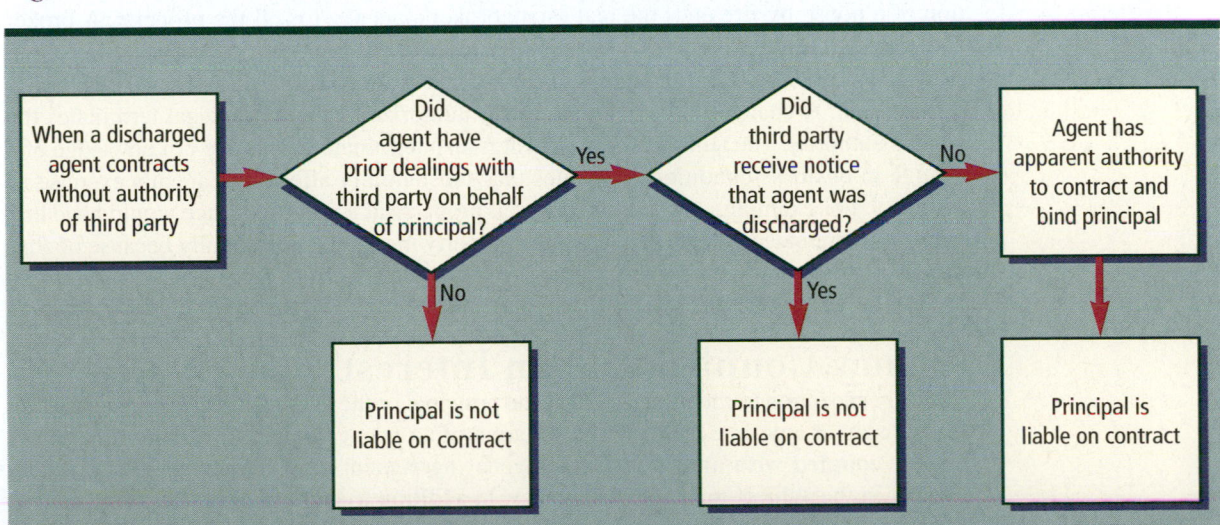

and a third party is ineffective upon the death of the principal. Although the agent may be liable to third parties for breach of the implied warranty that the agent has authority to act, third parties cannot recover from the estate of the principal because the contract is not binding.

Insanity   The insanity of either the principal or the agent usually terminates the authority of the agent. In some states, however, the courts have held that an agent has power to bind a principal who has become insane if the principal has not been legally declared insane and if the third party had no knowledge of the insanity. If the principal is only incapacitated briefly, the agent's authority may be suspended rather than terminated.

Durable Power of Attorney   Generally, an agency relationship is terminated upon the incapacity of the principal. However, the trend in many states has been to enact statutes that permit the creation of a durable power of attorney. Under such statutes, a person can appoint an agent called an "attorney in fact" by signing a written durable power of attorney. A **durable power of attorney** preserves the authority of an agent should the principal become incapacitated. In some cases, the durable power of attorney may even activate the agent's power once the principal is incapacitated. The durable power of attorney should contain the following words: "This power of attorney shall not be affected by subsequent disability or incapacity of the principal," or "This power of attorney shall become effective upon the disability or incapacity of the principal."

Bankruptcy   In the event of the bankruptcy of the principal, the agency is ended. All of the principal's ordinary contracts are cancelled, and title to the principal's property passes to a trustee for the benefit of creditors. The bankruptcy of the agent sometimes terminates the agency for the same reasons, but the principal and the agent may continue the relationship if they choose. Usually, the bankruptcy of the agent does not prevent the agent from doing the job in the regular way, provided the agent is not using personal funds.

Impossibility of Performance   An agency relationship terminates when it is impossible for the agent to accomplish the purpose of the agency for any reason. Destruction of a house by fire ends the real estate broker's agency to sell the property. A broker authorized to sell a principal's boat loses that authority if the boat is destroyed in a storm. An agent's loss of a license required to conduct the principal's business ends the authority of the agent. A change in the law that causes authorized acts to be illegal terminates the agent's authority. The authority of the agent is also terminated by notice or knowledge of a change in business conditions or values that substantially affects the agent's exercise of authority. For example, an agent hired to sell property at a specified price would have that authority terminated when the value of the property increases substantially because of zoning changes.

Agency Coupled with an Interest

The only exception to the rule that either the principal or the agent may terminate an agency relationship at any time arises in the situation of an agency coupled with an interest. An **agency coupled with an interest** is an agency agreement in which the agent is given an interest in the subject matter of the agency, in addition to compensation for services rendered to the principal. The concept protects the agent's interest in specific property belonging to the principal. The principal lacks power to revoke agencies of this kind without the consent of the agent.

> ## EXAMPLE 34-5:   An Agency Coupled with a Lot of Interest
>
> James Heilman borrowed $9,000 from the National Security Specialty Bank of Louisville. He put up as security 200 shares of stock in the Actors' Theatre Group of Louisville. Heilman then authorized the bank to sell the shares to satisfy the loan obligation should he default on that loan. In the event that it becomes necessary to sell the stock, the bank serves as Heilman's agent. Heilman may not terminate the agency except by paying off the $9,000 loan (plus interest, as per his agreement with the National Security Specialty Bank).

Notice of Termination to Third Parties

The principal has the duty to notify third parties with whom the agent has done business when the agency relationship has been terminated by the act of the parties. The exception to this rule is when the agency is terminated by operation of the law. In such instances, the principal is not required to notify anyone, and no subsequent act by the agent will bind the principal.

LO10

The type of notice required depends on how the former business relations were conducted. When the third party has given credit to the principal through the agent, the third party is entitled to actual notice of termination of authority, which may be done by regular mail or by telephone. The safest way, however, is by certified mail, because the post office provides a receipt of the notice. A notice in the classified advertisement section in a newspaper of general circulation is sufficient for third parties who have never given credit but who have had cash transactions with the agent or know that other persons have dealt with the principal through the agent. The failure to give third parties appropriate notice would make the principal liable on contracts made by a former agent with third parties.

Quick Quiz 34-4 True or False?

1. The parties to an agency relationship may mutually agree to terminate their agreement at any time.

2. The death of the principal or agent ordinarily terminates the agency relationship automatically.

3. The failure to give third parties appropriate notice would make the principal liable on contracts made by the former agent.

Summary

34.1 An agent's authority may arise expressly from the written or spoken words of the principal to the agent or implied from the agent's reasonable effort to understand the meaning of the principal's words describing what the agent is to do. Apparent authority results from actions by the principal that give a third party reason to believe that an agent has the authority to act for the principal. Principals do not often give agents the power to delegate authority to subordinates.

34.2 As a result of the fiduciary relationship, the agent owes the principal the duty of obedience to instructions; loyalty; reasonable judgment, prudence, and skill; accounting for agency money and property; personal performance of agency work; and communication of all facts that affect the subject matter of the agency.

34.3 In addition to the duties that the principal owes to the agent under the agency agreement, there are certain implied obligations. These obligations include the duty to compensate the agent, reimburse the agent for authorized expenses incurred, indemnify the agent for losses caused by the agency relationship through no fault of the agent, and comply with the terms of the agency contract.

34.4   An agency agreement generally terminates when its purposes are accomplished. The agency may also terminate at any time by the principal's revocation of the agent's authority or by the agent's renunciation of the agency relationship. If either party dies, be-

comes insane, goes bankrupt, or ceases to be qualified to act, the agency relationship is terminated by operation of the law. The principal has the duty to notify third parties with whom the agent has done business when the agency relationship has been terminated by acts of the parties. Actual notice is required when the third party has given credit to the principal through the agent. A public notice in a newspaper of general circulation is sufficient for third parties who have never given credit but who have had cash transactions with the agent.

Key Terms

agency coupled with an interest, 716

apparent authority, 706

durable power of attorney, 716

express authority, 705

implied authority, 705

indemnification, 712

lingering apparent authority, 706

renunciation, 715

revocation, 715

scope of authority, 709

Questions for Review and Discussion

1. What is the difference between express and implied authority?
2. What is apparent authority?
3. What are the consequences of an unauthorized delegation of agency authority?
4. When can an agent legally appoint a subagent?
5. What are the duties of an agent to the principal?

6. What are the remedies available to a principal?
7. What are the duties that a principal has in relation to an agent?
8. What are the remedies of an agent?
9. What are the ways that an agency relationship can be terminated?
10. Who is entitled to notice that an agency has ended?

Investigating the Internet

Access the Web site for the National Conference of Commissioners on Uniform State Laws (NCCUSL) and conduct a search for the Uniform Athlete Agents Act (UAAA). Answer the following questions with regard to the act: (1) According to the Prefatory Note, what problems motivated the NCCUSL to write the Uniform Athlete Agents Act? (2) How does the UAAA define the term "athlete agent"? (3) How does the UAAA define "professional-sports-services contract"? (4) According to Section 5 of the UAAA, which state office should govern the registration of athlete agents? (5) According to Section 10 of the UAAA, what should the "Warning to a Student-Athlete" clause in an agency contract say?

Cases for Analysis

1. Darden Restaurants contracted with Trans-Pac Foods for the delivery of several shipments of frozen shrimp from Los Angeles to its restaurant in Indianapolis. Trans-Pac entered a contract with Gulf Atlantic and Pacific (GAP), a transportation agent, to arrange for the actual shipment. GAP entered a contract with C.A.R. Transportation, a second transport brokerage company, which actually hired the trucking companies that would ship the frozen shrimp to Indianapolis. One of those companies was All-American Transport. All-American drivers signed waivers stating that All-American and its contractor would not hold Darden or Trans-Pac liable for freight payments. GAP was paid by Trans-Pac and then GAP was billed by C.A.R. However, GAP went bankrupt and could not pay C.A.R., so C.A.R. then filed a lawsuit against Darden and Trans-Pac, both of which produced the waiver forms signed by the All-American Drivers. In turn, C.A.R. argued that the drivers had no actual authority to sign the waivers. Darden and Trans-Pac argued that the drivers had the apparent authority to bind both All-American and C.A.R. as the contractor who hired All-American. Did the All-American drivers have apparent authority sufficient to bind C.A.R. to the waivers? Explain. *C.A.R. Transportation Brokerage Company, Inc. v. Darden Restaurants, Inc.,* Case No. 98-56122 (U.S. Court of Appeals for the Ninth Circuit).

2. Sturgill gave his significant other the authority to write checks that were drawn on his personal checking account. After Sturgill passed away, she continued to write checks that were drawn on his account. The executor of Sturgill's estate objected to this practice and brought a lawsuit against the bank for continuing to honor the checks. The bank argued that because it had received no notice of Sturgill's death, it was within its rights when it honored her authority to cash the checks. The executor argued that the death of Sturgill automatically terminated the agency, and the bank therefore had no right to continue to cash the checks. Who is correct here? If the bank is found liable to the estate, does it have a cause of action against the agent? Explain. *Sturgill v. Virginia Citizens Bank Co.,* 291 S.E.2d 207.

3. Luken drove her car onto a parking lot owned and operated by the Buckeye Parking Corporation. She had been in the habit of using this particular parking lot at least once a week for about two years. The lot had a sign over the entrance that clearly indicated that it was a parking lot. About two dozen cars were in the lot. A young man who appeared to be the parking attendant and who had in his possession a handful of tickets approached Luken. Luken asked him to park her car, which he agreed to do. He then asked her how long it would be before she returned, and she answered that she would be back in about an hour. When she returned, the lot was unattended, and she could not find her car. Subsequently, Luken discovered that the apparent attendant had taken her car and had been involved in an accident that extensively damaged the vehicle. Luken sued Buckeye, claiming that the corporation had, by its actions, led her to believe that the young man was an attendant in its employ. Therefore, under the theory of apparent authority, she claimed that she deserved to be reimbursed for her loss. Was Luken correct? Explain your response. *Luken v. Buckeye Parking Inc.,* 68 N.E.2d 217 (OH).

4. George Jackson, purchasing agent for Ozan, Inc., using his own funds, purchased computer supplies from Lenwell Office Supply Store at a special discount. Each time Ozan needed additional computer supplies, Jackson took them from his personal stock and charged Ozan the regular price. He recorded the transaction as if the supplies were purchased from an acceptable supplier. He then pocketed the difference. What duties, if any, has Jackson breached by reselling the supplies to Ozan? Explain.

5. On April 11, Fred Chapman discharged Anna Savant, the manager of his store, the Super Electronic Supply Outlet. On April 12, Chapman called *The Barnard Crossings Chronicle* and had a notice printed to the effect that Savant no longer worked for Super. On that same day, Savant ordered twelve electronic games, two computers, two laser printers, a fax machine, and a car stereo from the Global Electronic Components Corporation. As she had frequently done in the past while acting as manager for Super, she told George Pierce, the owner of Global, to send the bill to Super. Pierce did so. Savant then kept these items for herself. Pierce did not have actual notice of Savant's discharge until April 28, when he saw the notice as he

was throwing out some old newspapers. Savant could not be located, so Pierce brought suit against Chapman and Super. Chapman argued that the newspaper notice was sufficient to warn Pierce not to deal with Savant. How would the court rule? Explain.

6. Stahl was having trouble with her Volkswagen. She brought it to the service station of LePage, where it was examined and the trouble was diagnosed. LePage informed Stahl that he would not be able to do the work, but that his employee Donley wanted to take the job on his own and could make use of the garage facilities for this purpose. A new engine was required, and Donley installed the wrong engine. The entire job had to be done over at a cost of hundreds of dollars. Stahl brought suit against LePage. She argued that she should be allowed to recover against LePage for the misdeed of Donley, because Donley had apparent authority to act as LePage's agent. LePage disputed this claim, arguing that the facts did not warrant a finding of agency under any theory. How did the court find in this dispute? Why? *Stahl v. LePage,* 352 A.2d 682 (VT).

7. Castle Fabrics, Inc., sold fabric to Fortune Manufacturers, Inc. A dispute arose as to the acceptability of the fabric received, and Fortune returned the fabric to Castle for full credit. Castle gave Fortune only partial credit and sued Fortune for recovery of its loss. In court, Fortune showed a credit memorandum from a Castle employee indicating that Fortune would be given full credit for the fabric. Although it was within the regular responsibility of the Castle employee to send the memorandum, on this occasion, management had specifically instructed the employee not to send one. Fortune agrued that the employee was an agent of Castle and thus chargeable with any mistake the agent made. Castle claimed it was not chargeable with the action of its employee because the employee had disobeyed specific instructions not to send the memorandum. The judgment was for whom and why? *Castle Fabrics, Inc., v. Fortune Furniture Mfrs. Inc.,* 459 F. Supp. 409 (N.D. MS).

8. Lloyd, an attorney, was appointed guardian of Ernest Parker. Two years later, he was appointed guardian of Virginia Hockenberry. That same year, he agreed to represent David Isaac in the purchase of a plot of real estate from Debra Taylor. On several occasions, Lloyd deposited client settlement checks into his own account. The funds received were therefore commingled with the funds in his personal account. He later used these funds to pay for his student loans, his automobile loan, his insurance, his taxes, his outstanding credit card bills, and his barber. Identify the duties that Lloyd has violated in relation to his principals, Parker, Hockenberry, and Isaac. *Office of Disciplinary Counsel v. Lloyd,* 643 N.E.2d 1086 (OH).

9. Ross needed a grinding mill and consulted Clifton, who on occasion repaired such mills but did not sell them. Ross and Clifton together selected a mill from a catalog, which Clifton happened to have on hand, that they decided would meet Ross's purposes. Ross instructed Clifton to order the mill they had selected, and Clifton did so in his own name and with his own money. When the mill arrived, Ross refused to accept it, stating that it was too small and would not do the job he intended it to do. Clifton brought suit to recover the amount he had spent. The judgment was for whom and why? *Clifton v. Ross,* 28 S.W. 1085 (AR).

Quick Quiz Answers

34-1		34-2		34-3		34-4	
1.	F	1.	T	1.	T	1.	T
2.	F	2.	F	2.	T	2.	T
3.	F	3.	T	3.	T	3.	T

Chapter 35 — Employment Law

The Opening Case
Dohme v. Eurand America, Inc.

Randall Dohme was working at Eurand America as an engineering supervisor when a fire broke out on the company's property. Dohme quickly located a fire alarm and tried to activate it. When the alarm failed to work properly, Dohme had to scramble to find a working alarm. By the time he had located and activated the second alarm, he had been over-come by smoke and had to be treated at a local hospital. Later, after his release, he was interviewed by a fire department inspector. During the interview, Dohme told the inspector about the concerns he had over fire safety at Eurand. Later, Dohme was designated as the new Facilities/Computerized Maintenance Management System Administrator, which required him to oversee the company's fire safety system. In this capacity, Dohme discovered that several fire alarm safety inspections were overdue. Despite being warned not to do so, Dohme reported his concerns to an insurance inspector who was conducting a risk management investigation at Eurand facilities. Dohme not only told the inspector about the fire safety problems but also showed the inspector a computer printout that confirmed that the fire alarm inspection process was behind schedule. Dohme also told the inspector that he was concerned that he was being set up as the fall guy for the problems with the fire safety system. Apparently Dohme's concerns were well founded because he was in fact discharged. He later brought a wrongful discharge lawsuit against the company. Dohme argued that because he was fired for informing the insurance inspector about the faulty fire warning system, his discharge violated public policy. The trial court disagreed and dismissed Dohme's case. The trial court argued that the only reason Dohme had notified the inspector about the fire system problems was that he was afraid he would be blamed for those problems. Therefore, he could not now claim that he was thinking about public safety when he made his original report to the inspector. The court of appeals discounted the trial court's argument, noting that an employee who reports a safety issue and is then fired as a result will have a wrongful discharge case against the former employer, regardless of that employee's motive in filing the original safety report. Motive, the court of appeals said, does not matter in a public policy wrongful discharge lawsuit. The only thing that matters is public safety. (See *Dohme v. Eurand America, Inc.*, 170 Ohio App.3d 593, Court of Appeals of Ohio for Montgomery County.)

Opening Case Questions

1. Why was Eurand confident that it would win this lawsuit? Explain.

2. Given Eurand's confidence, why did Dohme bother to file the lawsuit? Explain.

3. On what grounds did Dohme support his wrongful discharge lawsuit?

4. Should Dohme's motive for reporting the problem be relevant? Explain.

5. Should the fact that Dohme reported the problem to an insurance inspector rather than a government official, such as a fire department inspector, matter? Explain.

 Learning Objectives

1. Explain the doctrine of employment-at-will.
2. Itemize the situations that fall outside employment-at-will.
3. List the wrongful discharge exceptions to employment-at-will.
4. Explain the after acquired evidence rule.
5. Indicate the functions of the Occupational Safety and Health Act.
6. List the functions of the Fair Labor Standards Act.
7. Explain the difference between unemployment insurance and workers' compensation.
8. Identify the major provisions of the Family Medical Leave Act.
9. Distinguish between disparate treatment and disparate impact.
10. Distinguish between business necessity defenses and the defense offered by a bona fide occupational qualification (BFOQ).

35-1 The Employment Relationship

An employment relationship may be formed in many ways. It may result from a simple oral agreement between two individuals, or it may be created by a detailed written contract that is finalized after complex negotiations between a union and a corporation. In the United States, the dominant legal doctrine governing most employment relationships is employment-at-will. Many states, however, have come to the conclusion that employment-at-will must be changed to ensure justice for employees. For this reason, the at-will doctrine has been modified by the addition of several wrongful discharge exceptions.

Employment-at-Will

As noted, most jurisdictions in the United States still follow the doctrine of **employment-at-will**, which states that an employer can dismiss an employee at any time for any reason. Under this doctrine, the employer does not even have to give a reason for the firing. The rationale for the employment-at-will doctrine is that both the employer and the employee should be free to terminate the employment relationship at any time. This principle allows both parties to end an unsatisfactory relationship or take advantage of new opportunities. Unfortunately, the principle can be abused by unscrupulous employers. Therefore, the law has created certain exceptions to the general rule. Some of these exceptions actually eliminate an employee's at-will status. This elimination occurs when a group of employees forms a union that is recognized by the state or federal government as the official bargaining unit for those employees. Another exception is when an employee negotiates his or her own employment contract. At-will status has also been altered somewhat by the Worker Adjustment and Retraining Notification Act (WARN) and a variety of civil rights legislation. The doctrine also has been modified by a series of court-created exceptions, usually listed under the general heading of wrongful discharge.

EXAMPLE 35-1:   The Employment-at-Will Merry-Go-Round

Laura Farragher worked as a cashier for the Gentry Merry-Go-Round of Foods Company, a concessionaire business that worked the fair and festival circuit in Arkansas each summer. Generally, Farragher started work in May at the Memorial Day Festival at the Little Rock Airport and stayed with the company all summer, until the Arkansas Horse Show in October held at the state fairgrounds. One year, after the Independence Day Festival, Ben Gentry, the owner and operator of Gentry Merry-Go-Round, told Farragher that her services were no longer needed because he wanted his daughter to work to earn tuition for college. Under the doctrine of employment-at-will, Farragher had no legal recourse. Gentry had the ability to discharge her at any time with or without notice, with or without offering her a reason. Of course, the opposite was also true, so when Gentry's daughter quit to take a job at a local restaurant, he could do nothing about it except, perhaps, rehire Farragher. Not surprisingly, Farragher had already formed her own concessionaire business. Unfortunately for Gentry, Farragher's Fun House of Foods went on to compete with Gentry's Merry-Go-Round at almost every county fair and village festival in the state, eventually driving it out of business. The moral of the story should be self-evident.

Collective Bargaining Agreements

An early victory over employment-at-will was won by organized labor. As a result of some hard-fought battles during the 1930s and 1940s, those employees who belong to labor unions today are frequently protected by hiring and firing procedures written into their collective bargaining agreements. A **collective bargaining agreement** is a contract negotiated by the employer and the labor union that covers all issues related to employment. Such agreements prevent the unfair discharge of employees. The employer needs some legitimate, employment-related reason, or just cause, for the release. In general, collective bargaining contracts also provide a grievance procedure. Under a **grievance procedure**, employees have the right to appeal any employer's decision that they think violates just cause.

Often, economic conditions force layoffs or plant closings. When such events occur, some or all employees may lose their jobs. Still, most collective bargaining agreements provide a negotiated procedure by which such layoffs occur. In this way, employees are at least guaranteed that the layoffs will be handled in as fair a manner as possible.

Professional Employment Contracts

Individuals with unique abilities, special talents, or a highly specialized education often have the power to negotiate their own employment contracts. Such individuals would not be affected by employment-at-will. Generally, such people are in demand and can thus be selective in the choice of employers. Professional athletes, established scientists, top business executives, famous entertainers, and well-known artists and writers belong in this category.

Worker Adjustment and Retraining Notification Act

Many employers who contemplate mass layoffs and/or plant closings must comply with the provisions of the Worker Adjustment and Retraining Notification Act (WARN). Under this federal statute, employers with more than 100 full-time employees must give written notice to a union official 60 days before any plant closing or mass layoff. If the employees are not represented by a union, the advance notice must go directly to all

Talking Points

In his treatise, *Overcoming Law,* Richard Posner offers two opposing views on employment-at-will, both of which appear to emerge from the philosophy of Georg Wilhelm Friedrich Hegel.

According to Posner's interpretation, "Employment at will is a corollary of freedom of contract, and freedom of contract is a social policy with a host of economic and social justifications, even though nature is not one of them. Employment at will happens to be the logical terminus on the road that begins with slavery and makes intermediate stops at serfdom, indentured servitude, involuntary servitude, and guild restrictions. . . . Hegel himself . . . would have thought employment at will a fine idea."

On the other side of the employment fence is the American legal scholar, Drucilla Cornell, who proposes, according to Posner, that "employment at will should be outlawed. Every employee would be entitled after successful completion of a brief probationary period to retain his or her job for life unless economic adversity required layoffs or an arbitrator or some other neutral adjudicator determined that the employer had good cause to discharge the employee."

Which side of the argument makes the most sense to you? Is employment part of the right to contract, which allows both sides to enter and leave the agreement freely, or is it something that should bind one side, the employer, for the life of the employee, while allowing the employee to leave at any time, with or without reason or notice? Explain your position thoroughly and thoughtfully.

employees who will be affected by the layoff or closing. Written notice is not required if the layoff or closing is caused by a natural disaster, such as a flood or an earthquake. Notice is also not required if the closing is caused by an unpredictable business situation or if the notice might prevent the acquisition of business or capital that the employer is attempting to acquire.

Protected Classes and Civil Rights Law

The rule that says that an employer can discharge an employee at any time for any reason or for no reason is also limited by civil rights legislation, such as the Civil Rights Act, the Age Discrimination in Employment Act, and the Americans with Disabilities Act. As the prototype, the Civil Rights Act of 1964 provides a template that the other acts generally follow. The Civil Rights Act of 1964 acknowledges the existence of certain protected classes, including race, color, creed, gender, and national origin, and makes it illegal to use membership in one of those classes as a reason for employment-related decisions. Thus, it is not completely true to say that an employer can discharge an employee for "any reason or for no reason." Thanks to civil rights legislation, an employer cannot discharge an employee if the only reason for the discharge is membership in one or more of the protected classes. Civil rights legislation is covered at length later in this chapter.

Employers with 100 or more full-time employees must provide a 60-day notice to the union, or if there is no union, to the individual employees, regarding any planned layoffs or closings.

Wrongful Discharge

Despite the prevalence of labor unions in this country, most employees are not union members. Also, most workers are not in a position to dictate the terms of their own employment contracts. As a result, most workers are subject to the doctrine of employment-at-will and can be dismissed at any time for any reason or for no reason. These employees would have no protection were it not for the exceptions to employment-at-will that the courts have created under the heading of wrongful discharge. **Wrongful discharge**, which is also referred to as *unjust dismissal* in some states, gives employees legal grounds for a lawsuit against employers who have dismissed them unfairly. The courts have used several theories to judge the injustice of a dismissal. These theories include promissory estoppel, fraud, implied contract, implied covenant, public policy tort, and the intentional inflection of emotional distress.

Promissory Estoppel   Some courts use promissory estoppel to support wrongful discharge cases brought in employment-at-will jurisdictions. To make a case based on promissory estoppel, the employee must demonstrate that the employer or a representative of the employer, generally a supervisor or department head, promised the employee job security despite the apparent at-will nature of the employment relationship. In promissory estoppel cases, what matters is that someone in authority made a promise to the employee that the employee believed and relied on, to his or her detriment. Promissory estoppel thus involves four elements:

1. The employer makes a promise.

2. The employer can reasonably expect the employee to rely on the promise.

3. The employee really does rely on the promise and, as a consequence, does something or refrains from doing something.

4. The employee in turn is hurt by the action or inaction in reliance on the promise.

Under these circumstances, the employer cannot deny the promise made to the employee, and the doctrine of employment-at-will is unavailable as a defense.

> ## EXAMPLE 35-2:   The Power of Promissory Estoppel
>
> Bennett worked for Jameson for three years without incident. Unfortunately, on the eve of the beginning of his fourth year, Bennett was arrested for a drug-related felony, allegedly committed during his free time. Sonja Gephardt, Bennett's supervisor, told him in front of several witnesses, "We have to lay you off now, but the company bosses have promised that you can have your job back at full seniority, once the case is over. They've also promised that you'll get back pay too." When Bennett was acquitted, he attempted to be reinstated as per Gephardt's promise but was told that he was no longer needed. When Bennett brought a wrongful discharge suit against Jameson, the company filed a summary judgment motion for dismissal noting that because Bennett was an at-will employee, the company could discharge him at any time for any reason or for no reason with or without notice. The court, however, refused to grant the summary judgment motion because the judge believed that Bennett had presented a *prima facie* case for promissory estoppel. This case was established because:
>
> 1. Gephardt, representing Jameson, had made a promise to Bennett that his job with full seniority and back pay would be waiting for him after the case was resolved.
>
> 2. Gephardt, and therefore Jameson, could have reasonably expected Bennett to rely on the promise.

3. Bennett really did rely on the promise and, as a consequence, did not look for employment elsewhere.

4. Bennett was hurt by not looking for another job because he lost money while he was unemployed and while he sought a new job.

Under the circumstances of this case, the company cannot deny the promise that its agent, Gephardt, made to the employee, Bennett, and the doctrine of employment-at-will will be unavailable to it.

Fraud-Related Employment Cases Some states now permit an employee to bring a wrongful discharge based on fraud, a cause of action similar to promissory estoppel. A cause of action based on fraud generally applies only to false promises made by a prospective employer to a possible future employee who relies on those promises to his or her detriment. Often in such a situation, the employer induces a potential employee to take a job that the employer knows will last only a limited amount of time, without telling the employee about the short duration of that position. The employer thus exploits the employee for a limited period of time and then discharges the employee. Hiring an employee without informing him or her that the business is ending or that an office, store, or plant is about to close down are circumstances that could provide the basis for employment-related lawsuits based on fraud.

Implied Contract The facts that support implied contract are similar to those that validate a promissory estoppel, so the two arguments often appear in the same case. However, there are major differences. Implied contract actually takes promissory estoppel several steps beyond a promise made by an employer and applies the principle to a general pattern of behavior by the employer that creates certain reasonable expectations on the part of the employees. Thus, **implied contract** involves an employment relationship that would have been at-will, had the employer or an agent of the employer not said, done, written, or printed something that created a workplace environment that implies the existence of a contract.

When examining a case to determine whether the employer has created an implied contract, the court can look at all of the facts involved in that employment arrangement. The court can consider, for example, oral promises made by the employer, the nature of the employment relationship, the way the parties have dealt with each other in the past, the length of the employment relationship, the customary way the employer handles such situations, and the employer's policies and procedures. To determine the employer's policies and procedures, the court can examine various company documents, including the employee handbook; letters, memos, text messages, voice mail messages, and e-mails sent to the employee; the employee's evaluation record; and any oral promises made in face-to-face situations between the employer and the employee. The creation of the implied contract exception gives employees a fighting chance to have their day in court, a chance that previously did not exist in pure employment-at-will jurisdictions.

EXAMPLE 35-3: A Prima Facie Case for Implied Contract

When Cynthia Montalbano went to work for Holmes Enterprises, she was required to read the entire employee handbook and sign an acknowledgment indicating that she had read and understood all of the terms in that manual. One of the procedures involved a progressive disciplinary process that promised, when employees were to be disciplined for any problem, they would first receive an oral warning, followed by a written warning. Only on the third offense would employees be penalized by a suspension, and only on a fourth offense would an employee be subject to a possible discharge order. The first time Montalbano was absent without permission, she was immediately discharged. When Montalbano filed a wrongful discharge suit against Holmes Enterprises, the company filed a summary judgment motion for dismissal, noting that because Montalbano was an at-will employee, the company could discharge her at any time for any reason or for no reason with or without notice. The court would not grant the summary judgment motion because the judge believed that Montalbano had presented a *prima facie* case for the creation of an implied contract, as established by Holmes clearly indicating that the handbook was to be considered a part of the employment relationship.

Many jurisdictions that have recognized the implied contract exception still allow employers to preserve an employment-at-will arrangement by using a disclaimer. In effect, a **disclaimer** says that, regardless of provisions or policies in the employee handbook and regardless of any oral promises to the contrary, an employment-at-will situation still exists between the employer and its employees. A legally effective disclaimer must include the following statements:

1. Neither the employee policy manual nor any other communication to employees is intended to create a contract between the business and its employees.

2. The employer reserves the right to dismiss an employee at any time with or without reason and with or without notice.

3. No one other than the president of the firm (or some other specified executive) can make any oral or written change in this disclaimer.

To be an effective attempt to preserve employment-at-will, a disclaimer also must be written in clear, unequivocal language. Moreover, it must be placed somewhere conspicuous, such as within the opening pages of the employee handbook or on a centrally located bulletin board. Finally, an effective disclaimer must be communicated to the employees or at least acknowledged by them in some way. Even then, a disclaimer might prove ineffective if the employer has made some sort of specific promise. For instance, if an employer adds a disclaimer to a handbook that also includes a very specific plan for progressive discipline, that employer might still be required to follow that disciplinary plan. Employers who fail to follow their own progressive disciplinary plan may find themselves in the midst of a wrongful discharge lawsuit, despite the disclaimer.

State Variations in Handbook Rules
The basic law in relation to employment-at-will, implied contracts, and disclaimers is, with a few exceptions, essentially identical in most jurisdictions, at least in relation to the original presentation of an employment manual to employees. The same is not true about the law when employers make subsequent changes in the employee handbook. Because the law varies from jurisdiction to jurisdiction, this problem can become especially acute for businesses with offices, plants, and/or stores in several states. Nevertheless, a general statement of the law is possible in relation to a situation in which an employer alters an employee manual, after that manual already has been established as a part of the employment relationship. The general rule states that when an employer makes changes in an employee manual and the employee continues to work under the new terms, the employee has accepted the new terms, and the continued work by the employee amounts to that employee's consideration.

> ## A Question of Ethics
>
> Beth Waid was to receive a 15 percent commission on all sales she made for her employer, the Jian Computer Corporation. Waid sold a $10,000,000 computer system to the Defense Department. To avoid paying $1,500,000 to Waid, Jian fired her, despite her record as a terrific salesperson. In an employment-at-will state that did not recognize the implied covenant exception, such a discharge would be legal. However, would such a termination be ethical? Explain.

Some states say that the employee must work for a certain amount of time, such as three weeks, before the continued work is enough to constitute consideration for the changes. Others set no such minimum. Some jurisdictions adhere to the proposition that an implied contract requires a strong message from the employer that he or she intends that the handbook operate as a contract. When this is the case, any and all alterations must be clearly communicated to the employee, usually by having all employees sign a separate form indicating that they have seen the changes. A few states will not permit changes to enter the implied contract if those changes are so drastic that they considerably interfere with an employee's expectations, as established by the original working conditions.

Implied Covenant **Implied covenant** holds that there is an implied promise in any employment relationship that the employer and the employee will be fair and honest with each other. Therefore, neither party will unfairly or dishonestly cheat the other out of anything due to the other party because of the employment relationship. The existence of an implied covenant has nothing to do with anything that the employer has said, written, or done. The implied covenant exists because the employment relationship exists. Several legal experts argue convincingly that once a jurisdiction embraces implied covenant, that jurisdiction is no longer an at-will jurisdiction. These experts contend that if a jurisdiction has said that a promise of fairness exists within any employment relationship, it becomes impossible to discharge an employee for "no reason" or "without notice." A discharge without cause or without notice would be inherently unfair and thus a clear violation of the ever-present, inescapable implied covenant.

Public Policy Tort In states that still adhere to the at-will doctrine, an employee who can prove that his or her discharge somehow violated public policy may recover damages in tort. Public policy is the broad legal principle that says that the courts will not allow anyone to do anything that injures the public at large. For example, in many jurisdictions, if an employee is fired for refusing to violate the law, such a discharge would violate public policy. Public policy encourages people to obey the law. Firing someone who wants to obey the law would clearly violate public policy. Similarly, if the firing itself violates the law, public policy will provide a remedy for the employee.

To succeed in a wrongful discharge lawsuit grounded on the public policy tort exception to employment-at-will, the employee would have to prove the following elements: clarity, jeopardy, causation, and the lack of an overriding business justification for the discharge. Each of these elements can be explained in the following way:

1. Clarity requires the existence of a definite public policy, clearly created by the U.S. Constitution, the state constitution, a statute, an administrative regulation, a common law principle, or a general governmental policy.

2. Jeopardy requires that the public will be endangered if the court does not dissuade the type of firing involved in the case.

The Opening Case Revisited
Dohme v. Eurand America, Inc., Round 2

Recall that in The Opening Case at the beginning of this chapter, Randall Dohme worked at Eurand America as a supervisor responsible for the company's fire safety system. Consequently, when a safety inspector showed up at Eurand, Dohme felt compelled to report several safety problems resulting from a series of overdue fire alarm inspections. Dohme made this report even though he had been warned by management not to talk to the insurance inspector. Later, after he had been discharged, Dohme brought a public policy wrongful discharge case against Eurand. It is relatively clear that Dohme had a fairly good case against Eurand. However, the appeals court did not decide the case on the merits. Rather, it simply ruled that the trial court had been mistaken when it decided that Dohme's case should be thrown out before trial. Consequently, the appeals court sent the case back to the trial court so that Dohme would have his day in court. However, if we look at the elements required for a successful public policy wrongful discharge suit, it is plain to see that Dohme had an excellent case. Recall that to succeed in a public policy wrongful discharge lawsuit, the employee has to prove the existence of clarity, jeopardy, causation, and the lack of an overriding business justification. When we apply these elements to the Dohme case, we get the following results:

1. Clarity requires the existence of a definite public policy. In this case, the state has clear public policy supporting fire safety. To suggest otherwise would be utterly irresponsible.

2. Jeopardy requires that the public will be endangered if the court does not dissuade the type of firing involved in the case. In this case, if the court does not restrain the discharge of a safety-conscious employee, then that employee, and others like him, will not talk to fire inspectors about safety problems, and as a result, the safety of the public will be jeopardized.

3. Causation requires that the discharge be induced by actions that are related to the stated public policy issue. In this case, the evidence clearly indicates that Dohme's discharge was caused by his unauthorized talk with the insurance inspector.

4. The lack of an overriding business justification means that the employer had no legitimate business reason for the discharge of the employee. Eurand offered no plausible business reason for the firing of Dohme.

3. Causation requires that the discharge be induced by actions that are related to the stated public policy issue.

4. The lack of an overriding business justification means that the employer had no legitimate business reason for the discharge of the employee.

In a wrongful discharge lawsuit based on public policy, the judge is charged with determining whether the first two elements, clarity and jeopardy, exist. These two elements are considered questions of law. If the case is tried before a jury, the jurors, as the triers of fact, would determine the existence of causation and the absence of an overriding business justification. In the absence of a jury, the judge would make this determination.

Complex Adaptation and Public Policy Tort The interaction of the state legislature and the court system in the development of the public policy tort exception to employment-at-will demonstrates how the law works as a complex adaptive system. In this case, the interaction begins with the state legislature, which creates a statutory provision or promotes a state policy that is designed to further a social objective deemed necessary to promote harmony, stability, or justice in the state. The court then intervenes in reaction to an individual case whose facts are intertwined with that policy. The result of the case either promotes or thwarts the legislative objective, prompting or alleviating the need for further legislative action.

Public policy encourages employees to do what is right by promising them the full protection of the law. This protection sends a clear message to employees that those who take a risk by promoting the health, safety, and welfare of the general public rather than the private welfare of their employer will be supported by the courts in a wrongful discharge suit, despite the traditional doctrine of at-will employment.

Intentional Infliction of Emotional Distress Another tort claim that is being used more frequently in wrongful discharge lawsuits is the intentional infliction of emotional distress. An employee may attempt to recover damages for the intentional infliction of emotional distress if the conduct of the employer in the discharge of the employee caused serious mental and emotional suffering. To succeed in such a lawsuit, the plaintiff must prove that the employer's conduct was extreme, that the employer knew the conduct was extreme and would result in emotional distress, and that the conduct was the proximate cause of serious mental and emotional suffering.

After Acquired Evidence Defense

A relatively new defense that employers have used successfully in wrongful discharge cases is called the *after acquired evidence defense*. This defense is applied when an employer uncovers evidence, usually during the discovery process, that reveals that the employer could have legitimately discharged the employee, even if the employee's claims of wrongful discharge prove to be true. The defense is often raised as the grounds for the granting of a summary judgment.

EXAMPLE 35-4: An After Acquired License Problem

Frank Handley was discharged from his position as a test pilot for Coastline Aviation, Inc., when he was absent from work on one occasion without notifying his superior. The company's employment manual, which had no disclaimer, indicated that an employee would receive three warnings, one oral and two in writing, for unexcused absences before being suspended. Only after a fourth unexcused absence could an employee be discharged. Handley filed a wrongful discharge suit against Coastline based on a breach of the implied contract created by the promises in the employment manual. During the discovery process, attorneys for Coastline found out that Handley's pilot's license had been suspended several years before he was hired and that Handley had lied about his license on his job application. The court ruled that even though the lack of a license had not been the reason that he was discharged, under the circumstances, because he had falsified his application and was not qualified to fly an airplane, which is clearly the function of a test pilot, he would not be entitled to receive any damages.

The after acquired evidence defense has also been used by defendants in discrimination lawsuits. Consequently, the Equal Employment Opportunity Commission has issued a special rule that is to be applied when such a defense is raised. This rule is discussed later in the chapter.

Quick Quiz 35-1 True or False?

1. Employment-at-will has virtually disappeared as a legal doctrine in most states thanks to the development of wrongful discharge.

2. Generally, collective bargaining agreements have eliminated grievance procedures as cumbersome and outdated because of the development of wrongful discharge.

3. Fraud is no longer considered grounds for a lawsuit in any kind of wrongful discharge case.

35-2 Laws Regulating Employment Conditions

Employment conditions can be divided into two distinct areas: the actual physical situation in which employees must work and the compensation received by employees. Moreover, there is a national employment verification system that affects all newly hired employees. The federal government regulates these working conditions to protect workers.

Health and Safety Laws

Various state and federal laws and administrative rules and regulations are designed to reduce preventable hazards to employees in the workplace and to provide for safe and helpful working conditions. On the state level, departments of labor and health may be charged with determining whether an employer is complying with state health and safety laws. On the federal level, the Occupational Safety and Health Act assures all workers in a business, in or affecting interstate commerce, a safe and healthful place of employment.

Occupational Safety and Health Administration

The Occupational Safety and Health Administration (OSHA), an agency responsible to the Department of Labor, establishes and enforces occupational health and safety standards with which employers must comply. To withstand a court challenge, however, it must be shown that the OSHA standards and regulations reasonably reduce the frequency or severity of employee injuries or illnesses. Employers are required to keep records of illnesses, injuries, and deaths suffered by employees and submit requested reports to the secretary of labor.

A corps of OSHA inspectors enforce compliance with its many and varied health and safety regulations. Employees are permitted to request an inspection if they believe that a violation exists. The U.S. Supreme Court has ruled that an OSHA inspector must produce a search warrant if the employer refuses to admit an inspector to the job site voluntarily. When a violation of a standard is observed, the inspector issues a citation. A citation is a notice commanding the appearance of the employer in a proceeding. Employers may contest citations before the OSHA's Review Commission. If this effort fails, they may seek relief in the U.S. Court of Appeals.

Fair Labor Standards Act

The principal federal law affecting the wages and hours of employees is the Fair Labor Standards Act (FLSA), commonly referred to as the Wage-Hour Law. Frequently amended, the act provides that workers in interstate commerce or in an industry producing goods for sale in interstate commerce must be paid no less than a specified minimum wage. Furthermore, it specifies that employees cannot work for more than 40 hours per week unless they are paid time and a half for overtime. The act prohibits the employment of children under the age of 14 years or the employment of "oppressive child labor" in any enterprise engaged in commerce or in the production of goods for commerce. Provisions of the FLSA have been duplicated by a number of states to regulate intrastate commerce and industries not covered by the federal law.

Wage and Hour Exceptions and Exemptions   The wage and hour provisions of the FLSA permit the employment of learners, apprentices, and messengers at less than the minimum wage. However, the employer must obtain express permission from the Wage and Hour Division of the Department of Labor and is subject to conditions set by it governing wages and hours. Full-time students are permitted to be employed under the same conditions in retail and service stores outside of school hours.

The wage and hour provisions of the FLSA, with certain exceptions, do not apply to people employed in an executive, administrative, or professional capacity. The exempt workers are generally identified as those who manage other employees. At least 50 percent of their primary duties must be in the performance of office or nonmanual work relating to the operations of the company or in the performance of work requiring scientific or specialized study. State, local, and federal employees; self-employed persons; and armed forces personnel are exempted from the wage and hour provisions. Also exempted are outside salespeople, employees of certain seasonal amusement or recreational businesses, and employees of small retail or service establishments.

Identity and Employment Eligibility

The federal Immigration Reform Act of 1986 created a national employment verification system that placed responsibility for verification of the identity and employment of all employees on the employer. The act provided that alien workers hired on or before November 6, 1986, had until May 5, 1988, to seek temporary resident status. Those who do not have documentation of their right to work in this country are not entitled to help from the National Labor Relations Board (NLRB) in labor disputes.

Employers are required to request and examine documentation of identity and employment eligibility of all new hires and rehires, including U.S. citizens, permanent residents, and nonimmigrant visa holders. Job applicants must present original documentation. After the documents are reviewed by the employer, individuals who accept an offer of employment are required to complete and sign an employment eligibility verification form in the presence of a supervisor or a human resource officer.

Quick Quiz 35-2 True or False?

1. The Occupational Safety and Health Act is a model law created by the American Law Institute.

2. The minimum wage is set by OSHA.

3. The Immigration Reform Act of 1986 does not affect the job application process.

35-3 Worker Benefits

The law attempts to protect workers who have left a job because of retirement, injury, or disability. The law also assists workers who have been laid off or discharged. These objectives are accomplished through Social Security, unemployment insurance, and worker's compensation.

Social Security

Federal and state governments participate in programs designed to reduce the financial risk to workers caused by their unemployment, disability, hospitalization, retirement, or death. The primary federal law covering these risks is the Social Security Act of 1935. Under the Federal Insurance Contributions Act (FICA), both employers and employees are taxed equally to help pay for the worker's loss of income on retirement. The law provides that the employee's contribution is held back by the employer, who then provides a matching contribution. The amount that an employee is assessed is based on the employee's annual wage base. Each year the annual wage base is raised to accommodate changes that occur because of increases in the cost of living. The Social Security Administration will pay benefits to retired workers who are eligible under the plan. Each retired worker's benefit payments are set by law but are also raised automatically to match cost-of-living increases.

Unemployment Insurance

The unemployment insurance section of the Social Security Act provides for a joint federal and state system of unemployment insurance. Temporary financial assistance is available to individuals who are unemployed through no fault of their own and who have earned sufficient credits from prior employment. Under the Federal Unemployment Tax Act, each state operates its own unemployment insurance system, subject to conditions established by the federal government. In addition to meeting state requirements regarding length of time employed and amount of wages, former employees must be ready, willing, and able to take suitable full-time employment should it become available. Thus, claimants are ineligible to receive unemployment benefits when they refuse to work without good cause. Good cause for refusing to work must be real, not imaginary; substantial, not trivial; and reasonable, not whimsical. For example, a desire to avoid a small cut in pay does not constitute good cause to refuse an employer's offer of employment in a reasonably similar position.

EXAMPLE 35-5:   The Case of the Vacationing Administrative Assistant

Regina Pastoria, an administrative assistant with Jacksonville Contractors, was discharged when the firm was downsizing. She registered with the state unemployment agency and asked for unemployment compensation. The interviewing official at the unemployment office told her about an opening for an administrative assistant at the Rayfield Construction Corporation. Pastoria refused the position on the grounds that she needed a short vacation before accepting another job. Pastoria would be ineligible for benefits for any week in which she refused suitable employment without good cause.

To recover for work-related injuries under workers' compensation, a worker must be injured on the job. A worker traveling to work, traveling home, or traveling to some other non–work-related destination cannot recover for injuries. This restriction is also true of lunches and breaks when a worker leaves the workplace. The result is different, however, when a worker leaves the work site on a *special mission* for the employer. Then the employee would be eligible to recover if he or she is injured, especially if the trip involved a business-related lunch that the employee was required to attend away from the job site. Sometimes the distinction between a work-related injury and one that is not related to work is clear. Often, however, this distinction is not obvious. An examination of the surrounding circumstances will help make a determination when a close call must be made. One of the things to look for to make such a determination would be whether, from an objective point of view, the employee believed that he or she was required by the employer to perform the task involved in the injury. An additional piece of evidence would be the location of the injury. If the injury takes place on the job site and under the orders of the employer, for example, then the activities would be work related.

Unemployment benefits help those out of work, however, the recipient must be ready, willing, and able to work should suitable employment become available.

An employee who quits a job without cause or is discharged for misconduct or theft generally does not qualify for unemployment benefits. Most states disqualify workers from receiving benefits if they are on strike because of a labor dispute. Domestic workers, agricultural workers, and state and local government employees are not governed by the federal–state program. Separate federal unemployment programs exist for railroad workers and federal civilian workers.

Workers' Compensation

Workers' compensation laws are in effect in all states. These statutes compensate covered workers or their dependents for injuries, disease, or death that occur on the job or as a result of it. One form provides a fund operated only by the state government. Employers pay into a state-controlled fund. When employees suffer injuries, they apply to the state to receive their benefits.

If this worker is injured on the job, his state's workers' compensation insurance will pay benefits based on the severity and duration of the injury.

In another form of workers' compensation, companies are required to carry insurance for their workforce, but they have the option of contributing to the state fund or purchasing insurance from a private insurer. In the third form, all employers are required to purchase workers' compensation insurance from private insurers.

Pension Plan Regulation

The Employee Retirement Income Security Act (ERISA) provides necessary supervision over employee pension plans that are established by many employers. Under the act, employers must place their pension contributions on behalf of the employees into a pension trust, independent of the employer. Under the rules of vesting, workers are guaranteed the right to receive pension benefits, regardless of whether they are working under the plan at the time of retirement. The law requires all pension plans to have minimum vested benefits. All pension plans must provide vested benefits after a worker has been on the job for five years.

Family and Medical Leave Regulation

Under the provisions of the federal Family and Medical Leave Act (FMLA), employers who have 50 or more employees at the workplace (or within 75 miles of the workplace) must give those employees up to 12 weeks of leave time in a 12-month period for child, spousal, or parental care or for the employee's own serious medical condition if that condition necessitates either in-patient treatment or medical care on a continuing basis. The 12-month period can be calculated based on a calendar year or from the time the leave actually begins. The leave time may be unpaid, but it must not jeopardize the job of the employee. To qualify for the leave time guaranteed by the FLMA, the worker must have been employed by the firm for at least one year and worked for 1,250 hours over the 12-month period before the leave is requested. Employees can draw on the 12 weeks consecutively, at intervals, or as an adjusted work plan. For example, an employee might take a half-week of leave time now and another half-week later, or an employee might reduce his or her workweek from five to four days, or a worker might adjust his or her daily work schedule from eight to six hours, and so on.

Employer Responsibilities   Both the employee and the employer have responsibilities under the FMLA. For instance, the employer must keep the employee's group health insurance in effect while the employee is on leave. Furthermore, when the employee returns to work, the employer must reinstate the employee to his or her former job or a job equal to the former job. In addition, the employer must make certain that, upon returning to work, the employee receives the same pay and the same benefits that he or she received before going on leave. Employers are also forbidden to dismiss an employee or discriminate against a worker who exercises his or her leave rights under the FMLA. Similarly, the employer cannot retaliate against a worker who protests the employer's attempt to bypass the rights granted to employees under this act. Employers are also responsible for informing employees, in writing, when leave time under the FMLA has been activated.

Employee Responsibilities   The FMLA also imposes certain obligations on employees. For instance, employees are required by law to give notice of their intention to take an FMLA leave whenever they can foresee the need for the leave. This notice must be given to the employer at least 30 days before the employee intends to take the leave. If the need for a leave is unpredictable, the employee must give notice as soon as doing so is practical.

Enforcement of FMLA Rules   Employees who believe that their employer has violated FMLA rules can file complaints with the Labor Employment Standards Administration. Moreover, employees who believe that their rights have been violated may file a lawsuit against their employers. Finally, a state statute or a collective bargaining agreement that gives employees more comprehensive leave coverage would supersede FMLA.

Quick Quiz 35-3 True or False?

1. Most states have eliminated workers' compensation laws because they are too expensive to maintain.

2. Under the Federal Unemployment Tax Act, all state unemployment compensation systems were dismantled.

3. The Family Medical Leave Act provides for 12 weeks of paid leave for all employees in any 12-month period.

35-4 Equal Employment Opportunity

In recent years, the government has attempted to address the problem of discrimination in the workplace. One integral part of this attempt was the Civil Rights Acts of 1964 and 1991. Other facets of this attempt include the Equal Pay Act of 1963, the Age Discrimination in Employment Act, the Uniformed Services Employment and Reemployment Rights Act, and the Americans with Disabilities Act.

The Equal Pay Act of 1963

Under provisions of the federal Equal Pay Act of 1963, employers must pay women the same amount that they pay men for the same job. The underlying motto of those who support the Equal Pay Act was and is "equal pay for equal work." Such a rule is easy to follow when the work in question is exactly the same. Problems occur when the work done by the women in the workplace is comparable, but not identical, to the work done by the men. To deal with this issue, the courts have ruled that as long as the work in question requires the same level of effort, ability, and accountability and is rendered in a comparable work environment, it is considered substantially equal. Substantially equal work requires equal pay. When a worker brings a claim under the Equal Pay Act, she must first establish that the employer does not pay female workers the same as male workers for essentially the same work. The burden then moves to the employer, which must show that the different pay rate is based on some sort of nondiscriminatory criterion. Systems based on merit, training, and productivity are acceptable to the court as legitimate reasons for different pay rates. Remedies available under the Equal Pay Act include back wages and punitive damages. Employers might also be ordered to eliminate the unfair pay system. Since 1979, the Equal Pay Act has been administered by the Equal Employment Opportunity Commission (EEOC).

Civil Rights Act of 1964

LO9

LO10

The Civil Rights Act of 1964 prohibits discrimination on the basis of race, color, creed, gender, and national origin. Employees who believe that they have been discriminated against can file complaints with the Equal Employment Opportunity Commission (EEOC). Moreover, some state governments have equal employment agencies that have been designated as deferral agencies under Title VII. In those states, all discrimination charges filed with the EEOC must be sent by the EEOC to the state equal employment agency. Even so, an employee who has filed such a claim can ask the EEOC, rather than the state agency, to conduct the inquiry. Discrimination claims must be registered with the EEOC no later than 180 days after the prohibited activity. In states with deferral agencies, that deadline is lengthened to 300 days. Discrimination can be committed in one of two ways: disparate treatment and disparate impact.

Disparate Treatment In cases of **disparate treatment**, the employer intentionally discriminates against an individual or a group belonging to a protected class. The protected classes are race, color, creed, gender, and national origin. For instance, a business that advertised for "salesmen" or "saleswomen" rather than "salespersons" would be practicing this type of discrimination. A common misconception exists that this type of brazen discrimination has been eliminated from the workplace. Such is not the case. Even into the 1990s, the United States Supreme Court was still reviewing cases that dealt with companies that continued to discriminate in direct and obvious ways.

EXAMPLE 35-6:   The Johnson Battery Discrimination Case, for the First Time

Johnson Controls Inc., a battery manufacturer located in Wisconsin, had an employment policy that eliminated women younger than 70 years of age from performing certain jobs in the making of batteries unless they could produce proof that they were infertile. The company argued that it was just trying to protect its workers, because all the prohibited jobs involved prolonged exposure to lead. The U.S. Supreme Court disagreed and labeled the company's policy as a clear-cut example of sex discrimination.

Businesses have a defense against a charge of disparate treatment, called a *bona fide occupational qualification (BFOQ)*. The discrimination may be justified if the employer can prove that the job requirement is a BFOQ. Even so, a BFOQ defense can never be raised to justify racial discrimination. However, a BFOQ defense can work for some forms of sexual discrimination. For example, a requirement that all applicants for a job modeling women's bathing suits be female would be a BFOQ.

EXAMPLE 35-7:   The Johnson Battery Discrimination Case, Once Again

Could Johnson Controls Inc., in Example 35-6, argue that infertility in a woman is a valid BFOQ? The U.S. Supreme Court said no. A BFOQ must be related to the job performance. Both men and women can be competent battery makers, so excluding one sex or the other from that job cannot be justified.

Disparate Impact   In contrast to disparate treatment, disparate impact is a more subtle form of discrimination. Discrimination through **disparate impact** or *adverse impact* occurs when an employer has a policy that on the surface seems neutral but that has an unequal and unfair impact on the members of one or more of the protected classes. For instance, an employer who requires all employees who work in the warehouse to be six feet tall and weigh at least 180 pounds may have discriminated against women under the doctrine of disparate impact. Although the criteria seem neutral on the surface, they would exclude women disproportionately and thus have an unfair impact on them.

Businesses have a defense against a charge of disparate impact known as *business necessity*. A qualification may be permitted despite its disparate impact on a protected class if the employer can show that the qualification is needed to perform the job. For example, a requirement that all job applicants have a law degree for a job as an attorney might have a disparate impact on one or more of the protected classes. However, because a law degree is needed for the job, it will be allowed. Naturally, the claimant has an opportunity to demonstrate that the challenged practice is not really needed to perform the job in question.

Sexual Harassment   In recent years, the courts have witnessed an increase in the number of **sexual harassment** claims. There is no question that sexual harassment is a type of sexual discrimination and that it is forbidden by the Civil Rights Act. However, exactly what constitutes sexual harassment is misunderstood by many people. Although most people recognize *quid pro quo* harassment, they do not realize that the creation of a hostile work environment also constitutes sexual harassment. **Quid pro quo sexual harassment** occurs when a supervisor makes unwelcome sexual advances toward a subordinate or suggests that the subordinate trade sexual favors for preferential treatment. A hostile work environment occurs when misconduct, such as sexually explicit comments, photographs, pictures, cartoons, jokes, posters, or gestures, pervade the workplace to the extent that conditions become distressing, offensive, or hostile. The law also expressly forbids employers from retaliating against employees who file sexual harassment complaints.

Affirmative Action and Reverse Discrimination

The term **affirmative action** refers to a practice by which an employer actively pursues a policy that will reduce the effects of past discrimination in the workplace. The term "affirmative," in this context, means to go forth actively, and the word "action" means a definitive plan. Therefore, affirmative action occurs when an employer initiates a definitive plan to eliminate discriminatory practices. Affirmative action is not mandated by the Civil Rights Act of 1964. However, it is not prohibited either. Generally, affirmative action plans come from a court order as the result of a court case. Nothing, however, prevents an employer from pursuing an affirmative action plan voluntarily. An affirmative action declaration might also be issued by the chief executive, as was the case in 1965 when President Johnson issued an Executive Order to eliminate discrimination in businesses holding federal contracts.

Some people are opposed to affirmative action because they see it as a form of reverse discrimination. **Reverse discrimination** is a term that refers to a practice that is designed to eliminate discrimination against the members of a protected class but that has the opposite effect on other members of that class or on the members of another protected class. The Supreme Court has reacted to such complaints by requiring that affirmative action plans promote a "compelling state interest" and be finely drawn to minimize any harm to those workers not included in the plan. To preserve an affirmative action plan, the government must show that the plan is necessary to fight past discriminatory practices, has a specified termination date, and is the only way to reverse the discriminatory practice.

Civil Rights Act of 1991

Congress enacted the Civil Rights Act of 1991 to meet several objectives. One objective involves the doctrine of disparate impact. The second objective involves an expansion of the remedies available under the Civil Rights legislation.

Strengthening Disparate Impact
The first goal of the Civil Rights Act of 1991 was to strengthen the doctrine of disparate impact that had been weakened by the U.S. Supreme Court. The act makes it clear that in disparate impact cases, the employer has the burden of proving that a business necessity exists for the discriminatory practice that forms the basis of the complaint. The law also makes it clear that the employer must prove that the hiring or promotion qualification is directly related to the specific job in question rather than to general business needs. The party who files a complaint in a disparate impact case may also be victorious if he or she can show that the same business goal can be reached by using a nondiscriminatory employment practice.

Compensatory and Punitive Damages
A second objective was to expand the availability of compensatory and punitive damages. Prior to the passage of the new act,

Business Law in the News

Indiscretions: Harassers in High Places

Scott Stacy was driving home from work in late September when news of the Mark Foley sex scandal came over the car radio. The details were shocking. Foley had sent sexually charged e-mails and instant messages to former teenage pages, in which he made repeated references to sexual acts and body parts. But to Stacy, the story was all too familiar. He runs what is becoming an increasingly important fixture on the treatment scene for the professional class: a rehab for sexual harassers. "I work with so many people in positions of power," says Stacy, founder of Lawrence (Kan.)-based Acumen Assessments Inc. "When they fall, they fall real hard."

Companies have long packed off their troubled throngs to treatment centers for alcohol and drug addiction. But in recent years more and more have begun sending the serial workplace sex harasser, or "boundary violator," to get help, too. With jury awards for sexual misconduct in the office on the rise, companies figure it's better to spend the thousands of dollars on psychological treatment than to wait for a lawsuit that ultimately could cost millions. What's more, in the age of e-mail—as the Foley scandal demonstrated all too clearly—it's getting easier to prove that improper behavior has taken place. Shipping a manager off to rehab, says Garry Mathiason, a partner with the San Francisco employment law firm Littler Mendelson, "shows the employer took it seriously and did something about it."

In recent years, a half-dozen facilities have made the treatment of sexual harassers a specialty. Nestled in anonymity in such places as Mississippi and Georgia, they feature bucolic-sounding names like Pine Grove and Ridgeview. For his part, Foley checked into Sierra Tucson, a 160 acre spa-like treatment center, where a typical stay can cost up to $65,000. Foley's lawyer issued a statement that the former Republican congressman is being treated for alcoholism. But Sierra Tucson specializes in various maladies, including sexual addiction and compulsivity.

What can managers expect at one of these places? Following a psychological assessment, therapists tailor a recovery program to deal with the offender's underlying problems. In the case of graphic language and locker-room joshing, the manager may simply need a week's worth of assessment and education. In more serious cases, such as cyberstalking and predatory come-ons, therapists work to uncover the original trauma that is spurring the behavior. That process can take several months and includes both group and individual therapy. Patients learn what emotions trigger such things as "boundary drift" and "inappropriate channeling of unmet needs." Sexual harassers, therapists say, often have damage from childhood. The idea is to teach them how to cope with these issues.

Digital Tracks

Sometimes an accuser's account differs wildly from the accused's. That prompted the Professional Renewal Center in Lawrence, Kan., to put a polygrapher on staff. But as the world becomes one giant archive, the instances of he-said, she-said are fading. The disinhibiting power of e-mails and voice mails are seductive to sexual harassers, but also memorialize the wrong in writing. "Men, frankly, are still pretty dumb about this," says Dr. Paul M. Earley, director of adult addiction medicine and the impaired professionals program at Ridgeview Institute in Smyrna, Ga. Then again, all that data can be useful to therapists; companies often send rehabs reams of incriminating evidence scraped off a harasser's hard drive.

Most companies have some form of sexual harassment training these days. And the number of charges being filed with the Equal Employment Opportunity Commission fell from 15,549 in 1995 to 12,679 in 2005. But with jury awards and settlements headed in the opposite direction, experts expect rehabs to remain in demand. Employees who file complaints often won't sue if they feel the manager has changed and made an apology. Of course, recidivism does occur. In those cases, the backsliders, just like drug addicts, are often sent straight back into treatment.

Questions for Analysis

1. What conduct described in the article can be labeled direct sexual harassment?

2. What conduct in the article can be labeled the type of conduct that leads to the creation of a hostile work environment?

3. What role might e-mail and voice mail play in a sexual harassment lawsuit?

4. What trend is evident when we look at sexual harassment cases filed with the EEOC?

5. What trend is evident when we look at sexual harassment cases that make it to trial?

Source: Michelle Conlin, "Indiscretions: Harassers in High Places: With Legal Payouts Rising, More Managers Who Cross the Line Are Winding up in Rehab," _BusinessWeek,_ November 13, 2006, 44.

only victims of racial discrimination could collect compensatory and punitive damages. All other victims of discrimination were limited to collecting back pay only. Under the Civil Rights Act of 1991, compensatory and punitive damages are now available to people who have been discriminated against because of their sex, religion, or national origin. Other remedies that are available under Title VII are back pay, reinstatement, and attorney fees.

Other Effects of the Civil Rights Act of 1991   The 1991 Civil Rights Act also added a few other critical provisions designed to reinstate the actual intent of Congress in creating the original statute in 1964. For instance, the new law mandates that American businesses must give U.S. citizens working abroad the same protection against discrimination that they give workers in the United States. In addition, the new act makes it clear that an employment practice is illegal even if only a portion of the practice is discriminatory.

After Acquired Evidence in Relation to Discrimination Cases   The EEOC has adopted an approach for discrimination cases in which after acquired evidence reveals that the employer had a legitimate reason for discharging the employee. The rule, which applies only to cases involving the EEOC, states that the commission will not require that the employer rehire the claimant, nor will the commission attempt to recover backpay or compensatory damages that arise after the time that the after acquired evidence was obtained. However, to avoid frustrating the purposes of the Civil Rights Act of 1991, the EEOC will still seek punitive damages in such cases.

Age Discrimination in Employment Act

The Age Discrimination in Employment Act (ADEA) prohibits discrimination on the basis of age. ADEA covers employment agencies, employers of 20 or more employees, and labor unions of more than 25 members. This act protects any person aged 40 years or older from discrimination in hiring, firing, promotion, or other aspect of employment.

Like the Civil Rights Act, the ADEA is administered by the EEOC. Age discrimination claims must be registered with the EEOC no later than 300 days after the prohibited activity. Naturally, if age is a true job qualification, the law does not apply. For instance, if the job involves the modeling of junior miss fashions, it would not be discrimination to hire someone of suitable age to model the clothes. The courts, however, will carefully scrutinize all such requirements and generally be able to detect those that are merely a pretense covering age discrimination.

EXAMPLE 35-8:   Taggart, Time, and the ADEA

Thomas Taggart, aged 58 years, lost his position when the subsidiary he worked for was disbanded by Time, Inc., the parent corporation. All of the employees who were laid off as a result of the closing were promised preferential treatment for other jobs at Time, Inc. Taggart applied for more than 30 of these positions. He was never

rehired. Most of the time the reason given for his rejection was that he was overqualified. Taggart brought an age discrimination suit under the ADEA. Time, Inc.,
argued that Taggart was not rehired because of an overqualification barrier that had
nothing to do with his age. The court disagreed. The court ruled that calling Taggart
overqualified was just another way of saying he was too old.

In 1990, Congress amended the ADEA in response to a U.S. Supreme Court case that
held that the original ADEA did not cover employee benefit plans. The amendment, which
is called the Older Workers' Benefit Protection Act (OWBPA), makes it clear that the
ADEA forbids discrimination against older workers in the handling of their employee benefit and retirement plans. In addition, OWBPA gives older workers legal recourse if they
are forced or tricked into giving up their rights under the ADEA. Usually this situation occurs when the employee is asked to sign a waiver. A waiver of rights is valid only if it is
given freely and without force or coercion. The employer has the job of proving that the
waiver is valid if it is introduced as evidence in court.

Uniformed Services Employment and Reemployment Rights Act

Under provisions of the Uniformed Services Employment and Reemployment Rights Act
(USERA), an employee who has served in the armed forces and successfully completed his
or her tour of duty is entitled, upon returning to work, to be reinstated in his or her previous
position on the job. Unlike the Civil Rights Act, which is controlled by the EEOC, USERA
is administered by the Office of Veterans' Employment and Training Service (VETS). Also
unlike the Civil Rights Act, under USERA, employees may file a complaint with VETS, or
they can take the case directly to court. No statute of limitations is connected to USERA.
However, employees are not permitted to hold back on the filing of a case for an unreasonable length of time. Employees who succeed in a case might receive damages, an injunction
to prevent their termination, and sometimes, at the discretion of the judge, attorneys' fees.

Americans with Disabilities Act

The Americans with Disabilities Act (ADA) is designed to open the American workplace
to this country's disabled citizens. The ADA is divided into several titles. Title I lays out
the duties imposed on private-sector employers, whereas Title II covers public services and
public transportation. The ADA is administered by the EEOC. The ADA carefully outlines
what is considered a disability. It also explains who and what are covered by the act and
what practices are specifically forbidden.

Disabilities   The ADA defines **disability** as any physical or mental impairment that
substantially limits one or more of the major life activities. This definition includes paralysis, blindness, deafness, cancer, mental retardation, learning disabilities, and AIDS, among
others. Excluded from protection are people with kleptomania, pyromania, or gambling
disorders. Nor does the act extend to people who use illegal drugs. The definition of disability also does not include homosexuality or bisexuality. However, because the act forbids discrimination against people who are associated with a particular disability,
discrimination against homosexuals, on the basis of the claim that they are more likely to
contract AIDS, would be forbidden.

Activities and Individuals Covered by ADA   Discrimination is forbidden in
the screening of applicants, initial hiring, and on-the-job treatment. This protection against

discrimination also extends to apprenticeship programs, promotions, pay raises, and on-the-job training opportunities. Individuals, including both employees and applicants for employment, cannot be segregated or classified because of a disability. The ADA also protects an individual from discrimination because that individual is associated with someone who has a disability. As is true of other situations, a state statute that gives individuals with disabilities more protection than the ADA would supersede the federal statute.

Forbidden Practices The ADA forbids discrimination on the basis of a disability if the disabled individual can do the essential functions of the job with "reasonable accommodations." Exactly what would qualify as a reasonable accommodation in a given set of circumstances is, at best, problematic. Nevertheless, the statute does give some guidance in determining the extent of a **reasonable accommodation**. An accommodation will be reasonable if it permits the disabled individual to accomplish the essential functions of the job without imposing an undue hardship on the employer. Factors used in determining whether a proposed accommodation will cause **undue hardship** include the type of accommodation needed, the expense involved in providing the accommodation, the financial ability of the company to provide the necessary accommodation, and the size and nature of the company involved. Because of the innovative nature of the law and the lack of precedent, the EEOC has decided to follow a case-by-case evaluation of all claims filed by disabled individuals against employers.

Quick Quiz 35-4 True or False?

1. The term "affirmative action" refers to a practice by which an employer actively pursues a policy that will reduce the effects of past discrimination in the workplace.

2. American businesses working in other countries need not give U.S. citizens the same protection against discrimination under the Civil Rights Act as those afforded workers in the United States itself.

3. The Uniformed Services Employment and Reemployment Rights Act (USERA) is administered by the EEOC.

Summary

35.1   In the United States, the dominant legal doctrine governing most employment relationships is employment-at-will. This doctrine means that an employer can dismiss an employee at any time for any reason. Employees who belong to labor unions today are frequently protected by hiring and firing procedures written into their collective bargaining agreements. Individuals with unique abilities, special talents, or a highly specialized education often have the power to negotiate their own employment contracts and would not be affected by employment-at-will. Most employees would have no protection were it not for the exceptions to

employment-at-will that the courts have created under the heading of wrongful discharge. Wrongful discharge gives employees legal grounds for a lawsuit against employers who have dismissed them unfairly. The courts have used several theories to judge the injustice of a dismissal. These include promissory estoppel, fraud, implied contract, implied covenant, public policy tort, and intentional inflection of emotional distress.

35.2   OSHA establishes and enforces occupational health and safety standards with which employers must comply. The principal federal law affecting the wages and hours of employees is the Fair Labor Standards Act. The act provides that workers in interstate commerce or in an industry that produces goods for sale in interstate commerce must be paid no less than a specified minimum wage. Furthermore, it specifies that employees cannot work for more than 40 hours per week unless they are paid time and a half for overtime and prohibits the employment of children under the age of 14 years or the employment of oppressive child labor in any enterprise engaged in commerce or in the production of goods for commerce. The federal Immigration Reform Act of 1986 created a national employment verification system that placed responsibility on the employer for verifying the identity and employment of all employees. Employers are required to request and examine documentation of identity and employment eligibility of all new hires and rehires, including U.S. citizens, permanent residents, and nonimmigrant visa holders.

35.3 Federal and state governments participate in programs designed to reduce the financial risk to workers by reason of their unemployment, disability, hospitalization, retirement, and death. The principal federal law covering these risks is the Social Security Act of 1935. The unemployment insurance section of the Social Security Act provides for a joint federal and state system of unemployment insurance. Under the Federal Unemployment Tax Act, each state operates its own unemployment insurance system, subject to conditions established by the federal government. Workers' compensation laws are in effect in all states. These statutes compensate covered workers or their dependents for injuries, disease, or death that occurred on the job or as a result of it. ERISA provides needed supervision over employee pension plans established by many employers. Under the act, employers must place their pension contributions on behalf of the employees into a pension trust, independent of the employer. Under provisions of the Family and Medical Leave Act (FMLA), employers who have 50 or more employees must give those employees up to 12 weeks of leave time for child, spousal, or parental care. This leave time may be unpaid, but it must not jeopardize the job of the employee.

35.4 The Equal Pay Act mandates that workers receive equal pay for equal work. The Civil Rights Act of 1964 prohibits discrimination based on race, color, creed, gender, and national origin. Employees who believe they have been discriminated against can file a complaint with the EEOC. Discrimination can be committed in one of two ways: disparate treatment or disparate impact. Sexual harassment is also a type of sexual discrimination, and it is forbidden by the Civil Rights Act. The Civil Rights Act of 1991 was enacted by Congress to strengthen the doctrine of disparate impact and extend the availability of compensatory and punitive damages. Other steps toward equality in employment include the Age Discrimination in Employment Act, the Uniformed Services Employment and Reemployment Rights Act, and the Americans with Disabilities Act.

Key Terms

affirmative action, 739

collective bargaining agreement, 724

disability, 742

disclaimer, 728

disparate impact, 738

disparate treatment, 737

employment-at-will, 723

grievance procedure, 724

implied contract, 727

implied covenant, 729

quid pro quo sexual harassment, 739

reasonable accommodation, 743

reverse discrimination, 739

sexual harassment, 738

undue hardship, 743

workers' compensation, 735

wrongful discharge, 726

Questions for Review and Discussion

1. What is employment-at-will?
2. What situations fall outside employment-at-will?
3. What theories are offered under wrongful discharge?

4. What is the after acquired evidence rule?
5. What are the functions of the Occupational Safety and Health Act?
6. What are the functions of the Fair Labor Standards Act?
7. What are the differences between unemployment insurance and workers' compensation?
8. What are the major provisions of the Family Medical Leave Act?
9. What is the difference between disparate treatment and disparate impact?
10. What is the difference between the business necessity defense and the defense offered by a bona fide occupational qualification (BFOQ)?

Investigating the Internet

Information about employment law can be found on a Web site called the Employment Law Information Network or *EL infonet.com*. As a research assignment, access the Web site and answer the following questions: (1) What are the four main links noted at the top of the home page for *EL infonet.com*? (2) What are some of the topics listed as part of the main navigation link? (3) What are some of the "quick links" available on the *EL infonet.com* Web site? (4) What topics are available for research in the Federal Employment Law Articles Library located on this site? (5) What are the most current employment law seminars scheduled for upcoming months?

Cases for Analysis

1. The Equal Employment Opportunity Commission (EEOC) recently has been hit with many newly filed cases that allege discrimination based on caregiver status. The cases involve, for example, a police officer who was not promoted because she had young children at home, a man who was fired for taking time off to care for his sick father, a class action case against an employer that discriminated against workers who had applied for FMLA leave, and a case filed by a man who took leave time to take care of his elderly parents. Caregiver discrimination, which is officially known as family responsibility discrimination, or FRD, has caused some experts to suggest that the EEOC should create guidelines that are specifically aimed at defining and outlining the elements of FRD. Others argue that there really is no such thing as FRD and that each case must be treated for what it really is, that is, gender discrimination, age discrimination, disabilities discrimination, family leave discrimination, or some other form of specifically delineated discrimination. What existing statutes could be called upon to handle FRD cases, even if those cases must go by another, more traditional name? See Tresa Baldas, "EEOC Looks at Caregiver Bias: Suits Involving Family Care Rise," *The National Law Journal*, May 21, 2007, pp. 1 and 18.

2. Eugene Meade was offered a job by Cedarapids, Inc. The job required moving to Eugene, Oregon, where Cedarapids, Inc., had a facility called the El-Jay Plant. To entice Meade to join the Cedarapids staff, management representatives told him that business was improving, that they believed in the potential of the El-Jay plant, that El-Jay sales were growing, that production at the plant was also increasing, and that there were plans to bring in an even greater numbers of new employees. On the basis of these assurances, Meade left his job and moved to Oregon. He also signed an agreement that noted that he was an at-will employee who could be fired at any time. Meade later discovered that all of the statements about the financial health of the El-Jay plant were false. Furthermore, Meade believed that the management had known all along

that the statements were false. Meade learned that the El-Jay plant was actually caught in a downward economic spiral and was about to close. When Meade was discharged, he brought a lawsuit against Cedarapids, Inc., arguing that he had been defrauded into moving to Oregon. In response, the Cedarapids management team argued that they had no duty to disclose the plan to shut down the Oregon facility. The management team also pointed to the agreement that Meade had signed and concluded that, as an at-will employee, he could not complain about his firing. The trial court agreed and dismissed the case. Meade then filed an appeal. Is there enough evidence of fraud in this case to allow it to go to a jury? Explain. *Meade v. Cedarapids, Inc.* Case No. 97-35836 (The United States Court of Appeals for the Ninth Circuit).

3. Carla McFarland was an associate professor of English literature at Highland College. She was the only single person in her department. Consequently, she was frequently assigned classes late in the evening, on weekends, and during the summer semester. She was also called upon to pick up visiting professors and serve as their escort and guide during their stays at the college. She received extra duty as adviser to the *The Highland Review*, the college's literary magazine. When McFarland complained about the unequal treatment, she was told that the married professors had family responsibilities that she did not have, which took up much of their time and prevented them from having the flexibility that she had. Thus, she would continue to carry the extra load. McFarland filed a complaint with the EEOC. Can discrimination based on an employee's status as a single person be considered unlawful under the Civil Rights Act? Explain. Is this a case of disparate impact or disparate treatment? Explain. See Wilson, Robin. "Singular Mistreatment: Unmarried Professors Are Outsiders in the Ozzie and Harriet World of Academe." *The Chronicle of Higher Education* (23 April 2004): A10–A12.

4. Henderson worked as a chemical engineer for the Wannisky Chemical Corporation. McGuire, Henderson's supervisor, ordered him to remove the labels from several hundred steel drums that had once contained a severely corrosive acid. McGuire told Henderson that they intended to reuse the drums to ship a new chemical fertilizer. Henderson refused to remove the labels, because reusing the old drums would violate both state and federal laws. When McGuire told another employee to remove the labels

and reuse the drums, Henderson reported the company's activities to the state and federal authorities. Henderson was fired for his refusal to follow orders and for notifying the authorities. In a lawsuit against Wannisky, which legal exception to the employment-at-will doctrine did Henderson use? Explain.

5. Bennerson was employed by the Checker Garage Service Corporation as an auto mechanic. His duties included both assisting mechanics in the garage and making road calls to service vehicles owned and operated by his employer. During his lunch hour, Bennerson used one of his employer's taxi cabs to drive to a restaurant. En route to the restaurant, he was seriously injured when the taxi struck a pole. Bennerson filed a claim before the workers' compensation board. His claim was granted. Checker Garage appealed, arguing among other things that the taxi that Bennerson drove did not "go out of control" but that Bennerson had lost control. Was Checker correct? Explain. *Bennerson v. Checker Garage Service Corporation,* 388 N.Y.S.2d 374 (NY).

6. Nancy Barillaro and Nancy Fotia were employed in the inspection and trimming departments of Elwood Knitting Mills for approximately 16 years. Barillaro was laid off in September and Fotia in November. Both were offered the option of returning to work in March of the following year as knitting machine operators, but at an 18 percent reduction in pay. Neither accepted the offer. They argued that the offered work would have involved a loss in seniority and a substantial reduction in pay. In addition, Fotia claimed that she was not familiar with the operation of the machine. Barillaro claimed that she was too short to operate the machine. The Pennsylvania Unemployment Compensation Board decided that neither claimant was eligible to receive benefits because they refused offers of suitable work without good cause. Was the board correct in its ruling? Explain. *Barillaro v. Unemployment Compensation Bd. Of Review,* 387 A.2d 1324 (PA).

7. The Wynn Oil Company, which conducted an enormous amount of business with Latin American companies, argued that being male was a bona fide occupational qualification (BFOQ) for the position of sales executive. Wynn contended that because of certain Latin American customs, the hiring of a female sales executive would have a serious detrimental effect on the company's business. The contention was challenged in federal court. Will Wynn's argument succeed? Explain. *Fernandez v. Wynn Oil Co.,* 653 F.2d 1273 (9th Cir.).

8. The Spelling Entertainment Group hired actress Hunter Tylo to appear in the television show *Melrose Place*. Her role was to involve the seduction of another character's husband. When Tylo became pregnant, she dutifully reported her condition to Spelling. The entertainment company then discharged her, arguing that non-pregnancy was a bona fide occupational qualification (BFOQ) for the role designed for Tylo. Tylo challenged the contention that her condition disqualified her from performing her job. Can non-pregnancy be a BFOQ? Explain. *Tylo v. Superior Court,* 55 Cal. App. 4th 1379 (CA).

9. Rice, an African American woman, was denied employment as a public health representative by the city of St. Louis for lack of a college degree. Failing to obtain relief after filing a complaint with the EEOC charging racial discrimination, she filed a lawsuit in the federal district court. Rice took the position that the degree requirement had a disparate impact on African Americans and was invalid under the Civil Rights Act of 1964. She pointed out that blacks were only approximately 55 percent as likely as whites in the St. Louis area to have a college degree. Testimony showed that the satisfactory performance of public health representatives required the ability to communicate with others, frequently in emotional situations, and the ability to speak and write intelligibly. There was also a risk to the public health and safety in the employment of unqualified applicants. Did Rice prevail? Explain. *Rice v. The City of St. Louis,* 607 F.2d 791 (8th Cir).

10. The Commonwealth of Virginia required all applicants for state troopers to be between 21 and 29 years of age, at least 5 feet, 9 inches tall, and at least 156 pounds. The height and weight requirements eliminated 98 percent of the female applicants. The basic employment requirements also made it mandatory that all applicants, including applicants for civilian dispatcher positions, complete and pass written mental ability tests. The tests for dispatcher positions were not valid predictors of job performance. The tests for the trooper positions also were shown not to be predictors of job performance. The United States brought suit, charging that Virginia engaged in a pattern and practice of discrimination against African American applicants for the civilian positions and against both African American and women candidates for the trooper positions. Did the United States prevail? Explain. *United States v. Commonwealth of Virginia,* 620 F.2d 1018 (4th Cir).

11. Shirley Painter was the Chief Deputy Clerk in the Bookkeeping Department of the Civil Division of the Municipal Court of the City of Cleveland. She decided to run for city council and asked for a leave of absence to pursue that goal. At first she was granted the leave. However, two months later, she was terminated. Painter brought a wrongful discharge lawsuit against Charles Graley, the assistant personnel director in the municipal court clerk's office. Painter asked to be reinstated. She also asked for back pay and punitive damages. Her wrongful discharge suit was based on a violation of public policy. She argued that she had appropriate grounds for the suit because her termination violated the state constitution. Graley argued that a plaintiff can bring a wrongful discharge lawsuit based on public policy only if a statute exists that prohibits the firing in question. Has Painter stated sufficient legal grounds for her wrongful discharge lawsuit? Explain. *Painter v. Graley,* 639 N.E.2d 51 (OH).

Quick Quiz Answers

35-1	35-2	35-3	35-4
1. F	1. F	1. F	1. T
2. F	2. F	2. F	2. F
3. F	3. F	3. F	3. F

Chapter 36

Labor–Management Relations Law

The Opening Case

Laborers Union Local No. 324 v. National Labor Relations Board

One morning, as was his custom, Douglas Murray, an avid opponent of the leadership of Laborers Union Local No. 324, arrived at the Union Hall and distributed copies of his newsletter. A union official who was present at the time ordered Murray to leave the union hall. When Murray refused, the official sent for the police. The police, however, declined to arrest Murray because the union official could not produce any written rules that prohibited Murray from handing out literature. Four days after this incident, the union enacted a rule that prohibited handing out literature in the union hall. Not to be denied, Murray responded by passing out his newsletters in the parking lot of the hall. Again, he was threatened with arrest. This time however, the police were not called. Nevertheless, Murray registered a complaint against the union with the National Labor Relations Board (NLRB) arguing that both the new anti-literature rule and the arrest threat violated the anti-coercion provisions of federal labor law. The case was brought before an administrative law judge who ruled in favor of Murray. The union appealed to the NLRB, which also sided with Murray. The Ninth Circuit Court of Appeals had a slightly different take on the case, however. The appellate court decided that the rule itself was a perfectly legitimate way for the union to run its own business. The fact that union leadership created the rule because they were fed up with Murray's relentless criticism did not matter. However, the appeals court did think the union had gone too far in repeatedly threatening Murray with arrest. Therefore, the court declared that the NLRB's order compelling the union to announce that it would never harass members with arrest threats again was probably a good idea, and a notice to that effect went up as ordered. (See *Laborers Union Local No. 324 v. National Labor Relations Board*, Case No. 95-70700, U.S. Court of Appeals for the Ninth Circuit.)

Opening Case Questions

1. Which federal labor law added the anti-coercion provision?

2. What was the underlying purpose of this act?

3. What other provisions prohibiting unfair labor practices are included in that law?

4. When was this law passed by Congress?

5. Which federal labor law was passed by Congress after this act?

LO Learning Objectives

1. Relate the historical context in which unions developed.
2. Outline the congressional–judicial tug-of-war in union history.
3. List the basic aims of labor unions.
4. Identify the major provision of the Norris-LaGuardia Act.
5. Indicate the primary tenets of the Wagner Act.
6. List the functions of the Taft-Hartley Act.
7. Explain the provisions of the Landrum-Griffin Act.
8. Describe the jurisdiction of the National Labor Relations Board.
9. Identify the possible results of a complaint filed with the NLRB.
10. Distinguish between the public sector's right to strike in the states and at the federal level.

John L. Lewis (left), founder of the Congress of Industrial Workers (CIO), and Samuel Gompers (right), founder of the American Federation of Labor (AFL), combined to form the AFL-CIO in 1955. Labor unions continue to shape the way companies operate.

36-1 Labor Law and the Complex Adaptive System

A **labor union** is an organization that acts on behalf of all employees in negotiations with the employer regarding the terms of their employment. It is a lawful assembly that is protected by the First Amendment to the United States Constitution and by federal and state statutes. Americans have always had a love–hate affair with unions. On the one hand, they recognize that the marketplace should be allowed to fluctuate without undue interference from the government. On the other hand, they acknowledge that businesses, when left unregulated, often take advantage of that freedom and exploit the labor market. Americans also recognize that people ought to have the right to enter and leave the job market at will. Yet they also recognize that employers hold a great deal of power in the labor market and are therefore grateful when unions create a more level playing field. This seesaw-like relationship is evident in the historical development of the union movement in the United States.

A Complex Adaptive Tug-of-War

LO1

LO2

The history of union development in the United States affords us one of the most vivid examples of how the law operates as a complex adaptive system. In this case, two powerful agents in the legal system, the legislature and the courts, were at odds for a long period of time and thus played off one another in a lengthy and complicated tug-of-war. Although this legal tug-of-war really had no definitive beginning, for the sake of convenience, we can identify the passage of the Sherman Antitrust Act in 1890 as a logical starting point. This statute was designed to break up the great anticompetitive trusts of the nineteenth century. However, the act was also used by big business, with the support of the courts, to outlaw union activities in a way that had been neither anticipated nor sanctioned by Congress. One of the primary legal tools that the courts used against strikes was the injunction. Big business argued that the net effect of a strike was to hurt a company's ability to compete with rival companies. As such, it was an illegal restraint of trade under the Sherman Act. The courts agreed and willingly issued injunctions, even when a union simply threatened to strike against a company as a bargaining tactic.

Congress reacted to this example of judicial activism by passing the Clayton Act in 1914. One of the central objectives of the Clayton Act was to hamper the federal courts' ability to issue injunctions to stop union activities. The federal judicial system, however, effectively destroyed the Clayton Act when the Supreme Court created two criteria that allowed the courts to issue injunctions freely to stop labor activities. The first test was the objectives test. Under this test, a court could issue an injunction if it determined that the goal or the objective of a strike was unlawful. Under the second test, the means test, the courts could stop a strike if it was conducted in an unlawful manner. The two tests were easily manipulated by big business so that the courts routinely issued injunctions in ways that had not been foreseen nor intended by Congress. Not to be outdone, Congress reacted to this subterfuge by passing the Norris-LaGuardia Act in 1932. The net effect of the Norris-LaGuardia Act was to prohibit the federal courts completely from issuing injunctions against union-organized strikes. The law also forbids the courts from using injunctions to stop picketing or boycotts organized by unions.

LO3 LO4 The Objectives of Labor Organization

The Norris-LaGuardia Act was just one step down a long road of labor law development. Later labor laws both promoted the aims of labor unions and helped prevent unions from becoming too powerful. Many different types of unions have developed over the years since the advent of the Norris-LaGuardia Act. Whatever their form, however, labor unions have several objectives in common. These objectives include (1) creating a seniority system to protect workers' jobs from arbitrary layoffs and replacement with less demanding wage earners; (2) upgrading worker status through wage and fringe benefit increases; and (3) sponsoring laws that improve social, economic, and political conditions for workers.

Quick Quiz 36-1 True or False?

1. A labor union is an organization that acts on behalf of all employees in negotiations with the employer regarding the terms of their employment.

2. Labor union activity is not protected by the First Amendment.

3. One of the first successful union organizing efforts took place in 1886, when Samuel Gompers organized the Congress of Industrial Workers.

36-2 Major Federal Labor Legislation

After the Norris-LaGuardia Act was passed by Congress in 1932, several tough labor laws were enacted. The three most important legislative enactments are the National Labor Relations Act of 1935 (generally referred to as the Wagner Act); the Labor-Management Relations Act of 1947 (popularly referred to as the Taft-Hartley Act); and the Labor Management Reporting and Disclosure Act of 1959 (often simply called the Landrum-Griffin Act). The first of these was designed to support labor's attempt to organize. The last two were designed to curb some unanticipated problems that accompanied the growth of unions in the United States. (See Table 36-1.)

The Wagner Act

The passage of the National Labor Relations Act in 1935 (commonly known as the Wagner Act) opened the door for the rapid growth of the union movement. It is probably the most significant labor relations statute, in that it expressly sets forth the unfair labor practices prohibited for both employers and unions.

The Wagner Act gives workers the right to organize by allowing them to form, join, or aid labor unions. It also establishes procedures for representative elections and

Did You Know?

In the fourteenth century, a "Confraternity of Beggars," complete with by-laws, officers, and membership conditions, was established to benefit the blind in Strasbourg.

LO5

Table 36-1 Federal Laws Governing Labor-Management Relations

Year	Law	Major Provisions
1914	Clayton Act	Exempted union activity from the antitrust laws
1926	Railway Labor Act	Provided for supervision of collective bargaining for railroads and airlines Established the National Mediation Board to conduct union elections and mediate employer-union disputes
1932	Norris-LaGuardia Act	Outlawed yellow-dog contracts Limited the power of federal courts to issue injunctions to halt labor disputes Guaranteed employees the right to organize into unions and to engage in collective bargaining
1935	Wagner Act	Created the National Labor Relations Board (NLRB) Authorized NLRB to conduct representative elections and to determine the bargaining unit Outlawed certain conduct by employers as unfair labor practices Authorized NLRB to hold hearings on unfair labor practice petitions
1947	Taft-Hartley Act	Outlawed certain practices by unions as unfair labor practices Allowed states to legislate right-to-work laws Provided an 80-day cooling-off period in strikes that endangered national health or safety Created a mediation and conciliation service to assist in the settlement of labor disputes
1959	Landrum-Griffin Act	Established a bill of rights for union members Required unions to adopt constitutions and bylaws Required unions to submit annual reports detailing assets, liabilities, payments, and loans Added further provisions to the list of unfair labor practices

collective bargaining. After a union has been chosen to represent the employees of a business, only that union can bargain with management. After the union has been set up at a business, individual workers cannot, on their own initiative, negotiate with management. The union has the exclusive right to bargain with the management of the business, even if the employees do not agree with how the union is handling a matter. The Wagner Act is also known for its creation of the National Labor Relations Board (NLRB), which hears and rules on charges that unfair labor practices have been committed by employers or by unions.

Various activities are prohibited by the Wagner Act as **unfair labor practices**, that is, improper employment practices by either an employer or union. These activities include the following:

- Interference with employees' right to organize.
- Domination or interference with the formation or administration of any union.
- Discrimination to encourage or discourage union membership.
- Discharge for charges filed or testimony given.
- Refusal to bargain collectively.

Talking Points

No two intellectuals appear to be further apart than Adam Smith, the spiritual founder of capitalism, and Karl Marx, the principal architect of communism. Yet if we read the following two excerpts from their most influential treatises, they appear to be in agreement on at least one point: the propensity of workers to unite in a common cause and eventually become violent as a result.

> Such combinations, however, are frequently resisted by a contrary defensive combination of the workmen; who sometimes too, without any provocation of this kind, combine of their own accord to raise the price of their labour. Their usual pretences are, sometimes the high price of provisions; sometimes the great profit which their masters make by their work. But whether their combinations be offensive or defensive, they are always abundantly heard of. In order to bring the point to a speedy decision, they have always recourse to the loudest clamour, and sometimes to the most shocking violence and outrage.
>
> —Adam Smith, *Wealth of Nations,* p. 71.
>
> The unceasing improvement of machinery, ever more rapidly developing, makes their livelihood more and more precarious. The collisions between individual workmen and individual bourgeois take more and more the character of collisions between two classes. Thereupon the workers begin to form combinations (trade unions) against the bourgeois; they join together in order to keep up the rate of wages; they form permanent associations in order to make provision beforehand for these occasional revolts. Here and there the contest breaks out into riots.
>
> —Karl Marx and Frederick Engels, *Essential Works of Marxism,* p. 21.

Looking back from a historical perspective, were Marx and Smith correct in their predictions that unionization leads to violence? Is such violence ever justifiable from a moral perspective? If these two philosophers are convinced that unionization leads to violence, at what point do you suppose they part company? Explain.

See Karl Marx and Frederick Engels, "The Communist Manifesto," in *Essential Works of Marxism,* Arthur P. Mendel, ed. (New York: Bantam Books, 1961); Adam Smith, *An Inquiry into the Nature and Causes of The Wealth of Nations* (Amherst, NY: Prometheus Books, 1991).

Interference with Employees' Right to Organize   An employer cannot interfere with employees when they are forming a union, selecting their representatives, voting, striking, picketing, or engaging in any other protected and legal acts. For example, an employer cannot threaten to fire or discipline a worker for union activity or reward workers who do not participate in union activities. Threats to eliminate certain benefits or privileges, to close down the business, or to discharge workers for union activity also are prohibited.

EXAMPLE 36-1: Insubordination or Inconsistency: Which One Trumps the Other?

In his 10 years as a chef at the Imperial National Hotel in Houston, James Kirby might have been fired several times for violating work rules. He frequently refused to follow orders, disobeying direct instructions from his supervisor. When a union began organizing the kitchen service and housekeeping staff, Kirby strongly supported the effort. During the organizing campaign, Kirby apparently acted in an insubordinate manner and was discharged. At a subsequent NLRB hearing, his discharge was found to be tainted. On appeal, the court reasoned that, though Kirby was far from the valued and trusted employee the union claimed he was, the hotel had tolerated his insubordination for 10 years. The court held that Kirby's discharge was more the result of his union activities than his work performance and reinstated him with back pay.

Domination or Interference with the Formation or Administration of Any Union

An employer cannot form a company-run union for its employees. The purpose of this prohibition is to bar company-owned unions from bowing to the wishes of management. It is also an unfair practice to aid one union over another, place employer spies at union meetings, reward some union officials, or agree with a union that a closed shop will be maintained. A **closed shop** is a work site in which the employer, by agreement, hires only union members in good standing. It is usually lawful, however, to have a provision allowing a union shop in the employment contract. A **union shop** is a place of employment in which nonunion workers may be employed for a trial period of not more than 30 days, after which the nonunion workers must join the union or be discharged.

Discrimination to Encourage or Discourage Union Membership

Intentional discrimination by the employer toward an employee to encourage or discourage union membership is an unfair labor practice. Such discrimination may involve assigning an employee to less desirable work or denying an employee the opportunity to participate in overtime work. Also viewed as discriminatory is **constructive discharge**, which occurs when an employee is demoted to a job with lesser pay or authority or poorer working conditions than a previously held job or when the employee is subjected to supervisory harassment. To avoid employee complaints of intentional discrimination, employers must rely on meaningful business reasons when bestowing or denying employment opportunities.

EXAMPLE 36-2:   Constructive Discharge: Nothing Trivial About It

Teresa Remington was chosen by union members to serve as their representative in collective bargaining meetings with the Harrisburg Construction Company. After her selection, Remington was harassed by the general manager of her department for trivial matters pertaining to scheduled lunch breaks and the cleanliness of her locker in the break room. Remington has the right to file a complaint with the NLRB, charging constructive discharge due to her union activities.

Discharge for Charges Filed or Testimony Given

It is unlawful for employers to discharge or otherwise discriminate against employees because they file charges or give testimony under the Wagner Act. The courts interpret discrimination under this provision to include discharge, layoff, failure to rehire or recall, and transfer of covered employees.

Refusal to Bargain Collectively

An employer must negotiate with employee representatives over wages, hours, the effects of business changes on employees, grievance procedures, health benefits, seniority systems, dues checkoffs, and vacations. Issues must be discussed willingly, free of delaying tactics, coercion, or harassment by both sides. The employer has no duty to agree to any union demands but must meet with employee representatives at reasonable times and places to bargain in good faith. Neither party can bargain about a closed shop contract, politics, religious issues, management functions, or foreign affairs. The NLRB has no jurisdiction over religious schools, both on labor relations grounds and by virtue of the religion clauses of the First Amendment of the U.S. Constitution. The U.S. Supreme Court has ruled that the requirements of collective bargaining would represent an encroachment upon the freedom of church authorities to shape and direct teaching in accordance with the requirements of their religion.

The Taft-Hartley Act

The Labor-Management Relations Act of 1947, popularly named the Taft-Hartley Act, established a means to protect employers in collective bargaining and labor organization matters. The act also prohibits union officials from using coercive or abusive tactics against its own members. A detailed list of unfair labor activities that unions, as well as employers, were forbidden to practice was added to those of the Wagner Act.

State Right-to-Work Laws

State laws that prohibit labor–management agreements requiring union membership as a condition of getting or keeping a job are called **right-to-work laws**. These laws, in effect, outlaw both the closed shop and the union shop.

Ordinarily, state labor relations laws have not applied to unions and businesses that are involved in interstate commerce and that are governed by federal labor laws. The Taft-Hartley Act, however, has created special rules with regard to state right-to-work laws. It provides that union shop contracts are legal only in states that do not forbid them. As a result, state right-to-work laws, where they exist, are applicable to most unions and businesses. All employees in the **bargaining unit** (i.e., a unit formed for the purpose of collective bargaining) are benefited by the collective bargaining agreement negotiated by the union, even if they have not paid union dues. However, nonunion employees lose all right to vote on union officers or collective bargaining agreements.

Free Speech Provision

The Taft-Hartley Act includes a free speech provision that allows employers to comment freely on union organizing activities. The provision states that employers do not commit an unfair labor practice by speaking to employees about unions unless they threaten reprisal or promise some benefit to employees. For instance, an employer might properly inform its employees that they should not vote for a union, but a threat to fire anyone for favoring a union shop would be an unfair labor practice.

Employee Anti-Coercion Provision

It is also an unfair labor practice for a labor union to try to coerce employees to join the union, block the employment of individuals who refuse to support a union, or encourage an employee to withdraw an unfair labor practice charge. A union can set rules for its internal operations and punish any member who refuses to follow them, but it cannot use force, violence, or intimidation against an employee. A union is also not permitted to discipline one of its members without good cause. The union has a duty to represent all of its members on an equal basis.

Secondary Boycott

It is also prohibited for a union to engage in a **secondary boycott**. This action is a conspiracy in which a union places pressure on a neutral customer or supplier with whom the union has no dispute to cause the neutral entity to cease doing business with the employer with whom the union has a dispute. Under the Taft-Hartley Act provision, it is an unfair labor practice for a union (1) to strike against an employer because another employer uses nonunion employees, (2) to strike against a general contractor to force the contractor to stop dealing with a subcontractor, (3) to ask employees of another company not to load trucks carrying the products of a company the union is striking, or (4) to refuse to work on products made by nonunion employees.

The Opening Case Revisited

Laborers Union Local No. 324 v. National Labor Relations Board, Round 2

Recall that, in The Opening Case at the beginning of the chapter, Douglas Murray, a member of Local No. 324, was threatened by union officials with arrest on more than one occasion if he did not stop distributing his anti-leadership newsletter at the union hall. On one occasion when the police actually arrived on the scene, they refused to arrest Murray because the union had no rule that prohibited the activity that Murray was involved in. In reaction, the union passed a rule that prohibited the handing out of any literature at the union hall. When Murray registered a complaint with the NLRB, both the administrative law judge and the NLRB saw the rule for what it was—a direct reaction to Murray and his opposition to union leadership. The appeals court, however, was less concerned about the short-term motive for the passage of the rule and more with the actual substance of that rule. Thus, the court saw the rule simply as a way for the union to govern its own operation, something that was still protected under the law. However, the appeals court did regard the constant arrest threats against Murray as a violation of the anti-coercion tactics that had been outlawed by Taft-Hartley. Apparently, the union also saw the error of its ways in this regard, because union leadership did not contest that part of the NLRB's decision.

EXAMPLE 36-3:   Secondary Boycotts: Of Primary Concern

The Benning Oil Company sold fuel oil to the Monarchy Empire Hotel chain. The oil was shipped on tankers owned by the Metroliner Transport Corporation, whose employees were nonunion. The union representing Benning instructed its members to refuse to ship the fuel oil to the docks where the Metroliner tankers were docked to force Benning to stop using a nonunion shipper. This form of secondary boycott is an unfair labor practice, because it involved an innocent employer in a union tactic intended to harm another employer.

National Emergency Strikes   The Taft-Hartley Act gives the president of the United States special powers to deal with actual or threatened strikes that affect interstate commerce or that endanger the nation's health and safety. On the basis of a board of inquiry's findings, the president can order the attorney general to petition a federal district court to issue an injunction, stopping the strike for 60 days. The board of inquiry may then require the union members to vote on the most recent offer within an additional 15-day period and to send the results to the attorney general within 5 days after balloting. When the injunction ends after this 80-day period, the employees may strike. However, the president can then make legislative recommendations to Congress that would resolve the dispute.

Other Prohibited Union Practices   Under other provisions of the Taft-Hartley Act, unions cannot refuse to bargain collectively with an employer and must give notice to the employer of an intention to strike prior to the termination date of a collective bargaining contract. It is also an unfair labor practice for a labor union to require an employer to keep unneeded employees, pay employees for not working, or assign more employees to a given job than are needed (i.e., **featherbedding**). Another provision of the law prohibits a union from requiring employees who join a union to pay excessively high dues, fees, and related expenses. To determine what is excessive, the courts consider the amounts other unions charge and the employee's wages.

The Landrum-Griffin Act

The Labor Management Reporting and Disclosure Act of 1959, known as the Landrum-Griffin Act, is a tough anticorruption law. It is designed to clean up the corruption and violence that had been uncovered in the internal affairs of unions. The law requires all unions to adopt constitutions and bylaws and to register them with the secretary of labor. In addition, unions are required to submit annual reports detailing assets, liabilities, receipts, sources, payments to union members exceeding $10,000, loans to union members and businesses, and other monies paid out.

Bill of Rights Provision   An important part of the Landrum-Griffin Act is the bill of rights provision for union members. This provision assures all union members of the opportunity to participate in the internal affairs of their union. They are guaranteed the right to vote in union elections, to speak at union meetings, and to receive union financial reports.

Hot-Cargo Agreement   The Landrum-Griffin Act amended the Taft-Hartley Act, making it an unlawful labor practice to become involved in a **hot-cargo contract**. In this type of agreement, an employer voluntarily agrees with a union not to handle, use, or deal in nonunion-produced goods of another employer.

BusinessWeek **Business Law in the News**

Autos: A Deal That Could Save Detroit

Just a few weeks ago, United Auto Workers President Ron Gettelfinger had nothing but contempt for the "strip-and-flip" private equity investors bidding for Chrysler Group. So most people expected him to come out slugging when Cerberus Capital Management agreed to buy the struggling automaker on May 14. Instead Gettelfinger embraced Chrysler's new owner. "The status quo is off the table," he declared.

Attitudes are evolving rapidly in Detroit these days, and it is clear that the arrival of the bare-knuckle financial wizards from Cerberus is only going to hasten the pace of change in town. Managers and UAW leaders alike appear to accept that a time of reckoning is at hand. As they look ahead to landmark labor talks this summer, both sides finally appear set to face up to the most vexing problem of all: unsustainably high health-care costs. Thanks to luxe benefits handed over during the golden age of corporate largesse in the 1950s, the Big Three will have an estimated $120 billion in long-term medical liabilities, a crippling burden that puts them at a nearly insurmountable disadvantage to global rivals.

But General Motors, Ford Motor, and Chrysler's new owners at Cerberus believe they may have a cure for Detroit's epic health-care woes. Their idea: to propose handing over the companies' long-term liability to an independent fund managed by UAW, which would be financed by a huge one-time injection of cash and stock. Union workers would probably contribute more toward their own coverage costs but would gain protection from the devastating prospect of bankruptcy. The automakers, meanwhile, would wall off a risk that terrifies investors— and earn perhaps their final shot at becoming competitive again. "I think an independent health-care fund has to happen," says Sean McAlinden, chief economist at the Center for Automotive Research in Ann Arbor, Mich. "Ron Gettelfinger may even be resigned to doing it."

This radical idea already has some precedent in Detroit. In 2005 GM and the UAW created a so-called voluntary employee benefits association (VEBA) trust, for a small portion of the company's retiree health-care expenses. The union has also consented to VEBA funds for individual plants belonging to a few parts suppliers. Over the past few months, managers at all three car manufacturers have been closely studying a similar deal struck between the United Steelworkers and Goodyear Tire & Rubber Co. in December that relieved the tiremaker from most of its medical obligations without stiffing union workers.

While the Big Three have not been trumpeting the VEBA trust plan, expect to hear more about it as this summer's labor talks approach. Creating such a trust "for the whole industry [is the] primary objective of this year's round of bargaining," says one investment banker well-connected in Detroit. "That's clearly what the Big Three want." . . .

If it all sounds too good to be true, it may very well be. The devil will be in the plan's infinite details. The companies' ability to fund a big trust, first of all, depends upon how much money the UAW requests. If the union seeks assets totaling 80% of liabilities, then GM and Ford may not be able to afford it. Since GM already borrowed $18 billion in 2003 to shore up its pension fund and Ford borrowed $23.5 billion this year for restructuring, neither wants to shoulder much more long-term debt. Both have junk bond debt ratings, so the money would be quite expensive.

At some point, a judge would also have to sign off on a global Big Three trust, because Ford and GM face a legal impediment. When the union gave them concessions on health care last year, a lawsuit was filed to freeze retiree benefits. The courts upheld the deal, but froze the new benefits package until 2011. GM Chairman and CEO G. Richard Wagoner Jr. said in a December interview that further concessions made on behalf of those retirees would

need court approval. The same goes for Ford—but not Chrysler, which never won the same health-care concessions as its rivals. . . .

If giant independent trusts get established for all of the auto companies, one far-reaching implication of the move is that the UAW would become an enormous health-care provider. Another is that the union would be forced to manage benefits. That means if costs rise faster than investment returns, the union might have to offer weaker medical benefits to its own members. Right now, if health care gets more expensive, GM, Ford, and Chrysler just cut bigger checks. But it's possible the UAW may do just as well at managing the money as the companies do. Major union-run pension plans nationwide made nearly 14.6% returns last year, about half a point better than large corporate-run funds did, according to Wilshire Associates.

So there's reason to believe that the UAW, even though it will certainly negotiate aggressively, may be willing to go for the idea of a VEBA trust. Although the idea would have been a nonstarter in 2003, the last time the union contract was renegotiated, things have taken a powerful turn for the worse in the past few years. And the arrival of Cerberus may well increase Detroit's willingness to engage in complex financial engineering. "You bring in private equity, and the game changes," says Center for Automotive Research Chairman David E. Cole.

Questions for Analysis

1. What is the main collective bargaining problem currently involved in negotiations between the United Auto Workers (UAW) and Chrysler?

2. What course of action has been offered to solve this problem?

3. Which car makers would be involved in this solution?

4. Are there any precedents for this type of cooperation between labor and management?

5. What problems might yet derail this unusually optimistic labor–management plan?

Source: David Welch and Nanette Byrnes with Anthony Bianco, "News & Insights–Autos: A Deal that Could Save Detroit: A Chrysler Sale to Cerberus May Spark a Plan to Eliminate Most of the Health-Care Liabilities Crushing Carmakers," *BusinessWeek*, May 28, 2007, 30–33.

36-3 The Collective Bargaining Process

The Taft-Hartley Act established a system for helping labor and management settle their disputes without causing a major disruption in the economy or endangering the public health and safety. Central to this collective bargaining process is the NLRB and the procedures it follows in settling labor–management disputes.

The National Labor Relations Board

The NLRB is a governmental commission that has the exclusive jurisdiction to enforce the Taft-Hartley Act and related laws. It has the power to act when cases are brought before it, but only in cases in which the employer's operation or the labor dispute affects commerce. Like most government regulatory agencies, the NLRB has investigative, regulatory, administrative, enforcement, and judgmental powers. It can make its own rules of procedure, conduct investigations into unfair labor practice charges, compel individuals to appear with papers relevant to the controversy, hold hearings, and issue orders. Appeals from the five-member board go first to the appropriate U.S. Court of Appeals and then to the U.S. Supreme Court.

Unfair Labor Practice Procedure

A person, union, or employer can file notice with the NLRB of an alleged unfair labor practice within six months after it occurs. It is important to remember that unfair labor practices include not only those practices that occur between management and the labor union but also those between a union and its own members. This point is a crucial part of the union representation process, because once a collective bargaining unit is formed, the employees have only one recourse when they have a grievance, and that is through the union. Consequently, the law imposes an affirmative duty on the unions to be fair in their representation of all members. This rule does not mean that the union cannot monitor its own internal affairs, nor does it mean that unions must represent those outside of the bargaining unit. However, once a worker becomes a member of a union, he or she has the right to expect fair and equal treatment, and the union has the duty to deliver such treatment or be liable for not doing so.

If the charge has merit, a complaint is issued to notify the offending party that a hearing is to be held concerning the charges. Efforts are made through arbitration to resolve the dispute before the hearing date. **Arbitration** involves the submission of the dispute to selected persons and the substitution of their decision for the judgment of the NLRB. If arbitration efforts fail, the hearing is held. In the event that the complaint is found to be valid, a cease-and-desist order may be issued, restoring the parties to the state that existed before the unfair practice began. For example, wrongfully discharged employees may be reinstated with or without back pay. Evidence at the hearing that does not support the complaint is dismissed.

Either party to the hearing may subsequently appeal the NLRB action to the appropriate U.S. Court of Appeals and then to the Supreme Court.

Mediation   The Taft-Hartley Act encourages labor and management to agree freely on the settlement of disputes. To further this effort to preserve labor peace and promote prompt settlements, Congress has formed the Federal Mediation and Conciliation Service. This body can act by itself or upon the request of either side to a labor dispute. Its mediation role is to offer nonbinding suggestions for settling the dispute, require the parties to negotiate, and force a vote by employees on an employer's offers.

The Right to Strike in the Public Sector

Strikes, like the 2003 Chicago garbage strike, can cause major inconveniece and hardship for the general public. Unions often count on public pressure to get favorable concessions from management.

In the public sector, when the general welfare, safety, health, and morals of the public are involved, the right to strike is restricted. Consequently, strikes by police, firefighters, refuse collectors, air traffic controllers, postal workers, and other public employees who perform vital services are generally illegal, unless specifically authorized by statute. The U.S. Code states that "an individual may not accept or hold a position in the government of the United States or the government of the District of Columbia if he participates in a strike or asserts the right to strike against the government." The U.S. Supreme Court has affirmed lower court rulings that there is no constitutional right to strike against the federal government. Thus, strikes by federal employees are substantially more than merely unfair labor practices; they are crimes.

EXAMPLE 36-4:   Air Traffic Controllers: To Strike or Not To Strike

The air traffic controllers, employees of the Federal Aviation Administration, went on strike. The controller's union, the Professional Air Traffic Controllers Organization, demanded that the controllers be removed from the civil service designation that prohibited them from striking. They argued that prohibition of the right to strike was a violation of a fundamental civil liberty. A federal district court ruled that government employees did not have the right to strike because Congress had not given them such a right. The controllers persisted in their strike. As a result, all striking controllers were fired, and the union was fined $100,000 an hour for the duration of the strike. The union was subsequently decertified, removing its rights to bargain on behalf of the controllers.

A Question of Ethics

The air traffic controllers in Example 36-4 simply wanted rights that are guaranteed to many similarly situated workers. They argued that prohibition of the right to strike was a violation of a fundamental civil liberty. Nevertheless, the Court held that Congress had the authority to deny them that right. Consequently, the firing of the striking air traffic controllers was legal. Now consider whether the firing was ethical. Explain your response.

Did You Know?

Union membership in Great Britain surpassed 2 million at the beginning of the twentieth century.

(Continue)

This level made the British labor movement the most influential European union movement up to that time in history.

Quick Quiz 36-3 True or False?

1. There is no appeal permitted after a decision has been rendered by the National Labor Relations Board.

2. If a complaint is found valid under the NLRB procedures, a cease-and-desist order may be issued, restoring the parties to the state that existed before the unfair labor practice began.

3. The United States Supreme Court has repeatedly affirmed that federal employees have a constitutionally protected right to strike.

Summary

36.1   The first federal statute relating to labor was the Clayton Act, which attempted to prohibit federal courts from forbidding activities such as picketing and strikes. The Norris-LaGuardia Act specified acts, such as striking, picketing, and boycotting, that were not subject to federal injunctions.

36.2   The Wagner Act opened the door for the growth of labor unions. It set forth specific labor practices that were prohibited for employers and unions, established procedures for representative elections and collective bargaining, and created the NLRB. The Taft-Hartley Act outlaws specific conduct by unions as unfair labor practices and provides for an 80-day cooling off period in strikes that endanger national health or safety. The Act also provides a mediation and conciliation service to assist in the settlement of labor disputes. The Landrum-Griffin Act provides a bill of rights for union members, requires unions to report to the secretary of labor, and has added to the list of unfair labor practices.

36.3   The NLRB has exclusive jurisdiction to enforce labor–management relations laws with investigative, regulatory, administrative, enforcement, and judgment powers. Any person, union, or employer can file notice with the NLRB of an alleged unfair labor practice. If the complaint has merit, a hearing is held before the NLRB. If the complaint is found to be valid, an order may be issued restoring the parties to the state existing prior to the unfair practice. Appeals of NLRB actions can be taken to the appropriate U.S. Circuit Court of Appeals and then to the U.S. Supreme Court. The Federal Mediation and Conciliation Service was formed to encourage labor and management to agree freely on the settlement of their disputes. Its mediation role is to offer nonbinding suggestions for settling the dispute, require the parties to negotiate, and force a vote by employees on employers' offers. In the public sector, the right to strike is restricted. The U.S. Code states that "an individual may not accept or hold a position in the government of the United States or the government of the District of Columbia if he participates in a strike or asserts the right to strike against the government."

Key Terms

arbitration, 758

bargaining unit, 754

closed shop, 753

constructive discharge, 753

featherbedding, 756

hot-cargo contract, 756

labor union, 749

right-to-work laws, 754

secondary boycott, 754

unfair labor practices, 751

union shop, 753

Questions for Review and Discussion

1. In what historical context did unions develop?
2. What was the nature of the congressional–judicial tug-of-war in union history?
3. What are the basic aims of labor unions?
4. What was the major provision of the Norris-LaGuardia Act?
5. What are the primary tenets of the Wagner Act?
6. What are the functions of the Taft-Hartley Act?
7. What are the provisions of the Landrum-Griffin Act?
8. What is the extent of the jurisdiction of the National Labor Relations Board?
9. What possible results can come from filing a complaint with the NLRB?
10. What is the difference between the public sector's right to strike in the states and at the federal level?

Investigating the Internet

The Democratic Labor Movement maintains a Web site called *LaborNet*. Access the home page of *LaborNet* and, as a research project, answer the following questions: (1) What other labor nets can be accessed from the *LaborNet* home page? (2) What additional *LaborNet* resources can be found by accessing the "Resources" link on the home page? (3) What mainstream news media sources does *LaborNet* recommend? (4) What international labor information sources does *LaborNet* promote? (5) What general reference sources does *LaborNet* advocate?

Cases for Analysis

1. Nine longshoremen, all of whom were members of Local 13 of the International Longshoremen's and Warehousemen's Union, found that they were having difficulty getting jobs. The problem seemed to be that Local 13 had refused to place them on a hiring list at the union's hiring hall. Because this list was the only way that union members could get jobs as longshoremen, the nine union members were in effect being boycotted by the union and, as a result, by all potential employers. When the out-of-work union members filed grievances with Local 13, they were effectively ignored. To challenge these actions (as well as others not covered here), the out-of-work longshoremen filed a complaint with the National Labor Relations Board (NLRB). The NLRB and the District Court dismissed the complaint, and the longshoremen appealed. The union argued that the question of whether to place certain members on the hiring list was a purely in-

ternal union affair that could not be challenged by the NLRB or the courts. The longshoreman contended that by refusing to place them on the list and ignoring their grievances, the union was being unfair to them. Should the appeals court overturn this ruling by the NLRB and the District Court? Explain. *Richard Diaz, et al. v. International Longshoremen's and Warehousemen's Union, Local 13*, Case No. 04-56957 (U.S. Court of Appeals for the Ninth Circuit).

2. The union representing employees of the Consolidated Manufacturing Company elected Franco and Allanson to act on their behalf at a collective bargaining session with management. At the session, Franco and Allanson demanded that the new collective bargaining agreement include terms that would require management to hire only union members in good standing. Management disagreed with this proposal. Instead, management offered a

term in the agreement that would allow the company to hire nonunion workers for a trial period lasting no more than 30 days. After the 30-day trial period, the nonunion worker would have to join a union. Which of these terms in the proposed collective bargaining agreement would be allowed under federal labor law? Explain. Management also proposed that the employee union be disbanded and replaced by a company-run union. Management argued that the new company-run union would not only be more efficient but also more economical than the current union. Would this proposal be allowed under federal labor law?

3. An employee was discharged for violating the company's no-solicitation rule in its factory and offices. The employee had persisted in soliciting union membership on company property during lunch periods. The company argued that its no-solicitation rule would have been enforced against not merely union solicitation but any solicitation. How would you decide? Why? *Republic Aviation Corp. v. NLRB,* 324 U.S. 793 (U.S. Sup. Ct.).

4. Having advised Exchange Parts Co. that it was conducting an organizational campaign, the union petitioned the NLRB for an election to determine whether it would be certified as the bargaining agent of the company's employees. During the organizational campaign, while the granted certification election was pending, the company announced five additional benefits for the employees, two of which were announced only a few days before the election. In the election, the employees voted against being represented by a union. The union then filed a complaint with the NLRB, charging the company with an unfair labor practice because it granted benefits while the campaign was taking place and the election was pending. The union argued that the company's actions interfered with the freedom of choice of the employees to determine whether they wished to be represented by the union. For whom would you decide? Why? *NLRB v. Exchange Parts Co.,* 375 U.S. 405 (U.S. Sup. Ct.).

5. Darlington Manufacturing Co. operated one textile mill that was controlled by Deering Milliken, which operated 27 other such mills. The union began an organizational campaign, which Darlington resisted. The employees filed charges of unfair labor practices with the NLRB. The board found in a subsequent hearing that the different mills controlled by Deering Milliken represented an integrated enterprise and that the closing of the Darlington mill was due to the antiunion hostility of Deering Milliken.

The NLRB ordered Deering Milliken to provide back pay to the workers until they obtained similar work. The court of appeals denied enforcement of the NLRB order, holding that an independent employer has an absolute right to close a business, regardless of notice. On review by the U.S. Supreme Court, how should the Court rule on the question of whether an employer has the absolute right to close part of a business, no matter what the reason? Why? *Textile Worker's Union v. Darlington Mfg. Co.,* 380 U.S. 263 (U.S. Sup. Ct.).

6. The NLRB conducted an election among employees of Savair Manufacturing Co. to determine whether the union would represent the employees. During the election, recognition slips were distributed. The employees were told by the union that if they signed the slips before the election, they would not have to pay an initiation fee if the union won. At least 35 employees signed the slips before the election, which the union won by a vote of 22 to 20. The company refused to bargain with the union, contending that the union, by offering possible benefits to employees for signing the recognition slips, was guilty of an unfair labor practice. Did the practice of the union prevent a fair and free choice of a bargaining representative? Why or why not? *NLRB v. Savair Mfg. Co.,* 414 U.S. 270 (U.S. Sup. Ct.).

7. The Department Store Employees Union (union) was selected by the employees of the Emporium Capwell Company (company) as their exclusive bargaining unit. Charges of discrimination in the workplace were levied against the company through the union. The union followed the grievance procedure, as established in the collective bargaining agreement. Some of the employees became dissatisfied with the union's handling of the case. Accordingly, they asked the union to begin to picket the company. Union officials advised these dissatisfied employees that according to the collective bargaining agreement, the union was bound to follow the established grievance procedure. The employees refused to cooperate with the grievance procedure and demanded that company management deal with them directly to establish an overall anti-discrimination policy. Later the employees also picketed the store. Written notices were given to the picketing employees, telling them that they could be discharged if they repeated the conduct. The employees ignored the notices and, after picketing on the following weekend, were discharged. The employees filed a

complaint with the National Labor Relations Board, which found that it could not support the employees. The NLRB believed that such support would challenge the exclusive bargaining power of the union and thereby subvert the statutory intent of Congress. The appeals court hearing the case reversed the Board's findings, stating its belief that discrimination cases had a special posi-

tion and thus fell outside the guarantee to the union of exclusive bargaining power. The case was appealed to the United States Supreme Court. Should the Supreme Court uphold the union's exclusive right to engage in collective bargaining with the company? Explain. *Emporium Capwell, Co. v. Western Addition Community Organization,* 420 U.S. 50. (U.S. Sup. Ct.).

Quick Quiz Answers

36-1 1. T
2. F
3. F

36-2 1. F
2. F
3. T

36-3 1. F
2. T
3. F

Part 7 Case Study

Betty Dukes v. Wal-Mart, Inc.
United States Court of Appeals for the Ninth Circuit
Case Nos. 04-16688 and 04-16720 (CA)

Summary

Betty Dukes, one of the plaintiffs in this case, worked as an employee of Wal-Mart, Inc. Over the period of her employment with Wal-Mart, she is said to have experienced and witnessed a pattern of gender discrimination that allegedly permeates the entire corporate culture of Wal-Mart. Accordingly, Dukes and a number of other plaintiffs filed a class action lawsuit against Wal-Mart under Title VII of the Civil Rights Act of 1964. The allegations made by the plaintiffs are that women who have worked at Wal-Mart (1) are consistently paid at a rate that is under the rate paid to men who have analogous jobs, even though the women have better performance records and more seniority, and (2) are forced to postpone promotions and are not promoted as often as men. The plaintiffs also claim that this scheme of gender discrimination results from an inflexible, controlled organization that invites policies and procedures that promote the stereotyping of women. The result is a habitual pattern of unfair treatment of women throughout the corporate structure. The plaintiffs have asked for injunctive and declaratory remedies. They have also asked for exemplary damages. The size of the class is calculated to be approximately 1.5 million women, including not only full- and part-time hourly workers but also salaried administrators. Because the case is a class action lawsuit, the plaintiffs have the burden of demonstrating that it meets the class requirements, as delineated in the Federal Rules of Civil Procedure. Thus, the plaintiffs must show that (1) the class has so many members that they cannot all be brought into court at the same time; (2) the issues that will form the basis of the suit are common to all of those plaintiffs; (3) the claims and defenses that will be used in the case are characteristic of the claims and defenses that would be used by the absent members; and (4) the plaintiffs who are present will be able to represent the interests of those who are absent. The interesting thing about a class action lawsuit like this one is that so much evidence must be brought to convince the court that the case should be heard as a class action, it appears as if the case is being tried without actually going to trial. Consider the following brief portion of the court's 46-page opinion and see if there is enough preliminary evidence to convince you of the plaintiff's case—or if it seems as if the appellate court judges are talking themselves into a case that just does not exist.

The Court's Opinion

PREGERSON, Circuit Judge:

Plaintiffs filed a class action suit against Wal-Mart alleging sexual discrimination under Title VII of the 1964 Civil Rights Act. The district court certified the class with minor modifications to Plaintiffs' proposed class. We have jurisdiction under 28 U.S.C. Sec. 1292(e). . . .

A district court may certify a class only if: "(1) the class is so numerous that joinder of all members is impracticable; (2) there are questions of law and fact common to the class; (3) the claims or defenses of the representative parties are typical of the claims or defenses of the class; and (4) the representative parties will fairly and adequately protect the interests of the class." Fed. R. Civ. P. 23(a). . . .

[Note: The following edited portion of the court's decision focuses only on the second requirement, that is, the question of whether the case involves issues that would be common to all the members of the class. This point is referred to by the court as the issue of commonality.]

Commonality

Rule 23(a)(2) requires that "there are questions of law or fact common to the class." Fed. R. Civ. P. 23(a)(2). Commonality focuses on the relationship of common facts and legal issues among class members. . . .

The district court found that Plaintiffs had provided evidence sufficient to support their contention that significant factual and legal questions are common to all class members. After analyzing Plaintiffs' evidence, the district court stated:

> Plaintiffs have exceeded the permissive and minimal burden of establishing commonality by providing: (1) significant evidence of company-wide corporate practices and policies, which include (a) excessive subjectivity in personnel decisions, (b) gender stereotyping, and (c) maintenance of a strong corporate culture; (2) statistical evidence of gender disparities caused by discrimination; and (3) anecdotal evidence of gender bias. Together, this evidence raises an inference that Wal-Mart engages in discriminatory practices in compensation and promotion that affect all plaintiffs in a common manner. *Dukes I,* 222 F.R.D. at 166.

The court noted that Wal-Mart raised a number of challenges to Plaintiffs' evidence of commonality but held that such objections related to the *weight* of the evidence, rather than its validity, and thus should be addressed by a jury at the merits phase. . . . Wal-Mart renews a number of those challenges. We address each challenge below.

"Significant Proof" of a Corporate Policy of Discrimination

Plaintiffs presented four categories of evidence: (1) facts supporting the existence of company-wide policies and practices; (2) expert opinions supporting the existence of company-wide policies and practices; (3) expert statistical evidence of class-wide gender disparities attributable to discrimination, and (4) anecdotal evidence from class members around the country of discriminatory attitudes held or tolerated by management. *See Dukes I,* 222 F.R.D. at 145. Wal-Mart contends that this evidence is not sufficient to raise an inference of discrimination.

(1) Factual Evidence

Plaintiffs presented evidence of: (1) uniform personnel and management structure across stores; (2) Wal-Mart headquarter's extensive oversight of store operations, company-wide policies governing pay and promotion decisions, and a strong, centralized corporate culture; (3) consistent gender-related disparities in every domestic region of the company; and (4) gender stereotyping. Such evidence supports Plaintiffs' contention that Wal-Mart operates a highly centralized company that promotes policies common to all stores and maintains a single system of oversight. Wal-Mart does not challenge this evidence. . . .

(2) Expert Opinion

Plaintiffs presented evidence from Dr. William Bielby, a sociologist, to interpret and explain the facts that suggest that Wal-Mart has and promotes a strong corporate culture—a culture that may include gender stereotyping. . . . Dr. Bielby concluded: (1) that Wal-Mart's centralized coordination, reinforced by a strong organizational culture, sustains uniformity in personnel policy and practice; (2) that there are significant deficiencies in Wal-Mart's equal employment policies and practices; and (3) that Wal-Mart's personnel policies and practices make pay and promotion decisions vulnerable to gender bias. . . .

Wal-Mart challenges Dr. Bielby's third conclusion as vague and imprecise because he concluded that Wal-Mart is "vulnerable" to bias or gender stereotyping but failed to identify a specific discriminatory policy at Wal-Mart. . . .

(3) Statistical Evidence

Dr. Richard Drogin, Plaintiffs' statistician, analyzed data at a regional level. He ran separate regression analyses for each of the forty-one regions containing Wal-Mart stores. He concluded that "there are statistically significant disparities between men and women at Wal-Mart in terms of compensation and promotions, that these disparities are wide-spread across regions, and that they can be explained only by gender discrimination." *Dukes I,* 222 F.R.D. at 154. . . .

Wal-Mart challenges Dr. Drogin's findings and faults his decision to conduct his research on a regional level, rather than analyze the data store-by-store. . . .

(4) Anecdotal Evidence

In their declarations, the potential class members testified to being paid less than similarly situated men, being denied or delayed in receiving promotions in a disproportionate manner when compared with similarly situated men, working in an atmosphere with a strong corporate culture of discrimination, and being subjected to various individual sexist acts. The district court credited this evidence.

Wal-Mart contends that the district court erred because the 120 declarations cannot sufficiently represent a class of 1.5 million. . . .

Conclusion

Plaintiffs' expert opinions, factual evidence, statistical evidence, and anecdotal evidence present significant proof of a corporate policy of discrimination and support Plaintiffs' contention that female employees nationwide were subjected to a common pattern and practice of discrimination. Evidence of Wal-Mart's subjective decision-making policy raises an inference of discrimination and provides further evidence of a common practice. Accordingly, we conclude that the district court did not abuse its discretion in holding that Plaintiffs satisfied the commonality factor.

Questions for Analysis

1. Does this case involve a claim of disparate treatment or disparate impact? Explain

2. What changes to the Civil Rights Act made by Congress in 1991 would have affected the remedies sought by the plaintiffs in this case? Explain.

3. Why did the plaintiffs bring this case under the Civil Rights Act rather than the Equal Pay Act? Explain.

4. If the plaintiffs can demonstrate that only certain parts of the policies and procedures instituted by Wal-Mart are discriminatory, will they still prevail? Explain.

5. Is the statistical evidence convincing in this case? Explain.

Part Eight

Business Organization and Regulation

Chapter 37

Sole Proprietorships and Partnerships

The Opening Case
Robinson v. Kleinfeld

When Josef Kleinfeld first arrived in the United States in the late 1980s, he had no idea what to do with the small inheritance that he had acquired after his parents' deaths. As he wandered around the streets of lower Manhattan, it did not take him long to discover that one of the fastest growing businesses in the city was the video rental store. Kleinfeld used his inheritance to purchase a building in the East Village and opened his outlet store on the ground floor. Unfortunately, Kleinfeld was so inexperienced in business matters and so slow to adjust to the fast moving technology of the video market that he lost a great deal of money during his first year of operation. Things became so bad that he decided that he had to fire his only clerk, a young New York University student named Dawn Robinson. Robinson had other ideas. She prevailed upon Kleinfeld to keep her on as his clerk by convincing him that she would forego her hourly wages and instead take a percentage of the store's profits every two weeks. That way, Kleinfeld would not have to pay her anything at all if the store did not make any money during any given two-week period. Kleinfeld, who could see that Robinson had great knowledge about the video market and was very skillful in handling customers, gave her more and more responsibility in the operation of store matters. Eventually, Robinson was running the entire business. She hired and fired clerks, ordered tapes, set prices, balanced the books, handled payroll, wrote the firm's employee manual, and filled out the firm's tax returns every year. Her business acumen also led her to move Kleinfeld's store away from Beta tapes and into an exclusive VHS business much more quickly than any competitor in that part of the city. Later, she was quick to see that the DVD market would quickly overtake the VHS market and moved the store into DVDs, again ahead of all the local competition. The store eventually expanded until it occupied all three floors of Kleinfeld's building. During all of this time, Robinson continued to draw a percentage of the profits, periodically negotiating increases until the percentage reached 45 percent. Meanwhile, Kleinfeld did little more than check on Robinson's progress every two weeks—and sometimes not even then. Her work at the store enabled him to use his own profits to engage in other ventures not related to the DVD outlet. While working on one of these ventures, Kleinfeld met Gerry Ackerman, who offered to purchase Kleinfeld's business and his building for $50 million. Kleinfeld agreed. When Robinson was told about the deal, she expected to get a share of the sale price, based on her percentage of the profits. Kleinfeld was offended by Robinson's demand and refused to comply. Robinson sued Kleinfeld, claiming that she had been a partner in the video business in everything but name. She ran the business; she contributed her expertise in technology, customer relations, and business matters to the running of the store; and for 20 years she had taken only a fair share of the profits for pay. The judge ruled in Robinson's favor, declaring that over the course of their 20-year business arrangement, Kleinfeld had made her a partner, whether he knew it or not.

Opening Case Questions

1. What is the definition of a partnership?

2. What is the most crucial factor in the creation of a partnership?

3. What additional factor helped create a partnership in this case?

4. How can problems like the ones that occurred in this case be avoided?

5. What statute usually covers general partnership matters in most states?

Learning Objectives

1. List the most common forms of business associations.
2. Outline the advantages and disadvantages of a sole proprietorship.
3. Identify the two model acts that govern partnership law.
4. Describe the differences between the aggregate and the entity theories of partnership.
5. Explain the nature of a partnership agreement.
6. Explain when profit sharing does not create a partnership.
7. Explain what constitutes a person in partnership law.
8. Identify the different views of specific partnership property in partnership law.
9. Distinguish between dissociation and dissolution in partnership law.
10. Distinguish between a registered limited liability partnership and a limited partnership.

37-1 Sole Proprietorships

There are several forms of doing business available to people who are about to enter the economic arena for the first time. Here are some of the most common forms:

*   Sole proprietorships
*   General partnerships
*   Registered limited liability partnerships
*   Limited partnerships
*   Corporations
*   Limited liability companies

Formation of a Sole Proprietorship

The easiest business organization to form is a **sole proprietorship**. In most cases, businesspeople can initiate a sole proprietorship by simply opening their doors for business. Depending on the nature, location, and extent of the business, the sole proprietor may have to check zoning restrictions, licensing laws, and filing requirements. For example, some states require a formal filing if a sole proprietor chooses to use a fictitious name.

Advantages and Disadvantages of a Sole Proprietorship

Perhaps the greatest advantage to a sole proprietorship is that the owner has complete control over the business. Another major advantage is that the owner may keep all of the profits made by the sole proprietorship. A third advantage is that a sole proprietorship is relatively simple to begin and to end.

A major disadvantage to this type of business is that the owner of a sole proprietorship is subject to unlimited liability. For example, the sole proprietor is responsible for all of the debts incurred in running the business. This liability may even extend to the owner's personal assets. Another disadvantage is that the sole proprietorship's existence depends entirely upon the sole proprietor. Finally, owners of sole proprietorships often find it difficult to raise a lot of cash quickly for expansion purposes.

Quick Quiz 37-1 True or False?

1. Businesspeople can form a sole proprietorship only by going through the attorney general's office in the state capital.

2. The greatest advantage of a sole proprietorship is that the owner has complete control over the operation of the business.

3. A major disadvantage of a sole proprietorship is unlimited liability.

37-2 General Partnership Characteristics

Often a sole proprietor will decide to extend his or her business venture by joining with other people to create a partnership. The law of partnership has integrated principles associated with tort law, contract law, and agency law. However, because of its unique characteristics, it has also developed its own separate and distinct legal principles.

Revised Uniform Partnership Act

One of the most dependable sources of law affecting partnerships has been the National Conference of Commissioners on Uniform State Laws (NCCUSL), which developed the **Uniform Partnership Act (UPA)** in 1914. The UPA was so successful that it was put into practice by every state in the union but one. Only Louisiana, which is devoted to the Napoleonic Code, did not adopt the UPA. Nevertheless, the UPA has been the mainstay of partnership law, in relation to general partnerships, for more than 90 years. It does, however, have its limitations and shortcomings. For instance, it never made it clear whether a partnership should be considered an entity with an existence separate from the partners or whether it was in fact simply an aggregate of all of the partners. These problems motivated two agents within the complex adaptive legal system, the NCCUSL and the American Bar Association (ABA), to collaborate to develop an updated set of rules for partnerships, named the **Revised Uniform Partnership Act (RUPA)**.

The NCCUSL offers several reasons to support states' adoption of the RUPA. Chief among those reasons is that the new act solves several problems with the UPA, not the least of which is the old act's ambiguity about the status of a partnership as an entity or an aggregate. The new act also clarifies the nature of a partner's interest in partnership property, explains the duties partners have in relation to one another, and gives partners the power to pursue a remedy when those duties are violated. It grants partnerships continuity of life, a feature that is similar but not identical to the one enjoyed by corporations. Finally, the revised act solves one of the most troubling problems of the old partnership structure, that of joint and several liability. For these reasons, among others, the RUPA has been implemented in more than half the states. The RUPA will therefore be the basis of discussion for the remainder of this chapter.

Elements of a Partnership

The RUPA says that a **partnership** is "an association of two or more persons to carry on as co-owners a business for profit." The RUPA definition emphasizes the two most essential elements of a partnership. First, partnerships must involve at least two persons. As is often the case with legal terms, "person" can have multiple meanings. In this case, the term "person" can refer to a flesh-and-blood individual, a corporation, other partnerships, joint ventures, trusts, estates, and other commercial or legal institutions. Second, a partnership must involve a sharing of profits. This last point is so crucial that the sharing of profits is considered *prima facie* evidence of the existence of a partnership. *Prima facie* evidence in this context means that the law presumes, in the absence of evidence to the contrary, that an individual receiving profits is a partner.

Entity and Aggregate Theories

Under the Uniform Partnership Act, there was room to dispute whether a partnership should be considered an aggregate or an entity. According to the **entity theory**, a partnership exists as an individual person with its own separate identity. This unique, individual entity is separate from the identities of the partners. In contrast, under the **aggregate theory**, the partnership is seen simply as an assembly or collection of the partners who do business together. The RUPA has settled this dispute. Under the RUPA, a partnership is considered an entity in most situations. Thus, a partnership is an entity in its ability to own title to property, to sue or be sued, and to have its own separate bank accounts in its own name. Under the RUPA, partnerships also have continuity of existence. **Continuity of existence** permits a partnership to continue to operate as an entity even after the individual partners are no longer associated with it. In addition, the partners are considered agents of the partnership. However, the RUPA still considers a partnership an aggregate in relation to liability. Thus, even under the RUPA, partners still have unlimited liability for the obligations of the partnership. It is, however, possible to avoid even this problem if the partners elect to form a registered limited liability partnership. The concept of registered limited liability partnerships is discussed subsequently in this chapter.

LO4

Quick Quiz 37-2 True or False?

1. The Revised Uniform Partnership Act has yet to be adopted by any state legislature.

2. Under the RUPA, a partnership is usually considered an aggregate.

3. Under the RUPA, partners are seen as agents of the partnership.

37-3 Partnership Formation

The problem with a partnership is that it can emerge simply because of the way that two or more parties are doing business with one another. That is why it is essential that business-people be aware of their relationships with other businesspeople with whom they work on a daily basis (see Table 37-1). Certainly the best way to form a partnership is to enter a contractual relationship by drawing up a partnership agreement. Consequently, we will examine this approach first. However, we will also look at the circumstances that can automatically create a partnership as a matter of law.

Formation of a Partnership by Contract

One of the most common ways to form a partnership is by an express agreement between the parties. Although the agreement can be oral, it is generally best to put the terms in writing to prevent misunderstanding and disputes that might arise later in the life of the partnership. The written agreement that establishes a partnership is called a partnership agreement. The RUPA is quite specific about the nature of a partnership agreement. In fact, the RUPA defines a partnership contract as "the agreement, whether written, oral, or implied, among the partners concerning the partnership, including amendments to the partnership agreement." It is of course still possible for the partners to enter agreements subsequent to the creation of a partnership that would not be considered part of the partnership agreement. Thus, partners might enter a loan or a rental agreement that would be separate from the partnership agreement itself.

Both the RUPA and UPA are default statutes, which means that the partners are free to enter any type of agreement that they desire. However, if the partners neglect to include something in the agreement or are unsure of the interpretation of some point, the RUPA (or UPA in those states that still follow it) will "fill in the gaps." It is advisable for a partnership agreement to include the following provisions:

1. The name and duration of the partnership.
2. The names of the partners.
3. The amount of capital that each partner has contributed to the partnership.
4. The character and the extent of the business of the partnership.
5. The way that profits will be divided.
6. The way that any loss will be shared.
7. The duties of the partners.
8. Any limitations placed on the partners.
9. A section on salaries, if so desired.

Table 37-1 Partnership Formation

Form	Definition
Partnership by contract	Express agreement drawn up by partners Articles of partnership
Partnership by proof of existence	Individuals form partnership because of their method of doing business Sharing of profits is *prima facie* evidence

10. An explanation of the dissolution process, if it is to be different from the process outlined in the RUPA.

11. A provision for determining the value of a partner's interest in the partnership.

It is also wise to recall that, though the RUPA does not require that a partnership agreement be in writing, the Statute of Frauds does dictate that certain types of contracts, such as those that will take longer than one year to complete, must be in writing. Thus, it is best to cross-reference with the Statute of Frauds just to make certain that none of those provisions apply.

Formation of a Partnership by Proof of Existence

The definition of a partnership offered by the RUPA establishes the parameters within which a partnership will be formed. The definition states that a business arrangement will be considered a partnership if it involves two or more persons, in association with one another, who are carrying on a business as co-owners for profit. Therefore, to show that a business is operating as a partnership by proof of existence, we must be able to point to three elements: (1) an association of two or more persons, (2) who are co-owners of (3) a business for profit.

LO6

LO7

An Association of Two or More Persons   In the case of a partnership, a "person" can be a living flesh-and-blood individual, a corporation, another partnership, a joint venture, a trust, an estate, or some other commercial enterprise or legal institution. Any two of these persons working together would be sufficient to create an association.

Co-Ownership of the Business

There are certain signs that indicate that the parties in a venture are co-owners. One such sign is the existence of management power. Of course, management power by itself is not

The Opening Case Revisited, Part I
Robinson v. Kleinfeld, Round 2

The lawsuit between Robinson and Kleinfeld at the opening of this chapter is a classic case of the formation of a partnership by proof of existence. As is often true in a situation like this, neither Kleinfeld nor Robinson ever used the term "partnership" to describe their business relationship, except perhaps in the most casual and off-handed way. Nor had they drawn up a contract to delineate their roles and responsibilities in the running of the video outlet. Instead, the business simply evolved from one between an employer and his employee to one between partners. The most telling piece of evidence was, of course, the sharing of profits. This sharing was never questioned by either party. In fact, profit sharing was so ingrained in their relationship that the percentage that Robinson received grew annually until it reached an almost equal arrangement. The court also noted, however, that Robinson brought more to the table than just the profit-sharing arrangement. She also brought several valuable assets to the enterprise—her time, her talent, and her expertise. It is quite likely that Kleinfeld would never have made the video outlet a success without Robinson's business know-how, her grasp of the video marketplace, her easygoing way with customers, and her powers of persuasion. Kleinfeld could not profit from that talent and energy for 20 years without realizing that their association had made a quantum leap from an employer–employee relationship to one of partners.

enough. Employees who are not partners and even independent contractors who have control over certain projects conducted for the business may have management power without being co-owners. Still, the power to make management decisions is a persuasive piece of evidence that is helpful in establishing co-ownership. Co-ownership is also established by the sharing of profits among the partners. However, the RUPA also says that certain types of profit sharing, though real enough, will not rise to the level needed to create a partnership. These profit-sharing activities include the following:

1. The repayment of a debt.
2. Wages to an employee.
3. Payments to an independent contractor.
4. Rent payments to a landlord.
5. Annuity payments or health benefit payments to a beneficiary, representative, or designee of a retired or deceased partner.
6. Interest payments on a loan, even if the level of payments is tied to profit fluctuations.
7. Consideration for the sale of goodwill or for the sale of other property even if the payments are made in installments.

Although the sharing of profits is *prima facie* evidence of the existence of a partnership, parties can receive profits in any of the ways on this list without being saddled with the label of partner.

Carrying on a Business for Profit   Finally, it is not enough for two or more persons to simply be co-owners of property, even if the property does make a profit. The association must also have the goal of running the business together. It is, of course, essential that the business in question be run for a profit. This point means that the venture cannot involve an unincorporated nonprofit venture. It is also unlikely that a solitary profit-making business transaction by itself will be enough to establish a partnership.

The Opening Case Revisited, Part II
Robinson v. Kleinfeld, Round 3

Once Robinson has demonstrated to the court's satisfaction that she and Kleinfeld were sharing profits, the burden would shift to Kleinfeld. He would then have to show that the sharing of profits was of a type not associated with partnership activity and that it therefore could not be used by Robinson as proof of the partnership's existence. However, to accomplish this, he would have to demonstrate that Robinson's profit sharing was located in the list outlined above. A quick look at that list reveals that none of them, save one, even remotely relates to the type of payments that Robinson received. The one that comes the closest is the payment of wages. Unfortunately for Kleinfeld, the payments that Robinson received were clearly not wages, which was apparent from the original conversation between Robinson and Kleinfeld. During that discussion, she expressly gave up the right to receive an hourly wage in exchange for the right to receive profits. Moreover, the fluctuations in the amount of money that Robinson actually took home would verify that the payments that she received could not possibly be wages.

BusinessWeek Business Law in the News

Stopping Reform Before It Starts:
Small Biz Is Emerging as a Powerful Opponent of Universal Health Care

Big business CEOs are lining up left and right in favor of health insurance coverage for all Americans. But there's a big barrier to a sweeping overhaul of the U.S. health-care system: small business.

While activist CEOs of major corporations have changed the debate over health care by entertaining the idea of comprehensive reform and universal coverage, small-business groups remain committed to blocking broad government involvement. And small businesses have a surprising amount of political muscle. "When small-business owners feel threatened by major governmental intervention, they really show their strength," says Karen Kerrigan, president of the Small Business & Entrepreneurship Council, a conservative advocacy group. "If any health-care plan includes government mandates or costs on the small business sector, it's going to be very difficult to pass."

Fear of reflexive resistance is one reason why Charles N. "Chip" Kahn III, president of the Federation of American Hospitals, and Ron Pollack, director of the liberal advocacy group Families USA, invited the National Federation of Independent Business to join secret talks in 2005 to create a bipartisan coalition to push for universal health coverage. The NFIB, the nation's largest small-business organization, with a half-million members, turned them down cold.

NFIB Executive Vice-President Dan Danner says his group steered clear of the talks because it worried the coalition would back government-run health care. Only about 50% of small businesses pay for workers' health insurance, and the NFIB feared that all of its members would be forced to bail out old-line manufacturers saddled with billions of dollars in legacy costs. "At the end of the day, that's always the rub with these proposals: How are you going to pay for them?" observes Danner. "It's the proverbial whose-ox-gets-gored, who pays for what."

Many small-business owners agonize over health care. Joe Balsarotti, who has owned a computer consulting business in St. Louis since 1983, provided health care for his four employees until the coverage costs quadrupled for one, a diabetic. When that employee left the company, Balsarotti ended the benefit.

"It was either that, or cost exceeds profits," he says. Balsarotti knows that reform is necessary in health care but worries what kind of remedies Washington might apply. "I can't run a business if I don't know what my costs are," he says. "I also don't like the idea of a government bureaucracy running things."

With small business conflicted or opposed to change, big businesses are moving ahead. Even without the NFIB, the Kahn-Pollack talks resulted in a 16-organization coalition for universal insurance coverage. Members include the U.S. Chamber of Commerce, the American Hospital Assn., and America's Health Insurance Plans as well as large companies such as Johnson & Johnson, Kaiser Permanente, and Pfizer. . . .

Advocates of change realize they can't succeed without persuading small business to join them or remain neutral. Says one business coalition representative: "Small business has a lot of power and helped to kill Bill Clinton's health-care plan" in 1994, when many big businesses were open to government action.

Republican consultant Frank I. Luntz, whose client list includes both large and small businesses, says elected officials see small-business owners as "the American Dream occupation. Politicians want to help them."

Maybe so, but small businesses also deftly deploy campaign contributions to friendly lawmakers and cooperate to pressure their hometown representatives. Small businesses know, "it's crazy not to be actively participating in the debate at this time," Danner says. . . .

But what small businesses really want, says Kerrigan, is for Congress to pass a series of small measures that would give small businesses more insurance choices and make the system more affordable.

Among the top priorities: allowing entrepreneurs to lower their insurance premiums by buying into larger pools of multiple small firms; breaking down regulatory barriers by allowing small businesses to pick insurance offerings in any state, not just in their home base; giving sole proprietors the same kind of health-care tax break that larger employers get; and expanding health savings accounts and giving small

(Continued)

Business Law in the News *(Continued)*

employers more tax incentives to offer HSAs to their workers.

Ed Gillespie, a Washington lobbyist who is set to direct a coalition of CEO reformers led by Safeway Inc.'s Steven A. Burd, thinks entrepreneurs can be brought to the table. "Small businesses always have to be leery of mandates," says Gillespie, a former Republican National Committee chairman. "But they want to be part of the solution, too."

Questions for Review

1. What two advocacy groups work to promote the interest and concerns of small businesses?

2. Why are small businesses opposed to government-run health care?

3. How do small businesses manage to get their voices heard in the government?

4. What are the top priorities for small businesses in relation to health insurance?

5. What health care plan did a small business coalition defeat in the 1990s?

Source: Richard S. Dunham and Keith Epstein, "Stopping Reform Before It Starts: Small Biz Is Emerging as a Powerful Opponent of Universal Health Care," *BusinessWeek,* April 16, 2007, 55–56.

Quick Quiz 37-3 True or False?

1. A partnership can emerge simply because of the way two or more parties are doing business with one another.

2. A "person" can be a living flesh-and-blood individual, a corporation, another partnership, a joint venture, a trust, an estate, or some other commercial enterprise or legal institution.

3. The sharing of profits is *prima facie* evidence of the existence of a partnership.

37-4 Partnership Property Rights and Duties

Property is an extremely critical element in partnership law, because virtually every decision made by a partner deals with the disposition of partnership property. Decisions involving the use of partnership property, such as machinery, equipment, furniture, and vehicles; the purchase of raw materials; and the sale of finished products all involve the disposition of property. Even service-oriented partnerships such as shipping firms and restaurants involve the disposition of property in one way or another. Therefore, partnership duties and rights always involve partnership property. This point is also why it is critical to determine whether a given piece of property belongs to the partnership entity or to an individual partner as his or her personal property. At times it is relatively easy to distinguish between partnership property and property that belongs to individual partners. For instance, the capital contributions of all partners are considered the property of the partnership. **Capital contributions** are sums that are contributed by the partners as permanent investments and that the partners are entitled to have returned when the partnership is dissolved. In contrast, loans or later advances that partners make to the partnership and accumulated but undivided profits belong to the partners on an individual basis. Other forms of partnership property belong only to the partnership in its status as an entity.

Partnership Property

The fact that the RUPA has established the existence of a partnership as an entity has alleviated some of the difficulties once associated with identifying partnership property. The RUPA states that partnership property is any and all property that has been obtained by the partnership itself. For instance, if the property was obtained in the partnership's name, it is partnership property. If the property was obtained by a partner in his or her role as a partner, it is partnership property. If the instrument of title for the property includes the name of the partnership, it is partnership property. Finally, if the instrument of transfer indicates that the property was obtained by a partner in his or her role as a partner or if the partnership is referred to in the instrument, the property belongs to the partnership.

When it is difficult to determine whether a piece of property belongs to the partnership or to a partner, the court may ask the following questions: Has the partnership included the property in its account books? Has the partnership expended its own funds to improve or repair the property? Has the partnership paid taxes on the property? Has the partnership paid other expenses, such as maintenance costs, for the property? The more of these questions that can be answered in the affirmative, the more likely it is that the property is partnership property.

Specific Partnership Property

The RUPA has made a significant change in the rule with regard to individual pieces of partnership property. Under the UPA, each partner had a property interest in all specific items of partnership property. Each partner was therefore a co-owner of that property. This form of ownership was known as tenancy in partnership. Under the UPA, a tenancy in partnership had the following characteristics:

1. A partner had an equal right with all other partners to possess and use specific partnership property for partnership purposes but not for that partner's personal use.

2. A partner's interest in partnership property could not be assigned (i.e., transferred by sale, mortgage, pledge, or otherwise) to a nonpartner, unless the other partners agreed to the transfer.

3. Partners' rights in partnership property were not subject to attachment (i.e., taking a person's property and bringing it into the custody of the law) for personal debts or claims against the partners themselves.

4. A deceased partner's interest in real property held by the partnership passed to the surviving partners.

5. Partners' rights in specific partnership property were not subject to any allowances or rights to widows, heirs, or next of kin.

Under the RUPA, all of this has changed. The RUPA states that "A partner is not co-owner of partnership property and has no interest in partnership property which can be transferred, either voluntarily or involuntarily." Of course, partners will still be able to use partnership property. However, their right to hold and use such property is limited to partnership purposes. This significant change in relation to partnership law actually brings partnership property rights in relation to individual pieces of partnership property in line with the way property rights operate for other business associations, such as corporations.

Interest in the Partnership

The RUPA establishes that a partner has an interest in the partnership as a firm. That right consists of two parts: (1) a transferable economic interest and (2) a nontransferable interest in management rights.

Transferable Economic Interest   The partner's economic interest is his or her share of the profits and losses and his or her share of the surplus. **Surplus** includes any funds that remain after the partnership has been dissolved and all other debts and prior obligations have been paid. Partners can voluntarily assign their economic interest to another party. The assignee in such an action, however, is not entitled to take part in the management of the partnership. The assignee also cannot gain access to the partnership books or the partnership financial records. Nor can an assignee demand to receive information concerning the transactions of the partnership.

Management of the Firm   Participation in management decision making is not limited to the partner's proportional share of the firm. Instead, all partners have equal rights in the management of the partnership business. The day-to-day decisions of the firm are decided by a majority vote of the partners. If a vote is split evenly, then the status quo remains. If such deadlocks persist, and the very operation of the business is threatened, it may be time to dissolve the partnership. Occasionally, a unanimous vote is required in a business decision. However, such decisions must involve actions that fall outside the regular, daily operation of the business. Decisions that involve amendments to the partnership agreement also require unanimous consent.

It is, of course, possible for a partner to reduce his or her part in management voluntarily by becoming a silent partner. A **silent partner** is one who does not participate in the day-to-day business of the firm. This role is in contrast to a **secret partner**, whose identity and existence are not known outside the firm but who nevertheless can participate in the management of the firm. Some partnerships create their own hierarchy of partners. Thus, a firm may be divided into *junior* and *senior partners* or into *managing* and *nonmanaging partners*.

Partnership Rights and Duties

We have already pinpointed most of the individual rights that partners possess by virtue of their participation in the partnership. These rights include: (1) the right to use partnership property, as long as the property is held and used for partnership purposes; (2) the right to receive the partner's share of the profits (and losses) and his or her share of the surplus; (3) the right to manage the regular day-to-day operation of the partnership business; (4) the right to approve of serious matters outside the ordinary course of business; and (5) the right to approve of amendments to the partnership agreement. In addition, partners have certain enforcement rights, should the need arise to implement the other rights.

Enforcement Rights   Under the UPA, a partner's enforcement rights are few. In fact, partners have only three enforcement rights: (1) the right to see the firm's financial records, (2) the right to compel an accounting, and (3) the right to compel a dissolution of the entire partnership. Under the RUPA, those enforcement rights are enhanced. The three rights previously noted are retained, but in addition, a partner can sue another partner directly or, under the entity theory, the partnership itself to enforce his or her partnership rights as expressed in the RUPA or granted by the partnership agreement. In such an action, the partner can ask for damages or for an equitable remedy, such as an injunction or specific performance. Of course, the reverse is also true; that is, the partner can be sued by another partner or by the partnership itself.

Partnership Duties   The RUPA notes that partners have three critical duties: (1) loyalty, (2) obedience and (3) due care. The first of these three, the duty of loyalty, is based on the fact that the partners are in a fiduciary relationship.

The Duty of Loyalty   The duty of loyalty has become centrally important under the RUPA, unlike its position under the UPA, which devoted only a very small amount of space to the topic. According to the RUPA, the duty of loyalty includes the following items:

1. To account to the partnership for any property, profits, or benefit that comes from the partner's use of partnership property or from the winding up process after dissolution.

2. To refrain from dealing with people who may have an interest that is adverse to the best interests of the partnership.

3. To refrain from entering any competition with the partnership in the operation of partnership business.

A partner does, however, retain the right to look after himself or herself during the formation of the partnership, because the duty of loyalty does not arise until the partnership entity actually exists.

The Duty of Obedience   Simply stated, the duty of obedience means that a partner must follow faithfully all the arrangements made in the partnership agreement. The partner must also honor all decisions made by the partnership, provided those decisions were made following proper protocols. If a partner disobeys the partnership agreement or disregards a decision lawfully made by the other partners, he or she will be liable for any loss that befalls the partnership as a result of that disobedience.

Talking Points

One of the premiere economists of the last century was a Harvard professor named Joseph Schumpeter, who wrote a treatise entitled *Capitalism, Socialism, and Democracy* in which he foretold the ultimate end of the capitalist economic system. Oddly, Schumpeter was himself a confirmed capitalist, so when he predicted the end of the capitalist economy, it was without joy or pleasure. In fact, it was more of a warning than a prediction, offered with the hope that something could be done to divert the path of destruction. Schumpeter's affection for capitalism is described in the following passage, penned by Allen M. Sievers in his study, *Revolution, Evolution, and the Economic Order*:

> The capitalist, for one thing, wishes to provide for his family, and indeed capitalism is really not individual-centered but family-centered. Further, the capitalist shares in lesser degree the romantic adventuresomeness which characterized feudal society, or there would be no risky innovation or entrepreneurial exploit. Capitalism also requires a kind of symbiosis with the aristocracy and other non-bourgeois elements to run the state, and this depends on a kind of loyalty by these classes to capitalism. The masses must also be awed by the glamor or prestige of capitalist success in order to submit to the discipline necessary for business production. The business classes themselves must have an *esprit de corps* and a devotion to their way of life, as well as a code of ethics if the contract and property system is to work. We might say in sum, that Schumpeter believed that capitalist civilization is based on a rationalism qualified just a bit by other human qualities.
>
> Allen M. Sievers, *Revolution, Evolution, and the Economic Order*, p. 41

We can distill from this quotation five essential qualities of the capitalist: (1) family-centeredness, (2) a willingness to take risks, (3) loyalty to the capitalist ideal, (4) awe at the success of capitalistic ventures, and (5) a code of ethics that permits the rules of contract and property law to work. Which of the business organizations described in this chapter is best suited to realizing these ideals? Explain.

The Duty of Due Care   Basically, the duty of due care means that partners must do their best in the business, based on their talents, education, and abilities. It does not mean that partners must be infallible. On the contrary, the standard recognizes that partners may make mistakes and allows for those mistakes, provided the partner acted with an ordinary level of skill and competence and in the best interests of the partnership.

Quick Quiz 37-4 True or False?

1. Under the RUPA, each partner has a property interest in all specific items of partnership property.

2. The RUPA states that partnership property is any and all property that has been obtained by the partnership itself.

3. A partner's economic interest in the partnership is nontransferrable.

37-5 Dissociation and Dissolution

One of the objectives of the National Conference of Commissioners on Uniform State Laws and the American Bar Association in rewriting the UPA and developing the RUPA was to make certain that the new law coincided as much as possible with commercial realities. Under the UPA, whenever a partner ceased to be associated with the partnership, technically, that partnership went through the dissolution process. In present commercial realities, it no longer makes sense for partners to have to deal with the dissolution technicalities when the only thing that is really happening is the buyout of a partner who wants to leave the firm. Consequently, the RUPA now includes two methods by which a partner becomes dissociated with partnership: dissociation and dissolution.

Dissociation of a Partnership

Under RUPA, a **dissociation** takes place whenever a partner is no longer associated with the running of the firm. It is always possible for partners to leave a partnership firm when they want. However, sometimes, a partner leaves the firm wrongfully because he or she does not have the legal right to do so. A partner's right to withdraw from a partnership may depend on whether the partnership is a term partnership or a partnership at will. A **term partnership** is one that has been set up to run for a certain set time period or to accomplish a task of some sort. A partner who leaves a term partnership before the term expires or before the task is accomplished has acted wrongfully. A **partnership at will** is one that any partner may leave without liability. The RUPA establishes the circumstances in which it is proper to leave a partnership. Some rules affect both types of partnerships; others apply only to partnerships at will. These include (1) a partner's death in either type of partnership; (2) a partner's leave-taking from a partnership at will; (3) a partner's leave-taking from either type of partnership under the rules set up by the partnership agreement; or (4) a partner's leave-taking from either type of partnership, if a court has decided that a partner cannot do what he or she is supposed to do under the partnership agreement.

Dissolution of a Partnership

The **dissolution** of a partnership occurs when a partner ceases to be associated with the partnership and the partnership ends. The dissolution of a partnership can occur in one of three ways: (1) by an action committed by the partners, (2) by operation of law, or (3) by the decree of a court of law.

An Action by the Partners Whenever a partnership at will exists, that partnership can be dissolved whenever a partner notifies the other partners that he or she intends to leave the firm. Partnerships at will, however, are not dissolved when a partner dies or enters bankruptcy. Whenever a term partnership is involved, the RUPA says that there are several ways to dissolve the firm: (1) when the time limit has passed; (2) when the task of the partnership has been accomplished; (3) when there is express agreement among all partners to end the partnership; (4) when a partner dies; (5) when a partner becomes incapacitated; (6) when a partner goes bankrupt; and (7) when a partner produces a wrongful dissociation from the partnership and, within 90 days of that leave-taking, at least half the other partners agree to end the business.

This partnership is in the "winding up" stage and is selling its assets and inventory to satisfy creditors and hopefully distribute surplus to the former partners.

By Operation of Law Dissolution becomes effective by operation of law if some event occurs that makes it illegal to continue the business of the firm. If, for instance, at some time in the distant future it became illegal to manufacture and sell tobacco products, a partnership formed to produce and market cigarettes would dissolve by operation of law.

By a Court Order When a partner has engaged in some sort of wrongdoing and, on those grounds, another partner petitions the court for a dissolution, the court may dissolve the partnership by court order. When a continuation of the business would be economically foolish, the court may dissolve the firm. Finally, when a partner does something that makes it impractical to continue the business with that partner, the court may order the dissolution of the business.

Winding Up the Partnership Business When a partnership terminates, there must be a winding up of the partnership affairs. This action includes the orderly sale of the partnership's assets, the payment of creditors, and the distribution, if any, of the remaining surplus to partners according to their profit-sharing rations.

Quick Quiz 37-5 True or False?

1. The RUPA includes two methods by which a partner becomes dissociated with a partnership: dissociation and dissolution.

2. A partnership at will is one that any partner may leave without liability.

3. When partnership terminates, there must be a winding up of the partnership affairs.

37-6 Other Forms of Partnership Business

The changing needs of the modern marketplace and the development of new ideas in the law have combined to allow for a new form of partnership, the registered limited liability partnership. Those same forces have also cooperated to update one of the more traditional forms of the partnership business, the limited partnership.

Registered Limited Liability Partnerships

Recent statutory developments in several states have produced a new type of business organization known as the registered limited liability partnership (RLLP or LLP). A **registered limited liability partnership** is a general partnership in all respects except one—liability. In a traditional general partnership, the liability for the torts committed by a partner or an employee of the partnership is joint and several. This stance means that each partner is liable and may be sued in a separate action or in a joint action. A judgment may be levied against one or more partners. The release of one partner in one action does not necessarily release the others.

The statutes usually require that the registration statement be filed by all of the partners or at least by those partners holding a majority interest in the partnership. Limited liability partnerships must update their registration statement each year or risk the loss of registration. As far as the tax laws are concerned, LLPs are considered general partnerships. When an LLP has been created, partners can no longer be held jointly or severally liable for the torts, wrongful acts, negligence, or misconduct committed by another partner or by any representative of the partnership. Naturally, partners would still be liable for their own wrongful acts and for the wrongful acts committed by other partners or employees who are under the direct control of that partner. The Revised Uniform Partnership Act includes the provisions necessary for obtaining limited liability status. Thus, states that have adopted the RUPA in its entirety do not need to pass a separate statute to allow for the creation of an LLP.

Limited Partnerships

Limited partnerships are governed by the Revised Uniform Limited Partnership Act (RULPA). The revised act defines a **limited partnership** as "a partnership formed by two or more persons . . . having one or more general partners and one or more limited partners." **General partners** take an active part in the management of the firm and have unlimited liability for the firm's debts. **Limited partners** are nonparticipating investors. They contribute cash, property, or services to the partnership but do not take part in the management of the firm.

A limited partnership is advantageous for both the limited partner and the general partner. The general partner can accumulate additional capital without admitting another general partner who would be entitled to management rights. Thus, the general partner maintains control while strengthening the firm's treasury. The limited partner also benefits because a limited partnership means limited liability. **Limited liability** in turn means that the limited partner's nonpartnership property cannot be used to satisfy any debts owed by the partnership. Thus, limited partners receive a return on their investment while risking only that original investment.

Limited partnerships must follow strict filing requirements. Usually, a certificate of limited partnership must be filed with the secretary of state's office. The purpose of the certificate is to warn third parties of the limited liability of some partners. However, some state statutes indicate that neither the names of the limited partners nor the amounts of their capital contributions must be included in the certificate. This provision simplifies the formation of a limited partnership because it allows limited partners to remain anonymous.

Failure to file a certificate of limited partnership will deprive a limited partner of limited liability if third parties attempting to hold the limited partner liable did not know that they were dealing with a limited partnership. Moreover, if in the certificate of limited partnership, a limited partner is incorrectly identified as a general partner, he or she would not have limited partner status. To correct such an error, the limited partner would have to refile an amended certificate of limited partnership or leave the limited partnership altogether. Such drastic actions would be necessary unless the state statute under which the

Did You Know?

Because the dissolution of a partnership occurs whenever a partner becomes disassociated with the carrying on of partnership business, the dissolution of every partnership is inevitable. Therefore, the dissolution of a partnership is not a question of "if" but of "when."

limited partnership was formed allows a limited partner who has been incorrectly named as a general partner to file with the appropriate state office a unilateral **disclaimer of general partner status**. Limited partners must also guard against becoming too involved in the business. A limited partner who exercises too much control over partnership affairs may lose the protective mantle of limited liability. Recently, however, many state legislatures have greatly expanded the types of activities that a limited partner can perform without losing the shelter provided by limited partnership status.

Quick Quiz 37-6 True or False?

1. A registered limited liability partnership is like a general partnership in all respects except liability.

2. In most states, to become a registered limited liability partnership, the partners must file with the auditor's office in the county courthouse.

3. Limited partnerships must have at least three limited partners and no general partners.

Summary

37.1   The easiest business organization to form is a sole proprietorship. All that businesspeople have to do is open their doors for business, and a sole proprietorship is created. The greatest advantage to a sole proprietorship is that the owner has complete control over the business. The major disadvantage is that the sole proprietor is subject to unlimited liability.

37.2   The Revised Uniform Partnership Act states that a partnership is "an association of two or more persons to carry on as co-owners a business for profit." Under the RUPA, a partnership is considered an entity, or an individual unit that exists separate from the partners. A partnership is an entity in its ability to own title to property, sue or be sued, and have its own separate bank accounts in its own name. Under the RUPA, partnerships also have continuity of existence.

37.3   One of the most common ways to form a partnership is by an express agreement between the parties. It is generally best to put the terms in writing to prevent misunderstanding and disputes that might arise later in the life of the partnership. The written agreement that establishes a partnership is called a partnership agreement. To show that a business is operating as a partnership by proof of existence, three elements must exist:

(1) an association of two or more persons (2) who are co-owners of (3) a business for profit.

37.4   Capital contributions are sums that are contributed by the partners as permanent investments and that the partners are entitled to have returned when the partnership is dissolved. Loans or later advances that partners make to the partnership and accumulated but undivided profits belong to the partners on an individual basis. Other forms of partnership property belong only to the partnership in its status as an entity. The RUPA states that "A partner is not co-owner of partnership property and has no interest in partnership property which can be transferred, either voluntarily or involuntarily." Partners can use a partnership only for partnership purposes. The RUPA establishes that a partner has an interest in the partnership as a firm. That interest consists of two parts: (1) a transferable economic interest and (2) a nontransferable interest in management rights.

37.5   Under the RUPA, a dissociation takes place whenever a partner is no longer associated with the running of the firm. Partners can leave a partnership firm whenever they want. A partner leaves a firm wrongfully if he or she does not have the legal right to do so. The dissolution of a partnership occurs when a partner ceases to be associated with the partnership and the partnership ends. The dissolution of a partnership can occur in one of three ways: (1) by an action committed by the partners, (2) by operation of law, or (3) by the decree of a court of law.

37.6 The changing needs of the modern marketplace and the development of new ideas in the law have combined to allow for a new form of partnership, the registered limited liability partnership. Those same forces have cooperated to update one of the more traditional forms of the partnership business, the limited partnership.

Key Terms

aggregate theory, 771

capital contribution, 776

continuity of existence, 771

disclaimer of general partner status, 783

dissociation, 780

dissolution, 780

entity theory, 771

general partner, 782

limited liability, 782

limited partner, 782

limited partnership, 782

partnership, 771

partnership at will, 780

registered limited liability partnership, 782

Revised Uniform Partnership Act (RUPA), 770

secret partner, 778

silent partner, 778

sole proprietorship, 769

surplus, 778

term partnership, 780

Uniform Partnership Act (UPA), 770

Questions for Review and Discussion

1. What are the most common forms of business associations?
2. What are the advantages and disadvantages of a sole proprietorship?
3. What are the two model acts that govern partnership law?
4. What are the differences between the aggregate and entity theories of partnership?
5. What is the nature of a partnership agreement?
6. When does profit sharing not create a partnership?
7. What constitutes a person in partnership law?
8. What are the different views of specific partnership property in partnership law?
9. What is the difference between dissociation and dissolution in partnership law?
10. What is the difference between a registered limited liability partnership and a limited partnership?

Investigating the Internet

One of the most vocal groups providing advocacy for small businesses is the Small Business Entrepreneurship (SBE) Council. The SBE Council offers an internship for qualified college students. Access the SBE Council's Web site and answer the following questions about the SBE Council and its internship program: (1) What is the SBE Council, and how many members belong to it? (2) What does the SBE internship program involve? (3) What are the requirements for becoming an intern for the SBE Council? (4) What must applicants send to the SBE Council to be considered for the internship program? (5) Can a student who becomes an intern get college credit for his or her time as an intern with the SBE Council?

Cases for Analysis

1. Jennifer Yauger owned a loft in uptown Silverton. Robert Tomba and Gary Jorgen were partners in a mail-order business in Middletown called NASCAR Collectibles. To open an outlet in Silverton, Tomba and Jorgen leased the loft from Yauger. As part of the agreement, Yauger received $2,650 in rent each month. Later Tomba and Jorgen set up a Web site and began an online auction house for NASCAR collectibles, similar to eBay. They were successful beyond their highest expectations, making over $2 million in their first year of operation. When another online auction house offered Tomba and Jorgen $60 million for their site, they accepted the offer without hesitation. When Yauger heard about the deal, she claimed that she was a partner and demanded a $20 million payment, a sum equal to a one-third share of the sale price. When the case went to court, Yauger pointed to her monthly payments and labeled those payments a share of the profits. She argued that this payment demonstrated that she was a partner, based on proof of existence. Should the court grant Yauger partner status and give her a share of the proceeds from the sale of the business? Explain.

2. Kerry Taylor owned a warehouse in the industrial flats of Parke Central City. Yale Roberts and William Hull were partners in a chain of restaurants called Pirate's Seafood Carousel. Roberts and Hull leased Taylor's warehouse for their restaurant. As part of the agreement, Taylor received $7,500 in rent each month. Taylor retained office space on the top floor of the warehouse. She also agreed to allow Roberts and Hull to remodel the rest of the warehouse to meet the needs of their new restaurant. Taylor occasionally offered advice about the remodeling of the warehouse. In addition, after the restaurant opened for business, Taylor frequently signed for shipments that Roberts and Hull had ordered for the restaurant. After five years in this location, and after selling their other restaurants, Roberts and Hull decided to dissolve their partnership. During the winding up process, they were surprised to learn that Taylor claimed that she should receive a share of the surplus cash after the dissolution of the partnership, because she claimed to be a partner in Pirate's Seafood Carousel. Is Taylor correct in her claim? Will Roberts and Hull have to pay her a share of their surplus cash? Explain.

3. When the father of Stephen and Chris Nuss died, the two boys, aged 15 and 12 years, began to work the family farm. While the boys were still under the age of majority, their mother, Lois, kept the books for the farm. As the boys grew older, they took more and more responsibility in running the farm. They also rented and worked additional acres of farmland. They financed these rental agreements on their own, but their mother cosigned for the arrangements. The boys also purchased additional farmland. Again, their mother helped in this purchase by cosigning. When Chris decided to leave farming, Stephen paid him $100,000, and in exchange, Chris signed over the deed to the newly purchased land. Lois was not involved in this transaction. Stephen's farming business grew. He eventually amassed more than 1,200 acres. He and his wife, Linda, kept their own financial records and maintained their own checking account for the running of the farm. Stephen's mother was not involved in any of this detail. However, Stephen continued to pay many of the expenses involved on the original farm, where his mother still maintained her residence. Stephen also paid the insurance, maintenance, and repair expenses on all buildings and equipment on the original farm. Because Stephen continued to farm this land, in addition to the land he had subsequently purchased, these payments were always characterized as rent. No other payments went to Stephen's mother. When Stephen died, Linda, his widow and executor, claimed that a partnership existed and that the farm equipment on the original acreage and original acreage itself belonged to that partnership. Lois argued that no partnership between Stephen and her existed. Is Linda or Lois correct? Did a partnership exist? Explain. *In re Estate of Nuss,* 646 N.E.2d 504 (OH).

4. McCoy and Gugelman borrowed money from State Security Bank for their partnership, Antiques, Etc. When McCoy and Gugelman failed to pay back the debt, the bank sued them as individuals. At trial, McCoy and Gugelman argued that their partnership, Antiques, Etc., was an entity, not an aggregate, of the partners. Therefore, they concluded, the bank would have to show that the partnership funds were insufficient to answer the judgment before it could proceed against them individually. Are they

correct? Why or why not? *Security State Bank v. McCoy,* 361 N.W.2d 514 (NE).

5. Shane ran a liquid fertilizer business. As part of the operation of the business, Shane paid Svoboda a specified amount per acre to spread the fertilizer on his clients' crops. Svoboda's per acre payments remained steady, despite Shane's profits or losses. Frisch was injured while filling a tank truck that was supposed to haul the fertilizer to Svoboda's tractor. Frisch sued both Shane and Svoboda, claiming that Svoboda was sharing in Shane's profits and was therefore a partner. Was Frisch correct? Explain. *Frisch v. Svobada,* 157 N.W.2d 774 (NE).

6. Summers and Dooley formed a partnership for the purpose of operating a trash collection business. The business was operated by the two men, and when either was unable to work, the nonworking partner provided a replacement at his own expense. Summers approached Dooley and requested that they hire a third worker. Dooley refused. Notwithstanding Dooley's refusal, Summers, on his own initiative, hired a worker. Summers paid the employee out of his own pocket. Dooley, upon discovery that a third person had been hired, objected. He stated that the additional labor was not necessary and refused to allow partnership funds to be used to pay the new employee. After paying out more than $11,000 in wages without any reimbursement from either partnership funds or his partner, Summers brought suit in the Idaho state courts. The trial court held that Summers was not entitled to reimbursement for the wages he had paid the employee. On appeal, did the Supreme Court of Idaho uphold the trial court's decision? Explain. *Summers v. Dooley,* 481 P.2d 318 (ID).

Quick Quiz Answers

37-1	37-2	37-3	37-4	37-5	37-6
1. F	1. F	1. T	1. F	1. T	1. T
2. T	2. F	2. T	2. T	2. T	2. F
3. T	3. T	3. T	3. F	3. T	3. F

Chapter 38 | The Corporate Entity

The Opening Case

Valley Victory Church v. Darvin Struck and Bonnie Struck

Darvin and Bonnie Struck donated a parcel of land to the Valley Victory Church. Because the Strucks were keen on using the donation as a tax deduction, they asked for and received assurances that the Valley Victory Church was incorporated. These assurances turned out to be false. The attorney who had been responsible for filing the church's yearly reports with the secretary of state's office had left the state and neglected to notify the church of his move. When the report was not filed, the secretary of state revoked Valley Victory's standing as a corporation and sent a letter to that effect to the now-absent attorney. The attorney, of course, neither received the letter nor alerted church officials, who continued to act as if the church were a corporation. This confusion may not have mattered all that much had there not been a problem with the donated land. Church officials wanted to build a new church, but to do so, they needed to even out the land. Accordingly, they advertised for and received several shipments of landfill. By chance, some of this "landfill" was laced with asphalt and trash. As a result, the Department of Environmental Quality (DEQ) ordered the church to clean up the mess. In the meantime, Jeremy Juntunen, who was apparently under the mistaken impression that Struck still owned the land, asked Struck if he could dump some asphalt on the property. Struck, who appears to have been unaware of the DEQ order, approved the request. Juntunen dumped the asphalt on the property until a church official asked him to stop. After the mess was removed, there was a dispute over the clean up costs. The Strucks, who were now aware of the church's noncorporate status, decided to take back the land. To support this claim, the Strucks argued that at the time of the gift, the church's corporate standing had been revoked, and it could not have accepted the gift of the land. Therefore, the land was still theirs. Church officials made two counterarguments. First, at the time of the gift, church officials testified that they had a good faith belief that the church was in fact a corporation. Therefore, under the doctrine of *de facto* corporation, they continued to operate as a corporation. Second, church officials argued that the Strucks had given the land to the congregation, not to the church. Because of a technicality in state law, the court was forced to reject the church's first argument on the *de facto* doctrine. However, the court noted that, under Montana statutory law, once the secretary of state had restored the church's corporate status, all previous acts were ratified.

That meant that the church's acceptance of the land was valid when it had occurred. The court also supported the church's second argument as far as it could,
saying that under corporation by estoppel, the Strucks could not recognize the
church as a corporation when they transferred the land and then change their
minds when it suited them. As a result, the church won the day; in retrospect, perhaps that was the way it was supposed to be all along. (See *Valley Victory Church
v. Darvin Struck and Bonnie Struck*, Case No. 04-618, 2005MT72, The Supreme
Court of Montana.)

Opening Case Questions

1. What is a *de jure* corporation?

2. What is a *de facto* corporation?

3. Why did the court reject Valley Victory's *de facto* argument?

4. What is the doctrine of corporation by estoppel?

5. Why could the court accept the estoppel claim even though it rejected the *de
    facto* argument?

Learning Objectives

1. Describe the evolution of associative corporativism.
2. Explain the nature of a corporation.
3. List the constitutional rights of a corporation.
4. Describe the differences among a private, a public, and a quasi-public corporation.
5. Distinguish between a close and an S corporation.
6. List the typical elements within the articles of incorporation.
7. Distinguish between the articles of organization and the operating agreement of a
   limited liability company.
8. Distinguish between a *de jure* and a *de facto* corporation.
9. Identify the objective of piercing the corporate veil.
10. Distinguish between common and preferred stock.

38-1 The Corporation in the Complex Adaptive System

Corporations are a product of capitalism. Although capitalism originated in Europe, it
flourished in the United States in the nineteenth century, because the American economic
system at that time provided the perfect engine for capitalistic progress. Much of this
progress occurred because there was an enormous amount of land that needed to be developed in the United States and an influx of energetic immigrants who were willing to
improve that land. Capitalism grew in response, because those businesspeople who
worked the land as farms, factories, railroads, and stores needed an efficient way to raise
capital to finance land development projects. The corporation was the perfect means of
raising capital quickly and using it effectively. The corporation of today, however, bears
little resemblance to the corporation as it was born in the nineteenth century, and the

development of the corporate form of doing business is a vivid example of the complex adaptive system at work.

The Beginnings of Corporativism

A **corporation** is a legal entity created under the authority of a state or federal statute that gives certain individuals the capacity to operate an enterprise. The statutory template that most states follow in developing their corporate law statutes is the Model Business Corporation Act, often referred to as the Model Corporation Act and sometimes simply as the MBCA. The MBCA is a relatively young statute, and is therefore not quite as settled as older, more traditional statutes, such as the Uniform Commercial Code and the original Uniform Partnership Act. In addition. the model act has been revised since its original inception, making some of its provisions even more recent and therefore less fully developed than similar provisions in other comparable statutes. Also, many states have a long history of common law decisions in relation to corporate law, some of which must be preempted when a state legislature adopts the MBCA. Even in the face of explicit instances of preemption however, some state courts have been reluctant to surrender long-term common law principles and sometimes have found creative ways to interpret the MBCA within the context of that state's long-standing legal tradition. Therefore, the study of corporate law must always be tempered by a look at the state law of the jurisdiction in which a dispute is located. The process of doing business as a self-governing business association, that is, as a corporation, is called **associative corporativism**, or simply **corporativism**. In the nineteenth century, each corporation was individually created by a unique legislative enactment. Each corporation had its own charter that outlined the powers and abilities of that corporation.

Corporate Limited Liability

Today one of the most attractive features of the corporate way of doing business is its limited liability. **Limited liability** means that the corporate investors cannot be held personally liable for the debts of the corporation. Thus, the most that an investor can lose is the amount of money used to purchase his or her **shares** of the corporation.

Corporate Entity Status

A corporation exists apart from its owners and is taxed directly on the income it earns. As a legal entity, a corporation can own property and sue or be sued, just as an individual can. Moreover, the existence of a corporation is not affected by the death, incapacity, or bankruptcy of a manager or shareholder.

Corporate Constitutional Rights

Under provisions of the U.S. Constitution, a corporation is also considered an artificially created legal person. Within the context of the Fourteenth Amendment, a corporation—like a natural person—may not be deprived of life, liberty, or property without due process of law. Also, a corporation may not be denied equal protection of the laws within the jurisdiction of a state.

Corporate Citizenship

A corporation is considered a citizen of both the state in which it is incorporated and the state where it has its principal place of business. It can also be sued as a citizen of both these states. By virtue of the due process clause of the Fourteenth Amendment, a state court may also exercise jurisdiction over a noncitizen corporate defendant, as long as that corporation has had an appropriate contact with that state. Such contact can include owning property within the state, doing business in the state, or committing a tort within the state.

U.S. Const. Amendment 14

38-2 Types of Corporate Entities

Corporations may be classified in various ways to emphasize a purpose or characteristic. For clarity, this chapter is limited mainly to a discussion of the major kinds of corporations created by statute and authorized by state-granted charters to incorporate.

Private, Public, and Quasi-Public

A **private corporation** is a corporation formed by private persons to accomplish a task best undertaken by an entity that can raise large amounts of capital quickly or that can grant the protection of limited liability. Private corporations can be organized for a profit-making business purpose or for a nonprofit charitable, educational, or scientific purpose. If the corporation is organized for profit-making purposes, those profits may be distributed to the shareholders in the form of dividends. **Dividends** are the net profits, or surplus, set aside for the shareholders. **Shareholders** (or stockholders, as they are also known) are the persons who own units of interest (shares of stock) in a corporation.

Large private corporations generally sell their stock to the public at large and are therefore often referred to as public corporations. When the owners of a private corporation decide to sell stock to the public at large, financial experts report that the corporation is about to "go public." This designation can be confusing because the term **public corporation** is more properly used to describe a corporation created by the federal, state, or local government for governmental purposes. When used in the latter sense, the term includes incorporated cities, sanitation districts, school districts, transit districts, and so on. Corporations that are privately organized for profit but also provide a service on which the public depends are generally referred to as **quasi-public corporations**. In most instances, they are public utilities, which provide the public with such essentials as water, gas, and electricity. (Note: Unless specified otherwise, the discussion in this chapter and those that follow will focus on private corporations.)

Google, Inc., headquartered in Menlo Park, California, maintains 17 corporate offices in the United States and 38 corporate offices in 23 countries throughout Asia, Europe , and North and South America.

Domestic, Foreign, and Alien

A corporation is a **domestic corporation** in the state that grants its charter. It is a **foreign corporation** in all other states. The right to do business in other states (subject to reasonable regulation) is granted by the commerce clause of the U.S. Constitution. To qualify to do business in another state, a foreign corporation must obtain a certificate of authority by providing information similar to the information provided by a domestic corporation applying for a charter. A **certificate of authority** is a document that grants a foreign corporation permission to do business in another state. A registered office and agent must be maintained

within the state upon which service of process (notice of a lawsuit) may be made on behalf of the corporation. An **alien corporation** is one that, though incorporated in a foreign country, is doing business in the United States.

Close and S Corporations

A business corporation may be designated as a **close corporation** when the outstanding shares of stock and managerial control are closely held by fewer than 50 shareholders (often members of the same family) or by one person. State business corporation statutes generally accommodate closely held corporations by allowing them to have a few directors or a sole director and president, with no voting shares in the hands of the public.

The Subchapter S Revision Act of 1982 gives small, closely held business corporations the option of obtaining special tax advantages by becoming an S corporation. An **S corporation** is a corporation in which shareholders have agreed to have the profits (or losses) of the corporation taxed directly to them rather than to the corporation. In this way, they avoid double taxation. There are, however, several restrictions on S corporations. These restrictions include limits on the number and types of owners that can be involved in such an entity. Consequently, many individuals now look to limited liability companies to escape double taxation.

Limited Liability Companies

The **limited liability company (LLC)** is best thought of as a cross between a partnership and a corporation. Like a corporation, the LLC offers the protection of limited liability to its owners. However, unlike a corporation, the LLC's tax liability flows through the LLC and to the owners. In this way, an LLC, like a partnership and an S corporation, escapes the double taxation penalty that falls on corporate entities. In addition, LLCs are statutory, which means that they may come into existence only if the owners follow the precise steps laid out in the state code by the state legislature. The owners of an LLC are called members. The people who run the LLC are called managers. Later in this chapter, we discuss the formation details of an LLC. Chapter 39 also includes a discussion of the duties and responsibilities of the members and the managers of an LLC.

Quick Quiz 38-2 True or False?

1. A private corporation is one that is formed under the authority of a state statute to perform a governmental function.

2. A certificate of authority is issued only to S corporations that have passed the test of associative liability.

3. Limited liability companies have been outlawed in most states because they limit the tax revenue that is due to the government.

38-3 Corporate Formation

A corporation may be incorporated in any state that has a general incorporation statute. Keep in mind that corporations are also subject to court decisions and the state constitution. Federal agencies such as the Securities and Exchange Commission (SEC) also

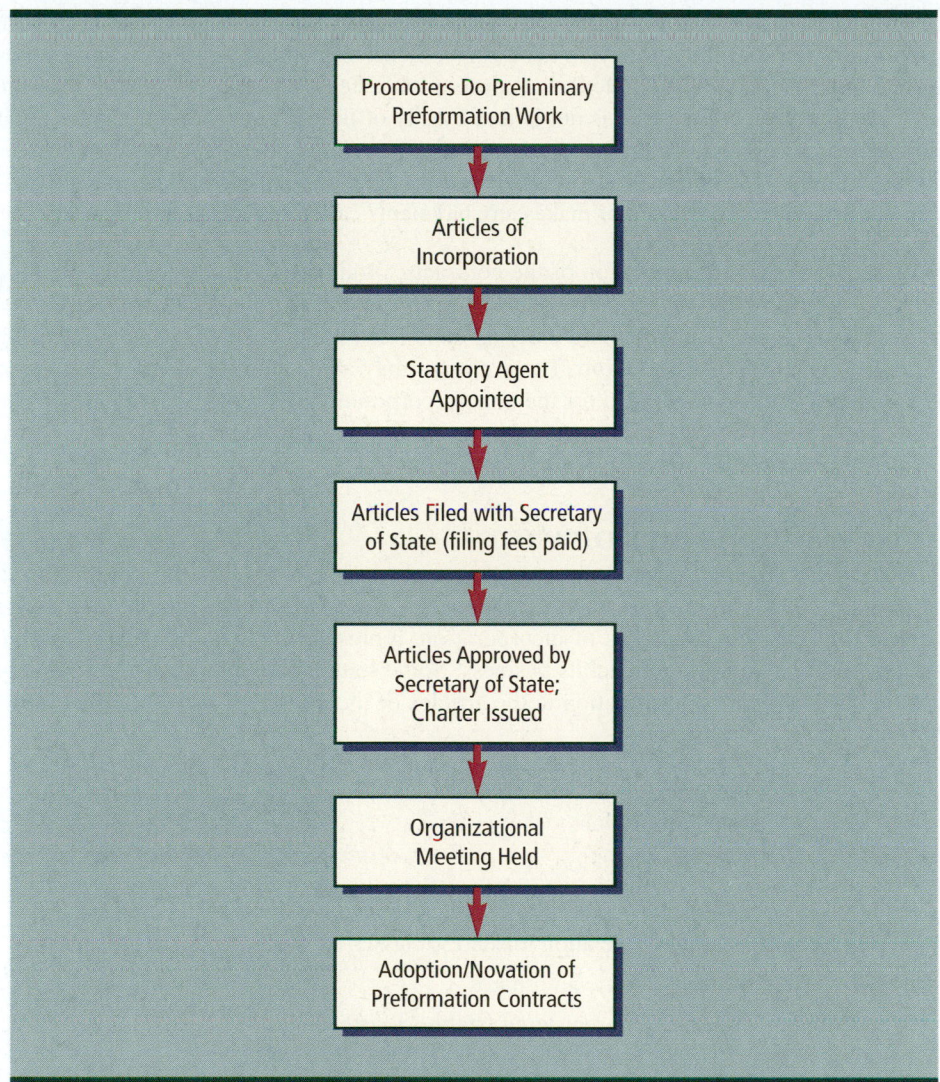

Figure 38-1   This chart shows the steps in the incorporation process.

regulate corporate activity. A proper understanding of effective corporate formation necessitates an examination of promoters, the articles of incorporation, the corporate name, the approval of the articles, and commencement of business. Figure 38-1 illustrates the steps of the incorporation process.

Promoters

The people who want to begin a new corporation or incorporate an existing business are called **promoters**. These people do the actual day-to-day work involved in the incorporation process. **Incorporators** are the people who actually sign the articles of incorporation and submit them to the appropriate state officials. The promoters may also be the incorporators, who later become shareholders and directors of the corporation. Promoters occupy a fiduciary relationship with the nonexistent corporation and its future shareholders. Therefore, the promoter must act in the best interests of the new corporation and its shareholders. The promoter must be honest and loyal and fully reveal all information about any contracts made for the corporation.

Preformation Contracts   Often, promoters will enter contracts for the unborn corporation. For example, it may be necessary to lease office and warehouse space, purchase equipment, and hire employees as preliminary steps in preparing the way for the new corporation. A corporation is not bound by any of the promoter's contracts unless it adopts those contracts. Adoption occurs expressly if the directors pass a resolution agreeing to be bound by a contract. Adoption can also occur implicitly if the corporation accepts the benefits of a contract or makes any payments called for by the agreement.

Novation   Even after adoption of the contracts, promoters are still potentially liable under the preincorporation contracts. One way for promoters to escape potential liability is to have the corporation and the third party agree to release them. The agreement releasing a promoter is known as a **novation**. The promoter may also include an automatic release clause in all contracts negotiated for the unborn corporation. However, the release clause must do more than simply include the corporation as a party to the contract. It must also specifically release the promoters from liability.

Articles of Incorporation

The **articles of incorporation** are the written applications to the state for permission to incorporate. This written application is prepared by the corporation's incorporators. The articles, together with the status of incorporation, represent the legal boundaries within which a corporation must conduct its business. Some state incorporation statutes are very strict, requiring detailed information in the articles of incorporation. Typically this information includes the following:

- The corporation's name
- The duration of the corporation
- The purpose(s) of the corporation
- The number and classes of shares
- The shareholders' rights in relation to shares, classes of shares, and special shares
- The shareholders' right to buy new shares
- The addresses of its original registered (statutory) office and its original registered (statutory) agent
- The number of directors plus the names and addresses of the initial directors
- Each incorporator's name and address

A Question of Ethics

Frank Klesner served as a promoter for the formation of a corporation that eventually came to be known as Aerospin, Inc. The board of directors of Aerospin, Inc., held an initial organization meeting at which they were asked to ratify several contracts that Klesner had made on behalf of the corporation before the corporation had actually been formed. One of the contracts involved the purchase of an office building in downtown Billings, Montana. Rudy Lawnbridge, one of the directors, knew of an office building that Aerospin, Inc., could get for much less than the price paid for the building purchased by Klesner. Lawnbridge also knew that because the contract for the Billings building did not include a release clause, Aerospin, Inc., did not have to adopt the contract. Legally Lawnbridge is correct, but is it ethical for the board of Aerospin, Inc., to abandon Klesner in this manner? Explain.

The newer version of the MBCA has simplified this list somewhat, requiring only the name of the corporation, the number of shares originally authorized, the address of the original registered (statutory) office, the address of the original registered agent, and the incorporators' names and addresses.

The Corporate Name

One of the first steps in forming a corporation is to choose a corporate name. Usually, the words or an abbreviation of the words *corporation*, *company*, or *incorporated* must appear somewhere in the corporate name. Also, the corporation cannot choose a name that some other corporation already uses or a name that would confuse the new corporation with one already in existence. Even in situations in which a specific state statute does not prohibit the use of similar names, the courts will prevent such duplication if confusion or unfair competition results. Often the secretary of state's office can tell promoters whether a name has been taken. It is also possible to reserve a name. Usually, there is a small fee for this service. Promoters also must make certain that they check the availability of a corporate name in not only the state of incorporation but also any state within which they plan to have the corporation do business.

Approval of Articles

After the articles of incorporation are submitted to the state, the appropriate state officer, often the secretary of state, will examine them to make certain that they meet all legal requirements. The secretary of state will also make certain that all filing fees have been paid and that a registered or statutory office and a registered or statutory agent have been appointed. The registered or **statutory agent** is an individual who is designated to receive service of process when a lawsuit is filed against the corporation. Once satisfied that all legal formalities have been met, the secretary of state will issue the corporation's charter, or certificate of incorporation. The charter, or **certificate of incorporation**, is the corporation's official authorization to do business in the state. After the charter is issued, the corporation becomes a fully and legally incorporated entity. The work of the promoters and incorporators ends, unless they become directors or officers of the corporation.

> ***Did You Know?***
>
> A quick reference to corporate law is a book entitled *Corporations: Laws of the United States*, published by Nova Publishing.

Commencement of the Business

Most state statutes provide that the first order of business upon incorporation is holding an organizational meeting. Some states require that the meeting be run by the initial directors designated in the articles. In contrast, those states that do not require naming the directors in the articles allow the organizational meeting to be run by the incorporators. Nevertheless, the first order of business at an incorporator-run meeting is to elect the directors. In addition to the appointment of the first directors, the adoption of bylaws, or regulations, also occurs at the organizational meeting. **Bylaws** or **regulations** are the rules that guide the corporation's day-to-day internal affairs. Bylaw provisions usually stipulate the time and place of shareholders' and directors' meetings, quorum requirements, qualifications and duties of directors and officers, and procedures for filling board vacancies.

Formation of a Limited Liability Company

Similar to a corporation, a limited liability company requires only one person to incorporate. However, the term "person" is liberally defined to include not only people but also corporations and other legal entities, such as partnerships, limited partnerships, trusts, estates, and so on. The term "person" can even include another LLC. Because not all states

Talking Points

One of the central problems of the law is the question of justice. How do jurists know when a decision is just? Is there some sort of internal voice of human nature that tells them they are doing the right thing? Or does the standard for judgment emerge from within the social system? Is it experience, education, or intuition that forms the seat of judgment in these matters? This issue is placed before us by Arnold Brecht in his essay, "Relative and Absolute Justice." Brecht describes this ethical–legal battle in the following way:

> What is just, what is unjust? . . . In examinations of these old questions a modern school of relativity has evolved during the last three or four decades, in this as in other fields of the social sciences. This school has advanced the doctrine that justice, the idea or feeling of justice (or, as some would say, the idea of right, or the ends of law and justice) are conceptions or phenomena of a relative character, because the postulates of justice cannot be ascertained apart from the system of values accepted in a certain period and locality by a certain person or group of persons. Especially will these postulates vary according to whether one regard(s) the individual or the group as the highest value.
>
> —Arnold Brecht, "Relative and Absolute Justice," pp. 21–22

Over the last century, progress has led to pollution, energy shortages, unemployment, new diseases, and, preventative war. In this context, is progress as highly valued in the twenty-first century as it was in the nineteenth? Which value system is correct? Does such a question even make sense in a system of relative justice? Do you believe in the concept of relative justice or the principle of absolute justice? Explain your answers to each of these questions.

recognize the tax advantage usually granted to limited liability companies, it is wise for persons contemplating the formation of an LLC to check the legal status of such entities in all of the states in which they intend to do business.

The Articles of Organization   The **articles of organization** are the written application to the state for permission to form a limited liability company. These articles must include the name of the LLC, the duration of the LLC, and the address where the LLC's operating agreement and bylaws are to be kept. If neither the articles nor the operating agreement, as discussed below, include a duration statement, then some state statutes set an automatic duration period, generally of 30 years. In contrast, in the absence of a duration statement, other state statutes set an unlimited duration. The name of the LLC must include the term "Limited Liability Company" or those words abbreviated, followed by the word "Limited" or the abbreviation "Ltd." In addition, the name of the LLC must not be the same as the name of another LLC or corporation.

However, a problem may arise when a general partnership is transformed into an LLC. An existing general partnership may discover that it has been using a name that is reserved for a corporation or for an already existing LLC. This transformation will require changing the name of the existing partnership before it becomes an LLC. Such a change can be bothersome and complicated, not to mention expensive. The only other alternatives in such a situation would be to acquire authorization to use the common name or to abandon the effort to form an LLC. In addition, a statutory agent for the service of process must be named at the time that the articles are filed in the office of the secretary of state. Finally, proper filing fees must also be paid. Such fees are generally not exorbitant.

The Operating Agreement It is also beneficial for the members of an LLC to draw up an **operating agreement**. Such an agreement, though not required by law in all states, is still very helpful in establishing the bylaws of the LLC, which outline the structure and operation of an LLC. Typically the articles of organization include formation provisions, operating provisions, the nature of the business to be conducted by the LLC, distribution of profits and losses, the powers of the managers, voting rights of the members, admission and withdrawal procedures, provisions regarding the transfer of a member's interest in the LLC, and provisions involving the termination of the LLC, among others. Provisions not covered by the operating agreement are determined by the statute authorizing the creation of LLCs in that state.

Oral Modifications of the Operating Agreement Some state LLC statutes specify that operating agreements can be oral. Under such a provision, certain procedures may inadvertently be added to the operating relationship between the members simply because of a conversation among those members. For this reason, operating agreements should be written even if state law does not require a writing. Moreover, it is wise to add a provision to the written operating agreement that asserts there can be no oral modifications to the agreement. Fortunately, even those statutes that allow oral additions to the operating agreement specify that certain things, such as an agreement to make a capital contribution to the LLC, must be in writing to be binding on the members.

Taxation of an LLC Under Internal Revenue Service (IRS) regulations, the status of a business under state law is not the determining factor in establishing whether a firm, such as an LLC, should be taxed as a partnership or a corporation. Rather, the tax status of such an entity depends on an election made by the owners of that entity. Under the regulations, an entity with two or more members can elect to be treated for tax purposes as an association or as a partnership. An entity owned by one person can elect either association status or a status that will, in effect, hold that the owner and the entity are identical. Election as an association in either situation means that the entity will be taxed as a corporation. The other choice will avoid the corporate tax status.

Quick Quiz 38-3 True or False?

1. An agreement that releases a promoter is called a novation.

2. Bylaws are the rules that guide the corporation's day-to-day internal affairs.

3. Operating agreements for LLCs are required in all states.

38-4 Defective Incorporation

For various liability reasons, the courts may be called upon to decide whether a business entity is a *de jure* corporation, a *de facto* corporation, or a corporation by estoppel.

De Jure and *De Facto* Corporation

A corporation whose existence is the result of the incorporators having fully or substantially complied with the relevant corporation statutes is a *de jure* **corporation**. Its status as a corporation cannot be challenged by private citizens or the state. Sometimes an error is made in the incorporation process. When this occurs, the corporation does not exist legally.

Nevertheless, as long as the following conditions have been met, a ***de facto* corporation** (a corporation in fact) will exist:

1. A valid state incorporation statute must be in effect.
2. The parties must have made a *bona fide* (good faith) attempt to follow the statute's requirements for incorporation.
3. The business must have acted as if it were a corporation.

Usually, if only some minor requirement has been left unsatisfied, the court will hold that there has been a good faith attempt to incorporate. Only the state can directly challenge the existence of a *de facto* corporation. Thus, a *de facto* corporation has the same rights, privileges, and duties as a *de jure* corporation as far as anyone other than the state is concerned. The doctrine of *de facto* corporation is in a state of flux at the present time. The doctrine is itself a common law principle and, as such, can be altered by the courts and by statutory law. Moreover, it seems that the Model Business Corporation Act eliminates the doctrine altogether. Nevertheless, some states have either altered that proposition or ignored it. Montana, for example, has added a section to its version of the MBCA, which states that a corporation that forfeits its corporate status, and then recovers it, will be treated as a corporation retroactively to the day that it lost its corporate status. In effect, what this statute does is to validate the use of the *de facto* doctrine when the secretary of state retroactively reactivates a corporation's corporate status. This application is not exactly the reestablishment of the *de facto* doctrine, but it is a reasonable facsimile. Other states have found other ways around the MBCA by reinstituting a frequently ignored doctrine called corporation by *estoppel*. Given the uncertainty surrounding this issue, however, it is best to check the most recent version of a state's corporate law statute should the question ever arise.

Corporation by Estoppel

In some states, if a group of people act as if they are a corporation when in fact and in law they are not, any parties who have accepted that counterfeit corporation's existence will not be allowed to deny that acceptance. Similarly, individuals who acted as if they were a corporation will not be able to deny that the corporation exists. This doctrine has been labeled **corporation by estoppel**. Corporation by estoppel does not create a real corporation. Instead, it is a legal fiction used by the courts on a case-by-case basis to prevent injustice. Generally, but not always, it is applied in contract cases rather than in tort cases. Some states may have also abolished corporation by estoppel, and so, as with *de facto* corporation, it is best to check the most recent version of a state's corporate law statute.

The Opening Case Revisited

Valley Victory Church v. Darvin Struck and Bonnie Struck, Round 2

Recall that in The Opening Case at the beginning of this chapter, the Valley Victory Church lost its *de jure* corporate standing when the attorney who was responsible for filing the church's yearly reports with the secretary of state's office left the state without filing that crucial report. When the report was not filed, the secretary of state revoked Valley Victory's corporate standing and sent a letter to that effect to the truant attorney. The attorney, of course, neither received the letter nor alerted church officials, who continued to act as if the church were a corporation. When, in the middle of the lawsuit, Darvin Struck discovered this oversight, he argued that the church had no corporate existence at the time of his gift and so the property was still his. Church officials made two counterarguments. First, they said that at the time of the gift, they had a good faith belief that the church was a corporation operating under the authority of a valid state incorporation statute. Therefore, under the doctrine of *de facto* corporation, they continued to operate as a corporation. Second, church officials argued that the Strucks had given the land to the congregation, not to the church. Although the court clearly wanted to accept the church's first argument, it reluctantly rejected that line of reasoning. The court, however, did decide that, under Montana statutory law, once the secretary of state had restored the church's corporate status, all previous corporate acts were ratified. That meant that the church's acceptance of the land was valid when it had occurred. The court also supported the Church's second argument as far as it could, saying that under corporation by estoppel, the Strucks could not recognize the church as a corporation when they transferred the land and then change their minds when it suited them.

Quick Quiz 38-4 True or False?

1. The legal status of a *de jure* corporation cannot be challenged by private citizens or the state.

2. The doctrine of the *de facto* corporation requires that there be a *bona fide* attempt to incorporate under an existing incorporation statute and an exercise of corporate power.

3. Corporation by estoppel does not create a real corporation.

38-5 Piercing the Corporate Veil

Sometimes the court will disregard corporate status to impose personal liability on those who have used the corporation to commit fraud or crimes or to harm the public. In such cases, the court will **pierce the corporate veil** and hold the wrongdoers (usually the controlling shareholders) personally liable for activities committed in the corporation's name. The shareholders of close corporations are more likely to fall victim to piercing the corporate veil than are the shareholders of large corporations, because the shareholders of a close corporation are often also the original incorporators, as well as the directors and officers of the corporation, and thus may neglect to follow the corporate formalities required by statute and/or fail to keep corporate property and business separate from their personal property and business. Thus, the court will sometimes find that the corporation is nothing more than the **alter ego** (other self) of the original incorporators.

LO9

EXAMPLE 38-1:   Jamestown Beauty and Tanning's Alter Ego

For 12 years, Laurie Bostic ran the Jamestown Beauty and Tanning Salon by herself. On advice from her financial planner, she decided to incorporate. She named herself president and chairperson of the board. She was also the sole shareholder. Despite the incorporation of Jamestown, Bostic continued to run her salon as if it were a sole proprietorship. She failed to keep a separate bank account for the salon and usually simply commingled her personal funds with funds that actually belonged to the corporation. She also used all of the property in the salon as her own personal property. She held no directors' meetings and kept no corporate records. When she was sued by a creditor, the court allowed that creditor to pierce the corporate veil and hold Bostic personally liable. Bostic had failed to maintain a distinction between herself and the corporation so that, even though on paper in the secretary of state's office, they appeared to be different, in reality, they were not. Therefore, the court concluded that the Jamestown Beauty and Tanning Salon was actually Bostic's alter ego.

Veil piercing by the courts is less likely to occur with an LLC because corporate formalities are not required by law for LLCs as they are with a corporation. However, in many states, the shareholders of a small corporation can enter a close corporation agreement, which would allow them to escape the need to follow many corporate formalities. Large corporations can also fall victim to piercing the corporate veil if they set up subsidiaries, completely control those subsidiaries, and then commit fraud through the subsidiary. In such cases, however, it is the parent corporation, rather than the individual shareholders, that the courts will hold liable. The test used to determine whether the corporate veil should be pierced to reach the parent corporation is called the *instrumentality test*. This test requires that the parent corporation so dominate the subsidiary that the subsidiary has become a "mere instrumentality of the parent." In this situation, the courts will allow the veil of the instrumentality to be pierced to reach the dominant corporation and to hold that corporation liable for any harm that has been committed through the instrumentality. The courts, however, do not engage in such veil piercing lightly. Still, while the courts respect the separate corporate identity of most subsidiaries, they cannot allow a subsidiary to be used by the parent so that the parent can escape liability, especially if the instrumentality was set up in the first place to commit fraud. When a corporation is set up as a mere instrumentality of a parent, it is sometimes referred to as a **dummy corporation** or a **corporate shell**.

Quick Quiz 38-5 True or False?

1. Most courts have decided that the practice of corporate veil piercing is actually a form of corporation by estoppel.

2. Large corporations are never subject to veil piercing.

3. The standard used to determine whether the corporate veil should be pierced to reach the parent corporation is called the instrumentality test.

 **BusinessWeek** **Business Law in the News**

A Carmaker with Silicon Valley Spark

It takes a big car manufacturer four years to develop a new model. In that period of time, Tesla Motors, Inc. has created a brand-new kind of car company—not to mention plenty of buzz.

Filling the niche for a green vehicle that isn't virtuously homely, Tesla has buyers standing in line to buy its sleek $98,000 electric sports car, which starts coming off the assembly line in October. The wait list now includes George Clooney, California Governor Arnold Schwarzenegger, and Google Inc. founders Larry Page and Sergey Brin. They want to be the first in their neighborhoods to own the eerily quiet machine that can rocket from 0 to 60 in four seconds.

But once the short list of environmentally conscious tycoons trades in their Toyota Priuses for Tesla Roadsters, will there be enough business for the company to survive? Boutique automakers have a grim history. The last car startup to make it was Walter Chrysler's namesake company in 1925. Many auto industry insiders are impressed with Tesla's technology, but question whether the 250-employee San Carlos (Calif.) company will be able to sell enough cars to thrive in the ultracompetitive global car industry. "These guys look undercapitalized to build cars in real numbers," says James N. Hall, vice-president of AutoPacific Inc., an auto industry consulting firm. "They can sell cars until other, bigger manufacturers start selling vehicles that aren't pure electrics but are green enough."

So what makes Tesla think it has a chance? The very fact that it has been built by outsiders. After all, Detroit is hardly a model of corporate efficiency. Tesla bills itself as Silicon Valley's version of a car company. Importing executives and management ideas from the technology industry, it is handing out stock options to every employee, doing away with independent dealers, and outsourcing the manufacturing of its cars. Almost all of Tesla's $105 million in startup capital has come from wealthy California idealists and venture investors. "Silicon Valley is the best in the world at everything it does," boasts Elon Musk, the PayPal founder who sold the company for $1.5 billion before becoming Tesla's chairman and chief source of funds. "The corporate culture [in the Valley] is extremely efficient and very competitive."

Startup energy radiates from Tesla's converted warehouse space on a side street in middle-class San Carlos. All of the top executives—except Musk, who isn't involved in the day-to-day operations—work together in small, cheaply decorated offices. If big decisions need to be made, no one needs to schedule big meetings, write up proposals, or go through any chains of command.

Battery Power

Tesla CEO, Martin Eberhard, a former computer engineer, says he is trying to build a car manufacturer that is also a technology company. By outsourcing mundane parts like brakes and seat belts, Tesla engineers are able to focus on a few core technologies: the battery, the computer software, and the proprietary motor that make the car go. . . .

The company, which plans to go public next year, has created a second division, Tesla Energy, to sell its energy storage technology the same way Toyota licenses its hybrid systems. Its first customer is Think Nordic, a Norwegian producer of small city cars. Some investors believe this unit may have more potential than the car side of the business. . . .

Compared with Big Auto, Tesla's near-term sales goals are modest—just 1,000 a year for the Roadster and 10,000 annually for the future sedan. Eberhard believes they should be easily reachable. He notes that owners of Toyota's Prius earn on average well in excess of $100,000 a year. That means they can afford something much nicer than Toyota's $22,000 hybrid. If necessary, the company would be willing to use a small gas engine to boost Blue Star's range and broaden its appeal.

Musk is convinced there are plenty of customers, like him, who will want something faster or flashier than a Prius. At the moment, in fact, he drives a Porsche and his wife drives a 14-mpg Maserati Quattroporte sedan. "I just can't get into the Prius," Musk says.

Questions for Analysis

1. What are the steps in forming a new corporation like Tesla Motors?

2. When a corporation is created, when does corporate financing begin?

3. Who was the source of Tesla's startup capital?

4. What does it mean when a company plans to "go public"?

5. What part of Tesla Motors' corporate name reveals whether it is a corporation or a limited liability company?

Source: David Welch, "A Carmaker with Silicon Valley Spark: The Tech Veterans behind Tesla Think They Know a Better Way to Build an Electric Car," *BusinessWeek*, July 30, 2007, 73–74.

38-6 Corporate Financing

Corporate financing begins when the original investments are made to set up the corporation. Once the corporation is operating, additional corporate financing may be obtained from earnings, loans, and the issuance of additional shares of stock. The issuing and selling of shares of stock to raise capital is known as *equity financing*, and equity securities give their owners a legal interest in the assets, earnings, and control of the corporation. The part of a corporation's net profits or surplus set aside for the shareholders is known as dividends.

Classes of Corporate Stock

The number of shares and classes of stock that a corporation is authorized to issue are established in its certificate of incorporation. A shareholder who purchases corporate stock invests money or property in the corporation and receives a stock certificate. A **stock certificate** is written evidence of ownership of a unit of interest in the corporation.

Dividends

The most common type of dividend is the **cash dividend**, declared and paid out of current corporate earnings or accumulated surplus at regular intervals. A corporation's board of directors has the sole authority to determine the amount, time, place, and manner of dividend payment. Typically, the directors' declaration of a dividend sets a cutoff date—the date by which a shareholder must hold corporate stock of record to receive payment. In a few instances, a distribution of earnings is made in shares of capital stock, called a **stock dividend**.

Common Stock   The most usual type of corporate stock is **common stock**. Common stock carries with it all the risks of the business, inasmuch as it does not guarantee its holder the right to profits. The shareholder is usually entitled to one vote for each share of stock held. The holders of common stock are paid dividends when the corporation elects to make such a distribution. Holders of common stock risk whatever they invest.

Preferred Stock   Those classes of stock that have rights or preferences over other classes of stock are known as **preferred stock**. These preferences generally involve the payment of dividends and/or the distribution of assets on the dissolution of the corporation. Preferred stock may be either cumulative or noncumulative. Generally, dividends on cumulative preferred stock are paid every year. However, if the dividends are not paid in one year, they will be paid in later years if any dividends at all are paid by the corporation. Dividends on noncumulative preferred stock are also usually paid each year. However, with noncumulative preferred stock, dividends that are not paid in one year are lost forever.

Stock Valuation   **Par value** is the value placed on the shares of stock at incorporation. This value, which is the same for each share of stock of the same issue, is stated on the corporation's certificate of incorporation. In the case of par value shares, the amount of the capital stock or stated capital is the total par value of all the issued stock.

   The practice of placing a par value on a share of stock has been criticized as misleading. Uninformed buyers often interpret par value printed on the face of the certificate as the actual market value of the shares. To correct this condition, all states have authorized the issuance of no par value stock. *No par value stock* is corporate stock issued without any stated price. In fact, par value stock has been eliminated completely under provisions found in the newest version of the MBCA.

Quick Quiz 38-6 True or False?

1. Corporate financing cannot begin until six months after the certificate of incorporation has been issued.

2. The most common type of dividend is the stock dividend.

3. The practice of placing a par value on a share of stock has been approved of and is now mandated by the American Federated Banking Commission.

Summary

38.1 The process of doing business as a self-governing business association, that is, as a corporation, is called associative corporativism, or simply corporativism. A corporation is a legal entity (also referred to as a legal person), the creation of which is empowered by a state or a federal statute authorizing individuals to operate an enterprise. A corporation is a legal person and therefore has certain constitutional rights, such as the right to equal protection of the law and the right not to be deprived of property without due process. Corporations also have dual citizenship. They are citizens of the states in which they are incorporated and in which they have their principal place of business.

38.2 Corporations can be classified in many ways, including private, public, and quasi-public corporations; domestic and foreign corporations; and close and S corporations. The limited liability company offers the protection of limited liability but allows tax liability to flow through the LLC and to its owners.

38.3 A corporation can be incorporated in any state that has a general incorporation statute. The people who actually start the corporation are the promoters. Promoters are liable on preformation contracts until those contracts are adopted by the corporation. The articles of incorporation are drawn up by the corporation's incorporators. After reviewing the articles of incorporation,

the secretary of state will issue a corporate charter, and the corporation becomes a legally incorporated entity. The members of a limited liability company must also follow precise formation procedures.

38.4 A *de jure* corporation is a legally formed corporation. Two doctrines, *de facto* corporation and corporation by estoppel, have been developed to deal with the problem of defective incorporation. A *de facto* corporation exists if there has been a good faith attempt to comply with an existing incorporation statute and an exercise of corporate power. The doctrine of corporation by estoppel prevents later denial of corporate existence by parties willing to deal with an entity as if it were a corporation.

38.5 Under the doctrine of piercing the corporate veil, courts can refuse to recognize a legally formed corporation to prevent injustice and to impose personal liability on the wrongdoers.

38.6 Corporate financing begins when the incorporators give money to set up the business. Subsequent financing takes many forms. The issuing and selling of shares of stock to raise capital is called equity financing. The two most popular classes of stock are common stock and preferred stock. Stock can also be par value or no par value stock. Dividends can be issued as cash or as stock.

Key Terms

Questions for Review and Discussion

1. How did the concept of corporativism evolve?
2. What is the nature of a corporation?
3. What are the constitutional rights of a corporation?
4. What are the differences among a private, a public, and a quasi-public corporation?
5. What is the difference between a close and an S corporation?
6. What are the typical elements within the articles of incorporation?
7. What is the difference between the articles of organization and the operating agreement of a limited liability company?
8. What is the difference between a *de jure* and a *de facto* corporation?
9. What is the objective of piercing the corporate veil?
10. What is the difference between common and preferred stock?

Investigating the Internet

The full text of the Model Business Corporation Act (MBCA) can be found on the Web site of the American Bar Association. Access that Web site and, as a research project, answer the following questions: (1) How does the Model Business Corporation Act (MBCA) define the following terms: "corporation," "foreign corporation," "shareholder," and "shares"? (2) According to Section 2.02 of the MBCA, what items *must* be included in the articles of incorporation? (3) According to Section 2.03 of the MCA, what constitutes conclusive proof that the incorporators have satisfied all the conditions precedent necessary to demonstrate that they have successfully incorporated? (4) Is there any exception to the rule set down in Section 2.03? Explain. (5) According to Section 2.05 of the MBCA, what is the purpose of the organizational meeting held by the incorporators?

Cases for Analysis

1. Dr. Steven A. Pottschmidt was employed by Dr. Thomas J. Klosterman, who was doing business as a corporation named Thomas J. Klosterman, M.D., Inc. Once Pottschmidt's original employment agreement ended, he decided to bring a breach of contract suit against Klosterman alleg-

ing that he, Pottschmidt, had not been paid the amount that was actually owed him under the agreement. Within two months of the lawsuit, Klosterman created a new corporation, called Klosterman Family Practice, Inc. Klosterman Family Practice, however, did not employ anyone other than the staff of the first corporation, Thomas J. Klosterman, M.D., Inc. In addition, the second corporation had not moved from the original office, had not changed its phone number, had not purchased new equipment or new furniture, and had not taken on any new patients. For a while, the two corporations held separate accounts at one bank. Eventually, however, the first company's bank account was terminated, and income for bills sent out by the first company were placed in the account of the second company. Pottschmidt wants the court to permit him to pierce the corporate veil of both Thomas J. Klosterman, M.D., Inc., and Klosterman Family Practice, Inc., to hold Dr. Klosterman directly liable for the money owed to him. Is there enough evidence here to permit the veil piercing requested by the plaintiff? Explain. *Pottschmidt v. Thomas J. Klosterman, M.D., Inc.*, 169 Ohio App.3d 824 (Court of Appeals of Ohio, Ninth District, Medina County).

2. The Aerenthal Financial Loan Corporation lent $578,000 to Raymond Viviani and secured the loan with a mortgage on Viviani's ski lodge, which was located south of Burlington, Vermont. Vermont decided to build a new state highway along a route that cut right through Viviani's lodge. Viviani contested the state's decision and attempted to get the highway rerouted. After several months of unsuccessful battles with the state, Viviani decided to settle for the offer from the government. The state then paid Viviani the market value for the property. Unfortunately, the state failed to notify Aerenthal Financial Loan Corporation about the transaction. When Aerenthal discovered that it had not been notified, it filed a formal protest with the state. The state sent its apologies but argued that Aerenthal had no right to be notified about what was essentially a contractual matter between Viviani and the government. Aerenthal disagreed, arguing that the government had violated its constitutional right not to be deprived of property without due process of law. The state responded by noting that under the state constitution, it had operated properly and Aerenthal was not entitled to due process. Who is correct here? Explain.

3. General Housing Assistance was incorporated as a nonprofit organization that provides low-cost housing for families who have been economically dislocated because of the downsizing of a company or the outsourcing of jobs. One year after the formation of General Housing Assistance, General Mutual Housing Assistance was incorporated in the same state. General Mutual Housing Assistance sold housing shares in condominiums to subscribers. General Mutual ran an aggressive, often obnoxious advertising campaign. After this campaign, General Housing found that people were confusing the two entities. The resulting mix-up damaged General Housing Assistance's image and threatened its charitable funding sources. Consequently, it filed suit to stop General Mutual from using the name because of the confusion between the two entities. Are the names similar enough to cause the court to order General Mutual to change its name? Explain.

4. Through Langham Engineering, Michael Langham marketed his invention, the cross-slope monitor (CSM), as an accessory to John Deere equipment. He had a plan to expand his business to include the CSM as an accessory to Caterpillar Tractor (CAT) equipment. To do this, Langham and Clark Balderson of Balderson, Inc., entered a preincorporation agreement (PIA), in which Langham agreed to contribute his technical abilities, and Balderson agreed to contribute his leadership capabilities to manufacture and market the CSM to CAT. No release clause was included in the PIA. The resulting corporation was named Illinois Controls, Inc. Balderson was designated the president and chairman of the board, and Langham was named vice president. Over the next two years, Balderson failed to train and motivate the sales staff about the proper techniques for selling the CSM to CAT dealers. Balderson also neglected to arrange demonstrations and consignment sales, failed to employ properly trained personnel, and disregarded the need to develop, print, and distribute installation manuals for the CSM. Finally, Balderson set up another corporation named the Dymax Corporation, which dealt with CAT's competitors, thereby undermining Illinois Control's relationship with CAT. As a result, Illinois Controls was forced to shut down operations. Langham sued Balderson personally for the losses that he incurred as a result of Balderson's failure to meet his obligations as outlined in the PIA. Balderson argued that the PIA was a promoter's contract and that the corporation had adopted it. Therefore, Illinois Controls

should be held liable. Was Balderson correct? Explain. *Illinois Controls, Inc., v. Langham,* 639 N.E.2d 771 (OH).

5. Harry and Kay Robinson of New York purchased a new Audi automobile from World Wide Volkswagen (WWV) in New York. After having an accident in Oklahoma, they brought a product liability action against WWV. The case was brought to court in Oklahoma. The Robinsons claimed that the injuries they suffered were caused by the defective design and placement of their automobile's gas tank and fuel system. WWV, which was incorporated in New York and did business there, contended that the Robinsons could not sue WWV in Oklahoma because it was not a citizen of Oklahoma. WWV further contended that it performed no services, owned no property, and closed no sales in Oklahoma. It solicited no business in Oklahoma either through salespersons or through advertising. It also did not indirectly through others serve or seek to serve the Oklahoma market. Did the Oklahoma state court have jurisdiction over WWV? Explain. *World Wide Volkswagen Corporation v. Woodson,* 100 S.Ct. 559 (U.S. Sup. Ct.).

6. Spence was a promoter in the incorporation of a new business. The new corporation had not yet been formed when he bought Huffman's employment agency to serve as the nucleus of that corporation. Eventually, the corporation was formed, but it never generated enough cash to pay Huffman for the employment agency. Huffman sued Spence, attempting to hold him personally liable for the amount due. Spence claimed that the corporation was liable and that his personal assets were not a proper target of the suit. Was Spence correct? Explain. *Spence v. Huffman,* 486 P.2d 211 (AZ).

7. MBI filed its original articles of incorporation under the name Montana Public Employees Benefit Services Co., Inc. After filing the articles, the corporation entered a contract with the Montana Department of Administration. Under the contract, the new corporation would have exclusive administrative control over Montana's public employee deferred-payment pension plan. The articles were not approved by the secretary of state, who requested a name change. After the corporation's name was changed to MBI, the charter was issued, and the corporation became a legal entity. The Montana Association of Underwriters, a private corporation that wanted a share in administering the state pension plan, challenged the validity of the contract, arguing that at the time the contract was signed,

MBI did not legally exist. Was the Montana Association of Underwriters correct? Explain. *Montana Association of Underwriters v. Department of Administration and MBI,* 563 P.2d 577 (MT).

8. Lamas Company, Inc., was incorporated in Georgia. Baldwin negotiated with Lamas, sole owner of Lamas Company, Inc., to finish some electrical work on a construction site. When Baldwin was dissatisfied with the work, he decided to sue. Unfortunately, the statute of limitations ran out before he could sue Lamas Company, Inc., so he sued Lamas individually. Baldwin argued that he had dealt only with Lamas, that he did not know Lamas was an agent of the company, that Lamas did not tell him about the company, and that he understood the contract to be with Lamas individually. Lamas pointed out that Baldwin made out and sent checks directly to Lamas Company, Inc., and that Lamas Company, Inc., always appeared as the payee on those checks. Lamas claimed that this evidence alone would be enough to stop Baldwin from denying that he had dealt with Lamas Company, Inc. The trial court rendered judgment against Lamas. On appeal, did the appellate court reverse? Explain. *Lamas v. Baldwin,* 230 S.E.2d 13 (GA).

9. Boafo was allegedly injured while giving birth at Parkway Regional Hospital. Boafo sued both Parkway Regional and Hospital Corporation of America (HCA), asking the court to pierce the corporate veil to reach HCA, which Boafo claimed was a parent company. Boafo showed that the two corporations shared the same offices, that they purchased hospital equipment together, that HCA owned 100 percent of Parkway stock, that major financing for Parkway was performed by HCA through a national accounting system, and that Parkway was insured by another wholly owned subsidiary of HCA. In answer, HCA emphasized that Parkway handled its own daily financing, that it was free to negotiate and enter its own contracts, that it had an adequate amount of money in its treasury, and that it was not formed to promote fraud, conceal crime, or evade legal liability. The trial court granted summary judgment, dismissing the claim against HCA. Did the appellate court uphold the trial court's ruling? Explain. *Boafo v. Hospital Corporation of America,* 338 S.E.2d 477 (GA).

10. The Northeastern Corporate Institute of Technology (NCIT), a profit-oriented corporation engaged in nuclear research projects, owned and operated an experimental station in a remote region of Alaska. The Alaskan Chemical Disposal Corpora-

tion, a subsidiary of NCIT, disposed of all chemical and nuclear waste products produced by NCIT's experimental station. On a routine disposal route, an Alaskan Chemical Disposal transport convoy collided with a North Coast moving van. The lead truck in the convoy spilled chemical waste into a lake owned by Kenneth Ridgeway. Ridgeway sued both NCIT and Alaskan Chemical Disposal. NCIT argued that the disposal of NCIT's chemical was the sole responsibility of Alaskan Chemical Disposal, which it characterized as an independent contractor. Ridgeway's attorney, however, had discovered that Alaskan Chemical Disposal had no business other than providing waste disposal services to NCIT. The attorney also discovered that Alaskan Chemical Disposal was listed as a division of NCIT, was financed by NCIT, and shared the same board of directors and officers as NCIT. Moreover, the attorney found out that Alaskan Chemical Disposal was badly undercapitalized. In addition, all decisions in the running of Alaskan Chemical Disposal were made by NCIT. In light of all of this evidence, Ridgeway's attorney began to suspect that Alaskan Chemical Disposal might have been formed to allow NCIT to escape liability in just this type of situation. Will Ridgeway be allowed to maintain its suit against NCIT? Explain.

Quick Quiz Answers

38-1	38-2	38-3	38-4	38-5	38-6
1. T	1. F	1. T	1. T	1. F	1. F
2. T	2. F	2. T	2. T	2. F	2. F
3. F	3. F	3. F	3. T	3. T	3. F

Chapter 39 — Corporate Governance

The Opening Case

American Federation of State, County, & Municipal Employees (AFSCME), Employees Pension Plan v. American International Group (AIG), Inc.

The American Federation of State, County, & Municipal Employees (AFSCME) is a union that represents governmental workers. The AFSCME manages a pension plan for its members that is enhanced by investments in a number of corporations. One of those corporations is the American International Group (AIG). The AFSCME owns 26,965 shares of voting stock in AIG. As a shareholder, the AFSCME developed a shareholder proposal in which it recommended that the rules of the corporation be changed so that shareholders like AFSCME could propose candidates for the board of directors. The names of candidates named by the shareholders would then be placed on the ballot along with the candidates put forward by the directors of the corporation and voted on at the shareholder' meeting. The rules of AIG permitted changes to be made in the operating procedures of the corporation by a majority vote of the shareholders, which is what AFSCME sought with this proposal. The law says that to be qualified to make a proposal, a shareholder must meet certain preliminary requirements under Rule 14 (a) of the Securities Exchange Act of 1934. According to that rule, a proposal, which cannot be greater than 500 words, can only be submitted by a shareholder who owns at least 1 percent of the company's shares or, failing that, at least $2,000 in market value of those shares. The shareholder must also have owned those shares continuously for at least one year before the proposal was submitted to the corporation. It was clear from the outset that AFSCME easily met these preliminary requirements. Nevertheless, AIG sought to block the proposal from being placed on the ballot. To do this, AIG asked the Securities and Exchange Commission (SEC) to disallow the proposal on the grounds that it could be excluded under Rule 14a-8(i)(8), which states that a corporation can refuse to honor any proposal that "relates to an election for membership on the company's board of directors." Now this sounds relatively straightforward, and the court might have also seen it that way, had it not been for the fact that the SEC itself had issued two conflicting interpretations of the exclusion under Rule 14a-8(i)(8). One interpretation, dating back to the latest revision of the rule in 1976, said that the provision was meant to eliminate only shareholder proposals that affected a single election. According to this interpretation, AIG could not exclude the AFSCME proposal. The other interpretation, presented by the SEC in response to a specific request made by the trial court in this case, said that the exclusion was meant to apply to a proposal that affected not just one election but the entire election process, at least insofar as that proposal involved a proxy solicitation contest. The trial court bought this interpretation, but the appellate court did not. The appellate court preferred to endorse the interpretation that was issued by the SEC at the time that the exclusion was actually written. For that reason, the AFSCME shareholder proposal was approved by the court. (*American Federation of State, County, & Municipal Employees (AFSCME), Employees Pension Plan v. American International Group (AIG), Inc.*, Case No. 05-2825-cv., United States Court of Appeals for the Second Circuit.)

Opening Case Questions

1. What is a shareholder proposal?

2. What are the requirements for a shareholder proposal?

3. What was the reason that AIG sought to exclude this proposal?

4. Why did the trial court ask the SEC for its interpretation of the rule?

5. Why did the court find for the plaintiff in this case?

LO Learning Objectives

1. Explain the central dilemma of corporate governance.
2. Describe the functions of directors, officers, and shareholders.
3. List the five theories of corporate governance.
4. Describe cumulative voting and proxy solicitation.
5. Explain shareholder proposals.
6. Distinguish between voting trusts and pooling agreements.
7. Contrast shareholder direct suits with shareholder derivative suits.
8. Contrast the business judgment rule with the fairness rule.
9. List the rights that belong to shareholders.
10. Explain the management of a limited liability company.

39-1 Management of the Corporation

Most state incorporation statutes provide that a corporation's business affairs are to be managed under the direction of a board of directors. The board of directors establishes broad policies, and the officers and other employees implement those policies. The shareholders are the owners of the corporation. How to keep the role of the board separate from that of executive management and that of shareholders is related to the challenge of how best to organize the board and select its members. The issues are even more complex today because a single individual often functions as a director, an officer, and a shareholder. Nevertheless, the three roles have distinct functions and should be examined separately.

LO1

LO2

Directors of the Corporation

The business affairs of a corporation are managed by a board of directors elected by the shareholders. The board's responsibility is to take whatever actions are appropriate, in keeping with the corporation's rules and regulations, to further the corporation's business. Individual board members are supposed to use their own judgment in the corporate decision-making process.

Qualifications of Directors   State law and corporate rules set up the qualifications that a person must have to be a corporate director. Unless prohibited by the corporation's certificate of incorporation, membership on the board of directors can be extended to anyone, including aliens, minors, and nonshareholders. Often the certificate stipulates that at least one director must be a state resident and at least one is a shareholder.

Time Commitment of Directors   Directors are elected at the annual meeting of the shareholders. Generally, directors hold office for one or two years. The number of directors on the board varies between eight and twelve. Usually, several directors are elected as a group to maintain continuity; this procedure permits one-third of the board to be elected annually. The basic time commitment for a director is approximately 30 days per year, but depending upon need, availability, and interest, it can be 40, 60, 80, or even more days. Naturally, directors can resign from the board. However, many states require written notice of the director's resignation to the corporation.

Meetings of Directors   The directors of most large corporations meet on a regular basis at a precise time and place of their choosing. The directors of many smaller corporations meet only when specific items are to be considered. Some states allow small corporations with fewer than 50 shareholders to eliminate the board of directors entirely, as long as someone is assigned the duties that the board would have performed.

Directors are not entitled to be notified about regular board meetings unless notice is required by the corporation's bylaws. (The bylaws, or regulations of a corporation, determine how that corporation will operate.) However, directors must be notified of special meetings of the board. For example, a special meeting of the directors might be called to decide whether the corporation should institute a lawsuit. If any director is not notified of a special meeting, all actions taken at the meeting are void. A director may not specify another person to vote in her or his place. The quorum, or minimum number of directors necessary to conduct business, is usually one more than half of the total number of directors. Bylaws may require more than a quorum, perhaps 70 percent of the directors, to conduct certain types of business. This supermajority might be needed, for instance, to remove a director or sell a significant portion of the business. Generally though, the actions of a quorum constitute the official actions of the board.

EXAMPLE 39-1:   Meeting the Quorum

The board of directors of Barber Enterprises, Inc., consisted of seven persons. At a properly called meeting, one of the directors presented a motion calling for a stock-option purchase plan for Barber's president, vice presidents, secretary, and treasurer. Five directors attended the meeting. This constituted a quorum. Three of the five voted for the plan. This vote would constitute an official act by the board.

Officers of the Corporation

Directors are not expected to spend all of their time and energy managing the corporation. They have the authority to appoint officers and agents to run the day-to-day affairs of the corporation. By statute, the usual officers are a president, several vice presidents, a secretary, and a treasurer. Other officers, such as a comptroller, cashier, and general counsel, are often provided. The bylaws of the corporation describe the duties of each officer. Officers have the authority of general agents for the operation of the normal business of the corporation. They in turn delegate duties to various department heads. Although the roles of directors and officers differ, they are frequently assumed by the same people. An individual may be both chief executive officer and chair of the board of the same corporation. Directors and officers can also be shareholders in the corporation.

Shareholders of the Corporation

The shareholders are the owners of the corporation. The more shares that a shareholder owns, the more voting power that shareholder has in the running of the corporation. Therefore, the most effective way for a shareholder to obtain corporate power is to purchase more stock. Unfortunately, purchasing additional stock is not always possible, either because the shareholder does not have the financial leverage needed to purchase enough shares to gain corporate control or because there are no shares available to purchase. Another way to gain operating power is to work with the shares that the shareholder already owns but increase voting power in other ways. Before looking at those voting techniques, it is important to remember that though many shareholders are individuals, others are large institutions such as union pension funds that have invested large sums of money in corporate stock to gain a return for their retirees.

Quick Quiz 39-1 True or False?

1. The business affairs of a corporation are managed by a board of directors elected by the shareholders.

2. Membership on a board of directors can never be extended to aliens, minors, or nonshareholders.

3. Directors have authority to appoint officers and agents to run the day-to-day affairs of the corporation.

39-2 Issues in Corporate Governance

Under the original concept of a corporation, the shareholders are the primary reason that a corporation exists. This image has evolved over the years, so the shareholders often take a back seat to consumers, employees, environmentalists, politicians, social science engineers, and economists. For this reason, the corporate landscape has come to resemble a battlefield in recent years. There are those who believe that the battle is a good thing because it helps make corporations more responsible. There are others, however, who believe that the battle has weakened and in some cases completely dismantled corporate power. Which side has correctly diagnosed the problem remains to be seen. For the present, we can examine five different points of view about how a corporation ought to be governed. These include special interest group control, governmental control, independent director control, managerial control, and shareholder democratic control.

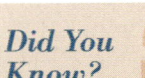

Did You Know?

Although the shareholders of a corporation are the actual owners of the corporation, they are not agents of the corporation, as are the directors and officers, and therefore cannot commit the corporation to any contractual arrangements.

Theories of Corporate Governance

As noted previously, five theories have been put forth by legal scholars and business experts regarding how corporations should be managed: special interest group control, governmental control, independent director control, managerial control, and shareholder democracy.

Special Interest Group Control

Special interest group control is based on the idea that corporate decision making affects more individuals and groups than just the shareholders and the managers of the corporation. The people who support special interest group control argue that many corporate decisions, such as a decision to open or close a factory, affect the community through consumers, suppliers, employees, and community neighbors. Consequently, all of these groups and more should be represented on the boards of directors of all major corporations. Individuals who support special interest group control would like to see representatives from employees' unions, consumer protection organizations, and environmental protection groups on these boards. Opponents of the theory point out the impracticality of this approach to corporate management.

Governmental Control

Support for the **governmental control** theory of corporate management is based on the belief that because corporate decision making influences more individuals and groups than just the shareholders and the managers, corporate decisions should be made by an impartial group of corporate outsiders. Usually, the corporate outsiders named are government officials. These specially educated government officials would make corporate decisions in an objective manner, based on the needs of the entire society and the economy as a whole. Opponents of this theory label such an approach socialistic and point to the relatively poor record of many socialist economies as evidence of the impracticality of this approach.

Of course, those who support governmental control do not always go so far as to demand that the government have a seat in every corporate boardroom in America. A less dramatic and perhaps more effective technique is to use governmental control indirectly through regulatory legislation. One particularly effective piece of Congressional legislation in this regard is the Sarbanes-Oxley (SarbOx) Act of 2002. SarbOx was passed by Congress in the wake of a series of corporate scandals, some of which were caused by the failure of the board and the chief corporate officers to oversee activities properly within their corporations. Thus, Congress placed certain strict requirements on officers and directors and added severe penalties for the failure to meet those requirements. For example, under SarbOx, chief executive officers (CEOs), chief operating officers (COO's), and chief financial officers (CFOs) are required to present declarations that confirm the accuracy of their corporation's financial statements. They must indicate that the statements do not misrepresent the company's economic situation. The penalties for violating this particular provision include possible incarceration and monetary penalties that run into the millions.

Other regulations under SarbOx prevent individual loans from the corporation to board members or officers and require that the participants on a corporation's audit team consist of impartial outside directors. There is also a regulation against altering evidence that prohibits the revision, destruction, or suppression of records needed in a government investigation of the corporation. Similar to the penalty for filing a misleading financial statement, the punishment for violating this rule also involve incarceration. On a more positive note, the SarbOx encourages companies to develop ethical rules and regulations and promote efficient monetary management procedures. The act also shields any employees who must provide information to federal authorities about any corporate violations of these provisions. Employees are not alone in this campaign, however, because SarbOx also set up a Public Accounting Oversee Board to regulate corporate auditing procedures.

Not everyone in the corporate community is happy about the passage of SarbOx or about the extra regulatory responsibilities that it places on corporate directors, officers, and auditors. Some financial experts, for instance, predict that the United States will soon

BusinessWeek **Business Law in the News**

SarbOx Isn't Really Driving Stocks Away

The U.S. capital markets are being suffocated by regulation. So argue politicians from both parties, who have joined forces in the past year with various business groups to bolster American competitiveness. In town meetings, op-ed pieces, and industry gatherings, they have attacked the Sarbanes-Oxley Act of 2002 and other corporate reforms for driving companies away from U.S. stock exchanges to other, more business-friendly locales.

The statistics, however, paint a somewhat different picture. It turns out that a record number of non-U.S. companies are flocking to NYSE Euronext and NASDAQ to make their initial public offerings. So far this year, 22 companies, many from China and Israel, have raised nearly $4.4 billion on U.S. exchanges, according to Thomson Financial. That's more than even the first half of 2000, when 17 foreign companies collected nearly $4.2 billion. If the pace continues, the foreign IPOs will handily surpass the record $10.9 billion raised last year by 34 companies.

The conventional thinking is that Sarbanes-Oxley's tough restrictions on corporate audit practices and internal controls will lead foreign companies to list elsewhere. But companies such as RRSat Global Communications Network Ltd. aren't being frightened off. When the $43 million-a-year Israeli provider of services for TV and radio systems shopped for a place to take its stock public, it bypassed Tel Aviv and London in favor of NASDAQ. The company, which went public seven months ago, came to the U.S. partly because of—not despite—the regulatory requirements. "It's positive for the company," says Gil Efron, RRSat's chief financial officer. "It supports the confidence of the shareholder in the [financial] reporting by the company, and it improves [our] internal processes."

To be sure, the less regulated London market is attracting its share of foreign IPOs, too. So far this year, the London Stock Exchange has helped 12 non-British outfits raise nearly $18 billion on its market, according to Thomson. Last year, 16 non-British companies raised $22.7 billion on the main market. The LSE's alternative market, where small companies that generally wouldn't qualify for U.S. listings

go, has clocked 19 non-British IPOs so far this year, raising nearly $2 billion.

But London has an edge over New York in that its time zone is much closer to those in Russia and Eastern Europe, two IPO hotbeds that have accounted for five of London's offshore-based IPOs, raising nearly $5.6 billion this year. London banks and investors have much more expertise in these regions than New York has. Where the geographical playing field is level—Chinese listings, for instance—New York is strong and getting stronger. What's more, whereas the Chinese have long tapped British investors by way of Hong Kong, now they're keen to solicit American money. "They're saying: 'We don't need to bother with London,'" says G. Andrew Karolyi, a finance professor at Ohio State University who closely tracks the exchanges.

Indeed, for Chinese entrepreneurs especially, qualifying for a U.S. listing is a badge of honor. Ten of this year's offshore-based IPOs on U.S. markets so far are from China, up from seven in all of last year. NYSE Euronext "provides us access to high-quality investors world-wide," says Ma Tao, vice-president of investor relations for Qiao Xing Mobile Communication Co., a maker of mobile handsets that raised $160 million on the New York exchange in May.

Critics of U.S. regulations still argue that the IPO surge could be even stronger if the stringent rules were eased. "Sarbanes-Oxley is an issue in every single listing," says Skadden, Arps, Slate, Meagher & Flom lawyer Michael V. Gisser, who works with Asian companies on going public. "There is reason to be concerned," adds John A. Thain, chief executive of NYSE Euronext, who has long pressed for change. But, he concedes, "we're still doing pretty well."

Questions for Analysis

1. What is the conventional wisdom about the effects of the SarbOx regulations?

2. What evidence contradicts the conventional wisdom?

(Continued)

Business Law in the News (*Continued*)

3. What is an IPO?

4. Corporations from which unlikely country prefer a U.S. listing to a U.K. listing?

5. What counterargument to the increase in IPO listings is offered by the anti-SarbOx coalition?

Source: Joseph Weber with Xiang Ji in Hong Kong, "Finance, The Market: SarbOx Isn't Really Driving Stocks Away: Despite the Doomsayers, Many Foreign Companies Are Rushing to List on U.S. Exchanges," *BusinessWeek,* July 2, 2007, 87.

experience a serious loss of foreign business because of the strict rules enforced under SarbOx. These pundits fear that some global alien corporations that have the chance to place their stock for sale on an American stock exchange will move instead to a foreign exchange in search of a more lenient approach to corporate governance. Although some evidence of this trend has been detected, other causes may explain why a foreign corporation might choose to list in London rather than New York. Some analysts argue that the epidemic of anti-corporate lawsuits rather than regulatory legislation is what actually drives foreign firms away from the United States. Others suggest that the American insistence that all disputes be fashioned under American law, a trend known as **legal imperialism**, makes listing in the United States unpopular today. In contrast, some experts see no crisis at all, and still others suggest that the problem of attracting foreign firms to an American exchange is less troublesome than dealing with the type of widespread corruption that sparked the passage of SarbOx in the first place.

Independent Director Control   A third theory of corporate control involves the establishment of independent directors. Those theorists who support the use of independent directors argue that the most effective way to ensure that corporate decisions are made in the best interests of those affected is to make certain that the decision makers themselves are not affected by those decisions. Some groups have already implemented requirements to ensure the addition of independent directors to the boards of many corporations. **Independent directors** are defined as directors who have no family members employed by the corporation, who are not themselves employed by the corporation, or, if they were at one time employed by the corporation, have not been on the staff for at least three years. There is, of course, an "opt out" rule that permits some corporations to sidestep the independent directors' rule if they are a "controlled" company. A **controlled company** is one that has more than half its voting power concentrated in one person, or a small group of persons, who always vote together. The opt out provision is designed to give parent companies that are already controlled by independent boards a technique for eliminating a duplication of the independence restriction in their subsidiaries.

Managerial Control   The fourth approach to corporate governance is **managerial control**. Those who favor managerial control point out that the officers and the directors of a corporation are in the best position for judging not only the needs of the corporation but also the needs of the community and the needs of society at large. Individuals who favor managerial control would insulate the managers from shareholders by limiting the shareholders' power to vote and making it difficult for shareholders to sue managers. Opponents of managerial control argue that corporate managers may tend to be self-interested and, as a result, make relatively short-sighted decisions.

Shareholder Democracy   Individuals who favor **shareholder democracy**, or **corporate democracy** as it is also known, believe that the shareholders have the right to run the corporation, because without their money, the corporation would not be able to survive. As the real owners of the corporation, the shareholders have a right to say how their money and their property should be used. Supporters of shareholder democracy would make management more responsive to shareholders by giving shareholders greater voting control and making it easier for them to take managers to court. Opponents of this theory point out that most shareholders are removed from the center of corporate activity and therefore cannot make the same type of informed decisions that the managers can make.

Today there is a delicate balance between the theories of managerial control and shareholder democracy. Therefore, this chapter will focus on the battle between these two positions as it examines the subject of corporate control. The two most significant areas of this conflict lie in shareholder voting control and shareholder lawsuits. Shareholders can influence corporate decision making through their voting powers and through their right to initiate a lawsuit against managers (see Table 39-1).

Shareholder Voting Control

Shareholders usually receive one vote per share of common stock held. Shareholders who are dissatisfied with management can attempt to buy more shares to increase their voting power. With this increased voting power, the dissatisfied or dissident shareholders can influence the election of the board of directors. However, shareholders are not always able to buy more shares of the corporation, either because they cannot afford them or because the other shareholders are not willing to sell. In such cases, shareholders can resort to one of the other voting methods available:

LO4

LO5

LO6

- Cumulative voting
- Proxy solicitation
- Shareholder proposals
- Voting trusts

- Pooling agreements
- Shareholder nominations
- Unanimous voting restrictions

Table 39-1   Shareholder Control

Votes and Lawsuits	Explanation
Voting control:	
Cumulative voting	Each share of stock has as many votes as there are directors to be elected
Proxy voting	The right to vote another shareholder's stock
Voting trusts	An agreement among shareholders to transfer their voting rights to a trustee
Pooling agreements	Shareholders join together in a temporary arrangement, agreeing to vote the same way on a particular issue
Shareholder proposals	A suggestion about a broad company policy or procedure submitted by a shareholder and included in management's proxy solicitation
Shareholder suits:	
Direct suit	A suit brought by shareholders who have been deprived of a right
Derivative suit	A suit brought by shareholders based on an injury to the corporation

Cumulative Voting   Ordinarily, each share of common stock is worth one vote. Therefore, only a majority of shareholders can elect directors of the corporation. To give minority shareholders an opportunity to elect one or more directors, some states permit **cumulative voting**. This system allows shareholders to multiply the number of their voting shares by the number of directors to be elected. All these votes may be cast for one candidate or distributed among several candidates. This procedure allows minority shareholders an opportunity to be represented on the board of directors.

EXAMPLE 39-2:   Cumulative vs. Straight Voting

Beth General, James Garrett, Ken Collins, and Heather Gilliam were presented to the shareholders as candidates for the board of directors of Shopton Enterprises, Inc. Three of the four were to be chosen. Because cumulative voting was authorized, the minority shareholders cast all their weighted votes for Gilliam, who had promised to represent the minority voice in corporate affairs. Had the minority voters been allowed only one vote for each share instead of three, they might have failed in their effort to elect a favored director.

Proxy Voting   A **proxy** is the authority given to one shareholder to cast another shareholder's votes. **Proxy solicitation** is the process by which one shareholder asks another for his or her voting right. Proxy solicitation also refers to the actual document that is used to request the right to vote the other shareholders' votes. The minority shareholder's voting power increases as the number of proxies held rises. Because majority shareholders, including management, can also solicit proxies, a struggle between the two groups, known as a **proxy contest**, often results. Proxy contests involving large, publicly held corporations are closely regulated by the Securities and Exchange Commission (SEC). The primary federal law that controls the operation of a proxy contest is Section 14 (a) of the Securities Exchange Act of 1934. Section 14 (a) is designed to prevent fraud by requiring a complete revelation of certain facts by any individual or group that gets involved in the proxy solicitation process. Specifically, the law requires that anyone soliciting a proxy must disclose the identity of the solicitor, the reason behind the solicitation, and all other crucial facts that the shareholders will need to make an informed decision about the proxy. The document that communicates this information to the shareholders is called a **proxy statement**, which is delivered to SEC and then sent to shareholders before the shareholders' annual meeting. Generally, the solicitation includes a card called a proxy card that can be returned to the solicitor. Rule 14 (a) of the Securities Exchange Act has recently become the focus of heated debate among shareholders and management alike. The dispute covers the question of what corporate management can and cannot exclude from proxy materials that are to be sent to shareholders.

Stockholders exercise their control through votes at annual meetings and through proxies.

Shareholder Proposals   Another way for shareholders to exercise their voting power to shape corporate decision making is the shareholder proposal. Because shareholder proposals are placed in the proxy materials that are sent from corporate management to shareholders, they are closely allied with the proxy solicitation process and also governed by the Securities Exchange Act of 1934. A shareholder proposal allows shareholders to influence corporate affairs because, under SEC guidelines, shareholders of large, publicly owned corporations can compel management to include their proposals in management's proxy solicitation prior to the next shareholder meeting. A **shareholder proposal** is a suggestion about a broad company policy or procedure that is submitted by a shareholder. The proposal cannot be about the ordinary business operation of the corporation. It must concern something that affects all shareholders. A proposal to hire or fire a particular employee would not qualify, whereas a proposal to amend the corporate charter would. The rules also prohibit proposals that concern only dividend payments.

To qualify as a valid shareholder proposal under SEC rules, the proposal must be no more than 500 words long and must be submitted to management at least 120 days before the shareholders' meeting. In addition, the shareholder must have owned at least 1 percent or $2,000 in market value of the voting stock of the corporation for one year and may submit only one proposal at a time. Even then, managers can reject the proposal if they feel that it does not qualify as a valid shareholder proposal according to a lengthy list of disqualifying characteristics cataloged by the SEC. Included on this list are proposals that are personal grievances, those beyond the corporation's power, and proposals that relate to a corporate election. However, some of these limitations recently have been challenged in a series of lawsuits filed by high-powered corporate shareholders.

Shareholder proposals, sometimes referred to as **shareholder resolutions**, have traditionally been among the weakest of shareholder voting tactics. One reason is that for many years, such proposals were not taken seriously by the directors and officers of most corporations, a situation that was exacerbated by the fact that the courts did not appear to take them seriously either. Much of this attitude was caused by the open-ended nature of the

The Opening Case Revisited, Part I

American Federation of State, County, & Municipal Employees (AFSCME), Employees Pension Plan v. American International Group (AIG), Inc., Round 2

In The Opening Case at the beginning of this chapter, the American Federation of State, County, & Municipal Employees (AFSCME) developed a shareholder proposal in which it recommended that the rules of the AIG be changed so that shareholders like AFSCME could propose candidates for the board of directors. The law says that to be qualified to make a proposal, a shareholder must meet certain preliminary requirements in Rule 14 (a) of the Securities Exchange Act of 1934, namely, that a proposal, which cannot exceed 500 words in length, can only be submitted by a shareholder who owns at least 1 percent of the company's shares or, failing that, at least $2,000 in market value of those shares. The shareholder must also have owned those shares continuously for at least one year before the proposal was submitted to the corporation. It was clear from the outset that AFSCME easily met these preliminary requirements. Nevertheless, AIG sought to block the proposal from being placed on the ballot, under Rule 14a-8(i)(8), which states that a corporation can refuse to honor any proposal that "relates to an election for membership on the company's board of directors." The court ultimately disallowed the exclusion.

A Question of Ethics

In the twenty-first century, it has become increasingly popular for shareholders to press their corporate demands through the use of shareholder proposals. Many of these proposals are filed by large institutional shareholders. Nevertheless, corporate boards continue to resist such proposals. Is it ethical for corporate directors to resist the will of the shareholders in this way? Explain your position by referring to the section on corporate social responsibility in Chapter 1.

Table 39-2 Strengthening Shareholders

>> End supermajority votes, the rule that up to 80% of owners back some proposals:	>> Reelect all directors each year rather than hold staggered elections:	>> Let shareholders approve golden parachutes if they exceed three times pay:	>> Allow investors to cast a nonbinding vote on executive pay:	>> Link executive pay to performance of the company:
2006 **63%**	2006 **66%**	2006 **52%**	2006 **40%**	2006 **30%**
2007 **73%**	2007 **72%**	2007 **66%**	2007 **43%**	2007 **35%**

Data: Institutional Shareholder Services. 2007 averages are based on preliminary vote counts and are not final.

Source: Jena McGregor, "Activist Get More Respect: Boards Are Listening, and Shareholder Proposals Are Making Headway," *BusinessWeek,* June 11, 2007, 34–35.

Table 39-3 Shareholder Proposals

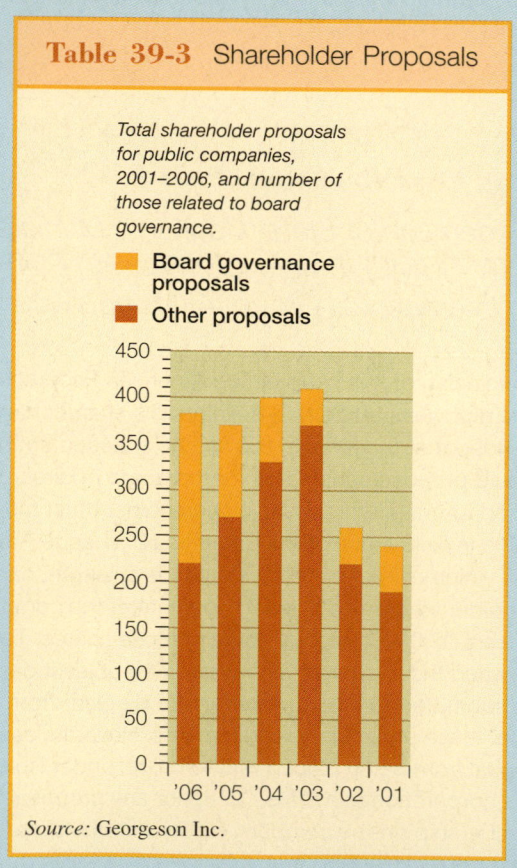

Total shareholder proposals for public companies, 2001–2006, and number of those related to board governance.

- Board governance proposals
- Other proposals

Source: Georgeson Inc.

Source: Sheri Qualters, "Dissident Shareholders Up Demands," *The National Law Journal,* March 5, 2007, 1 and 9.

rules which permitted the corporate directors to reject most proposals made by shareholders. Moreover, many of the proposals that did make it to the ballot were filed by people with a political agenda and demanded such things as a cessation of business dealings with South African companies, a boycott of Defense Department contracts, or a campaign to redistribute shareholder dividends among needy Third World nations.

Shareholder proposals have become more effective in recent years, partly because the shareholder proposal has become less a soapbox for political dissidents and more a tool for large institutional shareholders. These institutional shareholders, such as the American Federation of State County & Municipal Employees or Boston Common Asset Management, press claims against corporations asking not for political actions but for a share in corporate governance (see Table 39-2). Typically, such proposals demand that the corporation make some sort of amendment in voting procedures, such as change in the bylaws to require a majority rather than a plurality vote on directors, to allow shareholders to cast advisory votes on executive salaries, or to permit shareholders to vote on antitakeover tactics, such as the use of a white knight or a lockup agreement strategy (see Chapter 40). Corporate directors have become more amenable to such shareholder proposals in light of the Sarbanes-Oxley Act and the outside support that has been provided by newly formed expert support groups, such as the Institutional Shareholder Services and Global Advisors, Inc., to help shareholder activists.

Voting Trusts   A **voting trust** is an agreement among shareholders to transfer their voting rights to a trustee. A **trustee** is a person who is entrusted with the management and control of another's property or the rights associated with that property. Sometimes, the trustee is one of the shareholders; at other times, the trustee is an outsider. The trustee votes those shares at the annual shareholders' meeting at the direction of the shareholders. Shareholders surrender only their voting rights. All other rights, including the right to receive profits, remain with them. Generally, once a voting trust has been created, it cannot be ended until the specified time period has run its course. However, state statutes usually place a maximum time limit on the duration of a voting trust. Most state time limits run from 10 to 21 years. Voting trusts must be in writing and must be filed with the corporation.

Pooling Agreements   Sometimes, shareholders join together in a temporary arrangement and agree to vote the same way on a particular issue. Such agreements are known as **pooling agreements**, shareholder agreements, or voting agreements. They differ from proxies and voting trusts because the shareholders retain control of their own votes. In this sense, pooling agreements are also the weakest voting arrangement because shareholders can change their votes at the last minute. If a member of a pooling agreement changes her or his vote, however, the other members may bring a lawsuit against the shareholder who broke the agreement. In general, pooling agreements are interpreted by the court under the principles of contract law.

Shareholder Nominations   Another way to increase the voting power of shareholders is to augment their ability to elect a director or directors who will represent their point of view in crucial issues facing the company. Several ways to do this include enacting state statutes, altering SEC rules, or changing stock exchange regulations so that certain events will trigger the ability of shareholders to elect board members. One such triggering event might be coupled with a shareholder proposal to permit shareholders to nominate their own directors. The rules might permit this nomination process to go forward as long as 50 percent of the votes cast (not 50 percent of the available votes, but 50 percent of those votes actually used in an election) support such a proposal. Another triggering event might be the ability of the minority shareholders to reach a 35–50 percent (depending on how the rule is worded) margin of voters who block the election of a management-nominated board candidate. Should either of these events occur, the minority shareholders would be permitted to place their own director on the next ballot at the expense of the corporation.

Talking Points

Corporate risk takers will be successful only if they can avoid the inclination to move from a simple, practical operation to one that is strangled by unnecessarily formal procedures. This is the issue that is placed before us by Robert Lekachman in his essay, "The Analysis of Capitalism." In this essay, Lekachman describes the economic philosophy of Joseph Alois Schumpeter in the following way:

> Schumpeter identified four major changes in capitalism, all of them by-products of success. Increasingly, corporate bureaucracy had substituted itself for the entrepreneur. This was the most important change. Invention had become a social process, the product of group research supported and controlled in great laboratories, administered by large corporations. . . . With the replacement of the entrepreneur by the salaried employee, the organization man, the dynamic of capitalism vanished. For the salaried administrator will work just as readily for the state after industry has been nationalized. He may scarcely know the difference.
>
> —Robert Lekachman, "The Analysis of Capitalism," pp. 398–399

Is Schumpeter correct that the ultimate future of corporate governance is corporate bureaucracy? If Schumpeter is correct, is this necessarily a bad thing? Can you think of situations in which corporate bureaucracy might be a good thing, that is, when it might actually fuel progress rather than hamper it? Or is bureaucracy always destructive? Explain your answers to each of these questions.

Unanimous Voting Restrictions An additional approach to strengthening the power of the shareholders involves a change in the corporate bylaws that makes it more difficult for the board to approve crucial issues that affect the fate of the corporation. The new voting bylaws would require unanimous agreement among all directors when the issue before the board involves a critical matter such as a merger, the sale of corporate assets, or a large increase in the salary of a top officer. Under current bylaws, one director with one vote on a board of twelve persons is of little consequence. However, under the revised regulations that require the unanimous approval of the board when

The Opening Case Revisited, Part II

American Federation of State, County, & Municipal Employees (AFSCME), Employees Pension Plan v. American International Group (AIG), Inc., Round 3

In The Opening Case at the beginning of this chapter, the American Federation of State, County, & Municipal Employees (AFSCME) developed a shareholder proposal in which it recommended that the rules of the AIG be changed so that shareholders like AFSCME could propose candidates for the board of directors. Understandably, AIG sought to exclude the proposal from the ballot. Ultimately, the appeals court disallowed the exclusion and permitted the proposal to go through. However, the new rules of AIG will permit shareholders to propose board candidates only if the proposal is approved by the shareholders.

major issues are decided, a single board member would have the power to block any material change contemplated by the rest of the board. The fact that a single director would have the power to stop major changes in corporate structure and policy might encourage minority shareholders to join forces in a campaign to elect their own director to the board.

Combinations   Although each of these voting techniques has been discussed separately, in practice, they can be combined to increase shareholder voting power. For example, a group of minority shareholders could enter a pooling agreement in which they all agree to cast their cumulative votes for a single board candidate. It is even possible for one of the voting techniques to be used to institute another of those techniques.

Shareholder Lawsuits

The battle between management and dissident shareholders may also be waged on a front other than the annual shareholders' meeting. That front is the courtroom. Shareholders can sue management to compel a change in direction or to force management to overturn a decision. The two types of suits available to shareholders are direct suits and derivative suits.

Direct Suits   A **direct suit** is brought by shareholders who have been deprived of a right that belongs to them as shareholders. These rights include the right to vote, the right to receive dividends, the right to transfer shares, the right to purchase newly issued stock, and the right to examine corporate books and records. If shareholders have been denied any of these rights, they can bring a direct suit to make up for any loss they have suffered.

Derivative Suits   A **derivative suit** allows shareholders to sue corporate management on behalf of the corporation. Unlike a direct suit, a derivative suit is not based on a direct injury to a shareholder. Instead, the injury is to the corporation. The shareholders' right to sue is derived from the corporate injury. Shareholders who bring a successful derivative suit are entitled to recover attorney fees. To bring a derivative suit, shareholders must meet certain prerequisites. One prerequisite is the exhaustion of internal remedies. Before bringing suit, the shareholder must attempt to solve the problem by communicating with the board of directors and with other shareholders. In their original complaint commencing the derivative action, the shareholders must state the steps that they took to exhaust all internal remedies. If the shareholders have not exhausted internal remedies and still insist on bringing the lawsuit, the court will dismiss the case and deny any request from the shareholders for the payment of attorney fees.

To bring a derivative suit, a shareholder must own stock at the time of the injury and at the time of the suit. This requirement is known as the **rule of contemporary ownership**. Frequently, state corporate laws also require derivative suit plaintiffs to pay a security deposit to cover the corporation's potential expenses in defending the derivative suits. All of these requirements make it difficult for a shareholder to bring a derivative lawsuit.

Quick Quiz 39-2 True or False?

1. Under the original concept of the corporation, the shareholders are the primary reason that a corporation exists.

2. Pooling agreements have been outlawed in all states.

3. A controlled company is one that has more than half its voting power concentrated in one person, or a small group of persons, who always vote together.

Table 39-4 Management Responsibilities		
Rule	**Situation**	**Explanation**
Business judgment rule	Manager does not profit from decision	The decision stands if it is made (1) in good faith, (2) with due care within the law, and (3) in the corporation's best interests.
Fairness rule	Manager profits from decision	The decision must be fair to the corporation because managers must remain loyal to the corporation.

39-3 Governance Responsibilities

When the court hears a case challenging a manager's decision, it will turn to one of two rules in judging that conduct: the business judgment rule or the fairness rule (see Table 39-4).

The Business Judgment Rule

Under the **business judgment rule**, the court will not interfere with most business decisions. The rule protects managers who act with due care and in good faith, as long as their decisions are lawful and in the best interests of the corporation. The rule results from the commonsense belief that, based on their education, experience, and knowledge, managers are in the best position to run the corporation. In contrast, shareholders and judges are far removed from the day-to-day operations of the business and should not be allowed to second-guess most management decisions. Protecting directors and officers in this way encourages people to become corporate managers and reassures them that they will be protected when they make difficult business decisions. The business judgment rule emerges from the duty of due diligence that a manager owes to the corporation. The **duty of due diligence** consists of three parts. It says that when acting on behalf of the corporation, a manager must act (1) in good faith, (2) using the same level of care that an ordinarily prudent individual would use in a comparable situation, and (3) in the reasonable belief that the best interests of the company are being met.

EXAMPLE 39-3:   The Business Judgment Rule in Action

Donald Young was chair of the board and chief executive officer of the Sterling Software Corporation. On September 9, a Connecticut software company went on the market for $590 million. The Connecticut company appeared to be a guaranteed money-maker. In considering the plant's purchase, Young had to act before September 12. After careful examination of the plant's financial records, consultation with the corporation's legal and financial experts, and a detailed study of the marketplace, Young decided to buy. According to the business judgment rule, if the Connecticut software company proves to be an unprofitable investment, Young will be protected because he acted (1) with due care, (2) in good faith, (3) within the law, and (4) in the best interests of the corporation.

The Fairness Rule

The business judgment rule assumes that managers do not personally profit from business decisions. If managers do profit, then the decision is suspect, because all managers owe a

duty of loyalty to the corporation. To fulfill this duty, managers must place the corporation's interests above their own. When managers enter contracts with the corporation or when they are on the boards of two corporations that do business with each other, a different standard is used to judge their conduct. This standard, known as the **fairness rule**, requires managers to be fair to the corporation when they personally benefit from their business decisions. Managers who benefit from their own decisions are said to be self-dealing. The fairness rule does not automatically declare managers disloyal if they profit from a corporate decision. Rather, it allows the court to examine the decision to determine its basic fairness to the corporation. How to measure fairness is, at best, problematic. At a minimum, it requires corporate managers to disclose all crucial information when they enter contracts with the corporation.

EXAMPLE 39-4:   Upholding Corporate Fairness

Amy Myers was the chair of the board of the Ural-Orenburg Shipping Corporation. The corporation leased a shipping depot from Denikin, Inc. Myers was also the majority shareholder and CEO of Denikin. Before finalizing the lease agreement, Myers revealed her relationship with Denikin to the other board members of Ural-Orenburg. The rental rate for the warehouse was in keeping with current market rates. Consequently, if the lease were challenged by shareholders of either corporation, a court, using the fairness rule, would uphold its validity.

Two rules that are offshoots of the fairness rule and the duty of loyalty are the insider trading rule and the corporate opportunity doctrine. Both rules give specific ways to measure a corporate manager's fairness in certain types of situations.

The Insider Trading Rule   Because of their role in corporate affairs, directors and officers often possess inside information. **Inside information** is material, nonpublic, factual data that can be used to buy or sell securities at a profit. Directors, officers, and other key individuals in a corporation, such as major shareholders, who are not directors or officers, qualify as insiders. In fact, under current SEC rules, any individual who holds such information, including corporate employees such as administrative assistants, researchers, public relations executives, human resource personnel, marketing directors, and so on, can be insiders. Even nonemployees such as financial planners, accountants, auditors, and attorneys who, by virtue of their contact with a company, have material nonpublic data about the company's stock can be insiders. Corporate "outsiders," such as spouses, family members, and friends, may be considered insiders if they receive corporate information about corporate stock without being involved in any actual business need to have the information. Such "outside" insiders are generally referred to as **tippees**. Nevertheless, the most common actual corporate insiders are directors and officers.

Inside information clearly gives directors and officers an advantage over corporate outsiders in the buying and selling of stock. This advantage must not be abused when dealing with the corporation or with individuals outside the corporation. Corporate managers act unfairly when they use their inside information to either cheat the corporation or take unfair advantage of corporate outsiders. Such transactions, which are referred to as **insider trading**, are forbidden by law. According to the **insider trading rule**, when managers possess important inside information, they are obligated to reveal that information before trading on it themselves. The rule also states that when inside information is revealed, the managers must use that information when trading with the corporation or with those outside the corporation.

The Corporate Opportunity Doctrine
As noted previously, along with the duty of due diligence and the duty of actual authority (see the next section), corporate managers also owe a duty of loyalty to the corporation. The duty of loyalty requires that corporate managers place the corporation's well-being ahead of their own interests. One offshoot of this duty is the idea of the corporate opportunity doctrine. The **corporate opportunity doctrine** states that corporate managers cannot take a corporate business opportunity for themselves if they know that the corporation would be interested in that opportunity as well. Before taking such an opportunity, a manager must first offer it to the corporation by informing other managers and shareholders. If the corporation rejects the opportunity, then the manager is free to take that opportunity.

The Actual Authority Rule
Corporate managers are also held to a third duty, that is, the duty to act within actual authority. The authority spoken of here includes those powers that have been granted to managers by virtue of their position within the corporation. The duties of the directors and officers of the corporation are outlined in the appropriate state statutes, in the articles of incorporation, in the regulations issued by government bodies such as the SEC, in relevant case law, and in the bylaws of the company. The **actual authority rule** states that a manager may be held liable if he or she exceeds his or her authority and the corporation is harmed as a result. Some states say that the managers will be liable for any violation of the limits of their authority on the basis of absolute or strict liability; some jurisdictions will consider the managers responsible only if the violation results in negligent or intentional conduct. This duty is also sometimes referred to as the **duty of obedience**. It is, of course, possible for a vote of the board or of the shareholders to approve a previously unauthorized act by a manager through the process of **ratification**.

Efforts to Limit Liability
Corporate managers have come under very close scrutiny by regulators and the courts in recent years. As a result, many otherwise well-qualified individuals have avoided serving as corporate managers in general but, in particular, as corporate directors. To counteract this trend, some states have enacted legislation that is designed to help protect the good faith and due diligent activities of such managers. These legislative enactments take three forms: (1) voluntary protective measures, (2) automatic protective measures, and (3) protective measures that limit the amount of damages that can be recovered against directors. A voluntary protective measure is one that permits corporate shareholders to fashion their bylaws so as to limit or eliminate the liability of directors for decisions made while carrying out their duties. Such measures would allow recovery of damages only if the director deliberately broke the law, deliberately violated the duty of loyalty, deliberately violated the duty of good faith, or improperly benefited from the transaction in question. Automatic protective measures grant the same type of immunity by state law, regardless of the action or inaction of corporate shareholders. The final measure would allow lawsuits against managers even in the cases noted above but would place a cap on the amount of money damages that can be recovered against directors.

Efforts to Increase Responsibility
At the same time that state governments are attempting to ease the liability of directors, the federal government has enacted efforts to increase director responsibilities for catching and stopping the wrongdoing of others within the corporation. One such measure is the **Sarbanes-Oxley Act**, which places an affirmative duty on the directors of publicly traded corporations to monitor whether their corporation is conforming to all legal requirements. A second measure involves the **United States Sentencing Commission**, which has issued a set of rules that control the discretion of the federal courts in issuing fines against corporations found guilty of criminal activi-

ties. Under the new rules, if the directors of a corporation did not do their best to discover and stop illegal activities, the court can place very severe penalties on the corporation, once it has been found guilty of those violations. The idea behind the new rules is to force directors to pay more attention to what is going on within their own companies, especially in relation to crime-stopping activities.

The new rules have led some legal commentators to suggest a series of steps that corporate directors should take when faced with suspected wrongdoing within their company. Seven steps are recommended: (1) Once a legal violation has been uncovered (or even suspected), the activity must cease instantly; (2) any and all consequences that have flowed from the violation should be uncovered and stopped immediately; (3) any attempt to engage in a cover-up, and in fact any actions that can be remotely perceived as a cover-up, must be avoided religiously; (4) notification of the violation must be made to the proper authorities; (5) investigations must be made to uncover any similar or related activities that may be illegal; (6) the cause or causes of the legal violations must be determined; and (7) an action plan must be created and executed to punish the violators and to prevent any future violations.

Quick Quiz 39-3 True or False?

1. The business judgment rule states that a manager's decision will stand as long as it was legal, was made with due care and in good faith, and was made in the best interests of the corporation.

2. The fairness rule states that a decision made by a manager will stand if it is fair to the corporation.

3. The business judgment rule is used by the courts when the manager is disinterested, that is, he or she does not personally gain from the decision.

39-4 Shareholder Rights

LO9

In addition to their voting rights and their right to sue, shareholders are entitled to examine certain corporate records, share in dividends, transfer shares of stock, and buy newly issued stock.

Right to Examine Corporate Records

A shareholder's right by statute to inspect the records of the corporation is usually limited to inspections for proper purposes at an appropriate time and place. Idle curiosity and an intent that unreasonably interferes with or embarrasses corporate management would prompt officers or directors to refuse shareholders' requests to examine corporate accounts, minutes, and records. When the purpose of inspection is proper, it may be enforced by a court order.

Right to Share in Dividends

Shareholders have the right to share in dividends after they have been declared by the board of directors. Once declared, a dividend becomes a debt of the corporation and enforceable by law, as is any other debt. However, shareholders cannot force the directors to declare a dividend unless the directors are not acting in good faith in refusing to do so. Courts are not inclined to order directors to meet and declare a dividend if the court must substitute its own business judgment for that of the directors.

Right to Transfer Shares of Stock

Shareholders have the right to sell or transfer their shares of stock. The person to whom stock shares are transferred has the right to have the stock transfer entered on the corporate books. The transferee becomes a **shareholder of record** and is entitled to vote, receive dividends, and enjoy all other shareholder privileges.

Preemptive Rights

Unless the right is denied or limited by the corporate charter or by state law, shareholders have the right to purchase a proportionate share of every new offering of stock by the corporation. This right is known as the shareholder's **preemptive right**. Preemptive rights are more prevalent in small, closely held corporations than in large, publicly owned corporations. This right prevents management from depriving shareholders of their proportionate control of a corporation simply by increasing the number of shares in the corporation.

Quick Quiz 39-4 True or False?

1. Assuming a request by a shareholder to inspect the corporate books is a proper one, the courts will enforce that request.

2. Today the courts will readily substitute their own judgment and declare a dividend on corporate stock, even when the directors of the corporation have voted against such a move.

3. Preemptive rights are more common in large, publicly held corporations than in small, closely held corporations.

39-5 Governance of a Limited Liability Company

LO10

The members of a limited liability company can choose to manage the business themselves, or they can hire outside management. An LLC that is run by the members themselves is called a member-managed LLC, whereas one operated by outside managers is referred to as a manager-managed LLC.

Member-Managed LLCs

If the managers choose to run the LLC on their own, management rights are apportioned among the members, according to the capital contributions made by each member to the LLC. Like the partners in a general partnership, the members of the LLC act as agents of the LLC. Accordingly, whenever a member performs a function within his or her apparent authority, the LLC will be bound by that action. However, as is true of a partnership, some actions fall outside the member's apparent authority. These include but are not limited to disposing of the firm's goodwill and submitting a claim of the LLC to arbitration. Naturally, the operating agreement can alter any of these statutory provisions.

Manager-Managed LLCs

If the members hire outside managers, then the LLC is run like a corporation. In the absence of an operating agreement, a single manager operates much like the CEO of a

Did You Know?

Limited liability companies became more popular in the United States in 1988 when a ruling by the Internal Revenue Service declared that they could be treated as partnerships for tax purposes.

corporation, while a group of managers acts as a board of directors. Nevertheless, regardless of the number of managers involved in an LLC, both the business judgment rule and the fairness rule apply to their decisions in the same way that those rules apply to the directors of a corporation.

Fiduciary Duties

Regardless of whether the members or the managers ultimately run the LLC, both groups have a fiduciary duty to the LLC and to its members. However, as noted in the previous chapter, it would be wise to outline the specific management duties in the written operating agreement.

Quick Quiz 39-5 True or False?

1. The members of an LLC have no choice in the matter of who will manage their firm.

2. An operating agreement established by the LLC is not permitted to alter statutory provisions regarding governance in any way.

3. Regardless of whether the members or the managers ultimately run the LLC, fiduciary duties have been suspended by provisions outlined in the latest version of the Uniform Limited Liability Company Act.

Summary

39.1 The business affairs of a corporation are managed by a board of directors elected by the shareholders. The directors have the authority to appoint officers and agents to run the day-to-day affairs of the corporation.

39.2 Five theories have been put forth by legal scholars and business experts concerning how corporations should be managed. These theories are special interest group control, governmental control, independent director control, managerial control, and shareholder democracy. Shareholders can increase their voting power by purchasing additional stock. If they cannot purchase additional stock, they may use another device to increase their voting power, such as cumulative voting, proxies, voting trusts, pooling agreements, shareholder proposals, shareholder nominations, and unanimous voting restrictions. Shareholders can also sue the corporation. Direct suits are brought by shareholders to protect their own rights. Derivative suits are brought by shareholders when they feel that the corporation has been damaged by a management decision.

39.3 Under the business judgment rule, the court will not interfere with most management decisions as long as those decisions are made with due care, in good faith, within the law, and in the best interests of the corporation. If the manager profits personally from a business decision, then the court will use the fairness rule to judge the manager's conduct.

39.4 Shareholder rights include the right to examine corporate records, the right to share dividends, the right to transfer shares of stock, and the right to buy newly issued stock.

39.5 The members of a limited liability company can choose to manage the business themselves or hire outside management. Regardless of whether the members or the managers ultimately run the LLC, both groups have a fiduciary duty to the LLC and to the members of the LLC. Nevertheless, it would be wise to outline specific management duties in the operating agreement.

Key Terms

actual authority rule, 824	independent director, 814	rule of contemporary ownership, 821
business judgment rule, 822	inside information, 823	Sarbanes-Oxley Act, 824
controlled company, 814	insider trading, 823	shareholder democracy, 814
corporate democracy, 814	insider trading rule, 823	shareholder of record, 826
corporate opportunity doctrine, 824	legal imperialism, 814	shareholder proposal, 817
cumulative voting, 816	managerial control, 814	shareholder resolutions, 817
derivative suit, 821	pooling agreement, 819	special interest group control, 812
direct suit, 821	preemptive rights, 826	tippee, 823
duty of due diligence, 822	proxy, 816	trustee, 819
duty of loyalty, 823	proxy contest, 816	United States Sentencing Commission, 824
duty of obedience, 824	proxy solicitation, 816	
fairness rule, 823	proxy statement, 816	voting trust, 819
governmental control, 812	ratification, 824	

Questions for Review and Discussion

1. What is the central dilemma of corporate governance?
2. What are the functions of directors, officers, and shareholders?
3. What are the five theories of corporate governance?
4. What is the difference between cumulative voting and proxy solicitation?
5. What is a shareholder proposal?
6. What is the difference between a voting trust and a pooling agreement?
7. What is the difference between a shareholder direct suit and a shareholder derivative suit?
8. What is the difference between the business judgment rule and the fairness rule?
9. What are the rights that belong to shareholders?
10. How does the management of a limited liability company operate?

Investigating the Internet

The National Conference of Commissioners on Uniform State Laws (NCCUSL) maintains a Web site on which it is possible to access a summary of every act worked on by the commissioners. Access the NCCUSL Web site, locate a summary of the Uniform Limited Liability Company Act, and, as a research project, answer the following questions: (1) What is the purpose of the Uniform Limited Liability Company Act (ULLCA)? (2) How does the ULLCA define a limited liability company? (3) What are the noteworthy features of the act, according the NCCUSL? (4) When did the UCCUSL complete work on the ULLCA? (5) What organization has endorsed the ULLCA?

Cases for Analysis

1. United Missionary Baptist Church, a not-for-profit corporation, held an election for the new church pastor. Several members of the church were dissatisfied with the results of the election and with the procedures that were followed during the election. They claimed that the inclusion of absentee balloting violated the church's constitution. Without making any parliamentary moves to correct the alleged misapplication of the constitution, and despite the fact that they had used their own absentee ballots during the election, these unhappy members brought a derivative lawsuit, asking the court to compel the church to follow its own constitution. The suit was dismissed. However, the members who brought the lawsuit claimed that because the lawsuit was a derivative action, they were entitled to attorney's fees, just as the shareholders of a profit corporation were entitled to attorney's fees. The court agreed that the same rules that apply to profit corporations in derivative actions apply to derivative suits brought for nonprofit corporations. However, the court still refused to grant the request for attorney's fees. Why? *Russell v. United Missionary Baptist Church,* 637 N.E.2d 82 (OH).

2. The bylaws of Jameson Enterprises, Inc., required a 70 percent supermajority to establish a quorum sufficient to hold a meeting to remove a director from the board. The bylaws also designated a meeting with such a purpose as a special meeting. The board consisted of ten directors. Six showed up at the meeting. Of the four who failed to attend, three were in Europe. The fourth, Weinberger, was not notified of the meeting because he was the one to be removed. The six directors attending the meeting first voted to change the bylaws to require only 60 percent of the directors to establish a quorum sufficient to hold a special meeting. The six directors then unanimously voted to remove Weinberger. When Weinberger found out about the meeting, he objected to the vote and claimed that the entire procedure was void. Was Weinberger correct? Explain.

3. Smith, a shareholder, filed suit against the board of directors of a corporation in which he had owned stock. Smith claimed that he and other shareholders had not received top dollar for their shares when their corporation had merged with another. Consequently, they sought either a reversal of the merger or payment from the directors to make up for their losses. The directors, Smith argued, had violated their duty of due care because they based their decision on a 20-minute speech by the CEO. Also, the directors had not even looked at the merger documents, let alone studied them. Furthermore, the directors had not sought any independent evaluation by outside experts. For their part, the directors argued that because their decision was made in good faith and was legal, they were protected by the business judgment rule. Were the directors correct? *Smith v. VanGorkon,* 488 A.2d 858 (DE).

4. Donald Lewis was a shareholder in S.L.&E., Inc., a corporation that owned land and a complex of buildings in Rochester, New York. The land and buildings were leased to LGT, a tire manufacturer. Donald's brothers were shareholders and directors of both S.L.&E. and LGT. Donald had no financial or managerial interest in LGT. S.L.&E. leased the land to LGT at a rate that Donald considered damaging to S.L.&E. He pointed out that S.L.&E. collected only $14,000 per year in rent from LGT while paying out $11,000 in taxes. This rate, he argued, meant that S.L.&E. could never be a profit-making corporation. Should the directors of LGT and S.L.&E. be judged by the business judgment rule or the fairness rule? Explain. *Lewis v. S.L.&E., Inc.,* 629 F.2d 764 (2nd Cir.).

5. Jackson set up a trust for his seven children. Most of the assets in the trust consisted of stock in the two newspapers owned and run by Jackson. Over the course of 18 years, Jackson transferred all but two shares of voting stock in the newspapers. The trustee was given full power to manage the assets in the fund and sell or otherwise dispose of the newspaper stock. State law places a strict 10-year limit on voting trusts. The plaintiffs claimed that the trust, which had lasted 18 years, was no longer valid, having passed the 10-year limit. The defendants claimed that the 10-year limit did not apply to this trust. Were the defendants correct? Explain. *Jackson v. Jackson,* 402 A.2d 893 (CT).

6. Klinicki and Lundgren incorporated to form an air taxi service known as Berlinair, Inc. Each of them owned one-third interest in the corporation. The final third was owned by Lelco, Inc., a company owned by Lundgren. In his capacity as president

of Berlinair, Lundgren learned that the Berlinair Flug Ring (BFR), a business association of Berlin's travel agents, was looking for an air charter service. Lundgren incorporated a new corporate entity called Air Berlin Charter (ABC). ABC then negotiated an air charter contract with BFR. Klinicki brought suit, demanding that Lundgren reimburse Berlinair for any profits made by ABC on the BFR contract. Was this a direct or derivative suit? Explain. Should the business judgment rule or the fairness rule be used by the court to measure Lundgren's performance? Explain. Who should have won the suit? Defend your choice. *Klinicki v. Lundgren,* 695 P.2d 906 (OR).

7. Naquin, Dubois, and Hoffpauir incorporated to form Air Engineered Systems and Services, Inc. Dubois became president and Hoffpauir became secretary-treasurer. Naquin was employed by the company. Conflicts among the three caused a breakdown in the working relationship. Dubois and Hoffpauir offered Naquin $2,000 a month for 10 years for his share of the business if he would sign a noncompetition agreement. Naquin refused to sell until he could examine the corporate records. Dubois and Hoffpauir refused to allow Naquin to see the books until he signed the noncompetition agreement. Could Dubois and Hoffpauir attach such a condition to Naquin's request? Explain. *Naquin v. Air Engineered Systems and Services, Inc.,* 463 So.2d 992 (LA).

8. Snodgrass, a minority shareholder in the 21st Century Broadcasting Network, Inc., was dissatisfied with management's decision to cancel several long-running news shows and replace them with several sitcoms and talk shows. She was also disturbed that management had decided to discharge several editorial writers and newscasters, including one who had recently won a major award for investigative journalism. Finally, she believed that a change in policy that would phase out foreign broadcast efforts would eventually cost the company an enormous amount of money. Assuming that Snodgrass does not want to sue the corporation, what options does she have if she wants to increase her influence over the board of directors of 21st Century Broadcasting Network, Inc.? Explain.

9. Keith Harris, a shareholder of Fastway Airlines, Inc., discovered that Donald Fleure, chief executive officer of Fastway, had sold some of his own land to the corporation at what Harris believed to be excessive prices. Can Harris bring a direct or a derivative suit in this situation? Explain. Would the fairness rule or the business judgment rule be used to evaluate the activities of Fleure? Explain.

Quick Quiz Answers

39-1		39-2		39-3		39-4		39-5	
1.	T	1.	T	1.	T	1.	T	1.	F
2.	F	2.	F	2.	T	2.	F	2.	F
3.	T	3.	T	3.	T	3.	F	3.	F

The Opening Case

The AT&T Buyout of Baby Bell South

Buyout fever among corporations returned with a vengeance in the twenty-first century, when scores of corporations and investors began to bid for, sell, buy, and renegotiate deals among corporate competitors, allies, and enemies. One such deal, which was foreseen by a few experts but scoffed at by most, was the buyout that AT&T aimed at Bell South. A buyout or merger like the one contemplated between AT&T and Bell South must be reviewed by several federal agencies. These agencies include the Securities and Exchange Commission, the Federal Trade Commission, the Antitrust Division of the Department of Justice, and, because both companies are key players in the communications industry, the Federal Communications Commission (FCC). In this case, the AT&T–Bell South merger easily passed muster under Justice Department rules, but it did not do as well when it ran into the FCC. Some experts saw the interference of the FCC as unnecessary meddling by an agency that was more concerned with social engineering than genuine antitrust issues. Others argued that the FCC played a vital role in the negotiation process because it secured certain compromises between AT&T and Bell South. Whatever the case, what is clear is that the FCC did not hesitate to flex its regulatory muscles as it pushed the two communications giants into actions that the regulators saw as socially beneficial. Thus, the FCC was instrumental, for example, in extracting an agreement from AT&T to provide a greater customer link to broadband, including a plan to give residential customers the use of independent broadband service at bargain-basement prices. Perhaps even more significant was the FCC's concern with the social ramifications of the merger. At one point, the FCC grabbed a chance to strengthen domestic employment rates by convincing AT&T to bring thousands of paying jobs back to the United States. What is truly significant about this deal is not that AT&T and Bell South agreed to the concessions stipulated by the FCC but that they did so without objecting to the fact that most of them fell outside the agency's legislative power. The question that remains is whether AT&T's and Bell South's willingness to submit to the influence of the FCC represents a one-time deal or a trend that will affect all such future buyouts. (See Emily Heller, "AT&T Buyout of Bell South: Top '06 Deal," *The National Law Journal*, February 5, 2007, pp. S-1 and S-6.)

Opening Case Questions

1. What is a corporate merger, and how does it differ from a consolidation?

2. Why is this merger subject to Federal Communications Commission (FCC) rules?

3. What tactics did the FCC employ in this merger?

4. What other agencies might be involved in the regulation of a merger?

5. What is significant about the fact that AT&T and Bell South agreed to the concessions engineered by the FCC?

 Learning Objectives

1. Explain the development of the federal government's power to regulate business.
2. Describe the source of state power to regulate business.
3. Explain how the Securities and Exchange Commission prevents unfair practices.
4. Contrast per se antitrust violations with rule-of-reason violations.
5. Define the various techniques of corporate expansion.
6. Contrast the interest of the Securities and Exchange Commission with that of the Federal Trade Commission in corporate expansion.
7. Contrast the role of the Environmental Protection Agency with that of the Federal Energy Regulatory Commission.
8. Identify the rights guaranteed to workers under the Employee Retirement Income Security Act and the Worker Adjustment and Retraining Notification Act.
9. Identify the two ways that a corporation may undergo dissolution.
10. Explain the circumstances under which a limited liability company may undergo dissolution.

40-1 Business and the Constitution

Despite the beliefs of many theorists, it is not possible to separate the world of the law from the world of economics. In the real world, the two systems interact with each other in such a way that they become, at times, one single system, the **judicial–economic system**.

The Commerce Clause of the Constitution

Sometimes the law must adapt to economic realities, as seen in the way the law has adjusted to economic realities to give the federal courts the power to regulate economic activity. The process worked something like this: The **Commerce Clause** is found in Article I, Section 8, Clause 3, of the Constitution. Clause 3 states that "Congress shall have the Power . . . To regulate Commerce with foreign nations, and among the several States." At first the courts interpreted this clause to mean that the federal courts could only regulate commercial activity if the activity passed between two or more states.

U.S. Const. Article I
(see page 945)

However, changing economic needs demanded a revision of this narrowly drawn interpretation. The federal government, which had entered the land-granting business, determined that it needed a way to enforce the distribution of this land. To meet this and other related economic needs, the Supreme Court in an 1824 case, *Gibbons v. Ogden,* held that any commercial activity that affected commerce among the states could be regulated by the federal government. This ruling included the activity that occurred within a single state, so long as that completely in-state activity affected interstate commerce. The extent of this interpretation was not felt until 1942, when in the case of *Wickard v. Filburn,* the Supreme Court upheld the doctrine so thoroughly that a farmer's production of wheat for use only on his own farm was held to affect interstate commerce. The Court reasoned that if the farmer used his own wheat, he would not buy wheat in interstate commerce, thus weakening the entire interstate market. The justices emphasized that it was the cumulative effect of many such farmers that concerned them rather than the effect of a single farmer.

The Judicial–Economic System

Several dynamic factors work together in the judicial–economic system to make this type of revolutionary adjustment to the realities of the marketplace palatable to the culture as a whole. These factors include (1) the need to reason by analogy in the common law system, (2) the desire to balance individual justice with regulatory justice, and (3) the inclination on the part of jurists to control legal change so that the revolutionary process is almost imperceptible from case to case.

Reasoning by Analogy Whenever a judge must decide a case, he or she is faced with a conflict that involves real people embroiled in a series of real events. In such cases, the judge must make a decision based on precedent. When a judge applies the law of an old case to the facts of the new case, the match between the two is rarely exact. Therefore, the judge must reason by analogy. Reasoning by analogy gives the judge a certain degree of flexibility. Generally, if there is a deviation from precedent, the judge will justify this slight change in the law by explaining how the present case can be distinguished from the past case.

Balancing Individual and Regulatory Justice The inclination to reason by analogy is driven by the perceived need to balance individual justice with regulatory justice. **Individual justice** is justice meted out to the people in the case before the judge. It is important that the parties in the case believe that the judge has entered a fair ruling that is tailor-made to their situation. However, the judge must also promote regulatory justice. **Regulatory justice** is a fair and balanced interpretation of the law that evolves from and is consistent with previous law. When a judge deviates too much from regulatory justice, he or she risks a political upheaval. As a result, in most cases, the judge balances the two goals and creates a new ruling that is in line with regulatory justice but that fine-tunes the rule enough to fit the particular case, thus introducing a small measure of change into the system.

Controlling Legal Change What results from the judge's need to reason from analogy and his or her desire to balance individual justice with regulatory justice is a system that promotes change at a slow and measured rate. For this reason, it is possible for the judicial–economic system to adjust legal rules to changing economic realities. The parties to the case welcome change because it reassures them that the law is flexible enough to deal with their individual problems. Other jurists welcome the new precedent as an added weapon in their arsenal of past cases. Legislators welcome the new case as long as it offers a change that is so small it manages to preserve the judicial–economic status quo.

EXAMPLE 40-1: The Interstate Effects of Intrastate Commerce

The Lafayette Nuclear Research and Development Corporation owned and operated DeBroglie Plutonium Processing Plant, Inc. Both corporations were based in Louisiana. DeBroglie supplied Lafayette with about 25 percent of its plutonium needs and did no other plutonium business with anyone. The other 75 percent of Lafayette's plutonium came from one in-state producer and two out-of-state suppliers. When the federal government imposed new safety regulations on all plutonium processing plants, DeBroglie argued that the regulations did not apply to it because its business was totally within the borders of Louisiana. The court disagreed. The court said that

A Question of Ethics

The Framers of the U.S. Constitution clearly wanted to limit the legislative power of the national government. They made this desire quite clear by enumerating the powers that Congress would possess and by specifically starting Article I of the Constitution with the following words, "All legislative Powers herein granted shall be vested in a Congress of the United States." Now reread Example 40-1. In that case, the court allowed Congress to regulate DeBroglie, a corporation that did business totally within a single state. Is it ethical for the courts, in their interpretation of the Commerce Clause, to ignore the deliberate attempt by the Framers to limit Congressional power to the regulation of commerce "among the several states" and to extend that power, allowing Congress to regulate a commercial activity that takes place completely within one state? Explain.

the fact that 25 percent of Lafayette's plutonium was purchased from DeBroglie meant that Lafayette did not buy that 25 percent from other corporations, including the two corporations from outside Louisiana. Because the two corporations outside Louisiana could have sold more plutonium to Lafayette had DeBroglie not sold its plutonium to Lafayette, DeBroglie's business was affecting interstate commerce, and could therefore be regulated by Congress.

State Regulatory Power

LO2

In contrast to the convoluted and indirect way that the judicial–economic system has developed federal commerce power, the system had no problem accommodating state economic power, because the states automatically have the power to regulate economic activities. This power comes from a state's police power. **Police power** is the state's authority to restrict private rights to promote and maintain public health, safety, welfare, and morals. A state has police power simply by virtue of its existence as a legitimate governmental authority. Today we take for granted that all business activity, even that of the sole proprietor, is subject to state regulation. The state government and the various subdivisions of the state government, from countries to cities to zoning districts, all play a role in this regulatory process.

Did You Know?

Since the Constitution was ratified, more than 10,000 amendments have been proposed by Congress. Despite all this activity, only 27 amendments have been ratified.

Quick Quiz 40-1 True or False?

1. The world of the law and the world of economics often interact in such a way that the two become, at times, one single system, the judicial–economic system.

2. Police power is the state's authority to restrict private rights to promote and maintain public health, safety, welfare, and morals.

3. The Contracts Clause is found in Article I, Section 8, Clause 3, of the Constitution.

40-2 Securities Regulation

LO3

Two pieces of federal legislation that affect business are the Securities Act of 1933 and the Securities Exchange Act of 1934 (see Table 40-1). The primary purpose of these acts is to protect business investors by making certain that they are informed about the securities they purchase. The independent regulatory agency that carries out this function is the Securities and Exchange Commission (SEC). The SEC regulates the issuance of securities by corporations and partnerships. A **security** has been defined as a monetary investment that expects a return solely because of another person's efforts. As the following example demonstrates, a security is a security even if it is called something else.

EXAMPLE 40-2:   A Security by Any Other Name

Osgood Minerals, Inc., had to raise an enormous amount of capital quickly. One of the directors devised a scheme whereby Osgood would sell to investors parcels of land owned by the corporation and used for mining purposes. In return, the investors would be entitled to a return on their investment. The return would be calculated in relation to the amount of land owned by each investor. To avoid having to comply with SEC regulations, Osgood labeled each sale a land contract rather than a security. Because the sales were land contracts, Osgood argued, it did not have to follow SEC regulations. The SEC disagreed and brought suit to stop the sale of unregulated securities. The court held that because each investor's profits would be derived solely from the efforts of others, the investments were securities and therefore subject to SEC regulations.

Securities Act of 1933

The Securities Act of 1933 regulates the issuance of new securities by corporations and partnerships. Offers of securities by mail or through interstate or foreign commerce must be registered with the SEC. A registration statement and a prospectus must be filed with the SEC. A **registration statement** contains detailed information about the corporation, including data about its management, capitalization, and financial condition. A **prospectus** contains much of the same information but in a condensed and simplified form. The registration statement is designed for the experts at the SEC, whereas the prospectus is designed for potential investors.

Securities Exchange Act of 1934

The Securities Exchange Act of 1934, which actually established the SEC, deals with the subsequent trading in securities. It requires periodic reports of financial information concerning registered securities, and it prohibits manipulative and deceptive actions in the sale and purchase of securities. The act prohibits insiders, including officers and directors, from realizing profit from any purchase and sale of securities within any period of less than six months. The courts have held that insiders are not permitted to trade on information until that information has been made available to the public.

According to Section 14 (a) of the 1934 act, shareholders, including majority shareholders, who solicit proxies (see Chapter 39) must also follow strict reporting requirements. The SEC requires a written proxy solicitation to include the identity of the individual or individuals seeking the proxy, any potential conflicts of interest, and specific information about any corporate changes to be voted

The Securities and Exchange Commission (SEC) regulates the issuance of securities by corporations and partnerships and assures that the public is protected by enforcing mandatory reporting requirements and other 1933 and 1934 Act mandates.

on. When management solicits proxies, the solicitation must also include information about management salaries. The SEC regulations also state quite specifically that all material information must be stated in readable language and be displayed prominently, rather than buried in small type somewhere in the back of the document. The regulations also explicitly forbid false or misleading information.

Quick Quiz 40-2 True or False?

1. The Securities and Exchange Commission regulates the issuance of securities by corporations and partnerships.

2. The Securities Exchange Act of 1934 actually established the Securities and Exchange Commission.

3. Under the Securities Exchange Act of 1934, majority shareholders are exempt from proxy solicitation reporting requirements.

40-3 Antitrust Regulation

Both the federal government and the states have antitrust laws to preserve the values of competition and to discourage monopolies. A **monopoly** is the exclusive control of a market by a business enterprise. At the federal level, the four principal antitrust statutes are the Sherman Antitrust Act, the Clayton Act, the Robinson-Patman Act, and the Federal Trade Commission Act.

Sherman Antitrust Act

LO4

The Sherman Antitrust Act (1890) prohibits contracts, combinations, and conspiracies in restraint of trade. It also prohibits monopolization, attempts to monopolize, and combinations or conspiracies to monopolize any part of interstate or foreign commerce. Violations of the Sherman Antitrust Act must involve at least two people acting together. The courts use two tests to judge antitrust offenses: per se violations and the rule-of-reason standard. The two tests, however, sometimes represent moving targets that are easy to articulate but difficult to implement in a consistent and fair fashion. In fact, the line of distinction between the two standards is sometimes so small that the two tests can, at times, seem as indistinguishable from each other as a set of identical twins.

Per Se Violations Some restraint-of-trade practices are so serious that they are prohibited, whether or not they harm anyone. These practices are labeled **per se violations**, which means that the practice is so contrary to antitrust policy that harm is presumed, and the practice is prohibited. For example, price fixing is inherently unreasonable and therefore considered a per se violation. An agreement between competitors to divide territories among themselves to minimize competition would also be unlawful, even if the agreement helps the parties compete against other parties outside the agreement. Similar unlawful activities include agreements among competitors to stop competing with one another in prices, customers, or products.

Rule-of-Reason Standard If an alleged antitrust practice is not considered a per se violation, then the courts will judge the legality of that practice with the rule-of-reason approach. The **rule-of-reason standard** will stop certain practices only if they are an

Table 40-1   Securities and Antitrust Regulations

Regulation	Explanation
Securities regulation:	
Securities Act of 1933	Regulates the issuance of new securities
Securities Exchange Act of 1934	Established the Securities and Exchange Commission; act deals with subsequent trading in securities
Antitrust regulations:	
Sherman Antitrust Act	Prohibits contracts, combinations in restraint of trade; also prohibits monopolies, attempts to monopolize, and conspires to monopolize
Clayton Act	Prohibits specific practices such as tying agreements and interlocking directorates
Robinson-Patman Act	Deals with product pricing, advertising, and promotional allowances
Federal Trade Commission Act	Established the Federal Trade Commission

unreasonable restriction of competition. As a result, some practices that in fact limit competition may be legal. To determine if an anticompetitive practice is legal, the court considers such facts as the history of the restraint, the harm that results, the reason for the practice, and the purpose to be attained.

The Evolving Nature of the Twin Standards   The per se and rule-of-reason standards have been part of antitrust law for decades, so the line of distinction between the two is usually very clear. However sometimes, as the law evolves, that line of distinction becomes less and less distinct. A case in point involves the court's distinction between resale price maintenance (RPM) agreements and quasi-RPM arrangements. An **RPM agreement** occurs when a retailer and a manufacturer decide that the retailer will sell certain products at a price set by the manufacturer. These RPMs have been outlawed by the court as a per se violation of antitrust law. In contrast, a **quasi-RPM arrangement** occurs when a manufacturer lets retailers know the price that it expects to see on an item and then declines to sell that item to any retailer that does not list the item at that price. Such arrangements are legally permissible under antitrust law because the law cannot take away the rights of manufacturers to pick those sellers they want to deal with. The distinction between the two seems, at best, artificial and, at worst, nonexistent.

Post-Sherman Antitrust Legislation

Three principal antitrust statues made the Sherman Act more specific and, as a result, more effective. The Clayton Act of 1914, the Robinson-Patman Act of 1936, the Foreign Trade Antitrust Improvements Act, and the Federal Trade Commission Act of 1914 sought to prevent practices that reduced competition or favored the creation of monopolies.

Clayton Act   Congress passed the Clayton Act to police specific business practices that could be used to create a monopoly. One practice outlawed by the act is tying agreements. A **tying agreement** occurs when one party refuses to sell a product unless the buyer also purchases another product tied to the first product. The issue is the effect of the tie-in on the seller's competitors.

Interlocking directorates are also outlawed by the Clayton Act. **Interlocking directorates** occur when individuals serve as directors of two corporations that are competitors. This provision is not entirely foolproof, however, because banks and common carriers are exempt. To fall under this part of the Clayton Act, at least one of the corporations must have an aggregate worth (capital, surplus, and individual profits) of more than $1 million.

Robinson-Patman Act   The Robinson-Patman Act deals with product pricing, advertising, and promotional allowances. It specifically prohibits a seller from charging different prices to different customers for the same product when such differences might injure competition. However, nothing in the law is intended to prevent price differences due to cost of manufacture, sale, delivery, or bulk purchases.

Federal Trade Commission Act   In addition to establishing the Federal Trade Commission (FTC), the Federal Trade Commission Act, as amended, declares that "unfair methods of competition, and unfair or deceptive practices in or affecting commerce are hereby declared unlawful." The act did not name specific unfair methods of competition. Instead, it has allowed the courts and the FTC to determine those unfair practices. The Federal Trade Commission Act was amended by the Wheeler-Lea Act and amendments in 1938 and 1975. This legislation authorized the FTC to act against unfair or deceptive acts without first proving the existence of anticompetitive behavior. The FTC was also granted the power to challenge false advertising of food, drugs, and cosmetics, regardless of the advertiser's knowledge of the advertisement's truth or falsity.

The Foreign Trade Antitrust Improvements Act (FTAIA)   Another antitrust measure passed by Congress is the Foreign Trade Antitrust Improvements Act (FTAIA). Unlike the other antitrust provisions supported by Congress, the FTAIA is designed to circumvent some of the restrictions placed on American companies by the Sherman Antitrust Act. The objective of the FTAIA is to permit American companies operating in foreign markets to have a fighting chance against foreign competitors that are not subject to the strict antimonopoly provisions of the act. Under terms of the bill, if an American company is operating totally in a foreign market, that company is not subject to American antitrust law.

Antitrust Revisionism

In recent years, Congress has paid close attention to developments in antitrust law and, as a result, has inaugurated a congressional think tank known as the **United States Antitrust Modernization Committee**. Four members of this twelve-member bipartisan group are appointed by the president, while the remaining eight are appointed by Congress. The stated objective of the group is to examine antitrust law and report recommendations on how to modernize the law. The group must hold public hearings, attended by those constituents who are affected by the law. Those parties affected include large corporations, consumer advocate groups, and government regulators. Many large corporations favor several proposed reforms, including the elimination, or at least the streamlining, of the list of per se violations now outlawed by the act. Another reform promoted by the companies is the elimination of triple damage awards that are now permitted under law.

Talking Points

In his treatise, *Overcoming Law*, the legal scholar Richard Posner spends a great deal of time exploring the relationship between economics and the law. In doing so, he focuses on the ideas of two economists, Ronald Coase, who won the Nobel Memorial Prize for Economic Sciences in 1991, and George Stigler, the author of *The Citizen and the State: Essays on Regulation*. Posner explains their points of view in the following way:

> The Swedish Academy had also emphasized Stigler's theory of regulation . . . as "treating *political behavior as utility-maximizing* [and] *political parties as firms supplying regulation,* with *what is supplied being what is wanted* by those groups (or coalitions) which are able to outbid others in the political market.
> —Posner, *Overcoming Law,* pp. 411–412 (italics added)

> These terms, and the vast bodies of formal theory that have grown up around them, assume the *fragility of markets* and the *robustness of government,* whereas Coase believes that careful observation of markets and government discloses the *robustness of markets* and the *fragility of government.*
> —Posner, *Overcoming Law,* p. 413 (italics added)

Of the two economists, which one would appear to support government regulation? Summarize the theory of that economist. What is the major objection that the other economist has for opposing government intervention? Which view supports the idea that the judicial–economic system is a flexible and responsive system? Explain your answers to each of these questions.

In contrast, consumer advocates want to make it easier for plaintiffs to bring antitrust lawsuits against certain types of defendants, but especially against manufacturers. Plaintiffs frequently complain that retailers rarely bring antitrust claims against manufacturers, because retailers can avoid the effects of any antitrust scheme, such as a price-fixing conspiracy, by passing the increased cost of doing business on to the consumers. The consumers, who under current rules are frequently barred from bringing lawsuits against manufacturers, have no recourse other than to pay the higher prices. For this reason, consumer advocacy groups favor making it easier for plaintiffs to file class-action lawsuits against all manufacturing firms that violate antitrust law but especially against those large cartels that are the worst offenders. Finally, state and local regulators would also like to see changes in the law. These regulators favor changes that would transfer more antitrust enforcement authority from the federal government to the states.

Quick Quiz 40-3 True or False?

1. Price fixing is an example of a rule-of-reason practice under the Sherman Antitrust Act.

2. Per se violations must involve actual harm to be actionable under the Sherman Antitrust Act.

3. The Robinson-Patman Act has been repealed by the United States Antitrust Modernization Committee.

40-4 Tactics of Corporate Expansion

No other area of corporate activity has been scrutinized by the government more closely in recent years than the area of corporate expansion (see Table 40-2). As noted previously, several governmental agencies may be involved in any given corporate expansion venture, including the Department of Justice and the Federal Communications Commission. However, the two agencies that have the primary responsibility for regulating this activity are the SEC and the FTC. The two commissions have different interests in the expansion process. The SEC is concerned with regulating the expansion tactics themselves, whereas the FTC is more concerned with the competitive effects of those expansion tactics.

Expansion Tactics and Securities Law

All corporations change in size. Some grow and expand, while others shrink until they dissolve completely or are absorbed by a larger, more successful enterprise. Like all other corporate activities, corporate expansions are looked at very closely by government. The primary expansion techniques include mergers and acquisitions (M&A).

Merger and Consolidation   Traditionally, a **merger** involves two corporations, one which is absorbed by the other. One of the two corporations continues to carry on business under its original name, and the other simply disappears into the first. In contrast, in a **consolidation**, both companies disappear, and a new company carries on the business under a new name. Today, most legal scholars do not make any distinction between merger and consolidation. In fact, many state incorporation statutes make no reference to consolidation, preferring the term *merger* instead. A merger requires advance approval from the boards and shareholders of both corporations. In general, a two-thirds majority vote of the shareholders will be required before a merger can be approved, though some states require a supermajority of four-fifths. Shareholders who dissent are entitled to be paid for their stock if they do not wish to be a part of the merger. Written notice of a dissent is required so that the cost of purchasing the dissenter's stock can be figured as a part of the expense involved in the merger.

Table 40-2   Securities Law and Corporate Expansion

Technique	Explanation	Regulation
Merger and consolidation	In a merger, one company is absorbed by another; in a consolidation, two companies join and a new company results.	Most antifraud provisions of the SEC apply here.
Asset acquisition	One corporation buys all the property of another.	Antifraud provisions of the SEC apply here if a proxy solicitation is involved or if insider information is used to profit from the sale.
Stock acquisition (takeover)	One corporation (suitor) makes a tender offer to the shareholders of another corporation (target).	Whenever a suitor makes an offer to acquire more than 5 percent of the target, the suitor must file with the SEC.

Most antifraud provisions of the SEC apply to the merger process. Often the merger vote will be preceded by a proxy solicitation battle. All material facts about the merger must be included in the proxy solicitation. In addition, the solicitation must not contain any false or misleading information. Similarly, the SEC prohibits insiders who know of merger plans from taking advantage of that knowledge to profit personally before the knowledge is revealed to the public.

Some state statutes apply different rules to mergers that involve a limited liability company (LLC). Under some state statutes, a merger involving an LLC requires the unanimous approval of the members rather than the two-thirds majority required of corporations. However, as is true in other circumstances, the operating agreement of an LLC could cancel this unanimous vote requirement. If the operating agreement specifies that a merger vote may be approved by less than a unanimous vote, many states give those members who are opposed to the merger the right to withdraw from the LLC and receive the cash value of their investment. However, once again, the operating agreement can alter this statutory right.

Asset Acquisition In an **asset acquisition**, one corporation purchases all the property of a second corporation. However, as in the case of mergers, SEC antifraud regulations can be applied to asset acquisitions if a proxy solicitation process is involved or if insider information is used to profit from the sale. Asset acquisition is easy and efficient, because the only formality required is approval by the directors and shareholders of the corporation that is selling its assets. A second advantage is that the buyer need not purchase all of the assets of the seller. The buyer may choose to purchase some assets while rejecting others.

Another advantage of asset acquisition is that, in general, no debts or other liabilities are transferred from seller to buyer. There are exceptions to this rule however. In certain situations, the debts of the selling corporation will transfer to the buying corporation. For instance, if the buyer is simply a continuation of the selling corporation, the buyer will not escape the liabilities of the seller. Similarly, if the sale is structured fraudulently to escape the liabilities of the selling corporation, the debts will transfer to the buyer. It is also possible for the buyer to either expressly or implicitly assume the debts and liabilities of the seller. Finally, if, despite its label as an asset acquisition, the sale is actually a merger, the liabilities will transfer to the buyer.

Stock Acquisition In a **stock acquisition**, the buyer purchases enough stock in a corporation to gain voting control of that corporation. Stock acquisitions come in many shapes and sizes (see Table 40-3). One type of stock acquisition is the leveraged buyout (LBO). In a **leveraged buyout**, a controlling portion of the stock in a corporation is purchased by a group of shareholders, often several outsiders but sometimes a team of officers and directors of the company. The potential buyers can then collect the money needed to purchase the outstanding

Table 40-3   Stock Acquisition Techniques

Technique	Explanation
Leveraged buyout	A controlling portion of stock purchased by shareholders; leveraged by loans and junk bonds.
Tender offer	Suitor makes a public offer to buy voting stock in a target corporation.
Takeover bid	Tender offer opposed by the management of the target corporation.
Corporate raid	Takeover bid opposed by management of target because corporate raider intends to dismantle target.

shares by enlisting the support of a bank. The bank will lend a good portion of the money to the buyers, taking an enormous payment to support that loan. If the amount produced by the bank proves inadequate, the buyers will seek the assistance of an investment firm. The investment firm produces the remainder of the needed money by issuing **junk bonds**, or bonds that are unstable but offer an elevated level of return to large, powerful investors. Because the stock purchase is made possible by these high-stakes loans, the buyout is referred to as "leveraged." The shareholders are motivated to sell because the buyout team offers them an inflated price for their shares. Sometimes after the buyers have purchased control of the corporation, they ensure their continued control by transforming the company into a private corporation. This action is referred to as "taking the company private."

A second form of stock acquisition is the tender offer. In a **tender offer**, the buyer or suitor, whether it is an individual, a consortium of like-minded individuals, or another corporation, makes a public offer to buy voting stock in a **target corporation**. A successful tender offer occurs once the buyer or buyers have purchased enough of the voting stock to satisfy the original goal, whatever that might have been. One advantage of the stock acquisition process is that it sidesteps the board of directors. The buyer deals directly with the shareholders. Usually, the shareholders are motivated to sell because the buyer has made an offer that is above the current market price of the stock.

Sometimes a tender offer is welcomed by the directors and the officers of the target because they see it as a way to strengthen the corporation and enhance their own positions within the company. At other times, however, the tender offer is seen as a corporate **take-over bid** by an **unfriendly buyer**. In a takeover bid, the unfriendly buyer, also known as an **unfriendly suitor** or a **hostile bidder**, intends to purchase enough stock to control the corporation. Often the goal of the hostile bidder is to change management and shake up the corporation after the takeover. If the suitor intends to dismantle the corporation totally or somehow integrate the target into an existing corporation to such an extent that the target ceases to exist, the suitor is referred to as a **corporate raider** and the tender offer a **corporate raid**. In both cases, hostile bidder and corporate raider, the target's management is expected to fight the takeover with every tactic available.

To avoid being taken over by a hostile bidder, the management of a corporation can institute both post-offer and pre-offer tactics. Post-offer tactics include, but are not limited to, public relations initiatives, greenmail, the white knight gambit, lockup agreements, and targeted shareholder agreements (see Table 40-4). In contrast, pre-offer tactics could involve supermajority voting and accelerated loans, among others (see Table 40-5).

Post-Offer Techniques

Post-Offer Techniques Probably the least problematic post-offer technique is the public relations initiative. Such an initiative is aimed at convincing shareholders that it is in their best interests not to sell their shares to the hostile bidder. News releases, advertisements, press conferences, and even personal letters would attempt to convince shareholders that present management should be retained. The difficulty with this approach is that many arguments pale to insignificance when placed alongside a bid that is above the current market price of the stock.

Sometimes the most effective way for a target to shake off a bidder's hostile suit is to offer the bidder **greenmail**. A corporation that activates the greenmail defense has offered to buy the portion of the target's stock that the bidder already owns. Naturally, such an approach will work only if the target's offer is significantly higher than the amount that the bidder paid for the stock in the first place. Such an approach is disfavored because it robs the shareholders of the opportunity to make a profit by selling their shares and may seriously devalue the target's remaining stock, thereby victimizing the shareholders a second time.

Another post-offer technique that can be used by the target company is the white knight gambit. To implement this tactic, the target invites another suitor to outbid the hostile bidder. The second suitor is known as a **friendly suitor** or a **white knight**, because the invited suitor agrees that it will retain existing management. The white knight also frequently agrees not to disrupt the smooth running of the target by selling off key assets, closing down plants,

BusinessWeek **Business Law in the News**

Topps Accepts $385.4M Takeover Bid

The Topps Co., maker of baseball cards and Bazooka bubble gum, said Tuesday it accepted a $385.4 million takeover offer from a buyout group that includes former Disney CEO Michael Eisner, but the deal drew immediate opposition from one of its own board members.

Topps director Arnaud Ajdler, along with the investment firm Crescendo Partners II, launched a campaign to kill the deal. Crescendo owns about 6.6 percent of the company's shares, according to filings with the Securities and Exchange Commission. Ajdler is also a managing partner of Crescendo.

Ajdler said Tuesday he had not yet been in touch with other major shareholders but he thought the deal should be abandoned because negotiations did not go through a proper process and that the Eisner-led offer undervalues the company.

"I believe that the process that led to the signing of the merger agreement was flawed in that the board of directors did not shop the company and thus failed to maximize the competitive dynamics of a sale transaction that would have garnered the highest price available," Ajdler wrote in a letter sent to the board members on Tuesday.

The deal was approved in a 7-3 vote by the board with Ajdler and two others voting against the deal. Ajdler was joined by Timothy Brog, president of Pembridge Capital Management LLP, and another board member, John Jones. Pembridge had earlier pressed the company to solicit acquisition proposals.

The buyout group, which includes the Tornante Co. LLC, founded by Eisner, and the Chicago-based private equity firm Madison Dearborn Partners LLC, has agreed to pay $9.75 for each Topps share, which represents a premium of 9.4 percent over the stock's Monday closing pricing of $8.91 on the Nasdaq Stock Exchange.

In a sign that some investors think the bidding could go higher, Topps shares rose 90 cents, or 10 percent, to close at $9.81 on the Nasdaq Stock Market. Its shares have traded between $7.50 and $10 over the past 52 weeks.

The company said in its announcement that it will solicit better offers over the next 40 days.

The deal requires regulatory approval and a vote by Topps shareholders, but the company said it could close by the third quarter.

As part of the merger agreement, Chief Executive Arthur T. Shorin agreed to retire within 60 days of the close of the deal. He would remain as a consultant, according to an SEC filing. Shorin, 70, has been CEO of Topps and its predecessor since 1980, according to the company Web site.

Eisner was CEO of The Walt Disney Co. for two decades until he stepped down in 2005. Disney owns theme parks, movie studios, and the ABC, ESPN and Disney TV networks.

Topps, founded in 1938, makes trading cards featuring athletes of Major League Baseball, the NFL and NBA. In addition to Bazooka bubble gum, it owns the Ring Pop and Push Pop brands.

Questions for Review

1. Is the buyout discussed in the story an asset acquisition or a stock acquisition?

2. Is the buyout discussed in the story a leveraged buyout or a tender offer?

3. Is the buyout discussed in the story a hostile takeover?

4. What federal agency is involved in the oversight of this buyout?

5. Which corporation is the target in this story?

Source: Vinnee Tong, "Topps Accepts $385.4M Takeover Bid," *BusinessWeek.com,* March 6, 2007.

or laying off employees. A takeover battle usually follows. The winner is generally the suitor that can offer the highest price for the target's outstanding stock.

A fourth post-offer technique is the **lockup agreement**. A lockup agreement might be used by target management if the target owns an irreplaceable piece of property, the sale of which would seriously devalue the overall worth of the target. Such property might include rich timberland or an extremely productive coal mine. Provided that the sale of that property

Table 40-4 Post Offer Antitakeover Tactics

Post-Offer Tactics	Explanations
Public relations campaign	Target corporation uses news releases, advertisements, and press conferences to convince shareholders to retain present management.
Greenmail	Target corporation offers to buy target's stock already owned by suitor.
White knight	Target corporation invites friendly suitor to outbid a hostile bidder.
Lockup agreement	Target corporation tags irreplaceable property for sale when hostile bidder succeeds in takeover.
Targeted shareholder agreement	Target corporation makes deal with suitor to protect management of target.

does not deplete virtually all the assets of the target, management could enter a contract with a white knight, giving the knight an option to buy that valuable piece of property should the hostile bidder gain control of the target corporation. The idea is to discourage the hostile bidder from buying the now-devalued target.

A fifth post-offer technique is the **targeted shareholder agreement**. Strictly speaking, a targeted shareholder agreement is not an anti-acquisition tactic as much as it is an executive protection strategy. Under the provisions of a targeted shareholder agreement, the suitor negotiates a deal with certain targeted shareholders, generally the CEO, the CFO, the CTO, and other high-ranking officers. These agreements will provide the officers/shareholders with handsome employment-related deals that supplement the price that they will receive for the sale of their stock. Such deals might include a salary increase, a severance package, a non-compete agreement, and so on. The strategy behind negotiating a targeted shareholder agreement is not to stop the acquisition but to protect key employees who might be financially damaged or even discharged in the post-acquisition culture.

Targeted shareholder agreements were hampered in the late 1990s and early in the twenty-first century by two rules instituted by the SEC. These rules, known collectively as the **best-price rule**, prohibited suitors from offering different prices to different shareholders during a tender offer process. Unfortunately, the best-price rule was interpreted differently by different federal courts. Some courts, using what was called the **integral-part test**, decided that any type of price enhancement, including employment-related packages, would violate the best-price rule—period. The other rule, known as the **bright-line test**, was used by those courts that saw a violation of the best-price rule only during the actual tender offer. Thus, if an employment agreement was negotiated with a targeted shareholder before or after the actual tender offer, and the actual price that the suitor paid for the stock remained unaffected, then there was no violation of the best-price rule. The SEC eventually amended the rule to make it clear that targeted shareholder agreements that involved *only* employment-related agreements would not be subject to the best-price rule. This decision is likely to pave the way for the increased use of the targeted shareholder agreement in the future.

Pre-Offer Techniques Sometimes post-offer techniques are instituted too late to prevent takeover. For this reason, many corporations plan ahead by instituting certain pre-offer measures even before any unfriendly suitors have appeared on the horizon (see Table 40-5). For example, a corporation could institute a supermajority provision into its bylaws that would require a 90 percent affirmative vote by all shareholders for the approval of any merger. Such a move would mean that any suitor would have to acquire 90 percent of the stock of the target to assure a takeover. A back-up provision requiring a supermajority to change the supermajority

Table 40-5 Pre-Offer Antitakeover Tactics

Pre-Offer Tactic	Explanation
Supermajority provision—for takeover bids	Target corporation rewrites bylaws to require 90 percent vote to approve any takeover.
Supermajority provision—for amendments	Target corporation rewrites bylaws to require 90 percent vote to amend the bylaws.
Accelerated loans	Target corporation enters loan agreements which are due in full when the target is subject to a successfull takeover.

bylaws would also be necessary to ensure that the suitor does not simply take 51 percent of the target and then use that majority control to eliminate the supermajority merger vote provision.

An additional pre-offer technique involves the corporation in a series of accelerated loans. Under the provisions of an accelerated loan program, all major loans taken out by the corporation are due in full immediately upon the takeover of the target by an unfriendly suitor. The plan is to place the suitor in a precarious financial position because, once the target has been acquired, the suitor would be forced to pay off a series of expensive loans, thus straining the treasury of the target. The accelerated loan gambit is often unsuccessful because the financial institutions that made the loans are often willing to renegotiate the terms of the accelerated loans with the target's new owner to avoid getting a poor return on their investments.

Takeover Bids and the SEC   Takeover bids are closely scrutinized by the SEC. Under recent amendments to federal securities law, whenever a suitor makes an offer to acquire more than 5 percent of a target, that suitor must file a statement with the SEC. The statement must indicate (1) where the money for the takeover originates, (2) why the suitor is buying the stock, and (3) how much of the target the suitor already owns. These procedures are designed to let shareholders know the identity and intention of a takeover bidder. Bidders who falsify any information on their statement may find their takeover bid stopped by a court order.

Expansion Tactics and Antitrust Law

As noted previously, antitrust law is designed to preserve competition and discourage monopolies. One way that companies can create monopolies is through a corporate expansion effort. Antitrust law does not focus on corporate expansion techniques. Instead, it looks at how an expansion attempt will affect competition in the marketplace (see Table 40-6). Section 7 of the Clayton Act forbids any corporate expansion if that expansion sets up a monopoly or otherwise hurts competition. The Clayton Act applies to horizontal, vertical, or conglomerate expansion attempts.

Expansion Attempts   Because horizontal expansion occurs between companies that are involved in the same business, such attempts often result in monopolies. Consequently, horizontal expansion schemes are closely scrutinized by the FTC and are more likely to be labeled illegal. A vertical expansion occurs between companies that were in a customer–supplier relationship. If a manufacturer of designer jeans were to buy a chain of department stores that carried its jeans, a vertical expansion would result. A conglomerate expansion joins two companies that were not in competition with each other, either because they dealt in different products or services or because they operated in different geographical areas.

Hart-Scott-Rodino Antitrust Act   Like the SEC, the FTC has a chance to step into expansion situations even before they become an established fact. This opportunity is provided by the Hart-Scott-Rodino Antitrust Act. Hart-Scott-Rodino is designed to police

Table 40-6 Antitrust Law and Corporate Expansion

Technique	Explanation	Regulation
Horizontal expansion	Occurs between companies that are involved in the same business	Closely scrutinized by the FTC because of the likelihood of a monopoly
Vertical expansion	Occurs between companies that are in a customer–supplier relationship	Less likelihood of monopoly, therefore less FTC scrutiny
Conglomerate expansion	Occurs between two companies that are not in competition with each other	Least likelihood of monopoly, therefore least FTC scrutiny

any expansion attempts that might harm competition in the marketplace. The act requires corporations that are setting up an expansion attempt to notify the FTC before the deal is completed. This advance notice allows the FTC to investigate the anticompetitive effects of the planned expansion. Should the FTC decide that the expansion will hurt competition, it can go to court and ask for an injunction to prevent the expansion.

The Tunney Antitrust Act   The federal government also regulates corporate expansion through the activities of the Antitrust Division of the Department of Justice (DOJ) and through the activities of specialized agencies, such as the Federal Communications Commission (FCC). The DOJ's Antitrust Division is charged with policing mergers that affect antitrust law to ensure that in carrying out a corporate combination, the participants have not violated those laws. The primary goal of the DOJ, however, is not to stop such mergers outright but instead to help the parties negotiate a merger that can be completed without violating the law. Such agreements are referred to as **consent decrees**. The Justice Department's antitrust consent decrees are, in turn, regulated by a federal statute known as the **Antitrust Procedures and Penalties Act** or simply as the **Tunney Act**.

The Tunney Act requires that the DOJ defend its support of a consent decree by sending the decree to the federal court along with a complaint and a **competitive impact statement (CIS)**. The CIS is a document that clarifies any potential antitrust problems inherent within the expansion and the solutions to those problems suggested by the decree. The law requires that 60 days before concluding the agreement, the DOJ publish the complaint, the decree, and the CIS in the *Federal Register*. Publishing the documents gives people a chance to have input into the nature, purpose, and effects of the agreement. The *Federal Register* will then print these statements and observations. A judge must also approve the decree. In doing so, the judge takes into account two elements: (1) the effect of the decree on competition and (2) the decree's effect on the community and on any parties who might be hurt separately. The Tunney Act was amended in 2004 to make it clear that the courts have the authority to challenge consent decrees negotiated by the Justice Department.

The corporate expansion process is sometimes regulated by specialty agencies that are charged with overseeing the socioeconomic activities of the corporations involved in the expansion process. Thus, for instance, the Federal Communications Commission would be responsible for reviewing merger plans proposed by corporations involved in the communications industry. Some agency officials take this responsibility very seriously and use their power to negotiate concessions within merger agreements that permit the agency to engage in an unofficial, but effective, brand of social engineering. The FCC is one such agency. In recent years, it has exercised its review power in merger cases to protect consumers, set prices, and return jobs to the United States. Agencies that use their regulatory powers to advance social agendas that are technically outside their legislative authority are referred to as **activist agencies**.

The Opening Case Revisited

The AT&T Buyout of Baby Bell South, Round 2

The AT&T–Bell South merger discussed in The Opening Case ran into some difficulty when it was reviewed by the Federal Communications Commission. The FCC, it seems, was intent on using the merger as an opportunity to flex its regulatory muscles. Some experts applauded the FCC's actions as a long overdue venture into socio-political activism, whereas others saw it as an unwelcome abuse of power. Whatever the case, the FCC clearly secured some very serious compromises from the corporations. Specifically, the FCC managed to extract an agreement from AT&T to provide a greater customer link to broadband and a promise to bring thousands of lucrative jobs back into the United States. However, the most intriguing aspect of the case was that both AT&T and Bell South agreed to the FCC's demands without objecting that most of those demands fell outside the agency's legislative power. The question that remains is whether AT&T's and BellSouth's willingness to submit to the influence of the FCC represents a one-time deal or a trend that will affect all such future buyouts.

Quick Quiz 40-4 True or False?

1. Most antifraud provisions of the Securities and Exchange Commission apply to the merger process.

2. Greenmail is the least effective anti-hostile takeover technique.

3. The Hart-Scott-Rodino Act is designed to police any expansion attempts that might harm competition in the marketplace.

40-5 Other Forms of Regulation

Corporations are regulated by the government in a variety of ways that extend beyond their involvement in the securities market, the antitrust arena, and the corporate expansion game. Many of these controls have been discussed in previous chapters, including labor regulations in Chapter 35, bankruptcy and debt adjustment in Chapter 32, commerce regulation in Chapter 22, and consumer protection regulation in Chapter 20. Three areas of regulation as yet unmentioned include energy regulation, environmental protection, and employment regulation.

Energy Regulation

The Arab Oil embargo of 1973 and the subsequent energy crisis focused national attention on the power industry. In answer to these concerns, Congress created the Department of Energy and the Federal Energy Regulatory Commission. National concerns with the problems of nuclear energy have also recently focused attention on the Nuclear Regulatory Commission.

Federal Energy Regulatory Commission   The Federal Energy Regulatory Commission (FERC) is responsible for regulating the transportation and the wholesale price of natural gas and electricity sold for use in interstate commerce. State utility commissioners regulate intrastate prices. Rates are calculated to allow companies a specific rate of return on investments (earnings divided by total assets), which they may not exceed. When utilities are confronted with increased costs due to higher fuel prices, they can apply to the commission for permission to pass these increased costs on to customers through fuel adjustment charges.

Nuclear Regulatory Commission Mandated by the Energy Reorganization Act, the Nuclear Regulatory Commission (NRC) is responsible for the licensing, construction, and operation of nuclear reactors. It is also responsible for regulating the possession, use, transportation, handling, and disposal of nuclear material. The NRC develops and implements rules and regulations governing licensed unclear activities.

Environmental Protection Regulation

The Environmental Protection Agency (EPA) is an independent agency in the executive branch of the federal government. It was created to carry out the provisions of the National Environmental Policy Act and other major environmental laws and executive orders dealing with air, water, solid waste, toxic substance, and noise pollution.

The Environmental Protection Agency administers all major antipollution programs and can enforce program standards against businesses for both intentional and unintentional infractions.

National Environmental Policy Act The purpose of the 1969 National Environmental Policy Act is to establish a national policy that will combat pollution and improve the environment. The legislation encourages efforts that prevent or eliminate damage to the environment and that stimulate the health and welfare of the public. The act requires a detailed statement of environmental consequences in every recommendation or proposal for legislation and other major federal actions significantly affecting the quality of the human environment. These environmental impact statements describe in detail the expected adverse environmental consequences of a proposed action. The alternatives to the action are also described.

Environmental Protection Agency All major antipollution programs dealing with air, noise, solid wastes, toxic substances, and pesticides were placed under the administrative control of the EPA in 1970. The EPA's primary responsibilities are to conduct research on all aspects of pollution, set and enforce pollution control standards, monitor programs to determine whether pollution abatement standards are being met, and administer grants to assist states in controlling pollution.

The EPA has the power to enforce the standards and programs it initiates. It encourages voluntary compliance by industry and communities and supports state and local governments' efforts to conduct enforcement actions of their own. When such efforts fail, the EPA conducts enforcement proceedings. Often the EPA must act against companies that pollute the environment, even if the pollution activity is unintentional. For example, the Federal Water Pollution Control Act forbids "any addition of any pollutants to navigable waters from any source." The courts have interpreted this broad prohibition to include even accidental pollution, because to hold otherwise would weaken the statute.

Employment Protection Regulation

In Chapters 35 and 36, employment law and labor-management relations law were discussed at length. However, those discussions do not describe the full extent of the law regarding employment matters. The law has taken several steps to protect employees who are affected by the sale, merger, or closing of a business. Two key pieces of legislation in this regard are the Employee Retirement Income Security Act (ERISA) and the Worker Adjustment and Retraining Notification Act (WARN).

Employee Retirement Income Security Act   As noted in Chapter 35, ERISA employers must place their pension contributions into a pension trust on behalf of their employees, independent of the employer. Under the rules of vesting detailed in the statute, workers are guaranteed the right to receive their pension benefits, regardless of whether they are working under the plan at the time of retirement. However, what happens if a business is sold or merges with another business? The answer to this question depends on whether the sale is a stock acquisition or an asset acquisition.

If the sale is a stock acquisition, in most cases the employee benefit plan is assumed by the purchasing corporation. However, if the sale involves an asset acquisition, then the buyer may or may not adopt the plan. The purchasing corporation may also elect to assume the plan after it has amended the plan to its satisfaction. Another alternative is for the purchaser to adopt an entirely new employee benefit plan that is similar but not identical to the plan of the selling corporation. Whatever the case, it is incumbent upon the purchaser to examine all pertinent records regarding the seller's employee benefit plan. These records include but are not limited to the annual report that is given to all participants in the plan, all insurance and annuity contracts, all Internal Revenue Service forms associated with the benefit plan, and the writing that describes the plan.

Worker Adjustment and Retraining Notification Act   If the sale of a business involves a plant closing or a mass layoff, then provisions of the Worker Adjustment and Retraining Notification Act (WARN) must be considered. The WARN Act requires employers with at least 100 full-time employees to give those employees 60 days' notice before all plant closings and mass layoffs. The notice must be in writing and be given to every affected worker unless the workers are represented by a union, in which case the notice must be given to a representative of the union. In addition, WARN requires that written notice of all plant closings and mass layoffs be given to the highest elected official of the local political subdivision in which the layoff or closing will happen. However, WARN's provisions do not apply if a state statute or a collective bargaining agreement requires a longer period of advance notice.

Quick Quiz 40-5 True or False?

1. The Arab Oil Embargo of 1973 and the subsequent energy crisis focused national attention on environmental protection and resulted in the establishment of the Environmental Protection Agency.

2. The Nuclear Regulatory Commission replaced the Federal Energy Regulatory Commission.

3. The Worker Adjustment and Retraining Notification Act repealed the Employee Retirement Income Security Act.

40-6 The Government and Corporate Dissolution

Just as the government is involved in the birth and growth (expansion) of a corporation, it is also involved in its death, or dissolution. Whether a corporation ends involuntarily or voluntarily, the government is somehow involved.

Involuntary Dissolution

If a corporation has repeatedly conducted business in an unlawful manner, the secretary of state can ask the state attorney general to bring a *quo warranto* action against that corporation. Under a *quo warranto* proceeding, the state revokes the corporation's charter. Common examples of illegal actions forming the grounds for revocation include a failure to file annual reports, a failure to pay franchise taxes, or a failure to maintain a registered or statutory agent for service of process. Corporations formed fraudulently and those exceeding their authority may also be subject to a *quo warranto* proceeding.

Courts have the power to liquidate the assets of a corporation when an action is brought by a shareholder. Grounds for involuntary dissolution at the request of a shareholder include the following:

- Evidence of illegal, oppressive, or fraudulent acts.
- A misapplication or waste of corporate assets.
- A deadlock of directors that threatens irreparable harm.
- Evidence that a dissolution is necessary to protect the rights of the complaining shareholder.

Voluntary Dissolution

Because the government grants corporate charters and regulates corporate activity, it must be informed when a corporation voluntarily dissolves. A corporation can be dissolved voluntarily by the unanimous approval of the shareholders or by a positive vote of the directors with the approval of two-thirds of the shareholders. Once the decision to dissolve has been approved, a statement of intent must be filed with the state government. The corporation will then cease business and notify creditors (by certified mail) and the public (by publication). After all claims have been received, corporate assets will be used first to pay creditors, with the surplus going to shareholders. If the existing assets cannot meet all claims, a receiver may be called in to handle matters. A *receiver* is a person appointed by law to hold property subject to diverse claims. The receiver would divide assets fairly among creditors. Following the distribution of all assets, the corporation must prepare articles of dissolution and present them to the secretary of state.

Quick Quiz 40-6 True or False?

1. If a corporation has repeatedly conducted business in an unlawful manner, the secretary of state can require the Federal Justice Department to revoke its charter.

2. Courts no longer have any power to liquidate the assets of a corporation when an action is brought by a shareholder.

3. Corporations are no longer permitted to engage in voluntary dissolution.

40-7 Dissolution of a Limited Liability Company

Because limited liability companies are created by state statutory law, the dissolution of a LLC is also regulated by state statutory law. Most state LLC statutes outline the circumstances that will trigger the dissolution of an LLC.

Circumstances of Dissolution

The dissolution of an LLC can be initiated by the unanimous agreement of all of its members. Similarly, the dissolution can be triggered by the expulsion, bankruptcy, or withdrawal of a member. However, many state statutes now declare that in both member-managed and manager-managed LLCs, a member may not leave the LLC unless such a departure is authorized by the operating agreement. Naturally, the articles of organization or the operating agreement can also specify other events that would cause a dissolution. Some state statutes also assert that the death of a member does not trigger a dissolution. Instead, the death of a member is classified as a disassociation.

Effects of Dissolution

As is true with a partnership, a limited liability company does not stop business immediately upon the dissolution event. Dissolution must be distinguished from the winding up of the LLC, which effectively puts it out of business. Winding up involves completing all of the business of the LLC and selling its property to satisfy all of the debts of the firm. As is the case with the dissolution of a partnership, the dissolution of an LLC need not be followed by a winding up of the LLC. If all of the remaining members of the LLC want to continue the LLC, they may do so. It is also possible for the operating agreement to specify that the vote to continue need not be unanimous among the remaining members. The operating agreement should also indicate that the LLC will dissolve when the number of members within the LLC falls below the number required by state law.

Quick Quiz 40-7 True or False?

1. The dissolution of an LLC is regulated by the federal government only.

2. Once an LLC has engaged in a dissolution procedure, the business does not stop immediately.

3. If all the remaining members of an LLC want to continue the LLC, they may do so.

Summary

40.1   The federal government, the state government, and various subdivisions of the state government all play a role in the regulation of business. The state government and it subdivisions all come by their power along traditional lines. The regulatory power of the state government is based on the state's police power. Police power is the state's authority to restrict private rights to promote and maintain public health, safety, welfare, and morals. A state has police power simply by virtue of its existence as a legitimate governmental authority. The federal government, however, has no inherent police power, because it is a government of limited powers. The federal government exercises power over commercial activities through the Commerce Clause of the Constitution (Article I, Section 8, Clause 3).

40.2   The primary objective of the Securities Act of 1933 and the Securities Exchange Act of 1934 is to protect investors by informing them about the securities they purchase. The Securities and Exchange Commission carries out this objective.

40.3   To preserve the value of competition and to discourage monopolies, the government has enacted several antitrust statutes. The Sherman Antitrust Act prohibits contracts, combinations, and conspiracies in restraint of trade. The Clayton Act, the Robinson-Patman Act, the Foreign Trade Improvements Act, and the Federal Trade Commission Act make the Sherman Antitrust Act more specific and more effective.

40.4   Although both securities law and antitrust law pertain to monopolies, they have different areas of focus. Securities law is concerned with regulating corporate expansion techniques, including mergers, consolidations, asset acquisitions, and stock acquisition.

Antitrust law is concerned with how corporate expansion affects competition in the marketplace. Antitrust law applies to horizontal, vertical, or conglomerate expansion attempts.

40.5 Through the Federal Energy Regulatory Commission and the Nuclear Regulatory Commission, the government regulates businesses involved in energy production. By means of the Environmental Protection Agency, the government also regulates businesses that pollute the environment.

40.6 Corporations can dissolve involuntarily or voluntarily. A corporation that has repeatedly conducted business in an unlawful manner may be subject to involuntary dissolution by the state. A corporation can be voluntarily dissolved by unanimous approval of the shareholders or by a positive vote of the directors with the approval of two-thirds of the shareholders. The government is involved in both involuntary and voluntary dissolution.

40.7 Because limited liability companies are created by state statutory law, the dissolution of a limited liability company is also regulated by state statutory law. Most state LLC statutes outline the circumstances that will trigger the dissolution of an LLC.

Key Terms

activist agencies, 847

Antitrust Procedures and Penalties Act, 847

asset acquisition, 842

best-price rule, 845

bright-line test, 845

Commerce Clause, 833

competitive impact statement (CIS), 847

conglomerate expansion, 846

consent decree, 847

consolidation, 841

corporate raid, 843

corporate raider, 843

friendly suitor, 843

greenmail, 843

horizontal expansion, 846

hostile bidder, 843

individual justice, 834

integral-part test, 845

interlocking directorates, 839

judicial–economic system, 833

junk bonds, 843

leveraged buyout (LBO), 842

lockup agreement, 844

merger, 841

monopoly, 837

per se violation, 837

police power, 835

prospectus, 836

quasi-RPM arrangement, 838

registration statement, 836

regulatory justice, 834

RPM agreement, 838

rule-of-reason standard, 837

security, 836

stock acquisition, 842

takeover bid, 843

target corporation, 843

targeted shareholder agreement, 845

tender offer, 843

Tunney Act, 847

tying agreement, 839

unfriendly buyer, 843

unfriendly suitor, 843

United States Antitrust Modernization Committee, 839

vertical expansion, 846

white knight, 843

Questions for Review and Discussion

1. What is the source of the federal power to regulate business?
2. What is the source of state power to regulate business?
3. How does the Securities and Exchange Commission prevent unfair practices?
4. How do per se antitrust violations differ from rule-of-reason violations?
5. What are the various techniques of corporate expansion?
6. How does the interest of the Securities and Exchange Commission in corporate expansion differ from that of the Federal Trade Commission?
7. How does the role of the Environmental Protection Agency compare with that of the Federal Energy Regulatory Commission?

8. What are the rights that are guaranteed to workers under the Employee Retirement Income Security Act and the Worker Adjustment and Retraining Notification Act?

9. What are the two ways that a corporation may undergo dissolution?

10. What are the circumstances under which a limited liability company may undergo dissolution?

Investigating the Internet

Access the Web site of the *Mergers and Acquisitions Report* and, as a research project, answer the following questions: (1) What is the purpose of the *Mergers and Acquisitions Report*? (2) What is the "Source Media" function of the *Mergers and Acquisitions Report*? (3) What additional resources are available for professionals who access the *Mergers and Acquisitions Report* Web site? (4) What are some of the current news stories being covered by the *Mergers and Acquisitions Report*? (5) What is the home city and state of the *Mergers and Acquisition Report*?

Cases for Analysis

1. The following lead paragraph was published in an article entitled, "Why the *Times* Could Go Private," in the December 11, 2006 issue of *Business-Week*: "Even before restive shareholders began ramping up pressure on The New York Times Co. and insurance mogul Maurice R. 'Hank' Greenberg started buying shares, Chairman Arthur O. Sulzberger Jr. was thinking about taking the company private. In recent months, he has been quietly soliciting advice from trusted friend and financial adviser Steven Rattner, according to sources familiar with those discussions." Later, the article adds that "Rattner met with members of the Ochs-Sulzberger family, who control the voting shares of the parent company through a trust and hold 9 of the company's 13 director seats. He offered various strategic alternatives, say sources, including a leveraged buyout." What does the phrase "taking the company private" mean? What is a leveraged buyout? See Tom Lowry and Jon Fine, "Why the *Times* Could Go Private: An LBO Would Be a Long Shot, but Sulzberger and an Adviser Are Talking It Over," *BusinessWeek*, December 11, 2006,. p. 40.

2. Filburn, a farm owner in Ohio, raised winter wheat primarily to feed his livestock and poultry and to make flour for home use. Under the provisions of the Agricultural Adjustment Act, Filburn was given notice of a wheat acreage and yield allotment. Filburn, however, sowed more acreage and harvested more wheat than he was allowed. As a result, the government fined him $117.11. Filburn sued the government to prevent it from collecting the fine. He argued that the production and consumption of wheat on his own land for his own purposes are outside the reach of Congress because, at most, this activity had an indirect effect upon interstate commerce. Was Filburn correct? Explain. *Wickard v. Filburn,* 63 S.Ct. 82 (U.S. Sup. Ct.).

3. The W. J. Howey Co. owned a large citrus grove in Florida. The citrus grove was serviced by Howey-in-the-Hills, Inc., a corporation owned and operated by the same people who ran the Howey Co. When the Howey Co. needed money, it sold tracts of land in the grove. Each buyer had to purchase both land from the Howey Co. and a service contract from Howey-in-the-Hills. The purchasers had no right to enter the land or to market the crop. All cultivating and marketing was done by the service company. Most of the buyers were from out of state. In return for their purchase, they received a share of the profits after the crops were harvested and sold. The SEC brought suit against both companies, arguing that the land and service contracts were actually securities that should have been registered with the commission. Was the SEC correct?

Explain *Securities and Exchange Commission v W. J. Howey Co.*, 66 S.Ct. 1100 (U.S. Sup. Ct.).

4. Topco Associates, Inc., is a cooperative association of small and medium-sized regional supermarket chains. Each of its member chains operates independently. All members are required to operate under exclusive territorial licenses issued by Topco. These licenses provide that members will sell Topco-controlled brands only within the marketing territory given them. The government filed suit in federal district court. It argued that this scheme of dividing markets among competing chains violated the Sherman Antitrust Act because it prohibited competition in Topco-brand products among grocery chains engaged in retail operations. Topco defended by arguing that the association actually increased competition between the smaller and the larger chains. Was Topco correct? Defend your answer. *United States v. Topco Associates, Inc.*, 92 S.Ct. 1126 (U.S. Sup. Ct.).

5. Enstrom purchased an aircraft from the Interceptor Corporation. When the aircraft crashed due to a design defect, Enstrom sued Interceptor. However, when Enstrom found out that Interceptor's assets had been purchased by the Interceptor Company (IC), it asked the court to join IC as a new defendant. IC argued that it was a different corporation involved in a different business. IC further argued that it had simply purchased the assets of Interceptor and was now involved in selling those assets, like the aircraft, to other buyers, like Enstrom. IC concluded that it was therefore not liable to Enstrom. Was IC correct? Why or why not? *R. J. Enstrom Corporation v. Interceptor Corporation*, 555 F.2d 277 (10th Cir.).

6. Earth Sciences, Inc., conducted gold-leaching operations in Colorado. The process involved spraying gold ore with a toxic substance. To prevent pollution, Earth Sciences had installed a reserve sump to catch any toxic runoff. An unexpected early thaw melted a snowbank, covering the ore heap. As a result, the reserve sump overflowed, dumping toxic waste into the Rito Seco Creek. The United States brought suit, alleging that Earth Sciences had violated pollution laws. Earth Sciences argued that it should not be held liable for an unintentional pollution accident. Was Earth Sciences correct? Explain. *United States v. Earth Sciences, Inc.*, 559 F.2d 368 (10th Cir.).

7. C. E. Stumpf & Sons, Inc., was formed to conduct a masonry and general contracting business. The corporation was owned in equal shares by Stumpf and his two sons, who had previously operated the same business as partners. Hostility between the two sons grew so extreme that one, Donald, ended contact with his family and was allowed no say in the operation of the business. After Donald's withdrawal from the business, he received no salary, dividends, or other revenue from the company. He brought suit seeking involuntary dissolution of the corporation. Should the court of appeals of California uphold the trial court's dissolution order? Why or why not? *Stumpf v. C. E. Stumpf & Sons, Inc.*, 120 Cal. Rptr. 671 (CA).

8. Image Technical Services, Inc. (ITS), an independent service organization (ISO), provides services for companies with copying machines made by the Eastman Kodak Co. In response to such competition, Kodak tied the sale of any of its parts to an agreement not to contract for services from any ISO. Under the terms of such an agreement, a customer who wished to buy Kodak parts had to agree not to purchase service from an ISO. ITS brought a lawsuit against Kodak under the Sherman Antitrust Act. In the suit, ITS alleged that such arrangements amounted to the type of tying agreement that was specifically outlawed by the Sherman Act. Kodak filed a motion for a summary judgment, arguing that the purchase of parts and the service of the machines with those parts did not represent the purchase of two separate products. Kodak concluded that it was therefore entitled to a judgment as a matter of law. Should the Court grant the summary judgment motion, or is there enough evidence of a tying agreement here to allow the matter to proceed to trial? Explain. *Eastman Kodak Co. v. Image Technical Services, Inc., et al.*, 504 U.S. 451 (U.S. Sup. Ct.).

Quick Quiz Answers

40-1	40-2	40-3	40-4	40-5	40-6	40-7
1. T	1. T	1. F	1. T	1. F	1. F	1. F
2. T	2. T	2. F	2. F	2. F	2. F	2. T
3. F	3. F	3. F	3. T	3. F	3. F	3. T

Part 8 Case Study

Gries Sports Enterprises, Inc. v. Cleveland Browns Football Co., Inc.
Supreme Court of Ohio 496 N.E.2d 959

Summary

Arthur Modell, president, CEO, and a director of the Cleveland Browns Football Co., Inc., (Browns) owned 53 percent of that corporation. Other members of the board at that time included Pat Modell, Modell's wife; James Bailey, who was also chief counsel for and an employee of the Browns; James Berick, who was outside counsel representing the corporation and a Browns shareholder; Richard Cole; and Nate Wallack, who was also an employee of the Browns. The final member of the board of directors was Robert Gries, who owned 43 percent of the Browns and also owned Gries Sports Enterprises, Inc. (GSE). Modell also owned 80 percent of the Cleveland Stadium Corporation (CSC), which leased Cleveland Stadium from the city and which then subleased the Stadium to the Browns and the Cleveland Indians. Other shareholders of CSC included Berick, Bailey, Cole, Wallack, Gries, and GSE. Modell was also president of CSC, and Bailey was both secretary and general counsel of that corporation.

CSC purchased 190 acres of land in Strongsville, Ohio, from Modell for $3,000,000 in cash and a promissory note for $1,000,000. Although Modell later canceled the $1,000,000 note, CSC still had debts exceeding $4,000,000. Modell decided that it would be expedient for the Browns to purchase CSC. Accordingly, he had CSC appraised by the brokerage and investment banking firm of McDonald and Company. Modell and Bailey, along with Michael Poplar, chief financial officer of CSC, determined that the Browns should pay $6,000,000 for the purchase of CSC. After this decision had been made, Modell, Bailey, Berick, and Poplar told Gries and Cole that CSC would be purchased by the Browns for $6,000,000. The purchase plan involved a payment of $120 per share of CSC to the minority shareholders, among whom were Berick, Bailey, Wallack, and Cole. Modell, the majority shareholder in CSC, was to receive a payment of $4,800,000 for his shares.

Subsequently, Gries did his own investigation into the value of CSC and concluded that Modell, Bailey, and Poplar had seriously overvalued the worth of that corporation. When the board met to consider the purchase, Modell made a presentation in support of the plan, and Gries explained his opposition. When the matter came to a vote, Bailey, Berick, Cole, and Wallack all voted for the plan. Neither Arthur nor Pat Modell participated in the vote, and Gries voted against the transaction. The following day, Gries filed a derivative lawsuit, the objective of which was to compel a reversal of the decision to purchase CSC. Gries stated that the transaction was unfair to the corporation, in that CSC was worth only $2,000,000 at the time that the Browns purchased it for $6,000,000. Gries argued that the fairness rule rather than the business judgment rule should be used to evaluate the directors' conduct because the directors who voted for the purchase were either "interested" directors due to their stock ownership or were dominated by Modell and had simply "rubber stamped" his decision.

Moreover, Gries contended that the overvaluation of CSC was prompted by Modell's need to secure the money to pay off outstanding debts to several banks.

Modell and the other directors argued that the decision to buy CSC should be evaluated by the business judgment rule. The trial court agreed with Gries, but the appeals court reversed that decision. The case then went to the Ohio Supreme Court.

The Court's Opinion

Justice Wise

The appellees-directors herein claim that they are protected by the presumption of good faith and fair dealing that arises from the business judgment and, therefore, they do not have the burden of proving that their decision to purchase CSC was intrinsically fair to the Browns' minority shareholders.

The issue before us, then, centers on the applicability of the business judgment rule. The business judgment rule is a principle of corporate governance that has been part of the common law for at least one hundred fifty years. It has traditionally operated as a shield to protect directors from liability for their decisions. If the directors are entitled to the protection of the rule, then the courts should not interfere with or second-guess their decisions. If the directors are not entitled to the protection of the rule then the courts scrutinize the decision as to its intrinsic fairness to the corporation and the corporation's minority shareholders. . . . A party challenging a board of directors' decision bears the burden of rebutting the presumption that the decision was a proper exercise of the business judgment of the board. . . .

In a stockholders' derivative action challenging the fairness of a transaction approved by a majority of directors of a corporation a director must be (1) disinterested, (2) independent, and (3) informed in order to claim benefit of the business judgment rule. If a director fails to pass muster as to any one of these three, he is not entitled to the business judgment presumption. This does not mean that the director's decision is necessarily wrong; it only removes the protection provided by the business judgment presumption. Once this presumption is removed, the court must then inquire into the fairness of the director's decision.

(A) [A] director is interested if (1) he appears on both sides of the transaction or (2) he has or expects to derive a personal financial benefit not equally received by the stockholders; (B) a director is independent if his decision is based on the corporate merits of the subject before the board rather than extraneous considerations or influences; a director is not independent when he is dominated by or beholden to another person through personal or other relationship; and (C) a director is informed if he makes a reasonable effort to become familiar with the relevant and reasonably available facts prior to making a business judgment.

Browns' directors Modell, Gries, Bailey, Berick, Cole, and Wallack, were all stockholders in CSC. Modell was the fifty-three percent majority stockholder in the Browns and the eighty percent majority stockholder in CSC (one hundred percent after March 2, 1982). [These facts convinced the court that the directors were interested in the challenged decision and were therefore not entitled to the protection of the business judgment rule. The court then went on to apply the fairness rule to the purchase of CSC by the Browns.]

(W)hen the transaction ". . .involves insiders dealing with their corporation the test of validity of the transaction is fairness. That our courts have frequently so held is without question . . . the substance of our decisions that 'when the persons, be they stockholders or directors, who control the making of a transaction and the fixing of its terms, are on both sides, then the presumption and deference to sound business judgment are no longer present.'"

In the instant case, no arms length negotiations as to price, terms, the elements to be included (or not to be included), or any other aspect of the proposed acquisition ever took place between the Browns and CSC. The $6,000,000 price was arrived at by Messrs. AMA (Modell), Bailey and Poplar . . . prior to any disclosure to plaintiffs of the possibility of such an acquisition, and never changed despite plaintiff's objections and despite the valuations furnished the defendants by plaintiffs. The manner in which the subject transaction was initiated, structured and disclosed to plaintiffs therefore did not satisfy the reasonable concept of fair dealing. . . .

The judgment of the court of appeals is reversed, and the judgment of the trial court is reinstated.

Judgment reversed.

Questions for Analysis

1. Which party had the burden of proof in this case?

2. According to the court's opinion, what factors should be taken into consideration in determining whether a director has an interest in a transaction that is challenged by a shareholder in a derivative lawsuit?

3. According to the court's opinion, when is a director independent, and under what circumstances does the director lose that independence?

4. What circumstances does the court say will make a director informed?

5. When the business judgment rule cannot be used, as occurred in this case, what standard is applied by the court to determine whether to reverse a challenged decision made by the directors?

6. Did the court consider the purchase of the Cleveland Stadium Corporation by the Cleveland Browns to be fair to the corporation and the minority shareholders in this case? Why or why not?

Part Nine

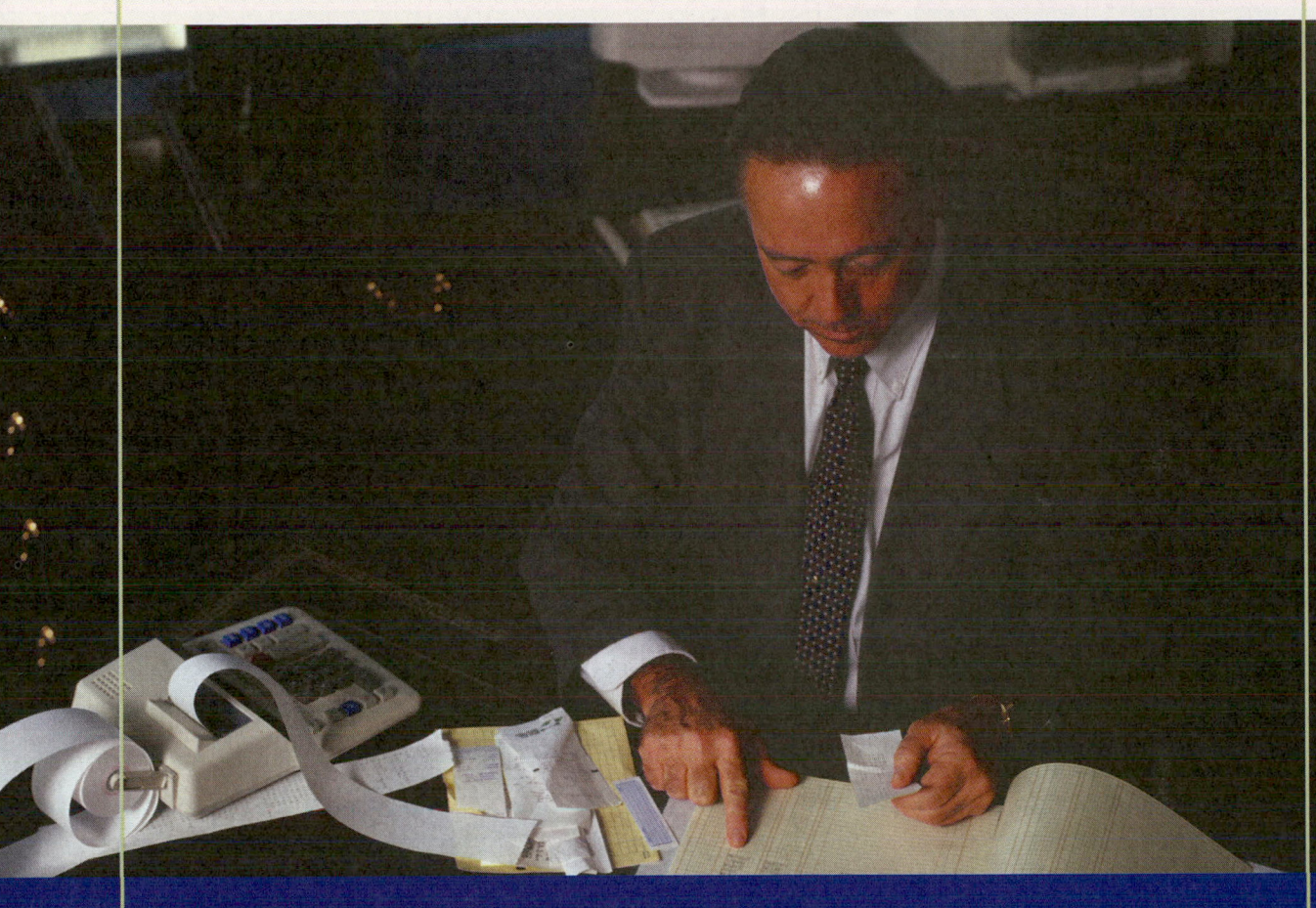

Chapter 41 Professional Liability

The Opening Case
Gambling with Malpractice

Sometimes when an attorney makes a mistake, no one notices. Sometimes only the client notices, and if the error is not too severe, the case goes forward. Sometimes, however, the mistake is so serious, and the damage so dreadful, that a malpractice suit, or two, or three, result. Such was the case when the law firm of Dorsey & Whitney helped engineer a deal that permitted a group of entrepreneurs to open a casino in upstate New York. The law firm represented an investment bank that was based in Minnesota. The Minnesota bank provided funds for the deal and enlisted the support of 31 additional banks that also lent money to the new casino. All in all, the loans topped $28 million. Things moved along rather well until, after 12 months of effort, the casino had failed to make any money. At that point, the Minnesota bank decided it was time to compel the casino owners to pay up. The process still might have moved along easily enough—had a major defect not surfaced. That defect was that the law firm had never received proper authorization from the National Indian Gaming Commission to open the casino in the first place. Because the deal was not officially authorized by the Commission, the contract between the casino owners, on the one hand, and the Minnesota investment bank and the additional lenders, on the other, was not enforceable. When the members of the law firm discovered their error, they tried to renegotiate the loans without telling anyone that the casino had not been authorized properly. In addition, the firm represented both the investors and the Minnesota bank in the same deal as it attempted to renegotiate the deals with the casino owners. As a result, the law firm found itself sitting in the defendant's seat in state court. The lawsuit had been filed by the 31 investors who found they could not collect any money from the casino owners and therefore believed that they had been misrepresented by the law firm. Fortunately for the law firm, the court dismissed the case because the plaintiffs did not have the necessary qualifications to bring the lawsuit in the first place. However, that did not mean that its problems were over. In fact, they were just beginning. When the Minnesota investment bank went bankrupt, its new trustee also brought a malpractice action against the law firm, as did another of the investors, a lender called Bremer Business Finance Group. The federal bankruptcy court judge found against the law firm in both lawsuits. This decision forced the firm to file an appeal in the Minnesota bank case and an objection to the judge's proposals in the Bremer case. One moral of the story seems to be that it is best to avoid gambling with the reputation of your firm. Another is when you find out you did something wrong, 'fess up before things get worse. (See Leigh Jones, "Indian Casino a Bad Bet for Dorsey & Whitney," *The National Law Journal*, March 19, 2007, p. 10.)

Opening Case Questions

1. Who is the client of the law firm?

2. What duties did the law firm violate in this case?

3. What is one lesson that the firm should have learned from this case?

4. What are the steps that should be filed in a malpractice case against a law firm?

5. Would any expert witnesses need to be called in this case?

 Learning Objectives

1. Distinguish between a certified public accountant and a public accountant.
2. Differentiate between generally accepted accounting principles and generally accepted auditing standards.
3. Identify the types of auditing opinions that can be issued by auditors.
4. Indicate the duties that accountants owe to their clients.
5. Outline the registration requirements imposed on architects by the state.
6. Identify the duties that an architect owes to his or her clients.
7. Determine the duties that an attorney owes to his or her clients.
8. State the standard of care used to judge health care professionals.
9. Contrast the locality rule with the national standard in determining a health care provider's liability.
10. Explain the circumstances in which hospitals can be held liable for the torts of independent contractor physicians.

41-1 The Liability of Accountants

As we've seen in the commercial world, the legal system and the economic culture interact with each other in such a way that they become, at times, one single system, the judicial–economic system. In the last chapter, we also examined how the judicial–economic system acts as another aspect of the complex adaptive system of the law. Now we turn our attention to one of the key players in the judicial–economic system, the accountant.

The Regulation of Accounting and Auditing

Accountants, like all professionals, must meet certain basic standards that are defined by the nature of their profession. A **professional** is a person who can perform a highly specialized task because of his or her special abilities, education, experience, and knowledge. Often the term professional is reserved for those individuals who perform a service for the public good. An **accountant** is a professional who can plan, direct, and evaluate a client's financial affairs. Although many accountants are charged with keeping a client's financial records, their responsibilities often go far beyond such routine tasks. Moreover, the nature of accounting means that an accountant's activities may have an impact on investors who exist outside the accountant's inner circle of clients. For these reasons, among others, accountants are regulated by the government. The federal government's power to regulate business, in general, and accounting, in particular, emerges from the Commerce Clause of the Constitution. The regulation of accounting by the state is part of the state's police power. The state's police power permits the state to regulate various activities to promote the general health, safety, welfare, and morals of the people.

Accountant Registration

The regulation of accounting is part of the state's police power. There are many different types of accountants. Some accountants work only for one employer. British Petroleum, for example, employs hundreds of accountants to chart the financial fortunes of the corporation. Other accountants hire themselves out to work for a wide variety of different clients. Such accountants generally belong to two categories: certified public accountants and public accountants.

Certified public accountants (CPAs) have met certain age, character, education, experience, and testing requirements. These requirements are generally established by the state. For example, the state government may require CPAs to be at least 18 years of age and of good moral character. The state may also require a bachelor's degree, two years of experience, and a passing score on a written examination that covers accounting, auditing, and other related subject areas. **Public accountants (PAs)** are accountants who work for a variety of clients but are not certified. Frequently, states will not allow individuals to call themselves public accountants unless they have met certain requirements that are not as strict as the requirements for CPAs. State registration requirements are designed to shield citizens against people who practice accounting without the education or experience necessary to do a competent job. The state cannot, however, prevent someone from practicing accounting as a profession. The state can only stop such individuals from calling themselves CPAs, PAs, or any other title that might mislead a client into thinking the nonregistered accountant is registered.

Accounting and Auditing

Accountants perform a number of functions for their clients. They may balance accounts, reconcile bank records with account books, handle the payroll, fill out income tax returns, and handle other tax matters. Another important job that falls to the accountant is the task of auditing.

Auditing   An **audit** is an examination of the financial records of an organization to determine whether those records are a fair representation of the actual financial health of the institution. To be effective, an audit is usually conducted by an outside, independent auditor. An **auditor** is an accountant who conducts an audit. The dilemma that auditors face is that they are responsible at two levels of accountability. Traditionally, auditors are hired by and work for the organization that is being audited. This is the first level of accountability. At the second level of accountability, auditors are responsible to the investors, lenders, shareholders, and others who rely on the financial statements made by those auditors. Ideally, auditors ought to be loyal to both groups of individuals. Realistically, auditors do not always overlook the fact that the organization is the one that hired them and that writes out their paycheck. As a result, there is a tendency, probably unconscious in most cases, to help the organization rather than the outside investors.

Accounting Principles   An independent group known as the Financial Accounting Standards Board (FASB) has established **generally accepted accounting principles (GAAP)**. The rules established by the FASB are followed by the American Institute of Certified Public Accountants (AICPA). The rules outline the procedures that accountants must use in accumulating financial data and preparing financial statements. In general, the procedures facilitate the preparation of reports that are useful, understandable, reliable, verifiable, and comparable.

Auditing Standards   The **Auditing Standards Board of the AICPA** has set up **generally accepted auditing standards (GAAS)**. These auditing standards measure the quality of the performance of auditing procedures. In short, the auditing standards explain how an auditor can determine whether proper accounting procedures have been used. There are ten auditing standards. Three of them relate to the auditors, three relate to their work in the field, and four relate to the opinions that they issue.

Types of Opinion   An auditor's opinions may be unqualified or qualified. When auditors conclude that the financial records of the company are an accurate reflection of the company's financial status, they will issue an **unqualified opinion**. When auditors issue a **qualified opinion**, they are saying that the books represent the company's financial health as of a given date. However, auditors may qualify the opinion in one of two ways. One type of qualified opinion is the "subject to" opinion. In this case, auditors state that the books represent the company's financial health subject to some uncertainty, such as a pending lawsuit, which may affect the company in the future. The second type of qualified opinion is an "except for" opinion. Such an opinion indicates that the financial statements are an accurate reflection of the company's financial health except for some minor deviation from GAAP, not serious enough to warrant an adverse opinion. Auditors may also issue adverse opinions and disclaimers. An **adverse opinion** is rendered when the deviations from GAAP are so serious that an unqualified opinion is impossible and a qualified opinion is not justified. An adverse opinion would be rendered in the following cases:

LO3

- The financial statements do not fairly present the financial health of the organization.
- Generally accepted accounting principles are consistently ignored.
- Financial information has not been adequately disclosed.
- There are major uncertainties that could have a serious impact on the organization, and the auditor disagrees with management's presentation of those uncertainties.

A **disclaimer** declares that the auditor has decided not to give any opinion on the company's financial records. This situation generally occurs because the auditor has not had enough time to examine the books properly or was denied access to crucial records. An auditor might also issue a disclaimer if the books indicate that the organization exercised no control over the accounting process.

Accountants have a fiduciary duty with their clients and must adhere to the AICPA Code of Professional Ethics as well as GAAP and GAAS standards for the profession.

Ethical Rules of Accountants   The AICPA has also established a **Code of Professional Ethics**, which outlines rules that govern the ethical conduct of accountants. These rules are frequently used by the courts to determine whether an accountant has breached a duty to the client in nontechnical matters not covered by GAAP and GAAS. For example, the AICPA's code has established that accountants owe their clients a duty of confidentiality even after the relationship has terminated. In this regard, an accountant cannot reveal information about a client's business to anyone outside of the accountant–client relationship unless authorized to do so

by the client. Although this privilege does not extend to a court's request for information, it does cover most other situations. The ethical code also encompasses contingent fees, the independence of the auditor, promotional practices, operational practices, and quality reviews by peers.

The Sarbanes-Oxley Act

In response to some of the difficulties that can be traced to the dual identity that auditors must assume, Congress enacted the **Sarbanes-Oxley Act**. Although the Sarbanes-Oxley Act has many targets, one of the most crucial is to restore the confidence of the investment community. A key feature of the act is the creation of the **Public Company Accounting Oversight Board (PCAOB)**. This new regulatory agency is charged with the task of making certain that correct, unbiased, and comprehensive data find their way to potential investors, so that they can make informed decisions about investment opportunities. To accomplish this task, Congress gave the board responsibility for the supervision of public accounting firms. With this power came the ability to set up practical instructions for auditing procedures and philosophical canons for the ethical values that such firms must follow. To give the new federal board proper authority, the act requires the registration of all public accounting firms that are involved in auditing publicly traded corporations. The board has the authority to inspect those companies and their procedures on a regularly established schedule. The board consists of five members, only two of whom are permitted to be certified public accountants. The hope is that this approach will keep the agency objective and unbiased as it evaluates both the accounting firms and the procedures by which they operate.

The Sarbanes-Oxley Act also enacted several additional features. For example, the act specifically prohibits conflicts of interest that might arise when former auditors are hired by a company, if that company is still being audited by the same firm that once employed the former auditor. The prohibition lasts for one year and covers only the uppermost management positions of the audited company. Sarbanes-Oxley also requires that corporate audit committees receive timely and comprehensive reports from the accounting firm that is auditing the company. Alternative approaches to the way that financial data are packaged must be included in these regular reporting sessions. Under the provisions of the act, Congress has ordered a probe into the recent merging of the Big Eight accounting firms into the Big Four. The aim of the probe is to find out what led to the mergers, what fallout will result from the new configuration, and what ways exist to improve the competitive atmosphere in the accounting profession.

Conflicting Jurisdictional Problems

Although auditors and accountants are regulated by several different authorities, those authorities coexist peacefully as long as they agree with one another. Trouble results, however, when different agencies promote different agendas. This problem is further complicated whenever accountants interact with other professionals. Many of these professionals, notably attorneys, are also regulated by professional authorities, some of which promote duties that conflict with those of the accounting profession. Thus, for example, the FASB might require auditors to perform a task that calls for information that is in the hands of a client's attorney. The AICPA might support the auditor's need to obtain such information from their clients' attorneys, but the American Bar Association (ABA) might direct attorneys to withhold information from auditors to preserve attorney–client privilege or the work product privilege or both. At that point, no matter what happens, someone will violate his or her professional code and someone—the auditor, the attorney, or the client—will have to suffer the consequences.

EXAMPLE 41-1:   The Hazards of Serving Too Many Masters

In the mid 1970s, in the midst of a growing litigation epidemic, the FASB released a decision that required auditors to make sure that they accrued certain losses to income while auditing any client's books, including losses that might result from possible lawsuits. To do this properly, the auditors had to get information from their clients' attorneys. To help auditors accomplish this task, the AICPA announced that auditors were now permitted to ask clients to obtain certain information from their attorneys. In reaction, the ABA declared that attorneys ought to be very careful about providing auditors with too much information, lest they violate the attorney–client or the work product privilege or both. The AICPA responded by assuring the ABA that their auditors would never go so far as to violate either the attorney–client or the work product privilege. Everything might have rested there, had the Public Company Accounting Oversight Board (PCAOB) of Sarbanes-Oxley not gotten into the act. The PCAOB muddied the waters considerably by warning auditors that they would be severely disciplined for not insisting that attorneys provide them with the necessary information, regardless of whatever arguments those attorneys might make. Does this conflict give the auditors a license to demand that attorneys violate the attorney–client privilege and the work product privilege? Certainly the ABA does not think so, but the PCAOB insists that it does. Whatever the ultimate outcome of this dispute might be, it serves to illustrate the problems that arise when too many governmental agencies regulate the same activity. (See Peggy A. Heeg, "Auditors Are Increasingly at Odds with Attorneys," *The National Law Journal*, November 20, 2006, pp. S-1 and S-6–S-7.)

Duties Owed by the Accountant to the Client

A client often hires an accountant to take care of all the client's financial affairs. Therefore, the client and the accountant have a contractual arrangement. If an accountant fails to fulfill the terms of the contract, the client could bring a breach of contract suit against the accountant. For this reason, it is very important that the terms of the contract include express duties that outline the task of the accountant and the time limits, if any, within which the tasks must be performed. Naturally, certain implied duties are included in any contract between an accountant and the client. These implied duties arise because the relationship exists. Thus, the accountant's agreement to work for the client implies an agreement to use the appropriate level of skill and due care that would be expected of any similarly situated accountant. An accountant might also be liable to clients under common law for negligence and fraud.

Negligence/Malpractice   The client has the right to expect the accountant to do a good job in whatever task has been assigned. From this right arises the accountant's duty of due care. The duty of due care means that the accountant must perform the job with the same skill and competence that a reasonable accounting professional would use in the same situation. **Negligence** or **malpractice** occurs whenever an accountant fails to meet his or her duty of due care. Although the term malpractice is usually reserved for health care professionals and attorneys, it could also be applied to any form of professional negligence. How a reasonable accounting professional would handle a given situation, and thus avoid a charge of malpractice, would be determined by reference to GAAS or GAAP.

Whenever accountants ignore the rules established by GAAS and GAAP, they do so at their own risk. It is fairly certain that ignoring or remaining ignorant of these principles and procedures is a one-way ticket to a malpractice suit, and there is little question that in such

Talking Points

The passage of the Sarbanes-Oxley Act caused a great deal of furor and consternation among companies that have had to comply with its strict reporting requirements, as well as among the accounting and auditing firms that must carry out the actual financial analyses of such companies. Some experts see the changes brought by the Sarbanes-Oxley Act as a chance to make things better by improving internal operations and boosting investor confidence. Others see these changes as additional requirements imposed as a punishment on an entire industry as the result of the malfeasance of a few bad apples. These two points of view are expressed in the following ways.

In a speech before the National Press Club, Securities and Exchange Chairman William Donaldson remarked, "Simply complying with the rules is not enough. They should, as I have said before, make this approach part of their companies' DNA. For companies that take this approach, most of the major concerns about compliance disappear. Moreover, if companies view the new laws as opportunities—opportunities to improve internal controls, improve the performance of the board, and improve their public reporting—they will ultimately be better run, more transparent, and therefore more attractive to investors."

In contrast, in a recent publication, representatives of the financial consulting firm Deloitte & Touche LLP suggested that "Few will publicly admit it but many have come to view the Sarbanes-Oxley Act . . . as an unwelcome requirement. Cost, effort and energy poured into complying with new regulations, all caused by a tiny minority of unethical individuals. Most will agree that the law was needed to restore investor confidence. But few will acknowledge that they themselves need it. Or can benefit from it. This is someone else's problem—and, like schoolyard justice, the whole class gets punished."

Which of these two views do you think is the most accurate view of the situation? Have companies and auditors welcomed the changes introduced by Sarbanes-Oxley, or have they done their best to get around the law? Explain. Does the analogy of "schoolyard justice" accurately describe the wide target area hit by Sarbanes-Oxley? Why or why not?

A Question of Ethics

Samuel Sorrell works as a CPA for the accounting firm of Morris, Miller, and Kierns. He has just completed an audit of the Randall-Cassidy Sports Wear Corporation. The audit revealed that Randall-Cassidy is in serious financial difficulty. Moreover, Sorrell feels obligated to issue an adverse opinion because Randall-Cassidy's financial statements do not fairly reflect the financial status of the corporation, generally accepted accounting principles have not been followed properly, and major uncertainties about the sportswear market could cause a serious slump in corporate sales. Sorrell learns that Thomas Keifer, the CEO of Randall-Cassidy, plans to make a presentation to a group of potential investors. The presentation contains figures that are technically accurate but that will actually mislead the investors as to the true financial state of the corporation. Ethically, what should Sorrell do now? Would your answer change if one of the investors directly asked Sorrell about the company's financial condition? Why or why not?

circumstances, the accountant would be found liable for negligence. Unfortunately, the opposite precept is not always true; that is, just because an accountant follows the GAAS or GAAP guidelines does not automatically lead to his or her vindication in a court of law. It is always possible that an accountant can follow the proper principles and procedures yet still make other errors that lead to liability. Thus, an accountant might follow GAAS, yet file a return after a required deadline, or the accountant might make a calculation error, or send the forms to the wrong agency, and so on.

Fraud Accountants must perform their duties with the best interests of their client in mind. If an accountant *deliberately* misrepresents the client's financial condition or in some way *deliberately* falsifies a statement or an auditing report, that accountant may be liable to the client for fraud. Accountants may also be liable for fraud if they compile a financial report or conduct an audit recklessly. To make a proper case for fraud, it is not enough for the plaintiff to show that the accountant deliberately or recklessly attempted to falsify records and statements. In addition, the plaintiff must demonstrate that he or she actually relied on the false statements or reports. The extra effort is worth it, however, because if the plaintiff succeeds in proving that he or she was defrauded by the accountant, that plaintiff can ask for and will often be awarded punitive damages.

The Accountant's Liability to Third Parties

Under common law, an accountant can be held liable to some third parties who are damaged by a negligently prepared financial statement. Accountants are also liable to some third parties if they deliberately make fraudulent statements.

Negligence/Malpractice The right to bring suit for a negligently prepared financial statement will always extend to actually named third parties. Most states also extend this right to any limited classes of specifically foreseen third parties. A few states extend the right to bring suit protection to reasonably foreseeable classes of third parties (see Table 41-1).

Actually Named Third Parties If an accountant prepares a financial statement with the actual knowledge that the client is going to show the statement to a particular third party, then the accountant is clearly liable to that *known* third party. If, for example, the client tells the accountant that the statement is for Mr. X, then Mr. X can recover if he suffers actual financial loss due to the accountant's negligence.

Table 41-1 Accountants' Liability to Third Parties Under Common Law

Liability Theory	Explanation
Actually named third parties	When accountants prepare financial statements knowing that the client will show the statement to a named third party, then those accountants will be liable to that known third party if through their negligence the third party is injured. Only a few states limit recovery to actually named third parties.
Specifically foreseen third parties	Accountants may also be liable to certain third parties for negligently prepared financial statements if those third parties are members of a limited class that is specifically foreseen when the financial statement is drawn up. Most states follow this theory.
Reasonably foreseeable third parties	Accountants may also be liable for negligently prepared financial statements if those third parties can be reasonably foreseen as recipients of the statements. Only a few states extend recovery this far.

Specifically Foreseen Third Parties Most states have extended this rule even further, holding that accountants are also liable to the limited class of third parties that is specifically foreseen when the financial statement is drawn up. Thus, an accountant who prepares a financial statement knowing that the client intends to show it to investors would be liable to any investor in that same class of specifically foreseen third parties. To recover from the accountant, the investors would have to rely on the statements and suffer financial loss.

Reasonably Foreseeable Third Parties Some courts have become very strict in holding accountants liable to third parties. These jurisdictions have adopted a test that depends on whether the plaintiff in the case was foreseeable as a possible recipient of the accountant's report. For instance, if it is reasonable for the accountant to foresee that the financial statement would be shown to bankers, suppliers, and potential investors, then the accountant is liable to anyone of these reasonably foreseeable classes of individuals. This ruling would be true even if the class were not specifically mentioned when the accountant was hired by the client. This version is the strictest of the three tests that the courts have adopted for determining the extent of an accountant's liability to third parties in negligence cases.

Fraud Because fraud involves a deliberate deception, the courts have no difficulty extending protection to a wide class of third parties. Thus, an accountant who prepares a fraudulent financial statement is liable to anyone who can be reasonably foreseen as relying on that statement.

EXAMPLE 41-2:   Foreseeing the Effects of the Specifically Foreseen Rule

Isaac Berryman brought suit against the accounting firm of Dowling, Krueger, and McBride when it failed to detect the poor financial condition of New Design Software, Inc. Berryman was an investor who lost his life savings when New Design collapsed. The accountants argued that Berryman could not sue them because New Design, not Berryman, was their client. Under the named third party test, the accountants would be correct because Berryman was not actually named as a recipient of the financial reports prepared by the accountants. However, under the specifically foreseen rule, the accountants would be wrong because Berryman is a member of a limited class of third parties that was specifically foreseen as a recipient of the information. Significantly, if Berryman could show fraud, it would not matter whether he was actually named as a recipient or simply the member of a specifically foreseen class. If fraud is involved, anyone who can be reasonably foreseen as a recipient of those reports could hold Dowling, Krueger, and McBride liable for any actual loss caused by reliance on those reports.

An Accountant's Statutory Liability

Accountants may also be sued for violating statutory laws governing their activities. Such suits can arise under the Securities Act of 1933, the Securities Exchange Act of 1934, and various state laws.

Securities Act of 1933 Under the Securities Act of 1933, the first time a corporation issues stock for sale, it must file a registration statement (see Chapter 40). Such statements are prepared by accountants. The 1933 act allows purchasers who have lost money after buying corporate stock based on misleading or false registration statements to sue the accountants who prepared the statements. To succeed in such a lawsuit, the plaintiff must show that the registration statement included a false or misleading statement about a material matter and that he or she suffered a measurable financial setback as a result of relying on that statement. However, the accountant has a defense in such cases. Usually, if the accountant can show that he or she used due diligence in preparing the report, he or she will escape liability. Due diligence is generally demonstrated by reference to the proper application of GAAS and GAAP standards. However, the accountant will also have to show that he or she committed no additional negligent actions and made no other avoidable mistakes.

Securities and Exchange Act of 1934   A second federal law, the Securities and Exchange Act of 1934, also contains some provisions that affect accountants. These provisions are designed to prevent the fraudulent filing of various documents with the SEC and the fraudulent manipulation of the securities market. Both acts also contain provisions that impose criminal liability on accountants in some situations.

State Statutes   In addition to these federal statutes, most states have enacted similar statutes regulating the activities of accounts as they relate to the sale of stock. State statutes that regulate the sale of stock are frequently referred to as blue sky laws because they are set up to stop the sale of securities that are as empty as several feet of blue sky.

Quick Quiz 41-1 True or False?

1. An accountant is a professional who can plan, direct, and evaluate a client's financial affairs.

2. An auditor's report and the accompanying financial statements will always guarantee an institution's financial health.

3. Whenever certified public accountants ignore the rules established by GAAS and GAAP, they do so with little or no risk, because of their certified status.

41-2 The Liability of Architects and Attorneys

In addition to accountants, two other frequently contracted business professionals are architects and attorneys. Both are regulated by the states, and both must follow certain clearly stated duties.

The Liability of Architects

An architect is a professional who plans the construction or alteration of a variety of structures, from small, single-family dwellings to enormous skyscrapers. Generally, architects do not actually construct the building. However, they may manage the construction according to their detailed plans.

State Regulation   Under its police power, the state can regulate the conduct of architects. States often establish an agency that makes the rules that architects must follow to be officially recognized as professionals in their field of expertise. The state will usually establish age, character, education, experience, and testing requirements. Often a state will maintain a list of all architects officially registered as having met all of these legal requirements.

Duties of the Architect   Like any other professional, an architect owes a duty to exercise due care and skill in carrying out professional duties. This standard of care requires the architect to use the same methods, techniques, and procedures that any architect of ordinary skill would use in a similar situation. The standard does not demand that the architect's design be perfect or that the execution of the design be faultless. Architects can make mistakes, as long as those mistakes do not result from a failure to use appropriate skill and good judgment according to accepted professional standards.

Contractual Liability   Sometimes the final version of a building differs from the original plan at the time the contract was made. If the deviation is actually an error caused by the architect's failure to use due care and skill, the architect may have to reimburse the client for any extra money spent to correct the error. This requirement is known as the **cost of repair rule**. A different rule is followed if the design is so defective that the structure is unusable for its originally intended purpose. In such situations, the court may declare that the architect owes the client the difference between the market value of the building as it stands and the market value of the intended structure.

Tort Liability   Unlike mistakes made by accountants, errors made by architects may injure people or damage property. If the architect has failed to exercise the appropriate standard of care and if, as a result, property is damaged or people are injured, the architect may have to compensate the victims. Note, however, that the architect's mistake must cause injury or damage.

> ## EXAMPLE 41-3:   The Ironic Puzzle of Causation
>
> Architects Lefkowitz and Rudman were hired to plan the new Convention Center to be located in Las Vegas. Rudman failed to check the stress specs on a balcony on the second level of the convention center's main exhibition floor. Had he made the check, his inspection would have revealed that an error had been made that could cause the balcony to collapse under its own weight. The construction firm of McMahon-Fulton, Inc., ignored the Lefkowitz-Rudman specs and used their own plans. However, the McMahon-Fulton plan contained the same error that the architects' plan had contained. On the night that the convention center opened, the balcony suffered a partial collapse that injured several people. Because the contractor had ignored the Lefkowitz-Rudman plan, the architects were not held liable, despite their error.

The Liability of Attorneys

Next to the accountant, one of the most sought-after professionals by a businessperson is the attorney. An attorney is a professional because of expert knowledge, ability, and education in finding, understanding, interpreting, and, ultimately, applying the law. Attorneys advise their clients in a variety of different ways, all of which require good faith, loyalty, and the exercise of due care.

State Regulation of Attorneys   Like accountants and architects, attorneys are regulated by the state's police power. Also like accountants and architects, attorneys are normally required to be of a certain age (usually 18) and of good moral character. They are required to possess a certain educational background and to pass a special examination, demonstrating minimum competency. Unlike architects and accountants, attorneys often do not have any experience requirements, because architects and accountants usu-

Talking Points

In his essay, "The Chaotic Indeterminacy of Tort Law: Between Formalism and Nihilism," Denis J. Brion, professor of law at Washington and Lee University School of Law, explains that two very distinct interpretations of the law have existed side by side for a number of years. He calls one of these two theories formalism and the other nihilism. Brion explains the two theories in the following way:

> In "Legal Formalism: On the Immanent Rationality of Law," Ernest Weinrib offers . . . the idea that the law can be accurately described in terms of . . . its "inner coherence." He argues that the law is altogether distinct from politics and that it can only be understood from within itself. The function of judges is to "make transactions and distributions" in the social world conform to the "latent unity" of the law. The function of legal scholars is to make explicit the internal coherence and intelligibility of the law.
>
> In *The Disorder of Law: A Critique of Legal Theory,* Charles Sampford sets out to criticize the various theories of law that seek to describe it as systematic. His principal thesis is that society itself is without system—his term is the "social melee"—and that the law, as an integral part of society, is correspondingly disordered—the "legal melee." He concludes that, because of this disorder, the impact of legal doctrine on social and individual practices is strongly attenuated.

Of the two theorists, which one has the more accurate view of the legal system? Which view supports the idea that the judicial–economic system is a flexible and responsive system? Explain your answers to each of these questions. A third alternative is offered by Lawrence Friedman in his treatise *Law in America*. The law, Friedman says, is not a separate autonomous system. Rather, the law "is, essentially, a product of society; and as society changes, so does its legal system. Feudal societies have feudal legal systems; socialist societies have socialist systems; tribal societies have tribal systems; capitalist societies have capitalist legal systems. How could it be otherwise?" Of the three theorists, which one reflects your own personal view? Which view is supported by the evidence in this chapter concerning the regulation of the legal profession? Explain your answers.

ally are required to have only a bachelor's degree, whereas attorneys obtain an advanced degree in law. This extra education often takes three to four years beyond the bachelor's degree. The experience requirement of architects and accountants frequently amounts to two years.

Ethical Rules of Attorneys   The American Bar Association has established a set of ethical standards entitled the ABA Model Rules of Professional Conduct. These rules have been officially adopted and implemented in 47 states. Only California, New York, and Maine have rejected the new rules. California and Maine elected to create rules peculiar to their own jurisdictions, while New York prefers to operate under the old Model Code of Professional Responsibility. The new Model Rules of Professional Conduct simplify the old rules by dividing professional responsibility into eight different areas. These areas include the client–lawyer relationship, the lawyer's duty as a counselor, the lawyer's responsibilities as an advocate, the lawyer's obligations to third parties, the responsibilities of lawyers to one another in law firms and in partnerships, the lawyer's duty to perform public service, and the lawyer's responsibilities in relation to the legal profession.

Negligence/Malpractice An attorney has the duty to represent clients with good faith, loyalty, and due care. An attorney who does not fulfill these duties may be liable for malpractice. Usually, however, an attorney is not liable to a third party who is not a client.

Duties of the Attorney When a client hires an attorney, the client has the right to expect the attorney to act in *good faith*, which means that the attorney's duty is to act in the best interests of the client. In the absence of such good faith conduct, the attorney may face a lawsuit brought by the client and disciplinary action brought by the state.

An attorney also has a duty of *loyalty* to protect the client and to make certain that the client receives advice and representation that is free of conflicting interests. Thus, an attorney cannot represent two clients on opposite sides of the same dispute, unless both sides have been completely informed of the dual representation and consent to it. Similarly, an attorney violates the duty of loyalty if he or she takes advantage of a client for personal profit. The duty of loyalty also gives rise to certain privileges that exist between clients and their attorneys. One of the most fundamental privileges is the attorney–client privilege. The **attorney–client privilege** guarantees that information that passes between clients and their attorneys will remain secret. The rationale that supports the attorney–client privilege is the belief that clients must feel free to tell their attorneys everything that is involved in a case so that the attorney can do his or her best as an advocate of that client. The privilege can be waived if a third party unrelated to the client is present during a discussion with the attorney, provided that third party is not a person involved in the case, such as another attorney in the firm, a paralegal, or a legal assistant.

Closely related to attorney-client privilege is the work product privilege. The **work product privilege** protects all notes, recordings, research documents, Q&As, voice mails, faxes, e-mails, computer records, memos, letters, flash drives, disks, DVDs, CDs, and so on that are prepared in anticipation of litigation. So, for instance, if an attorney interviews a client about the facts in a pending lawsuit and takes notes during that interview, those notes are protected by the work product privilege. Or if a client sends an e-mail to his or her attorney after an interview, saying something like, "Oh, by the way, when we talked yesterday, I forgot to tell you this or that about the lawsuit," that e-mail is also protected by the work product privilege. Like the attorney–client privilege, the work product privilege can be waived if the work product is revealed to a third party not related to the client or not involved in the preparation of the client's case. Moreover, the work product privilege is not an absolute privilege. This distinction means that the content of the work product may have to be disclosed if a party who needs the information wrapped up in that work product can convince a judge that he or she has a substantial need for that information and cannot obtain that information some other, more legitimate, less intrusive way.

Like all other professionals, an attorney owes a duty of *due care* to clients. This duty means that in giving legal advice, negotiating claims, litigating suits, making out wills, negotiating divorce settlements, and performing any number of other legal tasks, an attorney must exercise the same skill and care that would be expected of other attorneys in the same situation.

Steps in a Legal Malpractice Case

For a plaintiff to succeed in a malpractice case against an attorney, that plaintiff must demonstrate the existence of four specifically drawn elements. First, the plaintiff must show that the attorney owed a duty to that plaintiff. Generally, this proof is not a problem, because when the client consults the attorney, a contract is created by which the attorney assumes the duty to represent that client with the appropriate level of care. The question of duty can arise, however, when there is a factual discrepancy about whether the client actually hired the attorney to represent him or her. Thus, the duty clearly arises when the client comes to the attorney's

The Opening Case Revisited
Gambling with Malpractice, Round 2

The duty of due care is one of the most fundamental duties that an attorney owes to his or her client. In fact, some might argue that it is the most fundamental duty of all. In *The Opening Case* at the beginning of this chapter, the law firm breached this duty by not ensuring that the new casino was properly authorized by the National Indian Gaming Commission. As it turned out, this error was the most serious blunder in this case. Had the law firm checked the details of the deal properly in the first place, all of the additional problems that flowed from this one error would have been avoided.

office and asks the attorney to help him or her deal with a legal problem. In contrast, if a student were to ask a law professor a hypothetical question during a class discussion, then no duty has arisen because there is no client-attorney relationship created in such a situation.

Second, the attorney must have breached the duty that is owed to the client. The attorney's duty is measured by his or her compliance with a standard that holds that an attorney must represent a client in a way that demonstrates enthusiasm and dedication to the client's best interests. The attorney cannot, however, file claims or advance arguments that have no realistic chance of succeeding or that are not firmly grounded in acceptable legal principles. The attorney must act as a reasonable professional would in the same circumstances. This standard does not mean that attorneys are not permitted to make mistakes. On the contrary, mistakes are tolerated as an inevitable part of the legal profession, just as a long as they do not result from carelessness, inattention, laziness, or ignorance. Third, the plaintiff must show that the attorney's questionable behavior caused the resulting harm to the plaintiff. Moreover, it is not enough that there is a factual connection between the behavior and the injury. There must also be a legal connection between the two. Such a legal connection requires foreseeability. Fourth, the plaintiff must show that he or she suffered actual harm as a result of the attorney's breach of duty.

Because attorneys are professionals and because the intricacies of the law are often mystifying to the layperson, the law requires that the elements of malpractice must be supported by expert testimony. Expert testimony can only be overlooked when the relationship between the injury suffered by the client and the behavior by the attorney is so obvious that the experience of the plaintiff is within the everyday experience of the jury. As we shall see, a very similar—in fact, an almost identical—standard is used to guide the question of whether expert testimony is needed in the case of malpractice claims that are filed against health care professionals.

Third-Party Liability   In contrast to accountants and architects, attorneys are rarely held liable to third parties because the attorney's responsibilities are tied closely to the interests of the client and the client alone.

EXAMPLE 41-4:   The Phantom Zone of Third-Party Liability

William Zafris hired the Brooks Construction Company to replace the windows on his back patio. Four days after the job was finished, the windows began to crack. When Zafris called Brooks, the company refused to take any responsibility. Unable to get any satisfaction through normal channels, Zafris contacted Sarah Montgomery, a local attorney. Montgomery advised Zafris not to pay Brooks, pending a resolution of the dispute. Eventually, the matter was settled in Brooks's favor. Brooks then sued Montgomery for advising Zafris not to pay his bill. The court ruled that Brooks could not hold Montgomery liable for the advice she had given Zafris, even though that advice had proved to be incorrect, because she had acted in good faith and with due care.

Court-Driven Protection   As we've seen, attorneys who are negligent can be the target of a civil suit brought by a wronged client. There are other safeguards within the legal system, however, that are designed to make certain that attorneys do not file phony lawsuits, promote unwarranted legal arguments, conduct unnecessary investigations, file unjustifiable motions, or make allegations that lack evidentiary support. The Federal Rules of Civil Procedure, for example, specifically forbid such objectionable conduct and impose severe penalties should that rule be broken. Many states have similar civil rules that are designed to deter unprofessional conduct on the part of unscrupulous attorneys. Penalties can include a payment of money to the court or to the other party. These payments may even include attorneys' fees in appropriate cases.

Criminal Liability   Attorneys are not immune to criminal liability, especially when they act in collusion with their clients. Fortunately, most of the time, attorneys know what is going on within the attorney-client relationship because they are responsible for most, if not all, of the legal decisions made in that relationship. Sometimes, however, an attorney, especially an in-house attorney, might not know everything about a transaction that he or she is handling for a client. An **in-house attorney** is one who is part of the officer corps of a business and, as an employee of that business, does what he or she is told to do by his or her supervisor. Therefore, the attorney might know very little about the details behind a particular deal. Thus, the attorney might draft a contract between a manufacturer and a retailer that appears legitimate but involves a series of unrecorded kickbacks about which the attorney knows nothing. Or an attorney might transcribe the details of a contract that involves a stock transaction based on insider trading without knowing anything about that insider's involvement in the deal. In the past, prosecuting attorneys were willing to give attorneys the benefit of the doubt. Today, however, such favoritism is fast becoming a thing of the past. In the current climate, prosecutors are less likely to be forgiving when an attorney should have known better about a suspicious contract or should have asked certain crucial questions that remained unspoken.

BusinessWeek **Business Law in the News**

Legal Affairs: In-House Attorneys, Watch Your Step

For most executives, a Chicago jury's decision on July 13 to convict former Hollinger International Inc. Chairman Conrad Black of fraud is a matter of curiosity, not concern. After all, the verdict matters little to managers who aren't busy ripping off their companies. But lawyers, particularly those employed by corporations, may find the results more troubling. That's because the same jury also convicted an in-house attorney—a comparatively rare event.

That attorney, Mark Kipnis, worked for Hollinger's U.S. unit in Chicago. By all accounts, he was a dedicated scrivener who followed orders while preparing a wide variety of documents. Among those transactions were the ones ultimately targeted by federal prosecutors: noncompete agreements connected with the sale of Hollinger publications that channeled millions directly into the pockets of Black and others. While Kipnis was charged as a participant in the fraud, he was never accused of helping conceive of it or of getting a penny of the payments. Essentially, Kipnis, 59, was charged as an enabler of deals he knew were crooked.

In most prosecutions of attorneys, the lawyer plays a more central role in the scheme than Kipnis did. Of 1,236 convictions obtained by a federal Corporate Fraud Task Force in the last five years, 23 were of corporate counsel. "There's a reluctance, usually, to go after lawyers," says George M. Cohen, a legal ethics expert at the University of Virginia School of Law. In part, he says, that's because it's hard to show that lawyers know all the details about the deals they work on.

For some observers, the Kipnis case sets disturbingly high expectations for in-house attorneys when it comes to recognizing when transactions are being used for corrupt purposes. Special-purpose entities like those used by Enron Corp. and noncompete deals like those in the Hollinger case can serve legitimate ends. Corporate counselors have long argued that they should not be presumed to be omniscient simply because they drafted documents. "I think this jury essentially criminalized Mark Kipnis' negligence for failing to ask questions of his client, and I think it sends a very frightening message to corporate counsel," says Hugh Totten, a litigation partner at Perkins Coie in Chicago who observed much of the trial in order to provide commentary to the media.

'A Real Challenge'

Now 59, Kipnis joined Hollinger in 1998. Prosecutors alleged Black concocted a scheme to demand noncompete payments from buyers of Hollinger publications, and then he and others pocketed the money without telling the board. Kipnis' role in drafting the noncompetes was so extensive, says juror Tina Kadisak, that "we definitely came to the conclusion that he did know what was going on." But jurors also felt bad for him, she says. "He got himself into something and then couldn't find a way out."

Indeed, Kipnis' predicament captures why Stephen Gillers, a New York University School of Law ethics professor, calls the job of in-house attorney "the most ethically challenged position in the American legal profession." That's because the client is the corporation, but the counselor gets told what to do by executives. "They have to be aware of the risk that their bosses are violating a duty to their clients, and it's a real challenge, because you don't want to accuse your boss of illegal activity," Gillers says.

Kipnis, who hasn't been able to find work as a lawyer since leaving Hollinger (now Sun-Times Media Group Inc.) in 2003, operates a Sign-A-Rama franchise in suburban Chicago. His attorney, Ronald S. Safer, plans to ask the judge to overturn the jury's verdict. The only legitimate criticism of his client, Safer says, "is that he was not as diligent as he should have been in getting all the ins and outs of every one of these transactions before the audit committee." The fact a jury considered that criminal conduct, he says, "is a frightening thought."

Juror Kadisak says the verdict sends a different message: "As much as you need to follow directions and do your job, if something doesn't seem right to you, you have to speak up or not do it."

Questions for Analysis

1. What criminal charges were brought against the attorney in this case?

2. Why has it been rare for prosecutors to bring charges against attorneys?

3. What is especially disturbing about this case?

4. Why has the job of an in-house council been labeled as "the most ethically challenged position in the American legal profession"?

5. What is the real underlying message in this case?

Source: Michael Orey, "Legal Affairs: In-House Attorneys, Watch Your Step: The Conviction of Conrad Black's Corporate Counsel Sends a Chilling Message," *BusinessWeek*, August 6, 2007, 36.

41-3 The Liability of Health Care Providers

Health care providers are professionals who possess the specialized knowledge, abilities, education, and experience that make it possible for them to answer some aspect of a patient's health care needs. Some businesspeople must deal with health care providers on a daily basis. Such contact is routine for hospital administrators, risk-management experts, pharmaceutical salespeople, hospital accountants, insurance adjusters, and biomedical equipment salespeople. Even individuals who do not deal regularly with health care providers in the business world may one day have to deal with them as patients. Knowledge of the liability of such professionals may be helpful in these situations.

The Professional Status of Health Care Providers

It should be obvious that physicians are professionals, because they must possess the specialized knowledge, abilities, education, and experience needed to perform their jobs. However, dentists, podiatrists, chiropractors, nurses, nurse practitioners, nurse technicians, radiologic technologists, respiratory therapists, and laboratory technicians are also considered health care professionals. All these professions are regulated by the state. In addition, most are regulated by independent professional organizations such as the American Society of Clinical Pathologists.

The Health Care Standard of Care

Unlike accountants, architects, and attorneys, health care professionals frequently must physically touch their patients. This physical touching can involve routine tests and examinations, as well as dangerous and painful procedures. To avoid liability for the intentional tort of battery, health care providers frequently must obtain the patient's written consent. In addition to intentional torts, health care providers might be vulnerable to charges of negligence if they do not follow the appropriate standard of care.

Consent Patients who undergo tests and treatment have the right to know about those procedures and the right to refuse to undergo them if they so desire. These rights impose a duty on the health care professional to seek the patient's consent. Consent takes two forms: general consent and informed consent. Upon entering a hospital, a patient automatically gives **general consent** for the routine tests and procedures that are needed for diagnosis and treatment. Although such consent is implied in the situation, many hospitals require patients to sign general consent forms (see Figure 41-1).

```
CONSENT UPON ADMISSION TO HOSPITAL


Patient _____    Date _____ a.m. _____ p.m. _____


(or _____ for _____ )
knowing that I, or the patient (am) (is) suffering from an illness requiring hospital care do hereby
voluntarily consent to such hospital care requiring an operation, diagnostic tests or therapeutic
treatment by Dr. _____ , his/her
assistant or his/her designee or as necessary according to his/her judgment.


I also recognize that during the course of my operation, tests, or therapy unforeseen conditions may
necessitate additional or different procedures and I am aware that inasmuch as the practice of
medicine and surgery is not an exact science, there have been no guarantees made to me as the
result of treatments or examinations to be performed in this hospital.


I have read the above statements and I certify that I understand them.




_____    _____
Witness                              Signature of Patient
```

Figure 41-1   Many hospitals today require patients to sign general consent forms like this one upon admission.

When a diagnostic test or a procedure will be dangerous or painful, the treating physician must obtain the patient's **informed consent**. For this type of consent, the physician must tell the patient in advance about the procedure and the risks involved. Informed consent must be in writing on a form that is signed by the patient and witnessed by a third party. Generally, a written consent form is considered valid by the court and precludes any suit based on battery, unless the patient can prove a lack of understanding of the information on the form or a deliberate misrepresentation as to its content.

Negligence   For a patient to succeed in a negligence case against a health care professional, the patient must show that the four elements of negligence exist in the case. First, the patient must demonstrate that the health care provider owed a duty to that patient. Usually, the question of duty is not at issue in such cases. However, the question will arise whenever the relationship between the patient and the health care provider is not clear-cut or obvious. In such cases, the court may be asked to determine whether the health care provider owed a duty to the plaintiff.

Second, after establishing the existence of a duty between the health care provider and the patient, the plaintiff must show that the health care professional breached that duty. The health care professional's duty is measured by his or her compliance with a standard of care. The health care provider must act with the same level of skill, care, and knowledge that any reasonable health care provider would display in a similar situation.

Determining how a reasonable health care provider would act in a given situation can be determined in several ways. One way is to refer to the hospital's policy and procedure manual. When professionals follow the standard policies and procedures as written in the manual, they are performing as any reasonable professional would, unless the procedure in the manual can be shown to be out of date, incompetently written, or incomplete in some way.

If a hospital's manual does not address a situation, if the manual is outdated, if the procedure is incompetently written, or if the steps in the procedure are incomplete, the court may judge the performance by going outside the hospital and looking at the manuals or procedures used at other hospitals. Many states today use a rule called the locality rule. The **locality rule** judges a health care provider's behavior on the basis of how other health care professionals in the same community would have acted in the same situation. Thus, rural physicians are compared to other rural physicians in the same rural community, city physicians with other city physicians in the same city, and so on. The rationale behind the locality doctrine is the commonsense notion that it is unfair to judge the professional conduct of a small-town general practitioner (GP) who is involved in a case involving a heart attack victim by comparing him or her to a big city cardiologist involved in a similar case. In such a comparison, the small-town GP will always be judged poorly, because he or she will have neither the educational opportunities nor the up-to-date facilities that are available to the big city cardiologist.

Despite the widespread use of the term "locality rule," there is no single locality doctrine. Instead, there are variations on the same theme. The most rigorous version of the doctrine is the true locality rule. The **true locality rule** requires the court to look at the standard of care used in the exact locality of the physician. This standard makes it very difficult for the plaintiff, who must use an expert witness from the same area as the defendant. Such experts are rarely forthcoming because the fraternity of local physicians is generally a closed group. A second variation on the locality rule is the **similar locality rule**. This rule permits the court to judge the actions of a local physician against those of a physician in a community of comparable size and socioeconomic character. Thus, a physician in New York would be compared to one in Chicago or Los Angeles, a physician in Cleveland with one in Pittsburgh or Buffalo, and a physician in Green Bay, Wisconsin, with one in South Bend, Indiana, or Dayton, Ohio. This rule permits the plaintiff to find an expert in one of those analogous localities an easier task because there are fewer fraternal ties among that class of physicians.

The third version of the locality rule is the **same state locality rule**. This rule, perhaps the least logical of the four variations, ignores the socioeconomic character of the physician's home base and concentrates instead on the geographical limits of a state border. Thus, a plaintiff who finds him- or herself in a state that honors the same state locality rule (there are only three: Arizona, Virginia, and Washington) can call an expert from any region in that state to testify as an expert witness. The final variation of the locality rule is known as the **similar practitioner rule**. This rule actually rests on a double standard that permits GPs to be judged by one criterion and specialists by another. Thus, GPs, who are apparently expected to stay close to home, are judged by other GPs in the same community, whereas specialists, who are expected to be more cosmopolitan and therefore more educated, more up-to-date, and more competent, are judged by a standard that can be applied anywhere in the country.

Those states that no longer use the locality rule have adopted another rule called the **national rule** or the **national standard**. These states have recognized that with the advent of continuing education requirements and the presence of mass communication, online continuing education programs, and the like, there is rarely any good reason for a health care professional to be unaware of the development of medical trends on a national, or, at times, even an international basis.

Causation in a Malpractice Suit A crucial element in any malpractice case is the issue of causation. In such a case, the plaintiff must prove not only that the defendant's conduct did not conform to acceptable medical practices but also that this failure to follow acceptable procedures was the cause of the plaintiff's injury. Much of the difficulty in supplying this proof arises because the fact finder in a malpractice case must attempt to understand medical evidence that is frequently beyond his or her experience.

Expert Testimony Because many of the tasks performed by the health care provider are highly specialized, determining how the professional should act often requires expert testimony. However, expert testimony is not required if the action under examination is within the common knowledge of all people.

EXAMPLE 41-5:   Experts Need Not Apply

Nurse Noel Grady was called away from Kurt Yarborough's room by another nurse. Yarborough was sedated but restless. He was thrashing about and had attempted to leave the bed several times. Despite this state, Grady left him alone, failing to raise the siderails or restrain Yarborough in any way. While Grady was absent, Yarborough tried to get out of bed. He fell and broke his leg. At Grady's negligence trial, the judge ruled that no expert testimony was needed to measure Grady's standard of care. The judge felt that the issue of whether a sedated and restless patient should be left unsupervised and unrestrained was well within the common knowledge of the jurors.

Medical Records and the Patient's Rights

In recent years, concerns about privacy matters have come to the forefront of the law. In no area of the law is this truer than in health care law. Physicians once effectively guarded the secrecy of their files by arguing that patients were apt to misinterpret or misunderstand notations made in medical jargon or hospital shorthand. These arguments are no longer acceptable. To ensure the patient's right to see his or her records, Congress passed the **Health Insurance Portability and Accountability Act (HIPAA)**. Under HIPAA, Congress has guaranteed that patients have the right to see their medical records and parents have the right to see the medical records of their children. The act also gives both groups the right to obtain duplicates of the records. There are, of course, exceptions to this rule. For instance, records that result from psychotherapy sessions receive a higher level of protection under the act. Patients are permitted to see such records only if the patient has the physician's permission. Even with permission, the patient must look through the records along with the physician. These extra limitations are placed on psychotherapy records because they are seen as somewhat emotional and open to a wide variety of false impressions.

The Health Insurance Portability and Accountability Act (HIPAA) gives patients the right to review their medical records and the records of their children.

41-4 Hospital Liability

Hospitals can be held liable for the negligence of a physician, even if that physician is not an employee of the hospital. Hospitals routinely grant physicians, who are not employed by the hospital, the privilege to treat their patients at that hospital. The granting of such **staff privileges** can be troublesome for the hospital if the staff physician becomes the defendant in a malpractice lawsuit, because the patient frequently sues not only the physician but also the hospital. Two legal theories that have been used successfully to add the hospital to the list of defendants in a malpractice lawsuit are ostensible authority and negligent credentialing.

Ostensible Authority and Hospital Liability

Ostensible authority, also known as agency by estoppel and apparent authority, has been successfully used by plaintiffs to hold the hospital, as well as the physician, liable for malpractice. **Ostensible authority** is created when a hospital presents itself to the public at large as a provider of health care services and in some way leads the patient to believe that a physician with staff privileges is an employee of the hospital. This authority can be shown if the hospital allows the physician to wear a hospital identification tag, use hospital equipment, dispense medication at the hospital, issue orders to hospital employees, and so on. Under such circumstances, the courts have been willing to hold that, because it is reasonable to believe that these representations would lead the patient to the conclusion that the physician is an employee of the hospital, the patient can add the hospital to the malpractice suit as a defendant.

Negligent Credentialing by Hospital Authorities

Negligent credentialing occurs if the hospital has retained a physician that the governing body of the hospital knew or should have known was incompetent. Another form of negligent credentialing occurs if a previously competent physician with staff privileges loses that competence and the hospital governing body knows or should have known about the changed circumstances but takes no remedial action. This form of negligent credentialing is sometimes referred to as **negligent retention**. In either situation, a patient injured by the malpractice of the incompetent physician can also hold the hospital liable.

Tort Reform and Litigation

In recent years, some states have attempted to lessen the burden placed on hospitals by ostensible authority and negligent credentialing. This movement has been motivated by the belief that such lawsuits frequently pull the hospital into a lawsuit unjustly. To alleviate this injustice, tort reform provisions often place the burden of proof on the plaintiff to prove both ostensible authority and negligent credentialing. For instance, in the area of ostensible authority, some states say that the plaintiff must prove that the hospital held itself out to the public at large as a provider of health care services and that the hospital gave no notice that nonemployee staff physicians, rather than hospital employees, would render services to the patient. Moreover, these statutes also allow the hospital to escape liability by posting notices that inform patients of the independent status of staff physicians. In states that have established such a statutory protection for hospitals, a patient can hold a hospital that posts such notices liable only if the hospital directed the negligent actions that injured the patient. In negligent credentialing, some states have created a rebuttable presumption that says a hospital is presumed to have properly credentialed staff physicians if the hospital is accredited by the Joint Commission of Accreditation of Health Care Organizations. If the hospital can show that it is accredited, the burden of proof shifts to the plaintiff to show that the hospital did not follow the credentialing procedures of the Joint Commission, that the hospital knew or should have known of the physician's incompetence and did nothing to limit the physician's privileges, or that the credentialing process did not apply to this hospital, this physician, or the type of case that formed the basis for the lawsuit.

Quick Quiz 41-4 True or False?

1. A hospital can never be held liable for the torts of a physician unless that physician is an employee of that hospital.

2. Ostensible authority applies only to hospitals in large urban areas.

3. Negligent credentialing and negligent retention have been outlawed under the Restatement (Second) of Torts.

Summary

41.1 Accountants are business professionals who can plan, direct, and evaluate the complex financial affairs of their clients. The most common types of accountants are certified public accountants and public accountants. Accountants must follow generally accepted accounting principles. Auditors must follow generally accepted auditing standards. They must also follow the Code of Professional Ethics of the AICPA. Accountants may be liable to both their clients and third parties.

41.2 Architects and attorneys are considered professionals and are regulated by the state. Architects may find themselves liable to clients and to third parties, whereas attorneys are generally responsible to their clients alone. Both architects and attorneys must exercise due care and skill in carrying out their professional duties.

41.3 The term *health care provider* includes not only physicians but also dentists, chiropractors, podiatrists, nurses, nurse practitioners, nurse technicians, radiologic technologists, respiratory therapists, and laboratory technicians. Like other professionals, health care providers must act with the same skill, care, and level of knowledge that a reasonable health care professional would display in a similar situation.

41.4   Hospitals can be held liable for the negligence of a physician, even if that physician is not an employee of the hospital. The granting of staff privileges can be troublesome for the hospital if the staff physician becomes the defendant in a malpractice lawsuit, because the patient can sue both the physician and the hospital. Two legal theories that have been used successfully to add the hospital to the list of defendants in a malpractice lawsuit are ostensible authority and negligent credentialing.

Key Terms

accountant, 861

adverse opinion, 863

attorney–client privilege, 872

audit, 862

Auditing Standards Board of the AICPA, 863

auditor, 862

certified public accountant (CPA), 862

Code of Professional Ethics, 863

cost of repair rule, 870

disclaimer, 863

general consent, 876

generally accepted accounting principles (GAAP), 862

generally accepted auditing standards (GAAS), 863

Health Insurance Portability and Accountability Act (HIPAA), 879

informed consent, 877

in-house attorney, 874

locality rule, 878

malpractice, 865

national rule, 878

national standard, 878

negligence, 865

negligent credentialing, 880

negligent retention, 880

ostensible authority, 880

professional, 861

public accountant (PA), 862

Public Company Accountability Oversight Board (PCAOB), 864

qualified opinion, 863

same state locality rule, 878

Sarbanes-Oxley Act, 864

similar locality rule, 878

similar practitioner rule, 878

staff privileges, 880

true locality rule, 878

unqualified opinion, 863

work product privilege, 872

Questions for Review and Discussion

1. What is the difference between a certified public accountant and a public accountant?
2. What is the difference between generally accepted accounting principles and generally accepted auditing standards?
3. What are the various types of auditing opinions that can be issued by auditors?
4. What duties do accountants owe to their clients?
5. What are the registration requirements imposed on architects?
6. What are the duties that an architect owes to his or her clients?
7. What are the duties that an attorney owes to his or her clients?
8. What is the standard of care used to judge health care professionals?
9. What is the difference between the locality rule and the national standard in determining a health care provider's liability?
10. What are the circumstances in which hospitals can be held liable for the torts of independent contractor physicians?

Investigating the Internet

Access the Web site of the American Bar Association and search for the link to the ABA's Center for Professional Responsibility. Once there, search the site for answers to the following questions regarding the ABA's new Model Rules of Professional Conduct: (1) When were the ABA Model Rules of Professional Conduct first adopted by the ABA House of Delegates? (2) What was the name of the preceding set of professional rules used by the ABA, and what was the name of the first such set of rules? (3) Which states have not adopted the new ABA Model Rules of Professional Conduct? (4) Which state was the first to adopt the ABA Model Rules, and when did that state adoption occur? Which state was the most recent state to adopt the ABA Model Rules, and when did that state adoption occur? (5) What is the title of the book that the ABA recommends as the definitive history of the Model Rules of Professional Conduct?

Cases for Analysis

1. While she was under investigation by a grand jury, Martha Stewart penned an e-mail that explained the circumstances that led to the ImClone scandal. Stewart then dispatched the e-mail to her attorney, and sent a copy to her daughter, Alexis Stewart. The e-mail was inadvertently provided to the government, along with a number of other files that had been delivered in response to a subpoena. When the e-mail was identified, government attorneys went back to the court and asked the judge to decide whether they could use the e-mail as evidence. Stewart's attorneys argued that the e-mail was under the protection of the attorney–client privilege and the work product privilege. On the other side of that argument, it is clear that the intended recipient of the e-mail was Stewart's daughter, not her attorney. Should the judge uphold the protection granted by the attorney–client privilege and the work product privilege, or should she allow the government to use the e-mail, because Stewart sent it to a third party? Explain. *United States v. Stewart*, 03 Cr. 717 (United States District Court Southern District of New York).

2. Fred Stern and Company applied to the Ultramares Loan Corporation for a credit advance in support of its import business. As was its custom, Ultramares asked Stern for a detailed financial statement that included an audited balance sheet. Stern agreed and supplied Ultramares with a report from its auditors, Touche, Niven, and Company. When Stern went to Touche, Niven, and Company, the import corporation did not reveal to the accounting firm that Ultramares would see the report. The only thing that the importers told the auditors was that the report would be shown to some possible creditors. Touche, Niven, and Company filed an audit report that stated Stern had a net worth of $1 million. Satisfied with the statement, Ultramares loaned the money to Stern. The report turned out to be completely false. Fred Stern and Company was not only worth less than $1 million; it was actually completely worthless. The auditors had filed the erroneous report because Stern had shown them a phony set of books that misrepresented the company's value. The importer, of course, could not hope to pay Ultramares back for the money it had borrowed, so the loan company went after someone who actually had enough money to make up for their loss, and that was the accounting firm of Touche, Niven, and Company. The firm argued that the report had been prepared for Stern, and because it had no knowledge that Ultramares would see the report, it could not be liable to the loan company. Apply each of the standards used to evaluate an accounting firm's liability to third parties and report on the results for each test in this case. *Ultramares Corp. v. Touche*, 255 N.Y. 70, 174 N.E. 441.

3. The Consolidata Services Company (CDS) was established to provide small businesses with payroll services. All CDS clients were required to provide CDS with an advance deposit equal to the amount of one payroll. When CDS got into a cash flow problem, it tapped into some of this deposit money to cover its own debts. Eventually, the accounting firm of Alexander Grant, which had been hired by CDS to advise it on taxes and other financial matters, discovered that the deposit account was $150,000 short. CDS assured Grant that it was devising a plan to cover the missing $150,000. Accordingly, CDS asked Grant not to reveal the deficit. Nevertheless, Grant informed several of its own clients using the CDS payroll services and other nonclients of CDS's problem. Was Alexander Grant correct in revealing the information? What guidelines did the court use to answer this question? Explain. *Wagenheim v. Alexander Grant and Co.,* 482 N.E.2d 955 (OH).

4. Burke, an energy tycoon, hired the accounting firm of Arthur Young and Company to audit several of his operations. The SEC brought an action against Burke for fraud and for failure to meet certain SEC reporting requirements. The SEC also named Arthur Young as a defendant, claiming that the accounting firm should have discovered the fraud. Arthur Young argued that it had followed GAAS when it had audited Burke. The accounting firm concluded that this strict adherence to GAAS immunized it from liability under securities law. The SEC argued that Arthur Young should have done more to discover the fraud than what was required under GAAS. Was the SEC correct? Explain. *Securities and Exchange Commission v. Arthur Young and Company,* 590 F.2d 785 (9th Cir.).

5. Hutchins and O'Neil, as general partners in the Haddon View Investment Co., became limited partners in Car Wash Investments. The general partner in Car Wash was the Minit Man Development Company. Coopers and Lybrand were the accountants who handled the accounting work for both Minit Man and Car Wash. They performed audits and prepared financial statements that allegedly revealed two healthy companies. Nevertheless, both Car Wash and Minit Man went out of business. As a result, Hutchins and O'Neil lost a total of $252,000. They sued Coopers and Lybrand, alleging malpractice, breach of contract, concealment, fraud, and deceit in the accountants' work for Car Wash and Minit Man. Coo-

pers and Lybrand argued that Hutchins and O'Neil could not sue them because Car Wash and Minit Man were their clients, not Hutchins and O'Neil. Were the accountants correct? *Haddon View Investment Co. v. Coopers and Lybrand,* 436 N.E.2d 212 (OH).

6. Bainbridge hired the architectural firm of Seymour, Shaefer, and Lashutke to draw up plans for the alteration of Bainbridge's office building in Albuquerque, New Mexico. The plans called for the removal of the paneling in parts of the building and its replacement with Maxwell-Plus, a new, more durable material. Maxwell-Plus was specifically recommended by the architects as the best product on the market. From the beginning, the contractor had difficulty with the installation of Maxwell-Plus. In addition, two months after the work was completed, the new paneling began to deteriorate rapidly. Investigation indicated that Seymour, Shaefer, and Lashutke had failed to consider the dry, arid climate of Albuquerque, for which Maxwell-Plus was totally unsuitable. Bainbridge had to have the paneling replaced at a cost of $122,532. Subsequently, he sued the architects. Seymour, Shaefer, and Lashutke argued that they were not liable to Bainbridge because the total value of the building had not been altered by their alleged error. Were the architects correct? Explain.

7. Craybaugh worked as a research scientist for National Research Industries, Inc. While conducting a field experiment involving a new solar energy converter, something went amiss and the converter exploded, injuring several bystanders. Craybaugh was also injured. While she was being treated in the company infirmary, several attorneys from National's legal department arrived on the scene, told Craybaugh they were representing her, and took her confidential statement. They later turned the statement over to the district attorney, and Craybaugh ended up facing criminal charges. Craybaugh and her mother joined as plaintiffs in a suit against the attorneys in the legal department. What duty or duties may have been violated by the attorneys? Was the mother a proper party in this lawsuit? Why or why not?

8. Malcolm was a physician who ran a small private practice in Harrison, Kansas. One evening, the Sandersons brought their young daughter in for treatment of what they thought was a minor throat infection. Dr. Malcolm treated her with a standard antibiotic and sent the child home. What neither

Dr. Malcolm nor the Sandersons knew was that the child had contracted a rare and often fatal blood disease. The disease, Seballian Syndrome, could only be treated with a new antibiotic called Veritrium. Had the Sanderson child been treated with Veritrium in a timely manner, her illness would have been short lived, and she would have suffered no permanent damage. As it was, the inaccurate diagnosis and the ill-advised treatment initiated by Dr. Malcolm actually made the child worse and almost caused her untimely death. Although the child eventually recovered, her hearing was permanently damaged. The Sandersons initiated a malpractice suit against Dr. Malcolm. The doctor argued that because of her location in the remote section of Kansas, she should not be expected to be as up to date on modern techniques as physicians who practice in large metropolitan areas. Furthermore, she argued that she could not have known about the new treatment and should therefore not be held liable. Is the physician correct? Explain.

Quick Quiz Answers

41-1	41-2	41-3	41-4
1. T	1. T	1. T	1. F
2. F	2. F	2. T	2. F
3. F	3. T	3. F	3. F

Chapter 42 Electronic Law

The Opening Case

Who Was Who in the "Whois" Database?

As is true of any newly developing area of the law, electronic law is filled with controversy. One recent controversy surrounds an electronic file called the "Whois" database. Despite its mysterious sounding name, the "Whois" database is nothing more than an "electronic phonebook" that catalogs the identities of people and businesses that own domain names. A domain name is the Internet address of a business or an individual. The names begin with the letters "www" and are completed with the familiar ".com," ".edu," or ".net" endings, among others. The agency that controls the content and the availability of the "Whois" database is the Internet Corporation for Assigned Names and Numbers, or ICANN. The "Whois" database has always been completely open and easily accessible on the Web. Thus, anyone who wanted to know the identity of the owner of a domain name could simply tap into the database to get the owner's identity. Some domain name owners have objected to this process however, so ICANN has considered the advisability of concealing that information and forcing a searcher to go to an in-between connection to obtain the identity of the domain name owner. Supporters of the new protective measures indicate that the current system is so open and accessible that it amounts to a direct and undeniable invasion of privacy. Those who oppose the new protections, however, see the "Whois" database as an invaluable tool in the campaign to find and punish cybersquatters and other electronic offenders who either extort money from the real owners of certain trademark names or use the domain name to lead buyers to phony merchandise, X-rated Web sites, or other Internet locations for personal profit. Yet legitimate domain name holders who are listed in the "Whois" database frequently find themselves victimized by unreasonable inquiries, spying, cyberstalking, and in some extreme cases even identity theft. Those who prefer the openness of the present system point to the costly setbacks and postponements that would occur should trademark holders be forced to go after cybersquatters and other illegitimate domain name holders in an indirect and roundabout way. Regardless of who is correct in this debate, one thing is certain—someone will be unsatisfied with the result. (See L. Marek, "Web Site Owners May Get Tougher to Find: Proposal Could Aid Infringers on Net," *The National Law Journal*, February 26, 2007, pp. 1, 18.)

Opening Case Questions

1. What is a domain name?

2. What is the "Whois" database?

3. What is the traditional policy regarding listings in the "Whois" database?

4. What are the arguments supporting a change?

5. What are the arguments supporting the status quo?

 Learning Objectives

1. Clarify the basic nature of electronic law.
2. Explain the nature of electronic trespass.
3. List electronic crimes that are committed with a computer and those committed against computers.
4. Describe the nature of an electronic tort.
5. Distinguish between electronic defamation and electronic invasion of privacy.
6. List statutes that are involved in electronic contract law.
7. Describe how trademark infringement relates to e-law.
8. Judge when trade secret protection will be provided for computer programs.
9. List statutes that are involved in electronic copyright protection.
10. Judge when patent protection can be obtained for a computer program.

42-1 Electronic Crimes

Computers have become an integral part of our lives, and the law has been forced to deal with this reality. The area of law that pertains to computers and their related difficulties is known as **electronic law** or **e-law**. Electronic law is so new that it still has a variety of different names. Legal experts refer to it variously as **cyberlaw**, e-law, and **computer law**. A decade ago, there was no such thing as e-law. Instead, the law governing computers was a mismatched hodge-podge of principles, doctrines, and theories, loosely hammered together from other legal disciplines. Today, though e-law is not yet completely autonomous, it has nevertheless begun to develop its own rules, statutes, and precedents. Thus, it is becoming more and more common to talk about e-law as if it were *sui generis*, that is, a law unto itself. Even though e-law has a long way to go before it is officially *sui generis*, it can be thought of today as having its own identity.

The term "electronic crime" is fast becoming a part of our everyday vocabulary. More-over, the increased attention that politicians, the media, and law enforcement agencies have given to crimes against computers and those committed using computers means that most people are aware of this type of criminal activity, even if they do not know what to call it. A cursory glance at any newspaper or newsmagazine will reveal articles, columns, editorials, and letters to the editor that touch daily on a wide variety of computer issues. To initiate an exploration of electronic crime, it is best to begin by defining a few essential terms.

Electronic Crimes and Electronic Trespass

Because of the multijurisdictional nature of the American legal system, there is no single way to deal with electronic crime. It is safe to begin, however, by noting that an **electronic crime** is any criminal activity that is associated with a computer. This definition includes crimes that are committed by using a computer, such as electronic blackmail, and crimes that are committed against a computer, such as electronic terrorism or electronic germ warfare. Some states have dealt with the problem of defining electronic crimes by simply folding the traditional criminal code into the electronic crime lexicon. This approach is termed electronic trespass. **Electronic trespass** is the use of a computer or other electronic device to commit any crime defined within the conventional criminal code. In any jurisdiction using the electronic trespass approach, there is no need to have a separate definition for a crime like electronic extortion. The electronic trespass statute simply assumes that if extortion is committed using a computer, then the rules, definitions, and penalties associated with extortion by nonelectronic means apply to extortion committed by computer.

Electronic Crimes Executed with Computers

The second way to deal with electronic crime is to create individual crimes associated directly with the computer. Although this technique is time consuming and difficult, some jurists prefer it over the electronic trespass approach because criminal law must involve narrowly drawn and specifically written statutes, because some crimes are punishable by imprisonment and others by death. Specificity and exactness are also required in criminal law, because the accused has the right to know exactly what behavior is prohibited by the criminal code. For this reason, some states have added crimes to their criminal codes that heretofore existed only in law review articles. Such innovative crimes include electronic extortion, electronic stalking, electronic spoofing, and electronic piracy.

Electronic Extortion
Electronic extortion, **e-extortion**, or **cyberextortion**, as it is sometimes called, can happen when a hacker gains access to the computer records of an individual, a business firm, or some other type of organization and uncovers illegal, reckless, negligent, unethical, or embarrassing conduct that would damage the image or the financial status of that individual, company, or institution. Often the hacker contacts the victim and threatens to reveal the damaging information unless he or she receives a payoff of some sort. A talented but unprincipled hacker could make an enormous amount of money from those people and institutions willing to meet his or her unscrupulous demands. Computer users who spend a great deal of time in chatrooms are especially susceptible to the tricks of the electronic blackmailer. Electronic blackmailers will gain the confidence of a fellow chatroom regular and then elicit private information that can be used to extort money from the victim. Electronic blackmailers might also demand payments from a business to prevent the hacker from shutting down the company's computer system and thus effectively destroying the ability of that firm to do business.

Electronic Stalking
Electronic stalking is closely associated with electronic extortion. Electronic stalking sometimes comes before, after, or during the electronic extortion process. **Electronic stalking** involves targeting vulnerable individuals by tracking their computer transactions, personal records, and communication habits and then using those transactions, records, and habits to victimize the innocent party. Again, chatroom regulars are the target of choice for the electronic stalker, who acts as the victim's confidant and then arranges a face-to-face meeting with the victim to take advantage of him or her in some way.

Electronic Spoofing
Although electronic spoofing may sound harmless, it is actually a very serious crime. In **electronic spoofing**, the perpetrator uses a computer to assume another computer user's identity to carry out a crime. A simple form of electronic spoofing involves adopting the identity of an e-mailer to defraud recipients of the original e-mailer's messages. Another type of electronic spoofing involves creating a phony Web site to obtain credit card numbers, debit card numbers, passwords, and other confidential information to

commit a wide variety of crimes, such as investment fraud, credit card fraud, pyramid schemes, and so on. Sometimes electronic spoofers create their own Web sites. More often, however, they find a way to divert consumers from a legitimate Web site to one with a similar name or address. The electronic spoofer can then promise to send merchandise that appears on the genuine Web site while confiscating the funds used to "buy" the actual merchandise. Another form of electronic spoofing involves online auction houses such as eBay. Although most auction house sellers and buyers are legitimate, some are not. Phony sellers can promise merchandise that they never deliver. Some electronic spoofers may actually bid on their own phony items, thus raising the final bid on items that are never sent to the auction winner. Another electronic spoofing method involves sending out phony e-mails that solicit buyers and, in the process, obtaining credit card information, account numbers, passwords, and the like. This last technique, for obvious reasons, is called **phishing**.

Mark Nichols sits in his home office in Crosby, N.D., Friday, March 26, 2004. Nichols was duped by an e-mail scam that fooled him into submitting his eBay password and other personal information to a phony Web site.

Electronic Piracy   The crime of **electronic piracy** involves using a computer or other electronic device to create at least one, but usually more than one, illegal duplicate of data stored in a digital format. The copied data can include, but are not strictly limited to, software. The downloading or transmission of unauthorized copies over the Internet or within an intranet would also be considered electronic piracy. Stripped down to its simplest form, electronic piracy is nothing more than theft. The fact that electronic piracy is the theft of intellectual property rather than the theft of money or goods probably makes it more, rather than less, reprehensible.

Electronic Crimes That Focus on Computers

Another way to deal with electronic crime is to single out those crimes that target computers to disable the entire system that they operate or steal secret information or data stored within the system. Sometimes the data are stolen, and then the original computer's memory is erased. This procedure makes the stolen data that much more important to the innocent computer user. Crimes that target computers include electronic terrorism, identity theft, electronic vandalism, and electronic germ warfare.

Electronic Terrorism   An act of **electronic terrorism** involves operating a computer to disrupt or destroy one or more of the critical elements of the national electronic infrastructure. These elements include the national or a regional power grid, the air traffic control system, any urban water or sanitation system, ground transportation systems such as railroad or subway systems, national stock markets, the national weather service, the postal service, the banking system, a harbor system, and/or the national defense system. Electronic terrorists can use any number of techniques to enter and disrupt these systems. They might, for instance, send a virus into a vital computer network that causes the entire infrastructure to collapse. Or hackers might enter a single system to establish false Web sites, to misdirect or falsify e-mails, to destroy data streams, to disrupt calendaring programs, to erase stored data, or to vandalize Internet service providers. Hackers might also enter a system to destroy a Web site so that legitimate users can no longer access that site. The banking system and the stock market are obvious targets for such attacks. Electronic terrorists might also seek out crucial corporate electronic systems for attack to shut down vital national industries.

Identity Theft In **identity theft**, the electronic criminal, using one of the techniques noted previously, steals credit card information, financial and personal data, passwords, access code numbers, and debit card information. The e-criminal then uses this stolen information to impersonate the innocent party. Using this technique, the identity thief can clean out bank accounts, run up credit card transactions, divert cash transfers, and generally disrupt the financial and the personal life of the victim. What is especially insidious about identity theft is that it sometimes takes the victim months or even years to reestablish his or her own credit, employment, housing, and personal history with banks, credit unions, department stores, credit card companies, schools, and even the government itself. The damage done by identity theft can therefore last far beyond the immediate monetary loss in such transgressions. Often overlooked in identity theft is the fact that the innocent party is not the only victim. Those banking institutions, credit card companies, and department stores involved in the theft are also victims, because they can be left "holding the bag."

Electronic Vandalism Gifted but unprincipled electronic vandals can disrupt a computer system so thoroughly that an entire Web site crashes or is so totally paralyzed that the legitimate owner of the Web site can no longer function properly. This type of operation is referred to as **electronic vandalism**. E-vandalism might be implemented to undermine the operation of a business as revenge for real or imaginary transgressions, to exercise power, or to injure the owner of a business. Unlike e-terrorism, which often has a political end, and electronic extortion and electronic spoofing, which have financial goals, electronic vandalism, like other forms of vandalism, is often performed on a dare, to gain attention, or just to show that the electronic vandals can get away with it.

BusinessWeek **Business Law in the News**

How Secure Is Your Domain?

When Kevin Medina and John Naruszewicz joined forces nine years ago, the Internet was like an untamed frontier. There was little to discourage Medina, the owner of an office-cleaning business in New Jersey, from joining the dot-com gold rush. The tiny company they started, RegisterFly.com Inc., ultimately became a midsize registrar of Internet addresses for more than 200,000 customers, including entertainer Michael Jackson. Now a messy fight between the two for control has brought RegisterFly to its knees and prompted angry calls for better oversight of the Web registry industry.

The RegisterFly.com saga sheds light on a little-understood but vital corner of the Internet. Domain-name registrars receive fees from individuals and businesses to record Web names that start with "www" and end with ".com," and ".net" or the like. The registration industry has grown at a gallop, from 145 players in 2000 to more than 860 last year. Many operate smoothly, charging a few dollars to register new names, renew annual registrations, or transfer them, then pass that information on to a handful of registries that keep master lists of names.

But some unruly outfits have also appeared, while the industry goes virtually unregulated. "We need to tame the wild West and bring control and regulation to this business," says Sam Flanders, president of 2wmc.com Consulting Group Inc. and a RegisterFly.com customer.

After months of customer complaints about poor service, RegisterFly's problems came to a boil in February when Naruszewicz and another company director fired Medina as chief executive. They accused him of stealing from customers to pay for luxury cars, a penthouse apartment in Miami's posh South Beach, and a liposuction operation.

Medina, who denies the accusations, regained the helm on Mar. 9 after a U.S. Disrict Court judge ruled that he was the sole owner. But in the meantime the company Web site was operating fitfully. Some 75,000 customers had lost control or their domain names, according to a court filing. Many are trying to transfer their accounts to other registrars but haven't been able to get RegisterFly to respond.

"Train Wreck"

RegisterFly customers aren't just mad at the company. They fault the International Corporation for Assigned Names & Numbers (ICANN), a private nonprofit organization sanctioned by the U.S. and other nations to accredit registrars, for not moving fast enough to investigate and take action. It was only after a year of eroding service that ICANN on Feb. 21 threatened to revoke RegisterFly's accreditation. "ICANN knew what was going on, yet they waited and let this train wreck happen," says Philip J. Corwin, counsel for the International Commerce Assn., which represents companies that own domain names.

   ICANN insists it acted as quickly as possible. Until February, the organization lacked evidence that RegisterFly had violated its contract with ICANN by failing to pay fees and by replacing the names of the registrees with Kevin Medina's name, according to ICANN. The group gave RegisterFly a deadline of Mar. 14 to set things right or face de-accreditation. But ICANN, based in Marina del Rey, Calif., has limited powers. The U.S. Commerce Dept. asked it to monitor the operations of registrars, not oversee customer consumer complaints.

   Still, the organization sees the RegisterFly mess as a call to action. Paul Twomey, ICANN's chief executive, plans on proposing reforms at a meeting of ICANN's board and interested parties in Lisbon during the week of Mar. 26. For one thing, he would like ICANN to have more say over the actvities of companies . . . known as resellers, who also sell domain names.

Questions for Analysis

1. What wrongful, perhaps even criminal, acts is the owner and chief executive of RegisterFly.com accused of committing? Explain.

2. What additional, computer-related wrongful acts or crimes might be related to the domain name problem? Explain.

3. Because it acts as an accrediting body, could ICANN be resonsible for any crimes that might have been committed by the chief executive while he was working for RegisterFly? Explain.

4. Because it acts as an accrediting body, could ICANN be resonsible for any torts that might have been committed by the chief executive while he was working for RegisterFly? Explain.

5. Do you see any potential privacy issues in this case? Explain.

Source: Steve Hamm and Megan Tucker, "How Secure is Your Domain? Problems at RegistryFly.com Shed Light on Loose Oversight of Net Addresses," *BusinessWeek,* March 26, 2007, 118.

Electronic Germ Warfare   When perpetrators use viruses to enter and destroy a computer system, they are engaged in **electronic germ warfare**. Clearly, viruses can be employed to attack a computer system and commit several of the electronic crimes explained previously. An electronic extortionist can, for example, threaten to unleash a virus that might cripple a company's computer system unless that company pays a certain sum of money to the e-criminal. In effect, the electronic extortionist is using the virus to extract a ransom from the business. Likewise, an e-terrorist or e-vandal could employ a virus to upset a computer system for psychological motives or political reasons. However, unleashing a virus into a system for no reason other than personal viciousness is also an e-crime. Viruses are especially destructive because they are often undetectable until the damage has been done. Viruses are also particularly treacherous because they can affect a single computer, a business intranet, or even the entire Internet itself.

Quick Quiz 42-1 True or False?

1. Electronic trespass is the use of a computer or other electronic device as an instrumentality to victimize through any crime as defined within the conventional criminal code.

2. Phishing involves sending out phony e-mails that solicit buyers and, in the process, obtaining credit card information, account numbers, and passwords.

3. E-blackmail includes operating a computer to disrupt or destroy one or more of the critical elements of the national electronic infrastructure.

42-2 Electronic Torts

The rapid development of computer science has changed the operation of the judicial–economic system in many ways, from the way we communicate to the way we conduct ourselves in the marketplace. Computers and their technological cousins, the mobile phone, the videocam, the fax machine, and the phonecam, have made our lives more convenient, more efficient, and, in many situations, easier. However, these innovations have also inspired the villainous among us to create new and different tactics for committing torts. The term electronic tort has been coined to cover those torts that either use or target a computer.

The Basics of Electronic Tort Law

A tort is a private wrong that injures another party. Generally, such injuries involve bodily harm, emotional suffering, property damage, and/or the ruin of the victim's reputation. The objective of tort law is to compensate the victim for the harm caused by the tortfeasor. The tortfeasor is the one who commits a tort. In electronic law, electronic torts are different from most other torts, because they are always somehow entangled with information. An **electronic tort** or **e-tort** can be described as the invasion, distortion, theft, falsification, destruction, misuse, deletion, or exploitation of data stored in or associated with an electronic mechanism, including desktop PCs, laptops, notebooks, mobile phones, phonecams, videocams, personal digital assistants (PDAs), mainframes, and home computers that are isolated or integrated into an intranet or the Internet. It would be highly unusual for an electronic tort to involve a physical injury to the victim. However, it can often happen that the victim's reputation is damaged because of a false report distributed via e-mail, that the victim's emotional health is disturbed because of an invasion of his or her privacy, or that the innocent party's financial condition is disrupted because his or her identity has been confiscated. The focus here will be on two intentional torts: electronic defamation and electronic invasion of property.

Electronic Defamation

Like all forms of defamation, electronic defamation is the communication of false and destructive data about a person that harms that person's reputation. The essential difference between defamation and cyberdefamation is that, in **electronic defamation**, the false and destructive information is transmitted by an electronic device. What is most interesting about e-defamation is that in most cases, the courts have limited, rather than expanded, liability for defamation using a computer. Such was not always the case. When the courts first faced these issues, they usually ruled in favor of the victim. For instance, in the now famous Prodigy case, the court easily extended liability for defamation from the instigating party to the Prodigy Service Company, the firm that had set up and controlled the defendant's Internet service.

This case, however, represented only the first volley fired in the battle over e-defamation. The second round was fired by Congress, which passed the Communications Decency Act (CDA). One of the express objectives of the CDA is to protect Internet service providers (ISPs) from future defamation lawsuits for false statements posted by other individuals on the Internet. Still, the law by itself has not halted the proliferation of electronic defamation lawsuits that attempt to hold ISPs liable for defamatory statements. In one especially telling case, America Online was found not responsible for defamation, even though the plaintiff clearly demonstrated that the provider knew about the defamatory nature of a posting and had not removed the posting with proper haste. In addition, the protection granted to ISPs has gone beyond protecting those who post defamatory comments. The courts have also decided that ISPs are not responsible when hackers introduce viruses into a computer system, when piracy is permitted to occur, and when an invasion of privacy takes place via the ISP's link.

Electronic Invasion of Privacy

An **electronic invasion of privacy** results from an unwelcome and unwanted intrusion into the private matters of an individual when the intrusion is carried out or sustained by an electronic device. Because computer science is itself in a constant state of change, it should not be a surprise to discover that the principles of e-law, as they relate to privacy, are also in a highly unsettled state. Nevertheless, there are still some general points that can be made in relation to e-invasion of privacy. The first of these points explores the principles of privacy.

Principles of Privacy   The right to privacy is not explicitly mentioned in the United States Constitution. Nevertheless, the law has long recognized the existence of a right to privacy in both common law and constitutional law.

Revelation of Private Computer Records   Today, the revelation of private records often involves an invasion of information stored in a computer file. Most invasions that affect private records pertain to employees who, because of their jobs, work closely with confidential files, such as medical, financial, scholastic, or employment records. A failure to protect such records, whether they are stored in a computer or on paper, can result in an invasion of privacy lawsuit. Nevertheless, some courts have held that records stored as data in a computer require a degree of protection that is greater than the protection given to paper records because paper records can be hidden away or locked in a filing cabinet, whereas computer records are easy to retrieve, compile, and disseminate. Still, not every claim of a computer-related invasion of privacy automatically translates into a successful lawsuit. The law is still unsettled in several key areas, not the least of which is the question of whether ISPs are permitted to protect the privacy rights of their subscribers.

Private Privacy versus Public Privacy

Most of the time, **private information**, or **private-private information**, as it is sometimes called, includes reports on personal matters, family relationships, sexual habits, employment records, medical data, and financial records. However, the law also recognizes a fundamental difference between **private privacy** and **public privacy**. The law is familiar with private privacy concerns about matters such as health concerns, sexual preferences, family matters, and so on. However, the computer age has given rise to another privacy concern, that is, the concern over the publication of what is essentially public information, or what has been termed public-privacy matters. Some jurists and many private citizens are convinced that computer records require a higher degree of protection than paper records because paper records can be physically hidden in a drawer or locked in a safe, but computer records are easy to locate, retrieve, compile, and disseminate.

A very vivid example of the belief in the right to protect public-private matters occurred in the 1990s, when a company called Lotus Development suggested putting together a CD-ROM that would list over 120 million Americans. The proposed list would include the individuals' names, addresses, phone numbers, marital status, age, educational background, income, buying habits, employment status, and so on. All of the information that would have been included on the CD was essentially "public" information, easily obtained by examining public records. Yet there was a huge outcry from the public against the plan. The cry was so loud and so strong that Lotus never issued the CD-ROM package. The lesson to be learned from the Lotus case is that the computer age has given rise to new privacy concerns about how public-private matters are stored and disseminated. The public-privacy principle is based on two suppositions: (1) Privacy rules must be applied to some public information, or at least to the way information is compiled, stored, retrieved, and disseminated; and (2) there is a substantial difference between isolated bits of public information and the compilation of that same information in a database that can be easily stored, retrieved, and disseminated by businesses, educational institutions, and the government.

Data Mining of Public-Private Information

Data mining occurs when someone associates two or more pieces of public information to create information that the subject considers private, despite the public nature of the data from which the private information is obtained. The issue here is whether mining public information to uncover private matters is a violation of an individual's right to privacy. Some commentators have argued that an individual's privacy is invaded if, in obtaining the individually separate pieces of public information, the alleged tortfeasor ignores or bypasses the victim's consent and produces a piece of hybrid information, information referred to as **public-private information**, that embarrasses, disturbs, or financially injures the innocent party. In such a situation, these commentators argue that the innocent party should have a cause of action against the data miner, at least to the extent that the innocent party can show harm.

EXAMPLE 42-1:   ATMs, Video Cameras, and Data Mining

George Filmore was an avid biker who regularly rode his bicycle into town to do his daily errands. One of those errands involved stopping at the ATM outside a local branch of the Buckeye National Bank. The ATM contained a video camera that photographed individuals as they activated the computerized system. Shortly after one of his usual stops at the ATM, Filmore discovered that he was being inundated with advertisements, telemarketing phone calls, and e-mail spam, selling a wide variety of products for bicyclists. Eventually, Filmore discovered that one of the bank's subsidiaries owned and operated a sports equipment company that regularly accessed the videos produced at the ATMs around the country and used the information to target potential buyers. This particular instance of data mining may not have financially hurt Filmore, but it did annoy him enough for him to send a nasty letter of protest to the bank, to close all of his accounts, and to move his money into a bank that assured him it did not routinely data mine its customers.

In the Filmore case in Example 42-1, the various pieces of information that the bank mined included Filmore's address, phone number, e-mail address, bank account balance, and his hobby as a bicyclist. Arguably, all of these pieces of information taken individually are public. The privacy rights emerge because the public pieces of information have been mined to produce a valuable piece of public-private information that was exploited by the bank and its subsidiary without Filmore's approval and in a way that enraged him. Unfortunately, there is little case law concerning public-privacy rights. Moreover, the law that does exist militates against the firm establishment of a public-privacy right, at least at the present time.

Statutory Protections and Violations of Privacy

Despite appearances to the contrary, the government has not been totally oblivious to the computerized trafficking in public-private and private-private information that has occurred in recent years. In fact, the government has enacted several statutes to deal with certain aspects of these privacy invasions. These acts include the Fair Credit Reporting Act, the Right to Financial Privacy Act, the Electronic Communications Privacy Act, and the Driver's Privacy Protection Act. As is usually the case, however, the government has also found new ways to violate the privacy rights of its citizens. Perhaps the most controversial federal law responsible for many of these potential violations is the USA PATRIOT Act.

The Fair Credit Reporting Act
The Fair Credit Reporting Act involves records kept by credit bureaus, most of which now use computers to store data about consumers. Credit reports, by their very nature, include information that can be issued to businesses, insurance companies, banks, and employers. Under the act, credit bureaus must inform people about the nature of the information that is in their files. The act also gives people the right to change any inaccurate information found in their files. In addition, the credit bureau is responsible for sending notices to businesses and others who have received reports containing inaccurate data.

The Right to Financial Privacy Act
The Right to Financial Privacy Act forbids financial institutions from opening customer records, most of which are kept on computer files, to the government without appropriate authorization from the customer or without an official court order of some sort. In addition, if the government asks for a client's financial information, the institution must inform the client about the invasion of his or her records. The client then has the right to contest the intrusion as an unwarranted violation of his or her privacy rights. Naturally, none of these restrictions actually stops either the government or the financial institution itself from investigating allegations of wrongdoing on the part of the client.

The Electronic Communications Privacy Act
The Electronic Communications Privacy Act was designed to add additional electronic communication techniques, such as e-mail transmissions, to the list of illegal wire-tapping prohibitions. Unfortunately, a number of exceptions to this general rule were also added to the statute, allowing employers to monitor the e-mail transmissions of their employees. One of these exceptions permits an employer to monitor the e-mail transmissions of employees if those employees consent to the surveillance. Another exception allows surveillance if the e-mail transmissions are carried out in the ordinary course of business.

The Driver's Privacy Protection Act
The Driver's Privacy Protection Act was added to the Violent Crime Control and Law Enforcement Act of 1994. The goal of the statute was to give drivers the opportunity to pass up the "opportunity" to be placed on any lists that the motor vehicle bureau might distribute to businesses and other governmental agencies. The creation of such lists is an example of the type of data mining that has come to the attention of jurists as a new way to violate the privacy rights of American citizens.

The USA PATRIOT Act   One of the most far-reaching attempts by the federal government to expand its surveillance power was the passage of a federal statute entitled the Uniting and Strengthening America by Providing Appropriate Tools Required to Intercept and Obstruct Terrorism Act. Often referred to as the USA PATRIOT Act, or simply the Patriot Act, this statute involves several stipulations that encourage federal law enforcement organizations, including the Federal Bureau of Investigation (FBI) and the Secret Service, to undertake surveillance projects that involve communication transmissions by wire, voice, and other electronic means. These projects also include transmissions via computer lines using the Internet and e-mail capabilities. The statute alters other federal laws, including two of the laws mentioned previously, the Fair Credit Reporting Act and the Right to Financial Privacy Act. Under the USA PATRIOT Act, for example, the Fair Credit Reporting Act requires consumer reporting agencies to turn over to the federal government a consumer's records if a government agency says that those records *could* be related to an intelligence operation conducted by the government against suspected terrorist activities. Furthermore, the USA PATRIOT Act allows the FBI to compel libraries to turn over library circulation reports, information on library patrons, and records on patron Internet use.

The USA PATRIOT Act was renewed by Congress in 2006. Fortunately, the reauthorization added some safeguards to protect the civil rights of U.S. citizens. For example, under changes to the act, agencies like the Department of Justice (DOJ) must produce statements detailing their activities in relation to the act. These statements help, but by themselves, they simply reveal violations of the act after they have occurred. For instance, one statement revealed that the Federal Bureau of Investigation (FBI) had exploited national security letters (NSLs) to obtain evidence in an investigation. NSLs are issued by the FBI much like subpoenas are issued in garden variety investigations. NSLs are simpler to obtain than subpoenas, however, because the Bureau does not have to demonstrate that the desired information is linked to a terrorist organization or a hostile government. The NSLs are then presented to financial institutions, communication corporations, and Internet providers, among others, to compel them to produce the records of people suspected of being security risks. The statement indicated that the NSLs in question had been issued without following the specific procedures outlined by the act. As a result, some legal experts are calling for additional amendments to the act that will make NSLs harder to obtain, to require an official court review of NSLs, to empower financial institutions to resist such letters, and to allow the targets of the NSLs an opportunity to contest their validity. Moreover, some legal experts would like to eliminate the NSLs totally. These experts argue, rather convincingly, that, no matter how the NSLs are structured, unless they include the same safeguards as other warrants, they clearly violate the Fourth Amendment to the Constitution. The extensive damage done to civil rights, they argue, is not worth the small amount of information gained by issuing the letters. Others would prefer to abolish the USA PATRIOT Act altogether. These experts point to the NSL problem as a symptom of a much wider problem, that is, the very premise upon which the act is based—that Americans cannot be trusted.

The Computer Fraud and Abuse Act   Technically, the Computer Fraud and Abuse Act (CFAA) is a criminal law statute that outlaws obtaining national security information, compromising the confidentiality of a computer, trespassing in a government computer, accessing a computer to defraud, damaging a computer, damaging computer information, trafficking in passwords, or threatening to damage a computer. However, the statute also allows civil lawsuits in certain circumstances. Recently, in a series of cases, the courts have made it easier to bring such lawsuits under the CFAA. These lawsuits have clearly established three new principles. First, the CFAA can be used as the basis for an e-lawsuit against both profit-making and nonprofit corporations. The only requirement is that the target's computers must be linked to the Internet, which automatically means they engage in interstate commerce. Second, case law has demonstrated that all violations under

Talking Points

In his essay, "The Legal Protection of the Face We Present to the World," Richard Posner, chief justice for the Appeals Court of the United States Seventh Circuit, argues that the right to privacy is just a fancy way for people to cover up the truth and thus present a false face to those with whom they deal. Posner contends that if the false image that one presents in the marketplace fools people who have trusted that individual, then that false image must be destroyed.

Lucas D. Introna, reader in the Center for the Study of Technology and Organization, Lancaster University (UK), interprets Posner's position in the following way: "Posner, (1978) tend(s) to see the need for privacy as a way of hiding or covering up what ought to be exposed for scrutiny. He argues that exposure through surveillance would provide a more solid basis for social interaction because participants will be able to discern all the facts of the matter for themselves. Privacy, for him, creates opportunities for hiding information that could render many social interactions 'fraudulent.' To interact with someone without providing that person with all information would be to socially defraud that person, or so he argues. This is a very compelling argument, which has made Posner's paper one of the canons in the privacy literature."

In contrast, in his article "Workplace Surveillance, Privacy, and Distributive Justice," Introna argues that employees are "rightly concerned that the employer will only have 'part of the picture,' and that they may be reduced, in subsequent judgments, to that 'part of the picture' alone. They are also concerned that employers will apply inappropriate values when judging this 'part of the picture.' More than this, they will also be concerned by the fact that employers may implicitly and unbeknowingly bring into play a whole lot of other 'parts' of pictures that ought not be considered in that *particular context*."

Of the two positions, which one has the more accurate view of the results of workplace surveillance? Of the two legal theorists, which one reflects your own personal view? Which view is supported by the evidence in this chapter concerning the right of privacy? Explain your answers.

the CFAA can be tapped for the creation of civil liability. This intepretation of the CFAA opens the door to a wide variety of civil suits. Third, under the CFAA, garden-variety agency law principles can be used to establish that a user lacked authorization when he or she tappped into the computer involved in the lawsuit.

Privacy and the European Union

American courts have called upon both the common law tradition and the United States Constitution to create a new right to privacy. The courts, Congress, and various state legislatures have then defended that right in a variety of creative ways. In contrast, the Europeans have simply admitted that privacy is an inherently fragile concept that will be invaded by computers no matter what they try to do about it. Perhaps the most visible weapon against cyberinvasion in the European arsenal is the European Data Protection Directive, which assures the citizens of Europe that they will enjoy certain protections should they engage in commerce on the Internet. Among the protections granted to cyberconsumers in Europe are the ability to obtain any computer data stored on them, the opportunity to adjust any incorrect data, the authority to prevent some people from using certain types of data, and the chance to demand certain remedies for any unlawful activities that affect their own stored data. The EU privacy directive also prevents European firms from business dealings

The Opening Case Revisited, Part I

Who Was Who in the "Whois" Database? Round 2

The "Whois" database has been subject to claims of privacy invasion. As explained in The Opening Case at the beginning of the chapter, the "Whois" database is an "electronic phonebook" cataloging the identities of those people and businesses that own domain names. The agency that controls the content and the availability of the "Whois" database is the Internet Corporation for Assigned Names and Numbers (ICANN). The "Whois" database has always been completely open and easily accessible on the Web. Thus, anyone who wanted to know the identity of the owner of a domain name could simply tap into the database to get additional data about the owner. Recently, however, some of these domain name owners have objected to this process. They have complained, with good reason, that the current system is so open and accessible that it amounts to an invasion of privacy. Some of these innocent domain name holders have been subjected to unreasonable inquiries, spying, cyberstalking, and in some extreme cases even identity theft. "Enough is enough," has become their rallying cry.

in countries that do not grant similar protections. This prohibition is problematic to American firms, because the United States currently has no such guarantees.

Quick Quiz 42-2 True or False?

1. Electronic torts are different from most other torts because they are always somehow entangled with information.

2. The right to privacy is explicitly mentioned in Article VIII of the United States Constitution.

3. Data mining occurs when someone associates two or more pieces of public information to create information that the subject considers private, despite the public nature of the data from which the private information is obtained.

42-3 Electronic Contract Law

Electronic commerce, **e-commerce**, or **cybercommerce** involves the process of transacting business by electronic means. E-commerce can involve purchasing products using electronic credit and debit cards, extracting money from a checking account at a local ATM, transferring funds electronically from one financial institution to another, or buying and selling merchandise on the Internet. All of these new electronic techniques of carrying on business have led to changes in the law. The most important electronic commercial statutes in this regard are the federal E-Sign Act, the Uniform Electronics Transactions Act, and the Uniform Computer Information Transactions Act.

The E-Sign Act

The **E-Sign Act** was instigated by Congress as a way to make sure that any e-commerce document has the same credibility that its paper equivalent would receive. Briefly, the E-Sign Act guarantees that any e-contract created on the Internet or by e-mail will be considered completely legal, so long as the parties to the contract have agreed that electronic signatures will be used by all parties to the agreement. As long as the e-agreement can be duplicated and kept within a computer, it will be afforded the same validity as its paper counterpart. The statute clearly applies to sale-of-goods contracts, as covered by Article 2, and leases, as covered by Article 2A, of the Uniform Commercial Code. Some documents are intentionally excluded from the federal law. These exclusions are records of court proceedings, wills, health insurance cancellations, foreclosure notices, prenuptial agreements, eviction notices, and divorce agreements.

The Uniform Electronic Transactions Act

Like the E-Sign Act, the Uniform Electronic Transactions Act (UETA) makes certain that electronic documents and paper documents receive identical treatment in the marketplace. The act thus is concerned with the similarities among rather than the differences between paper and electronic documents. Once the parties to an e-contract have willfully entered an agreement using electronic means, the agreement will be just as valid as a similar one that is negotiated off the Web and is subsequently reduced to paper. The law also makes it clear that if another statute, such as the Statute of Frauds, requires a writing and a signature, then the electronic record and the electronic signature will meet that requirement. Under the UETA, an electronic signature is defined as "an electronic sound, symbol, or process attached to or associated with a record and executed or adopted by a person with intent to sign the record."

UETA 2 (8)

The Uniform Computer Information Transactions Act (UCITA)

The Uniform Computer Information Transactions Act (UCITA) handles such diverse agreements as database contracts, software licensing agreements, customized software formulation, and the rights associated with multimedia packages. The new act manages to respond to concerns involved in the making of any Internet-related contract. Despite the apparent strength of UCITA, it must be remembered that it is a **default statute**. As a result, under UCITA, the parties to a cybercontract are granted the freedom to indicate what they want when they enter into an agreement. It is only when the parties to an e-contract have overlooked some term, condition, clause, practice, or procedure that they are compelled to look at the provisions of the uniform statute.

Quick Quiz 41-3 True or False?

1. The E-Sign Act was instigated by the ALI as a way to make sure that any e-commercial document is given the same credibility that its paper equivalent has received for centuries.

2. The UETA makes certain that e-documents and paper documents receive different treatment in the marketplace.

3. The UCITA is a default statute.

42-4 Intellectual Property Rights and E-Protection Law

Computer technology has made personal computers in the home, office, factory, and store almost as indispensable as the telephone. Consequently, it has become imperative to protect the ownership of computer programs. Ownership can be protected in the law in four ways: securing trademark protection, establishing trade secret status, securing a copyright, or obtaining a patent.

Trademark Protection

LO7

A trademark is a symbol, picture, image, name, device, color, or word that a business uses to distinguish itself from its competitors. Once a business has established that it owns a trademark, that business has the exclusive right to use that mark to identify its products and services, as well as the business itself. The law provides businesspeople with several ways to establish trademark ownership: common law, state law, and federal law. Common law establishes trademark ownership after the fact. To claim that trademark ownership has been established by common law, the alleged owner must show that the trademark has been used with such intensity and for such a long time that the mark has come to be identified not only with the business's products but also with the business itself. Every state legislature has also passed state trademark laws to protect the use of trademarks in intrastate commerce.

The Trademark Act Despite the use of common law and state law to protect trademarks, most of the legal action in this area takes place at the federal level. The Trademark Protection Act, also known as the Lanham Act, was passed in 1946 to provide for the registration of trademarks with the federal government. The registration authority is the U.S. Office of Patents and Trademarks. Under the Lanham Act, once a trademark is properly registered with the office, it cannot be used by any other business. The act also protects trademark owners from businesses that use symbols, pictures, words, and so on that are so similar to the protected mark that consumers might be confused into thinking that the secondary mark is actually the original mark, thus leading those consumers from the owner's product to those of the competitor.

The Trademark Dilution Act As noted previously, trademark infringement causes economic damage because it takes customers away from the trademark owner. The customers are "stolen" from the legitimate trademark owner because they are confused by the unlawful appropriation of the trademark. However, sometimes customers are not confused, but damage still results. This situation is referred to as trademark dilution, because the effectiveness of the trademark is diluted or "watered down" by the unlawful infringement. The Trademark Dilution Act was created by Congress in 1995 to establish a standard for trademark infringement that would not involve direct and obvious consumer confusion. Unfortunately, the act has not always worked as well as it was supposed to, mainly because of the courts' often perplexing rules about how it ought to be interpreted. To remedy this situation, Congress amended the act in 2006.

The Trademark Dilution Revision Act The new act, referred to as the Trademark Dilution Revision Act, established several new provisions. First, the new act allows trademark owners to obtain an injunction to stop the use of a trademark, simply by demonstrating that the effectiveness of the original mark would probably be diminished. Second, the act strengthens the eligibility of certain marks for protection, especially expressive trademarks such as Quick Lube, Fresh Way Cleaners, or Complete Comfort Heating. Third, the act provides a series of characteristics that the courts can apply to determine if the unauthorized use of a trademark really does obscure the effectiveness of the original mark. Despite these changes, the act still manages to include provisions that provide a First Amendment shield for the use of trademarks in parodies, critiques, satire, and commentaries.

Trademark Infringement in E-Commerce: Domain Names Trademark infringement in e-commerce may occur in many ways, but the most troublesome has been in the area of domain names. A domain name is the Internet address of a business or an individual. The names begin with the letters "www" and finish with the familiar ".com," ".edu," and ".net" endings, for example. The domain names themselves cannot be copyrighted. Instead, they are distributed by registration companies that are certified and regulated by the International Corporation for Assigned Names and Numbers (ICANN). Domain names are really numbers, expressed in an understandable and comfortable way. Naturally, companies want to use domain names that are easily identifiable with their business and their products, which is possible if the name has not been registered with someone else. If someone else has registered that domain name, the company that owns the trade name may have to pay that individual or business for the right to use its own trade name. A party who takes a trade name as a domain name with the intention of holding that name to sell it back to the rightful owner is called a **cybersquatter**.

The Anticybersquatting Consumer Protection Act Some instances of cybersquatting are perfectly innocent. The fan of a television personality or a consumer who loves a particular make of car might have taken a domain name out of sense of loyalty to that person or product or just to have a little fun by identifying with the famous name. This type of cybersquatting is inadvertent and without malice, and such cases are therefore settled pretty quickly when the real owner shows up to make a claim. However, there are also premeditated cybersquatters. A **premeditated cybersquatter** is one who takes the domain name of a famous person or a well-known company to extort money from the

The Opening Case Revisited, Part II
Who Was Who in the "Whois" Database? Round 3

Despite its strange sounding name, the "Whois" database is simply an electronic phonebook listing certain details about those people and businesses that own domain names. Thus, the "Whois" database is a very helpful tool for legitimate trademark owners who are trying to stop premeditated cybersquatters. Several members of the ICANN board, however, would like to change the process by concealing the identities of domain name holders and forcing a searcher to go to an in-between connection to uncover their true identities. Those who oppose the new system see the "Whois" database as a critical tool in the effort to find and punish cybersquatters and other electronic offenders, who either extort money from the real owners of certain trademark names or use the domain name to lead buyers to phony merchandise, X-rated Web sites, or other Internet locations for their personal profit. Those who support the openness of the present system also point to the costly setbacks and postponements that will occur should trademark holders be forced to go after cybersquatters and other illegitimate domain name holders in an indirect and roundabout way.

actual owner. The ACPA was designed to deal with premeditated cybersquatters. The law allows the legitimate owners of trademarks and famous names to go to court to obtain an injunction that will stop the cybersquatter from using the domain name or to seek damages that will compensate the owners for the mischief caused by the cybersquatter.

Trademark Infringement in E-Commerce: Trademark Tapping

Trademark tapping is a technique used by some companies to increase the number of "hits" on their Web sites. To engage in **trademark tapping**, a company enters a "competitive-hit" agreement with a search engine. The agreement states that whenever a user inputs a set of key terms identified by the company, the search engine will post that company's Web site as a search option. The actual trademark tapping occurs when the original company includes another company's trademark name as one of its key terms. A variation of trademark tapping also occurs when an Internet software provider promises a client that whenever a cybersurfer enters a set of designated Web sites, the client's pop-up advertisements will appear on the surfer's screen. This type of agreement becomes problematic when one of the Web sites that triggers a pop-up belongs to the competition. (See Table 42-1.) Trademark holders believe that both trademark tapping tactics are unjust practices that infringe on their trademark ownership rights. Because federal law does not directly outlaw either form of trademark tapping though, some state legislatures have passed state laws that deal with the practice. A Utah statute, for example, permits businesses to obtain an electronic registration mark. The use of the registration mark empowers the owner to bring a lawsuit in state court against anyone who uses the registered electronic trademark in a trademark tapping campaign.

Trade Secret Protection

A **trade secret** is a plan, process, device, procedure, formula, pattern, compilation, technique, program, design, method, or improvement used in a business and disclosed only to those employees who need to know it to do their jobs. The Uniform Trade Secrets Act sets up two conditions that must be met for a plan, process, program, and so on to gain trade secret status. First, the plan, process, or program must gain financial worth simply because it is a secret and cannot be applied by others who might use it to compete with the owner of the secret. Second, the alleged secret must be the subject of reasonable attempts to protect it from those who would use it in a way that would financially hurt the owner of the secret.

Establishing Trade Secret Status   The right to characterize a computer program as a trade secret depends on the way the owners of the program treat it in relation to other people. In general, the easier it is for people to gain access to the program, the less likely it is that the program will be considered a secret should the matter be contested in

Table 42-1 Infringement in E-Commerce Trademark Tapping	
Offense	**Explanation**
Competitive hit agreement	An agreement between a client and search engine that whenever a cybersurfer inputs a competitor's trademark, the search engine will post the client's Web site as a search option.
Pop-up advertisement agreement	An agreement between a client and an Internet software provider by which the provider agrees to "pop" the client's ad whenever the competitor's Web site is used by a cybersurfer.

court. Therefore, to protect trade secret status, the owners of a program must make certain that the program is treated as a secret from the very beginning. The goal is to grant access to the secret only to those people who need to know it to carry out their duties in the ordinary course of business. Steps that can be taken to increase the likelihood that a court will rule that a program is a trade secret include the following: (1) label the program as secret in all documents related to the program, (2) limit employee access to the program on a need-to-know basis, (3) maintain tight security in the business in general but especially in any area where the program is required to be out in the open for business purposes, (4) keep the program and all related material under lock and key when it is not in use, (5) require employees who work with the program to sign secrecy agreements, (6) require customers who purchase the use of the program to sign licensing agreements, and (7) be especially vigilant in limiting any access to the program by competitors.

Computer Programs Denied Trade Secret Status

Computer programs that have been transferred to software and then placed on the open market for wide distribution cannot claim trade secret status. Software that is widely distributed can be easily copied. Thus, it becomes difficult to demonstrate that the company has taken extensive measures to protect the information on the software. Moreover, because the purpose of placing the software on the open market is to sell it to as many people as possible, the seller must make the software readily available in bookstores and video outlets. This availability on the open market defeats the whole trade secret concept.

Computer Programs Granted Trade Secret Status

Trade secret status is available to companies that distribute their software on a limited, highly selective basis. For example, a computer company that produces and sells a program used to control the distribution of drugs by pharmaceutical firms might be able to call that program a trade secret. Such a company would not actually sell the program to the pharmaceutical firm but would instead allow the firm to use the program through a licensing agreement. A **licensing agreement** occurs when the producer of a product, in this case a computer program, allows a purchaser to use the product only if the purchaser agrees to respect the producer's desire for secrecy. In this situation, to use the program, the pharmaceutical company would have to agree to respect the computer company's desire for secrecy. In this type of highly selective, strictly controlled transaction, trade secret status works.

State Statutory Trade Secret Protection

Various states have enacted trade secret statutes designed to protect trade secrets within the state's borders. Many of these statutes are patterned after the **Uniform Trade Secrets Act**, written by the National Conference of Commissioners on Uniform State Laws. Typically, these statutes define a trade secret, describe transgressions of the act, and provide for both damages and injunctive relief when there has been a trade secret infringement. The statutes also generally include a statute of limitations, typically about four years, and indicate that continuing use of a trade secret is a single rather than a series of transgressions. Some state statutes also allow for attorney's fees.

The Economic Espionage Act

The federal government also entered the trade secret arena with the passage of the **Economic Espionage Act** of 1996. The Espionage Act does not provide for any civil actions but instead outlines criminal sanctions for the theft of trade secrets and the use of fraud to obtain trade secrets. Persons convicted under the statute can face up to 10 years of imprisonment and fines that may reach as much as $500,000. The statute forbids the theft of trade secrets for distribution to a foreign government or an agent of a foreign government or for economic gain that does not benefit the actual owner of the trade secret.

Copyright Protection

A **copyright** is an intangible property right granted to authors of literary, artistic, and musical compositions. A copyright means that the owner has the exclusive right to reproduce, publish, and sell his or her work in a fixed, tangible medium of expression. Because a computer program is a fixed medium of expression, it is subject to copyright protection. The federal Copyright Act specifically lists the following as works that are subject to copyright protection: literary works, dramatic works, musical works, pantomimes, pictorial works, sculptures, graphic works, motion pictures, audiovisual works, sound recordings, architectural works, and choreographic works. Computer programs are also specifically covered by the Copyright Act of 1980, which includes computer programs in the category of "writings" or "literary" works to which exclusive rights can be granted.

The judicial–economic system has responded to the rapid changes that have occurred in computer technology. In fact, many of the recent alterations in the law were specifically designed to keep abreast of the effects of electronic communication on copyright privileges. Despite this effort, the high-speed, global, interactive nature of the Internet has caused unforeseen problems in copyright law. For example, computer technology now makes it possible for a single copy of a computer program or an individual copy of a literary work to be made available to millions of computer users, simply by placing that single copy on a Web site that is accessible to other users. This advance in computer technology may have been predictable to cyberneticists, but it went virtually unnoticed for quite some time by jurists and legislators. Nevertheless, despite the unpredictability of the problem, the law, as a complex adaptive system, has adapted to the problem and provided a few solutions.

The No Electronic Theft Act   One such solution came from Congress in the form of the **No Electronic Theft Act (NET Act)**, a federal law that granted limited immunity to persons who duplicate copyrighted works on the Internet, as long as those users do not profit from the copying process. The statute does not simply grant immunity to infringers, however. Instead, it imposes criminal penalties for the violation of certain provisions. Specifically, it makes it illegal to create a duplication (including an electronic duplication) of a copyrighted work for commercial profit or private financial gain by copying or handing out one or more copies of one or more copyrighted productions within a single 180-day period, if the productions in question have a complete retail value of over $1,000. Penalties can include fines of up to $100,000 and imprisonment of up to 10 years.

The Digital Millennium Copyright Act   To defend their copyright privileges, copyright holders have developed computer protection programs that prevent users from duplicating their copyrighted works. Thus, the copyright owner of a film or television show might place a protective program on a DVD to prevent users from creating a copy of that film or television show from the DVD. Not to be outdone, infringers then created software that would allow a user to sidestep the protective program and create a duplicate of the scrambled work. In response to this technological tug-of-war, Congress passed the **Digital Millennium Copyright Act (DMCA)**. The DMCA is designed to combat technological advances that permit users to override protection systems. The law makes it illegal to use technological means to bypass or override programs designed to prevent access to a copyrighted work. Another provision of the DMCA makes it illegal to use any means to circumvent a program intended to frustrate the copying of a copyrighted work. First-time offenders can be fined up to $500,000 and imprisoned for up to five years. Second-time offenders can be fined up to $1 million and receive a prison sentence that can reach as long as 10 years.

The World Intellectual Property Organization   It would be unfair and incomplete to close any discussion of the Digital Millennium Copyright Act without mentioning its connection with the **World Intellectual Property Organization (WIPO)**. WIPO is

part of the United Nations and supported the development of two international treaties specifically designed to deal with electronic copyright problems. Two separate but closely related treaties resulted from the efforts of the WIPO. The first treaty is known as the **World Intellectual Property Organization Copyright Treaty**. This treaty guarantees that copyright holders will be allowed to use the Internet to post their works with full copyright protection. The second WIPO treaty, the **World Intellectual Property Organization Phonograms Treaty**, gives copyright holders the right to copy, publish, and distribute their works in any way, including by making video copies, audio copies, and encrypted copies. The DMCA was written to implement the provisions of these treaties into law in the United States.

Peer-to-Peer Network Problems Computer technology generally has managed to stay several steps ahead of developments in the judicial–economic system. It seems as though each problem solved by the judicial–economic system leads to a new, heretofore unanticipated problem. Such was the case with developments in file-sharing technology. One file-sharing development that caused a great deal of concern among copyright holders was a system known as **peer-to-peer (P2P) networking**. P2P networking involved connections among personal computers joined to the same interconnected network. This technique eliminated the need to go through a core Web server. It also permitted the users to access and download files located on other personal computers on the same network. Although peer-to-peer systems have many legitimate purposes, they are also open to abuse. One abuse involved downloading music files. Copyright owners felt threatened by the use of these interconnected peer-to-peer systems to download music files. To protect their rights, several music industry firms joined together in a lawsuit to target a company named Napster, Inc., which ran a file-sharing network. Napster was accused of copyright infringement by providing a network that facilitated downloading music files. Napster provided the software, known as MusicShare, that permitted members of its system to download duplicates of music files via the Internet and aided members by providing them with technical support whenever it was needed. The court ruled that Napster was liable for infringement even though it did not directly infringe itself, because it clearly aided the illegal and abusive infringement activities of the members of its network.

LO10

Patent Protection

A *patent* is a property right granted by the federal government to an inventor. A patent gives the inventor the exclusive right to make, use, and sell that invention for a period of years. A patent differs from both a trade secret and a copyright. A patent is, in effect, a deal with the government. The inventor reveals the details of the invention in the patent application. In exchange, the inventor receives a guarantee from the government that it will protect the inventor's exclusive right to produce and profit from that invention for a specified period of time. In contrast, a trade secret is not revealed in any way in the open marketplace; the holder of the trade secret receives no guaranteed protection from the government. A copyright differs from a patent in that a copyright protects only the expression of an idea, whereas a patent protects the idea itself.

The Patent Application Process Unlike a copyright application process, which involves the use of preprinted forms provided by the Copyright Office, each patent application requires the creation of a unique technical document. The document is then filed with the Patent Office. To qualify for a patent, an invention must meet three requirements. First, the invention must fall within the limits defined by the statute as "patentable subject matter." Second, the invention must consist of some nonobvious, new, and useful feature not known or understood before the invention of this particular device. Third, the patent application must be so specific that individuals who are educated and experienced in the field can create the device on their own.

Patentable Subject Matter   The law states that for the subject of a patent application to be patentable, it must be a "process, machine, manufacturer or composition of matter." In contrast, such things as laws of nature, natural phenomena, and abstract ideas cannot be patented. Neither mathematical formulas nor mathematical algorithms are patentable, because they are actually laws of nature. An algorithm is a series of steps that, if followed properly, will reach a desired goal. Because many computer software programs are based on mathematical algorithms, problems arose when inventors first attempted to patent computer software. In fact, when patent applications for computer software programs began to appear in the Patent Office in the 1970s, most software programs were eventually found to be unpatentable. However, during the 1980s and the 1990s, the trend reversed itself. Today, more than 80 percent of all patent claims involving computers have been upheld, including those involving software alone. However, the law in this area remains somewhat unclear. Fortunately, some general guidelines can be laid down. For example, if a software program is only one part of a larger, more conventional process, the courts will allow patent protection for the whole process.

EXAMPLE 42-2:   Alison's Shatter-Proof Patent Problem

Alison Louise, the owner, operator, and CEO of Alison, Inc., "Home of the Best Shatter-Proof Glass Products in America," developed a new process for mass producing shatterproof glass goods. The new process allowed Alison, Inc., to produce a better quality glass at about half the cost of its closest competitors. Part of Alison's success was due to the use of lasers in the process. However, the lasers had to be timed so precisely that each one was controlled by a computer, following the directions of a computer program. This portion of the process was only about one-fourth of the entire operation, the rest of which was relatively conventional. The patent examiner denied Alison's patent application because part of the process involved an unpatentable computer program. A federal court reversed the refusal, because the process itself was new and could be patented. The use of the program was only one part of that process.

However, if the software stands alone, the question of whether the patent application will be granted is more difficult. The Court of Appeals for the Federal Circuit has addressed the issue in several cases and tends to affirm such patent applications. The appellate court generally upholds the patentability of software, even if it is based on a mathematical algorithm, because the software actually changes the operation of the computer. Thus, the software can be viewed as either a process or a change in the physical nature of the computer itself. In 1996, the U.S. Patent and Trademark Office established a set of guidelines for computer-related inventions. The objective of the guidelines is to help eliminate ambiguity in the law regarding the patentability of software.

EXAMPLE 42-3:   Cole's Infinity Bucks Tracker Tracks a Win

Cole Christopher, the owner-operator of Cole's Infinity Bucks, Inc., developed Cole's Infinity Bucks Tracker, a software program that allowed the user to overlay on a computer screen all available trajectories for any stocks that he or she wished to purchase or sell in the near future while simultaneously displaying all changes in the data related to each pictured stock. Such a program would be invaluable to investors as they planned investment strategies. The patent examiner refused to issue a patent, arguing that Cole's program was simply the expression of a mathematical algorithm. The Board of Patent Appeals supported the examiner's position. The Court of Appeals for the Federal Circuit, however, reversed the decision and stated that in effect, Cole's program transformed an ordinary, all-purpose computer into a specialized computer. Thus, the all-purpose computer had in effect become a new computer, capable of performing a new function by following the commands of the software program. Cole's Infinity Bucks Tracker can be viewed as either a process creating a change or an alteration in the physical nature of the computer itself.

Until recently a **business system** was also considered unpatentable because it was not a "process, machine, manufacturer, or composition of matter." However, in a recent court case, a computer system for analyzing information about a group of mutual funds was declared patentable by a federal court. This decision culminated in a slow erosion of the business systems category of unpatentable subjects. Even so, a computerized business system must still consist of some nonobvious, new, and useful feature not known or understood before the invention of this system. It must also be so specific that people who are educated and experienced in the field can recreate the system on their own.

Usefulness, Novelty, and Nonobviousness

The objective of patent law is to encourage inventiveness and promote progress for the benefit of all society. Thus, a device, to be patentable, must be useful. Many processes involving computer programs would pass the usefulness test. Passing the usefulness test alone, however, is not enough to qualify for a patent. The new invention must also be novel and nonobvious. To pass the novelty test, the new device or process must be original. Copying someone else's innovation, even unintentionally, will disqualify an invention from patent eligibility. Similarly, to pass the nonobviousness test, the changes or improvements must not be obvious to a person of ordinary skill in the field. If the changes are obvious, then a patent will not be issued.

Recent Developments in the Nonobviousness Test

The patent review process became more difficult for patent holders recently when the United States Supreme Court revised the traditional test of nonobviousness. The traditional test, which was referred to as the **teaching, suggestion, or motivation test** or the **TSM standard**, compelled those who challenged a patent to demonstrate that the so-called "innovation" would have been obvious to any one exposed to the same *teaching* session, the same off-hand *suggestion*, or the same *motivation* as the inventor had been exposed to. In essence, the test rests on the belief that any small innovation based on prior art in the field would not be patentable but that other innovations, even small ones beyond prior art, would be (see Table 42-2). **Prior art** refers to all relevant technical knowledge about the field to which the invention belongs. The test was difficult, however, because it also required the challenger to produce some sort of hard evidence to support the TSM challenge. Generally, the only factual data that the court would accept as hard evidence was information that had been printed in a professional journal or data that rose to that level of credibility.

The Supreme Court recently made it clear that previous courts had been too uncompromising in their use of TSM. Accordingly, the Court suggested that challengers ought to consider using other types of evidence to contest the validity of a patent claim. Such evidence might include economic requirements, the knowledge of other inventors in the same field, or progress in the relevant technology that might show that a person of ordinary skill could easily

Table 42-2 Recent Developments in Patent Law

Standard	Explanation
Teaching, suggestion, motivation	An invention is obvious and not patentable if anyone exposed to the same teaching, suggestion, or motivation would have come up with the same invention.
Obvious-to-try standard	An invention is obvious and not patentable if the innovation was so obvious that anyone of ordinary skill could see that it was obvious to try that innovation.
Possible legislative changes	Some *possible* legislative changes slated for the future may be (1) increased ease in obtaining injunctions; (2) an 18-month publication rule; and (3) a change in the burden of proof.

have developed the same innovation introduced in the challenged patent. If any of these features exist, the innovation is not patentable. In addition, the Supreme Court reintroduced a variation on the TSM test called the obvious-to-try standard, a test that had been outlawed by previous precedent. Under the newly reinstated **obvious-to-try standard**, if the challenger can demonstrate that anyone of ordinary skill could see that it would have been obvious to try such an innovation, the innovation would be labeled as obvious, and the invention would not be patentable.

Nonobviousness and E-Inventions The new rulings make it more difficult for inventors to obtain patents and easier for challengers to demonstrate that an innovation is obvious and therefore not patentable. The decision to make the test of patentability harder will have a direct effect on computer-related e-inventions. Many innovations in computer technology that might have been patentable under the old rules will not be patentable under the new obviousness tests. For instance, under the old rules that dealt exclusively with TSM, a small innovation in the component parts of a laptop or a PDA might have been patentable if the new component was not made clear by teaching, suggestion, or motivation. Now, if the challenger can show that trends in engineering made the innovation a logical next step, or that it was obvious to try the change in the component parts of that PDA or laptop, the innovation, no matter how clever, will be unpatentable.

Legislative Changes on the Horizon There are also some legislative reforms in the works for patent law. Some of these suggestions are aimed at introducing a more demanding procedure for inventors to secure a patent and an easier procedure for challengers to use to convince the court to reverse a patent that has been issued by the U.S. Patent and Trademark Office. Others are designed to help patent holders deal with patent infringers who have illegally appropriated a patented innovation. The three most probable suggestions include (1) a provision that will make it easier for patent holders to convince a court to issue an injunction to stop an alleged infringement; (2) a provision that would establish an 18-month publication rule that would require patent applicants to publish their patent materials within 18 months of filing, in order to stop other engineers, inventors, and scientists from traveling down the same road unnecessarily; and (3) a shift in the burden of proof in relation to a patent challenge. This last suggestion is the most controversial of the three. The current rule states that a patent that has been granted is assumed to be legitimate. This assumption requires the opposition to demonstrate that the patent is not legitimate. One suggested change would reverse the presumption completely. Such a radical change is unlikely, however. Another suggestion would make it easier for the opposition to attack the assumption successfully. The application of this new test is sometimes referred to as enhanced examination, advanced assessment, in-depth determination, or double-take testing.

The Double-Take Testing Controversy The patent review process is clearly overloaded. Would-be inventors filed more than 300,000 patent applications with the U.S. Patent and Trademark Office in 2006. These applications had to be handled by the 4,000 patent review officers who currently staff the agency. Those who support double-take testing requirements for patent eligibility point to these figures and argue that strengthening the patent evaluation process would lower expenses and increase the efficiency of the overall procedure. Supporters of the change also point out that innovations such as the 18-month rule would help fuel the progress of science and technology because the advanced notice given to other inventors by the early publication requirement would prevent them from wasting time on innovations that are already slated for patent approval. Others point out that stronger requirements are no longer as risky as they once were, because patent examiners have access to the Internet, which clearly accelerates the patent review process. Those who oppose a tougher review argue that a more stringent review process may result in some worthy patents being unjustly rejected. Opponents also note that only about 2 percent of the patents granted are ever contested in lawsuits or arbitration hearings, indicating that the process as it operates now really works quite well.

Specificity in the Application Federal law states that a patent application must describe the nature of the invention in "full, clear, concise, and exact terms." In fact, the application must be so clear that any person educated and experienced in that field can recreate the invention without having to engage in an extensive trial-and-error period. This requirement causes some difficulty in computer software patent applications, because the surest way to guarantee that someone else will be able to recreate the invention is to provide the source code in the patent application. However, many inventors are reluctant to include source code because such codes often contain trade secrets that they are unwilling to dump into the public domain. The usual compromise is to include in the patent application either a flowchart or some other visual diagram that reveals the details of the process.

Quick Quiz 42-4 True or False?

1. The right to characterize a computer program as a trade secret depends on the way the owners of the program treat it in relation to other people.

2. A copyright means that the owner has the exclusive right to reproduce, publish, and sell his or her work in a fixed tangible medium of expression.

3. A business system is not the proper subject of a patent application.

Summary

42.1 The area of law that pertains to computers and their related difficulties is known as electronic law. Electronic law is so new that it still has a variety of different names. Legal experts refer to it variously as e-law, cyberlaw, and computer law. An electronic crime is any criminal activity that is associated with a computer, including crimes committed using a computer, such as

electronic blackmail, and crimes committed against a computer, such as electronic terrorism or electronic germ warfare. Some states have dealt with the problem of defining e-crimes by simply folding the traditional criminal code into the electronic crime lexicon. This approach is termed electronic trespass. Electronic trespass is the use of a computer or other electronic device as an instrumentality of any crime, as defined within the conventional criminal code. Electronic trespass also includes crimes that target computers as victims.

42.2 An electronic tort is the invasion, distortion, theft, falsification, destruction, misuse, deletion, or exploitation of data stored in or associated with an electronic mechanism, including desktop PCs, laptops, mobile phones, phonecams, videocams, PDAs, mainframes, and home computers that are isolated or integrated into an intranet or the Internet. Generally, when an electronic tort has been committed, the victim complains of one or more of the following injuries: The victim's reputation has been damaged because of a false report distributed via e-mail or some other electronic text-messaging technique, the victim's emotional health is disturbed because of an invasion of his or her privacy, or the innocent party's financial condition has been disrupted because his or her identity has been confiscated via computer. Two e-torts are significant in this area: electronic defamation and electronic invasion of privacy.

42.3 New electronic techniques of carrying on business have led to changes in the law. The most important electronic commerce statutes in this regard are the federal E-Sign Act, the Uniform Electronics Transfer Act, and the Uniform Computer Information Act.

42.4 Ownership rights in computer programs and computer software can be protected by trademarks, trade secrets, copyrights, and patents. A trademark is a word, symbol, color, design, or device that identifies a business and its products. A trade secret is a plan, process, or device used in a business and known only to employees who need to know the secret to do their jobs. A program can be protected by a trade secret only if its distribution is tightly controlled. Copyrights are intangible property rights granted to authors of literary, artistic, and musical productions. Computer programs can be copyrighted. A patent is a property right that is granted by the federal government to an inventor. A computer program that is part of a larger, more conventional process can be patented.

Key Terms

business system, 907

computer law, 887

copyright, 904

cybercommerce, 898

cyberextortion, 888

cyberlaw, 887

cybersquatter, 901

data mining, 894

default statute, 899

Digital Millennium Copyright Act (DMCA), 904

e-commerce, 898

Economic Espionage Act, 903

e-extortion, 888

e-law, 887

electronic commerce, 898

electronic crime, 887

electronic defamation, 892

electronic extortion, 888

electronic germ warfare, 891

electronic invasion of privacy, 893

electronic law, 887

electronic piracy, 889

electronic spoofing, 888

electronic stalking, 888

electronic terrorism, 889

electronic tort, 892

electronic trespass, 888

electronic vandalism, 890

E-Sign Act, 899

e-tort, 892

identity theft, 890

licensing agreement, 903

No Electronic Theft Act (NET Act), 904

obvious-to-try standard, 908

peer-to-peer (P2P) networking, 905

phishing, 889

premeditated cybersquatter, 901

prior art, 907

private information, 893

private privacy, 893

private-private information, 893

public privacy, 893

public-private information, 894

teaching, suggestions, or motivation test, 907

trade secret, 902

trademark tapping, 902

TSM standard, 907

Uniform Trade Secrets Act, 903

World Intellectual Property Organization (WIPO), 904

World Intellectual Property Organization Copyright Treaty, 905

World Intellectual Property Organization Phonograms Treaty, 905

Questions for Review and Discussion

1. What is the basic nature of electronic law?
2. What is the nature of electronic trespass?
3. What electronic crimes can be committed with a computer, and what electronic crimes can be committed against a computer?
4. What is the nature of an electronic tort?
5. What is the difference between electronic defamation and electronic invasion of privacy?
6. What statutes are involved in electronic contract law?
7. How can a trademark be infringed in e-law?
8. When will trade secret protection be provided for a computer program?
9. What statutes are involved in electronic copyright protection?
10. When can a patent be obtained for a computer program?

Investigating the Internet

Access the Computer Professionals for Social Responsibility Web site and, as part of a research project, answer the following questions: (1) What does Computer Professionals for Social Responsibility promote as its primary goal? (2) What projects is CPSR currently running? (3) Where is the headquarters of CPSR located? (4) What five principles form the foundation of the philosophy of CPSR? (5) How many different countries have members who are part of CPSR?

Cases for Analysis

1. Officials at Semco, Inc., believed that some of their company's most important computer files, which they characterized as trade secrets, had been appropriated by Terry Hildreth, a former vice president of Semco. Semco officials accused Hildreth of using these programs to run his new limited liability company, Hildreth Manufacturing, LLC. Semco engaged in a series of harassing tactics designed to stop Hildreth's use of the alleged trade secrets. To protect himself and his new firm, Hildreth brought a lawsuit asking for a declaratory judgment that no trade secrets had been taken, despite Semco's allegations to the contrary. Semco then brought a second lawsuit alleging, among other things, that trade secrets had indeed been misappropriated by Hildreth. After the suits were decided in favor of Hildreth, the results were appealed. During both suits, the following facts came to light: Material that described the manufacturing steps that Semco now claimed were trade se-

crets had been routinely made available to vendors. Semco also regularly provided information about its "secret" manufacturing processes to people outside the company. Semco did not require employees to file nondisclosure or secrecy agreements. Visitors were not screened, the building was locked only after regular business hours, and the plant was open for public tours. On the basis of these facts, how should the appeals court rule on the issue of trade secrets? Explain. *Hildreth Mfg., LLC. v. Semco, Inc.,* 151 Ohio App. 3d 693.

2. Parrish and Chlarson worked for J&K Computer Systems, Inc. Parrish was a computer programmer, and Chlarson was a trainee. In his capacity as programmer, Parrish wrote an accounts receivable program. Customers of J&K were granted licenses to use the program. A label on the program noted that it was J&K's property and that it could not be used without authorization under a licensing agreement.

Parrish, Chlarson, and all other J&K employees were informed that the program was a secret. Nevertheless, Parrish copied it, left J&K's employ, and, along with Chlarson, opened a business similar to J&K. Parrish and Chlarson then sold the copied program to various customers. When J&K sued, Parrish and Chlarson argued that the fact that J&K had revealed the program to their customers meant it was no longer a trade secret. Were Parrish and Chlarson correct? Explain. *J&K Computer Systems, Inc., v. Parrish,* 642 P.2d 732 (UT).

3. Diehr and Latton applied for a patent to protect their development of a new process for molding raw, uncured synthetic rubber into cured products. Diehr and Latton argued that their unique contribution was to measure the temperature inside the mold and feed that temperature into a computer that was programmed to calculate the exact time needed for the curing process. The computer would then activate a mechanism to open the mold. The process, as conceived by Diehr and Latton, eliminated the guesswork usually associated with measuring the length of time for the mold to remain closed. The patent office denied the patent because it used a computer program in the process. The office said that the program was essentially a mathematical idea and was therefore unpatentable. Diehr and Latton argued that the mere fact that a computer program was used as part of a process did not mean that the whole process would be unpatentable. Were Diehr and Latton correct? Why or why not? *Diamond v. Diehr,* 101 S.Ct. 1048 (U.S. Sup. Ct.).

4. Hiroyuki Iwahashi, Yoshiki Nishioka, and Mitsuhiro Hakaridani applied for a patent for an autocorrelation unit for use in computers for pattern recognition, in this case to aid in voice recognition. To achieve this type of pattern recognition, computers must perform a lengthy multiplication cycle that requires intricate circuitry and a costly multiplier unit. The computer hardware involved in this process is also large and cumbersome. The purpose of the new invention is to streamline the multiplication cycle. The elimination of the multiplier and the intricate circuitry is made possible by an algorithm that allows the computer to obtain the needed result by detouring the time-consuming multiplication cycle and using instead the electronic equivalent of a multiplication table. The U.S. Patent and Trademark Office rejected the patent application, and the Board of Patent Appeals and Interferences upheld that decision. Both concluded that the alleged invention was nothing more than an algorithm and could not therefore be patented. The inventors appealed the decision, arguing that the algorithm is simply part of the apparatus, which altered the operation of the computer and was therefore subject to patentability. Can a patent be rejected solely on the argument that the invention involves an algorithm? Explain. *In re Iwahashi,* 888 F.2d 1370 (Fed. Cir.).

5. Stern Electronics, Inc., entered a licensing agreement with Konami Industry Co., Ltd., granting Stern exclusive rights to market the video game Scramble in the United States. Omni Video Games, Inc., wrote a new program that duplicated the sights and sounds of Scramble. Stern sued Omni in federal court, asking for an injunction to prevent Omni from marketing its knockoff of Scramble. Omni argued that Stern could not get a copyright for the Scramble audiovisual display because every time a player plays the game, the display is different. The display is not fixed in a tangible medium, as required by law. Because Omni had written its own program, Stern could not stop it from marketing the duplicate Scramble games. Was Omni correct? Explain. *Stern Electronics, Inc., v. Kaufman and Omni Video Games, Inc.,* 669 F.2d 852 (2nd Cir.).

Quick Quiz Answers

42-1	42-2	42-3	42-4
1. T	1. T	1. F	1. T
2. T	2. F	2. F	2. T
3. F	3. T	3. T	3. F

Chapter 43 — International Law

The Opening Case
The Sanchez Ultimatum

The story of the capture, arrest, and would-be prosecution of Diego Sanchez could easily have been torn out of the pages of a Robert Ludlum novel. Sanchez, a citizen of Argentina, was a political activist with a strong anti-Western agenda. At first he confined his activities to writing and distributing pamphlets and newsletters. However, Sanchez soon adopted twenty-first century tactics to publish an anti-Western political blog on the Internet. His notoriety on the Web caught the attention of a terrorist cell that had global ties to a network of anti-Western cells working in the European Union. One of these cells recruited Sanchez to work in France, Spain, and Portugal. Initially, Sanchez played a small role. However, his chameleon-like ability to blend into French, Spanish, and Portuguese gatherings made him an invaluable member of the organization. It was this ability that led to his involvement in a series of kidnappings and executions of Islamic clerics, the purpose of which was to place blame on the French government, which was accused of either ignoring the crimes or being actively involved in carrying them out. Sanchez later returned to Argentina. An investigation by French authorities led to the suspicion that Sanchez had actually been an agent provocateur employed by the Argentinean government. Accordingly, the French demanded that Argentina turn Sanchez over to the International Criminal Court in The Hague. The Argentinean government claimed that it had the right under the Rome Statute of the International Criminal Court to try Sanchez rather than turning him over to the ICC. The French argued that the Argentinean government had been granted sufficient time to prosecute Sanchez but had failed to do so, making the Sanchez case a matter for the ICC. The Argentinean government responded that Sanchez had not yet exhausted all domestic remedies, and until that happened, he would remain in their custody. At that point, the case became permanently stalled. Sanchez remained in Argentinean custody, the French continued to yell "foul," and the ICC remained silent on the issue.

Opening Case Questions

1. What is the Rome Statute?

2. What are the jurisdictional limits of the International Criminal Court?

3. Does the ICC have original jurisdiction over criminals like Sanchez?

4. What prevents a defendant from becoming a victim of a trumped-up political trial?

5. Where is the ICC located?

 **Learning Objectives**

1. Differentiate among the major new world orders.
2. List the criteria for a just war.
3. Explain the jurisdiction of the International Court of Justice.
4. Describe the mission of the International Criminal Court.
5. Identify the main goal of UNCITRAL.
6. State the differences between the UCC and the CISG.
7. Outline the structure of the World Trade Organization.
8. Relate the objectives of the Dispute Settlement Understanding.
9. Determine the major purpose of NAFTA.
10. Clarify the goals of the European Union.

43-1 The New World Order

The phrase "new world order" was used during the Paris Peace talks in 1919 to describe the remaking of the world map following World War I, and then again decades later by George H. W. Bush to describe the coalition of nations that fought to free Kuwait after the Iraqi invasion in 1990. It is a phrase frequently used to describe situations on the global stage that are unusual and unfamiliar. For that reason, among others, the phrase can be used to describe the situation in which we find ourselves today. A **new world order** is a set of initial conditions that describes how nation-states relate to one another on a global scale. The use of the word "new" to describe that order reveals that these initial conditions have just emerged from a tectonic shift in international relations. Generally, because the conditions are so new, no one is exactly certain what those conditions are and how they work. (See M. MacMillan, *Paris 1919: Six Months that Changed the World,* New York: Random House, 2001.)

Patterns within the New World Order

This description is not to say that global conditions do not follow certain patterns, but in the new world order, those patterns have yet to be determined. These patterns are not rules exactly, but neither are they unpredictable chance events. They instead have the status of indicators that are right more often than wrong. The trick then is to determine what the global initial conditions really are and what pattern those conditions can be expected to follow. What makes this trick so difficult is that the international players do not come into the game fresh but instead are steeped in their own expectations of what the pattern should be. When the pattern shifts, sometimes the players do not, which causes diplomatic errors, international incidents, and global conflicts, some of which can be solved easily but most of which cannot.

EXAMPLE 43-1:   The Global Shift on 9/11

One of the reasons that many government officials were slow to act in response to the hijackings that began the terror attacks of 9/11 was that they expected the hijackers to follow a set pattern. Up until that moment in time, hijackers, at least those who had taken American hostages on American planes, had had some sort of political bargaining in mind. Thus, they would demand political asylum in Cuba or Libya, the release of political prisoners being held in American prisons, a ransom to be paid to some foreign political party, or airtime during which they could broadcast their grievances against the United States. What American officials did not realize was that while they were looking in one direction, the world had moved in another. They were no longer facing hijackers with an agenda based on political bargaining but terrorists who had an entirely different plan in mind.

Our job during the remainder of this chapter will be to determine the nature of this new world order. It is not an easy task, because not everyone agrees about what that order might be. In fact, there are almost as many new world orders as there are political commentators to talk about them. Still, even within this confusing collection of political theories, common themes exist. Accordingly, we will divide our study in this chapter into four parts: (1) economic new world order theories; (2) civilizational new world order theories, (3) international new world order theories, and (4) globalized new world order theories. It is crucial to consider what each of these theories offers before looking at international law itself. To examine international law without taking a moment to understand the environment in which it operates is a little like trying to teach the rules of baseball to someone who has never seen a baseball diamond. Sure, it can be done—but why try, especially if there is a real diamond on the next block?

The World Order of Westphalia

Regardless of whether we ultimately adopt an economic, civilizational, international, or globalized new world order as a model, one thing is clear: Every one of these "new world orders" must work within the Westphalia system. The **Westphalia system**, as reflected originally in the terms of the Treaty of Westphalia, which ended the Thirty Years' War in 1648, describes the existence of **nation-states** as the central performers on the international scene. It describes certain qualities that functioning nation-states must have to be recognized as legitimate international players. These characteristics include the following:

1. Nation-states will govern a recognized area of land on the map. In other words, it is possible to point to a place on a world map and say something like, "There is Lithuania." It is also possible to travel to and enter a nation-state because it is a physical, geographical reality.

2. Nation-states have sovereignty. Sovereignty is the exclusive power of a nation-state to govern what happens within its own borders. Therefore, nation-states can create their own governing systems to run their own territory. They can also establish an internal police force to ensure domestic tranquility and a military arm to protect their people and territory from attack and invasion from other nation-states.

3. Nation-states have the sole and absolute ability to raise money within their own borders in the form of taxes, tariffs, bonds, fines, and investments. They also have the sole legal power to coin money and set its value.

4. Nation-states have a responsibility to provide for and play fair with their own citizens. Thus, a nation-state is responsible for providing or at least supporting the development of an infrastructure (i.e., a transportation system [roads, bridges, harbors, airports], a communication system [telephones, radio, television, Internet access, and so on], a sanitation system, an education system, and a health care system) for the safe and profitable operation of the economy of the state.

Although not explicitly part of the Westphalia formula, implied within this picture is the idea that nation-states exist because they are nation-states. In other words, nation-states control territory and govern the people of that territory, and then, if they have done this successfully, they are worthy of the title nation-state. It is not enough just to yell, "Hey! From now on, the six-block area on the east side of Cleveland from 66th Street on the west to 72nd Street on the east, and from St. Clair Ave. on the north to Superior Ave. on the south is now a nation-state." It just does not work that way. In fact, most of the time a nation-state is a nation-state before it calls itself a nation-state. As Lee Harris demonstrates in his perceptive study, *Civilization and Its Enemies: The Next Stage of History,* until the 20th century this requirement was not much of a problem. However, at times over the last 100 years or so, nation-states have been created by other nations-states or by the United Nations simply by cobbling parts of the map together like a jig-saw puzzle, or by giving territory to a group of people. Sometimes this works as it did with Israel in 1948, and sometimes, as in other parts of the Middle East, it does not. In fact, it would not be inaccurate to declare that earning the rank of a nation-state is what marks a functioning nation-state from a failed nation-state, or worse yet, a rogue nation-state. A true nation-state is answerable for its actions. Other entities, which are sometimes referred to as **worldwide organizations** like the World Trade Organization and the World Bank, and outlaw bands such as Al Qaeda and the Red Brigade, do not have the same rank, the same power, or the same respectability as nation-states, because they have neither earned their position nor demonstrated the ability, or even the willingness, to be answerable for their actions on the world stage. For this reason all of the following New World Order theories, save one, assume that nation-states are the key players on the international stage. (For a detailed analysis of the demise of the traditional nation-state see Lee Harris, *Civilization and Its Enemies: The Next Stage of History.* New York: Free Press, 2004, pp. 28-31.)

Post-9/11 New World Order Theories

As noted previously, political pundits have offered four new world orders for our consideration: the economic, the civilizational, the international, and the globalized. Each of these new world orders has several incarnations, each slightly different from the others. Nevertheless, within each category, the variations share more characteristics than differences, so we will focus on those common denominators.

The Economic New World Order

The economic new world order sees the international community as divided into two sectors: (1) those nations that have matured economically and thus have healthy, functioning, though not perfect economies and (2) those nation-states that are economically dysfunctional. Thomas Barnett, senior strategic researcher at the naval war college and author of *The Pentagon's New Map,* calls the functioning nations the Core and the dysfunctional nations the Gap. Richard Haass of the Council on Foreign Relations and author of *The Opportunity* refers to the economically secure nations as the "21st Century Concert," or simply, the Concert. Haass does not directly name the economically unstable nations. However, given his overall theoretical bend, calling them the unintegrated nations would not be out of line. Traditionally, economically sound nations have been referred to as developed nations and economically fragile nations as developing nations. Developed nations include such nation-states as the United States, the countries in Western Europe, China, Russia, Japan, Australia, New Zealand, Canada, South Africa, Israel, and India. The developing nations include nation-states in the Middle East, the Balkans, all of Africa except South Africa, South and Central America, Indonesia, and Southeast Asia.

Both Barnett and Haass insist that developed nation-states must find ways to overcome or eliminate disconnectedness (Barnett's word) or to integrate (Haass's term) the developing nation-states with the Core or Concert. Adopting this perspective dramatically alters the political map and therefore demands a change in tactics. Some nation-states, such as China and Russia, are no longer seen by the United States as "the enemy" as they were during the Cold War. Instead, they are seen as allies within the Concert, and as such, they share a common set of goals with all other Core nations. In contrast, the enemy is any individual, group, or set of circumstances that somehow separates a nation from the Concert or prevents it from developing to the extent that it can become a self-sufficient member of the Core. Under this version of the new world order, international law has certain clear and decisive objectives, namely, to promote the integration of developing nations within the functioning Concert and to fight the forces that keep nation-states underdeveloped, whether those forces are Al Qaeda, warlords in Somalia, drug runners in Columbia, a rogue government, disease, famine, or corporate irresponsibility. (See T. Barnett, *The Pentagon's New Map: War and Peace in the Twenty-first Century,* New York: Berkley Books, 2004; R. N. Haass, *The Opportunity: America's Moment to Alter History's Course,* New York: Public Affairs, 2005.)

The Civilizational New World Order   The civilizational new world order was so named by Samuel Huntington in his book, *The Clash of Civilizations.* This view sees the globe as divided into eight distinct civilizations that are more or less autonomous and more or less incapable of successfully cooperating with more than one, or at the most two, other civilizations at the same time. A **civilization** is a group of people in a series of different nation-states that share certain common characteristics, including their history, religion, traditions, beliefs, often language, and sometimes ancestry. The eight civilizations are Western Civilization (the United States, Canada, Western Europe, Israel, Australia, and New Zealand); the Sinic Civilization (China, North and South Korea, and most of Southeast Asia); the Orthodox Civilization (Russia and other states in Eastern Europe); the Latin American Civilization (South and Central America); the Islamic Civilization (Middle Eastern nation-states, the nation-states of northern Africa, and Indonesia); the African Civilization (the central and southern regions of Africa); the Hindu Civilization (India and Sri Lanka); and the Japanese Civilization.

Some of these civilizations contain powerful central states that serve as a sort of international "big brother" to the lesser states within a civilization. A civilization with a recognized central state is generally more stable, less war-like, and more economically prosperous than one without. The civilizations with central states include Western Civilization (the U.S.); the Sinic Civilization (China); the Hindu Civilization (India); the Orthodox Civilization (Russia); and the Japanese Civilization (Japan). Since most international conflicts occur between rather than within Civilizations, each Civilization is better off if it can limit its contact with other Civilizations. To this end, Huntington has outlined a number of rules that each civilization should follow in dealing with all other civilizations. These rules include (1) the prime directive of the civilizational world order, that is, that each civilization should never interfere with the internal affairs of another civilization; (2) the rule of collective mediation, which calls for dialogue and compromise whenever a dispute arises between civilizations; (3) the commonalities rule which encourages civilizations to emphasize those ideals that draw them together rather than those that drive them apart. Thus, it is healthier for Western Civilization, for instance, to share its focus on self-determination rather than to insist that all nations adopt Western-style democracy. Under this version of the New World Order, international law has two goals: to promote civilizational autonomy and to protect civilizational rights. (See: S. P. Huntington. *The Clash of Civilizations and The Remaking of World Order.* New York: Simon & Schuster, 1996.)

The International New World Order   Like the Economic New World Order, the International New World Order sees the nation-states of the world grouped into economic sectors, zones is the term used by Robert Cooper, author of *The Breaking of Nations: Order and Chaos in the 21st Century,* who is one of the primary supporters of this theory. Unlike the Economic New World Order, however, the International New World Order is divided into three such zones: the pre-modern, the modern, and the postmodern zones. The pre-modern zone resembles Barnett and Haass's disconnected or nonintegrated nations. However, there is a difference because Cooper uses the term "pre-modern" to refer to governments that have lost the ability to govern or have abused or overused their power in order to suppress their people. The modern and postmodern zones differ not so much in economic as in political outlook. Modern zone nation-states, such as Japan and the UK, are those that prefer to honor the Westphalian tradition, and thus emphasize national sovereignty. In contrast, the postmodern zone nations, such as France and Germany, are willing, even eager, to defer to what are called the **NGOs, non-governmental organizations,** such as the United Nations, the World Bank, and the International Criminal Court. Postmodern nations, thus, have a more global view. Some even have the ultimate goal of establishing a world government.

The downside of the international new world order is that it requires a global police force to protect the postmodern zone against the destructive and frequently warlike tendencies of the modern and the pre-modern zones. The NGOs are unable to perform that duty, because they lack the military strength needed to support global judicial declarations, such as the resolutions frequently issued by the UN Security Council. The responsibility for enforcing such orders has fallen on the shoulders of the only nation that has both the military capability and the political nerve to take up that responsibility. That nation-state is the United States, which, according to Cooper, even while operating as a modern zone nation-state must nevertheless stand separate from all other nation-states and all three zones. In effect then, in the international new world order, the United States takes on the role of the *de facto* global government, a role examined at length in a book entitled, *The Case for Goliath: How America Acts as the World Government in the 21st Century,* by Michael Mandelbaum. International law becomes somewhat muddied in this environment. Some global laws must be passed that permit NGOs to have more power and stronger enforcement abilities. Simultaneously, international law under this theory must grant the United States a certain degree of autonomy, especially when the Americans must apply their police power function. (See R. Cooper, *The Breaking of Nations: Order and Chaos in the Twenty-first Century,* New York: Grove Press, 2003; M. Mandelbaum, *The Case for Goliath: How America Acts as the World's Government in the Twenty-first Century,* New York: Public Affairs, 2005.)

The Globalized New World Order
The globalized new world order is the only theory that has abandoned the notion that the nation-state is the primary actor on the international stage. In the globalized world, the multinational corporation, not the nation-state, becomes the seat of ultimate economic, political, and military power. Globalization as a concept sees the world as having become more interconnected because of advances in transportation and communication that make instantaneous contact between parties on a global basis as easy, or perhaps even easier, than it ever was on a local basis. The growth of this instantaneous interconnectedness is the wellspring of all other forms of expansion, not least of which is the use of the Internet as a way to conduct business. Global interconnectedness has greatly benefited international businesses, which can now trade quickly, make contracts instantly, and ship raw materials and finished products from one part of the globe to another in hours.

This level of global integration has fueled other forms of interconnectedness as well. Because orders can be filled instantly and goods shipped almost as fast, products no longer have to be manufactured in the place where they are to be used. Thus, products manufactured in Beijing, China, on Monday can be on the shelves of stores in Willowick, Ohio, on Tuesday. This movement permits the manufacturer to outsource jobs to foreign countries such as China, where wages are lower, working conditions less regulated, and raw materials cheaper. For this reason, firms that moved onto the global scene early in the globalization process have grown rapidly and continued to do well in the international marketplace. Some of these corporations, or mega-corporations as they are sometimes called, have become as economically independent, if not as powerful, as some of the nation-states of the world. Moreover, the mega-corporations do not always suffer the same restraints placed on nation-states. Instead, they can operate on a global level without having to be tied down to a particular place or a particular set of national rules. Under this version of the new world order, international law has a set of unambiguous goals, all of which must ensure the smooth operation of the multinational mega-corporation.

43-2 International Law and War

Karl von Clausewitz, a nineteenth-century Prussian soldier and political scientist, is credited with one of the most often-quoted definitions of war. "War," Clausewitz claims, "is a continuation of politics by other means." In today's world of complex multinational corporations, delicate international relationships, and instantaneous Internet transactions, Clausewitz might have added that war is also the continuation of international business by other means. As we have seen recently, international business can be affected profoundly by war, especially when it is an unpopular war that lacks international legal authorization and when it results in a protracted campaign of attrition that drags on for months with no clear goals and no end in sight. Such a situation can increase costs, cause shortages of raw materials, endanger shipping, and render the execution of a contract commercially impracticable, if not impossible to perform. This scenario may be true even if the parties to a war are not citizens of the nations that are at war. Some of these problems can be solved by the internal law of a particular nation-state.

EXAMPLE 43-2:   The *S.S. Christos* and the Suez Crisis

The Transatlantic Financing Corporation operated the *S.S. Christos,* a cargo ship carrying wheat from Texas to Iran, for the United States government. While the *S.S. Christos* was en route to Iran, Israel invaded Egypt. Two days later, France and Great Britain invaded the Suez Canal Zone. The invasion and subsequent closing of the Suez Canal made it impossible for the *S.S. Christos* to use the canal. A 3,000-mile detour around the southern coast of Africa cost Transatlantic an unexpected $44,000 above the original estimated cost of $305,842.92. When the United States government refused to pay the additional amount, the company brought a lawsuit. Although the United States and Transatlantic were not directly involved in the Suez hostilities, their contract had been affected by the conflict. Nevertheless, the federal court did not allow Transatlantic to recover the additional payment from the government of the United States. The court's decision was based on a traditional rule of contract law in the United States. The court declared, "While it may be an overstatement to say that increased cost and difficulty of performance never constitute impracticability, to justify relief there must be more of a variation between the expected costs and the cost of performing by an available alternative than is present in this case."

The lesson to be learned from the case in Example 43-2 is a simple one: When entering a contract that relies on the international marketplace, it is wise for all parties to be aware of the international conditions in all areas of the globe that may affect the contract. This approach is

Talking Points

In her influential study of World War I, *The Guns of August*, the historian Barbara W. Tuchman writes that in 1910, two very different, yet equally popular, views on the prospect of future wars existed on both sides of the Atlantic. One of these views was represented by a book by Norman Angell entitled *The Great Illusion.* War, Angell argued, had become an untenable option because of the economic connections among the nations of the global community. Any war would have such devastating consequences that nations could no longer afford to engage in any sort of armed conflict.

In support of this view, a key British military leader, Viscount Esher, contended that a combination of factors, including "commercial disaster, financial ruin and individual suffering," made war in the twentieth century "more difficult and improbable" than ever before in the history of civilization (Tuchman, p. 10).

A contradictory position was represented by a German general named Friedrich von Bernhardi who, in a work entitled *Germany and the Next War,* argued that war was inevitable. In fact, Bernhardi argued, war was a consequence of "natural law." Bernhardi insisted that war was a "biological necessity" and actually the human expression of "the struggle for existence." Bernhardi wrote that, among nation-states, "there can be no standing still." He concluded that destruction awaits any country that fails to move up the evolutionary ladder of development (Tuchman, pp. 10–11). "

Of the two positions, which has been supported by the weight of world history in the twentieth century? Which view continues to be popular in the twenty-first century? Which view seems to have been adopted by the international community? Which view seems to be supported by most Americans? Which view seems to be in line with American political and military policy in the twenty-first century? Which view is morally correct? Explain.

crucial because courts in the United States will take into account the foreseeability of any international crisis, including not only war but also war-related events, such as blockades, quarantines, and border closings. If the court deems that the international crisis was foreseeable, the loss suffered by the parties affected by the crisis will not be offset by the court.

The Just War Theory

One central question that cannot be answered solely by the law of a single nation-state is whether a war is just. Ethical and legal philosophers in the West have developed criteria for determining when a war can be considered legally and morally correct. This theory, termed the **just war theory**, has been invoked to defend and question the morality of many armed conflicts. In its traditional form, the theory focuses on two main areas. First, it establishes the criteria that would justify going to war. Second, it institutes criteria for the proper conduct of a war that is already in progress. A third modern feature of justifiability adds a set of criteria that establish the rules of conduct that must be followed after a war ends.

Criteria for Going to War
The just war theory endorses six criteria for deciding whether a war can be morally justified: (1) just cause, (2) right intention, (3) competent authority, (4) probability of success, (5) proportionality, and (6) last resort. The first criterion, **just cause**, says that to be morally permissible, a war must be waged for honorable motives. Included among these motives are self-defense and the defense of a fellow sovereign nation-state that has been targeted by an aggressor and is unable to defend itself properly. The second criterion, **right intention**, declares that a war must be waged only if the combatant has the correct objective. The difference between the first and the second

criteria is the difference between an objective justification for war and the subjective intent of the actual combatants. A war may have an objectively justifiable cause and yet be fought for the wrong reasons. This situation could happen, for instance, if one country goes to the defense of another country but then uses that defensive campaign as a pretext to destroy the government and subjugate the civilian population of the aggressor nation-state.

The third criterion, **competent authority**, states that war can be declared and run only by legitimately recognized nation-states. This standard does not mean, however, as some people have suggested, that the United Nations must declare a war for that war to have been declared by competent authority. In fact, from a legal perspective, the UN cannot declare war. The UN Charter is founded on the belief that all member nations maintain their sovereign authority, including the authority to declare war. This criterion also means that it is not ethically permissible for individuals such as Osama Bin Laden to declare war on anyone. War is a function of nation-states in their relationships with one another, not the purview of individuals.

The fourth criterion, **probability of success**, declares that at the outset of a war, there must be a reasonable chance that the war will be successful; a suicidal war would fall outside this criterion. Fifth, **proportionality** holds that the good advanced by the war must exceed the negative consequences of entering the conflict. Thus, a war fought over an imaginary diplomatic insult must be considered unjust, because the objective of vindicating a spurious affront to national honor is not proportional to the death and destruction caused by war. Finally, the criterion of **last resort** means that a war can be fought only after all other means for the resolution of the dispute have been tried and failed. If both nations still have diplomatic options available for ending the crisis in a nonviolent way; if an international organization, such as the United Nations, is still willing to explore a negotiated settlement; or if time still exists to pursue a nonviolent solution, war cannot be waged as a solution to the conflict, and if one side insists on declaring war, that war will be an unjust conflict. However, the fact that all options have not been implemented is not decisive. What matters is that the nation-state that began the war gave authentic consideration to each available option, short of war.

Criteria for the Proper Conduct of War

It is not enough to advocate a set of ethical and legal criteria for entering war and then ignore the criteria for conducting the war or for conduct that must be followed after the end of a war. For this reason, many modern, legal, and moral theorists suggest several additional criteria that should guide conduct during a war and behavior after a war. The first of the criteria for conducting a war requires that the warring factions use only those military means that are proportional to the ends that they wish to achieve. Thus, because it was possible for the international coalition to subdue and eject the invading Iraqi army from Kuwait in Gulf War I by using conventional weapons, the use of nuclear weapons would have been considered a disproportionate tactic. The second criterion states that the war must be fought with discrimination. This restriction means that only combatants should be targeted in the war and that civilians must be kept out of harm's way.

Criteria for Proper Postwar Conduct

Three just war principles have been established for gauging the morality of conduct following the cessation of hostilities. The first of these principles is the principle of repentance. The **principle of repentance** calls for a genuine expression of remorse by the combatants for the death and destruction caused by war. Conduct that expresses either joy or satisfaction at the death of enemy combatants, even combatants involved in a war of aggression, would violate this principle. The second criterion, the **principle of honorable surrender**, requires the victor in a war to accept the surrender of the enemy and treat the defeated combatants with dignity and respect. Refusing a genuine offer of surrender, violating that surrender after it has been implemented, or mistreating enemy combatants after surrender would all be violations of this principle.

Actions that are motivated by revenge or retribution would also violate the principle of honorable surrender, as would conduct that injures or humiliates prisoners of war. Finally, the **principle of restoration** requires that the victor in a conflict act responsibly in rebuilding the defeated nation's physical environment, economy, and governmental structure.

The Strategy of Preemptive War

A nation-state starts a **preemptive war** to stop another nation-state's imminent attack on the first nation-state. A preemptive war is not the same as a preventative war, though the terms are often used as synonyms. A preemptive war is waged to stop an attack before it can begin. In contrast, a nation-state begins a **preventative war** to stop another nation-state from reaching a point that it would be capable of attacking the first nation. The doctrine adopted by the United States in 2002 was a doctrine of preemptive war, not one of preventative war. The concept of preemptive war goes back 500 years to Thomas More, who in his work *Utopia* noted that it would be wise to attack preemptively a force that was about to attack you. In the United States, two major military figures, General Leslie Groves, the head of The Manhattan Project, which developed the atomic bomb during World War II, and General Curtis LeMay, former commander of the Strategic Air Command (SAC), advocated preemptive war against the Soviet Union. In the 1950s, the Joint Chiefs of Staff commissioned a study that also recommended a preemptive strike against the Soviet Union. In all of these cases, cooler heads prevailed, and preemptive war was not at that time advocated as a strategic policy of the United States.

Times have changed, however, and preemptive war has become an active strategic policy of the United States and was the primary stated motivation for the invasion of Iraq in 2003. Although it is difficult to pinpoint the exact moment of this shift in policy, the move toward preemptive war as the national policy of the United States seems to have come about less than three months after September 11, 2001, when, in the aftermath of the attacks on the World Trade Center and the Pentagon, President George W. Bush asked then-Secretary of Defense Donald Rumsfeld about war plans for an attack against Iraq. Evidence indicates that President Bush had similar strategic planning discussions with Vice President Richard Cheney and National Security Advisor Condoleezza Rice. Nevertheless, the first conscious public declaration of this change in policy occurred in a presidential address to the graduating class of West Point on June 1, 2002.

Preemptive War and the Just War Theory

The just war theory is designed to help individuals and governments make judgments about the justifiability of particular wars rather than about the morality of war in general. Indeed, the very existence of a just war theory presumes that some wars are in fact justifiable. Therefore, it is difficult to characterize the morality of a war-making strategy, such as the strategy of preemptive war, without reference to the war's actual historical context. Nevertheless, all preemptive wars share certain characteristics that make it possible to judge such wars under the theory. First, preemptive wars rarely pass the requirement of last resort, because by definition, they are never a last resort and therefore can rarely be justifiable under that criterion. Second, it is doubtful that a war that is designed to prevent the future actions of an adversary can be proven to outweigh the negative consequences of an actual conflict. Because the actions contemplated by the enemy never actually take place, they can never be weighed accurately against the actions that actually do take place in a war. Thus, preemptive wars often fail the test of proportionality. Third, because preemptive wars are always based on preventing future events rather than dealing with events that have actually taken place, it is much too easy to conjure up a pretext that will allow a nation to go to war against another sovereign state. Such an abuse of power is what the just war theory is designed to prevent. Thus, preemptive wars also often fail the initial just cause test.

Of course, very few philosophical arguments are as clear-cut as the case against preemptive war seems at first. A case can certainly be made that preemptive wars do not automatically fail the just case test. To classify preemptive war automatically as unjust means ignoring the fact that a nation-state may have a valid reason for entering such a conflict. If, for example, one nation-state repeatedly commits a wide variety of human rights violations, especially violations that involve indiscriminate attacks on innocent victims, other nations may be justified in coming to the aid of such innocent victims. In fact, a nation-state that ignores evidence that a rogue nation-state has repeatedly victimized its own people may be morally culpable for failing to act against that rogue nation-state. Similarly, the argument that proportionality can never be judged when the wrong prevented is a future event fails to consider that the best judge of future behavior is usually past behavior. Thus, few reasons exist to believe that a nation-state that has consistently victimized innocent people in the past will change its policy in the future. Finally, the point at which a war becomes a last resort often depends on a number of factors, many of which are highly problematic. In gauging whether a war really was waged as a last resort, the fact that other options were not tried is not evidence that the war was not a last resort. It is generally enough that the other alternatives were authentically considered as viable options. If, after serious consideration, pursuing such alternatives seemed foolish at best and dangerous at worst, the preemptive war may have been justified.

Preemptive War and the New World Order Theories

The concept of preemptive war can also be viewed in relation to the four new world order theories. Such an examination would reveal, not surprisingly, that each theory approaches the problem of preemptive war in a different way. To clarify these differences, it will be helpful to view each theory within the context of a concrete hypothetical. Suppose, for example, that the rogue government of a Middle Eastern nation has been conducting a series of aggressive and unprovoked wars against its neighbors, wars that have killed hundreds of thousands of innocent victims, including citizens of the rogue nation itself. Suppose further that this rogue nation-state has been accused of and has not denied developing and stockpiling biological, chemical, and nuclear weapons, as well as a series of long-range delivery systems. In addition, suppose that in response to repeated resolutions issued by the UN Security Council, the rogue has misled, mistreated, and expelled UN inspectors. Suppose also that the rogue is now suspected of having illicit ties with a series of Middle Eastern terrorists groups, all of which have in the past made successful terror attacks against the United States, Israel, Egypt, Saudi Arabia, Spain, and the United Kingdom. Finally, suppose that the UN has issued one final resolution, ordering the rogue nation-state to cooperate with UN weapons inspectors immediately or face severe negative consequences. Consider each of the four new world orders and then determine how the nation-states of the world ought to deal with the hypothetical rogue. Remember to consider all four of the new world order theories: (1) the Barnett-Haass economic new world order; (2) the Huntington civilizational new world order; (3) the Cooper-Mandelbaum international new world order; and (4) the globalized new world order.

What happens when the deadline passes and the rogue has once again ignored the UN Security Council? The answer depends upon the nature of the new world order in which we find ourselves. If the economic theorists are correct, the rogue is clearly an agent of diviseness and must be dealt with accordingly. The rogue is responsible for the economic, political, and military destabilization of the entire region. This destabilized environment makes it difficult for the rogue's neighbors to focus on the economic and political development of their own people. In addition, the rogue has repeatedly victimized its own people, which further aggravates the region's instability. Moreover, the rogue's relationship with terror groups and its apparent development of chemical, biological, and nuclear weapons makes it dangerous and unpredictable. Given these conditions, the clear course of action for the nations of the Core, once the deadline has passed without compliance, is to wage a preemptive war against the rogue. Of course, the economic theorists would not favor such a move until, or unless, an economic recovery plan could be developed first. There is no point in toppling a regime if it cannot be replaced with a better, fairer, more effective regime. The point is to integrate the nation, not to destroy it. The economic theorists would also point out that it is essential that the people of the regime buy into the restructuring project. If the people oppose the effort, little will be accomplished.

In contrast, if the civilizational new world order is correct, we arrive at an entirely different conclusion. In a world divided into eight civilizations, each of which pursues its own best interests, the problems associated with a Middle Eastern rogue remains a Middle Eastern problem. If the region is unstable, then those nation-states victimized by the instability of the rogue, and only those nations, are charged with the responsibility of dealing with the rogue. The international new world order would see the problem as a global threat that requires the intervention of an international coalition of modern and postmodern nations. Once that coalition was duly authorized by the appropriate international agency, most likely the UN but perhaps NATO, it would be charged with launching a preemptive strike against the rogue. Its objective would be to eliminate the threat to the modern and postmodern zones.

Finally, if the globalized new world order is correct, the problem would be avoided until it threatened the economic stability of international trade. Once international trade was threatened, the response of the mega-corporations would be economic not military. Rather than mobilizing troops, the "megacorps" would mobilize economic sanctions against the rogue. These economic sanctions might include shutting down refineries, raising food prices, stopping shipments of raw materials and finished products, interfering with the flow of immigration, and so on. The goal would be to place a gentle squeeze on the economy of the rogue until it either collapsed under its own weight or changed its ways.

Substantive and Procedural Issues

Most of these just war requirements were established before the advent of contemporary warfare. In the modern age, the face of war has changed. Along with these changes have come alterations in the conduct of war, including ways of dealing with prisoners of war, occupation forces, and war crimes.

Substantive Legal Changes
Following World War II, in 1949, a major effort involving most of the nations of the world and sponsored by the American Red Cross was held in Geneva, Switzerland, to address the issues of prisoners of war, occupation forces, and war crimes. Out of this series of international meetings came the **Geneva Conventions**. These conventions attempt to deal with many of the problems brought on by the nature of warfare in the modern era. For instance, the first, second, and third conventions are concerned with prisoners of war, and the fourth deals with occupation forces.

Procedural and Analytical Problems
Substantive changes in the law of war and international relations, such as the Geneva Conventions, are frequently complicated by procedural and analytical questions. The mere fact that a convention has been written and adopted does not mean that it will be applied properly and consistently by the nations that signed the convention. Analytical questions nearly always plague any court faced with the application of an international agreement. To facilitate this analytical process, the U.S. courts have established some guidelines for interpreting international agreements such as the Geneva Conventions.

For instance, in determining the applicability of such international pacts, the courts will first look at the literal language of the agreement, especially any definitions contained within the agreement. Second, the court will examine any supporting documentation, such as the Red Cross Commentaries in the case of the Geneva Conventions, for assistance in interpreting the settlement. Third, U.S. courts will take a liberal view in the interpretation of such agreements. This guideline means that the court will broadly and openly interpret the convention to include as many cases and situations as are justly warranted.

Quick Quiz 43-2 True or False?

1. One central question that cannot be answered solely by the law of a single nation-state is whether a war is just.

2. The just war theory was developed in the twenty-first century to deal with problems of modern warfare.

3. The Geneva Conventions attempt to establish rules involving occupation forces and prisoners of war.

43-3 International Law and the United Nations

As World War II drew to a close, representatives of 50 nations met in San Francisco to work out the details of the formation of the United Nations. At that meeting, called the United Nations Conference on International Organization, the 50 nations adopted a charter that on June 26, 1945, established the United Nations. The stated purposes of the United Nations are to advance human rights, to end war, to enhance human achievement, to support peaceful international coalitions, and to promote truth, justice, and the rule of law. The promotion of international law has taken many forms within the structure of the United Nations, including the International Law Commission, International Court of Justice, the UN Commission on International Trade Law, and the UN Convention on Contracts for the International Sale of Goods. Although the International Criminal Court stands outside the official system of the UN, it nevertheless has an important role to play in the administration of global justice

The Structure of the United Nations

The United Nations is an enormous, complicated organization that consists of many agencies, organizations, courts, and commissions (see Table 43-1). The three major governing bodies are the Secretary General, the General Assembly, and the Security Council. The **Secretary General** is the chief administrator of the United Nations. He or she heads up the **Secretariat**, which is the administrative bureaucracy of the UN. The Secretary General also takes a leading role in promoting world peace. The Security Council recommends a candidate for the position of Secretary General, but the General Assembly votes that person into office. The **General Assembly** is made up of all the member nations of the UN. Each nation has one vote on resolutions and other matters presented to the assembly. The UN **Security Council** deals with crises that involve threats to international peace. The Council consists of 15 members. Five of these members hold permanent seats: China, France, Russia, the United Kingdom, and the United States. The General Assembly elects the remaining 10 members for two-year terms.

The United Nations Headquarters in New York City.

The International Law Commission

The International Law Commission is responsible for leading the way in the development and codification of international law. Because all UN member nations retain their sovereign identities, the codifications drawn up by the Commission must be joined voluntarily by each nation-state. The Commission meets every year at a time authorized by the General Assembly. A legal topic can make its way to the Commission in one of two ways. Either the General Assembly submits a legal issue to the Commision or the Commission itself decides to pursue a legal problem. After the Commission has examined a legal topic in depth, it may draw up a draft on that aspect of international law. That draft then goes to the General Assembly for further consideration. Once the General Assembly has accepted a draft, it is codified into a convention. That convention is then submitted to the member states for their adoption. Some of the conventions that have been suggested by the Commission and adopted by the General Assembly include the Convention on the Law of Treaties and the Convention on Diplomatic Relations. The General Assembly elects each of the 34 members of the International Law Commission, who each remain on the commission for five years. (See *Basic Facts about the United Nations,* New York: United Nations, 2003, pp. 269–270.)

The International Court of Justice

One of the principal vehicles for the establishment of international law and justice is the **International Court of Justice (ICJ)**. Like many of the agencies of the UN, the ICJ, which is popularly referred to as the World Court, is not located in New York City (see Figure 43-1). Situated at The Hague in the Netherlands, the ICJ was established under provisions within the UN Charter. Key features of the court include its structure and its jurisdiction.

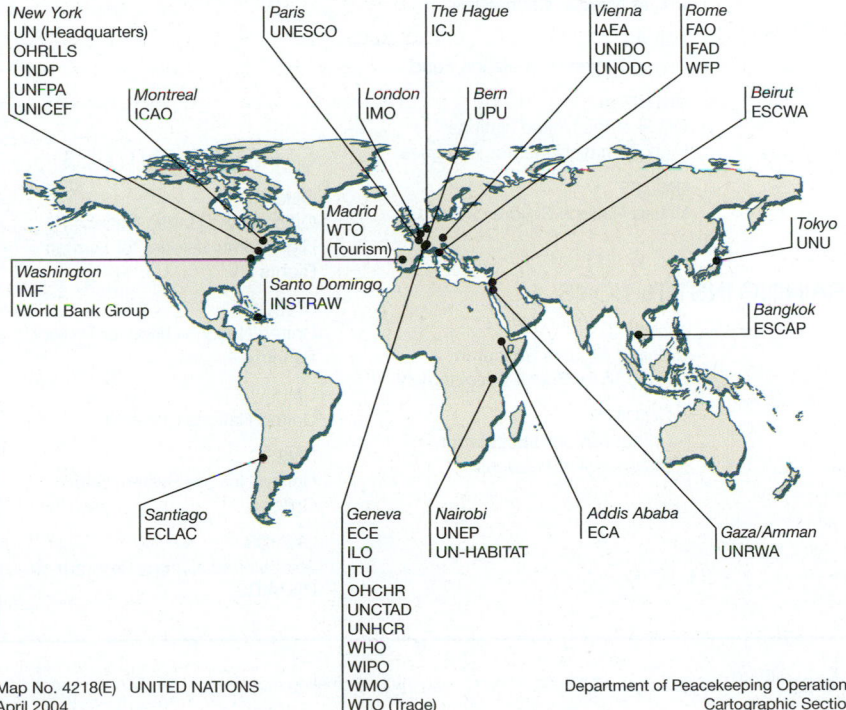

Figure 43-1 The Principal Offices of the United Nations.

Source: Department of Public Information, *Basic Facts about the United Nations* (New York: United Nations, 2003), p. 24.

Table 43-1   The United Nations System

THE UNITED NATIONS SYSTEM

P R I N C I P A L   O R G A N S   O F   T H E   U N I T E D   N A T I O N S

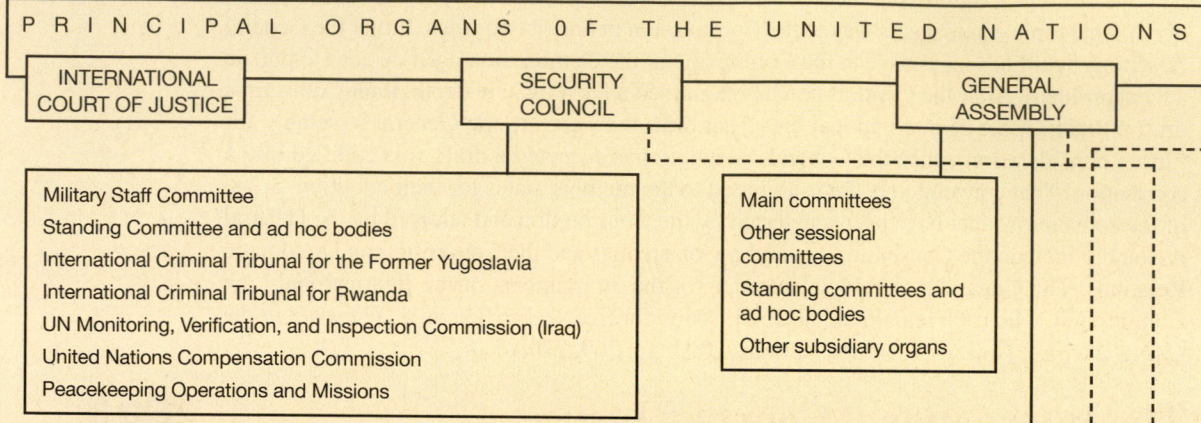

INTERNATIONAL COURT OF JUSTICE	SECURITY COUNCIL	GENERAL ASSEMBLY

Military Staff Committee

Standing Committee and ad hoc bodies

International Criminal Tribunal for the Former Yugoslavia

International Criminal Tribunal for Rwanda

UN Monitoring, Verification, and Inspection Commission (Iraq)

United Nations Compensation Commission

Peacekeeping Operations and Missions

Main committees

Other sessional committees

Standing committees and ad hoc bodies

Other subsidiary organs

PROGRAMS AND FUNDS

UNCTAD
United Nations Conference on Trade and Development

ITC
International Trade Center (UNCTAD,WTO)

UNDCP
United Nations Drug Control Program

UNEP
United Nations Environment Program

UNHSP
United Nations Human Settlements Program
(UN Habitat)

UNDP
United Nations Development Program

UNIFEM
United Nations Development Fund for Women

UNV
United Nations Volunteers

UNFPA
United Nations Population Fund

UNHCR
Office of the United Nations High Commissioner for Refugees

UNICEF
United Nations Children's Fund

WFP
World Food Program

UNRWA**
United Nations Relief and Works Agency for Palestine Refugees in the Near East

OTHER UN ENTITIES

OHCHR
Office of the United Nations High Commissioner for Human Rights

UNOPS
United Nations Office for Project Services

UNU
United Nations University

UNSSC
United Nations System Staff College

UNAIDS
Joint United Nations Program on HIV/AIDS

RESEARCH AND TRAINING INSTITUTIONS

INSTRAW
International Research and Training Institute for the Advancement of Women

UNICRI
United Nations Interregional Crime and Justice Research Institute

UNITAR
United Nations Institute for Training and Research

UNRISD
United Nations Research Institute for Social Development

UNIDIR**
United Nations Institute for Disarmament Research

*Autonomous organizations working with the United Nations and each other through the coordinating machinery of the Economic and Social Council.

**Report only to the General Assembly.

Source: L. Fasulo, *An Insider's Guide to the UN* (New Haven, CT: Yale University Press, 2004), pp. 6–7.

```
┌──────────────────────┐        ┌──────────────────┐        ┌──────────────────┐
│  ECONOMIC AND        │        │  TRUSTEESHIP     │        │  SECRETARIAT     │
│  SOCIAL COUNCIL      │        │  COUNCIL         │        │                  │
└──────────────────────┘        └──────────────────┘        └──────────────────┘
```

FUNCTIONAL COMMISSIONS

Commission for Social
  Development
Commission on Human Rights
Commission on Narcotic Drugs
Commission on Crime Prevention
  and Criminal Justice
Commission on Science and
  Technology for Development
Commission on Sustainable
  Development
Commission on the Status of
  Women
Commission on Population and
  Development
Statistical Commission

REGIONAL COMMISSIONS

Economic Commission for Africa (ECA)
Economic Commission for Europe (ECE)
Economic Commission for Latin
  America and the Caribbean (ECLAC)
Economic Commission for Asia
  and the Pacific (ESCAP)
Economic Commission for
  Western Asia (ESCWA)
United Nations Forum on Forestry
  Sessional and Standing
Committees Expert, ad hoc, and
  related bodies

RELATED ORGANIZATIONS

IAEA
International Atomic Energy Agency

WTO (trade)
World Trade Organization

WTO (tourism)
World Tourism Organization

CTBTO
Preparatory Commission for the
Comprehensive Nuclear-Test-Ban-
Treaty Organization

OPCW
Organization for the Prohibition of
Chemical Weapons

SPECIALIZED AGENCIES*

ILO
International Labor Organization

FAO
Food and Agriculture
Organization of the United Nations

UNESCO
United Nations Educational, Scientific,
and Cultural Organization

WHO
World Health Organization

WORLD BANK GROUP

  IBRD
  International Bank for Reconstruction
  and Development

  IDA
  International Development Association

  IFC
  International Finance Corporation

  MIG
  Multilateral Investment Guarantee
  Agency

  ICSID
  International Center for Settlement of
  Investment Disputes

IMF
International Monetary Fund

ICAO
International Civil Aviation Organization

IMO
International Maritime Organization

ITU
International Telecommunications Union

UPU
Universal Postal Union

WMO
World Meteorological Organization

WIPO
World Intellectual Property Organization

IFAD
International Fund for Agricultural
Development

OSG
Office of the Secretary-General

OIOS
Office of Internal Oversight
Services

OLA
Office of Legal Affairs

DPA
Department of Political Affairs

DDA
Department for Disarmament
Affairs

DPKO
Department of Peacekeeping
Operations

OCHA
Office for the Coordination of
Humanitarian Affairs

DESA
Department of Economic and
Social Affairs

DGAACS
Department of General
Assembly Affairs and Conference
Services

DPI
Department of Public Information

DM
Department of Management

OIP
Office of the Iraq Program

UNSECOORD
Office of the United Nations
Security Coordinator

ODC
Office on Drugs and Crime

UNOG
UN Office at Geneva

UNOV
UN Office at Vienna

UNON
UN Office at Nairobi

The Structure of the ICJ The ICJ is made up of fifteen judges. The Security Council and the General Assembly of the United Nations are jointly responsible for electing these judges, each of whom serves a nine-year term. All of the judges are also eligible for reelection. To ensure as much impartiality as possible, the UN Charter also specifies that no two judges can be citizens of the same country and that the judges may not have any additional employment while they sit on the Court. Ideally, the judges are chosen because of their legal qualifications. Every attempt is also made to ensure that the judges exemplify the foremost legal institutions in the world. When a nation is involved in a case presented to the ICJ, that nation is permitted to appoint a single judge to the court on a temporary basis.

Standing Within the ICJ Only sovereign nations have legal standing to initiate a case before the ICJ. Included within this category are nations that are member states of the United Nations. Nations that are not member states, however, may also have cases heard before the Court. Questions on the legal standing of nonmember states are left up to the determination of the General Assembly and the Security Council.

Subject Matter Jurisdiction in the ICJ Subject matter jurisdiction in the ICJ is outlined within the UN Charter. This jurisdiction includes legal questions specifically referred to within the charter, as well as any legal question raised by a member nation before the court. Such legal questions may involve the interpretation of treaties and international conventions. Unlike the courts of the United States, which can render opinions only when faced with an actual case, the ICJ is permitted to issue advisory opinions when requested by nation-states, the General Assembly, the Security Council, or other authorized agencies within the structure of the United Nations. Those judges who disagree with the advisory opinion of the majority are empowered to issue dissenting opinions. In an advisory case, sometimes a dissenting opinion can be just as vital as the majority opinion, because the dissenter's rationale may be used in other venues.

EXAMPLE 43-3: Jurisdiction, Advisory Opinions, and the ICJ

One source of advisory opinions involves the question of how the corporate body of the United Nations relates to individual member nations. For instance, in 1949, the General Assembly solicited an advisory opinion from the ICJ concerning the assassination of a UN mediator. The mediator had been killed on a mission to Palestine. The issue before the court was whether the United Nations could hold a member state liable for any harm that befell an agent of the United Nations. The Court found that the UN did indeed have that capacity.

The International Criminal Court

To deal with crimes against humanity, an official **International Criminal Court (ICC)** was set up by the Rome Statute of the International Criminal Court in 1998. Unlike the ICJ, the ICC is not an official agency of the United Nations, though the UN was instrumental in its establishment. The objective of the new court, which actually began operation in 2002, is to preside over trials involving genocide, war crimes, and other human rights violations. The International Criminal Court itself and its prison are physically situated in The Hague, along with the International Court of Justice. Eighteen judges, no two of whom may be citizens of a single country, serve on the ICC for a term of nine years. The judges are elected by the states who are parties to the statute. The Court also names one of the judges as President, as well as a registrar and an official prosecutor.

The Opening Case Revisited
The Sanchez Ultimatum, Round 2

In The Opening Case at the beginning of this chapter, we learned that the ren-
egade terrorist named Diego Sanchez had returned to Argentina, where a
French investigation concluded that Sanchez had been an agent provocateur
controlled by the Argentinean government. When the French investigators demanded that Argentinean officials turn Sanchez over to the International Criminal Court in The Hague, they refused, arguing that the Argentinean
government had the right under the Rome Statute to try Sanchez itself rather
than handing him to the ICC. The French claimed that the Argentinean government had been given enough time to prosecute Sanchez but had not done
so. That delay, it argued, had transformed the Sanchez case into a matter for
the ICC. The Argentinean government countered that Sanchez had not yet
been permitted to exhaust all Argentinean procedures, and until he did, he
would remain in their custody. At that point, the case became permanently
stalled. Sanchez continued to remain in Argentinean custody, the French continued to demand the release of Sanchez into their custody, and the ICC continued to remain silent.

One of the key differences between the ICJ and the ICC is that the ICC has jurisdiction over individual defendants. Interestingly enough, the ICC does not have original
jurisdiction over a defendant who has been charged with war crimes, genocide, or other
offenses against humanity. Rather, the defendant's own government must prosecute the
defendant before the ICC can claim jurisdiction. Should the government fail to bring
legal action against the defendant, the ICC can then step into the case. This feature has
caused some concern among opponents of the ICC, who argue that the Court could be
used as a tool for political persecution. Supporters counter this concern by pointing out
that even though the ICC is not an official arm of the UN, the UN Security Council is
empowered to intervene in a wrongful legal procedure perpetrated within or by the
Court. One major drawback is that the Court has very limited authority. Specifically, it
can hear only cases that involve the citizens of those countries that ratified the original
treaty that created the Court. Several major countries, including the United States, have
not ratified the treaty, which places their citizens outside the court's jurisdiction. (See
L. Fasulo, *An Insider's Guide to the UN*, New Haven, CT: Yale University Press, 2004,
pp. 100–104; *Basic Facts about the United Nations*, New York: United Nations, 2003,
p. 279.)

The UN Commission on International Trade Law

In 1996, the General Assembly of the United Nations authorized the creation of the UN
Commission on International Trade Law (UNCITRAL). The commission consists of
36 nations chosen to represent the primary social, economic, legal, and geographical areas
of the globe. The goal of the commission is to cultivate the organization and integration of
international law in relation to international trade. To this end, it coordinates the activities
of institutions involved in international trade, encourages continued commitment to current
treaties and conventions, and constructs new agreements for the community of international trade.

A Question of Ethics

The United States has repeatedly refused to ratify the Rome Statute of the International Criminal Court. Supporters of the international new world order might see this refusal as a puzzling development. After all, if the United States must act as the *de facto* world government, which is what the international order position seems to promote, it ought to benefit from any additional law enforcement support it can get. However, a closer look at this situation will reveal that this interpretation is not quite the case. If the United States must act as the *de facto* world government, the United States military must act as a *de facto* world police force. A police force, by its very nature, must enter dangerous, volatile, and potentially hazardous situations. Some of these police actions call for split-second decision making. Others may involve decisions that neither side in the action will approve or appreciate. As a result, the U.S. military will always be at risk of politically motivated prosecutions in the ICC. If, as the international order scenario suggests, the United States is to act above and beyond both the modern and the postmodern zones, then its military needs the type of legal protection from political retribution that the ICC cannot now promise to deliver.

The UN Convention on Contracts for the International Sale of Goods

One of these agreements is the **UN Convention on Contracts for the International Sale of Goods (CISG)**. This agreement became effective in 1988. It applies only to sales between businesses located in different countries. The agreement specifically excludes contracts involving goods purchased for use by individuals or families. The CISG affects the formation of an international trade contract, as well as the rights and duties that arise under such contracts. However, it deals neither with the validity of such contracts nor with the liability of the seller for harm caused by the goods. Application of the CISG is limited to businesses that are located in countries that have ratified the agreement or those that create contracts that expressly stipulate that the CISG will apply to the agreement.

The CISG governs contracts for goods within the international community in much the same way that the Uniform Commercial Code (UCC) applies to sale-of-goods contracts within the United States. There are some significant differences, however. For example, the UCC applies to contracts between merchants and to those that involve nonmerchants. The CISG, in contrast, involves only contracts between merchants. The UCC also involves not only sale-of-goods contracts but also other commercial agreements, such as leases. The CISG, in contrast, applies only to sale-of-goods contracts. Also, the UCC has modified the traditional mirror image rule to overcome problems caused by the battle of the forms. The CISG still applies the mirror image rule to the acceptance of a contractual offer. Finally, the UCC has a provision that says that any contract for the sale of goods valued at over $500 must be in writing to be enforceable. The CISG has no such provision.

Additional UN Economic Agencies

The efforts extended by the United Nations to monitor and regulate economic conditions in the global marketplace are evident in the existence of various organizations, each of which has its own mission in the financial structure of the worldwide economy. These agencies include global councils and conferences such as the Economic and Social Council (ECOSOC) and the UN Conference on Trade and Development (UNCTAD), as well as regional agencies such as the Economic Commission for Africa and the Economic

Commission for Europe. Other agencies include the International Labor Organization; the World Health Organization; the United Nations Educational, Scientific, and Cultural Organization (UNESCO); the World International Property Organization (WIPO); and the Food and Agriculture Organization. Each organization makes assessments and enters judgments that influence how international business is conducted. One such organization that has special significance in this regard is the Division for Science and Technology of UNCTAD.

The Division for Science and Technology of UNCTAD

The **Division for Science and Technology** was created in response to recommendations made by the eighth conference of UNCTAD and the Ad Hoc Working Group of the International Commission on Science and Technology. Both of these groups saw the need to improve the international sharing of science and technology among governments, businesses, and educational institutions, especially between developed and developing nations. The Division of Science and Technology was created to coordinate the activities of several agencies that previously had been charged with handling issues of international cooperation in the sharing of science and technology for economic development. Many experts see this creation as a step in the right direction but urge an even more unified response in this regard.

The Economic Security Council

The Commission on Global Governance, a 26-member international organization, has suggested streamlining the surveillance of international economic efforts under the auspices of an **Economic Security Council (ESC)**. The ESC would be a single, unified international agency under the management of the United Nations that would monitor the economic activities of the member nations of the UN. The ESC would evaluate the state of the international economy and implement long-term strategic planning to promote sustainable development across the planet. However, the ESC would not take the place of existing international agencies, such as the Economic and Social Council or the UN Conference on Trade and Development, but instead would coordinate their efforts in an efficient, effective, and economic manner.

Quick Quiz 43-3 True or False?

1. The Secretary General is the chief administrator of the United Nations.

2. When a nation is involved in a case presented to the ICJ, that nation must voluntarily eliminate any judge on the panel that is a citizen of that nation.

3. The UCC and the CISG are identical in every way.

43-4 International Law, Finance, and Trade

Not everyone who wants to enter a local business transaction has the ready cash to do so. This hurdle, however, does not necessarily prevent them from looking for ways to expand their financial base. Therefore, by their very nature, business transactions often involve buying on credit, borrowing money, and investing in risky ventures designed to make a fast profit. The same thing can be said about international business transactions. To deal with issues of finance and trade on a worldwide scale, several international organizations and agreements have emerged that are designed to make global dealings work as smoothly as local ones.

The International Monetary Fund and the World Bank

Two organizations that emerged in the aftermath of the Great Depression and World War II were the International Monetary Fund and the World Bank. Both institutions came out of a series of meetings held in Bretton Woods, New Hampshire, in the final months of World War II. The **International Monetary Fund (IMF)** is designed to serve as a way for financially strapped nations to secure loans that will help them engage in programs of sustainable economic growth and development. The IMF has 184 members, each of which has pledged to act responsibly in the pursuit of economic and developmental goals.

The **World Bank** has a mission that is quite similar to the mission of the IMF. The difference is that the IMF is dedicated to helping all nations, developed, developing, and undeveloped, with fiscal problems, whereas the World Bank works exclusively with the poorest nations in the international community. Even this mission is split between the two arms of the World Bank. The International Bank for Reconstruction and Development (IBRD) handles more conventional loans based on normal market provisions, whereas the International Development Association (IDA) handles loans to the world's most economically challenged nations.

The World Trade Organization

LO7

LO8

After the end of World War II, the primary trading nations of the international community met to work out the details of a major trade agreement. The agreement, named the **General Agreement on Tariffs and Trade (GATT)**, had as part of its original plan the creation of an International Trade Organization (ITO). Although the ITO was never established, GATT continued to function, frequently holding international conferences on the formation and execution of international trade law. The eighth conference, which came to be known as the Uruguay Round Agreements, resulted in the creation of the **World Trade Organization (WTO)**.

The Structure of the World Trade Organization

The World Trade Organization was designed to serve as the corporate nucleus for the management of international trade relationships. As such, the WTO replaced GATT as the focus of world trade talks. However, all agreements, treaties, and trade obligations created under GATT have been included in the WTO and thus remain in force. The structure of the WTO involves three levels: the Ministerial Conference, the General Council, and the Secretariat. The power to make key determinations under the authority of multinational trade agreements falls to the Ministerial Conference, which meets every two years. The responsibilities of the Ministerial Conference pass to the General Council whenever the Ministerial Conference is not assembled. Finally, the Secretariat, which is headed by a Director General, is responsible for the administration of the WTO.

The World Trade Organization is a constant target of controversy and its summits are frequently targeted by hostile and aggressive protesters.

The World Trade Organization Principles

The WTO has established certain overall principles that regulate how member nations must treat one another in the world of international trade. The first principle, the **national treatment principle**, states that WTO nations must apply the same standards to imports that they apply to domestic goods. The second principle, the **most-**

favored nation principle, maintains that all member nations must apply the same privileges, advantages, and benefits to all other member nations in relation to similar imports. The third principle, the **tariff-based principle**, asserts that the only way that member nations can regulate the imports of other nations is through tariffs. This rule eliminates the use of more drastic techniques, such as boycotts, quotas, and quantitative limits.

The Dispute Settlement Board   The **Dispute Settlement Board (DSB)** of the WTO was established to provide a forum for settling trade disputes among member nations. The DSB follows a commonly adopted procedure known as the **Dispute Settlement Understanding (DSU)**. All member nations can be held accountable under DSU regulations. According to those regulations, only member nations have standing to initiate a case. The DSU implements a number of measures designed to improve the way that quarrels are handled. For instance, the DSU has set up a series of precise time limits for the stages in a trade conflict. The DSU ensures that a network of comprehensive guidelines is followed consistently in all such controversies. The DSU also allows effective retaliatory measures that can be implemented by one nation against another if the offending nation refuses to adhere to a decision rendered under the DSU.

EXAMPLE 43-4:   The WTO, Germany, and the Korean Retaliation

Germany and Korea were involved in a dispute concerning trade in electronic appliances and automobiles. Korea claimed that in violation of trade agreements, Germany imposed a tariff on certain electronic appliances manufactured in Korea and imported to Germany. Korea followed proper DSU procedures and received a ruling from a panel that was supported by an appellate board. The ruling indicated that Germany had indeed violated the agreement. The WTO could not directly sanction Germany. Instead, it allowed Korea to impose an enormous tariff on luxury and sports model automobiles imported from Germany to Korea. This form of sanction is known as retaliation.

The North American Free Trade Agreement

The United States and many other similarly situated nations have entered comprehensive trade coalitions designed to open their borders to the free flow of international trade. The most famous of these comprehensive coalitions is the **North American Free Trade Agreement (NAFTA)**, a trading coalition that includes the United States, Canada, and Mexico. The goal of the coalition is to establish a trading market in North America, free from the burdens imposed by internal tariff barriers. Thus, each country within the agreement can take advantage of this free market by importing those goods that it cannot produce itself in exchange for the tariff-free exportation of the goods that it can produce.

LO9

The European Union

One of the most significant events to affect international law and commerce lately has been the inauguration of the **European Union (EU)**. The creation of the European Union, the attempt to formulate a common European economic policy, and the introduction of a common currency for most of Europe may transform the EU into a major competitor with the power to challenge American business interests in the global marketplace. Moreover, because many businesses within the EU have embraced cybercommerce, American firms may face unique challenges in that arena.

LO10

Business Law in the News

Disney World: The Great Walt of China

China's casual attitude toward product piracy costs foreign brands billions of dollars, has drawn withering international criticism, and prompted the U.S. to file a complaint with the World Trade Organization last month. Yet when a **You Tube** video clip of a Beijing area amusement park stocked with **Walt Disney**-like characters hit the Internet—and caught Disney's eye—Beijing took notice.

This isn't the sort of publicity China wants right now as Vice-Premier Wu Yi leads a trade mission to Washington on May 22–24. Waiting for her there: U.S. anger over the mainland's big trade surplus, restrictive currency policy, and intellectual-property rip-offs.

The Disney trouble started when a Japanese TV news crew visited Beijing's Shijingshan Amusement Park during China's spring holidays in early May and shot footage of characters that looked just like Mickey and Minnie Mouse, Snow White, Donald Duck, and other copyrighted properties. Disney lawyers, not amused, contacted Beijing's Copyright Bureau, pointing out that the park has no contractual rights to use the entertainment giant's characters.

Since then Shijingshan park officials have "enacted emergency measures" to resolve the matter, according to the bureau's deputy director, Wang Yefei. Even the Foreign Affairs Ministry weighed in, during a May 10 press briefing usually devoted to weightier matters. "We have noticed the media report," said spokeswoman Jiang Yu, adding that while attention focused on the fake Disneyland, "there are signs that not only are foreign brands such as Disney being hurt by copyright infringement, but also Chinese brands."

By May 12, there were no Disney-like creatures at the park, though attractions with titles like the Adventures of Cinderella were still running. Park General Manager Liu Jingwang said he didn't understand all the fuss. "We have our own mascots," he said. "We don't need to imitate other people." Disney officials seem satisfied for now. "The protection of intellectual property and the guarantee of a quality Disney experience for consumers is vital to our business," said Disney Asia spokeswoman Alannah Goss in an e-mail statement to *BusinessWeek,* adding that "we appreciate the efforts of the Beijing Copyright Bureau in dealing with this situation."

Questions for Analysis

1. What agreement established the World Trade Organization (WTO)?

2. Why did the United States government, rather than the Walt Disney Corporation, bring the infringement case to the WTO?

3. What procedures would be used to handle this type of dispute in the WTO?

4. Which of the new world order theories does this story appear to support the most? Explain.

5. Which of the new world order theories does this story appear to support the least? Explain.

Source: Chi-Chu Tschang and Ron Grover, "Disney World: The Great Walt of China," *BusinessWeek,* May 28, 2007, 16.

The Introduction of the Euro To adopt the **euro**, Europe's common currency, a country must first belong to the European Union. Membership in the EU alone, however, is not enough to allow a nation to adopt the euro. In addition, a nation must have a stable inflation rate, a history of interest rate convergence that falls within certain guidelines, and a pattern of fiscal responsibility. Of those nations that have qualified, eleven, including Austria, Belgium, France, Germany, Ireland, Italy, Luxembourg, the Netherlands, and Spain, elected to join the effort. Several nations, including the United Kingdom, Denmark, and Sweden, opted out of the program. The use of the euro is designed to lower costs by eliminating the need to change currencies when firms in the member states deal with one another across national boundaries.

Electronic Commerce and the European Union

The EU has been active in the development of electronic commerce directives in an attempt to head off proposed legislative initiatives in the individual member nations. Such individualized rules would complicate the rules of European e-commerce and defeat the purpose of a unified EU economic policy. One example of a unified directive is the Data Protection Directive. This directive assures all citizens of Europe that they will enjoy certain definitive privacy rights when they engage in e-commerce. Among the rights held by consumers in Europe are the right to obtain any computer data stored about them, the right to adjust any incorrect data, the right to deny another party the use of computer data, and the right to a legal remedy for any unlawful activities in relation to computer data. Another EU directive that affects e-commerce is the Directive on the Protection of Consumers in Respect of Distance Contracts (ECD). This directive gives specifically enumerated privileges to consumers who deal with companies selling goods and services within the EU by electronic means. The ECD allows consumers to cancel any electronic commerce transaction without penalty within seven working days.

The euro became the common currency used by European Union member states in 2002, replacing many of the individual currencies and providing consistency for the EU.

EXAMPLE 43-5:   The Case of the Dissatisfied European e-Consumer

Clay Joseph, a British citizen, was in the process of creating a new corporation that he hoped would revolutionize the comic book industry. To implement his business plan, he ordered a set of display cases from Volkmann Displays Unlimited, a German firm. On the same day, he also ordered a set of office furniture from IKEA in Sweden. When Joseph received the package from Volkmann, he discovered that the display cases could not hold the material that he wanted to store. One day later, the IKEA shipment arrived. Again he was dissatisfied, not because of any flaw in the furniture but because he had misjudged how the color of the chairs would fit into his office decor. As a European e-consumer, Clay Joseph's purchase of the books and the office furniture would be protected by the Directive on the Protection of Consumers in Respect of Distance Contracts (ECD), and he could rescind both deals within seven business days with no penalty whatsoever.

Did You Know?

The official symbol for the euro looks like this: €. The symbol itself is usually printed in yellow with a blue background.

Quick Quiz 43-4 True or False?

1. Two organizations that emerged in the aftermath of the Great Depression and World War II were the International Monetary Fund and the World Bank.

2. None of the agreements, treaties, or trade obligations created under GATT have been included in the WTO.

3. NAFTA is a trading coalition that includes the United States, the United Kingdom, and Greenland.

Summary

43.1   It is important to define the new world order and explain how it works because international law exists within that global order. The problem of defining the new world order is made more difficult because it is unfamiliar and difficult to understand. Four theories have been offered to describe the new world order: (1) the economic new world order, (2) the civilizational new world order, (3) the international new world order, and (4) the globalized new world order.

43.2   War has many significant effects on the transaction of business in the international marketplace. One of the key questions concerning the nature of war as it relates to international business is whether the war is just. Ethical and legal philosophers in the West have developed criteria for determining when a war can be considered legally and morally correct. This theory is termed the just war theory.

43.3   The stated purposes of the United Nations are to advance human rights, to end war, to enhance human achievement, to support peaceful international coalitions, and to promote international fidelity to truth, justice, and the rule of law. The promotion of international law has taken many forms within the structure of the United Nations, including the International Court of Justice, the UN Commission on International Trade Law, and the UN Convention on Contracts for the International Sale of Goods. The International Criminal Court also plays a key role in policing international justice.

43.4   To deal with issues of finance and trade on a worldwide scale, several international organizations and agreements have emerged that are designed to make global dealings work as smoothly as local ones. These include the International Monetary Fund, the World Bank, the World Trade Organization, the North American Free Trade Agreement, and the European Union.

Key Terms

civilization, 918

competent authority, 922

Dispute Settlement Board (DSB), 935

Dispute Settlement Understanding (DSU), 935

Division for Science and Technology, 933

Economic Security Council (ESC), 933

euro, 936

European Union (EU), 935

General Agreement on Tariffs and Trade (GATT), 934

General Assembly, 926

Geneva Conventions, 925

International Court of Justice (ICJ), 927

International Criminal Court (ICC), 930

International Monetary Fund (IMF), 934

just cause, 921

just war theory, 921

last resort, 922

most-favored nation principle, 934

national treatment principle, 934

nation-state, 916

new world order, 915

nongovernmental organization (NGO), 918

North American Free Trade Agreement (NAFTA), 935

preemptive war, 923

preventative war, 923

principle of honorable surrender, 922

principle of repentance, 922

principle of restoration, 923

probability of success, 922

proportionality, 922

right intention, 921

Secretariat, 926

Secretary General, 926

Security Council, 926

tariff-based principle, 935

UN Commission on International Trade Law (UNCITRAL), 931

UN Convention on Contracts for the International Sale of Goods (CISG), 932

Westphalia system, 916

World Bank, 934

World Trade Organization (WTO), 934

Worldwide organization, 917

Questions for Review and Discussion

1. What are the four new world order theories?
2. What are the criteria for a just war?
3. What is the extent of the jurisdiction of the International Court of Justice?
4. What is the mission of International Criminal Court?
5. What is the main goal of UNCITRAL?
6. What are the differences between the UCC and the CISG?
7. What is the structure of the World Trade Organization?
8. What are the objectives of the Dispute Settlement Understanding?
9. What is the major purpose of NAFTA?
10. What is the European Union?

Investigating the Internet

Access the Web site of the International Law Commission of the United Nations and, in a brief report, answer the following questions: (1) When was the International Law Commission established? (2) How many members sit on the Commission? (3) When and where does the International Law Commission hold its annual session? (4) What activities are held during the annual session? (5) How can the International Law Commission be contacted?

Cases for Analysis

1. After General Manuel Noriega had come under the authority of the United States forces following the invasion of Panama, his attorneys argued that he should be treated as a prisoner of war (POW) under the Geneva Conventions. The United States government agreed to treat Noriega as a POW but refused to give him official POW status. Noriega's attorneys argued that this treatment as POW could be withdrawn by the government at any time. They asked the court to declare their client a POW under the Geneva Conventions. The government argued that the events in Panama were considered hostilities rather than a war. Consequently, the government pointed out, Noriega could not be a POW. Article II of Geneva Convention III states that "the present convention shall apply to all cases of declared war and of any other armed conflict which may arise between two or more of the High Contracting Parties, even if the state of war is not recognized by one of them." Moreover, the International Red Cross Commentary on Convention III says, "Any difference between two states leading to the intervention of the armed forces is an armed conflict within the meaning of Article II." Finally, Article IV of the Convention defines POWs as "persons belonging to one of the following categories, who have fallen into the power of the enemy: (1) members of the armed forces of a Party to the conflict. . . ." Taking all of this into account, as well as the United States courts' intent to construe the Geneva Conventions liberally, should the court declare Noriega a POW? Explain. *United States of America v. Manuel Antonio Noriega*, 808 F. Supp. 791 (S.D. FL).

2. American Rice, Inc., a U.S. corporation, sold its goods in Saudi Arabia under the trade name of ABU BINT, which means "of the girl." Another American corporation, the Arkansas Rice Growers Cooperative Association, marketed similar products in Saudi Arabia using the name BINT

ALARAB, which in English means "Gulf Girl." American Rice sued Arkansas in federal district court under the Lanham Act, alleging an infringement by Arkansas of American Rice's exclusive trademark. None of the Arkansas rice products that American Rice complained of had entered any market within the United States. Arkansas argued that the federal district court had no extra-territorial power to mediate this international trade dispute. Was Arkansas correct? Explain. *American Rice, Inc., v. Arkansas Rice Growers Coop. Ass'n.,* 701 F.2d 414 (5th Cir.).

3. Gulf Oil Corporation and Eastern Air Lines entered a contract under the terms of which Gulf Oil was obligated to supply Eastern with jet fuel according to an established pricing system. In 1973, the Organization for Petroleum Exporting Countries (OPEC) established an oil embargo that precipitated the now-famous energy crisis of the 1970s. As a result of the oil embargo and the energy crisis, the price of crude oil skyrocketed. Gulf Oil asked Eastern to consent to a price increase over the price agreed to under the original contract. Eastern refused to comply with the increase. Gulf Oil then vowed to stop all jet fuel shipments to Eastern unless Eastern would reconsider its refusal to go along with the price increase. Eastern filed a lawsuit in federal district court alleging a breach of contract on Gulf Oil's part. Did the American court have jurisdiction over an exclusively American contract affected by an international incident, such as the 1973 oil embargo? Did the court agree that Gulf breached its contract with Eastern Airlines? Explain. *Eastern Air Line, Inc., v. Gulf Oil Corporation,* 415 F. Supp. 429 (S.D. FL).

4. Kenneth Armstrong, an American citizen, purchased the component parts of computers in Germany, Japan, and the United States. He took those parts to Bolivia, where he constructed the computers, stamped them with the name Starlight

Computers, and sold them. Armstrong had a Bolivian registration that allowed him to use the trade name Starlight. Although none of the computers were imported into the United States by Armstrong himself, many of the counterfeit computers eventually found their way into the U.S. marketplace. Starlight Computers, Inc., an American corporation, brought a lawsuit against Armstrong in United States District Court under the Lanham Act. Armstrong moved for a dismissal of the case, arguing that the American court did not have the authority to enforce the Lanham Act against his Bolivian operation. Is Armstrong correct? Explain.

5. France and Japan are involved in a dispute regarding trade in aircraft parts. France claims that in violation of certain trade agreements, Japan is imposing a tariff on certain types of aircraft parts that are manufactured in France and imported to Japan. France follows proper DSU procedures and receives a ruling from a panel that is supported by an appellate board. The ruling indicates that Japan has indeed violated the agreement. France asks the WTO to apply punitive sanctions directly against Japan. Will France's request be granted? Explain.

6. Helga Godel, a German citizen, placed an order for certain software items from Pascal Enterprises, a French firm. On the same day, she ordered a silverware set from Silverwings Ltd., an Austrian company. When Godel received the package from Pascal, she unwrapped the software and attempted to download the program into her computer. When she accessed the program, however, she found that though the program worked well, it was not what she had expected. Later that day, she received the silverware set. Again she was dissatisfied, this time with the quality of the product. As a European e-consumer, what rights does Godel have under the EU Directive on the Protection of Consumers in Respect of Distance Contracts? Explain.

Quick Quiz Answers

43-1		43-2		43-3		43-4	
1.	T	1.	T	1.	T	1.	T
2.	T	2.	F	2.	F	2.	F
3.	F	3.	T	3.	F	3.	F

Part 9 Case Study

Legal Consequences of the Construction of a Wall in the Occupied Palestinian Territory (Request for Advisory Opinion)
The International Court of Justice
Order of 30 January 2004

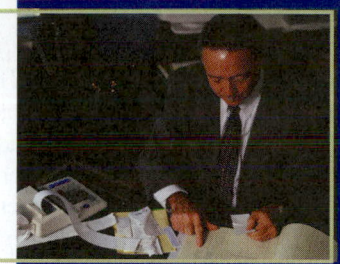

Summary

The International Court of Justice is an agency of the United Nations, established under a statute within the UN Charter. Fifteen judges sit on the ICJ. The judges are elected by the Security Council and the General Assembly of the United Nations for nine years. The judges are also eligible for reelection. To ensure as much impartiality as possible, no nation-state can have more than a single judge on the Court at the same time. The statute also says that judges must work exclusively for the Court during their term on the bench. Ideally, the judges on the Court are chosen because of their legal qualifications. Every attempt is also made to make certain that the judges exemplify the foremost legal institutions in the world.

The statute establishing the ICJ also includes provisions to ensure the impartiality of the judges. One such provision is Article 17, paragraph 2, which states, "No Member [of the ICJ] may participate in the decision of any case in which he has previously taken part as agent, counsel, or advocate for one of the parties, or as a member of a national or international court, or of a commission of enquiry, or in any other capacity."

The present case involves the question of whether one of the judges on the ICJ ought to be permitted to participate in the case or be disqualified under this provision because of his previous involvement in the issue before the Court. The case was brought to the ICJ by the Government of Israel in a letter addressed to the Court Registrar, dated December 31, 2003. In that letter, the government asserted:

> Resolution A/RES/ES-10/14 requesting the advisory opinion locates the request squarely in the context of the wider Arab-Israeli/Israeli-Palestinian dispute. The essentially contentious nature of the proceedings is also recognised by the Court's invitation to Palestine to participate in the case. It is inappropriate for a Member of the Court to participate in decisions in a case in which he has previously played an active, official and public role as an advocate for a cause that is in contention in this case. Israel will be writing to the President of the Court separately on this matter pursuant to Article 34 (2) of the Rules of Court.

Israel objected to the connection that Judge Nabil Elaraby of Egypt had to the case because of his involvement in a number of initiatives that touched on several sensitive issues involved in the dispute. Specifically, Israel pointed to the judge's contributions to the Tenth Emergency Session of the General Assembly of the United Nations, his employment as a legal counselor to the Egyptian Ministry of Foreign Affairs, his work as a legal consultant to the Egyptian Delegates to the Middle East Peace Initiative at Camp David in 1978, and his connection to certain actions resulting from the 1979 Israeli–Egypt Peace Treaty, especially the development of independent West Bank and Gaza Strip territories. Finally, and perhaps most significantly, the government of Israel pointed to an interview printed in a newspaper in Egypt in which the judge discussed his personal political views in relation to the nation-state of Israel.

A majority of the judges on the ICJ saw no problem with Judge Elaraby's involvement in the activities to which Israel objected. Specifically, they saw no problem with his role as legal advisor for Egypt, because in that capacity, the judge had been speaking and acting as an agent of his government. In relation to the published interview, the majority pointed to the fact that Article 17, paragraph 2, detailed certain roles that a judge was prohibited from performing in a case that was before the court. Nothing on the list, the Court concluded, mentioned giving interviews or publishing private political views. Therefore, the majority upheld the judge's participation in the case.

The sole dissenter was Judge Thomas Buergenthal of the United States. While Judge Buergenthal agreed with the court in relation to Judge Elaraby's official governmental roles, he disagreed about the private interview and objected to the Court's strict and limited interpretation of Article 17, paragraph 2. This point is critical because, as noted previously, in an advisory case, a dissenting opinion can sometimes be just as vital as the majority opinion, because the dissenter's rationale may be used in other venues.

Dissenting Opinion of Judge Buergenthal

1. I have voted against the instant Order because I believe that the Court's decision is wrong as a matter of legal principle.

2. Israel challenges Judge Elaraby's participation in these proceedings on the ground that his previous professional involvement and personal statements on matters which go to the substance of the question before the Court in this advisory opinion request require that he not participate in these proceedings.

3. As far as Judge Elaraby's professional activities as diplomatic representative of his country and its legal adviser are concerned, the Court rejects Israel's objection by concluding that these activities, having been performed many years before the question of the construction of the wall now submitted to the Court first arose, do not fall within the activities contemplated by Article 17, paragraph 2, of the Statute to justify that he be precluded from participation in the case.

4. With regard to the newspaper interview that Judge Elaraby gave two months before his election to this Court at a time when he was no longer his country's diplomatic representative, the Court finds no basis for precluding Judge Elaraby's participation in these proceedings, because Judge Elaraby "expressed no opinion on the question put in the present case."

5. Israel seeks Judge Elaraby's disqualification on the ground, *inter alia*, that the views expressed by Judge Elaraby in the interview bear directly on issues that will have to be addressed in the advisory opinion request and that, given their nature, they create an appearance of bias incompatible with the fair administration of justice.

6. In principle, I share the Court's opinion that Judge Elaraby's prior activities, performed in the discharge of his diplomatic and governmental functions, do not fall within the scope of Article 17, paragraph 2, of the Statute of the Court so as to prevent his participation in these proceedings. . . .

7. I part company with the Court's conclusions, however, with regard to the interview Judge Elaraby gave in August of 2001, two months before his election to the Court, when he was no longer an official of his Government and hence spoke in his personal capacity. See *Al-Ahram Weekly Online*, 16–22 August 2001, issue No. 547. . . .

10. It is clear, of course, that the language of Article 17, paragraph 2, does not apply in so many words to the views Judge Elaraby expressed in the above interview. That does not mean, however, that this provision sets out the exclusive basis for the disqualification of a judge of this Court. It refers to what would generally be considered to be the most

egregious violations of judicial ethics were a judge falling into one of the categories therein enumerated to participate in a case. At the same time, Article 17, paragraph 2, reflects much broader conceptions of justice and fairness that must be observed by courts of law than this Court appears to acknowledge. Judicial ethics are not matters strictly of hard and fast rules—I doubt that they can ever be exhaustively defined—they are matters of perception and of sensibility to appearances that courts must continuously keep in mind to preserve their legitimacy.

11. A court of law must be free and, in my opinion, is required to consider whether one of its judges has expressed views or taken positions that create the impression that he will not be able to consider the issues raised in a case or advisory opinion in a fair and impartial manner, that is, that he may be deemed to have prejudged one or more of the issues bearing on the subject-matter of the dispute before the court. That is what is meant by the dictum that the fair and proper administration of justice requires that justice not only be done, but that it also be seen to be done. In my view, all courts of law must be guided by this principle, whether or not their statutes or other constitutive documents expressly require them to do so. That power and obligation is implicit in the very concept of a court of law charged with the fair and impartial administration of justice. To read them out of the reach of Article 17, paragraph 2, is neither legally justified nor is it wise judicial policy.

12. In paragraph 8 of this Order, the Court declares that, "whereas in the newspaper interview of August 2001, Judge Elaraby expressed no opinion on the question put in the present case; whereas consequently Judge Elaraby could not be regarded as having 'previously taken part' in the case in any capacity."

13. What we have here is the most formalistic and narrow construction of Article 17, paragraph 2, imaginable, and one that is unwarranted on the facts of this case. It is technically true, of course, that Judge Elaraby did not express an opinion on the specific question that has been submitted to the Court by the General Assembly of the United Nations. But it is equally true that this cannot be examined by the Court without taking account of the context of the Israeli/Palestinian conflict and the arguments that will have to be advanced by the interested parties in examining the "Legal Consequences of the Construction of a Wall in the Occupied Palestinian Territory." Many of these arguments will turn on the factual validity and credibility of assertions bearing directly on the specific question referred to the Court in this advisory opinion request. And when it comes to the validity and credibility of these arguments, what Judge Elaraby has to say in the part of the interview I quoted above creates an appearance of bias that in my opinion requires the Court to preclude Judge Elaraby's participations in the proceedings.

14. What I consider important in reaching the above conclusion is the appearance of bias. That, in my opinion, is what Article 17, paragraph 2, properly interpreted, is all about and what judicial ethics are all about. And that is why I dissent from this Order, even though I have no doubts whatsoever about the personal integrity of Judge Elaraby for whom I have the highest regard, not only as a valued colleague but also a good friend.

(*Signed*) Thomas Buergenthal

Questions for Analysis

1. Why did Israel bring this case rather than a private party? Explain.
2. What is the central issue in this case?
3. What legal statutory provision provided grounds for the complaint lodged by Israel?
4. What was the decision of the majority? Explain.
5. On what point did the dissent contest the majority opinion? Explain.

Appendix A The Constitution of the United States

Preamble

We the People of the United States, in Order to form a more perfect Union, establish Justice, insure domestic Tranquility, provide for the common defence, promote the general Welfare, and secure the Blessings of Liberty to ourselves and our Posterity, do ordain and establish this Constitution for the United States of America.

Article I

Section 1. All legislative Powers herein granted shall be vested in a Congress of the United States, which shall consist of a Senate and House of Representatives.

Section 2. [1] The House of Representatives shall be composed of Members chosen every second Year by the People of the several States, and the Electors in each State shall have the Qualifications requisite for Electors of the most numerous Branch of the State Legislature.

[2] No Person shall be a Representative who shall not have attained to the Age of twenty-five Years, and been seven Years a Citizen of the United States, and who shall not, when elected, be an Inhabitant of that State in which he shall be chosen.

[3] Representatives and direct Taxes shall be apportioned among the several States which may be included within this Union, according to their respective Numbers, which shall be determined by adding to the whole Number of free Persons, including those bound to Service for a Term of Years, and excluding Indians not taxed, three fifths of all other Persons. The actual Enumeration shall be made within three Years after the first Meeting of the Congress of the United States, and within every subsequent Term of ten Years, in such Manner as they shall by Law direct. The Number of Representatives shall not exceed one for every thirty Thousand, but each State shall have at Least one Representative; and until such enumeration shall be made, the State of New Hampshire shall be entitled to chuse three, Massachusetts eight, Rhode Island and Providence Plantations one, Connecticut five, New York six, New Jersey four, Pennsylvania eight, Delaware one, Maryland six, Virginia ten, North Carolina five, South Carolina five, and Georgia three.

[4] When vacancies happen in the Representation from any State, the Executive Authority thereof shall issue Writs of Election to fill such Vacancies.

[5] The House of Representatives shall chuse their Speaker and other Officers; and shall have the sole Power of Impeachment.

Section 3. [1] The Senate of the United States shall be composed of two Senators from each State, chosen by the Legislature thereof, for six Years; and each Senator shall have one Vote.

[2] Immediately after they shall be assembled in Consequence of the first Election, they shall be divided as equally as may be into three Classes. The Seats of the Senators of the first Class shall be vacated at the Expiration of the Second Year, of the second Class at the Expiration of the fourth Year, and of the third Class at the Expiration of the sixth Year, so that one third may be chosen every second Year; and if Vacancies happen by Resignation, or otherwise, during the Recess of the Legislature of any State, the Executive thereof may make temporary Appointments until the next Meeting of the Legislature, which shall then fill such Vacancies.

[3] No Person shall be a Senator who shall not have attained to the Age of thirty Years, and been nine Years a Citizen of the United States, and who shall not, when elected, be an Inhabitant of that State for which he shall be chosen.

[4] The Vice President of the United States shall be President of the Senate, but shall have no Vote, unless they be equally divided.

[5] The Senate shall chuse their other Officers, and also a President pro tempore, in the Absence of the Vice President, or when he shall exercise the Office of President of the United States.

[6] The Senate shall have the sole Power to try all Impeachments. When sitting for that Purpose, they shall be on Oath or Affirmation. When the President of the United States is tried, the Chief Justice shall preside: And no Person shall be convicted without the Concurrence of two thirds of the Members present.

[7] Judgment in Cases of Impeachment shall not extend further than to removal from Office, and disqualification to hold and enjoy any Office of honor, Trust, or Profit under the United States: but the Party convicted shall nevertheless be liable and subject to Indictment, Trial, Judgment, and Punishment, according to Law.

Section 4. [1] The Times, Places and Manner of holding elections for Senators and Representatives, shall be prescribed in each State by the Legislature thereof; but the Congress may at any time by Law make or alter such Regulations, except as to the Places of chusing Senators.

[2] The Congress shall assemble at least once in every Year, and such Meeting shall be on the first Monday in December, unless they shall by Law appoint a different Day.

Section 5. [1] Each House shall be the Judge of the Elections, Returns, and Qualifications of its own Members, and a Majority of each shall constitute a Quorum to do Business; but a smaller Number may adjourn from day to day, and may be authorized to compel the Attendance of absent Members, in such Manner, and under such Penalties as each House may provide.

[2] Each House may determine the Rules of its Proceedings, punish its Members for disorderly Behavior, and, with the Concurrence of two thirds, expel a Member.

[3] Each House shall keep a Journal of its Proceedings, and from time to time publish the same, excepting such parts as may in their Judgment require Secrecy; and the Yeas and Nays of the Members of either House on any question shall, at the Desire of one fifth of those Present, be entered on the Journal.

[4] Neither House, during the Session of Congress, shall, without the Consent of the other, adjourn for more than three days, nor to any other Place than that in which the two Houses shall be sitting.

Section 6. **[1]** The Senators and Representatives shall receive a Compensation for their Services, to be ascertained by Law, and paid out of the Treasury of the United States. They shall in all Cases, except Treason, Felony and Breach of the Peace, be privileged from Arrest during their Attendance at the Session of their respective Houses, and in going to and returning from the same; and for any Speech of Debate in either House, they shall not be questioned in any other Place.

[2] No Senator or Representative shall, during the Time for which he was elected, be appointed to any civil Office under the Authority of the United States, which shall have been created, or the Emoluments whereof shall have been increased during such time; and no Person holding any Office under the United States, shall be a Member of either House during his Continuance in Office.

Section 7. **[1]** All Bills for raising Revenue shall originate in the House of Representatives; but the Senate may propose or concur with Amendments as on other Bills.

[2] Every Bill which shall have passed the House of Representatives and the Senate, shall, before it becomes a Law, be presented to the President of the United States; If he approve he shall sign it, but if not he shall return it, with his Objections to the House in which it shall have originated, who shall enter the Objections at large on their Journal, and proceed to reconsider it. If after such Reconsideration two thirds of that House shall agree to pass the Bill, it shall be sent together with the Objections, to the other House, by which it shall likewise be reconsidered, and if approved by two thirds of that House, it shall become a Law. But in all such Cases the Votes of both Houses shall be determined by yeas and Nays, and the Names of the Persons voting for and against the Bill shall be entered on the Journal of each House respectively. If any Bill shall not be returned by the President within ten Days (Sundays excepted) after it shall have been presented to him, the Same shall be a Law, in like Manner as if he had signed it, unless the Congress by their Adjournment prevent its Return in which Case it shall not be a Law.

[3] Every Order, Resolution, or Vote, to Which the Concurrence of the Senate and House of Representatives may be necessary (except on a question of Adjournment) shall be presented to the President of the United States; and before the Same shall take Effect, shall be approved by him, or being disapproved by him, shall be repassed by two thirds of the Senate and House of Representatives, accord-

ing to the Rules and Limitations prescribed in the Case of a Bill.

Section 8. **[1]** The Congress shall have Power To lay and collect Taxes, Duties, Imposts and Excises, to pay the Debts and provide for the common Defence and general Welfare of the United States; but all Duties, Imposts and Excises shall be uniform throughout the United States;

[2] To borrow money on the credit of the United States;

[3] To regulate Commerce with foreign Nations, and among the several States, and with the Indian Tribes;

[4] To establish an uniform Rule of Naturalization, and uniform laws on the subject of Bankruptcies throughout the United States;

[5] To coin Money, regulate the Value thereof, and of foreign Coin, and fix the Standard of Weights and Measures;

[6] To provide for the Punishment of counterfeiting the Securities and current Coin of the United States;

[7] To Establish Post Offices and Post Roads;

[8] To promote the Progress of Science and useful Arts, by securing for limited Times to Authors and Inventors the exclusive Right to their respective Writings and Discoveries;

[9] To constitute Tribunals inferior to the supreme Court;

[10] To define and punish Piracies and Felonies committed on the high Seas, and Offenses against the Law of Nations;

[11] To declare War, grant Letters of Marque and Reprisal, and make Rules concerning Captures on Land and Water;

[12] To raise and support Armies, but no Appropriation of Money to that Use shall be for a longer Term than two Years;

[13] To provide and maintain a Navy;

[14] To make Rules for the Government and Regulation of the land and naval Forces;

[15] To provide for calling forth the Militia to execute the Laws of the Union, suppress Insurrections and repel Invasions;

[16] To provide for organizing, arming, and disciplining, the Militia, and for governing such Part of them as may be employed in the Service of the United States, reserving to the States respectively, the Appointment of the Officers, and the Authority of training the Militia according to the discipline prescribed by Congress;

[17] To exercise exclusive Legislation in all Cases whatsoever, over such District (not exceeding ten Miles square) as may, by Cession of particular States, and the Acceptance of Congress, become the Seat of the Government of the United States, and to exercise like Authority over all Places purchased by the Consent of the Legislature of the State in which the Same shall be, for the Erection of Forts, Magazines, Arsenals, dock-Yards and other needful Buildings;—And

[18] To make all Laws which shall be necessary and proper for carrying into Execution the foregoing Powers, and all other Powers vested by this Constitution in the Government of the United States, or in any Department or Officer thereof.

Section 9. [1] The Migration or Importation of Such Persons as any of the States now existing shall think proper to admit, shall not be prohibited by the Congress prior to the Year one thousand eight hundred and eight, but a Tax or duty may be imposed on such Importation, not exceeding ten dollars for each Person.

[2] The privilege of the Writ of Habeas Corpus shall not be suspended, unless when in Cases of Rebellion or Invasion the public Safety may require it.

[3] No Bill of Attainder or ex post facto Law shall be passed.

[4] No Capitation, or other direct, Tax shall be laid, unless in Proportion to the Census or Enumeration herein before directed to be taken.

[5] No Tax or Duty shall be laid on Articles exported from any State.

[6] No Preference shall be given by any Regulation of Commerce or Revenue to the Ports of one State over those of another: nor shall Vessels bound to, or from, one State be obliged to enter, clear, or pay Duties in another.

[7] No money shall be drawn from the Treasury, but in Consequence of Appropriations made by Law; and a regular Statement and Account of the Receipts and Expenditures of all public Money shall be published from time to time.

[8] No Title of Nobility shall be granted by the United States: And no Person holding any Office of Profit or Trust under them, shall, without the Consent of the Congress, accept of any present, Emolument, Office, or Title, of any kind whatever, from any King, Prince, or foreign State.

Section 10. [1] No State shall enter into any Treaty, Alliance, or confederation; grant Letters of Marque and Reprisal; coin Money; emit Bills of Credit; make any Thing but gold and silver Coin a Tender in Payment of Debts; pass any Bill of Attainder, ex post facto Law, or Law impairing the Obligation of Contracts, or grant any Title of Nobility.

[2] No State shall, without the Consent of the Congress, lay any Imposts or Duties on Imports or Exports, except what may be absolutely necessary for executing its inspection Laws: and the net Produce of all Duties and Imposts, laid by any State on Imports or Exports, shall be for the Use of the Treasury of the United States; and all such Laws shall be subject to the Revision and Control of the Congress.

[3] No State shall, without the Consent of Congress, lay any Duty of Tonnage, keep Troops, or Ships of War in time of Peace, enter into any Agreement or Compact with another State, or with a foreign Power, or engage in War, unless actually invaded, or in such imminent Danger as will not admit of delay.

Article II

Section 1. [1] The executive Power shall be vested in a President of the United States of America. He shall hold his Office during the Term of four Years, and, together with the Vice President, chosen for the same Term, be elected, as follows:

[2] Each State shall appoint, in such Manner as the Legislature thereof may direct, a Number of Electors, equal to the whole Number of Senators and Representatives to which the State may be entitled in the Congress; but no Senator or Representative, or Person holding an Office of Trust or Profit under the United States, shall be appointed an Elector.

[3] The Electors shall meet in their respective States, and vote by Ballot for two Persons, of whom one at least shall not be an Inhabitant of the same State with themselves. And they shall make a List of all the Persons voted for, and of the Number of Votes for each; which List they shall sign and certify, and transmit sealed to the Seat of the Government of the United States, directed to the President of the Senate. The President of the Senate shall, in the Presence of the Senate and House of Representatives, open all the Certificates, and the Votes shall then be counted. The Person having the greatest Number of Votes shall be the President, if such Number be a Majority of the whole Number of Electors appointed; and if there be more than one who have such Majority, and have an equal Number of Votes, then the House of Representatives shall immediately chuse by Ballot one of them for President; and if no Person have a Majority, then from the five highest on the List the said House shall in like Manner chuse the President. But in chusing the President, the Votes shall be taken by States the Representation from each State having one Vote; A quorum for this Purpose shall consist of a Member or Members from two thirds of the States, and a Majority of all the States shall be necessary to a Choice. In every Case, after the Choice of the President, the Person having the greater Number of Votes of the Electors shall be the Vice President. But if there shall remain two or more who have equal Votes, the Senate shall chuse from them by Ballot the Vice President.

[4] The Congress may determine the Time of chusing the Electors, and the Day on which they shall give their Votes; which Day shall be the same throughout the United States.

[5] No person except a natural born Citizen, or a Citizen of the United States, at the time of the Adoption of this Constitution, shall be eligible to the Office of President; neither shall any Person be eligible to that Office who shall not have attained to the Age of thirty-five Years, and been fourteen Years a Resident within the United States.

[6] In case of the removal of the President from Office, or of his Death, Resignation or Inability to discharge the Powers and Duties of the said Office, the Same shall devolve on the Vice President, and the Congress may by Law provide for the Case of Removal, Death, Resignation or Inability, both of the President and Vice President, declaring what Officer shall then act as President, and such Officer shall act accordingly, until the Disability be removed, or a President shall be elected.

[7] The President shall, at stated Times, receive for his Services, a Compensation, which shall neither be increased nor diminished during the Period for which he shall have been elected, and he shall not receive within that Period any other Emolument from the United States, or any of them.

[8] Before he enter on the Execution of his Office, he shall take the following Oath or Affirmation: "I do solemnly swear (or affirm) that I will faithfully execute the Office of President of the United States, and will to the best of my Ability, preserve, protect, and defend the Constitution of the United States."

Section 2. [1] The President shall be Commander in Chief of the Army and Navy of the United States, and of the militia of the several States, when called into the actual Service of the United States; he may require the Opinion, in writing, of the principal Officer in each of the Executive Departments, upon any subject relating to the Duties of their respective Offices, and he shall have Power to grant Reprieves and Pardons for Offenses against the United States, except in Cases of Impeachment.

[2] He shall have Power, by and with the Advice and Consent of the Senate to make Treaties, provided two thirds of the Senators present concur; and he shall nominate, and by and with the Advice and Consent of the Senate, shall appoint Ambassadors, other public Ministers and Consuls, Judges of the supreme Court, and all other Officers of the United States, whose Appointments are not herein otherwise provided for, and which shall be established by Law; but the Congress may by Law vest the Appointment of such inferior Officers, as they think proper, in the President alone, in the Courts of Law, or in the Heads of Departments.

[3] The President shall have Power to fill up all Vacancies that may happen during the Recess of the Senate, by granting commissions which shall expire at the End of their next Session.

Section 3. He shall from time to time give to the Congress Information of the State of the Union, and recommend to their Consideration such Measures as he shall judge necessary and expedient; he may, on extraordinary Occasions, convene both Houses, or either of them, and in Case of Disagreement between them, with Respect to the Time of Adjournment, he may adjourn them to such Time as he shall think proper; he shall receive Ambassadors and other public Ministers; he shall take Care that the Laws be faithfully executed, and shall commission all the Officers of the United States.

Section 4. The President, Vice President and all civil Officers of the United States, shall be removed from Office on Impeachment for, and Conviction of, Treason, Bribery, or other high Crimes and Misdemeanors.

Article III

Section 1. The judicial Power of the United States, shall be vested in one supreme Court, and in such inferior Courts as the Congress may from time to time ordain and establish. The Judges, both of the supreme and inferior Courts, shall hold their Offices during good Behaviour, and shall, at stated Times, receive for their Services a Compensation, which shall not be diminished during their Continuance in Office.

Section 2. [1] The judicial Power shall extend to all Cases, in Law and Equity, arising under this Constitution, the Laws of the United States, and Treaties made, or which shall be made, under their Authority;—to all Cases affecting Ambassadors, other public Ministers and Consuls;—to all Cases of admiralty and maritime Jurisdiction;—to Controversies to which the United States shall be a Party;—between a State and Citizens of another State; between Citizens of different States;—between Citizens of the same State claiming Lands under the Grants of different States, and between a State, or the Citizens thereof, and foreign States, Citizens or Subjects.

[2] In all Cases affecting Ambassadors, other public Ministers and Consuls, and those in which a State shall be a Party, the supreme Court shall have original Jurisdiction, In all the other Cases before mentioned, the supreme Court shall have appellate Jurisdiction, both as to Law and Fact, with such Exceptions, and under such Regulations as the Congress shall make.

[3] The trial of all Crimes, except in Cases of Impeachment, shall be by Jury; and such Trial shall be held in the State where the said Crimes shall have been committed; but when not committed within any State, the Trial shall be at such Place or Places as the Congress may by Law have directed.

Section 3. [1] Treason against the United States, shall consist only in levying War against them, or, in adhering to their Enemies, giving them Aid and Comfort. No Person shall be convicted of Treason unless on the Testimony of two Witnesses to the same overt Act, or on Confession in open Court.

[2] The Congress shall have Power to declare the Punishment of Treason, but no Attainder of Treason shall work Corruption of Blood, or Forfeiture except during the Life of the Person attainted.

Article IV

Section 1. Full Faith and Credit shall be given in each State to the public Acts, Records, and judicial Proceedings of every other State. And the Congress may by general Laws prescribe the Manner in which such Acts, Records and Proceedings shall be proved, and the Effect thereof.

Section 2. [1] The Citizens of each State shall be entitled to all Privileges and Immunities of Citizens in the several States.

[2] A Person charged in any State with Treason, Felony, or other Crime, who shall flee from Justice, and be found in another State, shall on demand of the executive Authority of the State from which he fled, be delivered up, to be removed to the State having Jurisdiction of the Crime.

[3] No Person held to Service or Labour in one State, under the Laws thereof, escaping into another, shall, in Consequence of any Law or Regulation therein, be discharged from such Service or Labour, but shall be delivered up on Claim of the Party to whom such Service or Labour may be due.

Section 3. **[1]** New States may be admitted by the Congress into this Union; but no new State shall be formed or erected within the Jurisdiction of any other State; nor any State be formed by the Junction of two or more States, or Parts of States, without the Consent of the Legislatures of the States concerned as well as of the Congress. **[2]** The Congress shall have Power to dispose of and make all needful Rules and Regulations respecting the Territory or other Property belonging to the United States; and nothing in this Constitution shall be so construed as to Prejudice any Claims of the United States, or of any particular State.

Section 4. The United States shall guarantee to every State in this Union a Republican Form of Government, and shall protect each of them against Invasion; and on Application of the Legislature, or of the Executive (when the Legislature cannot be convened) against domestic Violence.

Article V

The Congress, whenever two thirds of both Houses shall deem it necessary, shall propose Amendments to this Constitution, or, on the Application of the Legislatures of two thirds of the several States, shall call a Convention for proposing Amendments, which, in either case, shall be valid to all Intents and Purposes, as part of this Constitution, when ratified by the Legislatures of three fourths of the several States, or by Conventions in three fourths thereof, as the one or the other Mode of Ratification may be proposed by the Congress; Provided that no Amendment which may be made prior to the Year One thousand eight hundred and eight shall in any Manner affect the first and fourth Clauses in the Ninth Section of the first Article; and that no State, without its Consent, shall be deprived of its equal Suffrage in the Senate.

Article VI

[1] All Debts contracted and Engagements entered into, before the Adoption of this Constitution shall be as valid against the United States under this Constitution, as under the Confederation.
[2] This Constitution, and the Laws of the United States which shall be made in Pursuance thereof; and all Treaties made, or which shall be made, under the Authority of the United States, shall be the supreme Law of the Land; and the Judges in every State shall be bound thereby, any Thing in the Constitution or Laws of any State to the Contrary notwithstanding.
[3] The Senators and Representatives before mentioned, and the Members of the several State Legislatures, and all executive and judicial Officers, both of the United States

and of the several States, shall be bound by Oath or Affirmation, to support this Constitution; but no religious Test shall ever be required as a Qualification to any Office or public Trust under the United States.

Article VII

The Ratification of the Conventions of nine States shall be sufficient for the Establishment of this Constitution between the States so ratifying the Same.

Amendments

Articles in addition to, and in amendment of, the Constitution of the United States of America, proposed by Congress, and ratified by the Legislatures of the several States pursuant to the Fifth Article of the original Constitution.

Amendment 1 [1791]

Congress shall make no law respecting an establishment of religion, or prohibiting the free exercise thereof; or abridging the freedom of speech, or of the press; or the right of the people peaceably to assemble, and to petition the Government for a redress of grievances.

Amendment 2 [1791]

A well regulated Militia, being necessary to the security of a free State, the right of the people to keep and bear Arms, shall not be infringed.

Amendment 3 [1791]

No Soldier shall, in time of peace be quartered in any house, without the consent of the Owner, nor in time of war, but in a manner to be prescribed by law.

Amendment 4 [1791]

The right of the people to be secure in their persons, houses, papers, and effects, against unreasonable searches and seizures, shall not be violated, and no Warrants shall issue, but upon probable cause, supported by Oath or affirmation, and particularly describing the place to be searched, and the persons or things to be seized.

Amendment 5 [1791]

No person shall be held to answer for a capital, or other infamous crime, unless on a presentment or indictment of a Grand Jury, except in cases arising in the land or naval forces, or in the Militia, when in actual service in time of War or public danger; nor shall any person be subject for the same offence to be twice put in jeopardy of life or limb; nor shall be compelled in any criminal case to be a witness against himself, nor be deprived of life, liberty, or property, without due process of law; nor shall private property be taken for public use, without just compensation.

Amendment 6 [1791]

In all criminal prosecutions, the accused shall enjoy the right to a speedy and public trial, by an impartial jury of the State and district wherein the crime shall have been committed, which district shall have been previously ascertained by law, and to be informed of the nature and cause of the accusation; to be confronted with the witnesses against him; to have compulsory process for obtaining witnesses in his favor, and to have the Assistance of Counsel for his defence.

Amendment 7 [1791]

In Suits at common law, where the value in controversy shall exceed twenty dollars, the right of trial by jury shall be preserved, and no fact tried by jury, shall be otherwise re-examined in any Court of the United States, than according to the rules of common law.

Amendment 8 [1791]

Excessive bail shall not be required, nor excessive fines imposed, nor cruel and unusual punishments inflicted.

Amendment 9 [1791]

The enumeration in the Constitution, of certain rights, shall not be construed to deny or disparage others retained by the people.

Amendment 10 [1791]

The powers not delegated to the United States by the Constitution, nor prohibited by it to the States, are reserved to the States respectively, or to the people.

Amendment 11 [1798]

The Judicial power of the United States shall not be construed to extend to any suit in law or equity, commenced or prosecuted against one of the United States by Citizens of another State, or by Citizens or Subjects of any Foreign State.

Amendment 12 [1804]

The Electors shall meet in their respective states and vote by ballot for President and Vice President, one of whom, at least, shall not be an inhabitant of the same state with themselves; they shall name in their ballots the person voted for as President, and in distinct ballots the person voted for as Vice President, and they shall make distinct lists of all persons voted for as President, and of all persons voted for as Vice President, and of the number of votes for each, which lists they shall sign and certify, and transmit sealed to the seat of the government of the United States, directed to the President of the Senate;—

The President of the Senate shall, in the presence of the Senate and House of Representatives, open all the certificates and the votes shall then be counted;—The person having the greatest number of votes for President, shall be the President, if such number be a majority of the whole number of Electors appointed; and if no person have such majority, then from the persons having the highest numbers not exceeding three on the list of those voted for as President, the House of Representatives shall choose immediately, by ballot, the President. But in choosing the President, the votes shall be taken by states, the representation from each state having one vote; a quorum for this purpose shall consist of a member or members from two thirds of the states, and a majority of all states shall be necessary to a choice. And if the House of Representatives shall not choose a President whenever the right of choice shall devolve upon them before the fourth day of March next following, then the Vice President shall act as President, as in the case of the death or other constitutional disability of the President.—The person having the greatest number of votes as Vice President, shall be the Vice President, if such number be a majority of the whole number of Electors appointed, and if no person have a majority, then from the two highest numbers on the list, the Senate shall choose the Vice President; a quorum for the purpose shall consist of two thirds of the whole number of Senators, and a majority of the whole number shall be necessary to a choice. But no person constitutionally ineligible to the office of President shall be eligible to that of Vice President of the United States.

Amendment 13 [1865]

Section 1. Neither slavery nor involuntary servitude, except as a punishment for crime whereof the party shall have been duly convicted, shall exist within the United States, or any place subject to their jurisdiction.

Section 2. Congress shall have power to enforce this article by appropriate legislation.

Amendment 14 [1868]

Section 1. All persons born or naturalized in the United States, and subject to the jurisdiction thereof, are citizens of the United States and of the State wherein they reside. No State shall make or enforce any law which shall abridge the privileges or immunities of citizens of the United States; nor shall any State deprive any person of life, liberty, or property, without due process of law; nor deny to any person within its jurisdiction the equal protection of the laws.

Section 2. Representatives shall be apportioned among the several States according to their respective numbers, counting the whole number of persons in each State, excluding Indians not taxed. But when the right to vote at any election for the choice of electors for President and Vice President of the United States, Representatives in Congress, the Executive and Judicial officers of a State, or the members of the Legislature thereof, is denied to any of the male inhabitants of such State, being twenty-one years of age, and citizens of the United States, or in any way abridged, except for participation in rebellion, or other crime, the basis of representation therein shall be reduced in the proportion which the number of such male citizens shall bear to the whole number of male citizens twenty-one years of age in such State.

Section 3. No person shall be a Senator or Representative in Congress, or elector of President and Vice President, or hold any office, civil or military, under the United States, or under any State, who having previously taken an oath, as a member of Congress, or as an officer of the United States, or as a member of any State legislature, or as an executive or judicial officer of any State, to support the Constitution of the United States, shall have engaged in insurrection or rebellion against the same, or given aid or comfort to the enemies thereof. But Congress may by a vote of two thirds of each House, remove such disability.

Section 4. The validity of the public debt of the United States, authorized by law, including debts incurred for payment of pensions and bounties for services in suppressing insurrection or rebellion, shall not be questioned. But neither the United States nor any State shall assume or pay any debt or obligation incurred in aid of insurrection or rebellion against the United States, or any claim for the loss or emancipation of any slave; but all such debts, obligations and claims shall be held illegal and void.

Section 5. The Congress shall have power to enforce, by appropriate legislation, the provisions of this article.

Amendment 15 [1870]

Section 1. The right of citizens of the United States to vote shall not be denied or abridged by the United States or by any State on account of race, color, or previous condition of servitude.

Section 2. The Congress shall have power to enforce this article by appropriate legislation.

Amendment 16 [1913]

The Congress shall have power to lay and collect taxes on incomes, from whatever source derived, without apportionment among the several States, and without regard to any census or enumeration.

Amendment 17 [1913]

[1] The Senate of the United States shall be composed of two Senators from each State, elected by the people thereof, for six years; and each Senator shall have one vote. The electors in each State shall have the qualifications requisite for electors of the most numerous branch of the State legislatures.

[2] When vacancies happen in the representation of any State in the Senate, the executive authority of such State shall issue writs of election to fill such vacancies: *Provided,* That the legislature of any State may empower the executive thereof to make temporary appointments until the people fill the vacancies by election as the legislature may direct.

[3] This amendment shall not be so construed as to affect the election or term of any Senator chosen before it becomes valid as part of the Constitution.

Amendment 18 [1919]

Section 1. After one year from the ratification of this article the manufacture, sale, or transportation of intoxicating liquors within, the importation thereof into, or the exportation thereof from the United States and all territory subject to the jurisdiction thereof for beverage purposes is hereby prohibited.

Section 2. The Congress and the several States shall have concurrent power to enforce this article by appropriate legislation.

Section 3. This article shall be inoperative unless it shall have been ratified as an amendment to the Constitution by the legislatures of the several States, as provided in the Constitution, within seven years from the date of the submission hereof to the States by the Congress.

Amendment 19 [1920]

[1] The right of citizens of the United States to vote shall not be denied or abridged by the United States or by any State on account of sex.

[2] Congress shall have power to enforce this article by appropriate legislation.

Amendment 20 [1933]

Section 1. The terms of the President and Vice President shall end at noon on the twentieth day of January, and the terms of Senators and Representatives at noon on the third day of January, of the years in which such terms would have ended if this article had not been ratified; and the terms of their successors shall then begin.

Section 2. The Congress shall assemble at least once in every year, and such meeting shall begin at noon on the third day of January, unless they shall by law appoint a different day.

Section 3. If, at the time fixed for the beginning of the term of the President, the President elect shall have died, the Vice President elect shall become President. If the President shall not have been chosen before the time fixed for the beginning of his term, or if the President elect shall have failed to qualify, then the Vice President elect shall act as President until a President shall have qualified; and the Congress may by law provide for the case wherein neither a President elect nor a Vice President elect shall have qualified, declaring who shall then act as President, or the manner in which one who is to act shall be selected, and such person shall act accordingly until a President or Vice President shall have qualified.

Section 4. The Congress may by law provide for the case of the death of any of the persons from whom the House of Representatives may choose a President whenever the right of choice shall have devolved upon them, and for the case of the death of any of the persons from whom the Senate may choose a Vice President whenever the right of choice shall have devolved upon them.

Section 5. Sections 1 and 2 shall take effect on the fifteenth day of October following the ratification of this article.

Section 6. This article shall be inoperative unless it shall have been ratified as an amendment to the Constitution by the legislatures of three fourths of the several States within seven years from the date of its submission.

Amendment 21 [1933]

Section 1. The eighteenth article of amendment to the Constitution of the United States is hereby repealed.

Section 2. The transportation or importation into any State, Territory, or possession of the United States for delivery or use therein of intoxicating liquors, in violation of the laws therefore, is hereby prohibited.

Section 3. This article shall be inoperative unless it shall have been ratified as an amendment to the Constitution by conventions in the several States, as provided in the Constitution, within seven years from the date of the submission hereof to the States by the Congress.

Amendment 22 [1951]

Section 1. No person shall be elected to the office of the President more than twice, and no person who has held the office of President, or acted as President, for more than two years of a term to which some other person was elected President shall be elected to the office of President more than once. But this Article shall not apply to any person holding the office of President when this Article was proposed by the Congress, and shall not prevent any person who may be holding the office of President, or acting as President, during the term within which this Article becomes operative from holding the office of President or acting as President during the remainder of such term.

Section 2. This article shall be inoperative unless it shall have been ratified as an amendment to the Constitution by the legislatures of three fourths of the several States within seven years from the date of its submission to the States by the Congress.

Amendment 23 [1961]

Section 1. The District constituting the seat of Government of the United States shall appoint in such manner as the Congress may direct:

A number of electors of President and Vice President equal to the whole number of Senators and Representatives in Congress to which the District would be entitled if it were a State, but in no event more than the least populous state;

they shall be in addition to those appointed by the states, but they shall be considered, for the purposes of the election of President and Vice President, to be electors appointed by a state; and they shall meet in the District and perform such duties as provided by the twelfth article of amendment.

Section 2. The Congress shall have power to enforce this article by appropriate legislation.

Amendment 24 [1964]

Section 1. The right of citizens of the United States to vote in any primary or other election for President or Vice President, for electors for President or Vice President, or for Senator or Representative in Congress, shall not be denied or abridged by the United States, or any State by reason of failure to pay any poll tax or other tax.

Section 2. The Congress shall have power to enforce this article by appropriate legislation.

Amendment 25 [1967]

Section 1. In case of the removal of the President from office or of his death or resignation, the Vice President shall become President.

Section 2. Whenever there is a vacancy in the office of the Vice President, the President shall nominate a Vice President who shall take office upon confirmation by a majority vote of both Houses of Congress.

Section 3. Whenever the President transmits to the President pro tempore of the Senate and the Speaker of the House of Representatives his written declaration that he is unable to discharge the powers and duties of his office, and until he transmits to them a written declaration to the contrary, such powers and duties shall be discharged by the Vice President as Acting President.

Section 4. Whenever the Vice President and a majority of either the principal officers of the executive departments or of such other body as Congress may by law provide, transmit to the President pro tempore of the Senate and the Speaker of the House of Representatives their written declaration that the President is unable to discharge the powers and duties of his office, the Vice President shall immediately assume the powers and duties of the office as Acting President.

Thereafter, when the President transmits to the President pro tempore of the Senate and the Speaker of the House of Representatives his written declaration that no inability exists, he shall resume the powers and duties of his office unless the Vice President and a majority of either the principal officers of the executive department or of such other body as Congress may by law provide, transmit within four days to the President pro tempore of the Senate and the Speaker of the House of Representatives their written declaration and the President is unable to discharge the powers and duties of his office. Thereupon Congress shall decide the issue, assembling within forty-eight hours for that purpose if not in session. If the

Congress, within twenty-one days after receipt of the latter written declaration, or, if Congress is not in session, within twenty-one days after Congress is required to assemble, determines by two thirds vote of both Houses that the President is unable to discharge the powers and duties of his office, the Vice President shall continue to discharge the same as Acting President; otherwise, the President shall resume the powers and duties of his office.

Amendment 26 [1971]

Section 1. The right of citizens of the United States, who are eighteen years of age or older, to vote shall not be denied or abridged by the United States or by any State on account of age.

Section 2. The Congress shall have power to enforce this article by appropriate legislation.

Amendment 27 [1992]

No law varying the compensation for the services of Senators and Representatives shall take effect, until an election of Representatives shall have intervened.

Appendix B — Uniform Commercial Code (Articles 1, 2, 2a, and 3)

Article 1: General Provisions

Part 1: Short Title, Construction, Application and Subject Matter of the Act

§1-101. Short Title. This act shall be known and may be cited as Uniform Commercial Code.

§1-102. Purposes; Rules of Construction; Variation by Agreement.

(1) This Act shall be liberally construed and applied to promote its underlying purposes and policies.

(2) Underlying purposes and policies of this Act are
  (a) to simplify, clarify and modernize the law governing commercial transactions;
  (b) to permit the continued expansion of commercial practices through custom, usage and agreement of the parties;
  (c) to make uniform the law among the various jurisdictions.

(3) The effect of provisions of this Act may be varied by agreement, except as otherwise provided in this Act and except that the obligations of good faith, diligence, reasonableness and care prescribed by this Act may not be disclaimed by agreement but the parties may by agreement determine the standards by which the performance of such obligations is to be measured if such standards are not manifestly unreasonable.

(4) The presence in certain provisions of this Act of the words "unless otherwise agreed" or words of similar import does not imply that the effect of other provisions may not be varied by agreement under subsection (3).

(5) In this Act unless the context otherwise requires
  (a) words in the singular number include the plural, and in the plural include the singular;
  (b) words of the masculine gender include the feminine and the neuter, and when the sense so indicates words of the neuter gender may refer to any gender.

§1-103. Supplementary General Principles of Law Applicable.

Unless displaced by the particular provisions of this Act, the principles of law and equity, including the law merchant and the law relative to capacity to contract, principal and agent, estoppel, fraud, misrepresentation, duress, coercion, mistake, bankruptcy or other validating or invalidating cause shall supplement its provisions.

§1-104. Construction Against Implicity Repeal.

This Act being a general act intended as a unified coverage of its subject matter, no part of it shall be deemed to be impliedly repealed by subsequent legislation if such construction can reasonably be avoided.

§1-105. Territorial Application of the Act; Parties' Power to Choose Applicable Law.

(1) Except as provided hereafter in this section, when a transaction bears a reasonable relation to this state and also to another state or nation the parties may agree that the law either of this state or of such other state or nation shall govern their rights and duties. Failing such agreement this Act applies to transactions bearing an appropriate relation to this state.

(2) Where one of the following provisions of this Act specifies the applicable law, that provision governs and a contrary agreement is effective only to the extent permitted by the law (including the conflict of laws rules) so specified:

Rights of creditors against sold goods. Section 2-402.

Applicability of the Article on Leases. Sections 2A-105 and 2A-106.

Applicability of the Article on Bank Deposits and Collections. Section 4-102.

Bulk transfers subject to the Article on Bulk Transfers. Section 6-102.

Applicability of the Article on Investment Securities. Section 8-106.

Perfection provisions of the Article on Secured Transactions. Section 9-103.

§1-106. Remedies to Be Liberally Administered.

(1) The remedies provided by this Act shall be liberally administered to the end that the aggrieved party may be put in as good a position as if the other party had fully performed but neither consequential or special nor penal damages may be had except as specifically provided in this Act or by other rule of law.

(2) Any right or obligation declared by this Act is enforceable by action unless the provision declaring it specifies a different and limited effect.

§1-107. Waiver or Renunciation of Claim or Right After Breach.

Any claim or right arising out of an alleged breach can be discharged in whole or in part without consideration by a written waiver or renunciation signed and delivered by the aggrieved party.

§1-108. Severability.

If any provision or clause of this Act or application thereof to any person or circumstances is held invalid, such invalidity shall not affect other provisions or applications of the Act which can be given effect without the invalid provision or application, and to this end the provisions of this Act are declared to be severable.

§1-109. Section Captions. Section captions are parts of this Act.

Part 2: General Definitions and Principles of Interpretation

§1-201. General Definitions.

Subject to additional definitions contained in the subsequent Articles of this Act which are applicable to specific Articles or Parts thereof, and unless the context otherwise requires, in this Act.

(1) "Action" in the sense of a judicial proceeding includes recoupment, counterclaim, set-off, suit in equity and any other proceedings in which rights are determined.

(2) "Aggrieved party" means a party entitled to resort to a remedy.

(3) "Agreement" means the bargain of the parties in fact as found in their language or by implication from other circumstances including course of dealing or usage of trade or course of performance as provided in this Act (Sections 1-205 and 2-208). Whether an agreement has legal consequences is determined by the provisions of this Act, if applicable; otherwise by the law of contracts (Section 1-103). (Compare "Contract".)

(4) "Bank" means any person engaged in the business of banking.

(5) "Bearer" means the person in possession of an instrument, document of title, or certificated security payable to bearer or indorsed in blank.

(6) "Bill of lading" means a document evidencing the receipt of goods for shipment issued by a person engaged in the business of transporting or forwarding goods, and includes an airbill. "Airbill" means a document serving for air transportation as a bill of lading does for marine or rail transportation, and includes an air consignment note or air waybill.

(7) "Branch" includes a separately incorporated foreign branch of a bank.

(8) "Burden of establishing" a fact means the burden of persuading the triers of fact that the existence of the fact is more probable than its non-existence.

(9) "Buyer in ordinary course of business" means a person who in good faith and without knowledge that the sale to him is in violation of the ownership rights or security interest of a third party in the goods buys in ordinary course from a person in the business of selling goods of that kind but does not include a pawnbroker. All persons who sell minerals or the like (including oil and gas) at wellhead or minehead shall be deemed to be persons in the business of selling goods of that kind. "Buying" may be for cash or by exchange of other property or on secured or unsecured credit and includes receiving goods or documents of title under a pre-existing contract for sale but does not include a transfer in bulk or as security for or in total or partial satisfaction of a money debt.

(10) "Conspicuous": A term or clause is conspicuous when it is so written that a reasonable person against whom it is to operate ought to have noticed it. A printed heading in capitals (as: NON-NEGOTIABLE BILL OF LADING) is conspicuous. Language in the body of a form is "conspicuous" if it is in larger or other contrasting type or color. But in a telegram any stated term is "conspicuous". Whether a term or clause is "conspicuous" or not is for decision by the court.

(11) "Contract" means the total legal obligation which results from the parties' agreement as affected by this Act and any other applicable rules of law. (Compare "Agreement".)

(12) "Creditor" includes a general creditor, a secured creditor, a lien creditor and any representative of creditors, including an assignee for the benefit of creditors, a trustee in bankruptcy, a receiver in equity and an executor or administrator of an insolvent debtor's or assignor's estate.

(13) "Defendant" includes a person in the position of defendant in a cross-action or counterclaim.

(14) "Delivery" with respect to instruments, documents of title, chattel paper or certificated securities means voluntary transfer of possession.

(15) "Document of title" includes bill of lading, dock warrant, dock receipt, warehouse receipt or order for the delivery of goods, and also any other document which in the regular course of business or financing is treated as adequately evidencing that the person in possession of it is entitled to receive, hold and dispose of the document and the goods it covers. To be a document of title a document must purport to be issued by or addressed to a bailee and purport to cover goods in the bailee's possession which are either identified or are fungible portions of an identified mass.

(16) "Fault" means wrongful act, omission or breach.

(17) "Fungible" with respect to goods or securities means goods or securities of which any unit is, by nature or usage of trade, the equivalent of any other like unit. Goods which are not fungible shall be deemed fungible for the purposes of this Act to the extent that under a particular agreement or document unlike units are treated as equivalents.

(18) "Genuine" means free of forgery or counterfeiting.

(19) "Good faith" means honesty in fact in the conduct or transaction concerned.

(20) "Holder" means a person who is in possession of a document of title or a certificated instrument or an investment security drawn, issued or indorsed to him or to his order or to bearer or in blank.

(21) To "honor" is to pay or to accept and pay, or where a credit so engages to purchase or discount a draft complying with the terms of the credit.

(22) "Insolvency proceedings" includes any assignment for the benefit of creditors or other proceedings intended to liquidate or rehabilitate the estate of the person involved.

(23) A person is "insolvent" who either has ceased to pay his debts in the ordinary course of business or cannot pay his debts as they become due or is insolvent within the meaning of the federal bankruptcy law.

(24) "Money" means a medium of exchange authorized or adopted by a domestic or foreign government as part of its currency.

(25) A person has "notice" of a fact when
   (a) he has actual knowledge of it; or
   (b) he has received a notice or notification of it; or
   (c) from all the facts and circumstances known to him at the time in question he has reason to know that it exists.

A person "knows" or has "knowledge" of a fact when he has actual knowledge of it. "Discover" or "learn" or a word or phrase of similar import refers to knowledge rather than to reason to know. The time and circumstances under which a notice or notification may cease to be effective are not determined by this Act.

(26) A person "notifies" or "gives" a notice or notification to another by taking such steps as may be reasonably required to inform the other in ordinary course whether or not such other actually comes to know of it. A person "receives" a notice or notification when
   (a) it comes to his attention; or
   (b) it is duly delivered at the place of business through which the contract was made or at any other place held out by him as the place for receipt of such communications.

(27) Notice, knowledge or a notice or notification received by an organization is effective for a particular transaction from the time when it is brought to the attention of the individual conducting that transaction, and in any event from the time when it would have been brought to his attention if the organization had exercised due diligence. An organization exercises due diligence if it maintains reasonable routines for communicating significant information to the person conducting the transaction and there is reasonable compliance with the routines. Due diligence does not require an individual acting for the organization to communicate information unless such communication is part of his regular duties or unless he has reason to know of the transaction and that the transaction would be materially affected by the information.

(28) "Organization" includes a corporation, government or governmental subdivision or agency, business trust, estate, trust, partnership or association, two or more persons having a joint or common interest or any other legal or commercial entity.

(29) "Party", as distinct from "third party", means a person who has engaged in a transaction or made an agreement within this Act.

(30) "Person" includes an individual or an organization (See Section 1-102).

(31) "Presumption" or "presumed" means that the trier of fact must find the existence of the fact presumed unless and until evidence is introduced which would support a finding of its non-existence.

(32) "Purchase" includes taking by sale, discount, negotiation, mortgage, pledge, lien, issue or re-issue, gift or any other voluntary transaction creating an interest in property.

(33) "Purchaser" means a person who takes by purchase.

(34) "Remedy" means any remedial right to which an aggrieved party is entitled with or without resort to a tribunal.

(35) "Representative" includes as agent, an officer of a corporation or association, and a trustee, executor or administrator of an estate, or any other person empowered to act for another.

(36) "Rights" includes remedies.

(37) "Security interest" means an interest in personal property or fixtures which secures payment or performance of an obligation. The retention or reservation of title by a seller of goods notwithstanding shipment or delivery to the buyer (Section 2-401) is limited in effect to a reservation of a "security interest". The term also includes any interest of a buyer of accounts or chattel paper which is subject to Article 9. The special property interest of a buyer of goods on identification of those goods to a contract for sale under Section 2-401 is not a "security interest", but a buyer may also acquire a "security interest" by complying with Article 9. Unless a consignment is intended as security, reservation of title thereunder is not a "security interest", but a consignment in any event is subject to the provisions on consignment sales (Section 2-326).

Whether a transaction creates a lease or security interest is determined by the facts of each case; however, a transaction creates a security interest if the consideration the lessee is to pay the lessor for the right to possession and use of the goods is an obligation for the term of the lease not subject to termination by the lessee, and

(a) the original term of the lease is equal to or greater than the remaining economic life of the goods,

(b) the lessee is bound to renew the lease for the remaining economic life of the goods or is bound to become the owner of the goods,

(c) the lessee has an option to renew the lease for the remaining economic life of the goods for no additional consideration or nominal additional consideration upon compliance with the lease agreement, or

(d) the lessee has an option to become the owner of the goods for no additional consideration or nominal additional consideration upon compliance with the lease agreement.

A transaction does not create a security interest merely because it provides that

(a) the present value of the consideration the lessee is obligated to pay the lessor for the right to possession and use of the goods is substantially equal to or is greater than the fair market value of the goods at the time the lease is entered into,

(b) the lessee assumes risk of loss of the goods, or agrees to pay taxes, insurance, filing, recording or registration fees, or service or maintenance costs with respect to the goods,

(c) the lessee has an option to renew the lease or to become the owner of the goods,

(d) the lessee has an option to renew the lease for a fixed rent that is equal to or greater than the reasonably predictable fair market rent for the use of the goods for the term of the renewal at the time the option is to be performed, or

(e) the lessee has an option to become the owner of the goods for a fixed price that is equal to or greater than the reasonably predictable fair market value of the goods at the time the option is to be performed.

   For purposes of this subsection (37):

(x) Additional consideration is not nominal if (i) when the option to renew the lease is granted to the lessee the rent is stated to be the fair market rent for the use of the goods for the term of the renewal determined at the time the option is to be performed, or (ii) when the option to become the owner of the goods is granted to the lessee the price is stated to be the fair market value of the goods determined at the time the option is to be performed. Additional consideration is nominal if it is less than the lessee's reasonably predictable cost of performing under the lease agreement if the option is not exercised;

(y) "Reasonably predictable" and "remaining economic life of the goods" are to be determined with reference to the facts and circumstances at the time the transaction is entered into; and

(z) "Present value" means the amount as of a date certain of one or more sums payable in the future, discounted to the date certain. The discount is determined by the interest rate specified by the parties if the rate is not manifestly unreasonable at the time the transaction is entered into; otherwise, the discount is determined by a commercially reasonable rate that takes into account the facts and circumstances of each case at the time the transaction was entered into.

(38) "Send" in connection with any writing or notice means to deposit in the mail or deliver for transmission by any other usual means of communication with postage or cost of transmission provided for and properly addressed and in the case of an instrument to an address specified thereon or otherwise agreed, or if there be none to any address reasonable under the circumstances. The receipt of any writing or notice within the time at which it would have arrived if properly sent has the effect of a proper sending.

(39) "Signed" includes any symbol executed or adopted by a party with present intention to authenticate a writing.

(40) "Surety" includes guarantor.

(41) "Telegram" includes a message transmitted by radio, teletype, cable, any mechanical method of transmission or the like.

(42) "Term" means that portion of an agreement which relates to a particular matter.

(43) "Unauthorized" signature or indorsement means one made without actual, implied or apparent authority and includes a forgery.

(44) "Value". Except as otherwise provided with respect to negotiable instruments and bank collections (Sections 3-303, 4-208 and 4-209) a person gives "value" for rights if he acquires them

   (a) in return for a binding commitment to extend credit or for the extension of immediately available credit whether or not drawn upon and whether or not a chargeback is provided for in the event of difficulties in collection; or

   (b) as security for or in total or partial satisfaction of a pre-existing claim; or

   (c) by accepting delivery pursuant to a pre-existing contract for purchase; or

   (d) generally, in return for any consideration sufficient to support a simple contract.

(45) "Warehouse receipt" means a receipt issued by a person engaged in the business of storing goods for hire.

(46) "Written" or "writing" includes printing, typewriting or any other intentional reduction to tangible form. As amended 1962 and 1972.

§1-201. General Definitions (1977 Amendments). Subject to additional definitions contained in the subsequent Articles of this Act which are applicable to specific Articles or Parts thereof, and unless the context otherwise requires, in the Act:

* * *

1. (5) "Bearer" means the person in possession of an instrument, document of title or certificated security payable to bearer or indorsed in blank.

* * *

2. (14) "Delivery" with respect to instruments, documents of title chattel paper or certificated securities means voluntary transfer of possession.

* * *

3. (20) "Holder" means a person who is in possession of a document of title or an instrument or a certificated investment security drawn, issued or indorsed to him or his order or to bearer or in blank.

* * *

§1-202. Prima Facie Evidence by Third Party Documents.

A document in due form purporting to be a bill of lading, policy or certificate of insurance, official weigher's or inspector's certificate, consular invoice or any other document authorized or required by the contract to be issued by a third party shall be prima facie evidence of its own authenticity and genuineness and of the facts stated in the document by the third party.

§1-203. Obligation of Good Faith. Every contract or duty within this Act imposes an obligation of good faith in its performance or enforcement.

§1-204. Time; Reasonable Time; "Seasonably".

(1) Whenever this Act requires any action to be taken within a reasonable time, any time which is not manifestly unreasonable may be fixed by agreement.

(2) What is a reasonable time for taking any action depends on the nature, purpose and circumstances of such action.

(3) An action is taken "seasonably" when it is taken at or within the time agreed or if no time is agreed at or within a reasonable time.

§1-205. Course of Dealing and Usage of Trade.

(1) A course of dealing is a sequence of previous conduct between the parties to a particular transaction which is fairly to be regarded as establishing a common basis of understanding for interpreting their expressions and other conduct.

(2) A usage of trade is any practice or method of dealing having such regularity of observance in a place, vocation or trade as to justify an expectation that it will be observed with respect to the transaction in question. The existence and scope of such a usage are to be proved as facts. If it is established that such a usage is embodied in a written trade code or similar writing the interpretation of the writing is for the court.

(3) A course of dealing between parties and any usage of trade in the vocation or trade in which they are engaged or of which they are or should be aware give particular meaning to and supplement or qualify terms of an agreement.

(4) The express terms of an agreement and an applicable course of dealing or usage of trade shall be construed wherever reasonable as consistent with each other; but when such construction is unreasonable express terms control both course of dealing and usage of trade and course of dealing controls usage of trade.

(5) An applicable usage of trade in the place where any part of performance is to occur shall be used in interpreting the agreement as to that part of the performance.

(6) Evidence of a relevant usage of trade offered by one party is not admissible unless and until he has given the other party such notice as the court finds sufficient to prevent unfair surprise to the latter.

§1-206. Statute of Frauds for Kinds of Personal Property not Otherwise Covered.

(1) Except in the cases described in subsection (2) of this section a contract for the sale of personal property is not enforceable by way of action or defense beyond five thousand dollars in amount or value of remedy unless there is some writing which indicates that a contract for sale has been made between the parties at a defined or stated price, reasonably identifies the subject matter and is signed by the party against whom enforcement is sought or by his authorized agent.

(2) Subsection (1) of this section does not apply to contracts for the sale of goods (Section 2-201) nor of securities (Section 8-319) nor to security agreements (Section 9-203).

§1-207. Performance or Acceptance Under Reservation of Rights.

A party who with explicit reservation of rights performs or promises performance or assents to performance in a manner demanded or offered by the other party does not thereby prejudice the rights reserved. Such words as "without prejudice", "under protest" or the like are sufficient.

§1-208. Option to Accelerate at Will. A term providing that one party or his successor in interest may accelerate payment or performance or require collateral or additional collateral "at will" or "when he deems himself insecure" or in words of similar import shall be construed to mean that he shall have power to do so only if he in good faith believes that the prospect of payment or performance is impaired. The burden of establishing lack of good faith is on the party against whom the power has been exercised.

§1-209. Subordinated Obligations. An obligation may be issued as subordinated to payment of another obligation of the person obligated, or a creditor may subordinate his right to payment of an obligation by agreement with either the person obligated or another creditor of the person obligated. Such a subordination does not create a security interest as against either the common debtor or a

subordinated creditor. This section shall be construed as declaring the law as it existed prior to the enactment of this section and not as modifying it. Added 1966.

Note: *This new section is proposed as an optional provision to make it clear that a subordination agreement does not create a security interest unless so intended.*

Article 2: Sales

Part 1: Short Title, General Construction and Subject Matter

§2-101. Short Title. This Article shall be known and may be cited as Uniform Commercial Code—Sales.

§2-102. Scope; Certain Security and Other Transactions Excluded from this Article.
Unless the context otherwise requires, this Article applies to transactions in goods; it does not apply to any transaction which although in the form of an unconditional contract to sell or present sale is intended to operate only as a security transaction nor does this Article impair or repeal any statute regulating sales to consumers, farmers or other specified classes of buyers.

§2-103. Definitions and Index of Definitions.
(1) In this Article unless the context otherwise requires
  (a) "Buyer" means a person who buys or contracts to buy goods.
  (b) "Good faith" in the case of a merchant means honesty in fact and the observance of reasonable commercial standards of fair dealing in the trade.
  (c) "Receipt" of goods means taking physical possession of them.
  (d) "Seller" means a person who sells or contracts to sell goods.
(2) Other definitions applying to this Article or to specified Parts thereof, and the sections in which they appear are:
  "Acceptance". Section 2-606.
  "Banker's credit". Section 2-325.
  "Between merchants". Section 2-104.
  "Cancellation". Section 2-106(4).
  "Commercial unit". Section 2-105.
  "Confirmed credit". Section 2-325.
  "Conforming to contract". Section 2-106.
  "Contract for sale". Section 2-106.
  "Cover". Section 2-712.
  "Entrusting". Section 2-403.
  "Financing agency". Section 2-104.
  "Future goods". Section 2-105.
  "Goods". Section 2-105.
  "Identification". Section 2-501.
  "Installment contract". Section 2-612.
  "Letter of Credit". Section 2-325.
  "Lot". Section 2-105.
  "Merchant". Section 2-104.

  "Overseas". Section 2-323.
  "Person in position of seller". Section 2-707.
  "Present sale". Section 2-106.
  "Sale". Section 2-106.
  "Sale on approval". Section 2-326.
  "Sale or return". Section 2-326.
  "Termination". Section 2-106.
(3) The following definitions in other Articles apply to this Article:
  "Check". Section 3-104.
  "Consignee". Section 7-102.
  "Consignor". Section 7-102.
  "Consumer goods". Section 9-109.
  "Dishonor". Section 3-507.
  "Draft". Section 3-104.
(4) In addition Article 1 contains general definitions and principles of construction and interpretation applicable throughout this article.

§2-104. Definitions: "Merchant"; "Between Merchants"; "Financing Agency".
(1) "Merchant" means a person who deals in goods of the kind or otherwise by his occupation holds himself out as having knowledge or skill peculiar to the practices or goods involved in the transaction or to whom such knowledge or skill may be attributed by his employment of an agent or broker or other intermediary who by his occupation holds himself out as having such knowledge or skill.
(2) "Financing agency" means a bank, finance company or other person who in the ordinary course of business makes advances against goods or documents of title or who by arrangement with either the seller or the buyer intervenes in ordinary course to make or collect payment due or claimed under the contract for sale, as by purchasing or paying the seller's draft or making advances against it or by merely taking it for collection whether or not documents of title accompany the draft. "Financing agency" includes also a bank or other person who similarly intervenes between persons who are in the position of seller and buyer in respect of the goods (Section 2-707).
(3) "Between merchants" means in any transaction with respect to which both parties are chargeable with the knowledge or skill of merchants.

§2-105. Definitions: Transferability; "Goods"; "Future" Goods; "Lot"; "Commercial Unit".
(1) "Goods" means all things (including specially manufactured goods) which are movable at the time of identification to the contract for sale other than the money in which the price is to be paid, investment securities (Article 8) and things in action. "Goods" also includes the unborn young of animals and growing crops and other identified things attached

to realty as described in the section on goods to be severed from realty (Section 2-107).

(2) Goods must be both existing and identified before any interest in them can pass. Goods which are not both existing and identified are "future" goods. A purported present sale of future goods or of any interest therein operates as a contract to sell.

(3) There may be a sale of a part interest in existing identified goods.

(4) An undivided share in an identified bulk of fungible goods is sufficiently identified to be sold although the quantity of the bulk is not determined. Any agreed proportion of such a bulk or any quantity thereof agreed upon by number, weight or other measure may to the extent of the seller's interest in the bulk be sold to the buyer who then becomes an owner in common.

(5) "Lot" means a parcel or a single article which is the subject matter of a separate sale or delivery, whether or not it is sufficient to perform the contract.

(6) "Commercial unit" means such a unit of goods as by commercial usage is a single whole for purposes of sale and division of which materially impairs its character or value on the market or in use. A commercial unit may be a single article (as a machine) or a set of articles (as a suite of furniture or an assortment of sizes) or a quantity (as a bale, gross, or carload) or any other unit treated in use or in the relevant market as a single whole.

§2-106. Definitions: "Contract"; "Agreement"; "Contract for Sale"; "Sale"; "Present Sale"; "Conforming" to Contract; "Termination"; "Cancellation".

(1) In this Article unless the context otherwise requires "contract" and "agreement" are limited to those relating to the present or future sale of goods. "Contract for sale" includes both a present sale of goods and a contract to sell goods at a future time. A "sale" consists in the passing of title from the seller to the buyer for a price (Section 2-401). A "present sale" means a sale which is accomplished by the making of the contract.

(2) Goods or conduct including any part of a performance are "conforming" or conform to the contract when they are in accordance with the obligations under the contract.

(3) "Termination" occurs when either party pursuant to a power created by agreement or law puts an end to the contract otherwise than for its breach. On "termination" all obligations which are still executory on both sides are discharged but any right based on prior breach or performance survives.

(4) "Cancellation" occurs when either party puts an end to the contract for breach by the other and its effect is the same as that of "termination" except that the cancelling party also retains any remedy for breach of the whole contract or any unperformed balance.

§2-107. Goods to Be Severed from Realty: Recording.

(1) A contract for the sale of minerals or the like (including oil and gas) or a structure or its materials to be removed from realty is a contract for the sale of goods within this Article if they are to be severed by the seller but until severance a purported present sale thereof which is not effective as a transfer of an interest in land is effective only as a contract to sell.

(2) A contract for the sale apart from the land of growing crops or other things attached to realty and capable of severance without material harm thereto but not described in subsection (1) or of timber to be cut is a contract for the sale of goods within this Article whether the subject matter is to be severed by the buyer or by the seller even though it forms part of the realty at the time of contracting, and the parties can by identification effect a present sale before severance.

(3) The provisions of this section are subject to any third party rights provided by the law relating to realty records, and the contract for sale may be executed and recorded as a document transferring an interest in land and shall then constitute notice to third parties of the buyer's rights under the contract for sale.

Part 2: Form, Formation and Readjustment of Contract

§2-201. Formal Requirements; Statute of Frauds.

(1) Except as otherwise provided in this section a contract for the sale of goods for the price of $500 or more is not enforceable by way of action or defense unless there is some writing sufficient to indicate that a contract for sale has been made between the parties and signed by the party against whom enforcement is sought or by his authorized agent or broker. A writing is not insufficient because it omits or incorrectly states a term agreed upon but the contract is not enforceable under this paragraph beyond the quantity of goods shown in such writing.

(2) Between merchants if within a reasonable time a writing in confirmation of the contract and sufficient against the sender is received and the party receiving it has reason to know its contents, it satisfies the requirements of subsection (1) against such party unless written notice of objection to its contents is given within ten days after it is received.

(3) A contract which does not satisfy the requirements of subsection (1) but which is valid in other respects is enforceable
  (a) if the goods are to be specially manufactured for the buyer and are not suitable for sale to others in the ordinary course of the seller's business and the seller, before notice of repudiation is received and under circumstances which reasonably indicate that the goods are for the buyer, has made

either a substantial beginning of their manufacture of commitments for their procurement; or

(b) if the party against whom enforcement is sought admits in his pleading, testimony or otherwise in court that a contract for sale was made, but the contract is not enforceable under this provision beyond the quantity of goods admitted; or

(c) with respect to goods for which payment has been made and accepted or which have been received and accepted (Section 2-606).

§2-202. Final Written Expression: Parol or Extrinsic Evidence.

Terms with respect to which the confirmatory memoranda of the parties agree or which are otherwise set forth in a writing intended by the parties as a final expression of their agreement with respect to such terms as are included therein may not be contradicted by evidence of any prior agreement or of a contemporaneous oral agreement but may be explained or supplemented

(a) by course of dealing or usage of trade (Section 1-205) or by course of performance (Section 2-208); and

(b) by evidence of consistent additional terms unless the court finds the writing to have been intended also as a complete and exclusive statement of the terms of the agreement.

§2-203. Seals Inoperative.
The affixing of a seal to a writing evidencing a contract for sale or an offer to buy or sell goods does not constitute the writing a sealed instrument and the law with respect to sealed instruments does not apply to such a contract or offer.

§2-204. Formation in General.

(1) A contract for sale of goods may be made in any manner sufficient to show agreement, including conduct by both parties which recognizes the existence of such a contract.

(2) An agreement sufficient to constitute a contract for sale may be found even though the moment of its making is undetermined.

(3) Even though one or more terms are left open a contract for sale does not fail for indefiniteness if the parties have intended to make a contract and there is a reasonably certain basis for giving an appropriate remedy.

§2-205. Firm Offers.
An offer by a merchant to buy or sell goods in a signed writing which by its terms gives assurance that it will be held open is not revocable, for lack of consideration, during the time stated or if no time is stated for a reasonable time, but in no event may such period of irrevocability exceed three months; but any such term of assurance on a form supplied by the offeree must be separately signed by the offeror.

§2-206. Offer and Acceptance in Formation of Contract.

(1) Unless otherwise unambiguously indicated by the language or circumstances

(a) an offer to make a contract shall be construed as inviting acceptance in any manner and by any medium reasonable in the circumstances;

(b) an order or other offer to buy goods for prompt or current shipment shall be construed as inviting acceptance either by a prompt promise to ship or by the prompt or current shipment of conforming or nonconforming goods, but such a shipment of nonconforming goods does not constitute an acceptance if the seller seasonably notifies the buyer that the shipment is offered only as an accommodation to the buyer.

(2) Where the beginning of a requested performance is a reasonable mode of acceptance an offeror who is not notified of acceptance within a reasonable time may treat the offer as having lapsed before acceptance.

§2-207. Additional Terms in Acceptance or Confirmation.

(1) A definite and seasonable expression of acceptance or a written confirmation which is sent within a reasonable time operates as an acceptance even though it states terms additional to or different from those offered or agreed upon, unless acceptance is expressly made conditional on assent to the additional or different terms.

(2) The additional terms are to be construed as proposals for addition to the contract. Between merchants such terms become part of the contract unless

(a) the offer expressly limits acceptance to the terms of the offer;

(b) they materially alter it; or

(c) notification of objection to them has already been given or is given within a reasonable time after notice of them is received.

(3) Conduct by both parties which recognizes the existence of a contract is sufficient to establish a contract for sale although the writings of the parties do not otherwise establish a contract. In such case the terms of the particular contract consist of those terms on which the writings of the parties agree, together with any supplementary terms incorporated under any other provisions of this Act.

§2-208. Course of Performance or Practical Construction.

(1) Where the contract for sale involves repeated occasions for performance by either party with knowledge of the nature of the performance and opportunity for objection to it by the other, any course of performance accepted or acquiesced in without objection shall be relevant to determine the meaning of the agreement.

(2) The express terms of the agreement and any such course of performance, as well as any course of dealing and usage of trade, shall be construed whenever reasonable as consistent with each other; but when such construction is unreasonable, express terms shall control course of performance and course of performance shall control both course of dealing and usage of trade (Section 1-205).

(3) Subject to the provisions of the next section on modification and waiver, such course of performance shall be relevant to show a waiver or modification of any term inconsistent with such course of performance.

§2-209. Modification, Rescission and Waiver.

(1) An agreement modifying a contract within this Article needs no consideration to be binding.

(2) A signed agreement which excludes modification or rescission except by a signed writing cannot be otherwise modified or rescinded, but except as between merchants such a requirement on a form supplied by the merchant must be separately signed by the other party.

(3) The requirements of the statute of frauds section of this Article (Section 2-201) must be satisfied if the contract as modified is within its provisions.

(4) Although an attempt at modification or rescission does not satisfy the requirements of subsection (2) or (3) it can operate as a waiver.

(5) A party who has made a waiver affecting an executory portion of the contract may retract the waiver by reasonable notification received by the other party that strict performance will be required of any term waived, unless the retraction would be unjust in view of a material change of position in reliance on the waiver.

§2-210. Delegation of Performance; Assignment of Rights.

(1) A party may perform his duty through a delegate unless otherwise agreed or unless the other party has a substantial interest in having his original promisor perform or control the acts required by the contract. No delegation of performance relieves the party delegating of any duty to perform or any liability for breach.

(2) Unless otherwise agreed all rights of either seller or buyer can be assigned except where the assignment would materially change the duty of the other party, or increase materially the burden or risk imposed on him by his contract, or impair materially his chance of obtaining return performance. A right to damages for breach of the whole contract or a right arising out of the assignor's due performance of his entire obligation can be assigned despite agreement otherwise.

(3) Unless the circumstances indicate the contrary a prohibition of assignment of "the contract" is to be construed as barring only the delegation to the assignee of the assignor's performance.

(4) An assignment of "the contract" or of "all my rights under the contract" or an assignment in similar general terms is an assignment of rights and unless the language or the circumstances (as in an assignment for security) indicate the contrary, it is a delegation of performance of the duties of the assignor and its acceptance by the assignee constitutes a promise by him to perform those duties. This promise is enforceable by either the assignor or the other party to the original contract.

(5) The other party may treat any assignment which delegates performance as creating reasonable grounds for insecurity and may without prejudice to his rights against the assignor demand assurances from the assignee (Section 2-609).

Part 3: General Obligation and Construction of Contract

§2-301. General Obligations of Parties. The obligation of the seller is to transfer and deliver and that of the buyer is to accept and pay in accordance with the contract.

§2-302. Unconscionable Contract or Clause.

(1) If the court as a matter of law finds the contract or any clause of the contract to have been unconscionable at the time it was made the court may refuse to enforce the contract, or it may enforce the remainder of the contract without the unconscionable clause, or it may so limit the application of any unconscionable clause as to avoid any unconscionable result.

(2) When it is claimed or appears to the court that the contract or any clause thereof may be unconscionable the parties shall be afforded a reasonable opportunity to present evidence as to its commercial setting, purpose and effect to aid the court in making the determination.

§2-303. Allocation or Division of Risks. Where this Article allocates a risk or a burden as between the parties "unless otherwise agreed", the agreement may not only shift the allocation but may also divide the risk or burden.

§2-304. Price Payable in Money, Goods, Realty or Otherwise.

(1) The price can be made payable in money or otherwise. If it is payable in whole or in part in goods each party is a seller of the goods which he is to transfer.

(2) Even though all or part of the price is payable in an interest in realty the transfer of the goods and the seller's obligations with reference to them are subject to this Article, but not the transfer of the interest in realty or the transferor's obligations in connection therewith.

§2-305. Open Price Term.

(1) The parties if they so intend can conclude a contract for sale even though the price is not settled. In such a case the price is a reasonable price at the time for delivery if

(a) nothing is said as to price; or

(b) the price is left to be agreed by the parties and they fail to agree; or

(c) the price is to be fixed in terms of some agreed market or other standard as set or recorded by a third person or agency and it is not so set or recorded.

(2) A price to be fixed by the seller or by the buyer means a price for him to fix in good faith.

(3) When a price left to be fixed otherwise than by agreement of the parties fails to be fixed through fault of one party the other may at his option treat the contract as cancelled or himself fix a reasonable price.

(4) Where, however, the parties intend not to be bound unless the price be fixed or agreed and it is not fixed or agreed there is no contract. In such a case the buyer must return any goods already received or if unable so to do must pay their reasonable value at the time of delivery and the seller must return any portion of the price paid on account.

§2-306. Output, Requirements and Exclusive Dealings.

(1) A term which measures the quantity by the output of the seller or the requirements of the buyer means such actual output or requirements as may occur in good faith, except that no quantity unreasonably disproportionate to any stated estimate or in the absence of a stated estimate to any normal or otherwise comparable prior output or requirements may be tendered or demanded.

(2) A lawful agreement by either the seller or the buyer for exclusive dealing in the kind of goods concerned imposes unless otherwise agreed an obligation by the seller to use best efforts to supply the goods and by the buyer to use best efforts to promote their sale.

§2-307. Delivery in Single Lot or Several Lots.
Unless otherwise agreed all goods called for by a contract for sale must be tendered in a single delivery and payment is due only on such tender but where the circumstances give either party the right to make or demand delivery in lots the price if it can be apportioned may be demanded for each lot.

§2-308. Absence of Specified Place for Delivery.

Unless otherwise agreed

(a) the place for delivery of goods is the seller's place of business or if he has none his residence; but

(b) in a contract for sale of identified goods which to the knowledge of the parties at the time of contracting are in some other place, that place is the place for their delivery; and

(c) documents of title may be delivered through customary banking channels.

§2-309. Absence of Specific Time Provisions; Notice of Termination.

(1) The time for shipment or delivery or any other action under a contract if not provided in this Article or agreed upon shall be a reasonable time.

(2) Where the contract provides for successive performances but is indefinite in duration it is valid for a reasonable time but unless otherwise agreed may be terminated at any time by either party.

(3) Termination of a contract by one party except on the happening of an agreed event requires that reasonable notification be received by the other party and in agreement dispensing with notification is invalid if its operation would be unconscionable.

§2-310. Open Time for Payment or Running of Credit; Authority to Ship Under Reservation.

Unless otherwise agreed

(a) payment is due at the time and place at which the buyer is to receive the goods even though the place of shipment is the place of delivery; and

(b) if the seller is authorized to send the goods he may ship them under reservation, and may tender the documents of title, but the buyer may inspect the goods after their arrival before payment is due unless such inspection is inconsistent with the terms of the contract (Section 2-513); and

(c) if delivery is authorized and made by way of documents of title otherwise than by subsection (b) then payment is due at the time and place at which the buyer is to receive the documents regardless of where the goods are to be received; and

(d) where the seller is required or authorized to ship the goods on credit the credit period runs from the time of shipment but post-dating the invoice or delaying its dispatch will correspondingly delay the starting of the credit period.

§2-311. Options and Cooperation Respecting Performance.

(1) An agreement for sale which is otherwise sufficiently definite (subsection (3) of Section 2-204) to be a contract is not made invalid by the fact that it leaves particulars of performance to be specified by one of the parties. Any such specification must be made in good faith and within limits set by commercial reasonableness.

(2) Unless otherwise agreed specifications relating to assortment of the goods are at the buyer's option and except as otherwise provided in subsections (1)(c) and (3) of Section 2-319 specifications or arrangements relating to shipment are at the seller's options.

(3) Where such specifications would materially affect the other party's performance but is not seasonably made or where one party's cooperation is necessary to the agreed performance of the other but is not seasonably forthcoming, the other party

(a) is excused for any resulting delay in his own performance; and

(b) may also either proceed to perform in any reasonable manner or after the time for a material part of his own performance treat the failure to specify or to cooperate as a breach by failure to deliver or accept the goods.

§2-312. Warranty of Title and Against Infringement; Buyer's Obligation Against Infringement.

(1) Subject to subsection (2) there is in a contract for sale a warranty by the seller that

(a) the title conveyed shall be good, and its transfer rightful; and

(b) the goods shall be delivered free from any security interest or other lien or encumbrance of which the buyer at the time of contracting has no knowledge.

(2) A warranty under subsection (2) will be excluded or modified only by specific language or by circumstances which give the buyer reason to know that the person selling does not claim title in himself or that he is purporting to sell only such right or title as he or a third person may have.

(3) Unless otherwise agreed a seller who is a merchant regularly dealing in goods of the kind warrants that the goods shall be delivered free of the rightful claim of any third person by way of infringement or the like but a buyer who furnishes specifications to the seller must hold the seller harmless against any such claim which arises out of compliance with the specifications.

§2-313. Express Warranties by Affirmation, Promise, Description, Sample.

(1) Express warranties by the seller are created as follows:

(a) Any affirmation of fact or promise made by the seller to the buyer which relates to the goods and becomes part of the basis of the bargain creates an express warranty that the goods shall conform to the affirmation or promise.

(b) Any description of the goods which is made part of the basis of the bargain creates an express warranty that the goods shall conform to the description.

(c) Any sample or model which is made part of the basis of the bargain creates an express warranty that the whole of the goods shall conform to the sample or model.

(2) It is not necessary to the creation of an express warranty that the seller use formal words such as "warrant" or "guarantee" or that he have a specific intention to make a warranty, but an affirmation merely of the value of the goods or a statement purporting to be merely the seller's opinion or commendation of the goods does not create a warranty.

§2-314. Implied Warranty: Merchantability; Usage of Trade.

(1) Unless excluded or modified (Section 2-316), a warranty that the goods shall be merchantable is implied in a contract for their sale if the seller is a merchant with respect to goods of that kind. Under this section the serving for value of food or drink to be consumed either on the premises or elsewhere is a sale.

(2) Goods to be merchantable must be at least such as

(a) pass without objection in the trade under the contract description; and

(b) in the case of fungible goods, are of fair average quality within the description; and

(c) are fit for the ordinary purposes for which such goods are used; and

(d) run, within the variations permitted by the agreement, of even kind, quality and quantity within each unit and among all units involved; and

(e) are adequately contained, packaged and labeled as the agreement may require; and

(f) conform to the promises or affirmations of fact made or the container or label if any.

(3) Unless excluded or modified (Section 2-316) other implied warranties may arise from course of dealing or usage of trade.

§2-315. Implied Warranty: Fitness for Particular Purpose.

Where the seller at the time of contracting has reason to know any particular purpose for which the goods are required and that the buyer is relying on the seller's skill or judgment to select or furnish suitable goods, there is unless excluded or modified under the next section an implied warranty that the goods shall be fit for such purpose.

§2-316. Exclusion or Modification of Warranties.

(1) Words or conduct relevant to the creation of an express warranty and words or conduct tending to negate or limit warranty shall be construed wherever reasonable as consistent with each other; but subject to the provisions of this Article on parol or extrinsic evidence (Section 2-202) negation or limitation is inoperative to the extent that such construction is unreasonable.

(2) Subject to subsection (3), to exclude or modify the implied warranty of merchantability or any part of it the language must mention merchantability and in case of a writing must be conspicious, and to exclude or modify any implied warranty of fitness the exclusion must be by a writing and conspicuous. Language to exclude all implied warranties of fitness is sufficient if it states, for example, that "There are no warranties which extend beyond the description on the face hereof".

(3) Notwithstanding subsection (2)

(a) unless the circumstances indicate otherwise, all implied warranties are excluded by expressions like "as is", "with all faults" or other language which in common understanding calls the buyer's attention to the exclusion of warranties and makes plain that there is no implied warranty; and

(b) when the buyer before entering into the contract has examined the goods or the sample or model as fully as he desired or has refused to examine the goods there is no implied warranty with regard to defects which an examination ought in the circumstances to have revealed to him; and

(c) an implied warranty can also be excluded or modified by course of dealing or course of performance or usage of trade.

(4) Remedies for breach of warranty can be limited in accordance with the provisions of this Article on liquidation or limitation of damages and on contractual modification of remedy (Sections 2-718 and 2-719).

§2-317. Cumulation and Conflict of Warranties Express or Implied.

Warranties whether express or implied shall be construed as consistent with each other and as cumulative but if such construction is unreasonable the intention of the parties shall determine which warranty is dominant. In ascertaining that intention the following rules apply:

(a) Exact or technical specifications displace an inconsistent sample or model or general language of description.

(b) A sample from an existing bulk displaces inconsistent general language of description.

(c) Express warranties displace inconsistent implied warranties other than an implied warranty of fitness for a particular purpose.

§2-318. Third Party Beneficiaries of Warranties Express or Implied.

Note: If this Act is introduced in the Congress of the United Sates this section should be omitted. (States to select one alternative.)

Alternative A—A seller's warranty whether express or implied extends to any natural person who is in the family or household of his buyer or who is a guest in his home if it is reasonable to expect that such person may use, consume or be affected by the goods and who is injured in person by breach of the warranty. A seller may not exclude or limit the operation of this section.

Alternative B—A seller's warranty whether express or implied extends to any natural person who may reasonably be expected to use, consume or be affected by the goods and who is injured in person by breach of the warranty. A seller may not exclude or limit the operation of this section.

Alternative C—A seller's warranty whether express or implied extends to any person who may reasonably be expected to use, consume or be affected by the goods and who is injured by breach of the warranty. A seller may not exclude or limit the operation of this section with respect to injury to the person of an individual to whom the warranty extends. As amended 1966.

§2-319. F.O.B. and F.A.S. Terms.

(1) Unless otherwise agreed the term F.O.B. (which means "free on board") at a named place, even though used only in connection with the stated price, is a delivery term under which

(a) when the term is F.O.B. the place of shipment, the seller must at that place ship the goods in the manner provided in this Article (Section 2-504) and bear the expense and risk of putting them into the possession of the carrier; or

(b) when the term is F.O.B. the place of destination, the seller must at his own expense and risk transport the goods to that place and there tender delivery of them in the manner provided in this Article (Section 2-503);

(c) when under either (a) or (b) the term is also F.O.B. vessel, car or other vehicle, the seller must in addition at his own expense and risk load the goods on board. If the term is F.O.B. vessel the buyer must name the vessel and in an appropriate case the seller must comply with the provisions of this Article on the form of bill of lading (Section 2-323).

(2) Unless otherwise agreed the term F.A.S. vessel (which means "free alongside") at a named port, even though used only in connection with the stated price, is a delivery term under which the seller must

(a) at his own expense and risk deliver the goods alongside the vessel in the manner usual in that port or on a dock designated and provided by the buyer; and

(b) obtain and tender a receipt for the goods in exchange for which the carrier is under a duty to issue a bill of lading.

(3) Unless otherwise agreed in any case falling within subsection (1)(a) or (c) or subsection (2) the buyer must seasonably give any needed instructions for making delivery, including when the term is F.A.S. or F.O.B. the loading berth of the vessel and in an appropriate case its name and sailing date. The seller may treat the failure of needed instructions as a failure of cooperation under this Article (Section 2-311). He may also at his option move the goods in any reasonable manner preparatory to delivery or shipment.

(4) Under the term F.O.B. vessel or F.A.S. unless otherwise agreed the buyer must make payment against tender of the required documents and the seller may not tender nor the buyer demand delivery of the goods in substitution for the documents.

§2-320. C.I.F. and C.&F. Terms.

(1) The term C.I.F. means that the price includes in a lump sum the cost of the goods and the insurance and freight to the named destination. The term C.&F. or C.F. means that the price so includes cost and freight to the named destination.

(2) Unless otherwise agreed and even though used only in connection with the stated price and destination, the term C.I.F. destination or its equivalent requires the seller at his own expense and risk to

   (a) put the goods into the possession of a carrier at the port for shipment and obtain a negotiable bill or bills of lading covering the entire transportation to the named destination; and

   (b) load the goods and obtain a receipt from the carrier (which may be contained in the bill of lading) showing that the freight has been paid or provided for; and

   (c) obtain a policy or certificate of insurance, including any war risk insurance, of a kind and on terms then current at the port of shipment in the usual amount, in the currency of the contract, shown to cover the same goods covered by the bill of lading and providing for payment of loss to the order of the buyer or for the account of whom it may concern; but the seller may add to the price the amount of the premium for any such war risk insurance; and

   (d) prepare an invoice of the goods and procure any other documents required to effect shipment or to comply with the contract; and

   (e) forward and tender with commercial promptness all the documents in due form and with any indorsement necessary to perfect the buyer's rights.

(3) Unless otherwise agreed the term C.&F. or its equivalent has the same effect and imposes upon the seller the same obligations and risks as a C.I.F. term except the obligation as to insurance.

(4) Under the term C.I.F. or C.&F. unless otherwise agreed the buyer must make payment against tender of the required documents and the seller may not tender nor the buyer demand delivery of the goods in substitution for the documents.

§2-321. C.I.F. or C.&F.; "Net Landed Weights"; "Payment on Arrival"; Warranty of Condition on Arrival.

Under a contract containing a term C.I.F. or C.&F.

(1) Where the price is based on or is to be adjusted according to "net landed weights", "delivered weights", "out turn" quantity or quality or the like, unless otherwise agreed the seller must reasonably estimate the price. The payment due on tender of the documents called for by the contract is the amount so estimated, but after final adjustment of the price a settlement must be made with commercial promptness.

(2) An agreement described in subsection (1) or any warranty of quality or condition of the goods on arrival places upon the seller the risk of ordinary deterioration, shrinkage and the like in transportation but has no effect on the place or time of identification to the contract for sale or delivery or on the passing of the risk of loss.

(3) Unless otherwise agreed where the contract provides for payment on or after arrival of the goods the seller must before payment allow such preliminary inspection as is feasible; but if the goods are lost delivery of the documents and payment are due when the goods should have arrived.

§2-322. Delivery "Ex-Ship".

(1) Unless otherwise agreed a term for delivery of goods "ex-ship" (which means from the carrying vessel) or in equivalent language is not restricted to a particular ship and requires delivery from a ship which has reached a place at the named port of destination where goods of the kind are usually discharged.

(2) Under such a term unless otherwise agreed

   (a) the seller must discharge all liens arising out of the carriage and furnish the buyer with a direction which puts the carrier under a duty to deliver the goods; and

   (b) the risk of loss does not pass to the buyer until the goods leave the ship's tackle or are otherwise properly unloaded.

§2-323. Form of Bill of Lading Required in Overseas Shipment; "Overseas".

(1) Where the contract contemplates overseas shipment and contains a term C.I.F. or C.&F. or F.O.B. vessel the seller unless otherwise agreed must obtain a negotiable bill of lading stating that the goods have been loaded on board or, in the case of a term C.I.F. or C.&F., received for shipment.

(2) Where in a case within subsection (1) a bill of lading has been issued in a set of parts, unless otherwise agreed if the documents are not to be sent from abroad the buyer may demand tender of the full set; otherwise only one part of the bill of lading need be tendered. Even if the agreement expressly requires a full set

   (a) due tender of a single part is acceptable within the provisions of this Article on cure of improper delivery (subsection (1) of Section 2-508); and

   (b) even though the full set is demanded, if the documents are sent from abroad the person tendering an incomplete set may nevertheless require payment upon furnishing an indemnity which the buyer in good faith deems adequate.

(3) A shipment by water or by air on a contract contemplating such shipment is "overseas" insofar as by usage of trade or agreement it is subject to the commercial, financing or shipping practices characteristic of international deep water commerce.

§2-324. "No Arrival, No Sale" Term. Under a term "no arrival, no sale" or terms of like meaning, unless otherwise agreed,

(a) the seller must properly ship conforming goods and if they arrive by any means he must tender them on arrival but he assumes no obligation that the goods will arrive unless he has caused the nonarrival; and

(b) where without fault of the seller the goods are in part lost or have so deteriorated as no longer to conform to the contract or arrive after the contract time, the buyer may proceed as if there had been casualty to identified goods (Section 2-613).

§2-325. "Letter of Credit" Term; "Confirmed Credit".

(1) Failure of the buyer seasonably to furnish an agreed letter of credit is a breach of the contract for sale.

(2) The delivery to seller of a proper letter of credit suspends the buyer's obligation to pay. If the letter of credit is dishonored, the seller may on seasonable notification to the buyer require payment directly from him.

(3) Unless otherwise agreed the term "letter of credit" or "banker's credit" in a contract for sale means an irrevocable credit issued by a financing agency of good repute and, where the shipment is overseas, of good international repute. The term "confirmed credit" means that the credit must also carry the direct obligation of such an agency which does business in the seller's financial market.

§2-326. Sale on Approval and Sale or Return; Consignment Sales and Rights of Creditors.

(1) Unless otherwise agreed, if delivered goods may be returned by the buyer even though they conform to the contract, the transaction is

(a) a "sale on approval" if the goods are delivered primarily for use, and

(b) a "sale or return" if the goods are delivered primarily for resale.

(2) Except as provided in subsection (3), goods held on approval are not subject to the claims of the buyer's creditors until acceptance; goods held on sale or return are subject to such claims while in the buyer's possession.

(3) Where goods are delivered to a person for sale and such person maintains a place of business at which he deals in goods of the kind involved, under a name other than the name of the person making delivery, then with respect to claims of creditors of the person conducting the business the goods are deemed to be on sale or return. The provisions of this subsection are applicable even though an agreement purports to reserve title to the person making delivery until payment or resale or uses such words as "on consignment" or "on

memorandum". However, this subsection is not applicable if the person making delivery

(a) complies with an applicable law providing for a consignor's interest or the like to be evidenced by a sign, or

(b) establishes that the person conducting the business is generally known by his creditors to be substantially engaged in selling the goods of others, or

(c) complies with the filing provisions of the Article on Secured Transactions (Article 9).

(4) Any "or return" term of a contract for sale is to be treated as a separate contract for sale within the statute of frauds section of this Article (Section 2-201) and as contradicting the sale aspect of the contract within the provisions of this Article on parol or extrinsic evidence (Section 2-202).

§2-327. Special Incidents of Sale on Approval and Sale or Return.

(1) Under a sale on approval unless otherwise agreed

(a) although the goods are identified to the contract the risk of loss and the title do not pass to the buyer until acceptance; and

(b) use of the goods consistent with the purpose of trial is not acceptance but failure seasonably to notify the seller of election to return the goods is acceptance, and if the goods conform to the contract acceptance of any part is acceptance of the whole; and

(c) after due notification of election to return, the return is at the seller's risk and expense but a merchant buyer must follow any reasonable instructions.

(2) Under a sale or return unless otherwise agreed

(a) the option to return extends to the whole or any commercial unit of the goods while in substantially their original condition, but must be exercised seasonably; and

(b) the return is at the buyer's risk and expense.

§2-328. Sale by Auction.

(1) In a sale by auction if goods are put up in lots each lot is the subject of a separate sale.

(2) A sale by auction is complete when the auctioneer so announces by the fall of the hammer or in other customary manner. Where a bid is made while the hammer is falling in acceptance of a prior bid the auctioneer may in his discretion reopen the bidding or declare the goods sold under the bid on which the hammer was falling.

(3) Such a sale is with reserve unless the goods are in explicit terms put up without reserve. In an auction with reserve, the auctioneer may withdraw the goods at any time until he announces completion of the sale. In an auction without reserve, after the auctioneer calls for bids on an article or lot, that article

or lot cannot be withdrawn unless no bid is made within a reasonable time. In either case a bidder may retract his bid until the auctioneer's announcement of completion of the sale, but a bidder's retraction does not revive any previous bid.

(4) If the auctioneer knowingly receives a bid on the seller's behalf or the seller makes or procures such a bid, and notice has not been given that liberty for such bidding is reserved, the buyer may at his option avoid the sale or take the goods at the price of the last good faith bid prior to the completion of the sale. This subsection shall not apply to any bid at a forced sale.

Part 4: Title, Creditors and Good Faith Purchasers

§2-401. Passing of Title; Reservation for Security; Limited Application of this Section.

Each provision of this Article with regard to the rights, obligations and remedies of the seller, the buyer, purchasers or other third parties applies irrespective of title to the goods except where the provision refers to such title. Insofar as situations are not covered by the other provisions of this Article and matters concerning title become material the following rules apply:

(1) Title to goods cannot pass under a contract for sale prior to their identification to the contract (Section 2-501), and unless otherwise explicitly agreed the buyer acquires by their identification a special property as limited by this Act. Any retention or reservation by the seller of the title (property) in goods shipped or delivered to the buyer is limited in effect to a reservation of a security interest. Subject to these provisions and to the provisions of the Article on Secured Transactions (Article 9), title to goods passes from the seller to the buyer in any manner and on any conditions explicitly agreed on by the parties.

(2) Unless otherwise explicitly agreed title passes to the buyer at the time and place at which the seller completes his performances with reference to the physical delivery of the goods, despite any reservation of a security interest and even though a document of title is to be delivered at a different time or place; and in particular and despite any reservation of a security interest by the bill of lading

  (a) if the contract requires or authorizes the seller to send the goods to the buyer but does not require him to deliver them at destination, title passes to the buyer at the time and place of shipment; but

  (b) if the contract requires delivery at destination, title passes on tender there.

(3) Unless otherwise explicitly agreed where delivery is to be made without moving the goods,

  (a) if the seller is to deliver a document of title, title passes at the time when and the place where he delivers such documents; or

  (b) if the goods are at the time of contracting already identified and no documents are to be delivered, title passes at the time and place of contracting.

(4) A rejection or other refusal by the buyer to receive or retain the goods, whether or not justified, or a justified revocation of acceptance revests title to the goods in the seller. Such revesting occurs by operation of law and is not a "sale".

§2-402. Rights of Seller's Creditors Against Sold Goods.

(1) Except as provided in subsections (2) and (3), rights of unsecured creditors of the seller with respect to goods which have been identified to a contract for sale are subject to the buyer's rights to recover the goods under this Article (Sections 2-502 and 2-716).

(2) A creditor of the seller may treat a sale or an identification of goods to a contract for sale as void if as against him a retention of possession by the seller is fraudulent under any rule of law of the state where the goods are situated, except that retention of possession in good faith and current course of trade by a merchant-seller for a commercially reasonable time after a sale or identification is not fraudulent.

(3) Nothing in this Article shall be deemed to impair the rights of creditors of the seller

  (a) under the provisions of the Article on Secured Transactions (Article 9); or

  (b) where identification to the contract or delivery is made not in current course of trade but in satisfaction of or as security for a pre-existing claim for money, security or the like and is made under circumstances which under any rule of law of the state where the goods are situated would apart from this Article constitute the transaction a fraudulent transfer or voidable preference.

§2-403. Power to Transfer; Good Faith Purchase of Goods; "Entrusting".

(1) A purchaser of goods acquires all title which his transferor had or had power to transfer except that a purchaser of a limited interest acquires rights only to the extent of the interest purchased. A person with voidable title has power to transfer a good title to a good faith purchaser for value. When goods have been delivered under a transaction of purchase the purchaser had such power even though

  (a) the transferor was deceived as to the identity of the purchaser, or

  (b) the delivery was in exchange for a check which is later dishonored, or

  (c) it was agreed that the transaction was to be a "cash sale", or

  (d) the delivery was procured through fraud punishable as larcenous under the criminal law.

(2) Any entrusting of possession of goods to a merchant who deals in goods of that kind gives him power to transfer all rights of the entruster to a buyer in ordinary course of business.

(3) "Entrusting" includes any delivery and any acquiescence in retention of possession regardless of any condition expressed between the parties to the delivery or acquiescence and regardless of whether the procurement of the entrusting or the possessor's disposition of the goods have been such as to be larcenous under the criminal law.

(4) The rights of other purchasers of goods and of lien creditors are governed by the Articles on Secured Transactions (Article 9), Bulk Transfers (Article 6) and Documents of Title (Article 7).

Part 5: Performance

§2-501. Insurable Interest in Goods; Manner of Identification of Goods.

(1) The buyer obtains a special property and an insurable interest in goods by identification of existing goods as goods to which the contract refers even though the goods so identified are non-conforming and he has an option to return or reject them. Such identification can be made at any time and in any manner explicitly agreed to by the parties. In the absence of explicit agreement identification occurs
  (a) when the contract is made if it is for the sale of goods already existing and identified;
  (b) if the contract is for the sale of future goods other than those described in paragraph (c), when goods are shipped, marked or otherwise designated by the seller as goods to which the contract refers;
  (c) when the crops are planted or otherwise become growing crops or the young are conceived if the contract is for the sale of unborn young to be born within twelve months after contracting or for the sale of crops to be harvested within twelve months or the next normal harvest season after contracting, whichever is longer.

(2) The seller retains an insurable interest in goods so long as title to or any security interest in the goods remains in him and where the identification is by the seller alone he may until default or insolvency or notification to the buyer that the identification is final substitute other goods for those identified.

(3) Nothing in this section impairs any insurable interest recognized under any other statute or rule of law.

§2-502. Buyer's Right to Goods on Seller's Insolvency.

(1) Subject to subsection (2) and even though the goods have not been shipped a buyer who has paid a part or all of the price of goods in which he has a special property under the provisions of the immediately preceding section may on making and keeping good a tender of any unpaid portion or their price recover them from the seller if the seller becomes insolvent within ten days after receipt of the first installment on their price.

(2) If the identification creating his special property has been made by the buyer he acquires the right to recover the goods only if they conform to the contract for sale.

§2-503. Manner of Seller's Tender of Delivery.

(1) Tender of delivery requires that the seller put and hold conforming goods at the buyer's disposition and give the buyer any notification reasonably necessary to enable him to take delivery. The manner, time and place for tender are determined by the agreement and this Article, and in particular
  (a) tender must be at a reasonable hour, and if it is of goods they must be kept available for the period reasonably necessary to enable the buyer to take possession; but
  (b) unless otherwise agreed the buyer must furnish facilities reasonably suited to the receipt of the goods.

(2) Where the case is within the next section respecting shipment tender requires that the seller comply with its provisions.

(3) Where the seller is required to deliver at a particular destination tender requires that he comply with subsection (1) and also in any appropriate case tender documents as described in subsections (4) and (5) of this section.

(4) Where goods are in the possession of a bailee and are to be delivered without being moved
  (a) tender requires that the seller either tender a negotiable document of title covering such goods or procure acknowledgement by the bailee of the buyer's right to possession of the goods; but
  (b) tender to the buyer of a non-negotiable document of title or of a written direction to the bailee to deliver is sufficient tender unless the buyer seasonably objects, and receipt by the bailee of notification of the buyer's rights fixes those rights as against the bailee and all third persons; but risk of loss of the goods and of any failure by the bailee to honor the non-negotiable document of title or to obey the direction remains on the seller until the buyer has had a reasonable time to present the document or direction, and a refusal by the bailee to honor the document or to obey the direction defeats the tender.

(5) Where the contract requires the seller to deliver documents
  (a) he must tender all such documents in correct form, except as provided in this Article with respect to bills of lading in a set (subsection (2) of Section 2-323); and

(b) tender through customary banking channels is sufficient and dishonor of a draft accompanying the documents constitutes non-acceptance or rejection.

§2-504. Shipment by Seller.
Where the seller is required or authorized to send the goods to the buyer and the contract does not require him to deliver them at a particular destination, then unless otherwise agreed he must

(a) put the goods in the possession of such a carrier and make such a contract for their transportation as may be reasonable having regard to the nature of the goods and other circumstances of the case; and

(b) obtain and promptly deliver or tender in due form any document necessary to enable the buyer to obtain possession of the goods or otherwise required by the agreement or by usage of trade; and

(c) promptly notify the buyer of the shipment.

Failure to notify the buyer under paragraph (c) or to make a proper contract under paragraph (a) is a ground for rejection only if material delay or loss ensues.

§2-505. Seller's Shipment Under Reservation.
(1) Where the seller has identified goods to the contract by or before shipment:

(a) his procurement of a negotiable bill of lading to his own order or otherwise reserves in him a security interest in the goods. His procurement of the bill to the order of a financing agency or of the buyer indicates in addition only the seller's expectation of transferring that interest to the person named.

(b) a non-negotiable bill of lading to himself or his nominee reserves possession of the goods as security but except in a case of conditional delivery (subsection (2) of Section 2-507) a non-negotiable bill of lading naming the buyer as consignee reserves no security interest even though the seller retains possession of the bill of lading.

(2) When shipment by the seller with reservation of a security interest is in violation of the contract for sale it constitutes an improper contract for transportation within the preceding section but impairs neither the rights given to the buyer by shipment and identification of the goods, to the contract nor the seller's powers as a holder of a negotiable document.

§2-506. Rights of Financing Agency.
(1) A financing agency by paying or purchasing for value a draft which relates to a shipment of goods acquires to the extent of the payment or purchase and in addition to its own rights under the draft and any document of title securing it any rights of the shipper in the goods including the right to stop delivery and the shipper's right to have the draft honored by the buyer.

(2) The right to reimbursement of a financing agency which has in good faith honored or purchased the draft under commitment to or authority from the buyer is not impaired by subsequent discovery of defects with reference to any relevant document which was apparently regular on its face.

§2-507. Effect of Seller's Tender; Delivery on Condition.
(1) Tender of delivery is a condition to the buyer's duty to accept the goods and, unless otherwise agreed, to his duty to pay for them. Tender entitles the seller to acceptance of the goods and to payment according to the contract.

(2) Where payment is due and demanded on the delivery to the buyer of goods or documents of title, his right as against the seller to retain or dispose of them is conditional upon his making the payment due.

§2-508. Cure by Seller of Improper Tender or Delivery; Replacement.
(1) Where any tender or delivery by the seller is rejected because non-conforming and the time for performance has not yet expired, the seller may seasonably notify the buyer of his intention to cure and may then within the contract time make a conforming delivery.

(2) Where the buyer rejects a non-conforming tender which the seller had reasonable grounds to believe would be acceptable with or without money allowance the seller may if he seasonably notifies the buyer have a further reasonable time to substitute a conforming tender.

§2-509. Risk of Loss in the Absence of Breach.
(1) Where the contract requires or authorizes the seller to ship the goods by carrier

(a) if it does not require him to deliver them at a particular destination, the risk of loss passes to the buyer when the goods are duly delivered to the carrier even though the shipment is under reservation (Section 2-505); but

(b) if it does require him to deliver them at a particular destination and the goods are there duly tendered while in the possession of the carrier, the risk of loss passes to the buyer when the goods are there duly so tendered as to enable the buyer to take delivery.

(2) Where the goods are held by a bailee to be delivered without being moved, the risk of loss passes to the buyer

(a) on his receipt of a negotiable document of title covering the goods; or

(b) on acknowledgment by the bailee of the buyer's right to possession of the goods; or

(c) after his receipt of a non-negotiable document of title or other written direction to deliver as provided in subsection (4)(b) of Section 2-503.

(3) In any case not within subsection (1) or (2), the risk of loss passes to the buyer on his receipt of the goods if the seller is a merchant; otherwise the risk passes to the buyer on tender of delivery.

(4) The provisions of this section are subject to contrary agreement of the parties and to the provisions of this Article on sale on approval (Section 2-327) and on effect of breach on risk of loss (Section 2-510).

§2-510. Effect of Breach on Risk of Loss.

(1) Where a tender or delivery of goods so fails to conform to the contract as to give a right of rejection the risk of their loss remains on the seller until cure or acceptance.

(2) Where the buyer rightfully revokes acceptance he may to the extent of any deficiency in his effective insurance coverage treat the risk of loss as having rested on the seller from the beginning.

(3) Where the buyer as to conforming goods already identified to the contract for sale repudiates or is otherwise in breach before risk of their loss has passed to him, the seller may to the extent of any deficiency in his effective insurance coverage treat the risk of loss as resting on the buyer for a commercially reasonable time.

§2-511. Tender of Payment by Buyer; Payment by Check.

(1) Unless otherwise agreed tender of payment is a condition to the seller's duty to tender and complete any delivery.

(2) Tender of payment is sufficient when made by any means or in any manner current in the ordinary course of business unless the seller demands payment in legal tender and gives any extension of time reasonably necessary to procure it.

(3) Subject to the provisions of this Act on the effect of an instrument of an obligation (Section 3-802), payment by check is conditional and is defeated as between the parties by dishonor of the check on due presentment.

§2-512. Payment by Buyer Before Inspection.

(1) Where the contract requires payment before inspection non-conformity of the goods does not excuse the buyer from so making payment unless
   (a) the non-conformity appears without inspection; or
   (b) despite tender of the required documents the circumstances would justify injunction against honor under the provisions of this Act (Section 5-114).

(2) Payment pursuant to subsection (1) does not constitute an acceptance of goods or impair the buyer's right to inspect or any of his remedies.

§2-513. Buyer's Right to Inspection of Goods.

(1) Unless otherwise agreed and subject to subsection (3), where goods are tendered or delivered or identified to the contract for sale, the buyer has a right before payment or acceptance to inspect them at any reasonable place and time and in any reasonable manner. When the seller is required or authorized to send the goods to the buyer, the inspection may be after their arrival.

(2) Expenses of inspection must be borne by the buyer but may be recovered from the seller if the goods do not conform and are rejected.

(3) Unless otherwise agreed and subject to the provisions of this Article on C.I.F. contracts (subsection (3) of Section 3-221), the buyer is not entitled to inspect the goods before payment of the price when the contract provides
   (a) for delivery "C.O.D." or on other like terms; or
   (b) for payment against documents of title, except where such payment is due only after the goods are to become available for inspection.

(4) A place or method of inspection fixed by the parties is presumed to be exclusive but unless otherwise expressly agreed it does not postpone identification or shift the place for delivery or for passing the risk of loss. If compliance becomes impossible, inspection shall be as provided in this section unless the place or method fixed was clearly intended as an indispensable condition failure of which avoids the contract.

§2-514. When Documents Deliverable on Acceptance; When on Payment.

Unless otherwise agreed documents against which a draft is drawn are to be delivered to the drawee on acceptance of the draft if it is payable more than three days after presentment; otherwise, only on payment.

§2-515. Preserving Evidence of Goods in Dispute. In furtherance of the adjustment of any claim or dispute
   (a) either party on reasonable notification to the other and for the purpose of ascertaining the facts and preserving evidence has the right to inspect, test and sample the goods including such of them as may be in the possession or control of the other; and
   (b) the parties may agree to a third party inspection or survey to determine the conformity or condition of the goods and may agree that the findings shall be binding upon them in any subsequent litigation or adjustment.

Part 6: Breach, Repudiation and Excuse

§2-601. Buyer's Rights on Improper Delivery. Subject to the provisions of this Article on breach in installment contracts (Section 2-612) and unless otherwise agreed under the sections on contractual limitations of remedy (Sections 2-718 and 2-719), if the goods or the tender of delivery fail in any respect to conform to the contract, the buyer may
   (a) reject the whole; or
   (b) accept the whole; or

(c) accept any commercial unit or units and reject the rest.

§2-602. Manner and Effect of Rightful Rejection.

(1) Rejection of goods must be within a reasonable time after their delivery or tender. It is ineffective unless the buyer seasonably notifies the seller.

(2) Subject to the provisions of the two following sections on rejected goods (Sections 2-603 and 2-604)

    (a) after rejection any exercise of ownership by the buyer with respect to any commercial unit is wrongful as against the seller; and

    (b) if the buyer has before rejection taken physical possession of goods in which he does not have a security interest under the provisions of this Article (subsection (3) of Section 2-711), he is under a duty after rejection to hold them with reasonable care at the seller's disposition for a time sufficient to permit the seller to remove them; but

    (c) the buyer has no further obligations with regard to goods rightfully rejected.

(3) The seller's rights with respect to goods wrongfully rejected are governed by the provisions of this Article on Seller's remedies in general (Section 2-703).

§2-603. Merchant Buyer's Duties as to Rightfully Rejected Goods.

(1) Subject to any security interest in the buyer (subsection (3) of Section 2-711), when the seller has no agent or place of business at the market of rejection a merchant buyer is under a duty after rejection of goods in his possession or control to follow any reasonable instructions received from the seller with respect to the goods and in the absence of such instructions to make reasonable efforts to sell them for the seller's account if they are perishable or threaten to decline in value speedily. Instructions are not reasonable if on demand indemnity for expenses is not forthcoming.

(2) When the buyer sells goods under subsection (1), he is entitled to reimbursement from the seller or out of the proceeds for reasonable expenses of caring for and selling them, and if the expenses include no selling commission then to such commission as is usual in the trade or if there is none to a reasonable sum not exceeding ten percent on the gross proceeds.

(3) In complying with this section the buyer is held only to good faith and good faith conduct hereunder is neither acceptance nor conversion nor the basis of an action for damages.

§2-604. Buyer's Options as to Salvage of Rightfully Rejected Goods.

Subject to the provisions of the immediately preceding section on perishables if the seller gives no instructions within a reasonable time after notification of rejection the buyer may store the rejected goods for the seller's account or reship them to him or resell them for the seller's account with reimbursement as provided in the preceding section. Such action is not acceptance or conversion.

§2-605. Waiver of Buyer's Objections by Failure to Particularize.

(1) The buyer's failure to state in connection with rejection a particular defect which is ascertainable by reasonable inspection precludes him from relying on the unstated defect to justify rejection or to establish breach

    (a) where the seller could have cured it if stated seasonably; or

    (b) between merchants when the seller has after rejection made a request in writing for a full and final written statement of all defects on which the buyer proposes to rely.

(2) Payment against documents made without reservation of rights precludes recovery of the payment for defects apparent on the face of the documents.

§2-606. What Constitutes Acceptance of Goods.

(1) Acceptance of goods occurs when the buyer

    (a) after a reasonable opportunity to inspect the goods signifies to the seller that the goods are conforming or that he will take or retain them in spite of their non-conformity; or

    (b) fails to make an effective rejection (subsection (1) of Section 2-602), but such acceptance does not occur until the buyer has had a reasonable opportunity to inspect them; or

    (c) does any act inconsistent with the seller's ownership; but if such act is wrongful as against the seller it is an acceptance only if ratified by him.

(2) Acceptance of a part of any commercial unit is acceptance of that entire unit.

§2-607. Effect of Acceptance; Notice of Breach; Burden of Establishing Breach After Acceptance; Notice of Claim or Litigation to Person Answerable Over.

(1) The buyer must pay at the contract rate for any goods accepted.

(2) Acceptance of goods by the buyer precludes rejection of the goods accepted and if made with knowledge of a non-conformity cannot be revoked because of it unless the acceptance was on the reasonable assumption that the non-conformity would be seasonably cured but acceptance does not of itself impair any other remedy provided by this Article for non-conformity.

(3) Where a tender has been accepted

    (a) the buyer must within a reasonable time after he discovers or should have discovered any breach notify the seller of breach or be barred from any remedy; and

(b) if the claim is one for infringement or the like (subsection (3) of Section 2-312) and the buyer is sued as a result of such a breach he must so notify the seller within a reasonable time after he receives notice of the litigation or be barred from any remedy over for liability established by the litigation.

(4) The burden is on the buyer to establish any breach with respect to the goods accepted.

(5) Where the buyer is sued for breach of a warranty or other obligation for which his seller is answerable over

(a) he may give his seller written notice of the litigation. If the notice states that the seller may come in and defend and that if the seller does not do so he will be bound in any action against him by his buyer by any determination of fact common to the two litigations, then unless the seller after seasonable receipt of the notice does come in and defend he is so bound; or

(b) if the claim is one for infringement or the like (subsection (3) of Section 2-312) the original seller may demand in writing that his buyer turn over to him control of the litigation including settlement or else be barred from any remedy over and if he also agrees to bear all expense and to satisfy any adverse judgment, then unless the buyer after seasonable receipt of the demand does turn over control the buyer is so barred.

(6) The provisions of subsections (3), (4) and (5) apply to any obligation of a buyer to hold the seller harmless against infringement or the like (subsection (3) of Section 2-312).

§2-608. Revocation of Acceptance in Whole or in Part.

(1) The buyer may revoke his acceptance of a lot or commercial unit whose non-conformity substantially impairs its value to him if he has accepted it

(a) on the reasonable assumption that its non-conformity would be cured and it has not been seasonably cured; or

(b) without discovery of such non-conformity if his acceptance was reasonably induced either by the difficulty of discovery before acceptance or by the seller's assurances.

(2) Revocation of acceptance must occur within a reasonable time after the buyer discovers or should have discovered the ground for it and before any substantial change in condition of the goods which is not caused by their own defects. It is not effective until the buyer notifies the seller of it.

(3) A buyer who so revokes has the same rights and duties with regard to the goods involved as if he had rejected them.

§2-609. Right to Adequate Assurance of Performance.

(1) A contract for sale imposes an obligation on each party that the other's expectation of receiving due performance will not be impaired. When reasonable grounds for insecurity arise with respect to the performance of either party the other may in writing demand adequate assurance of due performance and until he receives such assurance may if commercially reasonable suspend any performance for which he has not already received the agreed return.

(2) Between merchants the reasonableness of grounds for insecurity and the adequacy of any assurance offered shall be determined according to commercial standards.

(3) Acceptance of any improper delivery or payment does not prejudice the aggrieved party's right to demand adequate assurance of future performance.

(4) After receipt of a justified demand failure to provide within a reasonable time not exceeding thirty days such assurance of due performance as is adequate under the circumstances of the particular case is a repudiation of the contract.

§2-610. Anticipatory Repudiation.
When either party repudiates the contract with respect to a performance not yet due the loss of which will substantially impair the value of the contract to the other, the aggrieved party may

(a) for a commercially reasonable time await performance by the repudiating party; or

(b) resort to any remedy for breach (Section 2-703 or Section 2-711), even though he has notified the repudiating party that he would await the latter's performance and has urged retraction; and

(c) in either case suspend his own performance or proceed in accordance with the provisions of this Article on the seller's right to identify goods to the contract notwithstanding breach or to salvage unfinished goods (Section 2-704).

§2-611. Retraction of Anticipatory Repudiation.

(1) Until the repudiating party's next performance is due he can retract his repudiation unless the aggrieved party has since the repudiation cancelled or materially changed his position or otherwise indicated that he considers the repudiation final.

(2) Retraction may be by any method which clearly indicates to the aggrieved party that the repudiating party intends to perform, but must include any assurance justifiably demanded under the provisions of this Article (Section 2-609).

(3) Retraction reinstates the repudiating party's rights under the contract with due excuse and allowance to the aggrieved party for any delay occasioned by the repudiation.

§2-612. "Installment Contract"; Breach.

(1) An "installment contract" is one which requires or authorizes the delivery of goods in separate lots to be separately accepted, even though the contract

contains a clause "each delivery is a separate contract" or its equivalent.

(2) The buyer may reject any installment which is non-conforming if the non-conformity substantially impairs the value of that installment and cannot be cured or if the non-conformity is a defect in the required documents, but if the non-conformity does not fall within subsection (3) and the seller gives adequate assurance of its cure the buyer must accept that installment.

(3) Whenever non-conformity or default with respect to one or more installments substantially impairs the value of the whole contract there is a breach of the whole. But the aggrieved party reinstates the contract if he accepts a non-conforming installment without seasonably notifying of cancellation or if he brings an action with respect only to past installments or demands performance as to future installments.

§2-613. Casualty to Identified Goods.
Where the contract requires for its performance goods identified when the contract is made, and the goods suffer casualty without fault of either party before the risk of loss passes to the buyer, or in a proper case under a "no arrival, no sale" term (Section 2-324) then

(a) if the loss is total the contract is avoided; and

(b) if the loss is partial or the goods have so deteriorated as no longer to conform to the contract the buyer may nevertheless demand inspection and at his option either treat the contract as avoided or accept the goods with due allowance from the contract price for the deterioration or the deficiency in quantity but without further right against the seller.

§2-614. Substituted Performance.
(1) Where without fault of either party the agreed berthing, loading, or unloading facilities fail or an agreed type of carrier becomes unavailable or the agreed manner of delivery otherwise becomes commercially impracticable but a commercially reasonable substitute is available, such substitute performance must be tendered and accepted.

(2) If the agreed means or manner of payment fails because of domestic or foreign governmental regulation, the seller may withhold or stop delivery unless the buyer provides a means or manner of payment which is commercially a substantial equivalent. If delivery has already been taken, payment by the means or in the manner provided by the regulation discharges the buyer's obligation unless the regulation is discriminatory, oppressive or predatory.

§2-615. Excuse by Failure of Presupposed Conditions.
Except so far as a seller may have assumed a greater obligation and subject to the preceding section on substituted performance:

(a) Delay in delivery or non-delivery in whole or in part by a seller who complies with paragraphs (b) and (c) is not a breach of his duty under a contract for sale if performance as agreed has been made impracticable by the occurrence of a contingency the non-occurrence of which was a basic assumption on which the contract was made or by compliance in good faith with any applicable foreign or domestic governmental regulation or order whether or not it later proves to be invalid.

(b) Where the causes mentioned in paragraph (a) affect only a part of the seller's capacity to perform, he must allocate production and deliveries among his customers but may at his option include regular customers not then under contract as well as his own requirements for further manufacture. He may so allocate in any manner which is fair and reasonable.

(c) The seller must notify the buyer seasonably that there will be delay or non-delivery and, when allocation is required under paragraph (b), of the estimated quota thus made available for the buyer.

§2-616. Procedure on Notice Claiming Excuse.
(1) When the buyer receives notification of a material or indefinite delay or an allocation justified under the preceding section he may by written notification to the seller as to any delivery concerned, and where the prospective deficiency substantially impairs the value of the whole contract under the provisions of this Article relating to breach of installment contracts (Section 2-612), then also as to the whole,

(a) terminate and thereby discharge any unexecuted portion of the contract; or

(b) modify the contract by agreeing to take his available quota in substitution.

(2) If after receipt of such notification from the seller the buyer fails so to modify the contract within a reasonable time not exceeding thirty days the contract lapses with respect to any deliveries affected.

(3) The provisions of this section may not be negated by agreement except in so far as the seller has assumed a greater obligation under the preceding section.

Part 7: Remedies

§2-701. Remedies for Breach of Collateral Contracts not Impaired.
Remedies for breach of any obligation or promise collateral or ancillary to a contract for sale are not impaired by the provisions of this Article.

§2-702. Seller's on Discovery of Buyer's Insolvency.
(1) Where the seller discovers the buyer to be insolvent he may refuse delivery except for cash including payment for all goods theretofore delivered under the contract, and stop delivery under this Article (Section 2-705).

(2) Where the seller discovers that the buyer has received goods on credit while insolvent he may reclaim the goods upon demand made within ten days after the receipt, but if misrepresentation of solvency has been made to the particular seller in writing within three months before delivery the ten-day limitation does not apply. Except as provided in this subsection the seller may not base a right to reclaim goods on the buyer's fraudulent or innocent misrepresentation of solvency or of intent to pay.

(3) The seller's right to reclaim under subsection (2) is subject to the rights of a buyer in ordinary course or other good faith purchaser under this Article (Section 2-403). Successful reclamation of goods excludes all other remedies with respect to them. As amended 1966.

§2-703. Seller's Remedies in General.
Where the buyer wrongfully rejects or revokes acceptance of goods, or fails to make a payment due on or before delivery or repudiates with respect to a part or the whole, then with respect to any goods directly affected and, if the breach is of the whole contract (Section 2-612), then also with respect to the whole undelivered balance the aggrieved seller may

(a) withhold delivery of such goods;
(b) stop delivery by any bailee as hereafter provided (Section 2-705);
(c) proceed under the next section respecting goods still unidentified to the contract;
(d) resell and recover damages as hereafter provided (Section 2-706);
(e) recover damages for non-acceptance (Section 2-708) or in a proper case the price (Section 2-709); or
(f) cancel.

§2-704. Seller's Right to Identify Goods to the Contract Notwithstanding Breach or to Salvage Unfinished Goods.

(1) An aggrieved seller under the preceding section may
  (a) identify to the contract conforming goods not already identified if at the time he learned of the breach they are in his possession or control; or
  (b) treat as the subject of resale goods which have demonstrably been intended for the particular contract even though those goods are unfinished.

(2) Where the goods are unfinished an aggrieved seller may in the exercise of reasonable commercial judgment for the purposes of avoiding loss and of effective realization either complete the manufacture and wholly identify the goods to the contract or cease manufacture and resell for scrap or salvage value or proceed in any other reasonable manner.

§2-705. Seller's Stoppage of Delivery in Transit or Otherwise.

(1) The seller may stop delivery of goods in the possession of a carrier or other bailee when he discovers the buyer to be insolvent (Section 2-702) and may stop delivery of carload, truckload, planeload or larger shipments of express or freight when the buyer repudiates or fails to make a payment due before delivery or if for any other reason the seller has a right to withhold or reclaim the goods.

(2) As against such buyer the seller may stop delivery until
  (a) receipt of the goods by the buyer; or
  (b) acknowledgement to the buyer or by any bailee of the goods except a carrier that the bailee holds the goods for the buyer; or
  (c) such acknowledgement to the buyer by a carrier by reshipment or as warehouseman; or
  (d) negotiation to the buyer of any negotiable document of title covering the goods.

(3) (a) To stop delivery the seller must so notify as to enable the bailee by reasonable diligence to prevent delivery of the goods.
  (b) After such notification the bailee must hold and deliver the goods according to the directions of the seller but the seller is liable to the bailee for any ensuing charges or damages.
  (c) If a negotiable document of title has been issued for goods the bailee is not obliged to obey a notification to stop until surrender of the document.
  (d) A carrier who has issued a non-negotiable bill of lading is not obliged to obey a notification to stop received from a person other than the consignor.

§2-706. Seller's Resale Including Contract for Resale.

(1) Under the conditions stated in Section 2-703 on seller's remedies, the seller may resell the goods concerned or the undelivered balance thereof. Where the resale is made in good faith and in a commercially reasonable manner the seller may recover the difference between the resale price and the contract price together with any incidental damages allowed under the provisions of this Article (Section 2-710), but less expenses saved in consequence of the buyer's breach.

(2) Except as otherwise provided in subsection (3) or unless otherwise agreed resale may be at public or private sale including sale by way of one or more contracts to sell or of identification to an existing contract of the seller. Sale may be as a unit or in parcels and at any time and place and on any terms but every aspect of the sale including the method, manner, time, place and terms must be commercially reasonable. The resale must be reasonably identified as referring to the broken contract, but it is not necessary that the goods be in existence or that any or all of them have been identified to the contract before the breach.

(3) Where the resale is at private sale the seller must give the buyer reasonable notification of his intention to resell.

(4) Where the resale is at public sale
  (a) Only identified goods can be sold except where there is a recognized market for a public sale of futures in goods of the kind; and
  (b) it must be made at a usual place or market for public sale if one is reasonably available and except in the case of goods which are perishable or threaten to decline in value speedily the seller must give the buyer reasonable notice of the time and place of the resale; and
  (c) if the goods are not to be within the view of those attending the sale the notification of sale must state the place where the goods are located and provide for their reasonable inspection by prospective bidders; and
  (d) the seller may buy.
(5) A purchaser who buys in good faith at a resale takes the goods free of any rights of the original buyer even though the seller fails to comply with one or more of the requirements of this section.
  (a) The seller is not accountable to the buyer for any profit made on any resale. A person in the position of a seller (Section 2-707) or a buyer who has rightfully rejected or justifiably revoked acceptance must account for any excess over the amount of his security interest, as hereinafter defined (subsection (3) of Section 2-711).

§2-707. "Person in the Position of a Seller".

(1) A "person in the position of a seller" includes as against a principal an agent who has paid or become responsible for the price of goods on behalf of his principal or anyone who otherwise holds a security interest or other right in goods similar to that of a seller.
(2) A person in the position of a seller may as provided in this Article withhold or stop delivery (Section 2-705) and resell (Section 2-706) and recover incidental damages (Section 2-710).

§2-708. Seller's Damages for Non-Acceptance or Repudiation.

(1) Subject to subsection (2) and to the provisions of this Article with respect to proof of market price (Section 2-723), the measure of damages for non-acceptance or repudiation by the buyer is the difference between the market price at the time and place for tender and the unpaid contract price together with any incidental damages provided in this Article (Section 2-710), but less expenses saved in consequence of the buyer's breach.
(2) If the measure of damages provided in subsection (1) is inadequate to put the seller in as good a position as performance would have done then the measure of damages is the profit (including reasonable overhead) which the seller would have made from full performance by the buyer, together with any incidental damages provided in this Article (Section

2-710), due allowance for costs reasonably incurred and due credit for payments or proceeds of resale.

§2-709. Action for the Price.

(1) When the buyer fails to pay the price as it becomes due the seller may recover, together with any incidental damages under the next section, the price
  (a) of goods accepted or of conforming goods lost or damaged within a commercially reasonable time after risk of their loss has passed to the buyer; and
  (b) of goods identified to the contract if the seller is unable after reasonable effort to resell them at a reasonable price or the circumstances reasonably indicate that such effort will be unavailing.
(2) Where the seller sues for the price he must hold for the buyer any goods which have been identified to the contract and are still in his control except that if resale becomes possible he may resell them at any time prior to the collection of the judgment. The net proceeds of any such resale must be credited to the buyer and payment of the judgment entitles him to any goods not resold.
(3) After the buyer has wrongfully rejected or revoked acceptance of the goods has failed to make a payment due or has repudiated (Section 2-610), a seller who is held not entitled to the price under this section shall nevertheless be awarded damages for non-acceptance under the preceding section.

§2-710. Seller's Incidental Damages.
Incidental damages to an aggrieved seller include any commercially reasonable charges, expenses or commissions incurred in stopping delivery, in the transportation, care and custody of goods after the buyer's breach, in connection with return or resale of the goods or otherwise resulting from the breach.

§2-711. Buyer's Remedies in General; Buyer's Security Interest in Rejected Goods.

(1) When the seller fails to make delivery or repudiates or the buyer rightfully rejects or justifiably revokes acceptance then with respect to any goods involved, and with respect to the whole if the breach goes to the whole contract (Section 2-612), the buyer may cancel and whether or not he has done so may in addition to recovering so much of the price as has been paid
  (a) "cover" and have damages under the next section as to all the goods affected whether or not they have been identified to the contract; or
  (b) recover damages for non-delivery as provided in this Article (Section 2-713).
(2) Where the seller fails to deliver or repudiates the buyer may also
  (a) if the goods have been identified recover them as provided in this Article (Section 2-502); or
  (b) in a proper case obtain specific performance or replevy the goods as provided in this Article (Section 2-716).

(3) On rightful rejection or justifiable revocation of acceptance a buyer has a security interest in goods in his possession or control for any payments made on their price and any expenses reasonably incurred in their inspection, receipt, transportation, care and custody and may hold such goods and resell them in like manner as an aggrieved seller (Section 2-706).

§2-712. "Cover"; Buyer's Procurement of Substitute Goods.

(1) After a breach within the preceding section the buyer may "cover" by making in good faith and without unreasonable delay any reasonable purchase of or contract to purchase goods in substitution for those due from the seller.

(2) The buyer may recover from the seller as damages the difference between the cost of cover and the contract price together with any incidental or consequential damages as hereinafter defined (Section 2-715), but less expenses saved in consequence of the seller's breach.

(3) Failure of the buyer to effect cover within this section does not ban him from any other remedy.

§2-713. Buyer's Damages for Non-Delivery or Repudiation.

(1) Subject to the provisions of this Article with respect to proof of market price (Section 2-723), the measure of damages for non-delivery or repudiation by the seller is the difference between the market price at the time when the buyer learned of the breach and the contract price together with any incidental and consequential damages provided in this Article (Section 2-715), but less expenses saved in consequence of the seller's breach.

(2) Market price is to be determined as of the place for tender or, in cases of rejection after arrival or revocation of acceptance as of the place of arrival.

§2-714. Buyer's Damages for Breach in Regard to Accepted Goods.

(1) Where the buyer has accepted goods and given notification (subsection (3) Section 2-607) he may recover as damages for any non-conformity of tender the loss resulting in the ordinary course of events from the seller's breach as determined in any manner which is reasonable.

(2) The measure of damages for breach of warranty is the difference at the time and place of acceptance between the value of the goods accepted and the value they would have had if they had been as warranted, unless special circumstances show proximate damages of a different amount.

(3) In a proper case any incidental and consequential damages under the next section may also be recovered.

§2-715. Buyer's Incidental and Consequential Damages.

(1) Incidental damages resulting from the seller's breach include expenses reasonably incurred in inspection, receipt, transportation and care and custody of goods rightfully rejected, any commercially reasonable charges, expenses or commissions in connection with effecting cover and any other reasonable expense incident to the delay or other breach.

(2) Consequential damages resulting from the seller's breach include

(a) any loss resulting from general or particular requirements and needs of which the seller at the time of contracting had reason to know and which could not reasonably be prevented by cover or otherwise; and

(b) injury to person or property proximately resulting from any breach of warranty.

§2-716. Buyer's Right to Specific Performance or Replevin.

(1) Specific performance may be decreed where the goods are unique or in other proper circumstances.

(2) The decree for specific performance may include such terms and conditions as to payment of the price, damages, or other relief as the court may deem just.

(3) The buyer has a right of replevin for goods identified to the contract if after reasonable effort he is unable to effect cover for such goods or the circumstances reasonably indicate that such effort will be unavailing or if the goods have been shipped under reservation and satisfaction of the security interest in them has been made or tendered.

§2-717. Deduction of Damages From the Price.
The buyer on notifying the seller of his intention to do so may deduct all or any part of the damages resulting from any breach of the contact from any part of the price still due under the same contract.

§2-718. Liquidation or Limitation of Damages; Deposits.

(1) Damages for breach by either party may be liquidated in the agreement but only at an amount which is reasonable in the light of the anticipated or actual harm caused by the breach, the difficulties of proof of loss, and the inconvenience or non-feasibility of otherwise obtaining an adequate remedy. A term fixing unreasonably large liquidated damages is void as a penalty.

(2) Where the seller justifiably withholds delivery of goods because of the buyer's breach, the buyer is entitled to restitution of any amount by which the sum of his payments exceeds

(a) the amount to which the seller is entitled by virtue of terms liquidating the seller's damages in accordance with subsection (1), or

(b) in the absence of such terms, twenty percent of the value of the total performance for which the buyer is obligated under the contract or $500, whichever is smaller.

(3) The buyer's right to restitution under subsection (2) is subject to offset to the extent that the seller establishes

    (a) a right to recover damages under the provisions of this Article other than subsection (1), and

    (b) the amount or value of any benefits received by the buyer directly or indirectly by reason of the contract.

(4) Where a seller has received payment in goods their reasonable value or the proceeds of their resale shall be treated as payments for the purposes of subsection (2); but if the seller has notice of the buyer's breach before reselling goods received in part performance, his resale is subject to the conditions laid down in this Article on resale by an aggrieved seller (Section 2-706).

§2-719. Contractual Modification or Limitation of Remedy.

(1) Subject to the provisions of subsections (2) and (3) of this section and of the preceding section on liquidation and limitation of damages,

    (a) the agreement may provide for remedies in addition to or in substitution for those provided in this Article and may limit or alter the measure of damages recoverable under this Article, as by limiting the buyer's remedies to return of the goods and repayment of the price or to repair and replacement of non-conforming goods or parts; and

    (b) resort to a remedy as provided is optional unless the remedy is expressly agreed to be exclusive, in which case it is the sole remedy.

(2) Where circumstances cause an exclusive or limited remedy to fail of its essential purpose, remedy may be had as provided in this Act.

(3) Consequential damages may be limited or excluded unless the limitation or exclusion is unconscionable. Limitation of consequential damages for injury to the person in the case of consumer goods is prima facie unconscionable but limitation of damages where the loss is commercial is not.

§2-720. Effect of "Cancellation" or "Rescission" on Claims for Antecedent Breach.

Unless the contrary intention clearly appears, expressions of "cancellation" or "rescission" of the contract or the like shall not be construed as a renunciation or discharge of any claim in damages for an antecedent breach.

§2-721. Remedies for Fraud.
Remedies for material misrepresentation or fraud include all remedies available under this Article for non-fraudulent breach. Neither rescission or a claim for rescission of the contract for sale nor rejection or return of the goods shall bar or be deemed inconsistent with a claim for damage or other remedy.

§2-722. Who Can Sue Third Parties for Injury to Goods.

Where a third party so deals with goods which have been identified to a contract for sale as to cause actionable injury to a party to that contract

(a) right of action against the third party is in either party to the contract for sale who has title to or a security interest or a special property or an insurable interest in the goods; and if the goods have been destroyed or converted a right of action is also in the party who either bore the risk of loss under the contract for sale or has since the injury assumed that risk as against the other;

(b) if at the time of the injury the party plaintiff did not bear the risk of loss as against the other party to the contract for sale and there is no arrangement between them for disposition of the recovery, his suit or settlement is, subject to his own interest, as a fiduciary for the other party to the contract; and

(c) either party may with the consent of the other sue for the benefit of whom it may concern.

§2-723. Proof of Market Price: Time and Place.

(1) If an action based on anticipatory repudiation comes to trial before the time for performance with respect to some or all of the goods, any damages based on market price (Sections 2-708 or Sections 2-713) shall be determined according to the price of such goods prevailing at the time when the aggrieved party learned of the repudiation.

(2) If evidence of a price prevailing at the times or places described in this Article is not readily available the price prevailing within any reasonable time before or after the time described or at any other place which in commercial judgment or under usage of trade would serve as a reasonable substitute for the one described may be used, making any proper allowance for the cost of transporting the goods to or from such other place.

(3) Evidence of a relevant price prevailing at a time or place other than the one described in this Article offered by one party is not admissible unless and until he has given the other party such notice as the court finds sufficient to prevent unfair surprise.

§2-724. Admissibility of Market Quotations.
Whenever the prevailing price or value of any goods regularly bought and sold in any established commodity market is in issue, reports in official publication or trade journals or in newspapers or periodicals of general circulation published as the reports of such market shall be admissible in evidence. The circumstances of the preparation of such a report may be shown to affect its weight but not its admissibility.

§2-725. Statute of Limitations in Contracts for Sale.

(1) An action for breach of any contract for sale must be commenced within four years after the cause of action has accrued. By the original agreement the parties may reduce the period of limitation to not less than one year but may not extend it.

(2) A cause of action accrues when the breach occurs, regardless of the aggrieved party's lack of knowledge of the breach. A breach of warranty occurs when tender of delivery is made, except that where a warranty explicitly extends to future performance of the goods and discovery of the breach must await the time of such performance the cause of action accrues when the breach is or should have been discovered.

(3) Where an action commenced within the time limited by subsection (1) is so terminated as to leave available a remedy by another action for the same breach such other action may be commenced after the expiration of the time limited and within six months after the termination of the first action unless the termination resulted from voluntary discontinuance or from dismissal for failure or neglect to prosecute.

(4) This section does not alter the law on tolling of the statute of limitations nor does it apply to causes of action which have accrued before this Act becomes effective.

Article 2A—Leases (Revised 1990)

Part 1: General Provisions

§2A-101. Short Title. This Article shall be known and may be cited as the Uniform Commercial Code—Leases.

§2A-102. Scope. This Article applies to any transaction, regardless of form, that creates a lease.

§2A-103. Definitions and Index of Definitions.—

(1) In this Article unless the context otherwise requires:

(a) "Buyer in ordinary course of business" means a person who in good faith and without knowledge that the sale to him [or her] is in violation of the ownership rights or security interest or leasehold interest of a third party in the goods, buys in ordinary course from a person in the business of selling goods of that kind but does not include a pawnbroker. "Buying" may be for cash or by exchange of other property or on secured or unsecured credit and includes receiving goods or documents of title under a pre-existing contract for sale but does not include a transfer in bulk or as security for or in total or partial satisfaction of a money debt.

(b) "Cancellation" occurs when either party puts an end to the lease contract for default by the other party.

(c) "Commercial unit" means such a unit of goods as by commercial usage is a single whole for purposes of lease and division of which materially impairs its character or value on the market or in use. A commercial unit may be a single article, as a machine, or a set of articles, as a suite of furniture or a line of machinery, or a quantity, as a gross or carload, or any other unit treated in use or in the relevant market as a single whole.

(d) "Conforming" goods or performance under a lease contract means goods or performance that are in accordance with the obligations under the lease contract.

(e) "Consumer lease" means a lease that a lessor regularly engaged in the business of leasing or selling makes to a lessee who is an individual and who takes under the lease primarily for a personal, family, or household purpose [if the total payments to be made under the lease contract, excluding payments for options to renew or buy, do not exceed $(WOL)].

(f) "Fault" means wrongful act, omission, breach, or default.

(g) "Finance lease" means a lease with respect to which:

(i) the lessor does not select, manufacture, or supply the goods;

(ii) the lessor acquires the goods or the right to possession and use of the goods in connection with the lease; and

(iii) one of the following occurs:

(A) the lessee receives a copy of the contract by which the lessor acquired the goods or the right to possession and use of the goods before signing the lease contract;

(B) the lessee's approval of the contract by which the lessor acquired the goods or the right to possession and use of the goods is a condition to effectiveness of the lease contract;

(C) the lessee, before signing the lease contract, receives an accurate and complete statement designating the promises and warranties, and any disclaimers of warranties, limitations or modifications of remedies, or liquidated damages, including those of a third party, such as the manufacturer of the goods, provided to the lessor by the person supplying the goods in connection with or as part of the contract by which the lessor acquired the goods or the right to possession and use of the goods; or

(D) if the lease is not a consumer lease, the lessor, before the lessee signs the lease contract, informs the lessee in writing (a) of the identity of the person supplying the goods to the lessor, unless the lessee has selected that person and directed the lessor to acquire the goods or the right to possession and use of the goods from that person, (b) that the lessee is entitled under this Article to the promises and warranties, including those of any third party, provided to the lessor by the person supplying the goods in connection with or as part of the contract by which the lessor acquired the goods or the right to possession and use of the goods, and (c) that the lessee may communicate with the person supplying the goods to the lessor and receive an accurate and complete statement of those promises and warranties, including any disclaimers and limitations of them or of remedies.

(h) "Goods" means all things that are movable at the time of identification to the lease contract, or are fixtures (Section 2A-309), but the term does not include money, documents, instruments, accounts, chattel paper, general intangibles, or minerals or the like, including oil and gas, before extraction. The term also includes the unborn young of animals.

(i) "Installment lease contract" means a lease contract that authorizes or requires the delivery of goods in separate lots to be separately accepted, even though the lease contract contains a clause "each delivery is a separate lease" or its equivalent.

(j) "Lease" means a transfer of the right to possession and use of goods for a term in return for consideration, but a sale, including a sale on approval or a sale or return, or retention or creation of a security interest is not a lease. Unless the context clearly indicates otherwise, the term includes a sublease.

(k) "Lease agreement" means the bargain, with respect to the lease, of the lessor and the lessee in fact as found in their language or by implication from other circumstances including course of dealing or usage of trade or course of performance as provided in this Article. Unless the context clearly indicates otherwise, the term includes a sublease agreement.

(l) "Lease contract" means the total legal obligation that results from the lease agreement as affected by this Article and any other applicable rules of law. Unless the context clearly indicates otherwise, the term includes a sublease contract.

(m) "Leasehold interest" means the interest of the lessor or the lessee under a lease contract.

(n) "Lessee" means a person who acquires the right to possession and use of goods under a lease. Unless the context clearly indicates otherwise, the term includes a sublessee.

(o) "Lessee in ordinary course of business" means a person who in good faith and without knowledge that the lease to him [or her] is in violation of the ownership rights or security interest or leasehold interest of a third party in the goods leases in ordinary course from a person in the business of selling or leasing goods of that kind but does not include a pawnbroker. "Leasing" may be for cash or by exchange of other property or on secured or unsecured credit and includes receiving goods or documents of title under a pre-existing lease contract but does not include a transfer in bulk or as security for or in total or partial satisfaction of a money debt.

(p) "Lessor" means a person who transfers the right to possession and use of goods under a lease. Unless the context clearly indicates otherwise, the term includes a sublessor.

(q) "Lessor's residual interest" means the lessor's interest in the goods after expiration, termination, or cancellation of the lease contract.

(r) "Lien" means a charge against or interest in goods to secure payment of a debt or performance of an obligation, but the term does not include a security interest.

(s) "Lot" means a parcel or a single article that is the subject matter of a separate lease or delivery, whether or not it is sufficient to perform the lease contract.

(t) "Merchant lessee" means a lessee that is a merchant with respect to goods of the kind subject to the lease.

(u) "Present value" means the amount as of a date certain of one or more sums payable in the future, discounted to the date certain. The discount is determined by the interest rate specified by the parties if the rate was not manifestly unreasonable at the time the transaction was entered into; otherwise, the discount is determined by a commercially reasonable rate that takes into account the facts and circumstances of each case at the time the transaction was entered into.

(v) "Purchase" includes taking by sale, lease, mortgage, security interest, pledge, gift, or any other voluntary transaction creating an interest in goods.

(w) "Sublease" means a lease of goods the right to possession and use of which was acquired by the lessor as a lessee under an existing lease.

(x) "Supplier" means a person from whom a lessor buys or leases goods to be leased under a finance lease.

(y) "Supply contract" means a contract under which a lessor buys or leases goods to be leased.

(z) "Termination" occurs when either party pursuant to a power created by agreement or law puts an end to the lease contract otherwise than for default.

(2) Other definitions applying to this Article and the sections in which they appear are:

"Accessions". Section 2A-310(1).
"Construction mortgage". Section 2A-309(1)(d).
"Encumbrance". Section 2A-309(1)(e).
"Fixtures". Section 2A-309(1)(a).
"Fixture filing". Section 2A-309(1)(b).
"Purchase money lease". Section 2A-309(1)(c).

(3) The following definitions in other Articles apply to this Article:

"Account". Section 9-106.
"Between merchants". Section 2-104(3).
"Buyer". Section 2-103(1)(a).
"Chattel paper". Section 9-105(1)(b).
"Consumer goods". Section 9-109(1).
"Document". Section 9-105(1)(f).
"Entrusting". Section 2-403(3).
"General intangibles". Section 9-106.
"Good faith". Section 2-103(1)(b).
"Instrument". Section 9-105(1)(i).
"Merchant". Section 2-104(1).
"Mortgage". Section 9-105(1)(j).
"Pursuant to commitment". Section 9-105(1)(k).
"Receipt". Section 2-103(1)(c).
"Sale". Section 2-106(1).
"Sale on approval". Section 2-326.
"Sale or return". Section 2-326.
"Seller". Section 2-103(1)(d).

(4) In addition, Article 1 contains general definitions and principles of construction and interpretation applicable throughout this Article. As amended in 1990.

§2A-104. Leases Subject to Other Law.—

(1) A lease, although subject to this Article, is also subject to any applicable:

(a) certificate of title statute of this State: (list any certificate of title statutes covering automobiles, trailers, mobile homes, boats, farm tractors, and the like);

(b) certificate of title statute of another jurisdiction (Section 2A-105); or

(c) consumer protection statute of this State, or final consumer protection decision of a court of this State existing on the effective date of this Article.

(2) In case of conflict between this Article, other than Sections 2A-105, 2A-304(3), and 2A-305(3), and a statute or decision referred to in subsection (1), the statute or decision controls.

(3) Failure to comply with an applicable law has only the effect specified therein.

§2A-105. Territorial Application of Article to Goods Covered by Certificate of Title.—

Subject to the provisions of Sections 2A-304(3) and 2A-305(3), with respect to goods covered by a certificate of title issued under a statute of this State or of another jurisdiction, compliance and the effect of compliance or noncompliance with a certificate of title statute are governed by the law (including the conflict of laws rules) of the jurisdiction issuing the certificate until the earlier of (a) surrender of the certificate, or (b) four months after the goods are removed from that jurisdiction and thereafter until a new certificate of title is issued by another jurisdiction.

§2A-106. Limitation on Power of Parties to Consumer Lease to Choose Applicable Law and Judicial Forum.—

(1) If the law chosen by the parties to a consumer lease is that of a jurisdiction other than a jurisdiction in which the lessee resides at the time the lease agreement becomes enforceable or within 30 days thereafter or in which the goods are to be used, the choice is not enforceable.

(2) If the judicial forum chosen by the parties to a consumer lease is a forum that would not otherwise have jurisdiction over the lessee, the choice is not enforceable.

§2A-107. Waiver or Renunciation of Claim or Right After Default.—

Any claim or right arising out of an alleged default or breach of warranty may be discharged in whole or in part without consideration by a written waiver or renunciation signed and delivered by the aggrieved party.

§2A-108. Unconscionability.—

(1) If the court as a matter of law finds a lease contract or any clause of a lease contract to have been unconscionable at the time it was made the court may refuse to enforce the lease contract, or it may enforce the remainder of the lease contract without the unconscionable clause, or it may so limit the application of any unconscionable clause as to avoid any unconscionable result.

(2) With respect to a consumer lease, if the court as a matter of law finds that a lease contract or any clause of a lease contract has been induced by unconscionable conduct or that unconscionable conduct has occurred in the collection of a claim arising from a lease contract, the court may grant appropriate relief.

(3) Before making a finding of unconscionability under subsection (1) or (2), the court, on its own motion or that of a party, shall afford the parties a reasonable opportunity to present evidence as to the setting, purpose, and effect of the lease contract or clause thereof, or of the conduct.

(4) In an action in which the lessee claims unconscionability with respect to a consumer lease:

(a) If the court finds unconscionability under subsection (1) or (2), the court shall award reasonable attorney's fees to the lessee.

(b) If the court does not find unconscionability and the lessee claiming unconscionability has brought or maintained an action he [or she] knew to be groundless, the court shall award reasonable attorney's fees to the party against whom the claim is made.

(c) In determining attorney's fees, the amount of the recovery on behalf of the claimant under subsections (1) and (2) is not controlling.

§2A-109. Option to Accelerate at Will.—

(1) A term providing that one party or his [or her] successor in interest may accelerate payment or performance or require collateral or additional collateral "at will" or "when he [or she] deems himself [or herself] insecure" or in words of similar import must be construed to mean that he [or she] has power to do so only if he [or she] in good faith believes that the prospect of payment or performance is impaired.

(2) With respect to a consumer lease, the burden of establishing good faith under subsection (1) is on the party who exercised the power; otherwise the burden of establishing lack of good faith is on the party against whom the power has been exercised.

Part 2: Formation and Construction of Lease Contract

§2A-201. Statute of Frauds.—

(1) A lease contract is not enforceable by way of action or defense unless:
  (a) the total payments to be made under the lease contract, excluding payments for options to renew or buy, are less than $1,000; or
  (b) there is a writing, signed by the party against whom enforcement is sought or by that party's authorized agent, sufficient to indicate that a lease contract has been made between the parties and to describe the goods leased and the lease term.

(2) Any description of leased goods or of the lease term is sufficient and satisfies subsection (1)(b), whether or not it is specific, if it reasonably identifies what is described.

(3) A writing is not insufficient because it omits or incorrectly states a term agreed upon, but the lease contract is not enforceable under subsection (1)(b) beyond the lease term and the quantity of goods shown in the writing.

(4) A lease contract that does not satisfy the requirements of subsection (1), but which is valid in other respects, is enforceable:
  (a) if the goods are to be specifically manufactured or obtained for the lessee and are not suitable for lease or sale to others in the ordinary course of the lessor's business, and the lessor, before notice of repudiation is received and under circumstances that reasonably indicate that the goods are for the lessee, has made either a substantial beginning of their manufacture or commitments for their procurement;
  (b) if the party against whom enforcement is sought admits in that party's pleading, testimony or otherwise in court that: a lease contract was made, but the lease contract is not enforceable under this provision beyond the quantity of goods admitted; or
  (c) with respect to goods that have been received and accepted by the lessee.

(5) The lease term under a lease contract referred to in subsection (4) is:
  (a) if there is a writing signed by the party against whom enforcement is sought or by that party's authorized agent specifying the lease term, the term so specified;
  (b) if the party against whom enforcement is sought admits in that party's pleading, testimony, or otherwise in court a lease term, the term so admitted; or
  (c) a reasonable lease term.

§2A-202. Final Written Expression: Parol or Extrinsic Evidence.—

Terms with respect to which the confirmatory memoranda of the parties agree or which are otherwise set forth in a writing intended by the parties as a final expression of their agreement with respect to such terms as are included therein may not be contradicted by evidence of any prior agreement or of a contemporaneous oral agreement but may be explained or supplemented:
(a) by course of dealing or usage of trade or by course of performance; and
(b) by evidence of consistent additional terms unless the court finds the writing to have been intended also as a complete and exclusive statement of the terms of the agreement.

§2A-203. Seals Inoperative.—

The affixing of a seal to a writing evidencing a lease contract or an offer to enter into a lease contract does not render the writing a sealed instrument and the law with respect to sealed instruments does not apply to the lease contract or offer.

§2A-204. Formation in General.—

(1) A lease contract may be made in any manner sufficient to show agreement, including conduct by both parties which recognizes the existence of a lease contract.

(2) An agreement sufficient to constitute a lease contract may be found although the moment of its making is undetermined.

(3) Although one or more terms are left open, a lease contract does not fail for indefiniteness if the parties have intended to make a lease contract and there is a reasonably certain basis for giving an appropriate remedy.

§2A-205. Firm Offers.— An offer by a merchant to lease goods to or from another person in a signed writing that by its terms gives assurance it will be held open is not revocable, for lack of consideration, during the time stated or, if no time is stated, for a reasonable time, but in no event may the period of irrevocability exceed 3 months. Any such term of assurance on a form supplied by the offeree must be separately signed by the offeror.

§2A-206. Offer and Acceptance in Formation of Lease Contract.—

(1) Unless otherwise unambiguously indicated by the language or circumstances, an offer to make a lease contract must be construed as inviting acceptance in any manner and by any medium reasonable in the circumstances.

(2) If the beginning of a requested performance is a reasonable mode of acceptance, an offeror who is not notified of acceptance within a reasonable time may treat the offer as having lapsed before acceptance.

§2A-207. Course of Performance or Practical Construction.—

(1) If a lease contract involves repeated occasions for performance by either party with knowledge of the nature of the performance and opportunity for objection to it by the other, any course of performance accepted or acquiesced in without objection is relevant to determine the meaning of the lease agreement.

(2) The express terms of a lease agreement and any course of performance, as well as any course of dealing and usage of trade, must be construed whenever reasonable as consistent with each other; but if that construction is unreasonable, express terms control course of performance, course of performance controls both course of dealing and usage of trade, and course of dealing controls usage of trade.

(3) Subject to the provisions of Section 2A-208 on modification and waiver, course of performance is relevant to show a waiver or modification of any term inconsistent with the course of performance.

§2A-208. Modification, Rescission and Waiver.—

(1) An agreement modifying a lease contract needs no consideration to be binding.

(2) A signed lease agreement that excludes modification or rescission except by a signed writing may not be otherwise modified or rescinded, but, except as between merchants, such a requirement on a form supplied by a merchant must be separately signed by the other party.

(3) Although an attempt at modification or rescission does not satisfy the requirements of subsection (2), it may operate as a waiver.

(4) A party who has made a waiver affecting an executory portion of a lease contract may retract the waiver by reasonable notification received by the other party that strict performance will be required of any term waived, unless the retraction would be unjust in view of a material change of position in reliance on the waiver.

§2A-209. Lessee Under Finance Lease as Beneficiary of Supply Contract.—

(1) The benefit of a supplier's promises to the lessor under the supply contract and of all warranties, whether express or implied, including those of any third party provided in connection with or as part of the supply contract, extends to the lessee to the extent of the lessee's leasehold interest under a finance lease related to the supply contract, but is subject to the terms of the warranty and of the supply contract and all defenses or claims arising therefrom.

(2) The extension of the benefit of a supplier's promises and of warranties to the lessee (Section 2A-209(1)) does not: (i) modify the rights and obligations of the parties to the supply contract, whether arising therefrom or otherwise, or (ii) impose any duty or liability under the supply contract on the lessee.

(3) Any modification or rescission of the supply contract by the supplier and the lessor is effective between the supplier and the lessee unless, before the modification or rescission, the supplier has received notice that the lessee has entered into a finance lease related to the supply contract. If the modification or rescission is effective between the supplier and the lessee, the lessor is deemed to have assumed, in addition to the obligations of the lessor to the lessee under the lease contract, promises of the supplier to the lessor and warranties that were so modified or rescinded as they existed and were available to the lessee before modification or rescission.

(4) In addition to the extension of the benefit of the supplier's promises and of warranties to the lessee under subsection (1), the lessee retains all rights that the lessee may have against the supplier which arise from an agreement between the lessee and the supplier or under other law.

§2A-210. Express Warranties.—

(1) Express warranties by the lessor are created as follows:
   (a) Any affirmation of fact or promise made by the lessor to the lessee which relates to the goods and becomes part of the basis of the bargain creates an express warranty that the goods will conform to the affirmation or promise.
   (b) Any description of the goods which is made part of the basis of the bargain creates an express warranty that the goods will conform to the description.
   (c) Any sample or model that is made part of the basis of the bargain creates an express warranty that the whole of the goods will conform to the sample or model.

(2) It is not necessary to the creation of an express warranty that the lessor use formal words, such as "warrant" or "guarantee", or that the lessor have a specific intention to make a warranty, but an affirmation merely of the value of the goods or a statement purporting to be merely the lessor's opinion or commendation of the goods does not create a warranty.

§2A-211. Warranties Against Interference and Against Infringement; Lessee's Obligation Against Infringement.—

(1) There is in a lease contract a warranty that for the lease term no person holds a claim to or interest in the goods that arose from an act or omission of the lessor, other than a claim by way of infringement or the like, which will interfere with the lessee's enjoyment of its leasehold interest.

(2) Except in a finance lease there is in a lease contract by a lessor who is a merchant regularly dealing in goods of the kind a warranty that the goods are delivered free of the rightful claim of any person by way of infringement or the like.

(3) A lessee who furnishes specifications to a lessor or a supplier shall hold the lessor and the supplier harmless against any claim by way of infringement or the like that arises out of compliance with the specifications.

§2A-212. Implied Warranty of Merchantability.—

(1) Except in a finance lease, a warranty that the goods will be merchantable is implied in a lease contract if the lessor is a merchant with respect to goods of that kind.

(2) Goods to be merchantable must be at least such as
 (a) pass without objection in the trade under the description in the lease agreement;
 (b) in the case of fungible goods, are of fair average quality within the description;
 (c) are fit for the ordinary purposes for which goods of that type are used;
 (d) run, within the variation permitted by the lease agreement, of even kind, quality, and quantity within each unit and among all units involved;
 (e) are adequately contained, packaged, and labeled as the lease agreement may require; and
 (f) conform to any promises or affirmations of fact made on the container or label.

(3) Other implied warranties may arise from course of dealing or usage of trade.

§2A-213. Implied Warranty of Fitness for Particular Purpose.—

Except in a finance lease, if the lessor at the time the lease contract is made has reason to know of any particular purpose for which the goods are required and that the lessee is relying on the lessor's skill or judgment to select or furnish suitable goods, there is in the lease contract an implied warranty that the goods will be fit for that purpose.

§2A-214. Exclusion or Modification of Warranties.—

(1) Words or conduct relevant to the creation of an express warranty and words or conduct tending to negate or limit a warranty must be construed wherever reasonable as consistent with each other; but, subject to the provisions of Section 2A-202 on parol or extrinsic evidence, negation or limitation is inoperative to the extent that the construction is unreasonable.

(2) Subject to subsection (3), to exclude or modify the implied warranty of merchantability or any part of it the language must mention "merchantability", be by a writing, and be conspicuous. Subject to subsection (3), to exclude or modify any implied warranty of fitness the exclusion must be by a writing and be conspicuous. Language to exclude all implied warranties of fitness is sufficient if it is in writing, is conspicuous and states, for example, "There is no warranty that the goods will be fit for a particular purpose".

(3) Notwithstanding subsection (2), but subject to subsection (4),
 (a) unless the circumstances indicate otherwise, all implied warranties are excluded by expressions like "as is", or "with all faults", or by other language that in common understanding calls the lessee's attention to the exclusion of warranties and makes plain that there is no implied warranty, if in writing and conspicuous;
 (b) if the lessee before entering into the lease contract has examined the goods or the sample or model as fully as desired or has refused to examine the goods, there is no implied warranty with regard to defects that an examination ought in the circumstances to have revealed; and
 (c) an implied warranty may also be excluded or modified by course of dealing, course of performance, or usage of trade.

(4) To exclude or modify a warranty against interference or against infringement (Section 2A-211) or any part of it, the language must be specific, be by a writing, and be conspicuous, unless the circumstances, including course of performance, course of dealing, or usage of trade, give the lessee reason to know that the goods are being leased subject to a claim or interest of any person.

§2A-215. Cumulation and Conflict of Warranties Express or Implied.—

Warranties, whether express or implied, must be construed as consistent with each other and as cumulative, but if that construction is unreasonable, the intention of the parties determines which warranty is dominant. In ascertaining that intention the following rules apply:

(a) Exact or technical specifications displace an inconsistent sample or model or general language of description.

(b) A sample from an existing bulk displaces inconsistent general language of description.

(c) Express warranties displace inconsistent implied warranties other than an implied warranty of fitness for a particular purpose.

§2A-216. Third-Party Beneficiaries of Express and Implied Warranties.—

Alternative A—A warranty to or for the benefit of a lessee under this Article, whether express or implied, extends to any natural person who is in the family or household of the lessee or who is a guest in the lessee's home if it is reasonable to expect that such person may use, consume, or be affected by the goods and who is injured in person by breach of the warranty. This section does not displace principles of law and equity that extend a warranty to or for the benefit of a lessee to other persons. The operation of this section may not be excluded, modified, or limited, but an exclusion, modification, or limitation of the warranty, including any with respect to rights and remedies, effective against the lessee is also effective against any beneficiary designated under this section.

Alternative B—A warranty to or for the benefit of a lessee under this Article, whether express or implied, extends to any natural person who may reasonably be expected to use, consume, or be affected by the goods and who is injured in person by breach of the warranty. This section does not displace principles of law and equity that extend a warranty to or for the benefit of a lessee to other persons. The operation of this section may not be excluded, modified, or limited, but an exclusion, modification, or limitation of the warranty, including any with respect to rights and remedies, effective against the lessee is also effective against the beneficiary designated under this section.

Alternative C—A warranty to or for the benefit of a lessee under this Article, whether express or implied, extends to any person who may reasonably be expected to use, consume, or be affected by the goods and who is injured by breach of the warranty. The operation of this section may not be excluded, modified, or limited with respect to injury to the person of an individual to whom the warranty extends, but an exclusion, modification, or limitation of the warranty, including any with respect to rights and remedies, effective against the lessee is also effective against the beneficiary designated under this section.

§2A-217. Identification.— Identification of goods as goods to which a lease contract refers may be made at any time and in any manner explicitly agreed to by the parties. In the absence of explicit agreement, identification occurs:

(a) when the lease contract is made if the lease contract is for a lease of goods that are existing and identified;

(b) when the goods are shipped, marked, or otherwise designated by the lessor as goods to which the lease contract refers, if the lease contract is for a lease of goods that are not existing and identified; or

(c) when the young are conceived, if the lease contract is for a lease of unborn young of animals.

§2A-218. Insurance and Proceeds.—

(1) A lessee obtains an insurable interest when existing goods are identified to the lease contract even though the goods identified are nonconforming and the lessee has an option to reject them.

(2) If a lessee has an insurable interest only by reason of the lessor's identification of the goods, the lessor, until default or insolvency or notification to the lessee that identification is final, may substitute other goods for those identified.

(3) Notwithstanding a lessee's insurable interest under subsections (1) and (2), the lessor retains an insurable interest until an option to buy has been exercised by the lessee and risk of loss has passed to the lessee.

(4) Nothing in this section impairs any insurable interest recognized under any other statute or rule of law.

(5) The parties by agreement may determine that one or more parties have an obligation to obtain and pay for insurance covering the goods and by agreement may determine the beneficiary of the proceeds of the insurance.

§2A-219. Risk of Loss.—

(1) Except in the case of a finance lease, risk of loss is retained by the lessor and does not pass to the lessee. In the case of a finance lease, risk of loss passes to the lessee.

(2) Subject to the provisions of this Article on the effect of default on risk of loss (Section 2A-220), if risk of loss is to pass to the lessee and the time of passage is not stated, the following rules apply:

(a) If the lease contract requires or authorizes the goods to be shipped by carrier (i) and it does not require delivery at a particular destination, the risk of loss passes to the lessee when the goods are duly delivered to the carrier; but (ii) if it does require delivery at a particular destination and the goods are there duly tendered while in the possession of the carrier, the risk of loss passes to the lessee when the goods are there duly so tendered as to enable the lessee to take delivery.

(b) If the goods are held by a bailee to be delivered without being moved, the risk of loss passes to the lessee on acknowledgment by the bailee of the lessee's right to possession of the goods.

(c) In any case not within subsection (a) or (b), the risk of loss passes to the lessee on the lessee's receipt of the goods if the lessor, or, in the case of a finance lease, the supplier, is a merchant; otherwise the risk passes to the lessee on tender of delivery.

§2A-220. Effect of Default on Risk of Loss.—

(1) Where risk of loss is to pass to the lessee and the time of passage is not stated:
    (a) If a tender or delivery of goods so fails to conform to the lease contract as to give a right of rejection, the risk of their loss remains with the lessor, or, in the case of a finance lease, the supplier, until cure or acceptance.
    (b) If the lessee rightfully revokes acceptance, he [or she], to the extent of any deficiency in his [or her] effective insurance coverage, may treat the risk of loss as having remained with the lessor from the beginning.
(2) Whether or not risk of loss is to pass to the lessee, if the lessee as to conforming goods already identified to a lease contract repudiates or is otherwise in default under the lease contract, the lessor, or, in the case of a finance lease, the supplier, to the extent of any deficiency in his [or her] effective insurance coverage may treat the risk of loss as resting on the lessee for a commercially reasonable time.

§2A-221. Casualty to Identified Goods.— If a lease contract requires goods identified when the lease contract is made, and the goods suffer casualty without fault of the lessee, the lessor or the supplier before delivery, or the goods suffer casualty before risk of loss passes to the lessee pursuant to the lease agreement or Section 2A-219, then:

(a) if the loss is total, the lease contract is avoided; and
(b) if the loss is partial or the goods have so deteriorated as to no longer conform to the lease contract, the lessee may nevertheless demand inspection and at his [or her] option either treat the lease contract as avoided or, except in a finance lease that is not a consumer lease, accept the goods with due allowance from the rent payable for the balance of the lease term for the deterioration or the deficiency in quantity but without further right against the lessor.

Part 3: Effect of Lease Contract

§2A-301. Enforceability of Lease Contract.— Except as otherwise provided in this Article, a lease contract is effective and enforceable according to its terms between the parties, against purchasers of the goods and against creditors of the parties.

§2A-302. Title to and Possession of Goods.— Except as otherwise provided in this Article, each provision of this Article applies whether the lessor or a third party has title to the goods, and whether the lessor, the lessee, or a third party has possession of the goods, notwithstanding any statute or rule of law that possession or the absence of possession is fraudulent.

§2A-303. Alienability of Party's Interest Under Lease Contract or of Lessor's Residual Interest in Goods; Delegation of Performance; Transfer of Rights.—

(1) As used in this section, "creation of a security interest" includes the sale of a lease contract that is subject to Article 9, Secured Transactions, by reason of Section 9-102(1)(b).
(2) Except as provided in subsections (3) and (4), a provision in a lease agreement which (i) prohibits the voluntary or involuntary transfer, including a transfer by sale, sublease, creation or enforcement of a security interest, or attachment, levy, or other judicial process, of an interest of a party under the lease contract or of the lessor's residual interest in the goods, or (ii) makes such a transfer an event of default, gives rise to the rights and remedies provided in subsection (5), but a transfer that is prohibited or is an event of default under the lease agreement is otherwise effective.
(3) A provision in a lease agreement which (i) prohibits the creation or enforcement of a security interest in an interest of a party under the lease contract or in the lessor's residual interest in the goods, or (ii) makes such a transfer an event of default, is not enforceable unless, and then only to the extent that, there is an actual transfer by the lessee of the lessee's right of possession or use of the goods in violation of the provision or an actual delegation of a material performance of either party to the lease contract in violation of the provision. Neither the granting nor the enforcement of a security interest in (i) the lessor's interest under the lease contract or (ii) the lessor's residual interest in the goods is a transfer that materially impairs the prospect of obtaining return performance by, materially changes the duty of, or materially increases the burden or risk imposed on, the lessee within the purview of subsection (5) unless, and then only to the extent that, there is an actual delegation of a material performance of the lessor.
(4) A provision in a lease agreement which (i) prohibits a transfer of a right to damages for default with respect to the whole lease contract or of a right to payment arising out of the transferor's due performance of the transferor's entire obligation, or (ii) makes such a transfer an event of default, is not enforceable, and such a transfer is not a transfer that materially impairs the prospect of obtaining return performance by, materially changes the duty of, or materially increases the burden or risk imposed on, the other party to the lease contract within the purview of subsection (5).
(5) Subject to subsections (3) and (4):
    (a) if a transfer is made which is made an event of default under a lease agreement, the party to the lease contract not making the transfer, unless that party waives the default or otherwise agrees, has the rights and remedies described in Section 2A-501(2);

(b) if paragraph (a) is not applicable and if a transfer is made that (i) is prohibited under a lease agreement or (ii) materially impairs the prospect of obtaining return performance by, materially changes the duty of, or materially increases the burden or risk imposed on, the other party to the lease contract, unless the party not making the transfer agrees at any time to the transfer in the lease contract or otherwise, then, except as limited by contract, (i) the transferor is liable to the party not making the transfer for damages caused by the transfer to the extent that the damages could not reasonably be prevented by the party not making the transfer and (ii) a court having jurisdiction may grant other appropriate relief, including cancellation of the lease contract or an injunction against the transfer.

(6) A transfer of "the lease" or of "all my rights under the lease", or a transfer in similar general terms, is a transfer of rights and, unless the language or the circumstances, as in a transfer for security, indicate the contrary, the transfer is a delegation of duties by the transferor to the transferee. Acceptance by the transferee constitutes a promise by the transferee to perform those duties. The promise is enforceable by either the transferor or the other party to the lease contract.

(7) Unless otherwise agreed by the lessor and the lessee, a delegation of performance does not relieve the transferor as against the other party of any duty to perform or of any liability for default.

(8) In a consumer lease, to prohibit the transfer of an interest of a party under the lease contract or to make a transfer an event of default, the language must be specific, by a writing, and conspicuous.

§2A-304. Subsequent Lease of Goods by Lessor.—

(1) Subject to Section 2A-303, a subsequent lessee from a lessor of goods under an existing lease contract obtains, to the extent of the leasehold interest transferred, the leasehold interest in the goods that the lessor had or had power to transfer, and except as provided in subsection (2) and Section 2A-527(4), takes subject to the existing lease contract. A lessor with voidable title has power to transfer a good leasehold interest to a good faith subsequent lessee for value, but only to the extent set forth in the preceding sentence. If goods have been delivered under a transaction of purchase, the lessor has that power even though:
(a) the lessor's transferor was deceived as to the identity of the lessor;
(b) the delivery was in exchange for a check which is later dishonored;
(c) it was agreed that the transaction was to be a "cash sale"; or

(d) the delivery was procured through fraud punishable as larcenous under the criminal law.

(2) A subsequent lessee in the ordinary course of business from a lessor who is a merchant dealing in goods of that kind to whom the goods were entrusted by the existing lessee of that lessor before the interest of the subsequent lessee became enforceable against that lessor obtains, to the extent of the leasehold interest transferred, all of that lessor's and the existing lessee's rights to the goods, and takes free of the existing lease contract.

(3) A subsequent lessee from the lessor of goods that are subject to an existing lease contract and are covered by a certificate of title issued under a statute of this State or of another jurisdiction takes no greater rights than those provided both by this section and by the certificate of title statute.

§2A-305. Sale or Sublease of Goods by Lessee.—

(1) Subject to the provisions of Section 2A-303, a buyer or sublessee from the lessee of goods under an existing lease contract obtains, to the extent of the interest transferred, the leasehold interest in the goods that the lessee had or had power to transfer, and except as provided in subsection (2) and Section 2A-511(4), takes subject to the existing lease contract. A lessee with a voidable leasehold interest has power to transfer a good leasehold interest to a good faith buyer for value or a good faith sublessee for value, but only to the extent set forth in the preceding sentence. When goods have been delivered under a transaction of lease the lessee has that power even though:
(a) the lessor was deceived as to the identity of the lessee;
(b) the delivery was in exchange for a check which is later dishonored; or
(c) the delivery was procured through fraud punishable as larcenous under the criminal law.

(2) A buyer in the ordinary course of business or a sublessee in the ordinary course of business from a lessee who is a merchant dealing in goods of that kind to whom the goods were entrusted by the lessor obtains, to the extent of the interest transferred, all of the lessor's and lessee's rights to the goods, and takes free of the existing lease contract.

(3) A buyer or sublessee from the lessee of goods that are subject to an existing lease contract and are covered by a certificate of title issued under a statute of this State or of another jurisdiction takes no greater rights than those provided both by this section and by the certificate of title statute.

§2A-306. Priority of Certain Liens Arising by Operation of Law.—

If a person in the ordinary course of his [or her] business furnishes services or materials with respect to goods subject to a lease contract, a lien upon those goods in the possession of that person given by statute or rule of law for those materials or services takes priority over any interest of the lessor or lessee under the lease contract or this Article unless the lien is created by statute and the statute provides otherwise or unless the lien is created by rule of law and the rule of law provides otherwise.

§2A-307. Priority of Liens Arising by Attachment or Levy on, Security Interests in, and Other Claims to Goods.—

(1) Except as otherwise provided in Section 2A-306, a creditor of a lessee takes subject to the lease contract.
(2) Except as otherwise provided in subsections (3) and (4) and in Sections 2A-306 and 2A-308, a creditor of a lessor takes subject to the lease contract unless:
   (a) the creditor holds a lien that attached to the goods before the lease contract became enforceable,
   (b) the creditor holds a security interest in the goods and the lessee did not give value and receive delivery of the goods without knowledge of the security interest; or
   (c) the creditor holds a security interest in the goods which was perfected (Section 9-303) before the lease contract became enforceable.
(3) A lessee in the ordinary course of business takes the leasehold interest free of a security interest in the goods created by the lessor even though the security interest is perfected (Section 9-303) and the lessee knows of its existence.
(4) A lessee other than a lessee in the ordinary course of business takes the leasehold interest free of a security interest to the extent that it secures future advances made after the secured party acquires knowledge of the lease or more than 45 days after the lease contract becomes enforceable, whichever first occurs, unless the future advances are made pursuant to a commitment entered into without knowledge of the lease and before the expiration of the 45-day period.

§2A-308. Special Rights of Creditors.—

(1) A creditor of a lessor in possession of goods subject to a lease contract may treat the lease contract as void if as against the creditor retention of possession by the lessor is fraudulent under any statute or rule of law, but retention of possession in good faith and current course of trade by the lessor for a commercially reasonable time after the lease contract becomes enforceable is not fraudulent.
(2) Nothing in this Article impairs the rights of creditors of a lessor if the lease contract (a) becomes enforceable, not in current course of trade but in satisfaction of or as security for a pre-existing claim for money, security, or the like, and (b) is made under circumstances which under any statute or rule of law apart

from this Article would constitute the transaction a fraudulent transfer or voidable preference.
(3) A creditor of a seller may treat a sale or an identification of goods to a contract for sale as void if as against the creditor retention of possession by the seller is fraudulent under any statute or rule of law, but retention of possession of the goods pursuant to a lease contract entered into by the seller as lessee and the buyer as lessor in connection with the sale or identification of the goods is not fraudulent if the buyer bought for value and in good faith.

§2A-309. Lessor's and Lessee's Rights When Goods Become Fixtures.—

(1) In this section:
   (a) goods are "fixtures" when they become so related to particular real estate that an interest in them arises under real estate law;
   (b) a "fixture filing" is the filing, in the office where a mortgage on the real estate would be filed or recorded, of a financing statement covering goods that are or are to become fixtures and conforming to the requirements of Section 9-402(5);
   (c) a lease is a "purchase money lease" unless the lessee has possession or use of the goods or the right to possession or use of the goods before the lease agreement is enforceable;
   (d) a mortgage is a "construction mortgage" to the extent it secures an obligation incurred for the construction of an improvement on land including the acquisition cost of the land, if the recorded writing so indicates; and
   (e) "encumbrance" includes real estate mortgages and other liens on real estate and all other rights in real estate that are not ownership interests.
(2) Under this Article a lease may be of goods that are fixtures or may continue in goods that become fixtures, but no lease exists under this Article of ordinary building materials incorporated into an improvement on land.
(3) This Article does not prevent creation of a lease of fixtures pursuant to real estate law.
(4) The perfected interest of a lessor of fixtures has priority over a conflicting interest of an encumbrancer or owner of the real estate if:
   (a) the lease is a purchase money lease, the conflicting interest of the encumbrancer or owner arises before the goods become fixtures, the interest of the lessor is perfected by a fixture filing before the goods become fixtures or within ten days thereafter, and the lessee has an interest of record in the real estate or is in possession of the real estate; or
   (b) the interest of the lessor is perfected by a fixture filing before the interest of the encumbrancer or owner is of record, the lessor's interest has

priority over any conflicting interest of a predecessor in title of the encumbrancer or owner, and the lessee has an interest of record in the real estate or is in possession of the real estate.

(5) The interest of a lessor of fixtures, whether or not perfected, has priority over the conflicting interest of an encumbrancer or owner of the real estate if:

(a) the fixtures are readily removable factory or office machines, readily removable equipment that is not primarily used or leased for use in the operation of the real estate, or readily removable replacements of domestic appliances that are goods subject to a consumer lease, and before the goods become fixtures the lease contract is enforceable; or

(b) the conflicting interest is a lien on the real estate obtained by legal or equitable proceedings after the lease contract is enforceable; or

(c) the encumbrancer or owner has consented in writing to the lease or has disclaimed an interest in the goods as fixtures; or

(d) the lessee has a right to remove the goods as against the encumbrancer or owner. If the lessee's right to remove terminates, the priority of the interest of the lessor continues for a reasonable time.

(6) Notwithstanding subsection (4)(a) but otherwise subject to subsections (4) and (5), the interest of a lessor of fixtures, including the lessor's residual interest, is subordinate to the conflicting interest of an encumbrancer of the real estate under a construction mortgage recorded before the goods become fixtures if the goods become fixtures before the completion of the construction. To the extent given to refinance a construction mortgage, the conflicting interest of an encumbrancer of the real estate under a mortgage has this priority to the same extent as the encumbrancer of the real estate under the construction mortgage.

(7) In cases not within the preceding-subsections, priority between the interest of a lessor of fixtures, including the lessor's residual interest, and the conflicting interest of an encumbrancer or owner of the real estate who is not the lessee is determined by the priority rules governing conflicting interests in real estate.

(8) If the interest of a lessor of fixtures, including the lessor's residual interest, has priority over all conflicting interests of all owners and encumbrancers of the real estate, the lessor or the lessee may (i) on default, expiration, termination, or cancellation of the lease agreement but subject to the lease agreement and this Article, or (ii) if necessary to enforce other rights and remedies of the lessor or lessee under this Article, remove the goods from the real estate, free and clear of all conflicting interests of all owners and encumbrancers of the real estate, but the lessor or lessee must reimburse any encumbrancer or owner of the real estate who is not the lessee and who has not

otherwise agreed for the cost of repair of any physical injury, but not for any diminution in value of the real estate caused by the absence of the goods removed or by any necessity of replacing them. A person entitled to reimbursement may refuse permission to remove until the party seeking removal gives adequate security for the performance of this obligation.

(9) Even though the lease agreement does not create a security interest, the interest of a lessor of fixtures, including the lessor's residual interest, is perfected by filing a financing statement as a fixture filing for leased goods that are or are to become fixtures in accordance with the relevant provisions of the Article on Secured Transactions (Article 9).

§2A-310. Lessor's and Lessee's Rights When Goods Become Accessions.—

(1) Goods are "accessions" when they are installed in or affixed to other goods.

(2) The interest of a lessor or a lessee under a lease contract entered into before the goods became accessions is superior to all interests in the whole except as stated in subsection (4).

(3) The interest of a lessor or a lessee under a lease contract entered into at the time or after the goods became accessions is superior to all subsequently acquired interests in the whole except as stated in subsection (4) but is subordinate to interests in the whole existing at the time the lease contract was made unless the holders of such interests in the whole have in writing consented to the lease or disclaimed an interest in the goods as part of the whole.

(4) The interest of a lessor or a lessee under a lease contract described in subsection (2) or (3) is subordinate to the interest of

(a) a buyer in the ordinary course of business or a lessee in the ordinary course of business of any interest in the whole acquired after the goods became accessions; or

(b) a creditor with a security interest in the whole perfected before the lease contract was made to the extent that the creditor makes subsequent advances without knowledge of the lease contract.

(5) When under subsections (2) or (3) and (4) a lessor or a lessee of accessions holds an interest that is superior to all interests in the whole, the lessor or the lessee may (a) on default, expiration, termination, or cancellation of the lease contract by the other party but subject to the provisions of the lease contract and this Article, or (b) if necessary to enforce his [or her] other rights and remedies under this Article, remove the goods from the whole, free and clear of all interests in the whole, but he [or she] must reimburse any holder of an interest in the whole who is not the lessee and who has not otherwise agreed for the cost of repair of any physical

injury but not for any diminution in value of the whole caused by the absence of the goods removed or by any necessity for replacing them. A person entitled to reimbursement may refuse permission to remove until the party seeking removal gives adequate security for the performance of this obligation.

§2A-311. Priority Subject to Subordination. Nothing in this Article prevents subordination by agreement by any person entitled to priority.

Part 4: Performance of Lease Contract: Repudiated, Substituted and Excused

§2A-401. Insecurity: Adequate Assurance of Performance.—

(1) A lease contract imposes an obligation on each party that the other's expectation of receiving due performance will not be impaired.

(2) If reasonable grounds for insecurity arise with respect to the performance of either party, the insecure party may demand in writing adequate assurance of due performance. Until the insecure party receives that assurance, if commercially reasonable the insecure party may suspend any performance for which he [or she] has not already received the agreed return.

(3) A repudiation of the lease contract occurs if assurance of due performance adequate under the circumstances of the particular case is not provided to the insecure party within a reasonable time, not to exceed 30 days after receipt of a demand by the other party.

(4) Between merchants, the reasonableness of grounds for insecurity and the adequacy of any assurance offered must be determined according to commercial standards.

(5) Acceptance of any nonconforming delivery or payment does not prejudice the aggrieved party's right to demand adequate assurance of future performance.

§2A-402. Anticipatory Repudiation.—

If either party repudiates a lease contract with respect to a performance not yet due under the lease contract, the loss of which performance will substantially impair the value of the lease contract to the other, the aggrieved party may:

(a) for a commercially reasonable time, await retraction of repudiation and performance by the repudiating party;

(b) make demand pursuant to Section 2A-401 and await assurance of future performance adequate under the circumstances of the particular case; or

(c) resort to any right or remedy upon default under the lease contract or this Article, even though the aggrieved party has notified the repudiating party that the aggrieved party would await the repudiating party's performance and assurance and has urged retraction.

In addition, whether or not the aggrieved party is pursuing one of the foregoing remedies, the aggrieved party may suspend performance or, if the aggrieved party is the lessor, proceed in accordance with the provisions of this Article on the lessor's right to identify goods to the lease contract notwithstanding default or to salvage unfinished goods (Section 2A-524).

§2A-403. Retraction of Anticipatory Repudiation.—

(1) Until the repudiating party's next performance is due, the repudiating party can retract the repudiation unless, since the repudiation, the aggrieved party has cancelled the lease contract or materially changed the aggrieved party's position or otherwise indicated that the aggrieved party considers the repudiation final.

(2) Retraction may be by any method that clearly indicates to the aggrieved party that the repudiating party intends to perform under the lease contract and includes any assurance demanded under Section 2A-401.

(3) Retraction reinstates a repudiating party's rights under a lease contract with due excuse and allowance to the aggrieved party for any delay occasioned by the repudiation.

§2A-404. Substituted Performance.—

(1) If without fault of the lessee, the lessor and the supplier, the agreed berthing, loading, or unloading facilities fail or the agreed type of carrier becomes unavailable the agreed manner of delivery otherwise becomes commercially impracticable, but a commercially reasonable substitute is available, the substitute performance must be tendered and accepted.

(2) If the agreed means or manner of payment fails because of domestic or foreign governmental regulation:

(a) the lessor may withhold or stop delivery or cause the supplier to withhold or stop delivery unless the lessee provides a means or manner of payment that is commercially a substantial equivalent; and

(b) if delivery has already been taken, payment by the means or in the manner provided by the regulation discharges the lessee's obligation unless the regulation is discriminatory, oppressive, or predatory.

§2A-405. Excused Performance.—

Subject to Section 2A-404 on substituted performance, the following rules apply:

(a) Delay in delivery or nondelivery in whole or in part by a lessor or a supplier who complies with paragraphs (b) and (c) is not a default under the lease contract if performance as agreed has been made impracticable by the occurrence of a contingency the nonoccurrence of which was a basic assumption on which the lease contract was made or by compliance in good faith with any applicable foreign or domestic governmental regulation or order, whether or not the regulation or order later proves to be invalid.

(b) If the causes mentioned in paragraph (a) affect only part of the lessor's or the supplier's capacity to perform, he [or she] shall allocate production and deliveries among his [or her] customers but at his [or her] option may include regular customers not then under contract for sale or lease as well as his [or her] own requirements for further manufacture. He [or she] may so allocate in any manner that is fair and reasonable.

(c) The lessor seasonably shall notify the lessee and in the case of a finance lease the supplier seasonally shall notify the lessor and the lessee, if known, that there will be delay or nondelivery and, if allocation is required under paragraph (b), of the estimated quota thus made available for the lessee.

§2A-406. Procedure on Excused Performance.—

(1) If the lessee receives notification of a material or indefinite delay or an allocation justified under Section 2A-405, the lessee may by written notification to the lessor as to any goods involved, and with respect to all of the goods if under an installment lease contract the value of the whole lease contract is substantially impaired (Section 2A-510):

(a) terminate the lease contract (Section 2A-505(2)); or

(b) except in a finance lease that is not a consumer lease, modify the lease contract by accepting the available quota in substitution, with due allowance from the rent payable for the balance of the lease term for the deficiency but without further right against the lessor.

(2) If, after receipt of a notification from the lessor under Section 2A-405, the lessee fails so to modify the lease agreement within a reasonable time not exceeding 30 days, the lease contract lapses with respect to any deliveries affected.

§2A-407. Irrevocable Promises: Finance Leases.—

(1) In the case of a finance lease that is not a consumer lease the lessee's promises under the lease contract become irrevocable and independent upon the lessee's acceptance of the goods.

(2) A promise that has become irrevocable and independent under subsection (1):

(a) is effective and enforceable between the parties, and by or against third parties including assignees of the parties; and

(b) is not subject to cancellation, termination, modification, repudiation, excuse, or substitution without the consent of the party to whom the promise runs.

(3) This section does not affect the validity under any other law of a covenant in any lease contract making the lessee's promises irrevocable and independent upon the lessee's acceptance of the goods.

Part 5: Default

A. In General

§2A-501. Default: Procedure.—

(1) Whether the lessor or the lessee is in default under a lease contract is determined by the lease agreement and this Article.

(2) If the lessor or the lessee is in default under the lease contract, the party seeking enforcement has rights and remedies as provided in this Article and, except as limited by this Article, as provided in the lease agreement.

(3) If the lessor or the lessee is in default under the lease contract, the party seeking enforcement may reduce the party's claim to judgment, or otherwise enforce the lease contract by self-help or any available judicial procedure or nonjudicial procedure, including administrative proceeding, arbitration, or the like, in accordance with this Article.

(4) Except as otherwise provided in Section 1-106(1) or this Article or the lease agreement, the rights and remedies referred to in subsections (2) and (3) are cumulative.

(5) If the lease agreement covers both real property and goods, the party seeking enforcement may proceed under this Part as to the goods, or under other applicable law as to both the real property and the goods in accordance with that party's rights and remedies in respect of the real property, in which case this Part does not apply.

§2A-502. Notice After Default.—
Except as otherwise provided in this Article or the lease agreement, the lessor or lessee in default under the lease contract is not entitled to notice of default or notice of enforcement from the other party to the lease agreement.

§2A-503. Modification or Impairment of Rights and Remedies.—

(1) Except as otherwise provided in this Article, the lease agreement may include rights and remedies for default in addition to or in substitution for those provided in this Article and may limit or alter the measure of damages recoverable under this Article.

(2) Resort to a remedy provided under this Article or in the lease agreement is optional unless the remedy is expressly agreed to be exclusive. If circumstances cause an exclusive or limited remedy to fail of its essential purpose, or provision for an exclusive remedy is unconscionable, remedy may be had as provided in this Article.

(3) Consequential damages may be liquidated under Section 2A-504, or may otherwise be limited, altered, or excluded unless the limitation, alteration, or exclusion is unconscionable. Limitation, alteration, or exclusion of consequential damages for injury to the

person in the case of consumer goods is prima facie unconscionable but limitation, alteration, or exclusion of damages where the loss is commercial is not prima facie unconscionable.

(4) Rights and remedies on default by the lessor or the lessee with respect to any obligation or promise collateral or ancillary to the lease contract are not impaired by this Article.

§2A-504. Liquidation of Damages.—

(1) Damages payable by either party for default, or any other act or omission, including indemnity for loss or diminution of anticipated tax benefits or loss or damage to lessor's residual interest, may be liquidated in the lease agreement but only at an amount or by a formula that is reasonable in light of the then anticipated harm caused by the default or other act or omission.

(2) If the lease agreement provides for liquidation of damages, and such provision does not comply with subsection (1), or such provision is an exclusive or limited remedy that circumstances cause to fail of its essential purpose, remedy may be had as provided in this Article.

(3) If the lessor justifiably withholds or stops delivery of goods because of the lessee's default or insolvency (Section 2A-525 or 2A-526), the lessee is entitled to restitution of any amount by which the sum of his [or her] payments exceeds:
   (a) the amount to which the lessor is entitled by virtue of terms liquidating the lessor's damages in accordance with subsection (1); or
   (b) in the absence of those terms, 20 percent of the then present value of the total rent the lessee was obligated to pay for the balance of the lease term, or, in the case of a consumer lease, the lesser of such amount or $500.

(4) A lessee's right to restitution under subsection (3) is subject to offset to the extent the lessor establishes:
   (a) a right to recover damages under the provisions of this Article other than subsection (1); and
   (b) the amount or value of any benefits received by the lessee directly or indirectly by reason of the lease contract.

§2A-505. Cancellation and Termination and Effect of Cancellation, Termination, Rescission, or Fraud on Rights and Remedies.—

(1) On cancellation of the lease contract, all obligations that are still executory on both sides are discharged, but any right based on prior default or performance survives, and the cancelling party also retains any remedy for default of the whole lease contract or any unperformed balance.

(2) On termination of the lease contract, all obligations that are still executory on both sides are discharged but any right based on prior default or performance survives.

(3) Unless the contrary intention clearly appears, expressions of "cancellation", "rescission", or the like of the lease contract may not be construed as a renunciation or discharge of any claim in damages for an antecedent default.

(4) Rights and remedies for material misrepresentation or fraud include all rights and remedies available under this Article for default.

(5) Neither rescission nor a claim for rescission of the lease contract nor rejection or return of the goods may bar or be deemed inconsistent with a claim for damages or other right or remedy.

§2A-506. Statute of Limitations.—

(1) An action for default under a lease contract, including breach of warranty or indemnity, must be commenced within 4 years after the cause of action accrued. By the original lease contract the parties may reduce the period of limitation to not less than one year.

(2) A cause of action for default accrues when the act or omission on which the default or breach of warranty is based is or should have been discovered by the aggrieved party, or when the default occurs, whichever is later. A cause of action for indemnity accrues when the act or omission on which the claim for indemnity is based is or should have been discovered by the indemnified party, whichever is later.

(3) If an action commenced within the time limited by subsection (1) is so terminated as to leave available a remedy by another action for the same default or breach of warranty or indemnity, the other action may be commenced after the expiration of the time limited and within 6 months after the termination of the first action unless the termination resulted from voluntary discontinuance or from dismissal for failure or neglect to prosecute.

(4) This section does not alter the law on tolling of the statute of limitations nor does it apply to causes of action that have accrued before this Article becomes effective.

§2A-507. Proof of Market Rent: Time and Place.—

(1) Damages based on market rent (Section 2A-519 or 2A-528) are determined according to the rent for the use of the goods concerned for a lease term identical to the remaining lease term of the original lease agreement and prevailing at the times specified in Sections 2A-519 and 2A-528.

(2) If evidence of rent for the use of the goods concerned for a lease term identical to the remaining lease term of the original lease agreement and prevailing at the times or places described in this Article is not readily available, the rent prevailing within any reasonable time before or after the time described or at any other

place or for a different lease term which in commercial judgment or under usage of trade would serve as a reasonable substitute for the one described may be used, making any proper allowance for the difference, including the cost of transporting the goods to or from the other place.

(3) Evidence of a relevant rent prevailing at a time or place or for a lease term other than the one described in this Article offered by one party is not admissible unless and until he [or she] has given the other party notice the court finds sufficient to prevent unfair surprise.

(4) If the prevailing rent, or value of any goods regularly leased in any established market is in issue, reports in official publications or trade journals or in newspapers or periodicals of general circulation published as the reports of that market are admissible in evidence. The circumstances of the preparation of the report may be shown to affect its weight but not its admissibility.

B. Default by Lessor

§2A-508. Lessee's Remedies.—

(1) If a lessor fails to deliver the goods in conformity to the lease contract (Section 2A-509) or repudiates the lease contract (Section 2A-402), or a lessee rightfully rejects the goods (Section 2A-509) or justifiably revokes acceptance of the goods (Section 2A-517), then with respect to any goods involved, and with respect to all of the goods if under an installment lease contract the value of the whole lease contract is substantially impaired (Section 2A-510), the lessor is in default under the lease contract and the lessee may:

  (a) cancel the lease contract (Section 2A-505(1));
  (b) recover so much of the rent and security as has been paid and is just under the circumstances;
  (c) cover and recover damages as to all goods affected whether or not they have been identified to the lease contract (Sections 2A-518 and 2A-520), or recover damages for nondelivery (Sections 2A-519 and 2A-520);
  (d) exercise any other rights or pursue any other remedies provided in the lease contract.

(2) If a lessor fails to deliver the goods in conformity to the lease contract or repudiates the lease contract, the lessee may also:

  (a) if the goods have been identified, recover them (Section 2A-522); or
  (b) in a proper case, obtain specific performance or replevy the goods (Section 2A-521).

(3) If a lessor is otherwise in default under a lease contract, the lessee may exercise the rights and pursue the remedies provided in the lease contract, which may include a right to cancel the lease, and in Section 2A-519(3).

(4) If a lessor has breached a warranty, whether express or implied, the lessee may recover damages (Section 2A-519(4)).

(5) On rightful rejection or justifiable revocation of acceptance, a lessee has a security interest in goods in the lessee's possession or control for any rent and security that has been paid and any expenses reasonably incurred in their inspection, receipt, transportation, and care and custody and may hold those goods and dispose of them in good faith and in a commercially reasonable manner, subject to Section 2A-527(5).

(6) Subject to the provisions of Section 2A-407, a lessee, on notifying the lessor of the lessee's intention to do so, may deduct all or any part of the damages resulting from any default under the lease contract from any part of the rent still due under the same lease contract.

§2A-509. Lessee's Rights on Improper Delivery; Rightful Rejection.—

(1) Subject to the provisions of Section 2A-510 on default in installment lease contracts, if the goods or the tender or delivery fail in any respect to conform to the lease contract, the lessee may reject or accept the goods or accept any commercial unit or units and reject the rest of the goods.

(2) Rejection of goods is ineffective unless it is within a reasonable time after tender or delivery of the goods and the lessee seasonably notifies the lessor.

§2A-510. Installment Lease Contracts: Rejection and Default.—

(1) Under an installment lease contract a lessee may reject any delivery that is nonconforming if the nonconformity substantially impairs the value of that delivery and cannot be cured or the nonconformity is a defect in the required documents; but if the nonconformity does not fall within subsection (2) and the lessor or the supplier gives adequate assurance of its cure, the lessee must accept that delivery.

(2) Whenever nonconformity or default with respect to one or more deliveries substantially impairs the value of the installment lease contract as a whole there is a default with respect to the whole. But, the aggrieved party reinstates the installment lease contract as a whole if the aggrieved party accepts a nonconforming delivery without seasonably notifying of cancellation or brings an action with respect only to past deliveries or demands performance as to future deliveries.

§2A-511. Merchant Lessee's Duties as to Rightfully Rejected Goods.—

(1) Subject to any security interest of a lessee (Section 2A-508(5)), if a lessor or a supplier has no agent or place of business at the market of rejection, a merchant lessee, after rejection of goods in his [or her] possession or control, shall follow any reasonable

instructions received from the lessor or the supplier with respect to the goods. In the absence of those instructions, a merchant lessee shall make reasonable efforts to sell, lease, or otherwise dispose of the goods for the lessor's account if they threaten to decline in value speedily. Instructions are not reasonable if on demand indemnity for expenses is not forthcoming.

(2) If a merchant lessee (subsection (1)) or any other lessee (Section 2A-512) disposes of goods, he [or she] is entitled to reimbursement either from the lessor or the supplier or out of the proceeds for reasonable expenses of caring for and disposing of the goods and, if the expenses include no disposition commission, to such commission as is usual in the trade, or if there is none, to a reasonable sum not exceeding 10 percent of the gross proceeds.

(3) In complying with this section or Section 2A-512, the lessee is held only to good faith. Good faith conduct hereunder is neither acceptance or conversion nor the basis of an action for damages.

(4) A purchaser who purchases in good faith from a lessee pursuant to this section or Section 2A-512 takes the goods free of any rights of the lessor and the supplier even though the lessee fails to comply with one or more of the requirements of this Article.

§2A-512. Lessee's Duties as to Rightfully Rejected Goods.—

(1) Except as otherwise provided with respect to goods that threaten to decline in value speedily (Section 2A-511) and subject to any security interest of a lessee (Section 2A-508(5)):
  (a) the lessee, after rejection of goods in the lessee's possession, shall hold them with reasonable care at the lessor's or the supplier's disposition for a reasonable time after the lessee's seasonable notification of rejection;
  (b) if the lessor or the supplier gives no instructions within a reasonable time after notification of rejection, the lessee may store the rejected goods for the lessor's or the supplier's account or ship them to the lessor or the supplier or dispose of them for the lessor's or the supplier's account with reimbursement in the manner provided in Section 2A-511; but
  (c) the lessee has no further obligations with regard to goods rightfully rejected.

(2) Action by the lessee pursuant to subsection (1) is not acceptance or conversion.

§2A-513. Cure by Lessor of Improper Tender or Delivery; Replacement.—

(1) If any tender or delivery by the lessor or the supplier is rejected because nonconforming and the time for performance has not yet expired, the lessor or the supplier may seasonably notify the lessee of the lessor's or the supplier's intention to cure and may then make a conforming delivery within the time provided in the lease contract.

(2) If the lessee rejects a nonconforming tender that the lessor or the supplier had reasonable grounds to believe would be acceptable with or without money allowance, the lessor or the supplier may have a further reasonable time to substitute a conforming tender if he [or she] seasonably notifies the lessee.

§2A-514. Waiver of Lessee's Objections.—

(1) In rejecting goods, a lessee's failure to state a particular defect that is ascertainable by reasonable inspection precludes the lessee from relying on the defect to justify rejection or to establish default:
  (a) if, stated seasonably, the lessor or the supplier could have cured it (Section 2A-513); or
  (b) between merchants if the lessor or the supplier after rejection has made a request in writing for a full and final written statement of all defects on which the lessee proposes to rely.

(2) A lessee's failure to reserve rights when paying rent or other consideration against documents precludes recovery of the payment for defects apparent on the face of the documents.

§2A-515. Acceptance of Goods.—

(1) Acceptance of goods occurs after the lessee has had a reasonable opportunity to inspect the goods and
  (a) the lessee signifies or acts with respect to the goods in a manner that signifies to the lessor or the supplier that the goods are conforming or that the lessee will take or retain them in spite of their nonconformity; or
  (b) the lessee fails to make an effective rejection of the goods (Section 2A-509(2)).

(2) Acceptance of a part of any commercial unit is acceptance of that entire unit.

§2A-516. Effect of Acceptance of Goods; Notice of Default; Burden of Establishing Default After Acceptance; Notice of Claim or Litigation to Person Answerable Over.—

(1) A lessee must pay rent for any goods accepted in accordance with the lease contract, with due allowance for goods rightfully rejected or not delivered.

(2) A lessee's acceptance of goods precludes rejection of the goods accepted. In the case of a finance lease, if made with knowledge of a nonconformity, acceptance cannot be revoked because of it. In any other case, if made with knowledge of a nonconformity, acceptance cannot be revoked because of it unless the acceptance was on the reasonable assumption that the nonconformity would be seasonably cured. Acceptance does not of itself impair any other remedy provided by this Article or the lease agreement for nonconformity.

(3) If a tender has been accepted:

    (a) within a reasonable time after the lessee discovers or should have discovered any default, the lessee shall notify the lessor and the supplier, if any, or be barred from any remedy against the party not notified;

    (b) except in the case of a consumer lease, within a reasonable time after the lessee receives notice of litigation for infringement or the like (Section 2A-211) the lessee shall notify the lessor or be barred from any remedy over for liability established by the litigation; and

    (c) the burden is on the lessee to establish any default.

(4) If a lessee is sued for breach of a warranty or other obligation for which a lessor or a supplier is answerable over the following apply:

    (a) The lessee may give the lessor or the supplier, or both, written notice of the litigation. If the notice states that the person notified may come in and defend and that if the person notified does not do so that person will be bound in any action against that person by the lessee by any determination of fact common to the two litigations, then unless the person notified after seasonable receipt of the notice does come in and defend that person is so bound.

    (b) The lessor or the supplier may demand in writing that the lessee turn over control of the litigation including settlement if the claim is one for infringement or the like (Section 2A-211) or else be barred from any remedy over. If the demand states that the lessor or the supplier agrees to bear all expense and to satisfy any adverse judgment, then unless the lessee after seasonable receipt of the demand does turn over control the lessee is so barred.

(5) Subsections (3) and (4) apply to any obligation of a lessee to hold the lessor or the supplier harmless against the infringement or the like (Section 2A-211).

§2A-517. Revocation of Acceptance of Goods.—

(1) A lessee may revoke acceptance of a lot or commercial unit whose nonconformity substantially impairs its value to the lessee if the lessee has accepted it:

    (a) except in the case of a finance lease, on the reasonable assumption that its nonconformity would be cured and it has not been seasonably cured; or

    (b) without discovery of the nonconformity if the lessee's acceptance was reasonably induced either by the lessor's assurances or, except in the case of a finance lease, by the difficulty of discovery before acceptance.

(2) Except in the case of a finance lease that is not a consumer lease, a lessee may revoke acceptance of a lot or commercial unit if the lessor defaults under the lease contract and the default substantially impairs the value of that lot or commercial unit to the lessee.

(3) If the lease agreement so provides, the lessee may revoke acceptance of a lot or commercial unit because of other defaults by the lessor.

(4) Revocation of acceptance must occur within a reasonable time after the lessee discovers or should have discovered the ground for it and before any substantial change in condition of the goods which is not caused by the nonconformity. Revocation is not effective until the lessee notifies the lessor.

(5) A lessee who so revokes has the same rights and duties with regard to the goods involved as if the lessee had rejected them.

§2A-518. Cover; Substitute Goods.—

(1) After a default by a lessor under the lease contract of the type described in Section 2A-508(1), or, if agreed, after other default by the lessor, the lessee may cover by making any purchase or lease of or contract to purchase or lease goods in substitution for those due from the lessor.

(2) Except as otherwise provided with respect to damages liquidated in the lease agreement (Section 2A-504) or otherwise determined pursuant to agreement of the parties (Sections 1-102(3) and 2A-503), if a lessee's cover is by a lease agreement substantially similar to the original lease agreement and the new lease agreement is made in good faith and in a commercially reasonable manner, the lessee may recover from the lessor as damages (i) the present value, as of the date of the commencement of the term of the new lease agreement, of the rent under the new lease agreement applicable to that period of the new lease term which is comparable to the then remaining term of the original lease agreement minus the present value as of the same date of the total rent for the then remaining lease term of the original lease agreement, and (ii) any incidental or consequential damages, less expenses saved in consequence of the lessor's default.

(3) If a lessee's cover is by lease agreement that for any reason does not qualify for treatment under subsection (2), or is by purchase or otherwise, the lessee may recover from the lessor as if the lessee had elected not to cover and Section 2A-519 governs.

§2A-519. Lessee's Damages for Non-Delivery, Repudiation, Default, and Breach of Warranty in Regard to Accepted Goods.—

(1) Except as otherwise provided with respect to damages liquidated in the lease agreement (Section 2A-504) or otherwise determined pursuant to agreement of the parties (Sections 1-102(3) and 2A-503), if the lessee elects not to cover or a lessee elects to cover and the cover is by lease agreement that for any reason does not qualify for treatment under Section 2A-518(2), or is by purchase or otherwise, the measure of damages

for non-delivery or repudiation by the lessor or for rejection or revocation of acceptance by the lessee is the present value, as of the date of the default, of the then market rent minus the present value as of the same date of the original rent, computed for the remaining lease term of the original lease agreement, together with incidental and consequential damages, less expenses saved in consequence of the lessor's default.

(2) Market rent is to be determined as of the place for tender or, in cases of rejection after arrival or revocation of acceptance, as of the place of arrival.

(3) Except as otherwise agreed, if the lessee has accepted goods and given notification (Section 2A-516(3)), the measure of damages for non-conforming tender or delivery or other default by a lessor is the loss resulting in the ordinary course of events from the lessor's default as determined in any manner that is reasonable together with incidental and consequential damages, less expenses saved in consequence of the lessor's default.

(4) Except as otherwise agreed, the measure of damages for breach of warranty is the present value at the time and place of acceptance of the difference between the value of the use of the goods accepted and the value if they had been as warranted for the lease term, unless special circumstances show proximate damages of a different amount, together with incidental and consequential damages, less expenses saved in consequence of the lessor's default or breach of warranty.

§2A-520. Lessee's Incidental and Consequential Damages.—

(1) Incidental damages resulting from a lessor's default include expenses reasonably incurred in inspection, receipt, transportation, and care and custody of goods rightfully rejected or goods the acceptance of which is justifiably revoked, any commercially reasonable charges, expenses or commissions in connection with effecting cover, and any other reasonable expense incident to the default.

(2) Consequential damages resulting from a lessor's default include:
   (a) any loss resulting from general or particular requirements and needs of which the lessor at the time of contracting had reason to know and which could not reasonably be prevented by cover or otherwise; and
   (b) injury to person or property proximately resulting from any breach of warranty.

§2A-521. Lessee's Right to Specific Performance or Replevin.—

(1) Specific performance may be decreed if the goods are unique or in other proper circumstances.

(2) A decree for specific performance may include any terms and conditions as to payment of the rent, dam-ages, or other relief that the court deems just.

(3) A lessee has a right of replevin, detinue, sequestration, claim and delivery, or the like for goods identified to the lease contract if after reasonable effort the lessee is unable to effect cover for those goods or the circumstances reasonably indicate that the effort will be unavailing.

§2A-522. Lessee's Right to Goods on Lessor's Insolvency.—

(1) Subject to subsection (2) and even though the goods have not been shipped, a lessee who has paid a part or all of the rent and security for goods identified to a lease contract (Section 2A-217) on making and keeping good a tender of any unpaid portion of the rent and security due under the lease contract may recover the goods identified from the lessor if the lessor becomes insolvent within 10 days after receipt of the first installment of rent and security.

(2) A lessee acquires the right to recover goods identified to a lease contract only if they conform to the lease contract.

C. Default by Lessee

§2A-523. Lessor's Remedies.—

(1) If a lessee wrongfully rejects or revokes acceptance of goods or fails to make a payment when due or repudiates with respect to a part or the whole, then, with respect to any goods involved, and with respect to all of the goods if under an installment lease contract the value of the whole lease contract is substantially impaired (Section 2A-510), the lessee is in default under the lease contract and the lessor may:
   (a) cancel the lease contract (Section 2A-505(1));
   (b) proceed respecting goods not identified to the lease contract (Section 2A-524);
   (c) withhold delivery of the goods and take possession of goods previously delivered (Section 2A-525);
   (d) stop delivery of the goods by any bailee (Section 2A-526);
   (e) dispose of the goods and recover damages (Section 2A-527), or retain the goods and recover damages (Section 2A-528), or in a proper case recover rent (Section 2A-529);
   (f) exercise any other rights or pursue any other remedies provided in the lease contract.

(2) If a lessor does not fully exercise a right or obtain a remedy to which the lessor is entitled under subsection (1), the lessor may recover the loss resulting in the ordinary course of events from the lessee's default as determined in any reasonable manner together with incidental damages, less expenses saved in consequence of the lessee's default.

(3) If a lessee is otherwise in default under a lease contract, the lessor may exercise the rights and pursue

the remedies provided in the lease contract, which may include a right to cancel the lease. In addition, unless otherwise provided in the lease contract:

   (a) if the default substantially impairs the value of the lease contract to the lessor, the lessor may exercise the rights and pursue and remedies provided in subsections (1) or (2); or

   (b) if the default does not substantially impair the value of the lease contract to the lessor, the lessor may recover as provided in subsection (2).

§2A-524. Lessor's Right to Identify Goods to Lease Contract.—

(1) A lessor aggrieved under Section 2A-523(1) may:

   (a) identify to the lease contract conforming goods not already identified if at the time the lessor learned of the default they were in the lessor's or the supplier's possession or control; and

   (b) dispose of goods (Section 2A-527(1)) that demonstrably have been intended for the particular lease contract even though those goods are unfinished.

(2) If the goods are unfinished, in the exercise of reasonable commercial judgment for the purposes of avoiding loss and of effective realization, an aggrieved lessor or the supplier may either complete manufacture and wholly identify the goods to the lease contract or cease manufacture and lease, sell, or otherwise dispose of the goods for scrap or salvage value or proceed in any other reasonable manner.

§2A-525. Lessor's Right to Possession of Goods.—

(1) If a lessor discovers the lessee to be insolvent, the lessor may refuse to deliver the goods.

(2) After a default by the lessee under the lease contract of the type described in Section 2A-523(1) or 2A-523(3)(a) or, if agreed, after other default by the lessee, the lessor has the right to take possession of the goods. If the lease contract so provides, the lessor may require the lessee to a semble the goods and make them available to the lessor at a place to be designated by the lessor which is reasonably convenient to both parties. Without removal, the lessor may render unusable any goods employed in trade or business, and may dispose of goods on the lessee's premises (Section 2A-527).

(3) The lessor may proceed under subsection (2) without judicial process if it can be done without breach of the peace or the lessor may proceed by action.

§2A-526. Lessor's Stoppage of Delivery in Transit or Otherwise.—

(1) A lessor may stop delivery of goods in the possession of a carrier or other bailee if the lessor discovers the lessee to be insolvent and may stop delivery of carload, truckload, planeload, or larger shipments of express or freight if the lessee repudiates or fails to make a payment due before delivery, whether for rent, security or otherwise under the lease contract, or for any other reason the lessor has a right to withhold or take possession of the goods.

(2) In pursuing its remedies under subsection (1), the lessor may stop delivery until

   (a) receipt of the goods by the lessee;

   (b) acknowledgment to the lessee by any bailee of the goods, except a carrier, that the bailee holds the goods for the lessee; or

   (c) such an acknowledgment to the lessee by a carrier via reshipment or as warehouseman.

(3) (a) To stop delivery, a lessor shall so notify as to enable the bailee by reasonable diligence to prevent delivery of the goods.

   (b) After notification, the bailee shall hold and deliver the goods according to the directions of the lessor, but the lessor is liable to the bailee for any ensuing charges or damages.

   (c) A carrier who has issued a nonnegotiable bill of lading is not obliged to obey a notification to stop received from a person other than the consignor.

§2A-527. Lessor's Rights to Dispose of Goods.—

(1) After a default by a lessee under the lease contract of the type described in Section 2A-523(1) or 2A-523(3)(a) or after the lessor refuses to deliver or takes possession of goods (Section 2A-525 or 2A-526), or, if agreed, after other default by a lessee, the lessor may dispose of the goods concerned or the undelivered balance thereof by lease, sale, or otherwise.

(2) Except as otherwise provided with respect to damages liquidated in the lease agreement (Section 2A-504) or otherwise determined pursuant to agreement of the parties (Sections 1-102(3) and 2A-503), if the disposition is by lease agreement substantially similar to the original lease agreement and the new lease agreement is made in good faith and in a commercially reasonable manner, the lessor may recover from the lessee as damages (i) accrued and unpaid rent as of the date of the commencement of the term of the new lease agreement, (ii) the present value, as of the same date, of the total rent for the then remaining lease term of the original lease agreement minus the present value, as of the same date, of the rent under the new lease agreement applicable to that period of the new lease term which is comparable to the then remaining term of the original lease agreement, and (iii) any incidental damages allowed under Section 2A-530, less expenses saved in consequence of the lessee's default.

(3) If the lessor's disposition is by lease agreement that for any reason does not qualify for treatment under subsection (2), or is by sale or otherwise, the lessor may recover from the lessee as if the lessor had elected not to dispose of the goods and Section 2A-528 governs.

(4) A subsequent buyer or lessee who buys or leases from the lessor in good faith for value as a result of a disposition under this section takes the goods free of the original lease contract and any rights of the original lessee even though the lessor fails to comply with one or more of the requirements of this Article.

(5) The lessor is not accountable to the lessee for any profit made on any disposition. A lessee who has rightfully rejected or justifiably revoked acceptance shall account to the lessor for any excess over the amount of the lessee's security interest (Section 2A-508(5)).

§2A-528. Lessor's Damages for Non-Acceptance, Failure to Pay, Repudiation, or Other Default.—

(1) Except as otherwise provided with respect to damages liquidated in the lease agreement (Section 2A-504) or otherwise determined pursuant to agreement of the parties (Sections 1-102(3) and 2A-503), if a lessor elects to retain the goods or a lessor elects to dispose of the goods and the disposition is by lease agreement that for any reason does not qualify for treatment under Section 2A-527(2), or is by sale or otherwise, the lessor may recover from the lessee as damages for a default of the type described in Section 2A523(1) or 2A-523(3)(a), or, if agreed, for other default of the lessee, (i) accrued and unpaid rent as of the date of default if the lessee has never taken possession of the goods, or, if the lessee has taken possession of the goods, as of the date the lessor repossesses the goods or an earlier date on which the lessee makes a tender of the goods to the lessor, (ii) the present value as of the date determined under clause (i) of the total rent for the then remaining lease term of the original lease agreement minus the present value as of the same date of the market rent at the place where the goods are located computed for the same lease term, and (iii) any incidental damages allowed under Section 2A-530, less expenses saved in consequence of the lessee's default.

(2) If the measure of damages provided in subsection (1) is inadequate to put a lessor in as good a position as performance would have, the measure of damages is the present value of the profit, including reasonable overhead, the lessor would have made from full performance by the lessee, together with any incidental damages allowed under Section 2A-530, due allowance for costs reasonably incurred and due credit for payments or proceeds of disposition.

§2A-529. Lessor's Action for the Rent.—

(1) After default by the lessee under the lease contract of the type described in Section 2A-523(1) or 2A-523(3)(a) or, if agreed, after other default by the lessee, if the lessor complies with subsection (2), the lessor may recover from the lessee as damages:

(a) for goods accepted by the lessee and not repossessed by or tendered to the lessor, and for conforming goods lost or damaged within a commercially reasonable time after risk of loss passes to the lessee (Section 2A-219), (i) accrued and unpaid rent as of the date of entry of judgment in favor of the lessor, (ii) the present value as of the same date of the rent for the then remaining lease term of the lease agreement, and (iii) any incidental damages allowed under Section 2A-530, less expenses saved in consequence of the lessee's default; and

(b) for goods identified to the lease contract if the lessor is unable after reasonable effort to dispose of them at a reasonable price or the circumstances reasonably indicate that effort will be unavailing, (i) accrued and unpaid rent as of the date of entry of judgment in favor of the lessor, (ii) the present value as of the same date of the rent for the then remaining lease term of the lease agreement, and (iii) any incidental damages allowed under Section 2A-530, less expenses saved in consequence of the lessee's default.

(2) Except as provided in subsection (3), the lessor shall hold for the lessee for the remaining lease term of the lease agreement any goods that have been identified to the lease contract and are in the lessor's control.

(3) The lessor may dispose of the goods at any time before collection of the judgment for damages obtained pursuant to subsection (1). If the disposition is before the end of the remaining lease term of the lease agreement, the lessor's recovery against the lessee for damages is governed by Section 2A-527 or Section 2A-528, and the lessor will cause an appropriate credit to be provided against a judgment for damages to the extent that the amount of the judgment exceeds the recovery available pursuant to Section 2A-527 or 2A-528.

(4) Payment of the judgment for damages obtained pursuant to subsection (1) entitles the lessee to the use and possession of the goods not then disposed of for the remaining lease term of and in accordance with the lease agreement.

(5) After a lessee has wrongfully rejected or revoked acceptance of goods, has failed to pay rent then due, or has repudiated (Section 2A-402), a lessor who is held not entitled to rent under this section must nevertheless be awarded damages for non-acceptance under Sections 2A-527 and 2A-528.

§2A-530. Lessor's Incidental Damages.— Incidental damages to an aggrieved lessor include any commercially reasonable charges, expenses, or commissions incurred in stopping delivery, in the transportation, care and cus-

tody of goods after the lessee's default, in connection with return or disposition of the goods, or otherwise resulting from the default.

§2A-531. Standing to Sue Third Parties for Injury to Goods.—

(1) If a third party so deals with goods that have been identified to a lease contract as to cause actionable injury to a party to the lease contract (a) the lessor has a right of action against the third party, and (b) the lessee also has a right of action against the third party if the lessee:
   (i)   has a security interest in the goods;
   (ii) has an insurable interest in the goods; or
   (iii) bears the risk of loss under the lease contract or has since the injury assumed that risk as against the lessor and the goods have been converted or destroyed.

(2) If at the time of the injury the party plaintiff did not bear the risk of loss as against the other party to the lease contract and there is no arrangement between them for disposition of the recovery, his [or her] suit or settlement, subject to his [or her] own interest, is as a fiduciary for the other party to the lease contract.

(3) Either party with the consent of the other may sue for the benefit of whom it may concern.

§2A-532. Lessor's Rights to Residual Interest.— In addition to any other recovery permitted by this Article or other law, the lessor may recover from the lessee an amount that will fully compensate the lessor for any loss of or damage to the lessor's residual interest in the goods caused by the default of the lessee.

Article 3: Negotiable Instruments (Revised 1990)

Part 1: General Provisions and Definitions

§3-101. Short Title.— This Article may be cited as Uniform Commercial Code—Negotiable Instruments.

§3-102. Subject Matter.—

(a) This Article applies to negotiable instruments. It does not apply to money, to payment orders governed by Article 4A, or to securities governed by Article 8.
(b) If there is conflict between this Article and Article 4 or 9, Articles 4 and 9 govern.
(c) Regulations of the Board of Governors of the Federal Reserve System and operating circulars of the Federal Reserve Banks supersede any inconsistent provision of this Article to the extent of the inconsistency.

Note: The previous version of Article 3, Commercial Paper, is found in the Instructor's Resource Guide. You may wish to photocopy it for your students' use.

§3-103. Definitions.—

(a) In this Article:
  (1) "Acceptor" means a drawee who has accepted a draft.
  (2) "Drawee" means a person ordered in a draft to make payment.
  (3) "Drawer" means a person who signs or is identified in a draft as a person ordering payment.
  (4) "Good faith" means honesty in fact and the observance of reasonable commercial standards of fair dealing.
  (5) "Maker" means a person who signs or is identified in a note as a person undertaking to pay.
  (6) "Order" means a written instruction to pay money signed by the person giving the instruction. The instruction may be addressed to any person, including the person giving the instruction, or to one or more persons jointly or in the alternative but not in succession. An authorization to pay is not an order unless the person authorized to pay is also instructed to pay.
  (7) "Ordinary care" in the case of a person engaged in business means observance of reasonable commercial standards, prevailing in the area in which the person is located, with respect to the business in which the person is engaged. In the case of a bank that takes an instrument for processing for collection or payment by automated means, reasonable commercial standards do not require the bank to examine the instrument if the failure to examine does not violate the bank's prescribed procedures and the bank's procedures do not vary unreasonably from general banking usage not disapproved by this Article or Article 4.
  (8) "Party" means a party to an instrument.
  (9) "Promise" means a written undertaking to pay money signed by the person undertaking to pay. An acknowledgment of an obligation by the obligor is not a promise unless the obligor also undertakes to pay the obligation.
  (10) "Prove" with respect to a fact means to meet the burden of establishing the fact (Section 1-201(8)).
  (11) "Remitter" means a person who purchases an instrument from its issuer if the instrument is payable to an identified person other than the purchaser.

(b) Other definitions applying to this Article and the sections in which they appear are:

"Acceptance"	Section 3-409
"Accommodated party"	Section 3-419
"Accommodation party"	Section 3-419

(c) The following definitions in other Articles apply to this Article:

(d) In addition, Article 1 contains general definitions and principles of construction and interpretation applicable throughout this Article.

§3-104. Negotiable Instrument.—

(a) Except as provided in subsections (c) and (d), "negotiable instrument" means an unconditional promise or order to pay a fixed amount of money, with or without interest or other charges described in the promise or order, if it:

   (1) is payable to bearer or to order at the time it is issued or first comes into possession of a holder;

   (2) is payable on demand or at a definite time; and

   (3) does not state any other undertaking or instruction by the person promising or ordering payment to do any act in addition to the payment of money, but the promise or order may contain (i) an undertaking or power to give, maintain, or protect collateral to secure payment, (ii) an authorization or power to the holder to confess judgment or realize on or dispose of collateral, or (iii) a waiver of the benefit of any law intended for the advantage or protection of an obligor.

(b) "Instrument" means a negotiable instrument.

(c) An order that meets all of the requirements of subsection (a), except paragraph (1), and otherwise falls within the definition of "check" in subsection (f) is a negotiable instrument and a check.

(d) A promise or order other than a check is not an instrument if, at the time it is issued or first comes into possession of a holder, it contains a conspicuous statement, however expressed, to the effect that the promise or order is not negotiable or is not an instrument governed by this Article.

(e) An instrument is a "note" if it is a promise and is a "draft" if it is an order. If an instrument falls within the definition of both "note" and "draft", a person entitled to enforce the instrument may treat it as either.

(f) "Check" means (i) a draft, other than a documentary draft, payable on demand and drawn on a bank or (ii) a cashier's check or teller's check. An instrument may be a check even though it is described on its face by another term, such as "money order".

(g) "Cashier's check" means a draft with respect to which the drawer and drawee are the same bank or branches of the same bank.

(h) "Teller's check" means a draft drawn by a bank (i) on another bank, or (ii) payable at or through a bank.

(i) "Traveler's check" means an instrument that (i) is payable on demand, (ii) is drawn on or payable at or through a bank, (iii) is designated by the term "traveler's check" or by a substantially similar term, and (iv) requires, as a condition to payment, a countersignature by a person whose specimen signature appears on the instrument.

(j) "Certificate of deposit" means an instrument containing an acknowledgment by a bank that a sum of money has been received by the bank and a promise by the bank to repay the sum of money. A certificate of deposit is a note of the bank.

§3-105. Issue of Instrument.—

(a) "Issue" means the first delivery of an instrument by the maker or drawer, whether to a holder or non-holder, for the purpose of giving rights on the instrument to any person.

(b) An unissued instrument, or an unissued incomplete instrument that is completed, is binding on the maker or drawer, but nonissuance is a defense. An instrument that is conditionally issued or is issued for a special purpose is binding on the maker or drawer, but failure of the condition or special purpose to be fulfilled is a defense.

(c) "Issuer" applies to issued and unissued instruments and means a maker or drawer of an instrument.

§3-106. Unconditional Promise or Order.—

(a) Except as provided in this section, for the purposes of Section 3-104(a), a promise or order is unconditional unless it states (i) an express condition to payment, (ii) that the promise or order is subject to or governed by another writing, or (iii) that rights or obligations with respect to the promise or order are stated in another writing. A reference to another writing does not of itself make the promise or order conditional.

(b) A promise or order is not made conditional (i) by a reference to another writing for a statement of rights with respect to collateral, prepayment, or acceleration, or (ii) because payment is limited to resort to a particular fund or source.

(c) If a promise or order requires, as a condition to payment, a countersignature by a person whose specimen signature appears on the promise or order, the condition does not make the promise or order conditional for the purposes of Section 3-104(a). If the person whose specimen signature appears on an instrument fails to countersign the instrument, the failure to countersign is a defense to the obligation of the issuer, but the failure does not prevent a transferee of the instrument from becoming a holder of the instrument.

(d) If a promise or order at the time it is issued or first comes into possession of a holder contains a statement, required by applicable statutory or administrative law, to the effect that the rights of a holder or transferee are subject to claims or defenses that the issuer could assert the original payee, the promise or order is not thereby made conditional for the purposes of Section 3-104(a); but if the promise or order is an instrument, there cannot be a holder in due course of the instrument.

§3-107. Instrument Payable in Foreign Money.—

Unless the instrument otherwise provides, an instrument that states the amount payable in foreign money may be paid in the foreign money or in an equivalent amount in dollars calculated by using the current bank-offered spot rate at the place of payment for the purchase of dollars on the day on which the instrument is paid.

§3-108. Payable on Demand or at Definite Time.—

(a) A promise or order is "payable on demand" if it (i) states that it is payable on demand or at sight, or otherwise indicates that it is payable at the will of the holder, or (ii) does not state any time of payment.

(b) A promise or order is "payable at a definite time" if it is payable on elapse of a definite period of time after sight or acceptance or at a fixed date or dates or at a time or times readily ascertainable at the time the promise or order is issued, subject to rights of (i) prepayment, (ii) acceleration, (iii) extension at the option of the holder, or (iv) extension to a further definite time at the option of the maker or acceptor or automatically upon or after a specified act or event.

(c) If an instrument, payable at a fixed date, is also payable upon demand made before the fixed date, the instrument is payable on demand until the fixed date and, if demand for payment is not made before that date, becomes payable at a definite time on the fixed date.

§3-109. Payable to Bearer or to Order.—

(a) A promise or order is payable to bearer if it:
(1) states that it is payable to bearer or to the order of bearer or otherwise indicates that the person in possession of the promise or order is entitled to payment;
(2) does not state a payee; or
(3) states that it is payable to or to the order of cash or otherwise indicates that it is not payable to an identified person.

(b) A promise or order that is not payable to bearer is payable to order if it is payable (i) to the order of an identified person or (ii) to an identified person or order. A promise or order that is payable to order is payable to the identified person.

(c) An instrument payable to bearer may become payable to an identified person if it is specially indorsed pursuant to Section 3-205(a). An instrument payable to an identified person may become payable to bearer if it is indorsed in blank pursuant to Section 3-205(b).

§3-110. Identification of Person to Whom Instrument is Payable.—

(a) The person to whom an instrument is initially payable is determined by the intent of the person, whether or not authorized, signing as, or in the name or behalf of, the issuer of the instrument. The instrument is payable to the person intended by the signer even if that person is identified in the instrument by a name or other identification that is not that of the intended person. If more than one person signs in the name or behalf of the issuer of an instrument and all the signers do not intend the same person as payee, the instrument is payable to any person intended by one or more of the signers.

(b) If the signature of the issuer of an instrument is made by automated means, such as a check-writing machine, the payee of the instrument is determined by the intent of the person who supplied the name or identification of the payee, whether or not authorized to do so.

(c) A person to whom an instrument is payable may be identified in any way, including by name, identifying number, office, or account number. For the purpose of determining the holder of an instrument, the following rules apply:

  (1) If an instrument is payable to an account and the account is identified only by number, the instrument is payable to the person to whom the account is payable. If an instrument is payable to an account identified by number and by the name of a person, the instrument is payable to the named person, whether or not that person is the owner of the account identified by number.

  (2) If an instrument is payable to:

    (i) a trust, an estate, or a person described as trustee or representative of a trust or estate, the instrument is payable to the trustee, the representative, or a successor of either, whether or not the beneficiary or estate is also named;

    (ii) a person described as agent or similar representative of a named or identified person, the instrument is payable to the represented person, the representative, or a successor of the representative;

    (iii) a fund or organization that is not a legal entity, the instrument is payable to a representative of the members of the fund or organization; or

    (iv) an office or to a person described as holding an office, the instrument is payable to the named person, the incumbent of the office, or a successor to the incumbent.

(d) If an instrument is payable to two or more persons alternatively, it is payable to any of them and may be negotiated, discharged, or enforced by any or all of them in possession of the instrument. If an instrument is payable to two or more persons not alternatively, it is payable to all of them and may be negotiated, discharged, or enforced only by all of them. If an instrument payable to two or more persons is ambiguous as to whether it is payable to the persons alternatively, the instrument is payable to the persons alternatively.

§3-111. Place of Payment.— Except as otherwise provided for items in Article 4, an instrument is payable at the place of payment stated in the instrument. If no place of payment is stated, an instrument is payable at the address of the drawee or maker stated in the instrument. If no address is stated, the place of payment is the place of business of the drawee or maker. If a drawee or maker has more than one place of business, the place of payment is any place of business of the drawee or maker chosen by the person entitled to enforce the instrument. If the drawee or maker has no place of business, the place of payment is the residence of the drawee or maker.

§3-112. Interest.—

(a) Unless otherwise provided in the instrument, (i) an instrument is not payable with interest, and (ii) interest on an interest-bearing instrument is payable from the date of the instrument.

(b) Interest may be stated in an instrument as a fixed or variable amount of money or it may be expressed as a fixed or variable rate or rates. The amount or rate of interest may be stated or described in the instrument in any manner and may require reference to information not contained in the instrument. If an instrument provides for interest, but the amount of interest payable cannot be ascertained from the description, interest is payable at the judgment rate in effect at the place of payment of the instrument and at the time interest first accrues.

§3-113. Date of Instrument.—

(a) An instrument may be antedated or postdated. The date stated determines the time of payment if the instrument is payable at a fixed period after date. Except as provided in Section 4-401(c), an instrument payable on demand is not payable before the date of the instrument.

(b) If an instrument is undated, its date is the date of its issue or, in the case of an unissued instrument, the date it first comes into possession of a holder.

§3-114. Contradictory Terms of Instrument.— If an instrument contains contradictory terms, typewritten terms prevail over printed terms, handwritten terms prevail over both, and words prevail over numbers.

§3-115. Incomplete Instrument.—

(a) "Incomplete instrument" means a signed writing, whether or not issued by the signer, the contents of which show at the time of signing that it is incomplete but that the signer intended it to be completed by the addition of words or numbers.

(b) Subject to subsection (c), if an incomplete instrument is an instrument under Section 3-104, it may be enforced according to its terms if it is not completed, or according to its terms as augmented by completion. If an incomplete instrument is not an instrument under Section 3-104, but, after completion, the requirements of Section 3-104 are met, the instrument may be enforced according to its terms as augmented by completion.

(c) If words or numbers are added to an incomplete instrument without authority of the signer, there is an alteration of the incomplete instrument under Section 3-407.

(d) The burden of establishing that words or numbers were added to an incomplete instrument without authority of the signer is on the person asserting the lack of authority.

§3-116. Joint and Several Liability; Contribution.—

(a) Except as otherwise provided in the instrument, two or more persons who have the same liability on an instrument as makers, drawers, acceptors, indorsers who indorse as joint payees, or anomalous indorsers are jointly and severally liable in the capacity in which they sign.

(b) Except as provided in Section 3-419(e) or by agreement of the affected parties, a party having joint and several liability who pays the instrument is entitled to receive from any party having the same joint and several liability contribution in accordance with applicable law.

(c) Discharge of one party having joint and several liability by a person entitled to enforce the instrument does not affect the right under subsection (b) of a party having the same joint and several liability to receive contribution from the party discharged.

§3-117. Other Agreements Affecting Instrument.—

Subject to applicable law regarding exclusion of proof of contemporaneous or previous agreements, the obligation of a party to an instrument to pay the instrument may be modified, supplemented, or nullified by a separate agreement of the obligor and a person entitled to enforce the instrument, if the instrument is issued or the obligation is incurred in reliance on the agreement or as part of the same transaction giving rise to the agreement. To the extent an obligation is modified, supplemented, or nullified by an agreement under this section, the agreement is a defense to the obligation.

§3-118. Statute of Limitations.—

(a) Except as provided in subsection (e), an action to enforce the obligation of a party to pay a note payable at a definite time must be commenced within six years after the due date or dates stated in the note or, if a due date is accelerated, within six years after the accelerated due date.

(b) Except as provided in subsection (d) or (e), if demand for payment is made to the maker of a note payable on demand, an action to enforce the obligation of a party to pay the note must be commenced within six years after the demand. If no demand for payment is made to the maker, an action to enforce the note is barred if neither principal nor interest on the note has been paid for a continuous period of 10 years.

(c) Except as provided in subsection (d), an action to enforce the obligation of a party to an unaccepted draft to pay the draft must be commenced within three years after dishonor of the draft or 10 years after the date of the draft, whichever period expires first.

(d) An action to enforce the obligation of the acceptor of a certified check or the issuer of a teller's check, cashier's check, or traveler's check must be commenced within three years after demand for payment is made to the acceptor or issuer, as the case may be.

(e) An action to enforce the obligation of a party to a certificate of deposit to pay the instrument must be commenced within six years after demand for payment is

made to the maker, but if the instrument states a due date and the maker is not required to pay before that date, the six-year period begins when a demand for payment is in effect and the due date has passed.

(f) An action to enforce the obligation of a party to pay an accepted draft, other than a certified check, must be commenced (i) within six years after the due date or dates stated in the draft or acceptance if the obligation of the acceptor is payable at a definite time, or (ii) within six years after the date of the acceptance if the obligation of the acceptor is payable on demand.

(g) Unless governed by other law regarding claims for indemnity or contribution, an action (i) for conversion of an instrument, for money had and received, or like action based on conversion, (ii) for breach of warranty, or (iii) to enforce an obligation, duty, or right arising under this Article and not governed by this section must be commenced within three years after the [cause of action] accrues.

§3-119. Notice of Right to Defend Action.—
In an action for breach of an obligation for which a third person is answerable over pursuant to this Article or Article 4, the defendant may give the third person written notice of the litigation, and the person notified may then give similar notice to any other person who is answerable over. If the notice states (i) that the person notified may come in and defend and (ii) that failure to do so will bind the person notified in an action later brought by the person giving the notice as to any determination of fact common to the two litigations, the person notified is so bound unless after reasonable receipt of the notice the person notified does come in and defend.

Part 2: Negotiation, Transfer, and Indorsement

§3-201. Negotiation.—

(a) "Negotiation" means a transfer of possession, whether voluntary or involuntary, of an instrument by a person other than the issuer to a person who thereby becomes its holder.

(b) Except for negotiation by a remitter, if an instrument is payable to an identified person, negotiation requires transfer of possession of the instrument and its indorsement by the holder. If an instrument is payable to bearer, it may be negotiated by transfer of possession alone.

§3-202. Negotiation Subject to Rescission.—

(a) Negotiation is effective even if obtained (i) from an infant, a corporation exceeding its powers, or a person without capacity, (ii) by fraud, duress, or mistake, or (iii) in breach of duty or as part of an illegal transaction.

(b) To the extent permitted by other law, negotiation may be rescinded or may be subject to other remedies, but those remedies may not be asserted against a subsequent holder in due course or a person paying the instrument in good faith and without knowledge of facts that are a basis for rescission or other remedy.

§3-203. Transfer of Instrument; Rights Acquired by Transfer.—

(a) An instrument is transferred when it is delivered by a person other than its issuer for the purpose of giving to the person receiving delivery the right to enforce the instrument.

(b) Transfer of an instrument, whether or not the transfer is a negotiation, vests in the transferee any right of the transferor to enforce the instrument, including any right as a holder in due course, but the transferee cannot acquire rights of a holder in due course by a transfer, directly or indirectly, from a holder in due course if the transferee engaged in fraud or illegality affecting the instrument.

(c) Unless otherwise agreed, if an instrument is transferred for value and the transferee does not become a holder because of lack of indorsement by the transferor, the transferee has a specially enforceable right to the unqualified indorsement of the transferor, but negotiation of the instrument does not occur until the indorsement is made.

(d) If a transferor purports to transfer less than the entire instrument, negotiation of the instrument does not occur. The transferee obtains no rights under this Article, and has only the rights of a partial assignee.

§3-204. Indorsement.—

(a) "Indorsement" means a signature, other than that of a signer as maker, drawer, or acceptor, that alone or accompanied by other words is made on an instrument for the purpose of (i) negotiating the instrument, (ii) restricting payment of the instrument, or (iii) incurring indorser's liability on the instrument, but regardless of the intent of the signer, a signature and its accompanying words is an indorsement unless the accompanying words, terms of the instrument, place of the signature, or other circumstances unambiguously indicate that the signature was made for a purpose other than indorsement. For the purpose of determining whether a signature is made on an instrument, a paper affixed to the instrument is a part of the instrument.

(b) "Indorser" means a person who makes an indorsement.

(c) For the purpose of determining whether the transferee of an instrument is a holder, an indorsement that transfers a security interest in the instrument is effective as an unqualified indorsement of the instrument.

(d) If an instrument is payable to a holder under a name that is not the name of the holder, indorsement may be made by the holder in the name stated in the instrument or in the holder's name or both, but

signature in both names may be required by a person paying or taking the instrument for value or collection.

§3-205. Special Indorsement; Blank Indorsement; Anomalous Indorsement.—

(a) If an indorsement is made by the holder of an instrument, whether payable to an identified person or payable to bearer, and the indorsement identifies a person to whom it makes the instrument payable, it is a "special indorsement". When specially indorsed, an instrument becomes payable to the identified person and may be negotiated only by the indorsement of that person. The principles stated in Section 3-110 apply to special indorsements.

(b) If an indorsement is made by the holder of an instrument and it is not a special indorsement, it is a "blank indorsement". When indorsed in blank, an instrument becomes payable to bearer and may be negotiated by transfer of possession alone until specially indorsed.

(c) The holder may convert a blank indorsement that consists only of a signature into a special indorsement by writing, above the signature of the indorser, words identifying the person to whom the instrument is made payable.

(d) "Anomalous indorsement" means an indorsement made by a person who is not the holder of the instrument. An anomalous indorsement does not affect the manner in which the instrument may be negotiated.

§3-206. Restrictive Indorsement.—

(a) An indorsement limiting payment to a particular person or otherwise prohibiting further transfer or negotiation of the instrument is not effective to prevent further transfer or negotiation of the instrument.

(b) An indorsement stating a condition to the right of the indorsee to receive payment does not affect the right of the indorsee to enforce the instrument. A person paying the instrument or taking it for value or collection may disregard the condition, and the rights and liabilities of that person are not affected by whether the condition has been fulfilled.

(c) If an instrument bears an indorsement (i) described in Section 4-201(b), or (ii) in blank or to a particular bank using the words "for deposit", "for collection", or other words indicating a purpose of having the instrument collected by a bank for the indorser or for a particular account, the following rules apply:

(1) A person, other than a bank, who purchases the instrument when so indorsed converts the instrument unless the amount paid for the instrument is received by the indorser or applied consistently with the indorsement.

(2) A depositary bank that purchases the instrument or takes it for collection when so indorsed converts the instrument unless the amount paid by the bank with respect to the instrument is

received by the indorser or applied consistently with the indorsement.

 (3) A payor bank that is also the depositary bank or that takes the instrument for immediate payment over the counter from a person other than a collecting bank converts the instrument unless the proceeds of the instrument are received by the indorser or applied consistently with the indorsement.

 (4) Except as otherwise provided in paragraph (3), a payor bank or intermediary bank may disregard the indorsement and is not liable if the proceeds of the instrument are not received by the indorser or applied consistently with the indorsement.

(d) Except for an indorsement covered by subsection (c), if an instrument bears an indorsement using words to the effect that payment is to be made to the indorsee as agent, trustee, or other fiduciary for the benefit of the indorser or another person, the following rules apply:

 (1) Unless there is notice of breach of fiduciary duty as provided in Section 3-307, a person who purchases the instrument from the indorsee or takes the instrument from the indorsee for collection or payment may pay the proceeds of payment or the value given for the instrument to the indorsee without regard to whether the indorsee violates a fiduciary duty to the indorser.

 (2) A subsequent transferee of the instrument or person who pays the instrument is neither given notice nor otherwise affected by the restriction in the indorsement unless the transferee or payor knows that the fiduciary dealt with the instrument or its proceeds in breach of fiduciary duty.

(e) The presence on an instrument of an indorsement to which this section applies does not prevent a purchaser of the instrument from becoming a holder in due course of the instrument unless the purchaser is a converter under subsection (c) or has notice or knowledge of breach of fiduciary duty as stated in subsection (d).

(f) In an action to enforce the obligation of a party to pay the instrument, the obligor has a defense if payment would violate an indorsement to which this section applies and the payment is not permitted by this section.

§3-207. Reacquisition.— Reacquisition of an instrument occurs if it is transferred to a former holder, by negotiation or otherwise. A former holder who reacquires the instrument may cancel indorsements made after the reacquirer first became a holder of the instrument. If the cancellation causes the instrument to be payable to the reacquirer or to bearer, the reacquirer may negotiate the instrument. An indorser whose indorsement is canceled is discharged, and the discharge is effective against any subsequent holder.

Part 3: Enforcement of Instruments

§3-301. Person Entitled to Enforce Instrument.— "Person entitled to enforce" an instrument means (i) the holder of the instrument, (ii) a nonholder in possession of the instrument who has the rights of a holder, or (iii) a person not in possession of the instrument who is entitled to enforce the instrument pursuant to Section 3-309 or 3-418(d). A person may be a person entitled to enforce the instrument even though the person is not the owner of the instrument or is in wrongful possession of the instrument.

§3-302. Holder in Due Course.—

(a) Subject to subsection (c) and Section 3106(d), "holder in due course" means the holder of an instrument if:

 (1) the instrument when issued or negotiated to the holder does not bear such apparent evidence of forgery or alteration or is not otherwise so irregular or incomplete as to call into question its authenticity; and

 (2) the holder took the instrument (i) for value, (ii) in good faith, (iii) without notice that the instrument is overdue or has been dishonored or that there is an uncured default with respect to payment of another instrument issued as part of the same series, (iv) without notice that the instrument contains an unauthorized signature or has been altered, (v) without notice of any claim to the instrument described in Section 3-306, and (vi) without notice that any party has a defense or claim in recoupment described in Section 3-305(a).

(b) Notice of discharge of a party, other than discharge in an insolvency proceeding, is not notice of a defense under subsection (a), but discharge is effective against a person who became a holder in due course with notice of the discharge. Public filing or recording of a document does not of itself constitute notice of a defense, claim in recoupment, or claim to the instrument.

(c) Except to the extent a transferor or predecessor in interest has rights as a holder in due course, a person does not acquire rights of a holder in due course of an instrument taken (i) by legal process or by purchase in an execution, bankruptcy, or creditor's sale or similar proceeding, (ii) by purchase as part of a bulk transaction not in ordinary course of business of the transferor, or (iii) as the successor in interest to an estate or other organization.

(d) If, under Section 3-303(a)(1), the promise of performance that is the consideration for an instrument has been partially performed, the holder may assert rights as a holder in due course of the instrument only to the fraction of the amount payable under the instrument equal to the value of the partial performance divided by the value of the promised performance.

(e) If (i) the person entitled to enforce an instrument has only a security interest in the instrument and (ii) the person obliged to pay the instrument has a defense, claim in recoupment, or claim to the instrument that may be asserted against the person who granted the security interest, the person entitled to enforce the instrument may assert rights as a holder in due course only to an amount payable under the instrument which, at the time of enforcement of the instrument, does not exceed the amount of the unpaid obligation secured.

(f) To be effective, notice must be received at a time and in a manner that gives a reasonable opportunity to act on it.

(g) This section is subject to any law limiting status as a holder in due course in particular classes of transactions.

§3-303. Value and Consideration.—

(a) An instrument is issued or transferred for value if:
  (1) the instrument is issued or transferred for a promise of performance, to the extent the promise has been performed;
  (2) the transferee acquires a security interest or other lien in the instrument other than a lien obtained by judicial proceeding;
  (3) the instrument is issued or transferred as payment of, or as security for, an antecedent claim against any person, whether or not the claim is due;
  (4) the instrument is issued or transferred in exchange for a negotiable instrument; or
  (5) the instrument is issued or transferred in exchange for the incurring of an irrevocable obligation to a third party by the person taking the instrument.

(b) "Consideration" means any consideration sufficient to support a simple contract. The drawer or maker of an instrument has a defense if the instrument is issued without consideration. If an instrument is issued for a promise of performance, the issuer has a defense to the extent performance of the promise is due and the promise has not been performed. If an instrument is issued for value as stated in subsection (a), the instrument is also issued for consideration.

§3-304. Overdue Instrument.—

(a) An instrument payable on demand becomes overdue at the earliest of the following times:
  (1) on the day after the day demand for payment is duly made;
  (2) if the instrument is a check, 90 days after its date; or
  (3) if the instrument is not a check, when the instrument has been outstanding for a period of time after its date which is unreasonably long under the circumstances of the particular case in light of the nature of the instrument and usage of the trade.

(b) With respect to an instrument payable at a definite time the following rules apply:
  (1) If the principal is payable in installments and a

due date has not been accelerated, the instrument becomes overdue upon default under the instrument for nonpayment of an installment, and the instrument remains overdue until the default is cured.
  (2) If the principal is not payable in installments and the due date has not been accelerated, the instrument becomes overdue on the day after the due date.
  (3) If a due date with respect to principal has been accelerated, the instrument becomes overdue on the day after the accelerated due date.

(c) Unless the due date of principal has been accelerated, an instrument does not become overdue if there is default in payment of interest but no default in payment of principal.

§3-305. Defenses and Claims in Recoupment.—

(a) Except as stated in subsection (b), the right to enforce the obligation of a party to pay an instrument is subject to the following:
  (1) a defense of the obligor based on (i) infancy of the obligor to the extent it is a defense to a simple contract, (ii) duress, lack of legal capacity, or illegality of the transaction which, under other law, nullifies the obligation of the obligor, (iii) fraud that induced the obligor to sign the instrument with neither knowledge nor reasonable opportunity to learn of its character or its essential terms, or (iv) discharge of the obligor in insolvency proceedings;
  (2) defense of the obligor stated in another section of this Article or a defense of the obligor that would be available if the person entitled to enforce the instrument were enforcing a right to payment under a simple contract; and
  (3) a claim in recoupment of the obligor against the original payee of the instrument if the claim arose from the transaction that gave rise to the instrument; but the claim of the obligor may be asserted against a transferee of the instrument only to reduce the amount owing on the instrument at the time the action is brought.

(b) The right of a holder in due course to enforce the obligation of a party to pay the instrument is subject to defenses of the obligor stated in subsection (a)(1), but is not subject to defenses of the obligor stated in subsection (a)(2) or claims in recoupment stated in subsection (a)(3) against a person other than the holder.

(c) Except as stated in subsection (d), in an action to enforce the obligation of a party to pay the instrument, the obligor may not assert against the person entitled to enforce the instrument a defense, claim in recoupment, or claim to the instrument (Section 3-306) of another person, but the other person's claim to the instrument may be asserted by the obligor if the other person is joined in the action and personally asserts the claim against the person entitled to enforce the instrument. An obligor is not obliged to pay the instrument if the person seeking enforcement of the instrument does not have rights of a holder in due course and the obligor proves that the instrument is a lost or stolen instrument.

(d) In an action to enforce the obligation of an accommodation party to pay an instrument, the accommodation party may assert against the person entitled to enforce the instrument any defense or claim in recoupment under subsection (a) that the accommodated party could assert against the person entitled to enforce the instrument, except the defenses of discharge in insolvency proceedings, infancy, and lack of legal capacity.

§3-306. Claims to an Instrument.—

A person taking an instrument, other than a person having rights of a holder in due course, is subject to a claim of a property or possessory right in the instrument or its proceeds, including a claim to rescind a negotiation and to recover the instrument or its proceeds. A person having rights of a holder in due course takes free of the claim to the instrument.

§3-307. Notice of Breach of Fiduciary Duty.—

(a) In this section:
  (1) "Fiduciary" means an agent, trustee, partner, corporate officer or director, or other representative owing a fiduciary duty with respect to an instrument.
  (2) "Represented person" means the principal, beneficiary, partnership, corporation, or other person to whom the duty stated in paragraph (1) is owed.
(b) If (i) an instrument is taken from a fiduciary for payment or collection or for value, (ii) the taker has knowledge of the fiduciary status of the fiduciary, and (iii) the represented person makes a claim to the instrument or its proceeds on the basis that the transaction of the fiduciary is a breach of fiduciary duty, the following rules apply:
  (1) Notice of breach of fiduciary duty by the fiduciary is notice of the claim of the represented person.
  (2) In the case of an instrument payable to the represented person or the fiduciary as such, the taker has notice of the breach of fiduciary duty if the instrument is (i) taken in payment of or as security for a debt known by the taker to be the personal debt of the fiduciary, (ii) taken in a transaction known by the taker to be for the personal benefit of the fiduciary, or (iii) deposited to an account other than an account of the fiduciary, as such, or an account of the represented person.
  (3) If an instrument is issued by the represented person or the fiduciary as such, and made payable to the fiduciary personally, the taker does not have notice of the breach of fiduciary duty unless the taker knows of the breach of fiduciary duty.
  (4) If an instrument is issued by the represented person or the fiduciary as such, to the taker as payee, the taker has notice of the breach of fiduciary duty if the instrument is (i) taken in payment of or as security for a debt known by the taker to be the personal debt of the fiduciary, (ii) taken in a transaction known by the taker to be for the personal benefit of the fiduciary, or (iii) deposited to an account other than an account of the fiduciary, as such, or an account of the represented person.

§3-308. Proof of Signatures and Status as Holder in Due Course.—

(a) In an action with respect to an instrument, the authenticity of, and authority to make, each signature on the instrument is admitted unless specifically denied in the pleadings. If the validity of a signature is denied in the pleadings, the burden of establishing validity is on the person claiming validity, but the signature is presumed to be authentic and authorized unless the action is to enforce the liability of the purported signer and the signer is dead or incompetent at the time of trial of the issue of validity of the signature. If an action to enforce the instrument is brought against a person as the undisclosed principal of a person who signed the instrument as a party to the instrument, the plaintiff has the burden of establishing that the defendant is liable on the instrument as a represented person under Section 3-402(a).
(b) If the validity of signatures is admitted or proved and there is compliance with subsection (a), a plaintiff producing the instrument is entitled to payment if the plaintiff proves entitlement to enforce the instrument under Section 3-301, unless the defendant proves a defense or claim in recoupment. If a defense or claim in recoupment is proved, the right to payment of the plaintiff is subject to the defense or claim, except to the extent the plaintiff proves that the plaintiff has rights of a holder in due course which are not subject to the defense or claim.

§3-309. Enforcement of Lost, Destroyed, or Stolen Instrument.—

(a) A person not in possession of an instrument is entitled to enforce the instrument if (i) the person was in possession of the instrument and entitled to enforce it when loss of possession occurred, (ii) the loss of possession was not the result of a transfer by the person or a lawful seizure, and (iii) the person cannot reasonably obtain possession of the instrument because the instrument was destroyed, its whereabouts cannot be determined, or it is in the wrongful possession of an unknown person or a person that cannot be found or is not amenable to service of process.
(b) A person seeking enforcement of an instrument

under subsection (a) must prove the terms of the instrument and the person's right to enforce the instrument. If that proof is made, Section 3-308 applies to the case as if the person seeking enforcement had produced the instrument. The court may not enter judgment in favor of the person seeking enforcement unless it finds that the person required to pay the instrument is adequately protected against loss that might occur by reason of a claim by another person to enforce the instrument. Adequate protection may be provided by any reasonable means.

§3-310. Effect of Instrument on Obligation for Which Taken.—

(a) Unless otherwise agreed, if a certified check, cashier's check, or teller's check is taken for an obligation, the obligation is discharged to the same extent discharge would result if an amount of money equal to the amount of the instrument were taken in payment of the obligation. Discharge of the obligation does not affect any liability that the obligor may have as an indorser of the instrument.

(b) Unless otherwise agreed and except as provided in subsection (a), if a note or an uncertified check is taken for an obligation, the obligation is suspended to the same extent the obligation would be discharged if an amount of money equal to the amount of the instrument were taken, and the following rules apply:

(1) In the case of an uncertified check, suspension of the obligation continues until dishonor of the check or until it is paid or certified. Payment or certification of the check results in discharge of the obligation to the extent of the amount of the check.

(2) In the case of a note, suspension of the obligation continues until dishonor of the note or until it is paid. Payment of the note results in discharge of the obligation to the extent of the payment.

(3) Except as provided in paragraph (4), if the check or note is dishonored and the obligee of the obligation for which the instrument was taken is the person entitled to enforce the instrument, the obligee may enforce either the instrument or the obligation. In the case of an instrument of a third person which is negotiated to the obligee by the obligor, discharge of the obligor on the instrument also discharges the obligation.

(4) If the person entitled to enforce the instrument taken for an obligation is a person other than the obligee, the obligee may not enforce the obligation to the extent the obligation is suspended. If the obligee is the person entitled to enforce the instrument but no longer has possession of it because it was lost, stolen, or destroyed, the obligation may not be enforced to the extent of the amount payable on the instrument, and to that extent the obligee's rights against the obligor are

limited to enforcement of the instrument.

(c) If an instrument other than one described in subsection (a) or (b) is taken for an obligation, the effect is (i) that stated in subsection (a) if the instrument is one on which a bank is liable as maker or acceptor, or (ii) that stated in subsection (b) in any other case.

§3-311. Accord and Satisfaction by Use of Instrument.—

(a) If a person against whom a claim is asserted proves that (i) that person in good faith tendered an instrument to the claimant as full satisfaction of the claim, (ii) the amount of the claim was unliquidated or subject to a bona fide dispute, and (iii) the claimant obtained payment of the instrument, the following subsections apply.

(b) Unless subsection (c) applies, the claim is discharged if the person against whom the claim is asserted proves that the instrument or an accompanying written communication contained a conspicuous statement to the effect that the instrument was tendered as full satisfaction of the claim.

(c) Subject to subsection (d), a claim is not discharged under subsection (b) if either of the following applies:

(1) The claimant, if an organization, proves that (i) within a reasonable time before the tender, the claimant sent a conspicuous statement to the person against whom the claim is asserted that communications concerning disputed debts, including an instrument tendered as full satisfaction of a debt, are to be sent to a designated person, office, or place, and (ii) the instrument or accompanying communication was not received by that designated person, office, or place.

(2) The claimant, whether or not an organization, proves that within 90 days after payment of the instrument, the claimant tendered repayment of the amount of the instrument to the person against whom the claim is asserted. This paragraph does not apply if the claimant is an organization that sent a statement complying with paragraph (1)(i).

(d) A claim is discharged if the person against whom the claim is asserted proves that within a reasonable time before collection of the instrument was initiated, the claimant, or an agent of the claimant having direct responsibility with respect to the disputed obligation, knew that the instrument was tendered in full satisfaction of the claim.

§3-312. Lost, Destroyed, or Stolen Cashier's Check, Teller's Check, or Certified Check.—

(a) In this section:

(1) "Check" means a cashier's check, teller's check, or certified check.

(2) "Claimant" means a person who claims the

right to receive the amount of a cashier's check, teller's check, or certified check that was lost, destroyed, or stolen.

(3) "Declaration of loss" means a written statement, made under penalty of perjury, to the effect that (i) the declarer lost possession of a check, (ii) the declarer is the drawer or payee of the check, in the case of a certified check, or the remitter or payee of the check, in the case of a cashier's check or teller's check, (iii) the loss of possession was not the result of a transfer by the declarer or a lawful seizure, and (iv) the declarer cannot reasonably obtain possession of the check because the check was destroyed, its whereabouts cannot be determined, or it is in the wrongful possession of an unknown person or a person that cannot be found or is not amenable to service of process.

(4) "Obligated bank" means the issuer of a cashier's check or teller's check or the acceptor of a certified check.

(b) A claimant may assert a claim to the amount of a check by a communication to the obligated bank describing the check with reasonable certainty and requesting payment of the amount of the check, if (i) the claimant is the drawer or payee of a certified check or the remitter or payee of a cashier's check or teller's check, (ii) the communication contains or is accompanied by a declaration of loss of the claimant with respect to the check, (iii) the communication is received at a time and in a manner affording the bank a reasonable time to act on it before the check is paid, and (iv) the claimant provides reasonable identification if requested by the obligated bank. Delivery of a declaration of loss is a warranty of the truth of the statements made in the declaration. If a claim is asserted in compliance with this subsection, the following rules apply:

(1) The claim becomes enforceable at the later of (i) the time the claim is asserted, or (ii) the 90th day following the date of the check, in the case of a cashier's check or teller's check, or the 90th day following the date of the acceptance, in the case of a certified check.

(2) Until the claim becomes enforceable, it has no legal effect and the obligated bank may pay the check or, in the case of a teller's check, may permit the drawee to pay the check. Payment to a person entitled to enforce the check discharges all liability of the obligated bank with respect to the check.

(3) If the claim becomes enforceable before the check is presented for payment, the obligated bank is not obliged to pay the check.

(4) When the claim becomes enforceable, the obligated bank becomes obliged to pay the amount of the check to the claimant if payment of the check has not been made to a person entitled to enforce the check. Subject to Section 4-302(a)(1), payment to the claimant discharges all liability of the obligated bank with respect to the check.

(c) If the obligated bank pays the amount of a check to a claimant under subsection (b)(4) and the check is presented for payment by a person having rights of a holder in due course, the claimant is obliged to (i) refund the payment to the obligated bank if the check is paid, or (ii) pay the amount of the check to the person having rights of a holder in due course if the check is dishonored.

(d) If a claimant has the right to assert a claim under subsection (b) and is also a person entitled to enforce a cashier's check, teller's check, or certified check which is lost, destroyed, or stolen, the claimant may assert rights with respect to the check either under this section or Section 3-309.

Part 4: Liability of Parties

§3-401. Signature.—

(a) A person is not liable on an instrument unless (i) the person signed the instrument, or (ii) the person is represented by an agent or representative who signed the instrument and the signature is binding on the represented person under Section 3-402.

(b) A signature may be made (i) manually or by means of a device or machine, and (ii) by the use of any name, including a trade or assumed name, or by a word, mark, or symbol executed or adopted by a person with present intention to authenticate a writing.

§3-402. Signature by Representative.—

(a) If a person acting, or purporting to act, as a representative signs an instrument by signing either the name of the represented person or the name of the signer, the represented person is bound by the signature to the same extent the represented person would be bound if the signature were on a simple contract. If the represented person is bound, the signature of the representative is the "authorized signature of the represented person" and the represented person is liable on the instrument, whether or not identified in the instrument.

(b) If a representative signs the name of the representative to an instrument and the signature is an authorized signature of the represented person, the following rules apply:

(1) If the form of the signature shows unambiguously that the signature is made on behalf of the represented person who is identified in the instrument, the representative is not liable on the instrument.

(2) Subject to subsection (c), if (i) the form of the signature does not show unambiguously that the

signature is made in a representative capacity or (ii) the represented person is not identified in the instrument, the representative is liable on the instrument to a holder in due course that took the instrument without notice that the representative was not intended to be liable on the instrument. With respect to any other person, the representative is liable on the instrument unless the representative proves that the original parties did not intend the representative to be liable on the instrument.

(c) If a representative signs the name of the representative as drawer of a check without indication of the representative status and the check is payable from an account of the represented person who is identified on the check, the signer is not liable on the check if the signature is an authorized signature of the represented person.

§3-403. Unauthorized Signature.—

(a) Unless otherwise provided in this Article or Article 4, an unauthorized signature is ineffective except as the signature of the unauthorized signer in favor of a person who in good faith pays the instrument or takes it for value. An unauthorized signature may be ratified for all purposes of this Article.

(b) If the signature of more than one person is required to constitute the authorized signature of an organization, the signature of the organization is unauthorized if one of the required signatures is lacking.

(c) The civil or criminal liability of a person who makes an unauthorized signature is not affected by any provision of this Article which makes the unauthorized signature effective for the purposes of this Article.

§3-404. Impostors; Fictitious Payees.—

(a) If an impostor, by use of the mails or otherwise, induces the issuer of an instrument to issue the instrument to the impostor, or to a person acting in concert with the impostor, by impersonating the payee of the instrument or a person authorized to act for the payee, an indorsement of the instrument by any person in the name of the payee is effective as the indorsement of the payee in favor of a person who, in good faith, pays the instrument or takes it for value or for collection.

(b) If (i) a person whose intent determines to whom an instrument is payable (Section 3-110(a) or (b)) does not intend the person identified as payee to have any interest in the instrument, or (ii) the person identified as payee of an instrument is a fictitious person, the following rules apply until the instrument is negotiated by special indorsement:

(1) Any person in possession of the instrument is its holder.

(2) An indorsement by any person in the name of the payee stated in the instrument is effective as the indorsement of the payee in favor of a person who, in good faith, pays the instrument or takes it

for value or for collection.

(c) Under subsection (a) or (b), an indorsement is made in the name of a payee if (i) it is made in a name substantially similar to that of the payee or (ii) the instrument, whether or not indorsed, is deposited in a depositary bank to an account in a name substantially similar to that of the payee.

(d) With respect to an instrument to which subsection (a) or (b) applies, if a person paying the instrument or taking it for value or for collection fails to exercise ordinary care in paying or taking the instrument and that failure substantially contributes to loss resulting from payment of the instrument, the person bearing the loss may recover from the person failing to exercise ordinary care to the extent the failure to exercise ordinary care contributed to the loss.

§3-405. Employer's Responsibility for Fraudulent Indorsement by Employee.—

(a) In this section

(1) "Employee" includes an independent contractor and employee of an independent contractor retained by the employer.

(2) "Fraudulent indorsement" means (i) in the case of an instrument payable to the employer, a forged indorsement purporting to be that of the employer, or (ii) in the case of an instrument with respect to which the employer is the issuer, a forged indorsement purporting to be that of the person identified as payee.

(3) "Responsibility" with respect to instruments means authority (i) to sign or indorse instruments on behalf of the employer, (ii) to process instruments received by the employer for bookkeeping purposes, for deposit to an account, or for other disposition, (iii) to prepare or process instruments for issue in the name of the employer, (iv) to supply information determining the names or addresses of payees of instruments to be issued in the name of the employer, (v) to control the disposition of instruments to be issued in the name of the employer, or (vi) to act otherwise with respect to instruments in a responsible capacity. "Responsibility" does not include authority that merely allows an employee to have access to instruments or blank or incomplete instrument forms that are being stored or transported or are part of incoming or outgoing mail, or similar access.

(b) For the purpose of determining the rights and liabilities of a person who, in good faith, pays an instrument or takes it for value or for collection, if an employer entrusted an employee with responsibility with respect to the instrument and the employee or a person acting in concert with the employee makes a fraudulent indorsement of the instrument, the indorsement is effective as the indorsement of the person to whom the instrument is payable if it is made in the name of that person. If the person paying the instrument or taking it for value or for collection fails to exercise ordinary care in paying or taking the instrument and that failure substantially contributes to loss resulting from the fraud, the person bearing the loss may recover from the person failing to exercise ordinary care to the extent the failure to exercise ordinary care contributed to the loss.

(c) Under subsection (b), an indorsement is made in the name of the person to whom an instrument is payable if (i) it is made in a name substantially similar to the name of that person or (ii) the instrument, whether or not indorsed, is deposited in a depositary bank to an account in a name substantially similar to the name of that person.

§3-406. Negligence Contributing to Forged Signature or Alteration of Instrument.—

(a) A person whose failure to exercise ordinary care substantially contributes to an alteration of an instrument or to the making of a forged signature on an instrument is precluded from asserting the alteration or the forgery against a person who, in good faith, pays the instrument or takes it for value or for collection.

(b) Under subsection (a), if the person asserting the preclusion fails to exercise ordinary care in paying or taking the instrument and that failure substantially contributes to loss, the loss is allocated between the person precluded and the person asserting the preclusion according to the extent to which the failure of each to exercise ordinary care contributed to the loss.

(c) Under subsection (a), the burden of proving failure to exercise ordinary care is on the person asserting the preclusion. Under subsection (b), the burden of proving failure to exercise ordinary care is on the person precluded.

§3-407. Alteration.—

(a) "Alteration" means (i) an unauthorized change in an instrument that purports to modify in any respect the obligation of a party, or (ii) an unauthorized addition of words or numbers or other change to an incomplete instrument relating to the obligation of a party.

(b) Except as provided in subsection (c), an alteration fraudulently made discharges a party whose obligation is affected by the alteration unless that party assents or is precluded from asserting the alteration. No other alteration discharges a party, and the instrument may be enforced according to its original terms.

(c) A payor bank or drawee paying a fraudulently altered instrument or a person taking it for value, in good faith and without notice of the alteration, may enforce rights with respect to the instrument (i) according to its original terms, or (ii) in the case of an incomplete instrument altered by unauthorized completion, according to its terms as completed.

§3-408. Drawee Not Liable on Unaccepted Draft.—

A check or other draft does not of itself operate as an assignment of funds in the hands of the drawee available for its payment, and the drawee is not liable on the instrument until the drawee accepts it.

§3-409. Acceptance of Draft; Certified Check.—

(a) "Acceptance" means the drawee's signed agreement to pay a draft as presented. It must be written on the draft and may consist of the drawee's signature alone. Acceptance may be made at any time and becomes effective when notification pursuant to instructions is given or the accepted draft is delivered for the purpose of giving rights on the acceptance to any person.

(b) A draft may be accepted although it has not been signed by the drawer, is otherwise incomplete, is overdue, or has been dishonored.

(c) If a draft is payable at a fixed period after sight and the acceptor fails to date the acceptance, the holder may complete the acceptance by supplying a date in good faith.

(d) "Certified check" means a check accepted by the bank on which it is drawn. Acceptance may be made as stated in subsection (a) or by a writing on the check which indicates that the check is certified. The drawee of a check has no obligation to certify the check, and refusal to certify is not dishonor of the check.

§3-410. Acceptance Varying Draft.—

(a) If the terms of a drawee's acceptance vary from the terms of the draft as presented, the holder may refuse the acceptance and treat the draft as dishonored. In that case, the drawee may cancel the acceptance.

(b) The terms of a draft are not varied by an acceptance to pay at a particular bank or place in the United States, unless the acceptance states that the draft is to be paid only at that bank or place.

(c) If the holder assents to an acceptance varying the terms of a draft, the obligation of each drawer and indorser that does not expressly assent to the acceptance is discharged.

§3-411. Refusal to Pay Cashier's Checks, Teller's Checks, and Certified Checks.—

(a) In this section, "obligated bank" means the acceptor of a certified check or the issuer of a cashier's check or teller's check bought from the issuer.

(b) If the obligated bank wrongfully (i) refuses to pay a cashier's check or certified check, (ii) stops payment of a teller's check, or (iii) refuses to pay a dishonored teller's check, the person asserting the right to enforce the check is entitled to compensation for expenses and loss of interest resulting from the nonpayment and may recover consequential damages if the obligated bank refuses to pay after receiving notice of particular circumstances giving rise to the damages.

(c) Expenses or consequential damages under subsection (b) are not recoverable if the refusal of the obligated bank to pay occurs because (i) the bank suspends payments, (ii) the obligated bank asserts a claim or defense of the bank that it has reasonable grounds to believe is available against the person entitled to enforce the instrument, (iii) the obligated bank has a reasonable doubt whether the person demanding payment is the person entitled to enforce the instrument, or (iv) payment is prohibited by law.

§3-412. Obligation of Issuer of Note or Cashier's Check.—

The issuer of a note or cashier's check or other draft drawn on the drawer is obliged to pay the instrument (i) according to its terms at the time it was issued or, if not issued, at the time it first came into possession of a holder, or (ii) if the issuer signed an incomplete instrument, according to its terms when completed, to the extent stated in Sections 3-115 and 3-407. The obligation is owed to a person entitled to enforce the instrument or to an indorser who paid the instrument under Section 3-415.

§3-413. Obligation of Acceptor.—

(a) The acceptor of a draft is obliged to pay the draft (i) according to its terms at the time it was accepted, even though the acceptance states that the draft is payable "as originally drawn" or equivalent terms, (ii) if the acceptance varies the terms of the draft, according to the terms of the draft as varied, or (iii) if the acceptance is of a draft that is an incomplete instrument, according to its terms when completed, to the extent stated in Sections 3-115 and 3-407. The obligation is owed to a person entitled to enforce the draft or to the drawer or an indorser who paid the draft under Section 3-414 or 3-415.

(b) If the certification of a check or other acceptance of a draft states the amount certified or accepted, the obligation of the acceptor is that amount. If (i) the certification or acceptance does not state an amount, (ii) the amount of the instrument is subsequently raised, and (iii) the instrument is then negotiated to a holder in due course, the obligation of the acceptor is the amount of the instrument at the time it was taken by the holder in due course.

§3-414. Obligation of Drawer.—

(a) This section does not apply to cashier's checks or other drafts drawn on the drawer.

(b) If an unaccepted draft is dishonored, the drawer is obliged to pay the draft (i) according to its terms at the time it was issued or, if not issued, at the time it first came into possession of a holder, or (ii) if the drawer signed an incomplete instrument, according

to its terms when completed, to the extent stated in Sections 3-115 and 3-407. The obligation is owed to a person entitled to enforce the draft or to an indorser who paid the draft under Section 3-415.

(c) If a draft is accepted by a bank, the drawer is discharged, regardless of when or by whom acceptance was obtained.

(d) If a draft is accepted and the acceptor is not a bank, the obligation of the drawer to pay the draft if the draft is dishonored by the acceptor is the same as the obligation of an indorser under Section 3-415(a) and (c).

(e) If a draft states that it is drawn "without recourse" or otherwise disclaims liability of the drawer to pay the draft, the drawer is not liable under subsection (b) to pay the draft if the draft is not a check. A disclaimer of the liability stated in subsection (b) is not effective if the draft is a check.

(f) If (i) a check is not presented for payment or given to a depositary bank for collection within 30 days after its date, (ii) the drawee suspends payments after expiration of the 30-day period without paying the check, and (iii) because of the suspension of payments, the drawer is deprived of funds maintained with the drawee to cover payment of the check, the drawer to the extent deprived of funds may discharge its obligation to pay the check by assigning to the person entitled to enforce the check the rights of the drawer against the drawee with respect to the funds.

§3-415. Obligation of Indorser.—

(a) Subject to subsections (b), (c), and (d) and to Section 3-419(d), if an instrument is dishonored, an indorser is obliged to pay the amount due on the instrument (i) according to the terms of the instrument at the time it was indorsed, or (ii) if the indorser indorsed an incomplete instrument, according to its terms when completed, to the extent stated in Sections 3-115 and 3-407. The obligation of the indorser is owed to a person entitled to enforce the instrument or to a subsequent indorser who paid the instrument under this section.

(b) If an indorsement states that it is made "without recourse" or otherwise disclaims liability of the indorser, the indorser is not liable under subsection (a) to pay the instrument.

(c) If notice of dishonor of an instrument is required by Section 3-503 and notice of dishonor complying with that section is not given to an indorser, the liability of the indorser under subsection (a) is discharged.

(d) If a draft is accepted by a bank after an indorsement is made, the liability of the indorser under subsection (a) is discharged.

(e) If an indorser of a check is liable under subsection (a) and the check is not presented for payment, or given to a depositary bank for collection, within 30 days after the day the indorsement was made, the liability of the indorser under subsection (a) is discharged.

§3-416. Transfer Warranties.—

(a) A person who transfers an instrument for consideration warrants to the transferee and, if the transfer is by indorsement, to any subsequent transferee that:

(1) the warrantor is a person entitled to enforce the instrument;

(2) all signatures on the instrument are authentic and authorized;

(3) the instrument has not been altered;

(4) the instrument is not subject to a defense or claim in recoupment of any party which can be asserted against the warrantor; and

(5) the warrantor has no knowledge of any insolvency proceeding commenced with respect to the maker or acceptor or, in the case of an unaccepted draft, the drawer.

(b) A person to whom the warranties under subsection (a) are made and who took the instrument in good faith may recover from the warrantor as damages for breach of warranty an amount equal to the loss suffered as a result of the breach, but not more than the amount of the instrument plus expenses and loss of interest incurred as a result of the breach.

(c) The warranties stated in subsection (a) cannot be disclaimed with respect to checks. Unless notice of a claim for breach of warranty is given to the warrantor within 30 days after the claimant has reason to know of the breach and the identity of the warrantor, the liability of the warrantor under subsection (b) is discharged to the extent of any loss caused by the delay in giving notice of the claim.

(d) A [cause of action] for breach of warranty under this section accrues when the claimant has reason to know of the breach.

§3-417. Presentment Warranties.—

(a) If an unaccepted draft is presented to the drawee for payment or acceptance and the drawee pays or accepts the draft, (i) the person obtaining payment or acceptance, at the time of presentment, and (ii) a previous transferor of the draft, at the time of transfer, warrant to the drawee making payment or accepting the draft in good faith that:

(1) the warrantor is, or was, at the time the warrantor transferred the draft, a person entitled to enforce the draft or authorized to obtain payment or acceptance of the draft on behalf of a person entitled to enforce the draft;

(2) the draft has not been altered; and

(3) the warrantor has no knowledge that the signature of the drawer of the draft is unauthorized.

(b) A drawee making payment may recover from any warrantor damages for breach of warranty equal to the amount paid by the drawee less the amount the drawee received or is entitled to receive from the drawer because of the payment. In addition, the drawee is entitled to compensation for expenses and loss of interest resulting from the breach. The right of the drawee to recover damages under this subsection is not affected by any failure of the drawee to exercise ordinary care in making payment. If the drawee accepts the draft, breach of warranty is a defense to the obligation of the acceptor. If the acceptor makes payment with respect to the draft, the acceptor is entitled to recover from any warrantor for breach of warranty the amounts stated in this subsection.

(c) If a drawee asserts a claim for breach of warranty under subsection (a) based on an unauthorized indorsement of the draft or an alteration of the draft, the warrantor may defend by proving that the indorsement is effective under Section 3-404 or 3-405 or the drawer is precluded under Section 3-406 or 4-406 from asserting against the drawee the unauthorized indorsement or alteration.

(d) If (i) a dishonored draft is presented for payment to the drawer or an indorser or (ii) any other instrument is presented for payment to a party obliged to pay the instrument, and (iii) payment is received, the following rules apply:

(1) The person obtaining payment and a prior transferor of the instrument warrant to the person making payment in good faith that the warrantor is, or was, at the time the warrantor transferred the instrument, a person entitled to enforce the instrument or authorized to obtain payment on behalf of a person entitled to enforce the instrument.

(2) The person making payment may recover from any warrantor for breach of warranty an amount equal to the amount paid plus expenses and loss of interest resulting from the breach.

(e) The warranties stated in subsections (a) and (d) cannot be disclaimed with respect to checks. Unless notice of a claim for breach of warranty is given to the warrantor within 30 days after the claimant has reason to know of the breach and the identity of the warrantor, the liability of the warrantor under subsection (b) or (d) is discharged to the extent of any loss caused by the delay in giving notice of the claim.

(f) A [cause of action] for breach of warranty under this section accrues when the claimant has reason to know of the breach.

§3-418. Payment or Acceptance by Mistake.—

(a) Except as provided in subsection (c), if the drawee of a draft pays or accepts the draft and the drawee acted on the mistaken belief that (i) payment of the draft had not been stopped pursuant to Section 4-403 or (ii) the signature of the drawer of the draft was authorized, the drawee may recover the amount of the draft from the person to whom or for whose benefit payment was made or, in the case of acceptance, may revoke the acceptance. Rights of the drawee under this subsection are not affected by failure of the drawee to exercise ordinary care in paying or accepting the draft.

(b) Except as provided in subsection (c), if an instrument has been paid or accepted by mistake and the case is not covered by subsection (a), the person paying or accepting may, to the extent permitted by the law governing mistake and restitution, (i) recover the payment from the person to whom or for whose benefit payment was made or (ii) in the case of acceptance, may revoke the acceptance.

(c) The remedies provided by subsection (a) or (b) may not be asserted against a person who took the instrument in good faith and for value or who in good faith changed position in reliance on the payment or acceptance. This subsection does not limit remedies provided by Section 3-417 or 4-407.

(d) Notwithstanding Section 4-215, if an instrument is paid or accepted by mistake and the payor or acceptor recovers payment or revokes acceptance under subsection (a) or (b), the instrument is deemed not to have been paid or accepted and is treated as dishonored, and the person from whom payment is recovered has rights as a person entitled to enforce the dishonored instrument.

§3-419. Instruments Signed for Accommodation.—

(a) If an instrument is issued for value given for the benefit of a party to the instrument ("accommodated party") and another party to the instrument ("An accommodation party") signs the instrument for the purpose of incurring liability on the instrument without being a direct beneficiary of the value given for the instrument, the instrument is signed by the accommodation party "for accommodation".

(b) An accommodation party may sign the instrument as maker, drawer, acceptor, or indorser and, subject to subsection (d), is obliged to pay the instrument in the capacity in which the accommodation party signs. The obligation of an accommodation party may be enforced notwithstanding any statute of frauds and whether or not the accommodation party receives consideration for the accommodation.

(c) A person signing an instrument is presumed to be an accommodation party and there is notice that the instrument is signed for accommodation if the signature is an anomalous indorsement or is accompanied by words indicating that the signer is acting as surety or guarantor with respect to the obligation of another party to the instrument. Except as provided in Section 3-605, the obligation of an accommodation party to pay the instrument is not affected by the fact that the person enforcing the obligation had notice when the instrument was taken by that person that the accommodation party signed the instrument for accommodation.

(d) If the signature of a party to an instrument is accompanied by words indicating unambiguously that the party is guaranteeing collection rather than payment of the obligation of another party to the instrument, the signer is obliged to pay the amount due on the instrument to a person entitled to enforce the instrument only if (i) execution of judgment against the other party has been returned unsatisfied, (ii) the other party is insolvent or in an insolvency proceeding, (iii) the other party cannot be served with process, or (iv) it is otherwise apparent that payment cannot be obtained from the other party.

(e) An accommodation party who pays the instrument is entitled to reimbursement from the accommodated party and is entitled to enforce the instrument against the accommodated party. An accommodated party who pays the instrument has no right of recourse against, and is not entitled to contribution from, an accommodation party.

§3-420. Conversion of Instrument.—

(a) The law applicable to conversion of personal property applies to instruments. An instrument is also converted if it is taken by transfer, other than a negotiation, from a person not entitled to enforce the instrument or a bank makes or obtains payment with respect to the instrument for a person not entitled to enforce the instrument or receive payment. An action for conversion of an instrument may not be brought by (i) the issuer or acceptor of the instrument or (ii) a payee or indorsee who did not receive delivery of the instrument either directly or through delivery to an agent or a co-payee.

(b) In an action under subsection (a), the measure of liability is presumed to be the amount payable on the instrument, but recovery may not exceed the amount of the plaintiff's interest in the instrument.

(c) A representative, other than a depositary bank, who has in good faith dealt with an instrument or its proceeds on behalf of one who was not the person entitled to enforce the instrument is not liable in conversion to that person beyond the amount of any proceeds that it has not paid out.

Part 5: Dishonor

§3-501. Presentment.—

(a) "Presentment" means a demand made by or on behalf of a person entitled to enforce an instrument (i) to pay the instrument made to the drawee or a party obliged to pay the instrument or, in the case of a note or accepted draft payable at a bank, to the bank, or (ii) to accept a draft made to the drawee.

(b) The following rules are subject to Article 4, agreement of the parties, and clearing-house rules and the like:

(1) Presentment may be made at the place of payment of the instrument and must be made at the place of payment if the instrument is payable at a bank in the United States; may be made by any commercially reasonable means, including an oral, written, or electronic communication; is effective when the demand for payment or acceptance is received by the person to whom presentment is made; and is effective if made to any one of two or more makers, acceptors, drawees, or other payors.

(2) Upon demand of the person to whom presentment is made, the person making presentment must (i) exhibit the instrument, (ii) give reasonable identification and, if presentment is made on behalf of another person, reasonable evidence of authority to do so, and (iii) sign a receipt on the instrument for any payment made or surrender the instrument if full payment is made.

(3) Without dishonoring the instrument, the party to whom presentment is made may (i) return the instrument for lack of a necessary indorsement, or (ii) refuse payment or acceptance for failure of the presentment to comply with the terms of the instrument, an agreement of the parties, or other applicable law or rule.

(4) The party to whom presentment is made may treat presentment as occurring on the next business day after the day of presentment if the party to whom presentment is made has established a cut-off hour not earlier than 2 p.m for the receipt and processing of instruments presented for payment or acceptance and presentment is made after the cut-off hour.

§3-502. Dishonor.—

(a) Dishonor of a note is governed by the following rules:

(1) If the note is payable on demand, the note is dishonored if presentment is duly made to the maker and the note is not paid on the day of presentment.

(2) If the note is not payable on demand and is payable at or through a bank or the terms of the note require presentment, the note is dishonored if presentment is duly made and the note is not paid on the day it becomes payable or the day of presentment, whichever is later.

(3) If the note is not payable on demand and paragraph (2) does not apply, the note is dishonored if it is not paid on the day it becomes payable.

(b) Dishonor of an unaccepted draft other than a documentary draft is governed by the following rules:

(1) If a check is duly presented for payment to the payor bank otherwise than for immediate payment over the counter, the check is dishonored if the payor bank makes timely return of the check or sends timely notice of dishonor or nonpayment under Section 4-301 or 4-302, or becomes accountable for the amount of the check under Section 4-302.

(2) If a draft is payable on demand and paragraph (1) does not apply, the draft is dishonored if presentment for payment is duly made to the drawee and the draft is not paid on the day of presentment.

(3) If a draft is payable on a date stated in the draft, the draft is dishonored if (i) presentment for payment is duly made to the drawee and payment is not made on the day the draft becomes payable or the day of presentment, whichever is later, or (ii) presentment for acceptance is duly made before the day the draft becomes payable and the draft is not accepted on the day of presentment.

(4) If a draft is payable on elapse of a period of time after sight or acceptance, the draft is dishonored if presentment for acceptance is duly made and the draft is not accepted on the day of presentment.

(c) Dishonor of an unaccepted documentary draft occurs according to the rules stated in subsection (b)(2), (3), and (4), except that payment or acceptance may be delayed without dishonor until no later than the close of the third business day of the drawee following the day on which payment or acceptance is required by those paragraphs.

(d) Dishonor of an accepted draft is governed by the following rules:

(1) If the draft is payable on demand, the draft is dishonored if presentment for payment is duly made to the acceptor and the draft is not paid on the day of presentment.

(2) If the draft is not payable on demand, the draft is dishonored if presentment for payment is duly made to the acceptor and payment is not made on the day it becomes payable or the day of presentment, whichever is later.

(e) In any case in which presentment is otherwise required for dishonor under this section and presentment is excused under Section 3-504, dishonor occurs without presentment if the instrument is not duly accepted or paid.

(f) If a draft is dishonored because timely acceptance of the draft was not made and the person entitled to demand acceptance consents to a late acceptance, from the time of acceptance the draft is treated as never having been dishonored.

§3-503. Notice of Dishonor.—

(a) The obligation of an indorser stated in Section 3-415(a) and the obligation of a drawer stated in Section 3-414(d) may not be enforced unless (i) the indorser or drawer is given notice of dishonor of the instrument complying with this section or (ii) notice of dishonor is excused under Section 3-504(b).

(b) Notice of dishonor may be given by any person; may

be given by any commercially reasonable means, including an oral, written, or electronic communication; and is sufficient if it reasonably identifies the instrument and indicates that the instrument has been dishonored or has not been paid or accepted. Return of an instrument given to a bank for collection is sufficient notice of dishonor.

(c) Subject to Section 3-504(c), with respect to an instrument taken for collection by a collecting bank, notice of dishonor must be given (i) by the bank before midnight of the next banking day following the banking day on which the bank receives notice of dishonor of the instrument, or (ii) by any other person within 30 days following the day on which the person receives notice of dishonor. With respect to any other instrument, notice of dishonor must be given within 30 days following the day on which dishonor occurs.

§3-504. Excused Presentment and Notice of Dishonor.—

(a) Presentment for payment or acceptance of an instrument is excused if (i) the person entitled to present the instrument cannot with reasonable diligence make presentment, (ii) the maker or acceptor has repudiated an obligation to pay the instrument or is dead or in insolvency proceedings, (iii) by the terms of the instrument presentment is not necessary to enforce the obligation of indorsers or the drawer, (iv) the drawer or indorser whose obligation is being enforced has waived presentment or otherwise has no reason to expect or right to require that the instrument be paid or accepted, or (v) the drawer instructed the drawee not to pay or accept the draft or the drawee was not obligated to the drawer to pay the draft.

(b) Notice of dishonor is excused if (i) by the terms of the instrument notice of dishonor is not necessary to enforce the obligation of a party to pay the instrument, or (ii) the party whose obligation is being enforced waived notice of dishonor. A waiver of presentment is also a waiver of notice of dishonor.

(c) Delay in giving notice of dishonor is excused if the delay was caused by circumstances beyond the control of the person giving the notice and the person giving the notice exercised reasonable diligence after the cause of the delay ceased to operate.

§3-505. Evidence of Dishonor.—

(a) The following are admissible as evidence and create a presumption of dishonor and of any notice of dishonor stated:

(1) a document regular in form as provided in subsection (b) which purports to be a protest;

(2) a purported stamp or writing of the drawee, payor bank, or presenting bank on or accompanying the instrument stating that acceptance or

payment has been refused unless reasons for the refusal are stated and the reasons are not consistent with dishonor;

(3) a book or record of the drawee, payor bank, or collecting bank, kept in the usual course of business which shows dishonor, even if there is no evidence of who made the entry.

(b) A protest is a certificate of dishonor made by a United States consul or vice consul, or a notary public or other person authorized to administer oaths by the law of the place where dishonor occurs. It may be made upon information satisfactory to that person. The protest must identify the instrument and certify either that presentment has been made or, if not made, the reason why it was not made, and that the instrument has been dishonored by nonacceptance or nonpayment. The protest may also certify that notice of dishonor has been given to some or all parties.

Part 6: Discharge and Payment

§3-601. Discharge and Effect of Discharge.—

(a) The obligation of a party to pay the instrument is discharged as stated in this Article or by an act or agreement with the party which would discharge an obligation to pay money under a simple contract.

(b) Discharge of the obligation of a party is not effective against a person acquiring rights of a holder in due course of the instrument without notice of the discharge.

§3-602. Payment.—

(a) Subject to subsection (b), an instrument is paid to the extent payment is made (i) by or on behalf of a party obliged to pay the instrument, and (ii) to a person entitled to enforce the instrument. To the extent of the payment, the obligation of the party obliged to pay the instrument is discharged even though payment is made with knowledge of a claim to the instrument under Section 3-306 by another person.

(b) The obligation of a party to pay the instrument is not discharged under subsection (a) if:

(1) a claim to the instrument under Section 3-306 is enforceable against the party receiving payment and (i) payment is made with knowledge by the payor that payment is prohibited by injunction or similar process of a court of competent jurisdiction, or (ii) in the case of an instrument other than a cashier's check, teller's check, or certified check, the party making payment accepted, from the person having a claim to the instrument, indemnity against loss resulting from refusal to pay the person entitled to enforce the instrument; or

(2) the person making payment knows that the instrument is a stolen instrument and pays a person it knows is in wrongful possession of the instrument.

§3-603. Tender of Payment.—

(a) If tender of payment of an obligation to pay an instrument is made to a person entitled to enforce the instrument, the effect of tender is governed by principles of law applicable to tender of payment under a simple contract.

(b) If tender of payment of an obligation to pay an instrument is made to a person entitled to enforce the instrument and the tender is refused,. . . .

§3-604. Discharge by Cancellation or Renunciation.—

(a) A person entitled to enforce an instrument, with or without consideration, may discharge the obligation of a party to pay the instrument (i) by an intentional voluntary act, such as surrender of the instrument to the party, destruction, mutilation, or cancellation of the instrument, cancellation or striking out of the party's signature, or the addition of words to the instrument indicating discharge, or (ii) by agreeing not to sue or otherwise renouncing rights against the party by a signed writing.

(b) Cancellation or striking out of an indorsement pursuant to subsection (a) does not affect the status and rights of a party derived from the indorsement.

§3-605. Discharge of Indorsers and Accommodation Parties.—

(a) In this section, the term "indorser" includes a drawer having the obligation described in Section 3-414(d).

(b) Discharge, under Section 3-604, of the obligation of a party to pay an instrument does not discharge the obligation of an indorser or accommodation party having a right of recourse against the discharged party.

(c) If a person entitled to enforce an instrument agrees, with or without consideration, to an extension of the due date of the obligation of a party to pay the instrument, the extension discharges an indorser or accommodation party having a right of recourse against the party whose obligation is extended to the extent the indorser or accommodation party proves that the extension caused loss to the indorser or accommodation party with respect to the right of recourse.

(d) If a person entitled to enforce an instrument agrees, with or without consideration, to a material modification of the obligation of a party other than an extension of the due date, the modification discharges the obligation of an indorser or accommodation party having a right of recourse against the person whose obligation is modified to the extent the modification causes loss to the indorser or accommodation party with respect to the right of recourse. The loss suffered by the indorser or accommodation party as a result of the modification is equal to the amount of the right of recourse unless the person enforcing the instrument proves that no loss was caused by the modification or that the loss caused by the modification was an amount less than the amount of the right of recourse.

(e) If the obligation of a party to pay an instrument is secured by an interest in collateral and a person entitled to enforce the instrument impairs the value of the interest in collateral, the obligation of an indorser or accommodation party having a right of recourse against the obligor is discharged to the extent of the impairment. The value of an interest in collateral is impaired to the extent (i) the value of the interest is reduced to an amount less than the amount of the right of recourse of the party asserting discharge, or (ii) the reduction in value of the interest causes an increase in the amount by which the amount of the right of recourse exceeds the value of the interest. The burden of proving impairment is on the party asserting discharge.

(f) If the obligation of a party is secured by an interest in collateral not provided by an accommodation party and a person entitled to enforce the instrument impairs the value of the interest in collateral, the obligation of any party who is jointly and severally liable with respect to the secured obligation is discharged to the extent the impairment causes the party asserting discharge to pay more than that party would have been obliged to pay, taking into account rights of contribution, if impairment had not occurred. If the party asserting discharge is an accommodation party not entitled to discharge under subsection (e), the party is deemed to have a right to contribution based on joint and several liability rather than a right to reimbursement. The burden of proving impairment is on the party asserting discharge.

(g) Under subsection (e) or (f), impairing value of an interest in collateral includes (i) failure to obtain or maintain perfection or recordation of the interest in collateral, (ii) release of collateral without substitution of collateral of equal value, (iii) failure to perform a duty to preserve the value of collateral owed, under Article 9 or other law, to a debtor or surety or other person secondarily liable, or (iv) failure to comply with applicable law in disposing of collateral.

(h) An accommodation party is not discharged under subsection (c), (d), or (e) unless the person entitled to enforce the instrument knows of the accommodation or has notice under Section 3-419(c) that the instrument was signed for accommodation.

(i) A party is not discharged under this section if (i) the party asserting discharge consents to the event or conduct that is the basis of the discharge, or (ii) the instrument or a separate agreement of the party provides for waiver of discharge under this section either

Appendix C

United Nations Convention on Contracts for the International Sale of Goods

THE STATES PARTIES TO THIS CONVENTION,
BEARING IN MIND the broad objectives in the resolutions adopted by the sixth special session of the General Assembly of the United Nations on the establishment of a New International Economic Order,
CONSIDERING that the development of international trade on the basis of equality and mutual benefit is an important element in promoting friendly relations among States,
BEING OF THE OPINION that the adoption of uniform rules which govern contracts for the international sale of goods and take into account the different social, economic and legal systems would contribute to the removal of legal barriers in international trade and promote the development of international trade,
HAVE AGREED as follows:

Part I Sphere of Application and General Provisions

Chapter I Sphere of Application

Article 1
(1) This Convention applies to contracts of sale of goods between parties whose places of business are in different States:
  (a) when the States are Contracting States; or
  (b) when the rules of private international law lead to the application of the law of a Contracting State. [Pursuant to the reservation permitted by Article 95, the United States has excluded applicability of the Convention under this subparagraph.]
(2) The fact that the parties have their places of business in different States is to be disregarded whenever this fact does not appear either from the contract or from any dealings between, or from information disclosed by, the parties at any time before or at the conclusion of the contract.
(3) Neither the nationality of the parties nor the civil or commercial character of the parties or of the contract is to be taken into consideration in determining the application of this Convention.

Article 2 This Convention does not apply to sales:
(a) of goods bought for personal, family or household use, unless the seller, at any time before or at the conclusion of the contract, neither knew nor ought to have known that the goods were bought for any such use;
(b) by auction;
(c) on execution or otherwise by authority of law;
(d) of stocks, shares, investment securities, negotiable instruments or money;
(e) of ships, vessels, hovercraft or aircraft;
(f) of electricity.

Article 3
(1) Contracts for the supply of goods to be manufactured or produced are to be considered sales unless the party who orders the goods undertakes to supply a substantial part of the materials necessary for such manufacture or production.
(2) This Convention does not apply to contracts in which the preponderant part of the obligations of the party who furnishes the goods consists in the supply of labour or other services.

Article 4 This Convention governs only the formation of the contract of sale and the rights and obligations of the seller and the buyer arising from such a contract. In particular, except as otherwise expressly provided in this Convention, it is not concerned with:
(a) the validity of the contract or of any of its provisions or of any usage;
(b) the effect which the contract may have on the property in the goods sold.

Article 5 This Convention does not apply to the liability of the seller for death or personal injury caused by the goods to any person.

Article 6 The parties may exclude the application of this Convention or, subject to Article 12, derogate from or vary the effect of any of its provisions.

Chapter II General Provisions

Article 7
(1) In the interpretation of this Convention, regard is to be had to its international character and to the need to promote uniformity in its application and the observance of good faith in international trade.
(2) Questions concerning matters governed by this Convention which are not expressly settled in it are to be settled in conformity with the general principles on which it is based or, in the absence of such principles, in conformity with the law applicable by virtue of the rules of private international law.

Article 8
(1) For the purposes of this Convention statements made by and other conduct of a party are to be interpreted according to his intent where the other party knew or could not have been unaware what that intent was.
(2) If the preceding paragraph is not applicable, statements made by and other conduct of a party are to be interpreted according to the understanding that a reasonable person of the same kind as the other party would have had in the same circumstances.

(3) In determining the intent of a party or the understanding a reasonable person would have had, due consideration is to be given to all relevant circumstances of the case including the negotiations, any practices which the parties have established between themselves, usages and any subsequent conduct of the parities.

Article 9

(1) The parties are bound by any usage to which they have agreed and by any practices which they have established between themselves.
(2) The parties are considered, unless otherwise agreed, to have impliedly made applicable to their contract or its formation a usage of which the parties know or ought to have known and which in international trade is widely known to, and regularly observed by, parties to contracts of the type involved in the particular trade concerned.

Article 10 For the purposes of this Convention:

(a) if a party has more than one place of business, the place of business is that which has the closest relationship to the contract and its performance, having regard to the circumstances known to or contemplated by the parties at any time before or at the conclusion of the contract;
(b) if a party does not have a place of business, reference is to be made to his habitual residence.

Article 11 A contract of sale need not be concluded in or evidenced by writing and is not subject to any other requirement as to form. It may be proved by any means, including witnesses.

Article 12 Any provision of Article 11, Article 29 or Part II of this Convention that allows a contract of sale or its modification or termination by agreement or any offer, acceptance or other indication of intention to be made in any form other than in writing does not apply where any party has his place of business in a Contracting State which has made a declaration under Article 96 of this Convention. The parties may not derogate from or vary the effect of this article.

Article 13 For the purposes of this Convention "writing" includes telegram and telex.

Part II Formation of the Contract

Article 14

(1) A proposal for concluding a contract addressed to one or more specific persons constitutes an offer if it is sufficiently definite and indicates the intention of the offeror to be bound in case of acceptance. A proposal is sufficiently definite if it indicates the goods and expressly or implicitly fixes or makes provision for determining the quantity and the price.

(2) A proposal other than one addressed to one or more specific persons is to be considered merely as an invitation to make offers, unless the contrary is clearly indicated by the person making the proposal.

Article 15

(1) An offer becomes effective when it reaches the offeree.
(2) An offer, even if it is irrevocable, may be withdrawn if the withdrawal reaches the offeree before or at the same time as the offer.

Article 16

(1) Until a contract is concluded an offer may be revoked if the revocation reaches the offeree before he has dispatched an acceptance.
(2) However, an offer cannot be revoked:
    (a) if it indicates, whether by stating a fixed time for acceptance or otherwise, that it is irrevocable; or
    (b) if it was reasonable for the offeree to rely on the offer as being irrevocable and the offeree has acted in reliance on the offer.

Article 17 An offer, even if it is irrevocable, is terminated when a rejection reaches the offeror.

Article 18

(1) A statement made by or other conduct of the offeree indicating assent to an offer is an acceptance. Silence or inactivity does not in itself amount to acceptance.
(2) An acceptance of an offer becomes effective at the moment the indication of assent reaches the offeror. An acceptance is not effective if the indication of assent does not reach the offeror within the time he has fixed or, if no time is fixed, within a reasonable time, due account being taken of the circumstances of the transaction, including the rapidity of the means of communication employed by the offeror. An oral offer must be accepted immediately unless the circumstances indicate otherwise.
(3) However, if, by virtue of the offer or as a result of practices which the parties have established between themselves or of usage, the offeree may indicate assent by performing an act, such as one relating to the dispatch of the goods or payment of the price, without notice to the offeror, the acceptance is effective at the moment the act is performed, provided that the act is performed within the period of time laid down in the preceding paragraph.

Article 19

(1) A reply to an offer which purports to be an acceptance but contains additions, limitations or other modifications is a rejection of the offer and constitutes a counter-offer.
(2) However, a reply to an offer which purports to be an acceptance but contains additional or different terms which do not materially alter the terms of the offer

constitutes an acceptance, unless the offeror, without undue delay, objects orally to the discrepancy or dispatches a notice to that effect. If he does not so object, the terms of the contract are the terms of the offer with the modifications contained in the acceptance.

(3) Additional or different terms relating, among other things, to the price, payment, quality and quantity of the goods, place and time of delivery, extent of one party's liability to the other or the settlement of disputes are considered to alter the terms of the offer materially.

Article 20

(1) A period of time for acceptance fixed by the offeror in a telegram or a letter begins to run from the moment the telegram is handed in for dispatch or from the date shown on the letter or, if on such date is shown, from the date shown on the envelope. A period of time for acceptance fixed by the offeror by telephone, telex or other means of instantaneous communication, begins to run from the moment that the offer reaches the offeree.

(2) Official holidays or non-business days occurring during the period for acceptance are included in calculating the period. However, if a notice of acceptance cannot be delivered at the address of the offeror on the last day of the period because that day falls on an official holiday or a non-business day at the place of business of the offeror, the period is extended until the first business day which follows.

Artcle 21

(1) A late acceptance is nevertheless effective as an acceptance if without delay the offeror orally so informs the offeree or dispatches a notice to that effect.

(2) If a letter or other writing containing a late acceptance shows that it has been sent in such circumstances that if its transmission had been normal it would have reached the offeror in due time, the late acceptance is effective as an acceptance unless, without delay, the offeror orally informs the offeree that he considers his offer as having lapsed or dispatches a notice to that effect.

Article 22

An acceptance may be withdrawn if the withdrawal reaches the offeror before or at the same time as the acceptance would have become effective.

Article 23

A contract is concluded at the moment when an acceptance of an offer becomes effective in accordance with the provisions of this Convention.

Article 24

For the purposes of this Part of the Convention, an offer, declaration of acceptance or any other indication of intention "reaches" the addressee when it is made orally to him or delivered by any other means to him personally, to his place of business or mailing address or, if he does not have a place of business or mailing address, to his habitual residence.

Part III Sale of Goods

Chapter I General Provisions

Article 25 A breach of contract committed by one of the parties is fundamental if it results in such detriment to the other party as substantially to deprive him of what he is entitled to expect under the contract, unless the party in breach did not foresee and a reasonable person of the same kind in the same circumstances would not have foreseen such a result.

Article 26 A declaration of avoidance of the contract is effective only if made by notice to the other party.

Article 27 Unless otherwise expressly provided in this Part of the Convention, if any notice, request or other communication is given or made by a party in accordance with this Part and by means appropriate in the circumstances, a delay or error in the transmission of the communication or its failure to arrive does not deprive that party of the right to rely on the communication.

Article 28 If, in accordance with the provisions of this Convention, one party is entitled to require performance of any obligation by the other party, a court is not bound to enter a judgment for specific performance unless the court would do so under its own law in respect of similar contracts of sale not governed by this Convention.

Article 29

(1) A contact may be modified or terminated by the mere agreement of the parties.

(2) A contact in writing which contains a provision requiring any modification or termination by agreement to be in writing may not be otherwise modified or terminated by agreement. However, a party may be precluded by his conduct from asserting such a provision to the extent that the other party has relied on that conduct.

Chapter II Obligations of the Seller

Article 30 The seller must deliver the goods, hand over any documents relating to them and transfer the property in the goods, as required by the contract and this Convetion.

Section I. Delivery of the goods and handing over of documents

Article 31 If the seller is not bound to deliver the goods at any other particular place, his obligation to deliver consists:

(a) if the contract of sale involves carriage of the goods—in handing the goods over to the first carrier for transmission to the buyer;

(b) if, in cases not within the preceding subparagraph, the contract relates to specific goods, or unidentified goods to be drawn from a specific stock or to be manufactured or produced, and at the time of the conclusion of the contract the parties knew that the goods were at, or were to be manufactured or produced at, a particular place—in placing the goods at the buyer's disposal at the place;

(c) in other cases—in placing the goods at the buyer's disposal at the place where the seller had his place of business at the time of the conclusion of the contract.

Article 32

(1) If the seller, in accordance with the contract or this Convention, hands the goods over to a carrier and if the goods are not clearly identified to the contract by markings on the goods, by shipping documents or otherwise, the seller must give the buyer notice of the consignment specifying the goods.

(2) If the seller is bound to arrange for carriage of the goods, he must make such contracts as are necessary for carriage to the place fixed by means of transportation appropriate in the circumstances and according to the usual terms for such transportation.

(3) If the seller is not bound to effect insurance in respect of the carriage of the goods, he must, at the buyer's request, provide him with all available information necessary to enable him to effect such insurance.

Article 33 The seller must deliver the goods:

(a) if a date is fixed by or determinable from the contract, on that date;

(b) if a period of time is fixed by or determinable from the contract, at any time within that period unless circumstances indicate that the buyer is to choose a date; or

(c) in any other case, within a reasonable time after the conclusion of the contract.

Article 34 If the seller is bound to hand over documents relating to the goods, he must hand them over at the time and place and in the form required by the contract. If the seller has handed over documents before that time, he may, up to that time, cure any lack of conformity in the documents, if the exercise of this right does not cause the buyer unreasonable inconvenience or unreasonable expense. However, the buyer retains any right to claim damages as provided for in this Convention.

Section II. Conformity of the goods and third party claims

Article 35

(1) The seller must deliver goods which are of the quantity, quality and description required by the contract and which are contained or packaged in the manner required by the contract.

(2) Except where the parties have agreed otherwise, the goods do not conform with the contract unless they:

    (a) are fit for the purposes for which goods of the same description would ordinarily be used;

(b) are fit for any particular purpose expressly or impliedly made known to the seller at the time of the conclusion of the contract, except where the circumstances show that the buyer did not rely, or that it was unreasonable for him to rely, on the seller's skill and judgment;

(c) possess the qualities of goods which the seller has held out to the buyer as a sample or model;

(d) are contained or packaged in the manner usual for such goods or, where there is no such manner, in a manner adequate to preserve and protect the goods.

(3) The seller is not liable under subparagraphs (a) to (d) of the preceding paragraph for any lack of conformity of the preceding paragraph for any lack of conformity of the goods if at the time of the conclusion of the contract the buyer knew or could not have been unaware of such lack of conformity.

Article 36

(1) The seller is liable in accordance with the contract and this Convention for any lack of conformity which exists at the time when the risk passes to the buyer, even though the lack of conformity becomes apparent only after that time.

(2) The seller is also liable for any lack of conformity which occurs after the time indicated in the preceding paragraph and which is due to a breach of any of his obligations, including a breach of any guarantee that for a period of time the goods will remain fit for their ordinary purpose or for some particular purpose or will retain specified qualities or characteristics.

Article 37 If the seller has delivered goods before the date for delivery, he may, up to that date, deliver any missing part or make up any deficiency in the quantity of the goods delivered, or deliver goods in replacement of any non-conforming goods delivered or remedy any lack of conformity in the goods delivered, provided that the exercise of this right does not cause the buyer unreasonable inconvenience or unreasonable expense. However, the buyer retains any right to claim damages as provided for in this Convention.

Article 38

(1) The buyer must examine the goods, or cause them to be examined, within as short a period as is practicable in the circumstances.

(2) If the contract involves carriage of the goods, examination may be deferred until after the goods have arrived at their destination.

(3) If the goods are redirected in transit or redispatched by the buyer without a reasonable opportunity for examination by him and at the time of the conclusion of the contract the seller knew or ought to have known of the possibility of such redirection or redispatch, examination may be

deferred until after the goods have arrived at the new destination.

Article 39

(1) The buyer loses the right to rely on a lack of conformity of the goods if he does not give notice to the seller specifying the nature of the lack of conformity within a reasonable time after he has discovered it or ought to have discovered it.

(2) In any event, the buyer loses the right to rely on a lack of conformity of the goods if he does not give the seller notice thereof at the latest within a period of two years from the date on which the goods were actually handed over to the buyer, unless this time-limit is inconsistent with a contractual period of guarantee.

Article 40 The seller is not entitled to rely on the provisions of Articles 38 and 39 if the lack of conformity relates to facts of which he knew or could not have been unaware and which he did not disclose to the buyer.

Article 41 The seller must deliver goods which are free from any right or claim of a third party, unless the buyer agreed to take the goods subject to that right or claim. However, if such right or claim is based on industrial property or other intellectual property, the seller's obligation is governed by Article 42.

Article 42

(1) The seller must deliver goods which are free from any right or claim of a third party based on industrial property or other intellectual property, of which at the time of the conclusion of the contract the seller knew or could not have been unaware, provided that the right or claim is based on industrial property or other intellectual property:

   (a) under the law of the State where the goods will be resold or otherwise used, if it was contemplated by the parties at the time of the conclusion of the contract that the goods would be resold or otherwise used in that State; or

   (b) in any other case, under the law of the State where the buyer has his place of business.

(2) The obligation of the seller under the preceding paragraph does not extend to cases where:

   (a) at the time of the conclusion of the contract the buyer knew or could not have been unaware of the right or claim; or

   (b) the right or claim results from the seller's compliance with technical drawings, designs, formulae or other such specifications furnished by the buyer.

Article 43

(1) The buyer loses the right to rely on the provisions of Article 41 or Article 42 if he does not give notice to the seller specifying the nature of the right or claim of the third party within a reasonable time after he has

become aware or ought to have become aware of the right or claim.

(2) The seller is not entitled to rely on the provisions of the preceding paragraph if he knew of the right or claim of the third party and the nature of it.

Article 44 Notwithstanding the provisions of paragraph (1) of Article 39 and paragraph (1) of Article 43, the buyer may reduce the price in accordance with Article 50 or claim damages, except for loss of profit, if he has a reasonable excuse for his failure to give the required notice.

Section III. Remedies for breach of contract by the seller

Article 45

(1) If the seller fails to perform any of his obligations under the contract or this Convention, the buyer may:

   (a) exercise the rights provided in Articles 46 to 52;

   (b) claim damages as provided in Articles 74 to 77.

(2) The buyer is not deprived of any right he may have to claim damages by exercising his right to other remedies.

(3) No period of grace may be granted to the seller by a court or arbitral tribunal when the buyer resorts to a remedy for breach of contract.

Article 46

(1) The buyer may require performance by the seller of his obligations unless the buyer has resorted to a remedy which is inconsistent with this requirement.

(2) If the goods do not conform with the contract, the buyer may require delivery of substitute goods only if the lack of conformity constitutes a fundamental breach of contract and a request for substitute goods is made either in conjunction with notice given under Article 39 or within a reasonable time thereafter.

(3) If the goods do not conform with the contract, the buyer may require the seller to remedy the lack of conformity by repair, unless this is unreasonable having regard to all the circumstances. A request for repair must be made either in conjunction with notice given under Article 39 or within a reasonable time thereafter.

Article 47

(1) The buyer may fix an additional period of time of reasonable length for performance by the seller of his obligations.

(2) Unless the buyer has received notice from the seller that he will not perform within the period so fixed, the buyer may not, during that period, resort to any remedy for breach of contract. However, the buyer is not deprived thereby of any right he may have to claim damages for delay in performance.

Article 48

(1) Subject to Article 49, the seller may, even after the date for delivery, remedy at his own expense any failure to perform his obligations, if he can do so

without unreasonable delay and without causing the buyer unreasonable inconvenience or uncertainty of reimbursement by the seller of expenses advanced by the buyer. However, the buyer retains any right to claim damages as provided for in this Convention.

(2) If the seller requests the buyer to make known whether he will accept performance and the buyer does not comply with the request within a reasonable time, the seller may perform within the time indicated in his request. The buyer may not, during that period of time, resort to any remedy which is inconsistent with performance by the seller.

(3) A notice by the seller that he will perform within a specified period of time is assumed to include a request, under the preceding paragraph, that the buyer make known his decision.

(4) A request or notice by the seller under paragraph (2) or (3) of this article is not effective unless received by the buyer.

Article 49

(1) The buyer may declare the contract avoided:
   (a) if the failure by the seller to perform any of his obligations under the contract or this Convention amounts to a fundamental breach of contract; or
   (b) in case of non-delivery, if the seller does not deliver the goods within the additional period of time fixed by the buyer in accordance with paragraph (1) of Article 47 or declares that he will not deliver within the period so fixed.

(2) However, in cases where the seller has delivered the goods, the buyer loses the right to declare the contract avoided unless he does so:
   (a) in respect of late delivery, within a resonable time after he has become aware that delivery has been made;
   (b) in respect of any breach other than late delivery, within a reasonable time:
      (i) after he knew or ought to have known of the breach;
      (ii) after the expiration of any additional period of time fixed by the buyer in accordance with paragraph (1) of Article 47, or after the seller has declared that he will not perform his obligations within such an additional period; or
      (iii) after the expiration of any additional period of time indicated by the seller in accordance with paragraph (2) of Article 48, or after the buyer has declared that he will not accept performance.

Article 50 If the goods do not conform with the contract and whether or not the price has already been paid, the buyer may reduce the price in the same proportion as the value that the goods actually delivered had at the time of the delivery bears to the value that conforming goods would have had at that time. However, if the seller

remedies any failure to perform his obligations in accordance with Article 37 or Article 48 or if the buyer refuses to accept performance by the seller in accordance with those articles, the buyer may not reduce the price.

Article 51

(1) If the seller delivers only a part of the goods or if only a part of the goods delivered is in conformity with the contract, Articles 46 to 50 apply in respect of the part which is missing or which does not conform.

(2) The buyer may declare the contract avoided in its entirety only if the failure to make delivery completely or in conformity with the contract amounts to a fundamental breach of the contract.

Article 52

(1) If the seller delivers the goods before the date fixed, the buyer may take delivery or refuse to take delivery.

(2) If the seller delivers a quantity of goods greater than that provided for in the contract, the buyer may take delivery or refuse to take delivery of the excess quantity. If the buyer takes delivery of all or part of the excess quantity, he must pay for it at the contract rate.

Chapter III Obligations of the Buyer

Article 53 The buyer must pay the price for the goods and take delivery of them as required by the contract and this Convention.

Section I. Payment of the price

Article 54 The buyer's obligation to pay the price includes taking such steps and complying with such formalities as may be required under the contract or any laws and regulations to enable payment to be made.

Article 55 Where a contract has been validly concluded but does not expressly or implicitly fix or make provision for determining the price, the parties are considered, in the absence of any indication to the contrary, to have impliedly made reference to the price generally charged at the time of the conclusion of the contract for such goods sold under comparable circumstances in the trade concerned.

Article 56 If the price is fixed according to the weight of the goods, in case of doubt it is to be determined by the net weight.

Article 57

(1) If the buyer is not bound to pay the price at any other particular place, he must pay it to the seller:
   (a) at the seller's place of business; or
   (b) if the payment is to be made against the handing over of the goods or of documents, at the place where the handing over takes place.

(2) The seller must bear any increase in the expenses incidental to payment which is caused by a change in

his place of business subsequent to the conclusion of the contract.

Article 58

(1) If the buyer is not bound to pay the price at any other specific time, he must pay it when the seller places either the goods or documents controlling their disposition at the buyer's disposal in accordance with the contract and this Convention. The seller may make such payment a condition for handling over the goods or documents.

(2) If the contract involves carriage of the goods, the seller may dispatch the goods on terms whereby the goods, or documents controlling their disposition, will not be handed over to the buyer except against payment of the price.

(3) The buyer is not bound to pay the price until he has had an opportunity to examine the goods, unless the procedures for delivery or payment agreed upon by the parties are inconsistent with his having such an opportunity.

Article 59 The buyer must pay the price on the date fixed by or determinable from the contract and this Convention without the need for any request or compliance with any formality on the part of the seller.

Section II. Taking delivery

Article 60 The buyer's obligation to take delivery consists:

(a) in doing all the acts which could reasonably be expected of him in order to enable the seller to make delivery; and

(b) in taking over the goods.

Section III. Remedies for breach of contract by the buyer

Article 61

(1) If the buyer fails to perform any of his obligations under the contract or this Convention, the seller may:
  (a) exercise the rights provided in Articles 62 to 65;
  (b) claim damages as provided in Articles 74 to 77.

(2) The seller is not deprived of any right he may have to claim damages by exercising his right to other remedies.

(3) No period of grace may be granted to the buyer by a court or arbitral tribunal when the seller resorts to a remedy for breach of contract.

Article 62 The seller may require the buyer to pay the price, take delivery or perform his other obligations, unless the seller has resorted to a remedy which is inconsistent with this requirement.

Article 63

(1) The seller may fix an additional period of time of reasonable length for performance by the buyer of his obligations.

(2) Unless the seller has received notice from the buyer that he will not perform within the period so fixed, the seller may not, during that period, resort to any remedy for breach of contract. However, the seller is not deprived thereby of any right he may have to claim damages for delay in performance.

Article 64

(1) The seller may declare the contract avoided:
  (a) if the failure by the buyer to perform any of his obligations under the contract or this Convention amounts to a fundamental breach of contract; or
  (b) if the buyer does not, within the additional period of time fixed by the seller in accordance with paragraph (1) of Article 63, perform his obligation to pay the price or take delivery of the goods, or if he declares that he will not do so within the period so fixed.

(2) However, in cases where the buyer has paid the price, the seller loses the right to declare the contract avoided unless he does so:
  (a) in respect of late performance by the buyer, before the seller has become aware that performance has been rendered; or
  (b) in respect of any breach other than late performance by the buyer, within a reasonable time:
    (i) after the seller knew or ought to have known of the breach; or
    (ii) after the expiration of any additional period of time fixed by the seller in accordance with paragraph (1) of Article 63, or after the buyer has declared that he will not perform his obligations within such an additional period.

Article 65

(1) If under the contract the buyer is to specify the form, measurement or other features of the goods and he fails to make such specification either on the date agreed upon or within a reasonable time after receipt of a request from the seller, the seller may, without prejudice to any other rights he may have, make the specification himself in accordance with the requirements of the buyer that may be known to him.

(2) If the seller makes the specification himself, he must inform the buyer of the details thereof and must fix a reasonable time within which the buyer may make a different specification. If, after receipt of such a communication, the buyer fails to do so within the time so fixed, the specification made by the seller is binding.

Chapter IV Passing of Risk

Article 66 Loss of or damage to the goods after the risk has passed to the buyer does not discharge him from his obligation to pay the price, unless the loss or damage is due to an act or omission of the seller.

Article 67

(1) If the contract of sale involves carriage of the goods and the seller is not bound to hand them over at a particular place, the risk passes to the buyer when the goods are handed over to the first carrier for transmission to the buyer in accordance with the contract of sale. If the seller is bound to hand the goods over to a carrier at a particular place, the risk does not pass to the buyer until the goods are handed over to the carrier at that place. The fact that the seller is authorized to retain documents controlling the disposition of the goods does not affect the passage of the risk.

(2) Nevertheless, the risk does not pass to the buyer until the goods are clearly identified to the contract, whether by markings on the goods, by shipping documents, by notice given to the buyer or otherwise.

Article 68 The risk in respect of goods sold in transit passes to the buyer from the time of the conclusion of the contract. However, if the circumstances so indicate, the risk is assumed by the buyer from the time the goods were handed over to the carrier who issued the documents embodying the contract of carriage. Nevertheless, if at the time of the conclusion of the contract of sale the seller knew or ought to have known that the goods had been lost or damaged and did not disclose this to the buyer, the loss or damage is at the risk of the seller.

Article 69

(1) In cases not within Article 67 and 68, the risk passes to the buyer when he takes over the goods or, if he does not do so in due time, from the time when the goods are placed at his disposal and he commits a breach of contract by failing to take delivery.

(2) However, if the buyer is bound to take over the goods at a place other than a place of business of the seller, the risk passes when delivery is due and the buyer is aware of the fact that the goods are placed at his disposal at that place.

(3) If the contract relates to goods not then identified, the goods are considered not to be placed at the disposal of the buyer until they are clearly identified to the contract.

Article 70 If the seller has committed a fundamental breach of contract, Articles 67, 68 and 69 do not impair the remedies available to the buyer on account of the breach.

Chapter V Provisions Common to the Obligations of the Seller and of the Buyer

Section 1. Anticipatory breach and installment contracts

Article 71

(1) A party may suspend the performance of his obligations if, after the conclusion of the contract, it becomes apparent that the other party will not perform a substantial part of his obligations as a result of:

(a) a serious deficiency in his ability to perform or in his creditworthiness; or

(b) his conduct in preparing to perform or in performing the contract.

(2) If the seller has already dispatched the goods before the grounds described in the preceding paragraph become evident, he may prevent the handing over of the goods to the buyer even though the buyer holds a document which entitles him to obtain them. The present paragraph relates only to the rights in the goods as between the buyer and the seller.

(3) A party suspending performance, whether before or after dispatch of the goods, must immediately give notice of the suspension to the other party and must continue with performance if the other party provides adequate assurance of his performance.

Article 72

(1) If prior to the date for performance of the contract it is clear that one of the parties will commit a fundamental breach of contract, the other party may declare the contract avoided.

(2) If time allows, the party intending to declare the contract avoided must give reasonable notice to the other party in order to permit him to provide adequate assurance of his performance.

(3) The requirements of the preceding paragraph do not apply if the other party has declared that he will not perform his obligations.

Article 73

(1) In the case of a contract for delivery of goods by installments, if the failure of one party to perform any of his obligations in respect of any installment constitutes a fundamental breach of contract with respect to that installment, the other party may declare the contract avoided with respect to that installment.

(2) If one party's failure to perform any of his obligations in respect of any installment gives the other party good grounds to conclude that a fundamental breach of contract will occur with respect to future installments, he may declare the contract avoided for the future, provided that he does so within a reasonable time.

(3) A buyer who declares the contract avoided in respect of any delivery may, at the same time, declare it avoided in respect of deliveries already made or of future deliveries if, by reason of their interdependence, those deliveries could not be used for the purpose contemplated by the parties at the time of the conclusion of the contract.

Section II. Damages

Article 74 Damages for breach of contract by one party consist of a sum equal to the loss, including loss of profit, suffered by the other party as a consequence of the breach. Such damages may not exceed the loss which the party in breach foresaw or ought to have foreseen at the time of the conclusion of the contract, in the light of the facts and matters of which he then knew or ought to have known, as a possible consequence of the breach of contract.

Article 75 If the contract is avoided and if, in a reasonable manner and within a reasonable time after avoidance, the buyer has bought goods in replacement or the seller has resold the goods, the party claiming damages may recover the difference between the contract price and the price in the substitute transaction as well as any further damages recoverable under Article 74.

Article 76
(1) If the contract is avoided and there is a current price for the goods, the party claiming damages may, if he has not made a purchase or resale under Article 75, recover the difference between the price fixed by the contract and the current price at the time of avoidance as well as any further damages recoverable under Article 74. If, however, the party claiming damages has avoided the contract after taking over the goods, the current price at the time of such taking over shall be applied instead of the current price at the time of avoidance.
(2) For the purposes of the preceding paragraph, the current price is the price prevailing at the place where delivery of the goods should have been made or, if there is no current price at that place, the price at such other place as serves as a reasonable substitute, making due allowance for differences in the cost of transporting the goods.

Article 77 A party who relies on a breach of contract must take such measures as are reasonable in the circumstances to mitigate the loss, including loss of profit, resulting from the breach. If he fails to take such measures, the party in breach may claim a reduction in the damages in the amount by which the loss should have been mitigated.

Section III. Interest

Article 78 If a party fails to pay the price or any other sum that is in arrears, the other party is entitled to interest on it, without prejudice to any claim for damages recoverable under Article 74.

Section IV. Exemptions

Article 79
(1) A party is not liable for a failure to perform any of his obligations if he proves that the failure was due to an impediment beyond his control and that he could not reasonably be expected to have taken the impediment into account at the time of the conclusion of the contract or to have avoided or overcome it or its consequences.
(2) If the party's failure is due to the failure by a third person whom he has engaged to perform the whole or a part of the contract, that party is exempt from liability only if:
(a) he is exempt under the preceding paragraph; and
(b) the person whom he has so engaged would be so exempt if the provisions of that paragraph were applied to him.
(3) The exemption provided by this article has effect for the period during which the impediment exists.
(4) The party who fails to perform must give notice to the other party of the impediment and its effect on his ability to perform. If the notice is not received by the other party within a reasonable time after the party who fails to perform knew or ought to have known of the impediment, he is liable for damages resulting from such non-receipt.
(5) Nothing in this article prevents either party from exercising any right other than to claim damages under this Convention.

Article 80 A party may not rely on a failure of the other party to perform, to the extent that such failure was caused by the first party's act or omission.

Section V. Effects of avoidance

Article 81
(1) Avoidance of the contract releases both parties from their obligations under it, subject to any damages which may be due. Avoidance does not affect any provision of the contract for the settlement of disputes or any other provision of the contract governing the rights and obligations of the parties consequent upon the avoidance of the contract.
(2) A party who has performed the contract either wholly or in part may claim restitution from the other party of whatever the first party has supplied or paid under the contract. If both parties are bound to make restitution, they must do so concurrently.

Article 82
(1) The buyer loses the right to declare the contract avoided or to require the seller to deliver substitute goods if it is impossible for him to make restitution of the goods substantially in the condition in which he received them.
(2) The preceding paragraph does not apply:
(a) if the impossibility of making restitution of the goods or of making restitution of the goods substantially in the condition in which the buyer received them is not due to his act or omission;
(b) if the goods or part of the goods have perished or deteriorated as a result of the examination provided for in Article 38; or
(c) if the goods or part of the goods have been sold in the normal course of business or have been consumed or transformed by the buyer in the course of normal use before he discovered or ought to have discovered the lack of conformity.

Article 83 A buyer who has lost the right to declare the contract avoided or to require the seller to deliver substitute goods in accordance with Article 82 retains all other remedies under the contract and this Convention.

Article 84
(1) If the seller is bound to refund the price, he must also pay interest on it, from the date on which the price was paid.
(2) The buyer must account to the seller for all benefits which he has derived from the goods or part of them:
    (a) if he must make restitution of the goods or part of them; or
    (b) if it is impossible for him to make restitution of all or part of the goods or to make restitution of all or part of the goods substantially in the condition in which he received them, but he has nevertheless declared the contract avoided or required the seller to deliver substitute goods.

Section VI. Preservation of the goods

Article 85 If the buyer is in delay in taking delivery of the goods or, where payment of the price and delivery of the goods are to be made concurrently, if he fails to pay the price, and the seller is either in possession of the goods or otherwise able to control their disposition, the seller must take such steps as are reasonable in the circumstances to preserve them. He is entitled to retain them until he has been reimbursed his reasonable expenses by the buyer.

Article 86
(1) If the buyer has received the goods and intends to exercise any right under the contract or this Convention to reject them, he must take such steps to preserve them as are reasonable in the circumstances. He is entitled to retain them until he has been reimbursed his reasonable expenses by the seller.
(2) If goods dispatched to the buyer have been placed at his disposal at their destination and he exercises the right to reject them, he must take possession of them on behalf of the seller, provided that this can be done without payment of the price and without unreasonable inconvenience or unreasonable expense. This provision does not apply if the seller or a person authorized to take charge of the goods on his behalf is present at the destination. If the buyer takes possession of the goods under this paragraph, his rights and obligations are governed by the preceding paragraph.

Article 87 A party who is bound to take steps to preserve the goods may deposit them in a warehouse of a third person at the expense of the other party provided that the expense incurred is not unreasonable.

Article 88
(1) A party who is bound to preserve the goods in accordance with Article 85 or 86 may sell them by any appropriate means if there has been an unreasonable delay by the other party in taking possession of the goods or in taking them back or in paying the price or the cost of preservation, provided that reasonable notice of the intention to sell has been given to the other party.
(2) If the goods are subject to rapid deterioration or their preservation would involve unreasonable expense, a party who is bound to preserve the goods in accordance with Article 85 or 86 must take reasonable measures to sell them. To the extent possible he must give notice to the other party of his intention to sell.
(3) A party selling the goods has the right to retain out of the proceeds of sale an amount equal to the reasonable expenses of preserving the goods and of selling them. He must account to the other party for the balance.

Part IV Final Provisions

Article 89 The Secretary-General of the United Nations is hereby designated as the depositary for this Convention.

Article 90 This Convention does not prevail over any international agreement which has already been or may be entered into and which contains provisions concerning the matters governed by this Convention, provided that the parties have their places of business in States parties to such agreement.

Article 91
(1) This Convention is open for signature at the concluding meeting of the United Nations Conference on Contracts for the International Sale of Goods and will remain open for signature by all States at the Headquarters of the United Nations, New York, until 30 September 1981.
(2) This Convention is subject to ratification, acceptance or approval by the signatory States.
(3) This Convention is open for accession by all States which are not signatory States as from the date it is open for signature.
(4) Instruments of ratification, acceptance, approval and accession are to be deposited with the Secretary-General of the United Nations.

Article 92
(1) A Contracting State may declare at the time of signature, ratification, acceptance, approval or accession that it will not be bound by Part II of this Convention or that it will not be bound by Part III of this Convention.
(2) A Contracting State which makes a declaration in accordance with the preceding paragraph in respect of Part II or Part III of this Convention is not to be considered a Contracting State within paragraph (1) of Article 1 of this Convention in respect of matters governed by the Part to which the declaration applies.

Article 93

(1) If a Contracting State has two or more territorial units in which, according to its constitution, different systems of law are applicable in relation to the matters dealt with in this Convention, it may, at the time of signature, ratification, acceptance, approval or accession, declare that this Convention is to extend to all its territorial units or only to one or more of them, and may amend its declaration by submitting another declaration at any time.

(2) These declarations are to be notified to the depositary and are to state expressly the territorial units to which the Convention extends.

(3) If, by virtue of a declaration under this article, this Convention extends to one or more but not all of the territorial units of a Contracting State, and if the place of business of a party is located in that State, this place of business, for the purposes of this Convention, is considered not to be in a Contracting State, unless it is in a territorial unit to which the Convention extends.

(4) If a Contracting State makes no declaration under paragraph (1) of this article, the Convention is to extend to all territorial units of that State.

Article 94

(1) Two or more Contracting States which have the same or closely related legal rules on matters governed by this Convention may at any time declare that the Convention is not to apply to contracts of sale or to their formation where the parties have their places of business in those States. Such declarations may be made jointly or by reciprocal unilateral declarations.

(2) A Contracting State which has the same or closely related legal rules on matters governed by this Convention as one or more non-Contracting States may at any time declare that the Convention is not to apply to contracts of sale or to their formation where the parties have their places of business in those States.

(3) If a State which is the object of a declaration under the preceding paragraph subsequently becomes a Contracting State, the declaration made will, as from the date on which the Convention enters into force in respect of the new Contracting State, have the effect of a declaration made under paragraph (1), provided that the new Contracting State joins in such declaration or makes a reciprocal unilateral declaration.

Article 95 Any State may declare at the time of the deposit of its instrument of ratification, acceptance, approval or accession that it will not be bound by subparagraph (1)(b) of Article 1 of this Convention. [The United States has made such reservation.]

Article 96 A Contracting State whose legislation requires contracts of sale to be concluded in or evidenced by writing may at any time make a declaration in accordance with Article 12 that any provision of Article 11, Article 29, or Part II of this Convention, that allows a contract of sale or its modification or termination by agreement or any offer, acceptance, or other indication of intention to be made in any form other than in writing, does not apply where any party has his place of business in that State.

Article 97

(1) Declarations made under this Convention at the time of signature are subject to confirmation upon ratification, acceptance or approval.

(2) Declarations and confirmations of declarations are to be in writing and be formally notified to the depositary.

(3) A declaration takes effect simultaneously with the entry into force of this Convention in respect of the State concerned. However, a declaration of which the depositary receives formal notification after such entry into force takes effect on the first day of the month following the expiration of six months after the date of its receipt by the depositary. Reciprocal unilateral declarations under Article 94 take effect on the first day of the month following the expiration of six months after the receipt of the latest declaration by the depositary.

(4) Any State which makes a declaration under this Convention may withdraw it at any time by a formal notification in writing addressed to the depositary. Such withdrawal is to take effect on the first day of the month following the expiration of six months after the date of the receipt of the notification by the depositary.

(5) A withdrawal of a declaration made under Article 94 renders inoperative, as from the date on which the withdrawal takes effect, any reciprocal declaration made by another State under that article.

Article 98 No reservations are permitted except those expressly authorized in this Convention.

Article 99

(1) This Convention enters into force, subject to the provisions of paragraph (6) of this article, on the first day of the month following the expiration of twelve months after the date of deposit of the tenth instrument of ratification, acceptance, approval or accession, including an instrument which contains a declaration made under Article 92.

(2) When a State ratifies, accepts, approves or accedes to this Convention after the deposit of the tenth instrument of ratification, acceptance, approval or accession, this Convention, with the exception of the Part excluded, enters into force in respect of that State, subject to the provisions of paragraph (6) of this article, on the first day of the month following the expiration of twelve months after the date of the deposit of its instrument of ratification, acceptance, approval or accession.

(3) A State which ratifies, accepts, approves or accedes to this Convention and is a party to either or both the Convention relating to a Uniform Law on the

Formation of Contracts for the International Sale of Goods done at The Hague on 1 July 1964 (1964 Hague Formation Convention) and the Convention relating to a Uniform Law on the International Sale of Goods done at The Hague on 1 July 1964 (1964 Hague Sales Convention) shall at the same time denounce, as the case may be, either or both the 1964 Hague Sales Convention and the 1964 Hague Formation Convention by notifying the Government of the Netherlands to that effect.

(4) A State party to the 1964 Hague Sales Convention which ratifies, accepts, approves or accedes to the present Convention and declares or has declared under Article 92 that it will not be bound by Part II of this Convention shall at the time of ratification, acceptance, approval or accession denounce the 1964 Hague Sales Convention by notifying the Government of the Netherlands to that effect.

(5) A State party to the 1964 Hague Formation Convention which ratifies, accepts, approves or accedes to the present Convention and declares or has declared under Article 92 that it will not be bound by Part III of this Convention shall at the time of ratification, acceptance, approval or accession denounce the 1964 Hague Formation Convention by notifying the Government of the Netherlands to that effect.

(6) For the purpose of this article, ratifications, acceptances, approvals and accessions in respect of this Convention by States parties to the 1964 Hague Formation Convention or to the 1964 Hague Sales Convention shall not be effective until such denunciations as may be required on the part of those States in respect of the latter two Conventions have themselves become effective. The depositary of this Convention shall consult with the Government of the Netherlands, as the depositary of the 1964 Conventions, so as to ensure necessary co-ordination in this respect.

Article 100

(1) This Convention applies to the formation of a contract only when the proposal for concluding the contract is made on or after the date when the Convention enters into force in respect of the Contracting States referred to in subparagraph (1)(a) or the Contracting States referred to in subparagraph (1)(b) of Article 1.

(2) This Convention applies only to contracts concluded on or after the date when the Convention enters into force in respect of the Contracting States referred to in subparagraph (1)(a) or the Contracting State referred to in subparagraph (1)(b) of Article 1.

Article 101

(1) A Contracting State may denounce this Convention, or Part II or Part III of the Convention, by a formal notification in writing addressed to the depositary.

(2) The denunciation takes effect on the first day of the month following the expiration of twelve months after the notification is received by the depositary. Where a longer period for the denunciation to take effect is specified in the notification, the denunciation takes effect upon the expiration of such longer period after the notification is received by the depositary.

DONE at Vienna, this day of eleventh day of April, one thousand nine hundred and eighty, in a single original, of which the Arabic, Chinese, English, French, Russian and Spanish texts are equally authentic.

IN WITNESS WHEREOF the undersigned plenipotentiaries, being duly authorized by their respective Governments, have signed this Convention.

Glossary

abandoned In contract law, the condition that exists when a minor has left home and given up all rights to parental support.

abandoned property Property that has been discarded by the owner without the intent to reclaim ownership of it. Courts require clear and convincing evidence of both the desertion by the owner and the owner's intent never to return.

abandonment of contractual obligations The situation that exists when a party to a contract stops performance once it has begun.

abuse of discretion The determination that the judge in the lower court has misused his or her authority.

abuse of process The use of a legal procedure for a purpose other than that for which it is legitimately intended.

acceleration A provision in a mortgage agreement that allows the mortgagee to demand the entire balance due when the mortgagor misses a single installment payment.

acceptance A promise or act on the part of an offeree indicating a willingness to be bound by the terms and conditions contained in an offer. Also, the acknowledgment of the drawee that binds the drawee to the terms of a draft.

acceptor A drawee of a draft who has promised to honor the draft as presented by signing it on its face.

accommodation party A person who signs an instrument in any capacity for the purpose of lending his or her name to another party to the instrument. That person then assumes the same liability as the marker.

accord The implied or expressed acceptance of less than what the creditor billed the debtor.

accord and satisfaction An agreement (accord) whereby a creditor accepts as full payment an amount that is less than the amount due.

accountant A professional who can plan, direct, and evaluate a client's financial affairs.

accounting A statement detailing the financial transactions of a business and the status of its assets.

acknowledgment The official recognition by a notary public that another's signature was made by that party's free will. The acknowledgment is accomplished when the notary has signed the document and added the official seal to it.

active data Data in a computer system that are actually being used at the present time.

active fraud A false statement made or an action actually taken by one party with the intent to deceive a second

party and thus lead that second party into a deceptively based agreement.

activist agencies Agencies that use their regulatory powers to advance social agendas that are technically outside their legislative authority.

actual authority rule A rule that states a manager may be liable for exceeding his or her authority if the corporation is harmed as a result.

actual damages A sum of money equal to the real financial loss suffered by an injured party. Also called *compensatory damages*.

actual eviction An eviction in which the tenant is physically deprived of the leasehold.

actual malice The legal test used by the courts to determine defamation against a public official or a public figure. The actual malice test requires the public official or public figure to prove not only that the statement was false but also that it was made with the knowledge that it was false or with a reckless disregard for its truth or falsity.

actual malice test A defense against libel cases that states public officials must prove not only that the statement was false but that it was made with actual malice.

adhesion contract A contract drawn by one party that must be accepted as is on a take-it-or-leave-it basis.

administrative law That body of law, including decrees and legal decisions, generated by administrative agencies.

administrator (male); administratrix (female) A person appointed by the court to do the work of an executor if none is named in a will or if the executor either refuses to perform or is incapable of performing the duties.

ADR contract clause A clause that specifies that the parties to the agreement have promised to use an alternative dispute resolution technique when a disagreement arises rather than litigating the issue.

advance directives Written statement in which people gives instructions for their future medical care.

adversarial system The system on which the American legal process is built. An orderly and aggressive way to settle disputes in which attorneys for each side attempt to persuade a judge or jury of the veracity of his or her case.

adverse opinion An auditor's opinion that states that deviations from generally accepted accounting principles are so serious that an unqualified opinion is impossible and a qualified opinion is not justified.

adverse possession Title to real property obtained by taking actual possession of the property openly, notoriously, exclusively, under a claim of right, and continuously for a period of time set by state statute.

affirmance See *ratification*.

affirmative action A policy designed to reduce the effects of past discrimination.

affirmative defense A set of circumstances that indicates that a defendant should not be held liable, even if the plaintiff proves all of the facts in a complaint.

agency A legal agreement between two persons, whereby one is designated the agent of the other.

agency coupled with an interest An irrevocable agency agreement in which the agent is given an interest in the subject matter of the agency. Also called *irrevocable agency*.

agent A person authorized to act on behalf of another and subject to the other's control in dealing with third parties.

aggregate theory A theory in partnership law that holds that a partnership is actually a conglomeration of the partners rather than a separate legal person with its own legal identity.

agreements in restraint of trade Agreements that remove competition, deny to the public the services it would otherwise have, or result in higher prices and hardship.

algorithm A series of mathematical steps that, if followed properly, will reach a desired goal.

alien corporation A corporation that though incorporated in a foreign country does business in the United States.

allonge A strip of paper attached to a negotiable instrument for the writing of indorsements.

alternative dispute resolution (ADR) A process that occurs whenever individuals attempt to resolve a disagreement by stepping outside the usual adversarial system and applying creative settlement techniques, many of which have fact finding and the discovery of truth as their goal.

American Law Institute (ALI) test A test under which a criminal defendant will be judged not guilty by reason of insanity "as a result of mental disease or defect he lacks substantial capacity either to appreciate the criminality of his conduct or to conform his conduct to the requirements of the law."

annual percentage rate (APR) The true rate of interest on a loan.

annuity A guaranteed retirement income.

anomalous indorsement An indorsement made by an accommodation party.

answer A defendant's official response to a complaint.

anticipatory breach A breach that occurs when a party to a contract either expresses or clearly implies an intention not to perform the contract even before being required to act. Also called *constructive breach*.

apparent authority An accountability doctrine whereby a principal, by virtue of words or actions, leads a third party to believe that an agent has authority but no such authority was intended. Also called *ostensible authority*.

appeal The referral of a case to a higher court for review.

appeal bond The payment of a set sum of money into a protected account to secure the payment of that money to the plaintiff should the defendant be defeated.

appellate jurisdiction The power of a court to review a case for errors.

arbitration The process by which an outside party settles a dispute between two other parties.

arbitrator The third party in the arbitration procedure whose job is to settle the dispute.

arraignment A formal court proceeding, during which the defendant, after hearing the indictment or information read, pleads either guilty or not guilty.

arson The willful or malicious act of causing the burning of another's property.

articles of Confederation The first constitution of the United States; replaced by the U.S. Constitution in 1787.

articles of incorporation A written application to a state for permission to incorporate.

articles of organization The written application to the state for permission to form a limited liability company.

articles of partnership A written agreement that establishes a partnership.

assault An attempt to commit a battery.

asset acquisition The purchase of all the property of a corporation by another corporation.

assign To transfer property by sale, mortgage, pledge, or otherwise.

assignee A person to whom an assignment is made.

assignment The transfer of a contract right from one person to another.

assignor A person who assigns rights or delegates duties under an assignment.

associative corporativism The process of doing business as a self-governing business association, that is, as a corporation. Also known as *corporativism*.

assume the mortgage An agreement whereby the buyer of real property already mortgaged agrees to pay the mortgage.

assumption of the risk A defense against negligence that states the victim voluntarily exposed him- or herself to a known risk.

ATM card A card used together with a personal identification number (PIN) to gain access to an automatic teller machine.

attachment The act of taking a person's property and bringing it into the custody of law.

attorney-client privilege The guarantee that information that passes between clients and attorneys remains secret.

auction A sale that is open to the public, during which potential buyers compete for the right to purchase certain items by placing higher and higher bids until the highest bid is reached and the auctioneer accepts on behalf of the seller

auction with reserve An auction at which the auctioneer has the right to withdraw goods and not sell them if acceptable bids are not made.

auction without reserve An auction at which the auctioneer cannot withdraw goods unless no bid is made within a reasonable time.

audit An examination of the financial records of an organization to determine whether those records are a fair representation of the actual financial health of the institution.

auditor The accountant who examines the financial records of an organization to determine whether those records are a fair representation of the actual financial health of the institution.

authenticate (*a*) to sign; or (*b*) with the intent to sign a record, otherwise to execute or adopt an electronic symbol, sound, message, or process referring to, attached to, included in, or logically associated or linked with, that record.

automatic stay A self-operating postponement of collection proceedings against a debtor who has filed a petition for bankruptcy.

automatic suspension A court order that stops a debtor's creditors from making any further moves to collect the money that the debtor owes them.

back-up data Data associated with a computer system that have been duplicated for safekeeping at another location.

bailee The person to whom personal property is transferred under a contract of bailment.

bailment The transfer of possession and control of personal property to another with the intent that the same property will be returned later.

bailment by necessity Arises when a customer must give up possession of property for the benefit of both parties; for example, when one purchases a suit or dress and is required to give up possession of one's own property while being fitted.

bailment for the sole benefit of the bailee A bailment in which the bailee receives all the benefits of the transaction.

bailment for the sole benefit of the bailor A bailment in which the bailor receives all the transaction.

bailor The person who transfers personal property under a contract of bailment.

bait-and-switch confidence game An illegal promotional practice in which a seller attracts consumers by promoting a product (bait) that he or she does not intend to sell and then directs the consumers' attention to a higher-priced product (switch).

balloon payment A large final payment on a mortgage that has relatively low fixed payments during the life of the mortgage.

balloon-payment mortgage A mortgage that has relatively low fixed payments during the life of the mortgage followed by one large final (balloon) payment.

bank draft A check drawn by one bank on another bank in which it has funds on deposit in favor of a third person, the payee. Also called *teller's check*.

bankruptcy The legal process by which the assets of a debtor are sold to pay off creditors so that the debtor can make a fresh start financially.

bankruptcy trustee A person appointed by the court who is charged with the responsibility of liquidating the assets of the debtor for the benefit of all interested parties.

bargain-and-sale deed A deed that transfers title to real property but contains no warranties. This type of deed is not valid without consideration.

bargained-for exchange In reference to agreements, when a promise is made in exchange for another promise, in exchange for an act, or in exchange for a forbearance to act.

bargaining unit Employees joined together for the purpose of collective bargaining.

bartering An exchange of services and/or goods that are equal in value.

battered spouse syndrome A defense to criminal liability available to defendants if they can prove that they believed the only way to escape death or severe bodily injury was to use force against their tormentors.

battery The unlawful touching of another person.

bearer A person who is in possession of a negotiable instrument that is payable to the "bearer" or "cash" or that has been indorsed in blank.

bearer paper An instrument payable to bearer or cash that may be negotiated by delivery only.

beneficiary A third party receiving benefits from a contract made between two other parties. Also, the person named in an insurance policy to receive benefits paid by the insurer in event of a claim.

bequest Personal property left in a will. Also called *legacy*.

best evidence rule The legal rule that holds that the courts generally accept into evidence only the original of a writing, not a copy.

best-price rule Rules that prohibit suitors from offering different prices to different shareholders during a tender offer process.

bilateral contract A contract in which both parties make promises.

bilateral mistake In contract law, a mistake made by both parties to a contract. Bilateral mistake allows rescission by either party. Also called *mutual mistake*.

bill of exchange See *draft*.

bill of lading A document evidencing the receipt of goods for shipment and issued by a person engaged in the business of transporting or forwarding goods.

bill of sale A written statement evidencing the transfer of personal property from one person to another.

binder An oral or a written memorandum of an agreement for insurance intended to provide temporary insurance coverage until the policy is formally accepted.

binding precedent A previous cause that a particular court must follow.

blank indorsement An indorsement made by a signature alone, with no particular indorsee, written on a negotiable instrument.

blue laws State statutes and local ordinances that regulate the making and performing of contracts on Sunday.

bodily injury liability insurance A type of automobile insurance that covers the risk of bodily injury or death to pedestrians and to the occupants of other cars arising from the negligent operation of the insured's motor vehicle.

bond A certificate of indebtedness that obligates a government or corporation to pay the bondholder a fixed rate of interest on the principal at regular intervals and to pay the principal on a stated maturity date. Also, a promise by the executor or administrator (and the sureties, if any) of a will to pay the amount of the bond to the probate court if the duties of the position are not faithfully performed.

borrowed servant A servant loaned to another master.

bot A type of cyberagent that searches cyberspace for the lowest price in a contract, sifts through the net for the best accommodations, hunts cyberspace for the most economical plan, or spontaneously responds to a bidding process. Also known as *robot, shopping bot, cyberbot,* and *e-bot*.

boycott A concerted refusal to have dealings with someone to force the acceptance of certain conditions.

breach of contract The failure of one of the parties to a contract to do what was previously agreed upon.

bribery The act of offering, giving, receiving, or soliciting something of value to influence official action or the discharge of a public duty.

bright-line test Test used by the courts that establishes violations of the best-price rule occur only during the actual tender offer.

bulk transfer Any transfer of a major party of the materials, supplies, merchandise, or other inventory of an enterprise that is not in the ordinary course of the transferor's business.

burglary The break-in of a dwelling or building for the purpose of carrying out a felony.

business compulsion See *economic duress*.

business judgment rule The rule that a corporate manager's decisions will not be interfered with by a court as long as the decision was made with due care, is in good faith, is lawful, and is in the best interest of the corporation.

business system Until recently, business systems were considered unpatentable because they were not a "process, machine, or composition of matter." Recently, however, some computerized business systems have been patented if they consist of some nonobvious, new, and useful feature not known or understood before the invention of this system.

buyer in the ordinary course of business A person who in good faith and without knowledge that the sale is in violation of ownership rights or security interests of a third party buys goods in ordinary course from a person in the business of selling goods of that kind, not including a pawnbroker.

Buyer's Guide A window sticker that is required by the Federal Trade Commission Act to be placed in the window of each used car offered for sale by a used car dealer. The sticker discloses the warranties that are made with the sale of the car and other consumer protection information.

bylaws Rules that guide a corporation's day-to-day internal affairs. Also known as *regulations*.

c.f. Cost and freight. Terms instructing a carrier to collect the cost of goods shipped and freight charges.

c.i.f. Cost, insurance, and freight. Terms instructing a carrier to collect the cost of goods shipped, insurance, and freight charges.

c.o.d. Cash on delivery. Instructs a carrier to retain goods until he or she has collected the costs of the goods.

Can Spam Act A federal law designed to reduce the use of unsolicited email, commonly known as spam, on the Internet.

capacity In contract law, the legal ability to enter into a contractual relationship.

capital The money and property that a business needs to operate.

capital contribution The sum contributed by a business partner as a permanent investment in the business. It is then considered to be the property of the partnership.

carrier A business that undertakes to transport persons, goods, or both.

case in chief The collection of evidence that will prove a plaintiff's version of case to a jury.

case trustee A person appointed by a bankruptcy court to meet with creditors and report whether the case should proceed.

cash dividend Dividend paid to shareholders in the form of cash.

cashier's check A check drawn by a bank upon its own funds.

certificate of authority A document that grants a foreign corporation permission to do business within another state.

certificate of deposit (CD) An acknowledgment by a bank of the receipt of money and a promise to pay the money back on the due date, usually with interest.

certificate of incorporation A corporation's official authorization to do business in a state. Also called *charter* or *corporate charter*.

certification authority (CA) It is the job of the CA to provide businesses with digital signatures and to make certain that those signatures are kept current.

certified check A check that has been marked, or certified, by the bank on which it was drawn, guaranteeing payment to the holder.

certified public accountant (CPA) An accountant who has met certain age, character, education, experience, and testing requirements.

chattels Property that has substance and that can be touched.

check A draft drawn on a bank and payable on demand.

Check 21 Act A law that makes check clearing much quicker by the use of a *substitute check* in place of the original check for electronic check processing.

chemical abuse The use of drugs or alcohol to such an extent that a person's judgment is impaired or his or her physical body is harmed.

chemical dependency The state a person reaches when she or he can no longer function normally without regularly consuming drugs or alcohol.

chose in action Evidence of the right to property but not the property itself.

civil litigation The process of bringing a case to court to enforce a right.

civilization A group of people in a series of different nation-states that share certain common characteristics, including history, language, religion, traditions, beliefs, and sometimes blood.

class-action lawsuit A lawsuit that is brought by one or more plaintiffs on behalf of a class of persons.

clearly erroneous standard The determination that the decision made in the lower court was undeniably wrong, given the facts and evidence in the case.

click-on acceptance A method of acceptance used in Internet contracts in which a party manifests acceptance by clicking on an icon on the computer screen that states that he or she agrees to the terms of the contract.

close corporation A corporation whose shares of stock and managerial control are closely held be fewer than 50 shareholders (often members of the same family) or by one person.

close-end credit Credit that is extended only for a specific amount of money, such as to buy a car or other expensive item.

closed shop A place of employment in which the employer, by agreement, hires only union members in good standing.

code A compilation of all the statutes of a particular state or of the federal government.

Code of Federal Regulations (CFR) Annual listing of finalized federal rules and regulations.

Code of Professional Ethics A set of rules established by the American Institute of Certified Public Accountants that outlines rules that govern the ethical conduct of accountants.

codicil A formal document used to supplement or change an existing will.

coinsurance An insurance policy provision under which the insurer and the insured share costs, after the deductible is met, according to a specific formula.

collateral The property that is subject to a security interest.

collecting bank Any bank handling an item for collection except the payor bank.

collective bargaining A good faith meeting between representatives of employees and employers to discuss the terms and conditions of employment.

collective bargaining agreement A contract negotiated by an employer and a labor union that covers all issues related to employment.

collision insurance A type of automobile insurance that protects the insured against any loss arising from damage to the insured's automobile caused by accidental collision with another object or with any part of the roadbed.

comaker A person obligated, along with at least one other person, as a payor on a promissory note.

commerce Trade among the several states or between any foreign country and any state or territory.

Commerce Clause The clause in the U.S. Constitution that gives the federal government the power to regulate business.

commercial impracticability A doctrine under which the courts may excuse the performance of one party to a contract because an unforeseen and very severe hardship has arisen that would place an enormous amount of hardship on that party.

commercial unit A single whole for the purpose of sale, the division of which impairs its character or value on the market, such as a set of furniture.

commingled Mixed together, as in goods stored at a warehouse.

common carrier A company that transports goods or persons for compensation and offers its facilities to the general public without discrimination. Compare *contract carrier.*

common law The body of recorded decisions that courts refer to and rely upon when making later legal decisions.

common stock The most usual type of corporate stock. It carries with it all the risks of the business and does not guarantee its holder the right to profits.

community property Property that is acquired by the personal effects of either spouse during marriage and which, by law, belongs to both spouses equally.

comparative negligence A form of contributory negligence that requires the court to assign damages according to the degree of fault of each party.

compassion Respect for others and their rights. Compassionate people are sympathetic to the suffering of others and are understanding of their shortcomings.

compensatory damages See *actual damages.*

competent authority The requirement that just war may be declared and run only by legitimately recognized nation-states.

complaint A legal document filed by a plaintiff to begin a lawsuit. The complaint sets forth the names of the parties, the facts in the case, and the relief sought by the plaintiff.

complete performance In contract law, the situation that exists when both parties to a contract have fully accomplished every term, condition, and promise to which they agreed.

complex adaptive system A network of interacting conditions that reinforce one another while at the same time adjusting to changes from agents both inside and outside of the system.

comprehensive coverage A type of automobile insurance that provides protection against loss when the insured's car is damaged or destroyed by fire, lightning, flood, hail, windstorm, riot, vandalism, or theft.

computer firmware Computer software that is written to be used with only one type or brand of computer.

computer hardware The actual device known as a computer and its components, including the keyboard, screen, disk drive, and printer.

computer information Information in a form directly capable of being processed or used by, or obtained from or through, a computer.

computer package The combination of the computer hardware and the computer software when sold together.

computer program The instructions that tell the computer hardware what to do and when to do it.

computer software The card, tape, disk, or silicon chip that contains the computer program.

concealment In insurance, the intentional withholding of a fact that would be of material importance to the insurer's decision to issue a policy. See also *passive fraud.*

condemnation See *eminent domain.*

condition concurrent A condition in a contract that requires both parties to perform at the same time.

condition precedent In contract law, an act or promise that must take place or be fulfilled before the other party is obligated to perform his or her part of the agreement.

condition subsequent A condition in a contract in which the parties agree that the contract will be terminated depending on a prescribed event occurring or not occurring.

conditional indorsement An indorsement that makes the rights of the indorsee subject to the happening of a certain event or condition.

confidential relationship A relationship of trust and dependence between persons in a continued relationship, as between doctor and patient or between parent and child.

confirmation In bankruptcy law, the official approval of a reorganization plan.

conforming goods Goods that are in accordance with the obligations under the contract.

conglomerate expansion The joining of two companies that were not in competition with each other either because they dealt in different products or services or because they operated in different geographical areas.

consensual An agreement to act.

consent decree Agreements created by the Department of Justice to help parties negotiate a legal merger.

consent order Under the Federal Trade Commission Act, an order under which a company agrees to stop a disputed practice without necessarily admitting that the practice violated the law.

consequential damages Losses that do not flow directly and immediately from an act but only from some of the consequences or results of the act.

consideration In contract law, the mutual promise to exchange benefits and sacrifices between parties.

consignee One to whom goods are entrusted under a *consignment contract* for the purpose of selling them.

consignment contract A type of mutual benefit bailment in which the *consignor* entrusts goods to the *consignee* for the purpose of selling them.

consignor One who entrusts goods under a *consignment contract* to a *consignee* for the purpose of selling them.

consolidation The joining of two corporations.

conspiracy The crime that occurs when people get together with others to talk about, plan, or agree to the commission of a crime.

constitution The basic law of a nation or state.

constitutional law That body of law that involves a constitution and its interpretation.

constructive discharge Discriminatory action whereby an employee is demoted to a job with less pay, authority, or poorer working conditions than the job that person previously held or is subjected to supervisory harassment.

constructive eviction An eviction that occurs by the act of the landlord depriving the tenant of something of a substantial nature that was called for under the lease.

consumer Someone who buys or leases real estate, goods, or services for personal, family, or household purposes.

consumer goods Goods normally used for personal, family, or household purposes.

consumer products Tangible personal property normally used for personal, family, or household purposes.

continuity of existence doctrine A concept promoted by the Revised Uniform Partnership Act that permits a partnership to continue to operate as an entity even after individual partners are no longer associated with it.

contract An agreement based on mutual promises between two or more competent parties to do or to refrain from doing some particular thing that is neither illegal nor impossible. The agreement results in an obligation or a duty that can be enforced in a court of law.

contract carrier A company that transports goods or persons for compensation only for those people with whom it desires to do business. Compare *common carrier*.

contract for sale Either a present sale of goods or a contract to sell goods at a future time.

contract of record A special type of formal contract usually confirmed by a court with an accompanying judgment issued in favor of one of the parties.

contributory copyright infringement A violation of copyright law in which one party provides a way for a second party to violate the copyright protection granted to the third party even though the first party never violates the copyright himself or herself.

contributory negligence A legal defense that involves the failure of an injured party to be careful enough to ensure personal safety.

controlled company A corporation that has more than half its voting power concentrated in one person or a small group of persons, who always vote together.

Convention on Contracts for the International Sale of Goods (CISG) A United Nations treaty designed to govern commercial transactions between parties whose places of business are in different countries.

conventional mortgage A mortgage that involves no government backing by either insurance or guarantee.

conversion The wrongful exercise of dominion and control over another's personal property.

conveyance in trust A trust in which the settlor conveys away the legal title to a trustee to hold for the benefit of either the settlor or another as beneficiary.

Cooling-off Rule A Federal Trade Commission rule under which sales of consumer goods or services over $25 made away from the seller's regular place of business may be canceled within three business days after the sale occurs.

copyright A right granted to an author, composer, photographer, or artist to exclusively publish and sell an artistic or literary work for the life of the author plus 70 years.

corporate democracy See *shareholder democracy*.

corporate opportunity doctrine A principle that states corporate managers cannot take a business opportunity for themselves if they know their corporation would be interested in that opportunity.

corporate raid An unfriendly takeover, designed to dismantle the target corporation.

corporate raider An unfriendly suitor that intends to dismantle the target corporation after obtaining it.

corporation A legal entity (or a legal person) created by either a state or federal statute authorizing individuals to operate an enterprise.

corporation by estoppel The doctrine by which parties who have benefited by dealing with a business as though it were a corporation—though in law it is not—cannot deny its existence as a corporation. Similarly, individuals who have acted as if they were a corporation would not be able to deny that the corporation existed.

cost-benefit thinking A system of thought that focuses on the consequences to one person or institution and then weighs the cost against the benefits of performing the action under scrutiny.

cost of repair rule The principle that states that an architect or contractor may have to reimburse a client for any extra money spent by the client to correct an error initially made by the architect or contractor.

cost-plus contract A contract in which the price is determined by the cost of labor and materials plus an agreed percentage markup.

cotenancy The quality or state of more than one owner of a single property.

cotenants Two or more persons who own real property together.

counteroffer A response to an offer in which the terms and conditions of the original offer are changed.

courts Judicial tribunals that meet in a regular place and apply the law in an attempt to settle disputes by weighing the arguments presented by advocates for each party.

cover Buying similar goods from someone else when a seller breaches a contract.

creditor beneficiary A third party to whom one or both contracting parties owe a continuing debt of obligation arising from a contract.

crime An offense against the public at large punishable by the official governing body of a nation or state.

cross-appeal An appeal filed by a party that has prevailed at trial.

cross-examination The questioning of witnesses by an opposing attorney.

cumulative voting A system of voting for corporate directors that is designed to benefit minority shareholders by allowing shareholders to multiply their voting shares by the number of directors to be elected.

cure The correction of a defect in goods that caused the goods to be rejected by a buyer.

current market price contract An agreement in which the prices are determined with reference to the market price of the goods on a specified date.

curtesy Under common law, the right that a widower had, if children of the marriage were born alive, to a life estate in all real property owned by the wife during the marriage.

cyberagent (AKA electronic agent and e-agent) A computer program that acts without human intervention to begin an activity, to answer cybermessages, to deliver or accept cybermail, or to enter cybercontracts.

cybercontract A contract involving the sale or licensing of information in a digital format.

cybercrime Any criminal act that includes a computer.

cyberdefamation The communication of false and destructive information about an individual through the use of a computer or other electronic device.

cyberdiscovery A search for evidence using a computer. Also called *cyberspace discovery*.

cyberevidence Any and all types of computer-generated data.

cyberextortion Gaining access to the computer records of a business or other institution and, in the process, uncovering the illegal, unethical, or negligent conduct of that organization and using that information to commit extortion. Also called *cyberblackmail*.

cybergerm warfare Using viruses to attack a computer system.

cyberinvasion of privacy The unwelcome intrusion into private matters initiated or maintained by a computer.

cyberjurisdiction The authority of a court to hear a case based on Internet-related transactions.

cyberlaw A single law or a series of laws that deals exclusively with some aspect of computers and their attendant elements, such as their hardware and software.

cyberpirate Someone who registers a trademark or trademarks as a domain name with little or no intention of actually using the domain name in the hope that the actual holders of the trademark will buy the domain name for enormous sums.

cyberprincipal A principal who places authority in the hands of a cyberagent.

cyberspoiler See *cyberpirate*.

cyberspoofing Falsely adopting the identity of another computer user or creating a false identity on a computer Web site to commit fraud.

cyberspyware (AKA cybersnoopware) A program which, once it is installed in a computer, can keep a record of the keyboarding patterns established by the computer user.

cybersquatter See *cyberpirate*.

cyberstalking Targeting an individual for exploitation using that person's computer connections.

cyberterrorism Using a computer to disrupt or destroy one of the critical elements of the nation's electronic infrastructure.

cybertort The invasion, distortion, theft, falsification, misuse, destruction, or financial exploitation of information stored in a computer.

cybertrespass Gaining access to a computer with the intent to commit a crime.

cybervandalism Attacking a computer system so that a Web site is completely destroyed or paralyzed.

damage cap A limit on the amount of money that juries can award in certain types of tort law cases.

damages Money recovered by a party in a court action to compensate that party for injury or loss.

database The compilation of information in a form that can be understood and used by a computer.

data mining Searching for and placing together two or more pieces of public information to create information that the victim considers private.

de facto **corporation** A corporation defectively incorporated in good faith that exists in fact though not in law.

de jure **corporation** A corporation whose existence is the result of incorporators having fully or substantially complied with the relevant corporation statutes.

debit card A card used to electronically subtract money from a bank account to pay for goods or services.

debtor-in-possession A debtor who continues to operate his or her business after filing for bankruptcy.

declaration of trust A trust in which the settlor holds the legal title to the property as trustee for the benefit of some other person (the beneficiary) to whom the settlor now conveys the equitable title.

deductible An amount of any loss that is to be paid by the insured.

deed of trust A formal written instrument that transfers legal ownership of real property to a third party while the mortgagor remains on the property. The third party holds certain rights to that property as security for the mortgagor's creditors.

defamation The intentional tort that occurs when a false statement is communicated to others that harms a person's good name or reputation.

default statute A statute used to fill in the gaps when the parties to an agreement have failed to consider some matter in their agreement.

defective agreement An apparent contract in which mutual assent has been destroyed, thus rendering the alleged contract void.

defective condition A condition that makes a product unreasonably dangerous to the consumer, user, or property. See *product liability*.

defendant The person against whom a lawsuit is brought and from whom recovery is sought.

defense of others A defense to criminal liability to defendants if they can show they used force to rescue another person who was the victim of an apparent attack. The rescuer must have good reason to believe the victim was in danger of severe bodily injury or death.

del credere **agent** (del·KREH·de·reh) A factor who guarantees the credit of a third party to a principal and guarantees the solvency of the purchaser and the performance of the contract.

delegation The transfer of a contractual duty.

demand note A promissory note that is payable whenever the payee demands payment.

demurrage charge A fee charged by a carrier for the storage of goods still remaining in its possession beyond the time allowed for unloading by the cosignee.

demurrer A motion for dismissal of a case on the grounds that a plaintiff has failed to state a claim for which relief can be granted.

depositary bank The first bank to which an item is transferred for collection; the depositary bank may also be the payor bank.

deposition An oral question-and-answer session conducted under oath during which an attorney questions parties or witnesses from the opposition in a lawsuit.

derivative suit A lawsuit brought by shareholders on behalf of the corporation.

descriptive theory A system of ethical thought that describes the values at work within a social system.

design patent A patent granted to someone who invents a new, original, and ornamental design for an article of manufacture.

destination contract A contract under which the seller is required to deliver goods to a place of destination. The title and risk of loss remain with the seller until the goods reach the place of destination.

detriment In contract law, doing (or promising to do) something that one has a legal right not to do, giving up (or promising to give up) something that one has a legal right to keep, or refraining from doing (or promising not to do) something that one has a legal right to do.

devise Real property that is left in a will. In states that have adopted the Uniform Probate Code, the term refers to both real and personal property.

devisee One who receives the real property under a will. In states that have adopted the Uniform Probate Code, the term refers to a person who receives a gift of either real or personal property under a will.

devolution When courts redefine a right and transfer the power and the obligation to enforce that right from a higher legal authority to a lower one.

digital information contract A contract involving the sale or licensing of information in a digital format.

Digital Millennium Copyright Act (DMCA) A law that makes it illegal to use technological means to bypass or override programs designed to prevent access to a copyrighted work.

digital signature An encoded message that appears at the end of a contract created online.

direct examination The questioning of witnesses by the lawyer who has called them.

direct suit A suit brought by shareholders who have been deprived of a right that belongs to them as shareholders.

disability Any physical or mental impairment that substantially limits one or more of the major life activities.

disaffirm In contract law, to indicate by a statement or act an intent not to live up to the terms of the contract.

disclaimer In employment law, a statement that regardless of provisions or policies in an employment handbook and regardless of oral promises to the contrary, an employment-at-will situation still exists between an employer and its employees. Also, a statement declaring that an auditor has decided not to give any opinion on a firm's financial records.

disclaimer of general partner status A document filed with the appropriate state office when a limited partner has been incorrectly named as a general partner.

disclosed principal The person known by a third party to be the principal of an agent.

discounting System by which a bank will buy an instrument at a price below its face amount with the aim of ultimately collecting the face amount.

discovery The process by which parties to a civil suit search for information relevant to the case.

dishonor To refuse to accept or pay a negotiable instrument when it is presented.

disparagement Any false statement made to others that questions the legal ownership or raises doubts as to the quality of merchandise.

disparate impact A type of discrimination in an employer's policy seems neutral on the surface but has an unequal or unfair impact on members of one or more of the protected classes.

disparate treatment Intentional discrimination against an individual or group belonging to a protected class. The protected classes are sex, race, color, religion, and national origin.

disposable income The amount of money left from a person's income, after subtracting certain allowable deductions.

Dispute Settlement Board (DSB) See *Dispute Settlement Understanding*.

Dispute Settlement Understanding (DSU) A series of measures administered by an international Dispute Settlement Board that are designed to improve the way trading quarrels are handled.

disputed amount Consideration on which parties to a contract never agree.

dissociation A process authorized under the Revised Uniform Partnership Act that takes place whenever a partner is no longer associated with the running of the partnership firm.

dissolution of a partnership A change in the relation of partners caused by any partner ceasing to be associated in the carrying on of the business.

diversity cases Federal lawsuits that are between persons from different states, between citizens of the United States and a foreign government, or between citizens of the United States and citizens of a foreign nation. Diversity cases must involve an amount over $50,000.

dividends Net profits, or surplus, set aside for shareholders.

division for Science and Technology A United Nations agency created to coordinate activities regarding international cooperation in the sharing of science and technology for economic development.

document of title A paper that serves as evidence that the person holding the paper has title to the goods mentioned in the document.

domain name The Internet address of a business, institution, or individual.

domain name dispute Arises when an individual or organization has registered a domain name that is actually the protected trademark of a business or institution.

domestic bill of exchange A draft that is drawn and payable in the United States.

domestic corporation A corporation created by or organized under the laws of the state where it is operating.

domestic violence statute State laws that outlaw physical violence directed at any family member.

dominant tenement The property to which the right or privilege of an easement attaches.

donee One to whom a gift is given.

donee beneficiary A third party who provides no consideration for the benefits received and who owes the contracting parties no legal duty.

donor One who gives a gift.

double indemnity An optional provision in life insurance policies that provides that the insurer will pay double the amount due to a beneficiary if the insured dies from accidental causes.

dower By common law, the vested rights of the wife to a one-third lifetime interest in the real property owned by her spouse. Compare *curtesy*.

draft A written order by which the party creating it orders another party to pay money to a third party. Also called *bill of exchange*.

drawee The party named in a draft who is ordered to pay the money to the payee.

drawer The party who draws a draft, that is, the party who orders that the money be paid.

drug trafficking The unauthorized manufacture or distribution of any controlled substance or the possession of such a substance with the intention of manufacturing or distributing it illegally.

dummy corporation A corporation that is set up as a mere instrumentality of a parent corporation. Also called *corporate shell* and *empty shell*.

dunning letter A letter representing payment for goods.

durable power of attorney A document that authorizes an agent to act on another's behalf, with the power either surviving incapacity or becoming effective upon incapacity.

duress An action by one party that forces another party to do what need not be done otherwise.

duty An obligation placed on individuals because of the law.

duty of due diligence A duty that says that corporate managers when acting on behalf of the corporation must act (1) in good faith; (2) using the same level of care that an ordinarily prudent person would use in a comparable situation, and (3) in the reasonable belief that the best interests of the corporation are being met.

duty of loyalty A duty that states managers must place the corporation's interests above their own.

duty of obedience Managers' duty to ensure their exercise of authority is not excessive and does not harm the corporation.

e-911 location identifier system An electronic chip located in a mobile phone that sends out a signal that is designed to ensure that EMS personnel can locate people who are unable or unwilling to reveal their location when making an emergency call.

early neutral evaluation (ENE) A process similar to that of a settlement hearing, which may result in a final decision or be used to help shape the final decision.

easement The right to use the land of another for a particular purpose.

easement by prescription An easement that is obtained by passing over another's property without permission openly and continuously for a period of time set by state statute (20 years in many states).

e-check (sometimes called *electronic check conversion*) A system in which funds are electronically transferred from a customer's checking account, eliminating the need to process a paper check.

e-commerce Involves transacting business by any one of several types of electronic communication, from debit card purchases to buying and selling goods on the Internet.

economic compensatory damages Damages that are directly quantifiable, including damages awarded for lost wages, medical expenses, and expenses incurred in the repair or replacement of property.

economic duress Threats of a business nature that force another party without real consent to enter a commercial agreement. Also called *business compulsion.*

Economic Espionage Act Legislation that outlines criminal sanctions for the theft of trade secrets and the use of fraud to obtain trade secrets.

Economic Security Council (ESC) A single, unified international agency under the management of the United Nations that would monitor the economic activities of member nations.

e-consumer Someone who buys something on the Internet.

ejectment The common law name given to the lawsuit brought by a landlord to have a tenant evicted from the premises.

elective share See *forced share.*

electronic contracts Contracts made using computers, either via e-mail or the Internet, or that involve computer-related products, such as databases and software.

electronic crime Any criminal activity associated with a computer.

electronic data interchange (EDI) An electronic process used to negotiate contracts.

electronic defamation False and destructive information transmitted by an electronic device.

electronic fund transfer (EFT) A method of banking that uses computers and electronic technology as a substitute for checks and other banking methods.

electronic germ warfare The use of viruses to enter and destroy a computer system.

electronic invasion of privacy An unwelcome and unwanted intrusion into the private matters of an individual, carried out or sustained by an electronic device.

electronic jurisdiction The authority of a court to hear a case based on Internet-related transactions.

electronic piracy Using a computer or other electronic device to create at least one, but usually more than one, illegal duplicate of data stored in a digital format.

electronic spoofing A crime in which the perpetrator uses a computer to assume another computer user's identity to carry out a crime.

electronic stalking A crime in which the perpetrator targets vulnerable individuals by tracking their computer transactions, personal records, and communication habits and then using that information to victimize the innocent party.

electronic terrorism Operating a computer to disrupt or destroy one or more of the critical elements of the national electronic infrastructure.

electronic tort The invasion, distortion, theft, falsification, misuse, destruction, or financial exploitation of information stored in or related to an electronic device, including but not limited to desktop PCs, laptops, mobile phones, mainframes, phonecams, personal digital assistants (PDAs), and home computers that stand alone or are part of a network.

electronic trespass The use of a computer or other electronic device to commit any crime defined within the conventional criminal code.

electronic vandalism Disrupting a computer system so thoroughly the Web site crashes or can no longer function properly.

electronically stored information (ESI) Computerized evidence.

emancipated In contract law, the condition that exists when minors are no longer under the control of their parents and are responsible for their contracts.

embedded niche Levels of influence within a complex adaptive system.

embezzlement The act of wrongfully taking property entrusted into one's care.

eminent domain The right of federal, state, and local governments, or other public bodies, to take private lands, with compensation to their owners, for public use. Also called *condemnation*.

emotional duress Acts or threats that create emotional distress and lead a person into a contract against his or her will.

employment-at-will A doctrine followed by most jurisdictions in the United States that says an employer can dismiss an employee at any time for any reason.

end user A purchaser who is not involved in the production or assembly of the product.

endowment insurance Insurance protection that combines life insurance and investment so that if the insured outlives the time period of the policy, the face value is paid to the beneficiary.

entity theory A theory in partnership law that holds that a partnership is actually a separate legal person with its own legal identity.

entrapment A defense to criminal liability that claims that a previously law-abiding citizen was induced to commit a crime by a law enforcement officer.

equal dignities rule The legal rule that provides that when a party appoints an agent to negotiate an agreement that must be in writing, the appointment of the agent must also be in writing.

equal value theory A theory that insists a contract is valid only if the things exchanged are of equal value.

equipment Goods that are used or bought for use primarily in business.

equitable estoppel See *part performance*.

equitable remedy The requirement that a party do something or refrain from doing something, beyond the payment of money.

equity financing The issuing and selling of shares of stock to raise capital.

equity of redemption A mortgagor's right to pay off the mortgage in full, including interest.

escheat To revert to the state; to become property of.

E-Sign Act A federal statute, officially known as the Electronic Signatures in Global and National Commerce Act, which states that if the parties to a contract have voluntarily agreed to transact business electronically, then the electronic contract that results will be just as legally acceptable as a paper contract.

espionage The gathering or transmitting of information pertaining to the national defense of a nation for the political or military use of any foreign nation.

estate in fee simple An estate in which the owner owns the land for life with the right to use it or dispose of it freely.

estoppel A legal bar to denying acts, statements, or promises that are relevant and material to the validity of an insurance contract.

ethical relativism A system of ethical thought that says there is no objective or absolute standard of right and wrong.

ethics Rules of conduct that transcend legal rules, telling people how to act when the law does not.

euro Europe's common currency.

European Central Bank (ECB) The bank was established by provisions within the Maastricht Treaty and is the central hub of the European System of Central Banks.

European System of Central Banks (ESCB) A system of banks including the European Central Bank and the National Central Banks.

European Union (EU) A group of countries in Europe that have joined together to formulate a common European economic policy, minimize trade barriers, and introduce a common currency with the goal of making the EU a major global competitor.

eviction An act of the landlord that deprives the tenant of the enjoyment of the premises.

exculpatory agreement A clause that says one of the parties to a contract, generally the one who wrote the contract, is not liable for any economic loss or physical injury, even if that party caused the loss or injury.

exculpatory clause A clause in a contract that releases a party from liability for his or her wrongful acts. These clauses are not favored by law.

executed contract A contract whose terms have been completely and satisfactorily carried out by both parties.

executor (male); executrix (female) The party named in a will to carry out the terms of the will.

executory contract A contract that has not yet been fully performed by the parties.

exempt property Property of a decedent that passes to the surviving spouse or children and is beyond the reach of creditors.

express authority An agent's authority that the principal voluntarily and specifically sets forth as oral or written instructions in an agency agreement.

express contract A contract in which both parties accept mutual obligations through either oral discussion or written communication.

express warranty An oral or written statement, promise, or other representation about the quality of a product.

extant data Data that are difficult to retrieve because they are hidden within a computer system.

extortion The act of taking another's property with consent when such consent is coerced by threat to injure a victim's person, property, or reputation.

f.a.s vessel Free alongside vessel. Indicates that the seller must deliver goods, at the seller's own risk, alongside the vessel or at a dock designated by the buyer.

f.o.b. Free on board.

f.o.b. the place of destination Terms indicating that goods will be delivered free to the place of destination.

f.o.b. the place of shipment Terms indicating that goods will be delivered free to the place of shipment.

factor A special agent who is employed to sell merchandise consigned for that purpose.

failure of consideration A personal defense that may be used by a maker or drawer of a negotiable instrument when the party with whom the maker dealt breaches the contract by not furnishing the agreed consideration.

fair use doctrine An exception to the copyright protection rights granted to copyright holders that permits individuals to reproduce items for purposes of criticism, comment, news reporting, teaching, scholarship, and research.

fairness The ability to treat people with justice and equality.

fairness rule The rule that requires managers to be fair to the corporation when they personally benefit from their business decisions.

false imprisonment An intentional tort involving the unjustified confinement or detention of a person.

family allowance An amount of money taken from a decedent's estate and given to the family to meet its immediate needs while the estate is being probated.

family farmer Under Chapter 12 of the Bankruptcy Code, a farmer who receives more than half the total income from the farm. In addition, to qualify as a family farmer, 80 percent of the farmer's debt must result from farm expenses.

farm products Crops, livestock, or supplies used or produced in farming operations.

featherbedding Requiring an employer, usually by a union, to keep unneeded employees, to pay employees for not working, or to assign more employees to a given job than are needed.

federal question A matter that involves the U.S. Constitution, a federal statute or statutes, or a treaty; handled by federal district courts.

federal register Publication that produces a daily compilation of new regulations issued by federal administrative agencies.

felony A crime punishable by death or by imprisonment in a federal or state prison for a term exceeding one year.

fiduciary A person who acts in a position of trust or confidence.

fiduciary relationship A relationship based on trust such as exists between an attorney and a client, a guardian and a ward, a trustee and a beneficiary, or a director and a corporation.

field warehousing The practice of using goods that are stored in a warehouse as security for a loan.

finance charge The actual cost of a loan in dollars and cents.

firm offer A rule that no consideration is necessary when a merchant agrees in writing to hold an offer open for the sale of goods.

fixture An article of personal property physically attached to real property in such a way that an interest arises in it under real estate law.

flexible-rate mortgage A mortgage that has a rate of interest that changes according to fluctuations in the index to which it is tied. Also called *variable-rate mortgage*.

floater policy A policy that insures property that cannot be covered by specific insurance because the property is constantly changing in either value or location.

floating lien A provision, placed by the creditor, in a security agreement that a security interest of the creditor also applies to goods the debtor acquires at a later time.

forbearance The act of refraining from doing (or promising not to do) something that a person has a legal right to do.

forced share The portion of a decedent's estate assured to the family by state statute.

foreclosure The right of a mortgagee to apply to a court to have property sold when the mortgagor defaults or fails to perform some agreement in the mortgage.

foreign corporation A corporation created by or organized under the laws of a state other than the one in which it is operating.

foreign draft See *international bill of exchange*.

forgery The false making or alteration of a writing with the intent to defraud.

formal contract Under common law, a contract that is written; signed, witnessed, and placed under the seal of the parties; and delivered.

formalist theory A theory of legal interpretation under which the court will look to see if certain elements (offer, acceptance, mutual assent, consideration, capacity, and legality) exist before concluding whether or not the parties in a lawsuit have actually entered a legally binding contract.

forum shopping The process of locating a jurisdiction that has a friendly track record for the type of lawsuit that is about to be filed.

fraud A wrongful statement, action, or concealment pertinent to the subject matter of a contract knowingly made to damage the other party.

fraud in the inception Fraud that occurs when one party tricks another into a contract by lying to the innocent party about the actual nature of the contract.

fraud in the inducement Fraud that occurs when one party tricks another into a contract by lying about the terms of the agreement to get the innocent party to enter the contract under false pretenses.

fraudulent conveyance A transfer of property with the intent to defraud creditors.

friendly suitor See *white knight*.

frustration-of-purpose doctrine In contract law, the doctrine that releases a party from a contractual obligation when performing the obligations would be thoroughly impractical and senseless.

full warranty A warranty under which a defective product will be repaired or replaced without charge within a reasonable time after a complaint has been made about it.

fungible goods Goods of which any unit is, by nature or usage of trade, the equivalent of any like unit; wheat, flour, sugar, and liquids of various kinds are examples.

future goods Goods that are not yet in existence or under the control of people; they include fish in the sea, minerals in the ground, goods not yet manufactured, and commodities futures.

general agent A person who is given broad authority to act on behalf of the principal in conducting the bulk of the principal's business activities on a daily basis.

General Agreement on Tariffs and Trade (GATT) A nonstatic agreement among the principal trading countries to reduce or eliminate tariffs and to promote free trade on a global basis.

General Assembly The member nations of the United Nations.

general consent Consent that arises automatically when a patient enters a hospital for routine tests and procedures needed for diagnosis and treatment.

general jurisdiction The power of a court to hear any type of case.

general partner A partner who takes an active part in running a business and has unlimited liability for the firm's debts.

general release A document expressing the intent of a creditor to release a debtor from obligations to an existing and valid debt.

general warranty deed A deed that contains express warranties under which a grantor guarantees property to be free of encumbrances created by the grantor or by others who had title previously. Also called *full convenant* and *warranty deed*.

generally accepted accounting principles (GAAP) Rules established by the Financial Accounting Standards Board (FASB) that outline the procedures that accountants use in accumulating financial data and in preparing financial statements.

generally accepted auditing standards (GAAS) Standards set up by the Auditing Standards Board of the American Institute of Certified Public Accountants (AICPA) that measure the quality of the performance of the auditing procedures.

Geneva Conventions International meetings that attempted to deal with many of the contemporary complications brought on by the nature of warfare in the twentieth century.

gift *in causa mortis* (in·KAWS·ah·MORE·tes) A gift given during one's lifetime in contemplation of death from a known cause.

gift *inter vivos* (IN·ter·VY·vose) A gift between the living. For an exchange to be valid, the donor must intend to make a gift, the gift must be delivered to the donee, and the donee must accept it.

good faith Honesty in fact and observance of reasonable commercial standards of fair dealings in the trade.

goods All things (other than money, stocks, and bonds) that are movable.

goodwill The expected continuance of public patronage of a business.

government control A theory of corporate control based on the belief that because corporate decision making impacts upon more individuals and groups than just shareholders and managers, those decisions should be made by a group of corporate outsiders, usually government officials. Also called *state control*.

graduated-payment mortgage A mortgage that has a fixed interest rate during the life of the mortgage; however, the monthly payments made by the mortgagor increase over the term of the loan.

grantee A person to whom title to real property is transferred in a deed.

grantor A person who transfers title to real property in a deed.

gratuitous agency A situation in which a contract does not create an agency relationship

gratuitous agent An agent who is under contract but is not involved in an agency relationship

gratuitous bailment A bailment for the sole benefit of either the bailor or the bailee, in which the other party receives no consideration for benefits bestowed.

greenmail A strategy used to shake off a bidder's hostile suit by offering to buy, at significantly higher cost, the portion of stock already owned by the bidder who is trying to take over the company.

grievance procedure A procedure that allows employees to appeal any decision an employer makes that employees feel violates just cause.

gross negligence Very great negligence.

guaranteed insurability An optional provision in an insurance contract that allows the insured to pay an extra premium initially in exchange for a guaranteed option to buy more insurance at certain specified times later on with no questions asked and no medical examination required.

guarantor The promisor.

guaranty of payment A promise to pay another's bills or to settle wrongful acts if that party does not settle them personally.

health care proxy A written statement authorizing an agent to make health care decisions for another in the event of incapacity.

Health Insurance Portability and Accountability Act (HIPAA) Legislation that guarantees patients the right to see their medical records and those of their underage children.

heir One who inherits property either under a will or through someone's dying without a will.

holder A person who is in possession of a negotiable instrument that is issued or indorsed to that person's order or to bearer.

holder in due course rule A rule adopted by the FTC that states that holders of consumer credit contracts who are holders in due course are subject to all claims and defenses that the buyer could use against the seller, including personal defenses.

holder in due course A holder who has taken a negotiable instrument for value, in good faith, without notice that it is overdue or has been dishonored and without notice of any defenses against it or claim to it.

home equity loan A line of credit made available to homeowners based on the value of the property over and above any existing mortgages.

homeowner's policy A type of insurance that gives protection for all types of losses and liabilities related to home ownership. Items covered include losses from fire, windstorm, burglary, vandalism, and injuries suffered by others while on the property.

homestead exemption A provision in the Bankruptcy Code that allows debtors to exclude a statutory amount of equity in the debtor's place of residence and in property used as a burial ground when filing for bankruptcy.

homicide The killing of one human being by another.

honesty A character trait of a person who is open and truthful in his or her dealings with other people.

horizontal expansion The joining of companies involved in the same business.

hostile bidder See *unfriendly suitor*.

hot-cargo contract An agreement whereby an employer voluntarily agrees with a union not to handle, use, or deal in nonunion-produced goods for another employer.

identified goods Specific goods that are selected as the subject matter of a contract.

identity theft Using a computer to steal confidential information to clean out a person's bank account, to run up credit card debt, to divert cash transfers, and to disrupt the financial and personal life of the victim.

illusory promise A promise that does not obligate the promisor to anything.

implied authority The authority of an agent to perform acts that are necessary or customary to carry out expressly authorized duties.

impaired classes Creditors who receive less than the full value of their claims in bankruptcy proceedings.

implied contract A contract created by the actions or gestures of the parties involved in the transaction.

implied covenant An implied promise in any employment relationship that the employer and the employee will be fair with each other.

implied warranty A warranty that is imposed by law rather than by statements, descriptions, or samples given by the seller.

implied-in-fact contract A contract implied by direct or indirect acts of the parties.

implied-in-law contract A remedy imposed by a court in a situation in which the parties did not create a written, oral, or implied-in-fact agreement but one party has unfairly benefited at the innocent expense of another. Also called *quasi-contract*.

in pari delicto (in pah·ree de·LIK·toh) In equal fault. A contract relationship when both parties to an illegal agreement are equally wrong, in the knowledge of the operation and effect of their contract.

inactive data Data in a computer system that are not being used at the present time but that can be easily retrieved.

incidental beneficiary A third party for whose benefit a contract was not made but who would substantially benefit if the agreement were performed according to its terms and conditions.

incidental damages Damages awarded for losses indirectly, but closely, attributed to a breach to cover any expenses paid out by an innocent party to prevent further loss.

incorporators The people who actually sign the articles of incorporation to start a corporation.

indemnification Payment for loss or damage suffered.

indemnify To compensate for loss or damage or insure against future loss or damage.

independent contractor One who contracts to do a job and who retains complete control over the methods employed to obtain completion.

independent directors Directors who have no family members employed by the corporation, who are not themselves employed by the corporation, or, if they were once employed by the corporation, have not been on staff for at least three years.

independent director control A theory of corporate control that states that the best way to make certain that corporate decisions are made in the best interests of the corporation is to make sure that the decision makers themselves are not affected by the decisions.

indictment A set of formal charges against a defendant issued by a grand jury.

individual justice Justice that is meted out to the people on a case-by-case basis.

indorsee A person to whom a draft, note, or other negotiable instrument is transferred by indorsement.

indorsement in full See *special indorsement*.

indorser A person who indorses a negotiable instrument.

infliction of emotional distress The intentional tort that allows those injured emotionally by the wrongful acts of others to recover damages even without the accompanying physical injury.

informal contract An oral or written contract that is not under a seal or is not a contract of record. Also called *simple contract*.

information A set of formal charges against a defendant drawn up and issued by the prosecutor or district attorney.

informed consent Written consent given by patients for diagnostic tests or treatments that will involve danger or pain after being told about the procedure and the risks involved.

in-house attorney A member of the officer corps of a business who is instructed in his or her duties by a supervisor.

injunction A court order preventing someone from performing a particular act or commanding the defendant to do some positive act to alleviate a problem.

inland marine insurance An insurance contract that covers goods that are moved by land carriers such as rail, truck, and airplane.

innkeeper An operator of a hotel, motel, or inn that holds itself out to the public as being ready to accommodate travelers, strangers, and transient guests.

inside information Material, nonpublic, factual data that can be used to buy or sell securities at a profit.

insider trading Using inside information to either cheat the corporation or take unfair advantage of corporate outsiders.

insider trading rule A rule of corporate governance that states that when managers possess important inside information, they are obligated to reveal that information before trading on it themselves.

insolvent Inability of a business entity to pay its debts as they become due in the usual course of business.

installment note A promissory note in which the principal together with interest on the unpaid balance is payable in installments at specified times.

insurable interest The financial interest that a policyholder has in the person or property that is insured.

insurance A contract whereby one party pays premiums to another party who undertakes to pay compensation for losses resulting from risks or perils specified in the contract.

insured A party that is protected by an insurer against losses caused by the risks specified in an insurance policy.

insurer A party that accepts the risk of loss in return for a premium (payment of money) and agrees to compensate the insured against a specified loss.

integral-part test A finding that any type of price enhancement violates the best-price rule.

integrity The quality of having the courage to do what is right regardless of personal consequences.

intellectual property An original work fixed in a tangible medium of expression.

intended beneficiary A third party in whose favor a contract is made.

intentional or reckless infliction of emotional distress A tort involving someone who intentionally or recklessly causes another to undergo emotional or mental suffering.

interference with a contract The international tort that results when a person, out of ill will, entices a contractual party into breaking the contract.

interlocking directorates In antitrust law, a situation that occurs when individuals serve as two corporations that are competitors.

intermediary bank Any bank to which an item is transferred in the course of collection except the depository or payor bank.

international arbitration agreement A pledge to use arbitration if parties find themselves in disagreement about enforcement rights under an original contract.

international bill of exchange A draft that is drawn in one country but is payable in another. Also called *foreign draft*.

International Court of Justice (ICJ) One of the principal vehicles for the establishment of international law and justice.

International Criminal Court (ICC) International court that presides over trials involving genocide, war crimes, and other human rights violations.

International Law Commission A thirty-four-member panel of judges who seek to codify international law in as objective a manner as possible.

International Monetary Fund (IMF) A nongovernmental organization that is designed to help financially strapped nations to secure loans that will help them engage in programs of sustainable economic growth and development.

international terrorism Acts transcending national boundaries that violate a state's criminal laws and are intended to intimidate that country's civilians or influence the policy or conduct of the government.

interrogatories Written questions to be answered in writing under oath by the opposite party in a lawsuit.

interstate commerce Business activities that touch more than one state.

interstate shipment A shipment that goes beyond the borders of the state in which it originated.

intestacy The quality or state of one who dies without having prepared a valid will.

intestate Having died without leaving a valid will. Compare *testate*.

intestate succession The process by which property passes to others when people die without a will.

intrastate commerce Business activities that have no out-of-state connections.

intrastate shipment A shipment that is entirely within a single state.

invasion of privacy The intentional tort that occurs when one person unreasonably denies another person the right to be left alone.

inventory Goods held for sale or lease, or raw materials used or consumed in a business.

invitation to trade An announcement published for the purpose of creating interest and attracting a response by many people.

involuntary bailment A bailment arising from the leaving of personal property in the possession of a bailee through an act of God, accident, or other uncontrolled phenomenon.

irresistible impulse test Under this rule, criminal defendants are judged not guilty by reason of insanity if, at the time of the action in question, they suffered from a mental disease that either prevented them from knowing right from wrong or compelled them to commit the criminal act.

irrevocable offer A rule that no consideration is necessary when a merchant agrees in writing to hold an offer open for the sale of goods. Also called *firm offer*.

issue Descendants (children, grandchildren, great-grandchildren).

issuer Either a maker or a drawer of an instrument.

joint tenants Two or more persons who own property where the right of any deceased owner is automatically transferred to other surviving owners.

joint tenants with the right of survivorship See *joint tenants*.

judicial review The process by which a court determines the constitutionality of various legislative statutes, administrative regulations, and executive actions.

judicial–economic system The interaction of the legal system and the economic system so as to become, in effect, a single system.

junior mortgage A mortgage subject to a prior mortgage.

junk bonds Bonds with high risk but also a high rate of return.

junk science The distorted, exaggerated, misapplied, or misrepresented use of scientific evidence.

jurisdiction The authority of a court to hear and decide cases.

just cause A criterion under the just war theory, which states that to be morally permissible, a war must be waged only for honorable motives.

just war theory A theory for determining when a war can be considered legally and morally correct.

kidnapping The unlawful abduction of an individual against that individual's will.

knowledge In criminal law, the awareness that a particular result will probably occur.

labor union An organization that acts on behalf of all employees in negotiations with the employer regarding terms of their employment.

laches The equitable doctrine that a delay or failure to assert a right or claim at the proper time, which causes a disadvantage to the adverse party, is a bar to recovery.

lack of consideration A personal defense that may be used by a maker or drawer of a negotiable instrument when no consideration existed in the underlying contract for which the instrument was issued.

landlord A person who owns real property and who rents or leases it to someone else. Also called *lessor*.

larceny The act of taking and carrying away the personal property of another without the right to do so.

larceny by false pretenses The taking of someone's money or property by intentionally deceiving that person.

last resort A criterion under the just war theory that states that a war must be waged only as a final course of action.

last will and testament A formal document that governs the transfer of property at death.

law A set of rules created by the governing body of a society to maintain harmony, stability, and justice in that society.

law merchant In England, the commercial law developed by merchants who needed a set of rules to govern their business transactions.

lease A contract granting the use of certain real property to another for a specified period in return for the payment of rent.

lease option A contract that permits a party to lease real property while holding an option to purchase that property.

leasehold estate The creation of an ownership interest in the tenant. An interest in real estate that is held under a lease. Also called *tenancy*.

legal imperialism American insistence that all disputes be resolved under American law.

legal tender Money that may be offered legally in satisfaction of a debt and that must be accepted by a creditor when offered.

legatee One who receives personal property in a will.

lessee See *tenant*.

lessor See *landlord*.

leveraged buyout The purchase of a controlling portion of the stock in a corporation by a group of shareholders, usually officers and directors of the company.

liability The legal responsibility of an individual for his or her actions.

liable Legally responsible.

libel Any false statement that harms another person's good name or reputation made in a permanent form, such as movies, writing, and videotape, and communicated to others.

license A grant of permission to do a particular thing, to exercise a certain privilege, to carry on a particular business, or to pursue a certain occupation; an agreement that gives no property right or interest in land but merely allows the licensee to do certain acts that would otherwise be a trespass; a privilege granted by a state or city upon payment of a fee, which is not a contract and may be revoked for cause, conferring authority to perform a designated task, such as operating a motor vehicle.

licensing agreement An agreement in which one party is given permission from another party to do a particular thing in exchange for consideration.

lien A claim that one has against the property of another.

life estate An estate in which the owner owns real property for his or her life or for the life of another.

life insurance An insurance contract that provides monetary compensation for losses suffered by another's death.

limited defense See *personal defense*.

limited liability Status that specifies that an individual's liability will not go beyond his or her original investment.

limited liability company (LLC) A business organization that borrows elements from a partnership and a corporation. LLCs may come into existence only through following the steps laid out in the state code.

limited partner A partner who does not take part in the management of a firm and whose liability does not extend beyond his or her investment.

limited partnership A partnership formed by two or more persons having one or more general partners and one or more limited partners.

limited-payment life insurance Insurance that provides that the payment will stop after a stated length of time—usually 10, 20, or 30 years.

limited warranty A warranty that does not meet all of the requirements of a full warranty.

lingering apparent authority Apparent authority that stays with an agent if the principal has terminated the agent but has failed to give proper notice to third parties entitled to such notice.

liquidated damages Damages agreed to by the parties to a contract in the event of a breach.

liquidation The conversion of property into cash.

litigant A person involved in litigation.

living trust A trust that comes into existence while the person who establishes it is alive. Also called *inter vivos trust*.

living will A document in which individuals can indicate their desire not to be kept alive by artificial means if there is no hope for recovery.

local option The practice in a state of eliminating uniform statewide laws regulating Sunday activities and allowing the local counties, cities, towns, and villages to adopt their own special Sunday ordinances.

locality rule A means to judge a health care provider's actions on the basis of how other health care professionals in the same community would have acted in the same situation.

lockup agreement A contract between a target corporation and a white knight, giving the knight an option to buy valuable property should a hostile bidder gain control of the target corporation.

locus sigilli The place of the seal. The abbreviation L.S. is often used in place of the seal itself on formal written contracts.

lodger A person who has the use of property without actual or exclusive possession of it.

M'Naughten Rule The oldest test for insanity whereby a criminal defendant is declared not guilty by reason of insanity if, at the time of the criminal act, he or she suffered from a mental disease that prevented him or her from understanding the nature of the act and that the act was wrong.

Maastricht Treaty The outcome of a conference held in Maastricht, the Netherlands. The objectives of the treaty were to create a general European economic policy as well as a foreign policy acceptable to all member states.

majority A term used to describe persons who have reached the legal age of adulthood.

maker A person obligated as the payor on a promissory note. See also *comaker*.

malicious prosecution Bringing false criminal charges against an innocent victim.

malpractice Occurs when a professional accountant, health care professional, and attorney—fails to meet his or her duty of care.

managerial control A theory of corporate management that favors insulating managers from shareholders by limiting the shareholders' power to vote and by making it difficult for the shareholder to sue managers.

master An outdated term signifying an individual who has the right to control the physical conduct of a servant or employee.

material fact An essential or important fact; a fact of substance.

means test Three steps used to qualify someone for Chapter 7 bankruptcy.

med-arb A form of ADR that combines the best aspects of both mediation and arbitration. The parties first submit to a mediation session. If the matter cannot be settled, it moves to an arbitration hearing.

mediation The process by which an outside party attempts to help two other parties settle their differences.

mediator The third party in mediation whose job is to convince the contending parties to adjust or settle their dispute.

Medicaid A healthcare plan for low-income people that is administered by state governments but funded by both state and federal funds.

medical payments insurance A type of automobile insurance that pays for medical (and sometimes funeral) expenses resulting from bodily injuries to anyone occupying the policyholder's car at the time of an accident.

Medicare A federally funded health insurance program for people 65 years and over who are eligible for Social Security.

memorandum A written agreement containing the terms of an agreement, an identification of the subject matter of the agreement, the consideration promised, the names and identities of the parties to the agreement, and the signature of the party charged to the agreement.

merchant A person who deals in goods of the kind sold in the ordinary course of business or who otherwise claims to have knowledge or skills peculiar to those goods.

merger The acquisition of one corporation by another.

midnight deadline The deadline by which banks must settle or return checks or be responsible for paying them. If the payor bank is not the depository bank, it must settle for an item by midnight of the banking day of receipt. If the payor bank is also the depository bank, the deadline is midnight of the next banking day following the banking day on which it receives the relevant item.

minimum contacts The doctrine of minimum contacts identifies the fewest number of contacts that will permit a court to exercise personal jurisdiction over an out-of-state defendant.

minority A term used to describe persons who have not reached the legal age of adulthood.

mirror image rule In contract law, the rule that an acceptance must duplicate the terms in the offer.

misdemeanor A crime less serious than a felony that is generally punishable by a prison sentence of not more than one year.

misrepresentation A false statement innocently made by one party to a contract with no intent to deceive. Also, in insurance, giving false answers to questions in an insurance application that materially affect the risk undertaken by the insurer.

misuse of legal procedure Bringing legal action without probable cause and with malice.

mitigation A principle that states an innocent party cannot take advantage by deliberately raising the level of damages that the other party will have to pay as a consequence of a breach.

money order A type of draft that may be purchased from banks, post offices, telegraph companies, and express companies as a substitute for a check.

monopoly The exclusive control of a market by a business enterprise.

morals Values that govern society's attitude toward right and wrong.

mortgage A transfer of an interest in property for the purpose of creating a security for a debt.

mortgagee The party who lends money and takes back a mortgage as security for the loan.

mortgagor The party who borrows money and gives a mortgage to the lender or mortgagee as security for the loan.

most favored nation principle A principle that states that the World Trade Organization nations must apply the same privileges, advantages, and benefits to all other member nations in relation to similar imports.

mutual assent In contract law, the state of mind that exists between an offeror and an offeree once a valid offer has been accepted and once the parties know what the terms are and have agreed to be bound by them. Also known as "a meeting of the minds."

mutual-benefit bailment A bailment in which both the bailor and the bailee receive some benefit.

mutual mistake See *bilateral mistake.*

mutual recession A condition in which both parties to a contract agree to rescind the contract and return to the other any consideration already received or pay for any services or materials already rendered.

mutuum (MYOO·choo·um) A loan of goods with the intention that the goods may be used and later replaced with an equal amount of different goods.

National Central Banks (NCB) Part of the European System of Central Banks, the NCBs are located within the member nations of the EU.

national standard A rule that allows a court to judge a health care provider's degree of care by determining how the same procedure is performed on a national basis.

national treatment principle A principle that states that the World Trade Organization nations must apply the same standards to imports that they apply to domestic goods.

nation-states Sovereign divisions that govern a recognized area of land on a map, may raise money within their borders, and have a responsibility to provide for their citizens.

natural law theory A system of ethical thought that sees an unbreakable link joining the law and morality.

navigable airspace The space above 1,000 feet over populated areas and above 500 feet over water and unpopulated areas.

necessaries Goods and services that are essential to a minor's health and welfare.

negligence The failure to use that amount of care that a reasonably prudent person would have used under the same circumstances and conditions.

negligent credentialing Occurs if a hospital has retained a physician that the governing body of the hospital knew or should have known was incompetent.

negligent hiring The proprietor's liability for the hiring of an incompetent contractor who consequently harms an innocent third party while performing the hired-for work.

negligent retention The failure of a proprietor to dismiss an incompetent contractor after the proprietor has learned of the contractor's incompetence.

negotiable instrument A written document that is signed by the maker or drawer and that contains an unconditional promise or order to pay a certain sum of money on delivery or at a definite time to the bearer or to order.

negotiated rule making Occurs when an agency that is about to create a new rule or revise existing rules enters into a cooperative process by which all parties affected by the rule have a chance to shape the final form that the rule will take.

negotiation The transfer of a negotiable instrument in such form that the transferee becomes a holder.

new world order A set of initial conditions that describes how nation-states relate to one another on a global scale.

next of kin Those who are most nearly related by blood.

No Electronic Theft Act (NET Act) A federal law that grants limited immunity to persons who duplicate copyrighted works on the Internet, as long as those users do not profit from the copying process.

no-fault insurance A type of automobile insurance that allows drivers to collect damages and medical expenses from their own insurance carriers regardless of who is at fault in an accident.

nominal damages Token damages awarded to parties who have experienced an injury to their legal rights but no actual loss.

nonconforming goods Goods that are not the same as those called for under a contract or that are in some way defective.

nonconforming uses Uses of land permitted to continue even though newly enacted zoning laws no longer permit similar uses.

nondelegable duty A duty that the proprietor cannot delegate, or pass off, to another party.

nondisclosure See *passive fraud*.

nondisclosure agreement An agreement that requires employees to promise that, should they leave their employment with their present employer, they will not reveal any confidential trade secrets that they may learn at their current job.

noneconomic compensatory damages Damages that result from injuries that are intangible and, therefore, not directly quantifiable. Examples include damages resulting from pain and suffering, mental anguish, and loss of companionship.

nongovernmental organization (NGO) An organization that functions beyond the boundaries of any one governmental body.

North American Free Trade Agreement (NAFTA) A trading coalition that includes the United States, Canada, and Mexico

note A written promise by one party to pay money to another party. Also called *promissory note*.

novation The substitution, by mutual agreement, of another party for one of the original parties to a contract.

object code A computer program after it has been translated by the computer into a language that only the computer can comprehend.

obligee In contract law, the party to whom another party owes an obligation.

obligor In contract law, the party who is obligated to deliver on a promise or to undertake some act.

obvious-to-try standard A patent challenge that asserts anyone of ordinary skill could see the invention was obvious to try, which makes the invention not be patentable.

ocean marine insurance A type of insurance that covers ships at sea.

offer In contract law, a proposal made by one party to another indicating a willingness to enter into a contract.

offeree In contract law, the person to whom an offer is made.

offeror In contract law, the person who makes the offer.

open-end credit Credit that can be increased by the debtor, up to a limit set by the creditor, by continuing to purchase goods on credit.

open-price terms A contract for the sale of goods that is established even though the price is not settled.

operating agreement An agreement containing various rights, provisions, and powers that aid in establishing the bylaws of an LLC.

option In contract law, the giving of consideration to support an offeror's promise to hold an offer open for a stated or reasonable length of time. Also called *option contract*.

order bill of lading A negotiable bill of lading.

order for relief In bankruptcy law, a court's command that the liquidation begin.

order paper A negotiable instrument that is payable to someone's order.

ordinary life insurance See *straight life insurance*.

ordinary negligence Failure to use that amount of care that a reasonable person would use under the same circumstance.

original jurisdiction The authority of a court to hear a case when it is first brought to court.

ostensible authority Occurs when a hospital leads a patient to believe that a physician with staff privileges is an employee of the hospital.

output contract An agreement in which a seller agrees to sell "all the goods we manufacture" or "all the crops we produce" to a particular buyer. See also *requirements contract*.

outside party See *third party*.

overdraft A payment by a bank on behalf of a customer for more than the customer has on deposit.

paper data Data in a computer system that have been printed out in a hard copy for storage or filing in a conventional way.

par value The value that is placed on the shares of stock at incorporation.

parol evidence rule The rule that states that evidence of oral statements made before signing a written agreement is usually not admissible in court to change or to contradict the terms of a written agreement.

part performance An exception to the rule that contracts for the sale of land must be in writing. It applies when a person relies on an owner's oral promise to sell real estate and then makes improvements on the property or changes his or her position in an important way. Also called *equitable estoppel*.

partially disclosed principal A person, in a transaction conducted by an agent, whose existence is known to the third party but whose specific identify is unknown.

partnership An association of two or more persons to carry on a business for profit.

partnership at will A partnership in which any partner may leave without liability.

partnership by estoppel A partnership that occurs when someone says or does something that leads a third party to reasonably believe that a partnership exists.

passenger A person who enters the premises of a carrier with the intention of buying a ticket for a trip. One continues to be a passenger as long as the trip continues.

passive fraud A failure to reveal some material fact about the subject matter of a contract that one party is obligated to reveal to the other party and that intentionally deceives that second party, leading him or her into a damaging contract. Also called *concealment* and *nondisclosure*.

past consideration A promise to give another something of value in return for goods or services rendered and delivered in the past.

patent A grant from the government that gives an inventor the exclusive right to make, use, and sell an invention for a period set by Congress.

patent infringement Any unauthorized making, using, or selling of a patent invention during the term of the patent.

pawn See *pledge*.

payee The party named in a note or draft to whom payment is to be made.

payor bank A bank by which an item is payable as drawn or accepted. It includes a drawee bank.

peer-to-peer networking Connections among personal computers joined to the same interconnected network. Also called *P2P networking*.

per se violation In antitrust law, a restraint of trade practice so serious that it is prohibited whether or not it actually harms anyone.

perfected The state of a security interest when the secured party has done everything that the law requires to give the secured party greater rights to the goods than others have.

performance In contact law, the situation that exists when the parties to a contract have done what they had agreed to do.

periodic tenancy A leasehold estate, or tenancy, that continues for successive periods until one of the parties terminates it by giving notice to the other party.

personal defense In negotiable-instruments law, a defense that can be used against a holder but not against a holder in due course of a negotiable instrument. Also called *limited defense*.

personal jurisdiction A court's authority over the parties to a lawsuit.

personal property Everything that can be owned other than real estate.

personal representative Executors and administrators of wills in states that have adopted the Uniform Probate Code.

persuasive precedent A previous case that a court is free to follow or to ignore.

phishing A cyberspoofing method that involves sending out phony e-mails that solicit buyers and, in the process, obtaining credit card information, account numbers, passwords, and the like.

physical duress Violence or the threat of violence against an individual or that person's family, household, or property that is so serious that it forces a person into a contract against his or her will.

picketing The placement of persons for observation, patrol, and demonstration at the site of employment as part of employee pressure on an employer to meet a demand.

pierce the corporate veil The doctrine holding shareholders of a corporation personally liable when they have used the corporation as a facade to defraud or commit some other misdeed.

plaintiff The person who begins a lawsuit by filing a complaint in the appropriate trial court of general jurisdiction.

plant patent A patent granted to someone who invents or discovers and asexually reproduces any distinct and new variety of plant.

pledge The giving up of personal property as security for performance of an act or repayment of a debt.

pledgee A person to whom property is given as security for a loan.

pledgor A person who gives property to another as security for a loan.

plenary review The process by which appellate courts determine if lower courts have made errors of law.

police power A state's authority to restrict private rights to promote and maintain public health, safety, welfare, and morals.

policy The contract of insurance.

pooling agreement An agreement made by shareholders whereby they promise to vote the same way on a particular issue. Also called *shareholder agreements* and *voting agreements*.

post-appelate procedures The process of taking a case that has been rejected or dismissed by a domestic court to an international organization, such as the Inter-American Commission on Human Rights of the Organization of American States.

power of attorney An instrument in writing by which one person, as principal, appoints another as agent and confers the authority to perform certain specified acts on behalf of the principal.

precedent A model case that a court can follow when facing a similar situation.

preemption The process by which the courts decide that a federal statute must take precedence over a state statute.

preemptive right A shareholder's right to purchase a proportionate share of every new offering of stock by the corporation.

preemptive war A conflict waged when one nation attacks a sovereign nation to stop that nation from engaging in activities that the attacking nation has decided are against its national interests. Also called *preventive war.*

preexisting duty An obligation that a party is already bound to by law or by some other agreement. The party may not use this as consideration in a new contract.

preferred stock A class of stock that carries with it the right to receive payment of dividends and/or the distribution of assets on the dissolution of the corporation before other classes of stock receive their payments.

preliminary hearing A court procedure during which the judge decides whether probable cause exists to continue holding a defendant for a crime.

premeditated cybersquatter Someone who takes the domain name of a famous person or well-known company to extort money from the actual owner.

premium The consideration paid by the insured to the insurer for insurance protection.

prenuptial agreement An agreement between two people who are planning marriage and who agree to change the property rights they possess by law in a marriage.

prescriptive theory A system of ethical thought that describes how to come up with the values at work within a social system.

presenting bank Any bank presenting an item except a payor bank.

presentment A demand for acceptance or payment of a negotiable instrument made upon the maker, acceptor, or drawee by or on behalf of the holder of the instrument.

preventative war A war waged to prevent another nation-state from reaching a point that it would be capable of attacking the first nation.

prima facie **evidence** (PRY·mah FAY·shee) Evidence that is legally sufficient to prove a fact in the absence of evidence to the contrary.

primary committee In bankruptcy law, a committee of creditors set up to work with a debtor in drawing up a reorganization plan.

principal A person who authorizes an agent to act on her or his behalf and subject to her or his control.

principal objective The main goal that the parties to a contract hoped to meet by entering the contract in the first place.

primary objective test A rule that states a writing is not needed for enforcement if the promise to pay another party's debt is made to obtain a gain for the guarantor.

principle of honorable surrender A criterion under a modern version of the just war theory that requires a victor to accept the surrender of the enemy and to treat the defeated combatants with dignity and respect.

principle of repentance A criterion under a modern version of the just war theory that calls for a genuine expression of remorse for the death and destruction caused by war.

principle of restoration A criterion under a modern version of the just war theory that requires a victor in a conflict to act responsibly in rebuilding the defeated nation's physical environment, economy, and governmental structure.

prior art All relevant technical knowledge about the field to which the invention belongs.

private carriers Companies, not in the transportation business, that operate their own trucks and other vehicles to transport their own goods.

private civil trial Trials run according to the same rules of procedure and evidence as trials run under the official auspices of the court. In a private trial, the parties can hold the trial when and where they choose, and they can choose the judge. Lengthy civil cases are well-suited to this approach.

private corporation A corporation formed by private persons to accomplish a task best undertaken by an entity that can raise large amounts of capital quickly or that can grant the protection of limited liability.

private information Reports on personal matters, family matters, sexual habits, employment records, medical data, and financial records. Also called *private-private* information.

private warehouser A warehouser whose warehouse is not for general public use.

privity In contract law, the relationship that exists between two parties to a contract giving each a recognized interest in the subject matter of the contract so that they are bound to that contract.

probability of success A criterion under the just war theory that states that a war must be waged only when there is a reasonable chance of success.

probate To settle the estate of a decedent under the supervision of a court.

product liability A law that imposes liability on the manufacturer and the seller of a product produced and sold in a defective condition.

professional An individual who can perform a highly specialized task because of special abilities, education, experience, and knowledge.

promisee In the making of a contract, the party to whom a promise is made.

promisor In the making of a contract, the party who makes a promise.

promissory estoppel The legal doctrine that restricts an offeror from revoking an offer under certain conditions, even though consideration has not been promised to bind the agreement. To be effective, promissory estoppel requires that the offeror know, or be presumed to know, that the offeree might otherwise make a definite and decided change of position in contemplation of promises contained in the offer.

promoters The people who do the day-to-day work involved in creating a corporation.

property damage liability insurance A type of automobile insurance that provides protection when other people bring claims or lawsuits against the insured for damaging property such as a car, a fence, or a tree.

proportionality A criterion under the just war theory that states that the good advanced by the war must exceed the negative consequences of entering the conflict.

proprietor An owner, as of a business. The party for which an independent contractor works.

prosecutor An attorney that represents the government in a criminal procedure.

prospectus A document published by a corporation explaining, in simplified fashion for potential investors, the details of a stock issuance and the business making the offer.

protest A certificate of dishonor that states that a draft was presented for acceptance or payment and was dishonored.

provisional Not final.

proximate cause In tort law, the connection between the unreasonable conduct and the resulting harm. Proximate cause is determined by asking whether the harm that resulted from the conduct was foreseeable at the time of the original negligent act.

proxy The authority given to one shareholder to cast another shareholder's votes.

proxy contest A struggle between two factions in a corporation, usually management and a group of dissident shareholders, to obtain the votes of the other shareholders.

proxy solicitation The process by which one shareholder asks another for his or her voting right.

proxy statement A document that communicates information about the identity of a solicitor, the reason for a solicitation, and all other crucial information that shareholders need to make an informed decision about a proxy.

public accountant (PA) An accountant who works for a variety of clients but who is not certified.

Public Company Accounting Oversight Board A regulatory agency that is charged with the task of making certain that correct, unbiased, and comprehensive data finds their way to potential investors, so that they can make informed decisions about investment opportunities.

public corporation A corporation created by the federal, state, or local government for governmental purposes. Also, a large private corporation that generally sells its stock to the public at large.

public domain Owned by the public, not protected by copyright.

public offer An offer made through the public media but intended for only one person whose identity or address is unknown to the offeror.

public policy The general legal principle that says no one should be allowed to do anything that tends to injure the public at large.

public privacy Essentially public information that subjects consider private, such as names and addresses.

public-private information The association of two or more pieces of public information to create information that the victim considers private.

public warehouser A warehouser who owns a warehouse where any member of the public who is willing to pay the regular charge may store goods.

pump and dump scheme A scheme designed to lure unsuspecting investors into the trap of investing in what is essentially an empty shell, that is, a poorly financed corporation that appears to be more valuable than it really is.

punitive damages Damages in excess of actual losses suffered by the plaintiff awarded as a measure of punishment for the defendant's wrongful acts. Also called *exemplary damages.*

purchase money security interest A security interest that arises when someone lends money to a consumer and then takes a security interest in the goods that the consumer buys.

purpose In criminal law, the intent to cause the result that does, in fact, occur.

qualified indorsement An indorsement in which words, such as "without recourse," have been added to the signature to limit the liability of the indorser.

qualified opinion An opinion issued by an auditor saying that, as of a given date, the books of a firm represent its financial health; however, the auditor may qualify the opinion either because the firm is facing some uncertainty that might affect the company in the future or because the firm has deviated from generally accepted accounting principles (GAAP) in some minor way.

quasi-contract See *implied-in-law contract.*

quasi-public corporation A corporation that is privately organized for profit but also provides a service upon which the public is dependent.

quid pro quo **sexual harassment** A supervisor's unwelcome advancement or suggestion to a subordinate to trade sexual favors for preferential treatment.

quiet enjoyment The right of a tenant to the undisturbed possession of the property that he or she is renting.

quitclaim deed A deed that transfers to the buyer only the interest that the seller may have in a property and that contains no warranties.

racial profiling The act of targeting a person for criminal investigation primarily because of racial or ethnic characteristics.

radio frequency identity device A tiny electronic tracking chip that can be implanted in any physical object from clothing to canned goods.

ratification The principal's approval of an unauthorized act performed by an agent or by one who has no authority to act as an agent. Also, an approval of a contract made by a minor after reaching maturity.

rational ethics A system of ethical thought that uses reason as the basis for making ethical judgments.

real defense In negotiable-instruments law, any defense that can be used against everyone, including holders in due course. Also called *absolute defense* and *universal defense.*

real property The ground and everything permanently attached to it including land, buildings, and growing trees and shrubs; the air space above the land is also included.

reasonable accommodation The quality of accommodation that allows a disabled worker to accomplish essential functions in the workplace without imposing undue hardship on the employer.

reasonable care The degree of care that a reasonably prudent person would have used under the same circumstances and conditions.

reasonable time In contract law, the time that may fairly, properly, and conveniently be required to do the task that is to be done, with regard to attending circumstances.

rebuttable presumption A disputable presumption that a defending party has the right to attack.

rebuttal The presentation of evidence to discredit the evidence by the opposition and to reestablish the credibility of his or her own evidence.

recklessness In criminal law, a perverse disregard for a known risk of a negative result.

Registered Limited Liability Partnership (RLLP or LLP) A general partnership in which partners are not jointly or severally liable for partnership liabilities caused by the act or omission of another partner or employee unless the partner had supervision over the other partner or employee.

registration statement A statement required by the Securities and Exchange Commission to indicate details about a business selling securities.

reg-neg See *negotiated rule making.*

regulatory justice A fair and balanced interpretation of the law that evolves from and is consistent with previous law.

rejection The express or implied refusal by an offeree to accept an offer.

release In contract law, a promise made by one party agreeing to sue a second party.

remainder estate A future interest in property when title is to pass to someone other than the grantor or grantor's heirs at the expiration of a life estate.

remitting bank Any payor or intermediary bank remitting for an item.

removal A request to a U.S. District Court to accept a case that was first filed in a state court.

renter's insurance An insurance policy that protects tenants against loss of personal property, against liability for a visitor's personal injury, and against liability for negligent destruction of the rented premises.

renunciation A legal act by which a person abandons a right acquired, but without transferring it to another.

reorganization In bankruptcy law, a plan created by a qualified debtor that alters his or her repayment schedule and allows the debtor to stay in business.

request for admission A request made to secure a statement from a party that a particular fact is true or that a document or set of documents is genuine.

request for physical or mental examination A request for a party to undergo a physical or a mental examination.

request for real evidence A discovery device that asks the opposing party in a lawsuit to produce papers, records, accounts, correspondence, photographs, or other tangible evidence.

requirements contract An agreement in which one party agrees to purchase all of his or her requirements of a particular product from another party. See also *output contract.*

rescission A remedy in contract law that returns both parties to a contract back to their original positions before the contract was entered into.

reserve funds Earnings from a business that are held in reserve.

respondeat superior (re·SPOND·ee·yat se·PEER·ee·or) The legal doctrine that imposes liability on employers and makes them pay for torts committed by their employees within the scope of the employer's business. Literally translated, it means "Let the master respond."

restraint of trade A limitation on the full exercise of doing business with others.

restrictive covenant A promise by an employee in an employment contract not to work for anyone else in the same field of employment for a specified time period within a particular geographical area.

restrictive indorsement An indorsement in which words have been added to the signature of the indorser that specify the purpose of the indorsement or the use to be made of the commercial paper, such as "for deposit only."

reverse discrimination A practice designed to eliminate discrimination against a protected class but that has the opposite effect on members of another protected class.

reverse mortgage A type of loan that allows home owners, over the age of 62, to convert some of the equity in their home into cash while retaining ownership of their home.

reversion estate A future interest in property when title is to return to the grantor or grantor's heirs upon expiration of a life estate.

revocation The calling back of an offer by the offeror.

revolving charge account A charge account with an outstanding balance at all times.

right intention A criterion under the just war theory that states that a war must be waged only if the combatant has the correct objective.

right of way See *easement.*

right-to-work laws State laws that prohibit labor-management agreements requiring union membership as a condition of getting or keeping a job.

riparian owners People who own land along the bank of a river or stream. They have certain rights and duties with respect to the water that flows over, under, and beside their land.

robbery The act of taking personal property from the possession of another against that person's will and under threat to do great bodily harm or damage.

role model ethics A system of ethical thought that examines people and their patterns of behavior in order to uncover examples of the proper way to act.

RPM agreement The agreement between a retailer and a manufacturer that the retailer will sell certain products at a price set by the manufacturer.

rule of contemporary ownership The rule that holds that shareholders must own stock at the time of the injury and at the time of the lawsuit if they wish to begin a derivative suit.

rule-of-reason standard In antitrust law, a doctrine that holds that a court should stop certain practices only if they are an unreasonable restriction of competition.

S corporation A corporation in which shareholders have agreed to have the profits (or losses) of the corporation taxed directly to them rather than to the corporation.

sale A contract in which ownership of goods is transferred by the seller to the buyer for a price.

sale on approval A conditional sale that becomes absolute only if the buyer approves or is satisfied with the article being sold.

sale or return A sale in which the buyer takes title to goods with the right to revest title in the seller after a specified period or reasonable time.

sales puffery Persuasive words or exaggerated arguments made by salespeople to induce customers to buy their product. As long as such comments are reserved to opinion and do not misstate facts, they are not actionable as fraud, even if they turn out to be grossly in error. Also called *puffery.*

salvage A reward given to persons who voluntarily assist a sinking ship to recover its cargo from peril or loss.

salvor A person who salvages. The law of salvage gives the salvor the right to compensation for assisting a foundering vessel.

same state locality rule A means to judge a health care provider's actions on the basis of the standard of care used in the same state in which that provider practices.

Sarbanes-Oxley Act Legislation that places an affirmative duty on the directors of publicly traded corporations to monitor whether they are conforming to all legal requirements.

satisfaction The agreed-to settlement as contained in an accord.

satisfactory performance In contract law, the situation that exists when either personal taste or objective standards determine the contracting parties have performed their contractual duties according to the agreement.

science court A proposed court that would act as a forum for disputes involving scientific and technological controversies.

scope of authority The range of acts done while performing agency duties. Also called *scope of employment*.

scope of employment See *scope of authority*.

screen display The audiovisual configuration that appears on the screen of the computer monitor.

seal A mark or impression placed on a written contract indicating that the instrument was executed and accepted in a formal manner.

second mortgage See *junior mortgage*.

secondary boycott Conspiracy in which a union places pressure on a neutral customer or supplier with whom the union has no dispute in order to cause the neutral entity to cease doing business with the employer with whom the union has a dispute.

second-level domain (SLD) name Indicates the actual name, trade name, or other identifying mark of the institution, organization, or business using the domain name.

secret partner A partner whose identity and existence are not known outside of the firm but who can participate in the management of the firm.

Secretariat The administrative bureaucracy of the United Nations.

Secretary-General of the United Nations The chief administrator of the United Nations.

secured loan A loan in which creditors have something of value, usually called collateral, from which they can be paid if the debtor does not pay.

secured party A lender or seller who holds a security interest.

security In secured transactions, the assurance that a creditor will be paid back for any money loaned or credit extended to a debtor. In corporate law, a money investment that expects a return solely because of another person's efforts.

security agreement A written agreement that creates a security interest.

Security Council The United Nations body that deals with international crises.

security interest A creditor's right to use collateral to recover a debt.

self-defense A defense to criminal liability available to defendants if they can demonstrate (1) that they did not start the altercation, (2) that they had good reason to believe they were in danger of death or severe bodily injury, and (3) that they used only enough force to repel the attack.

servant An outdated term signifying a person employed to perform services in the affairs of another and who,

with respect to the physical conduct in the performance of the service, is subject to the other's right to control.

service of process The act of giving the summons and the complaint to a defendant.

servient tenement The property through which an easement is created or through which it extends.

settlement week An ADR technique in which the court clears its docket of all business except settlement hearings.

severalty The quality or state of sole ownership of a single property.

sexual harassment A type of sexual discrimination.

shares Portions of a corporation that may be owned by the various shareholders.

shareholder democracy A theory of corporate management that favors making management more responsive to shareholders by giving shareholders greater voting power and by making it easier for shareholders to sue managers.

shareholder of record A person to whom stock has been transferred and whose name has been entered on the corporate books as the owner of that stock. Shareholders of record are entitled to vote, receive dividends, and enjoy all other privileges of being a shareholder.

shareholder proposal A suggestion submitted by a shareholder about a broad company policy or procedure.

shareholders Persons who own units of ownership interest called shares of stock in a corporation. Also called *stockholders*.

shelter provision A provision whereby a holder who receives an instrument from a holder in due course acquires the rights of the holder in due course even though he or she does not qualify as a holder in due course.

shipment contract A contract under which a seller turns goods over to a carrier for delivery to a buyer. Both the title and risk of loss pass to the buyer when the goods are given to the carrier.

shoplifting The act of stealing goods from a store.

sight draft A draft that is payable as soon as it is presented to the drawee for payment.

silent partner A partner who does not participate in the day-to-day business of the firm.

similar locality rule The rule that allows a court to judge a health care provider's degree of care by determining how the same procedure is performed at another hospital located in a similar locality.

similar practitioner rule A means to judge a health care provider's actions according to whether that provider is a general practitioner or a specialist.

situational ethics A system of ethical thought that argues that each of us can judge a person's ethical decisions only by initially placing ourselves in that person's position.

slamming The illegal practice of changing a consumer's telephone service without permission.

slander Any false statement that harms a person's good name or reputation made in a temporary form, such as speech, and communicated to others.

slight negligence The failure to use that degree of care that persons of extraordinary prudence and foresight are accustomed to use.

software contract A contract involving the sale or licensing of information in a digital format.

sole proprietorship A business formed by the sole proprietor. It is the easiest business organization to form.

source code A set of instructions that tells the computer what to do or how to perform a particular task.

source code escrow agreement An agreement in which the computer source code is deposited with a third party. Once the agreement is made, the code can be released only by following precisely outlined procedures and usually only if both the buyer and seller agree to the release.

sovereign immunity The somewhat discredited doctrine preventing a lawsuit against government authority without the government's consent.

spam Unsolicited e-mail.

special agent A person who is authorized to conduct only a particular transaction or to perform only a specified act for a principal.

special indorsement An indorsement made by first writing on the back of a negotiable instrument an order to pay a specified person and then signing the instrument. Also called *indorsement in full.*

special interest group control A corporate control theory that is based on the fact that because corporate decision making impacts special interest groups, those groups should participate in that decision-making process.

special jurisdiction The power of a court to hear only certain kinds of cases.

special warranty deed A deed containing express warranties under which the grantor guarantees that no defects arose in the title during the time that he or she owned the property.

specific performance A decree from a court ordering a contracting party to carry out the promises made in a contract.

speculative damages Damage computed on losses that have not actually been suffered and that cannot be proved; they are based entirely on an expectation of losses that might be suffered from a breach; the courts do not allow speculative damages.

staff privileges When a hospital grants physicians, who are not employed by the hospital, the privilege to treat their patients at that hospital.

stale check A check that is presented for payment more than six months after its date.

standard construction rule A theory of legal interpretation under which the court will determine the principal objective of the parties in the making of the contract.

state control A theory of corporate management that is based on the belief that because corporate decision making impacts upon more individuals and groups than just the shareholders and the managers, those corporate decisions should be made by an impartial group of corporate outsiders, usually government officials.

statute A law passed by a legislature.

Statute of Frauds A law requiring certain contracts to be in writing to be enforceable.

statute of repose An absolute time limit for bringing a cause of action regardless of when the cause of action accrues, such as a certain number of years after a defective product has been sold to an injured customer.

statutes of limitations State laws that restrict the time within which a party is allowed to bring legal action against another.

statutory agent An individual who is designated to receive service of process when a lawsuit is filed against a corporation.

statutory interpretation The process by which courts analyze aspects of a statute that are unclear or ambiguous or that were not anticipated at the time the legislature passed the statute.

stock acquisition The purchase of enough of the voting stock of a corporation to allow the buyer to control the corporation. Also called *takeover.*

stock certificate Written evidence of ownership of a unit of interest in a corporation.

stock dividends Dividends paid to shareholders in the form of shares of capital stock.

stoppage in transit A right of the seller, upon learning that the buyer is insolvent, to have the delivery of goods stopped before they reach their destination.

straight bill of lading A bill of lading that does not contain words of negotiability.

straight life insurance Insurance that requires the payment of premiums throughout the life of the insured and pays the beneficiary the face value of the policy upon the insured's death.

strict liability The doctrine under which people may be liable for injuries to others whether or not they have been negligent or committed an international tort. Also called *absolute liability*.

strike A stoppage of work by employees as a means of enforcing a demand made on their employers.

subjective ethics An ethical theory that holds that there are no objective or absolute standards of right and wrong.

subject matter jurisdiction The power of a court to hear a particular type of case.

subject to the mortgage An agreement whereby the seller of real property that is already mortgaged agrees to continue paying the mortgage payments.

sublease A lease given by a lessee to a third person conveying the same interest for a shorter term than the period for which the lessee is holding it. Also called *underlease*.

subordinate To place in a lower order.

subordinated mortgage A mortgage that is reduced in priority to a person holding a second mortgage.

subordination agreement An agreement made by holders of first mortgages to allow their mortgage to be reduced in priority to a person holding a second mortgage.

subrogation The right of one party to substitute itself for another party.

substantial performance In contract law, the situation that results when a party to a contract, in good faith, executes all the promised terms and conditions of the contract with the exception of minor details that do not affect the real intent of their agreement.

substantial similarity test A test to determine whether a work has violated a copyrighted work's integrity by determining whether the two are so like one another that an ordinary reasonable observer would have no recourse other than to conclude that the second was copied from the first.

substitute check A paper reproduction of both sides of an original check that can be processed electronically.

substitute transportation insurance Insurance that reimburses the insured up to specific limits for transportation costs while a car is undergoing covered repairs.

sui generis A law unto itself. An area of the law that has developed its own independent self-contained rules.

suitor A corporation or individual who offers to purchase the voting stock of a corporation with the objective of taking over the corporation.

summary judgment motion A motion that asks a court for an immediate judgment for the party filing the motion because both parties agree on the facts in the case

and because under law the party who introduced the motion is entitled to a favorable judgment.

summary jury trial A shortened version of a trial conducted in less than a day before a jury. The jury's verdict is advisory only.

surebuttal A reply to the defendant's rebuttal.

surety One who stands behind executors or administrators and becomes responsible for their wrongdoing.

surplus Funds that remain after a partnership has been dissolved and all other debts and prior obligations have been settled.

survival statute A state law that allows a lawsuit to be brought even if both the plaintiff and the defendant are deceased.

takeover bid In corporate law, the offer to buy the voting stock of a corporation.

target In corporate law, a corporation that is the object of a takeover bid.

target corporation The subject of a tender offer.

targeted shareholder agreement An agreement by which a suitor negotiates a deal with certain shareholders to provide them with employment-related deals that supplement the price they will receive for selling their stock.

tariff-based principle A principle that states that the only way that World Trade Organization nations can regulate the imports of other nations is through tariffs.

taxable expenses Legal expenses, such as those involved in filing a case and issuing subpoenas.

teaching, suggestion, or motivation test or TSM standard A traditional test that states patent challengers to demonstrate that the innovation would have been obvious to any one exposed to the same teaching session, the same off-hand suggestion, or the same motivation as the inventor had been exposed to.

teller's check See *bank draft*.

temporary public figures People who are placed against their will into the public view by some event beyond their control.

tenancy An interest in real estate that is held under a lease. Also called *leasehold estate*.

tenancy at sufferance A leasehold estate, or tenancy, that arises when a tenant wrongfully remains in possession of the premise after his or her tenancy has expired.

tenancy at will A leasehold estate, or tenancy, that continues for as long as both parties desire.

tenancy by entirety Ownership by husband and wife, considered by the law as one, with full ownership surviving to the living spouse on the death of the other.

tenancy for years A leasehold estate, or tenancy, for a fixed period of time.

tenancy from year to year See *periodic tenancy.*

tenancy in partnership Ownership in which each person has an interest in partnership property and is co-owner of such property.

tenant A person to whom real property is rented or leased. Also called *lessee.*

tenants in common Owners of an undivided interest in property, with each owner's rights going to his or her heirs upon death rather than to the surviving cotenants.

tender To offer to turn goods over to a buyer.

tender of delivery An offer by the seller of goods to turn the goods over to the buyer.

tender of payment An offer by the buyer of goods to turn the money over to the seller.

tender of performance An offer to do what one has agreed to do under the terms of a contract.

tender offer A public offer by a suitor to buy voting stock.

term insurance Insurance that is issued for a particular period, usually five or ten years.

term partnership A partnership that is set up to run for a set time period or in order to accomplish a task of some sort.

termination by waiver The situation that exists when a party to a contract with the right to complain of the other party's unsatisfactory performance or nonperformance fails to complain.

testamentary trust A trust that is created by a will.

testate Having made a valid will. Compare *intestate.*

testator (male); testatrix (female) A person who makes a will.

third party In contract law, a person who may, in some way, be affected by a contract but who is not one of the contracting parties. Also called *outside party.*

time draft A draft that is not payable until the lapse of a particular time period stated on the draft.

tippees People who receive inside information about corporate stock without being involved in any business need to obtain that information.

title The right of ownership to goods. Also, a subdivision of a code containing all the statutes that deal with a particular area of law.

top-level domain (TLD) name The portion of the domain name that identifies the addressee's zone, for example, .com, .org, or .edu.

tort A private wrong that injures another person's physical well-being, property, or reputation.

tortfeasor A person who commits a tort.

tortious bailee Any party unlawfully in possession of another's personal property.

towing and labor insurance Insurance that reimburses up to specified limits for towing and labor charges whenever a car breaks down, whether or not an accident is involved.

trade acceptance A draft used by a seller of goods to receive payment and also to extend credit. It is often used in combination with a bill of lading.

trade dress The total image or appearance of a product, such as size, shape, color, texture, design, and advertising and marketing techniques used to promote its sale.

trade fixtures Items of personal property brought upon the land by a tenant that are necessary to carry on the trade or business to which the premises will be devoted. Contrary to the general rule, trade fixtures remain the personal property of the tenant and are removable at the expiration of the terms of occupancy.

trade secrets A plan, process, or device that is used in a business and is known only to employees who need to know the secret to carry out their jobs.

trademark tapping A technique companies use to increase the number of "hits" on their Web sites.

trademark Any word, name, symbol, or device adopted and used by a manufacturer or merchant to identify goods and distinguish them from those manufactured or sold by others.

transactions in computer information A contract whose subject matter entails the acquisition, development, or distribution of computer information.

transient A person who accepts the service of a hotel or other public accommodation without any obligation to remain a specified length of time.

transnational organizations or transnats Nongovernmental organizations that have neither earned status nor demonstrated the ability, or even willingness, to be accountable for their actions on the world stage.

traveler's check A draft purchased from a bank or express company and signed by the purchaser at the time of cashing as a precaution against forgery.

treason The levying of war against the United States, or the giving of aid and comfort to the nation's enemies.

true locality rule A means to judge a health care provider's actions on the basis of the standard of care used in the exact same locality or community.

trust A legal device by which property is held by one person for the benefit of another.

trustee A person who is entrusted with the management and control of another's property or the rights associated with that property.

Tunney or Antitrust Procedures and Penalties Act The federal statute that regulates the Justice Department's antitrust consent decrees.

tying agreement In antitrust law, an illegal practice that occurs when one party refuses to sell a given product unless the buyer also purchases another product tied to the first product.

UN Convention on Contracts for the International Sale of Goods (CISG) International agreement governing sales of goods between businesses located in different countries.

unconscionable contract A contract that is so one-sided that it is oppressive and gives unfair advantage to one of the parties.

unconscionable Ridiculously inadequate.

underinsured-motorist insurance Insurance that provides protection against the risk of being injured by an underinsured motorist.

underlease See *sublease.*

undisclosed principal A person, in a transaction conducted by an agent, whose existence and identity are unknown to the third party.

undisputed amount An amount upon which the parties to a contract have mutually agreed.

undue hardship The amount of inconvenience beyond that which is required of an employer who seeks to provide reasonable accommodation for a disabled worker.

undue influence The use of excessive pressure by the dominant member of a confidential relationship to convince the weaker party to enter a contract that greatly benefits the dominant party.

unenforceable contract A contract that cannot be upheld by a court because of some rule of law.

unfair labor practices Improper employment practices by either an employer or a union.

unfriendly suitor A suitor of a corporation who intends to change management and shake up the corporation after its takeover.

Uniform Commercial Code (UCC) A unified set of statutes designated to govern almost all commercial transactions.

Uniform Computer Information Transactions Act A statute that establishes standards for digital information contracts.

Uniform Durable Power of Attorney Act (UDPA) Legislation that states a person may appoint an "attorney in fact" by signing a written durable power of attorney.

Uniform Electronic Transactions Act (UETA) A model code that declares that if the parties to a contract have voluntarily agreed to transact business electronically, then the electronic contract that results will be just as legally acceptable as a paper contract.

Uniform Facsimile Signatures of Public Officials Act A law that allows use of facsimile signatures of public officials when certain requirements are followed.

Uniform Power of Attorney Act A unified set of statutes designed to govern all aspects of the durable power of attorney agency relationship.

Uniform Trade Secrets Act Legislation written by the NCCUSL to define a trade secret, describe transgressions, and provide for both damages and injunctive relief when there has been a trade secret infringement.

unilateral contract An agreement in which one party makes a promise to do something in return for an act of some sort.

unilateral mistake In contract law, a mistake made by only one of the contracting parties. Unilateral mistake does not offer sufficient grounds for recession or renegotiation.

unimpaired class In bankruptcy law, a group of creditors whose collection rights are not impaired by a reorganization plan.

uninsured-motorist insurance A type of automobile insurance that provides protection against the risk of being injured by a motorist who does not have insurance.

union shop A place of employment where nonunion workers may be employed for a trial period of not more than 30 days, after which the nonunion workers must join the union or be discharged.

United Nations Commission on International Trade (UNCITRAL) A fraternity of 36 countries that seeks to cultivate the organization and integration of international law in relation to international trade.

United States Antitrust Modernization Committee A Congressional think tank designed to examine antitrust law and report recommendations on how to modernize the law.

United States Code (USC) A compilation of all the statutes passed by Congress.

United States Sentencing Commission The commission that issues rules regarding federal courts' discretion in issuing punishments for crimes.

universal defense See *real defense.*

universal life insurance A form of straight life insurance that allows the policy owner flexibility in choosing and changing terms of the policy.

unlawful detainer A legal proceeding that provides landlords with a quick method of evicting a tenant. Also called *summary process, summary ejectment, forcible entry and detainer,* and *dispossessory warrant proceedings.*

unqualified opinion An opinion issued by an auditor that indicates that the financial records of a firm are an accurate reflection of the firm's financial status.

unsecured loan A loan in which creditors have nothing of value that they can repossess and sell in order to recover the money owed to them by the debtor.

Uruguay Round Agreements (URA) The eighth round of GATT talks, lasting from 1986 to 1993, out of which the World Trade Organization and the Dispute Settlement Understanding were created.

usage of trade Any method of dealing that is commonly used in the particular field.

Used Car Rule A rule established by the Federal Trade Commission requiring used car dealers to place a sticker, called a *Buyer's Guide,* in the window of each used car they offer for sale. The sticker provides consumer protection information.

usury The practice of charging more than the amount of interest allowed by law.

utilitarianism A system of ethical thought that focuses on the consequences of an action.

utility patent A patent granted to someone who invents or discovers any new and useful process, machine, article of manufacture, or composition of matter, or any new and useful improvement thereof.

utility thinking A system of thought that focuses the consequences to one person or institution and then weighs the cost against the benefits of performing the action under scrutiny.

uttering The crime of offering a forged instrument to another person, knowing it to be forged.

valid contract A contract that is legally binding and fully enforceable by the court.

values A standard for determining what things hold central importance.

vandalism The act of willfully or maliciously causing damage to property.

variable-rate mortgage See *flexible-rate mortgage.*

variance An exemption that permits a use that differs from those allowed under the existing zoning law.

verdict A finding of fact by the jury in a court case; the jury's decision.

vertical expansion The joining of two companies that were in a customer–supplier relationship.

vicarious liability The concept of laying responsibility or blame upon one person for the actions of another.

video conference A conference that uses a televised connection to permit any number of people at widely diverse locations to discuss the details of a case.

voidable contract A contract that may be voided or canceled by one of the parties.

voidable title Title that may be voided if one of the parties elects to do so.

void contract A contract that has no legal effect whatsoever.

void title No title at all.

voting trust An agreement among shareholders to transfer their voting rights to a trustee.

waiver The voluntary surrender of some right, claim, or privilege.

waiver of premium An optional provision in an insurance contract that excuses the insured from paying premiums if the insured becomes disabled.

warehouse A building or structure in which any goods, but particularly wares or merchandise, are stored.

warehouser A person engaged in the business of storing goods for hire.

warehouse receipt A receipt issued by a person engaged in the business of storing goods for hire.

warehouser's lien The right of a warehouser to retain possession of goods stored in the warehouse until the satisfaction of the charges imposed on them.

warranty A promise, statement, or other representation that an item has certain qualities; also, an insured's promise to abide by restrictions, especially those written into an insurance policy. Also, an obligation imposed by law that an item will have certain qualities. Warranties made by means of a statement or other affirmation of fact are called *express warranties;* those imposed by law are *implied warranties.*

warranty of fitness for a particular purpose An implied warranty that goods will be fit for a particular purpose. This warranty is given by the seller to the buyer of goods whenever the seller has reason to know of any particular purpose for which the goods are needed and the buyer relies on the seller's skill and judgment to select the goods.

warranty of habitability The landlord warrants that the premises are fit for human habitation.

warranty of merchantability An implied warranty that goods are fit for the ordinary purpose for which such goods are used. Unless excluded, this warranty is always given by a merchant who sells goods in the ordinary course of business.

warranty of title A warranty given by a seller to a buyer of goods that states that the title being conveyed is good and that the transfer is rightful.

waste Substantial damage to premises that significantly decreases the value of the property.

Web conference A conference that is carried out online via the Internet using personal computers to permit any number of people at widely diverse locations to discuss the details of a case.

Westphalia system As outlines in the Treaty of Westphalia, a theory that describes nation-states as the primary international actors.

white knight A post-offer technique where a target company invites another suitor to outbid a hostile bidder. The second suitor agrees that it will retain the existing management.

whole life insurance See *straight life insurance*.

widow's allowance See *family allowance*.

will A legal document, not valid until the testator's death, expressing the testator's intent in distribution of all real and personal property.

will theory A theory of legal interpretation under which the court will look to see if the parties to a contract have freely assumed the obligations and benefits due them under the contract.

work product privilege The guarantee that all notes, recordings, research documents, Q&As, voice mails, faxes, e-mails, computer records, memos, letters, flash drives, disks, DVDs, CDs, and so on that are prepared in anticipation of litigation remain confidential.

worker's compensation Worker protection provided for by state statutes that compensates covered workers or their dependents for injury, disease, or death that occurs on the job or as a result of it.

World Bank A nongovernmental organization that works exclusively with the poorest nations in the international community to help them secure loans.

World Intellectual Property Organization (WIPO) A division of the United Nations that supported the development of two international treaties designed to deal with electronic copyright problems.

World Intellectual Property Organization Copyright Treaty A treaty that guarantees copyright holders can use the Internet to post their works with full copyright protection.

World Intellectual Property Organization Phonograms Treaty A treaty that gives copyright holders the right to copy, publish, and distribute their works in any way.

World Trade Organization (WTO) A corporate nucleus for the management of international trade relationships.

world wide organization Any international institution that transcends and unites nation-states in a common purpose on a global basis. Established worldwide organizations include diplomatic institutions such as the United Nations, legal organizations such as the International Criminal Court, and economic institutions such as the World Bank.

writ of certiorari An order from the U.S. Supreme Court to a lower court to deliver the records of a case to the Supreme Court for review.

writ of execution A court order directing the sheriff of a county to sell the property of a losing defendant to satisfy the judgment against that defendant.

writ of replevin A court order requiring a defendant to turn goods over to a plaintiff because the plaintiff has the right to immediate possession of the goods.

wrongful civil proceedings Filing a false civil lawsuit.

wrongful death statute A law that allows third parties affected by a death to bring a lawsuit only if the death is caused by the negligence or intentional conduct of the defendant.

wrongful discharge Exceptions to employment-at-will that give employees legal ground for lawsuits against employers who have dismissed them unfairly.

yellow-dog contract An agreement whereby an employer requires, as a condition of employment, that an employee promises not to join a union.

zoning law A local regulation or ordinance that restricts certain areas to specific uses; for example, areas zoned for residential, commercial, agricultural, industrial, or other uses.

Photo Credits

Case Index

Subject Index